ISSUES AND IDEAS IN AMERICA

UNIVERSITY OF OKLAHOMA PRESS : Norman

ISSUES
AND IDEAS
IN AMERICA

★★★

Edited by BENJAMIN J. TAYLOR
and THURMAN J. WHITE

Library of Congress Cataloging in Publication Data
Main entry under title:

Issues and Ideas in America

Includes bibliographies.
1. United States—Intellectual life—History.
I. Taylor, Benjamin J. II. White, Thurman J.
E169.1.E86   973   76-18769   4 OCt'79
ISBN 0-8061-1327-8
ISBN 0-8061-1376-6 pbk.

This book is in commemoration of all those in the past who dedicated a part of their lives to advancing knowledge. Their dedication provided a springboard for enthusiastic research and search for understanding in what may be generically called modern American education. New and developing fields of inquiry owe a debt of gratitude to all those who have previously labored to enrich life for all mankind.

PREFACE

This book is an outgrowth of the many activities undertaken by the University of Oklahoma in its commemoration of the nation's two hundredth year. The contributions are varied in subject and approach and come from many areas of particular concern to the nation as it looks back on its past and forward to its future.

The contributions are organized into five parts. Part I is concerned with legal, political, and economic developments in the nation over the two-hundred-year period. Part II is devoted to the development of aspects of social, educational, and psychological thought. Part III deals with the evolution of uniquely American philosophical trends. Part IV is concerned with developments in science and medicine. Part V is devoted to the evolution of the concepts popularly termed ecology. The division of the book into parts has been somewhat arbitrary. The parts, and also the chapters within the parts, should be considered as overlapping to some extent, since many of the disciplines share the same philosophical, historical, political, and scientific bases and concerns.

Throughout the book are provided insights into the growth of the United States to a position of world leadership in virtually every area of human concern. Attainment of that position has not been easy; it has been achieved largely through Americans' willingness to experiment with alternatives. The authors clearly illustrate the impressive results that relatively free inquiry and debate have produced, in law, in economics, in social concerns, and in science. The freedoms enjoyed by Americans—and taken for granted by so many—have not been maintained and expanded without cost. Careful watch must be kept over those freedoms, as the chapter on slavery makes clear.

The tradition of freedom of inquiry and debate is exemplified in varying forms on the campuses of America's colleges and universities. The tradition is not without powerful critics, particularly during periods of readjustment within and among the major institutions of society. Adjustments, reorganization, and change generally bring with them basic conflicts of interest. There will be "winners" and "losers" in the process, as is made clear in the chapter on anomie as an explanation of deviance in America. The goal of freedom and justice for all has yet to be attained, and each generation is responsible for deciding how best to protect the basic rights of man, how to expand them to groups other than their own, and how to apply them to the problems they confront. The exercise of that responsibility yields substantial benefits, as this book illustrates.

It was possible to present here only a few representative achievements of the various disciplines and institutions. Our purpose has been to offer a selective view of some of America's accomplishments since 1776. The result is, we believe, a significant statement of America's contribution to the evolution of thought.

A comment on annotation: Because of the diversity of disciplines to which the authors belong, we have generally retained the systems of annotation they have used, which are commonly employed in their fields.

A special word of appreciation is extended to the authors who have contributed their scholarship to this book and to the several individuals who have contributed support, sometimes financially and always in encouragement. Among the latter we have a great sense of gratitude to Paul F. Sharp, President of the University of Oklahoma; Mrs. Gladys Warren, Director, Oklahoma Bicentennial Commission; Mrs. Gena Mattox, Secretary, Division of Economics; and Boyd Gunning, Executive Director, University of Oklahoma Foundation.

Benjamin J. Taylor

Thurman J. White

Norman, Oklahoma

CONTENTS

ISSUES AND IDEAS IN AMERICA

PART I: History, Law, Government, Economics

The history of the United States is one of experimentation centering on conflict and tension among various interest groups. This general theme is set forth by H. Wayne Morgan in Chapter 1, "American History as Experiment." Attention is devoted to such problems as regionalism versus national unity, individualism versus social obligations, freedom versus control, representation versus special interests, the desire for national uniqueness versus a need for world culture, and a desire to lead the world versus contempt for the world. Mistakes in the quest for basic national ideals are noted as well as some solutions necessary to correct the mistakes. Social change always brings the risk that the cure may be divisive.

William F. Swindler reviews in Chapter 2, "The Rights of Man," the contribution America has made in articulating a twofold principle of political theory: the creation and control of government by the governed and the limitation of the power of the state as it affects the rights of individual citizens. The complex structure of social and economic rights that has emerged continues to seek a balance between the government's obligation to secure freedoms for the citizen and the tenet of private freedom balanced by civic duty. The question posed for 1976 is how the democratic propositions set forth from 1774 to 1791 may be affected by the collectivist and revisionist outlooks of contemporary world society.

In Chapter 3, "Legislative Authority and Executive Leadership: A Grudging Partnership," Murray C. Havens deals with some of the difficulties encountered in the partnership of the legislative and executive branches of government. He sets forth the background of that partnership, the struggle for supremacy between the two branches of government. The result has been that from time to time both bodies have behaved irresponsibly. Alternatives to the present system are explored in the search for effective responsibility in the presidency. The rights and responsibilities of Congress, the electorate, and the executive branch are emphasized.

As Robert R. Wright demonstrates in Chapter 4, "The Relation of Law in America to Socio-Economic Change," the triumph of a given set of ideals finds expression in the legal system, which ultimately must deal with the permissible limits to change. It was not an easy task for the judiciary to lay the basis for effective trade between America and other nations, as well as among the states themselves in the context of the United States Constitution, which set up dual sovereignty. Key court cases and documents indicate that the American preoccupation was that of providing the greatest possible sphere for individual initiative in the marketplace. It was hoped that the over-all result would be a greater rate of economic growth and national well-being.

Daniel A. Wren, in Chapter 5, "Business: The Changing Scene," explores the various attitudes held by Americans about business enterprise both large and small. He traces the struggle for a philosophy of business from the colonial period to modern times. The founding fathers preferred to limit government involvement in economic affairs because of England's mercantilistic policies during the pre-Revolutionary period. Later, as markets changed, the general public and the government changed their attitudes toward business from time to time, particularly with the growth of scientific management in the refinement of business practices.

The discussion then turns to the growing influence that the federal government has had on the economic system. Benjamin J. Taylor and W. Nelson Peach deal with the trial-and-error approach of the federal government in Chapter 6, "The Emerging Role of Government in Economic Affairs." The authors begin with the debate over the proper industry "mix" that the country should take and proceeds to examine the responses of government to business cycles. Considerable attention is given to governmental activities in the post-World War II era in the context of economic objectives developed from the Employment Act of 1946. The attempt to stabilize the country's economy has posed difficult problems for the federal government, and the prospect of a movement away from mercantilistic policies becomes less likely.

1

AMERICAN HISTORY AS EXPERIMENT

By H. Wayne Morgan

The central shaping fact of American history is so obvious that it eludes many people. It is the scope of the country, not merely in geographic terms, though they are impressive enough to both foreigner and native, but in cultural diversity.[1] From the facts of size and scope come most of the forces basic to shaping American institutions and that elusive but operative quality, "the American way of life."

Any understanding of American history begins with processes that involved distances and variety over time and space and reflected tensions and ambivalences basic to national life. The obvious facts are geographical. The country's sections are independent yet became interdependent through human actions. Varied cultural attitudes inevitably arose from these changes, derived from climate and topography, as well as from economics and politics. The southerner, westerner, and New Englander have differing concepts of themselves and of the nation's needs and purposes. These views are both inclusive, as when they concern economic development, and parochial, as when they involve food, clothing, speech patterns, or the rate of acceptance of social change or new ideas.

Nor do Americans even share a single sense of time. Virginia was established in 1607; Massachusetts, in 1620. California entered the Union in 1850; Alaska and Hawaii, in 1959. These variations of time, as well as the special circumstances that accompanied the incorporation of each part of the Union, inevitably produced various concepts of what America was and was not. The weight of time and thus the sense of direction differ from place to place.

The tensions inherent in this nation building were most prominent in the population. Most of the first settlers were British, though of many religious and cultural persuasions, and reproduced British aspects of life in their new homes. But by the early nineteenth century the population had begun to take on the mosaic pattern that ultimately triumphed. The revolutions of 1848 sent many northern Europeans to the New World. The potato famine of the 1830's and 1840's transferred virtually whole counties of Ireland to the United States. The importation of blacks profoundly affected southern and then national life as early as the seventeenth century. As the twentieth century dawned, the United States remained the promised land for millions of Europeans, with their many religious, ethnic, social, and economic backgrounds.

Eager to do well, if not for themselves then for future generations, these immigrants consistently sought to adapt to the established, basically British, models of law, custom, and public conduct that the power structure usually called Americanization. Yet each ethnic or cultural group hoped to retain some private identity while accepting and then promoting a more homogenized public identity as Americans. The melting-pot ideal, in which troublesome divergences from the public norm allegedly disappeared as the mixed population accepted Americanization, was a myth. Many distinct kinds of taste, conduct, and ideals did not "melt." Yet the problems in accommodating these disparate immigrants were basic to the American situation: how to promote the order, efficiency, and stability that came from centralization without suppressing the individual uniqueness that enriches life and supports individualism through change and variety.

Most American institutions and attitudes developed in response to the tensions and aspirations that this geographic, cultural, and ethnic diversity engendered in people. The economy is varied, yet interdependent, developing at different rates and places. The political system has steadily focused on national development, yet is rooted in localistic demands and tensions. The whole culture always celebrated individual rights, yet laid down many restraints against potential anarchy in the name of national harmony. It has praised diversity, while remaining suspicious of many "foreign" tastes and activities in the population.

Fear of and hostility to things "un-American" have often embroiled the United States in foolish and tragic events. On some level these responses, most vividly spelled out in foreign policy, reveal fears about the country's stability, destiny, or intrinsic merit. All the overt problems in American life at some level reflect the tensions arising from the country's history and patterns of settlement. This sense of tenuous unity, of enormous possible success or catastrophe, the idea of the United States as an ongoing experiment, dominates its history from 1607 onward. In emotional and incisive ways many American intellectuals and artists have perceived and elaborated on these basic tensions and conflicting aspirations.

Walt Whitman found the diversity tolerable:

> *Do I contradict myself:*
> *Very well then I contradict myself,*
> *(I am large, I contain multitudes.)*
> *"Song of Myself"*

Politicians and businessmen, wrestling with conflicting demands, were usually less cheerful. In any event the task of developing the individual while promoting social stability has dominated American thinking. The Founding Fathers chose an appropriate national motto: "E Pluribus Unum" ("One out of Many"). That has been the basic American search; it remains valid as the second century of independence ends.

Since formal ideology supposed a set of prescribed solutions to social problems and answers to human dilemmas, it did not appeal to a pragmatic people like Americans. They have generally thought that problems arose at random rather than as a result of anything basic or irremediable in the existing system. Ideology and formal systems of thought so dear to Europeans took little hold on the American imagination, outside of religion. American thought and tastes remained fluid, open to many possibilities, amenable always to new and untested formulas. Theorizing has also seemed to be the opposite of action, so dear to the national image, and thus suspect in the minds of men eager to exploit or rationalize the external world.

But from the first, Americans generally accepted a rhetorical Americanism to explain the nation's present state and future prospects. This body of thought held generally that the individual was superior to the state; government was essentially negative, since it hindered personal freedom. And from the competition of many individuals, each utilizing special skills and seeking success, would come general social progress in material terms. Most Americans have believed in the promise of upward mobility, both of income and of status, for their children and grandchildren, if not for themselves. The future has thus seemed worth sacrifice and at least minimal planning. Diverse thoughts, as in religion or politics, were acceptable, provided they did not involve violence against the central existing order. And unusual customs, acted out in daily life, were tolerable, however odd they might seem to "native" Americans, as long as they did not threaten majority rule. The other side of this rhetorical Americanism was often overlooked, though its implications were clear. Americanism meant *not* that all men were fully equal but that they were entitled to equal opportunity and equal legal treatment. It meant not acceptance of disorder but the chance to work through and reform the existing system. And it meant tolerance for the rights of minorities but no special treatment unless they became part of a functioning majority.

This rhetoric, whose remnants dot both the intellectual and the material landscape, grew from fundamental aspects of American settlement, and was well established in some form long before 1776:

The colonists had to be pragmatic idealists because in a wilderness things must be made to work, yet idealism is required to reinforce the courage to confront that wilderness: Calvinism combined with the frontier experience plus commercial expansion amidst rising capitalism.[2]

In addition to securing the widest possibilities for the unfettered but responsible individual, Americans always wished to avoid any formal hierarchical system that threatened to suppress native talent. Hence the historic insistence on deference to the common man, always, of course, with the understanding that the American common man was uncommon in both his abilities and his chances in life. As a Pennsylvanian noted in 1756:

The people of this Province are generally of the middling Sort, and at present pretty much upon a Level. They are chiefly industrious Farmers, Artificers or Men in Trade; they enjoy and are fond of Freedom, and the meanest among them thinks he has a right to Civility from the greatest.[3]

Along with these demands for recognition of talent and opportunities for the individual went a basic insistence on the uniqueness of all things "American." This long-standing attitude was a defensive cover for fears of inferiority and was also necessary to justify American departures from ancient codes of conduct and procedure in every sector of life. Raoul de Roussy de Sales, the prominent French newspaperman and social thinker, made the point with both perception and Gallic irony during World War II:

Nothing is more difficult for Europeans to understand than the fundamental anti-European sentiment of America. I sometimes think that it is in fact the cornerstone of Americanism, more important than attachment to democracy, the pioneer spirit or the national messianism; for everything finally comes back to this: to be American is to be against Europe. Why? Because Americans came from Europe, the motives which made them leave their country of origin must be rationalized. The theme of liberty, of opportunity for all, of a better future and a more abundant life had to be invented. Each American must be able to say to himself: If my ancestors left Europe, or if I left it, it was because Europe is a damned and condemned continent. If he did not say this he would lose faith in himself and in the destiny of America. To be American is an act of faith. America is a country in which one must believe.[4]

Another Frenchman, Alexis de Tocqueville, had earlier skillfully analyzed America's basic dilemmas. He perceived in the 1830's and 1840's that the United States was a new social system, based on a radical sense of man's potentialities but functioning in a conservative inherited ideal of man's limitations in daily life. The long-term problems were clear: could mass-oriented democracy avoid eliminating individual liberty; could competition fail to result in mass; could unpopular dissent survive majority rule? The hidden tensions, whose management touched every American and shaped every national institution, were clear from the nation's founding: an urge for security versus a desire for adventure in a new world; a love of individual freedom competing with collective needs; a concern for material success that might thwart the nebulous idealism in which most Americans believed; and a desire to tolerate the unusual opposed to a fear of potentially disruptive diversity.

So much of the nation's life has focused on politics that it has often seemed a peculiarly American obsession. Political contests have been the major arena where these basic cultural tensions confronted concrete demands and in which voters expressed frustrations and clarified their expectations of society. Political concern and action have been major ways in which Americans expressed individuality. Citizens of older nations, with longer histories of turmoil and disappointment, usually saw government and politics as either threatening to private liberty or irrelevant to individual development. The long-standing American belief that political action could solve or at least define major human problems usually struck foreigners as irritatingly naïve or amusing. De Tocqueville's analysis was once again acute. He noted that political agitation was not wholly, or perhaps even basically, the work of politicians but reflected pressures from a broad-based and concerned electorate:

The great political movement which keeps American legislatures in a state of continual agitation, and which alone is noticed from outside, is only an episode and a sort of extension of the universal movement, which begins in the lowest ranks of the people and there spreads successively through all classes of citizens.

The American voter saw politics as a way of dealing with problems or of getting favors. But de Tocqueville also knew that the democratic political process was a means for individual voters to express themselves on great questions in a dramatic way:

It is hard to explain the place filled by political concerns in the life of an American. To take a hand in the government of society and to talk about it is his most important business and, so to say, the only pleasure he knows. That is obvious even in the most trivial habits of his life; even the women go to public meetings and forget household cares while they listen to political speeches. For them clubs to some extent take the place of theaters. An American does not know how to converse, but he argues; he does not talk, but expatiates. He always speaks to you as if addressing a meeting, and if he happens to get excited, he will say 'Gentlemen' when addressing an audience of one.

De Tocqueville thought that this faith in politics was characteristic of new nations. But he knew that politics would assume unusual importance in a democratic society that lacked clearly defined and widely accepted centers of authority. Political activity could inflate the individual voter's sense of importance and power in the election process:

But if an American should be reduced to occupying himself with his own affairs, at that moment half his existence would be snatched from him; he would feel it as a vast void in his life and would become incredibly unhappy.[5]

Politics as happiness was an unusual idea for Europeans but an integral part of American beliefs.

The political process, whether in the public arena of campaigns or the more private one of legislating, involved both the worst and the best parts of American culture. The worst aspects—waste, graft, posturing—were clear for all to see. And from the beginning, violence was a hallmark of American politics. In the colonial era resistance to British authority became almost a definition of American status. The Revolution was an organized form of political violence, at least in the minds of its opponents. The level of disorder abated somewhat in the early years of the Republic but characterized most of the rest of the nineteenth century. Duels, disruption of public meetings, fistfights on the floor of legislative bodies, including Congress, were common. This turbulence reflected in part the high expectations voters had of politics, the scramble for distinction in an egalitarian society, and the desire of citizens to enhance their status through participation in the electoral process.

Nor have leading politicians been personally safe amid these passions. The Brooks-Sumner beating incident in the Senate in 1859 personalized the intense debates over slavery and States' rights. In the twentieth century many national politicians have been targets of violence. Theodore Roosevelt was wounded during the campaign of 1912. Franklin D. Roosevelt was fired at early in 1933 before taking office. President Harry S Truman was the object of a band of assassins who stormed his temporary residence in Washington in 1950. Puerto Rican nationalists wounded several members of the House of Representatives in a shooting spree in 1954. Presidential candidates have been sheathed in a cocoon of security in recent times, which has not prevented such shootings as those of Robert Kennedy in 1968 and George Wallace in 1972.

At the highest level the American record of assassination is worse than that of many countries that Americans traditionally consider "backward." Three presidents fell to assassins' bullets in a mere thirty-six years, Abraham Lincoln (1865), James A. Garfield (1881) and William McKinley (1901). These three and another, John F. Kennedy (1963), were killed in public within a single century.

The close attention the Founding Fathers gave to the form of American government showed that they glimpsed the possibilities of this disorder in their constituents. The national political system clearly revealed their concern to balance the country's tensions, soften popular demands, and maintain a high level of expectation from politics while moderating its actual procedures and results. The federal government was thus originally superimposed on the states with defined powers but with enough vagueness to allow it to grow. The system at every level was designed to prevent any single person, group, or section from domination, and rested on the assumption that in due course men would prefer compromise to disruption.

In general, the federal government was granted control over truly national problems, such as foreign policy, territorial development, and internal improvements. Great powers originally remained to the states, on the grounds that in so large and diverse a nation localism should prevail unless it threatened basic national rights. There has never been a national police force, for instance, since law and order traditionally were local questions. The federal government has regulated such matters as welfare, education, and voting rights only reluctantly and often at the bidding of courts outside the voters' control. The redefinition of national rights in the mid-twentieth century and the growth of federal power have vividly illustrated the nation's increasing homogeneity, which altered inherited views of both citizens' rights and the role of the national government. But most governmental operations are still carried out at local levels, and federal power has expanded most only in response to a clear emergency, such as the Great Depression or war, revealing the tenacity of localism.

Yet, despite this political turbulence, politics normally has been a unifying or at least harmonizing process. Except during the crisis over disunion the system generally allowed groups to vent anger, announce demands, and obtain at least partial satisfaction. Political passions usually subsided after an appropriate election or legislative action and voters accepted the results. There has been no revolution, save that of 1776, and no coup; all alterations of the Constitution have come through processes it prescribed. In celebrating their alleged youthful ideals, Americans tend to forget that theirs is the second-oldest continuous government in the world today, after Great Britain.

This might have surprised the Founding Fathers. Jefferson allegedly thought that the tree of liberty needed occasional watering with the blood of martyrs. Hamilton believed that the new government of 1789 would last a mere generation. Eighteenth-century men had reason to be skeptical of the republican experiment. A large electorate had never before been called upon to govern as diverse a society as the new United States. Slow communications, settled habits, and regional differences made the country's distances and sectional antagonisms seem stark. And not all eighteenth-century statesmen were committed to the Enlightenment ideal of man's innate rationality and social goodness. Realists such as John Adams feared parties more than anything else in the governmental process, since they were likely to coalesce around specific disruptive demands and ambitious leaders that threatened the whole. "There is nothing I dread so much as the division of the Republic into two great parties, each under its leader," he noted. "This, in my humble opinion, is to be feared as the greatest political evil under our Constitution."[6]

It was a logical view, and for a time it seemed operative. But in due course major political parties tended to duplicate the nation's basic patterns of interests. It soon became more convenient and successful to enter an established party composed of often competing interests than to found a new party dedicated to one concern or group. By mid-nineteenth century the Democratic and Republican parties resembled in form the diverse electorate and nation they presumed to represent. The cost of the Civil War reinforced the general electorate's desire to avoid final confrontations or extreme solutions and added impetus to the normal tendency of American parties to become coalitions seeking progress through moderation. The rising wave of industrial growth after 1865 promised

security, if not wealth, to multitudes of men, and the fear of disrupting it worked against radicalism in American politics. De Tocqueville was proved right again:

Not only do men in democracies feel no natural inclination for revolutions, but they are afraid of them. Any revolution is more or less a threat to property. Most inhabitants of a democracy have property. And not only have they got property, but they live in the conditions in which men attach most value to property.[7]

Yet a great deal of apparently radical rhetoric remained to veneer the conservative desire for orderly growth and stability that basically motivated politics. From time to time genuinely frustrated dissident groups moved into the political process with special demands that the usual procedures could not or would not satisfy. In the Age of Jackson some interests opposed tendencies toward centralization and economic privilege. The slaveholders finally pursued their ambitions outside the normal political system. After the Civil War industrialism and its innovative pressures created a new array of dissidents. Minor groups organized around various ideologies, such as communism, anarchism, and socialism, to press for fundamental changes in the social system when the established parties were clearly closed to their appeals. The so-called Populist Revolt of the 1890's pitted the agrarian sector of the South and West against the East, as staple-producing farmers sought to improve their lot. In more recent times amorphous but compelling incursions into "normal" politics have come from minorities such as young people, blacks, Indians, and women. Yet none has formed a lasting party; all have benefited in some measure from the existing system's favors.

Those who seek harmony and accommodation of diverse and often unsettling interests find this historic process of co-option and partial response the genius of American politics. They warn that its end would plunge the nation into its natural chaos, which is always lurking under the surface of apparent unity. They see compromise in politics as a major cement in the national structure. Those who find this view too sunny have larger expectations from the political process and condemn it for not fundamentally altering what they see as an unjust economic and social system. In their minds the long search for national unity is successfully completed, and there is no great danger in seeking new departures.[8]

Both views may have some ironic truth. Much of the current public apathy toward government and politics indicates that the era of political parties oriented toward mass enthusiasm is closing. Government, always something different from politics, now emphasizes continuing bureaucracy rather than unstable partisanship. The old politics, whether capitalistic or socialistic, gave masses of men a sense of participating, of having individual importance, and of being part of open-ended change for the better. The political agitation that broadened public life in modern times and made its actions seem hopeful and productive for the individual voter was slow and unpredictable, inefficiencies that the new post-industrial order cannot afford. In every country the coming era of government will reflect the sophisticated and interlocked needs of highly technical civilizations. It will rest on information, planning, and rules implemented through experts outside of political pressure or persuasion, though the forms of party activities will doubtless remain.

The presidency has become the focus of demands for action from all groups. Nothing is more striking in American political history than the growth of both the actual powers and the public expectations of this office. As with parties, the Founding Fathers glimpsed this possibility and hedged the executive with both restrictions and powers. They were eager to avoid a monarch but equally concerned not to create a nonentity. However checks and controls developed, this office was the only source of either balance or leadership in the total system.

The presidency has so captivated modern Americans that it deserves close scrutiny. The clear constitutional powers accorded the executive are specific and few. He was to function first and foremost as the head of state, receiving and sending ambassadors and conducting foreign policy. He was to command the national armed forces but could not make war without the express consent of Congress. He could create an administration beholden to his policies, but his major officials and legislative proposals were subject to congressional approval. And like all other citizens he was to obey the law; various devices removed the judiciary from his control. Nothing in his constitutional situation pointed toward tyranny. But everything in his political role pointed toward steadily enhanced power, because the rest of the system was geared to slower response to public demands for action.

The presidency's authority grew with each national emergency. People became accustomed to see the executive, not Congress, as the originator of plans. And national party politics centered on the presidency in dramatic contests involving famous and admired men. The central fact about the presidency took on added dimensions as historical forces placed new demands on the political system: the president and vice-president are the only leaders on whom all the electorate can vote. All other politicians represent either districts or states, and periodic demands for national political action have no focus except the White House.

As the country became more unified and as the magnitude of emergencies and electoral demands increased in the twentieth century, the powers of the office grew far beyond its original dimensions or purpose. Presidents naturally added to this momentum, whether to gain glory or to inaugurate special programs. Theodore Roosevelt was the first genuinely modern president in frankly seeking to enlarge his power through public appeal. He glamorized the office and made it interesting for nonpolitical reasons and the focus of national expectation by the sheer force of his personality and activities. Franklin D. Roosevelt altered the office more than any predecessor and not only increased its actual power but permanently established public acceptance of a strong executive. He is the only president to date to lead the nation through both an extended depression and a world war, a set of emergencies that, combined with his personal flair, expanded the office's authority immensely.

The state of semiemergency that has prevailed in foreign policy since 1940 has underwritten expanding presidential authority, and yet most Americans still expect balance of interests and moderation to accompany presidential leadership. The description Harriet Beecher Stowe gave of Lincoln in 1864 is still an acceptable model for presidential greatness:

Lincoln's strength is of a peculiar kind. It is not aggressive so much as passive and among passive things it is like the strength not so much of a stone buttress as of a wire cable. It is strength swaying to every influence, yielding on this side and on that to popular needs, yet tenaciously and inflexibly bound to carry its great end; and probably by no other kind of strength could our national ship have been drawn safely thus far during the tossings and tempests which beset her way. Surrounded by all sorts of conflicting claims, by traitors, by half-hearted timid men, by Border State men and free State men, by radical Abolitionists and Conservatives, he has listened to all, yielded now here and now there, but in the main kept an inflexible, honest purpose, and drawn the national ship through.[9]

Expectations such as these vividly illustrated the diversity of conflicting demands surrounding the presidency and the delicate balance necessary for any executive to innovate within the existing system except in times of widely accepted emergency.

The presidency has come under increasing attack in recent times for having exceeded its popular support, especially in the conduct of foreign relations. The nature and purposes of those foreign relations have occasioned more debate within and outside the United States than any other of its policies. Until the mid-twentieth century the United States pursued few consistent foreign policies that in fact affected the rest of the world. Its active entrance into the world arena happened to coincide with a range of economic, military, and diplomatic power unparalleled in modern times. In many ways American governments have been the first since the height of the Roman Empire with the power to act out either their plans or their fantasies.

Since the United States was among the first modern nations to leave successfully a stronger imperial system, her people and governments were always concerned with some aspects of world problems. The American Revolution also involved several attitudes of critical importance in later world affairs. The colonial leaders felt obliged not merely to justify their own secession in practical terms but also to express a broad and enduring moral basis for such actions. This rhetoric, given its most elegant expression in the writings of Thomas Jefferson, set the Revolution in radical Enlightenment terms, praising democracy against tyranny and implying human equality and freedom in all spheres of life. The American Revolution thus became both a practical and an emotional model for people seeking independence everywhere. A British colonial official could say irritably after World War II: "That damned American Revolution . . . is still giving us trouble."[10]

The successful Revolution drew into its wake an already well-established sense of special mission among colonists. This was rooted in the religious puritanism of some colonists. But it also grew out of the obvious special possibilities for men of talent to gain wealth and power in the new United

States. From the beginning colonial leaders had insisted that the new nation must be a "City upon a Hill," not only in religious or moral terms but as an example of material success and individual liberty for all mankind.

These were large ambitions often difficult to work out peacefully with other peoples. In the century that followed independence, most Americans were concerned with internal matters. Foreign policy and participation in world affairs became linked in the public mind with wars, which had specific causes within a framework of general justification. The War of 1812 seemed to concern national honor as well as specific commercial rights. The Mexican-American War seemed to involve the nation's manifest destiny as well as demands for new territory. And the Spanish-American War, which climaxed the century, was a congeries of material desires and emotional appeals.

As in domestic politics, many special-interest groups worked at specific points in American foreign policy. Commercial interests often sought access to overseas markets, as in demanding new relations with Japan and China. The navy wished to enhance its power and influence with new ships and duties after the 1880's. Diplomats such as Secretary of State William Seward wanted to make the United States a great power in Victorian terms by acquiring strategic territory in the Pacific in the 1860's. At the end of the nineteenth century another secretary of state, James G. Blaine, sought to make the United States the dominant influence in the Western Hemisphere through a system of Pan-Americanism. And every president since 1789 has spent an often-unexpected amount of time and energy on world affairs, and in the twentieth century no candidates have sought the office without taking stands on the major foreign-policy questions.

It is a common saying among politicians that to voters the price of eggs is more significant than all the world's troubles. Newsmen have long known that a neighborhood slaying receives more coverage than an earthquake in China. The nation's size, wealth, and insularity compounded the average man's indifference to both the world's troubles and its needs until recent times. This general ignorance, combined with a feeling of natural superiority to other peoples, allowed American statesmen to conduct foreign affairs without much public hindrance, unless war was involved. That attitude was characteristic of most nations until the late nineteenth century, when it became necessary to justify foreign policies to electorates.

Whatever the special interests at work, the American people as a whole generally accepted a minimal set of beliefs about the nation's goals and rights in world affairs. Those attitudes recapitulated many of the tensions and ironies in the total society. Most Americans, for instance, saw the country as a force for both liberalism and stability. They desired to support self-rule in other countries, but only on American models. Hence the official and public concern for the forms of representative self-government in other nations. Hence the desire to promote free speech, assembly, and voting in many nations lacking traditions to support such innovations. In the nineteenth century Americans expected their opinions and power to temper what they perceived as innate European conservatism. During most of the twentieth century they have equally expected their actions to prevent radical revolutions while promoting a middle way. Above all, Americans have betrayed a touching faith in the power of a rising standard of living to sustain long-term stability by giving more and more people in various nations property and status to protect against revolutionaries. Other statesmen have seen these changes as the entering wedges of the anarchism and disorder Americans thought they were avoiding by promoting change.

Though American leaders sought great-power status in the late nineteenth and early twentieth centuries, few desired large tracts of territory or rule over colonial peoples. It was one thing to acquire Pacific naval bases or to interfere in Caribbean affairs; it was quite another to seek large permanent possessions. Except for military bases, Puerto Rico, and the Philippines, all the territory the United States acquired after 1789 ultimately entered the Union as states. On the whole, American statesmen and their public have been more interested in acquiring influence than territory. This has well suited their concept of self-importance and American uniqueness.

But, like other aspects of human affairs, American foreign policies steadily outstripped basic material interests and the abilities of supporting electorates to comprehend world complexities. Presidents were thus prone to simplify their explanations of foreign policies, especially those relating to wars. This also led the American people to desire final and more tangible results from their sacrifices than were reasonable to expect. That in turn helped produce an alternating rhythm of public support and withdrawal in twentieth-century world affairs.

The difficulties of managing and shaping the electorate's views led some presidents to operate almost independently in foreign policy. Many executives have promised peace while apprehensive of war, as did Wilson in 1916, Roosevelt in 1940, and Johnson in 1964. The tendency has gained momentum recently but is hardly new, nor is it limited to presidents whom historians usually label "strong." McKinley, for instance, suppressed an insurrection in the Philippines without a congressional declaration of war. He also used the army to govern Cuba and Puerto Rico. Theodore Roosevelt "took Panama," in a famous phrase. Wilson intervened in Mexico. President Calvin Coolidge used American marines in Central American countries. President Truman intervened in Korea without prior congressional approval. And Presidents Kennedy, Johnson, and Nixon conducted a devastating war in Vietnam without full constitutional sanction.

While presidential leadership in foreign affairs has often been suspect or disastrous, it has nonetheless represented many basic popular attitudes. In the midst of World War II, Raoul de Russy de Sales privately mused over the American attitudes that would affect the world at some point. His judgment was harsh but perceptive:

America will believe it her duty to concern herself with the rest of the world [after the war is over], but she will not do this without being paid for it. The payment which she will demand will not be material but moral. No country is more convinced than this one that she is right, or is more arrogant in her moral superiority. If she intervenes in the affairs of the world it will be to impose her ideas, and she will consider her intervention a blessing for lost and suffering humanity. The prospect is cheerless.[11]

The chances of combining true idealism about man's lot and material or emotional self-interest thus seemed both slim and dangerous to a world-weary European. It would become easy to kill men to save them from an alternate vision and to assume that the world could be made over in an American mold.

Of course, most Americans found such foreign criticism astonishing or even embittering. They recalled the casualties of two world wars, rooted in European power politics; the immense cost of various kinds of foreign aid since 1941; and an expensive defense system that supposedly protected other people as well as Americans. In many ways, despite a generation of direct involvement in world affairs, Americans as a whole and many of their spokesmen have learned little about other people's ideas or ambitions. As an essentially optimistic and pragmatic people given to specific problem solving, Americans still desire two things beyond the reach of governments of the past: gratitude from those they help and an end to tension.

Whatever the often-conflicting currents that have dominated the dramatic events of foreign affairs, most Americans have worked out their lives in a web of customs and circumstances concerning economics, or "making a living" in popular parlance. The same tensions and needs for balanced interests that informed politics or diplomacy have molded much of the American economic experience. Since the seventeenth and eighteenth centuries increasing technology and industrialism have offered people an ever-expanding view of personal security and affluence. This process was bound to affect America deeply, given its abundance of natural resources and insistence on the merits of individual enrichment. De Tocqueville shrewdly perceived that economics would loom large in American history and would take form under the impact of the people's inherited idealism about material progress. He knew that most Americans admired bigness yet suspected monopoly and believed that every man deserved a chance, but not at the expense of similar men. And he perceived that, for all its vigor and innovativeness, the economic process would be an essentially conservative force in American history:

The passions that stir Americans most deeply are commercial and not political ones, or rather they carry the trader's habits over into the business of politics. They like order, without which affairs do not prosper, and they set an especial value in regularity of mores, which are the foundation of a sound business; they prefer the good sense which creates fortunes to the genius which often dissipates them; their minds, accustomed to definite calculations, are frightened by general ideas; and they hold practice in greater honor than theory.[12]

The American ideal in general insisted that men *do* things; the egalitarian ethic demanded that society *reward* doing as

an expression of individual merit outside a hierarchical social order. In a country so wealthy, building productive businesses and making things were bound to become more generally popular than systematic and analytical thinking.

The process of developing the American economy reflected the need for harmony within society as a whole. As in politics, economics was a sphere of life whose results had effects that could be criticized, attacked, and altered in public action. In the largest sense, the whole thrust of American economic development has been the effort to find a balance between a centralist, or Hamiltonian, ethic that relied on mass and efficiency and a Jeffersonian rhetoric that emphasized individual freedom, equality, and small operations. This tension was a rising curve in early American history, once commercialism and manufacturing enterprises had eroded social arrangements that depended upon agrarian life. The process was no less striking in the South than in the North or West, for much of cotton culture and slave economics in general was mechanized. By 1860 the South depended upon world as well as local markets, tastes, and needs that the centralizing forces of industrialism had transformed.

Throughout American history the central government sought to balance economic growth in the various sections of the country to make the whole stronger than the sum of its parts and to ensure that no part fell far behind in the "modernization" process. The federal government thus underwrote transportation systems designed to promote sectional cooperation and economic interdependence. It also lavished money on roads, ports, levees, and other facilities basic to a national economy. By 1900 those efforts had created at least the outline of an interdependent system into which new industrial techniques and popular demands for affluence could easily flow without destroying the nation's inherited ethics or actual viability.

Industrialism and the social changes that followed in its wake profoundly altered every society it touched in the nineteenth century. But these shocks were probably less severe in the United States than elsewhere, partly because American optimism, openness to innovation, pragmatism, and interest in science softened the process.

But the new industrial United States did not escape stresses and strains any more than did older countries. Americans reflexively supported something called "free enterprise," not as an economic system but as part of an attitude toward life that emphasized productivity, individual mobility, and expansion. The rapid industrial growth of the post–Civil War era challenged the ironies implicit in the inherited belief that wealth need not necessarily undo freedom.

These ironies were most evident in the realm of public policy, where people talked blithely of rugged individualism while subsidizing and protecting every nascent industrial activity. Heavy industry benefited from high tariff protection after 1789 and especially after 1862. Governments at all levels eagerly sought to ease the paths of railroad, mining, and agrarian enterprises. Government-protected patent rights became the source of many fortunes; public-supported education created experts for the new economy. Minimal taxation allowed the formation through profits and savings of large capital sums for investment and diversification. In the twentieth century government spending developed an interstate highway system and subsidized the aircraft industry. Less overtly but with equal economic benefit, it vastly increased the educationad system and channeled billions of new dollars into the economy through welfare systems. Military expenditures, of course, became a legendary source of both economic growth and waste. Whatever the rhetoric, there was never a "free-enterprise" system in the United States. Government aid in some form hastened and supported the development of every major sector of the economy.

These economic processes have periodically introduced profound uneasiness in the American people. Some men inevitably have been left behind or made envious. Other powerful spokesmen, such as the Populists of the 1890's, have chafed under what they considered distant and impersonal controls that weakened their sectional prosperity. During periods of depression or stagnation, as in the 1890's and 1930's, many people questioned the system's operations, and occasionally its basic wisdom.

Yet the thrust of American economic policy has been toward solving perceived inequities in the inherited system rather than replacing it. In doing so, politicians and special-interest groups have often engaged the unconscious ironies that underlie the American experience. They have regulated to save competition, have opposed bigness while seeking its efficiencies, and have sought to make a highly complex and interdependent economic system responsive to personal whims and demands.

In many ways, concern about the economic order reached its peak in the late nineteenth century. The desire of laborers to counterbalance corporate power with unions was probably the crucial event in solidifying general acceptance of the economic order, since it thwarted the rise of an alternative political ethic to oppose industrialism and its social impacts. The election of 1896, which signaled the supremacy of the proindustrial Republican party for a generation, confirmed the desire of most Americans to retain the new order with suitable modifications to alleviate tensions. The election of 1932, which inaugurated the New Deal, and successive palliative reforms reconfirmed that belief, as reformers opted to save rather than replace the system.

Now, nearly a century after the first great contests over the directions of the industrial-technological society, the country is embroiled in another set of long-term economic problems that will have profound effects on the society as a whole. The responses to them are rooted in human and emotional attitudes, quite as much as they are in economics or material self-interest. Americans have historically viewed work as a meaningful exercise for the individual as well as for society, as a form of self-expression meriting social reward whether in increased income or higher status. They have believed that progress comes from the clash of individuals, whose labors and ideas, even if unwittingly, create both growth and stability. That idea may be waning in the latter part of the twentieth century, as more and more people at all levels of society rebel against unsatisfying labor and become skeptical about the general direction of society. In individual

terms the attitude is symbolized in what one worker told an interviewer: "I believe we'd be a lot better off if people got paid for what they want to do. You would certainly get a bigger contribution from the individual. I think it would make for exciting change. It'd be great."[13] Whether any society can meet the rising demands for meaningful work is an open question. Whatever the solution, the demands attest to the great hopes Americans have attached to labor and economic productivity as a social process and as forms of self-expression. But widespread dissatisfaction with work may be a way of expressing disaffection about inherited ideals, bearing the threat of exposing the old national tendencies to dissolution unless they are satisfied.

The search for cultural outlets for self-expression broader and more lasting than individual action in the marketplace has concerned many Americans. The Founding Fathers, whether as politicians or as Enlightenment men committed to a world view, believed that their new republic would and should become an example for mankind in things of the mind as well as of the market. Colonial culture had produced some artifacts and ideas unique to the New World situation. But most of the overt aspects of culture—painting, literature, music—remained patterned on Continental and especially British models. In the eighteenth century many artists, such as John S. Copley, consciously sought to infuse inherited forms with whatever new qualities there were in the American situation. That search for both the unique aspects of national life and the larger verities it might illuminate remained the dominant theme in American cultural pursuits, whether in portraiture or in the novel.

American intellectuals and artists were acutely conscious of the need to demonstrate the cultural vitality in their democratic and pluralistic society. Like many statesmen, they wanted the Old World to see and admit that their society meant more than money or worldly power. Individualism and democracy could foster the arts as much as aristocracies and monarchies had. The City upon a Hill, which America was and must remain in that view, needed parlors as well as kitchens, studios and granaries, museums to complement factories, and a public consciousness of man's creative side to match its love of his material side.

The role of painter, writer, or philosopher was never easy in a turbulent and irreverent society that prized visible saints, whether in church or in the marketplace. The American people seldom if ever conceived of systematic thinking, painting, or writing as forms of action and have not rewarded them as readily or fully as similar activities in industry and politics. The fact that thinking may produce more social change than moneymaking escapes them. Intellectuals have thus tended to spend more energy defining their place in society than producing thought.

Creative artists, especially in literature and painting, have generally performed while feeling alienated from society. Painters have developed a double tradition, of trying to set their work in a cosmopolitan setting apart from nationalism or of trying to emphasize the allegedly unique "American" qualities of their subject matter. In painting this has led to parallel emphases on realism and on abstraction. Realism, whether that of Winslow Homer or Andrew Wyeth, rests on the tacit assumption that both the American scene and the angle of vision are unique. The parallel tendency toward abstractionism, whether in late-nineteenth-century impressionism or the forms of Jackson Pollock and Mark Rothko, is in some degree a way of emphasizing supranational aspects of both the subject matter and the form of painting. Similar tendencies have infused American poetry, the novel, and drama. Like Americans in other pursuits creative persons have alternated among the desires to reshape the world in American images or avoid the "Old World" or to join a stable, comforting, inherited world culture. Above all, Americans have been suspicious of aristocratic tendencies in the arts and culture. Artists have often tried to define a special role in society at large as well as in their art form without becoming elitists lacking an audience. The arts, like politics or economics, have faithfully reflected the tensions between old and new, central and peripheral, unity and diversity basic to an understanding of American life.

Concern for developing general culture through education designed to meet broad social, economic, and political needs has been a major factor in American history. Like the institutions it serves, the educational system has reflected the tensions and ambitions in American culture. The first colonists desired learning chiefly as an adjunct to religion, to ensure literate clergy and congregations. Yet education quickly became identified with good citizenship and then as an avenue of economic and social advancement with almost endless promises. In due course, in the wake of the industrialism and immigration that transformed American life after the Civil War, the school system steadily took over many functions previously intended for older institutions, such as the home and family. Its original mission was to promote literacy and inquiry as the adjuncts of the curious or troubled mind. Its secondary but steadily expanding missions have involved accommodation, standardization, and harmonizing of an increasing student population.

The educational process also took on certain tones and aims of special importance to a democratic society. As fortunes grew, it became an avenue for philanthropic expression, where successful men might help others, immortalize themselves, or contribute something to social growth. Education promised to expand culture and elevate general taste in a society that lacked the directions and patronage of academies or aristocracies. The people emerging from the educational system were presumably committed to culture, to expanding knowledge, to social efficiency, and to democratic processes.

So much for theory. In fact, of course, education was no better than the people who shaped it or the aspirations it enfolded. Democracy has always been inclined to eclecticism, whether in politics or architecture, since established standards smacked of overweening authority. And education, whether at kindergarten or university level, soon resembled a patchwork quilt rather than a single-hued blanket. In the nineteenth century spokesmen and innovators in the educational process gradually widened the range of subjects in the school curriculum, trying to retain a core of knowledge while offering training suited to expanding industrial life.

As in politics and economics, local pressures and differing idealisms warred for control of education, attesting again to the great faith Americans placed in the power of the system to form and direct the youths who passed through it. Until the early nineteenth century most elementary schooling rested on rote teaching of the three R's with perhaps a seasoning of history and geography. The college level emphasized curricula inherited from the ancients and more recently from the British.

The demands for expertise, together with the growing possibilities for individual enrichment that accompanied industrialization after the Civil War, altered this approach. Education for the masses underwent many liberalizing changes, and the "higher learning" was transformed in a generation from the old collegiate plan to a new university ideal based on world rather than parochial models. Many of the changes, especially in professional training, rested on innovations imported from Germany, Austria, France, and Italy. But the educational system continued to reflect the facts of American society. Its basic dilemma remained how to inculcate a general standard of citizenship and of expectations in all its students, without creating class animosities, suppressing eccentric individuality, or exposing the central tensions in national life.

No American institution, except perhaps politics, bore so many expectations or faced so many impossible tasks as education. Nor was public interest in education always selfless. Many parents obviously expected to work out their own ambitions or frustrations through improved careers and social status for their children. Interest groups, business in particular, obviously wanted society to support expensive special education for future employees. Religious and ethnic groups vied for recognition in shaping the curricula to their tastes. And educationists themselves quarreled vigorously about social theory, while establishing routes of professional advancement.

Sectional and social tensions were also obvious in the educational system. Foremost among them was probably the struggle for supremacy between agrarian and industrial needs. A farm spokesman said in 1901:

Grammar, history, geography are bundles of abstractions, while the child is interested in the world of realities. Rotation of crops is as inspiring as the position of the preposition; the fertilization of apples and corn as interesting as the location of cities and the course of rivers; the economy of the horse and cow and sheep as close to life as the duties of the President and the causes of the Revolutionary War.[14]

What such a prescription might mean to a child in Brooklyn was unstated. Such attitudes forcibly revealed the tenacity of agrarian ideals in American life.

The growing educational system also revealed in its form the popularity of demands that local control determine the content and aim of education, despite education's theoretical ambitions to meet and solve new national questions. Just as the electorate opposed a national police force, so they rejected a centralized educational system, such as the Napoleonic model. Funding, curriculum, standards of performance remained rooted in local custom and demands, even as the new university system produced teachers at all levels oriented to national and international standards. The federal government played no serious role in education until well into the twentieth century, and until recently was confined to granting funds to local systems.

The content of the American educational system puzzled foreign observers. Early in the nineteenth century one of Horace Mann's revolutionary suggestions was that children learned better in groups than as individuals. That was one step in the growing belief that for most students interpersonal relations were more important than abstract knowledge. This ideal, which steadily gained support among educationists, inevitably shifted the thrust of education from personal fulfillment and individual enrichment to concern for social harmony at the expense of specific knowledge. American education tended to emphasize the development of a reasonable well informed citizenry rather than the enlightened or inquisitive individual. It reflected devotion to utilitarianism, to "getting along" with one's fellows while pursuing one's special skills. It also revealed the nineteenth-century reformers' success at overthrowing education for social or gentlemanly elites. De Tocqueville saw this broad trend developing early in many aspects of democratic life:

In aristocracies every man has but one sole aim which he constantly pursues; but man in democracies has a more complicated existence; it is the exception if one man's mind is not concerned with several aims at the same time, and these aims are often very diverse. Unable to be an expert in all, a man easily becomes satisfied with half-baked notions.

In a democracy, if necessity does not urge a man to action, longing will do so, for he sees that none of the good things around him are completely beyond his reach. Therefore he does everything in a hurry, is always satisfied with 'more or less,' and never stops for more than one moment to consider each thing he does.

His curiosity is both insatiable and satisfied cheaply, for he is more bent on knowing a lot quickly than on knowing anything well.

He hardly has the time, and soon he loses the taste, for going deeply into anything.[15]

He might have added that optimism about change, which usually equaled progress in the American mind, made most Americans skeptical of received wisdom and ready to replace it with something better in due course. Hence an impatience with codified systems of thought, or concern for details, which soon might be outmoded.

Exceptions to these attitudes evolved in the professional schools, established after the Civil War, and in the general renovation of higher education in the same period, which marked the nation's growing sophistication and developing ties with the rest of the world. Until after World War II only a small percentage of young people went to college; a still smaller percentage went on to schools of law, medicine, education, or science. The system of instruction quickly passed into the hands of professionals committed to both expert knowledge of specific subjects and general cultural values. But the society at large, which paid the bills and received the product, always remained skeptical of the elitist tendencies of college education, especially in humanities and arts. Social needs for experts generally suppressed these doubts, as did the obvious material and social success of college graduates over periods of time. Yet public irritability with higher education often became vocal.[16]

The excessive faith in education as a solution for specific social ills probably dated from the turn of the twentieth century. Urbanization, the decline of religion, the rise of skeptical scientism, and the immigration of millions of Europeans to the United States combined with industrial wealth to increase the demands placed upon schooling. The school became the focus of reformers who wanted it to supplement the family or church in teaching the virtues of rationality and orderly thought. It became the hope of many who wished to develop awareness of social injustice, as well as solutions for social problems, through broader education. And many other people frankly wanted to use the school system to "Americanize" the immigrants. Education would somehow thus provide the means of ensuring growth and innovation without threatening order and the inherited social system. Such demands and expectations were placed on no other sector of American life, not even politics.

Educationists took up the challenge enthusiastically and steadily expanded the system's coverage of knowledge and of the students it enrolled and retained in classes. The optimistic view of education's role remained dominant until the 1950's, when parents and critical experts began questioning the soundness of public education. In the 1960's higher education in particular became embroiled in such emotion-charged and generally unpopular nonacademic issues as the Vietnam War and social problems. These issues and the enormous costs of modern education turned many Americans against the continuing experiment with education as a cure for man's ills.

The debate over the general purposes of education, despite all the new theories of instruction or changes of curriculum, has not changed much in the past hundred years. The basic tensions still involve parochial versus cosmopolitan ideals; pure knowledge versus applied skills; and individual enrichment versus social needs, as well as the problem of who is to define those needs. The solutions at hand remain unappetizing or at least filled with potential conflicts. Is the idea of education as the handmaiden of leisure and culture inferior to demands for narrowly trained experts? Will this specialization in turn jeopardize fresh thinking and innovation in the social system? As growth slows in the near future, can societies afford to educate everyone? Is it reasonable to expect society to support the diffuse ideal of interpersonal socialization over the ability to read, do arithmetic, and recall when Christopher Columbus discovered America? As the ties and appeals of family life, religion, and work decline, should schools "socialize" students with some kind of broad ethic even at the expense of teaching specific skills?

These are old questions, cutting to the heart of American expectations and ambitions. Answers remain easier than solutions. But if the growth rate of the world economy slows, as seems inevitable, and if population does not decline dramatically in the next generation, which seems doubtful, education will have to emphasize specific talents needed for planned growth and survival at the expense of "socialization." This is especially true of that "socialization" oriented toward ideals of affluence and leisure that cannot be fulfilled.

The twin ideals of affluence and leisure, so heavily emphasized throughout American history, are at the center of the debate over "environmentalism" that has come to the fore since 1960. Little is new in this discussion, except the impact on the public mind of thinking about the environment and ecology. The direst warnings have rapidly been accepted as at least possible if not probable. The solution of even minimal environmental problems will involve the rearrangement, and perhaps the abandonment, of many aspects of the inherited American ethic and ideal.

For Americans the heart of environmental problems involves their ambivalent attitudes toward nature. Older cultures have learned to live with both short-term and long-term natural processes, accommodate to natural rhythms and their inherent disappointments, and accept nature's processes with resignation or rejoicing.[17] But Americans have assumed that man's reason and energy could combine with science and technology to eliminate nature's detrimental workings, to control her disasters, and to use her secrets to enrich human life. This was part of their confidence in a special providence relating to the New World. At the same time, they have desired to preserve wilderness, and to establish parks, remaining torn between a desire to dominate and at the same time be a part of natural processes.[18]

Pouring across a fresh continent, armed with optimistic attitudes toward progress and man's ability, Americans steadily eroded nature's rule. Forests fell before the woodsman's ax, whether to provide lumber or to open the land to farming. Animals were slaughtered on a vast scale, and survivors were crowded onto preserves. Mining was an especially ruthless enterprise throughout American history, leaving permanent scars on the land and the people involved in it. Riverways were altered to suit industrial needs. People crowded into cities, and by the late nineteenth century their personal as well as economic activities had created a whole range of unprecedented environmental and ecological problems.

Most observers saw these problems as specific difficulties that science and technology could solve or at least manage. The ever-growing need for water for both individual and industrial purposes, for example, could be met with a lavish system of dams, conduits, and channeled stream beds, bearing water from regions that did not need it to regions that did. Few people asked about the ultimate uses of the water, the effects these rearrangements of nature had on the ecosystem, or the problems that ever-expanding urban or agricultural needs posed for future water supply.

The same attitudes generally prevailed toward air pollution. By the end of the nineteenth century every industrial city wore a mantle of grime, resulting chiefly from the burning of soft coal in both homes and factories. Yet that cheap energy could not be disavowed lightly, whatever its ill effects, for it underlay prosperity. The smoky town was a busy town; the belching chimney signaled good times. Gas and oil were not yet available to replace coal. Some progress was made in abating the "smoke nuisance," but reform measures were chiefly aimed at reducing its color and ash content. Only a few experts realized that invisible gases were more dangerous than the soot that outraged housewives in their battle for cleanliness.

Until recently population growth, the basic problem confronting mankind in modern times, went unchallenged. As so often in American culture, size was equated with strength, and the large family remained in vogue well into the twentieth century. President Theodore Roosevelt devised special awards for parents of large families. Many Europeans, especially the French, worried about "race suicide," as the nineteenth-century birthrate stabilized in older countries in the throes of industrialization. The world food supply seemed limitless. Nineteenth-century farmers complained of overproduction and welcomed the expanding markets in the form of a growing population. Given the size and the natural wealth of the United States, few critics warned of overpopulation or of its attendant problems, such as crowding and regimentation.

These impacts on the environment, so often seen as "growth" or "progress" with manageable side effects, did not go entirely unchallenged. City reformers cleaned up a good many slums, eradicated or controlled disease, purified water and milk. At the turn of the century militant reformers insisted on preserving some wilderness areas from "progress." An occasional educator or a popular scientist like the geologist Nathaniel Shaler warned of the ill effects of destroying wildlife. "Each of these kinds we destroy is absolutely irreplaceable," Shaler warned. He thought it a part of American uniqueness and liberalism to abandon

the childish notion that the marvellous life of this world is fitly to be taken as a toy for man, to be carelessly rent away with his plow, or slain for his diversion. This establishment of a truly civilized state of mind, as regards man's duty by those creatures of all degree who share life with him, is the necessary foundation for such conduct as will keep our race and time from shame in the ages to come.[19]

Most such appeals were couched in moralistic or ethical terms, and the people had no comprehension of the ecological balances involved in altering nature to suit man's immediate needs.

A number of scientific breakthroughs and social demands fueled this progressive invasion of nature's processes. As in most environmental matters they often had ironic overtones and results. The appeals of the automobile were obvious. It almost ideally suited the American's deep-seated desire for personal control over his life, for expressing individuality through elaborate possessions, and for motion. It also promised to shorten the distance between country and city, to speed communication, and to cheapen the costs of transporting goods and people. But the main attractions of the internal combustion engine were environmental: it would end dependence on the horse. The age of manure, flies, and equine maintenance was over. The automobile, bus, and subway were thus ways of cleaning up American cities, of lessening the threat of disease, and of ending dependence on horse power, which was both expensive and uncertain.[20] Few experts or social critics warned of the new forms of pollution introduced by the automobile, of the vast public expense necessary to maintain roadways and bridges, or of the imbalances in the national economy resulting from emphasizing automobile production.

Similar ironies infused demands for new fuels. Coal was cumbersome to handle and noxious when burned. In due course both industry and householders switched to fuel oils and natural gas as they became inexpensive. Visible pollutants thus declined, to be replaced by invisible pollutants. The fuels remained cheap, which encouraged waste. The twentieth century also witnessed a rapid new emphasis on electricity, the energy of the future—clean, safe, efficient. But most electricity came from burning fossil fuels, which polluted the air and wasted much energy in conversion and transmission. Trapping water to generate electricity also affected the environment. New lakes altered plant and marine life, and the transmission lines that carried electricity to city users changed the landscape through which they passed.

Each success in meeting human demands created larger demands on the environment. A rapidly rising demand for beef, for instance, characterized the twentieth century. Steak was not merely tasty but also a sign of personal prosperity. Thus an enormous quantity of cereals that could have gone into bread went to fattening cattle for a luxury market. Industrial societies promised their members leisure time and mobility, which markedly raised demands for electricity and gasoline and caused gadgets, especially for the home, to proliferate wastefully.

These specific environmental demands and problems reflected a complex body of American ideals and attitudes that rapidly came to characterize advanced industrial countries and "emerging" nations alike in the twentieth century. Foremost among these ideals was the notion of abundance for all rather than for a few, as had characterized previous eras of history. Affluence became an aspect of democracy, modernism, and social justice, which governments everywhere quickly promoted. But the idea of abundance had a special hold on Americans, given their innate natural wealth, varied and skilled population, and high level of economic productivity. To alter the hope of plenty for all meant a fundamental shift away from the democratic ideal.

Americans have also believed fervently in the virtues of innovation, though often in relation to things rather than ideas. Inventiveness and pragmatic experimentation were two indelible aspects of the American character that fascinated foreign visitors. New processes, inventions, and additions to established products and ideas seemed welcome to Americans, whereas many older peoples feared the new as part of the unknown. A thing untried was more likely to be intriguing than threatening to an American. This open minded attitude led to many fruitful innovations but also promoted haste and waste, two major enemies of environmental order. American buildings, for example, were often consciously erected for one generation, on the assumption that new methods of the future would create a demand for better structures. Throwaway automobiles, toasters, or shirts became important parts of modern American life. The waste reflected a belief in the merit of anything "new and improved" and the equally powerful faith that natural resources were limitless and that technology would discover solutions to present problems.

To the average American democratic tone and representative institutions have always involved motion and change, in contrast to older orders in which social stratification has buttressed an accepted equilibrium. The search for self-expression and for equality of whatever kind, usually translated into visible wealth and social status, has thus accentuated growth and consumption. But in an important, if predictable, irony it has also left the lure of success and social status open-ended and continuous, producing an almost permanent dissatisfaction with stages of success among a people believing that all things are possible to him who tries. Enough is thus never enough. Anxieties arise from success as well as from failure.

As the twentieth century draws to a close, amid more doubts about man's condition than have prevailed since the Middle Ages, the inherited American ethic seems remarkably intact. Most Americans remain enamored of change, so often and easily confused with progress, chiefly because it provides novelty in life. At the same time, few Americans wish to de-emphasize individualism or to alter their expansive attitudes toward nature and man. For over two hundred years of independence they have almost consciously refused to develop a tradition and mechanism of social planning suitable to environmental problems. Their leadership, whether in politics, economics, advertising, or consumer consumption, continues to emphasize the attitudes that have produced these problems, and to assure people that they are temporary and soluble through refining the attitudes that have caused them.

America's egalitarian rhetoric and her visible success as an expansive culture have greatly exaggerated the expectations of her people and of much of the world for whom she became an example. The time when de Tocqueville's belief that Americans could correct mistakes and solve new problems is running out: "Therefore the great privilege enjoyed by the Americans is not only to be more enlightened than other nations but also to have the chance to make mistakes that can be retrieved."[21]

Social problems, such as racism, poverty, or environmental damage, have caused more tension in American life than overtly economic or political ones precisely because they lie outside the traditional problem-solving approach. They are continuous and cannot be abolished, like slavery, or managed, like smallpox. They have a compounding quality, as each "solution" put forward produces unforeseen side effects. Any substantial or final solution to them involves altering basic national ideals, demands, customs, and expectations flowing from past experience. This is always an uninviting prospect for politicians and rule makers of all persuasions, who naturally prefer promises to denials.

One hundred years ago the United States celebrated its

first centenary of independence with lavish ceremonies in Philadelphia. The economy was depressed; the echoes of the "southern question" lingered strongly. Both politicians and the public wrestled with concrete issues arising from the abstraction of "industrial change." Yet the birthday celebrations were exactly that—celebrations. Few commentators doubted the vitality or validity of American life as a whole. People still believed in their ability to surmount temporary troubles and to ensure long-term success. The curve of energy rose upward in both popular and expert imaginations.

The celebration of the second centenary of independence will produce much similar rhetoric, but it will not fall on such receptive ears. More than ever before in American history, doubts are widespread about the nation's ability to fulfill its inherited ideals. Prediction is a risky business, and historians are no better prophets than any other experts. But students of the past can at least show the directions and trends. Few turning points in history have actually come suddenly, however unexpected they seem. Every layer of history and life rises on its predecessors in time, just as every day in a man's life reflects all he knew before that dawn. Nations, like people, need accurate memories as precedents and guidelines. Lack of a sense of historical process is one explanation for the American's inability to see warning signs and his refusal to question ideals that may be unattainable.

From its inception the American experiment has been an effort in some degree to overcome history. The "New World" could avoid repeating the mistakes and imbalances its settlers left behind. "From the beginning Americans have been anticipating and projecting a better future," Herbert Croly said in 1909. "From the beginning the land of Democracy has been figured as the Land of Promise."[22] If America was a new dispensation, it had no need of history. Accompanying this sense of uniqueness was equally strong faith in progress, registered in material success, and in the final triumph of man's rationality over the irrationality the Old World represented. Americans thus devoted their energies to constructing a society to promote unity and orderly growth without stifling creativity and hoped to combine personal freedom with at least minimal responsibility for others and the society of which all were composed.

These were formidable tasks. Efforts to pursue them revolved around living with many tensions and ironies in rhetoric and practice, in the hope that time would allow homogenizing processes to triumph over potentially divisive trends.

Those tensions and ironies have reasserted themselves, like neurotic symptoms, just at the point in modern history when technological civilization seemed able to cover them with material well-being. Resolving the dilemmas will severely test every basic American ideal. The ethic of hard work, for instance, cannot in fact overcome either shortages in nature or divisive imbalances in the distribution of wealth and power. The cherished belief in individual action is in large measure responsible for the environmental crises, especially those relating to population growth and consumption of raw materials. The jerry-built system of government has failed to prevent, and is unable to manage, these social crises and must be overhauled. Its new orientation will have to rest on rational planning for minimal needs, regardless of individualistic claims. The greatest single challenge to American ideals is the redefining of equality. Satisfying the ambitions of those so far excluded from these rewards and retaining the support and status of those who now possess them is clearly impossible. Raising well-being for the excluded elements at the expense of affluent groups will not be achieved without destructive tension, and only then at the expense of inherited ideas of merit and reward. Freedom of any kind is the great problem for the future, when an unexpected or eccentric action may threaten entire systems.

Whatever system of ideals arises from the present tendencies will naturally be rooted in past experience. Whether man can alter his aspirations and meet new challenges without repeating old mistakes is open to question. But the questions must be raised, and raised in the full historical context that makes them relevant. Americans will need an altered set of ideals and principles, for unity and hope if for nothing else. Pessimism is now fashionable, just as optimism has been in the past. Both attitudes may conform to the reality of the moment and thus promote reasonably useful guides. As Bernard De Voto reminded readers, the United States is always "a chaos of races, cultures, creeds, traditions, philosophies, political and economic systems that had only once or twice been a nation and then only in periods of danger."[23]

The American experiment continues.

NOTES

1. Frederick Jackson Turner, *The Significance of Sections in American History* (New York: Henry Holt, 1932), 196.

2. Michael Kammen, *People of Paradox* (New York: Alfred Knopf, 1972), 165.

3. Carl Degler, *Out of Our Past* (New York: Harper and Row, 1970), 47.

4. Raoul de Roussy de Sales, *The Making of Yesterday* (New York: Reynal and Hitchcock, 1947), 40–41.

5. J. P. Mayer and Max Lerner (eds.), Alexis de Tocqueville, *Democracy in America* (New York: Harper and Row, 1966), 224.

6. Wilfred Binkley, *American Political Parties* (New York: Alfred Knopf, 2d. ed., 1956), 19.

7. De Tocqueville, *Democracy in America*, 611.

8. Few subjects have been more vividly discussed among historians than the role of minor parties in the American political system. For an often conflicting but stimulating series of discussions

see Roy F. Nichols, *The Invention of American Political Parties* (New York: MacMillan, 1967); Richard Jensen, *The Winning of the Midwest* (Chicago: University of Chicago Press, 1971); H. Wayne Morgan, *From Hayes to McKinley: National Party Politics, 1877–1896* (Syracuse: Syracuse University Press, 1969); Richard Hofstadter, *The Age of Reform* (New York: Alfred Knopf, 1956); David Burner, *The Politics of Provincialism: The Democratic Party in Transition, 1918–1932* (New York: Alfred Knopf, 1968); and David A. Shannon, *The Socialist Party of America* (New York: MacMillan, 1955).

9. Quoted in Binkley, *American Political Parties*, 240.

10. Degler, *Out of Our Past*, 73.

11. Roussy de Sales, *The Making of Yesterday*, 259, diary entry for July 7, 1942.

12. De Tocqueville, *Democracy in America*, 262–63.

13. Studs Terkel, *Working* (New York: Pantheon Books, 1974), 347.

14. Cited in Lawrence Cremin, *The Transformation of the School: Progressivism in American Education, 1876–1957* (New York: Alfred Knopf, 1961), 48.

15. De Tocqueville, *Democracy in America*, 587.

16. See Laurence Veysey, *The Emergence of the Modern American University* (Chicago: University of Chicago Press, 1965), for an analysis of the various tensions in higher education during its reformation in the late nineteenth century. As late as 1914 a major spokesman for agrarian interests criticized the tendency toward intellectual elitism in higher education: "The old idea of culture was to have something the great mass of humanity did not have. Men possessing an understanding of Greek and Latin used to constitute the cultured people. How narrow and selfish was this conception." See Cremin, *Transformation of the School*, 45.

17. For a good cross-section of recent writing on various aspects of the environmental crisis, see Ian G. Barbour (ed.), *Western Man and Environmental Ethics* (Reading, Mass.: Addison-Wesley Publishing Co., 1973).

18. See two works by Roderick Nash, *Wilderness and the American Mind* (New Haven: Yale University Press, 1967); and "The State of Environmental History," in Herbert J. Bass (ed.), *The State of American History* (Chicago: Quadrangle Books, 1970), 249–60. See also Russell B. Nye, *This Almost Chosen People* (East Lansing: Michigan State University Press, 1966), 256–304, for a discussion of the intellectual manifestations of the American view of nature.

19. Nathaniel Southgate Shaler, *Man and the Earth* (Chautauqua, N.Y.: Chautauqua Books, 1905), 208.

20. The automobile's beginnings and social impacts are well presented in James J. Flink, *America Adopts the Automobile, 1895–1910* (Cambridge: Massachusetts Institute of Technology Press, 1970). An early-twentieth-century motorist believed that the automobile offered "the feelings of independence, the freedom from timetables, from fixed and inflexible routes, from the proximity of other human beings than one's chosen companions; the ability to go where and when one wills, to linger and stop where the country is beautiful and the way pleasant, or to rush through unattractive surroundings, to select the best places to sleep and eat; and the satisfaction that comes from a knowledge that one need ask favors or accommodation from no one, or trespass on anybody's property or privacy." Larry McKilwain, "Keeping the Land Yacht Shipshape," *Harper's Weekly*, 53 (January 2, 1909), 10.

21. De Tocqueville, *Democracy in America*, 208.

22. Herbert Croly, *The Promise of American Life* (New York: MacMillan, 1909), 3.

23. Quoted in Wallace Stegner, *The Uneasy Chair: A Biography of Bernard DeVoto* (New York: Doubleday, Inc., 1974), 183. Many of the themes dealt with in this chapter can be pursued in several notable studies: Daniel Boorstin's trilogy, *The Americans*, appeared as *The Colonial Experience* (New York: Random House, 1958); *The National Experience* (New York: Random House, 1965); and *The Democratic Experience* (New York: Random House, 1973). David Potter, *People of Plenty: Abundance and the American Character* (Chicago: University of Chicago Press, 1954), is a classic work. There is much of import in Seymour Martin Lipset, *The First New Nation: The United States in Historical and Comparative Perspective* (New York: Doubleday, Inc., 1963).

2

THE RIGHTS OF MAN: A BICENTENNIAL PERSPECTIVE

By William F. Swindler

Perhaps the most enduring contribution of the movement for American independence was its articulation of a twofold principle of political theory: the creation and control of government by the governed and the limitation of the power of the state as it affected the rights of individual citizens. The principle was not original with the revolutionaries of 1776; indeed, they insisted that their fundamental quarrel with Great Britain concerned the universality of the "rights of Englishmen" to which they as colonists were entitled. Thus the products of the English Revolution of the seventeenth century were claimed by Americans as their heritage in a New World in a new century. The universality concept was reasserted in the French Revolution within a generation and became the catchphrase of Latin-American and Continental European revolutions during much of the nineteenth century. It may be suggested that the declarations of rights made by Americans between 1774 and 1776 and again in the Constitution of 1787 and the first ten amendments in 1791 provided the galvanic force for an idea that has dominated western democratic thought to the present.

Theory and practice have been distinguishable, and often apparently incompatible, as the world has moved from 1776 to 1976. The political rights which were analyzed and identified by John Locke, Charles Montesquieu, and Thomas Jefferson by now have merged into a more complex structure of social and economic rights that often confounds jurists if not philosophers. As early as the French Revolution the Anglo-American constitutional propositions were becoming distinguishable from the rationale of revolutions and constitutions in other political systems. As one modern French scholar points out, eighteenth-century Englishmen and Americans spoke in terms of individual liberties defined and exercised by the individual, while the *philosophes* were already thinking in terms of social rights and obligations. It is perhaps more than a coincidence that English and American constitutional language expresses the idea in terms of "bills of rights," while the French (or noncommon law) phrase was "the rights of man and of the citizen."

The international concept of the twentieth century, or more particularly of the world since World War II, has been an amalgam of politico-socioeconomic principles expressed as "human rights" (*Menschenrechte*). The term is collective rather than individualistic, differing both from the Anglo-American eighteenth-century belief in the obligation of government to secure liberties to the subject and citizen and in the French tenet of private freedom balanced by civic duty. Since Englishmen, Americans, and Frenchmen are part of the twentieth-century world—in two global conflicts they helped create it and in the process destroyed all possibility of returning to any prior order—they and all other people have had to come to terms with the proclaimed international principle of human rights, however susceptible of propagandistic variations and definitions that principle may be.

Again, as far as Americans are concerned, it may be more than coincidence—it may, at least, be symbolic of the future state of affairs—that the year 1968, which was designated by the United Nations General Assembly as the International Year of Human Rights, was also the year of the Democratic party fiasco in Chicago and the passion of American politics that continued in cycles of magnifying crises to the Watergate denouements of 1973 and 1974. The democratic propositions of 1774 to 1791 were products of an Enlightenment variously defined by English and European philosophers. The question in 1976 is how those propositions have been or may be affected by the collectivist and revisionist outlooks of contemporary world society.

A TALE OF THREE REVOLUTIONS

Locke and the "Rights of Englishmen"

"Things of this world are in so constant a flux that nothing remains long in the same state," wrote Locke in 1690, reflecting upon a century that had seen one monarch beheaded and another driven from the throne. Yet he concluded, in his *Second Treatise on Civil Government,* that the Glorious Revolution of two years before had re-established a primal truth: governments were created by men who in a "state of nature" were completely free and equal. Therefore, those who created government expected it to serve their wants better than they could be served in the former state. Thus the test of legitimacy of government was its acceptance by the governed:

It being only with an intention in everyone the better to preserve himself, his liberty and property (for no rational creature can be supposed to change his condition with an intention to be worse), the power of the society or the legislature constituted by them can never be supposed to extend farther than the common good.

The English Bill of Rights, accepted by William and Mary in 1688 as a condition of their own accession, in Locke's view thus articulated the fundamental conditions upon which legitimate government rested:

That all and singular the rights and liberties asserted and claimed in the said declaration, are the true, ancient and indubitable rights and liberties of the people of this kingdom, and . . . that all and every the particulars aforesaid shall be firmly and strictly holden and observed, as they are expressed in the said declaration; and all officers and ministers whosoever shall serve their Majesties and their successors according to the same in all times to come.

Neither Locke nor the drafters of the Bill of Rights claimed that they were introducing strange new propositions to political society; on the contrary, they were cited as "ancient and indubitable." At the beginning of the revolutionary century Sir Edward Coke had traced them to the Magna Carta of 1215 (King John's charter) and of 1225 (the reissued and confirmed grant of Henry III). If Coke's finding was gratuitous, at least it had been ratified by the Long Parliament, and the excesses of the Commonwealth itself, resulting in the Restoration's Habeas Corpus Act of 1679, had been taken as corroborating Locke's contention that government could only act "according to discretion for the public good." For the Restoration as for the inglorious Commonwealth, Locke concluded, the manifest fact of "a long train of abuses, prevarications and artifices, all tending the same way," condemned these governments to termination.

"Certain unalienable rights," as the Declaration of 1776 was to call them, were hence under the Lockean thesis the responsibility of legitimate government to preserve. If, as Coke insisted, they could be traced back to the Magna Carta, they were the rights of "free men" as the thirteenth century defined such men (that is, freeholders, or tenants of feudal interests); in 1629, in the Petition of Right, Coke himself identified only the "golden passage" as surviving to modern times:

. . . by the statute called The great charter of the liberties of England, it is declared and enacted, That no freeman may be taken or imprisoned, or be disseised of his freehold or liberties, or his free customs, or be outlawed or exiled, or in any manner destroyed, but by the lawful judgment of his peers, or by the law of the land.

Other particulars among the inalienable rights were those enumerated in the statute of 1689 and echoed in various American charters from the Massachusetts Body of Liberties in 1641 to the state constitutions of the Revolution: renunciation of "the pretended power of suspending of laws, or the execution of laws, . . . without consent of parliament";

the guarantee of the right to assemble and petition the crown for redress of grievances; the prohibition of standing armies in peacetime; the right of free elections; the prohibition of excessive bail or fines; juries and judgments of peers; and frequent legislative sessions by which the majority will could be implemented.

By the end of the English Revolution, therefore, Englishmen everywhere assumed that their constitution guaranteed these things to them. Englishmen in America, who had migrated in successive waves created by the very events of the revolution, shared this assumption. In fact, the year before the accession of William and Mary, William Penn had published a book for his new proprietary entitled *The Excellent Privilege of Liberty & Property; Being the Birth-Right of the Free-born Subjects of England,* in which he recapitulated the rights that "at present they do (or of right as Loyal English Subjects, ought to) enjoy." In 1641 the draftsmen of the Massachusetts Body of Liberties quoted copiously from Coke's works and the Petition of Right; the Connecticut Code of 1650 in turn quoted the Body of Liberties; and in 1683 the New York Charter of Liberties (disallowed by Parliament) did likewise.

Not only historic memory of the circumstances under which their colonies were originally established—frequently by charters setting forth these rights—but the avid reading of the oligarchy of colonial leadership further fortified the assumptions of Englishmen in America. What Locke had written was corroborated (albeit qualified as well) by seventeenth-century French writers—Montesquieu, Voltaire, Jean Jacques Rousseau. As the intellectual forces of the West gradually coalesced into the Enlightenment of the last third of the eighteenth century, leading Whigs at home in England and leading colonists in English America shared the conviction that Locke had interpreted the English Revolution in retrospect as the age of discovery of universal truths of legitimate government.

The Enlightenment and the American Revolution

Jefferson in Virginia, Edmund Burke in England—and Thomas Paine on the hustings and barricades of two continents—took Locke's rationale as the ultimate test of legitimacy in government. For Jefferson it was "self-evident" truth that governments were established essentially to further certain inalienable rights of man. This proposition, in the Declaration of 1776, which Jefferson largely wrote, is the logical extreme of the arguments contained in the declarations of 1774 and 1775, which John Dickinson wrote. The bills of particulars in all three Declarations are essentially the same. For the "Pennsylvania Farmer" in 1774 it was assumed that the British government would ultimately recognize the particulars as the birthright of English subjects and as a matter of constitutional principle would be compelled to redress them. A year later Dickinson reluctantly conceded that when the incumbent government persisted in flouting these rights the subject had the lawful obligation to take up arms to preserve them. It remained for Jefferson in 1776 to carry the principle to its logical extreme: to secure the rights of Englishmen, it was ultimately necessary to "dissolve the political bonds" with England itself.

George Mason saw a declaration of rights as a constitutional concept separate from—indeed, perhaps unrelated to—a legal document framing a plan of government. This intellectual distinction was continued until the Virginia Constitution of 1851, when the two documents were joined into one text. The Massachusetts Constitution of 1780, substantially the work of John Adams, made a similar distinction between a declaration of rights and the frame of government as two parts of the same instrument. The absence of a bill of rights in the Federal Constitution of 1787 led Alexander Hamilton to offer a specific defense. Bills of rights were "stipulations between kings and their subjects," which therefore had "no application to constitutions professedly founded upon the power of the people, and executed by their immediate representatives and servants."

Hamilton's argument did not persuade the majority of Americans who had so recently won a revolution to create a government based on the guarantee of those liberties. The adoption of the federal Bill of Rights thus established as American constitutional theory that this obligation extended to any and all governments. Thus, within the first decade of national history, all American constitutions, state and national, had come to accept the Lockean concept of legitimacy—that the individual citizen had the right to require of government the protection of his individual privileges.

Hamilton had contended that, in essence, the national charter of 1787 had already provided for the fundamental guarantees of the English Constitution, in the preservation of the writ of habeas corpus, the outlawing of bills of attainder, the guarantee of jury trials in criminal cases, and the narrow definition of acts of treason. James Madison, more clearly perceiving the temper of the time, introduced into the First Congress the proposed amendments to accommodate the national desire. Some of the amendments, such as the First Amendment, went notably beyond the English privileges, while others, such as the Fifth, all but recited the "golden passage" from the Magna Carta.

The First Amendment combined provisions for the three media for discussion of the common concerns of the public: the pulpit, the printing press, and open meetings. The phrase "Congress shall make *no* law," as Supreme Court Justice Hugo Black was to insist in the 1950's and 1960's, stated an absolute guarantee; and indeed, in two of the three subject areas it went substantially beyond the English propositions and those of many state constitutions. Congress was prohibited from legislative enactment concerning either "establishment" or "free exercise" of religion, in contrast to the establishmentarianism of the Church of England and the lingering qualifications for dissenters in some of the early state charters. The press-freedom clause was similarly unequivocal; statutory reform of the common law of libel, as a means of effectuating press freedom, began in England only with Fox's Libel Act in 1792. State constitutions divided themselves between those qualifying the guarantee with a recitation of Blackstone's rules on libel and those echoing George Mason's generality that "the freedom of the press

is one of the great bulwarks of liberty, and can never be restrained but by despotick governments."

As for freedom of assembly, the First Amendment stated a fact of pre-Revolutionary colonial political behavior, which conservatives before and after warned against as real or potential "mobocracy." Parliament followed in a few years with Lord Gordon's act. The state constitutions essentially repeated the federal provisions, and it was not until the cold-war tensions of the mid-twentieth century that ideological doubts began to manifest themselves in the extension of rights of assembly to include rights of association and, conversely, when the term "peaceably" came to be equated with "non-violence."

In the Second and Third Amendments the English Constitution was clearly evident. The right to bear arms had been proclaimed, for Protestants, in the 1689 Bill of Rights, as well as in the constitutions of five states. In the gun-control advocacy and rebuttals of the late twentieth century, the Second Amendment has tended to be regarded (as has the First Amendment press-freedom clause) as preserving a personal property right, whereas its public purpose is indicated in the generally overlooked opening clause: ". . . a well-regulated Militia . . . necessary to the security of a free State." The prohibition against quartering of troops, quoted directly from the Petition of Right of 1629, had given the revolutionaries one of their strongest cases of constitutional violation in the quartering acts passed by Parliament in the decade before 1776.

The Fourth, Fifth, and Sixth Amendments formed part of a continuum, to be regarded as "virtually running into each other," as the Supreme Court later put it. Unreasonable searches and seizures, usually carried out under the authority of the general warrant, had been one of the early complaints against the first Stuarts, in 1618. The Fifth Amendment was a paraphrase of both Article 39 of the Magna Carta and of the Massachusetts Body of Liberties of Massachusetts, while the Sixth Amendment was an amalgam of the Constitutions of Delaware, New Hampshire, and Pennsylvania. So also, the Seventh and Eighth Amendments echoed the language of a half-dozen state constitutions.

Four decades later Joseph Story, writing his *Commentaries on the Constitution of the United States* concluded that the English and American insistence upon bills of rights was essential to the effective operation of constitutional government. For, he wrote, whenever "a general power exists, or is granted to a government, which may in its actual exercise or abuse be dangerous to the people, there seems a peculiar propriety in restraining its operations, and in excepting from it some at least of the most mischievous forms, in which it may be likely to be abused." Moreover, he pointed out, "it is not always possible to foresee the extent of the actual reach of certain powers, which are given in general terms."

Thus, in Story's view, the constitutional reform of the common-law, begun in the power struggles of Parliament and James I and given philosophical perspective in the writings of Locke, culminated in the written constitutions and declarations of liberties in the Revolutionary and post-Revolutionary American governments.

The French Restatement: Rights and Duties

The French Revolution, and the varying forms of quasianarchy or political ferment it bequeathed to the generation that followed, offered a substantial qualification to the Jeffersonian proposition that Lockean individualism should be the test of constitutional legitimacy. Both the English and the American revolutions claimed to have redeeming and preserving values that had a long history in England itself; the *ancien régime* in France had never conceded, except among eccentric philosophers, the existence of such values. Individual freedom, as one contemporary writer has put it, is an idea of recent origin in France. The *philosophes* may have shared the convictions of the Enlightenment, but they developed them as domestic theories against a different background of political history. It has been said of Abbé André Morellet, who lived from 1727 to 1819, that he witnessed the disappearance of an entire world between those dates—from the demise of absolute monarchy to the demise of the idea of absolute individualism.

It has also been frequently observed that the *philosophes*—Montesquieu before them, then Voltaire and Rousseau, and, in a secondary sense, Denis Diderot—were essentially skeptics and rationalists, committed to "the critical spirit that treats all positions as tentative." That would lead, with a certain inexorable logic, from the analysis and dissipation of the concept of monarchical absolutism to a similar treatment of individual absolutism by the end of the revolutionary era. "Liberty, fraternity, equality" was ultimately a slogan of interdependence, of rights and duties, that the twentieth century would call collective liberty. Burke himself, writing with second thoughts about the French Revolution, saw the fundamental difference between that revolution and the Anglo-American revolutions as a crisis "not of the affairs of France alone, but of all Europe, perhaps of more than Europe."

The *philosophes* themselves reflected this institutionalized view of rights of the *citizen*—not the *individual*—in the succession of their works. Montesquieu, the earliest, in *L'Esprit des Lois* (1748) emphasized the frame of government, or separation of powers, as the most practical means of guarding against despotism. Voltaire, the middle protagonist in point of time, appealed for a completeness of individual freedom that Locke would have dismissed as a state of nature and others shrugged aside as a form of theoretical anarchy. Rousseau, whose work *Le Contrat Social* completed the triumvirate in 1762, stressed principles that Jefferson echoed: the legitimacy of government measured in proportion to its ability to preserve the rights of the subject; but Rousseau's famous statement, "Man is born free, and everywhere he is in chains," became a Marxian catchphrase within the next century.

The French old order collapsed because it had no persuasive answers to the philosophical critics, no viable alternatives to offer. What the revolutionists proposed, in the Declaration of the Rights of Man and of the Citizen, was something at once more abstract and more categorical than the English and American bills of rights. Obviously, the Virginia Constitution and Declaration of Rights of 1776

offered models of thought and language; the Marquis de Lafayette and Jefferson exchanged drafts of proposed French variants several times. It is not without significance that several collections of the texts of American state constitutions appeared in French in the years between 1776 and 1789. But it is equally significant that the Declaration of 1789, for which counterparts could be cited in many American charters, did not find categorical endorsement in succeeding French constitutions for its Article 16: "No society in which the guarantee of rights is not assured, nor the separation of powers determined, has a [valid] constitution."

The Declaration of 1789 accepted Rousseau's basic premise: All men are born free and equal in legal rights. These rights include, *au fond,* liberty, property, security, and the right of "resistance to oppression." The third article indicates a potential variance from the Anglo-American concept that sovereignty vests in the nation, not in the individual. The fourth and fifth articles seek to return to Voltaire: individual freedom is limited only by the rights of others, and only acts harmful to the social body may lawfully be proscribed. Indeed, the sixth article adds the proposition that laws may only be enacted by the people equitably represented.

The remaining articles in the seventeen original provisions closely resembled Anglo-American statements securing due process, prohibiting ex post facto laws, and asserting freedom of conscience and expression. The policy of public security, Article 12 provided, was to be equitably applied, taxation was to be equitable and determined by representative bodies, all public officers were to be accountable to the electorate, and property was to be protected "as an inviolable and sacred right."

"Since 1789," writes a contemporary English scholar, "Frenchmen have never been able to agree" how far the tenets of the *ancien régime*—"authority, hierarchy and national supremacy"—were to be qualified or supplanted by the revolution's slogans of liberty, equality, and fraternity. From the early nineteenth century and its divisions of ultras, Orleanists, and republicans to the end of the century and its mixture of monarchists, centrists, and radicals, the balance continually vacillated regarding political, economic, and social authority, which meant different things at different times to each of these groups.

Four years after the first publication of the Declaration of the Rights of Man and of the Citizen—in the Constitution of 1793—the propositions in the original document had increased from seventeen to thirty-five. At once more conciliatory and more explicit, the constitutional document in one article or another succeeded essentially in providing the factions of the following century with something to serve their respective purposes. For example:

"Liberty," said the new declaration, "has for its example, nature; for its regulation, justice; for its safeguard, law; its moral limit is in this maxim: *Do not do to another what you do not want done to you.*" With this florid apostrophe in Article 6, the constitution restated the rights of man and citizen in Article 2 as "equality, liberty, security, property;" defined law in Article 4 as "the free and solemn expression of the general will;" and declared in Article 12 that perpetration of "arbitrary acts" was always subject to prosecution.

Thus the declaration of the revolutionary Year I; the next constitution, ratified in Year III, divided the statement of Rousseau's democratic ideals into twenty-two rights and nine duties. The latter sought to revive some of the moral values of earlier times, as witness Article 3: "The obligations of each [citizen] to society consist of defending it, serving it, submitting to its laws, and respecting those who are its agents." Article 5 added: "No one is a good [citizen] if he is not forthrightly and zealously an observer of the laws." Article 9 summed up the matter of duties: "Each citizen owes his services to the fatherland and to the maintenance of liberty, of equality and of property, whenever the law calls upon him to defend them."

By the end of the century, in Year VIII, the consuls of the Republic had promulgated a third constitution, in which the Declaration of Rights and Duties gave way to fourteen articles on "civic rights," which spoke of enforcement of obligation to the state and the suspension of individual guarantees in times of national crisis. In the dozen more constitutions France was to have between 1800 and the Fifth Republic, established in 1958, only the revolutionary document of 1848 and the post-Vichy constitution of 1946 would again speak as categorically for the rights proclaimed to the world in the constitutions of 1789, 1793, and 1795.

THE ORDEALS OF LIBERALISM

Post-Napoleonic Reaction and Reform

Two short-term legacies of the Enlightenment and the Napoleonic conversion of the French Revolution were the so-called congress system of international security and the alternating currents of reform and repression in the internal affairs of Britain and Western European nations. The Congress of Vienna frankly sought the *status quo ante bellum,* and its uncertain plans for enactment encouraged Bonaparte to leave Elba and seek to recapture the populist following of the revolutionary decade. Once the Hundred Days had gone, other congresses sought to complete the work of Vienna, but for another half-dozen years the efforts of Aix-la-Chapelle, Troppeau, and Verona fell equally short of restoring the *ancien régime.*

Translated into domestic constitutional terms, the basic premise of all these congresses was the curtailment of the individual and social rights that had been so fervently asserted in the revolutionary age. Reaction fed, too, upon the general economic decline that followed the Napoleonic Wars. The London riots in Spa Fields in 1816 resulted in the first suspension of habeas corpus since the Puritan Revolution, and was accompanied by a sweeping extension of the sedition statutes of the 1790's. Three years after the riots further radical unrest led Parliament to pass a half-dozen coercive acts. In the France of the restored monarchy, ultra-Royalists set about systematic nullification of the revolutionary propositions of the previous generation, culminating in the Ordi-

nances of July, 1830, which brought Louis Philippe to the throne.

Three decades after the proclamation of the rights of man and citizen, which democratic spokesmen had hailed as the legacy of all Europe, the struggle over the principles represented therein remained confused. In the Low Countries the union of Holland and Belgium attempted by Vienna led to the Belgian Revolution of 1830, and was substantially fomented by the repressive religious laws of the dual monarchy. In Spain the revolt of its New World empire, as well as that of Portugal, was getting under way, while the original hope of the victors in the Peninsular War, for an enlightened regime under the 1812 constitution, faded under the autocracy of Ferdinand VII and the war of succession waged by his brother, Don Carlos. France, after the liberal press law of 1831 spawned a number of radical organs of leftist parties, substituted a stern press-control law in 1835.

Yet in Britain the reaction of the post-Napoleonic decade provided the impetus for the great reforms that began in 1832. The decline of the monarchy—George III having been declared insane and George IV intriguing with his cabinet to obtain a divorce from his queen, Caroline—gave the House of Commons an opportunity for a return to power. The result was a sixteen-year sequence of modernizing legislation, accompanied by the rise of a new industrial power that in both Whig and Tory parties, reduced the influence of the old aristocracy. By the time Victoria came to the throne, broadened suffrage in England, Scotland, and Ireland; abolition of slavery throughout the empire; relatively more humane employee policies effected by the Factory Act; the Poor Laws of 1834 and 1838; and general reforms in municipal government had laid the foundations for economic democracy, and they were foundations strong enough to withstand the violent agitation of the Chartists, who came in at the same time.

The British Reform Act of 1832, as John Stuart Mill was to point out, was far more than a modernizing of parliamentary representation. It awakened the whole kingdom to the fact that governmental and social systems could be altered through the power of majority opinion. Indeed, the 1832 statute was the culmination of a series of legislative efforts which at last prevailed. In the late 1840's, and again in the period from 1867 to 1872, even greater reforms would be accomplished as political leaders rallied public opinion. Electoral reforms opened the way to reform of criminal law and procedure, always a basic standard for identifying the rights of the individual as against the state. Twentieth-century humanists might deprecate the relatively slow and small advances of nineteenth-century Britain, but compared to the conditions on the Continent, still torn between absolutist traditions and the ferment of new social and economic ideas, the advances were noteworthy.

The unique relationship between law and public opinion that developed in nineteenth-century Britain was the subject of a classic study by the distinguished Oxford scholar, A. V. Dicey. Significantly, Dicey identified three currents of public opinion in that century. The first, the period of post-Napoleonic fluctuation between reform and reaction, he called "old Toryism or legislative quiescence." The second period, from the Reform Act of 1832 to 1870, was the age of Benthamite individualism. Finally came the period of collectivism, or sovereign intervention in the interest of equitable opportunities and assurances of essential rights and needs.

Jeremy Bentham—and John Austin in a variant of the same jurisprudential principle—found the test of valid public opinion in utility, or the practical effectiveness of legislative enactments for the benefit of the greatest number. The shift of political power from the aristocracy to the middle classes, made possible by the parliamentary and local-government reforms of 1832 and 1836, in turn made possible the passage of utilitarian statutes aimed at broadening personal liberties and ensuring their protection. As Dicey points out, "The men who guided English legislation for the forty years which followed the great Reform Act, introduced modifications into every branch of the law."

The free-trade concept espoused by the Benthamites had direct benefits for the laboring classes, as statutory restraints on collective bargaining were modified or repealed in laws dating from as early as 1824. The Marriage Act of 1835 and the Divorce Act of 1857 gave the institution of matrimony a predominantly secular, contractual status. New enactments on wills, inheritances, and disposition of property steadily replaced the tenurial concepts dating from feudal times, in a succession of laws that extended into the 1920's. Among the many reforms of tort law—the law of personal and individual wrongs—were Lord Campbell's renowned acts of the late 1840's preserving or creating a right in survivors to recover for their own losses resulting from the wrongful death of a principal and ensuring the right of the press to offer truth as a defense to libel actions.

Individualistic liberalism waned in Britain after the decade of new revolutions and reaction that began on the Continent with the uprisings of 1848. The chain-lightning effect of the outbreaks in France, the old Hapsburg Empire, Italy, and Germany attested to the greatly enhanced speed of ideas and their communication; and the contrast between the retrogressions of the post-Napoleonic age and the age that followed the mid-century revolutions attested even more importantly to the permanence of the idea of the social contract. In Britain liberalism went into a temporary eclipse during the ministries of Lord Darby and Lord Palmerston—yet produced the second great Reform Act, in 1867, a kind of landholders' emancipation. Then came the liberal renaissance under Benjamin Disraeli and William Gladstone, marked by ballot reforms, a modern civil service, broadened public education, and the consolidation of the national courts in the Judicature Act of 1873.

The acceptance by the state of responsibility for social guarantees—a transformation of the social contract from individualism to collectivism—took the form of parliamentary initiative in Britain, at the same time exemplifying some benevolent aspects of the despotism in Continental Europe. In France, Napoleon III gave way in due course to the Third Republic, but in Germany and the Hapsburg Empire the recognition and enforcement of social rights was part of the absolutist administration of the state itself. In either case—industrial democracy or republicanism in Britain and France,

a new authoritarianism in Central Europe—by the last quarter of the nineteenth century the age of individualism had given place to a kind of nationalistic collectivism. The way was already being prepared for the logical next step to be taken in the twentieth century: the attempted substitution of an international collectivism.

Among the first advocates of such collectivism, and one of the most articulate, was Karl Marx, whose analytical description of nineteenth-century industrial society in *Das Kapital* relied heavily upon Hegelian philosophy. Tediously statistical as the summary appendices were, they did not prevent the book from becoming a best seller of sorts in both England and the United States. In Europe the Marxian analysis provoked a series of countertheses devised by John Stuart Mill and Herbert Spencer and the French and German exponents of a historical school of jurisprudence. These writings approached Marxianism obliquely; it was "social Darwinism"—survival of the fittest as a law of nature applied economically as well as genetically—that offered the most direct challenge.

In central Europe and in France to a somewhat lesser degree under the Third Republic the mounting conflict in ideologies was met by progressively more stringent press laws. They reflected a steady decline in enthusiasm for the values identified with the liberal revolutions of the turn of the century and later in 1830 and 1848. The old order might indeed have died in those revolutions, but the remnants survived and reassembled in the vacuum. It would require the global conflicts of the twentieth century to destroy these remnants, and by then the principles of liberalism had also changed definition.

Latin America: Ambivalent Democracy

The unsettling effects of the American and French revolutions, but even more of the Napoleonic disruption of the Continental imperial traditions, were inevitably felt in the Portuguese and Spanish colonies in the New World. Essentially, however, the heritage of the Portuguese and Spanish empires—absolutist and hierarchical—left revolutionary leaders in Latin America with few cultural guidelines for self-government. Like British North America, the newly independent states of Central and South America could claim a common historical background, but there was no Iberian equivalent of the "rights of Englishmen" in which the Americans of 1776 found a rallying point.

José de San Martín and Simón Bolívar might be seen as latter-day counterparts to Adams and Jefferson; but the Adams-Jefferson leadership in the new United States alternated between centralized and decentralized forms of republicanism, while San Martín and Bolívar advocated variant forms of monarchy. In any case, neither of these liberators was destined to see, as Adams and Jefferson saw, a practical testing of their theories of government. The long period of Latin-American wars of independence, from 1809 to 1825, bred a tradition of military authoritarianism that appeared to offer the only practical assurance of stability in the years that followed. This military tradition, moreover, ran parallel to the ecclesiastical authoritarianism that was the most pervasive feature of the former colonial administrations. With a New World population less than half of which was of European background, the constitutional beginnings in the first quarter of the nineteenth century had minimal claims on a past and few certainties for the future in Latin America.

The first generation after independence was almost uniformly a spectacle of disintegration of the first efforts at government. In 1821, Augustín de Iturbide had proclaimed an independent Mexican empire, but two years later it had broken in two, and by 1828 the Central American half had split into five small independent states. Bolívar's dream of a Gran Colombia fell apart in 1830 and was reshaped into Ecuador, Venezuela, and New Granada. In 1835, Andrés Santa Cruz formed a confederation of Peru and Bolivia that lasted only four years. San Martín's Argentine confederation, an outgrowth of the promising union of the Río de la Plata in 1810, was to be torn by seven decades of civil war, beginning with the independence of Paraguay as a buffer state in 1811 to 1813, the separation of Banda Oriental (Uruguay) in 1825, and finally the subjugation of the autonomous government of Buenos Aires in 1880. Linguistically and politically separate, Brazil maintained stability essentially by remaining an empire after its independence from Portugal in 1822 until the end of the reign of Pedro II in 1889, but its claims to be a constitutional monarchy hardly compared with the reality in nineteenth-century Britain.

It was under these heavy handicaps that Latin-American liberalism sought for a foothold. It appeared by the second quarter of the century that the wars on independence had been waged by a domestic hierarchy against an absentee hierarchy; victory in such struggles was not synonymous with democracy. Authoritarianism, whether military or ecclesiastic, was not conducive to vigorous exercise of individual liberties or collective social action. Moreover, such Latin-American reformers as there were saw with misgiving the successive failures of the first revolutions in Continental Europe, while the lack of homogeneity in the new societies—a fractional number of Europeans, an uneasy balance between creoles and mestizos, a vast preponderance of aborigines who neither knew nor cared about Western idealism—made the primacy of individual rights a quixotic concept.

Economic liberalism—specifically, land reform and redistribution—in a feudal society is more meaningful than political or social liberalism, and the successive waves of revolutionaries in most Latin-American nations aimed in this direction. Peonage and slavery and the fiefdoms of local *caudillos* perpetuated the feudal system and retarded the growth of a uniform political standard among the nations. For much of the nineteenth century the efforts of central governments were concentrated upon military subjugation of the autonomous districts within each nation rather than upon formulation of a standard of justice for the inhabitants.

Yet Latin-American leaders were not ignorant of the heritage of the Enlightenment or indifferent to the ultimate values of personal liberty. As one Argentine political historian has written, the opportunity to inculcate such values simply had to wait upon the final evolution of the nation itself. Men like Bartolomé Mitre, Domingo Sarmiento, and Nicolás Avel-laneda shared with Jefferson the zeal for popular education as the foundation stone for democracy. Other Latin-American scholars have pointed out that the written constitutions that periodically appeared, even though honored more often in the breach than in the observance, served to focus popular understanding of the principles of government. After all, the Magna Carta had survived four centuries of reissue and confirmation before the English Revolution finally made it a permanent principle of constitutional rights.

The harsh strictures that nineteenth-century Latin America laid upon political growth were epitomized in the history of Mexico after its initial independence. Under adventurers like Guadalupe Victoria and Antonio López de Santa Anna, it gained little but lost much, in the breaking away of Texas and the taking away of an empire west of Texas by the United States' own march of empire. The nation's pent-up frustrations were idealized by Benito Juárez, who overthrew the kaleidoscope of dictatorships and in 1858 proclaimed the long-sought constitutional regime—only to be driven into exile three years later by a European intervention led by Napoleon III. The puppet government of Maximilian I was eventually eliminated under pressure from the United States, but the opportunity that Juárez had offered was gone. In 1876, Porfirio Díaz began his thirty-five years of dictatorship, and until the revolution of 1911 the concepts of political and civil freedom languished.

The intervention of Napoleon III was only the most overt of a continuing series of efforts by European powers to regain control over the former colonial empire. Repeatedly Spain suggested to Latin Americans the wisdom of uniting themselves—under Spanish hegemony—to deal with the rest of the Old World. In addition, as millions of Italians poured across the south Atlantic into Argentina, Brazil, and other countries, the newly unified kingdom of Italy sought to continue its cultural and political claims on the immigrants. And even as the United States, affirming the Monroe Doctrine with the declaration that it was "virtually sovereign in this hemisphere," offered a tacit protection from a reviving Old World imperialism, many Latin-Americans saw this as a de facto domination by the "giant of the north."

Thus deprived of practical bases for developing stable domestic economies, torn by the recurrent opportunism of local militarists and the sporadic interest in European powers in a revived colonialism, democracy in nineteenth-century Latin America remained an elusive political goal. The intellectual leadership between the two world wars tended toward pessimism, some, like José Ingenieros of Argentina, accepting social Darwinism as the most practical philosophy for such a heterogeneous culture, and others, like Carlos Bunge of Argentina, discerning no systematic progress toward reform except through a variant of the benevolent despotism of Central Europe before 1914.

Laissez Faire and American Liberalism

The Civil War and Reconstruction in the United States produced new constitutional statements on civil liberties and privileges in the Fourteenth and Fifteenth Amendments; but within a decade after adoption of these articles the overriding interest of the nation (or the dominant forces in the nation) directed the general principles of the Fourteenth Amendment away from the social objectives it was aimed at, in favor of the economic demands of free-enterprise capitalism. When in 1873 the Supreme Court in the slaughterhouse cases frankly moved constitutional jurisprudence from the social to the economic interest, the libertarian provisions of the amendment became subordinated and remained so for a half century.

Thus the energies that had been poured into conquering a continent, from the Atlantic Seaboard to the Pacific, had epitomized the ideal of individualism and made the American creed the total freedom of the individual person from government restraints. But even as the ideal crystallized—"rugged individualism," it would be called until, in the economic and social holocaust of the 1930's, any counterview or criticism at first seemed like treason—the "person" to which the guarantees of the Fourteenth Amendment referred was coming to be understood as a "legal person" (corporation). And with the ascendancy of the individual rights of the legal person, the rights themselves were being converted into a private collectivism, the most dramatic form of which became the trust.

In the burgeoning capitalism of the last quarter of the century, the network of railroads began to bind together the enormous geographic expanse of the United States. The trust then proceeded to acquire control over the products of this vast area as they were collected by the railroads and delivered to central points of distribution. The individualists who acquired these controls, the Rockefellers and the Harrimans and the Morgans, saw this development as the culmination of the American ideal. Social critics like Henry Demarest Lloyd saw the process as the ultimate extinction of both the free-enterprise system and political individualism.

The fact was that government was at first ideologically inhibited from seeking to come to grips with the situation as it was developing. Freedom from government had been the political rallying cry of the late eighteenth century; now, in the late nineteenth century, it required time to develop a concept that government itself was the only means of ensuring freedom. Even that early-day activist, Justice John Marshall Harlan, sought to define the freedom that government should guarantee in terms of the political individualism of the Founding Fathers, and only Oliver Wendell Holmes, sitting on the turn-of-the-century Supreme Court, was capable of discerning the collective guarantees of the future. The Fourteenth Amendment, he warned his colleagues in a memorable phrase, did not incorporate Spencer's *Social Statics* into American law.

The fact was that the individual guarantees of the eighteenth century had been defined by and for a population totally changed by the Industrial Revolution and the Civil War. Under the circumstances both legislatures and courts at first were at a loss about how to restate these values in nineteenth-century terms; indeed, as the converted objectives of the Fourteenth Amendment demonstrated, the courts for

the most part were zealous to restate the entire constitutional relationship in favor of laissez-faire economics. The direction thus set would continue until the demonstrated bankruptcy of laissez faire itself, in the coming of the Great Depression.

Thus the ascendancy of "rugged individualism" qua free enterprise continued from the late 1880's to the end of the first New Deal. Combinations in restraint of trade, which the Sherman Act of 1890 sought to control, were tortuously defined (as in the Sugar Trust Case of 1895) to keep them outside the reach of the law. The rights of labor were systematically subordinated to the rights of ownership and management in a long series of decisions from the labor injunction decision *(in re Debs)* in 1896 to the child-labor cases in 1918 and the secondary-boycott decision *(Duplex Printing Company* v. *Deering)* in 1921. And from 1897, when state regulation of the insurance industry was ruled unconstitutional *(Allgeyer* v. *Louisiana)* to 1932, when the state of Oklahoma was denied a power to prevent ruinous competition in a near-bankrupt industry *(New State Ice & Coal Company* v. *Liebman),* the courts consistently denied government the power to try to balance the values in the economy.

In successive waves of frustration had come the Greenback party, the Populists, and the trust busters under Theodore Roosevelt. The widely heralded "New Freedom" of Woodrow Wilson had been short-circuited by the overriding demands of World War I. It was not until laissez faire came to its disastrous end in the early 1930's that the age of private collectivism passed into government control. In the process the liberalism of the Founding Fathers, enunciated in the eighteenth-century Bill of Rights, had to be renewed in the context of a twentieth-century international and interdependent society.

ONE WORLD MALGRÉ LUI

The United Nations and the Universal Declaration

For nearly ninety years—from the Treaty of Paris in 1856 to the Charter of the United Nations in 1945—the society of nations groped for a formula to provide both for collective security and for the collective guarantee of individual rights. In the Treaty of Berlin in 1878, at the first and second Hague conferences of 1899 and 1907, and in the Versailles Treaty, with its Covenant of the League of Nations, in 1919, the search continued. The permanent—but voluntary—International Court of Arbitration was established after the First Hague Conference, and the permanent—but still voluntary—Court of International Justice (the World Court) was added after 1922. The accomplishments of all these multination efforts were modest, to describe them in the most affirmative terms.

Essentially, the problem of collective security and collective protection of human (that is, socio-economic) rights contained inherent contradictions and anomalies. With few conspicuously successful peace-keeping arrangements between a few contiguous nations as examples, there was little reason to expect a worldwide arrangement to succeed within contemporary experience. As for the rights of the individual as a subject of international legislation, the concept flew in the face of traditional international law, a law of *nations*. A few tenuous analogies had been developed in the nineteenth century, but the rights touched upon in these cases—telecommunications, postal services, copyright—were institutionalized forms of individual rights.

While formal international law by definition excluded the individual from its jurisdiction, by the turn of the century scholars of international law were beginning to concede that the treatment of individuals by sovereign states did warrant judicial notice in the world forum. The individual states—which were consistent grandiloquence referred to themselves as "High Contracting Parties"—in many bilateral treaties and multilateral conventions bound themselves to treat each others' nationals according to the same standards that applied to their own nationals. As far as the conventional, or "classical," writers on the subject were concerned, that was the only solution to the problem: the nationals, as individuals, were objects of international law rather than principals. "It is through the medium of their nationality only that individuals can enjoy benefits from the existence of the Law of Nations," wrote Louis Oppenheim in 1912.

To move from this theory to one that accorded the individual both legal standing and a cause of action in an international forum was (and is) a complex process. The concept of joint international responsibility for the treatment of human beings by sovereign states was projected in shocking terms by the discoveries of Nazi atrocities in the concentration camps after World War II. It is significant that the United Nations draft convention outlawing genocide was promulgated in 1948, in the same year as the Universal Declaration of Human Rights. Somewhat anomalously, in view of the ambivalent course of democracy in Latin America already considered, the American Declaration of the Rights and Duties of Man was drafted by the Organization of American States (formerly the Pan-American Union), also in the same year.

The Universal Declaration of Human Rights was the first of a series of related proclamations, protocols, conventions, and rules of procedure that slowly moved from the general to the particular. In 1950 came the European Convention on Human Rights, followed in 1955 by the creation of the Commission and Court on Human Rights. In 1952 the United Nations drafted a convention on the political rights of women. Eight years later came the Declaration on the Granting of Independence to Colonial Countries and Territories, complemented by a 1947 agreement for a trusteeship for New Guinea and one the same year for the Japanese mandated islands.

The decade of the sixties saw a progression of drafts on human rights. A declaration against all forms of racism came in 1963, followed two years later by a convention on the subject and in 1970 by uniform rules of procedure for enforcing the convention. In 1966 came the covenant on economic, social and cultural rights agreed upon by the United Nations Educational, Scientific, and Cultural Organization. It was complemented in the same year by a covenant on civil and political rights. Thus, in the three decades since the United Nations Conference was held in San Francisco, the regime of international law has been virtually inundated by paper instruments undertaking to implement the rights of man.

How effective these instruments have been is another story, not only in terms of practical difficulties entailed in defining general concepts but also in terms of political opportunism in raising issues under them. Sporadic efforts to litigate in domestic courts alleged infractions of this new international law have been rebuffed, at least in the United States. The American Convention on Human Rights of 1969 has not yet been promulgated. Constitutional and political obstacles are considerable; indeed, a characteristic weakness in such (and perhaps in most) international draft instruments is their consistent failure to take into account the domestic realities that stand in the way of implementation.

Against this series of caveats the Universal Declaration of Human Rights remains a development of historic proportions. Time alone will tell whether it represents a turning point. Certainly the proclamation of the subscribers to the European declaration is eloquently representative of the objectives of all recent international efforts in this direction:

We desire a charter of Human Rights guaranteeing liberty of thought, assembly and expression as well as the right to form a political opposition;
We desire a Court of Justice with adequate sanctions for the implementation of this Charter; ...
And pledge ourselves in our homes and in public, in our political and religious life, in our professional and trade union circles, to give our fullest support to all persons and governments working for this lofty cause, which offers the last chance of peace and the one promise of a great future for this generation and those that will succeed it.

The effectiveness of the Universal Declaration of Human Rights may prove to lie in its function as a standard rather than in any attempt to make it self-executing or even to convert it into a convention. In 1971 the secretary-general of the United Nations suggested this: "[T]he use of the Declaration as a yardstick by which to measure the content and standard of observance of human rights; and . . . the reaffirmation of the Declaration and its provisions in a series of other instruments" may eventually make for universal acceptance of the standards.

As of this writing the record of progress has been uneven. The Universal Declaration obviously inspired the American Declaration of 1948 and the European Declaration of 1950. These responses were followed by implementing instruments in the European Commission of 1955 and the Inter-American Commission of 1960, which established fact-finding bodies. The final stage, the establishing of tribunals with enforcement powers, as always has been marked by delay. A European court began sitting in 1959, but an Inter-American court is still only a proposal.

How much such agencies can really achieve is also meaningful only in terms of particular expectations. As one British observer has written:

It must be an inescapable conclusion that the successes of the European Convention have in nearly every case been indirect and the individual has benefited either because of the mere presence of the treaty and its machinery or through the application of someone else in a similar position. . . .

Inter-State petition does not seem to have resulted in much improvement in the rights and freedoms of the individual but has the desired effect of bringing the situation prevailing in a State to the attention of the other European States and the world. One might, however, question whether it should stop there.

Richard Falk has called this the "external constituency" effect, and on the eve of the International Year of Human Rights he added this observation:

It happens to be the case that the status quo *powers, not being able to identify sufficiently with the victims, . . . are also not willing to make the kind of commitment that is needed to make these claims effectively realized, and therefore, it means acquiescing in the suppression of these rights in those countries.*

These are realistic appraisals of the essential problems of international government in general. Moral force is the only weapon in the arsenal of the society of nations, and to the extent that it is used effectively in the media of publicity— as, for example, in *The Yearbook of Human Rights*—the rights of man have been advanced as substantially as it is prudent to expect after two hundred years.

The Letter and Spirit of the Laws

In 1976 the Universal Declaration of Human Rights reflects what the American Declaration of 1776 called "a decent respect to the opinions of mankind," annealed in the horrifying records of the global conflict of the forties, the African ferment of the fifties, and the southeastern Asian experiences of the sixties. If it remains essentially an abstract statement, the possibilities of its eventual implementation or controlling effect may best be envisioned in the following recapitulation and commentary:

THE UNIVERSAL DECLARATION OF HUMAN RIGHTS

Approved by the United Nations General Assembly, December 10, 1948

Whereas *recognition of the inherent dignity and of the equal and inalienable rights of all members of the human family is the foundation of freedom, justice and peace in the world,*

Whereas *disregard and contempt for human rights have resulted in barbarous acts which have outraged the conscience of mankind, and the advent of a world in which human beings shall enjoy freedom of speech and belief and freedom from fear and want has been proclaimed as the highest aspiration of the common people.*

Whereas *it is essential, if man is not to be compelled to have recourse, as a last resort, to rebellion against tyranny and oppression, that human rights should be protected by the rule of law,*

Whereas *it is essential to promote the development of friendly relations between nations,*

Whereas *the peoples of the United Nations have in the Charter reaffirmed their faith in fundamental human rights, in the dignity and worth of the human person and in the equal rights of men and women and have determined to promote social progress and better standards of life in larger freedom,*

Whereas *Member States have pledged themselves to achieve, in co-operation with the United Nations, the promotion of universal respect for and observance of human rights and fundamental freedoms,*

Whereas *a common understanding of these rights and freedoms is of the greatest importance for the full realization of this pledge,*

Now, therefore,

The General Assembly

Proclaims *this Universal Declaration of Human Rights as a common standard of achievement for all peoples and all nations, to the end that every individual and every organ of society, keeping this Declaration constantly in mind, shall strive by teaching and education to promote respect for these rights and freedoms and by progressive measures, national and international, to secure their universal and effective recognition and observance, both among the peoples of Member States themselves and among the peoples of territories under their jurisdiction.*

Article 1. *All human beings are born free and equal in dignity and rights. They are endowed with reason and conscience and should act towards one another in a spirit of brotherhood.*

Article 2. *Everyone is entitled to all the rights and freedoms set forth in this Declaration, without distinction of any kind, such as race, colour, sex, language, religion, political or other opinion, national or social origin, property, birth or other status.*

Furthermore, no distinction shall be made on the basis of the political, jurisdictional or international status of the country or territory to which a person belongs, whether it be independent, trust, non-self-governing or under any other limitation of sovereignty.

Article 3. *Everyone has the right to life, liberty and the security of person.*

Article 4. *No one shall be held in slavery or servitude; slavery and the slave trade shall be prohibited in all their forms.*

Article 5. *No one shall be subjected to torture or to cruel, inhuman or degrading treatment or punishment.*

The opening provisions of the declaration incorporate what

Anglo-American law has asserted as "self-evident" truths, recited in the American Declaration of Independence as a list of grievances because they had not been accepted as "self-evident." The language, in these and most of the articles of the 1948 declaration, is strikingly parallel to the provisions of the French Constitution of 1946. The Fifth Republic, in its 1958 Constitution, followed the practice of earlier nineteenth-century French documents, preferring to treat these as "self-evident" in a more settled society of the post-war years. In this sense, the United Nations declaration is a revolutionary document, and as such the drafters found it necessary to spell out in great detail the particular rights to be guaranteed to members of the human family.

Article 6. *Everyone has the right to recognition everywhere as a person before the law.*

Article 7. *All are equal before the law and are entitled without any discrimination to equal protection of the law. All are entitled to equal protection against any discrimination in violation of this Declaration and against any incitement to such discrimination.*

Article 8. *Everyone has the right to an effective remedy by the competent national tribunals for acts violating the fundamental rights granted him by the constitution or by law.*

Article 9. *No one shall be subjected to arbitrary arrest, detention or exile.*

Article 10. *Everyone is entitled to full equality to a fair and public hearing by an independent and impartial tribunal, in the determination of his rights and obligations and of any criminal charge against him.*

Article 11.-1. *Everyone charged with a penal offence has the right to be presumed innocent until proved guilty according to law in a public trial at which he has had all the guarantees necessary for his defence.*

2. No one shall be held guilty of any penal offence on account of any act or omission which did not constitute a penal offence, under national or international law, at the time when it was committed. Nor shall a heavier penalty be imposed than the one that was applicable at the time the penal offence was committed.

Articles 6 to 11 of the declaration are significant because they project into an international document the fundamental Anglo-American provisions of due process. While the language of several of the clauses is general rather than specific, the provisions taken together represent a major accommodation in the noncommon-law world and have their closest parallels in the English and American Bills of Rights.

Article 12. *No one shall be subjected to arbitrary interference with his privacy, family, home or correspondence, nor to attacks upon his honour and reputation. Everyone has the right to the protection of the law against such interference or attacks.*

Article 13.-1. *Everyone has the right to freedom of movement and residence within the borders of each state.*

2. Everyone has the right to leave any country, including his own, and to return to his country.

Article 14.-1. *Everyone has the right to seek and to enjoy in other countries asylum from persecution.*

2. This right may not be invoked in the case of prosecutions genuinely arising from non-political crimes or from acts contrary to the purposes and principles of the United Nations.

Article 15.-1. *Everyone has the right to a nationality.*

2. No one shall be arbitrarily deprived of his nationality nor denied the right to change his nationality.

Article 16.-1. *Men and women of full age, without any limitation due to race, nationality or religion, have the right to marry and to found a family. They are entitled to equal rights as to marriage, during marriage and at its dissolution.*

2. Marriage shall be entered into only with the free and full consent of the intending spouses.

3. The family is the natural and fundamental group unit of society and is entitled to protection by society and the State.

Article 17.-1. *Everyone has the right to own property alone as well as in association with others.*

2. No one shall be arbitrarily deprived of his property.

Article 18. *Every one has the right to freedom of thought, conscience and religion; this right includes freedom to change his religion or belief, and freedom, either alone or in community with others and in public or private, to manifest his religion or belief in teaching, practice, worship and observance.*

Article 19. *Everyone has the right to freedom of opinion and expression; this right includes freedom to hold opinions without interference and to seek, receive and impart information and ideas through any media and regardless of frontiers.*

Article 20.-1. *Everyone has the right to freedom of peaceful assembly and association.*

2. No one may be compelled to belong to an association.

The third group of articles in the declaration (12 to 20) relate to the traditional personal and political rights of the individual, echoing specific provisions of the American Constitution and comparable passages in the various French declarations of rights. The provisions are expressed in contemporary terms: the right-to-privacy provisions in Article 12, for example, have been considered in American constitutional law only in the past decade (compare Justice William O. Douglas' opinion in *Griswold* v. *Connecticut*), although the words echo Articles 7 and 8 of the French Constitution of 1946. Similarly, Article 14 reiterates the language of Article 6 of the Constitution of the Fourth Republic. Articles 16 and 17 can be compared with Articles 24 and 38 of the French Constitution of 1946. Articles 18 to 20 reflect the propositions in the First Amendment to the American Constitution.

Article 21.-1. *Everyone has the right to take part in the Government of his country, directly or through freely chosen representatives.*

2. Everyone has the right of equal access to public service in his country.

3. The will of the people shall be the basis of the authority of government; this will shall be expressed in periodic and genuine elections which shall be by universal and equal suf-

frage and shall be held by secret vote or by equivalent free voting procedures.

Article 22. Everyone, as a member of society, has the right to social security and is entitled to realization, through national effort and international co-operation and in accordance with the organization and resources of each State, of the economic, social and cultural rights indispensable for his dignity and the free development of his personality.

Article 23.-1. Everyone has the right to work, to free choice of employment, to just and favourable conditions of work and to protection against unemployment.

2. Everyone, without any discrimination, has the right to equal pay for equal work.

3. Everyone who works has the right to just and favourable remuneration insuring for himself and his family an existence worthy of human dignity, and supplemented, if necessary, by other means of social protection.

4. Everyone has the right to form and to join trade unions for the protection of his interests.

Article 24. Everyone has the right to rest and leisure, including reasonable limitation of working hours and periodic holidays with pay.

Article 25.-1. Everyone has the right to a standard of living adequate for the health and well-being of himself and of his family, including food, clothing, housing and medical care and necessary social services, and the right to security in the event of unemployment, sickness, disability, widowhood, old age or other lack of livelihood in circumstances beyond his control.

2. Motherhood and childhood are entitled to special care and assistance. All children, whether born in or out of wedlock, shall enjoy the same social protection.

Article 26.-1. Everyone has the right to education. Education shall be free, at least in the elementary and fundamental stages. Elementary education shall be compulsory. Technical and professional education shall be made generally available and higher education shall be equally accessible to all on the basis of merit.

2. Education shall be directed to the full development of the human personality and to the strengthening of respect for human rights and fundamental freedoms. It shall promote understanding, tolerance and friendship among all nations, racial or religious groups, and shall further the activities of the United Nations for the maintenance of peace.

3. Parents have a prior right to choose the kind of education that shall be given to their children.

Article 27.-1. Everyone has the right freely to participate in the cultural life of the community, to enjoy the arts and to share in scientific advancement and its benefits.

2. Everyone has the right to the protection of the moral and material interests resulting from any scientific, literary or artistic production of which he is the author.

Article 28. Everyone is entitled to a social and international order in which the rights and freedoms set forth in this Declaration can be fully realized.

Article 29.-1. Everyone has duties to the community in which alone the free and full development of his personality is possible.

2. In the exercise of his rights and freedoms, everyone shall be subject only to such limitations as are determined by law solely for the purpose of securing due recognition and respect for the rights and freedoms of others and of meeting the just requirements of morality, public order and the general welfare in a democratic society.

3. These rights and freedoms may in no case be exercised contrary to the purposes and principles of the United Nations.

Article 30. Nothing in this Declaration may be interpreted as implying for any State, group or person any right to engage in any activity or to perform any act aimed at the destruction of any of the rights and freedoms set forth herein.

The final ten articles of the declaration reflect the socio-economic concerns of modern world society and significantly parallel in almost every instance the French Constitution of 1946. Equal opportunity is the recurrent theme—in government employment and government services, in the right to work and to leisure, in social security defined to cover the basic needs of the individual in contemporary industrial society. If these have become "self-evident" truths in English and American law, and thus require no explicit constitutional assurances, the necessity of setting them out in the Universal Declaration suggests the novelty of their character in most parts of the world.

The cumulation of eighteenth-, nineteenth-, and twentieth-century values in the Universal Declaration of Human Rights suggests the rights and duties inherent in world society, which rights and duties are the product of two hundred years of effort.

3

LEGISLATIVE AUTHORITY AND EXECUTIVE LEADERSHIP: A GRUDGING PARTNERSHIP

By Murray Clark Havens

Of all the institutions and processes of American government that have attracted scholarly attention, perhaps none has been examined as intently and as repeatedly as the relations between the executive and legislative branches. Productive of continuing controversy over much of American history, this relationship has been subjected to judgments that have varied dramatically from scholar to scholar, depending on the historical context and on personal predilections. The purpose of this chapter is an examination of the changes that have taken place in executive and legislative roles in two centuries of American history (as well as in several centuries of earlier British and European history). In addition, the possible future direction of executive-legislative conflict and cooperation will be assessed, as well as potential changes in the character of the institutions.

LEGISLATIVE AUTHORITY: THE HISTORICAL TRADITION

The precursors of contemporary legislative institutions are to be found very far back in Western history. There is no reason to try to pin down exact dates; much of the development is lost in the mists of antiquity. There have been many fruitless disputes among scholars, for instance, about the continuity between the ancient tribal council, or *witan*, of the Angles and the Saxons and subsequent parliamentary institutions. The later Curia Regis, or Royal Council, though clearer in its origins and its dimensions, is a far cry from anything we would recognize today as a representative body. Rather than losing ourselves in controversy over the nature and consequences of these institutions or in pointless argument about when the first real English Parliament met, let us simply say that by the thirteenth and fourteenth centuries English monarchs occasionally summoned a so-called parliament to meet at a central location.

These early parliaments bore some resemblance to present-day institutions of the same name, but there were also crucial differences. In addition to the nobles of the realm, two prominent and respected individuals, or "knights," were selected to represent each geographic area. However, only an almost infinitesimal part of the population was eligible to serve in these positions or to play any part in their selection. There was no notion of "parliament" as a continuing body. Parliaments were summoned at highly irregular intervals, usually to confer additional legitimacy on a royal decision to utilize a new source of revenue or, more rarely, on some other kind of policy departure. Once the business for which it had been called was completed, the parliament ceased to exist, and there might be no occasion for the monarch to have recourse to another for many years. In essence, a parliament would meet at the pleasure of the king, only for as long as he pleased, and only to deal with the agenda that he had set before it.

Furthermore, the authority of a parliament was strictly limited, and in any serious sense it had no political power at all. Not only was it restricted to considering the matters set before it by the king but for many centuries it could only say yes to his proposals, the idea that the power to approve a policy initiative carried with it the power to reject that suggestion having yet to become part of the political scene. By modern standards the only purpose of the institution was to ease the political problems of the monarch and his associates, particularly in the matter of revenue. It is easier to collect taxes if it can be claimed that those to be taxed have acquiesced in the levy. But the appearance is not necessarily the fact, and the pressure on members of such a parliament to help extract funds from their perhaps recalcitrant neighbors, once the parliament had voted the new taxes, occasionally led to a curious sort of negative campaigning. The result was that almost no one was anxious to attend a parliament and incur such responsibilities and the concomitant unpopularity back home.

As time passed, however, parliaments began to display signs of exerting, or at least of wanting to exert, some independent authority of their own. There are hints of this in the fifteenth century but far more in the sixteenth century under the Tudor monarchs, especially under Queen Elizabeth I. This development reflected an acceleration in the pace of political change. The Tudors were engaged in the difficult task of trying to transform a feudal society into a nation-state. The agrarian economic base of an earlier England was being modified by the growth of trade and commerce. This change brought the beginnings of a modern middle class into the political sphere, especially in London. The Protestant

Reformation introduced still another axis of political conflict. A previously more or less clear-cut political situation had become highly uncertain.

The Tudor monarchs had a greater variety of possible sources of political support than their predecessors. An able politician could play them off against each other to good effect, and Elizabeth was one of the most astute of political leaders. But more and more frequently it became necessary to appeal for such support, not merely to demand it. Often the focus for such appeals was Parliament, which was meeting more frequently and more regularly. And politically sophisticated leaders in Parliament seized the opportunity to make demands of their own, to bargain with the monarch, negotiating compromises with the queen, in the course of which her requests were modified or parliamentary suggestions were accepted in return for support for her policies.

Though the changes under the Tudors left Parliament with power still substantially inferior to that of the monarch and with no formal constitutional changes to reflect its increased role, Parliament had at least come to expect to be taken into account and to be consulted on some important policy changes, particularly those involving governmental finance. It was the reluctance of the early Stuart monarchs, James I and Charles I, to accept that modification of their relationship to Parliament that led in large part to the constitutional struggle of the seventeenth century. Their stubborn refusal to permit Parliament to play even the limited role it had gained under the Tudors forced the issue. The insistence of Charles I on having either all power or none led to his loss not merely of power but of his head. Out of this conflict came the demand that Parliament not merely be consulted but become the ultimate repository of political authority, that it possess the sovereignty previously held by the monarch.

Unfortunately, though Parliament gained military victory in the civil wars of the 1640's, it proved incapable of providing effective day-to-day political leadership. The problem was seldom that it made the wrong decisions but rather that it was often unable to make any decisions at all or unable to make them promptly enough for the results to produce any benefit. Though his motives, like those of most political leaders, were no doubt mixed, Oliver Cromwell, the great military leader of the parliamentary cause, may have suffered as much from sheer frustration at the failure of Parliament to provide clear-cut policy guidelines as from the ambitious drive for personal political power that is often attributed to him. In any event, he finally acted in as highhanded a fashion as any absolute monarch, sending Parliament home and governing as a military dictator for the remainder of his life.

Cromwell did not, however, deny the constitutional authority of Parliament, merely its ability to exercise that authority in practice. Hence the restoration of the monarchy under Charles II brought Parliament back to a relatively strong position. And when James II began to raise the same issues as Charles I had raised, Parliament acted decisively to drive him into exile, offering the throne to William and Mary of Orange. The sovereignty of Parliament was now fully established. The institution that could execute one king and exile another, deciding on its own authority who should henceforth be king and even whether there should be one, was clearly the ultimate source of authority within the political system. But as experience under Cromwell had demonstrated, the possession of ultimate authority did not guarantee the ability to use that authority effectively for ordinary policy making.

As late as the early eighteenth century policy initiatives continued to come largely from the monarch and from a circle of advisers working closely with the monarch, which came to be referred to as the cabinet. Parliament could reject their proposals and, at least on domestic questions, occasionally did so. As the eighteenth century progressed, the cabinet and its leader, the prime minister, shifted gradually to a posture of responsibility to Parliament, rather than to the monarch. This was partly the result of happenstance, the death of Queen Anne having brought a parliamentary invitation to George, Elector of Hanover, to assume the throne. Since George I was unfamiliar with British politics and did not speak English, his impact on the political process was necessarily more limited than that of his predecessors, and the cabinet and Parliament were left to negotiate policies between them. Not until George III did a member of the House of Hanover come to the throne with background and talents that might have qualified him to play the role of earlier British monarchs—and by then it was no longer feasible for a monarch to do so. The requirement that the cabinet resign if defeated on a parliamentary question of confidence had already been in effect for several decades. While the monarch might still exercise great influence in Parliament, he was forced to do so indirectly, relying on his ability and that of his ministers to act through such political techniques as persuasion, negotiation, and compromise, supplemented by patronage and bribery.

The late eighteenth century was in some aspects the nadir of British parliamentary politics. Corruption was rife, and the Whig and Tory party alignments that had developed from the constitutional conflict of the seventeenth century had become more or less meaningless as that conflict became less and less relevant to contemporary politics. For most political leaders in Parliament politics largely revolved about the prestige and financial rewards of office and the personal opportunities afforded by jobbery and graft. Real political power, the capacity to influence public policies in a meaningful way, was of secondary or no concern. To be sure, there were exceptions, notably in the leadership of William Pitt, Charles Fox, and Edmund Burke, but the over-all record was dismal indeed, and that record had much to do with bringing on the American Revolution and with ensuring the failure of British efforts to put down that first great colonial rebellion.

The principle of parliamentary sovereignty was widely accepted among Americans at the time of the Revolution; indeed, that struggle was misconstrued by many as a continuation of the fight for that principle and against absolute monarchy, though, as we have already seen, that battle had been fought and won a century earlier in Britain. The commitment to legislative dominance and the perception of recent British rule as personal tyranny by George III led directly to the weakness of American executive leadership before 1789. No executive was provided at the national level, and, while there were governors in the various states, the powers of most of them were so limited that their offices might as well have been omitted. Forceful and effective public policies were almost impossible to produce under such circumstances, a weakness that contributed to the demand for drastic overhaul of the political system under a new constitutional structure.

The powers assigned to Congress by the authors of the new Constitution were numerous and potentially broad. If one takes into account the possibility of subsequent expansion through the commerce power, the war powers, the tax power, and the elastic clause, those powers are surely broad enough to permit almost any action for which there might be sufficient public demand. Our seeming national predilection for looking at most questions in terms of constitutional powers and limitations may have caused us to lose sight of far more important questions: Does the possession of sufficient constitutional authority by Congress guarantee effective use of that power to solve national problems and promulgate effective national policies? If we cannot be sure that that will be the case, under what circumstances is Congress likely to act effectively? Given circumstances under which Congress cannot or will not act on critical problems, what alternatives exist, and how safe are those alternatives?

REPRESENTATION AND POLICY MAKING

The British and American examples already cited are by no means the only instances of the failure of representative bodies, functioning on their own, to perform adequately in the determination of public policy. Western Europe offers abundant similar illustrations, with Weimar Germany and France under the Third and Fourth Republics perhaps the most conspicuous. They are not isolated cases but form a consistent pattern, and there are fundamental reasons why we should expect such a pattern, regardless of what country is involved.

Much of the problem stems from fundamental contradictions between the role of representation and the responsibility for policy making. Both are vital in a democracy, and policy making is a necessity in any kind of political system. But the two tasks may not be congenial to each other, especially if they are to be performed by the same institution.

One of these contradictions relates to the size of the body in question. Satisfactory representation demands a relatively large institution, lest important segments of the population be slighted or neglected. Indeed, demands are often heard for further increases in the membership of representative assemblies, especially as populations continue to grow. The smaller the representative body the less representative it must be; the smaller the representative body the greater the variety of interests, opinions, values, and ideas that will receive inadequate representation or none at all. In most legislative bodies at least one house will have several hundred members. Even so, some important groups will almost inevitably be left out.

On the other hand, effective policy making demands that responsibility be vested in one individual or in a fairly small group. Almost anyone with very much experience in committee service is aware of this principle. A committee of three members, given reasonable intelligence, compatible personalities, and good will, can usually reach a decision fairly promptly. Expand the committee to thirty members, and lengthier meetings, and more of them may be necessary before action can be taken. Increase the size of the committee to three hundred members, and it may never be able to reach a decision at all, or the decision may be indefinitely delayed.

Related to the problem of size is the contradiction between deliberation and action. To secure adequacy of representation, not only must all significant parts of the population have spokesmen in the representative body but those spokesmen must in fact speak for their constituents. All the important views must be heard and taken into account. There must be adequate opportunity for the defenders of each position to seek to persuade those on the other side of the validity of that position. In one sense a silent representative is no representative at all, and as long as there is any possibility of bringing those with opposing perspectives and those as yet uncommitted into agreement with one's point of view, the representative is free, indeed obligated, to attempt to persuade them.

Yet the logic of deliberation conflicts with the necessity for action. Not all problems can wait indefinitely. Some cannot wait at all. As a decision is delayed, some of the possible solutions to the problem are foreclosed, and the best option originally available may be one that has been eliminated by institutional procrastination. Worse still, it may turn out that all the viable alternatives have become unavailable or irrelevant so that the problem becomes completely out of control. This is not to suggest that every issue must be dealt with instantly or not at all. In many cases there is no great rush, and further deliberation will be well worth the time devoted to it. But the time dimension does intrude on other occasions, precluding extended discussion if appropriate action is to be taken soon enough to be of benefit.

An extension of the emphasis on deliberation is the doctrine of the concurrent majority enunciated by John C. Calhoun. Calhoun argued that policies should not be established on the basis of numerical majorities alone but should require the consent of all the important elements of the population. Any one of these elements should have an effective veto over new policies or major changes in existing programs. As later analysis will indicate in detail, much of the American constitutional structure reflects this principle. This country stops short of the rule in the former kingdom of Poland, which, with a parliament of several thousand members, required unanimous agreement for any action at all. Needless to say, action was rarely possible. But even in the United States it is usually extremely difficult and sometimes impossible to deal promptly and effectively with urgent and controversial questions of public policy.

A further difficulty with assigning policy-making responsibilities to a representative body is the difficulty of achieving spontaneous action within any large group. Unless interaction takes place—in other words, unless political organization and leadership are present—substantial numbers of individuals do not come at one and the same time to support the same policy or even to consider the same problem. Only very small groups can get along without organized leadership, and even then any given action can usually be traced to the initiative of one person or a few. In the absence of effective leadership a large body becomes chaotic, with no consensus on the problems to be dealt with or the solutions to be employed. A skeptical reluctance to put absolute trust in any set of political leaders is certainly healthy. In a democracy leaders must be kept responsible to the public, accountable for their actions, and aware that they may be replaced at any time. But that is a very different matter from trying to get along without any leaders at all.

The essential democratic principle of majority rule also creates difficulties in policy making. Even those who do not question that principle in general are hard pressed to apply it in practice, and a careful study of important policy decisions often reveals that majority rule has been no more than a convenient fiction. Traditional majoritarian theory argues that, if 51 per cent of the population wants a particular course of action and 49 per cent is opposed, the policy in question should be adopted. So far so good. But that hypothetical situation almost never exists in fact. Instead we find a situation in which 5 per cent of the population (or members of Congress) desire policy A, 4 per cent prefer B, 2 or 3 per cent each are committed to C, D, E, and F, and 80 per cent have never heard of the issue, do not care about it one way or another, or do not know what they want done about it. The simple principle of majority rule does not help in this situation, for there is no real majority. And unfortunately this is a quite typical situation.

What is to be done under these circumstances? If policy decisions are to be forthcoming—and in the long run most major problems have to be dealt with through public policies of one kind or another—the only feasible approach is for political leadership to create a majority where none previously existed. Sometimes this can be done by attracting public attention to the nature and seriousness of the situation, a process of education and propaganda. Even if most people are unwilling to support the proposal advanced, they may eventually become committed to an alternative, and policy making can then proceed. But it may not be possible to convince most people that this particular problem is of any concern to them, or it may not be possible to do so soon enough to permit an adequate solution to the problem.

Political leaders must then have recourse to the creation of a fictitious majority. This may be done by convincing those who support alternative policies that their ideal preferences have no chance of being implemented and that the particular policy being urged is the best that has any chance of being adopted and is better than no policy at all. In addition, political leaders may engage in logrolling, in which they offer their support on other issues more important to those involved in return for the assistance of the latter on the problem. Compromises may make it possible for still others to support the proposed policy. As a result of one or all of these devices, an apparent majority may emerge, even though the policy ultimately decided on may be less than ideal from the perspective of most of the individuals involved—perhaps of all of them.

All in all, any representative body will have difficulties in dealing with the responsibility for policy making. At best it will be able to respond to effective and imaginative leadership, accepting some proposals, rejecting others, accepting still others with modifications. It may also provide useful criticism and demands for policy action. Finally, it may accept some form of ultimate responsibility for control of those who do exercise political leadership. But a representative body cannot govern on its own without organization or leadership.

THE INSTITUTIONAL PROBLEMS OF CONGRESS

In addition to the defects of all representative bodies as policy-making institutions, the United States Congress has a number of unique characteristics that add to its weakness in this respect. Some of these characteristics stem from the basic constitutional structure of the American political system. Others have developed over the years within Congress itself. And some are the result of features of American political culture over which Congress and its members have little direct control but which will inevitably influence the political behavior of the legislators.

Of the cultural influences on Congress one of the more noticeable is the highly parochial nature of American politics, and especially of legislative politics. Only in connection with the presidency do many American voters think and act in terms of truly national issues. Congressional elections tend to turn largely on local questions and problems. Congressmen are usually perceived rather as diplomatic representatives to a wealthy foreign government, from which it is hoped a competent ambassador will extract sufficient amounts of "foreign aid" for the benefit of the region he represents. It is a rare voter who informs himself about the voting records of the members of Congress from his state and district, even on the most important issues. But far more voters know the success or failure of their congressman in obtaining public-works projects for his district, gaining government contracts for firms in his community, locating military installations near his home town, and finding government jobs for his constituents. Such considerations as these primarily determine the success of an incumbent in seeking re-election.

The highly decentralized structure of the American political parties adds to the parochialism of Congress. Except during presidential election campaigns, national parties hardly exist. Only the local party organization can have a significant impact on the congressman's political future. The rise of the direct primary has reduced even this impact, for the local party organization can no longer be assured of determining the party's nominee. Even the congressional election campaigns, in most parts of the country, take place largely outside the party structure, the candidate putting together an ad hoc organization of his personal friends and supporters. This organization may overlap the formal party structure but is never identical with it. The funding of congressional campaigns is also external to the party and largely local, not a matter over which national political institutions have any control.

As long as congressmen are perceived largely in terms of errand running and favor mongering for constituents, they will have little choice but to conform to those expectations. Their political careers depend on it. Some members of Congress, especially some senators, successfully mesh effective care for constituency interests with impressive contributions to the solution of national problems. But it requires rare talents and contributes nothing to the success of the congressman in the profession of politics unless he has his eye on the White House. In any case the local orientation of congressional politics effectively prevents Congress as an institution from accepting responsibility for national policy making. For that matter it prevents it from serving even as a satisfactory representative body with regard to national questions.

The absence of integrated internal leadership in Congress also weakens it in the policy-making realm. That has not always been true, at least in the House of Representatives. For a time the speaker, usually carrying out decisions previously arrived at in the majority-party caucus, could try to assure effective and responsible compliance with public expectations and demands. The work of the celebrated Thomas Reed, Speaker of the House in the 1890's, exemplified this kind of forceful internal congressional leadership. But both decision making in the caucus and the dominance of the Speaker ended early in the twentieth century. For the last half century Congress has been dependent on totally inadequate internal leadership. Though some very able individuals have served in such party leadership positions as Speaker and floor leader, the party as an institution just does not carry sufficient weight in Congress to permit such leaders to provide coherence and disciplined support for legislative policy making. The real power of Congress resides in its committee structure, and there is no mechanism to tie these committees together effectively.

Bicameralism contributes further to the deficiencies of Congress as a central political institution. The United States is virtually the only country that retains two houses with roughly equal powers. Everywhere else the second chamber has been either abolished or reduced drastically in its authority and political power. But in this country, with the necessity for duplicating all the institutions and procedures involved in the legislative process, that process is much more cumbersome than would otherwise be the case. Each house is highly jealous of its prerogatives, resenting any action that makes it appear to be dominated by the other. The formal procedures for coordinating their work tend to be rigid and awkward, and any informal effort by members of one house to encourage action by the other is vociferously rejected. On important matters the two houses are usually brought together, if at all, through the initiative of interest groups or the executive branch.

Various inhibiting rules and procedures add to the complexity of congressional politics. The best known of these rules is the provision for unlimited debate in the United States Senate, which gave rise to the filibuster. That is merely an extreme example of the emphasis on deliberation at the expense of decision that is typical of representative bodies, and in practice it is less important than some of the other obstacles to effective policy making in Congress, but it dramatizes the difficulties facing anyone who demands that Congress accept greater responsibility.

The necessity for extraordinary majorities for many procedures in both houses of Congress is a hindrance to reliance on that institution as a national decision maker. It is difficult enough to persuade 50 per cent of the members of the House or Senate to support a particular bill or even to take an interest in its subject. But when the action desired can be accomplished only through procedures requiring a two-thirds vote or in some cases even a four-fifths vote, the difficulties may well be insuperable.

Still other elements of procedure complicate life for congressmen themselves and make congressional business almost impossible for most outsiders to follow. Only years of experience on Capitol Hill equip one to use House or Senate rules to maximum advantage, and even expert and diligent parliamentarians occasionally become lost in the intricacies of congressional maneuvering.

Perhaps the most important institutional problem of Congress, however, is its committee system. One aspect of that system, the seniority rule, has received a great deal of attention—perhaps too much. It is impossible to justify the seniority rule in theory, and, though it is an exaggeration to call its results government by gerontocracy, it does occasionally elevate to a chairmanship someone who ought to be disqualified by reason of alcoholism, senility, tyrannical disregard of his fellow citizens and even his fellow congressmen, general ineptitude, or sheer stupidity. But these failings are fortunately rare, and the typical chairman is both competent and conscientious. The real problem lies with the committee system itself, and even if the seniority rule were to be abolished altogether, that problem would remain.

The difficulty is that Congress has in effect delegated its powers to its own committees and abdicated its responsibilities in favor of those committees. Committee decisions carry great weight in subsequent deliberations, and negative decisions in committee are almost always decisive and final. A committee can prevent floor consideration of a bill merely by refusing to report on it. Most of the real decisions by Congress are made in committee. As Woodrow Wilson noted in his doctoral dissertation almost a century ago, Congress in formal session is Congress on public exhibition, while Congress in committee is Congress at work.

The problem would be less serious if it were not for the highly unrepresentative character of the committees. Unfortunately, committee members are not a random sample of the membership of Congress. Instead, each congressman gravitates toward the committee or committees in which he has the greatest personal interest or on which he will have the greatest opportunity to provide benefits for his state or district or favors for his constituents. Consequently committee action usually reflects the demands of the interests and geographic locations most directly affected by a given policy and most conspicuously aware of its impact on them rather than the needs and demands of a broader cross section of the public.

The committee system also contributes to the lack of policy integration and coordination in Congress. Each committee is an independent fiefdom, subject to little or no external authority. Since the decline of party leadership and caucus authority there has been no one in Congress capable of forcing committees to work together to produce a coherent set of policies and programs. Instead committees dealing with related subjects are often at cross purposes, producing conflicting and contradictory recommendations that negate each other. As with bicameralism, it requires pressure from outside Congress to produce the coordination of which Congress ought to be capable itself, and that outside pressure is not always available.

The inherent weaknesses of representative bodies and the problems peculiar to the United States Congress combine to produce a strong negative bias in the American legislative process. Those opposed to a particular change in public policy may achieve their victory at any of various points in the process; those favoring the change must prevail at all of them. This proposition is perhaps clearest in respect to committees. A typical policy change will require the concurrence of no less than five standing committees, almost as many subcommittees, and two conference committees before it can be implemented.

Consider a hypothetical proposal to develop a federal research program on alternative energy sources for transportation. Taking into account standing committees alone, the authorizing bill will require the approval of the committees on interstate and foreign commerce of both houses. Even with the approval of the committee in each house, the proposal will not reach the floor of the House of Representatives without clearance from the House Rules Committee. With favorable action by all three of these committees, the original bill may now become law. But by itself the law has no impact, for no funds have been provided to carry it out. For that purpose a separate legislative action is required, necessitating approval by the appropriations committees of both houses. Any one of the five committees mentioned can effectively kill the proposal; only the concurrence of all five can secure the desired change. And no one of these committees has power or authority over any of the others; each is essentially responsible to itself alone. On the whole, Congress is much better designed to defeat legislation than to pass it, to hinder needed policy changes than to achieve them.

LEGISLATIVE IRRESPONSIBILITY

Most Americans have tended to think of the legislative branch as central to our system of government, at least in the determination of public policy. We think of statutes as the natural form for such policies. And we are reluctant to admit that Congress may be incapable of playing this role effectively.

It should be stressed that the legislative irresponsibility discussed here has nothing to do with the qualities of individual congressmen, most of whom are intelligent, con-

scientious, and diligent, doing their jobs as best they can. The problem is not with the unwillingness of individual members to meet their responsibilities but with the way in which Congress as an institution has defined those responsibilities. What gains a congressman respect from his colleagues and approval from the voters back home may not be very useful to the American political system as a whole. It may leave voters pleased with some beneficial local improvements but profoundly frustrated by the failure of adequate national policies to emerge—or dependent on other institutions to formulate such policies.

Much of the problem stems from the absence of focused responsibility for action in the legislative branch. The decentralized committee structure and the lack of disciplined parties and strong party leaders in Congress is one cause of this. But another is the fact that, with 535 members of Congress, no one of them is going to be held accountable for any failure to deal adequately with a problem, no matter how urgent it may be. This is an open invitation to pass along the responsibility. By the nature of their political situation, congressmen are forced to concentrate on shifting the blame for failure rather than on achieving successful policies. The buck may be passed to other congressmen, to the president, the bureaucracy, the judiciary, or the other party. But it is very rare to find a congressman who admits that he is at fault because he could and should have done something about a national problem that has not been solved. It is equally rare to find a congressman who suffers a political penalty because of such failure.

The legislator is held accountable on local problems, of course. He must accept responsibility for those, and woe betide the incumbent who fails to produce results in the form of national assistance; his congressional career will be short. As far as it goes, the role of intermediary between the local community and the national government is a useful contribution. But it leaves Congress in a weakened position in dealing with more general problems, policies, and programs. The centrifugal force of localism rules out the use of Congress as a central institution to integrate national decision making.

Congress has come to concentrate on essentially trivial matters because that is where the political advantage of its members lies and because that is the way in which it can best avoid responsibilities it is not prepared to meet. Its stress is on local legislation, minor legislation, and technical legislation. These are matters on which congressmen have genuine competence and on which they do not usually have to compete for control with other political institutions. Bills that will produce specific benefits for constituencies—often in the form of so-called pork-barrel appropriations—receive careful attention on Capitol Hill. So on occasion do minor and technical attempts to improve various kinds of national programs. Thousands of such bills are introduced in Congress every year. Many of them are passed, often with beneficial and worthwhile results. But measured against the overriding need for policies to meet urgent national problems, this contribution by the legislative branch is insignificant indeed. For solutions to major problems Congress remains dependent on the initiative of the executive branch. In the absence of executive proposals Congress seldom acts about the really crucial problems and almost never acts with effectiveness.

The American political culture contributes further to the weakness of Congress by making a virtue of political independence, lack of organization, and defiance of political leadership. To be sure, this is sometimes very much to the good, for it permits the imposition of controls on corrupt, misguided, or tyrannical leaders that might not otherwise be possible. But it also ensures that Congress will not be able to pull itself together to function as a cohesive institution. A body as large as Congress would have difficulty enough in functioning as a unit if its members were willing to subordinate their individual personalities and interests for the sake of common action. This might be achieved along several organizational lines, though the political party is the most plausible of them. No such unified action is possible, however, as long as most members of Congress perceive their roles in semianarchistic terms, delighting in playing mavericks and in demonstrating that there is no political leader and no organization or set of leaders that can force them to cooperate to deal with public problems. Many congressmen reap political rewards from this behavior, gaining added stature with their constituents by vociferous refusal to work in any sort of common cause with their fellow congressmen or with other political leaders.

A final consideration relates to the stress on negativism discussed earlier. The characteristics of representative institutions in general, the institutional nature of Congress in particular, and the American political culture combine to emphasize the importance of defeating bad legislation, even at the cost of making it difficult or impossible to achieve good policies. The Constitution reflects this orientation, its intricate arrangement of checks and balances adding to the complexity of policy making and increasing the likelihood that any policies that arouse serious controversy will fail to be enacted or implemented.

For some reason many Americans have always assumed that harm results only from bad policies, and they have paid little attention to the evil consequences of taking no action at all to deal with serious problems. Of course, the opposite extreme—the assumption that any action is better than none—is equally dangerous. But in the course of American history the greatest crises and disasters have resulted from the failure to act on urgent problems, not from positive action that turned out to be mistaken. The Civil War ensued after several decades of attempts to ignore or avoid the issue of slavery. But the refusal to come to grips with the issue did not make it go away; it merely made the problem worse and necessitated the greatest of America's national tragedies before a solution could be achieved. Similarly, the refusal to deal with the urgent economic problems of a majority of the population in the 1920's led to the depression of the 1930's, and the failure to act on a progression of international crises contributed to the outbreak of World War II.

When serious problems arise (and it requires glasses of an exceptionally rosy hue to pretend in any society at any time that there are no such problems), the assumption that they will vanish if only no positive blunders are committed, if only

no risk is run of mistaken policies, is extremely dangerous. Indeed it almost inevitably leads to disaster. It is as important to promote effective action to avoid and correct situations that harm large numbers of our citizens as it is to prevent governmental action that may itself lead to such harm.

EXECUTIVE LEADERSHIP:
THE HISTORICAL TRADITION

Though much of the literature on the history of the modern executive branch emphasizes its growth from the background of monarchy, absolute monarchy had a fairly brief history in most of Western Europe and an even shorter one in Britain. During the feudal era, though the monarch's power varied depending on the occupant of the throne, royalty always had to contend for authority with the barons and was usually the loser in such struggles, John and Richard III being the most conspicuous examples. The more-or-less unchallenged authority of the king runs only from Henry VII to Charles I—a little more than a century and a half. After the civil wars of the seventeenth century the power of the monarch was clearly subject to the ultimate authority of Parliament.

With the eighteenth century and the development of the responsible ministry, crown powers were increasingly divorced from the person of the monarch. They were exercised by the prime minister and his colleagues, who were responsible to Parliament and could remain in office only as long as a majority of the House of Commons was willing for them to do so. Ministers were (and are) appointed by the monarch, and the personal preferences of the latter might occasionally have an impact on such choices, depending on the willingness of Parliament to accept the monarch's selection. Parliament could always force the appointment of the individual it preferred by refusing to accept anyone else. Despite Queen Victoria's notorious antipathy toward Gladstone, for example, it was never possible for her to prevent him from serving as prime minister whenever his party gained a majority in the House of Commons.

The shift to parliamentary sovereignty and the responsible ministry produced a peculiar situation at the time of the American Revolution. For propaganda purposes it was desirable to portray the Revolution as a struggle against absolute monarchy, and the supporters of the rebellion included some of the ablest propagandists ever known. In such documents as the Declaration of Independence and the writings of Thomas Paine, George III was cast as scapegoat, being blamed for all the evils of the colonists' plight. In fact, as noted earlier, absolute monarchy had long since passed from the scene in Britain, that conflict having been fought and won a century earlier. The policies against which the American patriots were aroused were in reality the results of decisions made by responsible ministers with the approval of a majority of the members of Parliament; they were not personal decisions by the king. The real complaint of the colonists was not against the form of British rule but against British rule of any kind. There were no longer enough common interests among British subjects on the two sides of the

Atlantic to make possible the indefinite continuation of close political ties. George III had had relatively little to do with the situation.

One of the characteristics of propaganda is that those who produce it may come to believe it along with those to whom it is directed. And a disadvantage of propaganda is that, if it is believed at all, it is likely to be believed not merely during the occasion for which it was produced but for an indefinite time afterward. The consequences of the propaganda of the American Revolution were to have a profound impact on the writing of the Constitution of the United States and on the later development of the American political system.

As a result of the focusing of colonial discontent on the person of George III, during and immediately after the Revolution there was a strong impetus toward reducing executive power. Such national government as existed under the Articles of Confederation had no chief executive at all. Most of the newly organized state governments reduced the office of governor to a position of political impotence. The lack of executive power was accompanied by the lack of effective political action. During the war military leadership, especially in the person of George Washington, was able to step into the gap to a considerable degree. But the conclusion of hostilities left a vacuum of leadership and a failure to deal with many of the urgent problems facing the new nation.

This critical situation led, of course, to the establishment of a new constitutional system. But the authors of the Constitution were ambivalent about the powers of the executive branch. Reluctant to allow the situation to drag along without a serious effort to ameliorate the increasingly pressing problems of the new society, most of them were inclined to experiment with stronger institutions of leadership. They learned, however, that the ways in which they could do so were severely circumscribed by the antimonarchical ideas disseminated at the beginning of the Revolution. Monarchy in any form, no matter how limited and constitutional, was ruled out. But so was a republican executive responsible to the legislative branch, on the ground that it would prove as powerless and ineffective as the state executives with which the authors of the Constitution were familiar. The only alternative was an independently elected executive. To limit the risks inherent in this course, the chief executive was to be elected indirectly by a body specially created for that purpose, the electoral college. That arrangement did not survive in practice for as much as a decade. And the powers of the president were to be restricted in their exercise by a complex system of checks and balances, an arrangement that has survived all too well and has often made effective government all but impossible.

Ambivalence toward executive power continues, not merely in the United States but in many other countries as well. People want their political leaders to be restricted to minimize the amount of harm that can be done if those leaders should turn out to be corrupt, inept, or tyrannical. But those same people, or most of them, also want effective action to solve the problems with which they are unable to contend as individuals. No one has yet discovered a perfect means of achieving both goals at the same time. To accomplish one is to jeopardize the other. Nevertheless, it may be possible to achieve a form of leadership that is consistently effective yet responsible. That possibility will be considered in greater detail later in this chapter.

THE NECESSITY OF EXECUTIVE LEADERSHIP

It has been suggested that the political process rarely functions effectively without an able and vigorous executive. A number of crucial needs in the political system relate to this requirement. One is a symbolic indication of national unity. Conflict exists in any society. There will always be diverse interests and values; there may even be differing ideologies. No two individuals share identical perspectives on all issues. There is nothing wrong with conflict as such; indeed it is natural and inevitable. One of the virtues of democracy is that it permits such conflicts to be expressed openly rather than repressed. But no society can long endure if the relationships among its various parts consist of nothing but conflict or if its citizens have no awareness that they have some interests in common as well as some that divide them.

Various symbols of national unity may be helpful—a common flag, a common language, a national anthem, a crown, important national documents, celebrated incidents in the nation's history, important cultural monuments, and so on. The chief executive can also be useful in this way. This is most obvious in a constitutional monarchy, where pageantry can reinforce the symbolism but where the royal family can remain aloof from most of the conflicts in which the political process abounds. Even in a republic, however, the president can stand for national unity among those who disagree with him as well as among his followers. This is especially true in wartime or other national emergencies. In a democracy, needless to say, acceptance of the chief executive's symbolic role does not imply that he should be free of opposition to the policies he initiates or criticism of the effectiveness with which he carries them out.

Another important role of the chief executive lies in attracting public attention to government and politics. Few people have much intrinsic interest in the political process except when it directly and immediately impinges on their own lives. Even when their own interests are vitally affected, most citizens prefer to ignore the situation until after the fact, when the consequences are most apparent. The vast majority of Americans read the political news—if they read it at all—only after they have scanned items of news that relate more obviously to their lives, and television newscasts attract far less attention than programs of entertainment. The attention attracted to politics because of the citizens' awareness of the president is one of the few means of keeping most of them involved in the governmental process, and a democracy is surely healthier with some public involvement in government than with none at all.

In addition the president may focus attention on particular issues of crucial importance. Can we deal with problems before they become crises and perhaps disasters? Often we cannot unless quite a few citizens and their representatives are made aware of the problems while solutions are still possible. In most countries, including the United States, only the chief executive has the resources of publicity necessary to make the people aware of problems and issues that most of them would otherwise be content to ignore for years to come.

Beyond calling attention to crucial issues, another task of executive leadership is to assure action on specific proposals to resolve those issues. Even when there is sufficient public concern about a particular problem, there may not be enough support for any one course of action. The president, once he has made up his own mind, can offer a proposal, calling it to the attention of Congress and encouraging public and congressional support. If Congress is reluctant to act, he can apply political pressure in various ways, making congressmen aware of possible political rewards for going along with his proposal or implying penalties for refusing to do so. The tools available to him are not always sufficient for the purpose, but legislators are certainly more likely to act under such circumstances than they are in the absence of executive encouragement.

Even if Congress acts in a direction contrary to the president's recommendation, his effort may have been worthwhile, for it might not have acted at all if he had not stimulated the process, thereby serving as a sort of political catalyst. And the solution that eventually emerges from Congress may even be superior to the president's recommendation. The important thing is not that the president gets exactly the solution he wants but that he provides the stimulus for political action without which no program can be developed.

Another task of the chief executive is to integrate the political system, relating its various institutions and processes to each other. This responsibility is especially important in the United States, for no other major country has such a loosely woven constitutional fabric. The federal pattern often necessitates cooperation at two or even three levels of government if problems are to be dealt with effectively. Furthermore, at each level of government the tendency to employ a system of separation of powers and a complicated arrangement of checks and balances makes necessary a serious effort to coordinate the work of a great number of individuals and political institutions.

Only the chief executive seems to be capable of furthering this kind of cooperative political endeavor. No other institution carries adequate weight elsewhere in the political system. Congress cannot coordinate itself, much less the rest of the government. The judiciary has more potential in this respect but not enough; even the Supreme Court has sometimes been frustrated in its efforts to produce concerted government action. State and local governments have demonstrated no ability to bring the agencies of national government into line with their programs. So once more the president is the only recourse—often an inadequate recourse and occasionally a dangerous one, but for many purposes the only one the system has.

One of the most important presidential functions is the enforcement of responsibility in the bureaucracy. Despite much that has been said to the contrary, the crucial problem with American bureaucracy is not dishonesty, incompetence, or tyranny of its members. Like the members of Congress most of the personnel of federal administrative agencies are honest, competent, and conscientious, and, while that high standard is not uniform in state and local government, we need not be ashamed of the over-all quality of administrative personnel at those levels. The real problem is seldom how bureaucrats carry out their responsibilities but rather how those responsibilities are perceived and defined.

In most administrative agencies the natural tendency is to be primarily concerned with protecting the interests of the organized segments of the population with which it deals most frequently and most directly. Those are the persons with whom administrators regularly interact, and it would be surprising if they were not influenced by them. Furthermore, they are organized to undertake political action in behalf of their interests—action that will inevitably influence the agency in question. Besides, most of the personnel of a given agency are persuaded through their professional training and their own convictions that the contributions of the groups with which they deal are valuable to the nation and should be encouraged—that the well-being of those groups is essential to the well-being of the whole population. The administrator who does not believe that is unlikely to seek employment with the particularly agency in the first place or will transfer elsewhere at the earliest opportunity.

How is this tendency to protect particular interests at the expense of the rest of the population to be controlled? Congress cannot undertake the task, though it is often assumed to be doing so, because its working structure is just as closely tied to particular interests as is that of the bureaucracy. A neat triangular relationship customarily exists among the interest group, the congressional committees that deal with its concerns, and the relevant administrative agency. They work well together in their conflicts with other political institutions and with the rest of the public. The judiciary occasionally intervenes to protect broader interests and values, but it often has no opportunity to do so.

The institution that has most frequently exerted countervailing political pressure in behalf of broader segments of the population and otherwise unrepresented elements is the presidency. Admittedly presidents cannot always be relied on to do this, and their lack of effective control over some bureaucratic institutions, especially the so-called independent regulatory commissions, and their inability to dominate certain aspects of the administrative process has always limited presidential effectiveness in this regard. Still the presidency comes closest to meeting the conviction that some effective political control over administration should be maintained.

Another useful feature of executive leadership is that it serves as a focus for the electoral process. We have already noted that congressional elections turn on local issues rather than on national ones. The only time at which most voters are reacting to national problems and issues is during the presidential election campaign. Then they have an opportunity to pass judgment on the performance of the administration in office and the government in general, re-electing the president or supporting his chosen successor if they are pleased with the course of events and shifting to the candidate of the other party if they are dissatisfied.

For a number of reasons, then, it is doubtful that the political system could function satisfactorily without a chief executive. There must be a central institution, a focus, to which other institutions and the voting public can relate. The presidency has played that role in the United States. Alternative forms of executive leadership exist, however, and if it is admitted that the presidency does not always function perfectly, consideration must be given to whether one or more of those alternatives might be superior.

CABINET SYSTEM OR ONE-MAN LEADERSHIP

One of the most frequently heard criticisms of the American presidency is that it concentrates too much power and responsibility in one fallible individual. The president's day has only twenty-four hours, and he can do only so much in that time. The president, like any other person, is subject to the limitations of his personality, intellect, training, and experience. There are some problems about which he knows little and other problems about which he is not much interested. Nor is he immune to the vicissitudes of ill health and nervous strain.

By its very nature leadership must be exercised by a small number of individuals. If the body of leaders becomes too large, it succumbs to the failings of representative bodies and becomes incapable of effective decision making, or it must defer to the leadership of a smaller group within its ranks. But if leadership has to be undertaken by a small group, it does not necessarily have to be the responsibility of one man alone. Certainly as many as four or five individuals, perhaps as many as ten or fifteen, can work together effectively to consider problems and reach decisions, providing their personalities and ideas are reasonably congenial.

In Great Britain policy leadership has been the responsibility of the cabinet, a group of the most important department heads and other ministers, originally designated by the monarch but for the last two centuries appointed by the prime minister. Though certain offices are invariably included in the cabinet, others may be brought in or left out as the prime minister prefers, depending on the political importance of the individual cabinet member and the significance of the problems for which that office is responsible. Any major public question is presumably discussed at length in one or more cabinet meetings, and a decision is reached when the prime minister perceives a consensus among his colleagues.

One of the fundamental rules of the British constitutional system is that of collective responsibility. Under this principle all members of the cabinet are obligated to support a cabinet decision, whether or not they personally agree with it and even if they argued bitterly against it during the cabinet's deliberations. The government speaks with one voice, and no member of the cabinet is free to criticize its actions unless he is willing to resign first and then speak or write as an ordinary citizen or member of Parliament. An extension of collective responsibility is that the entire government stands or falls as a unit. A motion of censure or no confidence passed by the House of Commons forces the resignation of all the ministers, not just one or a few. Hence it is difficult to secure political advantage by throwing one's colleagues to the wolves, and the responsibility for a serious blunder cannot readily be avoided by selecting a convenient scapegoat and sacrificing him to avert further criticism in Parliament and the press.

The prime minister has become increasingly important in twentieth-century Britain, however. He may not always dominate decision making in the cabinet; even Winston Churchill was occasionally on the losing side in the deliberations of that body. But the prime minister certainly dominates the electoral process, for most voters come to think of him as personifying the government, and they vote for or against the local parliamentary candidate of the prime minister's party as they approve or disapprove of the performance of the government he heads.

Though we have an institution with that title, the United States has never really employed the cabinet system. Recent presidents have felt no obligation even to consult the cabinet, and no president has ever felt himself bound to follow its recommendations. The celebrated (and perhaps apocryphal) occasion when Abraham Lincoln, discovering his cabinet to be unanimously opposed to him on a certain issue, announced the result as, "One aye, seven nays; the ayes have it," aptly illustrates the locus of power in the American executive. The president's voice, if he chooses to employ it, is the only one that counts. He may choose to consult the cabinet as a whole. Short of that, he may request advice from particular individuals in the cabinet whose opinions he values. Or he may ignore the cabinet altogether in making important policy decisions, instead obtaining advice from lesser administrators, members of the White House staff, or private citizens or making decisions alone.

If the presidency as one-man leadership has come in for criticism, so has the growth of the so-called institutionalized presidency, in which key presidential subordinates act in the name of the president and with his authority, enabling him to meet responsibilities indirectly that he could not conceivably find time or energy to deal with in person. The vast increase in demands on the president made this development necessary, but it could lead to irresponsibility in the presidency. For one thing, the president may not be able to keep track of all the uses that are being made of his power; certainly no one outside the White House can do so. Even worse, the president may seek to avoid blame for the failures of his administration by shifting responsibility to one or more of his subordinates, arguing that his mistakes were the result of the bad advice he has received or that the actions attributed to him were really taken by staff members acting without his knowledge or consent. The Watergate episode produced dramatic instances of this kind of behavior.

Is there any way to guard against this risk? One approach is congressional or judicial investigation into the sources of White House actions, attempting to pin down who was responsible for particular decisions that have turned out badly. A better solution might be to adopt the principle of collective responsibility. The difficulty in tracking down the miscreants when something does go wrong in the presidency and the near impossibility of penalizing them adequately when they have been discovered implies some alternative: making the political leadership of the entire executive branch responsible as a unit through the president. He can properly be held accountable for the misdeeds of his subordinates, for he has selected them and ought to have been overseeing their work. The energy now wasted on trying to find out who did what in the executive branch could then be devoted to consideration of the substantive merits of the actions of the executive. When those are found to be unsatisfactory, the administration as a whole can be called to account—by the public at the next election or by Congress through impeachment proceedings or lesser sanctions.

THE PARLIAMENTARY ALTERNATIVE

In the parliamentary system, as opposed to the presidential system, the prime minister, department heads, and other leading executives are responsible to the legislative branch. In Britain and most other countries they are required to be members of that branch. The administration can remain in office only as long as it enjoys the support of a majority of the members of Parliament. If it is defeated on a motion of no confidence or on any major piece of legislation, the prime minister has a choice of resigning, along with all his colleagues, and turning over the government to the leader of the other party or of calling a general election, after which he must resign unless he gains the support of a majority of the members of the new Parliament. Many critics, both European and American, argue that the parliamentary system is more democratic or at least more responsible than the presidential system with its separation of powers. In particular, it is easier to get rid of an incompetent, corrupt, or tyrannical executive before the next election, which may be several years away, if all that is needed is a simple motion of no confidence rather than the cumbersome process of impeachment, which is arduous and time-consuming and may require the proof of personal misconduct of a criminal nature.

It is certainly true that the parliamentary system has functioned very well in some countries, notably in Great Britain but also in the Scandinavian countries, several other Western European democracies, and Australia, Canada, and New Zealand. But the way in which it functions has often been misunderstood by Americans. Specifically, they have failed to note that parliamentary government works well only in the context of political parties that are cohesive and well disciplined. That discipline is effective because the failure of the majority party to support the government headed by its own leaders leads to a sudden general election in which every member of Parliament will be forced to campaign for his own re-election. If that member has been disloyal to his party in Parliament, his campaign will have to be conducted without party support and without even the privilege of running as the candidate of that party. Since most voters are concerned not with the individual member of Parliament from their area but with the performance of national party leaders, an independent candidate has little or no chance of victory, and the member of Parliament who tries to switch parties will

usually find that the other party has too many able members of long standing to nominate a Johnny-come-lately from the other side.

As a consequence the government in power, representing a party with a parliamentary majority, is almost never defeated in Parliament. Except in a special situation in which no party had a majority in the House of Commons, the last time a British government was forced to resign on a question of confidence was almost a century ago. Hence this mechanism for holding the executive accountable is not much more likely to be employed in practice than impeachment in the United States, though British political leaders, aware that this procedure can be used against them, may be more careful than American chief executives to avoid actions that would jeopardize their support within their own party.

The above characterization applies only to a parliamentary system with two political parties. A multiparty parliamentary system in which no party has an opportunity to gain a majority often becomes chaotic and ineffective, as in Germany in the 1920's, in France until 1958, and in Italy more recently. Government is then possible only if several parties join in a coalition, and, since no two parties agree on all the issues of the day, the members of the coalition cannot achieve decisive action on most major problems.

Another misconception of some observers is that the parliamentary system is superior because it provides for legislative supremacy. Theoretically and constitutionally this is true, but in practice it is not. With two parties the majority party must maintain its unity and discipline, subject to the policy decisions made by its own leaders in the cabinet, lest it lose its majority status and face the threat of a premature election. Tight party control makes the ordinary member of Parliament relatively powerless vis-à-vis the executive, whatever the theoretical constitutional position of Parliament may be. In a multiparty parliamentary system the legislative branch may be supreme, it is true, but only in a negative sense. It can and often does prevent the executive from making policies and even from remaining in office very long, but it cannot act effectively to establish policies itself.

There is a certain irony in the current criticism of governmental institutions on both sides of the Atlantic. American critics of excessive presidential power at the expense of Congress often point to the British system as the ideal in this respect. British critics of excessive executive power and tight party discipline at the expense of "backbenchers" in Parliament often suggest that the American system of separation of powers would be superior. Perhaps both sets of critics are misled by prevailing political myths. Probably no political system can function effectively without a powerful executive. In that case the real question is not how much power the executive should have but how to keep the executive responsible in its exercise of that power.

PARTY GOVERNMENT

Many American political scientists have been attracted by the idea of government through responsible political parties—

parties clearly indicating in advance the course of action they will pursue if successful at the polls and accepting responsibility for the satisfactory achievement of those goals if their members are elected to public office. Whatever the merits of this proposal, it is certainly aimed at correcting a real defect in the American democratic system: the difficulty the intelligent voter encounters in using his ballot rationally because he cannot anticipate the consequences for public policy of electing any given candidate to office. Only the election of the chief executive is a partial exception to this rule, and even at that level party platforms and campaign speeches are notoriously inadequate guides to the future actions of a successful presidential or gubernatorial candidate.

To a considerable degree parties already serve as useful cues to voters. The notion that party labels are meaningless, that there are no real differences between the two major parties in the United States, is not supported by a careful examination of the American political process. While there is certainly some overlap between the parties, there are real differences between them in their basic perspectives on many questions of public policy, especially those with economic implications. Policy directions do vary, depending on which party is in control of the White House and of Congress, and the same differences can be discerned among party members in the electorate. There may still be room, however, for demanding that parties become *more* meaningful and *more* responsible and perhaps for insisting that they take firmer positions on a greater variety of issues.

Discussion of parties in the United States has long been marked by confusion about the relationship between the party and the president. Some see the party primarily as a tool of the latter. The president, viewed as the dominant figure in the political system, uses the party to gain support for himself among voters and for his program among congressmen and voters. By this interpretation the party has no importance of its own and serves merely to add to the president's power and to help him accomplish the goals of his administration. The most effective presidents have tended to stress their party affiliation, appealing for the support of those identifying with that party. The president who did so most explicitly was Woodrow Wilson, but Jefferson, Jackson, Lincoln, both Roosevelts, Truman, and Kennedy utilized partisan appeals on many occasions.

There is another way of looking at this relationship, however. The president may be viewed as an instrument of his party, chosen to carry out its program and policy commitments. In that view the president may be held responsible by his party for his performance in office and for his effectiveness in meeting its demands upon him. This process obviously minimizes the risk of a tyrannical or dishonest chief executive, but it raises the question who is to enunciate the policy position of the party if the president is not to do so. We have never developed an adequate alternative to the presidency for this purpose. The national-party convention is sometimes thought of in this connection, but it meets only every four years, and its members are selected almost exclusively with an eye to the would-be presidential nominee they are likely to support. Party members in Congress have

not proved capable of meeting this responsibility, partly because it is difficult to get them to act in concert and partly because they are less representative of their party as a whole than is the president.

Those who critize the presidency and urge a responsible party system as an alternative to it or as a means of controlling it may not have thought through the implications of their alternative. If the problem with the presidential system lies merely in some of the characteristics of the office, responsible parties may be an adequate solution. But to most of the critics the faults of the Presidency are inherent in any exercise of political power and leadership, regardless of the nature of the institution. Decisions made by a prime minister would be no more acceptable than those emanating from a president, and policy initiatives coming from a small group of congressmen or party leaders would be rejected as indignantly as those coming from the White House.

Central to the problem is the tendency of many Americans to demand contradictory goals: on the one hand, effective public policies to solve national problems; on the other, avoidance of the concentration of political power. In a large and complex society, these goals cannot be reached at the same time. Problems can be solved only with the exercise of power, and difficult problems can be solved only with the exercise of concentrated power. We can change the location of that power within the political system.Steps can be taken to ensure that those who wield power are responsible to some or all of the rest of the population. But political power will still be there, and we will still be faced with the twin tasks of using it and controlling it.

EXECUTIVE IRRESPONSIBILITY

Several factors contribute to the potential irresponsibility of the presidency. One of the more important of these is the psychological isolation of the president. The extraordinary responsibilities associated with the office; the knowledge that his great constitutional power, while it may often be delegated, cannot in any serious sense be shared with anyone else; the awareness that he has achieved the highest political position, so that he can aspire to no higher office; the realization that those with whom he must work have their own interests and ambitions, which will usually influence them more than his wishes and demands, so that he can count on the absolute loyalty of few if any of those around him; the physical isolation necessary to provide minimal security against assassination; the need to present a façade for public consumption, especially on television, that may have little to do with his real personality—all these conditions tend to keep the president apart from his fellow citizens and increase the risk that he will lose his awareness of their needs and problems or fail to develop such an awareness.

Some presidents, such as the Roosevelts, Truman, and Kennedy, avoided the worst consequences of these strictures through their zest for the political process. Interacting with their fellow citizens, including those who disagree with them, is an enjoyable part of the job for such leaders. Others, such as Wilson in his first administration and Lincoln throughout his, maintained a realistic perspective of their situation, sometimes in spite of severe psychological problems (amounting in Lincoln's case to recurring bouts of acute melancholia). But some presidents neither enjoyed politics for its own sake nor derived satisfaction from it as a means of achieving goals to which they were intensely committed. For such individuals, who either drift into politics more or less by accident or climb the political ladder to demonstrate to themselves that they are not the failures they otherwise perceive themselves to be, the pressures of the office may produce emotional collapse or may cause them to act in dangerous and highly irresponsible ways.

The rise of what has been called the imperial Presidency may increase the risk. The pageantry and formality surrounding the presidency, the honor and acclaim heaped on him, the custom that even his closest personal friends and political associates address him not by name but as "Mr. President"—these customs are at variance with some aspects of the American tradition and may well have got out of hand. But they may be symptoms of the problem rather than its cause, and many presidents have been more amused or annoyed than impressed by them.

More important is the tendency for presidents to be surrounded by sycophants and yes men. George Reedy has described this tendency with perception. Among those working for the president there is a natural reluctance to give him information and advice that they know will be unwelcome. It is much easier to tell him that everything is going well, that there are no difficult problems, and that all his programs and policies are working perfectly. In the long run it is a dangerous practice for the country and harmful to the political interests of the president. Every leader makes mistakes, because every human being does so, and there is no possibility of correcting those mistakes if they are never pointed out to the one who has the power to correct them. The ablest presidents have therefore been willing to expose themselves to criticism, keeping people of varying views in their administrations, reading publications hostile to their programs, and retaining or developing contacts with a variety of people outside the administration. In this way the president may be able to minimize his isolation and maximize his capacity to influence events to the advantage of his country and his political career.

From 1787 to the present some have argued that the chief threat to the civil liberties of the American people lies in the power of the president. In the light of American history, especially in wartime situations, it would be foolish to scoff at the threat. There have been episodes that have had tragic effects on the individuals affected and that constitute shameful blots on the American record. Such great presidents as Lincoln, Wilson, and Franklin Roosevelt have been responsible for some of the worst of these acts. Yet the over-all picture suggests that presidents have been perhaps less prone to infringe civil liberties than have members of other institutions of government, including Congress, and that efforts to promote and defend civil liberties owe much to presidential leadership. That is especially true of steps taken to secure civil rights for racial minorities previously deprived of equal treatment.

Note too that the presidency may be the only institution capable of controlling those bureaucracies that on occasion have been known to ignore the rights of citizens. Notable examples are the armed services and other agencies concerned with national security, the FBI, other institutions for law enforcement, and various agencies with investigatory functions, such as the Internal Revenue Service. Occasionally the judiciary may be able to limit the intrusion of such institutions into the lives of law-abiding citizens, but the administrators have sometimes failed to respond to any external authority short of the chief executive. The presidency, with all the risks of irresponsible leadership, is also the best hope for controlling irresponsibility that originates elsewhere in the political system.

Problems of national security present special dangers for the maintenance of free government. A threat to national survival may necessitate the creation and support of powerful institutions that may menace the constitutional structure. While it is not possible to get along without them, armed services and police forces have often played a vital role in the subversion of democratic governments. Legislative institutions have never been able to thwart such threats. Even judges cannot consistently do so. Only the chief executive has enough authority, and the respect in which his office is held by most members of the military and of law-enforcement agencies aids him in this process. The president's clear-cut constitutional status as commander-in-chief of the armed forces is a considerable asset; it is far from sure that any other civilian authority could maintain effective control over the armed services in crises.

Having dealt with executive actions of a positive character that may prove dangerous and irresponsible, we should now consider the negative side of irresponsibility. Leaders who fail to lead are also a threat to responsible government. The public has a right to expect that its demands for the solution of urgent national problems will be met, and the populace naturally becomes frustrated and eventually alienated from the political process if such action is indefinitely delayed. The great powers of the presidency are of no value if the occupant of the office refuses to use them, and the leadership potential of the White House is important only if it is utilized.

THE PRESIDENT AND EXECUTIVE LEADERSHIP

Two centuries have witnessed a wide variety of politicians in the office of president—*almost* all of them honest and of good will, but some astute and some inept, some powerful and some weak. Americans have paid a high price for some of the failures in the executive branch—for example, for many years before and after the Civil War and again in the 1920's.

The consequences of ineffective presidential leadership are an impressive testimonial to the inability of other American political institutions to undertake the solution of major public problems on their own. The golden era of congressional greatness is often assumed to have been the 1840's and

1850's, when the Senate was enriched by such majestic figures as Thomas Hart Benton, John C. Calhoun, Henry Clay, Stephen A. Douglas, and Daniel Webster. By comparison the quality of congressmen in the early 1860's was clearly inferior. Yet the earlier period produced next to nothing in the way of successful policies for contending with the critical national problems of the day, while in the early 1860's successful large-scale legislative programs were instituted, not only in regard to the Civil War but also in the fields of agriculture, higher education, transportation, financial reform, and other issues. Why did less experienced and perhaps less able members of Congress produce better results than the most famous men who ever sat there? The answer is obvious: the presidential leadership of Abraham Lincoln.

Both historical evidence and theoretical analysis suggest that there is no substitute for effective executive leadership. From a theoretical standpoint, however, there are alternatives to the presidential form that leadership may take. Several other sources of policy initiative can be imagined, and even if we confine our analysis to Western democracies, the parliamentary system is more typical than is the concentration of executive power in a president. Nevertheless, it is doubtful that a change from the presidential system in the United States would satisfy its critics. And the feasibility of such a change is open to real question. For one thing, it would be flying in the face of two centuries of American experience and tradition, and an almost revolutionary reform of this kind would have to overcome both tremendous resistance and inertia. Furthermore, the parliamentary system, with two rigidly structured and tightly disciplined parties, dominated by a prime minister and cabinet whose powers would scarcely be weaker in practice than those of the president, would leave the United States with the same problems the presidential system has created. And the multiparty variant of parliamentary government tends to be accompanied by chaotic instability and stalemate over needed policies. What Americans now have is at least no worse and may on occasion serve them better.

Americans are not without constraints to keep the presidency responsible and under control. The most important of those constraints is the desire of a first-term president to appeal for re-election and the natural desire of a second-term president to be succeeded by a congenial figure from his own party. No president wants to be known as a political failure whose administration was repudiated at the next election. As long as a system of free elections is maintained, no sane president is going to become totally irresponsible. True, the president can seek to manipulate public opinion through his publicity resources and through imaginative use of the communications media. But there are limits to his ability to delude the public, especially on issues about which most voters are personally aware, and in the last analysis he must either produce results with which they will be satisfied or anticipate rejection at the ballot box.

The critical problem with the electoral process as a mechanism for maintaining presidential responsibility is the rigid schedule of elections. No matter how gross the failures of a president and his administration, the voters cannot retaliate until the next election, as long as four years away. Hence the necessity of control devices that can be employed during the long periods between elections.

One of these, in theory, is party control of the presidency. But political parties in the United States, weak, decentralized, and victims of a culture that considers politics unimportant and partisan politics evil, are in a singularly poor position to accept this responsibility. Most Americans, even if they disapprove of the strong presidency, would prefer it to strong, cohesive, tightly disciplined political parties. The notion of responsible parties has gained popularity among political scientists; it has made much less headway among active politicians and the general run of voters.

Judicial control of the presidency has been sporadic and often ineffective, especially in wartime or when considerations of national security are raised in defense of otherwise questionable presidential actions. In a direct confrontation even the Supreme Court is no match for the chief executive—witness its strenuous and successful efforts to avoid such a showdown at several points in American history. Still it is undoubtedly healthy to keep the president and his associates and subordinates aware that their actions may occasionally be subject to judicial scrutiny, particularly when allegations of criminal misconduct are involved.

Can other institutions in the executive branch control the president? Only rarely. The bureaucracy is perfectly capable of ignoring him, going its own way and paying no attention to his demands for administrative action in furtherance of his programs and policies. But that is a far cry from imposing positive control over the actions the president takes himself or that other administrative agencies take at his behest. Subordinate administrators may successfully resist being controlled by the president, but they are scarcely in a position to dominate him. The cabinet, with no independent political base of its own, is in an even weaker position vis-à-vis the president. Once in a great while an individual cabinet member criticizes or takes issue with his boss, but almost never successfully.

Congress is clearly the institution most readily capable of keeping the president responsible between elections. If Congress were to concentrate on this task, abandoning its vain effort to replace the president as the locus of national policy making and reducing its expenditure of time and effort on local legislation and favors for constituents, it might succeed very well in maintaining the accountability of the President. Furthermore, it is a much more important job than most tasks on which congressmen spend most of their time.

There are, however, problems in this approach to enforcing executive responsibility. Most congressmen will be reluctant to abandon the roles in which they have achieved political success with relatively high career security to accept a responsibility that will thrust them directly into the maelstrom of national political controversy with consequences to their future careers that can never be clearly anticipated. Furthermore, it means abandoning the pretense that Congress is the central policy-making institution of national government, and even though many congressmen recognize that it has never really measured up to that responsibility, it is embarrassing to have to admit it, either to constituents or to themselves.

A further problem is the need to overhaul the sanctions available for penalizing an irresponsible president. In particular, the almost forgotten remedy of impeachment must be restored to the constitutional apparatus. After the failure to convict President Andrew Johnson on impeachment charges in 1868, the process came to be regarded as almost illegitimate, tantamount to revolution. The constitutional provision on the subject came to be read as applying only to personal misconduct of a criminal nature, though the authors of the Constitution surely had the much broader traditional British usage in mind when they referred to "high crimes and misdemeanors"—terminology probably meant to cover almost any serious malfeasance in office. To argue otherwise is to insist that once a public official has been elected he must be left in office until the expiration of his term unless it can be demonstrated that he belongs in the penitentiary instead, whereas it should be obvious that we have occasionally had presidents who belonged neither in the White House nor in jail.

Finally, it should be remembered that most presidents are capable of self-control. We would be unwise ever to rely on that as our only safeguard, for Americans will no doubt encounter from time to time a president who lacks self-control, and he must be held responsible entirely through institutions and processes outside the presidency. But most presidents, with their sense of fitness and right, their oath of office, their respect for the constitutional system and various national political traditions, will place limits on actions they might otherwise find advantageous. As long as a president is capable of saying to himself and to his political allies, "Of course, that would be politically beneficial, but it cannot be done because it would not be right," the threat of judicial action, impeachment, or defeat at the polls will be employed only rarely.

In summary, *effective* executive leadership is probably a necessity in any political system. *Responsible* executive leadership is vital in a democracy. Without the first, decisive policy making cannot take place, and urgent national problems will go unsolved. Without the second, government may become corrupt, inept, or tyrannical. Alternatives to the present presidential system of executive leadership can be found; they exist in theory and have worked well in practice in some other countries. But there is no reason to assume that these alternatives can avoid most of the problems to which the presidential system is prone, and most Americans would be unlikely to support such a change unless drastic improvements could be expected in consequence. We will probably continue to make do with the presidency, electing an occasional great president and an occasional failure, and a great many somewhere in between. The results have been by no means perfect, but on balance the performance of the presidency has been about as satisfactory as any other system has been for providing national leadership and initiating public policies.

4

THE RELATION OF LAW TO SOCIOECONOMIC CHANGE

By Robert R. Wright

This . . . Constitution [is] intended to endure for ages to come and, consequently, to be adapted to the various crises of human affairs.

Chief Justice Marshall, in *McCulloch* v. *Maryland* (1819)

This oft-quoted statement by Chief Justice John Marshall in the McCulloch case illustrates the use which has been made of and the interpretation given to the Constitution of the United States in new situations and under new conditions during the years since its ratification. Early on it was decided that the Constitution would be a flexible document, interpreted broadly, its sweeping phraseology applied liberally as new situations arose.

While Marshall is generally credited with being the architect of this doctrine, and while he had a great deal to do with its construction, both the times that preceded him and the arguments of other leading contemporary lawyer-statesmen contributed significantly to the view that ultimately emerged.

First of all was the common-law tradition itself, its roots extending deep into English legal history and jurisprudence. The theory behind English common law was that it was an expanding doctrine—that, as events developed, common-law judges would "discover" the law that already existed and apply it and that decisions of other common-law judges would also help provide guidance in the growth of the law. In more recent times it has become popular in some circles to assert that judges do not make law or ought not to make law. That function, it is argued, is solely for legislative bodies or perhaps for administrative agencies exercising rule-making power under broad grants of authority emanating from the legislature. In fact, however, courts have always made law,[1] and the earliest law of England stemmed largely from judges limited only by a few great documents, such as the Magna Carta (1215), a few statutes enacted by Parliament, pronouncements or actions of the king, and the structure of the feudal system. The law that evolved was largely judge-made law, which was "common" in the sense that it applied throughout the kingdom. It reinforced and reinterpreted the feudal system. Over the centuries, as judges developed their

own rules and applied precedents from other cases, there was continuous evolving of legal principles. Use of precedents, which lawyers refer to as *stare decisis*, lent some stability to the law, and the continuous evolutionary process provided some flexibility. When flexibility slowed or ceased, it was reinstated through the development of equity as a separate system.

The greatest of all exponents of the common law was Sir Edward Coke, who lived in the late sixteenth and early seventeenth century.[2] Coke was not only the exponent of the common law but also its chief proponent, and he evidenced an extreme reverence for it. Before Coke equity had begun its rise as a separate system to accord justice in cases in which the common law, as the result of precedent and the rigidity of feudal custom, had become too fixed. The rise of equity renewed flexibility in English law and also introduced a separate set of values. In its early days it was administered by ecclesiastics appointed by the king as lord chancellors to dispense justice in the name of the king. They were principally charged with ameliorating some of the hardships occasioned by the application of the common law in certain cases.[3] In Coke's time the lord high chancellor was Francis Bacon, and Coke's reverence for the common law and his feeling that it should be supreme led him into conflict with Bacon (a conflict that also had roots in personal and political encounters between the two men). Bacon's eventual impeachment by the House of Commons and removal from office for bribery[4] led to Coke's triumph over him, but equity remained a very important adjunct to the common law to provide relief from its harshness in certain situations.

Coke was, in a large sense, a bridge between the medieval and the modern.[5] In his extensive writings he interpreted the Year Books and set forth the common law as it pertained to property in a manner that was definitive for well over two centuries and was followed by Blackstone and by early American lawyers and judges.[6] At the same time, he enunciated principles that would be later embodied in American law. The principle of judicial review, for example, is traceable back to Coke's opinion in *Dr. Bonham's Case*[7] that an act of Parliament or the king is subject to "right reason" as embodied in the common law. In other words, if an act of Parliament was contrary to "right reason," as found in the sum of the common law, it could be overturned by the courts. It is amazing that this concept, enunciated in the early seventeenth century, did not create more of a stir in England than it did. In his earlier career Coke served in many high offices under Elizabeth I and later under the Stuart kings. He served as attorney general, as chief justice of the Court of Common Pleas and the King's Bench, and later in Parliament.[8] In his later years he increasingly came into conflict with the assertion of power by the sovereign. As attorney for Elizabeth, he had been a staunch defender of the pre-eminence of the crown and governmental power, but when he became chief justice, he experienced a change in character not unlike that of Thomas à Becket when Becket became archbishop of Canterbury.[9] In 1608, James I asserted that the king had the power to decide cases as he might choose, and Coke's response was a quote from an earlier great English jurist, Henry de Bracton: "The King ought to be under no man, but under God and the law."[10] Later, after he had been dismissed from the bench by King James and had been elected to Parliament, the question once again arose about the sovereignty and power of the king. This was part of the debate that ultimately led to the Petition of Right. At one point during the debate a proposal of the House of Lords was rejected that would have added a clause to the petition recognizing the sovereignty of the crown. Coke addressed this point in Parliament in these words:

I know that prerogative is part of the law, but sovereign power is no Parliamentary word; in my opinion, it weakens Magna Carta and all our statutes; for they are absolute without any saving of sovereign power. And shall we now add to it, we shall weaken the foundation of Law, and then the building must needs fall; take we heed what we yield unto— Magna Carta is such a Fellow, he will have no Sovereign.[11]

The rejection by Parliament of the assertion of "sovereign power" has modern overtones in light of the assertion of "executive privilege" by former President Nixon and in view of the Supreme Court decision in *United States* v. *Nixon.*[12]

Thus in his conflicts with the king and in *Dr. Bonham's Case,* Coke established the primacy of the law. Both Parliament and the king were subject to the law, and when their actions conflicted with it, their actions had to give way. Even before the American experience had begun, the groundwork had been laid not only for judicial review but for the supremacy of the law as enunciated by judges.

Moreover, it is readily apparent that the English experience formed the basis for the concept of change in the law and for the idea that the law had to adapt itself to new social and economic conditions. That it did so in America in many striking instances and in various ways is not an illustration of the uniqueness of the American experiment but instead demonstrates the continuity and cultivated growth of seeds that had already come to fruition in English law and would become hardier and more vigorous in the new soil. One of the most unique aspects of the American experience has been the swiftness of change and the law's usually swift response.

THE RECEPTION OF THE ENGLISH EXPERIENCE IN AMERICA

We often forget that America was under English rule almost as many years as it has been an independent nation. In celebrating the two hundredth anniversary of the nation, dating from the Declaration of Independence, it is necessary to keep in mind the fact that by the time of the declaration almost 170 years had elapsed since the founding of Jamestown. During that time English common law and parliamentary enactments had become rooted in the American system. Moreover, as the legal profession developed in the Colonies, those involved in it naturally tended to look to English precedents as well as to Coke's *Institutes* and his earlier doctrinal writings and, somewhat later, to Sir William Blackstone's *Commentaries on the Laws of England.*[13] Blackstone's *Commentaries* were published in four volumes between 1765 and 1769, and partly because law books and collections of cases were scarce in the Colonies, his *Commentaries* had an important influence on the development of early American law.[14]

Before the publication of Blackstone's works the legal profession in the Colonies had struggled from a rather crude infancy to a position of great influence.[15] Edmund Burke, in discussing the influence of law and the legal profession in the Colonies stated: "In no country, perhaps, in the world, is the law so generally studied. The profession itself is numerous and powerful, and in most provinces it takes the lead. The greater number of the deputies sent to the [Continental] Congress were lawyers."[16] Although John Adams lamented the fact that, when he was admitted to practice in Massachusetts in the middle of the eighteenth century, the practice of the law was often in the hands of deputy sheriffs, constables, and the like, he also noted the existence of a reputable bar: "Boston was full of Lawyers and many of them established Characters for long Experience, great Abilities and extensive Fame."[17] Adams' statement was not exaggerated: Of the fifty-six signers of the Declaration of Independence, twenty-five were lawyers. Thirty-one of the fifty-five members who drafted the Constitution were lawyers, and in the First Congress ten of the twenty-nine senators and seventeen of the sixty-five representatives were lawyers.[18] Thus the great documents of the republic were largely the product of lawyers. The documents that would have to respond to social and economic change were drafted by men whose profession represented a historic process in which there had been a steady acclimation of legal doctrine and theories to deal with new social conditions. These leaders of the bar had been brought up on Coke and Blackstone. Burke noted that nearly as many of Blackstone's *Commentaries* had been sold in America as in England.[19] The same was surely true of Coke's *Commentary upon Littleton.* Jefferson commented that it was "the universal elementary book of law students and a sounder Whig never wrote nor of profounder learning in the orthodox doctrine of . . . British liberties."[20] Later doctrinal writing would develop in America through writings of such lawyers as Chancellor James Kent and Justice Joseph Story.[21] Doctrinal writing was extremely important in America because of the aforementioned absence of books containing reports of cases, and the influence of the writings of Coke and Blackstone cannot be overestimated.[22]

Those were not the only ways, however, in which English law was received in America. Another way was through the formality of "reception statutes," in which states adopted the common law of England and parliamentary enactments that were not contrary to the American system of government as of a certain date (usually 1607 or 1620 or 1776).[23] Thus, as Justice Story was later to write in a Supreme Court decision, the English common law was not adopted in all respects; only those parts which related to our form of government and our situation were absorbed into American law.[24] Nonetheless, it was a substantial acquisition. Thus, because of the experience of the colonial period, the adaptation of English cases and statutes to the American situation, the rather careful study and use of the writings of English scholars and jurists (principally Coke and Blackstone), the grounding of American lawyers in the principles of English law, the influence of American lawyers in the developmental instruments of the country, and finally the "reception statutes" adopted in the various states, the end result was that for all practical purposes Americans inherited in a somewhat modified version a more or less complete system of jurisprudence that had been developed over a period extending back at least seven hundred years, to 1066.

Needless to say, English precedents were cited by early American courts and often governed early American decisions. The basic English law of property, contracts, torts, and the like, modified somewhat to the particular situation, was ingested wholesale into the American system so that today we appropriately speak of the Anglo-American legal tradition.

THE MAKING OF A NATION: THE DECLARATION AND THE CONSTITUTION

It might be said that the Declaration of Independence could more profitably be studied by political scientists than by lawyers. It is not a part of the basic law, the Constitution. It is not a part of the federal statutes contained in the United States Code. But it was the theme document of the Revolution and second only to the Constitution and Bill of Rights as the greatest of all such documents in American history. The spirit of the Declaration of Independence and the philosophy underlying it has a direct interrelationship with the Bill of Rights, and in that respect it has substantial significance. Like the Bill of Rights, it is in the civil-libertarian tradition. The Constitution, exclusive of its amendments, is a more conservative document aimed at establishing a government that would be representative of the most enlightened Anglo-American legal and governmental views of the day, tempered by compromises that had to be made in order to obtain ratification.

The Declaration of Independence itself, as fiery as it may seem, was not written without compromise. A committee composed of Thomas Jefferson, John Adams, Benjamin Franklin, Robert Livingston, and Roger Sherman was appointed to write it, and Jefferson assumed that John Adams would prepare the draft. Adams declined, arguing that Jefferson was a Virginian and that a Virginian ought to do the work and observed that he himself was "suspected and unpopular" and that Jefferson could "write ten times better than I can."[25] Yet after Jefferson prepared his document, it went through a substantial number of changes. Aside from such minor matters as correcting Jefferson's penchant for using *it's* when he meant *its,* other deletions were made that reduced the length of the document by about one-fourth.[26] One clause on slavery was stricken to appease South Carolina and Georgia, and some stirring phrases excoriating George III were also removed.[27] The end result was the magnificent document with its familiar wording.

Although the Declaration of Independence was a revolutionary document and thus could be viewed as a radical document, its philosophy was neither as radical nor as revolutionary as might be thought. What Jefferson wrote was not wholly an invention of the American mind but had its roots deep in the philosophy and writings of John Locke. Some philosophical segments seem to have been lifted almost in their entirety from Locke's *Second Treatise of Civil Government.*[28] Moreover, Jefferson's thinking was undoubtedly affected by the fact that he had been a student of George Wythe, who had held the chair in law at William and Mary, the first law professorship in the United States. Finally, many of the ideas Jefferson expressed were current in the Colonies about that time. Thus Jefferson's work was not entirely innovative. He himself said that his object was

not to find out new principles, nor new arguments, never before thought of, not merely to say things which had never been said before; but to place before mankind the common sense of the subject, in terms so plain and firm as to command their assent. . . . It was intended to be an expression of the American mind, and to give to that expression the proper tone and spirit.[29]

Of course, as an expression of the American mind of the time (which in many respects has persisted until today), it was masterfully written. Thus we see in the declaration a document that conforms to the views of society and the principles of the day, couched in magnificent language.

As mentioned, the declaration had a direct philosophical correlation with the Bill of Rights, or at least with the first eight amendments. Jefferson spoke of "life, liberty, and the pursuit of happiness," which was converted in the Constitution to "life, liberty, and property"—the original language of John Locke in his *Second Treatise.*[30] The concept that all men are equal before the law and that they have certain rights that cannot be transferred or taken away are concepts embodied in the early amendments to the Constitution rather than in the original body of the Constitution.[31] Of course, the declaration differed even from the Bill of Rights in that its main object was to express the perfidy and abuses of George III and provide the justification for the severance of ties with the mother country. To do so, Jefferson had to establish a concept that is not found in the Constitution:

the right of revolution. This right was established logically, once again by relying upon arguments implicit in the writings of John Locke: government is supposed to protect and secure the basic rights of men, which is the reason for government, and, in order to exist effectively, governments have to be based upon the consent of those whom they govern.[32] If a government does not carry out the ends for which it is established or if it violates or impinges upon those basic rights, then the people have the power to change it or, if need be, to establish a new government that will be responsive to the people.[33] The Constitution never went that far but instead relied upon the broad guarantees contained in the Bill of Rights and other amendments and upon the ability to amend the Constitution from time to time as the need might arise. Nonetheless, the Declaration of Independence was true to its time. It was responsive to the conclusion at which most people had by that time arrived: that there was no effective way to deal with George III and that the time had come to sever ties. Although there was disagreement in the Colonies and although there were many loyalists among the colonials, by the time of the declaration events and thoughts had pretty well melded to lay the groundwork for Jefferson's "expression of the American mind." Thus, while not a formal legal document in the usual sense, for all practical purposes the declaration amounted to a legal document in that it lay the basis for the establishment of a new government and also in that its basic philosophy ultimately found more specific expression in the Bill of Rights.

After the war, as everyone knows, the infant nation briefly went through the untenable experience of attempting to exist under the Articles of Confederation. Even so, that form of government was obviously a response in a legal sense to the social demands of the time. The specter of a strong central government as embodied in the king and, to a lesser degree, in Parliament, was still before the people. They preferred something less rigid. The result was a confederation so loose that it had no power and was thus completely ineffective. The Constitutional Convention that followed was inevitable, although in itself it was a radical act in that it amounted to the peaceful overthrow of an existing government (assuming that one can dignify the Articles of Confederation as having created a "government" in any genuine or rational sense of the word). It operated peacefully and undisturbed, however, and its product was ratified by the states. That no one particularly challenged the work of the convention as it proceeded or arrested its delegates or ousted them from their convention hall illustrates that once again it had become apparent to at least the leaders of the infant country that something had to be done to correct the overreaction against centralized power represented by the articles. Thus persons, most of whom were lawyers, were once again responding in an orderly manner to a felt necessity of the time. It was obviously no longer feasible to have a working society and a developing economy under the Articles of Confederation. The Revolution had demonstrated that people did not want a king, and the ineffectiveness of the articles had demonstrated that a loose confederation of the former Colonies without any real power at the center would not work.

Thus the Constitution of the United States, the fundamental, basic law and guiding set of principles, was a response to the social demands of the time. It is not the purpose here to examine the Constitution at any length, but it is appropriate to make a few observations concerning the document. The Preamble illustrates the changing thought patterns that had emerged since the Articles of Confederation were adopted in 1781. The Preamble begins: "We, the People of the United States." Before that time each of the former Colonies had viewed itself and had largely functioned as a sovereign state, but it is implicit in the Preamble that a nation was being forged in which the people, or electorate, of the individual states were the people, or electorate, of the national government. In the debate in the Virginia ratification convention, Patrick Henry challenged the right of the federal convention delegates to use the phrase "We, the People," believing that they should use the words "We, the States." The answer from Governor Edmund Randolph and from Edmund Pendleton was that the people delegated powers and that the people, not the states had the right to form the government. Obviously, this reply circumvented the basic issue. "Light Horse Harry" Lee dealt with it more directly by pointing out that the document was being submitted to the people for their consideration because it was to operate upon them if it was adopted. Indeed, that was what was intended.[34] Moreover, they were trying to form "a more perfect Union," a concept that ran directly contrary to the concept of the articles. Another element of the federal Constitution of substantially greater importance is that it created a unique system—dual sovereignty—in which the individual states continued to exist and to exercise certain powers not delegated to the federal government. To have abolished the states and simply created a single governmental entity on a national basis would clearly have doomed the document to defeat. The states had to be preserved, and powers had to be reserved to the states operating within their own spheres. That much of the substance of the Articles of Confederation had to remain inviolate. Thus the delegates to the Constitution provided a framework for the central government to deal with national and international problems, as well as with problems between the states themselves. In so doing, they dealt directly with the failings of the Articles of Confederation and thereby responded to the social needs of the times. From an economic standpoint the end result was to lay the basis on which trade could function effectively not only between the new government and foreign nations but also among the states themselves. That was the significance of delegating to the national government the power to regulate interstate and foreign commerce.

Practically all of the compromises in the Constitutional Convention, even though they formed basic law, related to social and political necessities. The large-state–small-state controversy was resolved in the creation of the Senate, for the benefit of the smaller states. It was obviously a political necessity, and the example of a bicameral legislative body already existed in the English Parliament. Another response was represented in the creation of the office of president. The delegates had to respond to the need for a single executive to head the government, but at the same time they had to avoid even the appearance of creating anything approaching a monarchy. Thus they adopted the system of checks and balances under which there was substantial control over the office of the president. They vested in the Congress, among other powers, the power to pass laws, the power of the purse, the power of impeachment, the power to regulate commerce, and the power to declare war. The end result was to limit the power of the executive. Even more inventive genius was involved in the development of Article Two of the Constitution. Although the president was given the power to make treaties, he had to do it with the advice and consent of the Senate. Certain appointments, including diplomats and justices of the Supreme Court, had to be made with the Senate's advice and consent. While he was given command of the armed forces, the power to make war was vested in the Congress. Moreover, the president had from time to time to give the Congress "Information of the State of the Union" and recommend "such Measures as he shall judge necessary and expedient." The drafters recognized that an executive was needed and that he must have the power to perform certain acts, but the presidency could have become weak and almost wholly subject to the Congress except for the fact that the early presidents were generally strong ones—particularly Washington, Jefferson, and ultimately Andrew Jackson—and these men, in large part by the force of their personalities, as well as some of the actions performed by them (such as Jefferson's purchase of the Louisiana Territory), provided the office with the strength that was required. Less than two hundred years later it would be the Congress instead of the presidency that would be struggling to re-establish its power.

Many other provisions reflected ways in which the founders of the Constitution either compromised or catered to the social conditions of the time. One of the obvious compromises was on the slavery issue. While perhaps a majority of the delegates opposed traffic in slavery, some of the southern states would have refused to join the Union unless it was guaranteed by the Constitution.[35] The result was a portion of Section Nine of Article One, which prevented Congress from prohibiting the slave trade before 1808, although allowing a head tax on importation of slaves.

Thus it is apparent that the greatest of all documents in American legal history was pragmatic, responsive to the times, and designed to achieve the practical goal of creating a national government sufficiently strong at the center to keep its parts from fragmenting while at the same time retaining considerable power in the individual states. If principles were compromised from time to time, it was generally because such compromises were essential to passage within the convention and later ratification by the states.

While the Constitution was the product of many hands, a few men, such as James Madison, had particular influence in its drafting.[36] In the system of checks and balances which they created, they sought to establish a government in which power could not dominate at any one point, whether with regard to the national government as opposed to the states or with regard to one branch as opposed to another branch. Power was fractionalized with the hope of avoiding the de-

velopment of factions within the government that could dominate it. The concepts of men such as Madison and Alexander Hamilton involved a broad dispersion of power in keeping with the philosophy of Locke, which undergirded much of the system. The genius of the framers was that they were able to compromise successfully while responding to the societal demands of the time and yet put together a mechanism that not only would prove acceptable to the people but also would operate effectively when put to the test. The document was a product of this genius, although it was also essential to its success that those who would put it into practice and interpret it also have the gift of genius. American government may be a government of laws and not of men, but the laws are the product of men, and their effectiveness depends upon the men who employ them and control their use.

GOVERNMENTAL USE OF LAW IN THE EARLY YEARS

The United States in the late eighteenth and early nineteenth centuries was an agrarian society lacking industry, capital, skilled labor necessary to develop an urban economy, and economic stability in the modern sense. It was largely a rudimentary society of farmers with a merchant class limited to small shopkeepers and a few tradesmen. Most manufactured items were purchased and shipped from England or the Continent. Jefferson in his early years favored this kind of society. He viewed farmers as the chosen people of God, and he felt that there was a certain evil in urban society that should be avoided.[37] In his later years, however, he saw the need for an urban economy and for manufacturing.[38] He realized that an agrarian nation was too unstable and that without the ability to manufacture its own goods the nation would be at the mercy of Europe. To Jefferson, however, it was purely a political matter. Jefferson almost always saw things in political rather than economic terms. It is interesting to note, however, that he eventually came around to the same position as Hamilton, who viewed things more from an economic standpoint than from the standpoint of political power or the protection of civil rights. Yet a central characteristic of American society, one that was probably inherited in part from Locke, is that human liberty can be enlarged through economic activity. Certainly this was Hamilton's approach, although he seemed less interested in human liberty than did Jefferson. Nonetheless, in essence, Hamilton felt that if the nation could be placed on a sound economic basis the other problems would take care of themselves.

One of the great documents in American history is Hamilton's "Report on Manufactures,"[39] which he wrote in 1791. Although Hamilton had made a substantial contribution to the passage of the Constitution through his work on the *Federalist Papers,* his major contribution was in what he outlined and forecast for the Republic rather than what he did or what happened in his time.

Hamilton was a good secretary of the treasury, but he was not the effective politician that Jefferson was. He was most effective in working with small groups on a private basis—somewhat as a modern-day Wall Street lawyer works. "Report on Manufactures"[40] anticipated some of the main developments in the economy. If the nation could solve the problems of scarcity, encourage productivity, and provide a basis for the rapid growth of the means of production, then the other problems would largely be solved.[41] Few of Hamilton's ideas came to fruition until after his death; exceptions were the founding of the Bank of the United States and the funding of the public debt. Central emphasis in the report was to utilize machinery to promote production, and the development of machine industry would be provided by use of the protective tariff. If the taxing power was used essentially for a nonrevenue-producing purpose—to regulate importation—the United States might thereby establish manufacturing in the United States. England had benefited greatly from machine production, which had led to a division of labor. This development was also valuable, Hamilton argued, in that it would provide Americans with choices of vocation. The result was what an economist might refer to as a multiplier effect in that it served to promote the growth of private capital, to make people more creative and energetic through the division of labor and provide them with more choices in society, to develop an industrial economy, and ultimately to achieve a credit-oriented economy as the society became more industrialized. Actually, Hamilton's ideas about the benefit to be derived by individuals from economic development are not too far from Jefferson's interest in utilizing law to promote public education, but in these areas as elsewhere each approached things differently. Hamilton viewed Jefferson as preoccupied with political matters, while Jefferson viewed Hamilton as concerned only with economic affairs and with people of wealth. Fortunately, Americans eventually chose the best of each view: in the protection of civil liberties they largely followed Jefferson, and in the development of the economy, they were generally Hamiltonians.

Hamilton realized that manufacturing would not grow by itself because habit and custom tend to result in inertia and because the law should be utilized to provide the leverage to bring about change and produce economic growth. If the law provided the basis for change, if it permitted innovation, it could be an effective instrument to promote growth. He believed that the market could not be left alone to assume the risk and that government, through law, should shoulder a part of the risk. Unlike Adam Smith, Hamilton was unwilling to rely on the "unseen hand." His proposal would put in motion a course of dynamic economic growth leading to the development of industry and an increase in jobs. Thus he was prepared to use law to deal with maladjustments in the nation's needs and provide the means of correcting those needs. This use of the law would obviously allow business interests to hedge against risks and, to some degree, redistribute assets.

It is clear that the nation followed these fundamental Hamiltonian propositions not only in the early days in connection with the protective tariff but in later times as well. The railroad industry was developed to a large extent through western land grants. Not only could the railroads utilize the land in extending their tracks westward but they could also make loans on the land through eastern moneylenders. This practice aided in creating a credit-oriented economy and at the same time provided fluid capital for the railroads and the development of the industry. In the twentieth century the United States government essentially did the same thing for the automobile industry by using federal funds to construct highways. Similarly, in recent times, the aerospace industry and associated industries such as electronics have benefited from government programs. Particularly in the twentieth century, the government has not hesitated to use the income tax, including tax cuts, tax rebates, deductions, and other devices, to provide incentives for certain segments of the economy.

Thus Hamilton's "Report on Manufactures" is something of a seedbed of future policy because it was early recognized that the law can be used to produce multiple effects and that a *political* economy was a necessity if the nation was to develop economically. Political stability, in Hamiltonian terms, would be based on prosperity emanating from economic growth. In turn, peace would be maintained among competing interest groups in society by an ever-expanding material productivity. Thus society did not have to "keep order" but only had to provide an economic situation in which material wealth would allay the need for concern about order in society. The idea was that men are at peace when they are trading and dealing, balancing interests and promoting prosperity. This in turn produces social order and reduces the heat of competing economic and political groups. The development of a steady but constantly expanding market with the creation of additional submarkets and the establishment of a division of labor lowers the heat of competing economic groups and provides social order. As we have seen, Hamilton's views proved to be prophetic in that civil peace was achieved in America through the use of legal institutions and the application of law to the social and economic system, rather than through reliance on man's goodness. At times an aura of near sanctity tends to surround the authors of the Constitution. In fact, they were distrustful of man's basic nature, aware of his innate capacity for evil, and they tempered their idealism with a strong dose of pragmatism.

Even before the adoption of the Constitution, the law was used positively as a tool designed to shape the nation and deal with social conditions. Two important examples are the Ordinance of 1785 and the Northwest Ordinance of 1787. Both had strong socioeconomic overtones with respect to the new nation. There had been recurrent controversies in the 1760's and 1770's about purchases of land from the Indians, and an act passed in 1774 prevented further colonization west of the Appalachians because of these purchases.[42] Yet the demand for western land continued, leading to the problem of land titles. The Ordinance of 1785[43] provided the foundation of real-estate law in the unsettled area. It involved, in a very large sense, governmental intervention in the economy and demonstrated the relationship of law to the economy. The ordinance declared that the territories purchased from the Indians by individual states and later ceded to the United States should be disposed of in a certain way. It also provided for an arrangement whereby surveyors would divide the territory into townships of six square miles and for a method of measuring and platting the land. Each township would be marked by subdivisions into lots one mile square, or 640 acres, and numbered from 1 to 36. Various ranges of townships would be created, and the plats would ultimately be transmitted by a geographer to the "Board of Treasury" and recorded. The secretary of war had the power to retain a certain amount of the land for the use of the "late Continental Army." The land would be sold for an amount not less than one dollar an acre. The sixteenth lot in every township would be reserved for public schools. Also, one-third of all of the gold, silver, lead, and copper mined in the area was reserved, and certain designated lots out of every township were reserved for future sales.

The Ordinance of 1785 provided a system whereby land titles were derived entirely from the government. The intervention of the government eliminated the problems that would arise from allowing people to deal directly with the Indians. The perils to peace in the western area mandated that these land sales be handled through the government. In addition, the ordinance protected the regularity of titles, which was essential to economic development in the West. It was one of the great exercises of the police power in American history.[44]

Another policy established by the Ordinance of 1785 is illustrated in the holding of certain lands to pay off the moral obligation to the soldiers of the Continental Army. This was a direct forerunner of veterans' pensions, soldiers' bonuses, and GI bills. Another policy that was established was the reserving of the section in each township for schools. This represented an early government recognition of the importance of public education and of the need for government to support public education. Also the sale of land for a minimum price provided a basis for the production of government revenue, while at the same time it was not so high a price as to discourage development of the land or even land speculation. In fact, the Continental Army soldiers made a practice of trading land warrants to land speculators. In that respect the western lands represented marketable goods being traded in the private market.

The end result was that through the Ordinance of 1785 the United States used the lands in the West to do things that are often done today through taxes. Taxation is impossible outside a moneyed economy, and money was scarce in the early days, so that the land itself became a substitute for money.

Two years later, in 1787, the Northwest Ordinance[45] became the basic legal document for the Upper Mississippi Valley and Great Lakes states. It was in some ways a precursor of the federal Constitution since it is basically a Federalist document, although it contains basic guarantees that were forerunners of the Bill of Rights. The Northwest Ordinance served a number of purposes. It provided a method for western states to grow and develop and ultimately enter the Union while in the meantime retaining much of the power in Washington. For each state it provided for the appointment of a governor (although his appointment could be revoked by Congress) and for the appointment of other officials. Provisions were made for an elective general as-

sembly and a legislative council of a limited number. Only the lower house was responsible to the people.

With regard to the "Bill of Rights" protections contained in the ordinance, it must be remembered that it was merely a statute of Congress and was subject to amendment or repeal. It seems apparent that the region and its development were viewed with some fear and distrust by the states on the eastern seaboard, and the provisions were designed to protect them and also eastern creditors. The seaboard states wanted Americans to move into the Old Northwest and develop the nation, but they also wanted to protect themselves, and they were probably also worried to some degree because settled interests in the west were predominantly French. The Northwest Ordinance created a procedure for the admission of a state to the Union once it had attained a population of sixty thousand. It thereby provided a procedure for the enlargement and sharing of power in society.

In the Northwest Ordinance, the United States effected one of the great political compromises in that it provided for the development of this area and for sharing of power with the new states while at the same time protecting the interests of the existing states and of eastern creditors.

Another compromise also involved land. The central government obtained releases from the seaboard states to the land and thereby eliminated any internal conflicts over land claims. Congress would dispose of the land in those states, and thus a major resource and vital asset was retained by the central government. Like the Ordinance of 1785, the Northwest Ordinance assured the regularity of land titles.

The Northwest Ordinance represented a major balancing of interests. Although those who drafted it were distrustful and fearful of the western settlers, at the same time they created a framework to bring new states into the Union and open up the West. The limitations and controls they imposed were understandable in that they were creating a pattern of power whose future they did not know. It is perhaps significant that the drafters seemed to foresee that our system could flounder or shatter on the rock of States' rights. This was the intent behind the prohibition against secession, the retention of land ownership in the central government, equal taxation of land owned by nonresidents, and retention of navigable waterways as common, free highways for commerce. In a sense the document forecast the conflict between sectional and national markets or interests. As indicated earlier, the Northwest Ordinance was a Federalist document, and the danger to federalism was the fragmentation of its parts. To protect the system, power at the center had to be made secure.

The sum of the foregoing is that from the beginning of the new nation, and even before the Constitution, it was recognized that the law was an instrument that could and should be used to affect our particular situation. Law operates only on the margin of human experience. But law and legal institutions had to be responsive to the social conditions and economic problems of the new nation, and the Hamiltonian, or Federalist, concept involved the active use of law to shape and improve those conditions and advance societal and economic interests. Even Jefferson, despite his preoccupation with the protection of civil liberty and with political institutions, expanded the constitutional power of the executive dramatically in the Louisiana Purchase of 1803. At the time Jefferson did not know whether what he was doing was legitimate. But he felt that it was essential to the national interest to protect against foreign influences in the American west and protect commerce on the Mississippi River by purchasing the Louisiana Territory.[46] Thus, in the end, Jefferson, the States' righter and strict constructionalist, acted in such a way as to expand the power of the president as well as of the national government. Although he did so primarily for political reasons, viewing the matter as essential to the well-being and protection of the nation, the end result had enormous economic ramifications. Jefferson was thus prepared to use the power of the state in matters of great economic importance because he saw the political need for securing and protecting the Union.

THE EFFECT OF EARLY JUDICIAL DECISIONS

We need consider only a few landmark decisions of the United States Supreme Court to see the effect they have had in accommodating competing interests or in dealing with the effects of rapid, deep-seated socioeconomic change. America has experienced such an uncommonly rapid rate of change that at times in the past it has almost seemed to have occurred unnoticed. Yet a vital role of law is to permit change in such an orderly manner as to make it bearable. In an earlier book I wrote:

The law fosters change. It promotes orderly acclimation to the effects of change. This is implicit in American legal order from the early days of the Republic when the essential nature of federalism, dual sovereignty and the relative positions of institutions in our legal system were being determined on down to the present time. Law in America, when broadly viewed, could never be equated with the status quo or with vested interests or inflexible bastions of settled power. The very function of the law has been to channel and sanction change resulting from economic and technological growth or from new social values in such a way as to preserve and maintain legal order and promote continuity and the peaceful advance of our society. The fact of change, and the inescapable truth that ever-continuing change is the certainty with which the law must reckon in providing a collateral social stability in the midst of existing newness, is the central theme of American law. Law's conservatism, in the real and best sense of the word, has been manifested in its ability to accomplish the purpose of assimilating change into the broader fabric of our life and institutions without disturbing the basic framework or upsetting the momentum.[47]

Fletcher v. *Peck* has been viewed as a conservative decision, but it was actually a dynamic one in that it involved the protection of bona fide purchasers of land.[48] This case was a classic example of legislative corruption in which the Georgia legislature gave away most of what is now Alabama and Mississippi. The original grantees then sold the land to bona fide purchasers for value without notice. A later legislature tried to revoke the land sales, and the issue was presented to the United States Supreme Court for decision. The decision by Chief Justice John Marshall served to protect the market by protecting commerce in land, not only land titles or the holders of land titles as such. A fee-simple title carries with it the power to alienate the land, and it is in the social and economic interest of the nation to promote the sale of land and to protect innocent purchasers in all but extreme situations. Therefore, the decision to protect the rights of the bona fide purchasers of the land, who did not have notice of the bribery of the Georgia state legislature, served to protect title in the context of the marketplace.

While Marshall conceded in *Fletcher* v. *Peck* that one legislature cannot abridge the power of its successors and while he was protecting vested rights in one sense, he was at the same time safeguarding a very important social and economic value. It is primary in *Fletcher* v. *Peck* that, in a Lockeian kind of society in which there is a broad dispersal of power, there must be a basis for giving men a reasonable expectation that they may use the property they acquire and that they may contract with the expectation that the right to contract will be protected. In a sense this is a protection of "vested rights," but a central fact in *Fletcher* v. *Peck* is that we confront the necessity for change, for growth, and for transferability of assets in a free and competitive market. Thus, while we cannot allow one legislature to bind another as a basic presumption, still the reasonable expectations of men cannot be upset even in extreme situations involving the wholesale bribery of the legislature.

Fletcher v. *Peck* protects land titles and good-faith purchasers, but it also protects commerce, trade, and movement of goods. This was particularly essential in the context of the time because Marshall and his contemporaries lived in a land-rich, capital-poor society. Nonetheless, the value of protecting the market and the alienability of land is essential in social and economic terms in all generations. Jefferson, who was certainly not a Federalist and whose motivations were undoubtedly different, was nonetheless proud of his part in the abolition of land tenures, entail, and primogeniture in Virginia—the result being, of course, to make the land more freely alienable. In *Fletcher* v. *Peck*, since land had been defined in relation to law and made a free, bargainable commodity not unlike grain or personal property, it was easy for Marshall to apply the obligation of contracts clause to land transactions. Thus, said Marshall in his opinion:

A law annulling conveyances between individuals, and declaring that the grantors should stand seized of their former estates, notwithstanding those grants, would be as repugnant to the Constitution as a law discharging the venders of property from the obligation of executing their contracts by conveyances. It would be strange if a contract to convey was secured by the Constitution, while an absolute conveyance remained unprotected.[49]

Dartmouth College v. *Woodward*[50] deals with a different kind of title, the franchise. It expands the protection of *Fletcher* v. *Peck* to intangibles, again utilizing the obligation-of-contracts clause. The decision protected the integrity of a corporation created by the state to exercise autonomy and resolve its differences within its own framework on an indefinite basis. Dartmouth College had been incorporated under a royal charter just before the Revolution, and certain prerogatives contained in the charter later became the property of the state of New Hampshire. A community controversy subsequently involved the college, with the result that the college charter was ultimately modified to increase the number of trustees, add a board of overseers, and effectively convert the college into a state school. The trustees of the college brought an action of trover (a common-law action involving alleged misappropriation of property) against Woodward to obtain the records, corporate seal, and other corporate property to which they were alleged to be entitled. In this manner the question was raised whether the acts that had taken place violated the federal Constitution. Marshall's opinion held that they did because the Court viewed the royal charter as a contract (the state of New Hampshire having succeeded to the rights and obligations of the crown); and, as a contract for the security and disposition of property on the basis of which property had been conveyed to the corporation, it fell under the Constitution. The obligation of New Hampshire under the contract could not be altered without violating the federal Constitution.

The case, of course, had a much greater impact than the issue at hand. It was a landmark case in the development of the modern corporation and of modern corporate law. It protected the phenomenon of organization for collective action, which has been one of the nation's greatest economic assets. The origins of our productivity have been in working relations among men utilizing knowledge and skills and exchanging ideas and pooling and protecting the end product. Thus, in the Dartmouth case the Court moved from a protection of man's relation to land to a legal protection of organization and the right to control the organization that results, subject to general laws applying to all similarly situated organizations. As Marshall stated:

The objects for which a corporation is created are universally such as the government wishes to promote. They are deemed beneficial to the country; and this benefit constitutes the consideration and, in most cases, the sole consideration of the grant. In most eleemosynary institutions, the object would be difficult, perhaps unattainable, without the aid of a charter of incorporation.[51]

He concluded that

Dartmouth College is an eleemosynary institution incorporated for the purpose of perpetuating the application of the bounty of the donors, to the specified objects of that bounty; that its trustees or governors were originally named by the founder, and invested with the power of perpetuating themselves; that they are not public officers, nor is it a civil institution, participating in the administration of government; but a charity-school, or a seminary of education, incorporated for the preservation of its property, and the perpetual application of that property to the objects of its creation.[52]

Marshall realized that he was doing more in this opinion than just protecting "an eleemosynary institution." He indicated that it was quite

possible that the preservation of rights of this description was not particularly in the view of the framers of the Constitution, when the clause under consideration was introduced into that instrument [but that it] *is not enough to say that this particular case was not in the mind of the convention, when the article was framed, nor of the American people, when it was adopted* [because the] *case, being within the words of the rule, must be within its operation likewise, unless there be something in the literal construction, so obviously absurd or mischievous, or repugnant to the general spirit of the instrument, as to justify those who expound the Constitution in making it an exception.*[53]

Clearly he was providing a broad definition of the constitutional provision. He was also using the law in a dynamic way to protect societal organizations.

One of the great landmark decisions that had a major impact upon the power of the government to establish socioeconomic institutions and use them to deal with the economy was *McCulloch* v. *Maryland.*[54] This case and the Marshall Court's decision in *Gibbons* v. *Ogden*[55] came at the beginning of a period of extraordinary economic development in the country, something of a "take-off period" in terms of industrial growth in the North. The growth between 1820 and 1860 was not perhaps as dramatic as that of the late nineteenth and early twentieth centuries, but it was a period of substantial change as the northeastern seaboard states converted from a basically agrarian economy with cities that were not much more than towns to the beginning of an urban industrial society. As economic productivity increased, the fledgling industries of the North began to grow dynamically, while the South remained attached to an agricultural way of life with relatively little industrial development.

In *McCulloch* v. *Maryland,* the Court upheld the power of Congress to establish a national bank, and in *Gibbons* v. *Ogden* the Court sustained and strengthened the power of Congress in the area of interstate commerce. Both opinions were written by Marshall.

The policies of the Federalists had been directed toward protective tariffs that would permit infant industries to grow, toward internal improvements, and toward the establishment of a sound fiscal policy (all these policies were also, of course, designed to strengthen the power of the central government). Many of the fiscal aspects of federal policy centered around the establishment of the Bank of the United States. After Congress had incorporated the Second Bank of the United States, the Maryland legislature imposed a tax on the bank's branch in Baltimore, and it appeared that other states would take similar steps, as indeed Ohio did.[56] An action was brought by the state of Maryland against McCulloch, who was the cashier of the bank, to force payment of penalties for refusal to pay the state tax. In sustaining the power of Congress to incorporate the bank and in overturning the attempt by Maryland to tax it, Marshall was agreeing with an argument made earlier by Hamilton and disagreeing with early philosophy expressed by Jefferson.[57] In the McCulloch case Marshall pointed out that the Constitution had been submitted to the people and ratified by the people, not by the state legislatures. The Articles of Confederation were nothing more than an alliance, and the Constitution changed this alliance into an effective government "possessing great and sovereign powers, and acting directly on the people."[58] Thus, said Marshall, the Constitution emanated in form and substance from the people, and the powers granted by them to the central government were to be exercised directly on them and for their benefit. The national government, though limited in its powers, was supreme within its sphere of action—the principle of dual sovereignty.

While its enumerated powers did not specifically provide for the establishment of a bank or the creation of a corporation, the federal government was given other great fiscal powers, including the assessment and collection of taxes and the power to borrow money, the power to regulate commerce, and the like. Entrusted with such powers, a government also had to be entrusted with the means to exercise them. Therefore, to the enumeration of powers in the Constitution the framers added the power to make "all Laws which shall be necessary and proper for carrying into Execution the foregoing Powers, and all other Powers vested by this Constitution in the Government of the United States, or in any Department or Officer thereof."[59]

Marshall interpreted the words "necessary and proper" as including the power to employ "any means calculated to produce the end and not as being confined to those single means, without which the end would be entirely unattainable."[60] Thus a particular action did not have to be absolutely necessary in order to come within the ambit of this phrase. If it was convenient or useful in achieving the end to do a certain thing, then the action would be upheld. That was the broad principle of construction for which Hamilton had argued, as opposed to the strict construction Jefferson had espoused. Congress had the power to adopt any means that might be appropriate and were conducive to achieve the desired end.

"This provision," said Marshall, "is made in a constitution, intended to endure for ages to come, and, consequently, to be adapted to the various *crises* of human affairs."[61] If Maryland was able to abridge or annihilate a useful and necessary right of the Congress by enacting a crippling tax, it would in effect have the power to nullify and overrule the action of Congress. That could not be permitted, for there was a great principle that Marshall found to pervade the Constitution and to be "so intermixed with the materials which composed it, so interwoven with its web, so blended with its texture, as to be incapable of being separated from it without rending it to shreds."[62] This principle was that the Constitution and the laws made pursuant to it were supreme. Since "the power to tax involves the power to destroy," said Marshall, and since that power might defeat and render useless the power to create, then the action taken by the State of Maryland was contrary to the Constitution.[63]

If any case decided by the Supreme Court was more important than McCulloch, it would be difficult to find it. For

the McCulloch case made clear the supremacy of the national government in areas in which it could act, and it provided an interpretation of the "necessary and proper clause" that permitted very broad action to be taken by the Congress when such action was found to be useful and convenient in carrying out its enumerated powers. Moreover, the case emphasized that the federal government had to be a center of energy and to have the power to deal directly with the citizenry. The Marshall Court was ruling that the federal government had legitimate responsibility for the total scope of government in the United States and for the marshaling of resources.

From an economic standpoint, even though Andrew Jackson later destroyed the Bank of the United States, McCulloch remained as a precedent for the power of the Congress to exercise broad fiscal powers, and it anticipated the creation of the federal reserve system and other acts that would deal with the economy. In the time in which it was decided, the decision was essential to economic growth and development. A powerful central bank was needed at the time to control state banks, which were wholly unregulated by the states and which issued notes promiscuously and were creating an unstable currency. The Bank of the United States ultimately served to control state banks that overextended themselves. Moreover, the bank issued its own bank notes, which helped provide a sounder, more stable currency. This was discussed in 1830 in an extensive congressional report on the Second Bank of the United States by the House Ways and Means Committee.[64] The favorable report did not, however, save the bank. Andrew Jackson was worried about the bank as an institution of political power, and many of his backers were staunch supporters of state banks. In 1832 he vetoed the bill renewing the bank's charter. While Jackson's veto was a mistake, one moral concerning the destruction of the Second Bank of the United States is that, despite the functional efficiency of an institution, it is not sufficient to defend that institution on the basis of efficiency if it is not also demonstrated that there are adequate safeguards to prevent the abuse of power by the institution.

Nicholas Biddle, the head of the bank and the country's first central banker, was an efficient but arrogant man who had made the unfortunate remark that state banks exist at the forbearance of the Bank of the United States. That was true, but it was an unfortunate remark, and it illustrated a problem of power over which Jackson felt compelled to exercise control. Jackson's action illustrated an enduring fact of constitutional law: the fact that the Court in McCulloch had sustained the constitutionality of the bank did not remove the power or the duty of Congress and the President to approve or disapprove of a law acting under the Constitution. Jackson did not have to do what the Court said he could do, and his authority to make his own determination about the propriety of the bank remained. Nonetheless, the veto was a disaster because the bank was performing an important function that was based directly on socioeconomic needs, and it was not until the Civil War that the United States began to create a central banking system and not until 1913, with the passage of the Federal Reserve Act, that the country finally regained the economic power it needed to cope effectively with the national monetary system.

In *Gibbons* v. *Ogden,* Marshall acted with restraint. He could have struck down the New York statute in question under the commerce clause of the Constitution (and he did not completely pass over that ground), but he decided the case on the basis that the congressional coastal licensing statute implied a right to move freely in commerce between the states. In this way he avoided a confrontation between the power of the Supreme Court and state power and, in effect, said that Congress and not the Court had voided the New York statute. In this manner the Court overturned the act of the State of New York that gave Aaron Ogden a monopoly on steamboat travel between New York and New Jersey (rights that Ogden had purchased from Robert Fulton and his backer, Chancellor Robert R. Livingston). Ogden's opponent, Thomas Gibbons, who also operated a steamboat line between New York and New Jersey, asserted that he was protected under the federal license to engage in the trade. Ogden had sought to enjoin his competitor.

In the opinion Marshall pointed out that Congress had the power to regulate interstate and foreign commerce and that this power included navigation. Commerce was not something that stopped at the external boundary line of each state but that existed between people in different states in the case of interstate commerce or between people in different parts of the same state in the case of internal commerce. Said Marshall

The genius and character of the whole government seem to be that its action is to be applied to all the external concerns of the nation, and to those internal concerns which affect the states generally, but not to those which are completely within a particular state, which do not affect other states, and with which it is not necessary to interfere for the purpose of executing some of the general powers of the government.[65]

In other words, a state could regulate its own internal commerce, but Congress had the power to regulate external commerce. He once again applied the supremacy clause of the federal Constitution to acts passed by Congress pursuant to its enumerated or implied powers. An act of any state that was contrary to the exercise of one of the powers of Congress would violate the supremacy provisions of the federal Constitution, and that was true of an act that would inhibit an individual's use of a license under an act passed by Congress.

Once again Marshall squarely rejected an argument Jefferson had put forward with regard to commerce. The impact of the decision was to say in effect that the care and feeding of the national market, the fostering of all economic activity among the states or with foreign nations, was essential to the powers of a central government. *Gibbons* v. *Ogden* thus set the stage for future cases that would greatly broaden the commerce power. The decision was essential to national economic growth since it effectively prevented the states from passing crippling legislation hampering the transportation of goods outside the boundaries of the state. *Gibbons* v. *Ogden,* along with *McCulloch* v. *Maryland,* realized the Hamiltonian dream of a national government possessing all its necessary powers and the ability to create a nation and promote its economic development. It would be foolish to assume that Marshall was unaware of what he was doing when he wrote these opinions for the Court. He was perfectly aware of the kind of system he was creating when he stated in *McCulloch* v. *Maryland* that "we must never forget, that it is *a constitution* we are expounding."[66] It might also be said that he never forgot that it was a *national* constitution which he was interpreting and a national government with national implications for which he was providing. It may fairly be said that the system Madison and Hamilton contemplated, which would be strong enough at the center to keep the parts from flying to pieces, was firmly entrenched and established by these early landmark decisions of the Marshall Court.

We should not pass on without noting the influence in these decisions not only of Hamilton and Hamiltonian principles but also of the able statesman-lawyer Daniel Webster. Webster presented the winning arguments in the Dartmouth College case, *McCulloch* v. *Maryland,* and *Gibbons* v. *Ogden.* His arguments were often influential, particularly in *Gibbons* v. *Ogden* and the Dartmouth College case, and any attorney knows that when he is successful in a case his arguments help shape and affect the opinion of the court. Certainly that was true of Webster, who was fortunate in having clients who could carry cases to the United States Supreme Court and also in whose cases he believed.

While there were other important cases in this early period, one slightly later case stands out as one designed to promote a climate in which technological development and economic growth could take place. This was *Charles River Bridge* v. *Warren Bridge,* decided in 1837 by the Court under Chief Justice Roger B. Taney.[67] Unlike the Dartmouth College case, the issue involved a claim to a monopoly. The Charles River Bridge, a toll bridge providing access to Boston by the farmers on the other side, was owned by a company under a charter that would not expire until 1856. It had been in operation for over forty years in 1828, when Massachusetts authorized another company to build and operate a free bridge, the Warren Bridge, across the Charles River. The Charles River Bridge Company sought to enjoin the construction of the Warren Bridge, and the question ultimately came before the United States Supreme Court. Once again Daniel Webster was an attorney of record, but this time on the losing side.

Chief Justice Taney recognized that the Charles River Bridge Company was making a very substantial claim and that a great many people might be seriously affected by the decision of the Court. The case had broader implications than simply the concerns of the two competing groups. Taney observed that the "object and end of all government is to promote the happiness and prosperity of the community by which it is established."[68] He perceived the country as active and enterprising with continuous advancement in size and wealth and with new developments in communication and transportation being essential to its growth. This power could not be surrendered and this social phenomenon could not be impaired by the state because the entire community had an interest in preserving it. Thus, with regard to the rights of the holders of the Charles River Bridge charter: "While the rights of private property are sacredly guarded, we must not forget that the community also have rights and that the happiness and well-being of every citizen depends on their faithful preservation."[69] He concluded that no exclusive privilege had been given to the Charles River Bridge Company over the waters of the river, that the company could not prevent anyone else from erecting another bridge and that the state had not guaranteed that another one would not be erected. The legislature had not undertaken to revoke the franchise granted the Charles River Bridge Company; it could still take its tolls as granted by the charter. Although its income would be destroyed by the free Warren Bridge, Taney concluded that it could not be implied that any rights had been taken away and that the charter did not expressly grant the company an exclusive franchise. In connection with this decision Taney was worried about implications for the railroad industry, then in its infancy. He stated:

In some cases, rail roads have rendered the turnpike roads on the same line of travel so entirely useless, that the franchise of the turnpike corporation is not worth preserving. Yet in none of these cases have the corporation supposed that their privileges were invaded, or any contract violated on the part of the state.[70]

He went on to state that, if the Court should hold as the Charles River Bridge Company contended, "what is to become of the numerous railroads established on the same line of travel with turnpike companies and which have rendered the franchises of the turnpike corporations of no value?" In short, technological growth should not be impaired by a narrow and conservative definition of the charter.

The Charles River Bridge owners were in a special position because they had been given the right to build "the bridge" and collect tolls. The real argument was not about the corporate form but about the exclusiveness of the franchise. The bridge was essential to the economic relationship between Boston and the farmers across the river, and, therefore, the bridge owners occupied a controlling position at a key point of the socioeconomic activity in that particular area. Thus there was a problem of economic power, and the good Jacksonian point supporting this decision is that corporate powers should not be limited to a single group of individuals.

Although the effect of the denial of the exclusiveness of the charter was to take something away from the bridge owners, Taney found this outcome to be essential for the public welfare and for a nation of growing productive capacity. The police power also entered in, because the practical effect of the use of the police power has a cause-and-effect relationship to human activity. The police power deals with the relational activities of men and with their intersecting situations in society. It is a primary means of ordering relationships in society because it establishes a public interest base from which its exercise radiates. The Charles River Bridge decision was a recognition of the interest of the whole community and of the effect on other human activity of actions in the private economic sector. It has an integral and direct relationship with the police power.

In a dissenting opinion to the *Charles River Bridge* case Justice Joseph Story posed the other side of the question: When must the state pay for deprivation of certain rights? In other words, when does the use of the police power amount to a taking? The answer of the majority opinion was that, if the community by indirect action deprives an individual or group of individuals of the utility of his or their operations, payment does not have to be made. Payment has to be made only when there is a direct taking of property rights. In effect Story argued in dissent that it was not legitimate for the state to provide for the public welfare at the harm and loss of private individuals. Although Taney did not completely come to grips with this question in the majority opinion, the clear answer to Story's dissent is that to accomplish a taking one must actually acquire, damage, or impair the use of the property in question by acts that relate directly to the property rather than by acts that are indirect and extraneous.

This case was a prime example of the law being utilized to promote technological change and economic development. As mentioned earlier, Taney was primarily concerned not with the protection of later bridge builders but with not hampering the railroads or developments in communication or transportation. The economy of the early days was market- and producer-oriented, and in the value hierarchy of change Taney was putting a premium on protecting the market and encouraging the technological growth of the nation. American policy has foreseen a central role for technological change, and the courts are prepared to prefer it to vested rights except in situations in which there is a direct deprivation of vested rights or in which the protection of vested rights is essential to the protection of the market itself (as in *Fletcher* v. *Peck*). The costs of favoring competition and promoting growth are high; the cost of obsolescence is high. Taney espoused a dynamic conservatism of a type reminiscent of Marshall with technological growth rated so high on the scale of values that the cost would be allowed to fall where it might. Thus, through law, in effect the national government subsidized technological development by leaving development unimpeded. The contrary approach is manifested in Story's dissent, which would have limited change and impeded technological and economic growth.

The case also had a profound impact on capital investment. A new bridge might not be built if the old one had to be paid off, and in holding as he did, Taney was promoting capital investment by reducing the overhead and by encouraging competing interests to proceed. The *terms* of investment may often determine who can enter the field. Investment can be limited by making the costs too high or the risks too great. In a sense this case is an expression of a ruthless conservatism in which one is willing to allow economic growth and technological change to do what they may with regard to vested interests in order to promote economic progress. The law is not allowed to harm vested interests directly, as was illustrated in *Fletcher* v. *Peck,* although that may be a side effect of the free range given to economic growth and technological change, since the end result may necessarily destroy existing capital through obsolescence.

Later cases in American legal history bear a relationship to and sustain the Charles River Bridge case. One of them was *Munn* v. *Illinois*.[71] In that case with two justices dissenting, the Supreme Court held that there was no violation of the due process clause of the Fourteenth Amendment as the result of an Illinois statute regulating charges for the storage of grain in warehouses in Chicago and at other major collecting points. The case once again illustrates a situation in which enormous economic power is held by those who are able to control the economy at some key point along the line. According to evidence presented in the case, in 1874 there were fourteen warehouses in Chicago owned by about thirty persons and controlled by nine business firms. As a result, they managed to control the charges for the use of the elevators and warehouses and, in effect, control the price of grain and its transportation from the Middle West to the East Coast. That amounted to a virtual monopoly in which, to paraphrase the case, those few people stood in the very "gateway of commerce" and took their toll from all who had to pass their way. The court decided that, if any business could be clothed with a public interest and cease to be a private business only, this one had become just that. As such, it could be regulated.

The issue involved in *Munn* v. *Illinois* once again illustrates a basic activity upon which other activities depend and from which other activities radiate outward. The elevators and warehouses in Chicago had become like public utilities because the grain had to flow through Chicago in its transportation by rail to the east. Thus there was a great intersection of human activity upon which limited interests in Chicago had a stranglehold. The case also illustrates the beginning of or struggling toward a great new field of law, public-utility law, when it had become apparent that certain ventures must be controlled for the public good. By the time of *Munn* v. *Illinois* in the late nineteenth century, Americans were suffering a profound disquiet in relying on the marketplace because by that time they were feeling the power of economic concentration and the complexity and interdependence of the economy. These were the days when the "captains of industry" were emerging, and the Supreme Court in the Munn case was groping to enlarge the concept of a public utility to include a vital industry. Since the time of that case, the people have, of course, substantially broadened the base of public utility regulation, as well as the concept that a key industry occupies a place similar to that of a public utility. They have, moreover, come to recognize the importance of Justice Louis Brandeis' fear of bigness[72] in any form, whether it involves the concentration of economic power in big business, the concentration of economic power in big labor, the monopolistic aspects of public utilities or vital industries, or the concentration of societal and political power in individuals and organizations within society. Part of the greatness of the early American republic was the freedom given to organization and the high value placed on the protection of economic growth and technological change. But at the same time this priority served to permit the development of a situation in which organization and technological and economic growth produced enormous concentrations of economic power in the form of conglomerate corporations, interlocking capitalistic structures, and the control of the economy by a few. The ultimate response came in the form of the Sherman Antitrust Act, the Clayton Act, the Wagner Act, the Taft-Hartley Amendment, and the rise of large numbers of regulatory agencies designed to police corporate entities and other accumulations of power and to protect the public interest. These efforts have been only partly successful, but the success in overcoming the capital-poor situation of the early days and in establishing a credit-oriented economy with an enormous capacity for production and economic growth led Americans to realize, particularly during the Great Depression of the 1930's, the importance of the consumer. The result has been that in recent years these forces have increasingly driven the nation from the doctrine of caveat emptor to the doctrine of caveat venditor—from a producer-oriented society to a consumer-oriented society, or at least a society that places great importance upon the protection of the consumer.

CONCLUSION

The purpose of this chapter has not been to provide a comprehensive history of the early development of American law. The object has been to discuss certain key cases and documents, including the Declaration of Independence and the Constitution, as they relate to the social and economic growth of the United States. It would seem apparent from the foregoing that early in American history the people concluded that law, in whatever form it might take, was a vital instrument to be employed for the well-being of society and was to be used in a positive manner to promote and respond to economic growth and technological advance. Vested interests were protected because they had to be protected in the marketplace; but that was a direct protection, and when it came to allowing vested interests to be affected by outside economic and technological forces involving growth and change, the chips fell where they might. Except for the protection of individual rights, a movement that grew during the Civil War and its aftermath for a time before fading and then was revitalized after World War II, the national preoccupation has been with providing the widest possible sphere in which individual initiative can operate effectively and in which economic growth and social advance will occur.

In the early days when the central government imposed its authority, the end result, as in *Gibbons* v. *Ogden* and *McCulloch* v. *Maryland,* was to provide a situation in which the states would not destroy what was obviously destined to become a nationwide interlocking economic system. Only with the rise of the captains of industry or robber barons of the late nineteenth century did the nation come to a sudden realization that there was a certain legitimacy in the power problem that the Jacksonians foresaw but did not fully understand. The problem was one of huge concentrations of power. It resulted from the high value placed upon organization and economic growth in society and the overwhelming success that eventuated.

The problems at issue were monopoly as foretold by the

Charles River Bridge case and dealing with key points of intersection in the economic process as illustrated not only by the Bridge case but even more vividly by *Munn* v. *Illinois.* It was necessary to protect the personal and property rights of individuals who might become victims of the system. The Supreme Court began to provide such protection in approving statutes providing for maximum hours of work, minimum wages, and the like. A decision along these lines was *Holden* v. *Hardy*, sustaining a law providing maximum working hours for miners.[73] The tendency was presaged even more vividly by Justice Oliver Wendell Holmes's dissent in *Lochner* v. *New York,*[74] in which a majority of the Supreme Court struck down a New York law providing for maximum hours of work for bakers, and Holmes in dissent wrote that the Fourteenth Amendment "does not enact Mr. Herbert Spencer's *Social Statics*" and that "a Constitution is not intended to embody a particular economic theory, whether paternalism and the organic relation of the citizen to the state or of *laissez faire.*"[75] Instead a Constitution "is made for people of fundamentally differing views, and the accident of our finding certain opinions natural and familiar or novel and even shocking ought not to conclude our judgment upon the question whether statutes which embody them conflict with the Constitution of the United States."[76] Holmes's dissent was in keeping with the earlier decisions, previously dis-

cussed, giving free range to the marketplace and to economic growth and development but at the same time in preventing a few private individuals or corporations from controlling or attempting to control economic situations to the detriment of the public interest. By the late 1930's, after a spate of decisions striking down the early legislation of the New Deal, the Supreme Court eventually came around to Holmes's thinking in his dissent in Lochner. The ability of the federal government to deal with the national economy, barring a fundamental incursion upon the rights of individuals, would not, for the most part, be questioned seriously after that time.

The history of American law has in large measure been one of maximizing opportunities for socioeconomic growth and social and technological change, while at the same time attempting to control the side effects and confine this expansion of energy within a framework that is socially beneficial and not threatening to individual citizens or harmful to human initiative. We must not forget, said Marshall, that it is a Constitution we are expounding and that the Constitution is intended to endure for ages to come and to be adapted to the various crises of human affairs. And we must not forget, said Holmes, that, in this adaptation to crises, the Constitution must be sufficiently broad to accommodate people of fundamentally differing views.

NOTES

1. See generally Robert A. Leflar, "Sources of Judge-Made Law," 24 *Okla. L. Rev.* 319 (1971) and Leflar, "Appellate Judicial Innovation," 27 *Okla. L. Rev.* 321 (1974). In the latter article this leading American legal scholar states: "The common law system could not have survived through the centuries if it had been no more than a method of perpetuating its own past. It has survived and is healthy today because in the hands of wise judges it is a system that calls for growth, one that builds on the past to meet the needs of the present and the future. The system will not tolerate hog-wild innovation, but without innovation, it will die—it would have died long ago. Legislatures can aid the courts in updating the law, but much of the ultimate responsibility rests upon our appellate courts and, specifically, upon the judges who sit on those courts." 27 *Okla. L. Rev.* at 346.

2. Coke's life was the subject of C. Bowen, *The Lion and the Throne* (1956). Extensive discussions of Coke can be found in other works, one of the more generally utilized being T. Plucknett, *A Concise History of the Common Law* (5th ed. 1956). For an extensive, scholarly evaluation, see 5 W. Holdsworth, *A History of English Law* 423–493 (2d ed. 1937).

3. See J. Pomeroy, *1 Equity Jurisprudence* 18–32 (5th ed. 1941).

4. W. Swindler, *Magna Carta* 175 (1965).

5. T. Plucknett, *supra* note 2, at 283.

6. See the discussion in R. Wright, *The Law of Airspace* 32–36 (1968), and R. Pound, 3 *Jurisprudence* 387–388, 428–429 (1959).

7. 8 Co. Rep. 114a (1610), in which Coke stated: ". . . it appears in our books, that in many cases the common law will controul Acts of Parliament, and sometimes adjudge them to be utterly void: for when an Act of Parliament is against common right and

reason, or repugnant, or impossible to be performed, the common law will controul it and adjudge such Act to be void." This dictum probably reflected Coke's views rather than the law of England as of that moment. Ultimately, however, such great documents as the Magna Carta would come to be regarded as fundamental English law (having modern import in the nonfeudal segments). Thus Oliver Cromwell would later remark that "in every government there must be something fundamental, somewhat like a Magna Carta, which should be standing and unalterable." Coke's dictum was prescient.

8. See T. Plucknett, *supra* note 2, at 242.

9. W. Swindler, *supra* note 4, at 172.

10. Id.

11. Id. at 185.

12. 418 U.S. 683 (1974). In the course of the opinion Chief Justice Burger stated for the Court: "The impediment that an absolute, unqualified privilege would place in the way of the primary constitutional duty of the Judicial Branch to do justice in criminal prosecutions would plainly conflict with the function of the courts under Art. III. In designing the structure of our Government and dividing and allocating the sovereign power among three co-equal branches, the framers of the Constitution sought to provide a comprehensive system, but the separate powers were not intended to operate with absolute independence." To do what the President claimed, said the Chief Justice, "would upset the constitutional balance of 'a workable government' and gravely impair the role of the courts under Art. III." 418 U.S. at 707. As a predicate the Court stated: "We therefore reaffirm that it is the province and duty of this Court 'to say what the law is' with respect to the claim of privilege presented in this case. *Marbury* v. *Madison, supra,*

at 177." 418 U.S. at 705. See Raoul Berger, "The President and the Constitution," 28 *Okla. L. Rev.* 97 (1975).

13. Coke's *Commentary on Littleton* (his *First Institute*) was published in 1628. His *Second Institute,* dealing with the Magna Carta and the old statutes of Edward I, was published in 1642. His *Third* and *Fourth Institutes,* on court jurisdiction and criminal law, were published in 1644. See 3 R. Pound, *supra* note 6 at 428. The *Commentary on Littleton* and the *Second Institute* had major impact. The later volumes are of substantially less importance. Blackstone's *Commentaries* had tremendous influence in both England and the Colonies. They appeared only a few years before the American Revolution, and were accepted as "quasi authority" in America. 3 R. Pound, *supra* note 6 at 388.

14. See 3 R. Pound, *supra* note 6 at 428–429. Pound says that Blackstone's *Commentaries* were "much used in America in the contests between the colonies and the crown which culminated in the Revolution."

15. See discussion in *B. Schwartz, The Law in America* 17 (1974).

16. As quoted, id. at 16.

17. Id. at 17.

18. Id. On this general subject see F. Rodell, *Fifty-five Men* (1936).

19. B. Schwartz, *supra* note 15, at 27.

20. Id. at 28.

21. Kent's *Commentaries on American Law* (1826–1830) was viewed by Pound as a "clear and accurate . . . exposition of our common law as received after the Revolution" and one which "generally stood for a decisive statement of it." 3 R. Pound, *supra* note 6, at 428–429. M. Radin, *Anglo-American Legal History* 303 (1936) stated that Kent and Story "developed the institutional textbook to an extent that was not known in England and created an influence for it that had not been known before."

22. See M. Radin, *supra* note 21.

23. For example, *Ark. Stat. Ann.* § 1–101 (1956 Repl.) provides: "The Common Law of England, so far as the same is applicable and of a general nature, and all statutes of the British Parliament in aid of or to supply the defects of the common law made prior to the fourth year of James the First (that are applicable to our own form of government), of a general nature and not local to that kingdom, and not inconsistent with the Constitution and laws of the United States or the Constitution and laws of this State, shall be the rule of decision in this State unless altered or repealed by the General Assembly of this State." See also such statutes as *Mo. Ann Stat.* § 1.010 (1969) and *Tex. Rev. Civ. Stat. Ann.* art. 1 (1969).

24. Quoted in B. Schwartz, *supra* note 15, at 29.

25. 1 *200 Years* 72 (Newman ed. 1973).

26. Id. at 80.

27. Id. Jefferson was particularly irritated by deletion of his references to slavery.

28. J. Locke, *Second Treatise . . . of Civil Government,* which is reproduced in *English Philosophers from Bacon to Mill* (Burtt ed. 1939).

29. Quoted in 1 *200 Years, supra* note 25 at 73.

30. The Fifth Amendment of the Bill of Rights returns to the "life, liberty, or property" phrase in the due-process clause, and the language is repeated in the Fourteenth Amendment. In discussing why men enter into a political society, Locke stated that man in a state of nature is in danger and that "it is not without reason that he seeks out and is willing to join in society with others, who are already united, or have a mind to unite, for the mutual preservation of their lives, liberties, and estates, which I call by the general name, property." Quoted from excerpts of Locke's writ-

ings contained in 1 *The People Shall Judge* 92 (Univ. of Chicago, 1949).

31. The Fifth Amendment, particularly the due-process clause, is, of course, the most obvious example, although the first nine amendments address themselves to this general proposition.

32. Locke stated, among other things: "Absolute arbitrary power, or governing without settled standing laws, can neither of them consist with the ends of society and government, which men would not quit the freedom of the state of nature for, and tie themselves up under, were it not to preserve their lives, liberties, and fortunes; and by stated rules of right and property to secure their peace and quiet." Thus what government does "must be with . . . the consent of the majority giving it either by themselves or by their representatives chosen by them." *The People Shall Judge, supra* note 30, at 96, 97.

33. Although they did not say so expressly, the framers of the Constitution were in effect exercising that right when they created a new basic document and an instrument of government to replace that of the Articles of Confederation (although the loose-knit government under the articles had not impinged on any basic rights).

34. *An American Primer* 103–104 (Boorstin ed. 1966), in a chapter written by Clarence L. Ver Steeg.

35. Id. at 108, in a chapter written by C. Herman Pritchett.

36. See, *e.g.,* B. Schwartz, *supra* note 15, at 39, 47.

37. Jefferson wrote: "Those who labor in the earth are the chosen people of God, if he ever had a chosen people, whose breasts he has made his peculiar deposit for substantial and genuine virtue." But as for manufacturing: "Dependence begets subservience and venality, suffocates the germ of virtue, and prepares fit tools for the designs of ambition." *The People Shall Judge, supra* note 30 at 415.

38. In 1816, Jefferson stated: "Shall we make our own comforts, or go without them, at the will of a foreign nation? He, therefore, who is now against domestic manufacture must be for reducing us either to dependence on that foreign nation, or to be clothed in skins, and to live like wild beasts in dens and caverns. I am not one of these; experience has taught me that manufactures are now necessary to our independence as to our comfort." Id. at 416.

39. See I *Reports of the Secretary of the Treasury of the United States* 78 et seq. (1837).

40. Id.

41. As Willard Hurst has written: "We believed that we could build a freer life for more men from a steadily rising material productivity, and we bent public policy largely to this purpose. In this respect we were all Hamiltonians. It accorded with the culture that here law's support functions related more to the economy than to any other non-legal institution. Economic means were our main reliance for fashioning new ways of life. . . . The rush and scale of our economic growth made all forms of power specially dependent upon economic development; law thus naturally concerned itself largely with economic power. Social order here became peculiarly dependent upon economic order; in proportion as we used law to sustain social framework, we thus used law largely to support economic processes." J. Hurst, *Law and the Social Process in United States History* 224–226 (1960).

42. This was the Quebec Act of 1774.

43. The ordinance was enacted by the Congress under the Articles of Confederation on May 20, 1785.

44. The police power is the power of the state to enact laws designed to promote the health, morals, safety, and general welfare of the community. It is a broad power that, generally speaking, is invalid only when it is exercised arbitrarily, capriciously, or unreasonably or when it amounts to a taking of private property for

public use without just compensation, or when it is employed for some nonpublic use or purpose.

45. This ordinance was also enacted under the Congress of the Articles of Confederation on July 13, 1787. It is reproduced in *Documents Illustrative of the Formation of the Union of the American States* (69th Cong.; 1st Sess., House Document No. 238 (1927) at 47–54), as well as in a substantial number of reference works.

46. See *The People Shall Judge, supra* note 30, at 496–499.

47. R. Wright, *supra* note 6, at 277.

48. 6 Cranch 87 (1810).

49. Id. at 137.

50. 4 Wheaton 518 (1819).

51. Id. at 637.

52. Id. at 640–641.

53. Id. at 644–645.

54. 4 Wheaton 316 (1819).

55. 9 Wheaton 1 (1824).

56. See *The People Shall Judge, supra* note 30, at 465.

57. Id. at 417–426. Jefferson argued: "The second general phrase is 'to make all laws *necessary* and proper for carrying into execution the enumerated powers.' But they can all be carried into execution without a bank. A bank therefore is not *necessary* and consequently not authorized by this phrase." Id. at 419. To Jefferson "necessary" meant "those means without which the grant of power would be nugatory." Id.

58. 4 Wheaton at 404.

59. Art. I, Sec. 8, Constitution of the United States.

60. 4 Wheaton at 413–414.

61. Id. at 415.

62. Id. at 426.

63. Id. at 431.

64. See *Register of Debates in Congress . . . of the First Session of the Twenty-second Congress together with an Appendix Containing Important State Papers and Public Documents . . .* (1833) VIII, 132–139, 142–143.

65. 9 Wheaton at 195.

66. 4 Wheaton at 407.

67. 11 Peters 420 (1837).

68. Id. at 547. This is basic Lockeian philosophy, as discussed earlier.

69. Id. at 548.

70. Id. at 550–551.

71. 94 U.S. 113 (1876).

72. In this regard Brandeis dealt largely with concentrations of economic power held by large corporations and in that context wrote of "the curse of bigness." He was writing in the context of his time, but his philosophy would certainly lead him to apply it with equal vigor to all large concentrations of economic or governmental power without regard to the nature or source. On Brandeis see A. Mason, *Brandeis: A Free Man's Life* 610–613 (1946). See also *Mr. Justice Brandeis* 129–140 (F. Frankfurter ed. 1932).

73. 169 U.S. 366 (1898).

74. 198 U.S. 45 (1905).

75. Id. at 75.

76. Id. at 76.

5

BUSINESS: THE CHANGING SCENE

By Daniel A. Wren

Americans seem preoccupied with business: historians analyze it, journalists describe it, politicians debate it, labor unions bargain with it, novelists lampoon it, consumers buy from it, and detractors criticize its practices. Despite its blemishes, business furnishes every man's sustenance in one way or another. Business touches every facet of our life, and its well-being is tied closely to the progress of the nation. From the corner merchants who brings us bread and milk to the nultinational conglomerate, our activities, our livelihood, and our appetites are served by business. The history of business is more than a history of the businessman, it is a story of interlocking lives of producers, consumers, financiers, retailers, and all manner of citizens who are striving for economic and social betterment in a land of political opportunity. Part of the fascination business holds for many is the premise that it represents a way to span the turbulent waters of social class. That is the American dream of the self-made man who rises from poverty to wealth and success. Another part of our fascination resides in a love-hate, attraction-revulsion attitude toward business and businessmen. While business brings us our sustenance, it is feared, much as a father is feared, for the power it wields over us. It is this split character of the American (perhaps of all) people that has given business its unique flavor throughout history. In American history the businessman has seen his role in society defined, blurred, and redefined by various generations. Throughout all the two hundred years of America's existence as a nation, it is this changing scene of business that commands our attention.

ANTE-BELLUM ENTERPRISE, 1776–1860

The Colonial Setting

America was a colony for almost as many years as it has been a nation. For its foreign settlers the lure of America was manifold: social betterment, economic opportunity, religious freedom, and political separation. No one element explains the whole, for the nation that was to emerge was a conglomerate of parts that defy a separate identification and explanation. The newcomers to these alien and often hostile shores were aristocrats as well as felons, and tramps and tarts as well as budding tycoons.

While the emigrants to America had varied backgrounds and goals, their arrival was due in no small part to the economic policies of England. The English had many colonies that sustained its economic prowess and proved its maritime superiority. The East Indian Company, the South Sea Company, and the Hudson's Bay Company had demonstrated, with varying degrees of success, the importance of a colonial system to the English national well-being. The national policy was one of mercantilism, and its goal was that of providing an outlet for English manufactured goods in the colonies while using the colonies to produce and ship raw materials to the motherland. This philosophy of mercantilism injected the government into a central role of financing and protecting trade in order to build a strong economy. It meant that the government intervened in all economic affairs, engaged in state economic planning, and regulated private economic activity to a large degree.

The American colonies were thus essentially business ventures, founded for commercial purposes to serve the homeland. From Virginia and Maryland would come the tobacco; from the Carolinas rice and indigo (for dye), along with cotton, were expected; and from Massachusetts and other New England settlements were to come furs from trade with the Indians and fish and whale products. In the southern colonies attempts were made to grow grapes to make wine and thereby to sever England's dependence on her traditional continental enemies. Raw materials for England's mills would come from the vast land and abundant resources of America. It was the policy of mercantilism that brought settlers to America; yet in that settlement and in the English economic policy were the seeds of discontent. It was the yoke of English mercantile domination that incensed the settlers and spurred them to seek independence from a far away master.

The Economic Seeds of Revolution. While it is not possible to explain the American Revolution as primarily economically motivated, it is evident that the economic burdens imposed by England on the colonists provided manifest grievances for latent discontents. From the English viewpoint various restrictions had to be placed on colonial activities to ensure the protection of English industry, a favorable balance of trade, and full employment (the mercantile philosophy). For the Colonies these restrictions were straws accumulating over the years to break their backs in the service of England. The colonial trade acts passed by Parliament were many: a series of Navigation Acts from 1651 to 1763 controlled colonial imports, exports, and manufactures; the Hat Act of 1732 forbade colonial manufacture of beaver hats; the Iron Act of 1750 prohibited the finishing of iron products; and the Molasses Act of 1733 placed a heavy tax on the importation of molasses, a cornerstone of colonial commerce since it was used in the making of rum. Other acts, such as the Sugar Act (1764), the Stamp Act (1765), the Quartering Act (1765) and the Tea Act (1773) added to the colonists' burdens. While history romanticizes the Tea Act and the subsequent Boston Tea Party, this was only the final sip from a cup of bitter brew.

A Cultural Heritage. Despite the grievances against the British and the severance of ties with that nation, America remained uniquely English, not only in tongue but in manners, morals, customs, and most of its cultural heritage. England had given America a flavor that would endure and prosper in the New World. Those benefits were many and furnished an impetus to a people who were weak but growing stronger year by year. Not all colonists wanted to break with England. About one-third remained steadfastly loyal to the crown, and those persons, called Tories, were to lose a great deal when the Revolution succeeded. One-third were neutral, either undecided or uncaring about the course of human events. The Revolution was the product of the other one-third of the populace—perhaps radicals, perhaps visionaries, but activists nevertheless. When victory seemed imminent, those in the neutral camp joined the rebels, ensuring a severance of the umbilical cord that for 168 years had nurtured the narrow strip of colonies along the Atlantic Seaboard. The result was a nation new in its independence but old in its cultural heritage of political, social, and economic ideals.

The *political* heritage was a long acquaintance with democratic, representative government. While major world powers retained monarchical privileges, England had placed its monarch under a constitution and bound his rule by consent of the governed. In the history of human liberty John Locke's essay *Concerning Civil Government* (1690) must stand as a great contribution to political theory and as an effective instigator of political action. It stated the principles of the "bloodless Revolution" of 1688, which brought about substantial fundamental changes in the British constitution. It also set the stage for the American Revolution of 1776 by inspiring the authors of the Declaration of Independence. Locke attacked the "divine right of kings," whose proponents traced this right to Adam's God-given right to rule his children, and set forth some new concepts of authority:

. . . who shall be judge whether the prince or legislative body act contrary to their trust? . . . To this I reply, the people shall be judge.

This notion found more explicit support in the Declaration of Independence:

We hold these truths to be self-evident, that all men are created equal, that they are endowed by their Creator with certain unalienable Rights, that among these are Life, Liberty, and the pursuit of Happiness.—That to secure these rights, governments are instituted among Men, deriving their just powers from the consent of the governed.

From Locke's work would come America's political heritage: First, men are governed by a natural law of reason and not the arbitrary rules of tradition of the whims of a central authoritarian figure. Second, civil society is built upon private property. The law of nature and reason commands one not to harm another's possessions and men enter into a civil society in order to preserve more perfectly their liberty and property, and these are then protected by both natural law and civil law. Since man has a natural right to property, the state cannot take it away from him but must rather protect his right to it. Third, a government derives its powers from the governed. Fourth, liberty to pursue individual goals is a natural right.

These four ideas interwove in practice to form a solid political foundation for industrial growth. It sanctioned laissez-faire economics, assured the pursuit of individual rewards, guaranteed the rights of property, gave protection to contracts, and provided for a system of justice among men.

The *social* heritage was strongly Protestant, giving the new nation a gospel of work, thrift, and diligence. Founded in part by stoics, the Puritans, America retained much of this worldly asceticism throughout its colonial days and afterward. The Reverend Cotton Mather had said before the Revolution that man had two "callings": to serve the Lord Jesus Christ and to pursue a "particular employment by which his usefullness to his neighborhood is distinguished." Business was God's work too, and this Protestant ethic provided an earthly sanction for commercial activities. Max Weber stated the case for Protestantism as creating the spirit of capitalism. In Weber's view Martin Luther had developed the idea of a "calling" in the sense of a task set by God, a life task. That new idea had evolved during the Reformation and became a central dogma of Protestant denominations. It placed worldly affairs as the highest form of moral activity for the individual and gave the performance of earthly duties a religious significance and sanction. Every man's occupation was a calling and as such legitimate in the sight of God. Weber saw this view as a keystone in developing a spirit of effort and gain; man was no longer able to give free rein to irrational impulses but was required by dogma to exercise self-control over his every action. One proved his faith in worldly activity, and he did it with zeal and self-discipline.

This new Protestant asceticism, which Weber also characterized as Puritanism, did not condone the pursuit of wealth for its own sake, for wealth would lead to pleasure seeking and to all the temptations of the flesh. Instead activity became the goal of the good life. Many corollaries developed in practice: (1) that the waste of time was the deadliest of sins, since every hour wasted meant a loss of the opportunity to labor for the glory of God; (2) that man must be willing to work: "He who will not work shall not eat"; (3) that the division and specialization of labor was a result of divine will since it led to the development of a higher degree of skill and to improvement in the quality and quantity of production and hence served the good of all; and (4) that consumption beyond basic needs was wasteful and therefore sinful: "Waste not, want not."

The Protestant ethic postulated that God desired profitability, that that was a sign of grace, and that to waste anything and reduce profits, or to forgo what might be a profitable venture, worked against God's will. By not seeking luxury, each man created a surplus or profit from his labors. A person could not consume created wealth beyond his basic needs, and thus the surplus was to be reinvested in other ventures or the improvement of present ones. In short, the Protestant ethic provided a social base for industrial development.

Two documents of 1776 tolled the death of mercantilism, the American Declaration of Independence, and Adam Smith's *The Wealth of Nations*. America's economic heritage was largely mercantile, but the pressures for an escape from the policies of England were strong. Coincident with the Declaration of Independence in America, Smith's book appeared in England. It was a declaration of *economic* independence. In the eighteenth century the Physiocratic school of thought emerged to challenge mercantilism. It advocated laissez-faire capitalism: the government should "let alone" the mechanisms of the market. Economics had a natural order and harmony, and government intervention interfered with the natural course of events. Adam Smith, a Scottish political economist, was not a Physiocrat per se but was influenced by their view of a natural harmony in economics. In *The Wealth of Nations*, Smith established the "classical" school and became the father of liberal economics. Smith thought that the tariff policies of mercantilism were destructive and, rather than protecting industry, penalized efficiency by state fiat and consequently misallocated the nation's resources. Smith proposed that only the market and competition be the regulators of economic activity. The "invisible hand" of the market would ensure the flow of resources to their best consumption and most efficient reward, and the economic self-interest of each person and nation, acting in a fully competitive market, would bring about the greatest prosperity to all.

When his writing appeared in the early stages of the Industrial Revolution, Smith found a large number of supporters for his liberal economics. He was in tune with the philosophy of the Enlightenment and the newly emerging group of entrepreneurs who wanted to sweep away the restrictions of mercantilism and the controlling power of the landed aristocracy. Americans found in Smith's market ethic an economic sanction for private initiative rather than mercantilism, competition rather than protection, innovation rather than economic stagnation, and self-interest rather than state interest as the motivating force. The market ethic became an important element of the cultural environment in which the industrial system flowered.

In the years between 1776 and 1787 the ideas of Adam Smith were widely read and discussed by American business and political leaders. Smith's writings fit into the philosophical concept of the new nation held by those who protested the strong role of government in economic matters. Smith's laissez-faire inclinations were acceptable to the framers of the Constitution. Article I, Section 8, gave Congress the power to impose and collect taxes, borrow money, coin money, fix standards of weights and measures, punish counterfeiters, issue patents, and to "regulate commerce with foreign nations and among the several states." Except for those powers government was evidently to maintain a relatively hands-off approach to economic affairs and to act primarily to maintain uniformity and order among the states. The American experience with the mercantilistic restrictions and duties had led to a desire to limit the role of government in economic matters. The flexibility of the commerce clause would not be taken advantage of by legislators for some years.

In brief, England's cultural legacy to America provided for a constitutional government, property rights, means to redress grievances, and the consent of the governed in all affairs. The Protestant ethic provided a duty to work and to use one's wealth wisely. The acceptance of Adam Smith's economics placed government in the role of an arbitrator, promoting uniformity in but not interfering with the commerce of the states. This English heritage, coupled with rich land, abundant timber, teeming streams, and seemingly endless natural resources gave America's business interests a propulsion toward world leadership.

Early American Business

The Expansion of Markets. The new nation was not to be confined to its coastal boundaries for long. The Northwest Territory beckoned, and settlers faced uncharted trails and sometimes hostile natives as they moved into Ohio, Indiana, Illinois, Michigan, and the middle states Kentucky and Tennessee. An aggressive national policy led to new territories: Louisiana (1803), Florida (1819), Texas (1845), Oregon (1846), and California (1848). Despite the expanding areas, trade remained largely localized. The trading regions were small, primarily because of crude means of transportation. No one ventured far to exchange the products of his labors for the commodities of the local general store or a neighboring village. Peddlers, or hawkers, the early traveling salesmen, inspired a litany of American jokes, as they took their wares to isolated farms and communities. Along rivers and canals rose cities such as St. Louis, Memphis, and Cincinnati, which became primary trade centers and would remain so until the railroads expanded trading areas.

As long as the markets were local, the traditional method of producing to serve consumers, the *domestic system*, remained viable. Under the domestic, or "putting-out" system, a merchant procured the raw materials and farmed them out to individual workers or families, who, using their own equipment, completed the products in their homes and delivered them to the merchant for a wage. The faults of the domestic system lay in the simple tools and technology and the lack of incentive to improve them, and in the inefficiencies of small-scale production with a limited division of labor. As the volume of trade grew, the domestic system proved inefficient, and the need for more capital, the benefits to be gained from specializing labor, and the economies of scale of a centralized workplace led to the *factory system*. As late as 1820 two-thirds of the textiles used in American homes were made in American homes under the domestic system, but by 1830 it was clear that the domestic system could no longer serve the market needs of the expanding nation. Advances in transportation, power, and communications were soon to make possible the supplanting of the domestic system with the factory system, an outgrowth of the Industrial Revolution in England.

America's Industrial Revolution. The Industrial Revolution began in England. At the base of the revolution was a new source of power, the steam engine. The steam engine was not new. Hero of Alexandria (circa A.D. 200) developed one for amusement. Later inventors built models but were hampered by mechanical problems. The Englishman James Watt developed the first workable steam engine in 1765, but twelve years elapsed before the financial and experimental problems were resolved and the engine was installed in industry. During this time Watt formed a partnership with Matthew Boulton, a leading English ironmaker, and they perfected steam power for Boulton's foundry. Later harnessed to the wheels of a hundred industries, the steam engine provided efficient, cheap power for ships, trains, and factories, revolutionizing English commerce and industry. Steam power lowered production costs and therefore prices and expanded markets. The growing market called for more workers, more machines, and a larger production scale on a regular basis and led to a need for management and organization. Capital was needed to finance these larger undertakings, and the men who could command the capital began to bring together workers and machines under one common authority. Labor was divided, each man specializing in some task; parts of certain products had to become interchangeable so that the division of labor would lead to a common final result. Out of the division of labor would come the need for the direction and coordination of efforts. Thus was born the factory system as a method of production.

The Industrial Revolution came to America slowly owing to England's restrictions on allowing skilled labor to emigrate and on exporting technological information. The physical elements of the Industrial Revolution in America were coal, iron, transportation, machinery, power, and factories. The human elements were entrepreneurs with a zeal for innovation and profits and a largely agrarian and handicraft labor force. Organizations were being reshaped by the demands for heavy infusions of capital, by the division of labor, and by the need for economical, predictable performance. Organizations needed to innovate and compete in a market economy, and this need created pressures for growth and the economies to be obtained from large-scale production and distribution. The entrepreneur-manager performed a distinct role in combining the traditional three factors of production (land, labor, and capital) in the ever-growing factory system. With size came the need for managers; for a capable, disciplined, trained, motivated work force; and for rationalizing of the planning, organizing, and controlling of operations in the early enterprise.

The factory system brought a new thrust to the nation's ability to produce. In contrast to the domestic system, the characteristics of the factory system were a substantial output of relatively standardized products made for distribution over a wide geographical, rather than local, scale; operations to be carried on in one or a few adjacent buildings in which there were mechanized processes and a central power source; and the assembling of workers who performed various tasks under organized supervision.

England had sought to prevent industrial development in America by prohibiting the sale of manufacturing equipment and the emigration of skilled labor. Samuel Slater, a textile engineer for Richard Arkwright, listed his occupation as farmer on his emigration papers, memorized detailed blueprints of the English textile equipment, and upon his arrival in America reconstructed the necessary equipment. With Moses Brown, a Quaker merchant of means, he launched America's first textile factory in 1790 with a seventy-two-spindle mill at Pawtucket, Rhode Island. On a visit to England, Francis Cabot Lowell observed textile manufacturing. He copied the designs of mechanical weaving equipment, brought them surreptitiously to America, and established the Boston Manufacturing Company at Waltham, Massachusetts. Other factories and other entrepreneurs followed until the New England textile industry grew to rival that of England.

Early business firms were more often than not, products of inventors' fertile minds and the open pocketbooks of capitalists. Inventors were prolific: Eli Whitney and the cotton gin (1794), Paul Revere's method of producing rolled copper (1801), Robert Fulton's steamboat (1807), Jethro Wood's iron plow (1819), Cyrus McCormick's reaper (1831), Thomas Davenport's electric motor (1834), and Charles Goodyear's rubber-vulcanizing process (1839) were examples of American ingenuity at work. Eli Whitney also took a giant step forward when he manufactured firearms on the principle of interchangeable parts. This principle was later applied to the manufacture of clocks and watches, sewing machines, and agricultural implements. In 1846 Elias Howe invented a sewing machine that was later improved upon by Isaac Singer. Hand-made tin cans were in use as early as 1820, and in 1853, Gail Borden succeeded in tinning evaporated milk, reducing people's dependence on fresh food.

In step with advances in manufacturing, the role of the entrepreneur was changing from that of merchant to one of hiring and organizing labor, producing, financing, and selling products. Despite this growth firms remained relatively small. For example, in 1850 the McCormick Harvester Company of Chicago employed three hundred workers, but was managed entirely by Leander McCormick and four foremen. American capitalists began engaging in philanthropy during this time, following the lead of Moses Brown, who in 1770 had founded Rhode Island College in Providence (which became Brown

University in 1804). Of all the advancements and inventions none tells the story of American industrial growth better than the progress in steel. Steel is the sinew of any industrial economy. Iron, because of its impurities, caused many problems for early machine designers and factory owners. The race to improve iron production proceeded, as is often the history of invention, on parallel concurrent paths in England and America. William Kelly, of Kentucky, began his experiments in 1847 and perfected a system of refining iron by subjecting it to a blast of hot air in a specially built furnace. Unfortunately, Kelly did not apply for a patent until 1857, two years after Sir Henry Bessemer had obtained his patent in England. The Bessemer process, based on the same idea, was an improvement over the very slow process of puddling, the removal of carbon and other impurities by passing heated gases over the molten iron. Until 1908 and the perfection of the open-hearth method of making steel, the Bessemer process formed the basis for the world's steel industry. The Americans made the most of their ingenuity in production; in 1868 the United States produced 8,500 tons of steel, Britain 110,000; in 1879 the countries' outputs were nearly equal; and in 1902, America produced 9,188,000 tons, England, 1,826,000. American industry was showing its mettle.

The Status of Labor. Labor, especially skilled labor, was scarce in America and has remained relatively so to this day. American wages were higher than those of England and the American worker was better off in terms of working conditions. Charles Dickens, that outspoken critic of the English factory system, lavished praise on New England mills after his visit in 1842 (*American Notes*). There were sweat shops in the clothing industry, especially in New York, Philadelphia, and Boston, but, on the whole the Americans were better masters than the English.

In textiles and other industries labor posed a problem as it did in England. The labor force remained largely unskilled, owing to England's continuing efforts to prevent skilled workers from leaving the country. To attract labor, early textile manufacturers developed two distinct labor-relations policies: the "Rhode Island system," begun by Slater at Pawtucket and later at Fall River, Massachusetts; and the "Waltham system" begun by Lowell and his associates. The Rhode Island system, patterned after the English practice of employing the whole family if possible, resulted in more child workers. In contrast, the Waltham system was designed to attract female workers to the factory by establishing company boardinghouses. Workers in the textile factories, mainly "Yankee" girls, were brought to the factories from the neighboring farms by agents touring the countryside emphasizing the moral and educational advantages of factory work. The girls had to be in the boardinghouses at 10:00 P.M., and their moral conduct was carefully supervised by housemothers. The American factory did not demonstrate in the same depth the evils as did the English factory. Employers were paying high wages to attract and hold their workers, child labor was not as prevalent, and abuses were less frequent and less severe. The American worker was less resistant to the introduction

of machinery, and the Luddites of England found few followers in America, except in Pittsburgh, where some hand-loom weavers rioted and destroyed their machines. Guilds were less well entrenched, and the American employer found innovation more acceptable to his workers.

The immigration of Irish and Germans in the 1830's and 1840's added to a swelling population. Labor remained scarce, however, as the western frontier continued to open new opportunities. The hours of labor were long by today's standards, typically twelve hours a day. Some craft workers were successful in reducing the hours to ten a day, but sunrise to sunset remained the rule for most. Real wages (the purchasing power of the dollar) were rising an estimated ½ per cent a year. Women in the labor force declined as mechanization moved more heavily into textiles, where most of the women worked; of the 1,385,000 "hands" in industry in 1860 only 20 per cent were women.

Unions had a difficult time in early America. An American legacy from England was the view that combinations of workers were "conspiracies" in restraint of trade and therefore illegal. Local craft guilds made some headway in America but often ran into court-ordered injunctions when they sought to strike. In a landmark case in 1842 (*Commonwealth v. Hunt*), the Supreme Court of Massachusetts held that a combination of workers was not illegal per se. If the object of the combination was criminal, then it could be prohibited. The court held that seeking a closed shop (workers must be union members) and striking were not illegal goals, and worker alliances for those purposes were proper. Although the decision applied only to Massachusetts, it discouraged attempts in other states to prosecute worker organizations on conspiracy grounds. Despite the decision unions made few inroads into American labor, especially among unskilled workers, until later years. Unlike the workers of many European countries American labor never took the radical bent or sought a party of its own. In short, the American worker was highly paid, worked about the same number of hours as he would have elsewhere, and found his efforts constantly improved with better tools and machinery. If the sweat on his brow formed too quickly, the West beckoned with virgin lands and ample opportunities.

Finance and Banking. A growing economy requires a means of exchange between buyers and sellers. Early financial transactions were based on a *barter system* of exchanging commodities for commodities. Tobacco, fur pelts, and other items were means of paying for products or services. This "commodity money" represented a crude mechanism that could not flourish long in an expanding economy. Metal money was not new but was very scarce in early America. The Spanish pieces of eight was very common in colonial America, so common in fact that it was adopted early as a monetary unit. The piece of eight, called dollar by the colonists, was similar to the German thaler in size, as well in pronunciation. The piece of eight also gave rise to another American term "bit." "One bit" was one-eighth of the Spanish dollar, equivalent to twelve and one-half cents. "Two bits" equaled twenty-five cents; "four bits," fifty cents; and so on.

The Continental Congress had authorized the printing and issuance of Continental notes, or Continental dollars. Owing to the scarcity of metal, paper money lent itself readily to the printing-press method of financing government operations. The Revolutionary War was financed in such a manner—and galloping inflation was the result. As the value of the dollar declined to the point that it became worthless, another quaint American phrase appeared: "Not worth a Continental [dollar]." This early lesson in finance seems to have failed to reach many modern-day political leaders.

Coinage was empowered by the Constitution; it was the task of Robert Morris, Alexander Hamilton, and Thomas Jefferson to develop the American monetary unit. They decided on a decimal system in which one cent represented 1/100 of the Spanish dollar; a quint was five cents, and a mark ten cents. The nation was put on a bimetallic standard, and values were based on the ratio of gold to silver; the first ratio was fifteen to one; that is, one ounce of gold was the value equivalent of fifteen ounces of silver. The ratio was poorly established, and gold and silver were hoarded and paper money ("cheap money") drove the "dear money" out of circulation, verifying once again Gresham's Law. By 1860 more than nine thousand different kinds of paper bank notes (state, local, and federal) were in circulation. A trader often found his note from a local bank "discounted" when he tried to pay his bills. The result was chaotic by today's standards, but seems not to have limited a growing volume of transactions.

Banking was a hot political issue in early America. Secretary of the Treasury Hamilton sought a national bank like the Bank of England. It would lend money in times of distress, collect taxes, transfer funds to foreign nations, and act as the fiscal agent for the government (it was not the same role as that of central banking today). Amid cries of "Unconstitutional!" the bank bill passed Congress and lasted until 1811, when the charter failed to be renewed. In 1816 a Second Bank of the United States was chartered and in 1823 came under the capable leadership of Nicholas Biddle. This venture was successful until the administration of President Andrew Jackson, who had a long-standing antipathy towards banks in general. After a long political battle Jackson succeeded in abolishing the bank (1836); not until later did central banking become politically acceptable. Even without a national bank, however, private banking flourished; by 1850 there were at least eight hundred state chartered banks and an unknown number of private banks. However, the periodic panics and crises were the result of the absence of a central bank to moderate financial ups and downs.

In summary, the nation's financial system kept pace with the growth of commerce. Despite its shortcomings, the system provided the foundation for creating the corporate organization.

The Emerging Corporation. The corporate organization has a long history but one of spotty and limited use. The Romans made limited use of the system, but it was joint-stock ventures such as the East India and Hudson's Bay companies that provided models for American practice. The corporation is a unique creation that has many values for business ventures. Without this form of organization, a businessman has only two basic means of organizing legally: a sole proprietorship and a partnership. In both organizations the courts have repeatedly held that, should the venture fail, there is no separation between the businessman's personal and business property. He would be held in financial double jeopardy in case of default, and creditors could claim his personal property to satisfy their claims. In contrast, the corporate form of organization offers "limited liability."

In America the corporate form of organization developed slowly. Chief Justice John Marshall's opinion in the Dartmouth College case contributed to its legal basis when he wrote that Dartmouth's charter was a contract between the college and the state of New Hampshire and, as such, was beyond the power of that state to repeal or amend. Marshall's language was not as specific as that of Associate Justice Joseph Story, who wrote a concurring opinion extending this legal principle to business enterprise. It was Story's opinion that was to establish the corporation as a separate "person," a legal entity, apart from those investors who furnished the capital or other resources for its formation. The separation of those who owned the shares of the corporation from those who managed its operations provided the basis for "limited liability" for the shareholders. Their liability, in case of corporate failure, was limited to the loss of their business investment and no more.

In 1837, Connecticut allowed the right of incorporation, but other states were slow to follow; in 1860 a greater part of the nation's business firms continued to operate under proprietorships and partnerships. As commerce expanded and organizations grew in size and in their requirements for capital, the corporate form became more important. Shares could be sold, bonds issued, and loans obtained in the name of the corporation. Many enterprises, such as railroad and canal construction, required investments beyond the means of one or a few men. By incorporation not only could larger sums be raised but flexibility was assured to shareholders if they wanted to sell, and, perhaps more importantly, a continuity of organization was provided that could exist beyond the individuals who founded it.

Early Travel. To depict the early American transportation system as crude is to be overly generous. It was in fact primitive. Travel from England to America took three months in cramped and jolting quarters; once the traveler had reached America, he had to float down rivers on rafts or struggle upstream along narrow, dangerous trails. One could travel by horseback or in a Conestoga, the forerunner of the covered wagon of the plains. It took two days to go from New York to Philadelphia by stage, with few inns for respite in between.

The new government recognized the problems and encouraged the construction of turnpikes and canals. Although most roads were privately financed, some state and federal funds were occasionally available. The Cumberland Road, opened in 1811 from Cumberland, Maryland, to Wheeling, West Virginia, and eventually to Vandalia, Illinois, was one of the few federally financed roads. In 1792 the Philadelphia and Lancaster Turnpike had been financed entirely from private funds. The object of road building was trade, the opening of new markets by shipping to settlers as they moved westward.

River and canal transportation made use of nature's own paths to move products and people. George Washington and his friends put their money in the Potomac River Company in 1784, and in 1817 the most famous canal of all, the Erie, was authorized. It ran 364 miles from Albany to Buffalo, New York, and touched off a craze of canal building throughout the country. River travel was one way downstream until American ingenuity in the person of Robert Fulton came to the rescue. In 1807, Fulton's steamboat, the *Clermont*, made a trip from New York to Albany, New York, a distance of 150 miles, on the Hudson River in thirty-two hours. Steamboats came into wide use on inland waterways and provided key services to many cities. Riverboating had an aura of glamour and excitement. Who can forget Samuel Clemens' dream of becoming a riverboat captain on the Mississippi? For boats plying inland waterways that were sometimes shallow or filled with sunken trees that could snag the boat, the paddle wheel was necessary. Oceangoing ships required a steam-driven screw propeller. In 1848 Samuel Cunard opened the first trans-Atlantic steamship service, from New York to Liverpool. The tall masts and billowing sails of schooners and clippers were soon to be replaced by the smokestacks of steamers. Steam-powered ships and boats provided new freedom for the traveler as well as a means of transporting produce and products. An age of dynamic growth in transportation had begun.

While waterways and turnpikes made possible the extension of the national market, a new scheme of travel was on the horizon. Iron rails, the flanged wheels, and puffing locomotives began to appear around 1830. Opposed initially by the canal supporters who were fearful of its competition, by 1850 the rail industry had brought a new dimension to American life. It all started with Colonel John Stevens of Hoboken, New Jersey, who obtained from the New Jersey legislature America's first railroad charter in 1815. Deemed "eccentric," he could not obtain financial backing until 1830, when he built the twenty-three-mile Camden and Amboy Railroad. Stevens made many technical contributions to the railroad industry and earned the title "Father of American Engineering." From his wealth he endowed the Stevens Institute of Technology, in Hoboken, New Jersey.

After the Camden and Amboy, other lines, such as the Chesapeake and Ohio and the Baltimore and Ohio, were built and expanded, and by 1850 there were nine thousand miles of track in the United States, reaching all the way into Ohio. The new age of rails was sweeping away local trade barriers, opening new markets, and revolutionizing trade and communications.

The railroads were truly America's first "big business." The textile industry, though growing and dominating the Northeast, never developed into companies of the size and scope of the railroads. The textile firms were largely tied to England's early managerial methods. The railroads, however, posed new problems. Developing slowly in England concur-

rently with advances in America, railroading had no body of literature or fund of practical experience on which to draw. The railroad industry grew to such a size and complexity that new means had to be developed to cope with huge financial requirements, to provide integrated systems of trackage and stations, to spread large fixed costs, and to handle a labor force dispersed over a wide geographical area. Managers had to develop ways to handle America's first industry of larger than local scope. Railroad pioneers had to set up the first organizational structures of any size and substance—and also to provide the nation's first professional managers. Unlike textile and other industries, railroad operations were dispersed and could not be controlled by frequent personal inspection of the hundreds of stations and thousands of miles of track. Thus communications were a significant problem. The investments in track and rolling stock were immense and required extensive long-range planning to prevent large fixed capital outlays from being placed in the wrong market area. Passenger safety and the prevention of damage or loss in transit of cargo were critical to successful operations. Scheduling of service required planning and coordination, and policies had to be developed to guide the decisions of lower organizational elements.

Unlike canals and pikes, the early railroads were entirely privately financed, although land grants and subsidies would come later. The railroads were resisted by vested interests in the canal and pike business, as well as by well-meaning citizens who feared them and found no sanction for them in the Bible. Some railroads were taxed to provide funds for canals, and some were sued for damages when canals lost revenues to the iron horse. Despite the resistance the web of tracks continued to grow, probing the interior of lands where nature had furnished no natural pathways. The Baltimore and Ohio had thirteen miles of track in 1827, and in the period 1830 to 1840 many lines were built from one city to another. By 1840, America had 3,326 miles of canals and 2,818 miles of railroads; by 1850, railroad trackage exceeded 5,000 miles, in contrast to approximately 3,700 miles of canals. Between 1850 and 1860 all states east of the Mississippi River were connected by some 30,000 miles of track, and one could travel all the way from New York to Chicago in three days. Companies such as the Erie, the Pennsylvania, the Western and Atlantic, the Chesapeake and Ohio, and the Baltimore and Ohio were making heavy investments in rolling stock and tracks, and few towns were out of earshot of the train's whistle.

Samuel F. B. Morse's invention of the telegraph provided the beginnings of a nationwide communication system. An experimental line was completed between New York and Washington, D.C., in 1844, and by 1860 about 50,000 miles of wires and poles crisscrossed the eastern half of the country. Usually built along railroad rights of way, the telegraph facilitated the transportation system, as well as handling commercial and personal messages.

The railroads vastly improved the ability of American business to expand the sale of its products. Markets were no longer local, and the telegraph facilitated the coordination of commercial and financial transactions. As more customers were brought within the reach of the manufacturers, the growth of factories made better economic sense. The corporate organization could command the capital, and production on a large scale was becoming economically feasible. But business had to pause in 1861 for more serious matters, and the real growth of enterprise was to come later.

Antebellum Management. Before closing this section on business before the Civil War, it is necessary to examine, albeit briefly, some of the men and the mode of management during that era. The typical business firms were small and largely family-owned and operated. Larger firms were often partnerships of capitalist and inventor or idea man. These partnerships were managed on an egalitarian basis, with little or no hierarchy of authority. The essence of ante-bellum management lay in its personal base; the small number of employees and the personal leadership of the owner made the organization close-knit. Grievances could be heard, problems worked out, and benefits provided on a person-to-person basis. While the small family firm should not be romanticized, one must recognize that it was adequate to the task it faced at the time. Later would come factory growth, expanded markets, more complex rules and procedures, with the result that gaps would grow among those who owned, those who managed, and those who worked for the organization.

Many individuals played important roles in the development of the American economy; only a few can be mentioned to illustrate the beginnings of American firms and fortunes. Éleuthère Irénée Du Pont received his first order in 1801, when President Jefferson asked him to refine some saltpeter. Du Pont's gunpowder factory, called Eleutherian Mills, on Brandywine Creek, near Wilmington, Delaware, was the modest beginning of what was to become a significant family enterprise. Ezra Cornell pioneered in telegraphy and made a fortune out of Western Union; he was to provide the money to found a college in Ithaca, New York, which would naturally be named for him. Peter Cooper, an industrialist and inventor, built the first American locomotive, the *Tom Thumb*, and was instrumental in forming the firm that in 1866 laid the first trans-Atlantic cable. John Deere developed the first self-cleaning plow and pioneered in other agricultural machinery. Cyrus McCormick's reaper was a boon to the farmer and helped make America the breadbasket of the world. Of the earliest American fortunes perhaps none exceeded that of John Jacob Astor, who traded his way to wealth with his American Fur Company. William Colgate helped people get closer to godliness with his manufacture of soap; he and his heirs donated so much to a college that it changed its name to his.

Early American entrepreneurs faced in common the problems of financing expansion, of bringing a reluctant labor force into the new factory regimen, of finding capable salaried professional managers, of coping with a growing national market brought on by the transportation and communication revolutions, and of resolving the problems caused by the new machines and production processes. Appropriately enough, the first signs of systematic management arose in the railroad industry, where the first large accumulations of re-

sources appeared and where a system had to be developed to allocate and utilize those resources. The Industrial Revolution had established in America a number of enterprises that would form the basis of the nation's industrial might.

THE RISE OF BIG BUSINESS, 1861–1920

Business Comes of Age

The years of internecine strife from 1861 to 1865 were a tragic pause in the nation's move toward world industrial leadership. The Civil War was as much an economic struggle between agrarian and industrial societies as it was a political and social one. The South, predominantly agricultural, was dealt a harsh blow, leaving the industrialized North in control. In the years that followed would occur a concatenation of events and inventions that would help the American business system mature.

The early period of American business was one of marketing and merchandising the constantly proliferating products and services that industry could provide consumers. Manufacturing technology continued to advance, and significant progress was made in organizing and managing the nation's vast resources. Marketing and manufacturing are dependent on one another; what is produced must be sold so that more can be produced. Finance, banking, transportation, and communication facilitate both marketing and manufacturing. In such a period the nation's financial system reaches maturity and new modes of transporting, communicating, and creating energy are developed. Taken together, these facets of business activity interacted as big business became Big Business.

The Marketing Revolution. The *channel of distribution* is the path a product takes as it moves from the manufacturer to the ultimate user, the consumer. In colonial and early America, middlemen played important roles in this channel, as commission merchants, jobbers, brokers, and agents took the products of manufacturers and importers and transferred them to wholesalers. Wholesalers took large shipments and divided them to serve retailers, who sold to the ultimate customers. Many retailers were specialized; that is, they handled hardware or dry goods or other similar groups of products. Other retailers, especially those in rural areas, fell into a "general-store" category, and handled a wide range of products.

The marketing revolution that occurred after the Civil War lay in this channel of distribution. The first change came with the development of department stores, where one could do much, if not all, of his shopping, much like the country general store but on a grander scale. The first department store was the Marble Dry-Goods Palace of Alexander T. Stewart, founded in New York City in 1848. Stewart's store was unique in that all goods had a fixed price, and there was no haggling, which was contrary to previous practices of trading and bargaining over what one paid for an item. Potter Palmer and Marshall Field opened stores in Chicago in 1852, and Morris Rich began operations in Atlanta, Georgia, in 1867. The last part of the century brought the greatest growth and a list of master merchants: John Wanamaker (who innovated the money-back guarantee), William Filene, Lord and Taylor, Brooks Brothers, Macy's, Gimbel's, Penney's, and on and on. The advantage of department stores lay in the economies to be derived from mass merchandising. Stores could purchase in large quantities and use this leverage to elicit discounts from manufacturers. Middlemen, and their share of the profits, could be reduced in importance if not eliminated entirely from the channel. With these savings the merchants reduced prices to the consumer, generating more trade; with large volumes of sales and an increased stock turn (inventory turnover), the costs of stocking merchandise were reduced, and greater buying economies could be attained again as the cycle continued.

Other steps in this revolution were the establishment of mail-order houses, food and variety chain stores, and supermarkets. The 1880's were marked by the opening of the mail-order house, first by Sears and Roebuck and then by Montgomery Ward. Centrally located in Chicago to reduce mailing costs, these firms were able to lessen substantially the role of the middleman in the channel. Chain stores were of two kinds, food and variety. George Hartford started the Great Atlantic and Pacific Tea Company in 1859 to revolutionize food merchandising. Frank W. Woolworth pioneered the five-and-dime variety store in 1879. Imitators soon followed, indicating the worthiness of the ventures. Still another innovation requires mention: Clarence Saunders initiated the idea of a self-service supermarket in Memphis, Tennessee, in 1916. The store was named Piggly Wiggly, and Saunders issued franchises for other stores. The customer entered the store through a turnstile, passed up and down the lane of shelves where products were displayed, served himself, and paid as he passed through a checkout stand. The savings in clerical costs were again to the customer's benefit.

All these efforts were aided by another tool of the mass merchandiser, advertising. First in newspapers, then in magazines, and still later through radio, promotional activities were aimed at the consumer. Instead of waiting for a customer to appear, advertising urged him with specials, sales, and other blandishments. By 1920 advertising had become a billion-dollar industry. From its beginnings as local markets for products, the marketing revolution, aided by manufacturing advances, transportation networks, and communications media, had truly created a national market. By 1920 one could rise in the morning, shave with his Gillette Safety Razor, wash with Ivory Soap, pour Borden's Eagle Brand Condensed Milk on his Kellogg's Corn Flakes, don his Arrow Collar, and smoke a Camel on his way to the electric interurban trolley.

Finance and Banking. As the American people moved westward, American financial power remained in the East. Civil War paper greenbacks (so called because of the vivid color on the reverse) were issued in large amounts to finance the Union's war effort. They were not redeemable in silver or gold and were "easy money" in that sense. Agrarian interests

wanted to keep the greenbacks because they increased the money supply, increased prices for land and commodities, and enabled them to use cheaper money to repay debts. Fiscal conservatives wanted "hard money," backed by silver and gold, both of which became relatively abundant after the mineral discoveries in the West. Much of the rest of the nineteenth century was characterized by the struggle between these two forces. The conflict came to a head in the presidential-election campaign of 1896. William Jennings Bryan, the Democratic nominee, advocated "free silver" and easy money; William McKinley, the Republican candidate, opted for gold. Bryan's oratory resounds yet: "You shall not press down upon the brow of labor this crown of thorns; You shall not crucify mankind upon a cross of gold." Few recall what McKinley said, but he won the election. In 1900 the Gold Standard Act was passed, defining the value of the nation's money solely in terms of gold.

There was still no central bank of the United States in 1861, but the need for one remained. In 1864 the National Bank Act took a large step forward, partly fulfilling the earlier dreams of Hamilton and Biddle. The act provided the essential rules for banks and banking that are followed today: the procedures by which banks were to be organized and chartered; initial capital requirements; the issuance of bank notes; and reserve requirements, that is, cash reserves versus deposit and note liabilities. In 1913 came the long-needed central bank, with the establishment of the Federal Reserve System.

The investment banking houses formed in the 1870's furnished a means of financing corporate ventures by arranging the sale of securities. Life-insurance companies experienced phenomenal growth: the "big five" had assets of 400 million dollars in 1890, 1.5 billion dollars in 1900. The investment "banker of bankers" was J. P. Morgan and Company. The influence of Morgan and Company was legion: the Pujo Committee Report of 1913, in concluding its study of the concentration of financial power in New York City, called J. Pierpont Morgan the head of a "money trust" (he was called much worse things by others). Whatever his faults, Morgan's role was crucial in arranging for the massive investments needed to start new companies, combine old ones, and even, at one time, to lend the nation gold to save the United States Treasury by stemming a flow of gold to Europe. Another of Morgan's larger transactions was the combining in 1901 of Frick, Carnegie, and the interests of others into the United States Steel Corporation, which was capitalized at 1.4 billion dollars.

With the growth of the financial world came the income tax. The first peacetime federal income tax was imposed during this period. The Wilson-Gorman Tax of 1894 levied a 2 per cent personal tax on all incomes above $4,000 and a 2 per cent tax on all corporate net income. In 1895 the Supreme Court declared the act unconstitutional. Taxpayers could rest easy until the Underwood-Simmons Tariff Act of 1913. The act provided for a 1 per cent tax on personal incomes over $3,000 (a $1,000 exemption was allowed for married couples). A surtax was added progressively on incomes up to $20,000; the maximum rate was 7 per cent on incomes in excess of $500,000 and taxpayers reported their income on Form 1040. The Court let this act stand; only the rates have changed.

The Advent of Mass Production. Aided by advancing technology, the manufacturing sector of the economy continued to gain on agriculture until by 1900 manufacturing output was twice that of agriculture. Agriculture benefited from manufacturing as farming was increasingly mechanized. Research and development brought artificial fertilizers, fungicides, insecticides, and steam- and gasoline-powered tractors. In the mid-1890's the United States took over the helm in world industry; by 1913 the nation would account for one-third of the total world's industrial production. American inventiveness was unsurpassed, and, as we shall see shortly, the organization and management of this massive accumulation of resources posed new problems.

At the core of the industrial advancement was yet another innovation, *mass production.* Mass-production manufacturing involves (1) the continuous processing of a product from beginning to end by the step-by-step addition of one part or subassembly to another; (2) interchangeable parts; (3) power to move a belt or line as the product moves from one work station to another; and (4) a sophisticated organization to obtain the proper timing of parts arrivals and the performance of human labor. In the early manufacture of carriages, railroad cars and engines, and automobiles, the assembly was stationary; that is, the parts were brought to the frame. Henry Ford, like other manufacturers, at first used the stationary-assembly process, but in 1913 he and his associates conceived the notion of a moving assembly, in which the automobile chassis was pulled by a windlass down a line, flowing by the workers, who added the various parts as the chassis passed. In 1914 a chassis, which had previously taken twelve hours to assemble under the stationary method, could be put together in one and one-half hours under the new method. Perhaps this advancement should be called the Second Industrial Revolution. The practice of mass production by the assembly line spread to other manufacturers in the auto industry, to the electrical industry, to the manufacture of household appliances, the processing of food, and the making of cigarettes, to name but a few.

Mass production was manufacturing's counterpart of mass marketing. It brought lower costs and lower prices and enabled mass marketers to extend their sales; conversely, the greater sales volume permitted greater application of mass-production methods. Together, they served to bring the consumer a growing wealth of products at lower and lower prices. For example, in 1910, Ford's Model T cost the consumer $950; by 1924 the purchase price was $290, and Ford was selling more than one and one-quarter million cars a year. Using lowered product price to expand the market and the greater market to achieve greater production savings, Ford divided work into small elements and put into practice Adam Smith's theory that the extent of the market was the only force limiting the division of labor. Ford's startling announcement in 1914 of a $5-a-day wage (at a time when the average wage in the auto industry was $2.40 a day) operated on two premises: that the best workers could be attracted and

retained and that the worker needed the wherewithal to buy industry's output. Although Ford lost his domination of the automobile industry as consumer preferences changed, his introduction of the logic of mass production had a lasting impact on American industrial thought.

The growth in the size of American firms during this time was spectacular, especially as compared with the size of the family firms of the earlier age. Corporations had enormous potential and, as industrialization proceeded, they grew in size, scope, resources, and power. In his *Strategy and Structure*, Alfred Chandler developed an interesting thesis about the historical growth of large corporations and their subsequent organizational forms. By tracing the history of various firms, he delineated four phases in the history of the large American enterprise: (1) "the initial expansion and accumulation of resources"; (2) "the rationalization of the use of resources"; (3) "the expansion into new markets and lines to help assure the continuing full use of resources"; and (4) "the development of a new structure to make possible continuing effective mobilization of resources to meet both changing short-term market demands and long-term market trends." Hence the historical industrial cycle runs: to accumulate resources, rationalize resource utilization, expand resources, and rerationalize resource utilization, presumably ad infinitum. The cycle starts and ends at different times in different companies, depending upon the state of the technology and the firm's ability to react to and capitalize on market opportunities. During the latter part of the nineteenth century many major industries were forming and would fit into Chandler's phase 1, the resource-accumulation stage.

Chandler further noted two elements of industrial growth and the periods during which they came: *horizontal* growth, from 1879 to 1893, and *vertical* growth, from 1898 to 1904. Horizontal growth occurred when producers in similar fields combined through mergers, pools, and/or trusts to gain economies of scale in manufacturing. Examples were firms dealing in oil, beef, sugar, tobacco, rubber, distillery, and so on. These mergers into larger units enabled the firm or firms to *control* their market, gain financial leverage, and cut costs of production. Viewed as monopolistic by some, the producers saw this trend as necessitated by the chaos of cutthroat competition. During the vertical-growth period firms moved "backward" or "forward" in the production process. Moving backward meant acquiring raw-material sources or suppliers; moving forward meant establishing marketing outlets for one's own products. For example, a petroleum-refining company would move backward to explore, acquire oil leases, drill, and build pipelines to its refinery; it would move forward to acquire wholesale agents and perhaps its own retail stations.

As these forces of industrial concentration worked together new titles of companies emerged, such as the "Americans," the "Nationals," and even the "Internationals." Examples are the American Locomotive Company, the National Can Company, and International Harvester. By 1905, 40 per cent of American manufacturing was controlled by about three hundred companies with a capital investment of seven billion dollars. It was during this era that big business became

Big Business. The trend toward concentration was slowed during the period 1905 to 1920 by the Sherman Act, the administration of Theodore Roosevelt, and a series of spectacular dissolutions of various trusts. But more about that later.

Transportation, Communication, and Energy. The advances in marketing and manufacturing would not have been possible without concomitant progress in the transportation, communication, and energy industries. Binding the nation together with a web of steel had been a dream before the Civil War. The cessation of hostilities made it possible for a new dream that would perhaps provide balm for old wounds. To get to the golden promise of California, the seeker had three choices: (1) three months in a covered wagon across Indian territory, deserts, mountains, and plains; (2) six months in a ship (a clipper could do it in four) around Cape Horn and its stormy seas; or (3) by ship to the Isthmus of Panama, a traverse across land and by river through malaria-ridden jungles, and then by ship again up the coast. The Golden Lorelei attracted people by all three means. Some made it; some did not.

In 1862 a charter was granted the Union Pacific Railroad to build from Omaha, Nebraska, to Nevada; at that point the Central Pacific, building eastward from Sacramento, was to meet the Union Pacific. Because of the rugged Sierra Nevada, the Central Pacific met with difficulties, and Congress instructed the Union Pacific to keep going west until it connected with the Central Pacific. The two lines finally met May 10, 1869, at Promontory Summit, near Ogden, Utah. A golden spike commemorated the joining of East and West—the nation was united by two strands of track. Other coast-to-coast lines were to follow: the Southern Pacific, the Northern Pacific, and the Santa Fe, and one could travel from the Atlantic to the Pacific in only one week.

Congress granted the railroad companies ten (later twenty) sections of land on alternate sides of the track for each mile of track laid. The purpose was to encourage settlement and to provide an added incentive for railroad development. Scandals resulted from alliances between those who built the lines and those who authorized their construction, the members of Congress. The railroad barons will be introduced in later pages.

Technological advancements made rail travel more pleasurable: steel rails replaced iron ones, George Pullman introduced the sleeping car in 1865; and George Westinghouse developed the air brake in 1868. Westinghouse's first brake stopped the engine, and therefore the train, from front to rear, and braking was a jolting experience. It took Westinghouse twenty more years to perfect the idea of using connecting air lines to stop the locomotive and the cars simultaneously.

Forty thousand miles of track were laid in the 1870's, and another seventy thousand miles in the 1880's. The railroads were developing an excess capacity for passenger and freight hauling, and lines duplicated one another. The high fixed cost of miles of track and expensive rolling stock made the competition ruinous. To get more business and to spread the fixed costs, railroads turned to rate discrimination; lower rates were often given for return routes to avoid pulling empty cars. Discrimination was also practiced on short- versus long-haul shipments. Consumers, especially farmers, protested; the railroads' rate wars did not seem to benefit the farmers. Protests led to organizations such as the granges, and organized efforts were begun to regulate rates and operations. The commerce clause of the Constitution was soon to be extended.

Urban and suburban transportation made marked advances during this period. Intra- and interurban trolley cars were at first horse-drawn, and the tracks were laid in the streets. After 1890 and the appearance of the electric trolley the horses were retired, and street sweepers' jobs were less onerous, and pedestrians could walk with greater assurance. By 1920 there were 50,000 miles of urban and interurban streetcar tracks. Retail markets were extended, and suburban living was facilitated by these improvements in transportation.

The automobile was a technological advancement that brought about substantial economic and social change during this period. Developed in 1876 by the German Nikolaus Otto, the internal-combustion engine was destined to provide a new means of transportation. The automobile gave man a new mobility, a new freedom of movement, which led to a decentralization of the cities and suburban living and posed a new threat to older, established forms of transportation. The automobile was still a curiosity in 1900. Not many people took the belching backfiring horseless carriages very seriously, and those who did were considered daft. It was the task of men like Henry Ford, Walter Chrysler, Ransom Olds, Louis Chevrolet, and others to change America's mind and redraw the face of America's map. Henry Ford popularized the idea with auto races, and his 999, driven by Barney Oldfield, was a sure winner. Many companies were formed, and various sources of power were tried; the "electric" (battery-powered) and the steam engine, along with the gasoline-powered internal-combustion engine. Gasoline won the day, providing a ready outlet for the products of the newly discovered petroleum fields in Texas, Oklahoma, California, and Louisiana.

Mass production was the key to the success of the industry; Ford used it to lower costs, and thereby prices. The expanded market was impressive: 100,000 cars produced by the industry in 1910, 500,000 in 1914, and 2 million in 1917. Roads were crude and delayed the industry's development. Routes were often circuitous as one tried to get from one place to another. For instance, the 1909 auto race from New York to San Francisco covered 4,106 miles, a distance much greater than the straight-line coast-to-coast distance. The winning car traveled the distance in twenty-two days. The great organizers of the automobile industry, W. C. Durant and Alfred Sloan, were soon to put Americans behind the wheel in increasing numbers. The auto was a boon to many industries: petroleum, steel, rubber, glass, insurance, road construction, and motor hotels, to name just a few. America's romance with the motor car began not only in the rumble seat but also in the shops of many carriage makers.

Air transportation was also on the horizon. Man had

dreamed of flight for generations. Samuel Langley took a major step forward when he launched an unmanned steam-powered plane in 1896. The plane stayed aloft for one and one-half minutes. The experiments were abandoned on the advice of a wet pilot who had crashed into the Potomac River during Langley's first attempt at manned flight. Orville and Wilbur Wright succeeded where Langley had failed; at Kitty-hawk, North Carolina, Orville made a twelve-second flight in a gasoline-powered craft in 1903. Wilbur followed with a second flight, which lasted fifty-nine seconds. The infant industry grew rapidly, carrying the mail, fighting in World War I, and in time providing passenger service. After centuries man had wings.

Communication advancements were just as dramatic as those in transportation. For many years the telegraph was the main means of long-distance communication and the under-sea Atlantic cable, completed in 1866, permitted rapid international communication. The communication revolution began in the familiar story of Alexander Graham Bell's invention of the telephone. The Bell Telephone Association was formed in 1877, and shortly thereafter, Bell hired Theodore Vail, who was to become the great organizer of the Bell System (American Telephone and Telegraph). In 1881 the system had 170,000 subscribers, each of whom paid $240 a year for phone service. By 1900 there were 600,000 subscribers; by 1910 there were five million telephones, one for every 18 Americans. Guglielmo Marconi added another phenomenal communications device, the "wireless." Lee De Forest invented the vacuum tube to accompany the device, and soon messages were no longer confined to the wires and poles of the telegraph or telephone. John Wanamaker installed a wireless for communication between his New York and Philadelphia stores. The operator was young David Sarnoff, who was later to found and head the giant Radio Corporation of America and still later the National Broadcasting Company.

Movies also came on the scene. Thomas A. Edison developed the first motion-picture camera in 1893, and in 1896 the first public movie show was held. The Nickelodeon, the world's first all-moving-picture theater, opened its doors in Pittsburgh in 1905, admission, five cents. By 1910 there were ten thousand movie houses; by 1920 there were 17,000 theaters and an estimated weekly audience of ten million. Thus in communications three great industries appeared during this period: telephone, radio, and motion pictures. Advertising had new means to reach the public, leisure was enhanced, and the web that now bound the nation was one of wires and tubes as well as tracks and roads.

Energy developments of the period also merit mention. Coal was the primary source of energy for the steam-driven wheels of industry. While coal continued to dominate, new discoveries of petroleum deposits were soon to reshape the energy base. Electrical energy also entered the scene. While not "invented" in the usual sense, the principles of electricity were applied to generate a new power source for factory gears and home lights and appliances. Edison's central power plant in New York City was built in 1882. By 1920 one-third of the nation's industrial power came from electricity. Half of the urban homes had electricity. In the rural areas 98 per cent of the homes still relied on kerosene lamps and candles, but not for long. The automobile pushed into the country, and radio created a new awareness of an urban way of life. In transportation, communication, and energy, new developments in technology and business were bringing a new age to American society.

Scientific Management. The new economics of mass production demanded an even sharper focus on the development of management talent. Large accumulations of resources were requisite to meet the demands of mass markets and mass distribution. As the industrial giants grew, the men who had built the empires were passing from the scene and being replaced by a new breed of salaried managers. The personalized, informal structures of the family business yielded the administrative needs of large industry. No longer could the owner-entrepreneur depend upon personal supervision. Technology demanded specialized knowledge, and staff personnel were added to handle engineering, production, purchasing, legal affairs, and other activities. Motives changed from the risk of loss or possibility of gain in one's equity as an entrepreneur to those important to a salaried manager. This separation of ownership and management required the development of an enlarged fund of managerial talent trained and wise in the administration of industrial affairs.

Industrial growth in the later nineteenth century had created the giant enterprise, and in the first two decades of the twentieth century it was the task of the salaried manager to design and implement the appropriate administrative structures. The large corporation demanded a formal structure of relationships between the firm's activities and personnel and required also a formalization of administrative procedures. Culmination of the resource-accumulation phase meant that the typical corporation of the early twentieth century was faced with two basic problems: the need to reduce unit costs by improving production techniques and processes and the need to facilitate planning, coordination, and appraisal of performance.

With resources accumulated and technology developed, the major impediment to added industrial productivity lay in the crude forms of developing, organizing, controlling, and administering this mass of resources. At no place in the firm was this more crucial than in the production shop itself. Labor was highly specialized, standardized methods and procedures were in short supply, and there was little emphasis on coordinating, integrating, and systematizing work. It was no coincidence that engineers became the source of early efforts to systematize management. Engineers designed the equipment, supervised its installation, advised on its utilization, and provided the major source of assistance in solving management problems. Accordingly, the first management writers emphasized techniques and methods of shop efficiency, for those appeared at the time to be the major industrial problems. One engineer, Frederick Winslow Taylor, stood out during this era, and, although he had a strong supporting cast, he emerged as the "Father of Scientific Management."

Taylor's goal was to systematize management practices so

that they would be in accord with the size of the enterprise. He began with time study, using a stop watch, to determine proper work methods, reduce fatigue, conserve human energy, and establish fair standards of work. He sought to standardize and improve tools, work methods, and working conditions so that obstacles to more efficient human performance would be removed. Plant layout, improved routing of work, scheduling of orders, accounting schemes, and other techniques were developed by Taylor and his associates.

The concept of the "first-class man" and the scientific selection of personnel were attempts to provide a better match between people's abilities and job requirements. A piece-rate incentive sought to boost production and lower per unit labor costs even while paying higher wages. Organization of the work force was to be facilitated by the use of "functional foremen," who brought specialized advice and assistance to the workplace. Taylor's philosophy for the industrial age was a "mental revolution," in which labor and management stopped fighting over the division of the spoils and turned their efforts to cooperation to attain greater efficiency. In Taylor's view everyone would benefit from this efficiency: labor from higher wages and improved working conditions, management from increased efficiency and higher profits, and the public from lower prices. Taylor was not alone in this drive for better management: Harrington Emerson, Henry Gantt, Morris Cooke, and Frank and Lillian Gilbreth were associated at one time or another with Taylor's work.

Scientific management became the catch phrase of the era, and a national concern for efficiency in industry became prominent. Taylor's ideas attracted the Boston lawyer Louis D. Brandeis, who was becoming noted in the early twentieth century as the "people's lawyer." In 1910, when the eastern railroads asked the Interstate Commerce Commission for an increase in freight rates, Brandeis took up the cause of the shippers and brought about an unusual series of hearings that put Taylor's ideas in the public eye. At a loss for a name to apply to the Taylor system, Brandeis noted that Taylor frequently used the word "scientific" in his work, and the term "scientific management" was the outcome. Brandeis' argument before the Interstate Commerce Commission was based on the inefficiency of railroad management, and he proposed that no rate increase would be necessary if the railroads applied scientific management. To prove his case he introduced a parade of witnesses who testified to the efficiencies to be gained by adopting improved management methods based on the Taylor principles. The phrase scientific management caught on with the press, and Taylor gained the public spotlight. The decision went against the railroads. The hearings concluded that it was too early to judge the merits of the new management system, but the testimony that the railroads could save one million dollars a day by applying scientific management had great appeal to cost-conscious manufacturers and to the public. Scientific management met the requirements of industry in rationalizing resource utilization—phase 2 of American industrial history.

The new managers of industrial enterprise would adopt scientific management and bring about tremendous gains in industrial efficiency. While Taylorism was not the sole contributing factor (one should add the methods of mass production and electrical sources of power), industrial productivity rose during the heyday of scientific management. In manufacturing, the number of man hours' input per unit of output fell from an index number of 74 in 1919 to 42 in 1929 (1899 = 100), for a gain in efficiency of 43 per cent. While output per person was rising rapidly, unemployment remained low, wages were rising, and the purchasing power of the dollar was relatively stable. The prosperous 1920's held forth the promise of economic abundance for all. A great outpouring of products from the industrial machine and gains in real income gave the consumer more than ever.

Economically, America came of age in this period. Large-scale administrative structures were required to cope with the economies of mass production and mass distribution. Rationalization of resource usage was required, and scientific management became the conventional means to meet that need. It was an age of concern for economic efficiency. With a tremendously productive industrial system, rising real wages, low-level unemployment, and mass marketing and distribution, America had never known such abundance.

Business, Government, and Society

No nation can undergo a transformation of society as the United States did in the nineteenth century without substantial repercussions. An examination of America's response to industrialism is necessary in order to understand the forces that would shape the twentieth century. American economic conditions encouraged a rapid growth in corporate size, and mass markets and mass production ushered in an era of intense competition. Aggressive entrepreneurs responded by overbuilding capacity, further intensifying price competition. To protect themselves, businesses sought to combine through pools, trusts, mergers, and holding companies to insulate themselves from the market forces. The doctrine of laissez faire was a one-way street in practice; government should do nothing to regulate business but everything to aid it. Large land grants to the railroads and legislation protecting industry against foreign competition fostered domestic monopolies.

In essence, the new age threatened everyone with the unknowns of change. Workers, farmers, and businessmen alike organized for collective action. Producers joined to control the conditions under which they sold their products, distributors combined to wield influence over marketing and transportation, and laborers formed trade unions to bargain with management. This organizational revolution revealed the degree to which industrialism had shifted the context of economic decisions from personal relationships among individuals to a struggle for power among well-organized groups.

Social Darwinism: Business Fact or Social Myth? In 1859, Charles Darwin published his great work, *On the Origin of Species by Means of Natural Selection, or the Preservation of Favored Races in the Struggle for Life.* In this book he set forth his theories concerning evolution and natural selection through the struggle for existence. Social scientists seized upon Darwin's theories in an attempt to apply them to human society, and the result was Social Darwinism. Two men were primarily responsible for spreading the implications of Darwin's theories to fields other than biology. One was Herbert Spencer, an English philosopher who advocated the pre-eminence of the individual over society and of science over religion. The other was William Graham Sumner, a professor of political and social science at Yale, who became the most vigorous and influential social Darwinist in America. Since the most striking phrases of Darwinism were "struggle for existence" and "survival of the fittest," both Spencer and Sumner believed that nature would provide that the "most fit" in a competitive situation would win. That process would lead to the continuing improvement of mankind, since the progress of civilization depended upon natural selection, and that in turn depended upon the workings of unrestricted competition. According to Sumner, competition was a law of nature that "can no more be done away with than gravitation." In the struggle for existence in a competitive society money was the measure of success; this fact explained the huge fortunes that millionaires acquired in a competitive system. Since they were the most fit, their huge fortunes were the legitimate wages of efficiency. Through unrestricted competition the fittest would survive and move up the social ladder of success, while the unfit would occupy the lower class structures and would eventually be eliminated through evolution. This process would be slow and gradual, and society must not try to interfere with the process of nature.

In his *Social Darwinism in American Thought*, Richard Hofstadter tried to link Social Darwinism to managerial philosophy. To John D. Rockefeller he (mistakenly) ascribed these sentiments:

The growth of a large business is merely a survival of the fittest. . . . The American Beauty rose can be produced in the splendor and fragrance which brings cheer to its beholder only by sacrificing the early buds which grow up around it. This is not an evil tendency in business. It is merely the working out of a law of nature and law of God.

James J. Hill implied that the absorption of smaller railroads by larger railroads represented the industrial analogy to the victory of the strong. He also believed that "the fortunes of railroad companies are determined by the law of the survival of the fittest." After reading Darwin and Spencer, Andrew Carnegie, one of Spencer's most prominent disciples, stated: "I remember that light came as in a flood and all was clear. Not only had I got rid of theology and the supernatural, but I had found the truth of evolution. 'All is well since all grows better' became my motto."

Historians have charged that American society saw its own image in that tooth-and-claw version of natural selection and that its dominant groups were therefore able to dramatize the vision of competition as a thing good in itself. Ruthless business rivalry and unprincipled politics were to be justified by the survival philosophy.

Are these allegations true? Businessmen were pragmatic doers who worked out rules as they met them. They read or heard little of Spencer, Darwin, Sumner, or Adam Smith, and cared little for abstract social and economic theories. In his book *Darwinism and the American Intellectual*, Raymond J. Wilson wrote: "it is not true that this commitment [to competition] was grounded on Darwinian premises." Few knew enough of Spencer or Darwin "to turn biology to the uses of self-justification." Further, Wilson claimed that only Carnegie was a true social Darwinist businessman. Even as a Darwinist, Carnegie put forth a gospel of wealth and steward-ship that characterized many of the leaders of the day who accumulated fortunes and then endowed foundations, colleges, libraries, and other philanthropies. The "American Beauty rose" analogy attributed to John D. Rockefeller was made by his son in the early 1900's and not during the heyday of social Darwinism. James J. Hill did make the "survival of the fittest" statement but during an interview in 1922 for his memoirs, not while he was active in the railroad business.

What can be concluded about the effect of Social Darwinism on the thought and practices of the businessman? At the peak of the movement in America businessmen, farmers, and workers were trying to avoid competition through coopera-tive efforts of pools, granges, and unions instead of allowing the laws of nature to run their course. Businessmen, being of a practical bent, have never been noted for their interest in the social theories of the intellectuals; there again Social Darwinism fell short. Another strike against the proponents was the known pious nature of the entrepreneurs, at least on Sunday, and the thought that Darwinian concepts appealed to them raised doubts. Social Darwinism may have provided a rationale for some practices, but the conclusion that it was the businessman's dominant philosophy is tenuous.

The Businessman: Robber Baron or Public Benefactor? Vir-tuous conduct seldom makes news. Historians and journalists are awed by the extraordinary and more often than not over-stress it to the detriment of those quiet, sturdy, responsible people who, unheralded, are the true productive builders. Matthew Josephson, among others, developed the idea of "robber barons" to such a point that the public is quick to equate any businessman with a tycoon-tyrant. The robber barons are of interest for a number of reasons: they char-acterized a stage in the economic development of America, they reflected the rags-to-riches aspirations of many Ameri-cans, and their practices served to bring about changes in the relationship of business to government and of business to society.

It was not by coincidence that the most flagrant of corrupt business practices came in the railroad industry. Rail lines crisscrossed the nation, and, with large fixed costs, it was inevitable that there would be price wars. Government land grants and subsidies had encouraged building in marginal-return areas where greater economic pressures would be brought to bear. Duplicate lines served these areas and crossed at key terminals, increasing competition. Finally, the granting of operating franchises opened the gates to collusion between the railroad promoter and the legislator. Railroad expansion frequently became a political decision rather than an economic one. There were other "barons," of course, but the railroads characterized an economic age in which businessmen sought to evade the economics of Adam Smith and turned to collusion instead of competition and to bribery instead of service.

Josephson noted that honesty toward customers, respectability, and conservatism in business practices—all those characteristics of the early American entrepreneur—were beginning to depart by the 1840's. The new businessmen left home early to seek their fortune; for the most part they came from the aggressive Yankee strain of New England, had grown up in relative poverty, were immigrants or the sons of immigrants, were acquisition-motivated, and were puritanical and pious men who took their Calvinistic origins seriously. There were exceptions. Some were contradictions in character, such as Daniel Drew who spent his evenings, often drunk, in a cheap hotel room reading the Bible and chewing tobacco. The saw the potential of growth in the burgeoning economy and vowed to take advantage of it. It would be impossible to chronicle all their activities, but some thumbnail sketches reveal the often contradictory nature of the robber barons.

Commodore Cornelius Vanderbilt gained control of the New York and Harlem Railroad by bribing members of the New York State legislature and by stock manipulation. He later built the New York Central system, watered the stock, increased his fortune, and once remarked: "What do I care about the law? Hain't I got the power?" Historians have dealt the commodore's son, William, a low blow. William Vanderbilt has been frequently quoted as saying, "The public be damned," as proof of the consciencelessness of the businessmen of the era. Omitted in most accounts are the occasion and the rest of the quotation. William as being interviewed by a reporter after the announcement that Vanderbilt was eliminating the Chicago Limited, a fast mail train that charged a higher extra fare for passengers who wanted to get to their destination quicker. William was asked, "Don't you run it for the public benefit?" William's reply was, "The public be damned. I am working for my stockholders. If the public wants the train, why don't they pay for it?" In short, the higher fare was for faster service; if the public wanted faster service, they should pay extra for it.

Daniel Drew has the dubious honor of being the first to engage in the practice that came to be called "watering stock." He purchased a herd of cattle with an enlistment bonus he had received from his Civil War army days. In transporting the herd to market, he fed them salt to make them thirsty, and then offered them all the water they could drink and sold at a very large profit some temporarily overweight cattle. Together with Jay Gould and Jim Fisk, Drew turned to railroading and soon gave the Erie line a reputation for mismanagement. This deadly trio Drew, Fisk and Gould cared nothing for the operations of the railroad; they were simply after the money they could make from their financial scheming.

The western railroaders were especially malignant. Led by Collis P. Huntington and aided by Leland Stanford, Sr., they purchased the favors of legislators who could grant them free government, bestow franchises, and pass enabling legisla-

tion. One year Huntington paid $200,000 to get a bill through Congress. He later complained that bribes to Congressmen were costing up to a half a million dollars a session and moaned, "I am afraid this damnation Congress will kill us." Stanford used his office of governor of California to finance his own railroad and made profits from the construction companies that received government funds to build the roads. In 1885 he was elected to the United States Senate, then known as the "Millionaires Club," and fought government regulation of railroads, including refusing to appear for the vote on the Act to Regulate Commerce, which established the Interstate Commerce Commission.

Not all the barons were railroad men. John D. Rockefeller combined audacity and cunning in building his South Improvement Company and the Standard Oil colossus. By conspiring with the railroads, he was able to extract rebates on his freight and receive rebates on the oil that his rivals shipped. Andrew Carnegie was a steel baron who at one point owned or controlled two-thirds of the nation's young steel industry. The Homestead strike earned Carnegie a poor press when union organizers were met by a force of Pinkerton detectives hired to protect the plant. The organizers were brutally stoned and beaten by the striking workers; state troops moved in and secured the plant for a wholly nonunion crew. In the process 14 persons were killed and 163 wounded.

We should not dwell too long on the barons and in so doing overlook some heroes of the story of American industry. In contrast to the barons there lived in the last half of the century quiet Americans who were revolutionizing the industrial structure. Some had their faults, but to a large degree their lives were marked by production, not destruction, and by the creation and management of wealth, not its manipulation. Again we can only sample from their lives to see a more refreshing view of American entrepreneurship. Edison immediately emerges as one of the most dynamic. His early work on automatic printing equipment to go with Morse's telegraph led to the development of Western Union. Unfortunately, he was cheated by Jay Gould, who had gained control of Western Union; Edison emerged from a court suit with one dollar for his pains. Edison made improvements in Bell's telephone and was shortly engaged in a patent fight that eventually led to the sale of his ideas to the rapidly growing Bell System. He was more richly rewarded in this case, receiving $100,000 for American patent rights and $145,000 for English rights. At Menlo Park, his stream of inventions was unparalleled: the phonograph, the dictaphone, the electric light (initially financed by Morgan), the motion-picture camera, and a host of others. His work formed the basis for such modern giants as General Electric, Consolidated Edison, and all the other "Edisons."

Despite his faults Carnegie must be considered a creator and innovator. He built a management accounting system to parallel his integrated steel works because he recognized at an early stage that, with the proper information about costs, management could gain a competitive advantage. He used this information to lower costs and prices in order to enlarge his market and outstrip his competitors. Carnegie plowed back his profits, refused to speculate in stocks, scorned financiers, and ran a tight ship. Carnegie believed in high wages for he found that well-paid workers functioned at their most productive level: "I can't afford to pay them [the workers] any other way [than high wages]." He never understood the Homestead strike and blamed the trouble on Henry Clay Frick, his partner and president of Carnegie Steel. Frick closed the plant (Carnegie was touring abroad when the dispute arose), hired the Pinkertons, built a fence around the property, and refused to budge. Carnegie had a knack for developing managers, however. Charles Schwab and W. E. Corey, both Carnegie protégés, were to become presidents of United States Steel. Carnegie eventually sold out to the Morgan interests, and the result was the formation of United States Steel in 1901. Carnegie's philanthropies are legendary, but he was also a dominant figure who brought integrated management to the steel industry and made it the world leader.

The stories of these creative entrepreneurs effectively counter the robber barons, and there were others as well: Ford, Nash, Durant, and Chrysler in automobiles; Wanamaker, the Filenes, Sears, Montgomery Ward, and J. C. Penney in retailing; the DuPonts, Westinghouse, Eastman, and a host of others. These were the productive men who were building America. Relatively uninterested in speculative schemes to get rich quick, they operated in a manner designed to create useful products at lower costs and prices to serve a growing America. The creative entrepreneurs are the true heroes of the American industrial story.

The Status of Labor. To the landless peasants and underpaid workmen of Europe, America was a land of golden opportunity; thousands, then tens and hundreds of thousands tore their family roots from the soil of Europe to make America a cultural potpourri. Immigration to America remained open until an isolationist fever in the 1920's closed the door to some nationalities. Blacks were here before the Civil War, Chinese had been brought in to build the railroads, and Irish, Germans, and Swedes populated the coal fields, steel mills, auto factories, and farms of America. After 1880 another flow of Slavs, Poles, and Italians added to the swelling work force. The increased supply of workers did not result in lower wages for the American worker. Real wages (the purchasing power of the workers' incomes) *doubled* between 1865 and 1890. From 1890 to 1921 the annual compound increase in real wages was 1.6 per cent a year, enabling another doubling. In addition to gains in terms of real wages, the hours of labor were lessening: in 1890 the average industrial work week was sixty hours; in 1910, fifty-five hours; and in 1920, fifty hours.

The organization of labor by unions made little progress among industrial workers, although craft workers in the building trades and railroad brotherhoods were relatively strong. Despite earlier decisions that rules that unions per se were not a combination or conspiracy in restraint of trade, a relatively hostile public opinion retarded unionization. For the industrial workers (that is, noncraft workers such as those in the building trades), two abortive attempts were made to organize. They were labor's countervailing responses

to the growth of business. The National Labor Union, headed by William H. Sylvis, sought to supplant the wage system with cooperative production in which the workers would pool their resources, supply their own labor, and manage the factories. The Noble Order of the Knights of Labor, organized in 1867, sought an eight-hour day, the establishment of a bureau of labor statistics, protection of child labor, a graduated income tax, government ownership of railroads and telegraph lines, the abolition of national banks, and a system of cooperation to take the place of wages. Neither of these organizations was to survive. Labor violence in the 1880's and 1890's fueled public fears of unions. The Molly Maguires terrorized the populace with murders and other atrocities in the Pennsylvania coal fields. The Haymarket Affair (1886), in which the Knights of Labor tried to enforce a general strike in Chicago, led to several deaths. The Homestead strike (1892) mentioned earlier, and the Pullman strike (1894) were other examples of violence brought about by confrontations between labor and management. Public fear of "radicals" and "anarchists," who were often equated with ligitimate union organizers, kept the union movement at a relative standstill. One success was the American Federation of Labor, organized in 1886 as a federation of craft unions that concentrated on the pursuit of immediate economic gains for the worker on the job rather than on distant political reforms. Under Samuel Gompers' leadership, the union membership increased from fewer than 200,000 in 1886 to more than 2,865,000 at the time of Gompers' death in 1924. The industrial worker, however, had to await other times and a changing public opinion to legitimatize his attempts at organization.

The management of labor and personnel relations gained little headway until 1900. The recruitment, hiring, and handling of people were the purview of the entrepreneur or his surrogate, the foreman. As business grew, relationships between owner and worker grew less personal. Out of scientific management grew a new movement in industrial psychology, vocational guidance, and personnel management. Employers formed "labor departments" to administer benefit plans, clubs, cafeterias, and other worker-welfare-oriented schemes. It was an attempt to restore some of the former relations in business by establishing special departments to handle employment affairs. The B. F. Goodrich Company developed the first employment department in America (1900); the National Cash Register Company established a labor department in 1902; and Plimpton Press, a showcase for scientific management, had a personnel department in 1910.

The early developmental period had few well-developed tools and techniques for personnel administration. World War I led to greater refinement, and the postwar period was marked by great strides in the management of personnel relations. Henry Ford, faced with a tight labor market and a worker turnover rate of 10 per cent, formed a personnel department in 1914, called the Sociological Department. The five-dollar-a-day wage, announced the same year, was "neither charity nor wages, but profit sharing and efficiency engineering." Ford, fearing that the high wages would lead the workers astray, employed one hundred investigators—"advisers"—who visited the workers' homes to ensure that their houses were neat and clean, that they did not drink too much, that their sex life was without tarnish, and that they used their leisure time profitably. Ford's Sociological Department was a far cry from modern concepts of personnel management, but its formation symbolized the notion that concern for the human element was the very best investment a business firm could make.

Extending the Commerce Clause. Politically, America was undergoing a great transformation in the relationship between business and government. The Populist-Progressive era of reform was an attack on corporate wealth and an effort to promote greater economic opportunity for all. The reformers, attempting to cope with societal change, centered their fire on the business leader, who was a symbol of change, which they could conveniently attack rather than the fact of change itself. The businessman was a target in the age of Populist-Progressive reform.

Progressivism had its roots in the Populist movement of the 1870's and 1880's. Whereas populism was overwhelmingly rural and provincial, progressivism was urban, middle class, and nationwide. Both were reform movements, and progressivism picked up where the populism of William Jennings Bryan left off. For both movements the central problem was to "restore" equality of opportunity by removing the interventions of government that benefited large-scale capital and by replacing those interventions with ones that favored persons with little or no capital. Populism waned because it was based on support from a declining segment of the population, the farmers. Progressivism, both a social and a political force, succeeded because it was concerned with labor, small businessmen, and the urban population.

America of the late nineteenth century was seeking to perfect democracy, and dissatisfied groups and individuals were responding with an outpouring of legislation to change the relations between man and state and between business and government. Founded on the premises of limited government, private property, freedom of economic opportunity, stress on individual initiative, and a laissez-faire government, America was finding imbalances and imperfections between the ideals and practices of economic democracy. Instead of laissez-faire capitalism perpetuating itself as Adam Smith had envisioned, businessmen were taking collective action to ration and monopolize the market, organized labor took on economic and political objectives, and special-interest groups fought to expand their opportunities at the expense of other groups. Feeling powerless as individuals, men turned more and more to collective action.

The change in public attitude—that is, as espoused by the Progressives—was a conviction that government should look out for the interests of all the people, not just a privileged few. The first attempts to reform business practices came logically with the railroads. In 1869, Massachusetts passed the first statutes regulating railroads; the grange laws of the seventies brought regulation to others, and the Interstate Commerce Act of 1887, which proved generally ineffective in practice, became the first national regulation. Beyond the railroads the Sherman Antitrust Act of 1890 sought to check corporate trusts and monopoly practices "in restraint of trade." Poorly defined and narrowly construed, it was generally ineffectual.

A big change came in 1901, after the assassination of President William McKinley and the succession of Theodore Roosevelt. At first the new President gave businessmen and other financial interests no cause for alarm. His well-phrased first message to Congress balanced his own Progressive inclinations with a probusiness stance. Mr. Dooley, Peter Finley Dunne's fictional Irishman, aptly summarized President Roosevelt's position: "'Th' trusts,' says he, 'are heejust monsthers build up be th' inlightened intherprise in th' men that have done so much to advance progres in our beloved counthry he says.' On wan hand I wud stamp thim undher fut; on th' other hand not so fast."

The honeymoon was brief. In 1902, President Roosevelt brought suit to dissolve the Northern Securities Company by invoking the Sherman Act. This direct blow at Northern Securities, a holding company set up by J. P. Morgan and Edward H. Harriman to control three major railroads, opened a new era in government-business relations. Known as an ardent proponent of conservation of natural resources as well as a trust buster, Roosevelt placed government in a new role as a regulator of business activity. Antitrust suits were filed against the Beef Trust (1905), the Standard Oil Company of New Jersey (1906), and the American Tobacco Company (1907), and new legislation regulated the railroads (Elkin's Act, in 1903, and the Hepburn Act, 1906) and the telephone, telegraph, and wireless industries (the Mann-Elkins Act, 1910). Other state and federal legislative enactments sought to limit hours of work and regulate female and child labor. The Clayton Act and the Federal Trade Commission Act (1914) strengthened the Sherman Act and made more explicit other discriminatory business practices. The Federal Reserve Act of 1913 created a more elastic currency and weakened the hold of large New York City banks over cash and reserves. In each new enactment of legislation the commerce clause of the Constitution was being extended to bring about more regulation of business practices.

Some of the voices of reform earned the title "muckrakers." Their protests were not only against business but also against the practices of corrupt governments and their failure to provide justice. Lincoln Steffens unfolded a trail of political corruption in *The Shame of the Cities*; Ida Tarbell criticized the unethical practices of Standard Oil; Thomas Lawson exposed Wall Street in *Frenzied Finance*; Upton Sinclair aimed at the nation's heart and hit its stomach in *The Jungle* (which resulted in the passage of the Pure Food and Drug Act); and David Phillips described the close connection between industrialists and lawmakers in *The Treason of the Senate*.

In essence, the reform movement aimed at coping with the cultural upheaval caused by large-scale enterprise, "spoils" government, and the abuse of the many by the powerful few, whether in business or in government. The result was a decline in laissez faire and a growth in government regulation of business.

BUSINESS IN AMERICAN LIFE, 1921–76

The World of Business

From colony to world power is the story of the American business system during the past two hundred years. No other nation in history has experienced such a dramatic growth in such a short period. As the present draws near, the scene of business shifts from domestic and local markets to a global one, from handicraft production to mass production, and from log pike roads to concrete ribbons girding the nation.

The international aspects of marketing, finance, and manufacturing become more obvious as transportation and communication modes advance. America offers a challenge not to King George and his mercantilist policies but to the other industrial nations of the world. Superiority in technology, organization, and management places the American business enterprise in world dominance. But with industrial power comes responsibility, and with responsibility comes the interdependence of nations as they strive to achieve their own goals. The world of business develops and awaits the future with a sometimes hesitant confidence that is the product of past accomplishments.

Marketing: The Age of the Consumer. The marketing revolution continued, in both the structure of markets and the products marketed. Competition ruled, despite charges of monopoly or oligopoly, and the change in the form of competition came about because of new communications devices for reaching the minds and pocketbook of the consumer. While the mass-medium technique of radio had already entered the scene, television was an advertising man's boon. Products could be displayed more alluringly, and more of the consumer's senses could be bombarded by appeals to get his money. This expansion of the media enabled companies to reach more people but, simultaneously, required the company to make its product somehow "different" from other products. Products had to appear different or had to appeal to different desires of consumers. No firm worth its salt would simply sell gas and oil; it had to sell "trust," "service," "innovation," "mileage," or whatever. Brand X became more a part of every commercial message. Novel brand names, slogans, jingles, and eye-appealing packages became more important as marketing personnel fought to capture space on the retailer's shelves, as well as a place in the consumer's cart.

The structure of distribution was also to undergo a transformation, although not as drastically as before. Chain and department stores were fairly well established by the 1930's, as were supermarkets. The 1930's were bad years for marketing, and World War II slowed domestic consumption. A postwar boom of spending, coupled with wider use of consumer credit, touched off a spree of marketing innovations. The discount house was one of the unique changes in structure. Korvette's in New York City was one of the first of

many. The concept of the discount house was originally a cash-and-carry, low-overhead operation. By reducing services and eliminating fancy decorations and furnishings and other expensive practices, the discounter could sell at lower prices. These methods are reminiscent of the early department store, especially in regard to discounts on large-quantity purchases. But over the years the department stores had become fancier and offered more services, and prices had to reflect the added costs of doing business. The discount house was the hungry barracuda in the tank of fat tuna. As the discount houses evolved, they too fell prey to the imperatives of competition to offer a "little more of this or that" to woo the consumer. They started accepting credit cards, making deliveries, building fancy stores, and so on, renewing what seems to be a never-ending cycle of retailing. Perhaps the future will bring discount discount houses.

Another substantial marketing innovation took place in the field of franchising. Through a franchise a local businessman could buy into a nationally (or regionally) advertised product, including various services for assisting him in his business. Food products were especially important, and fastfood franchises, such as McDonald's, Dairy Queen, Chicken Delight, Shakey's Pizza, and, of course, Colonel Sanders and his Kentucky Fried Chicken, were established in nearly every community. Motor hotels, mostly franchised, became more popular as highways improved and the interstate-highway system progressed. Motel chains, such as Holiday Inn and Howard Johnson's beckoned the weary traveler to stop outside the central city to avoid traffic congestion, parking problems, and tips to bellhops.

Marketing outlets moved to the suburbs as the populace did. Even such venerable mail-order houses as Wards and Sears moved to the suburbs and opened retail stores. By 1971, Sears was the world's largest retailer in terms of sales, and the nation's fifth-largest employer. Credit cards, installment payment plans, and revolving charge accounts grew in popularity, countering the cash payment, "avoid debt" dictum of the preceding generations. The cornucopia of new products rivaled the new means of financing purchases, as well as the new retail outlets. Clarence Birdseye discovered the secret of fast-freezing foods and paved the way to a host of frozen products of all kinds. Convenience foods, such as mixes, instant coffee, and TV dinners, freed the housewife from the drudgery of cooking her mother had known. The wringer washing machine and outdoor-clothes-line drying was replaced by automatic washers and dryers; electric refrigerators replaced iceboxes; and air conditioning made home life cool enough to watch TV. A process for removing caffeine from coffee was discovered accidentally when a French merchant accepted a shipment of beans that had been soaked in sea water during a storm. He called the product *sans caffeine*, soon shortened to Sanka. A customer who complained about the cheap thin quality of the glue used for a tape product of the Minnesota Mining and Manufacturing Company also gave us the name for another product. The customer said that the company was stingy ("Scotch") in its use of glue.

Modern marketing had a wealth of new products to sell and an effective way of promoting on a grand scale. It was the age of the consumer, and a consumer revolt was soon to come. Consumers became activists, especially in the style of Ralph Nader and his coterie. Not only was product safety questioned but such marketing practices as labeling, packaging, advertising, and warranting fell into disfavor. The government, through a multitude of agencies, took a stiffer stance regarding caveat emptor ("let the buyer beware"), turning it into caveat vendor. The balance of market power was shifting, bringing to business a new set of partners.

Finance and Banking. An expanding financial system was essential to the growth of marketing and manufacturing. Whereas early entrepreneurs operated from the hundreds or thousands of dollars of their savings, the modern corporate firm needed millions from bankers and the public sale of securities. The idea of a national bank was slow to gain adherents, and when it finally did, it was slow to develop as a national monetary force. The Federal Reserve Act had created the Federal Reserve System and the Federal Reserve Board in 1914. National policy decisions allowed the bankers, especially those in New York City, to dominate the newly created banking system until 1935. Some argue that the failure of the federal banking system to provide a stabilizing and prudent monetary policy contributed to the collapse of the banking system in 1929. The Great Contraction could have been prevented, it is argued, by a closer watch by the Federal Reserve over the money supply. While that is correct, other factors contributed to the weakened structure of banking. From 1900 to 1920 the number of banks grew from nine thousand to thirty thousand, and some of these ventures must have been marginal with shaky capital structures. From 1921 to 1929, before the national crisis, about five thousand banks failed, lending credence to the contention that the banking system was overcrowded. The stock-market crash of 1929 led to hasty withdrawals from banks in efforts to cover stock losses. The ensuing financial panic threatened the nation and was a virus in the bloodstream of capitalism. In 1931, President Herbert Hoover formed the National Credit Corporation in an effort to rescue the smaller, weaker banks and restore national confidence. The stronger banks refused to cooperate, and the venture failed. Hoover tried again in 1932 with the Reconstruction Finance Corporation, which made loans to banks and indeed saved many from liquidation. But too much time elapsed, and the crisis continued into the administration of Franklin D. Roosevelt. Temporary bank closings ("holidays") helped, but it was obvious that new legislation was needed. The Emergency Banking Act of 1933 started a plan of insuring deposits, helped eliminate runs, and brought some stability. The Federal Deposit Insurance Corporation was created, originally insuring all deposits up to five thousand dollars, and later the Federal Savings and Loan Insurance Corporation brought surety and stability to that area of the nation's financial structure. The Banking Act of 1935 finally placed the Federal Reserve System under government control and removed it from the hands of the banking interests. From that date on, the Federal Reserve Board has played an often crucial role in controlling the money supply and regulating the economy, sometimes successfully, but sometimes to the detriment of the citizens.

The currency in circulation in the 1920's consisted of gold and gold certificates, silver and silver certificates, and United States bank notes. The hoarding of gold during the Depression led President Roosevelt to require that all citizens exchange their gold holdings for other cash. There was no more private gold, except for numismatists. In the 1960's silver became scarce, and the cheap money made of copper-clad coins helped drive it out of circulation. Gold and silver certificates (paper money backed by gold or silver) disappeared, to be replaced by Federal Reserve notes. Silver and gold coins became collector's items. The continued declining value of the dollar at home and abroad threatened national stability.

Manufacturing: The Cybernetic Age. Manufacturing continued to dominate the economic scene, although the "services" sector was making some headway. An examination of selected segments of national income sources illustrates this:

SELECTED NATIONAL INCOME FIGURES (in billions)

	1929	1950	1970
Manufacturing	$21.9	$74.3	$217.7
Wholesale and retail trade	13.4	42.7	122.1
Services	10.3	23.1	103.2

At the heart of this continued dominance of manufacturing was the alliance between science and industry. Scientific advances in the past fifty years have been dazzling: antibiotics, plastics, synthetic fibers, television, tape and cassette recorders, computers, dry copiers, jet planes, rockets, and microcircuitry are but a few of a host of developments. This age has seen the growth of research-and-development activities in many firms, as well as in government-sponsored projects. Products for space-exploration ventures have found their way into the home, the farm, and the factory. The marriage of pure scientists and the businessmen who apply their findings have led to remarkable results in a space-age economy. Organizations such as Bell Laboratories and Texas Instruments are examples of outstanding research-and-development programs. Edwin H. Land, a scientist, invented instant photography and applied it in his Polaroid Camera; Chester Carlson perfected the photoelectrical (dry) copying technique, leading to the Haloid Corporation and, later, Xerox. Everette Lee De Golyer took a scientific instrument, the seismograph, and turned it into a method of discovering petroleum deposits. Others, many others, took science from the laboratory and put it to industrial use.

If mass production was the Second Industrial Revolution, then the Third Industrial Revolution lies in *cybernation.* Cybernetics, a word coined by Norbert Wiener, of the Massachusetts Institute of Technology, involves the automatic control of machines by other machines. The basis for modern cybernetics is the computer, which, surprisingly, is not a modern invention. The English mathematician and philosopher Charles Babbage conceived a computer as early as 1833.

The idea lay dormant for over a century, awaiting more advanced power sources and improved technology. International Business Machines financed the "rediscovery" of the computer in the early 1940's, and the early models filled entire rooms with scores of vacuum tubes. Thomas J. Watson was IBM's guiding hand in the development of this modern marvel, although others played important roles. The computer industry grew rapidly, aided by advancing technology in the development of microcircuitry, and revolutionized computation as well as the handling of masses of data. The computer inaugurated the cybernetic-automated age: operating on the feedback of data, machines can be controlled, corrected, and guided by computer. Automated steel factories are in operation, and automated production processes are used in automobile assembly and a number of other operations. Automation was initially feared as a potential threat to employment, but that threat has yet to materialize. Automation has led to personnel displacement, but industrial and union cooperation have provided short-term protection and long-term retraining programs. In short, in two centuries of American industrial history the nation has moved from the domestic system of production to the age of cybernation.

Transportation, Communication, and Energy. Railroads began to decline in the 1920's. The appearance of automobiles, buses, trucks, and airplanes contributed to what was to become a hardening of one of the nation's transportation arteries. The railroads adapted to the new modes of competition slowly but as best they could in view of often adverse work rules of unions and punitive regulation by various state agencies and the federal government. Steam engines were still used, although some lines moved to diesel motive power, albeit reluctantly. The railroads enjoyed a resurgence of popularity during World War II, when a rubber shortage and gas rationing forced Americans out of their automobiles. The respite was brief, and there was further decline in the postwar period. Passengers posed a particular problem; railroads would have preferred to abolish passenger service to focus on freight, where they felt they could compete more profitably. Regulatory agencies insisted on these passenger services, saddling the lines, especially those in the East, with a non-profitable burden. Despite regulations that favored the trucking industry, the railroads continued to dominate the freight-hauling business. Innovations such as piggy-back service (long-distance hauling of trucks on trains) and "unit trains" (trains carrying only one commodity) helped the railroads compete. The railroads' reluctance to carry passengers led to the formation of Amtrak, a government corporation that leases existing cars and lines for passengers. Amtrak has not been a resounding success, for it requires a continuing and constantly increasing subsidy from the taxpayers' pockets, whether or not they ride the trains. A number of mergers have reshaped the railroad picture, but bankruptcies and near bankruptcies are all too common. The Penn Central, a merger of the Pennsylvania and the New York Central lines, lost five hundred million dollars in 1970 and declared bankruptcy. It was an outstanding sum of money, and perhaps only in America could a company lose that much money without causing a serious drain on the rest of the economy. The Rock Island Line was "a mighty fine line," but it too went into receivership. The future of rail travel is not entirely bleak; the rising price of gasoline may put the nation back on the iron wheels yet.

Air travel has been a pleasant alternative to rail travel, especially in the jet age, for cross-national as well as international travel. The airplane progressed steadily from military uses to mail carrying and eventually to passenger and freight service. By 1940 the airlines had captured from the railroads the lion's share of the long-distance passenger service. The government has had a continuing influence on air travel, ranging from aircraft development, financing of airport construction, and weather service, to control of the air lanes for safety. From three months' to six hours' travel time from New York to London is the measure of transportation's progress in the last two hundred years.

America's romance with the automobile continued to grow, making possible suburban living, as well as producing traffic congestion. In the beginning there were large numbers of car manufacturers, but the numbers have dwindled over the years to four. The lack of highways hindered early travel, but a national highway system begun in 1916 has continued to the present. In 1956, Congress authorized the interstate highway system which was to provide for 41,000 miles of limited-access multilane roads connecting the principle centers of the nation. The automobile fed other industries, such as steel, rubber, and petroleum, as well as creating new ones, such as motels and tourism. During the Depression the humorist Will Rogers said that America was the "only nation that ever drove to the poorhouse in an automobile." With gasoline prices on the rise, Americans may have to take the bus in the future.

Advancements in communications proceeded to a worldwide system of electronic wizardry. The telephone became a necessity, not a luxury, and direct-dialing nationwide was the result of years of development by the A.T.&T. Long Lines Division. Television was an innovation in communications that reshaped radio broadcasting and also led to the decline of the motion-picture industry. David Sarnoff, of the Radio Corporation of America and the National Broadcasting Company, and William Paley, of the Columbia Broadcasting System, pioneered in bringing color TV to the nation. The launchings of communication satellites, which maintain their position by matching the earth's revolution, have permitted communication on a global scale. The Vietnam War was the first to be brought into the family's living room, live and in color, by means of TV satellites.

A nation that runs on wheels and flicks a switch to power its homes, offices, and factories is heavily dependent upon energy. For many years America continued to depend primarily on coal for heat and generation of electricity; petroleum products fueled transportation. Natural gas, as well as fuel oil, began to replace coal in home heating. Hydroelectric power as yet accounts for no more than 4 per cent of the country's annual energy needs. Great dams, such as the Hoover Dam and those built by the Tennessee Valley Authority, were constructed during this period, and more were authorized. Atomic power became a reality but has had limited application owing to fears of possible thermal pollution, explosions, and other catastrophes. Growing public consumption, ecological concern and government intervention have seemed to make the energy problem more acute, rather than allaying it. Emission controls placed on cars in the name of pollution abatement increased fuel consumption. Offshore drilling was limited because fear of spills and spoilage of sea waters and beaches. Similar concerns about the ecology of the North delayed the development of the North Slope oil discoveries. Stringent air control measures made soft, high-sulfur coal unusable, thus denying access to one of the nation's most abundant resources. Middle Eastern countries rich in oil used their advantage to further their political goals. The nation's energy problem worsened, and the end is not in sight.

The Professional Managers. The entrepreneur could deal face to face with most of his employees—he knew them, their problems, their likes and dislikes. Growth made industry less intimate, replacing the personal style of the entrepreneur with the bureaucratic style of the administrator. The personal touch of leadership was gone only to be replaced with directives from technically trained specialists that an advanced industrial nation required. Social competence, the manipulation of people, began to assume a new importance, and technical skills were played down. The emerging body of managers based their authority upon knowledge gained through education in a business-school-oriented society, rather than upon their ability to invent new gadgets or command the acquisition of capital. When the personal style of the entrepreneur-manager was replaced by a growing hierarchy of managers and specialists, the age of organization began. It was an age of structure, a largely impersonalized set of policies, rules, and offices that was intended to assure performance and profitability.

The age of organizational geniuses was typified by the General Motors Corporation. William C. Durant had conceived the idea of creating General Motors out of an amalgam of motor-car and parts producers. The union was unwieldy, and General Motors was plucked from the brink of financial disaster by an infusion of Du Pont money in 1920. In 1923, Alfred P. Sloan, Jr., became president of General Motors. Influenced by the Du Pont system of management, he created the concept of decentralized administration and operations with centralized control and review. By decentralizing operations and centrally coordinating control, the separate parts of General Motors could work toward a common end. Establishment of this multidivisional structure enabled organizational units to grow larger without the encumbrances that come from organizing by function. The concept of decentralization into product divisions required yet another pioneering idea, that of profit-center accountability. Du Pont's treasurer, Donaldson Brown, created the system of controlling through accounting responsibility by linking the various organizational subunits to a planned rate of return on controllable expenses. Given a certain amount of resource investment, the performance of each division or unit could

then be measured and controlled on the basis of the rate of return on investment. The result was a correlation between efforts expended and results obtained that enabled central management to judge and compare the effectiveness of each product division. Donaldson Brown left Du Pont to join General Motors and instituted basically the same system for Sloan. Together they created an organizational style widely emulated as other organizations grew too large to follow the previous structure of centralized authority and responsibility by function.

But even as these giant organizational structures were developing, the need to bring in the human element was recognized. Elton Mayo and Fritz Roethlisberger, of Harvard University, were leaders in the movement to bring human relations into the workplace. The manager needed technical skills, but, more importantly, he needed social skills in leading, counseling, and guiding workers. Others advocated "bottom-up management," "multiple management," and participative leadership. Followers of Mayo saw the root of economic problems in the social problems of industry. For them men's loss of identity was manifested in pessimistic reveries, in obsessive-compulsive behavior, in group turning inward to protect themselves from management, and in expressed needs to find social satisfactions on the job. Once social solidarity was restored, primary groups rebuilt, communications channels opened, and social and psychological needs fulfilled, men could turn their efforts to being more productive.

It was in business schools and industrial training groups that managers learned how to manage the large organization and to cope with the human problems of an industrial civilization. The nation's first business school was the Wharton School of Finance and Commerce (endowed by Joseph Wharton, a prominent steelmaker), founded at the University of Pennsylvania in 1881. Such schools grew slowly at first; most businessmen felt that management could be learned only by experience on the job. Between 1919 and 1924, however, 117 colleges developed some form of business curriculum, and a business-school boom was in progress. By 1928 about 67,000 students were enrolled in business schools, and enrollment continued to climb, even during the Depression. By then it was recognized that the modern manager of a large organization needed an education in quantitative, human, and managerial skills.

This drive for educated managers must be understood in terms of the changing views of society toward the businessman and the manager. The businessman represented in fiction may or may not be a barometer of his social esteem. One must be warned that the fictional businessman is generally portrayed in an unrealistic manner because of the novelist's need to dramatize in contrasts and to gain sympathy for characters. While it would be impossible to hold the businessman to blame for the hard times of the Depression era, it was evident that he became through fictional writings the *symbol* of society's ills. The 1920's had canonized the businessman as hero and the symbol of prosperity and the good life. When times turned turbulent, was it not fair to heap the blame on the "bankster" who robbed people of their homes and savings? While such charges were not entirely just, the businessman as portrayed in fiction undoubtedly became a convenient focal point for public wrath.

The novels of the 1930's and 1940's were characterized by disillusionment with individualism. Individualism, as the novelists viewed the world, was futile and they shifted their emphasis to pleas for humanitarianism and collectivism. The businessman as "hero" vanished, to be replaced by a "they" who did things without reason and were beyond the control of mere mortals. "They" represented power, machines, and forces, not individual managers whom one could hold responsible. The corporation was a monster of oppression in which people and their lives were ground down piece by piece. Representative of this kind of fiction were John Steinbeck's *Grapes of Wrath* and Nathaniel West's *A Cool Million*. For Steinbeck, it was not individuals but "they" who gave the migrants a hard time. West's hero, of the Horatio Alger type, found himself caught between the contending forces of "international bankers" and "world revolutionists" who slowly but surely destroyed his spirit of individualism and quest for free enterprise.

As the 1940's and 1950's unfolded, the manager completed the shift from the hero image by becoming more and more an "organization man." In conformity lay security, and the manager became a hero not because of great or daring deeds but because he tolerated grinding mediocrity and conformity. In John P. Marquand's *The Point of No Return*, Ernst Pawel's *From the Dark Tower*, and Sloan Wilson's *The Man in the Gray Flannel Suit*, the emphasis was on conformity and the futility of rebelling against the organization as a system.

The businessman often finds his esteem affected by the ups and downs of the economy. When things go well, he is all but canonized. When things go poorly, he is held responsible for the ills of modern civilization. Intellectuals have always maintained an uneasy truce with industrial life by idealizing agriculture and denigrating business. Jeffersonian and Jacksonian democracy were examples of the praise of an agricultural, small-unit, family-owned, ideal base of society. To be big was to be bad, and to live in the "city" was a sign of the decline of man. Why have the intellectuals idealized agriculture and sullied business? The growth of cities is the history of business: the big-businessman is the symbol of the city, and the city became the symbol of degradation. The idea of noncity living still prevails as an ideal; the first sign of success is the ability to escape the city by moving to the suburbs.

If the businessman is held in such low esteem, what can he do? The idea of "profession" or of being a "professional" has always connoted status beyond the ordinary. Business has been considered a base occupation by many cultures, by the Greeks and Romans especially, and those associated with business would prefer to be regarded as an integral part of society and an essential part of carrying out the goals of society. If business or management were regarded as a profession, then the manager would feel that his role in society was held in high esteem. Some believed that the master's degree in business administration should be recognized as the minimum prerequisite for entering the profession of management. The MBA became the "glamour-stock" degree as young managers, as well as older ones, sought to elevate their

stature. Others believed that business needed a code of ethics, but no sense of general agreement has evolved from that idea. Still others felt that the businessman could take the wind out of the critics' sails by being more "socially responsible," as discussed below. In brief, the modern manager was the educated manager, the professional trained to assume the responsibilities of the large organization. He did not own but managed the property of others. He succeeded, and succeeded well, in placing American management at the helm of world management. As the Frenchman Jean-Jacques Servan-Schreiber said in *The American Challenge:* "The American challenge is not ruthless, like so many Europe has known, . . . but it may be more dramatic. . . . Its weapons are not simply in the field of science, but also in organization and management."

The New Partners of Business

If a single phenomenon were to be selected to illustrate the difference between modern business and its predecessors, it would be the role of other claimants on the traditional prerogatives of the businessman. The businessman traditionally ran his business as he saw fit, relatively unimpeded by unions, governmental agencies, consumer groups, ecologists, or other members of society. Profits were dividends, not higher taxes, higher wages, or societal-welfare matters. Some see those claimants on the traditional property rights of business as encroachments on the free-enterprise system, as indeed they are. Others see them as justifiable advancements in making the businessman a better member of society, as indeed they are. The dilemma lies in the relative balance of power. The claimants, the new partners of business, are labor, society, and government.

Labor. The 1920's witnessed an upswing in company paternalism and welfare schemes designed to woo worker loyalty. Man became the firm's most important asset, not because of sentimentality or a moral attitude but because of the view that concern for employee welfare would increase worker efficiency. Personnel departments proliferated, and worker-welfare plans were designed with the hope that workers would reciprocate by expressing their appreciation through higher productivity. Employers' goals were "industrial betterment" or "industrial welfare," which was an uneven mixture of philanthropy, humanitarianism, and business acumen. Industrialists such as John H. Patterson, of National Cash Register, set the pattern for the industrial-welfare movement. Such schemes for welfare and paternalism had the objectives of preventing labor problems and improving performance by providing hospital clinics, lunchrooms, bathhouses, profit-sharing plans, recreational facilities, and a host of other devices to woo worker loyalty. Human happiness was a business asset, and the wise, profit-minded employer nurtured worker loyalty to the firm through various employee-welfare schemes.

Organized labor was not a significant force in the 1920's; the craft unions (such as the AFL) maintained their strength, but industrial unions were weak. Company-sponsored unions were fairly common, but labor's voice was not strident. Various union-management schemes were developed to give unions a voice in factory operation, but the balance of power remained in the hands of the employer and his use of company-welfare-oriented devices. The Depression intensified labor's problems, as it did everyone's. From that time on, labor began to seek government intervention in labor-management relations through legislation and other assistance. The new president, Franklin D. Roosevelt, was to become the staunch ally of organized labor.

The Roosevelt era was a bottom-up view of society. The use of federal power achieved a new dimension in government-business relations that even the Progressives had not envisioned. The New Deal introduced a positive concept of public responsibility for relief of want, for employment, for individual security, for parity for farmers, for recognition of organized labor, for maintenance of industrial peace, and for enlarged responsibilities in the operation of the nation's credit system. It was a new age, calling for a new balance of power that promised to restore society.

Of all the changes in the redress of power, none had more immediate significance for business than the new role for labor. The promanagement legal environment that prevailed in the 1920's and the reliance on union-management cooperation was abruptly altered in the 1930's. During this period the New Deal addressed itself to remedying a perceived imbalance in labor-management relations and passed revolutionary legislation that greatly strengthened the position of organized labor. The first significant piece of labor legislation passed by Congress was the Federal Anti-Injunction Act of 1932, more commonly referred to as the Norris-LaGuardia Act. That act, for all practical purposes, divested federal courts of injunctive powers in cases growing out of labor disputes. In 1933, Congress passed the National Industrial Recovery Act, the first in a series of New Deal enactments designed to lift the nation out of the Depression. Section 7a of the NIRA, expressed in similar but stronger language than that already existing in the Norris-LaGuardia Act, specifically guaranteed that "employees shall have the right to organize and bargain collectively through representatives of their own choosing . . . free from the interference, restraint, or coercion of employers." It further provided that "no employee and no one seeking employment shall be required as a condition of employment to join any company union or to refrain from joining, organizing or assisting a labor organization of his own choosing."

When the NIRA was declared unconstitutional by the Supreme Court in 1935 (*Schecter* v. *United States*), Congress quickly replaced it with a law that was even more pleasing to organized labor. The National Labor Relations Act, more commonly known as the Wagner Act, was far more definite in what it expected of collective bargaining than was the NIRA. The Wagner Act guaranteed employees "the right to self-organization, to form, join, or assist labor organizations, to bargain collectively through representatives of their own choosing, and to engage in concerted activities for the purpose of collective bargaining." In addition, it placed specific restrictions on what management could do by specifying five "unfair" management practices. To implement these provisions, the act established the National Labor Relations Board, which was granted the authority not only to issue cease-and-desist orders against employers violating the restrictions but also to determine appropriate bargaining units and conduct representation elections.

The passage of the Wagner Act marked a critical turning point in labor-management relations and created a new style of industrial unionism to supplement craft unionism. John L. Lewis, president of the United Mine Workers, led the fight for industrial unionism within the American Federation of Labor. Rebuffed, Lewis formed the Committee for Industrial Organization (known after 1938 as the Congress of Industrial Organizations), whose purpose came to be that of bringing workers into unions regardless of occupation or skill level. The newly founded CIO enjoyed almost instant success and as early as 1937 was able to claim almost four million members. By 1941 virtually all the giant corporations in the mass-production industries had recognized the CIO-affiliated unions as bargaining agents for their employees. With the legal climate created by the New Deal legislation, union membership spurted from fewer than three million members in 1933 to more than eight million by 1939. Other legislation to help labor emerged from a belief that industry had failed to provide security for the working class and that government must fill the vacuum. The response to this craving for security was made manifest in a number of pioneering legislative acts: the Social Security Act of 1935 sought to provide for old-age income; the Fair Labor Standards Act of 1938 established a guaranteed minimum hourly wage for certain workers; and the Railroad Unemployment Insurance Act of 1938 was the first national unemployment protection.

Labor thus gained substantial power during the 1930's through legislation. The New Deal labor policy was part of a power-equalization drive designed to restore the voice of the "little man" in the industrial hierarchy. During the war all shoulders were turned to the wheels of industry, and differences were temporarily laid aside. Employment regulation, such as through the War Labor Board, prevailed and in general enhanced the power of labor. After the war many strikes led to the opinion that labor had too much power and resulted in the passage of the Labor-Management Relations Act (Taft-Hartley Act) in 1947. In the 1950's a series of congressional hearings disclosed many cases of corrupt union leadership, which had grown so accustomed to its power that it too had forgotten the worker. The result was the Labor-Management Reporting and Disclosure Act (the Landrum-Griffin Act) of 1959. Its intent was to guarantee democracy for the worker within his union as well as at his place of employment. These acts did bring about some redress in the balance of power; no longer was the employer able to pursue unilateral actions with respect to labor policies. In general the whole environment of business had changed, not just with respect to labor but also in all relations with government.

The condition of the workers continued to improve, sometimes because of, sometimes despite, the actions of union leaders. In 1930 the forty-eight-hour work week (six eight-hour days) was common practice; by 1950, the forty-hour (five-day) work week was the standard. The reduced time at work gave laborers, and others, more time for travel, recreation, and other leisure activities. Wages, including real wages, have continually improved: from 1926 to 1970 the average weekly earning in manufacturing quintupled while prices were only doubling. This increase in wages did not include fringe benefits for employees (employer-paid life and health insurance, pensions, and so on), which have become prevalent in industry since World War II. During the Depression, earnings fell, but so did prices—although that was little consolation for the estimated twelve million Americans who were without work. The Public Works Administration and the Work Projects Administration were established to provide public employment and thereby relieve the unemployment problem. The government committed itself to promoting "full employment" with the Employment Act of 1946. While "full" has never been adequately defined, it became the government's policy to stimulate the economy and provide jobs if recession threatened. Other state and federal enactments have provided for workmen's-compensation laws to assist disabled workers, unemployment benefits are provided by most states, and these programs have served to stabilize the employment situation and protect the wage earner and his family. Industrial safety practices have been improved, and the Occupational Safety and Health Act of 1970 was the first stringent federal legislation in this regard. In summary, organized labor has established itself as a potent force and a wielder of great political influence. Its "partnership" with business has taken away some traditional management perogatives, but it can provide a check on excessive industrial practices by giving the worker, through his union representative, a voice in the industrial democracy.

Society. "Social responsibility," a broader concept of "business and society," has come to represent another claimant on the traditional rights of business. The philanthropy of businessmen is as ancient as business itself. They have been patrons of arts and letters, provided funds for community projects, supported churches, and endowed educational institutions. No one questioned the right of successful businessmen to give away some or all of their fortunes; after all, it was their money to do with as they pleased. The Whartons, Colgates, Cornells, Browns, Carnegies, Fords, Mellons, and Rockefellers, to name a few families, were benefactors.

But what of this new phenomenon, the corporation? Could it have a conscience? Could its managers and directors give away a portion of its profits to nonbusiness-related endeavors? Or were the managers to work only in the interest of the owners, the stockholders? The legal question of corporate philanthropy was based on the precedent set in an 1883 British case, *Hutton* v. *West Cork Railway Corporation.* The court ruled that the corporation existed only as a profit-making enterprise and that its responsibility lay in the equitable distribution of its earnings to its owners, the stockholders. Because of this precedent officers of corporations were hesitant to dole out money to other claimants, fearing stockholders' lawsuits.

A historic revision of the Federal Revenue Act in 1935 included the famous "5 per cent" clause, which permitted corporations to deduct up to that amount from net income for contributions to eleemosynary institutions. Despite this provision deductions for corporate giving rarely reached 1 per cent of taxable income. Another landmark case appeared in 1953, *A. P. Smith Manufacturing Company* v. *Barlow, et. al.* The company had donated fifteen hundred dollars to Princeton University for general educational purposes. Some stockholders sued, claiming that this was an *ultra vires* act, outside the powers granted by the charter of incorporation. The New Jersey Supreme Court ruled for the company, reasoning that business support of higher education was in the best interest of a free-enterprise society. The case was not appealed, and the precedent for corporate involvement in social activities had been established.

To some extent post–World War II concern for social responsibility also grew out of the criticisms of business during the Depression and from those who felt that too much power was concentrated in the hands of too few businessmen. There has been increasing concern that business firms have been unmindful of their relationship with their public constituency and their impact on the physical and social environment. The debate over corporate involvement remained a hot one, and one could find both proponents and opponents of the notion of social responsibility.

The proponents of corporate social responsibility believe that business is more than an economic institution. Business activities are made legitimate by the legal system, and business interacts with its social environment in employing people, buying supplies, selling products, and disposing of its wastes. They also believe that the profitability of business should be limited to some extent (there is widespread disagreement about what extent) in order to protect the consumer, preserve the physical environment (ecology), and provide social products, programs, and services. One argument for corporate activity in the social realm is based on the belief that an improved community and society will lead to long-range positive benefits to the firm and to business in general. Hence it is in the long-run self-interest of business that companies undertake to solve social problems. Corporate philanthropic donations to universities and trade schools, for example, promote education and training and ensure a better-qualified graduate for future employment.

Another argument is that corporate involvement in social actions can not only improve the community but also mute the accusations of the critics. Social action creates a community awareness of the corporate conscience and at the same time inproves the community itself. Business needs a favorable corporate image and can enhance its position by community social involvement. Still another argument is that government would not need to regulate and intervene so much or so often if business took more initiative in solving social problems. Government moves into social vacuums when no action has been taken by others. To avoid further governmental intervention and regulation, business should fill the void in community problem areas. By being socially responsible, the business manager can prevent governmènt action, reduce the cost of government, lower taxes (a cost of doing business), and promote community welfare all at the same time.

Finally, problems may become profits. While most arguments have little or no direct appeal for the pecuniary instincts of the businessman, this one does. It is this argument that is supposed to reach the businessman's wallet, if his conscience has not responded. Since business has a long, outstanding record for innovations and improvements, why not encourage him to turn this creativity to social problems and thereby turn them into profitable ventures? If problems can become profits, then a host of other things happen: community betterment coupled with corporate prosperity, as well as lessening government intervening. Indeed, the idea has great appeal. While there are some social problems whose solutions may not be convertible to profits, there are enough to warm the heart of any businessman. The example of one company, Dow Chemical Company, should suffice to demonstrate the potential. By fine-tuning production processes and by recycling wastes to recover raw materials, Dow has been able to pay for its pollution control devices out of the profits from recovered chemicals while simultaneously reducing air and water pollution. In short, social problems can be solved and lead to corporate profits, satisfying both the communities' needs and corporate goals.

The opponents of corporate social responsibility are of the opinion that business is an economic institution and should confine its activities to that sphere. Profitability, essential to survival, is endangered when the corporation begins to redirect its energies into the social realm. In a modern corporate organization officers manage the property of others, the stockholders. They are responsible to the stockholders, who want a return on their investment undiluted with vague noneconomic-related actions. Despite rulings such as in the Smith case, there are some who feel that such corporate philanthropy deprives individuals of their right to use their returns on their investments as best they see fit. Thus corporate giving violates individuals' rights to give to whom they choose. Another counter argument is that social-action programs can endanger the welfare of marginal producers and upset the balance of competition. The issue of pollution abatement is an illustration. What happens when manufacturers are told to "clean up or close up"? If they clean up, they may or may not be able to recoup the costs of pollution control. If not, there is a squeeze on profits. Some producers are marginal, that is, their profit margins are so slim that an increase in costs may force them out of business, eliminating the jobs of their employees, raising unemployment levels, affecting local businesses, and so on. In a study of twelve thousand plants in fourteen industries, the Environmental Protection Agency estimated that two hundred to three hundred plants would have to close and that from 50,000 to 125,000 jobs would be lost because of pollution-control requirements. The EPA also forecast a slowdown in gross national product but believed that all of this was a "modest" price to pay for cleaning up the environment. Whether or not the out-of-business managers and the unemployed workers agree with this contention is a moot point. Finally, some

feel that social concern is an individual, not a corporate, matter. Those who hold to this argument are not against social responsibility per se but feel that it is a matter of individual rather than corporate involvement. The corporation should encourage individuals to pursue socially responsible activities and evaluate and reward them for meritorious performance. The Xerox Corporation, for instance, has a plan that allows an employee a year's leave of absence at full salary for social service. While this argument opens up many possibilities for broadening social involvement, it can lead to gaps in areas where individual efforts may be too weak to solve bigger problems.

From these conflicting views the businessman is expected to come to some decision. It is not an easy one, this current American dilemma. There will be no final universal resolution, but social groups have become more vocal in their claims to the surpluses created by business. Consumer advocates, civil-rights groups, stockholders, community groups, university fund raisers, and a host of others have asked to be included in the activities in business's decision-making process.

Government. After World War I Americans witnessed the decline of the Progressivism of Theodore Roosevelt and Woodrow Wilson and welcomed the "return to normalcy" of Warren Harding. They withdrew from the arena of world politics and turned inward to enjoy a decade of prosperity. Calvin Coolidge stated the tenor of the decade with his oft-quoted "The business of America is business." Congress and the Supreme Court relaxed controls over business, the influence of organized labor declined, sales were predominant over production, and company unions and industrial-welfare schemes abounded. Politically, the decade of the 1920's was a nonactivist period. There was a brief restoration of the philosophy of laissez faire and its belief in the self-regulating nature of economy. Judge Elbert Gary held his famous dinners at which the guests agreed on steel prices, and banks and lending institutions gave free rein to financing whatever speculative impulse, be it land or stocks, the public might have. Blissfully ignoring the Florida land bust in 1926 and a downturn in economic activity in 1927, Mr. and Mrs. America enjoyed their bathtub gin, rumble seats, jazz, and short skirts. The great collapse of 1929 signaled the end of an era. After that, America turned in desperation to the New Deal of Franklin D. Roosevelt in the hope that government could do something, anything, to pull America from its morass.

No other period in American history has seen a political administration begin in such dire times, endure for such a long period, and cope with as many adversities as that of Franklin Delano Roosevelt. Roosevelt, scion of a patrician family, cousin of former President Theodore Roosevelt, and paralyzed from the waist down by polio, brought a charismatic personality to a people in the depths of despair. In his acceptance speech for the Democratic nomination, he had said, "I pledge you, I pledge myself, to a New Deal for the American people." This became the slogan of the policies of the Roosevelt administration, which promised to reshuffle the old cards of society.

Roosevelt saw as his first task the restoration of confidence to a stricken nation. During the "first hundred days" (March 9 to June 16, 1933) Congress in special session passed a multitude of bills enabling emergency legislation and giving Roosevelt tremendous political and economic powers. Roosevelt's keynote phrase, "The only thing we have to fear is fear itself," helped instill confidence and hope in the people. In those first hundred days legislation was passed creating such agencies as the Agricultural Adjustment Administration (AAA), the Civilian Conservation Corps (CCC), the Securities Exchange Commission (SEC), the Tennessee Valley Authority (TVA), the Federal Deposit Insurance Corporation (FDIC), and the Home Owners Loan Corporation (HOLC), and also passed the Federal Relief Act, the Railway Reorganization Act, and the National Industrial Recovery Act (NIRA). The day of alphabet-soup government had come.

While some viewed the New Deal as "creeping socialism" and prophesied the end of capitalism, others saw the reforms as a necessary adjustment of capitalism while the motor was running in order to save free enterprise. Private enterprise endured, but in the process elements of socialism did creep in. The restacking of the social, political, and economic order was to bring government into an activist role. Hands off as a policy was defunct, and the role of government increased in an effort to shift the balance of power as people perceived it from the financiers of Wall Street to the farmer, organized labor, and the "little man." Rexford Tugwell, one of Roosevelt's braintrusters, wrote that the idyllic days when business did what it willed were gone and that the new leadership of industry must recognize unions, democratize industry by encouraging worker participation, and keep in mind the "greatest good for the greatest number."

In subsequent years, regardless of administrations, government continued its role as a partner to be consulted and considered when businessmen made decisions. From the administration of Harry S Truman to that of Gerald R. Ford, more government agencies were created, more legislation passed, and more administrative rulings delivered. Government has also increased its role as a consumer of the products of industry, as in space exploration and national defense. Government has in addition become a competitor of business, such as in public-power projects, the Armed Forces Exchange System, and elsewhere. It has aided business with subsidies and it has bailed firms out of financial difficulties. Whatever one's feelings might be about the role of government vis-à-vis business, one fact remains: the government has become increasingly involved in economic life. Though capitalism has been preserved in that ownership and management remain in the hands of private individuals, control and policy guidelines have become more and more firmly lodged in the dominant political party. The new concept of the corporation has tied it more closely than ever before to the public interest.

CONCLUSIONS

What, then, can be concluded from this journey through two hundred years of American business life? No nation in history has made as much progress, or perhaps faced as many problems, as has the United States in two brief centuries. It took the great civilization of Rome longer to fall than the American nation has been in existance. Yet in this brief span of time a nation was created from a scattering of colonies and became the world's economic and political leader. The businessman has played a crucial, often criticized, role in the nation's advance. From a domestic system of production the country advanced to a cybernetic age of mass production that is unrivaled in its manufacturing prowess. American products, once available in small quantities in local markets, have become abundant and available worldwide. Crude trails have been replaced with transportation and communication systems that link the nation, continents, and the world and probe the solar system.

Americans are the most affluent, the healthiest, and the best-educated in the world. Yet, despite the marvels made possible by the business system, doubts remain about what it has created. The poor are still with us, air and water pollution problems are yet unsolved, the value of the dollar is declining, some products are unsafe and mislabeled, minority groups and women still face problems of discrimination, the tax burden grows greater, and an energy shortage threatens to engulf the nation. While the pessimist may weep and wail and the optimist may cheerfully dismiss the problems, the historian can present another viewpoint: the problems we face are no greater than the problems we have faced and solved. In transportation, communication, energy, marketing, manufacturing, finance, and management, the businessman has a long history of accomplishments. The businessman is a pragmatist, a doer, an innovator, and an organizer who has been able to adapt to a changing world. There is no reason to believe that his role will change, if we read closely the lessons from two hundred years of history.

BIBLIOGRAPHY

Allen, Frederick L. *Only Yesterday.* New York: Harper & Row, 1931.

Baughman, James P., ed. *The History of American Management.* Englewood Cliffs, N.J.: Prentice-Hall, Inc., 1969.

Bruchey, Stuart. *The Roots of American Economic Growth, 1607–1861.* New York: Harper & Row, 1965.

Burlingame, Roger. *Machines That Built America.* New York: The New American Library, 1953.

Clark, Victor. *History of Manufactures in the United States, 1607–1860.* New York: McGraw-Hill Book Co., 1916.

Chamberlain, John. *The Enterprising Americans: A Business History of the United States.* New York: Harper & Row, 1963.

Chandler, Alfred, Jr. *Strategy and Structure.* Cambridge, Mass.: M.I.T. Press, 1966.

Chandler, Alfred D. *Giant Enterprise: Ford, General Motors, and the Automobile Industry.* Harcourt, Brace & World, Inc., 1964.

————. *The Railroads: The Nation's First Big Business.* Harcourt, Brace & World, Inc., 1965.

Cochran, Thomas C. *American Business in the Twentieth Century.* Cambridge, Mass.: Harvard University Press, 1972.

————. *Business in American Life.* McGraw-Hill Book Co., 1972.

————, and William Miller. *The Age of Enterprise.* New York: Harper & Row, 1961.

Dale, Ernest. *The Great Organizers.* New York: McGraw-Hill Book Co., 1960.

Douglas, Elisha P. *The Coming of Age of American Business, 1600–1900.* Chapel Hill: University of North Carolina Press, 1971.

Edwards, George W. *The Evolution of Finance Capitalism.* New York: Augustus M. Kelley Publishers, 1967.

Fite, Gilbert C., and Reese, Jim E. *An Economic History of the United States.* 3d ed. Boston: Houghton-Mifflin, 1973.

Galbraith, John Kenneth. *The New Industrial State.* Boston: Houghton-Mifflin Co., 1967.

Gras, N. S. B., and Henrietta M. Larson. *Casebook in American Business History.* New York: Appleton-Century-Crofts, 1939.

Greene, Theodore P. *America's Heroes: The Changing Models of Success in American Magazines.* New York: Oxford University Press, 1970.

Greenleaf, William (ed.). *American Economic Development Since 1860.* Columbia, South Carolina: University of South Carolina Press, 1968.

Groner, Alex. *The American Heritage History of American Business and Industry.* New York: American Heritage Publishing Co., 1972.

Hayek, Friedrich. *Capitalism and the Historians.* Chicago: University of Chicago Press, 1954.

Hays, Samuel P. *The Response to Industrialism: 1885–1914.* Chicago: University of Chicago Press, 1957.

Heald, Morrell. *The Social Responsibilities of Business: Company and Community, 1900–1960.* Cleveland: Case Western Reserve University Press, 1970.

Heilbroner, Robert L. *The Making of Economic Society.* Englewood Cliffs, N.J.: Prentice-Hall, 1962.

Hidy, Ralph W. and Muriel E. Hidy. *Pioneering in Big Business, 1882–1911.* New York: Harper & Brothers, 1955.

Hofstadter, Richard. *The Age of Reform: From Bryan to F.D.R.* New York: Random House, Inc., 1961.

————. *Social Darwinism in American Thought.* Boston: The Beacon Press, 1960.

Hughes, Jonathan. *The Vital Few.* Boston: Houghton Mifflin Co., 1966.

Jones, Peter D'A., ed. *The Robber Barons Revisited.* Massachusetts: D. C. Heath and Company, 1968.

Kavesh, Robert A. *Businessmen in Fiction.* Hanover, N.H.: Amos Tuck School, 1955.

Kemmerer, Donald L. *Economic History of the United States.* Patterson, N.J.: Littlefield, Adams & Co., 1954.

Kirkland, Edward C. *Industry Comes of Age: Business, Labor, and Public Policy, 1860–1897.* New York: Holt, Rinehart, and Winston, 1961.

Krooss, Herman E. *Documentary History of Banking and Currency in the United States.* New York: McGraw-Hill Book Co., 1969.

Larson, Henrietta. *Guide to Business History.* Cambridge, Mass.: Harvard University Press, 1948.

Leuchtenburg, William E. *The Perils of Prosperity, 1914–32.* Chicago: University of Chicago Press, 1958.

Lord, Walter. *The Good Years: From 1900 to the First World War.* New York: Harper & Brothers, 1960.

McClelland, David. *The Achieving Society.* New York: Van Nostrand-Reinhold Co., 1961.

Mahoney, Tom, and Leonard Sloane. *The Great Merchants.* New York: Harper & Row, 1974.

Mayo, Elton. *The Human Problems of an Industrial Civilization.* New York: Macmillan Co., 1933.

Miller, William, ed. *Men in Business.* New York: Harper & Row, 1952.

North, Douglas C., and Robert P. Thomas, eds. *The Growth of the American Economy to 1860.* Columbia, S.C.: University of South Carolina Press, 1968.

Oliver, John W. *History of American Technology.* New York: Ronald Press Co., 1956.

Perkins, Dexter. *The New Age of Franklin Roosevelt: 1932–1945.* Chicago: University of Chicago Press, 1957.

Porter, Glenn, and Harold C. Livesay. *Merchants and Manufacturers: Studies in the Changing Structure of Nineteenth Century Marketing.* Baltimore: The Johns Hopkins Press, 1971.

Riesman, David, *et al. The Lonely Crowd: A Study of the Changing American Character.* New Haven, Conn.: Yale University Press, 1950.

Robertson, Ross M. *History of the American Economy.* Harcourt Brace Jovanovich, Inc., 1973.

Shapiro, Stanley J., and Alton F. Doody, eds. *Readings in the History of American Marketing: Settlement to Civil War.* Homewood, Ill.: Irwin Publishers, 1968.

Smith, Adam. *An Inquiry into the Nature and Causes of the Wealth of Nations.* 2 vols. London: Printed for W. Strahan and T. Cadell, in the Strand, 1776.

Sobel, Robert. *The Age of Giant Corporations: A Microeconomic History of American Business (1914–1970).* Westport, Conn.: Greenwood Press, 1972.

Stover, John F. *American Railroads.* Chicago: University of Chicago Press, 1961.

Studenski, Paul, and Herman Krooss. *Financial History of the United States.* New York: McGraw-Hill Book Co., 1952.

Taylor, Frederick W. *The Principles of Scientific Management.* New York: Harper & Row, 1911.

Taylor, George Rogers. *The Transportation Revolution (1815–1860).* New York: Harper & Row, 1951.

Weber, Max. *The Protestant Ethic and the Spirit of Capitalism.* New York: Charles Scribner's Sons, 1958.

Whyte, William H., Jr. *The Organization Man.* Garden City, N.Y.: Doubleday & Co., 1956.

Wiebe, Robert H. *Businessmen and Reform: A Study of the Progressive Movement.* Cambridge, Mass.: Harvard University Press, 1962.

Wren, Daniel A. *The Evolution of Management Thought.* New York: The Ronald Press, 1972.

6

THE EMERGING ROLE OF GOVERNMENT IN ECONOMIC AFFAIRS

By Benjamin J. Taylor and W. Nelson Peach

From the beginning of the nation to the present time there has been bitter controversy over the proper role of the federal government in economic affairs. Should real power reside with the federal government, or should it reside in the independent states? In the period immediately following independence the view that there should be a strong central government was perhaps best exemplified in the views and policies of Alexander Hamilton. Fear of a strong central government and insistence that the real power should rest with the states was best expressed by Thomas Jefferson.

Not only has the controversy persisted for two hundred years but the sides have changed hands as new issues and new circumstances have arisen. For example, in the early days the Tories, or conservatives, were in favor of a strong central government. The Whigs, or liberals, favored strong states and a weak central government with limited powers. Today the two sides are reversed. Conservatives generally favor limits on the power of the federal government, while liberals generally favor more power for the central government.

One of the early tests of the power of the central government occurred in the 1790's. In 1791 an excise tax was placed on the manufacture of whisky, an important industry for the people of western Pennsylvania. Money was scarce in that area, and most exchange was through barter. One of the few ways the settlers had of getting money to buy the things they needed was through the sale of whisky to easterners. A pack horse could carry only about four bushels of rye across the mountains at a time. But if the grain was converted to whisky, one could carry the equivalent of twenty-four bushels.

The farmers in western Pennslyvania resented all taxes, but especially the tax on whisky. Generally they ignored it. The few who paid it immediately lost the friendship and respect of their neighbors. The height of the opposition was reached in the summer of 1794, when seven thousand militiamen threatened to burn Pittsburgh. President George Washington, at the strong urging of Hamilton, called out fifteen thousand militiamen to put down the rebellion. It was suppressed, but, more important, it demonstrated that the national government was supreme and could coerce the citizens of a state when it was acting within its proper sphere. Many other examples of the conflict between the power of the federal government and of state governments will be discussed in the following pages. The topics treated do not necessarily appear in chronological order.

EARLY GOVERNMENT INFLUENCE ON THE ECONOMY AND THE RISE OF POLITICAL ECONOMY

After the War of Independence the United States faced economic problems that were similar in many respects to those that confronted the developing countries of Asia, Latin America, and Africa after World War II. The American population was engaged mainly in subsistence agriculture. However, the country had an abundance of resources that could be developed, and this endowment made the new nation different from nation-states that emerged from World War II seeking avenues of growth. At the close of the Revolutionary War, there were some small shopcraft industries engaged in the production of such goods as brick and pottery, shoes, harnesses, furniture, candles, and crude farming instruments, but during the colonial period Britain had discouraged the growth of manufacturing except of those goods not produced in England. The result was that American industries could not compete with English producers during the early years of the Republic.

There was a small, literate elite, but the vast majority of the population was largely uneducated. Those who were well educated, including George Washington, Thomas Jefferson, Alexander Hamilton, Tench Coxe, and Daniel Webster, formed a relatively small group. Most of the people lived in rural areas or small towns and worked on farms. The first census, taken in 1790, showed that about 95 per cent of the population lived in rural areas. The demands of subsistence agriculture left the people time for little else, including education. The blueprint for future development was open to debate and ultimately to evolutionary trial and error.

Even today in those parts of the world where most of the people are engaged in agriculture, output per person is relatively low and so, in turn, is per capita income. The United

States was in that category when it became a new nation. Per capita income was probably less than $100 a year. By 1859 it was $137, and in 1914 it was estimated at about $303. It was not until about 1870 that half of the population depended on industries other than agriculture for employment. As agricultural productivity rose, a greater proportion of the population left agriculture and moved to urban areas where opportunities grew until by 1974 disposable personal income was $4,623 in current dollars.

During the past few decades many former colonies have emerged as new nation-states. One of the immediate, pressing problems that faced those countries was how to devise a tax system adequate to cover the current operating expenses of the new government. Complicating this problem was the strong likelihood that the new government had inherited massive debts. If the emerging country was to have a reasonable chance of survival, arrangements had to be made quickly for paying back debts and for collecting adequate revenue for current operating expenses or seeking substantial subsidies from other countries or both. Those problems faced the newly independent United States two centuries ago. Not only the federal government but also the states had substantial debts, all of which were incurred mainly to finance the War of Independence. The government was in debt to both foreign and domestic lenders. The foreign creditors were mainly in France, Spain, and Holland. Not only had the principal on the loans not been paid when due but interest was in arrears. The foreign debt amounted to about $12 million, the domestic debt amounted to about $40 million, and the states owed about $25 million, a grand total of about $77 million.

The first of six major depressions began in 1783, at the end of the Revolutionary War, when the nation was unsettled both in its politics and in its economics. It was necessary for the nation to shift from a wartime status under the Second Continental Congress to peacetime production. Also, the economy had been geared to the production of goods needed to carry on the war, and conditions prevented a smooth transition from war production to the production of peacetime goods and services. During the colonial period most trade, both export and import, was with England. A resumption of trade was at best difficult at the close of hostilities. In addition, most of the industries that had either raised crops or manufactured goods for trade to England in such categories as tobacco, bread, flour, dried fish, and rice were largely destroyed during the hostilities. The result was a serious imbalance of trade and the necessity to export gold on a large scale to pay for purchases made from foreign countries. Several states issued paper money as a substitute for specie (gold). There was considerable question about the value of a currency generally unbacked by gold, and prices tended to rise in terms of paper. A loss of gold should have resulted in a substantial decline in the price of goods and services, but the paper substitutes, discounted though they were, tended to check that tendency.

The early period was difficult, but it provided a platform on which federal and state governments could begin to define their respective roles in the management of the economy.

Federal supremacy had not yet been established as doctrine and was not to be pronounced until 1819 in the Supreme Court's *McCulloch* v. *Maryland* decision.[1] Even after that time severe limits were placed on the federal government's involvement in economic affairs. Hamilton had a significant influence on the future role of the federal government, and thus it is necessary to review a few of his ideas on political economy.

Hamilton, who had been appointed secretary of the treasury shortly after George Washington became president, proposed that the national government assume the task of paying off the foreign debt, the domestic debt of the federal government, and the debts that had been incurred by the states. In order to accomplish this as soon as possible, Hamilton proposed the establishment of a sinking fund into which a specific portion of the annual revenue of the federal government would be set aside for the retirement of the public debt. In this manner a precedent was set that was to remain one of the basic principles of public finance in the United States for the next century and a half. That principle was to keep the public credit unimpaired and repay the debt as soon as possible after an emergency had passed. This principle was to become more sophisticated after World War II, but the fact that it was accepted at all in the early years seems in retrospect spectacular.

There was only minor opposition to the principle of paying the foreign and domestic debt of the federal government, but the proposal that the federal government assume the debts of the states aroused violent controversy. Bonds were selling at substantial discounts, and there was considerable speculation in the debt. It was claimed that to pay off the debt at par value was to favor the speculator at the expense of the patriot. It was also claimed that some states were favored at the expense of others. Generally, northern states had incurred more debt than southern states.

Hamilton's views prevailed. The federal government took over the burden of paying off the federal foreign debt, the domestic federal debt, and most of the debts of the states. By 1835 the process was complete, and the federal debt had been entirely paid off. In 1837 the federal government found itself with no debt and a substantial surplus. Arguments over how to dispose of the surplus were as heated as the earlier arguments over what to do about the debt. The surplus was finally distributed to the states in the form of loans that were never collected.

Under the revenue system proposed by Hamilton (to which the systems set up by the developing countries during recent decades bear a resemblance), chief reliance was on import tariffs, which were raised four times between 1789 and 1794. In addition, excises were imposed on some domestic products, especially whisky, which led to the Whisky Rebellion in 1794.

The fundamental questions facing the Founding Fathers were: What kind of economic system should be promoted? Should the new country remain substantially agricultural or should efforts be made to stimulate manufacturing? If manufacturing was to be promoted, what specific steps should be taken to do so? What resources did the United States have, and what were some of the principal limitations? Hamilton, the Tory, and Tench Coxe, the Whig, were two of the leaders in the movement for the promotion of manufacturing. As secretary of the treasury, Hamilton had been directed by the Congress to prepare a report on manufactures. The United States at the time, as is true of most new countries, suffered from a lack of statistical data. Partly to relieve the situation, Hamilton wrote to customs officials throughout the land, asking each of them to send in detailed reports on the status of manufacturing in their respective areas and on problems faced by local firms. He asked them to seek information from other informed persons in their areas. Largely on the basis of these reports, he compiled his famous *Report on Manufactures.*[2] It has been termed the "first American Treatise on political economy."[3]

Those who advocated manufacturing in late-eighteenth-century America faced a formidable array of opponents. As indicated earlier, most of the people were engaged in subsistence agriculture. Among a large segment of the population there was acceptance of the physiocractic doctrine that agriculture was the only major industry that produced a net surplus. Manufacturing was well established in the older economies of western Europe, and Britain had discouraged the development of it in the Colonies. Moreover, there was a shortage of capital and skilled labor in the newly independent country. The prevailing sentiment was heavily in favor of continuing as an agricultural economy. But Hamilton, Coxe and others insisted that, in order to have a balanced economy and for national security, vigorous efforts should be made to stimulate manufacturing.

Out of deference to the prevailing agricultural sentiment, Hamilton acknowledged that the cultivation of the earth has intrinsically a strong claim to pre-eminence over every other kind of industry. But agriculture did not have an exclusive claim. Furthermore, he pointed out, agriculture was not necessarily more productive or more beneficial than other industries. As a matter of fact, the real interests of agriculture would be advanced rather than injured by the encouragement of production in other industries. Industry would promote a greater division of labor, an increased use of machinery, a fuller utilization of the potential activity of the labor of women and children, an increase in immigration, and a bigger market for domestically produced goods, especially agricultural products. Also, he said, manufacturing adds to national wealth because it provides a more adequate domestic market for goods produced within the nation, thereby reducing dependence on other countries and thereby rendering it more nearly self-sufficient.

Hamilton proposed that in general women and children were more useful in manufacturing establishments than in other employment. He was enthusiastic about putting young children to work in cotton factories. It was pointed out that the establishment of manufacturing enterprises might result in so much immigration from the Old World that the demand for factory hands might be met with an ample surplus left for agriculture. As we will see later, a more affluent and industrial society of the twentieth century arose from the early humble beginnings, but that growth was not without

displacement of labor and of other resources in the process.

There was an obvious inadequacy of capital to finance American manufacturing in the 1790's. Hamilton was of the opinion that the scarcity could be offset by the establishment of banks, by resorting to the use of foreign capital, and by using the debt as capital. He was criticized for his notion of using the national debt as money, and yet that was the main reason for establishing the national banking system during the Civil War, and monetizing the debt was the principal device used to finance World Wars I and II.

Hamilton argued that infant industries that showed promise of developing into mature industries in which the United States had a comparative advantage should be encouraged with protective duties. He conceded that this policy would temporarily raise the price of the commodities but maintained that in the long run it would mean reduced prices. He held that this was invariably the case and maintained that the government should grant patronage to domestic manufacturing only during its initial stages of development.

The lesson was brought home to the country again at the close of the War of 1812. The second major depression in the country's short history came at the end of the war. Business activity had been high as a result of exports to England, France, and other nations at war. The war was financed by borrowing and issuing treasury notes. When the charter of the First Bank of America elapsed in 1811, many state banks were chartered. They issued their own currency without gold backing. Wartime inflation ended around 1815, when British merchants flooded the market with cheap goods as they had at the close of the Revolutionary War. Relatively small and unprotected firms were vulnerable. By this time the United States economy had been subjected to the demands of war production for 15 years, and the economic system was geared to inflation and war. Suddenly conditions changed. A rapid decline in the price level resulted in a large number of business failures. Costs of production were relatively higher for American domestic firms than for foreign competitors. Readjustment to a peacetime economy was costly in terms of unemployed resources. In a new attempt to bring order to the financial community, in 1816 the Second Bank of America was chartered for a period of twenty years. There was considerable resistance to the charter, particularly from state banks and persons attempting to develop western parts of the country.

Hamilton's position was that countries that have both extensive agricultural activities and well-developed manufacturing industries are more prosperous than those that depend principally on agriculture. The reason given was that the two kinds of industries provide each other with a dependable home market and lessen the reliance upon less dependable foreign markets. It was stressed also that the two can afford a greater variety of goods to foreign customers and thereby increase exports, and that not only the wealth but also the independence and security of a nation are materially connected with the prosperity of manufactures. As we shall see later, his approach was one of greater national controls over economic development or a planned system of mercantilism in order to strengthen the economic base.

The view was advanced that American manufacturers could afford to pay higher wages than those prevailing in Europe because raw materials were cheaper at home, and the expense of bringing European manufactured goods to this country represented 15 to 30 per cent of their value. Hamilton's *Report On Manufactures* was an attempt to refute some of the assumptions of laissez faire as they applied to this country in 1790. There has always been a role for the federal government in the operation of the economy, but government intervention has always met resistance, and often the necessity of it is even denied. He claimed that the interest of manufacturers and agriculturalists were interlocked and mutually beneficial.

The United States Supreme Court was an even greater influence than opposition from the states in slowing the pace of the federal government's movement into the economic affairs of the country. Its emphasis on the definition of interstate commerce and private-property rights left the various states largely in control of most industrial activity until well into the twentieth century. Not until 1937 was interstate commerce defined as encompassing the manufacturing process. Only distribution fell within the meaning of "interstate commerce." Furthermore, the Supreme Court deemed it necessary to hold the states out of the regulatory process in many categories, such as child-labor laws and wage-and-hour controls. The Court's emphasis on private-property rights was decidedly more laissez faire than Hamilton's articulation of them in his *Report on Manufactures.* The process of accumulating capital was a well-protected activity before the Court. Generally, the legislative branch was more successful in providing subsidies to the various industries than they were in regulating competition during the early years of the Republic. The concept of property underwent a change in definition from a holding of physical objects for the owners' private use to a concept of intangible property arising solely out of rules of law controlling transactions. The one is private control, while the other deals with the rights of individuals as workers, consumers, and citizens along with the rights of the public over scarce resources. The web of rules for all parties is defined and redefined by the courts, and the result is known as "property."

The third major depression in the United States came in 1837. This time the depression was not the result of adjustment from war to peace. It occurred during a period of rapid expansion of the economy. Andrew Jackson vetoed a bill to renew the charter of the Second Bank of the United States in 1832, four years before it was due for renewal. He immediately proceeded to remove federal government deposits from it and transfer them to state banks. The result was that the bank was forced to contract its loans, which had the effect of decreasing the money supply. Government policies concerning deposits of federal funds obtained from the sale of public lands caused some sections of the country to lose funds. In short, a substantial part of the cause of the Panic of 1837 was the lack of stability among financial institutions. That was not the sole cause of the depression, however. Overexpansion of a number of ventures also took its toll. Canal building to accommodate steamboats and other

boats to haul freight and passengers, mostly in the northern part of the United States, proved to be generally unprofitable. Some railroads had been built by that time, which reduced the incentive to undertake additional canal building. A slowdown in such activity also had a dampening effect on such industries as homebuilding, iron- and steelmaking for boat construction and other products needed by a prosperous, growing, and, most important, changing or moving population. Nevertheless, development of the West proceeded rapidly during the period of relatively free banking (the "Wildcat Banking Era") than it might have with a more orderly and uniform approach to banking through a national banking system.

The Depression of 1873

A severe and prolonged depression was touched off by a financial crisis in 1873. The heavy concentration of deposits of many banks were held in seven large New York banks. The National Banking Act required national banks to keep a percentage of reserves against deposits, and part of those reserves could be kept in other banks. Of these deposits 70 to 80 per cent were held in seven New York banks. Smaller banks usually made a demand on those deposits in the fall to finance agricultural activities. When local activity subsided, they returned surplus funds to the large banks. The New York banks found themselves with huge deficits in the 25 per cent reserve requirement, which consisted of legal tender notes and gold held against deposits. The result was that they had to call in loans to repair their deficits. At the same time several brokerage houses failed and loans in their category of transactions were called in too. The result was a run on the banks, but even so only a few national banks failed.

Overexpansion of internal developments, particularly among railroads, caused the depression in 1873. Too many railroads were in competition for the traffic east of the Mississippi. Bridges over the Mississippi to permit westward expansion of rail and an increase in the flow of goods and services to the West had not been completed. It would be several years before this barrier could be removed and stimulation of new investment at higher rates occur. Railroads had been built at a faster rate than the economy was prepared to accommodate. Massive grants of land to railroads provided them with a rich subsidy that hastened the decline of alternative means of transportation and was no small factor in the tendency toward overexpansion in rail.

Major and Minor Cycles

The record of major business cycles reveals that financial difficulties usually accompanied them. It was the monetary system that caused problems after the Revolutionary War, the War of 1812, the Civil War, and, during peacetime, the cycles that began in 1837, 1873, 1882, 1890, and 1907. The money supply was too large before 1873 and not large enough from that time until 1914. After World War II general inflation was again a substantial feature of the major and minor cycles. A brief review of the development of the banking system in the United States is necessary at this point.

For a century and a half following independence the United States experimented with various measures designed to provide the nation with a workable banking and currency system. The efforts were disappointing in many respects. As mentioned, in 1791, Alexander Hamilton proposed the establishment of the First Bank of the United States. The bank, modeled closely after the Bank of England, was designed to serve as the fiscal agent of the Treasury Department and as a central bank. Hamilton believed that the bank should be mainly private. Therefore, it was provided that four-fifths of the capital was to be subscribed by private individuals or corporations. Three-fourths of the private subscription was to be in government bonds because there was not enough gold and silver in the country at the time to provide the bank a capital of ten million dollars. The remaining one-fifth of the capital was subscribed by the government in cash. The bank then gave the government a loan in an equal amount. The bank was managed by a group of directors chosen in such a way that the private interest was predominant. The bank was chartered for twenty years, beginning in 1791. Because of strong opposition to the bank on the grounds that it had or might have accumulated too much power, renewal of its charter was denied, and it went out of existence in 1811, just a year before the beginning of the War of 1812.

The Second Bank of the United States was chartered in 1816 for a period of twenty years. It was established mainly because the currency situation had deteriorated to such an extent that there really was no national currency. The second bank got off to a bad start. There was dishonesty on the part of the managers and their friends. In addition, the managers made serious mistakes. President Andrew Jackson, who was vigorously opposed to the bank, took steps to assure that the charter of the bank was not renewed. When the bank went out of existence in 1836, it had a capital of thirty-five million dollars, four-fifths of which had been provided by private individuals and one-fifth subscribed by the federal government.

The national banking system was established during the Civil War. It was hoped that the new system would provide a sounder currency than the greenbacks that had been issued by the federal government or the state bank notes that had been issued by individual private banks. It was also hoped that the system would create a demand for government bonds because the Union sorely needed that kind of support to pay for the cost of the war. But the national banking system did not establish a central banking system. That had to wait a half century more. The currency system established under the national banking system was an improvement over the notes issued by state banks, but the currency system was inelastic; that is, it did not expand and contract to meet the needs of agriculture, industry, and commerce.

Throughout the nineteenth century the United States toyed with the use of both gold and silver as a basis for its currency (bimetallism). A makeshift Gold Standard Act was finally passed in 1900. In 1907 there was a severe panic. Banking operations ceased across the nation, hundreds of banks failed, gold payments were suspended, and clearinghouse certificates and script were used as mediums of exchange. Following this crisis the National Monetary Commission was formed. It consisted of nine senators and nine representatives and continued its work until 1912. When the commission was dissolved, it had published twenty-three volumes of investigations of most of the banking systems of the world, particularly those of Western Europe.

The Federal Reserve Act, which set up the central banking machinery for the first time in the United States, was passed in 1913, and the reserve banks began operating in 1914. The important characteristic of elasticity was to be assured by the following means: When productive activity (agriculture, commercial, or industrial) rose or expanded, the commercial banks, which were members of the Federal Reserve System, could rediscount the notes of their customers at the Federal Reserve Bank. At first speculative loans were not permitted by the act, but in 1916 the act was modified to allow the bank to make direct loans for fifteen days to member banks. In 1932 the act was further amended, and by 1935 it simply provided that reserve banks could grant advances subject only to the rules and regulations prescribed by the Board of Governors. So far as elasticity of currency was concerned, it had become a moot question in any event, for currency was no longer the important element. Bank credit had taken over most of the operations of commercial banks.

THE UNITED STATES DEVELOPS INTO AN INDUSTRIAL POWER

During the later half of the nineteenth century the two most important minerals in the world were coal and iron. In 1900 coal accounted for 90 per cent of the inanimate energy used in the United States, and iron and steel accounted for about 90 per cent of all metals used in the nation's industries. So important are these minerals that only those countries that had coal and iron in abundant quantities (permitting the mining of millions and even hundreds of millions of tons annually) could aspire to become industrialized.

At the end of the American Civil War, England dominated the world in large part because she produced most of the coal and iron in the world. The United States and Germany (the two next-largest producers) lagged far behind. Together they produced less than one-half the output of England. Militarily, politically, and economically England ran the world because of her production year after year of vast amounts of coal and iron.

The third most important mineral was petroleum. Destined in the twentieth century to become the principal source of inanimate energy, petroleum was discovered in 1859 in Pennsylvania, and the United States dominated world oil production for most of the following century.[4] But the pattern of production of these and other minerals that prevailed at the end of the Civil War was not destined to last forever.

Within the next thirty-five years there were violent shifts in the pattern of production in petroleum, coal and iron. With those shifts there were corresponding shifts in military, political, and economic power. Production in England continued to grow but not nearly as fast as it did in America or Germany. At the end of the period the United States had emerged as the world's largest producer of petroleum, coal, and iron and the things made mainly from these minerals. As a consequence in 1950 the United States had come to dominate the world militarily and economically as completely as England had dominated the world a century earlier.

The period from the Civil War to the end of the nineteenth century was also the heyday of the robber barons and the amassing of the great American fortunes. The Du Pont family became famous for gunpowder and later for a wide range of chemicals. J. P. Morgan emerged as the leading financier. John D. Rockefeller was a leader in the petroleum industry. There were great American railroad builders and financiers, including such giants as Jay Gould, James Daniel Fisk, Drew, and Cornelius Vanderbilt. Toward the end of the period Andrew Mellon made a fortune in coal and aluminum. There were many others.

Antitrust and Industrial Combinations

The general public grew increasingly uneasy about the tactics used by large corporations to concentrate capital under the control of a few individuals. Pooling arrangements, price-fixing agreements, centralized selling, and even intimidation drove competitors out of the market. The first big merger wave took place during the period 1897 to 1905, when about twenty-eight hundred firms consolidated into trusts or holding companies. Standard Oil Company was one of the first great giant American industrial corporations to develop through a trust arrangement. The desire to eliminate competition was one of the motivating forces behind Standard's practices. As the tactics used by Standard Oil and other large combinations became known to the public, pressures were exerted on Congress to take action against them. The Grangers and Greenbackers demanded that measures be taken against railroads and other corporations. In 1884 a political antimonopoly party entered the political arena. Both major political parties promised to take action during the campaign of 1888, when pressures for reform had become too great to be ignored any longer.

The first measures to control large business organizations were taken in the states. Antitrust clauses were often placed in incorporation laws passed before 1890. Competition among the states for plant location led them either to ignore the antitrust laws or to modify them. The authority given to corporations to hold stock in other corporations led to state chartering of holding companies, especially in Delaware and New Jersey. The states proved unwilling to deal with the malpractices of big business, and it was up to the federal government to act if anything was to be done about the large corporations.

The Sherman Antitrust Act of 1890 was the response made by Congress to public demands. The law was designed to declare illegal all combinations in restraint of trade. However, many terms and phrases of the act were not defined, and no regulatory commission was created to enforce it. All these matters were left to the courts with the result that the law was generally ineffective.

The sugar-trust case came before the Supreme Court in 1895 in *United States* v. *E. C. Knight* Company. The American Sugar Refining Company, incorporated in New Jersey, bought four firms in the Philadelphia area which gave it control of more than 98 per cent of all sugar refining in the country. It was held that the manufacturing of sugar as well as the acquisition of sugar refineries in a state did not fall within the meaning of interstate commerce. It appeared that nothing would come of the 1890 antimonopoly law.

During the late 1920's more than forty-six hundred mergers took place. In the 1950's, 1960's, and early 1970's there was a substantial movement toward mergers, but the pattern was different from that of the earlier periods in that mergers took place among companies producing totally unrelated products. More than nineteen thousand mergers of this kind took place during the years 1965 to 1972. The resulting organization is known as a conglomerate. In many cases the status of the multinational corporation, that is, whether it falls under the provisions of the antitrust laws, is even less certain than the status of either horizontal or vertical mergers. The horizontal merger is the elimination of competing firms producing the same or a similar product. The vertical merger is the acquisition of the entire production process from, for example, raw-resources processing to finished product.

Even in the spectacular cases before the courts the results were not significant. The Northern Securities Company case was a victory for the government when the Court ruled that the Northern Securities Company was to be dissolved because it was a holding company whose purpose was to restrain trade. But the control of railroad stock in question remained in the same hands after dissolution. The decision increased President Theodore Roosevelt's popularity and gave the public a feeling that monopolies would be controlled. The Standard Oil of New Jersey case of 1911 actually accomplished very little even though the corporation was forbidden to control its thirty-seven subsidiary companies, which meant complete dissolution into independent competing companies. Standard Oil of New Jersey gave its stockholders pro rata shares in the newly dissolved companies, which meant that the Rockefeller interests remained in control. The case did elicit from the public a new demand for more effective legislation. More precise language detailing specific violations in order to halt judicial legislation was evidently required.

The Clayton Act was passed in 1914 to correct deficiencies in the Sherman Act. Price discrimination was prohibited where such action among producers lessened competition or tended to create a monopoly. Tying contracts were banned because they prevented the use or sale of products of competing corporations. Many other prohibitions were contained in the law. All in all, the act emphasized the maintenance of fair competition. Monopoly remained illegal, but Congress did not want to slow down the growth of large corporate enterprises. The mood of the public had shifted somewhat to one that viewed the large firm as a distinct advantage, no longer an evil. This view was even more obvious in the Federal Trade Commission Act, also passed in 1914. A five-member commission was created to administer the will of Congress, which was to prevent business firms from using unfair methods of competition in interstate commerce. Cease-and-desist orders were issued by the commission and were enforceable in the federal courts.

A new attempt to deal with mergers came in the form of the Celler-Kefauver Antimerger Act of 1950. It was designed to prohibit horizontal mergers by acquisitions or purchase of assets and has been upheld in the courts.[5] Thus, since 1950, the United States has had an effective antimerger law. The conglomerate movement, which produced the large, multimarket, multiproduct, and multinational corporation is receiving increasing attention. Information is being collected about such matters as interlocking directorships among large corporations and banks, the effect concentration has on prices, income distribution, and world competition.[6]

The Great Depression

The era of mild government regulation of large corporate enterprise to maintain fair competition changed to one designed to restrict competition. Confused by the economic crises of the 1930's, Americans were willing to engage in many forms of experimentation to induce greater output and employment. The severe depression that hit the United States in 1929 caused the unemployment rate to soar to the highest level in the country's history (although statistical data are lacking, it has been estimated that the unemployment rate rose to as high as 25 per cent in 1932).

Protective tariffs were enacted to deal with the depression. The Hawley-Smoot Tariff of 1930, passed to protect agriculture, is one example of measures taken to restrict competition. Other nations, also suffering economic depression, retaliated by enacting protective legislation of their own. In addition to protective tariffs substantial subsidies were made available to some industries, particularly agriculture. The result was that the average level of prices remained too high to move the economy rapidly back to high employment levels.

The National Industrial Recovery Act (NIRA), passed in 1933, was designed to encourage self-regulation of industry or to eliminate unfair competitive practices. The industry codes were to put a floor under wages and prices. The law was interpreted by some as suspending the antitrust laws. Many employers, however, refused to enter into price-fixing arrangements or to comply with the labor standards contained in the codes even though they had signed them. Dissension and strikes erupted as a result. In 1935 the Supreme Court declared the NIRA unconstitutional because of the delegation of lawmaking power to the executive and a federal invasion of intrastate commerce.[7] The Court still did not interpret interstate commerce as including the manufacturing process.

Collective bargaining was encouraged through the National Labor Relations Act of 1935 (the Wagner Act). It created the National Labor Relations Board to administer the five provisions relating to unfair employer labor practices and to those dealing with representation. Enforcement was through cease-and-desist orders enforceable by federal courts. The economic effect of the law is uncertain; however, many studies indicate that in this period unions were able to raise wages above those prevailing in nonunion firms. If this is true, relatively higher wages deterred a movement to higher employment levels.

The Miller-Tydings Act (1937) and the McGuire Act (1952) permitted states to establish fair-trade laws. Such laws prevent retail firms from selling merchandise at prices lower than the manufacturers' suggested retail prices. Retailers are thus not allowed to engage in price competition, and as a result consumers often pay higher prices.

The Robinson-Patman Act (1936) limits certain forms of price discrimination. The result is that relatively inefficient small firms are protected from competition by larger firms.

The early drive to use antitrust legislation to maintain fair competition was altered somewhat during the Great Depression and subsequent years, when exemptions were permitted through legislation. A renewal of antitrust activity and a raising of penalties when violations are found may restore competition somewhat. Certain activities have also been reclassified as felonies instead of misdemeanors. At the same time legislation such as the Miller-Tydings Act should be repealed before the antitrust laws will be able to deal with certain price-fixing activities that distort the resource-allocation process. The long period of high unemployment drew to an end only after the United States entered World War II. At the close of the war, fear of the return of widespread unemployment led to passage of the Employment Act of 1946.

ECONOMIC GOALS
OF THE AMERICAN ECONOMY

The Employment Act created the Council of Economic Advisers (CEA) and identified five broad economic objectives, stressing "maximum production, employment, and purchasing power." The CEA was directed to develop and recommend to the president national economic policies to "avoid economic fluctuations or to diminish the effects thereof." The five goals set forth were (1) sustained and balanced economic growth, (2) economic stability, (3) economic justice, (4) economic freedom, and (5) a reasonable record of balance of payments. It is of interest to note that, although the goals were implied, they were not articulated until the years of the Eisenhower Administration (1952 to 1960). These broad objectives need some elaboration. The first four are discussed below. The fifth goal, involving international trade, will be treated in a separate section.

Economic Growth

This goal refers to increases in output per capita over time. Basically, an increase in output per capita at a full employment level involves an increase in the quality and quantity of resources. An increase in the quality and quantity of resources includes the implementation of technological innovations, the discovery of raw materials, and the production of physical and human capital. The precise definition of full employment has varied in accordance with shifts in political control of the executive branch of government. In the early 1960's maximum employment was viewed as having been achieved when 96 per cent of the labor force was employed. A rapid expansion of output and employment beginning around 1964 had lowered the unemployment rate to 3.5 per cent by 1969. The unemployment rate has fallen to an annual average of 4 per cent or below in only nine years since 1946. The best performance was in the period 1966 to 1969. It is interesting to note that the high-employment objective has been met most consistently in wartime. Except for those periods the United States economy has generally operated at higher rates of unemployment. Many people have opposed the use of the peacetime federal budget for a range of domestic programs necessary to attain high employment levels. They believe that such programs are nothing more than welfare. Investment in human or physical capital is often not considered legitimate by the constituents of many politicians. As a result, most presidents since World War II have used the military budget as the primary means of stabilization.

The economic-growth record may be difficult to improve. Some estimates of the rate of output to the end of the century indicate a slowing of the rate experienced over the past few decades. The rate of growth of output has averaged 2.8 per cent since World War II, but growth in output per man hour has optimistically been projected at 3.5 per cent a year and as low as 2 per cent by the year 2000.[8] It should be emphasized that the rate of growth has been much higher for a few selected years, such as the average of 3.2 per cent for the five-year period preceding 1962. Several factors are identified to support the lower projection of output per man hour: the declining birth rate, which signals a decline in new workers entering the labor force; a decline in the labor-force-participation rate of males; and a decline in the work year. To offset those declines in part, there may be a rise in the participation rate of women during the 1970's and 1980's, but even there some expect a decline to set in about 1990.

A slowdown in output will undoubtedly raise additional social problems. Transfers of income to alleviate the pressing problems of relatively deprived groups will be far more difficult at lower rates of growth than at higher ones because the real income of some will have to fall to permit the transfer. The matter of federal spending, as well as state and local expenditures, will be far more suspect than it is when the economy is experiencing higher growth rates. The choices available now are to try to reduce the trend toward more leisure, to encourage an upward change in the birth rate, which will raise the rate of growth of the labor force, or to invest more heavily in physical outlays to offset the need for labor-force participation. An alternative may be to provide greater opportunity to groups that have been the object of discrimination. Barring that, bargaining over longer paid vacations and holidays may become more difficult. In fact, welfare programs of all kinds are under review with the aim of putting welfare recipients to work. Many believe that large numbers of people not now working can and should work. Additional government involvement in research and development may also prove beneficial but may not provide the level of economic growth necessary to hold social and political dissent within manageable bounds. For example, the development of alternative energy resources to natural gas and oil may well require substantially more federal investment. Private industry may be unable or unwilling to make the necessary investment, considering the risk of potential energy resources in the context of expected rates of return on investment. Failure to develop alternative sources may mean that the public must settle for considerably lower rates of growth and real income than those to which it is accustomed. Policies that do not maintain adequate rates of growth may result in more family members seeking work in order to remain at the same level of living they have experienced. Obviously taxation would be less acceptable at lower rates of growth than at higher rates.

Economic Stability

The goal of economic stability has several aspects. Price stability generally refers to some acceptable rate of inflation, about 3 to 4 per cent a year. The consumer price index increased an average of about 1.5 per cent a year during the period 1952 to 1967. After 1967 prices rose substantially with the result that more than usual political interference in the economy took place. For example, in 1974 prices increased 12.2 per cent. The desire to make aggregate expenditures during war in excess of output brought about a general inflationary problem. At the same time the consuming public was conditioned to much smaller annual average price increases and came to accept the smaller rate as normal. Not only was the rate of increase in annual prices stimulated by government outlays to conduct war and to fund domestic programs but from 1965 to 1973 the public expected prices to be greater in future periods. If the public expects prices to be greater in the next week or month than in the current one, it makes greater demands for the full range of goods it views important. Administered prices, whether by government or private interests, compound the problem.

The basic goal of fiscal and monetary policy is to bring the rate of price increase down from recent experience but at the same time not to let unemployment rise beyond acceptable limits. In the process of restricting the money supply or expenditures on domestic programs or, better, lowering their rates of growth, resources are reallocated that may impose substantial costs in the form of unemployment on low-productivity firms and even high-productivity firms and on individuals. Therefore, some economists are beginning to define full employment to mean 4 or more per cent unemployment. Indeed, some argue that the size of the economy makes this an acceptable frictional unemployment level. This means simply that there are always some people in the process of moving from one job to another and searching for a new job after either voluntarily or involuntarily leaving an old one. If the search goes on for some time, generally because the applicant has entered the job market for the first time, the individual is considered unemployed. A free peacetime society must have some frictional unemployment to permit workers to seek improvement in their situation. Indeed, search for better positions improves the over-all functioning of the economy, provided workers become more productive in their new positions than they were in previous ones. The same is true with all resources used in the production process.

But unemployment in excess of the defined frictional rate, is not unhealthy for stability and growth. Indeed, under certain conditions rates that rise above the defined frictional rate free marginal resources, bring about movement to more efficient uses and hold down the rate of price increases. Such cannot, however, continue for long periods of time, or political and institutional stability may be threatened. It may be, and is, argued by labor groups such as the AFL-CIO, that the burden of stability should not be placed inordinately upon American workers. In the post–World War II period government deficit expenditures have assumed a substantial share of the uncertainties and instabilities generally shouldered by the extended family in earlier periods. Families of earlier decades had a greater responsibility for the welfare of members than do those of the last generation, unless they have voluntarily assumed it. The highly mobile labor force of today has changed the family structure and its economic responsibilities from those of an agricultural setting. The transition has not been completely made, however; many families in industrial settings continue to cling to the economic responsibilities of a past era.

The situation may be summarized by quoting the inscription found under the head of the Roman god Janus: "Forward I look and backward." High rates of unemployment and underutilization lead to instability in many forms; certainly, if those rates persist, they combine to retard economic growth and progress. The danger of a fiscal policy undertaken to keep people at work in the private sector is that it may encourage continued production of goods and services that would not otherwise survive the market test.

Economic Justice

By economic justice is meant a fair distribution of income among the various sectors of the economy. Economic justice is often interpreted as meaning an income based on the productivity of the resource or the contribution it makes to output. Put differently, it is the money value of the contribution it makes to the value of the product it produces. Redistribution of income based on need is also included in the sphere of economic justice. It is here that we consider transfers of income from those who earn it to those who do not.

A continuing problem with income redistribution is the definition of need and, once a definition is found, the monitoring of the redistribution system to minimize abuse. Indeed, if the definition of need is set too high, it becomes economically rational to refrain from work and receive welfare. At what point does an individual decide that it is economically not in his best interest to work when the difference between what he can earn and what he can receive without working is small? When this occurs to any degree, marginal industries and certain categories of employment are in danger of extinction. The inability to obtain labor in certain categories generates an incentive to seek acceptable substitutes within some range of expenditure one is willing to make. Take, for example, domestic employment. If the wage of domestic workers rises above the value of the services rendered, it will no longer be prudent for large numbers of employers to demand the service. Middle- and upper-middle-income groups may move to substitutes such as appliances that decrease the time and effort of housework. Working couples may redefine home responsibilities in ways that amount to a substitute for what otherwise might be a demand for a market service. An increase in the household chores performed by men is a response to an improved job market for women. The quest for a solution to the concept of distributive justice continues in the American society and becomes more acute as the rate of growth of real family income either slows or declines.

Economic Freedom

Government policies have a substantial effect on individuals in their pursuit of economic goals. Those policies should be so designed that they do not improve the position of one member of society at the expense of another. In addition, individuals should be free to enter or leave markets at will.

The pursuit of economic freedom has not been without difficulty. The United States government shifts emphasis from time to time from the goal of stable employment to one of stable prices, with the result that less stability can be found in the search for economic freedom and economic justice. A trade-off between the annual rate of price change and unemployment rates does not work to the benefit of the other goals. In fact, they are in conflict. This trade-off will be discussed in greater detail later.

During the decade of the sixties there was a concerted attempt to achieve all five goals. The pressures of the Vietnam War placed severe limits on domestic progress; moreover, many of the goals to achieve economic justice and freedom were all but abandoned in practice. For example, Title 7 of the Civil Rights Act of 1964 was designed in part to deal with racial and sex discrimination in employment. It did not prove effective, however, because of the lack of enforcement machinery. The Equal Employment Opportunity Commission (EEOC) created to administer the act sought cooperation from the National Labor Relations Board (NLRB), which administers the Taft-Hartley Act, to enforce its regulations, but was not successful. The EEOC requested that the NLRB use its authorization to stop discriminatory employment practices. It could then go to the federal courts to seek enforcement. During the middle and late 1960's, the longest sustained period of peacetime economic growth in the history of the United States, minorities, including women who are not, numerically speaking, in the minority, made substantial gains in employment opportunities. Those gains were largely in positions with relatively lower wages and security. As long as rapid growth and high employment levels were maintained, relatively disadvantaged groups made progress in the economic system, though seniority systems posed some limits on their successes in the labor market. Once the economy slowed in growth or declined, the requirement that the last hired would be the first fired brought a deterioration in previous gains. Even federal government agencies did not comply with the spirit of the law, not to mention the letter of it.

The Equal Employment Opportunity Act of 1972 was an attempt to correct some of the deficiencies of the Civil Rights Act. In 1965 the EEOC had set forth guidelines to deal with discriminatory employment practices. Those guidelines became potentially far more meaningful with the passage of the 1972 law. They also became highly controversial, because some groups perceive fulfillment of the guidelines to mean a decline in their own employment security. A few of the guidelines will be discussed to emphasize the difficulties involved in attempts to achieve more economic freedom for some and the implications of the policies for other groups.

Title 7 of the Civil Rights Act requires the removal of any artificial, arbitrary, and unnecessary barriers to employment. The United States Supreme Court in the *Griggs* v. *Duke Power Company* decision held that to require an applicant to pass an unvalidated ability test or to require a high-school education as a condition of employment or prerequisite for promotion was in violation of Title 7 because such requirements discriminate against blacks and are not job-related.[9] A validated test that is job-related is legal. However, requirements imposed purely as initial screening devices to eliminate a large number of job applicants are illegal. The aim is to afford blacks and others an equal opportunity for a job. This is critical in an economy characterized by persistently excessive unemployment rates. A brief comparison of the unemployment-rate experiences of selected industrial

countries will illustrate the point. During the years 1973 to 1975 only Canada compared with the United States in high rates of unemployment, as may be seen in the table below.

If growth is inadequate to absorb those willing to join the labor force, as it has been in the past, at least discriminatory testing devices will not be available to disqualify potential employees. Employment discrimination, as it existed in the past, might become difficult to perpetuate in the future, except that there are institutional safeguards that are more or less capable of insulating older white persons from some dangers of unemployment. But some of those safeguards may also be in jeopardy.

Seniority systems came under attack after the Griggs case. It has been argued that such systems perpetuate discrimination that took place years ago in initial hiring. A better understanding requires a brief discussion of Affirmative Action Program requirements.

The 1972 amendments to the Civil Rights Act of 1964 added to its coverage all employers and labor unions with fifteen or more full-time employees. Also, employees of state and local governments and educational institutions were brought under the law. Affirmative Action Programs are required to fulfill the intent of the law.

The primary requirement is a written stipulation of good-faith efforts to achieve equal employment opportunity. As a minimum such efforts must include (1) an analysis of deficiencies of the utilization of minorities, (2) a timetable for correcting such deficiencies, together with their expected goals, and (3) a coherent and reasonable plan for achieving those goals. A company must actively recruit employees from minority groups. Internally, the company must analyze all job classifications in regard to minority opportunity and determine the amount of training the employer can reasonably be capable of providing to make all job classifications available to minorities. Affirmative Action Programs required of employers and unions alike have often come close to upsetting traditional seniority systems and in some instances have done so. In periods of high unemployment with few job alternatives facing both black and white workers, charges of reverse discrimination grow if blacks are made better off at the expense of another group. Some white workers with more seniority have been discharged and black workers with

UNEMPLOYMENT RATES FOR NINE INDUSTRIAL COUNTRIES, 1973–FIRST QUARTER, 1975

	U.S.	Canada	Australia	Japan	France	Germany	Great Britain	Italy	Sweden
1973	4.9	5.6	1.9	1.3	2.7	1.0	3.0	3.8	2.5
1974	5.6	5.4	2.2	1.4	3.1	2.1	2.0	3.1	2.0
1975, 1st qtr.	8.3	7.0	---	1.8	4.6	3.0	3.5	3.1	1.6

Source: U.S. Department of Labor, *Monthly Labor Review*, Vol. 98, No. 6 (June, 1975), p. 10.

less time on the job have been retained. Resentment breaks out on both sides. When this occurs, the goals of economic freedom and justice are violated. The single best way to resolve the dilemma is to seek policies that will provide more rapid sustained economic growth.

Institutions of higher education have found themselves in much the same dilemma. At a time when the rate of growth of their budgets has declined, affirmative-action requirements persist. Either the enforcement of the plans will be vacated or most new positions and replacements will be designated for women and minorities, if they can be found. Whatever the long-run outcome, with relatively few women and minorities qualified for some positions, their short-run market price has risen above that of white males with similar or in some cases superior qualifications. With limited budgets total employment must suffer. Again, gains by one group can be and often are made at the expense of another. The alternative is to abandon attempts to provide equal employment opportunity. Truly equal employment opportunity for all is a long run proposition which has already been too long in arriving.

Another Equal Employment Opportunity guideline is that a prospective female employee may not be disqualified because she is pregnant. She may not be refused employment on such a ground even though the pregnancy is illegitimate, she is in the later stages of pregnancy, she is immediately eligible for sickness and accident benefits, or she has no intention of working permanently on the job. The consequence of this guideline may be that industry will have to finance many more childbirths, in which case labor costs will rise with the result that full-employment definitions may have to be revised upward. Both direct and indirect wage costs constitute the total wage rate. If the wage rate rises, and other things such as productivity remain the same or do not rise as much, price must rise or unemployment will rise or both.

Over all, in terms of the economic goals mentioned, the role of government in pursuing these objectives becomes more and more complex. As government attempts to achieve goals for any given group to attain economic freedom for all, there are inevitable failures. Institutional arrangements must change and are changing, but the question is, How rapidly can economic institutions change and still provide economic freedom, justice, and stability? What are some of the problems that must be solved? We now turn to a discussion of some of the problems that have arisen.

Inequality and Insecurity

A substantial segment of the American population has not enjoyed equal treatment and opportunity in the economy. Indeed, the American Negro, of all minorities except the American Indian, has been so disadvantaged that unusual restorative measures were required in the form of legislation that should not have been necessary under the Bill of Rights of the Constitution. The four economic goals previously discussed have not been achieved by American blacks.

The growth of cotton production in the early nineteenth century was a major factor leading to the importation of black slaves. In the southern states slave codes were developed that held that slaves were things whose persons and labor belonged to their masters. They could be freely bought and sold and were without civil rights. Not even the self-serving court system was willing to disturb this arrangement. In fact, it was protected by the courts. The result has been that even today blacks, though legally free, continue at a disadvantage in most aspects of economic life.

Operation of the over-all economy at a high level of employment is critical to any improvement in the economic welfare of blacks, but this approach by itself is not enough. A brief review of the recent record emphasizes the point. In 1959 the median family income of blacks was $3,047, or 52 per cent that of whites. In 1970 it was 61 per cent of the median family income of whites but fell back to 59 per cent in 1972. In absolute-dollar figures blacks have declined relative to whites. In 1959 black-family median income was $2,846 below that of the white counterpart. In 1972 it was $4,685 below.[10]

The percentage changes in the black-white income differential have been due primarily to the changed condition of black women. The income of black women was only 40 per cent that of white women in 1950, but in 1970 it rose to 79 per cent. The improvement of black male income for the same period was only from 61 to 66 per cent.

The burden of unemployment falls heavily upon blacks and reflects the damage of discrimination of the past, even if it could be assumed that none exists at present. A rule of thumb is that the black unemployment rate since World War II is approximately twice that for whites. During the period 1948 to 1973 the unemployment rate averaged 8.6 per cent for blacks and 4.3 per cent for whites. In January, 1975, the rate for black males was 14.0 per cent and 7.9 per cent for white males. It may well be that the requirements of Affirmative Action Programs have altered the rule of thumb, but the difference in the two rates is still pronounced. For younger persons the American economic system must be considered one of the cruelest in the world. Opportunities for employment are severely restricted. In January, 1975, among sixteen-to-nineteen-year-olds the unemployment rate among black males was 42.7 per cent and 18.2 per cent among white males. Other industrial societies provide substantially more opportunities for teen-agers.

Approximately twenty-four million Americans (11 per cent of the population) live in poverty. Poverty has been defined in several ways. As of 1974 a nonfarm family of four with a male head of household and an income of $5,038 was at the poverty threshold. The size of the family alters this figure up or down. Poverty is unevenly distributed geographically. For example, according to the 1970 census it was nearly twice as high in the South as in any other region. The regional percentage breakdown was 20.3 in the South, 10.1 in the Northeast, 10.8 in the North-Central, and 11.7 in the West.

Poverty is also unequal along other than geographic lines.

In 1970 the poverty rate for all persons in families with a male head of household was 9 per cent but 33 per cent in families with a female head of household. Poverty is far more prevalent among blacks and persons of Spanish heritage than among whites. In this regard the poverty rate among whites was 9 per cent, 23 per cent among Spanish persons, and 34 per cent among blacks.

The poor are not as active in labor-market activities as those above the poverty threshold. While 82 per cent of all family heads were in the labor force in 1970, either employed or seeking work, only 48 per cent of low-income heads of household were so classified. The percentage of poor black women and women of Spanish heritage participating in the labor force is higher than that of white women. A lack of education and the occupations in which the working poor are concentrated operate to yield low wages.

The poverty condition of the American population has gradually improved. One-third of the country lived in poverty in the 1930's. During the period 1947 to 1957, poverty was reduced from 28 per cent to 19 per cent of the population. It was further reduced in the decade 1960 to 1970 from forty million to twenty-five million. There was one notable exception: The poverty rate of those aged sixty-five and over rose from 14 per cent in 1959 to 15 per cent in 1972. Even so, the reader will have observed that the social-security system is under vigorous attack from a growing number of sources.

It is difficult to continue gains in employment and earnings for minority groups unless high employment levels are sustained. When unemployment rates are high, improvement in the economic status of women, blacks and other races, and the young must be at the expense of some other group. Consequently, economic growth is imperative if the objectives of the Employment Act of 1946 as amended in 1972 and the Equal Pay Act are to be met. There was a decline in real per capita personal income between 1973 and 1974. Per capita real taxes increased at the same time, so that real per capita disposable income declined. Growth and stability are essential in the pursuit of economic justice and freedom. A principal device used to achieve stability has been wage and price controls. These controls have been used in both war- and peacetime.

WAGE AND PRICE CONTROLS IN WAR AND PEACE

Wartime Controls

Wages and prices are subject to indirect as well as direct control by government. At times attempts have been made to raise wages and prices. Some such attempts have been made through the Fair Labor Standards Act of 1938 as amended on several occasions and with the enactment of the National Industrial Recovery Act in 1933. In those laws the government attempted to put a floor under the wages of all workers, as well as under the minimum price that various industries could place on their products. During peacetime efforts at control have usually been made for the purpose of placing a floor under wages and prices and not a ceiling. Peacetime efforts were typically limited to voluntary constraint by parties tied to productivity gains. Moral suasion and "jawboning" were employed to obtain adherence to administrative desires. Equalitarian motives are partly at the base of such attempts, but the fear that inflation will seriously impair economic growth has substantial influence on the desire to hold the rate of price increases within some acceptable limit.

Wage and price ceilings were instituted during World War I. The beginning of these controls was in October, 1916, when the Council of National Defense was organized. The council was directed to study war problems and to establish such agencies as might be necessary to prepare the nation in the event of war. After a series of difficulties with agencies established by the Council and after the United States entered the war, President Woodrow Wilson reorganized the War Industries Board (WIB) in 1918. He made the board directly responsible to him and free from control by the Council of National Defense. As reorganized, the War Industries Board was a creature of the executive branch, not authorized by legislation. The experience of World War I set a precedent for strong executive involvement in the affairs of the economy, which had been relatively free from direct interference in earlier periods.

A price-fixing committee within the WIB attempted to stabilize prices through negotiated agreements with producers of some basic commodities. The agreements were usually for three months, subject to renewal or revision at the end of the period. Prices set forth in the agreements were maximum prices for government contracts. The WIB paid little attention to prices charged to private consumers.

The first consumer controls were placed on food. A food-control program was established by President Wilson without congressional authority. It was later followed by legislation. In 1917, Congress passed the Lever Act (The Food and Fuel Control Act), which provided broad regulatory powers. The Food Administration grew out of the Lever Act. It attempted to prevent waste and to reduce the consumption of relatively scarce goods. It had the power to license producers, manufacturers, distributors, and retailers of food products. Failure to obey orders could lead to a loss of license and to the right to remain in business.

Other regulatory agencies were set up to assist the war effort. The list was considerable but included the Sugar Equalization Board, the United States Fuel Administration, and the War Labor Board. It has been estimated that by 1918 between 20 and 25 per cent of the gross national product was devoted to the conduct of the war. Such a system of federal control was new to the nation. Cooperation was generally obtained during the war, but the controls were unpopular and were lifted immediately after the war, with the expected result of price inflation.

The World War II Experience. When World War II began in Europe in 1939, the United States wholesale commodity price index was lower than in any year since 1934. Substantial excess capacity in industry and ten million unemployed workers provided plenty of room for noninflationary expansion of production. Price increases were moderate during 1939 and 1940, but they increased substantially in 1941. Farm-product prices increased most among the major kinds of commodities, and the rise was least in metals and metal products. Ironically, it was government policy that prompted the rise in farm prices. It was the policy of government to raise agricultural prices to or above parity defined in terms of 1910-to-1914 relative prices. Also, stockpiling to meet anticipated European food demands caused the administration to hold substantial agricultural supplies from the market.

As the economy moved more and more into war production, prices and wages continued to rise rapidly. The greatest price advances occurred before the United States actually entered the war, as had been the case just before World War I. In both wars the rise of wholesale prices was eventually checked by controls directed at the stabilization of costs and profits. The price rise began and was greatest at the wholesale level.

During World War I industrial wage rates lagged behind wholesale prices and rose only slightly more rapidly than prices generally. During World War II wages rose more rapidly than both. There had been a substantial change in institutions between the two periods, plus the fact that the labor market was much tighter during the latter war, both of which accounted for the difference.

President Roosevelt created the Office of Price Administration in August, 1941. It did not have authority to control prices, however, until Congress passed the Emergency Price Control Act early in 1942. Farm prices were exempt from controls until they reached 110 per cent of parity, and there were no wage-control provisions. General price regulations were issued, which froze most nonfarm prices at the March, 1942, level.

In October, 1942, the Economic Stabilization Act was passed. It brought farm commodities under control along with nonfarm prices and wages. The Office of Economic Stabilization controlled prices, and the National War Labor Board regulated wages. Roosevelt issued his "hold the line" order in April, 1942, which continued until August, 1945. During that time consumer prices rose 4.2 per cent, wholesale prices less than 2 per cent, and wages by about 6 per cent. When the war ended, there was substantial pressure to abolish controls. In August, 1945, by executive order President Harry S Truman abolished government control over wage rates in deference to collective bargaining, including conciliation and voluntary arbitration. He vetoed an extension of the price-control law in June, 1946. As a result wholesale prices rose 10 per cent in twenty-five days. A new law was passed quickly and signed on July 25 to deal with inflation. However, by the end of 1946 most efforts to regulate prices had been abandoned.

The Korean War. The inflationary impact of the Korean War was immediate from the time it broke out in June, 1950, but the inflation was generally short-lived. The expectation that shortages would develop drove consumers to increase their demand for goods and services. Producers raised the level of inventories in anticipation of shortages and relatively higher future prices. Once controlling legislation was passed, it was administered by the Wage and Stabilization Board. General regulations were developed, but unions and managements could request permission for specific exceptions. Continued modification of the regulations resulted in successive deviations from them or in higher and higher wage and price levels. The mere existence of the Wage Stabilization Board tended to push wages to the top limits. Again, the top limits were continuously raised.

Wartime controls over wages and prices have never been popular in the United States. The success of attempts at control depends very largely on the timing of the effort, as well as on the psychological involvement in the war. In addition, the level of general employment at the time the nation moves into war is also important in determining the success or failure of controls. The experience with controls during the Korean War was a great deal different from that of both world wars, partly because of the general prosperity in 1950 and partly because the parties involved had learned from past experience to anticipate regulatory-agency responses.

During wartime the government attempts to stabilize the economy but has never been completely successful because of the various interests that must be balanced. The origins of recent regulations of wages and prices are found in the Employment Act of 1946. Voluntary compliance was emphasized in the 1950's and 1960's.

Guideposts

During the post–World War II period and before 1962 the Council of Economic Advisers (CEA) urged unions and management to keep wages and prices within the limits of productivity changes. Even in mild recession periods of the 1950's, however, prices continued to move upward. This observation prompted the CEA to search for a new mechanism to control the inflationary process. The general guide for noninflationary wage behavior was that those rates (including fringe benefits) in each industry should not exceed the trend rate of over-all productivity change. The over-all-trend rate of the five years up to 1962 was 3.2 per cent. Any industry with a higher productivity experience was to hold wages at 3.2 per cent and lower price by the excess. If the experiences were 3.2 per cent, a wage increase of that amount would be consistent with a zero price increase. Certain exceptions were made if wage increases in excess of productivity gains were necessary to attract labor. Declining industries were also considered exceptions; for those industries a wage increase in excess of productivity was approved.

Essentially the guideposts were developed to prevent cost-push inflation, and they were to deal with the new trend of price inflation during periods of high unemployment. They were to prove ineffective later, when inflation was caused by growing general demand for goods and services.

The guideposts broke down during 1966 and 1967 primarily because of vast increases in aggregate demand associated with the Vietnam War. Enforcement of the guideposts depended on moral suasion and jawboning from the executive branch of government. By 1967 this effort had become monumental because literally thousands of independent wage-price decisions were taking place that could not be monitored by an administration heavily involved in war. No legislation was available to monitor the major wage and price decisions.

A great deal of the argument about the effectiveness of the guideposts centers on union power. Just how much economic power do unions have, or, put differently, to what extent can unions raise wages over the dictates of the market place? Unless it can be demonstrated that there has been an increase in union power, it cannot be said that they cause cost-push inflation.[11] Over the years a number of scholarly studies have been undertaken to grapple with the issue of union power. Empirical studies centering on wage-rate comparisons of firms within a single industry and interindustry studies have also been published. The comparison of several industries with varying degrees of unionization have not conclusively supported the theory that the economic power of the unions is significant. During relatively short periods of time unionized firms may show an advantage over nonunion firms within the same industry, but this record does not seem to hold for relatively longer periods.[12] Or at least, conclusions differ on that point.[13] One study concluded that the average percentage difference between union and nonunion wages was probably about 10 per cent over long periods. Still another concluded that there was no clear relationship between the strength of unions and postwar wage changes. Others reached a series of conclusions ranging from considerable union advantage to very little, if any.

Several other facts should be considered when looking at the issue of union power. First, the over-all composition of industry has changed over time with shifts from declining industries to those demonstrating greater growth with respect to labor's share of income generated in the form of wages. Even within industries where unionized firms pay higher wages than nonunion firms, it may merely be because of greater efficiency of operation and thus higher productivity rather than because of the existence of a union. Unions may also be a factor in more efficient organization of production within a firm as opposed to nonunion firms. The reverse may also be the case; that is, a firm may be better organized and in turn efficient enough to keep unions out. If so, this represents some union power, even with respect to nonunion firms. But it would be a positive economic force if the firm were more efficient than it would be in the absence of the threat of unionization.

The data over all do not support the thesis that unions have excessive economic power and thus force wages up at the expense of price stability, economic growth, and full employment. Yet in 1976 there was growing acceptance of the unproved thesis that unions have a great deal to do with high rates of inflation and unemployment. Basically, substantial acceptance of the existence of union power may preclude a rigorous search for other problems that may be more troublesome. A very important problem is the growing role of government political involvement in the economy. Politicians may transfer expenditures from more productive sectors to less productive ones with the result that the prime incentive for employment and output growth occurs in the less productive pursuits. Employment in government and the service industries is considered to be substantially less productive than is employment in manufacturing. As shifts occur in the rate of government support for the various sectors in the economy, unions attempt to hold the line on the relative positions of certain groups of workers. Whether or not they are able to do so may depend far more upon the political influence they have than on any economic power different from what the market place would dictate in their absence. For example, General Motors Corporation could almost surely defeat the United Auto Workers (UAW) in an open conflict. However, it does not make sense to assume that General Motors could possibly defeat the UAW against the wishes of the government. As a result, any perceived union power may be in fact merely the marginal support received from government as opposed to any real economic force in and of itself.

As the economy moved to higher levels of aggregate demand for goods and services in 1966 and 1967, whatever effectiveness the guideposts may have had earlier was no longer evident. Unions were in all-out competition to maintain their share of the national income. Prices rose, and the various consuming groups tried to protect their previous real-income positions. As they attempted to anticipate the annual rate of price change and to hold or revise their position, the annual rate of price change moved upward quickly. The response was a political one that made the allocation problem even worse.

New Economic Policy

In August, 1971, the Nixon administration imposed a ninety-day freeze on wages and prices. The annual rate of price increase had risen to over 7 per cent in early summer, and the wholesale price index indicated an even higher rate for future months. The freeze had resulted in a slight decline in the wholesale price index by October, 1971. However, an economy that allocates resources on the basis of thousands of independent price decisions was headed for eventual trouble in the first massive peacetime effort to manage the economy. In fact, the freeze and subsequent control phases hid the major bottlenecks of the economy by proliferating bottlenecks throughout the allocative system. The short duration of the freeze gave the appearance of a successful experience to many observers, but time was not to be kind to the highly controversial policy.

On November 13, 1971, phase 2 had begun. The Price Commission was established to control prices, and the Pay Board performed the same function for wages. Wage increases were to be held at an over-all 5.5 per cent annual increase, with the major burden of enforcement placed on the large, pattern-setting employers and unions. The goal for over-all price increases was set at 2.5 per cent. Regula-lations were developed to monitor the various kinds of business by size. It was recognized that the large, powerful firms would require closer attention than the smaller ones in more competitive industries.

The rationale for holding the rate of annual price increases to 2.5 per cent was as follows: The trend of productivity increase was 3 per cent a year. If over-all wages were permitted to rise by 5.5 per cent, then a 2.5 per cent increase in price would be consistent with the excess of wages over the gain in productivity.

The phase 2 wage- and price-control procedures were not equitable from the beginning. If the question whether the government should have tried to regulate in this manner in the first place is ignored, the question of equitable administration of the procedures cannot be ignored. Exceptions to the guidelines led to gamesmanship on the part of powerful companies and unions. Above-normal profits developed that gave the general public the impression that inequity abounded in the implementation of the guidelines. Further, the money market was not regulated at all, and only later was health added to the list of regulated industries. The position of the consumer continued to deteriorate.

In the course of "gaming" with the administration, "shortages" developed. A series of unfortunate events also occurred. For example, bad weather led to crop failures, with the result that food prices rose dramatically, driving up the consumer price index substantially. The public and organized labor were concerned about the decline in real income in a large portion of the population. Furthermore, the income policy was highly inconsistent with the stated employment objective of the administration. As real income declined, the required level of aggregate demand to maintain a high level of employment could not be sustained. Indeed, the Nixon administration attempted to promote business expansion through investment tax credits in addition to the exceptions from the guidelines of the Price Commission, both of which were transfers of income from consumers to the business sector. The New Economic Policy was doomed. However, it did not die. As late as the summer of 1975 the Ford administration was engaged in combating inflation rather than recession, which was marked by a rising unemployment rate that reached 9.2 per cent in May, 1975. The Federal Reserve Board's tight regulation of credit expansion continued to hold down consumer expenditures and, in turn, employment in critical sectors, such as construction.

Administrative inflation has not received much attention since the Kennedy and Johnson administrations of the 1960's. When there is market power or the ability to set price, decision makers do so in the context of demand and cost considerations, but also with an attitude of expected continued inflation. Large suppliers set prices in the context of anticipated demand and cost and anticipated inflation. Users accept the price and, in turn, behave in the same manner. The result is found in a trade-off between inflation and unemployment.

THE TRADE-OFF BETWEEN INFLATION AND UNEMPLOYMENT

Until the mid-1950's inflation had seldom occurred in the United States except during and immediately after wars. The prospect of peacetime inflation was ignored because unemployment was generally the major peacetime problem. By the close of the 1950's attention was devoted to the relationship between inflation and unemployment. The economy had demonstrated inflationary pressures during a time of slack demand for consumer goods and slow growth rates, while unemployment rates were relatively high. In 1958 a study of the British economy presented evidence that the rate of increase in money wages and the rate of unemployment were inversely related. This means that a push for lower unemployment rates is associated with higher rates of price increase. Higher unemployment rates are associated with lower rates of price increase.[14] Similar studies of the American economy have suggested that the same trade-off exists between the two goals of relative price stability and high levels of employment. The relationship, which has come to be called the Phillips curve, relates various rates of inflation to hypothetical rates of unemployment.

What are some possible explanations for the relationship? One possibility often mentioned is that labor unions push up wages even during periods when unemployment is high. Supply bottlenecks in product markets command the attention of some, and the issue of union economic power is dismissed. Market imperfections exist, but in precisely what magnitude and in what locations by industry are under examination. Indeed, Congress has undertaken the task of attempting to obtain more and better information concerning the structure and performance of industry in order to produce legislation that will preserve or restore workable competition. As Congress considers the problem, it is heavily influenced by the international sector. It seeks a policy that might permit the huge American economy to move to full employment and at the same time maintain a reasonable balance of trade.

The Phillips curve presents a range of choices to policy makers. If a set of relationships is stable over time, the implication is that full employment is that rate which in combination with some expected rate of inflation will best coincide with the political preferences of society. This means that an objective of 4 per cent unemployment will not necessarily constitute the full-employment goal of society. The rate of inflation that coincides with the unemployment rate is a powerful force that influences the general public. An inflationary rate of 10 per cent probably will not be politically acceptable if this rate is required to keep the unemployment rate at 4 per cent or below. The cost to society in the form of inflation may be considered too dear in return for the low unemployment benefits they expect to derive from it. A basic criticism of the Phillips curve as an instrument of policy is that, if anticipated inflation is higher than the expectations built into the curve on the basis of past experience, workers will demand higher wages at any rate of unemployment. Thus only if expectations change slowly will the relationships of unemployment to inflation be useful for stabilization policy.

Criticisms of the trade-off relationship have prompted many economists to seek a reduction of unemployment through other tools besides expansionary monetary or fiscal policy. These include repeal of minimum-wage laws, elimination of Fair-Trade laws, and prohibition of monopolistic practices of labor and business. Even so, the problem of economic goals remains one of trade-offs. A little less of one goal, for example, lower unemployment, requires a little more of the other, higher prices and wages.

The Cost of Unemployment. Inflation imposes its cost on society in the form of a redistribution of income. Those hardest hit are the low-income groups and workers on fixed incomes. If deep depression is selected as the best policy to halt or slow down the rate of inflation, the cost of unemployment rises to a very high level. High rates of unemployment certainly bring forgone output and income but also substantial underemployment. Underemployment is a situation in which people work in jobs well below their capacity or fewer hours a week than they desire. It has been estimated that each 1 per cent of unemployment means 35 billion dollars in forgone output. On this basis the 9.2 per cent unemployment rate reached in 1975 sums to 322 billion dollars of output lost on an annual basis. Underemployment adds to the amount. The cost of unemployment, therefore, has an effect on every citizen, not only on those incurring the direct cost of unemployment. Fewer goods and services are available for all. Recognition of this cost reduces the importance of the size of peacetime deficit spending by government. Indeed, it seems apparent that the deficits are too low to reduce the actual costs imposed on the population. The country cannot afford to waste labor and material resources and cannot afford to use them inefficiently, but it cannot afford idleness or unemployment. The decade of the thirties cost 200 billion dollars in lost or forgone output and income. High rates of unemployment in the much larger economy of the present certainly cannot be afforded and, if sustained over time, are not likely to be accepted. The end result is more, not less, political regulation of the economy. And all of this must be placed in the context of growing influence from abroad. The international sector has become increasingly onerous in the pursuit of domestic economic goals. Because of this, some space is devoted to a discussion of recent international economic developments.

THE ROLE OF THE UNITED STATES IN INTERNATIONAL TRADE AND FINANCE

Until around the mid-eighteenth century, mercantilism dominated trade relations between nations, largely because of war but also because of the view that the resources of the world were fixed. Leaders of nation-states wanted to expand their wealth and strength. The prevailing opinion during the period 1500 to 1750 was that any expansion would have to be at the expense of other nations because of the static view of world resources. Gains could be achieved through foreign trade, but only if a favorable balance of trade prevailed. A favorable balance of trade is defined as an excess of exports over imports; the excess would be paid for with gold and silver. In 1630 it was recognized that a continued inflow of gold and silver would have the effect of raising domestic prices and a reversal of the favorable trade process. An important goal of the early mercantilists was to build a strong nation that would be militarily powerful. The strong economic base that was required to achieve the objective included expanded agricultural output, diversified manufacturing, and secured sources of raw materials. Success in developing a nation with a strong base militarily, politically, and economically under mercantilism required the protection of domestic industry and the regulation of trade.

There was hardly any unregulated international trade. Monopolies were licensed by the monarchies of many nations during the colonial period of exploration, the sixteenth and seventeenth centuries. The burdens imposed on consumers ultimately led to revolutions, beginning with the American Revolution.

The Wealth of Nations, published by Adam Smith in 1776, emphasized individual freedom in economic matters and not regulation of their interests, especially in international trade. Free trade was one method of increasing a nation's wealth. Because of vested interests through special privileges granted by the state, free trade without substantial interference had to evolve over the decades. In fact, the desire of nations to regulate international trade continues to receive the serious attention of government bodies. In the early period of United States history virtually all federal revenues came from international trade through tariffs and duties.

The doctrine of comparative advantage was developed to show why nations would be better off to permit trade. It is the comparative advantage that a nation has over another and not absolute advantage that should induce them to trade. Specialization of production in products that one nation produces most cheaply permitting another nation to produce other goods through exchange makes both nations better off. This occurs even though one nation might be able to produce both products more efficiently than the other. Specialization, therefore, permits a nation to concentrate on goods it can produce most cheaply and trade for other goods. In so doing, it raises its productive capacity above what it would be if it attempted to produce all goods for domestic consumption. Tariffs and quotas on imports make a nation's consumers worse off than they would be without such devices that raise the price to those who want the output of other countries.

World Economy

Leadership of the new world economy was centered in London. The gold standard set the convertibility of the currencies for purposes of trade. The gold standard, however, was abandoned after World War I. Widespread inflation forced abandonment of the gold standard, although there was a standing desire to return to the gold standard. In 1919 the United States restored the old gold parity. Other nations, including Britain, let their currencies float. Chronic unemployment developed in Britain. Gradually other nations returned to gold, with the result that by the end of 1928 the international currency system based on gold had been largely re-established. The establishment of the Federal Reserve System in 1914 gave the United States a central-banking structure that stabilized its money market and put it in a position to rival London as the center of international transactions.

After World War I various nations took independent action in monetary affairs. They substituted their national goals for reliance on the automatic operation of the international monetary system to determine currency convertibility. Once more government intervention increased in economic life because of dissatisfaction with some of the consequences of free trade. Government became concerned with such problems as long work days, child labor, worker insecurity, and living conditions in the cities.

Around 1870 tariffs began rising throughout the world, and World War I did nothing to alter the trend. Wartime duties continued in Britain even after the close of hostilities. The other leading international financial center, the United States, abandoned the policy of low duties contained in the Underwood Tariff of 1913 and in 1922 substituted a high-tariff policy. Economic nationalism raised barriers to trade and also to immigration.

The relative industrial strength of the world shifted after World War I, Britain declining and the United States increasing in importance. Greater international reliance was placed on the United States, and as a result access to the American market was vital for economic stability of the rest of the world. A downturn in industrial production in 1929 led to worldwide depression. As income fell domestically, the demand for imports fell also. Long-term lending to foreign nations stopped, and the United States began importing capital or repatriating of past loans. The drain on other countries was substantial, and dependence of the free world on the American economy was clear.

In 1930 the United States enacted an even higher tariff on imports with the passage of the Smoot-Hawley Tariff. Other nations retaliated, and external markets for American goods began to decline. In 1933 the United States devalued the dollar in hopes that the dollar prices of foreign goods would rise. However, foreign suppliers of American imports cut prices, with the result that relative prices between the United States and other nations remained unchanged.

Tariff reduction was made possible by the Reciprocal Trade Agreements Act of 1934. The act emphasized expansion of American trade through reductions in foreign duties and permitted the president to reduce duties by as much as 50 per cent in exchange for parallel concessions by other countries. Passage of the law marked an end to the trend toward higher tariffs and the insulation of nations from each other in world markets.

The destruction caused by World War II made most of the world dependent on the dollar. Countries dependent on American output needed loans and grants to recover. Military expenditures in Europe and Japan eased somewhat the demand for dollars. The average annual deficit of the United States balance of payments of approximately 1.5 billion dollars during the period 1950 to 1964 was due primarily to military expenditures and long-term foreign investment. These deficit expenditures were largely offset by trade surpluses, which continued until 1971.

In the meantime, the United States became more and more dependent upon foreign sources for copper, oil, iron ore, and other raw materials. Japan and Western Europe also became better able to compete effectively by rebuilding their industrial machines and because of the unresponsiveness of American manufacturers to a change in the tastes of the American consumer, such as from larger to smaller automobiles.

The dollar became overvalued relative to several currencies, but certainly to the West German mark and the Japanese yen. The products of these nations became cheaper than American-produced goods, and the result was a substantial deterioration in the United States balance of payments. A brief review of the United Nations Monetary and Financial Conference held at Bretton Woods, New Hampshire, in 1944 is necessary to evaluate the trade situation that developed thereafter.

Trade restrictions that had continued through World War II caused concern particularly in the United States and the United Kingdom. The two nations and then others established the International Monetary Fund (IMF), the details of which were worked out at the Bretton Woods conference. At the same time the International Bank for Reconstruction and Development was established. The IMF set forth agreed-upon goals for the nations to pursue in international monetary affairs.

The three main objectives of the IMF were (1) to seek complete convertibility of currencies in foreign-exchange markets, (2) to restore exchange-rate stability, and (3) to seek national independence in fiscal and monetary policy consistent with exchange-rate stability.

Drawing rights were established for member countries of up to 25 per cent of its quota. This meant that a country could purchase with its own currency the currency of another country with which it was running a deficit. Sums in excess of the 25 per cent were permitted if the country justified its position.

It was the purpose of the IMF to eliminate the wide swings in price increases and decreases associated with flexible exchange rates and to develop more stability of exchange rates. If serious disequilibrium in a member's balance of payments developed, it must consult with the IMF if the country intended to change its par in excess of 10 per cent. However, this requirement has never been functional.

The real intent of the Bretton Woods conference was to set up an adjustable peg among the currencies of members. That is, the intent was to permit flexibility of exchange rates between established limits.

The Eurodollar Market

The cold war brought with it a fear on the part of East European banks of holding deposits of dollars in New York banks. They deposited their dollars in other European banks, and those banks in turn made loans with the deposits as reserves. A Federal Reserve limit on interest rates paid on time deposits had the result of encouraging dollar transfers from New York to Europe when European interest rates were higher than the rates that could be paid in New York. In 1960, Eurodollar deposits totaled about one billion dollars. There is a controversy over the extent that Eurodollar loans create some multiple of the initial deposits in new credit.

The relationship between the growth of the Eurodollar system and deficits in the United States balance of payments is subject to debate. What the system does is make monetary policy more difficult because of the flows of short-term capital. For example, an outflow of deposits to Eurobanks when the monetary authorities are expanding the money supply makes it more difficult to lower the interest rate. An inflow during a period of tight-money policy makes it more difficult to raise the interest rate.

The Bretton Woods agreement did not establish gold as the sole form for holding reserves. As a result many countries held part of their reserves in foreign currencies that were convertible to gold. Because of the relative economic strength of the United States at the close of World War II, the dollar was widely held as a reserve currency. In fact, it was better than gold in many ways. Dollar reserves earned interest, while gold was costly to store.

After 1957 large deficits in the United States balance of payments increased the size of foreign claims on the dollar, as well as the proportion of those claims converted into gold. In 1960 foreign claims on the dollar were about equal to United States gold reserves. By 1965 short-term foreign claims on the dollar exceeded gold reserves by about one-third. The world, in effect, was on a dollar, not a gold, standard. Suspension of the dollar convertibility into gold terminated the Bretton Woods system in August, 1971.

The Smithsonian Agreement of 1971 set up a framework to control the floating of currencies and to remove wide-spread restrictions on capital movements. The dollar was to be devalued, and a band of permissible fluctuations of currencies against the dollar was set at 4½ per cent or 2¼ per cent above or below the par value of currencies in terms of gold and special drawing rights from IMF. The Smithsonian parities lasted for a little more than a year. In February, 1973, they were abandoned, and a system of managed floating exchange rates have prevailed since that date.

The IMF appointed a committee of finance ministers of twenty nations to recommend a complete reform of the international monetary system. From July, 1972, until 1974 the Committee of Twenty believed that it would not be possible to overhaul the system and made interim proposals. Essentially it was agreed that the exchange-rate system should be based on special drawing rights, with the role of gold and reserve currencies diminished.

The oil-price crisis imposed by the Organization of Petroleum Exporting Countries (OPEC) put the international monetary system in jeopardy. The fourfold increase in the price of oil in 1973 upset international-trade patterns, balance of payments, production, and monetary conditions. The OPEC nations generated a substantial volume of foreign exchange which they could opt to spend in the form of imports from oil-consuming nations. Basically, the oil-producing nations could not absorb such large increases in purchases from other nations. Instead, the surpluses were invested in the Eurodollar market and other money markets that partly financed the deficits of the oil-consuming nations. In addition, investments were made in industrial stocks and bonds, which raised another difficult problem, that of external ownership of the domestic industries of many countries.

The solution may well move the world full circle back to mercantilism, but this time with greater international cooperation on the control of trade and payments. The alternative will be trade warfare and the imposition of a mercantilistic policy upon each nation. The latter course is no more likely to succeed now than during the pre-World War II period. The linking of nations in closer economic relationships will likely occur, and when that happens, the economic welfare of the entire world should substantially improve through free trade.

NOTES

1. *McCulloch* v. *Maryland*, 4 Wheat. 316 (1819).
2. Harold C. Syrett (ed.), *The Papers of Alexander Hamilton*.
3. Broadus Mitchell and Louise P. Mitchell, *American Economic History*, p. 263.
4. A local preacher near Titusville, Pennsylvania, commented that the whole scheme to take oil out of the ground was immoral because the oil was needed down there to feed the fires of hell and to remove it was to protect the wicked from the punishment they so justly deserved.
5. F. M. Scherer, *Industrial Market Structure and Economic Performance*, pp. 475–78.
6. *Ibid.*, p. 283.
7. *Schecter Poultry Corp.* v. *United States*, 295 U.S. 495, 1935.
8. Joint Economic Committee, *Long-Term Economic Growth*, p. 260.
9. 401 U.S. 424 (1971).
10. Paul A. Brinker and Joseph J. Klos, *Poverty, Unemployment, and Social Security*, Chaps. 3, 23, 25.
11. Milton Friedman, "What Price Guideposts?" in George P. Shultz and Robert Z. Aliber (eds.), *Guidelines, Informal Controls, and the Market Place*.

12. Allen M. Carter and F. Ray Marshall, *Labor Economics,* pp. 299–325.

13. H. Gregg Lewis, *Unionism and Relative Wages in the United States*, Chaps. 3, 4. Also see *Postwar Movements of Prices and Wages in Manufacturing Industries* (Study Paper No. 21), Joint Economic Committee, 86th Cong., 2d Sess., Washington, D.C.: U.S. Government Printing Office, 1960.

14. A. W. Phillips, "The Relationship Between Unemployment and the Rate of Change of Money Wage Rates in the United Kingdom, 1861–1957," *Economica*, Vol. XXV (November, 1958), pp. 283–99. For the United States economy see Paul A. Samuelson and R. M. Solow, "Analytical Aspects of Anti-Inflation Policy," *American Economic Review*, Vol. L (May, 1960), pp. 144–94.

BIBLIOGRAPHY

Bailey, Martin J. *National Income and the Price Level: A Study in Macrotheory.* New York: McGraw-Hill Book Company, Inc., 1962.

Bailey, Ralph Edward. *An American Colossus: The Singular Career of Alexander Hamilton.* Boston: Lothrop, Lee and Shepard Co., 1933.

Balogh, Thomas. *The Economics of Poverty.* 2d ed. White Plains, N.J.: International Arts and Sciences Press, 1974.

Barner, Richard J., and Ronald E. Muller. *Global Reach.* New York: Simon & Schuster, 1975.

Beard, Charles A., and Mary R. Beard. *The Rise of American Civilization.* New York: The Macmillan Company, 1936.

Black Economic Development (Report of the Thirty-fifth American Assembly, April 24–27, 1969). Harriman, N.Y.: The American Assembly, Columbia University.

Blechman, Barry M., Edward M. Gramlich, and Robert W. Hartman. *Setting National Priorities: 1975 Budget.* Washington, D.C.: Brookings Institution, 1974.

Blinder, Alan S. *Toward an Economic Theory of Income Distribution.* Cambridge, Mass.: MIT Press, 1975.

Boulding, K. E., and Martin Pfaff (eds.). *Redistribution to the Rich and the Poor: the Grants of Economics of Income Distribution.* Belmont, Mass.: Wadsworth, 1972.

Brinker, Paul A., and Joseph J. Klos. *Poverty, Unemployment, and Social Security.* Austin, Texas: Austin Press, 1976.

Brunhild, Gordon, and Robert H. Burton. *Macroeconomic Theory.* Englewood Cliffs, N.J.: Prentice-Hall, Inc., 1974.

Buchanan, James M., and Marilyn R. Flowers. *The Public Finances.* Homewood, Ill.: Richard D. Irwin, 1975.

Budd, Edward C. (ed.). *Inequality and Poverty.* New York: W. W. Norton and Company, Inc., 1967.

Carter, Allen M., and F. Ray Marshall. *Labor Economics.* Homewood, Ill.: Richard D. Irwin, Inc., 1972.

Chow, Gregory C. *Analysis and Control of Dynamic Economic Systems.* New York: John Wiley & Sons, Inc., 1975.

Clark, Colin. *The Conditions of Economic Progress.* 3d ed. London: Macmillan and Co., Ltd., 1957.

The Collected Writings of John Maynard Keynes: Vol. IX (ed. by Royal Economic Society). London: Macmillan and Co., Ltd., 1972.

Conference on Economic Progress. *Jobs and Growth.* Washington, D.C., May, 1961.

———. *A National Program for 1955.* Washington, D.C., February, 1955.

———. *Poverty and Deprivation in the U.S.* Washington, D.C., April, 1962.

———. *Toward Full Employment and Full Production.* Washington, D.C., July, 1954.

Council on International Economic Policy. *Critical Imported Materials.* Washington, D.C.: U.S. Government Printing Office, 1974.

Fabricant, Solomon. *Labor Savings in American Industry, 1899–1939.* New York: National Bureau of Economic Research, Inc., 1945.

Facts and Figures on Government Finance (18th biennial ed.). New York: Tax Foundation, Inc., 1975.

Fatemi, Nasrollah S. (ed.). *Problems of Balance of Payment and Trade.* Canbury, N.J.: Fairleigh-Dickinson University Press, 1975.

Friedman, Irving S. *Inflation: A World-Wide Disaster.* New York: Doubleday, 1975.

Ginsburg, Helen, ed. *Poverty, Economics and Society.* Boston: Little, Brown and Company, 1972.

Glahe, Fred R. *Macroeconomics: Theory and Policy.* New York: Harcourt, Brace and Company, 1973.

Gramlich, E. M. *The Distributional Effects of Higher Unemployment* (Brookings Papers on Economic Activity, Vol. 2). Washington, D.C.: The Brookings Institution, 1972. (1974).

Gray, Ralph, and John M. Peterson. *Economic Development of the United States.* Rev ed. Homewood, Ill.: Richard D. Irwin, 1974.

Hahn, F. H. *The Share of Wages in the National Income: An Inquiry into the Theory of Distribution.* New York: Humanities Press, 1972.

Hansen, Alvin H. *Economic Policy and Full Employment.* New York: McGraw-Hill Book Company, Inc., 1947.

Harberger, Arnold C. *Taxation and Welfare.* Boston: Little, Brown and Company, 1974.

Hardy, C. O. *Wartime Control of Prices.* Washington, D.C.: The Brookings Institution, 1940.

Harris, Seymour E. *The Economics of America at War.* New York: W. W. Norton & Company, Inc., 1943.

Harrod, Jeffrey. *Trade Union Foreign Policy.* New York: Doubleday, 1973.

Haveman, R. H., and T. W. Mirer. "Price Controls and Income Redistribution in an Expanding Economy," in U.S. Congress, Joint Economic Committee, *Price and Wage Control: An Evaluation of Current Policies.* 92d Cong. 2d sess., 1972.

Inflation Outlook (hearing before U.S. Congress, Joint Economic Committee, Sept. 26, 1974). Washington, D.C.: U.S. Government Printing Office, 1974.

Jameson, Kenneth, and Roger Skurskiieds. *U.S. Trade in the Sixties and Seventies.* Lexington, Mass.: D. C. Heath and Company, 1974.

Jantscher, Gerald R. *Bread upon the Waters: Federal Aids to the Maritime Industries.* Washington, D.C.: Brookings Institution, 1975.

Johnson, Harry G. *The Theory of Income Distribution*. London: Gray-Mills, 1974.

Joint Economic Committee. *Long-Term Economic Growth*. Washington, D.C.: U.S. Government Printing Office, 1974.

Juster, F. Thomas, ed. *Education, Income and Human Behavior*. New York: National Bureau of Economic Research, 1975.

Kneese, Allen V., and Charles L. Schultze. *Pollution, Prices, and Public Policy*. Washington, D.C.: Brookings Institution, 1975.

Keynes, John Maynard. *The General Theory of Employment, Interest, and Money*. New York: Harcourt, Brace and Company, 1936.

Kuznets, Simon. *Capital in the American Economy*. Princeton, N.J.: National Bureau of Economic Research, Princeton University Press, 1961.

————. *Economic Growth and Structure: Selected Essays*. New York: W. W. Norton and Company, Inc., 1965.

————. *Modern Economic Growth: Rate, Structure, and Speed*. New Haven, Conn.: Yale University Press, 1966.

————. *Uses of National Income in Peace and War*. New York: National Bureau of Economic Research, Inc., 1942.

Law, Alton D. *International Commodity Agreements*. Lexington, Mass.: D. C. Heath and Co., 1975.

Lees, Francis A., and Maximo Eng. *International Financial Markets: Development of the Present System and Future Prospects*. New York: Praeger, 1975.

Leontieff, Wassily, *et al. Studies in the Structure of the American Economy*. New York: Oxford University Press, 1953.

Levitan, Sar A., William B. Johnston, and Robert Tappart. *Still a Dream: The Changing Status of Blacks Since 1960*. Cambridge, Mass.: Harvard University Press, 1975.

Lodge, Henry Cabot, ed. *The Works of Alexander Hamilton* (12 vols.). New York: G. P. Putnam's Sons, 1904.

Martin, Robert F. *National Income in the United States, 1799–1938*. New York: National Industrial Conference Board, Inc., 1939.

Miller, Herman P. *Income Distribution in the United States*. Washington, D.C.: U.S. Government Printing Office, 1966.

————. *Rich Man, Poor Man*. New York: Thomas Y. Crowell Company, 1971.

Mills, Fredrick C. *Prices in a War Economy: Some Aspects of the Present Price Structure of the United States*. New York: National Bureau of Economic Research, Inc., 1943.

Mitchell, Broadus, and Louise P. Mitchell. *American Economic History*. Boston: Houghton-Mifflin Company, 1947.

Mitchell, Wesley C. *Business Cycles: The Problem and Its Setting*. New York: National Bureau of Economic Research, Inc., 1927.

————. and A. F. Burns. *Measuring Business Cycles*. New York: National Bureau of Economic Research, Inc., 1946.

Moore, Geoffrey H. *Production of Industrial Materials in World Wars I and II*. New York: National Bureau of Economic Research, Inc., 1944.

National Industrial Conference Board. *Conference Board Studies in Enterprise and Social Progress*. New York: National Industrial Conference Board, 1939.

The New American State Papers: Manufacturers (Vols. I–IX). Wilmington, Del.: Scholarly Resources, Inc., 1972.

Phelps, Edmund S., ed. *Economic Justice*. Baltimore: Penguin, 1974.

————. *Microeconomic Foundations of Employment and Inflation Theory*. New York: W. W. Norton and Co., 1970.

Postwar Movements of Prices and Wages in Manufacturing Industries (Study Paper No. 21), Joint Economic Committee, 86th Cong., 2d Sess. Washington, D.C.: U.S. Government Printing Office, 1960.

Riddle, J. H. *British and American Plans for International Currency Stabilization*. New York: National Bureau of Economic Research, Inc., 1944.

Sample, C. James. *Patterns of Regional Economic Change: A Quantitative Analysis of U.S. Regional Growth and Development*. Cambridge, Mass.: Ballinger, 1974.

Scherer, F. M. *Industrial Market Structure and Economic Performance*. Chicago: Rand McNally and Company, 1970.

Schultz, George P., and Robert Z. Aliber, eds. *Guidelines, Informal Controls, and the Market Place*. Chicago: University of Chicago Press, 1966.

Scoville, James G. *Perspectives on Poverty and Income Distribution*. Lexington, Mass.: D. C. Heath and Company, 1971.

Smith, Adam. *The Wealth of Nations*. New York: Modern Library, 1937.

Smith, James D., ed. *The Personal Distribution of Income and Wealth*. New York: National Bureau of Economic Research, 1975.

Solow, Robert M. "What Happened to Full Employment?" *Quarterly Review of Economics and Business*, Vol. 13 (Summer, 1973).

Steiner, George A., ed. *Economic Problems of War*. New York: John Wiley & Sons, Inc., 1942.

Survey of Current Business (monthly). Washington, D.C.: U.S. Department of Commerce.

Syrett, Harold C., ed. *The Papers of Alexander Hamilton*. 18 vols. New York: Columbia University Press, 1961.

U.S. Bureau of the Census. *Historical Statistics of the United States, Colonial Times to 1957*. Washington, D.C.: U.S. Government Printing Office, 1960.

————. *Long Term Economic Growth, 1860–1965*. Washington, D.C.: U.S. Government Printing Office, 1966.

U.S. Congress, Joint Economic Committee. *Hearings, Review of Phase II of the New Economic Program*. 92d Cong., 2d sess. April 14, 1972.

U.S. Council of Economic Advisers. *Economic Report of the President*. Washington, D.C.: U.S. Government Printing Office, 1947 to date.

U.S. Department of Labor. *Manpower Report of the President*. Washington, D.C.: U.S. Government Printing Office, 1973.

Van Meerhaeghe, M. A. G. *International Economics*. New York: Crane, Russak, 1973.

Wilhite, Virgle G. *Founders of American Economic Thought and Policy*. New York: Bookman Associates, 1958.

PART II: Society, Education, Psychology

American Negro slavery has attracted wide discussion on the origins of the institution, reasons for continuing it, and the social effects of it. Raymond Dacey, in "A Historiography of American Negro Slavery: 1918–1976," concerns himself primarily with the quality of historical conclusions on the slavery issue. Attention is given to the economic and social facets of slavery centered on five main topics. The topics are (1) the profitability of slavery as an investment; (2) the economic viability of slavery as a system of production; (3) the efficiency of slavery as a labor system; (4) the economic effects of slavery upon the Southern economy; and (5) the nature and quality of life for the individual slave. The essay concludes with a discussion of relatively recent accounts of slavery in the Soviet Union.

The next chapter of Part II examines the proposition that the present status of crime and social unrest in America suggests that the source of the problem may very well lie in the organization of American society. Richard E. Hilbert examines social organization in his "Anomie as an Explanation for Deviance in America: Its Development and Implication for Change." After a thorough discussion of what anomie has come to mean to sociologists, the writer examines certain changes in the system which might be expected to reduce the degree of anomie and thus the consequences of deviance caused by failure to achieve cultural goals.

The American educational system has developed into a phenomenal institution from a vast range of opinions and motives. John D. Pulliam, in the chapter "Shifting Patterns of Educational Thought," presents those aspects of selected movements in the philosophy of education which made a unique impact on the modern educational system in the United States. One of the important philosophical positions reviewed is the position of the Puritans in using education as an instrument for social control, to preserve social values they held dear and to preserve the faith. Among others, the author deals with the debate over a federal system versus one controlled by local jurisdictions. After the essential structure is set, changes in the philosophy of how best to achieve educational objectives are addressed. The author makes it clear that the educational system is a reflection of accepted societal values, and it is not immune from social conflict. A review is made of some of the paths that selected observers consider imperative for the educational system to take if civilization is to survive. Clear cut solutions are not available, but a few of the options and concerns of current debate are offered for the reader's consideration.

Much of psychological history has its origins in Europe. Study of the child, however, has been dominated by Americans. John C. McCullers and John M. Love, in their chapter "The Scientific Study of the Child," set forth "some useful guidelines and generalizations" toward the writing of a history of scientific child study. Their contribution represents the first history of its kind, but a more detailed study remains to be written. Concern with children dates to antiquity and scientific study of them started about 200 years ago. Child research today is one of the most active branches of psychology. The authors point out how and why the child is studied, as well as what has been learned. Major emphasis is devoted to American psychologists who contributed to knowledge concerning children. The current state of research activity is provided in order to reveal the types of hypotheses under scrutiny.

In total, Part II presents some of the issues and ideas that are and have been debated within the American educational system. The search for new knowledge is a fundamental objective of the entire process.

7

A HISTORIOGRAPHY OF NEGRO SLAVERY, 1918-1976*

By Raymond Dacey

Slavery scholarship has repeatedly been drawn into the emotional court of public opinion as an expert witness. It has provided the foundation upon which white supremacists, basic racists (white and black), abolitionists, civil rights activists and the various and sundry combinations thereof have based their conflicting opinions and upon which they have built their respective views of the world.* Traditional slavery scholarship provides the elements of a widespread, and in some locales the presently dominant, view of slavery, the Civil War and American Negroes. Therein slavery is seen as moribund on the eve of the Civil War and as the cause of the post war economic woes of the South, the war as an unnecessary blood bath and the depiction of American Negroes as slow, lazy and inept but always happy individuals. What does contemporary slavery scholarship offer to dispel this myth? What view of the last 150 years does it support? What picture of American Negroes does it paint?

The direct answers to these questions will be supplied by future generations. We will trace the major themes in slavery scholarship from its origins in 1905–18 to the present. The emphasis here is not upon reciting the conclusions of historians but upon examining the methods whereby those conclusions were drawn. We are interested primarily in the quality of historical conclusions concerning slavery.

INTRODUCTION

Slavery scholarship shapes and supports popular societal views of slavery, slaves and their descendents, and the major

historical events surrounding the Civil War. A familiarity with the conclusions of slavery scholarship and a knowledge of their quality is important for an understanding of contemporary and future views of the largest American minority.

This chapter follows the intertwined paths of the historiography of American slavery and the methodological evolution of contemporary economic history. Because this is not a history of American slavery, our interest in slavery is secondary. The central point of interest is the evolution of the historian's view of slavery as induced by the evolution of the historiographic method. Slavery is the issue with which the "revolution" in economic history began; and it is the issue upon which the major methodological tools of the new history most recently have been brought to bear.

The economic aspects of slavery scholarship center on five main topics: (1) the profitability of slavery as an investment; (2) the economic viability of slavery as a system of production; (3) the efficiency of slavery as a labor system; (4) the economic effects of slavery upon the Southern economy; and (5) the nature and quality of life for the individual slave. Paralleling these economic properties of the slavery system is a more societal view of the slave and slavery. Herein the characteristics of the slave (i.e., the African Negro) personality are analyzed, characterized and considered in relationship to the economic factors of the system. Together, the economic and social facets constitute a view, or historical analysis, of the institution of slavery.

Our consideration of the historiography of American slavery begins with U. B. Phillips who published, in 1905, "The Economic Cost of Slaveholding in the Cotton Belt" and, in 1918, *American Negro Slavery*, the analyses of American plantation slavery which dominated scholarly and secular thinking for over thirty years. In what amounts to an apologetic portrayal of slavery as a mechanism of racial and social adjustment for the slave, Phillips concludes that: (1) slavery was an unprofitable investment for the plantation owner; (2) slavery was economically moribund; (3) slave labor was inefficient; (4) slavery stagnated the Southern antebellum economy; and (5) the individual slave enjoyed good, sometimes excellent, material conditions. Paralleling this analysis is Phillips's view of the Negro slave as a submissive, ingratiating, superstitious and nonchalant "darkie"—the nigger fond of display, docile and contented in his acceptance

*I have drawn on many existent reviews and analyses in tracing the evolution of slavery scholarship. The most important of these are: "The Economics of Slavery," Chapter 4 of *The Reinterpretation of American Economic History* by R. W. Fogel and S. L. Engerman; the basis for the foregoing, "The Effects of Slavery Upon the Southern Economy: A Review of the Recent Debate" by S. L. Engerman; the review of slavery scholarship presented in *Time on the Cross* by Fogel and Engerman; and finally, the review essay "Slavery: The Progressive Institution?" by P. A. David and P. Temin. Misinterpretations and inadequate presentation of sources remain the responsibility of the author. The serious reader is urged to consult the original works, and an extended bibliography is provided for that purpose. The Afterword draws on the work and reviews thereof of A. Solzhenitsyn. These are presented in an annotated bibliography.

of subordination, happy (always smiling) and well-fed beyond the level of his economic worth. In short, the slave was "Sambo." The foregoing economic view together with the Sambo myth became known as the Plantation Legend.

This legend, while dominant, did not go unchallenged. Phillips' position was attacked by historians Richard Hofstadter ("U. B. Phillips and the Plantation Legend," 1944), Kenneth Stampp (*The Peculiar Institution*, 1956), and Stanley M. Elkins (*Slavery: A Problem in American Institutional and Intellectual Life,* 1959). These attacks centered on the social view of the slave and slavery and avoided or gave superficial treatment to the economic view. Hofstadter attacked Phillips's exaggerated account of the paternalistic nature of the owners, his portrait of a carefree and comfortable lifestyle for the slaves, and his account of the slaves as contented and docile. Hofstadter offered an alternative analysis, concluding that the absentee owners, however benevolent, had left the slaves vulnerable to cruel treatment by those in actual possession of them, that the slaves' health and general material conditions were poor, and that slaves indeed demonstrated a resistance to slavery. Hofstadter concluded that slavery scholars ought to begin again from the viewpoint of modern cultural anthropology.

Stampp began his analysis with the assumption "that slaves were merely ordinary human beings, that innately Negroes *are*, after all, only white men with black skins, nothing more, nothing less." He concluded that slaves constituted a profitable investment for the plantation owner, that slavery would not have fallen under its own economic weight, and that institutionalized slavery had not stagnated the economy or prevented the industrialization of the South. Although Stampp mildly challenged the belief that slavery constituted an inefficient form of labor, he did not extend himself to the conclusion that slave labor was as efficient as free labor. Stampp did conclude that the output of slave labor equaled that of free labor only because slaves worked longer hours and because slave women and children were exploited. Thus Stampp failed to overthrow the myth of the imcompetence of slave labor, preferring instead to support and maintain the view that slaves were harshly treated and cruelly driven to produce. Furthermore, Stampp advanced the view that the slaves, though never rebelling like their counterparts in South America, did participate in subtle resistance which took the form of shirking duties, injuring crops, feigning illness, and disrupting the work routine.

Elkins adopted and elaborated the view that slavery was exceptionally cruel and was sure to have had a psychological impact upon the individual slave. The result of slavery, according to Elkins, was "Sambo, the typical plantation slave . . . docile but irresponsible, loyal but lazy, humble but chronically given to lying and stealing." Sambo's "bahavior was full of infantile silliness" and his "relationship with his master was one of utter dependence and childlike attachment."

Thus Stampp and Elkins offer distinct analyses which yield a common conclusion—the slave's behavior was that of a Sambo. Therefore, the net result of the attacks upon Phillips was a reappraisal of the *economic* view of slavery; Phillips's Sambo of the "Traditional View," i.e., the "Plantation Legend," remained, for the most part, intact. Indeed, while

Phillips was an apologist for the institution of slavery and white supremacy, his attackers Stampp and Elkins, and to a certain extent Hofstadter, were apologists for Negro inferiority. The myth of black incompetence was maintained.

Alfred H. Conrad and John R. Meyer published "Economic Theory, Statistical Inference, and Economic History" in 1957 and "The Economics of Slavery in the Antebellum South" in 1958. These two papers mark the beginning of contemporary economic history and slavery scholarship. The former paper is a methodological manifesto; the latter is the first application of the new methodology. Conrad and Meyer's 1957 paper lays the foundations for the "new" economic history, also known as "cliometrics." (Clio is the Greek muse of history. J. R. T. Hughes is generally credited as the source of the name; Hughes claims S. Reiter originated it. See Hughes, 1965, on this point.) "The Economics of Slavery in the Antebellum South" constitutes the first purely economic analysis of the profitability of slavery and is the initial work of the "new" economic history. Both papers are classics which will be examined later in greater detail.

During the period 1957–74, numerous studies employing the Conrad-Meyer methodology were produced which extended and refined the methodological tools available to the economic historian. Cliometrics, a quantitative-data oriented discipline, also produced valuable new data. In 1974 R. W. Fogel and S. L. Engerman published *Time on the Cross: The Economics of American Negro Slavery*, which utilized many of the methodological and evidential advances and contributions of the new economic history. They came to the following conclusions:

1. Slavery was highly profitable; the institution was maintained for profit, not social benevolence.

2. The slave system was not moribund on the eve of the Civil War; indeed, slavery was never stronger, and the trend was toward even further entrenchment.

3. Slave agriculture was not inefficient compared with free agriculture, and the typical field hand was not lazy, inept, and unproductive; on the average he was harder-working and more efficient than his white counterpart.

4. Far from stagnating, the economy of the antebellum South grew quite rapidly.

5. The material (not psychological) conditions of the lives of slaves compared favorably with those of free industrial workers. Slaves were exploited in the sense that part of the income which they produced was expropriated by their owners. Over the course of his lifetime, the typical field hand received about 90 per cent of the income he produced.

These conclusions constitute a severe contradiction of the traditional interpretation of slavery. How could the originators of the traditional interpretation be so wrong? The answer, according to Fogel and Engerman, "hinges, to a large extent on certain broad methodological questions, and particularly on the role of mathematics and statistics in historical analysis." Put simply, Fogel and Engerman argue that if earlier authors had benefited from the fruits of the cliometric revolution, their analyses would have produced the same conclusions as *Time on the Cross*.

THE PHILLIPS TRADITION:
THE ORIGINS OF SLAVERY SCHOLARSHIP

Phillips' economic view of slavery is essentially financial. The dominant wisdom of Wall Street at that time centered upon the price-to-earnings ratio, and knowledge of this ratio for a specific corporate stock determined the solution of the investment decision. Slaves, Phillips argued, should be viewed as investments; that is, the market for slaves should be analyzed in the same manner as the market for corporate securities. The slave investment decision is resolved by examining the ratio of slave prices to cotton prices. Phillips's analysis gives monopoly behavior a central role. In any market, control over supply produces a rapid, often wild rise in price, e.g., the OPEC oil cartel. The mechanism which produced monopoly control over the supply of slaves was the congressional ban on importing slaves that was instituted in 1807. The effect was to drive the price of slaves up at a far more rapid rate than the rise in cotton prices. Phillips puts it thus:

1815 began the "ante-bellum" regime, in which the whole economy of the South was governed by the apparently capricious play of the compound monopoly of cotton and slave labor. The price of cotton was governed by the American output and its relation to the European demand. And the price of slaves was governed by the profits in cotton and the relation of the labor demand to the monopolized labor supply.

Slaves, therefore, were greatly overvalued vis-à-vis cotton, according to Phillips. The primary reason for the overvaluation was speculation. Those speculators who had cornered the slave market were in a position to extract ever-increasing payments as long as demand held up. There are two reasons for a maintenance of demand. First, the production of cotton involves returns to scale, and thus growers demanded increasing numbers of slaves in order to gain the rewards of large-scale production. Second, individuals also kept slaves for noneconomic reasons—as symbols of wealth and status, i.e., as objects of conspicuous consumption. These forces produced a sufficient level of demand to guarantee windfall profits to those who held monopoly control over the supply of slaves.

The analogy between this situation and the contemporary oil monopoly (OPEC) and spiraling prices for petroleum is obvious, but how good an analogy is it? First, the supply of petroleum is fairly well monopolized. The analogue of the increasing returns to scale mechanism for the slavery example is the simple necessity of oil as a basic input to an industrialized economy. Finally, the conspicuous consumption theme transfers intact. In place of buying and displaying oil as a consumption good, contemporary Americans purchase oil and oil products to produce and feed their objects of conspicuous consumptions—large automobiles, etc.

However, Phillips' analysis of the slave market based upon the securities investment model has a flaw. In order to obtain monopoly control over a security, an investor or group of investors must actually corner the security, i.e., gain virtually complete control of it. Slaves, while in short supply, were not held by one individual but by tens of thousands of individuals. There was no collusion among these persons.

Thus Phillips' analogy of a cornered market is inaccurate; it rests on a confusion of monopoly control over supply with the existence of virtually fixed and inelastic short-run supply. Phillips' analysis of the cause of the rise in the ratio of slave price to cotton price is inadmissible; similarly, his analysis provided no insight into the profitability of slavery.

To assess profitability, the historian must collect the necessary data to compute the (average) rate of return to a planter investing in a slave. Several historians have produced the necessary computations based upon data gathered from the records of the larger plantations. Most of these studies, except that of Lewis, found slavery unprofitable and thus provided support for Phillips' view that slaves were overvalued. They showed the rate of profit to be around 2 or 3 per cent and were based upon flawed interpretations of economic and accounting concepts, primarily the latter.

If slavery was unprofitable to most planters, as Phillips and others argued, then clearly the system of slavery was dying. This view originated with Phillips' predecessors but received his support. The view that slavery was moribund on the eve of the Civil War was given its modern formulation by Charles W. Ramsdell. Ramsdell saw the excessive allocation of land to cotton planting and the decline in cotton prices as the cause of the imminent collapse of the slave system. Between 1857 and 1860 the cotton crop increased by about 70 per cent, due in part to the railroad connecting rural areas to markets and thus increasing cotton acreage and in part to the planting of new fields in Texas. He saw prices falling and output rising and concluded: "Had not the war intervened there is every reason to believe that there would have been a continuous overproduction and very low prices throughout the sixties and seventies."

Ramsdell's argument has a flaw. Indeed, vast amounts of new land were being planted in cotton, and if demand had held fairly constant, then of course prices would have fallen. However, if the new lands had been planted in cotton in anticipation of expanded demand and had that anticipation been realized, then not only would profits have increased but it is also possible that output would have increased. Although it is not clear that demand would have increased, Ramsdell never examined the possibility. He was content to conclude that an increase in the land/labor ratio had placed the slave system on its deathbed.

Ramsdell is thus a supporter of the Phillips view that slavery was unprofitable. However, if both Phillips and Ramsdell have misinterpreted the data on cotton price movements, then both their analyses can be overturned. This is accomplished by Robert W. Fogel and Stanley L. Engerman in their essay "The Economics of Slavery," published in 1971.

The third major facet of the Phillips tradition is the bipartite view that slavery caused the stagnation of the Southern economy. First, the argument posits that Southern capital was tied up in slave investment and was therefore not available for industrialization. Second, this view holds that slave labor is immobile, as Phillips put it, fixed "rigidly in one line of employment." Phillips's view that slavery was indeed the cause of southern economic stagnation has received support from numerous historians. Guy S. Callender argued that

Southerners' "lack of [a] disposition to save" inhibited Southern capital formation. Eugene D. Genovese offered a class structure argument, which holds that slavery produced a super rich upper class, a very poor lower class, and virtually no middle class. This skewed distribution of wealth led to a low level of demand for domestically manufactured goods. Unlike the West, where the large middle class supported manufacturing, the South's upper class made its purchases in Europe; the lower class was too poor to support a large-scale industry. Genovese's argument involves conspicuous consumption with a European twist, and its net result is that slavery prohibited the industrial advance of the South.

The foregoing analyses are interesting but flawed by a lack of evidence. The analyses are actually interesting hypotheses; they are not, however, explanations.

THE MANIFESTO OF THE "NEW" ECONOMIC HISTORY

A total review of the traditional analysis of plantation slavery required more than using new data in the same old analytical models. New techniques of analysis were required. Slavery scholarship until the late 1950's consisted of analyses based upon accounting theory and plantation records. Such studies do not, as noted previously, provide explanations. In order to explain past economic events, the historian must employ economic theory, not accounting theory. Conrad and Meyer provide both the motivation for explanatory history and the first major piece of the genre.

As noted above, contemporary economic history began in 1957–58 with the publication of Conrad and Meyer's papers "Economic Theory, Statistical Inference and Economic History" and the "The Economics of Slavery in the Antebellum South." The former served as the methodological manifesto of the "new" economic historians; the latter ended the 50-year dominance of Phillips' interpretation of the institution of slavery.

Most revolutions are begun by simple acts, and so it is with the revolution in economic history. "Economic Theory, Statistical Inference and Economic History" does not suggest the use of revolutionary techniques; rather it "is an attempt to examine critically the function of [economic] theory in historical research and particularly in economic history." Conrad and Meyer state: "We shall take as our starting point the assertion that the historian is not interested simply in collecting facts or true statements about some segment of previous experience. He wants to find causes and to explain what happened." Historians, for the most part, have always sought to "explain what happened," although some would argue that they did not seek causes. These same historians have, however, used various theories and pseudotheories implicitly to produce desired explanations. Very rarely did a historian overtly announce the theoretical superstructure of his explanation; indeed, very rarely did historical explanation possess a unified theoretical structure. More often than not, historical explanations were pieced together from *ad hoc* applications of many theories, and little care was given to the

quality of the theories or to their applicability to the phenomena to be explained. Conrad and Meyer attempted to rectify this situation and concluded the first paragraph of their paper by saying: "Our purpose here is to introduce some of the problems attached to the concepts of historical causality and explanation in a stochastic universe and to suggest how the analytic tools of scientific inference can be applied in economic historiography."

The crucial part of their statement of purpose is the last phrase. Their aim is to further the employment of already established analytic tools—economic theory, statistical inference, and the general laws of nature and causality—for the purpose of explaining past economic events and processes. There are no radical, untried procedures being proffered here. The emphasis is placed on suggesting the relevance and applicability of general scientific inference to economic historiography. The essence of scientific inference is the explicit use of explanatory theory and data. While scientific writing may not be literary, it is very rarely purposefully misleading, and is never subtle. There is a great difference, in both style and longevity, between a scientific explanation of a physical phenomenon and a politico-historical explanation of a past event. Traditional historical analysis mirrors the prose style and subtle reasoning of politico-historical explanation; contemporary economic history follows the blunt style and explicit (theoretical) reasoning of scientific explanation. Although traditional history may be more readable because of its style, it is less explanatory, due to its analytical technique. Perhaps a better title than "new economic history" would be "analytical economic history."

Conrad and Meyer do not proffer specific analytical procedures but argue for the relevance of general inferential analysis. The major thrust of their argument centers on the logic of explanation. Explanatory arguments have the structure of and invoke for their support the logical law *modus ponendo ponens:* from 'A,' and 'A implies B,' follows 'B.' An (analytical) explanation of an event E consists of a model (i.e., theory) M and factual evidence C such that E deductively follows from C and M. Thus M must be of the form C implies E, symbolically C→E. An explanation of E is a deductive argument of the form:

$$C$$
$$C \rightarrow E$$
$$\therefore E \quad .$$

This form of explanation, termed deductive-nomological, is immediately applicable in a deterministic universe. Conrad and Meyer, at the outset, concerned themselves with a stochastic universe. Thus the deductive nomological explanation form is not to be taken literally.

The economic model M is written in its statistical-econometric form, and probability tests are performed to determine if the consequent of the explanation, E, differs significantly from an observed or recorded phenomenon E*. If no significant difference exists, then the event E* has been explained by C and M. Conrad and Meyer note:

The agreement of certain actual conditions [E*] with deduced conditions [E] *does not imply, of course, that the initial hy-pothesis* [C & M] *is necessarily correct. This is so because there may be other initial hypotheses from which the same observed conditions can be deduced. We are able, in short, to reject a hypothesis but not to accept one hypothesis over all others.*

Conrad and Meyer thus accept classical empiricism, which provides the philosophical-methodological underpinnings of classical physics, in its entirety. They argue that the inference one makes based on such a procedure is as follows: "The empirical [significance] test in that case [i.e., E* agrees with E] serves essentially to strengthen at a minimum our subjective beliefs in the truth of the hypothesis. And that is no little or mean advance." No suggestion is made that compatibility between E and E* supports an acceptance of the explanatory model M; such compatibility only increases belief in M. With a slight misuse of the language of logical probability, a successful explanation is said to increase the degree of confirmation of M, i.e., to improve the epistemological status of M.

Conrad and Meyer allude to the potential absolute falsification of a model M. Suppose M is of the form C→E, and we observe C and not E. Then the model M is falsified, and the statement 'C & cfE' is called the falsifier.

A simple rearrangement of the negation sign, ⌐, yields an entirely new explanation form. Suppose we observe ⌐C and E, where E is deduced from C and M. Specifically, suppose we know C to be false but, on the presumption of C, that the model M provides an explanation of E. Such an explanation is called a counterfactual explanation, the conclusion of which is a counterfactual conditional statement, symbolized by C→cfE. Conrad and Meyer say, "For example, to assert that 'If the Civil War had not occurred, the South would have abolished Negro slavery in an orderly fashion within one generation' is to propose a counterfactual or subjunctive conditional statement for which no procedure of verification or falsification is possible." In all of the methodological writings of the new economic historians, no topic is as mistreated and misunderstood as the concept of a counterfactual conditional proposition, including the paper by Conrad and Meyer under discussion here.

Counterfactual conditional statements have always been used by historians. Indeed, counterfactual propositions are fundamental to historiography, both old and "new." Fogel, in a review of the "new" methodology, notes that:

Like it or not, counterfactual conditional statements are too integral a feature of [historical] discourse to be banished. Should we advocate that historians give up the practice of making judgements about mistakes? Do we mean to exclude from history such statements as: 'Woodrow Wilson miscalculated the consequences of his failure to appoint a prominant Republican to the delegation that represented America at the Paris peace conference' or 'Andrew Johnson played into the hands of his enemies by suspending Stanton and making Grant ad interim *Secretary of War'? There are few historians who would accept a ban on such judgements. To do so would transform history into mere chronology.*

Counterfactual arguments play a central role in both the new economic history and the contemporary historiography of slavery. The revolutionary paper on the profitability of slavery by Conrad and Meyer employs counterfactual methodology. Fogel's analysis of the indispensability of railroads for American economic growth employs the technique at the peak of its analytical power, making Fogel the acknowledged master of counterfactual historiography. Finally, and ironically, counterfactual analysis, or, more accurately, the lack of it, constitutes the major flaw and points to the general implausibility of the Fogel and Engerman analysis of slavery, *Time on the Cross.*

The new economic historians employed counterfactual arguments primarily to overthrow existent historical beliefs and explanations. The very first such use of an explicit counterfactual argument was by Conrad and Meyer in "The Economics of Negro Slavery in the Antebellum South." Easily the most popular and perhaps the most complete use of counterfactual analysis is Fogel's *Railroads and American Economic Growth,* which will now be considered in some detail.

The axiom of indispensability proclaims that the railroads were not only the mainstay of American growth but were indeed indispensable for that growth. Fogel cites historian Sidney Dillion as follows:

The growth of the United States west of the Alleghanies during the past fifty years [1814–1891] is due not so much to free institutions, or climate, or the fertility of the soil as to railways. If . . . railways had not been invented, the freedom and natural advantages of our Western States would have beckoned to human immigration and industry in vain. Civilization would have crept slowly on, in a toilsome march over the immense spaces that lie between the Appalachian ranges and the Pacific Ocean; and what we now style the Great West would be, except in the valley of the Mississippi, an unknown and unproductive wilderness.

To overthrow such a belief, one need only consider a hypothetical economy for, say, 1890, wherein there are no railroads and shipping is accomplished via wagons and canals. The question to be answered here is: Would the economy be significantly worse off (on some criterion) without railroads than it was with them? The criterion chosen by Fogel is the Gross National Product (GNP) for 1890. He hypothesized an (agricultural) economy for 1890 wherein shipments were made via roads and a hypothetically extended system of canals. He found that such an economy would have had a GNP at most 7 per cent lower than the actual GNP for 1890. The difference is not overwhelming, which suggests that the axiom of indispensability is less a valid historical conclusion and more a rhetorical creation of the prorailroad lobby of the Guilded Era.

Fogel, as the author of the boldest application of the counterfactual method, became its chief defender. There were, to be sure, no paucity of detractors, and the most vociferous among them was the respected historian Fritz Redlich. He termed counterfactual arguments mere "figments," announcing that their use amounted to "quasi-history." He argued that in some cases Fogel's analysis was justified, "but this does not make Fogel's product history." Redlich did not stop with Fogel. With respect to the slavery paper by Conrad and Meyer, he announced, "Nevertheless I am reluctant to consider the paper as a whole a work of history." Thus to Redlich the new economic history, insofar as it employed counterfactual analysis, was not history. Cliometrics, in Redlich's view, was a branch of economics or perhaps alchemy, but not of history.

Redlich's attack involved a strange and muddled view of philosophy, e.g.,:

The new approaches to economic history are definitely positivistic, in that for positivism nothing matters unless it can be counted, measured, or weighed. But the age-old empiricism also roots in positivism. Consequently, the lines are strangely drawn. The new approaches, while positivistic at their roots, are antiempiricistic through their reliance on economic theory. Thereby they come closer to analytical history than to the empiricistic approach to which they are related . . . .

Earlier in this article it was argued that the "new" economic history might better be termed "analytical" economic history, precisely because it so closely pursued the tenets of (analytical) empiricism.

In response to Redlich, Fogel states, "if historians are not prepared to expurgate judgements about 'what might have been' from their narrations, the real issue regarding counterfactual conditional statements is not whether we should make them, but how to establish criteria which enables one to determine the validity of such statements." After developing an unnecessarily complex and totally *ad hoc* model, he concludes: "From the foregoing discussion, it is obvious that the crucial step in the verification of a counterfactual statement is the determination of the empirical validity of the explicit or implicit equation (or set of equations) which is purported to describe a specified reality." That is, if the model M is empirically valid, then the counterfactual statement C→cfE supported by M is verified.

Fogel's argument rests on a classical view of counterfactual statements as mere reformulations of causal laws. When viewed this way, causal laws become very special beasts and require an if–then connective of unusual strength. Logics for such strong connectives are called modal. Economic "laws" are not nearly strong enough to be translated via modal connectives, and thus Fogel's causal law analysis of counterfactual arguments evaporates. Can the counterfactual methodology of contemporary economic history be given a sound (philosophical) foundation?

The answer is positive and the analysis presented by Dacey in "The Role of Economic Theory in Supporting Counterfactual Arguments." Fogel was on the right track—the central issue in the justification of a counterfactual argument involving the economic model M is the epistemological status of M. Fogel's mistake lies in asking too much of any economic model, i.e., that it be a causal law. The alternative analysis requires no notion of causality nor any modal connectives, and its solution involves defining the counterfactual if-then,

→cf, in terms of probabilities. Using the definition of the late philosopher and teacher H. A. Finch, the remainder of the analysis is child's play. In essence, a model M will support the counterfactual conditional statement C→cfE if: (1) M is weakly acceptable, i.e., the probability of M on the basis of established fact is greater than ½, (2) C is factually, though not logically, false and (3) M is necessary to deduce E from C. The three foregoing conditions are strikingly simple. No modal logics are invoked, and no notion of causality is required.

We will return to the logic of counterfactual analysis when we consider the Conrad and Meyer slavery paper in greater detail. Presently, we will consider the second major innovation and methodological facet of the new history, the process of indirect measurement. The historian engaged in indirect measurement is very much like the earthbound astronomer who attempts celestial measurement. The astronomer can measure, for example, the surface temperature of a distant planet only indirectly, via calculations based on received light signals and physical theory. Similarly, to determine an unknown magnitude, the historian invokes data, i.e., known magnitudes, and economic theory. The economic theory connects the existent data to the unknown magnitude and allows the historian to determine a value for the previously unknown magnitude. The indirectly measured magnitude will be used together with existent data and an economic model to generate either a direct or indirect (counterfactual) explanation. The methodological problem of indirect measurement consists of accounting for the quality, or the status, of the indirectly determined value.

A simple and somewhat apocryphal example of indirect measurement in economic history is the following. A historian was interested in the colonial American-British cotton trade. In order to complete his study, he needed to know the number of bales of cotton transshipped from New Orleans to Britain for a given year, but no such records had been kept. However, since the burlap used to wrap each bale was very valuable, shipping agents kept careful records of the wrappers as they were returned to their owners. Thus the available data consisted of the total number of returned wrappers. The model employed was simple: the number of bales of cotton shipped from New Orleans equals the number of wrappers returned therefrom plus 10 per cent. The 10 per cent increment was included to account for worn out and/or excessively damaged wrappers. Although most instances of indirect measurement are not so simple, they are structurally identical to the foregoing cotton example. They employ existent data (in this case, the number of wrappers) and an economic model (in this case, a trivial equation: bales = 1.1 × wrappers).

The problem of indirect measurement, i.e., accounting for the accuracy of indirectly determined magnitudes, is a part of the larger problem of prediction. Economic-historical explanations do not follow the deductive-nomological explanation form exactly, because economic theory is stated in its probabilistic form. Similarly, in making an indirect measurement, the economic model is typically probabilistic and yields a probability statement as a conclusion. The problem arises in attempting to assess the quality of the indirectly determined magnitude on the basis of the probability assigned to it by the predictive argument. This is no mean or trivial issue, since it leads to all the problems of induction.

The historian is usually uncertain about both the quality of the existent data and the economic model. The central issue of economic prediction is stated by Oskar Morgenstern as follows:

. . . the question then is to decide whether [inaccuracies in predicted values] are due to a faulty model or to lack of definition of the [factual] information. Most likely, one will encounter a combination of the two, namely some admixture . . . To put this issue in different words: Is the application of an economic program, i.e., of a particular economic theory, more sensitive to changes in the model or to changes in the data (the quality of our information)? This is a far from trivial question to which at present the answer is not obtainable in general.

Thus the quality of an indirect measurement is influenced by both the quality of the data and the quality of the model in an unknown admixture.

The resolution of the problem of indirect measurement consists of determining the admixture. Morgenstern made the preceding comments in 1950, and at that time there was no general solution to the issue. In "The Effects of Theory and Data in Economic Prediction," I present the desired general solution. This solution does not involve invoking an inductive logic, which is usually highly problematic. Like the resolution of the problem of counterfactuals, the formula for computing the admixture is arrived at via probabilistic reasoning. If the solution to the issue, as stated by Morgenstern, is extended to a general solution of the problem of economic prediction, then it does involve a limiting form of inductive logic. The general answer to Morgenstern's formulation of the issue provides a partial resolution of the much larger problem of economic prediction. The problem of indirect measurement, therefore, can be said to be resolved only in part, and it will remain so until the general problem of induction is resolved.

Here we leave the discussion of the two major facets of Conrad and Meyer's methodological manifesto, counterfactual argumentation and indirect measurement. Conrad and Meyer's analysis of profitability places greater emphasis on the former, while the Fogel and Engerman study makes greater use of the latter. Indeed, the irony of the latter study is its complete and incorrect avoidance of counterfactual analysis.

THE PROFITABILITY OF SLAVERY

The first major application of the new methodology is by Conrad and Meyer in "The Economics of Slavery in the Antebellum South." The work's major emphasis is upon the profitability of slavery; its major innovation is the use of economic (capital) theory. Their analysis provides a continuation of the critical evaluation of the Phillips tradition.

Phillips viewed slavery as unprofitable, moribund, and the cause of a stagnated Southern economy due to an increasing slave to cotton price ratio, the analogue of an accounting concept. Earlier attacks on the Phillips tradition by Lewis C. Gray and Robert R. Russel argued for the profitability and viability of slavery while agreeing that it had stagnated the economy. Later critics argued that previous studies showing the unprofitability of slavery rested on inadmissible uses of accounting techniques. Thomas P. Govan showed that, by correcting these mistakes, slavery was shown to be profitable. Stampp's encompassing study, *The Peculiar Institution*, correctly employed contemporary accounting procedures to deduce the profitability of slavery and argued against the proposition that slavery caused the Southern economy to stagnate. The common thread running through all of these analyses is the use of accounting procedures. Unlike economic theory, accounting theory is incapable of explaining events. It is designed to yield a consistent, coherent scheme for registering the financial and monetary aspects of complicated economic phenomena. Economic theory, on the other hand, is designed to explain and, in some cases, predict economic phenomena. Accounting is related to economics in the same way that a system of weights and measures, e.g., the English system of pound, foot, and second or the metric system of kilogram, meter, and second, is related to physics. The former simplifies the recording and description of events, while the latter explains the occurrence of events.

Conrad and Meyer's great innovation and the revolutionary aspect of their work is the explicit application of explanatory economic theory to the profitability issue of slavery. They viewed the purchase of a slave as a standard investment problem, much as Phillips has suggested, saying, "From the standpoint of the entrepreneur making an investment in slaves the basic problems involved in determining profitability are analytically the same as those met in determining the returns from any other kind of capital investment." Phillips had originally made this point but failed to pursue it.

The major analytical tool employed by Conrad and Meyer is the equation

$$C = \frac{Re + Ee}{i} \left[1 - \frac{1}{(1+i)^n} \right],$$

where: C = the (average) price of a slave plus the value of the (average) amount of land and equipment required to support and employ a slave,

Re = the expected annual net revenue derived from a slave,

Ee = the expected annual cost to the planter (rental value) of the land and equipment,

i = the rate of return that planters earned on their investment in slaves and the associated land and equipment, and

n = the expected life of a slave at the time of his purchase.

The value of i is obtained by estimating the values of C, Re, Ee and n and solving the equation for i. In order to facilitate the estimation of C, Re, Ee and n, Conrad and Meyer specialized their analysis to account for the (economically) different roles of male and female slaves. The contributions of slaves to the profit of slave owners depend upon their productivity and effort, i.e., their output. The different roles of male and female slaves are represented by separate production functions. Males are viewed as an input in the production of agricultural goods; females are seen as an input in the production of both agricultural goods and new slaves. Conrad and Meyer say:

. . . we shall define slavery in terms of two production functions. One function relates inputs of Negro slaves (and the materials required to maintain the slaves) to the production of the southern staple crops, particularly cotton. The second function describes the production of the intermediate good, slave labor—slave breeding, to use an emotionally charged term which has affected, even determined, most of the historical conclusions about this problem.

Traditional procedures of historical estimation, used within the context of the two production functions, yield the following conclusions. Depending primarily upon the going market price for cotton and the quality of the land under cultivation, the rate of return on a male slave ranged between 2.2 and 5.4 per cent on the poorest land to between 10 and 13 per cent on the best land. On the average, owners of male slaves earned about 6 per cent on their investment. Alternative investment opportunities, such as railroad and corporate securities, also paid an average rate of return of 6 per cent. Thus an investment in male slaves was as good as its alternatives.

Using similar though more encompassing data and estimation techniques within the context of the production function for female slaves, Conrad and Meyer found the average rate of return on an investment in a childbearing female slave to be between 7 and 8 per cent on lands of poor to medium quality. In this case, an investment in a male slave returned at a rate between 4 and 5 per cent. Thus, by employing slaves to produce both staples and salable slaves, an investor in the upper South could obtain a rate of return equal to that from alternative investment opportunities. A similar investment in the better lands of Mississippi, Alabama, and South Carolina produced a rate of return greater than that of alternative opportunities. Conrad and Meyer conclude: "In sum, it seems doubtful that the South was forced by bad statesmanship into an unnecessary war to protect a system that must soon have disappeared because it was economically unsound. This is a romantic hypothesis, which will not stand against the facts."

Conrad and Meyer present their findings as the (average) rate of return actually realized by slave owners during 1830 to 1860, and this is a widely accepted misinterpretation of their analysis. The question actually asked by Conrad and Meyer is, "If investors during 1840 to 1850 believed that a prime slave would continue to be as productive as such slaves had been on average during the previous decade and if they thought that the price of cotton as well as slave maintenance costs would also continue at the average level of the late forties, was the 1846 to 1850 price of a slave justified by business considerations alone?" The Conrad and Meyer analysis answers this question affirmatively for both male and female slaves.

Conrad and Meyer thus began the revolution in economic history, and their methodological manifesto suggested new techniques for analyzing old historical issues. Their study of slavery marks the end of the Phillips tradition vis-à-vis the profitability of slavery; however, it is open to two major critiques. First, by concentrating on the years 1846 to 1850, Conrad and Meyer severely delimit the scope of their conclusion that slavery was a profitable investment. Robert Evans extended their study to cover the period 1830 to 1860 and employed an advanced variant of the economic theory which they used. He showed that the basic conclusions of the Conrad and Meyer study hold for the whole period from 1830 to 1860.

Second, Edward Saraydar argued that Conrad and Meyer obtained their profitability conclusion by overestimating the productivity of slave labor. Clearly, if the productivity of slave labor is overvalued, then any conclusion of profitability is totally suspect. In response to Saraydar's argument, James Foust and Dale Swan and Raymond Battalio and John Kagel found that Conrad and Meyer underestimated, not overestimated, the productivity of slave labor. This finding, of course, reinforces the earlier conclusion of profitability.

The studies of Conrad and Meyer and Evans concentrate on the profitability of slavery as measured by the rate of return on an investment in a slave and do not consider the issues of the viability of and the stagnating effects of the slavery institution. The viability of slavery depends not only on its profitability over a given period but also on the expectations of actual and potential investors about the future condition of the institution. Yasukichi Yasuba extended the earlier studies by proposing that viability be treated as a bipartite concept. In order to be viable: (1) an institution must be profitable (in the usual sense) and (2) the cost of producing slaves must be covered by the price of slaves. Obviously, a process that is not profitable is not viable, and hence the first condition. But profitability (in the short run) does not guarantee viability. Thus Yasuba also requires that the source of slaves, which, due to the Congressional ban on importation of slaves, was the breeding component of the institution itself, also be profitable. Yasuba's empirical analysis yields the conclusion that the breeding of slaves was a profitable enterprise, which re-enforces the findings of Conrad and Meyer and Evans. Those slaveholders who bred their own mature slaves stood to benefit from the profitability of breeding since they paid to themselves, as opposed to someone else, the economic rent accruing to breeding. The research of Conrad and Meyer, Evans, and Yasuba shows that slavery was both profitable and viable on the eve of the Civil War, i.e., that slavery was *not* moribund in 1860.

The remaining issue is the role of slavery in stagnating the Southern economy. This issue was attacked in the 1971 paper by Fogel and Engerman, in which they note that the stagnation issue has two facets: "The first is that slavery caused the Southern economy to stagnate. The second is that slavery retarded the growth of the Southern economy . . . the available evidence contradicts the proposition that the antebellum economy was stagnant. Unfortunately the evidence needed to test the proposition that slavery retarded the economic growth of the South has not yet been compiled." We will not treat the Fogel and Engerman analysis in any detail here, since it reappears, in an extended and completed form, in the larger study *Time on the Cross.*

The economics of slavery has always centered on a financial view of the world. Phillips invoked the wisdom of his period and, on the basis of a price-earnings ratio, concluded that slavery was unprofitable, unviable, and generally moribund. Other historians have attacked Phillips' accounting and computation techniques, but none of them were able to displace this analysis from its position of dominance except Conrad and Meyer. They invoked explanatory economic theory (the theory of capital) where their predecessors had employed *ad hoc*, nonexplanatory accounting methods. Conrad and Meyer thus wrote the first economic history of slavery, although it was concerned only with profitability. They employed a "new" methodology—new in that it had not been used overtly in the past—based upon the traditional techniques of statistical inference and scientific explanation. The result of their analysis was to displace the findings of Phillips and his followers and to prove that the new methodological techniques were both practicable and effective.

Further applications of the new methodology by Evans, Yasuba, and Fogel and Engerman extended the view of the antebellum South and completed the overthrow of the Phillips tradition. What remained lacking was a coherent, unified analysis of American slavery in the style of the new economic history. That was provided by Fogel and Engerman's *Time on the Cross*, the capstone to contemporary slavery scholarship.

TIME ON THE CROSS:
THE END OF SLAVERY SCHOLARSHIP?

"*Time on the Cross* brings to a close an historiographic cycle that began with the publication of Ulrich Bonnell Phillips' *American Negro Slavery* (1918)," according to a major critical review of *Time on the Cross*. As noted earlier, Phillips and his followers employed accounting theory together with historical data to generate the traditional view of American Negro slavery. Conrad and Meyer overthrew the traditional view on the issue of profitability by using economic theory together with standard sources of data. The revolutionary aspect of the Conrad and Meyer study is the use of explanatory economic theory in place of nonexplanatory accounting theory. Economic theory is capable (in principle) of explaining past and present and of predicting future phenomena; accounting theory can only provide a systematic description of past or present events. Economic theory is dynamic and provides a moving picture of past events whereas accounting theory merely yields a snapshot. A similar distinc-

tion can be drawn in biology between the dynamic explanatory theory of genetic evolution and the static description provided in Genesis.

Fogel and Engerman's *Time on the Cross* extends the historiographic tradition begun by Conrad and Meyer in two ways. First, it employs fairly sophisticated economic theory where Conrad and Meyer use simple capital theory. Second, the analysis in *Time on the Cross* consumes a vast amount of economic data gathered directly from traditional sources and indirectly from nontraditional sources and by indirect measurement. Both facets of this bipartite expansion of Conrad and Meyer's original framework are revolutionary and, in some respects, rather dubious.

It is not our intent here to examine in detail the techniques imployed by Fogel and Engerman. The analysis is an expansion of that used by Conrad and Meyer, differing mainly in scale and scope; its revolutionary aspect is its magnitude, not its methodological structure. A major difference in the two studies lies in the intended audiences. The Conrad and Meyer analysis was written for professional historians, whereas *Time on the Cross* was prepared for a popular audience. The former is therefore unambiguous reading for a historian but unintelligible to the general reader. On the other hand, *Time on the Cross* (Vol. I) is free of technical details, but still is not thereby comprehensible to the general reader. Volume II is proffered as the storehouse of technical detail. Thus, Volumes I and II ought to be intelligible to professional historians. A sizable critical literature has developed which suggests that much of both volumes is simply unintelligible, and that what is intelligible is incorrect or misleading. The major elements of the critical literature are listed and briefly discussed in the References at the end of this chapter. In the first major critical and interpretive review of the book, Paul David and Peter Temin note that:

The broad argument [of Time on the Cross] *has been well projected to reach the general public, but the specific details of the author's historical research are presented in a way that precludes comprehension by that readership. Indeed, much of the underlying technical economic and statistical methodology has been made so unnecessarily difficult to follow that without further elucidation it will remain inaccessible to all but a tiny number of the book's readers.*

David and Temin argue that *Time on the Cross* proffers two "arrestingly bold and essentially novel propositions." First, the consumption levels of slaves compared favorably with those of free Southern agricultural workers and approached those of Northern industrial workers. Second, plantation slavery as a system constituted a more efficient means of production than the standard Northern family farm. These conclusions provide a complete overthrow of the traditional view of plantation slavery as a system of production and of the Sambo image of the individual slave, which was originally advanced by Phillips. Fogel and Engerman thereby place themselves in an unusual position. While they abhor slavery, their desire for a detached objective economic analysis leads them to view plantation slavery, "moral considerations aside, [as] a comparatively benign institutional arrangement worthy of a progressive America." David and Temin continue:

The paradox of Time on the Cross *is that its laudable announced aim of rectifying a historiographic injustice and restoring to American Negroes today a source of justifiable pride in their cultural heritage has led the authors to the excess of an utterly sanguine reappraisal of the peculiar institution. The commercial success of capitalistic slavery somehow emerges as the most fitting subject for modern black pride. Few readers will miss the irony that this book, whose passionate title is meant to convey the depth of the authors' moral condemnation of slavery, in substance actually transcends even U. B. Phillips' rehabilitative intentions.*

David and Temin provide a three-part analysis of *Time on the Cross.* They consider, in turn, the methods and the evidence used to adduce Fogel and Engerman's two arrestingly bold and essentially novel conclusions, and they critique the general economic framework that overlays the analysis in *Time on the Cross.* After detailed discussions, David and Temin conclude the following with respect to Fogel and Engerman's assertion concerning the high consumption levels of slaves:

All quantitative studies are subject to error in some degree. But the description of the comparative material conditions of American Negro slavery which emerges from Time on the Cross *contains a preponderance of errors that run in one direction, imparting an upward bias of undetermined magnitude. In the instance of the rate of exploitation or expropriation, the distortion has been seen to be so large as to negate the usefulness of Fogel and Engerman's published "findings."*

In regard to Fogel and Engerman's second novel assertion concerning the efficiency of plantation slavery as a means of production, David and Temin remark:

The conclusion seems inescapable: Fogel and Engerman's factor productivity measures at best can speak to the issue of the comparative "revenue-generating efficiency" of the southern agricultural system, not the comparison between the technical or "standard physical task" efficiency of agriculture using slaves and free family farming. Furthermore, as has been seen from the preceding discussion of the methods used to measure the land and labor inputs, their "findings" lean heavily toward exaggerating even the relative revenue-*efficiency of southern agriculture. Their inferences about the relative personal efficiency of slave workers, correspondingly are overdrawn.*

Thus the major conclusions of *Time on the Cross* are without merit; they are unwarranted and unacceptable as (scientifically) uncontrovertible "findings." The methods and evidence gathered in support of the two major assertions are thus shown to be misapplied, but they are misapplied in the wrong context. There is a double error. "No greater degree of analytical rigor or meticulousness of scholarship [on the part of Fogel and Engerman] could really have redeemed the claim to have arrived at an ethically neutral economic appraisal of the 'performance' of a social institution, let alone the institu-

tion of chattel slavery. For the ethical and behavioral premises upon which modern economic welfare analysis rests are immediately inconsonant with the degree of personal involition which remains the defining attribute of the institution in question." It is the whole economic framework that is incorrect; technical and methodological mistakes made therein are unimportant. Thus we will not consider the detailed analysis that produced David and Temin's conclusions, but will accept them without comment and move on to their review of the economic framework employed in *Time on the Cross.*

Fogel and Engerman employ traditional welfare, or exchange, theory together with existent market data to arrive at their conclusions. However, David and Temin note:

Modern Welfare economics is grounded on the supposition that all market and non-market transactions of interest between individual actors are voluntary. Involuntary transactions, in which goods are wrested from unwilling "sellers" or forced upon unwilling "buyers," amount to theft and extortion, respectively. Such a theory is not helpful for deriving any precise statements about the welfare consequences of changes which entail the introduction or further extension of involuntary transactions of the sort essential to slavery.

The economic theory employed by Fogel and Engerman is therefore inapplicable, for the presuppositions of that theory clash with the defining characteristics of slavery—involuntary servitude. David and Temin conclude their review as follows:

Economic theory is thus well set up to guide us in making coherent statements about the welfare efficiency of slavery from the standpoint of everyone but the slaves. If this were what Time on the Cross *had set out to do, it would be both a less arresting and a less misleading book.*

Time on the Cross is arresting but also misleading. How could the authors have been less misleading? The answer to this question contains the greatest irony surrounding their research effort. Fogel and Engerman encounter the following pitfalls in arriving at their conclusions:

The authors consider the diet of slaves as given and assess its caloric worth without asking whether blacks under freedom would have chosen to work hard enough to require so much food energy, or whether the intake allowed them was adequate for their actual energy needs. The authors do not inquire how poor a free man—say, a freed black in the Reconstruction period—might have to have been before he chose to obtain such a level of food energy in the carbohydrate-intensive way the slaves were compelled to obtain theirs. Now do the authors ask how impoverished a free family would have to have been in the nineteenth century before the husband, wife and children 'chose' to toil the number of hours expected of slave families.

The answers to these questions can be adduced only via counterfactual arguments, which would posit a hypothetical (and factually false) economy wherein all slaves were free and made their own decisions vis-à-vis working hours, food intake, etc.

The irony of *Time on the Cross* lies in the absence of the requisite counterfactual argument. Recall that Conrad and Meyer, in beginning contemporary slavery scholarship, employed a counterfactual argument, and that Fogel is the master practitioner of counterfactual analysis. Counterfactual methodology is both a mainstay in the area under investigation and the tool kit of the investigators. It is clear that the foregoing questions should be considered, but can they be answered?

The response to this last query is negative, and therein lies the second facet of the newfound irony. The answers to the questions posed by David and Temin can be adduced only from a counterfactual argument employing both the economic theory advanced by Fogel and Engerman and a hypothetical description of the Southern ante-bellum economy wherein all slaves are free men and are capable of making their own economic decisions. However, that would not be an analysis of American slavery but an indirect evaluation of black economic agents. Thus to save their study of plantation slavery, Fogel and Engerman must introduce a hypothetical free-agent economy which is of no immediate interest to the object of study. Similar to the rationale of destroying a village to save it, a process quite popular in the recent past, Fogel and Engerman can live in the village only by leaving it.

Fogel and Engerman extended the analysis of Conrad and Meyer beyond its capacity for expansion. Recall David and Temin's remark that "economic theory is thus well set up to guide us in making coherent statements about the welfare efficiency of slavery from the standpoint of everyone but the slaves." The data advanced by Conrad and Meyer reflect market transactions wherein the only agents are slave breeders, sellers, buyers, and users. The Conrad and Meyer analysis gives no role to the slaves as economic decision makers. Fogel and Engerman attempt to use the same kind of data to support their conclusions about slaves as agents, i.e., producers and consumers, and are caught in the trap of providing an analysis of plantation slavery that can be made complete only by studying a nonslavery system. The desired analysis is not impossible; it is, however, implausible. David and Temin make the following point in this regard:

When people are enslaved, welfare is necessarily transferred to their masters, and there is no ethically neutral [i.e., purely objective] way to compare the welfare efficiency of the resulting institution with the set of outcomes characterizing an alternative institution under which that particular interpersonal welfare transfer need not take place [i.e., a nonslave ante-bellum southern economy]. Any such comparison would require weighing the slaves' losses against the masters' gains.

We are thus left with the following conclusions. Contemporary slavery scholarship began in 1958 with the Conrad and Meyer study, which established that plantation slavery was not moribund, but was indeed profitable, and ends with *Time on the Cross*. However, while the Fogel and Engerman study marks the end of the cliometric analysis of slavery, it does not constitute a capstone of any kind. The arrestingly novel results adduced in the study do not enjoy the same epistemological status as Conrad and Meyer's conclusions or their immediate extensions. Recall that the revolution in economic history began not with Conrad and Meyer's slavery study but with their essay on the historiographic method. Fogel and Engerman have succeeded in establishing the limits of the new method by exceeding them.

AFTERWORD

We have considered the major elements of the historiography of American Negro slavery and presented some evaluation of their contributions and epistemological status. Clearly, slavery was profitable (Conrad and Meyer) and viable (Yasuba). Profitability and viability are, of course, properties of the slavery institution, and therefore easily analyzed. What of the effects on the individual slave, his health, personality, and general welfare? Conclusions reached via historical research pertaining to the individual slave are neither as clear nor of the same quality as those pertaining to the institution of slavery. The lack of clarity and (epistemological) quality are not due to faulty economic historiography but rather to the fundamental impossibility of reaching those conclusions via an analysis based upon contemporary economic theory. That theory, in order to be applicable to an analysis of the individual slave, must put the slave in the position of the decision maker. However, the essence of slavery is the forced, though legal, forfeiture of the individual's right to decide for himself all but the trivial issues of daily existence. Thus, as David and Temin correctly note, an economic-historical analysis of the slave is beyond the scope of contemporary analytical tools.

Do we necessarily encounter the same impasse if we investigate slavery in other societies? Although different from the antebellum Southern society, the social-economic structure of postrevolutionary Russia also supported a vast system of slavery. However, the historiography of slavery in Soviet Russia reveals very little, since practically no historiography exists. A standard reference is *Forced Labor in Soviet Russia*, by D. J. Dallin and B. I. Nicolaevsky, in which the authors note that the Soviet system of forced labor was very profitable to the NKVD—the Commissariat for Internal Affairs (see their footnote 3, p. 14, for a discussion of this commission and its evolution). Since the NKVD made no investment in capital, human or machine, the system of forced labor provided a large return on a small outlay. This type of profitability is naïve, however, because the Soviets did not account for the alternative uses of the laborers and their services. (A free or open labor market allocates labor services in accordance with the most efficient employment of a worker.) Clearly, forced labor was not profitable to individual investors, as was American slavery, for there were no individual investors in the Soviet Union.

To compensate for the lack of motivation inherent in an individual performing a task he did not choose to perform, any system of slavery must provide a source of motivation.

In the case of American Negro slavery, the popular view of abolitionists held that fear of beatings and deprivation at the hands of merciless overseers provided the necessary source of motivation. Fogel and Engerman, at the other extreme, contend that economic sources of motivation were employed. (Recall their finding that only 10 per cent of a slave's output was expropriated.) The actual mechanism of motivation was most likely mixed but was probably based more on economic considerations than on fear. This last conclusion is based upon the established fact that slave owners placed a high value on their human property.

Motivation in the Soviet forced labor system was very simple. Since laborers were viewed as virtually free goods, there was no need to resort to economic means of motivation. Dallin and Nicolaevsky note that:

Marx had naïvely assumed that a slave must receive the subsistence minimum of rations below which neither life nor work is possible. Now it was found that a differential could be introduced in food rations in slave labor camps and that the smallest ration, i.e., that alloted to "slackers" and "shirkers" and in general to inefficient laborers, might well fall below the minimum required for subsistence. Moreover, this deliberate undernourishment would of itself compel all in the labor camps to do their utmost for the national economy. Differentials in wages had been introduced by the government in all fields of economy. A similar system, with appropriate modifications, must be introduced in the labor camps. (pp. 100–101)

Motivation sprang from deprivation, i.e., from a daily food allotment that was *below* the minimum subsistence level. The motivation mechanism was based on the maxim, "He who does not toil does not eat." In the biblical sense, it represents a mere truism: "He who but sits on his ass will die on his ass." The Soviet system employs a somewhat different translation: "He who does not toil enough does not eat enough." As in all slavery systems, the decision as to what constitutes "enough" rests not with the slave but with his overseer.

The central view of contemporary writing on Soviet forced labor, notably that of Solzhenitsyn, reveals a barbaric and inhuman collective overseer. The major issues of contemporary writing on Soviet forced labor are naturally concerned with the source of this barbarity. The standard view, the analogue of the Plantation Legend (circa 1920–50), is presented in Khrushchev's report to the Twentieth Party Congress (February, 1956). Therein the thesis is argued that the extreme abuses of human life and legal rule practiced under Stalin were due entirely to the dictator's personality. The inhuman madness of the system was merely a reflection of Stalin's own madness. The central point of Solzhenitsyn's *The Gulag Archipelago* is the rejection of this view. He traces the origin of the Soviet system of forced labor and enslavement to Lenin in December, 1917, and January, 1918. Solzhenitsyn concludes that the resulting system of forced labor camps throughout Russia and her satellites (here see R. K. Carlton, *Forced Labor in the "Peoples Democracies"*) is due not at all to Stalin's madness but is intrinsic in the Marxist-Leninist *Weltanschauung*. David J. Dallin and Boris I. Nicolaevsky agree with this view and note that "The system is an *organic* element, a normal component, of the social structure." In Solzhenitsyn's opinion, slavery in Soviet Russia could never be abolished except by virtually uprooting the Socialist system and its view of the world.

Thus if we accept Solzhenitsyn's analysis as a historical analysis, which it is only in part, we find that slavery in the Soviet system is more than an institution based upon economic rationality. Any historiography of Soviet slavery, therefore, would have to be based upon a theory of politico-economical behavior, but no such theory exists which has the scope and coherence of standard economic theory. Furthermore, if Solzhenitsyn's (wider) view is valid, i.e., that secrecy is required for the Soviet state to function, then, although data and information of relevance for testing his thesis may exist, they will never be employed for an objective analysis of the system. We are left to conclude that the future historiography of Soviet slavery will be primarily literary, like Solzhenitsyn's *Gulag*, whose epistemological status we cannot appraise.

REFERENCES

The following citations are listed in chronological order to provide the reader with a visual presentation of the evolution of slavery literature together with the attendant methodology papers. The bibliography is partially annotated.

Ulrich B. Phillips. 'The Economic Cost of Slaveholding in the Cotton Belt," *Political Science Quarterly*, Vol. 20, June, 1905, pp. 257–75.

———. *American Negro Slavery*, D. Appleton and Co., N.Y., 1918. (Second edition published by Louisiana State University Press, Baton Rouge, 1966, with a foreword by E. Genovese).

W. E. B. DuBois. Review of U. B. Phillips' *American Negro Slavery, American Political Science Review*, Vol. 12, November, 1918, pp. 722–26. This is a very critical and highly accurate evaluation. DuBois announces that the book "is readable but curiously incomplete and unfortunately biased." He then goes on to prove his contention by quoting directly from Phillips. This is an excellent review.

Charles W. Ramsdell. "The Natural Limits of Slavery Expansion," *The Mississippi Valley Historical Review*, Vol. 16, September, 1929, pp. 151–71.

Robert R. Russel. "The General Effects of Slavery Upon Southern

Economic Progress," *The Journal of Southern History*, Vol. 4, February, 1938, pp. 34–54.

Thomas P. Govan. "Was Plantation Slavery Profitable?" *Journal of Southern History*, Vol. 8, November, 1942, pp. 513–35.

Richard Hofstadter. "U. B. Phillips and the Plantation Legend," *Journal of Negro History*, Vol. 29, April, 1944, pp. 109–24.

Oskar Morgenstern. *On the Accuracy of Economic Observations*, Princeton University Press, 1950.

Kenneth Stampp. *The Peculiar Institution: Slavery in the Ante-Bellum South*, Alfred A. Knopf, N.Y., 1956. This is the major traditional analysis of American slavery. Fogel and Engerman attempt to overthrow Stampp's findings, but they fail.

Alfred H. Conrad and John R. Meyer. "Economic Theory, Statistical Inference, and Economic History," *The Journal of Economic History*, Vol. 17, December, 1957, pp. 509–44.

Simon Kuznets. "Summary of Discussion and Postscript," a review of the above paper, *The Journal of Economic History*, Vol. 17, December, 1957, pp. 545–53.

Lewis C. Gray. *The History of Agriculture in the Southern United States to 1860*, Peter Smith, Inc., Gloucester, Massachusetts, 1958.

Alfred H. Conrad and John R. Meyer. "The Economics of Slavery in the Ante-Bellum South," *Journal of Political Economy*, Vol. 66, April, 1958, pp. 95–130.

Douglas Dowd. "Comment" on the above paper, *The Journal of Political Economy*, Vol. 66, October, 1958, pp. 440–42.

Alfred H. Conrad and John R. Meyer. "Reply" to Dowd, *The Journal of Political Economy*, Vol. 66, October, 1958, pp. 442–43.

Henry A. Finch. "An Explication of Counterfactuals by Probability Theory," *Philosophy and Phenomenonological Research*, Vol. 18, 1958, pp. 368–78.

Stanley M. Elkins. *Slavery: A Problem in American Institutional and Intellectual Life*, University of Chicago Press, 1959.

Lance Davis, J. R. T. Hughes, and Stanley Reiter. "Aspects of Quantitative Research in Economic History," *The Journal of Economic History*, Vol. 20, December, 1960, pp. 539–47. This is one of the earliest methodology papers. It reviews the results of cliometric research conducted at Purdue University from 1957–60 and introduces the term "cliometrics."

Yasukichi Yasuba. "The Profitability and Viability of Plantation Slavery in the United States," *The Economic Studies Quarterly*, Vol. 12, September, 1961, pp. 60–67.

Richard A. Easterlin. "Regional Income Trends," in Seymour Harris, ed., *American Economic History*, McGraw-Hill, N.Y., 1961, pp. 525–47. This is a major source of data.

Douglas C. North. *The Economic Growth of the United States: 1790–1860*, Prentice Hall, Englewood Cliffs, New Jersey, 1961.

Robert Evans, Jr. "The Economics of American Negro Slavery," in *Aspects of Labor Economics* (NBER), Princeton University Press, 1962, pp. 185–243.

Douglas C. North. "Quantitative Research in American Economic History," *The American Economic Review*, Vol. 53, March, 1963, pp. 128–30.

Robert W. Fogel. "Discussion," *The American Economic Review*, Vol. 54, May, 1964, pp. 337–89. Herein Conrad and Meyer's "The Economics of Slavery . . . ." is noted as the "first classic of the new economic history" (p. 379). This is also the first of many methodological reviews of the new history.

———. *Railroads and American Economic Growth*, Johns Hopkins Press, Baltimore, 1964. This is the first book-length classic of the new economic history. It marks Fogel as the master practitioner of counterfactual methodology.

Edward Saraydar. "A Note on the Profitability of Ante-Bellum Slavery," *Southern Economic Journal*, Vol. 30, April, 1964, pp. 325–32.

Richard Sutch. "The Profitability of Ante-Bellum Slavery—Revisited," *Southern Economic Journal*, Vol. 31, April, 1965, pp. 365–77, with a reply by Saraydar, pp. 377–83.

Robert W. Fogel. "The Reunification of Economic History with Economic Theory," *American Economic Review*, Vol. 55, May, 1965, pp. 92–98.

Carl G. Hempel. *Aspects of Scientific Explanation*, The Free Press, N.Y., 1965. This is a collection of major papers by Hempel and includes the foundational paper "Studies in the Logic of Explanation," 1948, by Hempel and Oppenheim.

Guy S. Callender. *Economic History of the United States*, A. M. Kelly, N.Y., 1965.

Robert L. Basmann. "The Role of the Economic Historian in Predictive Testing of Proffered 'Economic Laws,'" *Explorations in Entrepreneurial History* (Second Series), Vol. 2, Spring/Summer, 1965, pp. 159–86. This is a classic paper which provides a role for the economic historian in econometrics.

J. R. T. Hughes. "A Note in Defense of Clio," *Explorations in Entrepreneurial History* (Second Series), Vol. 2, Winter, 1965, p. 154. Hughes tells us that "cliometrics" came from "the fevered imagination of my colleague, S. Reiter . . . ."

Fritz Redlich. "'New' and Traditional Approaches to Economic History and Their Interdependence," *The Journal of Economic History*, Vol. 25, December, 1965, pp. 480–95. Redlich coins "figment" in describing counterfactual arguments. He also divides historians into the good guys and the bad guys (quasi-historians). Fogel and Conrad and Meyer are bad guys.

Eugene D. Genovese. *The Political Economy of Slavery*, Pantheon Books, N.Y., 1965. This is an interesting work written by a Marxist.

George G. S. Murphy. "The 'New' History," *Explorations in Entrepreneurial History* (Second Series), Vol. 2, Winter, 1965, pp. 132–46. This is the most philosophical of the early methodology papers.

Robert W. Fogel. "The New Economic History: Its Findings and Methods," *The Economic History Review*, Vol. 19, December, 1966, pp. 642–56. A general review of conclusions and methodology; contains a short response to Redlich.

Lance Davis. "The New Economic History: Professor Fogel and the New Economic History," *The Economic History Review*, Vol. 19, December, 1966, pp. 657–63. A continuation of the previous reference. The article focuses on the contributions of Fogel and Davis announces that "Professor Fogel is the best" (of the new economic historians).

Robert E. Gallman. "Gross National Product in the United States, 1834–1909," *Output, Employment and Productivity in the United States After 1800*, Columbia University Press, N.Y., 1966, pp. 3–76. This is a major source of data.

Louis M. Hacker. "The New Revolution in Economic History: A Review Article Based on *Railroads and Economic Growth: Essays in Econometric History*, by Robert William Fogel," *Explorations in Entrepreneurial History* (Second Series), Vol. 3, 1966, pp. 159–75. This is a very negative review of both Fogel, 1964, and Conrad and Meyer, 1958.

Robert W. Fogel. "The Specification Problem in Economic History," *The Journal of Economic History*, Vol. 27, September, 1967, pp. 283–308. This is the first attempt by a historian to phrase and resolve the problems of historical prediction and indirect measurement. Recall that Morgenstern phrased the issue in 1950.

Stanley L. Engerman. "The Effects of Slavery Upon the Southern Economy: A Review of the Recent Debate," *Explorations in*

Entrepreneurial History (Second Series), Vol. 4, 1967, pp. 71–97. This is an excellent review, which provides the foundation for Fogel and Engerman, 1970, 1974.

Alfred H. Conrad. "Econometrics and Southern History," *Explorations in Entrepreneurial History* (Second Series), Vol. 6, Fall, 1968, pp. 34–53. Conrad addresses the question "How do we test, or warrant, a counterfactual proposition?" His answer is incomplete and misleading. This is, however, the first attempt to analyze, not just describe, counterfactual methodology.

Robert W. Fogel. "Comment," *Explorations in Entrepreneurial History* (Second Series), Vol. 6, Fall, 1968, pp. 54–58. This as well as the following two papers are short comments on the preceding paper.

Stuart Briechey. "Comment," *Explorations in Entrepreneurial History* (Second Series), Vol. 6, Fall, 1968, pp. 59–65.

Alfred D. Chandler, Jr. "Comment," *Explorations in Entrepreneurial History* (Second Series), Vol. 6, Fall, 1968, pp. 66–74.

Lance Davis. "'And It Will Never Be Literature': The New Economic History: A Critique," *Explorations in Entrepreneurial History* (Second Series), Vol. 6, Fall, 1968, pp. 75–92. An overview of the new history. We are informed that J. R. T. Hughes coined "the new economic history."

Fritz Redlfch. "Potentialities and Pitfalls in Economic History," *Explorations in Entrepreneurial History* (Second Series), Vol. 6, Fall, 1968, pp. 93–108. A critical review of the new and the old histories. This paper is somewhat more sympathetic to the new history than Redlich, 1965, though not by much.

Raymond Dacey. "Aspects of the Counterfactual Controversy," (unpublished). Presented at the Ninth Purdue Conference on Quantitative Economic History, Fall, 1969. This is a somewhat formal revision of the analysis attempted by Conrad, 1968. The logic of explanation is invoked to resolve the issue; the attempt, like Conrad's, fails.

Maurice Lévy-Leboyer. "La 'New Economic History,'" *Annales* (Economics Sociétés Civilisations), 1969, pp. 1035–69. This paper, in French, presents an overview of the new history. It is interesting for what it deems important and unimportant. It also includes the only reference I know to Dacey, 1969, and includes an extensive bibliography.

George G. S. Murphy. "On Counterfactual Propositions," *History and Theory*, Beiheft 9, 1969, pp. 14–38. This paper is a classic of sorts. It attempts a symbolic and logical analysis of counterfactual propositions and is sufficiently confused and ambiguous to be accepted by many economic historians as supporting their point of view and thereby resolving the issue. Murphy, however, confuses counterfactual propositions, which are not themselves interesting to the historian, with counterfactual arguments, which are the crux of the issue.

J. D. Gould. "Hypothetical History," *The Economic History Review*, Vol. 22, August, 1969, pp. 195–207. This paper enlists the writings of philosophers of science and history. Gould correctly perceives counterfactual arguments, not propositions, to be the point of issue. However, he does not try to resolve the issue raised by Conrad, 1968; he merely tells us what others had to say.

Robert W. Fogel. "Historiography and Retrospective Econometrics," *History and Theory*, Vol. 9, 1970, pp. 245–59. This is an overview article, followed by questions and comments from other historians and Fogel replies thereto: pp. 260–64, same reference.

Robert W. Fogel and Stanley L. Engerman. "The Economics of Slavery," Essay No. 24 in their book *The Reinterpretation of American Economic History*, Harper and Row, N.Y., 1971. This is both a review of the slavery literature, based upon Engerman, 1967, and a preview of *Time on the Cross*. The book is an excellent collection of papers from the new economic history, together with interesting and informative commentary.

James D. Foust and Dale E. Swan. "Productivity of Ante-Bellum Slave Labor: A Micro Approach," *Agricultural History*, Vol. 44, January 1970, pp. 39–62.

Douglas C. North. "Beyond the New Economic History," *The Journal of Economic History*, Vol. 34, March, 1974, pp. 1–7. This is the presidential address presented to the *Economic History Association*. It is a review of the contributions and limitations of the new economic history. The major limitation is the relevance on neoclassical economic theory.

Robert W. Fogel and Stanley L. Engerman. *Time on the Cross;* Vol. I, *The Economics of American Negro Slavery*, Vol. II, *Evidence and Methods—A Supplement*, both by Little, Brown and Co., Boston, 1974.

Paul A. David and Peter Temin. "Slavery: The Progressive Institution?," *The Journal of Economic History*, Vol. 36, September, 1974, pp. 739–83. This is the major critical and evaluatory essay review of *Time on the Cross*.

Raymond Dacey. "The Role of Economic Theory in Supporting Counterfactual Arguments," *Philosophy and Phenomenological Research*, Vol. 35, March, 1975, pp. 402–410. This is, of course, the final analysis of counterfactual analysis in economic history. It provides an answer to the question originally raised by Conrad, 1968.

———. "The Effects of Theory and Data in Economic Prediction," *Kyklos*, Vol. 28, 1975, pp. 25–28. This paper provides a solution to the problem of economic prediction as posed by Morgenstern.

Herbert G. Gutman. *Slavery and the Numbers Game: A Critique of "Time on the Cross,"* University of Illinois Press, Urbana, 1975. This material first appeared as an issue of the *Journal of Negro History* (Winter, 1974). It mounts a successful attack on the nontechnical and nontheoretical facets of the Fogel and Engerman study.

Gary Walton (editor). "A Symposium on 'Time on the Cross'", *Explorations in Economic History*, Vol. 12, Fall, 1975. This is a collection of the papers presented at what has become known as the Rochester conference, a meeting of professional historians devoted solely to a review of *Time on the Cross*. The collection includes the major paper by Richard Sutch, wherein he concludes that *"Time on the Cross* is a failure." Sutch's criticism is thorough and devastating. The negative conclusions reached in the body of this chapter are very mild in comparison.

Paul David, H. Gutman, Richard Stuch, Peter Temin, and Gavin Wright. *Reckoning with Slavery: Critical Essays in the Quantitative History of American Negro Slavery*, Oxford University Press, forthcoming. This collection organizes, interrelates and extends the previously published criticisms of the authors. One of the two papers by David and Temin is a revision of their 1974 essay "Slavery: The Progressive Institution?"

Thomas L. Haskell. "The True and Tragical History of 'Time on the Cross,'" *The New York Review of Books*, Vol. 22, No. 15, October 2, 1975, pp. 33–39. This is a review of the three preceeding collections. Also see Haskell's review of *Time on the Cross*.

Reviews of *American Negro Slavery*

The following is a partially annotated listing of reviews of U. B. Phillips' *American Negro Slavery*.

W. E. DuBois. "Review," *American Political Science Review*, Vol. 12, November, 1918, pp. 722–26. This is the only major critical review. See the comments on this review in the main bibliography.

M. J. Lorente. "Review," *Public*, Vol. 22, February 8, 1919, p. 138.

Mary W. Ovington. "Review," *The Survey*, Vol. 40, September 28, 1918, p. 718. This review is very favorable and includes the comment ". . . this might be the last work on the subject."

C. P. Patterson. "Review," *Political Science Quarterly*, Vol. 33, September, 1918, pp. 454–56.

Reviews of *Time on the Cross*

The following is a partially annotated listing of reviews of Fogel and Engerman's *Time on the Cross*.

John W. Blassingame. "The Mathematics of Slavery," *Atlantic*, Vol. 234, August, 1974, pp. 78–82. This is a highly critical review. Blassingame is the author of *The Slave Community*, Oxford University Press, N.Y., 1972, which analyzes slavery and plantation life from the perspective of the slave. Both the review and the book are recommended.

Walter Clemmons. "A New Look at Slavery," *Newsweek*, Vol. 83, May 6, 1974, pp. 77–78. This is an extremely favorable review. Clemons begins, "*Time on the Cross* is dynamite. This study of the ways and means of American slavery overturns popular beliefs and traditional interpretations so drastically that 're-visionist' is a feeble description of its thrust." He concludes "Together the volumes represent a rare instance of seminal work nonspecialists can read with the most intense pleasure and interest."

Paul A. David and Peter Temin. "Slavery: The Progressive Institution?" *The Journal of Economic History*, Vol. 34, September, 1974, pp. 739–83. This is the major review and evaluation of the book.

Constance Holden. "Cliometrics: Book on Slavery Stirs up a Scholarly Storm," *Science*, Vol. 186, December 13, 1974, pp. 1004–1007. *Science* is the journal of the American Association for the Advancement of Science (AAAS) and is the major interdisciplinary journal of the physical sciences. Holden's article is as much a news analysis as a review.

Michael Flusche. "Clio and the Computer," *America* (published by the Jesuits of America and Canada), Vol. 131, September 7, 1974, pp. 95–96.

Timothy Foote. "Massa's in de Cold, Cold Computer," *Time*, June 17, 1974, pp. 98–100. This is representative "newsweekly" review.

Nathan Glazer. "A New View of Slavery," *Commentary* (published by the American Jewish Committee), Vol. 58, August, 1974, pp. 68–72. This is a very favorable review of *Time on the Cross*. It is the only review that draws extensive connections between the book's conclusions and views of contemporary society. Glazer asks ". . . what are the implications of these findings for our understanding of the position of blacks in the United States, the responsibility of whites for that condition, and the prospects of future relations between the races in the United States?" His review examines answers to these questions.

Thomas L. Haskell. "Were Slaves More Efficient? Some Doubts About *Time on the Cross*," *The New York Review of Books*, September 19, 1974, pp. 38–42. Haskell takes the book to task on the use and misuse of the index of factor productivity.

Nathan I. Huggins. "Soft Slavery," *Commonweal*, Vol. 100, August 23, 1974, pp. 459–61.

William Letwin. "Review," *The Journal of Economic Literature*, Vol. 13, March, 1975, pp. 57–60. This is a critical review directed at professional economists.

Alan J. Lichtman. "A Benign Institution," *The New Republic*, Vol. 171, July 6–13, pp. 22–24. This is a fair and accurate appraisal of the book. Lichtman concludes ". . . the book is seriously flawed, methodologically and conceptually."

Peter Passell. "An Economic Analysis of that Peculiarly Economic Institution," *The New York Times Book Review*, April 28, 1974, p. 4. This is an excessively favorable review. Passell begins, "If a more important book about American history has been published in the last decade I don't know it" he concludes, "Fogel and Engerman have with one stroke turned around a whole field of interpretation and exposed the frailty of history done without science." This is more an advertisement than a review.

Harold D. Woodman. "Uncle Tom Revisited—By Computer," *The Christian Science Monitor*, June 25, 1974, p. F1.

C. Vann Woodward. "The Jolly Institution," *The New York Review of Books*, Vol. 21, May 2, 1974, pp. 3–6. Woodward is an accomplished historian of slavery. See his *The Strange Career of Jim Crow*, Oxford University Press, 1955 (second revised edition, 1966), for a nontechnical analysis of the southern Negro vis-á-vis legislation and civil rights from Reconstruction to 1910. The speeches of Martin Luther King, Jr., during the 1965 Montgomery March invoked Woodward and his views.

The following citations are given in chronological order and constitute a small collection of existent works on forced labor in and under the rule of Soviet Russia. The bibliography is partially annotated.

David J. Dallin and Boris I. Nicolaevsky. *Forced Labor in Soviet Russia*, Yale University Press, 1947. This book documents the resurgence of slavery in Russia under Stalin's rule.

Solomon M. Schwartz. *Labor in the Soviet Union*, Prager, N.Y., 1952. This text considers both free and forced labor in the Soviet Union and documents its findings on the basis of official Russian publications. It thus provides an analysis of the standard (party) analysis.

Richard K. Carlton. *Forced Labor in the "Peoples Democracies,"* Prager, N.Y., 1955. This text was researched and published under the auspices of International League for the Rights of Man, an agency of the United Nations. It contains primary and secondary data on forced labor camps in Soviet Russia, the Eastern European satellite "Peoples' Democracies" (i.e., Hungary, Romania, Czechoslovakia, Bulgaria, Poland and Yugoslavia), and Communist China.

Otto Larsen. *Nightmare of the Innocents*, Philosophical Library, N.Y., 1957. One man's account of the Soviet system of trials and labor camps.

Robert Conquest. *The Great Terror: Stalin's Purge of the Thirties*, MacMillan Co., N.Y., 1968. This is a long (633 page), detailed account of Stalin's purges.

Aleksandr Solzhenitsyn. *The Gulag Archipelago, 1918–1956: An Experiment in Literary Investigation*, translated from the Russian by T. P. Whitney, Harper and Row, N.Y., 1974. This is the first in a three-volume account intended to reveal the truth about the workings of the Soviet state to the Russian people. It includes contributions from 227 individuals as well as the author's first-hand experience. It has been compared to H. B.

Stowe's *Uncle Tom's Cabin*—a hopeless comparison. It is like Phillips' *American Negro Slavery* in that both works employ practically no (economic) theoretical framework. In terms of its place in the historiography of Soviet slavery, it is like Conrad and Meyer's "The Economics of Slavery in the Antebellum South" in that the book attempts to overthrow the major conclusions of Khrushchev's "standard" view. Clearly, Khrushchev's analysis is thereby analogous to Phillips's *Slavery*. This three-part comparison is vastly superior to any scheme which relates *Gulag* to *Uncle Tom's Cabin*.

Reviews of *The Gulag Archipelago*

Robert Conquest. "Evolution of an Exile," *Saturday Review–World*, Vol. 1, pp. 22–30, April 20, 1974. This is a careful and detailed review by an expert on the history of forced labor in Soviet Russia. Conquest argues that Solzhenitsyn continues the work begun by Pasternak in *Sketch for an Autobiography* and is therefore the latter's literary heir.

"Islands of Slavery," *Time*, Vol. 103, pp. 48–49, June 24, 1974. This is a standard newsweekly review. It argues that Solzhenitsyn finds Soviet slavery unprofitable. It is misleading.

Robert Kirsch. "'The Gulag Archipelago,'" Los Angeles Times Syndicate, June 26, 1974. Kirsch pursues the comparison between Solzhenitsyn's *Gulag* and Stowe's *Uncle Tom's Cabin*.

Joseph Alsop. "'Gulag Archipelago' Must Reading," Los Angeles Syndicate, June 26, 1974. Alsop's column is subtitled "Nixon Luggage for Moscow Should Include Book." The article is interesting in that it draws a tangential connection between *Gulag* and Fogel and Engerman's *Time on the Cross*.

Timothy Foote. "Towering Witness to Salvation," *Time,* Vol. 104, pp. 90–94, July 15, 1974. Foote compares *Gulag* with Solzhenitsyn's *Letter to the Soviet Leaders* (Harper and Row, N.Y., 1974) and finds that he "resembles Tolstoy in a number of ways."

George Steiner. "The Forests of the Night," *The New Yorker*, Vol. 50, pp. 78–87, August 5, 1974. Steiner's is easily the best of the reviews. He (correctly) places *Gulag* in both literary and historical perspectives.

Peter Hibblethwaite. "The Slavic Soul's Fourth Dimension," *America*, Vol. 131, September 7, 1974, pp. 87–90.

Catharine Hughes. "The Sentence for Nothing is 10 Years," *America*, Vol. 131, September 7, 1974, pp. 89–90. These two reviews consider Andrei D. Sakharov's *Sakharov Speaks* and Solzhenitsyn's *Letter to the Soviet Leaders* and *The Gulag Archipelago*. The principal difference between the two dissenters is that Sakharov does not find that all the ills of Soviet society are intrinsic in the Marxist-Leninist view of the world; Solzhenitsyn, of course, finds the contrary to be true.

8

ANOMIE AS AN EXPLANATION FOR DEVIANCE: ITS DEVELOPMENT AND IMPLICATION FOR CHANGE

By Richard E. Hilbert

It is now a rather widely accepted fact that the United States of America, the most advanced of the great industrial societies, is beset with enormous problems in the areas of crime and social unrest. In addition to alarmingly high rates of adult criminal behavior and juvenile delinquency, there is the constant threat of riots in our urban centers and challenges to the social order from virtually every minority group within our borders.[1] Less widely accepted, but equally important, is the fact that, in varying degrees, these problems have been with us since the very beginning of America as a nation state. Although the data are not always reliable, it appears that throughout the nineteenth century, the high rate of violence within our borders is unmatched within the stable democracies.[2] The situation with respect to offenses against property and corruption in government throughout the same period is no less appalling. Writing over a hundred years ago, the poet Whitman, generally regarded as an optimist, had this to say about the American scene:

Never was there, perhaps, more hollowness at heart than at present, and here in the United States. Genuine belief seems to have left us. The underlying principles of the States are not believed in (for all this hectic glow, and these melodramatic screamings), nor is humanity itself believ'd in. What penetrating eye does not everywhere see through the mask? The spectacle is appalling. We live in an atmosphere of hypocrisy throughout. The men believe not in the women, nor the women in the men. A scournful superciliousness rules in our literature . . . . The depravity of the business classes of our country is not less than has been supposed, but infinitely greater. The official services of America, national, state, and municipal, in all their branches and departments, except the judiciary, are saturated in corruption, bribery, falsehood, maladministration; and the judiciary is tainted. The great cities reek with respectable as well as non-respectable robbery and scoundrelism . . . (Whitman, 1870)

INTRODUCTION

Taken together, these facts about the history and present status of crime and social unrest in America suggest (to a sociologist, at least) that the source of the problem may very well lie in the organization of American society and, further, that the problematic features of that organization may be among the time-honored traditions of the American way of life.

The present chapter is concerned with social organization and its impact on crime and social unrest. However, it is not our aim to review all (or even everything of significance) that has ever been said on the subject. Rather, it is to expose in some detail one important theoretical perspective relating deviance and social unrest to social organization. For a variety of reasons, not the least of which is the author's preoccupation with social theory, there will be no systematic concern with the results of various empirical tests of the theory, of which it might be noted there are a great many.[3] The emphasis will be on exposing the development of the perspective and its implications for social change. However, it will quickly become evident that even a self-consciously theoretical work must make some reference to empirical data, if only to illustrate the utility of a particular theoretical point.

Anomie as a theory of deviance may be said to have originated with the publication in 1938 of the now famous article by Robert K. Merton entitled "Social Structure and Anomie."[4] Although the term anomie was used as early as the sixteenth century (Merton, 1957, p. 135), it was not used widely until the latter part of the nineteenth century, when it was reintroduced into the literature by Emile Durkheim.[5] Literally, the term translates as "normlessness," but is conceived today as a condition in human society in which certain of its members develop a lack of respect for the goals of the society, or for the norms which prescribe the legitimate means by which those goals may be pursued, or for both. With respect to the meaning of the term, a great deal more will be said later, in the treatment of those persons who have contributed to the development of the theory. For now, it is sufficient to say that the concept has earned a significant place in the frame of reference of the professional sociologist.

The recentness of the development under review may puzzle many readers. It seems to be related to two modes of thought which were characteristic of much social theory prior to the twentieth century. The first was a tendency to see deviance as a product of something basic to man's nature. This is in contrast to the view prevalent today, which ascribes a great deal of causal significance to the organization of the system within which the deviance takes place. According to the earlier view, society played a part, but it was seen as a mechanism by which the nature of man was brought under control. Should deviance break out, according to this view, society might be said to be responsible, in so far as it failed to bring the motivation under control, but the motivation to commit deviant acts was believed to be present at birth or to develop naturally as the actor matures. The mode of thought involved here may well be a variant of the assumption in early Christian thinking that men are born with a propensity to sin. The second was a tendency to think that only evil causes evil; that evil consequences invariably have evil precedents.[6] Given this way of thinking, it was impossible to conclude that a condition defined as evil (deviance) might be the result of one that is defined as good (the American Way of Life).

As will be seen, the theory of anomie runs counter to both these modes of thought: It holds that deviant motivation is system-generated and thus implies (in the case of deviance in America) that a condition defined as evil may be a consequence of one that is defined as good. Moreover, it holds that the features of the system which are responsible cannot easily be altered or cast aside, because they lie at the heart of that system.

It should be evident at this point that this commentary is as much a critique of the American way of life as it is an historical treatment of the development of a body of theory. Moreover, in view of the fact that the ideas involved have come mainly from American sociologists, *it may be said to be a theory about America by Americans.* Its inclusion in the bicentennial collection is therefore particularly appropriate.

The subject matter of this chapter is divided into five parts. The first part is given over to the views of Emile Durkheim on the sources of anomie in modern societies and on certain of its consequences. Next is a rather detailed treatment of the reformulation of Durkheim's original ideas by Robert K. Merton. The third part explores the more significant contributions to the further development of the theory of three authors: Talcott Parsons, Albert K. Cohen, and Richard Cloward (writing with Lloyd Ohlin). Fourth, there are introduced several additional considerations which, in the opinion of this author, contribute to the further development of the theory. Finally, we take up the question of the implications of the theory for social reform, on the assumption that the consequences of anomie, in some cases at least, are sufficiently problematic to justify a consideration of social reform as a way of reducing the rates at which they now occur.

THE CONTRIBUTIONS OF EMILE DURKHEIM

Anomie and the Division of Labor

Durkheim (1964b) introduced the concept of anomie in his first major work, *The Division of Labor in Society,* pub-

lished in 1893. His thesis in that work may be seen as a highly polemical attack on several bodies of thought in the intellectual tradition of his day. One of these was a position, deriving from the work of Comte, which stressed the importance for social order of what Durkheim referred to as a "collective conscience"—a set of specific moral norms and supporting sentiments with respect to which there is a high degree of consensus. Another was a conclusion, associated with the utilitarian individualism of the political economists and English philosophers, concerning the integrating effects in modern societies of individual contracts. An understanding of Durkheim's early contribution to the theory of anomie requires that we examine his attacks on both these bodies of thought.

Durkheim readily agreed that a high degree of consensus on specific moral norms is necessary for social order, so long as the generalization is limited to the simpler societies, i.e., those that are relatively undifferentiated in terms of the division of labor. He agreed also with those critics of industrial societies who argued that, as the division of labor advances, we can expect the degree of consensus relative to the "collective conscience" to decline, if for no other reason than that the division of labor emphasizes differences rather than similarities in the way men think and act. However, he did not agree with the conclusion often drawn by these critics that the decline in the "collective conscience" necessarily leads to disorder. Rather, he believed that, in the "normal" case, advances in the division of labor lead to a new form of solidarity, one based on the complementary relationships which develop when work roles are specialized and men are functionally interdependent. Durkheim referred to this new form of solidarity as "organic solidarity," and much of his early work had to do with its character and development in human society.

It was in connection with his effort to expose this new form of solidarity that Durkheim was moved to attack the utilitarian individualism of the political economists and English philosophers. He argued that integration in advanced industrial societies was not, as suggested in utilitarian individualism, the result of a network of essentially economic contracts between formally free individuals in a market. On the contrary, such contracts would be quite impossible without prior commitment to a set of constraining norms or "rules of the game." In other words, the existence of contractual relations, according to Durkheim, presupposes a normative structure without which the formation of such relations could not proceed in an orderly fashion. Above all, a normative structure cannot be explained as an outgrowth of contractual relations, if the former is a necessary condition for the emergence of the latter.

Thus it is clear from the context of Durkheim's argument with the utilitarians, that he believed the division of labor leads to a new solidarity, but not simply by making men interdependent or by forcing them to deal with each other in a market. Rather, it does so by creating a new morality. In his own words (1964b, p. 406):

. . . if the division of labor produces solidarity, it is not only

because it makes each individual an exchangist, *as the economists say; it is because it creates among men an entire system of rights and duties which link them together in a durable way. Just as social similitudes* [in the simpler societies] *give rise to law and a morality which protects them, so the division of labor* [in modern societies] *gives rise to rules which assure pacific and regular concourse of divided functions.*

But if Durkheim was critical of utilitarian individualism as an accurate description of the basis for solidarity in modern societies, he was inclined to give it a prominent place in the thinking of modern men and in the development of the division of labor itself. Indeed, it may be seen as providing the moral support for the individualization which the division of labor involves. Particularly important in this regard is the "cult of the individual," a set of beliefs about the dignity and worth of the individual which had its origins in the Enlightenment and which figured significantly in the philosophical justification for the French Revolution.

Durkheim recognized that such beliefs may be conceived as an element within the common conscience, but—and here he returns to the dominant theme in his treatment of the subject—they contribute nothing to the development of solidarity.

It is thus, if one wishes, a common cult, but it is possible only by the ruin of all others, and, consequently, cannot produce the same effects as this multitude of extinguished beliefs. There is no compensation for that. Moreover, if it is common in so far as the community partakes of it, it is individual in its object. If it turns all wills towards the same end, this end is not social. It thus occupies a completely exceptional place in the collective conscience. It is still from society that it takes all its force, but it is not to society that it attaches us; it is to ourselves. Hence it does not constitute a true social link. (1964b, p. 172)

At this stage in the development of his argument, Durkheim found himself in a kind of bind. Having concluded that the position of the utilitarian individualists concerning the integrating effects of individual contracts was naïve (that, in fact, the existence of contracts presupposes a morality without which such contracts could not proceed) and, further, that advances in the division of labor gave rise to this morality (while at the same time undermining the basis for solidarity prior to such advances), Durkheim was at pains to explain the fact that conflict and social unrest are so often present in societies in which the division of labor has progressed to an advanced state. Indeed, it was precisely because of this fact that many critics of industrialism had concluded that the division of labor was the factor primarily responsible for the conflict and social unrest in industrial societies.

But Durkheim had an answer: He argued that where conflict and social unrest are associated with advances in the division of labor, it is because the latter has progressed more rapidly than the morality necessary for its regulation. It was in relation to this condition that Durkheim first used the term *anomie*. Translated literally, anomie means normlessness, but in the context of *The Division of Labor* it refers

to a condition in which relations between specialists are insufficiently regulated to produce functional unity (the essence of organic solidarity). Interestingly, this is precisely the kind of condition one would expect to find if men were in fact related to one another in the manner described by the utilitarian individualists; that is, in terms of individual contracts and nothing more. It may be argued that in the absence of such regulation men could be expected to operate in terms of norms of efficiency in the formation of contractual relations. Such norms do not preclude the use of coercive power and, depending upon the circumstances, may actually lead to the use of such power. As will be seen, it is precisely this implication of Durkheim's thesis which became the cornerstone of one aspect of Merton's formulation of the theory, that aspect having to do with anomie as a function of the emphasis on utilitarianism in modern societies.[7]

Durkheim referred to a condition in which there is insufficient regulation between specialists as the "anomic division of labor." A good illustration of such a condition is the conflict between capital and wage labor, which Durkheim saw as widespread and as having serious consequences for the development of class conflict. Nevertheless, he was optimistic about the eventual outcome. In time, he believed, norms adequate to the task of regulating such relations would develop, because they were needed. For Durkheim, at least in this stage of his intellectual development, this was the way all such norms developed, in response to the need for them.

But although optimistic concerning the eventual development of adequate normative regulation of the relations between specialties, Durkheim was concerned about the quality of the norms that were under development. Because of the unequal distribution of power ("external inequality"), especially in the relations between capital and labor, norms might develop which would regularize such relations, but which would be seen as unjust. Durkheim referred to such norms (and the contracts negotiated in terms of them) as the "forced division of labor." They are unjust because those who are subject to them do not always get what they deserve.

If one class of society is obliged, in order to live, to take any price for its services, while another can abstain from such action thanks to resources at its disposal which, however, are not necessarily due to any social superiority, the second has an unjust advantage over the first at law. (1964b, p. 384)

More important for understanding his contribution to the development of the modern theory of anomie, Durkheim was convinced that the "forced division of labor" was inherently unstable. The individualism which underlies the whole process of specialization fosters a tendency toward individual self-fulfillment which can be held in check only at great cost to the society, in terms of conflict and social unrest. Indeed, revolutions have been known to spring from precisely this source of instability. In the very beginning of his discussion of the subject, he states (1964b, p. 374):

It is not sufficient that there be rules, however, for sometimes the rules themselves are the cause of evil. This is what occurs in class-wars. The institution of classes and of castes constitutes an organization of the division of labor, and it is a strictly regulated organization, although it often is a source of dissention. The lower classes not being, or no longer being, satisfied with the role which was devolved upon them from custom or by law aspire to functions which are closed to them and seek to dispossess those who are exercising these functions. Thus civil wars arise which are due to the manner in which labor is distributed.

Several observations are worth noting before closing the discussion of Durkheim's early contribution to the theory of anomie. For Durkheim, a phenomenon is to be considered "normal" if it is an inevitable consequence of a particular species of society; "abnormal" if it is not. In *The Division of Labor,* anomie is treated as an abnormal phenomenon, an imperfection in the state of organic solidarity which can be expected to disappear as the evolution of regulatory norms proceeds. He was particularly concerned with demonstrating that it was not an inevitable consequence of advances in the division of labor. Thus in his early work, at least, Durkheim appeared to be a critic of the industrial way of life, but an optimistic one. Second, in the context of *The Division of Labor,* anomie is a condition in which there is inadequate regulation of the activities of the persons involved, *including the means which they use in relating to one another.* This is not the emphasis given to the concept of anomie in his later work, specifically in *Suicide,* as we shall see. Third, given this concept of anomie, it would not be appropriate to see it as a source of deviant behavior, however undesirable he may have considered the consequences, but rather as a defect in the solidarity of the emerging social order—in today's language, a kind of social disorganization.

In summary, then, Durkheim's early contribution to the theory of anomie had to do, first, with calling attention to the fact that society is a moral order, and that the form which that order takes varies considerably, depending on the level of specialization or the division of labor. It had to do, second, with showing that the conditions described as ideal by the utilitarian individualists could not possibly provide the solidarity necessary for the persistence of a complex industrial society, and that without some kind of normative structure to control the use of coercive means, life would approximate the Hobbesian "war of all against all." Thirdly, it had to do with the observation that in the development of the division of labor in human societies, the morality necessary for its regulation sometimes fails to develop, with anomie as the result. Finally, it had to do with the existence and significance for solidarity of "external inequality" (of power). Thus even when regulatory rules develop, solidarity may be impaired if the rules in question have been developed unilaterally as a result of this irregularity. Called the "forced division of labor," such a system of rules is inherently unstable because it does not take account of the pressure generated by the ideology of individualism, with its emphasis on self-fulfillment through the development of one's talents and abilities.

Anomie and Suicide

Durkheim's early work on the division of labor in human society is the foundation upon which the bulk of his later writing rests. Even his work on suicide should be seen as an elaboration of the theme set out in his early work on the division of labor. All of the "suicidal currents" with which he was concerned in *Suicide* are consequences of the moral orders introduced in *The Division of Labor.* Moreover, the substance of his critique of industrial society in *Suicide* extended and developed ideas which were treated originally in his earlier work.

Durkheim's study of suicide is significant in several respects apart from the substance of his critique of industrial society. First, it is a classic example of a type of approach to the understanding of social life which has come to be associated with the discipline of sociology, namely, the analysis of variations in the rates of social phenomena. So common is this type of analysis in sociology today that it is sometimes referred to as *the* "sociological" approach. It contrasts sharply with the "clinical" approach, which is concerned with incidence. In the latter, an attempt is made to explain why one person rather than another behaves in a given way.[8] Second, it explains suicide in the context of the larger society rather than by reference to variables on the level of biology or individual psychology. Durkheim was among the first sociologists to reject the tendency toward reductionism in psychology, political economy, and political philosophy. Social facts, though not unrelated to biological and psychological facts, have a reality of their own.

It has often appeared that these social phenomena, because of their extreme complexity, were either inhospitable to science or could be subject to it only when reduced to their elemental conditions, either psychic or organic, that is, only when stripped of their proper nature. We have, on the contrary, undertaken to establish that it is possible to treat them scientifically without removing any of their distinctive characteristics. We have even refused to identify the immateriality of psychological phenomena; we have, furthermore, refused to reabsorb it, with the Italian school, into the general properties of organized matter. (1964a, pp. 144–145)

It should be clear, then, that Durkheim's approach, on the level of theory as well as methodology, is pre-eminently sociological. This will become more apparent as the substance of his work on suicide is exposed.

In general terms, the thesis in *Suicide* is that rates of suicide vary as a function of system-generated "suicidal currents" to which the members of the society are subject, depending on the positions they occupy. These currents are called "altruism," "egoism" and "anomie." Suicide resulting primarily from any one of the above currents is given the name of that current. For example, suicide resulting primarily from "egoism" is given the name of "egoistic suicide." There is full recognition, however, that for a given category of persons, two or more currents may be operating, sometimes at cross-purposes, to determine the rate of suicide for that category.

Altruistic suicide, according to Durkheim, tends to occur when the interests of the group are so important to the individual that his private interests, including his own life, become secondary considerations. The classic example of altruistic suicide, as one might expect, is the soldier who knowingly gives his life for his country, although there are other examples as well to which one might point: the Hindu woman who kills herself upon the death of her husband and the Ashanti officer who kills himself upon the death of his chief. Durkheim was particularly fascinated with the statistics on suicide among military personnel, because they presented striking examples of support for his thesis. For instance, the rates for military personnel are higher than for similar civilian groups. This is true in times of peace as well as in times of war. To refute the argument that the rates of suicide among military personnel are high because of the hardships of military life, Durkheim pointed out that the rates are higher for officers than for enlisted men, whose lot is generally a more difficult one. Moreover, rates of suicide increase with length of service, which is exactly what one would *not* expect, if it may be assumed that the first few years of service are always the more difficult to endure.

At the other extreme from altruistic suicide is egoistic suicide. It was conceived as resulting from an inordinately low degree of concern for group interests and thus for precisely those elements of social organization which give meaning to life. Thus if altruistic suicide results from a situation in which death has too much meaning to offset the advantages of life, egoistic suicide results from a situation in which life has too little meaning to offset the advantages of death. Durkheim supported his thesis concerning egoistic suicide by reference to data drawn from a number of areas of social life. His analysis of the statistics in the area of domestic relations, for example, showed that married persons tend to have lower rates than single persons, or those who have been widowed or divorced. Moreover, differences in this regard tend to increase in proportion to the size of the family unit. The significant variable, of course, is commitment to group interests and the meaning which such commitment provides.

In his treatment of egoistic suicide, Durkheim spent a great deal of time with the differences in rates of suicide between various religious groups. His analysis in this regard is particularly instructive, because it points up the fact that there are special cases, of which Protestantism is one, in which it is not just the *absence* of norms favoring full participation in the group, but the *presence* of norms favoring autonomy which is responsible for the low level of integration. In developing his argument, he noted first that Protestants have significantly higher rates than Catholics, and that the relationship holds true when other variables are held constant. He then pointed out that for the Catholic, religious truth and proper conduct are prescribed by the church, so that the question of salvation can be solved by compliance with church doctrine. For the Protestant, the situation is quite different; the ultimate judge of truth and proper conduct is not the church, but the individual. The net result is freedom from the obligation to comply with church

doctrine, but it is a freedom which enjoins him to make his own decisions on matters of religion and morality. Thus, in so far as he is faithful, the Protestant must bear a burden of responsibility which, in the case of the Catholic, can be shifted to the church. It is this burden, of course, that creates the strain disposing him to suicide.[9]

Durkheim's discussion of the impact of religious individualism on egoistic suicide is instructive in another sense as well. It is clear from the context of that discussion that the ethic of individualism, of which religious individualism is but one specific case, is perhaps the most significant variable affecting the low degree of integration of industrial society. It might be noted that his views on this subject are so strong that it would not be going to far to say that Durkheim's treatment of egoistic suicide has all the earmarks of a polemic against unfettered individualism. Later we shall see that the same kind of point can be made about his treatment of anomic suicide.

The third of the types of suicide discussed by Durkheim is anomic suicide. As with the others, it is conceived to be the result of a certain state of the social order, in this case anomie.[10] In his discussion of the sources of anomie, Durkheim relied heavily on certain facts about the variation of rates of suicide by stages of the business cycle. He noted that the rate of suicide increases during periods of unusual prosperity as well as during periods of depression. The fact that the rate goes up during depression is not particularly surprising; common sense might suggest that disappointment and suffering are likely to follow from financial loss. What is surprising is that it also goes up during periods of unusual prosperity, a fact of considerable importance to Durkheim's explanation of its sources.

In working out his explanation, Durkheim observed first that poverty-stricken people are not always upset with their circumstances. From this fact he concluded that even the increase in suicide rates during depressions cannot be explained in terms of the deprivation of economic needs, if such needs are assumed to be absolute and unchanging. On the other hand, if they are conceived to be relative and changing, an explanation which makes reference to the deprivation of economic need might be quite satisfactory. What he concluded, finally, was that the increase in the rate of suicide at the extremes of the business cycle must be the result of disturbances in the relationship between what one expects, contingent upon a certain amount of effort, and what one gets. Specifically, he argued that in periods of economic depression, the problem is that the economic status of large numbers of people is out of line with expectations in the area of living standards. In periods of unusual prosperity, on the other hand, the problem is that expectations of large numbers of people tend to get out of line with what is realistically possible. As one authority (Parsons, 1949, p. 335) has put it:

At both extremes [of the business cycle] *the relation between means and ends, between effort and attainment, is upset. The result is a sense of confusion, a loss of orientation. People no longer have a sense of "getting anywhere."*

133

The significance of Durkheim's discussion of suicide during various stages of the business cycle is, first, in calling attention to the fact that to experience success one must not only have access to the means by which goals are reached, but in addition, one must have a clear definition of what the goal is. Above all, the goal cannot be constantly receding. "One does not advance when one walks toward no goal, or—which is the same thing—when the goal is infinity." (Durkheim 1951, p. 248). It is, second, in calling attention to the fact that deprivation is relative to one's aspirations. That is, to say what is deprivating varies from time to time and from group to group, and depends on what one wants, or comes to expect, as a consequence of one's position within the society. In summary, in the context of *Suicide,* anomie results when aspirations are out of line with reality factors in the situation of the actor and can be eliminated only through the provision of goals which limit the actor to what is realistically possible.

Durkheim's discussion of anomic suicide is significant for another reason as well. It was in his treatment of this subject that he began to see anomie as a normal rather than an abnormal phenomenon in industrial societies. It will be recalled that in *The Division of Labor,* anomie was treated as an abnormal phenomenon, one which is not inevitable in such societies and which in time would be eliminated by the development of normative controls over the relations between specialists. But in *Suicide,* in his discussion of the sources of anomie, he stated that it is sometimes the result of certain general features of the industrial way of life and presumably, therefore, inevitable. Specifically, he argued that it is related to rapid technological developments and the sudden expansion of markets—conditions which he saw as presenting seemingly unlimited opportunities for the accumulation of wealth. For this reason, "The sphere of trade and industry . . . is actually in a chronic state [of anomie]." (1951, p. 254) In elaborating his point in this regard, he argued as follows (1951, p. 256, emphasis added):

Now that [the producer] *may assume to have almost the entire world as his customer, how could passions accept their former confinement in the face of such limitless prospects? Such is the source of the excitement predominating in this part of society, and which has hence extended to the other parts. There,* the state of crisis and anomie is constant and, so to speak, normal. *From top to bottom of the ladder greed is aroused without knowing where to find ultimate foothold. Nothing can calm it, since its goal is far beyond all it can attain.*

Clearly his emphasis has shifted. What was earlier considered an abnormal development, an imperfection in the state of organic solidarity in industrial society, has become an inevitable consequence of the social organization of such societies and thus (by definition) normal. It is the latter theme which pervades the formulations of the theory of anomie which appeared in America, beginning in the late 1930's.

Underlying the discussion of anomie in *Suicide* is an assumption about human nature that should be made explicit. For Durkheim (1951, p. 247–248) "human activity naturally aspires beyond assignable limits and sets itself unattainable goals." This view of human nature, which has been called into question in more recent times, reflects a view of man that dominated much Western thought throughout the nineteenth century. According to this view, man is possessed not just with a capacity to crave comfort, luxury, and physical well-being, but with a tendency to do so. The "problem" for society, is to regulate this tendency, for there is nothing in man's biological or psychological makeup that can be expected to perform this function. A stable society, then, is one in which men at all levels within the social order aspire to no more than they can realistically hope to attain, producing a kind of harmony between man and the condition he faces. Here again, in his treatment of anomie, Durkheim can be seen as striking a major blow at utilitarian individualism, which assumed that there is a direct and universal relationship between increasing prosperity and the advance of human happiness. Clearly he is saying that this is not necessarily the case; that happiness in the face of increasing prosperity is a function of the adequacy of those mechanisms regulating man's aspirations, a variable the utilitarians tended to ignore.

A word needs to be said about the relationship between egoistic and anomic suicide. Both are the result of the "insufficient presence" of society in individuals. But whereas in egoistic suicide there is a deficiency in commitment to collective activity, depriving the individual of meaning, in anomic suicide the deficiency is in commitment to limiting goals, leaving the individual with unrealistic benchmarks, or none at all, for measuring success. Thus, the two types may and do vary independently of one another. Durkheim (1951, p. 258) specifically calls our attention to this fact. "We may offer society everything social in us, and still be unable to control our desires . . . and vice versa." Yet it is clear that both types of suicide can be traced to elements within the social organization of modern societies, not the least of which is the division of labor and the ethic of individualism which is associated with it.

In his later work, Durkheim continued to emphasize the inadequacy of psychological or biological reductionism for the development of social theory, stressing instead the importance of explanations of social phenomena which relate those phenomena to the larger society. He also argued that the social structure of modern societies makes it difficult to secure the kind of commitment to the interests of the collectivity which social order requires. This is so because the emphasis on individuality which the division of labor requires heightens the egoistic inclinations of the individual. Moreover, the problem of "restraining horizons" is difficult in such societies, if for no other reason than that they present seemingly unlimited opportunities for the accumulation of wealth. There is, therefore, a tendency toward a lack of regulation of the means which may be used in attaining one's goals (anomie in the context of *The Division of Labor*) and toward a lack of regulation of the tendency to aspire to unrealistic goals (anomie in the context of *Suicide*). Thus, in spite of the optimism concerning the prospects for stability in modern societies expressed in his early work, there is every reason to believe that, in the end, Durkheim saw in the structure of such societies, features that make the "war of all against all" a constant threat.

THE CONTRIBUTIONS OF ROBERT K. MERTON

Merton's statement of the theory of anomie as an explanation for deviant behavior has been acclaimed by A. K. Cohen (1965, p. 5) as "the most influential single formulation in the sociology of deviance in the last 25 years." That statement, published over 10 years ago, is as unchallenged today as it was when it was made. The original paper is still one of the most frequently quoted in American sociology and has been the basis for literally hundreds of critical commentaries, extensions, and empirical studies on the subject.

Social Structure, Anomie and Deviant Behavior

Merton's statement of theory constitutes a significant advance over Durkheim's original formulation, with respect both to the causes and consequences of anomie. But in developing his ideas, Merton remains solidly within the tradition of sociological thinking which Durkheim did so much to establish: he is concerned with variations in rates of human behavior, rather than in incidence, and he explains those variations within the context of the larger society rather than by reference to variables at the biological or psychological levels of analysis. Thus, following Durkheim, he uses the sociological approach and is opposed to any form of reductionism in his treatment of social phenomena. Merton's orientation is quite explicit in the following excerpt from the introduction to his 1938 paper (1957, p. 132):

Our primary aim is to discover how some social structures exert a definite pressure upon certain persons in the society to engage in non-conforming rather than conforming conduct. If we can locate groups, not because the human beings comprising them are compounded of distinctive biological tendencies but because they are responding normally to the social situation in which they find themselves. Our perspective is sociological. We look at variations in the rates of deviant behavior, not at its incidence. Should our quest be at all successful, some forms of deviant behavior will be found to be as psychologically normal as conformist behavior, and the equation of deviant and psychological abnormality will be put into question.

Basic to Merton's thesis is a distinction between "goals" and "means" as elements of the social structure of a society. The distinction between the two, it should be noted, is analytic, so that in concrete situations a particular goal may also be a means to a further goal, but this fact does not make the distinction any less important for theoretical purposes. By "goals" is meant those "purposes and interests" held out as desirable of attainment by a society. They are the things "worth striving for," according to its cultural tradition. By "means," on the other hand, is meant the legitimate ways by which the members of a society, individually or in groups,

may pursue the cultural goals. Such ways are defined by the institutions of a society and, depending upon the form of the definition, may be prescribed, preferred, or simply permitted.

Also basic to Merton's thesis is the idea that, although both of these elements of the social structure are present in all human societies, the relations between them are not necessarily constant. In fact, they can and do vary independently of one another. In some societies, for example, the emphasis placed on the attainment of cultural goals may be quite strong, while the emphasis placed on conformity to the norms prescribing legitimate means to these goals may be quite weak. In the latter, the choice of means tends to be dominated by norms of efficiency, and when the limiting case is reached, according to Merton (1957, p. 133), "any and all procedures which promise the attainment of the all-important goal would be permitted." Obviously, the limiting case is never reached. If it were, society as we know it would not exist. There would be no legitimate (or illegitimate) means and interaction would be characterized by a "war of all against all," which is the antithesis of society. But the concept of such a hypothetical limiting case is nevertheless useful for heuristic purposes. The way in which Merton uses it in his formulation of the theory of anomie will be discussed presently.

The above case is but one type of "malintegrated" society. At the other extreme is that type of society in which the emphasis on institutional means is so great that they tend to become ends-in-themselves. As such, they require no justification in utilitarian terms and conformity to them becomes "ritualistic." As might be expected, societies of this type tend to be highly stable and resistant to change, which in the short run may be quite functional. But in the long run, presumably, it is not, for there is too little flexibility to adapt to new life conditions. Between these extremes, says Merton (1957, p. 134):

. . . are societies which maintain a rough balance between emphases upon cultural goals and institutionalized practices, and these constitute the integrated and relatively stable, though changing societies.

Of these two polar types of malintegrated societies, Merton is concerned primarily with that type which emphasizes cultural goals rather more than institutional means. His concern in this regard stems first from the fact that he is interested in the phenomenon of anomie (which he argues is likely to be great in societies of this type) and, second, from the fact that he is interested in contemporary American society (which he feels approximates this type).

Merton is concerned in his formulation of the theory of anomie with variations in rates of deviance *between* the polar types just described, as well as variations rates *within* the polar type represented by the American case. It will be argued here that a thorough understanding of his work requires the separation of these two aspects of his theory. This is not an easy task to accomplish, it might be noted, because Merton does not distinguish clearly between the two aspects of his theory. Moreover, it can be accomplished only by a process of abstraction, which carries with it the risk of distortion. But the task is an important one and, on balance, justified in spite of the attendant risks.

Merton's thesis on variations in rates of deviant behavior between the polar types described above has received relatively little attention from those who have dealt with his work. Nearly all of it has centered on his explanation for variations in rates of deviance within the polar type represented by the American case. Why this is so is an intriguing question in the sociology of knowledge, but one which is beyond the scope of the present discussion.[11] The substance of Merton's thesis is this: One can expect higher rates of deviance in societies of the American type, as compared with societies of the "ritualistic" type, because the relatively greater stress on goal-attainment in the former renders the norms prescribing legitimate means ineffective in controlling the use of technically more efficient ones. Merton (1957, p. 135) put it as follows:

With such a differential emphasis on goals and institutional procedures, the latter may be so vitiated by the stress on goals as to have the behavior of individuals limited only by considerations of technical expediency. In this context, the sole significant question becomes: Which of the available procedures is most efficient in netting the culturally approved value? The technically most effective procedure, whether culturally legitimate or not, becomes typically preferred to institutionally prescribed conduct. As the process of attenuation continues, the society becomes unstable and there develops what Durkheim called "anomie" (or normlessness).

One implication of Merton's position seems clear: The greater the emphasis on goal-attainment in relation to the emphasis on institutional means, the greater will be the tendency for participants in the system to engage in deviant forms of behavior. Thus, in the case where the emphasis on goal-attainment is greater than the emphasis on institutional means, deviance is a function of the disparity between the two emphases. It follows also that the disparity can increase as a result of an increase in the emphasis on cultural goals in relation to institutional means, or of a decrease on institutional means in relation to cultural goals, or of both.

Another implication, and one which will be stressed because it is so often overlooked in evaluating Merton's thesis, is that societies of the American type, as compared with societies of the ritualistic type, are likely to have higher rates of deviance at all levels within the system, among the rich as well as the poor, among the powerful as well as the powerless, among those with high status as well as those with low status. On the assumption that Merton is correct in classifying American society as he does, his thesis should go a long way toward explaining the deviance in high places in America, e.g., among successful corporation executives, politicians in high office, and football coaches whose teams are ranked nationally.

It is this aspect of Merton's theory of anomie which relates most closely to the discussion of anomie by Durkheim in *The Division of Labor*. In that discussion, it will be recalled,

anomie is a condition in which the relations of men in the market are unregulated because the norms necessary for their regulation have not yet developed. Merton, on the other hand, starts with the assumption that such norms are already in existence, but too weak to control the tendency toward the use of technically more efficient means which the emphasis on goal-attainment generates. Thus they are both talking about situations in which the means which men use are unregulated. But there is a difference. With Durkheim the means are not in violation of established regulatory norms, whereas with Merton they are. This is why, given Merton's concept of anomie, it is quite appropriate to classify the resulting expediency as deviant behavior. In summary terms, then, the difference may be stated as follows: expediency in the context of *The Division of Labor* is due to an undeveloped state of normative regulation, while in the context of Merton's thesis, it is due to the inability of established norms to keep it under control.[12]

It should be clear that the kind of deviance with which Merton is concerned is that which results from *participation in* a system of institutionalized goals and means. One would not expect the kind of pressure to commit deviant acts of which Merton speaks except among persons who aspire to attain the culturally favored goals. Moreover, it is clear that Merton is talking about *deviation from* a set of institutionalized cultural elements. Thus the deviant is not an "outsider" who happens to violate the norms of the system, but an "insider" who violates them because of problems associated with being a participant in that system. All this does not preclude the possibility that a deviant may become an outsider, in our view. Old commitments can be replaced by new ones. But when they are, the actor is technically no longer a deviating member of the old system but a conforming member of the new one. Hwever, it is most important to understand that in such a case, the actor is a deviant *before* he becomes an outsider, not *because* he is an outsider, as some have argued. (Cf. Becker, 1963).

In this connection, it is worthy of note that Merton considers it very unlikely that old commitments will be completely extinguished, even in those cases where the actor is thoroughly alienated and highly motivated to reject the cultural elements which are the objects of old commitments. In a very revealing footnote to his discussion of the consequences of withdrawing emotional support from institutional norms, Merton (1957, p. 136) makes the following statement:

It appears unlikely that cultural norms, once interiorized, are wholly eliminated. Whatever residuum persists will induce personality tensions and conflict, with some measure of ambivalence. A manifest rejection of the once-incorporated institutional norms will be coupled with some latent retention of their emotional correlates. Guilt feelings, a sense of sin, pangs of conscience are diverse terms referring to this unrelieved tension.

Put another way, even when there is a manifest rejection of the troublesome cultural elements, the actor may possess a latent orientation to those very same elements. Moreover, this latent orientation may affect his behavior in such a way as to justify arguing he is "reacting against" the old cultural elements, even when he is conforming to new ones.

It seems appropriate at this time to comment further on the significance of the points just covered in relation to certain criticisms of the theory of anomie. It has been argued by Becker, (1963) that deviants are "outsiders" who are deviant because of a process of labelling by "insiders" who are powerful enough to make those labels "stick." Presumably, such outsiders are not motivated by system-generated pressures to react against cultural elements to which they are committed, as anomie theorists contend. Rather, they are conforming to a system of cultural elements which for any number of reasons just happen to be different from those of the established system. Thus they are deviant only because they are labelled as such by representatives of the established system. In other words, deviance is a function of a process of labelling, not a process of disaffection and adaptation. Under the labelling perspective the outsider is no different psychologically from the insider. Both are conformists. The difference lies in the fact that the norms to which the outsider conforms are classified as deviant by the insider.

Anomie theorists, it should be noted, recognize the existence of deviant norms (e.g., those found in delinquent gangs) to which persons conform and, as a result, acquire the label of deviant. But they tend to see such norms as the result of a process of disaffection, adaptation and, in time, institutionalization. Once they are established, they stand as ready-made solutions to problems presented by the conventional normative system.[13] As such, they are attractive to those who possess the problem for which they are a solution. Anomie theorists therefore not only recognize the existence of deviant norms, but also have an explanation for their existence which is consistent with their overall theoretical perspective. This is not the case with labelling theorists. For the most part they fail to deal with the question: why are the deviant norms there for persons to conform to?

Returning to the substance of Merton's thesis, it is, of course, an empirical question as to whether American society approximates the polar type in which the emphasis on goal-attainment so exceeds the emphasis on legitimate means as to make the control of expediency difficult. Merton's original paper proffers some support for his contention that it does, although his facts relate rather more to the emphasis in America on monetary success than to the de-emphasis on the use of legitimate means in achieving this success. Drawing from a variety of published works on the success theme in American society, he concludes the following (1957, pp. 136–139):

1. Although money is not the only success goal in America, it is an important one. This is true in part because of the function of money as a medium of exchange.

2. The source of one's money is a variable affecting one's status, but the anonymity of urban life makes it possible to translate money acquired by illegitimate means into high status—if not immediately, then "in the course of time."

3. The American Dream of monetary success is "indefinite and relative," i.e., no specific amount of money is designated as the amount one must acquire to be a success. As a result, no matter how much one acquires, there is almost always someone who has acquired more and who is therefore more successful. Thus with few exceptions we are all destined to be failures in relation to someone else.[14]

4. The goal of monetary success in America is accompanied by a number of ideological beliefs, which may be said to function to keep the motivation of the participants in the system high in relation to continued pursuit of that goal. Among the more important of these beliefs are the following: First, that the goal is available to all members of the society, regardless of birth; second, precisely because it is available to all, it is incumbent upon all to pursue it; and third, even in the face of repeated failure to reach the goal, all are duty bound to continue in its pursuit, i.e., one must not be a "quitter." In this connection, we are reminded that seeming failure is often only a way-station to eventual success and, further, that the cardinal sin in America is not failure to reach the goal, but failure to continue in one's efforts to do so.

The other aspect of Merton's theory—and the one which has received the most attention from American criminologists—has to do with rates of deviance *within* the polar type represented by the American case. If it may be said that the tendency toward deviance is generally great in societies which simultaneously emphasize the attainment of certain success goals and de-emphasize the norms prescribing legitimate means to those success goals, then one would expect the tendency toward deviance to be even greater among those classes of persons whose access to the means which may legitimately be used is limited. This is the logic of Merton's explanation for the higher rates of deviance in the lower classes, for it is in these classes, obviously, that access to legitimate means is most severely limited. So that there will be no misunderstanding of what Merton is saying, it should be noted that it is not simply the existence of a class structure (which provides unequal access to legitimate means) that explains the higher rates of deviance in the lower classes, but the combination of such a class structure *plus* an emphasis on goal attainment which transcends class lines. Merton (1957, p. 146) puts it this way:

It is only when a system of cultural values extols, virtually above all else, certain common *success-goals, for the population at large, while the social structure rigorously restricts or completely closes access to approved modes of reaching these goals* for a considerable part of the same population, *that deviant behavior ensues on a large scale.*

One obvious conclusion which may be drawn from all this is that whether one is focusing on the deviance which results from the emphasis on goals over means or from the commitment of lower class persons to goals which are difficult of attainment given their access to legitimate means, structural features of the social system which are considered "good" are responsible for conditions which are considered "bad." Merton saw this clearly and at one point argued (1957, p. 146): "a cardinal American virtue, 'ambition,' promotes a cardinal American vice, 'deviant behavior.'"

It should now be clear what Merton means by anomie. In the context of his theory of deviance, anomie is a state of social organization (or, if one prefers, disorganization) in which there is a rejection of prevailing cultural goals, or institutional means, or both. Its sources are several, as we have seen, but in all cases it is the result of participation in an institutional system of cultural elements. The persons involved can thus be expected to be ambivalent because they are motivated to reject elements of the culture to which they are committed by virtue of their participation. It will be remembered that if the actor is not to some extent committed to certain institutional elements within the society in question, he will not have the problem for which rejection of one or more of these elements is a solution. It follows from all this that *the theory of anomie, as a theory of deviance, explains only those departures from the norms of an institutionalized system that result from participation in that system.* All other departures are beyond its scope of explanation.

In summary, Merton's reasoning with respect to the motivation involved in rule-violation in societies represented by the American case is as follows: First, socialization in societies of this type produces more concern with attaining the cultural goals than with conforming to the norms prescribing legitimate means. It follows that satisfactions will be derived more from winning than from sheer participating in competitive activity. Put another way, societies of this type generate such intense pressures to attain the cultural goals that the choice of means tends to be determined mainly by considerations of technical efficiency, with little regard for what is institutionally approved. This polar type tends to be quite unstable and exemplifies what Merton means by anomie (or normlessness). Second, socialization in societies of this type produces concern for attaining the cultural goals even among those whose access to the means which may legitimately be used is limited, that is, even within the lower classes. This leads to disaffection with institutional means, or with the goals, or both, and thus to deviant forms of behavior. In all cases these deviant forms of behavior may be seen as "individual adaptations" to system-generated pressures.

Modes of Individual Adaptation

Merton lists four types of such individual adaptations. It is important to understand that all four modes of individual adaptation refer to "ways of behaving" and not to "personality types." A given individual may manifest two or more of these "ways" in relation to the pressures he faces. On the other hand, having said this does not preclude the possibility that a particular individual may respond rather consistently in a particular way to a wide range of pressures. That is, the behavior of an individual may become patterned and thus constitute a generalized tendency of the type referred to as a personality trait.

All types are considered deviant in that they involve behavior which departs in some sense from prevailing institutional arrangements. They are presented schematically in the following table, in which (+) stands for "acceptance,"

(−) stands for "rejection," and (∓) stands for "rejection of prevailing institutional arrangements and substitution of alternative ones."

	Institutional Means	Culturally Favored Goals
INNOVATION	−	+
RITUALISM	+	−
RETREATISM	−	+
REBELLION	∓	∓

Fig. 1. Merton's Modes of Individual Adaptation (Adapted from Merton, 1957, p. 140).

Innovation as a mode of individual adaptation involves the use of illegitimate means in the pursuit of prevailing cultural goals. Often such means are more effective than legitimate ones—which helps explain their attractiveness—but, of course they need not be. Innovation occurs, as Figure 1 indicates, when there is continued acceptance of prevailing cultural goals in combination with rejection of the norms prescribing legitimate means to these goals. On the question of its distribution, Merton contends that it is likely to be found at all economic levels within a society such as our own (because of the stress at all levels on the attainment of cultural goals), but that the rates will be higher in the lower strata than in the higher strata (because of the relative lack of access in the lower strata to the means which may legitimately be used in pursuing the cultural goals).

Support for his contention that innovation is likely to be found at all levels within a society such as our own may be seen in the historical accounts of the Robber Barons, the studies of white collar crime, and the self-report studies of illegal activity among the more "respectable" people in our society. Merton cites a number of studies in support of his claim, but it should be noted that the evidence available to him in 1938 was far less than it is now. Subsequent research leaves little doubt that Merton was correct in his somewhat speculative conclusions on the subject.[15]

Support for the contention that innovation is likely to be greater in the lower class than in the higher classes may be seen in the official statistics of law enforcement agencies. This source of data has been called into question by a number of sociologists, on the grounds that there is a "class bias" in the way law enforcement agencies operate. Specifically, it has been argued that were it not for this bias the rates would be similar from one class to another. But it might be argued that only what is treated officially as crime is crime in any realistic conception of the term. That is to say, if some men are typically not treated as criminals when they commit acts that are defined as crime by statute, then it would be better from the point of view of understanding patterns of criminality to eliminate such acts from the category of crime, rather than to argue that much crime is overlooked by the class bias in law enforcement. This is another way of saying the anticipated official response to a given act should be an element in the definition of that act as crime or non-crime, regardless of whether, in some technical sense, it is against the law. Cloward and Ohlin (1960, pp. 6–7), commenting on this very point, argue as follows concerning the definition of delinquency:

Acts that do not ordinarily lead to the initiation of delin-quency proceedings may constitute deviance from the norms of some group or organization, such as church, school, social agency, family and peer groups; but these acts are not [i.e., should not be treated as] delinquent unless they are likely to be defined as such by agents of criminal justice.

Their argument in support of an "official" definition of delinquency is simply this: an act which is perhaps frowned upon, but otherwise ignored by the officials of the criminal justice system, will not have the same meaning to the actor, and very likely to the community as well, as one which would ordinarily result in a charge of delinquency. The same logic, obviously, could be applied to crime. Thus, for sociological purposes, a meaningful definition of crime is "what is treated as crime by the officials of the system," and for sociological research on the subject, official statistics therefore may be quite appropriate.

Having made a case for the acceptance of an "official" definition of crime as the most meaningful one for sociological purposes, we should not conclude that "legal" definitions of crime (what is defined as crime by statute) are of no value whatsoever. In certain kinds of ideological disputes, for example, it might be quite useful to start with a "legal" definition of crime. Recent efforts to secure more rigorous enforcement of the laws pertaining to "white-collar crime" have done this. Arguments in this regard often take the following form: although there is a great deal of white-collar crime being committed, very little of it is being prosecuted, because of a bias in law enforcement; furthermore, this kind of bias in the enforcement of law should be corrected, in all fairness to other classes of persons now being treated harshly by the law. But, however useful for ideological purposes a legal definition of crime may be, it is not useful for sociological purposes, if one is interested in crime as a category of deviant behavior.

Merton's analysis of innovation helps explain the facts available to us concerning the relationship between poverty and crime. It is well known that in America, and in many other societies as well, the two are highly correlated, especially if one is focusing on property crime. It is also well known that in some societies, poverty is not highly correlated with crime. Even when it is found "in the midst of plenty," poverty is not always correlated with crime. Poverty is most likely to be associated with crime when, as already suggested, the symbols of success are the same for those who are in the poverty classes as for those who are not. Merton (1957, p. 147) argues that the relatively low rates of crime in southeastern Europe may well be a function of the fact that in this area of Europe the "rigid class structure is coupled with *differential class symbols of success.*"

One obvious implication of Merton's thesis, in fact, of anomie theory in general, is that the relatively high rates of deviance in the lower classes (as a result of the combination of a cultural emphasis on success and limited access to the means by which success is achieved) could be significantly reduced either by de-emphasizing success, or by providing greater access to the means by which success is achieved, or by some combination of the two. A reduction in anomie from this source thus can be accomplished by bringing into alignment what people want and the means for getting what they want. These alternatives will be explored in greater detail below.

It is well to keep in mind that not all innovation, however deviant it may be from the point of view of the norms prescribing legitimate means, qualifies as crime. Crime is a legal concept and covers only those acts that are in violation of the law. Moreover, not all crime qualifies as innovation. Crimes of violence, for example, do not qualify as innovation unless they are committed in connection with the attainment of culturally-approved goals. Even some property crime does not qualify as innovation; this is true, for example, of much vandalism, which seems to be an end-in-itself rather than a means to an end, especially if by end we mean one which is culturally approved. As will be seen, the fact that much delinquency does not qualify as innovation is the primary basis for a major qualification of Merton's version of the theory of anomie introduced some years later by Albert K. Cohen (1955).

The second of the modes of "individual adaptation" is ritualism. According to Merton (1957, pp. 149–50):

It involves the abandoning or scaling down of the lofty cul-tural goals of great pecuniary success and rapid social mobility to the point where one's aspirations can be satisfied. But though one rejects the cultural obligation to attempt "to get ahead in the world," though one draws in one's horizons, one continues to abide almost compulsively by institutional norms.

Ritualism, like innovation, is related inversely to social class, but it is most likely to be found among those lower-middle-class persons who are having difficulty attaining the culturally favored goals legitimately, but who are too committed to the norms prescribing legitimate means to use illegitimate ones. The compulsive quality of the adherence to institutional norms suggests a kind of reaction formation, so that conformity is not without ambivalence, but it is conformity nevertheless, and so the pattern can be considered deviant only in so far as it involves rejection of the obligation to continue striving for lofty goals.[16] Since the penalty for rejection of this obligation is not usually very great, ritualism as a solution is probably the most common of those treated in the scheme and the preferred adaptation among lower-middle-class persons. For Merton, ritualism can be expected in the lower middle class because it is here that deep commitments to the institutional norms are likely to develop. In Merton's own words on the subject (1957, p. 151):

It is in the lower middle class that parents typically exert continuous pressure upon children to abide by the moral mandates of the society, and where the social climb upward is less likely to meet with success than among the upper middle class. The strong disciplining for conformity with mores reduces the likelihood of innovation and promotes the likelihood of ritualism.

The third of the modes of "individual adaptation" discussed by Merton is retreatism. It involves the rejection of both cultural goals and institutional means. In this category, Merton (1957, p. 153) classifies the activities of "psychotics, autists, pariahs, outcasts, vagrants, vagabonds, tramps, chronic drunkards, and drug addicts" in so far as they manifest the pattern of rejection described. Sociologically, retreatists are the true aliens and may be seen as being "*in* the society but not *of* it." (Merton, 1957, p. 157) This does not mean that their activities are not the result of participation in the society, or that their activities are not problematic for the society and likely to be classified as deviant, but only that in "not sharing the common frame of values, they can be included as members of the *society* (in distinction from the *population*) only in a fictional sense" (Merton, 1957, p. 153). Nor does their status as aliens mean that all traces of commitment to the institutionalized cultural elements have been eliminated in the process of rejecting them. As mentioned earlier, Merton recognizes that it is difficult to completely eliminate all traces of commitment to such cultural elements once they have been "interiorized," which means that persons who choose to retreat may still face internal "strains" leading to feelings of guilt or doubt and the various defense mechanisms associated with such feelings.

The last of the four deviant modes of individual adaptation is called rebellion. Like retreatism, it involves a rejection of the cultural goals and institutional means, but, unlike retreatism, it involves an attempt to replace them with acceptable alternatives. Persons involved in a pattern of rebellion have a "cause" for which they are fighting. Because of this fact the pattern is often a collective one, for there are obvious advantages in collective action when social change is the objective. Concerning the distribution of rebellion, Merton has little to say, except to point out that "it is typically members of the rising class rather than the most depressed strata who organize the resentful and the rebellious into a revolutionary group" (1957, p. 157).

It is important to note that in the discussion of rebellion, Merton specifically excludes a category of behavior that could be traced to the disparity between goals and means with which he is concerned in his treatment of variations within societies of the American type. Referred to by the term *ressentiment,* it is a pattern of behavior in which the actor retains some considerable commitment to the objects of value against which he is rebelling. Thus, it is behavior in which the actor condemns what he secretly craves. He in effect solves his problem by a process of rationalization in which he argues that the goal is not worth having. Rebellion, on the other hand, is a type of behavior in which the actor has extinguished whatever commitments he may have had to the objects of value against which he is rebelling. Rebellion, for Merton (1957, p. 156) "involves a genuine transvaluation, where the direct or vicarious experience of frustration leads to full denunciation of previously prized values."[17]

It may be assumed that Merton recognized that *ressenti-* *ment* could be traced to the disparity between goals and means, but felt either that it was an insignificant category or that it was significant, but did not fit neatly into his analytic scheme. Whatever his feelings in this regard, he recognized that some individuals who condemn established goals and means do so before they have extinguished their commitments to those goals and means, leaving them ambivalent and inclined to react in the manner described. Later we shall see that it is precisely the type of response called *ressentiment* which became, for Cohen, the one which best describes the motivation of the gang delinquent.[18]

Earlier it was noted that Merton's thesis with respect to variations between the polar types treated in his 1938 paper has been largely ignored by American sociologists. In this connection, it is interesting to note that at least one critic goes further and specifically denies that Merton concerns himself with the consequences of self-interested striving (egoism, in Durkheim's terms) for expediency on the level of means in societies of the American type. Reference is to the words of Horton (1964, pp. 294–95).

Merton's anomie differs from that of Durkheim in one crucial respect—in its identification with the very groups and values which Durkheim saw as the prime source of anomie in industrial societies. For Durkheim, anomie was endemic in such societies not only because of inequality in the conditions of competition, but more importantly, because self-interested striving (the status and success goals) had been raised to social ends. The institutionalization of self-interest meant the legitimization of anarchy and amorality. Morality requires, according to Durkheim . . . social goals obeyed out of disinterest and altruism, not self-interest and egoism. To maximize opportunities for achieving success would in no way end anomie.

In the judgment of this writer, Horton is clearly wrong. One can only assume that Horton, like so many others, has failed to read Merton carefully. Merton, as indicated above, discusses two sources of anomie, one of which is precisely the source which Horton claims Merton failed to recognize.

In summary, then, Merton's theory of anomie is an attempt to explain variations in rates of deviance *between* societies of the American type and so-called "ritualistic" societies, as well as variations in rates of deviance *within* societies of the American type. As such, it involves two related sources of anomie: the emphasis on goals (as compared with institutionally approved means), and the relative lack of opportunity in the lower classes. Concerning the first of these sources, anomie results when the institutions are unable to control the tendency toward expediency in the choice of means, produced by the emphasis on cultural goals. Concerning the second of these sources, anomie results when persons in the lower strata come to realize the difficulties they face in attaining the approved goals by legitimate means and proceed to reject the approved goals, the institutional means, or both. The two sources are similar in that both involve a heavy emphasis on goal-attainment. What differentiates them is the fact that in the latter there is a recognition of the differences by class in access to the means which may legitimately be used in attaining the approved goals.

By recognizing both aspects of Merton's theory, it is possible to point up the continuity between Durkheim and Merton. *What Merton means by an emphasis on goals as compared with institutional means is what Durkheim meant by the egoistic tendenceis in individualism.* The fact that Merton saw anomie as resulting also from inequality of opportunity in combination with an emphasis on common success goals in no way denies this continuity, Horton's statement to this effect notwithstanding.

On the other hand, Merton's reformulation of the theory of anomie does involve one very important difference from the position taken by Durkheim. The tendency to aspire to higher and higher levels of goals is not, as in Durkheim's version of the theory, a natural one that societies sometimes fail to regulate. Rather, it is culturally induced. Thus Merton breaks with the nineteenth century tradition, which sees unsocialized men as having insatiable desires for money, power, and status, and the creature comforts which they afford. The difference between Merton and Durkheim in this regard may seem inconsequential, since the result in both cases is that men desire more than they can realistically expect to get, under existing institutional arrangements. But in terms of the implications for change, the differences are far from inconsequential. If men do not naturally possess a tendency to aspire to higher and higher levels of goals, the presence of unrealistic aspirations is not a problem in the area of social control but in the area of socialization. The "solution" implied in Merton's formulation of the theory of anomie, other things being equal, is not more control over appetites, but less emphasis on goal-attainment in the process of socialization. For Merton, if men are ambitious it is because society wants them to be, and if their ambition motivates them to want what by legitimate means is difficult to attain, the society, not the individual, is responsible. The basis for our judgment that Merton was a radical social critic should now be evident.

Our aim has been to expose the more important aspects of Merton's theory of anomie and to spell out some of the implications for understanding deviance generally, but particularly in America. We have also pointed out some of the shortcomings in Merton's formulation of the theory and some of the issues he left unresolved. As a kind of preface to dealing with various efforts at further development of the theory, it might be useful to list the more important of these shortcomings and issues, because, for the most part, they have become the focus of attention of those efforts.

One obvious shortcoming has to do with the question of the extent of the ambivalence present in those who have adapted to their circumstances through one or the other of the modes of individual adaptation to which Merton calls our attention. He recognizes the likelihood of ambivalence among those who have "interiorized" the cultural elements which they later reject, and the possibility that this fact may then lead to various defense mechanisms as ways of managing the guilt which is likely to accompany ambivalence; but he does not deal extensively with the subject and, in fact, almost ignores the psychodynamics of the reactions to system-generated pressures. As we shall see, this is an area in which Talcott Parsons makes a significant contribution.

Another (and not unrelated) shortcoming in Merton's formulation of the theory has to do with the status of *ressentiment* as a reaction to the perceived inability to reach one's goals by legitimate means. For reasons which are not apparent from a reading of his work, Merton has chosen not to include it within his scheme. He argues it should not be confused with rebellion, the only category into which it might logically be placed, depending of course on how broadly the category is defined. The fact that it is not covered by his scheme would be of little consequence if it could be shown that only a small percentage of all deviance is characterized by the kind of reaction which is involved. But a number of theorists have argued that the percentage of deviant acts which may be so characterized is quite large, so that to ignore *ressentiment* is to ignore an important category of deviance. In fact, Albert K. Cohen's theory of gang delinquency (treated below) includes the argument that much of what gang delinquents do cannot be explained except by reference to the kind of ambivalence and subsequent reaction which is implied in *ressentiment.*

Another shortcoming of Merton's formulation of the theory has to do with the extent to which the adaptations become institutionalized as ready-made solutions to certain problems of adjustment within the lower classes in America. Although much of what Merton says is not inconsistent with the idea that institutionalization of this type is quite common, he does not specifically deal with the subject. Cohen, on the other hand, does, and we shall be looking at his ideas in this regard as we deal with his theory of gang delinquency.

Still another shortcoming in Merton's formulation has to do with the role of social structure in determining the types of deviant adaptations which various categories of persons may choose in solving their problems. Merton places almost exclusive stress on factors internal to the actor in his discussion of how system-generated problems are solved. Cloward and Ohlin, on the other hand, stress structural features of the situation in which actors (individually or collectively) find themselves. The ideas of Cloward and Ohlin also will be dealt with below.

Perhaps the most important shortcoming of Merton's theory of anomie has to do, on the one hand, with the question of the functional significance (for industrial societies) of common success goals and, on the other, with the source of the inequality of opportunity which plays such an important part in his thinking about differences in rates of deviance within societies of the American type. Ideas on both these subjects have been developed by sociological theorists, but seldom have they been tied in with the theory of anomie in any systematic way. Thus, the full impact of the theory is often missed by those who use it to explain deviance. Put another way, unless one understands what lies behind the common success goals and the inequality of opportunity in industrial societies, one can hardly be expected to appreciate the magnitude of the problem faced by those who may want to deal with anomie and its consequences on the level of deviance.

EXTENSIONS AND REFORMULATIONS

The task in this part of the chapter is to expose certain contributions to the theory of anomie of Talcott Parsons, Albert K. Cohen, and two men who published together, Richard Cloward and Lloyd Ohlin. The emphasis will be on contributions which have resulted in significant advances in understanding deviance in America.

Talcott Parsons and the Theory of Deviance

To be considered first is Talcott Parsons' theory of deviance. The most elaborate statement of his views on the subject appeared in *The Social System* (1951). In that statement, Parsons was concerned with deviance in general, so that what is here conceived as a contribution to the theory of anomie may well have been inadvertent (from the point of view of his motivation for making it). The ideas of Parsons on which we shall concentrate have to do mainly with the genesis and direction of deviant motivation. His discussion of both subjects, as will be noted, involves more psychology than much of what passes for sociology in America, because, for Parsons, no matter how much of the actor's motivation may be explained by reference to the experiences he may have had as a member of various groups within the society, the motivation itself is an individual phenomenon. For Parsons, there is no such thing as group motivation. His discussion of the genesis of deviant motivation deals with how the motivation to engage in acts defined as deviant is built up. His discussion of the directions of deviant motivation deals with the ways in which that motivation becomes differentiated and, to some extent, why.

Throughout his discussion of both subjects, Parsons makes sharp analytic distinctions between *socialization, deviance,* and *social control.* He defines *socialization* as a process by which the cultural elements of the society (or any of its component parts) are transmitted. From the point of view of the actor, it is the process by which the actor acquires those cultural elements, including, in many cases, commitments to them. *Deviance* may be defined in two ways, depending upon whether the point of reference is the individual actor or the interactive system. In the first context, says Parsons (1951, p. 250) deviance is a "motivated tendency for an actor to behave in contravention of one or more institutionalized normative patterns," while in the second, it is a "tendency on the part of one or more of the component actors to behave in such a way as to disturb the equilibrium of the interactive process." In both contexts, deviance is defined in relation to the institutionalized norms of an interactive system. Moreover, and most important, the actor is motivated to contravene the norms of the system in which he is a participant. Thus with Parsons, as with Merton, the deviant is a member of the group whose norms he violates. In the terms used earlier, he is an "insider" not an "outsider."

Social control is defined as those motivated processes within the actor or among those with whom he is in interaction by which deviance is, or tends to be, counteracted. As not all attempts at counteraction succeed, deviance may be seen as resulting either in successful counteraction or in change in the structure of the interactive system.

For those who are not familiar with the orientation of modern sociology, it might be useful to note that conformity to established norms is not considered "good" in a moral sense any more than deviance is considered "bad." Questions of morality are outside the frame of reference of science, which has become the prevailing method by which modern sociology has attempted to understand its subject matter.

Parsons begins his discussion of the genesis of deviant motivation by reference to a hypothetical stable interactive system. In such a system the participants are interacting in terms of a normative pattern which they share and have internalized. They are, moreover, sufficiently attached to one another to be sensitive to each other's reactions to any violations of that normative pattern. Parsons then posits the introduction of a disturbance "from whatever source," creating a strain in the relationship. For example, "A" may fail to live up to the expectations of "B," presenting both with a problem of "adjustment." To simplify matters, we shall focus on the problem faced by "B" in attempting to adjust to the changed behavior of "A." On the most general level of analysis, there are a limited number of ways in which "B" can solve his problem, says Parsons (1951, p. 252):

He can first restructure his own need-dispositions, by inhibition and by one or more of the mechanisms of defense, such as simply repressing the needs which are no longer gratified. He can, secondly, seek to transfer his cathexis to a new object and relieve the strain that way and, finally, he can renounce or seek to redefine the value orientation pattern with which alter [in our terms, "A"] *is no longer conforming.*

Should "B" successfully move in any one of these three directions, the strain in the relationship would be resolved. It would be resolved also if "A" were to abandon his changed behavior. It should be apparent that resolution in the first case (through a process of learning by "B") would result in a changed state of the interactive system, in the second (through "A" abandoning his changed behavior) a restoration of the old state.

There is another possible outcome, says Parsons, and one which is quite likely, because of the difficulty in making changes when one is a committed participant in the interactive system. That is, in one or more of the areas of possible change, a "compromise" solution may be reached. To take one example, "B" may not be able to "transfer his cathexis to a new object" because of the strength of his attachment to "A." But where this is the case, the relationship can no longer continue undisturbed. As Parsons (1951, p. 253) puts it:

Ego ["B" in our example] *must have some reaction to the frustration which alter* ["A" in our example] *has imposed upon him, some resentment or hostility. In other words the* [attachment] *acquires an ambivalent character, there is still the need to love or admire alter, but there is also the product of his frustration in the form of negative and in some sense hostile attitudes toward alter.*

It is of course possible, says Parsons, for the negative or hostile attitudes to be directed, not toward the person or persons involved, but toward the normative pattern in terms of which the problematic expectations derive. In this case the resulting ambivalence would take the form of simultaneous positive and negative attitudes toward the same normative pattern.

The adaptations to which Merton points as at least partial solutions to the "problems of adjustment" presented to its members by societies of the American type, may be seen as more specific examples of the general solutions referred to by Parsons in his discussion of the directions of deviant motivation. Parson (1951, p. 257–59) makes this very point in his discussion of the genesis and directions of deviant motivation. But most important for present purposes is to recognize that both Merton and Parsons note the likelihood of ambivalence in the personalities of those who adapt by one or more of the modes covered by their analyses. Moreover, both feel that the greater the degree of internalization of elements of the shared normative system, the greater the likelihood of ambivalence, whatever the solution attempted.

Thus none of the above analysis of Parsons' views on the genesis of deviant motivation is inconsistent in any fundamental way with what Merton had to say in his original paper. However, in concerning himself with the psychodynamics of the genesis of deviant motivation, Parsons provides us with additional insight into the significance of commitment to persons and to normative elements in the development of the negative component of ambivalence. Moreover, his concerns in this regard have led to important conclusions about the *extent* of ambivalence among these same persons; for Parsons it is far greater than has been suggested by Merton, and, as we shall see, far more important in explaining subsequent responses.

Parsons' discussion of the directions of deviant motivation builds directly on his discussion of the genesis of deviant motivation. He argues that while there are many ways in which the strains inherent in an ambivalent motivational structure may be handled, they all fall into one of two general categories. The first involves repression of one side of the ambivalent motivational structure so as to permit a relatively undisturbed expression of the other side. The second involves an attempt to gratify both sides of the ambivalent motivational structure. Presumably the latter cannot be accomplished within the same concrete situation, because the two sides are in conflict. But in a complex society such as our own, there are all sorts of possibilities to gratify both sides, for example, by segregating contexts and occasions.

In discussing the directions of deviant motivation, Parsons concentrates on the first of these approaches. He begins by noting that although one side of the ambivalent motivation structure is repressed, this does not mean that it is of no consequence in explaining what the actor does. In fact, the repressed component figures prominently in Parsons' explanation of probable responses to ambivalence. But before

taking on that aspect of Parsons' treatment of the subject, it is necessary to define certain terms. Parsons refers to the negative component of the actor's ambivalent motivational structure as the *alienative* component, and to the positive component as the *conformative* component. When the alienative component is dominant, he speaks of an *alienative dominance* in the actor's need-disposition structure. When the conformative component is dominant, he speaks of a *conformative dominance* in the actor's need-disposition structure.

Depending upon which of the two components is dominant, Parsons speaks of a tendency toward *compulsive alienation* or *compulsive conformity*. His reasons for suggesting a tendency toward compulsion in responding to an alienative or a conformative dominance are simple and, it might be added, fundamental to much of his thinking on the subject of deviant motivation. What he argues is that no matter which of the two components is dominant, the actor has a problem of managing the one that is repressed. He must keep it under control, so to speak, or it will break through and present additional problems of adjustment. One important mechanism of defense against the repressed component breaking through is *reaction formation.* The overt manifestation of reaction formation is an exaggerated expression of the dominant side of the ambivalent motivational structure. The tendency in the case of compulsive conformity is to "accentuate the positive," to be "compulsively careful" to conform to the institutionalized expectations. In the case of compulsive alienation, the tendency is to "accentuate the negative," to be "compulsively careful" *not* to conform to the institutionalized expectations.

Parsons does not stop here in his effort to differentiate motivations arising out of ambivalence. Compulsive conformity and compulsive alienation are further differentiated according to a variable which is well-known in psychological theory, that having to do with more or less control over the situation than one would normally expect. Referred to by Parsons as the activity-passivity dimension, it is combined with compulsive conformity and compulsive alienation to produce four types of deviant motivation: a tendency toward compulsive performance, a tendency toward compulsive acquiescence, a tendency toward rebelliousness, and a tendency toward withdrawal. The four types of deviant motivation and the combinations of variables which give rise to them may be seen in Figure 2. By motivation, in this context, is meant simply a tendency or disposition to act in a certain way. It is important, according to Parsons, to separate deviant moti-

	Activity	Passivity
Conformative Dominance	Tendency Toward Compulsive Performance	Tendency Toward Compulsive Acquiescence
Alienative Dominance	Tendency Toward Rebelliousness	Tendency Toward Withdrawal

Fig. 2. Types of Deviant Motivation (Adapted from Parsons, 1951, p. 257)

vation from deviant behavior, because the former is not always expressed and the latter cannot be adequately explained without some reference to the siutation in which the person who presumably possesses deviant tendencies finds himself. It might be noted in passing that much early psychology failed to take this important distinction into account, and thus attempted to explain deviance in terms of motivational patterns alone.

Inspection of Figure 2 will reveal that there are a number of similarities between Parsons' four types of deviant motivation and Merton's four modes of individual adaptation discussed above. Merton's "retreatism" is similar to Parsons' "tendency toward withdrawal," and Merton's "rebellion" is similar to Parsons' "tendency toward rebellion." Merton's "innovation" and his "ritualism" are more difficult to relate to Parsons' scheme, because they involve elements of conformative as well as alienative motivation, depending on whether one focuses on the cultural goals or the institutional means. However, it is important to keep in mind that while Merton was talking about types of deviant behavior, Parsons is talking about types of deviant motivation. The two typologies could be "brought together," so to speak, if one were willing to assume that Parsons' scheme applies to behavior as well as motivation, and, further, if one were to assume that each of Parsons' categories could apply to "cultural goals" as well as "institutional means." We have attempted to do this in Figure 3.

The value of Parsons' typology lies mainly in the fact that it calls attention to the variables which combine to produce each of the four categories of deviant motivation. The tendency toward withdrawal, for example, is a combination of an alienative dominance (in the actor's ambivalent motivational structure) plus a tendency toward passivity, while the tendency toward rebellion is a combination of an alienative dominance plus a tendency toward activity. Put this way, it can be seen that the tendency toward withdrawal and that toward rebellion are differentiated, not by any difference in the strength of the alienative component in relation to the conformative—for in both cases they are the same—but by a difference on the activity-passivity dimension. If this seems

inconsequential, consider this: for Parsons the motivation for such criminal activity is the tendency toward rebellion, while the motivation for much mental illness is the tendency toward withdrawal. If he is correct, then the difference between the criminal and the mental patient is less a matter of alienation than it is of a tendency toward activity or passivity. What this means, when one starts thinking about solutions to the problem of crime, is that in deterring a person from committing a criminal act we may be inducing him not to conform to conventional norms but to withdraw into the sick role or some other state of dependency. For many people, withdrawal may be considered a desirable alternative, but it is not a solution to the problem of deviance, only to the problem of crime. On the other hand, given the existence of a high level of alienation, the existence of a sick role, into which alienated people can periodically "slide," may drain off a great deal of alienative motivation which might otherwise be expressed in quite damaging ways—for example, in the form of personal and property crime. Parsons makes this point and argues that there is precious little understanding of the sick role as a mechanism for "capturing" certain types of alienated people and for putting them into a position where they can do very little damage. He argues also that the system of medical practice, therefore, performs important social control functions in so far as it deals with the alienative motivation of those who withdraw into the sick role as a solution to their problems.

A similar analysis can be made of the differences between the tendency toward withdrawal, on the one hand, and that toward compulsive acquiescence, on the other. The difference lies not in the degree of emphasis on passivity—it is great in both cases—but in the fact that the former involves a dominance in the actor's motivational structure on the alienative side, while the latter involves a dominance on the conformative side. Thus a tendency toward withdrawal can be turned into a tendency toward compulsive acquiescence by decreasing the strength of the alienative component to a point where it is no longer dominant. The reverse is also true; a tendency toward compulsive acquiescence can be turned into a tendency toward withdrawal by increasing the strength of the alienative component.

Albert K. Cohen and Delinquent Subcultures

The work of Albert K. Cohen has been interpreted to be a rejection of Merton's formulation of the theory of anomie.[19] While it is true that Cohen calls attention to a number of shortcomings in the work of Merton, his criticisms are best seen as suggestions for revisions of the theory rather than a rejection of the theory itself. Moreover, there are several respects in which Cohen's work falls directly within the mainstream of thinking among anomie theorists. First, it is an attempt to explain differences in rates of behavior by reference to structural features of the larger society. Second, the features with which he is concerned are basically the same ones which attracted the attention of Durkheim and Merton, namely, the emphasis in modern societies on common success goals and the disadvantages associated with lower class status.

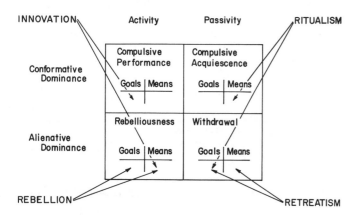

Fig. 3. Relationship of Merton's Modes of Individual Adaptation to Parsons' Directions of Deviant Motivations

Cohen's contributions to the development of the theory of anomie are to be found mainly in his treatment of the phenomenon of gang delinquency. They appeared for the first time in 1955 in a work entitled *Delinquent Boys: The Culture of the Gang.*[20] As the title suggests, the focus of attention is on the subculture around which the gang is organized. The theory which he develops relates mainly to that subculture. For Cohen an "adequate" theory of gang delinquency must explain at least the following: First, the content of the subculture (Why does it have the peculiar configuration of traits which it has?), and second, the distribution of the subculture within the society at large (Why is it found primarily among certain categories of persons and not others?). There are other questions as well, which Cohen considers important and which he attempts to answer, but those concerning the content of the subculture and its distribution are the ones to which he gives the most attention.

The delinquent subculture is described in terms of six general characteristics. Five have to do specifically with its content. The sixth has to do with the quality of the attachment of its members to the gang. The first of the characteristics is a tendency for gang members to prefer non-utilitarian activities over utilitarian ones. By non-utilitarian activities is meant activities that one values as ends-in-themselves, rather than as means to (culturally approved) ends. Much vandalism and violent behavior is seen by Cohen as non-utilitarian. Even the pattern of stealing seems to have a non-utilitarian quality to it, in that the items stolen are often discarded or given away, and those that are not seem to have value in part because they were stolen. "The stolen sweets are often sweeter than those acquired by more legitimate and prosaic means" (Cohen, 1955, p. 26). The second of the characteristics is the subculture's negativism. He argues that what is right by delinquent norms is defined by its negative polarity to conventional norms. Delinquent gang behavior is considered right, says Cohen (1955, p. 28), "precisely because it is wrong by the norms of the larger culture." The third characteristic considered by Cohen is its maliciousness. In whatever they do "there is a kind of *malice* apparent, an enjoyment in the discomfiture of others, a delight in the defiance of the taboo itself" (Cohen, 1955, p. 27).

The fourth, fifth, and sixth characteristics are a tendency toward short-run hedonism, an emphasis on versatility, and group autonomy. By short-run hedonism is meant a tendency toward immediate gratification. Cohen notes that a pattern of immediate gratification is common throughout the lower classes, but argues that it comes to "full bloom" in the delinquent gang. Under this pattern there is little concern for planning or for the long-run consequences of present acts— in a word, for the future. The tendency is to live in the present and let the future take care of itself. By versatility Cohen means simply a tendency to avoid specialization and to engage in a wide variety of activity. Lastly, by group autonomy is meant a tendency to resist being influenced by various agencies of control, (the family, the church, social work agencies, etc.) whose goals are often to regulate activities within the gang. As suggested earlier, Cohen is talking here not about the content of the subculture, but its attrac-tiveness to the gang in relation to alternative ways of thinking and acting.

Concerning the distribution of gang delinquency, Cohen contends that the pattern, as described, is found primarily among lower-class adolescent males. This is another way of saying that the rates of participation in the pattern vary by class, age, and sex. His thesis, to which we shall now turn, is an attempt to explain this variation.

In the simplest possible terms, the delinquent subculture exists because it is an attractive solution to a "problem of adjustment" faced by lower-class adolescent males. The distribution of the problem explains the distribution of the subculture. The nature of the problem explains the content of the subculture. According to Cohen, the problem of adjustment faced by lower-class adolescent males is primarily one of social status (or lack thereof), of not being able to compete successfully with middle-class boys. Like their middle-class counterparts, lower-class boys are interested in success in school and on the job; however, unlike their middle-class counterparts, they lack the ability to measure up to the standards by which success in these areas is measured. The ability to which Cohen refers as functional in school is the result of the way middle-class youth are socialized. It includes such things as ambition, good manners, industry, thrift, and the ability to defer immediate gratification, etc., none of which are likely to be as highly developed in the lower class as in the middle class.

The problem would not be at all serious, says Cohen, if lower-class boys did not care about the "good opinion" of middle class persons, (e.g., their teachers in school), or if they did not to some extent internalize the standards by which success within the middle class is measured. But they do, and so it is serious. Cohen, (1955, p. 119) summarizes his position as follows:

It may confidently be said that the [lower class] *boy, particularly if his training and values be those we have here defined as working-class, is more likely than his middle-class peers to find himself at the bottom of the status hierarchy whenever he moves in a middle-class world, whether it be of adults or of children. To the degree to which he values middle-class status, either because he values the good opinion of middle-class persons or because he has to some degree internalized middle-class standards himself, he faces a problem of adjustment and is in the market for a solution.*

As already noted, the problem of adjustment of the lower-class adolescent male is primarily a problem of social status, that is, he tends to end up in the "loser" category whenever he competes with his middle-class counterparts. But, to the extent that he internalizes the standards in terms of which he is being judged, he also faces a problem of self-esteem. The latter is a more serious problem in the sense that one cannot easily escape from it—for example, by withdrawing into a predominantly lower-class world. Being internal to the actor, the problem of self-esteem goes with him and can be solved only through a process of relearning, which is difficult to effect.

Cohen is not arguing that all lower-class adolescent males

have internalized the middle-class standards by which success is measured. Nor is he arguing that all who have internalized these standards have done so to the same extent, but only that some have done so to some extent, and to the extent that they have, they are faced with a problem of self-esteem, as well as one of social status. Depending upon the seriousness of the problem, Cohen reasons that failure is likely to produce alienative feelings in relation to these standards. In turn, this leads to ambivalence and, in some cases, the kind of compulsive reaction to which Parsons refers in his general theory of deviance and which has been observed among the members of delinquent gangs. His conclusions are all very tentative and involve a great many deductions, but that is how theories are built, and Cohen is confident enough about his approach to the subject matter not to be deterred from presenting his views by the possibility of being wrong.

Cohen recognizes that, depending upon the circumstances, the ambivalence to which he refers may lead not to gang delinquency but to a pattern of compulsive striving to escape from one's lower-class position. He refers to this pattern as the "college boy" response and argues that a certain number of lower-class youth can be expected to react this way. But it is obviously a difficult solution, and one that may be doomed to failure unless the boy is possessed of unusual talent and/or motivation. Ambivalence may lead also to what Cohen refers to as the "stable corner-boy" response. This response involves a passive acceptance of one's fate, based often on the belief that the future is not likely to be propitious. It is one which does not resolve the strains associated with failure, but then it does not involve the risks associated with being a delinquent either. The psychodynamics of both of these responses are rather well worked out by Cohen, but need not concern us here, except for noting that all involve deviant motivation and may be seen as responses to anomie.

For Cohen then, the delinquent subculture is best thought of as one of several possible solutions to the ambivalence that develops when one is judged a failure. The positive component of the ambivalent attitude structure is the result of having internalized, to some extent, those very standards. The compulsive quality of the delinquent solution is evidence of reaction formation. It will be recalled that reaction formation is a defense mechanism, born of ambivalence, in which the actor overemphasizes the dominant side of his ambivalent attitude structure in order to control the subordinate side, which is being repressed. At the same time that the delinquent subculture rejects the criteria in terms of which success is problematic, it substitutes a set of criteria in terms of which it is not. Thus the delinquent subculture is attractive in two respects: it expresses the lower-class male's negative feelings toward middle-class standards of success, and it provides him with an opportunity to be a success.

As noted earlier, the distribution of the delinquent subculture is explained in terms of the distribution of the problem of adjustment for which it is an attractive solution. It is found more among lower-class than middle-class persons, because the former are less able than the latter to measure up to the standards of success. It is found more among males than females, because it is still the male in our society who is under pressure to compete for status within the larger society. There is every reason to believe that as the female in our society comes to behave more like the male, she will face similar problems of adjustment and react in similar ways. Indeed, the dramatic increase in the arrest rates for females over the last ten years may be interpreted as a function of sex-role changes and the problems of adjustment which such changes present.

In summary, then, the content of the delinquent subculture is explained by reference to the nature of the problem faced by the lower-class adolescent male. The combination of early internalization of the standards of success to which he is subject and his subsequent alienation from those standards produces an internal problem which is managed by the mechanism of reaction formation. This leads to a wholesale rejection of the problematic middle class standards in favor of standards which can be met. Thus, deferred gratification is rejected in favor of immediate gratification, long-range planning in favor of short-run hedonism, utilitarian values in favor of non-utilitarian values, etc.

The pattern of behavior which results quite clearly does not fit into Merton's typology of deviant modes of individual adaptation. However, this should not be interpreted to mean, as some have argued (e.g., Clinard, 1964, pp. 30–33), that Cohen does not see his theory as a variant of the theory of anomie. What Cohen says (1955, p. 36) is that the "illicit means" thesis suggested by Merton as an explanation for much adult criminality does not explain the non-utilitarian emphasis within the delinquent subculture.

Were the participant in the delinquent subculture merely employing illicit means to the end of acquiring economic goods, he would show more respect for the goods he has thus acquired. Furthermore, the destructiveness, the versatility, the zest and the wholesale negativism which characterizes the delinquent subculture are beyond the purvue of this theory.

In Cohen's criticism of the "illicit means" thesis, the reference is to Merton's category of innovation (which involves the use of illegitimate means to conventional goals), and not to anomie theory in general. It might be noted in passing that the category of rebellion in Merton's typology *also* does not fit the facts about delinquent subcultures. Rebellion involves an attempt to substitute a new set of goals and means for those being rejected and is thus more "political" than the pattern described by Cohen. Actually, what Cohen describes comes very close to the category of *ressentiment* which Merton specifically excludes from his typology. On the other hand, it is identical with what Parsons calls rebellion. Cohen, for reasons which are not evident in his work, does not acknowledge either of these last two points.

Two other aspects of Cohen's thesis deserve comment. Both are ways of looking at the situation within which delinquent subcultures arise that were either de-emphasized or completely overlooked in Merton's original formulation. The first has to do with the process by which deviant solutions to problems of adjustment emerge. The general impression one gets in reading Merton is that the person beset with a problem of adjustment works out a solution to that problem independently of other persons. This model of what happens (referred to by Cohen as a psychogenic model) may suffice, for example, as an explanation for certain kinds of highly individualistic deviant behavior, but it will not suffice as an explanation for the emergence of a delinquent subculture or any other deviant subculture. For Cohen, a sufficient explanation for the emergence of a deviant subculture must recognize the possibility, indeed the probability, of collective problem-solving, involving a high degree of mutuality in the exploration and elaboration of alternatives. In Cohen's own words (1955, p. 61):

We may think of the process as one of mutual conversion. The important thing to remember is that we do not first convert ourselves and then others. The acceptability of an idea to oneself depends upon its acceptability to others. Converting the other is part of the process of converting oneself.

The second aspect of Cohen's thesis which deserves comment has to do with his recognition that there are class differences in the process of socialization, including the content of what is communicated, and that the degree to which these differences are institutionalized (shared and internalized) is fairly high. His position in this regard is evident in the fact that he does not hesitate to refer to the differences as cultural:

When we speak of "working-class culture" in the following pages, we shall be speaking of cultural characteristics and emphases which by no means characterize all working-class families but which do tend, in a gross statistical sense, to distinguish the cultural milieu of the working-class boy from that of the middle-class boy, and particularly which tend to characterize the least esteemed and economically most insecure levels of the working class. (Cohen, 1955, p. 95)

Put in other words, Cohen recognizes the existence of an established subculture within the lower classes, which has a bearing on the way children socialized in these classes learn to cope with the world. Furthermore, what they learn can affect their behavior independently of structural inequality (a lack of access to legitimate means).

The point at issue here can be approached in another way. If Cohen is correct in his assessment of the situation, it is not simply the lack of access to legitimate means in combination with common success goals which is the source of the problem of adjustment leading to gang delinquency among lower-class males. Also involved is an inbred inability on the part of these males to measure up to the standards of success which are being applied to them by people whose "good opinion" is important to them or which have been to some extent internalized. The point is important, for if Cohen is correct, access to legitimate means would not *immediately* solve the problem. The inability to which Cohen refers may include a lack of access to legitimate means, but it includes more than that. It involves an incapacity which is internal to the actor, a "defect of character," if you will, which puts the lower-class adolescent male at a disadvantage in the race

for status even under conditions of equality of opportunity.

On the other hand, much of what Cohen says implies that over the long haul many of the disabilities among lower-class adolescent males would disappear, if somehow we could eliminate (or even significantly reduce) the inequality of opportunity they face. Moreover, his reasoning, both on the level of general theory and in connection with specific substantive questions, suggests that the lower-class subculture which is responsible for the disabilities, is an adaptation to the relative lack of opportunity faced by lower-class persons:

There is good reason to believe that the modesty of working class aspirations is partly a matter of trimming one's sails to available opportunities and resources. (Cohen, 1955, p. 125)

Thus Cohen seems to be saying that the relative lack of access to means which may legitimately be used *is* a variable in the etiology of the response of the delinquent boy, but it enters the causal sequence in ways which Merton did not consider. It leads to adaptive responses (those associated with the lower classes generally), which then affect the development of ability (or lack thereof) among lower class adolescent males. In turn, this lack of ability becomes an internal factor, which, in combination with the desire to improve one's status, produces the problem of adjustment for which gang delinquency is one solution.

In summary, then, Cohen's contributions to the theory of anomie relate mainly to three aspects of Merton's original formulation. The first has to do with the adequacy of Merton's typology for the analysis of certain forms of deviant behavior, such as gang delinquency. Cohen argues that the category of innovation, involving the use of illegitimate means to conventional goals, does not fit the facts about gang delinquency—in particular, its emphasis on acts of a non-utilitarian or expressive nature. Our view is that the delinquent subculture fits very well into the category of *ressentiment*, which Merton specifically excludes from his typology. Because of the compulsive quality of the pattern which Cohen describes, and because it is admittedly a response to ambivalence, it would seem to fit also into Parsons' category of rebellion. On the other hand, it would be going too far to say, as at least one author has, that Cohen's criticism of the inadequacy of Merton's typology constitutes a rejection of the theory of anomie. In our view, Cohen's thesis is best seen as a variant of the theory of anomie as originally formulated by Merton.

The second aspect has to do with the inadequacy of the psychogenic model as an explanation for the emergence of the delinquent subculture or any deviant subculture. Cohen argues convincingly that the psychogenic model in terms of which Merton's theory is constructed does not sufficiently take into account collective problem solving, which for Cohen is the basic process by which subcultures are created. The psychogenic model views delinquency as the result of a process of problem solving, but the implication under this model is that each individual solves his problem independently of each other individual. For Cohen this is an inadequate picture of what happens. Indeed, according to Cohen's reasoning, few alterations in "frames of reference" of the type which we associate with social and cultural change would take place if problem solving were of this order. The need for support and the validity which comes from concensus almost require that each person contribute to the solution in a process of mutual conversion. Thus, for Cohen, the process by which subcultures are created is likely to be social or collective.

The third aspect has to do with several related ideas that Merton neglected to develop: First, the problem of adjustment of the lower-class adolescent male is not simply one of lacking the opportunity to compete for certain common success goals, but, in addition, involves a variable that is internal to the actor, namely, the inability to compete effectively even if the opportunity presents itself. Second, this inability to compete effectively is the result of a pattern of socialization within the lower classes, which is different in form and content from socialization in the middle classes. Third, this pattern of socialization is best seen as a response to the relative lack of opportunity faced by lower class persons generally. Thus Cohen's thesis recognizes a variable (the inability to compete effectively) in the development of gang delinquency which, although unrecognized by Merton, can be traced to the structural variable that figures so prominently in Merton's theory of anomie (inequality of opportunity).

Cloward and Ohlin and Illegitimate Opportunity Structures

It is generally conceded that Cloward and Ohlin are the most significant representatives of that group of anomie theorists who have taken their initial premises from the formulations of Merton (Cf. Clinard, 1964 and Taylor, Walton and Young, 1973). Merton himself (1964, p. 216) assessed their work as constituting the beginning of a new phase in the development of the theory of anomie:

It is no doubt too soon to say, but I am prepared to make the conjecture that a new phase in the developing theory of anomie was signalled in 1959 by Richard Cloward's paper, which extended the concept of access to the (implicitly legitimate) opportunity structure, a conception further developed in 1960 by Cloward and Lloyd, Ohlin in Delinquency and Opportunity.

Cloward and Ohlin make a number of important contributions to the further development of the theory of anomie. All are made in connection with three key questions which their theory attempts to answer. First, what is the source of the problem of adjustment for which delinquent subcultures are attractive solutions? Second, what are the conditions which result in the emergence of delinquent subcultures as solutions? Third, what accounts for the distinctive contents of various delinquent subcultures that have been observed? Our discussion of Cloward and Ohlin's contributions will deal briefly with all three questions, but our concern will be mainly with the third, for it is in connection with the question of the basis for the distinctive contents of various delinquent subcultures that the concept of illegitimate opportunity structure plays such a prominent part.

Like other anomie theorists, Cloward and Ohlin are concerned with variations in rates of deviance from one category of persons to another. Like Cohen, they start with the assumption that delinquent subcultures are found primarily among lower-class adolescent males. But unlike Cohen they recognize three types of delinquent subcultures, only two of which involve the kinds of expressive or non-utilitarian acts that Cohen argues are a key feature of the culture of the gang. Having recognized three types of delinquent subcultures, they are faced with a theoretical question that Cohen did not face, namely, what accounts for the distinctive contents of these subcultures? In answering this question they, in effect, answer the related question of why the several delinquent subcultures are distributed ecologically in the way that they are.

Most of the facts concerning the content and the distribution of the several delinquent subcultures were collected in the New York City area. In that area, the authors observed delinquent subcultures that emphasize utilitarian crime (the criminal), others that emphasize violence (the conflict), and still others that emphasize the use of drugs (the retreatist). The criminal subculture is broken down into two sub-types, those that emphasize the rackets (the sale of drugs, vice, and gambling) and those that emphasize conventional theft (burglary, larceny, and robbery). With respect to their distribution by neighborhoods (a most important set of facts, as it turns out), those criminal gangs that emphasize the rackets are found predominantly in Italian neighborhoods, while those that emphasize more conventional theft are found primarily in neighborhoods of mixed nationality. The conflict and retreatist gangs are found primarily in Black and Puerto Rican neighborhoods. In passing it might be noted that since the facts with which the theory deals were gathered almost exclusively in New York City, the theory may have limited applicability.

As already indicated, Cloward and Ohlin take their initial premises from the work of Merton. Indeed, their answer to the first of the questions which they pose (that having to do with the source of the problem of adjustment for which delinquent subcultures are attractive solutions) is substantially the same as that presented by Merton twenty-two years earlier.

Our hypothesis can be summarized as follows: The disparity between what lower-class youth are led to want and what is actually available to them is the source of a major problem of adjustment. Adolescents who form delinquent subcultures, we suggest, have internalized an emphasis upon conventional goals. Faced with limitations on legitimate avenues of access to these goals, and unable to revise their aspirations downward, they experience intense frustrations; the exploration of nonconformist alternatives may be the result. (Cloward and Ohlin, 1960, p. 86)

There are several differences between Cloward and Ohlin's "hypothesis" and the theory of anomie as developed by Merton which this general statement does not reflect. First, the conventional goals to which Cloward and Ohlin refer as having been internalized (and thus converted into aspirations) relate mainly to economic improvement. Lower-class youth who are motivated to join delinquent gangs are not particularly concerned with middle-class status, according to Cloward and Ohlin. Nor do they want to change their life-style. What they want is money and the kind of status within the lower classes which money can provide. Thus the goals with which delinquent types are concerned are conventional goals. Moreover, they are goals which are held in common with middle-class youth. But they do not include membership in the middle classes and all that such membership implies in terms of adopting middle-class values. It should be clear that, with respect to aspirations, Cloward and Ohlin take issue with Cohen.

Second, in elaborating upon their "hypothesis," the authors point out a fact that has been repeatedly substantiated over the years since Merton first presented his version of the theory: that aspirations, on the average, are somewhat lower in the lower classes than in the higher classes.[21] It should be understood that this fact does not in any sense invalidate the theory of anomie as an explanation for the higher rates of deviance within the lower classes. It is not the level of aspirations so much as it is the disparity between what persons at that level want and the means available to attain what they want, that is problematic. This is another way of saying that it is the relativity of aspirations which is significant for the theory of anomie, not the level of aspirations in any absolute sense.

But if the "disparity between what lower class youth are led to want and what is actually available to them," explains the problem of adjustment among lower-class adolescent males, it does not explain the emergence of delinquent subcultures as solutions to this problem. Cloward and Ohlin see four variables as having a bearing on the question of the emergence of deviant, including delinquent, subcultures. First, the persons involved must develop alienative feelings toward, and thus reduce their commitments to, the conventional normative system. The most significant step in the development of alienative feelings toward conventional norms is to come to see those norms as the cause of one's failure rather than, for example, personal inadequacy. Obviously, "awareness" of the part played by such norms in connection with an individual's success or failure is, therefore, a significant variable in the development of alienative feelings, and beyond that, in the emergence of delinquent subcultures.[22]

Second, the persons involved must be motivated to join with others in attempting to solve their problems rather than to "go it alone." Cloward and Ohlin's argument concerning the source of this motivation in the case of the frustrated lower-class youth is for all practical purposes identical with that presented by Cohen in his general theory of subcultural development. It comes down to this: There are definite advantages to collective problem solving whenever the solution is likely to involve a change in the actor's frame of reference. Specifically:

Collective support can provide reassurances, security, and needed validation of a frame of reference toward which the world at large is hostile and disapproving. (Cloward and Ohlin, 1960, p. 126)

Third, the persons involved must develop ways of handling the guilt which sometimes accompanies participation in activities which contravene conventional norms. It will be recalled that for Parsons and Cohen, the guilt was "handled" by the mechanism of reaction formation. For Cloward and Ohlin (1960, p. 131) the need for such a mechanism of defense is obviated by the process of alienation which, as they see it, involves a withdrawal of any feelings of legitimacy toward the conventional norms involved:

a person who places blame for failure on the unjust organization of the established social order and who finds support from others for his withdrawal of legitimacy from official norms . . . is psychologically protected against guilt feelings that would otherwise result from violation of those norms.

What they are saying is that the problem of guilt is solved in advance of the delinquent act, obviating the necessity for defense mechanisms of any kind. Obviously, if Cloward and Ohlin are correct, much of the reasoning of Parsons and Cohen (and Merton, also, to some extent) on the presence of reaction formation is called into question, for it assumes the presence of guilt. Clearly there is an urgent need for research on the question.

The fourth variable treated by the authors as having a bearing on the development of delinquent subcultures is the presence (or absence) of obstacles to the process of joint problem-solving. In addition to the motivation to solve problems jointly, there must be the opportunity to do so. At the very least there must be effective communication between those who are similarly troubled. This requires that they not be physically or socially isolated. By socially isolated, the authors are no doubt referring to the hostile feelings which often exists between members of different social and ethnic groups, and which serve as obstacles to the development of gangs that cut across social and ethnic lines.

Thus far, we have explained the source of the problem of adjustment for which delinquent subcultures are solutions and the conditions that must be met if the solution is to be a subcultural one. What remains is accounting for the distinctive content of the various delinquent subcultures—the criminal, the conflict, and the retreatist. As indicated earlier, it was in connection with this question that Cloward and Ohlin introduced the concept of "illegitimate opportunity structure."

Quite simply an "illegitimate opportunity structure" is an established and therefore stable pattern of illegitimate activity which provides opportunities for advancement for those who are associated with it. Such a pattern is most likely to exist in what Cloward and Ohlin call an "organized slum." By organized in this context is meant characterized by a high degree of integration between the non-criminal and criminal value systems, and between the upper-world and under-world residents of the area. It is this high degree of integration, of course, which makes the stable pattern of criminality possible.

Cloward and Ohlin account for the differences in context of delinquent subcultures in terms of differential access to illegitimate opportunity structures. In those lower-class neighborhoods where there are stable patterns of criminality by which young males can realistically expect to improve their economic status, the delinquent subculture most likely to emerge is the criminal. In such neighborhoods, there are opportunities not only to learn the roles associated with stable patterns of criminality but also to play such roles. There are, in other words, opportunities for engaging in crime as a career. In such neighborhoods, the problem of adjustment creating pressures toward delinquency is likely to be solved by taking advantage of such opportunities.

Conversely, in those neighborhoods where there is no stable pattern of criminality by which a young male can realistically expect to improve his economic status, the criminal pattern is not likely to emerge. In such neighborhoods the risks of getting caught are simply too great. The Harlem area of New York City is a prime example of a "disorganized slum." Even today, there are few, if any, opportunities for blacks to become racketeers. Organized crime is largely controlled by whites, and the police, with whom the racketeers are integrated, see to it that blacks do not become powerful enough to take over the territory. In January of 1960, the discriminatory practices of the police were exposed in a series of articles in the *New York Times,* at which time the Reverend Adam Clayton Powell is quoted as saying:

There is not operating in Harlem a single banker . . . The entire operation is totally in the hands of people who do not reside in nor are connected with this community. Here we find a community lower in income than any other in the city. And yet we spend $50,000,000 a year to support Italian and Jewish policy bankers. (quoted in Cloward and Ohlin, 1960, p. 201)

Earlier in that same month he proclaimed:

I am against numbers in any form. But, until the day when numbers is wiped out in Harlem—I hate to say this from the pulpit—I am going to fight for the Negro having the same chance as an Italian. (quoted in Cloward and Ohlin, 1960, p. 200)

Powell was calling attention to what had been known for some time, that in the New York City area, blacks and Puerto Ricans lack access to illegitimate as well as legitimate opportunity structures. Under such conditions, according to Cloward and Ohlin, one can expect the frustration to be particularly intense and conflict subcultures to emerge. The thesis is consistent with the facts, as noted earlier: it is in the predominantly black and Puerto Rican neighborhoods that the conflict subculture is most likely to be found.

The retreatist subculture, according to Cloward and Ohlin, develops among the "double failures," those aspiring lower-class youth who fail to achieve their goals either by illegitimate or legitimate means. Retreatism as a pattern involves the substitution of a "kick" (often in the form of drugs) for

the status which looms so large in the criminal and conflict gangs. According to Cloward and Ohlin (1960, p. 181) it arises:

from continued failure to near the goal by legitimate measures and from an inability to use the illegitimate route because of internalized prohibitions or socially structured barriers, *this process occurring while the supreme value of the success goal has not yet been renounced.*

One of the more important implications of the work of Cloward and Ohlin, especially with respect to their recognition of the significance of illegitimate opportunity structures, is that institutionalized patterns of criminality may be conceived as having positive functional significance for the society in at least two respects. First, they provide opportunities, albeit illegitimate ones, for ambitious lower-class youth to "work their way out of the slums," a fact of considerable significance, as it tends to support the ideology surrounding the American Dream that anybody can "make it" in America if he really tries. Second, were it not for these opportunities they might very well turn to violent activities, which are generally considered more serious, in that they violate personal rather than property rights. This is another way of saying that the existence of stable patterns of criminality perform "positive" functions for the society in "draining off" deviant motivation that might result in violence, which is generally considered more disruptive than property crime. An obvious conclusion from all this, of course, is that if we must have anomie, it might be better in terms of consequences, to permit adaptive criminal subcultures than to do away with them.

SOME ADDITIONAL CONSIDERATIONS

Earlier it was suggested that perhaps the most serious shortcoming of Merton's work on the theory of anomie has to do with his virtual neglect of two very important questions: what is the functional significance for industrial societies of the practice of emphasizing common success goals? And what is the source of the inequality of opportunity, which is so significant a variable in Merton's explanation of variations in rates of deviance within societies of the American type? The latter question actually has two parts to it: First, what is the source of the inequality in modern societies in the distribution of facilities and rewards? Second, how is this inequality translated into inequality of opportunity? Because of the complexity of the question on the source of inequality of opportunity, we shall deal with it first. Also, by so doing, the question of why modern societies emphasize common success goals will be less difficult to manage.

Achievement Values and Inequality of Rewards

It would seem of the first importance to understand the basis for social inequality if we are to appreciate the complexity of the "problem of anomie" in modern societies and, especially, if we "have a mind to do something about it." Perhaps the clearest statement on the subject may be found in the work of Parsons (1951, pp. 157–61). He argues that in modern (performance-oriented) societies such as our own, there is an "inherent tendency" within "instrumental achievement structures" (organizations producing goods and services) toward differentiation with respect to competence and responsibility, which has implications for social status. Concerning the tendency toward differentiation with respect to competence (defined as the capacity to do things well), Parsons (1951, p. 158) argues as follows:

achievement values cannot mean anything at all, if there is no discrimination between doing things "well" and doing them "badly". . . . With any at all elaborate system of the division of labor there will inevitably be a considerable range of differentiation of levels of competence, especially when a system of different technical roles and not just one role is considered.

Concerning the tendency toward differentiation with respect to responsibility, he argues (1951, p. 159) that:

beyond rather elementary levels, instrumental role-differentiation requires organization. Organization in turn differentiates roles along the axis of "responsibility" for the affairs of the collectivity. It seems to be one of the best attested empirical generalizations of social science that every continuous organization which involves at all complex cooperative processes, is significantly differentiated along this axis, informally if not formally.

He then goes on to argue that given differences in competence and responsibility we can expect differences in command over facilities, for it would be inefficient, to say the least, to put the best tools in the hands of the least skilled, or the most power (control over the affairs of the organization) into the hands of those with the least responsibility (impossible, actually, because of the relational quality of power). He thus concludes (1951, p. 159) that there is "an inherent tendency to allocate greater facilities to those on the higher levels of competence and responsibility."

There is a tendency toward differentiation, also, with respect to rewards, and for substantially the same reasons. To recognize competence and responsibility as contributing to efficiency is to recognize the value of competence and responsibility. There is thus a tendency for the allocation of rewards to be differentiated along the same lines as the allocation of facilities. In fact, says Parsons (1951, p. 159):

It is literally impossible to have an instrumental system sanctioned by the valuation of achievement without the internal differentiation of the role and facility structure coming also to be a differentiation of rewards, an internal stratification.

It follows from this that the only way to avoid differentiation in respect to facilities and rewards is to suppress the valuation of competence and responsibility. It follows also that this can be done only at the cost of efficiency. It might be noted in passing that Marxist ideology specifically denies that competence above that displayed by the ordinary worker

need be rewarded differentially. But the history of the Soviet experience demonstrates that with respect to both facilities and rewards there has been a high degree of differentiation. The factory manager in the Soviet Union, like his counterpart in the United States, makes substantially more than the ordinary worker. On the other hand, there have been some rather remarkable changes in the direction of equality in the reward structure (if not the facility structure) in the Israeli kibbutz and in the Chinese communes. All such experiments obviously deserve to be studied carefully for evidence that might contradict the theory here being elaborated.

It should be understood that the theory of stratification just described does not even remotely suggest that inequality is inevitable, but only that if a society should want something more than minimal efficiency in the performance of its workers, in whatever capacity they may be working, differentiation on the level of facilities and rewards is important, in fact, necessary. Nor does it suggest that those who possess high status are the best performers, for, as we shall see, status is affected by variables other than efficiency and effectiveness in instrumental achievement structures. Lastly, the rewards and facilities to which the theory makes reference need not be material ones (i.e., material goods or the equivalent in money). Stratification refers to differentiation in the structure of rewards and facilities of any kind. On the other hand, it should be obvious that, in America, material rewards are highly significant ones.

Ascriptive Values and Inequality of Opportunity

It has long been a fundamental feature of the theory of social systems that they are organized around values, and that there is a tendency in such systems toward consistency of action with respect to those values. Also, it is one of the most widely accepted generalizations in social science that the dominant subsystems in American society, the occupational and educational subsystems, are organized around a set of values which emphasize achievement rather than ascription (i.e., what a person *does* rather than who he *is*). Thus one of the crucially important questions for the theorist to answer is why, given the orientation toward achievement within the dominant structures in America and the tendency toward pattern consistency generally in human societies, do we tolerate structural arrangements, such as those associated with kinship systems, which emphasize ascription? We shall attempt to answer the question, but not just because it is of general theoretical significance. The inconsistency to which it refers is part of the reason for inequality of opportunity in modern societies.

The answer lies in understanding, first, that there are two bases for social structure, *any* social structure: the pattern of values by which actors are oriented, and the elements of the situation to which they are oriented. The most important of the situational elements are the so-called functional "exigencies" or "imperatives." In the simplest possible terms, these are the "reality factors" in the situation, the conditions which must be met if the structure is to persist through time.

An obvious implication of this position is that no social structure is derivable from the dominant values alone. Thus, says Parsons (1951, p. 168):

the extent to which the structure of social systems is not derivable from cultural elements is therefore a measure of the importance of the determinants underlying what we have called the functional "exigencies" or "imperatives" to which they are subject in the realistic conditions of their operation as systems. These resultants of these factors may be considered as patterns of deviation from what would be the model of "perfect integration" in terms of the dominant pattern of value-orientation.

An illustration may serve to illuminate the point Parsons is making. The social structure of American society is a product of certain values or ideals (e.g., men/women should be compensated according to their contributions in terms of goods and services) plus certain situational elements (e.g., the fact that some people are unable to contribute anything in terms of goods and services). The result is an "operating system" which includes a number of compromises with these values—for example, welfare programs under which men/women get "something for nothing." An important implication of Parsons' position in this regard is that in the absence of these compromises, the system would not survive, which is another way of saying the ideals, in their pure form, are not viable. Parenthetically, according to Parsons, there are no ideals which will meet all of the "needs" of any social system (i.e., all the conditions which must be met if the system is to survive). Parsons (1951, p. 168) refers to the structures which grow out of these compromises as *adaptive structures.* Technically, they are structures which differ in orientation from the dominant structures of the society, but which are nevertheless important (functionally speaking) for the preservation of these structures.

Turning now to the kinship system in modern societies, the reader should not be surprised to learn that it is classified as an adaptive structure. Why? First, because it is different in orientation from the values of the dominant structures of the society and, second, because it is functionally necessary to the preservation of those structures. Actually, it is not correct to say that the kinship system is functionally necessary. What is necessary is that certain functions associated with that system be performed.[23] The function to which we refer is generally thought of as a vital one, which means that the very existence of the society is dependent upon it.

The discussion thus far raises as many questions as it answers. For example, what is the vital function performed by the kinship system (defined as an interactive system based upon biological relatedness), and why must the system which performs this function be oriented around ascriptive rather than achievement values? Concerning the first of these questions, the function to which we refer is the socialization of children. It is generally conceived to be a vital one because no society can long exist without securing a certain level of commitment from new members to its values or, more specifically, to its role structure. Whether this function must be performed within what we have referred to as the kinship system is, of course, open to question. However, as Parsons (1951, p. 154) has pointed out, there are no known societies in which a major part of the training of children does not take place within a kinship unit. Moreover, the socializing agents are strategically important members of that unit, however it may be defined in a particular society.[24]

Concerning the second of these questions—that having to do with the organization of socialization around ascriptive values—the answer seems to lie in the fact that ascription is an outgrowth of the diffuse love attachments which play such a prominent role in the socialization of children and, indeed, may be necessary for the development of personality stability.[25] Such attachments, according to Parsons, produce a kind of solidarity in which the facilities and rewards available to one will have to be shared with the others. In other words, the solidarity of the kinship unit is likely to push the parents in the direction of treating their loved ones in terms of "who they are rather than what they do," which, in the last analysis, is all that is meant by ascription.

Whatever theoretical considerations one might bring to bear in explaining the universality of ascriptive values within kinship systems, the fact that they are present is of considerable importance to the explanation of inequality of opportunity in modern societies. In summary the argument is as follows: given the inequality in the facility and reward structure generated by the emphasis on achievement values within the productive subsystem, the tendency toward ascription within kinship units means that the children of the successful will have advantages over the children of the unsuccessful. In somewhat more eloquent terms, Parsons (1951, p. 161) puts it as follows:

In other words, these two basic components of the reward system of the society, occupational approval or esteem and the symbolic accoutrements thereof, and "emotional security" love and response in the kinship unit, must go together in some way. The consequence of this is that the combination of an occupationally differentiated industrial system and a significantly solidary kinship system must by a system of stratification in which the children of the more highly placed come to have differential advantages, by virtue of their ascribed kinship status, not shared by those lower down.

Before continuing it seems wise to emphasize several points that, until now, have been mentioned only briefly. First, facilities and rewards can be translated into opportunity by anyone who has access to them, not just by the individual who secured them through meritorious performance or the members of his family, with whom he is likely to share them. Secondly, in some societies of the modern type, notably those with socialist tendencies, the possibility of translating rewards and facilities into opportunities for advancement are far more circumscribed than they are in modern societies of the capitalist type. For example, it is more difficult in socialist than in capitalist societies to translate access to facilities and rewards into educational opportunities for one's children or into investments which by themselves would produce additional rewards. On the other hand, there is some evidence that men who are highly placed in socialist societies do use their power to secure advantages for friends and relatives. This fact is an important theme in a book on socialist bureaucracies (Djilas, 1958). Thus, although a wide range of variation is evident, complete separation of the kinship system from the occupational system, under present conditions, is impossible.

The qualification "under present conditions" in the last sentence is an important one. What we are saying is that we know of no way of socializing children independently of the kinship units which we have been discussing. Utopian thinkers have constructed "ideal" societies in which this is a central feature, Plato's *Republic* and Huxley's *Brave New World* being notable examples, but as yet none has been put into practice. Because of the perceptive way in which Huxley handled the "problem" with which we have been dealing, it deserves further consideration, which we shall give it below.

The Functional Significance of Common Success Goals

The last of the questions with which this part of the chapter is concerned is that having to do with the practice in modern societies of emphasizing common success goals. It will be remembered that the relative lack of opportunity within the lower classes in modern societies would not be problematic if the members of these classes did not share the success goals of the middle and upper classes. It might justifiably be asked, if common success goals are so problematic, if they lead to severe problems of adjustment within the lower classes, why are they emphasized?

The question is not nearly so difficult as it may at first seem. Quite simply, *common success goals provide the motivation for participation in the process by which it is determined who the best performers are.* It will be recalled that the emphasis on achievement values implies recognition of differences in competence and responsibility and, beyond that, in the allocation of rewards. It also implies that the participants in the system are motivated to compete for the rewards which are used to secure competent and responsible performance. This motivation can be guaranteed only if the persons involved have to some extent become committed to the acquisition of the commodities that have been defined as rewards. In the American case, these commodities are, in effect, the culturally favored goals. The line of reasoning involved here should not be taken to mean that all persons in America are committed to these goals. In fact, there is considerable evidence to suggest that they are not.[26] However—and this is the point at issue—those who are not committed are not motivated to compete, at least in terms of the goals in question. A good example of the type of person we have in mind here is the societal dropout, of which the hippie might be seen as an obvious example.

Where We Stand

Putting it all together, where do we stand? What is the present state of our thinking on the theory of anomie? The following series of propositions will serve to answer the question. Emphasis will be given to those ideas most relevant to the discussion in the last part of the chapter, on the implications for change.

1. Anomie is best conceived as a state of social organization involving widespread disrespect for one or more aspects of a society's normative system.

2. Anomie is the result of certain structural features of modern societies. The most important of these are the emphasis on achievement values within the productive subsystem and the emphasis on ascriptive values in the kinship subsystem.

3. The emphasis on achievement values within the productive subsystem, *in itself,* produces anomie by stressing goal-attainment rather more than conformity to the norms prescribing legitimate means. This source of anomie explains the higher rates of deviance in societies of the American type as compared with societies of the "ritualistic" type.

4. The emphasis on achievement values within the productive subsystem *in combination with* the emphasis on ascriptive values within the kinship subsystem also produces anomie, in this case, by stressing goal-attainment even among those who possess a relative lack of access to the means which may legitimately be used in pursuing the approved goals. The "relative lack of access" is a function in large part of the presence within the kinship system of ascriptive values. This source of anomie explains the higher rates of deviance in the lower as compared with the higher classes within societies of the American type.

5. The emphasis on achievement values within the productive subsystems of modern societies is by no means accidental. The stress in these subsystems on efficiency *requires* an emphasis on achievement values.

6. To say that a society emphasizes achievement values is to say simply that it stresses what a person does (his performance) rather than who he is (his qualities).

7. To stress performance means that the good performers must be given something more than the bad performers. What they are given could be a material reward or a nonmaterial reward or some combination of the two, but whatever they are given, the result will be some kind of inequality of status as between those who perform well and those who do not. On the other hand, one cannot infer from this statement that those who possess high status, even in an achievement oriented society, are the best performers.

8. A relative lack of opportunity by itself does not produce anomie. It is only when the disadvantages of class are combined with an emphasis on common success goals that anomie is likely to develop within the lower classes.

9. The function of common success goals is a point on which there is considerable agreement among anomie theorists. Common success goals provide the motivation for the competition without which it would be difficult (if not

indeed impossible) to ascertain who the best performers are.

10. The facilities and rewards associated with high status can usually be translated into some kind of opportunity for acquiring even greater rewards (i.e., for advancement within the status hierarchy). This is so not only for the person who receives the rewards, but for others as well, if he chooses to share them. In the American case, the ascriptive values within the kinship subsystem "push" the person who receives the rewards in the direction of sharing with his family, although obviously he is permitted to share them with anyone he chooses. Thus in the American case, particularly, the ascriptive values within the kinship subsystem lead to inequality of opportunity: the children of the successful have advantages over the children of the unsuccessful.

11. The rewards associated with high status can be more easily translated into opportunity for others in societies of the American (capitalistic) type than in societies of the socialist type. This kind of translation is a function of the freedom which exists in America to invest in education, in business enterprises, etc. Socialist societies greatly restrict this freedom, so that inequality of opportunity in socialist societies is less than in capitalistic societies. However, it is not unknown in such societies.

12. Inequality of opportunity (in combination with an emphasis on common success goals) produces anomie in part because the person who fails to attain the approved goals can (depending upon his level of awareness) "make a case" for that failure as being due to "structural features of the system" rather than his own incapacity. Thus his "level of awareness" must be regarded as a significant variable explaining differential rates of anomie by social class.

13. Regardless of the source of anomie, the state of anomie is likely to lead to deviance as a solution to the problems which it presents. It does not follow, however, that only anomie can lead to deviance. There are undoubtedly other causes of deviance.

14. The dynamics of the way in which anomie results in deviance is an area in which further development is needed, but the work of Parsons, Cohen, and Cloward and Ohlin constitutes an important step in the direction of solving the theoretical problems in this area.

15. Anomie theory implies that ambivalence is likely to be present in the motivational patterns of persons who have developed disrespect for one or more aspects of a society's normative pattern. This is because the disrespect is a function of *participation in* the society whose norms the actor comes to disrespect and, further, that participation implies some degree of internalization of the problematic normative pattern.

16. Agreement is not nearly so great on the question of how the negative component of the ambivalent motivational structure is managed. For Parsons and Cohen it is managed by a process of repression resulting in reaction formation; for Cloward and Ohlin it is managed by a process of learning involving the substitution of a new set of normative standards.

17. Until recently, discussions of the process by which solutions were arrived at made little reference to interaction between "kindred souls—persons similarly troubled. It was as if each person arrived at his solution independently of each person. Now, the weight of opinion is on the side of those who argue that, while some solutions may be arrived at in this way, those which become institutionalized as subcultures are created collectively.

18. In recognizing that some solutions become institutionalized as subcultures, anomie theorists have come to see the complexity of the process by which deviance is generated. The process is now conceived as involving, in addition to the basic problematic variables, one or more institutionalized subcultures which combine to produce the deviant solution. For example, lower-class culture, adaptive though it is, may be seen as contributing (in the way Cohen suggests) to the problems faced by lower-class adolescent males.

19. These institutionalized solutions are what sociologists call adaptive structures. They are structures which stress values that depart from the dominant theme in modern societies but which nevertheless perform important "functions" in relation to system maintenance. They co-opt, cool out, buy off the dissidents, often by providing outlets which are less disruptive than if the persons involved were to rebel.

20. Such structures, of course, become important variables in explaining why some persons do not succeed, even when opportunities develop. For example, if such structures reduce aspirations or promise rewards in the hereafter for suffering on earth, those who are involved in them are less likely to take advantage of any opportunities which may develop.

IMPLICATIONS FOR CHANGE

It is often said that sociologists are willing to analyze the situation surrounding social problems, but unwilling to propose solutions. True or not, the statement describes a position which should be understandable to anyone who is familiar with the limitations of science in connection with matters of social policy and with the role of scientist as neutral observer. Logically, as most philosophers will readily admit, science is a limited mode of cognition, which means that although science can tell us what is and what might be on the basis of what is, it cannot tell us what is right (or wrong) in any ultimate sense of the term. Because of this limitation, sociologists *as scientists* have been reluctant to get involved in matters of social policy, which in one way or another involve judgments of ultimate value. On the other hand, sociologists, *as citizens,* have been willing to discuss the implications of their theories for change whenever it appears that specific changes may eliminate a condition that is considered problematic for the society and whenever it is understood that in discussing such changes no judgments of ultimate value are intended, i.e., when it is understood that no one change is considered any better in an ultimate sense than any other. It is this latter set of considerations which underlies our motivation here.

Actually, the inclusion of a section on "implications for change" of the theory of anomie as an explanation for deviance in America is based upon several considerations. First, as already suggested, it would seem to be the responsible thing to do, given the seriousness of the problem of crime and social unrest in America today. But there is another reason as well, which might serve to justify the exercise. Any discussion of change as a solution is likely to reveal information on the costs involved in eliminating the conditions presumably responsible for the problem. Such information, it is felt, can be of value in at least two respects: it can help us make more rational judgments on solutions, and it can make us more aware of what one must "give up" in order to "solve" the problem—and give up something we must, whenever a social arrangement is altered. At the very least, we must give up an established way of doing things and the gratification which accompanies participation in such ways. More important, almost any change will have implications for the satisfaction of economic and political interests, by which is meant that the change will involve a shift in the distribution of money and power. Thus a discussion of the implications for change of the theory of anomie can be expected to reveal the political-economy of the problem. From our point of view, revelations of this sort are quite desirable, if for no other reason than that they suggest the probable sources, on the one hand, of resistance to a given solution and, on the other, of support for that solution.

Whatever the value of a section on "implications for change," the discussion will take the form of describing certain changes which can be expected to reduce the degree of anomie and thus the consequences in terms of deviance. There will be no concern with what is politically feasible, i.e., acceptable to a majority of the American people. Indeed, it is assumed that most of the changes to be discussed would not be politically feasible, at least at this stage in our history. More important, there will be no concern with measures of the type classified by sociologists as mechanisms of social control. Concern will be with changes in organization which can be expected to result in the production of less anomie, and not with measures which can be expected to control the expressions of that condition after it has been produced. For example, there will be no concern either with deterrence (through threats of punishment) or with therapy (through rehabilitation), both of which are strategies of control. This is not to imply that strategies of control do not in some sense "work," but only that our concern is with more "basic" solutions to the problem.

The first of the changes to be considered relates directly to Merton's contention that a major source of anomie in American society is the relatively greater emphasis on goal-attainment than on conformity to the norms prescribing legitimate means. It follows from this assumption that anomie and the tendencies toward deviance associated with it, in so far as they are a result of this combination of variables, can be reduced by changes in social structure which would produce a more "integrated" society, i.e., one in which there is a "rough balance between emphases upon cultural goals and institutionalized practices" (Merton, 1957, p. 134). In such a society, it will be recalled, the pressure to attain the cultural goals is less intense than in societies of the American

type, and there is a greater sense of satisfaction simply from participating in competitive activity.

It follows also that anomie and the tendencies toward deviance associated with it could virtually be eliminated by changes which would produce a ritualistic society. In such a society, it will be recalled, there is a relative lack of concern for goal-attainment, so that satisfactions are almost exclusively a function of participation in competitive activity. Actually, it is quite likely that in a ritualistic society there would be no competitive activity as we know it in America, because with a relative lack of concern for goal-attainment, "winning" would have little meaning.

In contemplating ritualism as a solution, it should be remembered that, according to Merton, societies at the ritualistic end of the continuum are no less "malintegrated" than societies of the American type. The difference lies in the problem they face. In ritualistic societies the problem is not one of anomie, but of rigidity and the consequences thereof in terms of the inability to adjust to changing life-conditions. The problem faced by ritualistic societies was very well put some years ago in *Time* (1964), in an analysis of the situation faced by India when China exploded its first atomic device.

Of all the Asian nations affected by Peking's nuclear explosion, India has the most to fear. Since Red China's humiliating walk through the Himalayas in 1962, the Indians have been obsessed by fear of renewed Communist aggression. Thus, though India was only recently the antinuclear Cassandra of the nonaligned world, the nation last week was earnestly debating whether to build A-bombs of its own.

Chief problem of India's nuclear advocates, of course, is their nation's deep emotional attachment to the principles of nonviolence, as practiced by Ghandi and internationally canonized by the late Jawaharlal Nehru. In a speech to students last week, Lal Bahadur Shastri, Nehru's successor, loyally insisted: "We cannot change our conviction because of China's action."

The fact that India subsequently proceeded to build A-bombs of its own and proved to be flexible enough to adjust to what was conceived to be a serious threat to the nation's survival does not invalidate the point at issue, namely, that ritualism, like anomie, may have serious consequences for a society.

Returning to the less radical move of structuring a more "integrated" society, the consequences, though less threatening to national survival, are no less important for present purposes. Because of the close functional relationship between goal-attainment and the average level of performance, one would expect a de-emphasis upon the former to have a depressing effect upon the latter. Indeed, if it may be argued that anomie is the cost of the relatively greater emphasis on goal-attainment than on conformity to legitimate means, then a reduction in the average level of performance is the cost of any change in social structure which would produce a more "integrated" society. Put somewhat differently, with less emphasis on goal-attainment and more emphasis on conformity to institutional means, the concern would be less with "winning," more with "how one plays the game."

The impact of such a change in emphasis is very likely

to be greatest within the productive subsystem of a society of the American type (also within the educational subsystem which is closely tied to it), although a change of this type is likely to affect all those subsystems in which there is a strong performance orientation. Moreover—and this is no less important a consideration—it is likely to affect persons at all class levels, since it involves a change in orientation of the society generally. Translated into economic terms, the change being discussed would, other things remaining equal, reduce the rate at which productivity has been increasing and, therefore, the level of material well-being. The level of productivity must certainly be highly dependent upon the emphasis on performance as measured by the norms of efficiency and effectiveness.

Less obvious perhaps, but equally important, is the depressing effect which such a change would have on the rate of innovation in American society. Whatever one's concept of moral and economic progress, the ability to innovate is essential to its attainment. The relationship between the variables involved can be seen in the following statement by Durkheim (1964a) who was particularly concerned with the conditions that facilitate change in the moral norms:

. . . in order that these transformations [in moral norms] *may be possible, the collective sentiments as the basis of morality must not be hostile to change, and consequently must have moderate energy. If they were too strong, they would no longer be plastic. Every pattern is an obstacle to new patterns, to the extent that the first is inflexible. (p. 70)*

Thus,

The authority which the moral conscience enjoys must not be excessive; otherwise no one would dare criticize it, and it would too easily congeal into an immutable form. To make progress, individuality must be able to express itself. In order that the originality of the idealist whose dreams transcend his century may find expression, it is necessary that the originality of the criminal, who is below the level of his time, shall also be possible. (p. 71)

In other words, the conditions which allow for desirable innovation also allow for undesirable innovation. Or what is the same thing, the conditions which prevent undesirable innovation also prevent desirable innovation.

Another change implied by our summary formulation of the theory relates directly to Merton's contention that a second source of anomie lies in the disparity between the commitment of lower-class persons to common success goals and their relative lack of access to the means which may legitimately be used in pursuing those goals. It follows from Merton's contention that anomie from this source (and the deviance associated with it) can be reduced either by reducing the commitment of lower-class persons to common success goals, or by increasing their access to the means which may legitimately be used in pursuing those goals or by some combination of the two.

Again, if our theory is correct, the first of these moves—reducing the commitment of lower-class persons to common success goals—can be expected to reduce the motivation of lower-class persons to succeed and, along with it, the quality of their performance. However, it might be expected to have a similar effect in the higher classes as well, if it results in a decline in the number of lower-class persons who are motivated to compete for the cultural goals. As the number of persons competing for these goals declines, the need to perform among those who remain would be reduced. In other words, as their status becomes more secure, higher-class persons can be expected to be less concerned with performance.

It should be obvious that any reduction in commitment among lower-class persons to common success goals will decrease the rate of upward social mobility of lower-class persons. In turn, this means a reduction in the rate at which talent (performance capabilities) within the lower classes will be developed and utilized. This probable consequence, it might be noted, has been seized upon by some theorists as the one which the emphasis on competition and on common success goals is designed to avoid.[27] It might be wise at this time to examine more closely what such theorists have been saying.

Their argument may be stated as follows: the pattern of competition and the emphasis on common success goals associated with it have arisen in industrial societies to meet a need in such societies for a high level of performance, especially in connection with the more technical work roles. Competition, although obviously not without drawbacks, appears on balance to be the most efficient way of allocating persons to such roles. How? By insuring a high degree of correspondence between the demands of such work roles and the performance capabilities of the persons being "allocated." Put another way, were an industrial society to depend upon a system of ascription, based, let us say, on kinship relationship, which is not necessarily related to performance, the allocation of persons to work roles would be much less efficient. There is no assurance, for example, that the son of a lab technician, by virtue of that fact, will be capable or willing to "fill his parent's shoes."

An interesting implication of this kind of reasoning is that if somehow one could predict at birth who would and who would not later on possess the talent and motivation necessary to perform effectively in various technical work roles, assignment to those roles could be made at birth, and the system of competition, with its emphasis on common success goals, could be eliminated. To get this kind of predictability, of course, would require far more knowledge of and/or control over the processes of reproduction and socialization than now exists.

The kind of knowledge and/or control required was described some years ago in Huxley's *Brave New World* (1932), apparently without any intention of suggesting a way one might solve the problem of anomie. Briefly, what he depicted was a society in which the reproduction and socialization of children were carried out "scientifically" on assembly-lines and in nurseries. The processes they used produced precisely the right number of qualified persons for each level of work role in the society. Everyone was able and willing to do the job he was assigned to do, and no one had more ability or motivation than was required for his job.

Clearly this is a kind of "ideal" solution to the problem of anomie in that it permits the elimination of the frustrations associated with the present system of competition without reducing the high average level of performance which it produces. Whether we shall ever acquire the degree of control over reproduction and socialization described by Huxley remains to be seen. This author thinks it is very unlikely, in spite of a great deal of speculation to the contrary. On the other hand, should the technology someday be developed which would permit a high level of control over these processes, there is little doubt in his mind that it will be utilized for the solution of problems such as the one with which we are here concerned.

Perhaps the most frequently proposed solution to the "problem" of anomie within the lower classes is that of increasing the access of persons at this level to the means which may legitimately be used in attaining the cultural goals. Logically, this can be done in at least two ways: by leveling all occupations, according them equal rewards, and by retaining inequality in the reward structure while making it difficult to translate this inequality in rewards into inequality of opportunity for oneself and others.

Concerning the first of these approaches, leveling all occupations, such a change could be expected to reduce inequality of opportunity, since there would be no inequality in rewards to translate into inequality of opportunity. However, because of the functional significance of inequality in the reward structure for the motivation of performance, it could be expected also to reduce the average level of performance within those subsystems emphasizing performance, and at all class levels. In addition, such a change would very likely make it more difficult to fill positions of responsibility at the top of the hierarchy of occupations, since to make the sacrifices involved in preparing for them would no longer "pay." As indicated earlier, equality in the reward structure is part of the program for reform of the Marxians, but seems to be inconsistent with their belief in industrialization and the related emphasis on performance.

Concerning the second of these approaches, retaining the emphasis on inequality within the reward structure while making it difficult to translate this inequality in rewards into inequality of opportunity, implementation would require that the successful performers be restricted in the use of the rewards for that performance to the purchase of consumer goods (and services). It would be necessary to control the use of rewards for "investments" which would yield some kind of advantage (in relation to various success goals) without additional effort by the investor. This could be accomplished in America only by the elimination of the private ownership of capital goods and by equalizing educational opportunities. It is this approach which is most consistent with the goals, if not the actual practices, of many socialist countries, notably the Soviet Union.

There is at least one additional point worth making with respect to this approach to the equalization of opportunity: it would not eliminate the frustrations associated with competition, especially for certain categories of individuals. As one author (Johnson, 1960, p. 574) put it some years ago:

. . . attempts to equalize opportunity, while desirable for their own sake within the American value system, would not necessarily reduce the competitive strain for those whose native endowments or unusual personal experiences unfit them for successful competition. Further, the social structure itself has a limited number of positions at the top, and some people would have to "fail" even all were equally able. (p. 547)

There is an implication of this line of reasoning which is worth exploring. It seems clear that the "advantage" of equality of opportunity for the society is that it makes difficult any attempt by those who fail to blame the system for that failure. The problem of adjustment for those who fail would very likely, therefore, be resolved in the direction of blaming oneself rather than the system. And while it may be assumed that a tendency toward blaming oneself is likely to result in higher rates of mental illness and of suicide, neither of these is as threatening to the society as the consequences of blaming the system.

It should not be forgotten that, in the American case, by eliminating the disparity between goals and means, only one of the two sources of anomie is removed; there remains the emphasis on goal-attainment which puts a strain on the institutional controls over the use of illegitimate means. Thus any serious effort to reduce the level of anomie in American society would of necessity involve a move toward a more "integrated" society in Merton's terms.

Before concluding the section on "implications for change," it is important to point out that to argue, as we have, that it is possible through changes in social structure to reduce the rates of deviant behavior, should not be taken to mean that we believe that through such changes (or any others, for that matter) deviance can be eliminated from human society. Society is a moral order, which means its boundaries are defined by moral norms, and so long as this is the case, what is defined as deviance at any given time can be eliminated only by the most successful kind of socialization. The norms would have to be implanted uniformly in all individuals and with sufficient intensity to deter the expression of all desires to the contrary. In his treatment of this very subject, Durkheim (1964a, p. 69) argued that:

. . . a uniformity so universal and absolute is utterly impossible; for the immediate physical milieu in which each one of us is placed, the hereditary antecedents, and the social influences vary from one individual to the next, and consequently diversify consciousnesses. It is impossible for all to be alike, if only because each one has his own organism and these organisms occupy different areas in space.

What is more important, even if it were possible through a process of socialization to deter the expression of all motivation to engage in what is now defined as deviant behavior, the very process by which this is accomplished would create new categories of deviance. Durkheim's discussion of the inevitability of crime provides us with the logic for this conclusion (1964a, p. 68).

One easily overlooks the consideration that these strong states of the common consciousness cannot be reinforced without reinforcing at the same time the more feeble states, whose violation previously gave birth to mere infraction of convention—since the weaker ones are only the prolongation, the attenuated form, of the stronger. Thus robbery and simple bad taste injure the same single altruistic sentiment, the respect for that which is another's. However, this same sentiment is less greviously offended by bad taste than by robbery; and since, in addition, the average consciousness has not sufficient intensity to react keenly to the bad taste, it is treated with greater tolerance. That is why the person guilty of bad taste is merely blamed, whereas the thief is punished. But if this sentiment grows stronger, to the point of silencing in all consciousnesses the inclination which disposes man to steal, he will become more sensitive to the offenses which, until then, touched him but lightly. He will react against them, then, with more energy; they will be the object of greater opprobrium, which will transform certain of them from the simple moral faults that they were and give them the quality of crimes.

What he is saying, in other words, is that by strengthening the sentiments supporting the moral norms, the result may well be a reduction in the number of acts which offend these norms, from the most serious to the least serious. But as a result of the very same process (i.e., by strengthening the sentiments supporting the moral norms) there is likely to be another result as well: the definition of what is criminal will change in the direction of including acts that were before "simple moral faults." By carrying this logic one step further, it may be concluded that by strengthening the sentiments supporting the moral norms, acts that were once tolerated as acceptable departures from the moral norms will take on the character of deviance.

What this means, if it is not already clear, is that deviance, like crime, is inevitable, a consequence of the institutionalization of a set of moral norms. Thus, it is the product of the very process by which order in human societies is secured. The "problem" stems from the fact that the institutionalization of moral norms not only functions to control behavior within the categories covered by those norms, it defines the categories. That is why attempts to reduce the number of violations under a given set of norms by strengthening the supporting sentiments may be quite successful, but at the same time may have the consequence of expanding the definition of what constitutes an intolerable violation. That is why

the process by which humans attempt to secure order appears doomed to failure; the gains made in one area of activity are lost in another.

Returning to our discussion of the implications of the theory of anomie for change (as a solution to the problem of deviance), it may be concluded from all this that even in a society not characterized by anomie, there will be a certain level of deviation from the norms. But by the same token it may be concluded that a society characterized by a high level of anomie will have a great deal more deviance. It is this added increment of deviance with which we are concerned in the present section, and to which the changes under discussion refer. Our concern is not with deviance in general, but with that deviance generated by the phenomenon of anomie.

If there is any one conclusion of this discussion that is worth stating, it is that the problems which societies face are sometimes a function of mechanisms which have been created by these societies to meet the conditions of their own existence. Anomie may be seen as one such problem. At the risk of being repetitious, anomie may be seen as a product of the attempt of industrial societies to meet their own needs for high levels of performance in connection with the more technical work roles. Industrial societies thus face a dilemma: they can eliminate anomie only by recreating the problem for which the pattern of competition is a solution. If it is indeed a dilemma, then there is no completely satisfactory solution; there is only the possibility of a "trade off" of one combination of good and evil for another. In this connection, science can be of some value in specifying the alternatives of action that are open to us and in estimating the costs associated with these alternatives, but it cannot resolve the questions of ultimate value involved in the trade-off decision. It is possible, of course, that science may produce the technology noted earlier in the discussion of *Brave New World*, but even if it does, decisions of ultimate value must be made regarding the use of such technology.

There is one other approach to the dilemma which should be noted. We can continue, as we have, to do nothing about the source of the motivation to deviance and concentrate on its control through the strategies of deterrence and therapy. Although costly, such an approach does have one distinct "advantage"; it requires no fundamental changes in the system which lies at the root of the problem.

NOTES

1. For summary statements of the statistics bearing on the magnitude of these problems, see the President's Commission on Law Enforcement and Administration of Justice, *Task Force Report: Crime and Its Impact—An Assessment* (Washington, U.S. Government Printing Office, 1967), *Report of the National Advisory Commission on Civil Disorders* (Washington, U.S. Government Printing Office, 1968) and *To Establish Justice, To Insure Domestic*

Tranquility (Washington, U.S. Government Printing Office, 1970).

2. For an excellent discussion of the history of violence in America, see *To Establish Justice, To Insure Domestic Tranquility* (Washington, U.S. Government Printing Office, 1970) Chapter I, "Violence in American History."

3. For an extended list of studies which utilize the concept of anomie, see the "Inventory of Empirical Studies," by Stephen Cole

and Harriet Zuckerman in *Anomie and Deviant Behavior,* edited by Marshall B. Clinard (New York, The Free Press of Glencoe, 1964), pp. 246–89.

4. The original version of the article was published in *The American Sociological Review,* Volume 3, pp. 672–82. It has been reprinted in Merton's *Social Theory and Social Structure* (Revised Edition, New York, The Free Press of Glencoe, 1957), pp. 131–60.

5. Two works by Durkheim are significant in this regard: *The Division of Labor in Society*, translated by George Simpson (New York, The Free Press of Glencoe, 1964) and *Suicide*, translated by John Spaulding and George Simpson (New York, The Free Press of Glencoe, 1951).

6. For discussion of the "evil-causes evil" fallacy and the impact of this kind of thinking on the development of sociological theory, see Albert K. Cohen, "Multiple Factor Approaches" in Wolfgang, Savitz, and Johnson, *The Sociology of Crime and Delinquency,* (New York, John Wiley and Sons, 1970) pp. 123–26.

7. Cf. Gouldner, 1970, pp. 65–73.

8. It might be noted that the "sociological" as compared with the "clinical" approach is not just another way of analyzing the same variables. Often the sociological approach will ignore variables considered important in the clinical approach, if it appears that they bear only on the explanation of the incidence of the phenomenon under examination. The point can perhaps best be made by reference to an illustration. Differences in GRE scores might well explain why one student gets into graduate school while another does not, but it is extremely unlikely that changes in GRE scores would explain the increases or decreases in graduate enrollment which can be observed from time to time.

9. It has been argued that what Durkheim in effect does in recognizing the dynamics of the Protestant case is abandon his claim in *The Division of Labor* that organic solidarity involves a significant reduction of the collective conscience, and move toward a position which permits us to see organic solidarity as involving not the absence of a collective conscience but the substitution of a new collective conscience for the old one. In the industrial west, it involves the doctrine of individualism, with its obligation to be free of all sorts of religious, domestic, or political restraints, but at the same time to be moral in ways that are consistent with the needs of an industrial society. For an elaboration of this view, see T. Parsons, *The Structure of Social Action* (New York, The Free Press of Glencoe, 1949) pp. 324–38.

10. It is important to keep in mind what was mentioned earlier: that anomie is conceived quite differently in *Suicide* than it is in *The Division of Labor.*

11. For the sociologist interested in such questions, it is suggested that the answer may lie in the fact that Merton's thesis in this regard implies that anomie is an inevitable consequence of the most basic features of the American Way, an idea which only the most detached observers of the American scene care to contemplate. It may lie also in the fact that many sociologists apparently believe that the structural features which give rise to deviant behavior *within* societies of the American type can be eliminated without making basic changes in the American Way. Indeed, they may feel that these features would not exist if the members of American society would only live up to its ideals, notably that of equality of opportunity. It is an implication of the thesis of the present chapter that this ideal can be realized, if at all, only by making radical changes in the American Way. Thus Merton's thesis on the consequences of inequality of opportunity in generating deviance is just as devastating a critique of the American Way, when all of its implications are made clear, as is his thesis on the consequences of the emphasis on success in societies of the American type without an equivalent emphasis on institutional means.

12. Other interpretations of Durkheim's concept of anomie are no doubt possible. For example, one could conceive of the expediency on the level of means as violating the norms which presumably existed prior to advances in the division of labor, which conception would justify arguing that even in the context of *The Division of Labor,* anomie involves deviance. But this interpretation rests on the assumption that the collective conscience underlying the solidarity of the preindustrial state of society has not been destroyed. If we take Durkheim at his word, advances in the division of labor inevitably lead to the destruction of the collective conscience.

13. See, for example, Cohen, 1955.

14. In this connection, one is reminded of the attitude toward success which surrounds big-time college football—namely, that there is only one "winner," the number one team in the nation, and that all the rest are "losers."

15. See, for example, Richard Austin Smith, "The Incredible Electrical Conspiracy," *Fortune* (April, 1961), pp. 132–80 and (May, 1961), pp. 161–244; Daniel Bell, "Crime as an American Way of Life," *The Antioch Review* (June, 1953), pp. 131–54; Edward H. Sutherland, *White Collar Crime,* New York, Holt, Rinehard and Winston, 1949; Robert A. Lane, "Why Business Men Violate the Law," *Journal of Criminal Law, Criminology and Police Science,* 44 (August, 1953), pp. 151–65.

16. The concept of reaction formation is discussed in detail below, in connection with the contributions to the theory of anomie of Talcott Parsons.

17. If this statement is to be taken literally, it would be more accurate to view rebellion not as deviance from the conventional system of values against which the actor is said to be rebelling, but conformity to an alternative system, as stated earlier. Indeed, Merton himself seems to be taking a position similar to this in a recent statement on the subject in which he classifies rebellion as non-conformity, while continuing to see the other modes of adaptation as aberrant forms of behavior. At the same time, the existence of the alternative system of values may be viewed as the result of reaction against the conventional normative system which is seen as problematic. (Merton, 1971, pp. 829–32)

18. See the discussion of Cohen's views below.

19. See, for example, Clinard, 1964, pp. 30–33 and Taylor, Walton and Young, 1973, pp. 135–38.

20. They appeared later in several other publications as well. (See, for example, Cohen, 1965 and 1966.)

21. Several of the more important studies on the subject are summarized in Cloward and Ohlin (1960, pp. 87–90).

22. System-blaming versus self-blaming has only recently received the attention it deserves as a variable affecting the development of alienative feelings, even though a case for research on the subject was made by Merton (1957, p. 240) some years ago. For a good summary of the literature bearing on the subject and for the results of an important piece of research on factors affecting the tendency toward system-blaming, see Kerbo (1972).

23. There may be other equally necessary functions performed by the kinship system, but for purposes of simplifying the discussion, only one such function will be treated. For an introduction to the more important concepts and issues surrounding functional analysis, see Johnson (1960, Chapter 3).

24. For data substantiating these generalizations, see Murdock (1949).

25. For evidence concerning the functional significance of diffuse love attachments, see Spitz (1945–46, Vols. I & II) and Davis (1940, pp. 554–64).

26. For a good discussion of the literature on the subject, see Cloward and Ohlin (1960, pp. 86–97).

27. See, for example, Cloward and Ohlin, 1960, pp. 80–82.

BIBLIOGRAPHY

Becker, Howard S.
 1963 *Outsiders: Studies in the Sociology of Deviance*, New York: Free Press.
Clinard, Marshall B.
 1964 *Anomie and Deviant Behavior*, New York: Free Press.
Cloward, Richard and Ohlin, Lloyd
 1960 *Delinquency and Opportunity: A Theory of Delinquent Gangs*, New York: Free Press.
Cohen, Albert K.
 1955 *Delinquent Boys: The Culture of the Gang*, New York: Free Press.
 1965 "The Sociology of the Deviant Act: Anomie Theory and Beyond," *American Sociological Review*, Vol. 30.
 1966 *Deviance and Social Control*, New Jersey: Prentice Hall.
Davis, Kinsley
 1940 "Extreme Isolation of a Child" in *American Journal of Sociology*, Vol. 45.
Djilas, Milovan
 1957 *The New Class: An Analysis of the Communist System*, New York: Praegar.
Durkheim, Emile
 1951 *Suicide: A Study in Sociology*, New York: Free Press.
 1964a *Rules of Sociological Method*, New York: Free Press.
 1964b *The Division of Labor in Society*, New York: Free Press.
Gouldner, Alvin W.
 1970 *The Coming Crisis of Western Sociology*, London: Heinemann Educational.
Horton, John
 1964 "The Dehumanization of Anomie and Alienation: A Problem in the Ideology of Sociology," *British Journal of Sociology*, Vol. 15.
Huxley, Aldous
 1932 *Brave New World*, New York: Doubleday, Doran and Company, Inc.

Johnson, Harry M.
 1960 *Sociology: A Systematic Introduction*, New York: Harcourt Brace and World, Inc.
Kerbo, Harold
 1973 *System Blaming as a Function of Density, Relative Deprivation, Ideology and Ethnicity*, University of Oklahoma, Unpublished Master's Thesis.
Merton, R. K.
 1957 *Social Theory and Social Structure* (revised edition), New York: Free Press.
 1964 "Anomie, Anomia and Social Interaction: Contexts of Deviant Behavior," in Marshall B. Clinard, *Anomie and Deviant Behavior*, New York: Free Press.
 1971 "Social Problems and Sociological Theory" in Merton, R. K. and Nisbet, Robert, *Contemporary Social Problems*, New York: Harcourt Brace Jovanovich, Inc.
Murdock, George P.
 1949 *Social Structure*, New York: Macmillan.
Parsons, Talcott
 1949 *The Structure of Social Action*, New York: Free Press.
 1951 *The Social System*, New York: Free Press.
Spitz, Rene
 1945– "Hospitalism" in *Psychoanalytic Study of the Child*, Vols.
 1946 I and II, New York: International Universities Press.
Taylor, Walton, and Young
 1973 *The New Criminology*, London: Routledge and Kegan Paul Lts.
Time Magazine
 1964 Vol. 84, November 6.
Whitman, Walt
 1870 *Democratic Vistas*, New York: J. S. Redfield.

9

SHIFTING PATTERNS OF EDUCATIONAL THOUGHT

By John D. Pulliam

PURITAN SHADOWS AND
REVOLUTIONARY VISTAS

The life of the mind in the American colonies before the Revolution set the tone for grandiose educational schemes, some of which were actually realized. Variation in climate of opinion was pronounced between individuals representing different cultural backgrounds and exposed to a variety of cultural influences. The broad scientific and secular issues which captured the imagination of Benjamin Franklin were poles apart from the narrow theological interests of Puritan divines. Few intellectual movements in history have been more opposite in thrust than the religious revival known as the Great Awakening and the humanistic-scientific movement of the eighteenth century called the enlightenment. While the enlightenment had a direct effect on many of the founding fathers and helped to provide a theoretical foundation for the American experiment in government, educational traditions in the United States extend back to the ideals and schools of early New England theocracies.

Colonial New England's Contribution
to American Education

Educational theory and practice varied widely in the thirteen English colonies on the American eastern coast. Southern plantation owners transplanted British secondary schools and used private tutors for the basic education of their sons and daughters. Schools in the middle colony urban centers reflected the diverse sectarian characteristics of settlers there. They were usually private, often denominational, and lacking in uniformity either of structure or curriculum. But by far the most significant contribution to educational ideas and practices came from the Puritan colonies, where schools received attention second only to and not divided from religion.

Having failed to purify the Anglican Church in England and subject to the persecution of their Calvinistic sect by Archbishop Laud, the Puritans migrated in large numbers, especially in the 1630's. They crossed an ocean and braved the wilderness in order to worship in their own way and to set up a new society for the regeneration of Christianity. It was not their intention to cast off civilization or the cultural values of Europe. For them, the church was the supreme institution on earth, and there was no tolerance of other religious sects or nonbelievers. The Puritans wanted a state church with secular as well as religious authority. That authority rested upon God's word as revealed in the Bible and was interpreted for the congregations by their ministers. Puritans opposed the divine right of kings and the rule of bishops; but that did not imply power equally distributed among all citizens. As John Cotton put it:

Democracy, I do not conceive that ever God did ordain as fit government either for church or commonwealth. If the people be governors, who shall be governed? As for monarchy, or aristocracy, they are both of them clearly approved, and directed in Scripture, yet so as referreth the sovereignty (God) himself, and setteth up theocracy in both, as the best form of government in the commonwealth as well as the church.

The aristocracy of the elect (those predestined for salvation) used education as an instrument for social control, the preservation of values, and the training of preachers to preserve the faith. This is clearly stated in *New England's First Fruits*:

After God had carried us safe to New-England, and we had builded our houses, provided necessaries for our liveli-hood, rear'd convenient places for God's worship, and settled the Civil Government; One of the next things we longed for, and looked after was to advance Learning and perpetuate it to Posterity; dreading to leave an illiterate Ministry to the Churches, when our present Ministers shall lie in the Dust.

Puritan ranks contained a large number of educated men, and some of the ministers were graduates of the best English universities. They were anxious for their children to enjoy the pracitcal advantage of schooling as well as moral training and religious instruction. Calvinistic doctrine rejected the concept that men could be saved through good works, pious beliefs,and upright behavior; but it was generally agreed that those who did not exhibit saintly conduct were not among the elect. Puritans despised materialistic exhibition as they despised the flesh; but they measured religious standing by conduct and worldly prosperity, both of which required education. An example of Puritan educational philosophy is contained in Thomas Hooker's story about a sick man in an apothecary shop in the dark of night. Although surrounded by the means to ease his condition, he is unable to cure himself because he cannot read the labels on the bottles of medicine and does not understand their use. So it is, Hooker said, with the ignorant sinner in the world. Without the guidance of approved Christian instruction he is totally lost.

In an effort to establish a model Christian community and a home for saints, the Puritan fathers were quick to put theory into practice. Harvard College, a theological seminary based on an imitation of Emmanuel College, Cambridge, was established in 1636. Its classical curriculum and attention to Scripture closely followed English precedent, with heavy stress on the Puritan doctrine of predestination and related theological concerns. New England authorities were quite willing to legislate rules of conduct, and Harvard had laws regulating every activity of its students. Its entrance requirements reflected the curriculum:

When any Schollar is able to understand Tully, or such like classical Latine Author extempore, and make and speake true Latine in Verse and Prose, suo ut aiunt Marte; and decline perfectly the Paradigm's of Nounes and Verbes in the Greek tongue; let him then and not before be capable of admission into the Colledge.

Once a college had been established, it was necessary that Latin grammar schools be provided, so that boys wishing to enter Harvard could get the necessary preparatory studies. A "fair grammar school" (Cambridge Latin School) was erected by the side of Harvard. Many New England towns established such classical secondary schools. Perhaps the best known was the Boston Latin Grammar School, where Ezekiel Cheever became the most famous New England schoolmaster.

Secondary and higher education was limited to a few boys who had both social status and intellectual ability; but Puritans were unwilling to leave basic education for all children to chance. Following the Protestant concept of the priesthood of all believers, New England Puritans felt it necessary to teach their sons and daughters to read. The family was a strong cultural institution and the basic economic unit. It was responsible for vocational skills extending through apprenticeship, religious training, and the transfer of the culture from one generation to another. Basic intellectual education, such as learning to read the Bible, was often accomplished within the closely-knit family units. To the individual child, it could not have mattered much whether the family, the community, or the church was in charge, for all exhibited the same values and characteristics. Indeed, the various elements of New England communities were bound together by isolation, religion, mutual dependence, and philosophy more than most historical social systems.

In 1642 the General Court of Massachusetts, "taking into consideration the neglect of parents and masters" ordered town officials to remove neglected children from those who were not responsible and place them as apprentices with someone who would see to their education and moral training. This law followed the theory of Cotton Mather, who dwelt upon the Christian duty of parents to instruct children for their salvation. Apparently the regulations went unheeded, for in 1647 the famous Old Deluder Satan Act was passed. This law required that every town set up a school or pay a sum of money to the next larger town for the support of a school and teacher. The following year a tax on property for the support of education was established in Dedham, Massachusetts. Although some towns were slow to comply, the early Massachusetts laws were responsible for establishing elementary schools for most children throughout the colony, and all Puritan communities eventually established schools. New England set the precedent of having universal, tax-supported, compulsory education for the masses, followed by secondary and college education for the selected few destined to become preachers.

Puritan Concepts of Psychology and Discipline. By modern standards, methods and discipline of Puritan schools seem unbelievably harsh. Fear and force were the chief instruments used to control discipline, and masters were proud of their ability to break the will of the child. A whipping post was commonly erected by the school door. Severe floggings were administered for any misbehavior or breaking one of the many rules. There are records of pupils being tortured by having a stick of flat wood (whispering stick) placed between their teeth, students made to kneel on hard pebbles or required to wear a dunce cap, a heavy wooden yoke, or a split twig fastened to the nose like a clothes-pin. Children could be confined to the stocks for major offenses. A Massachusetts law of 1646 provided that a stubborn and rebellious son of sufficient years to understand could be legally put to death, although this extreme was not practiced. There was no recognition of the right or the need for children to play or have recreation. Virtue came through obedience, performing unpleasant tasks, and being exposed to the rod. Cotton Mather's book *A Family Well-Ordered* (1699) emphasized obedience and labor as the proper virtues of children. He pointed out in very clear terms how the wayward child's soul would "burn in Hell for all eternity."

Puritan theology taught that the child was conceived in iniquity and born in sin. This concept of the bad, active, and evil nature of the child is the logical opposite of Rousseau's belief that man is good as he comes from "the Author of Nature." Puritans felt that the body was a source of corruption and that all "natural" interests must be suppressed. In order for the child to learn, it was first necessary to literally beat the "Devil" out of him. God was not bound by human standards of reason or justice. This is illustrated by Michael Wigglesworth's *Day of Doom*, a best-selling poem published in 1662. The theme of the poem concerns children who died at birth, and therefore could not have sinned by their own will. Wigglesworth concluded that such children were nevertheless guilty of original sin:

A crime it is, therefore in bliss
You may not hope to dwell;
But unto you, I shall allow
The easiest room in Hell.

Since the child was not only ignorant but also sinful by nature, schools were designed to instill proper beliefs and habits. Some of the materials used for this purpose seem morbid, sadistic, and even psychotic today. Children were expected to memorize passages such as:

I in the burying Place may see Graves shorter there than I;
From Death's Arrest no Age is free, Young Children too
*   must die.*
Oh God may such an Awful Sight Awakening to Me be,
That by Early Grace I shall, For Death Prepared be.

On the second morning of each week students were required to give a passage from the sermon of the previous Sunday. Sermon titles included "The Eternity of Hell Torments" and "Sinners in the Hands of an Angry God," by Jonathan Edwards, who called children "vipers" and told them that God was angry with them every day. The *New England Primer*, used widely in Puritan schools, contained such gems as John Cotton's "Spiritual Milk for American Babes drawn from Both Breasts of the Testaments for their Soul's Nourishment," and the following lines attributed to the English martyr John Rogers:

Thus ends the days of woeful youth
Who won't obey or mind the truth;
Nor harken to what preachers say,
But do their parents disobey.
They in their youth go down to hell,
Under eternal wrath to dwell.
Many don't live out half their days
For cleaving unto sinful ways.

Most of the Puritan emphasis on standards of behavior and rules of morality is unintelligible unless it is realized that, for them, every life experience represented God's test of human conduct. The Puritan devil was not a theoretical concept but a being manifestly real, ever present, and dangerous. It is hard for modern people with secular traditions, the mass media, and electric lights, to understand just how dramatic the spirit world must have seemed to New England's children. Youth were constantly plied with verses such as:

Youth forward slips
Death soonest nips

and

When wicked children mocking said,
To an old man, "Go up bald Head."
God was displeased with them and sent
Two bears which them to pieces rent.

Judge Samuel Sewall (the same judge who sentenced witches in Salem) recalled in his diary how his little daughter Betty burst into an "amazing cry of fear and anguish" because she was afraid that she might be sent to hell. Community attitudes and, certainly, the atmosphere of the Puritan schools must have been psychologically detrimental to sensitive children. Some of this influence may still be seen in teachers who do not trust children and always expect misbehavior.

Educational historian Elwood P. Cubberley's statement that Puritan educational laws are the foundation stones of the modern school system is probably too enthusiastic a claim; but it is certainly true that New England provided the educational model most copied in early America. For the preservation of their souls, Puritans demanded that both boys and girls be taught to read the Scriptures. They used schools as a means of preserving the faith and made public control and tax support American educational traditions. New England schools were open to all, at least on the primary level. Often, they were centers of community pride and a binding force on the towns. Teachers enjoyed high status in early Puritan schools, for often they were young ministers waiting upon a call, and most of them were college educated. Schools soon became a means of social and economic advancement as well as institutions for religious instruction. While no complete ladder system or comprehensive high school developed, the Puritans had both Latin grammar schools and colleges. The demand for a college-trained minister in every pulpit led to the continued support of secondary and higher education. Certainly the educational theory was narrow and intolerant. Crude methods, despicable psychology, harsh discipline, inadequate materials, and a very limited curriculum prevailed. Nevertheless, Puritan educational interest provided an example and a model for creation and development of one of the major institutions in the United States, the public schools.

Jonathan Edwards. American Puritan philosophy and educational theory found expression in the work of a number of ministers. John Cotton, Michael Wigglesworth, and the Mathers (Richard, Increase, and Cotton) were among the most conservative, while Thomas Hooker and John Wise sympathized with more liberal views. One Puritan theologian whose intellectual ability placed him among leading American philosophers, was Jonathan Edwards.

Born in East Windsor, Connecticut, in 1703, Edwards was descended from four generations of ministers. A precocious boy, he wrote a treatise on the habits of spiders at twelve years of age and entered Yale at thirteen. Graduating at the head of his class, he remained in New Haven studying theology for two more years. After serving a small church in New York for a few months, Edwards was called to be assistant pastor to his own grandfather, Solomon Stoddard, at Northampton. Two years later Stoddard died, leaving Edwards the sole minister of one of the largest and best-educated congregations in New England. Preaching fiery sermons against hell and damnation, Edwards noted a considerable increase in religious concern among members of his flock. By 1733, the power of his sermons had created a wave of religious fervor which grew into the revival called the Great Awakening.

Edwards wrote and published numerous pamphlets describing the more than 300 conversions at Northampton and his own very strict interpretation of the doctrine of predestination. His piety was so strict that there was no room for forgiveness. He attacked the young people in his own church for circulating "impure books." He also wanted an even more vigorous enforcement of the "halfway covenant," a curious rule by which church members not accepted as "converted" could have their children admitted to one sacrament. Finally, at the age of forty-seven, he was dismissed as pastor. For a time, he was minister at Stockbridge and missionary to the Housationic Indians. Since he was a strict theologian and lacked humanitarian skills, his missionary efforts were unsuccessful. In 1757, Edwards was elected president of the College of New Jersey (Princeton), which had been very supportive of the Great Awakening. The following year, he died after taking a crude vaccination during a smallpox epidemic.

Jonathan Edwards synthesized faith, reason, religion, and science into an idealism that was partly rational and partly mystical. As a young man he had a strong scientific bent; but he became perplexed about the conflict between scientific certainty and the belief that only God is absolute. This he resolved by claiming that time and space are finite (space, for example appears to be infinite, but for Edwards it is contained within the universe), whereas God transcends space and time. There is no present, past, and future for God, but man is confined to temporal limits. Following Calvin's thesis that God is absolute perfection and man is depraved, Edwards held that only God is real and man's reality is only secondary and dependent on God's will.

Because of the sin of Adam, man became eligible for eternal damnation. Since Adam's sin was against infinite perfection, it deserves infinite punishment through all the generations of human beings. Man therefore cannot perfect himself, but is totally dependent on God for his salvation and for his very being. Sinners should not expect mercy, for God's honor is at stake:

Their souls they think are precious: it would be a dreadful thing if they should perish, and burn in hell forever. They do not see through it, that God should make so light of their salvation. But then, ought they not to consider, that as their souls are precious, so is God's honor precious? The honor of the infinite God, the great King of heaven and earth, is a thing of as great importance (and surely may be so esteemed by God), as the happiness of you, a poor little worm.

For Edwards, epistemology begins with man's love of self, moves to the love of nature revealed through scientific laws, depends for higher knowledge on the truths revealed in Scripture, and attains its highest level in the contemplation of the nature of God. Like Locke, Edwards believed that first knowledge comes from sense experience; but contrary to the empirical tradition, he placed stress on intuition. Reason is useful, but revelation allows man to distinguish between truth and error. Human beings have an immediate awareness of spiritual truths. Even with the most extensive study of the Bible, man can grasp only partial understanding, for the mind of man is finite and imperfect.

In his 1754 essay on the "Freedon of the Will," Edwards attacked the Armenians who believed in the self-determination of will. He held that the will is controlled by environmental forces and volition. Previous associations, habits, and laws affect the choices we make, and, ultimately, man's will is determined by God. This led Edwards to the conclusion that education must form habits, control the environment, and provide for revelation.

Like all Puritan theologians, Edwards held the Bible to be an infallible source of Divine Providence and the mainstay of the school curriculum. Children must be taught to follow religious ideals and love righteousness, even though they might not be among the chosen elect. Physical punishment and the fear of burning eternally in hell were regarded by Edwards as the means of proper motivation and control in schools. He believed that children are naturally wicked and that the teacher, as servant of God's will on earth, must protect them from their own wayward tendencies. This could be done by purging desires, learning to fear God, forming habits of obedience and upright behavior, and careful attention to God's revealed word as a guide for man.

Educational Ideals of the Founding Fathers. Conservative religious traditions continued to have influence during the period of the American Revolution; but vast changes in culture also took place. Revolt against authority of revolutionary magnitude could hardly have been successful in the early New England theocracies. Intellectual life was stimulated by newspapers such as the *Boston News Letter* and periodicals like *Poor Richard's Almanac*, published by Franklin. There were thirty-seven newspapers in regular publication at the outbreak of hostilities in 1775. Bookstalls offered the works of Bacon, Locke, Boyle, Newton, Swift, Milton, Hume, Voltaire, and Addison, among others. European experiments in science and medicine were as popular as speculation in philosophy. Because John Locke provided the theoretical foundation for the American democratic experiment, his empirical views and educational ideas were especially popular among American intellectuals. The rational, liberal, scientific and humanistic movement known as the enlightenment had a profound influence on many of the founding fathers. The enlightenment was a protest against authority. It held that men as individuals have worth and dignity and are able to judge truth for themselves. It fostered a belief that the universe is governed by natural law, which reason and science can penetrate without divine revelation.

The scientific, practical, secular world-view found expression in the attitudes and actions of Benjamin Franklin. Franklin's belief in self-education for practical utility, his broad interest in empirical science, and his desire to provide educational opportunity for anyone who wanted to learn were all in keeping with Locke's theories. Eschewing the classics, Franklin's plan for his academy in Philadelphia (later the University of Pennsylvania) emphasized English and mathematics, although securing financial aid made it necessary to include a Latin school. Trusting in self-reliance, sound habit formation, and moderation, Franklin believed the classics to be obsolete for success in business and service to the community. He saw the sciences, especially mathematics and physics, as the most important part of the curriculum; but English usage and physical training were also important. History, he believed, would inspire patriotism and service, and discussion was the best tool of learning. His stress was always on utilitarian studies applicable to the real world. To this extent, Franklin anticipated the pragmatic philosophy of John Dewey.

An even more liberal expression of scientific and humanistic enlightenment thought is found in Thomas Paine's *Age of Reason*. Paine was a deist, who believed in a mechanical universe, the goodness of man, free inquiry, and human reason as a tool for man's advancement. Like Madison and Jefferson, Paine felt schools must be free of church control and tolerant of all views.

While George Washington was far more conservative than Paine, he felt that a national university was needed to combat foreign influences. His *Farewell Address* to the army called attention to the need for the promotion and diffusion of knowledge. James Madison also wanted to include a provision for a national university in the Constitution. The proposal failed, and later efforts by John Jay, James Monroe, and John Quincy Adams were also unsuccessful, partly because of legal and financial problems. Nevertheless, the best-known founding fathers were uniformly enthusiastic about the creation of a national institution for higher education.

John Adams frequently spoke and wrote about education as public policy. After graduating from Harvard in 1755, Adams served as master of a Latin school for three years. Like Jefferson, Adams believed that the best guard of the people against tyranny is the diffusion of knowledge through the whole body politic. He made a study of the number of college graduates and concluded that Massachusetts produced three times as many college trained men in proportion to the population as the rest of America. Adams believed that the educated should rule and hoped the schools of Massachusetts might be taken up as a model for the whole nation.

James Madison stated that "knowledge will forever govern ignorance, and a people who mean to be their own governors must arm themselves with the power which knowledge gives." Madison was in the forefront of the fight to separate church and state, for he feared the power and educational control of established religion. John Jay believed that knowledge was the very "soul" of a republic. Perhaps the sentiments of the founding fathers can best be summarized with the words supplied by Alexander Hamilton for Washington's *Farewell Address*: "Promote, then, as an object of primary importance, institutions for the general diffusion of knowledge. In proportion as the structure of government gives force to public opinion, it is essential that public opinion should be enlightened."

Plans for a National System of Education. One of Benjamin Franklin's many contributions to intellectual development in America was the creation, in 1743, of the organization which became the American Philosophical Society. Members of the Society were concerned about a number of problems which had arisen as a result of the Revolution, including the lack of a proper system of schools. The Society felt that only education could provide the protection needed for a republican government which would guarantee freedom to all posterity. Accordingly, the Society offered a prize for "the best system of liberal education and literary instruction, adapted to the genius of government of the United States;

comprehending also a plan for instituting and conducting public schools in this country, on principles of the most extensive utility."

Reaction to the offer was dramatic, for the subject was much on the minds of prominent national leaders. Plans were submitted by Du Pont de Nemours, French political leader in exile; James Sullivan, later governor of Massachusetts; Lafitte du Courteil, professor at Pennsylvania Academy; Nathaniel Chipman, army officer in the Revolutionary War; Pennsylvania pamphlet writer Samuel Harrison Smith; Maryland physician Samuel Knox; Benjamin Rush, who was surgeon-general of the army and a signer of the Declaration of Independence; Robert Coram, a political essay writer from Delaware; and Noah Webster, author of famous textbooks and dictionaries. The prize was shared by Knox and Smith in 1787. All of the plans called attention to the backwardness of education in the post-revolutionary period and suggested a comprehensive educational program—universal and tax-supported for both sexes and with public control.

While the plans were different, several basic themes were common to all of them. They were founded upon the theory that a free and self-governing republic requires a system of public education because its survival depends upon an enlightened electorate. Robert Coram spoke for many when he stated that it is a shame for only a small part of the people to have an opportunity to attend college. Education, he held, is just as important for one man as for another, and his plan called for rural schools equal in quality to those of cities. Samuel Knox listed seven objections to private schools, including their failure to provide equality of educational opportunity. Some of the plans limited free schools and tax support to basic elementary instruction; but all agreed that schools in a republic must be public. Coram believed that education which favored the wealthy would lead to a social caste system and destroy the liberties for which the Revolutionary War had been fought.

The education of children should be provided for in the constitutions of every state . . . . It is a shame, a scandal to civilized society, that part only of the citizens should be sent to colleges and universities to learn to cheat the rest of their liberties.

It was suggested that a national tax on property, or on commodities like tea and coffee, might be used to supplement local efforts to raise school revenues. The intellectuals and political leaders of the period all seemed to agree that tax-supported free schools for both sexes were the best guardians of political freedom.

Writers of the plans agreed that foreign schooling was dangerous for the American nation. They feared the exposure of impressionable youth to other political and social systems while seeking higher education. In "Thoughts upon the Mode of Education proper in a Republic," Benjamin Rush said:

The principle of patriotism stands in need of the reinforcement of prejudice, and it is well known that our strongest prejudices in favor of our country are formed in the first one and twenty years of life.

President Washington called attention to the serious danger of sending youth abroad before they had learned the value of the American system. Sullivan, Chipman and Knox all devoted several pages of their plans to a demand for keeping students in the United States and requiring studies aimed at developing the spirit of patriotism. Lafitte du Courteil understood well how ancient republics had used education to support their governmental systems and social attitudes. He believed it was absolutely necessary for a large nation composed of "diverse peculiar states" to develop a national system of education in order to foster unity and the bonds of patriotism.

Some attention was given in the plans to requiring compulsory attendance in public schools. The intent was not so much to force the closing of private and sectarian schools as it was to protect children from parents and masters who were indifferent or negligent. Courteil held that parents must be convinced that the state had a right to direct the education of all youth. Smith recommended punishment by law for any parent who failed to offer his child the opportunity of receiving instruction. Not all of the plans suggested compulsory education for both boys and girls, but they did insist that schools must be open to girls. Separation of church and state was hailed by the planners as another safeguard of liberty. Knox was outspoken in his argument that schools must remain emancipated from the tyranny of ecclesiastical authority.

All of the plans were founded on the belief that only education could make man fit to govern themselves. Unfortunately, the writers presented no practical solutions for the problem of how schools could be financed or administered. Little was said about how teachers might be secured and trained, or about buildings and materials. Whatever the possibilities might be for a national system of education today, proposals for a central school system in a decentralized nation before the new government was firmly established, must be regarded as utopian. The plans offer insight into the attitudes and philosophies of significant early national leaders; however, they offered no workable solutions to practical problems of education. Fear of a strong federal government and lack of adequate money probably would have prevented the adoption of any plan for a national system of education, even if the Congress had been favorable toward the idea.

By the first and tenth amendments to the Constitution, ecclesiastical domination over schools was prevented and educational authority vested in the separate states. The matter of a federal university was brought before the Constitutional Convention of 1787 by Charles Pinckney of South Carolina, but it was discarded. Washington provided an endowment of $25,000 in Potomac Company shares for such a university, but Congress did not act. The Constitution of the United States is silent on the subject of education, even though the men who wrote it had strong educational views.

Thomas Jefferson on Education. Jefferson provided the ideology for extending educational opportunity and argued that no democratic society is safe without an educated population. He saw no need for American youth to study in Europe and supported the development of colleges and universities in the United States. For more than fifty years, Jefferson was active as a legislator, drafting and submitting proposals to put his educational theories into practice. In youth, he worked to reform the schools of Virginia, while much of his old age was devoted to building the University of Virginia. The core of his educational philosophy is contained in the bills he drafted for Virginia, comprehending a blueprint for a complete educational system in that state. More than anything else, he wanted academic excellence, with equality of opportunity for all.

Jefferson was not, like Hamilton, a supporter of strong federal government or national social legislation. He believed in the principle of decentralization and considerable local control. While his plans were intended for a state, he suggested that control of the primary schools should be in the "ward," a geographical unit smaller than a county and about five miles square. Localization of financial control was also a Jeffersonian concept, but he thought poor wards should be aided from county or state revenues. The American pattern of educational control exercised today is quite in keeping with Jefferson's theory. Organization and administration of schools by districts, using a local board of elected citizens, but with overall authority vested in the state, is a reflection of his views.

Holding that education was "essentially necesary," Jefferson often said that only an educated nation could preserve freedom and promote general happiness. He wanted to make sure that those favored with wealth and status because of birth did not get the only chance at public positions. Being a great scholar himself, and also accomplished in many practical pursuits, Jefferson stressed both academic excellence and utility. He believed education could increase production, especially in agriculture, and that it could help save labor. The concept of improving both the individual and the society through practical education is much like the philosophy of the Moravian educator, Johann Amos Comenius.

Between 1776 and 1779, Jefferson offered three bills for a school system to the Virginia Assembly. The bill of 1779, known as "A Bill for the More General Diffusion of Knowledge," is the most famous statement of his educational policy. Fearing an ignorant population, the legislation called for a primary school in every hundred (ward), open to both sexes, free of charge, for three years. Reading, writing, arithmetic, and the history of Greece, Rome, England, and America were to be the curriculum. Work was to be given mostly by memory, since Jefferson, like Rousseau, did not believe that the power of reason developed much before the age of fifteen. No mention of the Bible is found in the bill, an expression of Jefferson's secular interests. Students might remain in the schools after three years, but at private expense. For each ten schools there was to be an administrative overseer to appoint teachers and supervise instruction. Jefferson seemed to feel that three years was enough to combat mass ignorance and that most people are not educable beyond minimal literacy.

Beyond the "primaries," there were to be twenty secondary schools distributed throughout Virginia. Worthy but indigent students selected from the elementary schools on the basis of ability were to be given scholarships for two or three years of classical education. English grammar, geography, and arithmetic through the cube root were also to be offered. It should be remembered that these secondary schools were to supplement existing Latin grammar schools, and that those able to afford tuition could attend regardless of their ability. Capable pupils without means were to be retained for the full six years of secondary education, and a few of the really outstanding ones were to be sent to William and Mary College, free of charge. Secondary and higher education was limited to males only. Jefferson wished to insure that any exceedingly able lad could get an education at state expense.

Control of the secondary schools was to be left to an independent board of public instruction. County magistrates were to appoint a visitor to supervise the primaries and to help in the selection of students for scholarships. Jefferson divided Virginia into districts, so that each geographical section would have a "college" (secondary school) close at hand. Both the development of modern lay school boards and the concept of delegating state authority to local school districts can be traced to Jefferson. While he thought only a handful of boys were capable of joining the few who make up "the natural aristocracy of talent," he believed their contribution would prove well worth the expense of education. He did not agree that free education is pure charity—the British view of the period.

While some have criticized Jefferson for offering only a modest three years of public instruction and fostering class distinctions by limiting most secondary education to those who could pay, his proposals were too advanced and liberal for the times. The Assembly did not consider the bill in 1779. In 1796 it was passed as an option, rendering it ineffective. Nevertheless, the Bill for a More General Diffusion of Knowledge became a model for state systems of education throughout the nation. For example, when Edward Coles became the first governor of the state of Illinois in 1818, he submitted an education bill based almost exactly on that of Jefferson. Coles had been secretary to James Madison and was quite familiar with Jefferson's writing. The Illinois frontier state legislature passed the bill; but two years later it repealed the mandatory tax support for it.

Jefferson supported personal religious beliefs; but he feared ecclesiastical authority. Stressing religious freedom, he was in the forefront of the fight to separate church and state. To this end, Jefferson opposed sectarian schools and efforts to use tax money for religious education.

The crowning achievement of Jefferson's educational efforts was the University of Virginia. After attempting to reform William and Mary, he became convinced that an entirely new university was needed. Jefferson was the driving force behind the university. He organized the curriculum, hired the faculty, planned many of the buildings, personally purchased and catalogued books for the library, and supervised the entire operation. In 1825, he saw his creation open, the first state university, with forty students and a "modern" curriculum.

Thomas Jefferson was the outstanding spokesman for the enlightenment. He had complete faith in the power of reason and science to improve the human condition and preserve democracy, provided that the people had access to education. Jefferson believed in peace, the deistic concept that moral disintegration leads to tyranny, and freedom from the control of elite classes or despotic institutions. Tolerant of other political and religious beliefs than his own, Jefferson defended the right of others to differ with him. He thought education would produce an enlightened population, which is the best protection for personal liberties. The people themselves, he argued, do incomparably better than a central government that which they are competent to understand. While Jefferson had very high standards and expected only a few boys to attain levels of scholarly excellence, he wanted to insure that the opportunity for such attainment was open to all and not limited by wealth. He despised the petty quarrels and bickerings characteristic of European states of his time and had little use for scholarly disputes over metaphysics. Education for practical utility, to guard individual freedom, and for the promotion of happiness and prosperity, was his goal. Perhaps Jefferson's most famous statement on education was, "If a nation expects to be ignorant and free, in a state of civilization, it expects what never was and never will be."

EUROPEAN INFLUENCES UPON AMERICAN EDUCATIONAL THOUGHT

Until the end of the nineteenth century, very little effort was made to create a native American pedagogy with a supporting philosophy of education. Schoolmen in the United States were absorbed in the practical concerns of building schools, devising administrative controls, securing teachers, passing school laws, and finding sufficient financial support. Leaders of the common school movement like James G. Carter, Horace Mann, and Henry Barnard were more interested in the mechanism for control and operation of free schools than in the aims, principles, and theories of education. When it was realized that a system of educational philosophy and a body of knowledge were necessary for the advancement of the educational profession, Americans turned to concepts and models already developed in Europe. It was not until the twentieth century that American educational theory gained enough strength to challenge the concepts of Pestalozzi and Herbart.

Failing in their efforts to get a federal system of education or a national university, educational leaders of the early national period attempted to obtain minimal schooling for the poor by using charity and European models. Monitorial schools, originated in England and India by Joseph Lancaster and Andrew Bell, appeared in New York City in 1806. The monitorial school offered cheap education to a large number of children by using a minimum teaching staff and depending on students to instruct one another. Students of ability were selected by the master and taught a simple exercise such as subtracting one single digit number from another. In turn, these "monitors" became responsible for teaching what they had learned to small groups of children. This system provided rudimentary charity education for children of the poor in urban centers before tax-supported schools were created. Lancaster himself visited the United States in 1818 to spread his school plan. He obtained support from existing free school societies and political leaders like DeWitt Clinton.

The Sunday school was another English educational program developed by Robert Raikes of Gloucester. In an effort to rescue the children of factory workers from filth, sin, and ignorance, he provided free schools on Sundays for youngsters who labored all week in the factories and mills. Philadelphia had a Sunday School Society in 1791 which offered primary instruction in reading and writing from six until ten o'clock on Sunday mornings and again from two to six in the afternoons. These were not church schools, but religious organizations often collected funds for their support. In the modern world, it seems incredible that children were expected to work long hours for six days and attend school on Sunday without any time for rest or recreation.

A third effort along similar lines was made by industrialist Robert Owen of New Lanark, Scotland. The infant school, originated by Owen and modified by Samuel Wilderspin, gave primary instruction to children who had attained their fourth birthday. In 1818 Boston made provisions for an infant school with an appropriation of five thousand dollars, and other American cities soon followed suit. Like the monitorial and Sunday schools, infant schools were designed to provide individual and social improvement for the poor, and were supported by philanthropy.

The Prussian Model

About the time that the first state laws authorizing public taxation for schools were being passed in eastern states, many Americans became aware of the educational programs offered by European nations. One of the early national attempts to reform education and build a uniform school system came in the kingdom of Prussia. Seventeen Prussian teachers were sent to work with Pestalozzi in 1808. On their return from Switzerland, they were given authority to create a centralized system of education, planned, financed, and controlled by the Prussian government. Using the most up-to-date methods of the times, the Prussians trained teachers, standardized textbooks, provided administrative supervision, organized efficient financing, built new and re-equipped old buildings, and provided high-quality materials such as maps, charts, and globes. The authority for all this came from the emerging belief that schools could be used as an instrument of nationalism.

The first report of Prussian schools to reach America was made by Victor Cousin, headmaster of the French Higher Normal School. Cousin's candid and detailed report on German and Prussian education was translated into English in 1834. Appearing soon afterward in American educational journals, the account of European progress stimulated great interest and caused Americans to go and look for themselves. Calvin Ellis Stowe, professor at Lane Theological Institute and husband of Harriet Beecher Stowe, had planned a trip to Europe to buy books for the college library. The Ohio legis-

lature commissioned him to observe and report on European schools. Stowe's *Elementary Education in Europe*, published in 1837, was widely distributed, not only in Ohio but throughout the nation. He was as much impressed with Prussian thoroughness and efficiency as Cousin, and called for American schools to follow the Pestalozzian methods and techniques of teacher training. Although the Ohio legislature did not act, Stowe's effort provoked a great deal of educational concern and was responsible for other visits. Alexander Bache, a grandson of Benjamin Franklin, toured Europe and published his observations of schools in 1839. Benjamin Smith of Virginia and Dr. Johannes Julius presented their accounts of Prussian education to American lawmakers. Even greater interest in European education came from the activities of Horace Mann and Henry Barnard.

Mann made the trip to Europe in 1843. As secretary of the Massachusetts Board of Education, his critical observations, especially of English schools, were quite influential. Mann agreed that German education and the Prussian schools were of excellent quality. In his famous *Seventh Report*, he showed how adequate governmental support of education made the difference between Prussian schools and those of the other European nations. While not suggesting a federal system, Mann was doing his best to get the state of Massachusetts to create a sound system of public education, and he used the European model as a lever. Henry Barnard visited Europe in 1835. His impressions of the schools there stimulated him to work for educational reform in Connecticut, Rhode Island, and later as the first United States Commissioner of Education. The extent of his interest is shown by his book, *Pestalozzi and His Educational System*, published in 1881.

Concepts of Rousseau, Pestalozzi, Froebel and their American Spokesmen

For most of educational history, the schools reflected the adult world like a mirror. Standardized and formal pedagogical practices were used to transmit the cultural heritage. The students were treated as miniature adults, while virtually no attention was paid to individual differences or creative capacities of pupils. Three Europeans led the protest against formalism and the benighted concepts of the nature of children. Their personalities could have hardly been more different, and their life-styles and attitudes were dissimilar, but all three made vast contributions to modernizing education. Jean-Jacques Rousseau (1712–78) was strictly a philosopher. Johann Heinrich Pestalozzi (1746–1827) and Friedrich Froebel (1782–1852) translated theory into actual practice.

Protest is the best word to describe the work of Rousseau. He provided the philosophic basis for the French Revolution as Locke had done for the American. Both Locke and Rousseau wrote about the social contract and the rights and liberties of human beings. Rousseau was at the forefront of the radical democratic movement of the eighteenth century. He was hostile to the conventionality of civilization and to its major institutions. He thought churches, governments, schools, and powerful families to be depraved and artificial.

Rejecting the concept of original sin, Rousseau held that human nature is basically good and that only civilization makes men evil. "Everything," he said, "is good as it comes from the hands of the Author of Nature; but everything degenerates in the hands of man."

Rousseau's spiritual rebellion against the structure and corrupting nature of social institutions is also found in his educational work. He treated the subject of public education in several essays, including "Considerations on the Government of Poland"; but his major position is contained in the educational classic *Emile*. Immediately after its publication in 1762, *Emile* was banned and ordered burned by the Archbishop of Paris. However, intellectuals like Kant read it with great interest. The book describes the education of a boy who is not sent to school, but trained by a tutor in a rural setting, where he can be protected from the evil influences of society (negative education). The boy is free to develop according to his own natural impulses, and he learns directly from experience with the environment. Curiosity, play, freedom, activity, growth, and natural interests are educational principles of the *Emile*. Rousseau insisted that teachers must study the child, for nothing in their own education provided them with the tools for understanding how youngsters grow and develop. To use books, memorization, logical distinctions, and set exercises in place of the child's own experience is to substitute the reasoning of others for the growth of the pupil's ability. The boy Emile is educated in a natural setting, where he has active contact with real objects and learns to be self-dependent through direct experience with the reality of the natural environment.

Rousseau's naturalism challenged rationalism and the heavy-handed authority of the dominant institutions. He believed that children pass through a series of natural or developmental stages as they pass from birth to maturity, and that these stages govern the educational process. During the stage of infancy (birth to five), physical growth, the perfection of motor activities, sense perception, and feelings prevail. In childhood (six to twelve), experience, games, physical work, and the child's own interests should direct educational activities and allow natural powers to grow. Books and the formal exercises of schools must be avoided at this stage; the student should not even be required to learn to read. The age of reason (thirteen to fifteen), is characterized by a great desire to learn and the ability to understand. During this stage, the student can learn so rapidly that he can master all useful knowledge, such as agriculture, geography, astronomy, and the manual arts. Here, the emphasis is not on the acquisition of facts, but upon the process of learning and the construction of materials or instruments. Defoe's *Robinson Crusoe* is suggested as proper literature for study at this stage. Finally, the social stage (sixteen to twenty), is dominated by an interest in human relationships, including sex. At this time the student learns about society through ethics, natural religion, and esthetics. In the social stage, the youth selects a mate and prepares for marriage. Rousseau's stages were crude and unscientific by modern standards; but his line of thinking foreshadowed the work of stage theorists like G. Stanley Hall and Jean Piaget.

Without making education purely vocational, Rousseau insisted that children should learn the manual arts in order to improve the mind and gain respect for those who work with their hands. At a time when rules of grammar and fine distinctions in logic were the mainstay of schools, he called for individual experience, natural development, health and physical education, freedom, and naturalism. He asserted that nothing, not even religion, should be taught until the student has developed the capability of understanding. He opposed emphasis on memory and the acquisition of facts. Rousseau's treatment of females was archaic, and his position on individualism was overstated; nevertheless, he started an educational revolution which could not be quelled.

Rousseau was much too radical to be accepted by many educators in Europe, and his ideas were not copied in America until the end of the nineteenth century. He did, however, stimulate the " psychological movement" in Europe, which soon spread on both sides of the Atlantic. One of the first to develop education on naturalistic lines was Johann Heinrich Pestalozzi. Born in Zurich, Pestalozzi became an enthusiastic supporter of Rousseau's ideas about the nature of man. He attempted to rear his own son according to some of the ideals of *Emile* and to translate theory into a system of instruction. A practical man, Pestalozzi understood that Rousseau was a visionary; however, he was convinced that the spirit of *Emile* could be combined with successful methods.

In 1774, Pestalozzi transformed part of his home at Neuhof (near Aargua, Switzerland) into a school for impoverished children. By building rapport with youngsters and helping them to understand that learning was to their own advantage, he both developed their academic skills and taught them vocational arts. This was a beautiful experiment in which youngsters learned to live together, contributed to the labor for the farm, and made considerable intellectual progress; but lack of capital made it impossible for the children to produce enough to sustain the venture, and Neuhof had to be abandoned.

Undaunted, Pestalozzi set down his views on education in *Leonard and Gertrude* (1781), which had an immediate success as a sentimental novel. The book deals with the widowed heroine's successful efforts to teach, provide for, and develop values in her children under very difficult conditions. In spite of the book's popularity, Pestalozzi was disappointed, because he felt that readers did not grasp his humanitarian concepts and educational theories. He wrote several other tracts explaining his points, but they were rather dull and achieved little popularity.

Times remained hard for Pestalozzi, although he was able to return to farming and try some unsuccessful agricultural experiments. His ideas gained some acceptance in Austria, Italy, and Germany. In 1792 he visited France and was made a "Citizen of the French Republic"; but his belief that education is the key to the progress of civilization was not understood. When the new Swiss government came to power, Pestalozzi was put in charge of an orphanage in the town of Stanz, which had been destroyed by the French army. Almost totally without support and housed in outbuildings of a ruined convent, Pestalozzi set up a school for eighty destitute and homeless children. Even under the most difficult conditions he was able to develop children into happy, cooperative, and well-disciplined students. One observation made at Stanz was that children with "blank" minds are much easier to teach than those who have already acquired inaccurate ideas or bad habits of learning. After only a year, the French returned and took over the convent for a hospital, leaving Pestalozzi without the means to continue his work.

For a time he was given a meager job as an assistant teacher in an infant school. So great was his success with little children that the Burgdorf School Commission gave him a letter of commendation, and in 1800 he was able to open a boarding school for boys in an old castle. Using funds from a Swiss society called "Friends of Education" and the aid of a local schoolmaster called Krusi, Pestalozzi built Burgdorf Castle into a model of the new education. There was an orphan school, a day school, and a "normal school for training teachers," as well as the boarding school for boys. Pestalozzi wrote *How Gertrude Teaches Her Children* snd several elementary textbooks while at Burgdorf. He advertised his methods and invited all to visit his schools to see it for themselves. The sponsoring society reported that Pestalozzi's students learned more spelling, reading, writing, and calculation in six months than could be expected in ordinary village schools in three years. During this period, most of Pestalozzi's concepts were made operational; but the political tide turned against him, and in 1804 he had to move his school to Yverdun. There he remained for twenty years, opening his school to the observation and scrutiny of all who wished to see his new methods.

For Pestalozzi, education involved the natural, harmonious development of all the child's natural abilities. He spoke of education of the hand, the heart, and the head, by which he meant vocational and moral, as well as intellectual, development. He believed that every individual could be educated to attain his own maximum potential, including a high degree of self-respect. With understanding of the process of growth and development, Pestalozzi believed that schools could perfect methods so that even the most humble and underprivileged could reach maximum success. His approach to social improvement was through individual growth and working relationships with others. Convinced that natural laws were violated by the formalism of existing schools, Pestalozzi exhorted his followers to experiment, discover, and test, rather than rely on tradition or written words. Accepting the evidence that children do indeed learn from direct experience, Pestalozzi introduced objects into the curriculum in order to enrich the student's environment. Rejecting the brutal punishment which had so long been part of schooling, he argued that discipline must be civilized and humane. With sympathy and understanding he was able to create an atmosphere in which the child wanted to learn. He saw no contradictions between learning manual skills and training the mind.

Although Pestalozzi was not a great scholar in the classical or philosophical tradition, he was able to absorb Rousseau's ideas without damage to his own imagination. Few educators have been less intrigued with mass education, yet the Prussians copied his methods for their government schools.

Democratic to the core, Pestalozzi was nevertheless decorated by the Czar of Russia, and his books were used in highly autocratic nations. Wishing to "teach beggars to live like men" and concerned about the needs of the underprivileged, Pestalozzi saw his methods and his techniques of teacher training used mainly to provide schools for the middle and upper classes. While many of his teachings are obsolete because of discovery in the fields of psychology and learning, his love of his fellow man and respect for the nature of the child cannot be discarded.

The most famous direct follower of Pestalozzi was Philip von Fellenberg, who established a school called the Institute at Hofwyl, Switzerland. Believing that farming activities and schools could be combined for the reduction of costs and the improvement of education, Fellenberg supported the teaching of handicrafts and vocational skills. There were a number of American advocates of Fellenberg's plan, and he had some influence on the creation of colleges for the teaching of agriculture and the mechanical arts.

In the United States, the most important early disciple of Pestalozzi was Joseph Neef. Neef had been a teacher in Pestalozzi's school and later became director of an orphanage in Paris, where he attracted the attention of a wealthy Philadelphian named Maclure. Neef was persuaded to establish a Pestalozzian school in Philadelphia and, later, in Louisville, Kentucky. Both failed, and Neef's influence in the United States was quite limited. Several other Swiss teachers accepted positions in America, including Hermann Krusi, the son of Pestalozzi's assistant. Maclure joined with Robert Owen to create the socialisitc colony in America at New Harmony, Indiana. While New Harmony was not a success, the principles behind it were taken from the writings of Rousseau and Pestalozzi. The influence of European educational theories had reached to a backwoods utopian experiment, in frontier Indiana.

A more widespread impact of Pestalozzi's methods was fostered by the work of Edward Austin Sheldon and the Oswego movement. Sheldon, secretary of the Board of Education at Oswego, New York, visited a number of cities in order to find ways of improving the schools. While attending an exhibition in Toronto in 1859, he came across a Pestalozzian program offered by the Home and Colonial Training Institution of London. Instruction was based on charts, pictures, manuals and objects brought together by Charles and Elizabeth Mayo, who had taught under Pestalozzi. Sheldon returned with $300 worth of materials and soon secured the services of Margaret E. M. Jones to demonstrate their use. Sheldon's success was spectacular, and in 1866 the New York legislature made Oswego a state normal school. Teachers flocked to the new program, and Oswego became the most famous teacher-training institution in the United States. Graduates of Oswego were hired in various parts of the nation, so that the concepts of Pestalozzi, especially object teaching, spread rapidly. Although not all of the concepts Pestalozzi had developed were used by Sheldon, the Oswego movement was very significant in making popular the educational theories of the Swiss pedagogue.

Friedrich Froebel was a shy and introspective mystic who

followed Pestalozzi, but created a new movement as well. His educational work began in a small Pestalozzian school in Frankfurt, and in 1808 he was able to teach under the master at Yverdon. Later, in Blankenburg, Froebel established his own experimental school for children between the ages of three and eight. The German term for the school was Klein-kinderbeschaftigungsanstalt (institution for the occupation of small children), later reduced to kindergarten.

Froebel was basically an idealist who viewed the child as an instrument for the realization of God's will in human nature. He believed that the spirit of the child could be linked with the absolute through a unity of experience and divine truth. Many of these mystical ideas are contained in his *The Education of Man*, which appeared in 1826.

From a practical viewpoint, the significance of Froebel was his belief that the educative process must begin in early childhood. Through play, self-activity, music, stories, and physical exercise, Froebel attempted to combine individual growth with social development. In addition to the use of objects, storytelling, and constructive social activities, Froebel emphasized respect for the individuality of the child and freedom of expression. About the time the project was in danger of collapse because of financial difficulties, Froebel was rescued by Baroness Bertha von Bulow-Wendhausen. Subsequently, the kindergarten spread rapidly in Europe. Froebel had a profound effect on early childhood education, and his ideas influenced both Maria Montessori and John Dewey.

The first American kindergarten appeared in Watertown, Wisconsin, in 1855. It was German and was conducted by Mrs. Carl Schurz, who had been a student of Froebel. Elizabeth Peabody created the first English-speaking kindergarten in 1860. Educational leaders like Henry Barnard were enthusiastic about the kindergarten idea; however, early efforts were private and limited to urban centers. In 1873, William T. Harris opened the first public kindergarten in St. Louis. From that time on, early childhood education became a major interest of the educational profession and the general public.

The ideas of Rousseau, Pestalozzi, Froebel, and their followers had an impact which gained momentum over the years. Sometimes the influence was extended through individuals or limited to changes in method; but the contribution to theory eventually was great. Although it was a long time in developing, the psychological movement in Europe and a new conception of human potential laid a foundation for the work of Parker, Dewey, and the progressives.

European Impact on Institutions of Higher Education

Before the Civil War, American colleges were usually denominational and under the control of clergymen. Even state universities had a strong theological base. Both colleges and universities offered a fixed curriculum selected by conservative philosophers and theologians. There was little opportunity for students to elect courses and almost no research activity. The collegiate way was practiced, and the classics held a dominant position.

Secularization, specialization, and the elective system were largely produced through the efforts of American college presidents, but not without European influence. When Daniel Coit Gilman assumed the presidency of the newly-founded Johns Hopkins University in 1876, he attempted to assemble the finest scholars to be found and invited outstanding college graduates to study under them. What he proposed was a graduate school on the German model, an idea that had been suggested by Henry P. Tappin (president of the University of Michigan) twenty years earlier. Before graduate education was offered in the United States, many American scholars had gone to the German universities, where research was emphasized and academic freedom reigned. Göttingen, Halle, Berlin, and Königsberg attracted numerous students from the United States. Gillman was well aware that college teachers and contributors to the existing body of knowledge had to be free of external restraint and provided with the time and equipment for research if they were to be effective. In a speech at the opening of the University, Thomas H. Huxley spoke on his idea of a university education which emphasized a broad curriculum and the importance of research instead of the inculcation of a set of accepted ideas.

Although new subjects were constantly acquiring status during the formative years of the American educational system, inclusion of the sciences in the curriculum received the greatest support from England. By the end of the eighteenth century, science had developed into a definite area of knowledge. Proponents of science argued for it on naturalistic and humanistic grounds; but there was great opposition by the classicists. Not only did they claim the older subjects were superior for training the mind, they also pointed out that science advocates did not agree concerning what should be taught. "Natural science" was a term used to cover a variety of subjects, only a few of which followed the modern analytical method. Meanwhile, new discovery and scientific interest were growing rapidly. The publication of Darwin's *Origin of Species* in 1859 marked the beginning of a new era.

Huxley, Spencer, and Ideas about the Curriculum. English biologist Thomas Henry Huxley (1825–95) was a strong supporter of the inclusion of science in the curriculum. Huxley was an ally of Darwin in the struggle to make evolution acceptable and was an important contributor to the field of physiology. It was a book by Huxley on that subject which injected the young John Dewey with an irresistible interest in the relationship between science and philosophy.

Huxley took the position that science was not only utilitarian, but also worthy of the attention of the best intellects. He argued that school children ought to begin with nature study in the elementary years and perfect their understanding of the scientific method thereafter. Mastering basic sciences as a foundation for later research was worthy of the best minds. Huxley held that the classicists concentrated on language and form, whereas the sciences provided an opportunity to study man directly. In order to acquire an intelligent understanding of the universe and the idea of causation, students must have work in scientific method. Huxley was one of the first to argue for science on the basis that it is impossible to be well educated without it. This belief found acceptance among some humanists, like John Ruskin. Ruskin was appalled at the ignorance of men of letters in the field of natural science and held that the curriculum must contain subjects upon which the creative capacity of the mind could be exercised.

An even more significant argument for science came from the efforts of Herbert Spencer (1820–1903). Like the great geologist Charles Lyell, Spencer made a direct contribution to the theory of evolution and must be credited with the concept of "survival of the fittest." As much a philosopher as a man of science, Spencer rejected metaphysical speculation in favor of studying unifying principles of knowledge. Due to his great reputation as a scholar, Spencer's ideas about the curriculum were highly acclaimed. His *What Knowledge is of Most Worth* provided proponents of science with the ammunition they needed to defend themselves against the classical tradition, and it quickly became an educational classic.

Interestingly enough, Spencer did not attempt to support science for scientific, or even for utilitarian, reasons. *What Knowledge is of Most Worth* does not deal with the question of the direct use of various subjects to persons in different walks of life. Instead, he argued that science is just as valuable as literature or classical languages for disciplining the mind, and that it has the further advantage of familiarizing the learner with rational relationships. Instead of offering a challenge to the traditionalists about the significance of their subjects for utility, Spencer attempted to beat them at their own game by saying that science could train the faculties of the mind as effectively as the classics. He said, "it is contrary to the beautiful economy of nature" that some subjects should be used for mental discipline and others for knowledge.

Spencer was a spokesman for a social theory which defended laissez-faire economics and social Darwinism. His individualism and materialism appealed to business concerns and the dominant forces in the American gilded age. Utilitarian interests found much-needed help in the ideas of Huxley and Spencer, just at a time when courses in technology, science, agriculture, and the mechanical arts were gaining momentum. While the rift between science and the classical humanists continued for decades (indeed, it is not yet healed), the arguments of English scientists were timely and therefore effective in altering the curriculum of American public schools and colleges. Inclusion of science in the curriculum owes a great deal to the influence of Spencer and Huxley.

Educational Ideas of Johann Friedrich Herbart

Johann Friedrich Herbart, born on the eve of the American Revolution (1776–1841), ultimately became one of the most significant European influences on American education in the late nineteenth and early twentieth centuries. A pioneering educator and philosopher, Herbart has been designated the "father of scientific pedagogy," as well as a major contributor to the development of educational psychology.

Trained as a philosopher, Herbart received his doctor's degree at Göttingen after formally opposing the doctrines of Kant. Later he was appointed to Kant's chair at the univer-

sity of Königsberg. His attention to educational concerns was stimulated by postenlightenment interests in child growth and development. Like Froebel, Herbart was heavily influenced by Rousseau; but in contrast with Froebel's mystical approach to education as a means of fulfilling God's divine will through each child, his interest centered on the social implications of educational practice. Herbart was interested in the moral development of the individual and the society. While Pestalozzi focused on education for the common and the poor, Herbart turned to psychology in an effort to relate learning to the former experience of the child. His associationism was an early effort to pull psychology away from philosophy and relate it to the known facts of physiology and growth.

The prevailing view of human perception in Herbart's time was "faculty psychology," the view that man's powers of reason consist of various separate "components" or faculties, each with a highly specialized function. Each faculty is connected only to the empirical senses as a data source by which one learns, and each requires expertise to fully develop the powers of reason, insight, memory, and the like. The curricula of classic educational institutions was designed to provide a varied but rigorous series of intellectual gymnastics which, faculty psychologists believed, sharpened the student's capability to reason in any situation. Faculties could be developed with subject content remote from situations in which reason was to be demonstrated.

While Herbart was grounded as a student in the "mental discipline" of Kant and Leibniz, he came to hold the view that the mind interacted with "ideas," or "reals," which were the sub-units of the absolute or ultimate "stuff" of the universe. Although he held that psychology was properly rooted in metaphysics, the a priori assumptions of which were not suitable for empirical testing, he believed that the learning process and the nature of the mind could be examined. Like many philosophers, Herbart was willing to accept Locke's thesis that sense impressions received by the mind were associated with each other because of factors like their mechanical similarity. The idea "cube," for example, was imagined to grow out of many impressions of a rectangular solid of equal proportions. The implication for education is that an idea must be presented many times if it is to be fixed firmly in the mind. Experience is the source of data or "ideas"; but the presentation and association of the data are the key to learning.

For Herbart, the mind was a unity with conscious and subconscious components, separated by a threshold called the "limen," active involvement of which is critical in the process of perception and learning. One "learns" by associating new sensory (or experience) data with ideas previously incorporated into the consciousness. The goal of the educator is to increase the number of "associated ideas" or "apperceptive mass" in the mind of the student, so that a reservoir of "co-relations" or "connections" based on previous experience would be available for each new situation.

While the number of ideas capable of being held in the consciousness was finite, those stored in the subconscious were not limited in number. They could be summoned at will, provided that the proper connections or associations had been made. Thus memory is not improved by memorization; but by association of the ideas to be remembered with other similar or connected ideas. Herbart believed that ideas of the greatest "force," or greatest momentary interest to the learner, would occupy the largest portion of the consciousness. Since the learner's interests were "many-sided" or varied, pedagogical techniques should focus on making and strengthening interconnections between various ideas already in the mind. Herbart suggested linking the subjects of history and geography, since both can be related easily to a time and space conceptual framework.

Herbart's *The Science of Education* (1806) and *Outlines of Educational Doctrine* (1835) were among the first efforts to apply psychology to pedagogy. The goal of the "cultured man" and moral development was to be reached by a broad range of experiences including the great ideas of human history and endeavor. Literature and models of outstanding human achievement were to be included in the curriculum. The two key pedagogical principles were the *frequency* with which an idea was presented and *interconnections* between clusters of ideas in the apperceptive mass. It was also necessary to be exposed to the most sophisticated and refined human knowledge if great ideas were to occupy the greatest portion of the consciousness.

Since ideas, regardless of their specific content, were apperceived by the learner in the same manner, Herbart designed a systematic technique for presentation or teaching. Ordering principles included from the familiar to the unfamiliar, from the concrete to the abstract, and a core curriculum consisting of the ideas of greatest significance in achieving moral development. There were four steps in Herbart's methodology, later extended to five by his American followers:

1. Preparation. Recalling by the student previously apperceived ideas or memories, co-related to his present interest, and heightening his sense of readiness for receiving the new material.

2. Presentation. Designed in logically sequential steps, the subject matter was used to fully and completely describe the new idea. Teacher's performance was critical.

3. Assimilation or Association. Contrast and comparison of the new idea to previously apperceived ideas in the learner's apperceptive mass.

4. Generalization. Principles were recognized as the greater force of amassed ideas occupied a larger portion of the finite consciousness than extraneous or "unconnected" ideas.

5. Application. Testing of the new principle with experiences to determine its completeness and usefulness. Success or failure increased the student's "interest" in co-related ideas.

Pestalozzi and Froebel heightened the interest of American educators with their alternative methods and techniques of discipline. By suggesting both the content appropriate to education and the means for organizing and teaching that content, Herbart made the next logical step toward a science of pedagogy. The Herbartian contribution to American education included emphasis on literature and history as a cultural core, logical structure of the curriculum and instructional planning, and methodology based on association of ideas.

Herbart's pedagogical concepts were imported wholesale during the late 1890's and early 1900's. They meshed well with the frontier spirit and social Darwinism, and there was little competition from American educational theory at the time. It was accepted that the individuality and creativity of the child were subservient to his capacity for making "right choices," and Herbart's theory suited the primary role of the teacher as the presenter of well-ordered explanations and predetermined ideas.

The American Herbartian Association, led by Charles and Frank McMurray and Charles de Garmo, helped to popularize Herbartian principles among American educators. A formal methodology tied to an emerging science of psychology offered the struggling American educators a much-needed rationale for standardizing practice. Herbart provided a systematic method of treating subject matter and organization for classroom instruction. His high status in Europe and explicit assumptions for pedagogical practice provided a means of incorporating education as a university discipline. His theories emerged at a time when the common school movement in America had created a demand for professional educators, who could adapt the educational process to the needs of the masses in a burgeoning nation. Further, the attempt to justify educational practice on the basis of "scientific psychology of learning" was attractive in the vacuum created by the release of public education from previous ecclesiastical restraints.

Unfortunately, Herbart's formalized method involved the student very little and placed great emphasis on the role of the teacher. The methods were often reduced to a rigid technique. Also, the concern for individual differences soon challenged the Herbartian belief that students perceive ideas in exactly the same way, or that the ultimate goal of education (i.e. personal character and social morality) was precisely the same for all.

Following the attack of Dewey and the associationists, Herbart's influence declined almost as rapidly as it had grown. Certainly he had little to say about purposes, emotions, values, and attitudes, which were quite important to later psychologists. Laboratory-based experimental psychology also began to discredit many of the assumptions upon which Herbart built his theories.

Students of education who devote their careers to promoting learning and the scientific study pedagogy owe a great debt to Herbart. His insights and interests in education were grounded in philosophy, psychology, and the known facts about child development. While he came too early to be influenced by Max Wundt and other scientific psychologists, Herbart was concerned about scientific development. But his practical experience as tutor to the sons of the governor of Interlacken (Switzerland) and his efforts to give practical education a respectable scientific base provided a transition between science making and the classroom. While his metaphysically-based psychology and its subsequent pedagogical practices have been superseded by a variety of new theoretical positions and discoveries about learning, motivation, and creative thinking, Herbart still stands as one willing to risk putting theory to the test of the practitioner. It is also true that, after generations of passionate research, the precise nature of learning is still illusive. The association of ideas is still a valid concept about learning at the present time.

PROGRESSIVE EDUCATION: ITS PHILOSOPHY AND CRITICS

The movement known as progressive education encompasses a large number of theoretical positions, some of which are hardly compatible. Early progressives in education were mindful of the reform movement in politics which bore the same name. Many were sympathetic with the efforts of Henry George, Eugene V. Debs, William Jennings Bryan, John Peter Atgeld, Robert M. La Follette, Lincoln Steffens, Upton Sinclair, and others who wished to legislate reform; but theoretical support for progressive education came from the work of Europeans like Pestalozzi and Froebel and the American pragmatic philosophy of Charles Peirce, William James, and John Dewey.

Educational philosopher Theodore Brameld classifies the progressive as an educational liberal. Instead of concentrating on the traditions of the past, the progressive looks to the present for a source of authority and cues about the future. Progressives reject the idea that man and society are in any way fixed or final. Recognizing the need for growth of the individual and evolution of the society, progressive educators are concerned about the process by which decisions are reached and problems solved. They do not see education as the absorption of a fixed body of knowledge, nor do they accept any particular set of systematic assumptions about human nature or ultimate reality. Stressing change, effective thinking, and the scientific method, they want schools to be places where children can learn how information can be utilized to meet personal and societal needs.

Although the progressive schools of the 1920's and 30's no longer exist, progressivism is still an influential American educational philosophy. It is opposed to authoritarianism in all forms and regards human experience as the basis of knowledge. The curriculum cannot, therefore, be limited to traditional subjects, but must include all fields of human endeavor. It allows for individual differences in belief and supports a tolerant, integrated, democratic social order. Solutions to problems may be sought in science and technology, and the stress is always on the process of learning rather than on ends. Since many of the most significant issues are social, the progressive sees schools as active participants in social change. Bringing students together in heterogeneous groups is thought to benefit the process of socialization, and schools are considered as working models of democracy. While not subject centered, progressive schools do include a wide variety of experiences, which are often organized around a core of related or associated topics. Progressives often assert that meeting needs of the individual child and interest in intellectual activity will motivate practice needed for learning, so

that outside rewards and the rote memorization of facts will be unnecessary. The learner is seen as an exploring, thinking, experiencing, developing organism.

Although many progressive schools have been criticized for being very permissive and failing to teach basic information or essential skills, there is little theoretical support for license. Progressives hold that freedom is necessary; but it must be organized and responsible freedom, not the haphazard release of energy. Progressives believe that students cannot be expected to support democracy unless they have had some experience with improving the way of life of the society or the community through the democratic process. The management of change and preparation for alternative future courses of action are seen as important educational functions.

Francis W. Parker as Father of Progressive Education

While there were several early innovators, Francis Wayland Parker stands out as a real pioneer in progressive education. Born in Bedford Township, New Hampshire, in 1837, Parker's own education was apprenticeship on a farm and a mere smattering of formal schooling. Still, at sixteen he became a teacher, and at twenty he was principal of schools in Carrolton, Illinois. At the beginning of the Civil War, Parker enlisted as a private in the Union forces. Although wounded and taken prisoner, he was discharged with the rank of colonel, which was no small feat for a man without wealth or political connections.

In 1872, Parker went to Germany to study philosophy and education. There, he observed schools based on the work of Pestalozzi, Froebel, and Herbart and read the most important theory available in Europe. On returning to America, he was appointed superintendent of schools in Quincy, Massachusetts. At Quincy he was able to lay the foundation for progressive schools by rejecting the formal, rigid, fact-centered program and approaching education from the standpoint of the child. From Quincy, Parker went to Boston and thence to Chicago, where he directed the Cook County Normal School for eighteen years. Shortly before his death in 1902, Parker founded the Chicago Institute. The Institute was created for experimentation in education. It was absorbed by the University of Chicago and directed by John Dewey after Parker died.

A practical individualist with a democratic outlook, Parker combined hard-headed common sense with profound faith in the human potential. He was an enemy of the old-time strict discipline; which he thought teachers leaned upon because they knew no other method of keeping order. Sensitive to the needs of childhood, Parker rejected conventional formalism and "unnatural order" in favor of freedom to develop naturally. Instead of requiring students to sit still and absorb words like a sponge, movement, creative activity, projects and field trips became the rule.

At Quincy, Parker encouraged the study of the natural environment, the substitution of personal experience for set exercises, and different rates of progress for different individuals. Following Froebel's respect for the child and the need for creative activity, Quincy students were allowed great freedom, so long as they showed evidence of growth and demonstrated a sense of responsibility. History and geography were combined into a core curriculum with the study of the local community as a starting point. Instead of devotion to the rules of grammar and the moods of verbs, students were encouraged to use language in reporting their own observations or creating their own stories. Parker introduced laboratory studies, vocational skills—including arts and crafts—artistic expression, and nature study. Indeed, Parker was the first American superintendent to encourage treks into surrounding communities, woodlands, fields, and streams to study both nature and the means of economic production. He often said that no urban school could teach so effectively as growing up on a well-managed efficient farm. Parker knew that traditional schools wasted vast amounts of time because students were bored, unmotivated, and learning was fact related. Using Herbart's concept of the many sidedness of interest, he kept a constant stream of new experiences before the student and attempted to relate each to the child's own perception of his life space. He created a set of conditions by which the child could develop full expression and keep interest alive. For Parker, the honest effort of the child, no matter how imperfect, was far more valuable than imitating a set copy or model. While he conceded that some facts—the multiplication tables for example—should be fully automatic, he saw no need for large amounts of memorization and drill. Teachers were to be mindful of the desires, hopes, fears, and aspirations of every pupil.

Quincy stirred up tremendous interest among educators and the lay public. Traditionalists looked upon Parker's schools with horror and indignation. Fearing the freedom and "lack of discipline," critics excoriated both Parker and his methods. The now familiar charge that students failed to learn fundamentals and that they would grow up more ignorant than their parents, was made from many quarters. Finally, in 1879, the Massachusetts Board of Education agreed to put the Quincy students through a special examination. To the profound dismay of the critics, Parker's students were able to read, write, spell, and calculate better than the majority of pupils in the state. Further, they were superior in history, geography, and mental arithmetic. Parker was lifted into fame, and visitors from all over the nation came to see the new programs. The *New York Times* (July 5, 1883) reported that Quincy schools led all the others in Massachusetts.

As principal of the Cook County Normal School, Parker brought together an outstanding group of teachers interested in new methods and techniques. There were weekly conferences in which practice teachers, supervisors, and professors discussed classroom problems. Parker continued to attack the strict discipline and mechanical methods of schools which pressed every child into a common mold. He called for "quality teaching" which emphasized activity, creative self expression, personality development, and the art of drawing out the student. While he was interested in the scientific study of education, Parker insisted that teaching is an art,

and every student bears the hallmark of those who have contributed to his learning. He continued to demand curriculum reform, including the introduction of science and physical education into the elementary school program.

In 1899, Mrs. Emmons Blaine gave one million dollars for the creation of the Chicago Institute. President William Rainey Harper offered to make the Institute part of the University of Chicago and thus create a School of Education. Shortly after Parker's death, Mrs. Blaine donated another million dollars for an experimental progressive school. Named for Colonel Parker, the school was a model of progressive education for thirty years, and was directed by Flora Cooke.

Francis Wayland Parker borrowed heavily from European educators; but his contribution included many of his own ideas. He combined a natural sensitivity to the needs of the child with profound faith in democracy and the belief that each individual could be educated to realize his natural potential. Although he lacked the sophisticated philosophic training of John Dewey, Parker was able to translate some of the best ideas of Pestalozzi, Froebel, and Herbart into practical methods for American Schools. Parker led the attack on dull, rigid, formalistic schools which were both anti-democratic and detrimental to the development of the personality of the child.

Parker was succeeded at Chicago by his friend and colleague John Dewey, who not only provided the major philosophic foundation for progressive education but also contributed a major educational experiment. In 1894, Dewey was invited to become chairman of the Department of Philosophy at the University of Chicago. Two years later he opened his Laboratory School with two teachers and sixteen students. Discarding traditional subjects, organization, and even furniture, Dewey offered the "activity program." In place of required work, the student was to engage in play, construction, artistic expression, communication, and whatever else normal healthy children like to do. Out of these natural activities (indeed Dewey said out of life itself) the child would reconstruct experience in the process of active learning. Dewey wanted to "train children in cooperative and mutually useful living," through natural life experience. Since other people exist in the life space of the individual, the school was to be a social institution, an embryonic society. A major feature of the Laboratory School was that it really was an experiment— Dewey wanted to test ideas rather than to establish a model. He was interested in knowing if subjects could be derived from the child's experience, rather than being logically prearranged. Although the school lasted only seven years, Dewey obtained important material for his major work, *Democracy and Education*, which he published in 1916.

Social Frontier and Social Reconstruction

However closely they may have followed Parker's example and Dewey's theory, the early progressives concentrated on the child. Freedom, creativity, natural interests, and stimulation of initiative, were dominant themes. Respect for the personality of the child and concentration on his needs meant that the school should concern itself with developing the whole child, not with subject matter. This is illustrated by the principles of the Progressive Education Association, organized in 1918, under the leadership of Stanwood of the Chevy Chase Country Day School:

1. *Freedom to develop naturally*
2. *Interest, the motive of all work*
3. *The teacher as a guide, not a taskmaster*
4. *Scientific study of student development*
5. *Greater attention to all the effects of the child's physical development*
6. *Cooperation between the school and home to meet the needs of child life*
7. *The Progressive School, a leader in educational movements.*

The organization grew rapidly, from a few hundred in 1920 to over 10,000 in the late thirties. Such a large group quite naturally consisted of persons who did not agree upon a number of educational matters. Charles W. Eliot, Harvard president and founder of the elective system, represented intellectual interests. William H. Kilpatrick and Elsworth Collings supported the project method of instruction. Hughes Mearns concentrated on developing the creative power of the child, as indicated by his books, *Creative Youth* and *Creative Power*. Boyd H. Bode forged a theoretical link between the philosophy of Dewey and experimentalist-progressive psychology. John Childs and George S. Counts held that the school must be very active as an instrument of social change. With the economic crisis of the 1930's, a storm broke out within the ranks of the progressives between those who emphasized social-democratic goals and those who were mostly interested in child development.

Fearing that the Depression would bring on a totalitarian regime unless emphasis could be placed on the moral life and the social aspects of democracy, some progressives called upon education to direct social and economic reconstruction. Kilpatrick insisted that it is the business of the school to help students think through a defensible social program. John Childs, reacting to the Oregon decision of 1925, which guaranteed the continued existence or private and parochial schools, called for reconsideration on the grounds that democracy required students to have some experience in a public school. It was Counts, however, who charged that progressive education had developed no theory of social welfare to combat anti-democratic forces or extreme individualism.

The Progressive Education Association did appoint a committee to study social and economic problems, with Counts as its chairman. Its report, "Call to the Teachers of the Nation," asked teachers to be aware of the contemporary order and urged the transfer of the democratic tradition "from individualist to collectivist economic foundations." The report contained many of the same ideas found in Counts' 1932 book, *Dare the School Build a New Social Order?*, which a number of his fellow progressives regarded as too radical. Many of those who were working with experimental

child-centered schools did not want to engage in a major conflict with powerful forces outside the profession. Professor Isaac Kandel, of Teachers College, pointed out that progressives could hardly advocate individualism and freedom on the one hand and call for social reconstruction through planning and the collective will on the other. However, social reconstruction appealed to a large number of progressives both within and without the Association. In a statement of its philosophy in 1938, the Progressive Education Association recognized the traditional and confused nature of the culture. It urged the free discussion of controversial issues in schools and held that the child should think reflectively about community problems. It supported an attitude of social sensibility, but rejected the creation of a blueprint for a new society. Nevertheless, a number of educators left the Association because of its image as an instrument for economic and social change.

In 1935, a number of professors and others interested in the reconstruction of society through education founded the John Dewey Society for the Study of Education and Culture. Its journal, *The Social Frontier*, was later renamed *Frontiers of Democracy* and adopted by the Progressive Education Association. The first issue led off with an article by Dewey entitled "Can Education Share in Social Reconstruction?" Later issues contained articles such as "Youth Versus Capitalism," and "W. R. Hearst—Epitome of Capitalist Civilization." It should surprise no one that George Counts was the editor.

Milder approaches to altering society through schooling were also used. For example, Harold Rugg wrote a series of books for social studies which included controversial issues. Although written for and popular with teachers, the books were attacked by conservative groups throughout the nation. One of the Daughters of Colonial Wars declared that Rugg's books "tried to give the child an unbiased viewpoint instead of teaching him real Americanism."

While Counts and the Social Frontier group publicly censured other progressives for their failure to develop a policy of social action, conservative reaction helped to split the progressives apart and contributed to the decline of the Progressive Education Association. The question of the role of the school in social change did not end with the progressives, however. It is a theme central to modern educational critics like Ivan Illich and the major concern of contemporary social reconstructionists like Theodore Brameld.

Meantime, various innovative or experimental schools were created. Many of these followed Dewey's theory, but some departed from the mainstream of the progressive fold to chart a new course. Junius Meriam, of the University of Missouri, threw out traditional time periods in favor of flexible scheduling and an activity curriculum. At Fairhope, Alabama, Marietta Johnson's school provided individualized instruction growing out of organic needs and creative abilities of children. Mrs. Johnson published *Youth in the World of Men* in 1929, and lectured on her methods all over the nation. Abraham Flexner's *Modern School* appeared in 1916, and it was followed by numerous reports on progressive educational reform.

One of the guiding lights of the progressive movement was Carleton Washburne, superintendent of schools in Winnetka, Illinois. He introduced individual instruction together with common group activities in the "Winnetka Plan." It was somewhat similar to the "Dalton Plan," which Helen Parkhurst described in 1922. The Dalton plan employed a contract system in which part of the day was spent in class activities and a portion reserved for activities for which each student had individually contracted with the teacher.

With the exception of programmed learning and computer assisted instruction, most of the contemporary "innovations" in modern education were tried by the progressives. Certainly there were programs which did not work, and much of the criticism directed toward "soft pedagogy, lax discipline, excessive freedom," and the like, had some basis in fact. Nevertheless, when the progressive movement ended in the 1940's, a great many promising alternatives had been tried in schools. The Eight-Year Study, published in 1942, was a detailed comparison of almost 1,500 matched pairs of college students. One member of each pair had attended a traditional school while the other received basic education in one of thirty participating progressive schools. The study indicated that students from progressive schools held their own on standard tests and were superior in intellectual curiosity and drive. Regardless of such factors, reaction against the progressives was so intense that almost all of their programs had been thrown out of public schools by 1950. Historical evidence shows that educators spend a great deal of time reinventing methods and approaches previously tried.

Essentialists and Perennialist Critics

Since the end of World War II, there has been increasing evidence of resurgence of conservative sentiment in America. A considerable portion of this conservative reaction has been directed toward education. Idealists, realists, neo-Scholastics, and other perennialist philosophers have always argued that the most significant and refined aspects of the culture, such as the great literary classics, should make up the bulk of the school curriculum. They found support from essentialists like William C. Bagley and from those who objected to the liberal social ideas of many progressives. The heaviest attack has been on the alleged excesses of progressive education and the theories of John Dewey. Conservatives have charged that Dewey and the progressives poisoned the minds of children and perverted the school system almost beyond recovery. Some of the venom was directed toward classroom teachers, but professors and colleges of education received the major blame. Historian Arthur Bestor Jr., in *Educational Wastelands* used the term "educationists" in reference to professors who train teachers. Another example of the biting critique of conservatives is Russell Kirk's *Prospects for Conservatives* published in 1956.

Essentialism may be treated both as a philosophy and as a protest. Under the leadership of William Bagley, one-time professor at Columbia and editor of *School and Society*, essentialists attacked progressives because of their failure to emphasize basic skills and teach "essential" facts. Bagley was not opposed to the methods of progressive educators, but he held discipline to be as important as democracy. He argued that progressive teachers:

condone and rationalize the refusal of the learner to attack a task that does not interest him. In effect, they open wide the lines of least resistance and least effort. Obedience they stigmatize as a sign of weakness. All this they advocate in the magic names of "democracy" and "freedom."

Essentialists see the purpose of education as the transmission of the most important parts of the cultural heritage. This involves training the individual through intellectual discipline and the rigorous application of the mind to traditional subjects. There must be a core of basic subjects which carry the major values of Western civilization. History, literature, natural sciences, and foreign languages are regarded as peripheral. Vocational skills, service, activities, and free choice for the students are generally opposed by essentialists. Society is logically prior to the individual and knowledge is logically prior to the knower. The conservative believes that the school is a vital institution, whose purpose is to give intellectual training to the young and preserve the cultural heritage. Rather than building a new social order, the school must preserve the status quo.

Not all essentialists are as critical or as outspoken as Bagley, Bestor, or Kandel. Albert Lynd and Bernard Iddings Bell take an extreme position; but James Conant supports a milder sort of essentialism. The Council for Basic Education is an example of a conservative educational organization which demands heavy emphasis on skills and "hard" subjects, but has no uniform theory base. Essentialists often disagree about what is essential. Nevertheless, they enjoy the support of the general public and a large number of public school administrators. Essentialism appears to be the dominant philosophy of education in practice today.

The Educational Philosophy of John Dewey

John Dewey was born in Burlington, Vermont, in 1859, the same year that *Origin of Species* was published. His boyhood was quite average, and he had not developed any special interests when he entered the University of Vermont. An edge was put on his intellectual appetite in his junior year, by a course in physiology. Dewey found it intellectually necessary to accept the theory of evolution, and he turned to philosophy as a means of bridging the gap between the new science and his earlier belief that the world was shaped by God's moral will. After two years of teaching school in rural Vermont and at Oiltown, Pennsylvania, Dewey entered Johns Hopkins University as a graduate student in philosophy. Although he studied with G. Stanley Hall and Charles Sanders Peirce, Dewey's major instructor was George Sylvester Morris. An idealist, Morris introduced Dewey to a system of thought which declared that matter was only an illusion, and mind-stuff or spirit was reality. For ten years after leaving Johns Hopkins to teach at the universities of

Michigan and Minnesota, Dewey remained under the spell of Hegel.

The vigorous pace of change in technology and society caused Dewey to become interested in democracy and the vitality of modern life. His concern shifted from psychology (in which field he had written his first book) to individual and social problems created by rapid political, economic, and social changes. As a critic of rugged individualism, free enterprise without controls, outmoded tradition, and institutions like schools, Dewey found himself disenchanted with a system of unchanging spiritual reality. He accepted the statement of William James that the universe was wide open and began to reconstruct his philosophy on pragmatic lines.

Charles S. Peirce derived the word "pragmatism" from the Greek term for action and first defined its meaning in an article called "How to Make Our Ideas Clear," which appeared in the *Popular Science Quarterly* in 1877. Peirce and a group of young men interested in philosophy, which included Chauncey Wright and William James, attempted to turn speculative theory into a practical plan for action. Peirce argued that in order to give ideas perfect clarity we need only consider the practical effects, immediate or remote, which the object of our conception may have for us. Pragmatism is a means of looking away from first principles, necessities, and categories and looking toward facts, consequences, and the fruits of action. It uses the scientific method as a way of analyzing problems and looking at all the evidence before any solution is considered. It is opposed to uncritically accepted authority, tradition, custom, intuition, or raw common-sense attitudes.

Peirce's early statements were largely ignored until William James reintroduced pragmatism in 1898. In essays like "What Pragmatism Means," James asked, "What difference would it practically make to any one if this notion rather than that notion were ture?" If no practical difference can be found, then the alternatives mean practically the same thing, and all disputes are idle. Since men can deal only with belief and doubt, when a belief becomes less and less contaminated by doubt, it approaches a type of truth. This truth is never infinite or ultimate in the metaphysical sense; but it serves as a guide for human activity. Thinking is always influenced by the human emotions, attitudes, and capabilities of the thinker. For pragmatists, that idea which is accepted as valid by all those who investigate and test it against experience is what is intended by "truth." Since thought processes are always carried on in relation to human purposes, truth does not exist apart from human action; it must change if life conditions are altered or new facts discovered. As James put it, we must live today by what truth we can get today and be prepared to call it falsehood tomorrow.

In the 1890's, Dewey was converted to the pragmatism of James. His own version of the philosophy, called instrumentalism or experimentalism, grew out of the ideas of Peirce and Dewey's own unique thought. It was Dewey who made pragmatism a comprehensive system of thought with which to deal with all problems generated by conflicts within the culture. Instrumentalism served to restore integration and cooperation between man's beliefs about the world in which he lives and his beliefs about the values and purposes that should direct his conduct. As much a method as a philosophy, instrumentalism concentrates on the scientific, experimental procedure as a tool for the clarification of ideas about social issues and moral conflicts in modern society.

Dewey saw the task of philosophy not as a vehicle to know the nature of ultimate reality; but to understand and control the world. For him, the human mind is an instrument which must be sharpened by experience for use in problem solving and adjustment to the practical situations of life. Human experience and collective human intelligence provide the best chance man has to cope with a world always in a state of flux. Anticipating Toffler and the futurists of today, Dewey held that problems cannot be solved with any degree of finality, because of the rapid rate of change. Real knowledge enables us to adapt our environment to our needs and to adapt our goals to the reality of the situation or life-space in which we exist.

Like Locke, Dewey became concerned about the origin of ideas and the problem of how the mind functions. He accepted the empirical concept that knowledge comes from experience, and, since action must precede knowledge, there can be no a priori ideas. Dewey's naturalism was drawn not only from Rousseau and Froebel, but also from biological sciences and Darwinian evolution. He saw human survival and the progress of the race tied to the means that men have available for solving essential problems. Natural intelligence and the reconstruction of past experience can be the means only if antecedent action is able to trigger a scientific, rational approach to problems. Past beliefs, grounded in tradition or drawn from authority, may actually inhibit the survival of man. For this reason, Dewey wanted to submit every tradition, attitude, belief, and institution to the experimental test with its corollary of verification in experience.

As a psychological functionalist, Dewey understood that the mind is set in motion by the organism's desire to meet its needs and solve its own problems. Although the human organism is of infinite complexity, intelligence can be defined as the use of experience in solving problems. The mind is an organic function used by man to reduce drives and satisfy needs in interaction with the environment. Human beings are not naturally passive, and the experiences they undergo become the materials out of which meaning is made. Clearly, Dewey understood that what people think about is related to what they do and the totality of environmental influence. Intelligence and learning can be made intelligible by equating them with the scientific method of problem solving. Since the individual is not isolated, intelligence must be directed toward social efficiency, or community issues, as well as individual needs.

Central to Dewey's educational theory is the complete act of thought. Although it is described in many of his works, the little book *How We Think* (1910) gives a detailed analysis of the problem-solving process. Dewey held that learning grows out of ongoing activity which means something to the learner. Activity is not merely muscular movement. It involves the individual in the relationships between the act and its consequences. This implies that schools must foster purposeful activity by building on the common interests of children, such as communication, inquiry, construction, and artistic expression. Although activity is necessary for learning, no progress is made so long as the activity is routine and the learner operates on the basis of habit.

Learning actually begins when a difficulty or problem creates a barrier and prevents an activity from continuing. The problem must be genuine (not imposed from outside by a teacher) and must be defined by the learner, so that he knows precisely what he is up against. The problem provides motivation, the driving force or interest needed in thinking. At this point, information or data concerning a possible solution is gathered. This may be done merely by reconstructing prior experience—How have I dealt with such a situation in the past?—or by more sophisticated means such as consulting an expert or using a library. The next step is forming an hypothesis—an educated guess as to how the problem may be resolved. The learner does not jump at once to any hypothesis, but first reflects on probable outcomes and the possibility of undesirable consequences if the hypothesis is accepted. Finally, the learner chooses the most likely hypothesis and puts it to the empirical test of experience. If it works, the problem is solved; if not, the learner has gained further data upon which to base later thought. The complete act of thought (activity, problem, data, hypothesis, testing) was taken directly from the research model of science.

Some of Dewey's statements on education are so often repeated as to be familiar:

Education may be defined as the process of continuous reconstruction of experience with the purpose of widening and deepening its social content, while, at the same time, the individual gains control of the methods involved.

Education . . . is a process of living and not preparation for future living.

Education is a growth and as long as growth continues, education continues.

Education is a social process, and to make this possible the school must be a democratic community.

Dewey once said that if we are willing to conceive education as the process of forming fundamental dispositions, philosophy may be defined as the general theory of education.

The philosophy of John Dewey continued to develop throughout his life. After leaving Chicago for Columbia, he devoted more of his attention to social and moral issues. Rejecting the idea that philosophy defines ends and education provides the means, Dewey held that ends must always be kept in view and adjusted as progress is made. Ends do not justify means. Dewey was an enemy of philosophic dualisms. He saw no conflict between the school and society, the child and the curriculum, or interest and effort in education. Although he was vitally interested in the concepts of community and democracy, Dewey insisted upon leaving open the possibility of different social relationships for the future. To view the democratic society as an end, or goal, would have violated his principle of continuous reconstruction of experience and constant adjustment to life conditions. Dewey supported a child-centered school without stiff authoritarianism,

but he also criticized the progressives for their failure to develop a sound theoretical foundation.

Until the end of his long life in 1952, Dewey remained an active and prolific philosopher. He was constantly attacked by idealists and other spokesmen for philosophic positions different from his own. His legions of followers often misunderstood him, and there is still controversy concerning exactly what some of his statements meant.

Nevertheless, John Dewey must be regarded as the most significant American educational philosopher. His realization that intelligent action is the ultimate resource of man in every field, his belief in the method of science as a means of progress in education, and his strong support of education viewed as a social process utilizing the continuous reconstruction of accumulated experience, remain among the most vital educational theories ever produced. Dewey is vigorously opposed and vigorously supported, but never ignored—a tribute to his greatness.

CURRENT CONTROVERSY IN EDUCATIONAL THEORY

It is obvious to even the most casual observer that American education is in a state of confusion. Clarification of purpose is badly needed in order that the school can effectively relate to the changing conditions of the larger society. Educational literature is full of issues concerning the professional role of teachers, methods, alternative patterns of school organization, meeting the needs of the disadvantaged, integration, finance, accountability, the influence of the mass media on schooling, and the curriculum. Even more controversial are problems arising out of debate over purposes and goals of education in a modern, industrial, technological, rapidly changing, and somewhat democratic state. Certainly the schools are in great difficulty. Notwithstanding the rhetoric, American schools appear to have followed the traditional subject curriculum supported by conservative educational policy and essentialist theory.

In spite of the progressive movement, the philosophy of Dewey, and widespread experimentation, American schools remain very much as they were generations ago. Certainly there is a new façade, complete with current catch-phrases and different plans of organization. However, under this shiny veneer there remains a hard core of basic information and essential skills still dominant in American schools. Success is measured in secondary education by the number of students who are able to enter the job market successfully and by the number of graduates who are able to cope with a college or university course.

In 1957, the Soviet success with Sputnik created public ferment which might have caused an educational revolution. Instead, essentialists like James B. Conant and Admiral Hyman Rickover led a movement for curriculum reorganization and higher standards in secondary schools. They called for more mathematics, science, and foreign language instruction, in order to produce the experts upon which an industrial society depends for technological progress and for winning wars, both hot and cold. The National Defense Education Act (1958) was a response to an almost evangelical appeal for excellence and accountability in traditional disciplines. Many professional educators were pleased with the funds, laboratories, teachers, and programs that were provided. While some called for effective and humanistic courses to meet the needs of all children, and many worried about equal educational opportunity, the educational reforms of the sixties were popular among school people. The effect was to reinforce the firm hold essentialism already had on education.

Recent educational changes have offered no new theory or alternative educational philosophy. It has generally been believed that a combination of adequate financial resources and reorganization would provide answers to all problems. So long as educational reforms are limited to innovations such as non-graded schools, team teaching, open classrooms, individualized instruction, and the use of instructional technology, they pose only minimal threats to conservatives. Many of these experiments are at the elementary level; but they have little effect on high schools and colleges, where academic disciplines and essentialistic beliefs are firmly entrenched. Conservatives can afford to give ground on methods, so long as there is no compromise on fundamental skills and acquisition of basic information. Organizational schemes such as changing junior high schools and upper elementary grades into middle schools are hardly a challenge to the conservative tradition.

Educational historian Michael Katz has concluded that very little change in the function and structure of American schools has taken place since the nineteenth century. In *Class, Bureaucracy, and Schools: the Illusion of Educational Change in America*, Katz charges that the purpose of formal education has been and is the transmission of dominant economic and social values through a bureaucratic structure. Another student of educational history who finds no fundamental alteration in educational aims is Clarence J. Karier. He believes that business values, social control, the protection of class privileges, and maintenance of the status quo have been dominant in the schools. Karier's position is well supported in a recent collection of documents published under the title *Shaping the American Educational State, 1900 to the Present*. While stressing sterility of the child's learning environment, aimlessness, and the mechanical nature of the curriculum, Charles E. Silberman indicated that there has been no real change in education. His widely read *Crisis in the Classroom* calls attention to the fact that the goals of education have not been altered significantly from those of the past.

Schools can hardly be expected to undergo any real or lasting change as long as no fundamental reassessment of the purposes of education is made. Educational innovation ranging from a systems approach in school reorganization to technological changes incorporating the media are often undertaken with little examination of basic aims and goals. Sometimes there is a tacit assumption that basic purposes are so well established and known that there is no point in discussing them at all. Attention given to slogans or the jargon of philosophic language is no substitute for an adequate theory base. Perhaps this is the reason some educational philosophers think reforms appear in stages and are repeated.

Using history as a guide, G. Max Wingo suggests that future events in education will very likely occur in a given order. First, there will be dissatisfaction and even profound hostility directed toward the school system and its established curriculum and methods. This may be linked to disenchantment with the social order, economic stress of inflation, changing youth attitudes, lack of faith in government, or the like. Whatever the cause, an attitude of discontent sets the stage and climate for reform. Second, "alternative" forms of education or experimental schools will be established outside of the public school system. These alternatives will be developed by a variety of individuals, including serious scholars, romantics, social radicals, and sundry "crackpots." Their schools are labeled "innovative, humanistic, open, progressive, child-centered," or whatever term is popular. They will vary greatly in programs, methods, and organization. Ecstatic reports of the uniform success of the innovative schools will be circulated with very little criticism and no objective evaluation. At the same time, critics of traditional education will fill journals with demands for change. In the third stage, public schools will adopt the educational reforms created by the private sector. Without a defining of objectives or a rigorous intellectual examination of the reforms, they will be accepted in the schools. It is expected that the reforms will do wonders for children and accomplish goals which traditional schools failed to achieve by traditional methods. However, it will be found that the claims of the reformers are exaggerated, and enthusiasm for the new programs will cool rapidly. Parents, teachers, and students will become disenchanted with the innovations and reforms. Finally, a wave of conservative reaction will set in. Another breed of critics will emerge to attack the reforms of the public schools. They will prove to everyone's satisfaction that students are ignorant of basic information and lacking in essential skills. Demands will be made for a return to time-tested methods and essentialist programs. The antagonists will fulminate against the soft pedagogy and soft-headedness of the reformers. They will call for intellectual rigor, discipline, and accountability. The circle will be closed, the reform finished. In good Hegelian terms, the cycle—thesis-antithesis-synthesis-thesis—will have occurred. It happened that way with progressive education and with the educational reforms of the 1960's. Only by overcoming the poverty of philosophy can the cycle be broken.

The School as Social Change Agent

If philosophy of education is to remain only an instrument to justify reoccurring cycles of essentialism, there is little hope that it can be productive. The strength of the conservative tradition rests upon the belief that social institutions and the nature of the culture will remain stable—that changes will not be revolutionary. For idealism, scholasticism, realism, and essentialism, the ends are established by authority outside and above the individual and the social system. Pre-twentieth-century philosophy developed metaphysical principles, axiological assumptions, and a priori statements from which the aims and goals of education could be logically derived. Their purpose was to make schooling reflect values already established as valid within a fixed philosophic system. Social change was seen as a gradual gravitation toward those fixed values—a realization of the philosophic "good."

There is always an organic connection between education and the cultural milieu. Modern philosophies of education stress this connection and insist that the question of educational aims and purposes has not been settled. To be sure, there are major conflicts between the several philosophic positions currently struggling for acceptance. Analytic philosophy is concerned with the clarification of meaning and rigorous care in the use of language and logic as tools for understanding basic problems. Existentialism deals with the meaning of individual experience and offers no clear guidance for schools as social institutions. Nevertheless, modern philosophies, including experimentalism, reconstructionism, existentialism, analytic philosophy, the Marxist protest, and futurism, represent the antithesis of the traditional point of view.

As we have seen, John Dewey and pragmatic-experimental theorists believe schools do have a major role in social change. Social reconstructionists like Theodore Brameld and futurists such as Kenneth Boulding see education as the major instrument for altering the society. Rapid advances in science and technology, rising aspirations of people throughout the world, economic growth, the population explosion, urbanization, increased leisure time, the knowledge explosion, international interdependence, alternative life-styles, and the like, have raised fundamental questions about education's relationship to society. Instead of using schools to help individuals reach eternal truth and established values, these philosophers hold that no values can be regarded as fixed and final.

The outstanding spokesman for altering society through education is Theodore Brameld. Brameld agrees with Karl Mannheim and Robert Heilbroner that we are about to witness the very end of civilization unless we can quickly and drastically reconstruct our priorities and behavior patterns. The crisis-culture theme is not new either in philosophy or education. What makes Brameld's theory worthy of serious consideration is the tremendous rate of change in the world today. By superimposing Alvin Toffler's *Future Shock* on the culture lag thesis of W. F. Ogburn and adding concepts like the population bomb and nuclear war, it becomes difficult *not* to accept the idea of worldwide crisis. Our salvation, Brameld believes, is nothing less than a reconstructed world order. The means for reaching this is through radical alteration of the purpose, function, and structure of education.

In *Education as Power*, Brameld takes the position that knowledge is power and that the reconstructionist value theory transmitted through schooling might produce a utopian "civilized civilization." Since Brameld thinks all values are man-made and relative to the contingencies of time, place, and culture, he believes it is possible to define ends through social consensus. It is assumed that world peace and economic cooperation might be such a goal; but all ends must be harmonious with culturological imperatives, and none may be imposed by outside authority such as national governments. Brameld offers a number of goals in various fields which he thinks would be agreed upon by free people everywhere. Such economic goals would include: satisfying basic wants of all consumers; assuring full employment under good working conditions; guaranteeing sufficient income to all families to meet reasonable standards of nourishment, shelter, dress, medical care, education, and recreation; utilizing all natural resources and large-scale enterprises in the interests of the majority of the people.

By the very volume and breadth of his writing, Brameld must be considered one of the most prolific contemporary educational philosophers. It is not intended here that his position, or even a summary of his views, be presented. Rather, Theodore Brameld is taken as an example of one of those who accepts the idea that schools can be used as instruments of social change. Critics of the position say that the schools are always reflections of the dominant power structure in society. They argue that schools can hardly become tools for massive, in-depth social revolution unless existing social control can be removed from them, and this itself implies major social revolution.

Deschool Society or Transmit Cultural Values?

A radical departure from the usual approach to the question, "What are schools for?" is taken by Ivan Illich. Born in Vienna, Illich was a Catholic priest in New York City, Puerto Rico, and Latin America before founding the Center for Intercultural Documentation in Cuernavaca, Mexico, in 1964. Although his cultural and intellectual background is similar to that of Jacques Maritain, Illich has developed a position diametrically opposed to the perennial philosophy of Neo-Thomism.

In his now famous (or infamous) book, *Deschooling Society*, Illich comprehensively denounces universal, compulsory, mass education supported by public taxation. Certainly Illich believes in the importance of education; but he thinks the structured, bureaucratic schools of modern society actually hinder the individual's opportunity to learn. Schools, he says, detach competence from the curriculum and emphasize the rituals of matriculation and acquiring degrees. Schools are used as screening devices to filter out a large number of students and to create an elite class for those who remain. In Latin America the poor are defined as those who failed to complete four years of formal schooling. Illich believes that a youngster in Mexico who drops out of school after three years would have been better off not to have entered at all. What he learned in his brief schooling is irrelevant for his needs, but he must carry the stigma of failure. He was tried by the educational system and found wanting. In the United States, Illich says that preventive concentration camps for predelinquents would be a logical improvement over the school system.

Illich compares modern bureaucratic schooling with two other enterprises in mass society, medicine and transportation. In Mexico, a simple mass transit system was developed, using rugged trucks and buses to provide cheap public transportation over poor roads from one village to another. In the 1960's the Mexican government decided to copy the interstate highway system model from the United States. Superhighways were built between major cities in Mexico at great cost to the taxpayers. Since few Mexicans own private automobiles, these highways did not benefit the majority. Furthermore, they used funds that might have gone to maintain and improve the local roads, trucks, and buses upon which most Mexicans depend. Highly sophisticated, very expensive hospitals served by professional doctors are the mainstay of modern medicine. Excellent care is provided for the wealthy, even to the extent of organ transplants and elaborate efforts to combat incurable sickness; but little attention is given to preventive medicine or basic health needs for the poor. Illich argues that schools are designed to help the privileged grow in power and affluence by attaining college degrees, while the basic educational needs of the masses are ignored. This contributes to problems in a world already divided into groups having more than they need and those who do not have enough.

In *Tools for Conviviality*, Illich says that people can be enslaved by their tools and institutions. He thinks it is economically absurd to pursue the goal of equal educational opportunity, and that school experience cannot overcome the educational disadvantage of the poor. For Illich, the escalation of schools is as destructive to society as the escalation of weapons, though less visibly so. The curriculum has become a sign of social rank, and school rituals are used to hide discrepancies between social principles and actual social organization. Like highways, schools appear to be open to all, but in reality they are open only to those who constantly renew their credentials. School failure is accepted as proof that education is complex, expensive, difficult to attain, and not within the ability of all people.

Illich especially objects to the hidden curriculum of "prejudice, guilt and discrimination" which society practices against its less fortunate members. The values passed on by schools serve as ritual initiation into the growth-oriented, materialistic, self-perpetuating, class conscious, business-dominated culture. Packaged values and myths are the stuff of which school programs are made. Illich defines the school as an "age-specific, teacher-related process requiring full-time attendance and an obligatory curriculum." He concludes that the United States should adopt a new constitutional amendment to the effect that "the state shall make no law with respect to the establishment of education."

Illich does not oppose education in general, but only institutionalized schools, which he feels foster suicidally distorted values. He proposes learning webs which would provide free access to all citizens to the educational tools of the community.

Learning webs would be supported by government through some sort of entitlements or vouchers. They would neither grant degrees nor provide for the accumulation of credit hours, a practice Illich likens to the body counts of the Vietnam war. Illich is aware that some tasks, such as the learning of basic skills, may benefit from the discipline of school-like drills; but mostly they would give motivated learners access to information. Teachers would be replaced with "facilitators," who would aid in the learning process when called upon. The facilitators would not be involved in controlling teachers and students to the satisfaction of legislatures and corporate executives. Mostly, they would keep out of the way of learning while fostering creative intercourse between persons. It is autonomous, creative intercourse between individuals and between persons and their environment that Illich calls "conviviality." He sees it as the opposite of industrial productivity.

Illich does not seem to feel that his program can be put into effect through political strategy. "With the possible exception of China under Mao, no present government could restructure society along convivial lines. The managers of our major tools—nations, corporations, parties, structured movements, professions—hold power." He does not expect schools to disappear from society until a new post-industrial economic theory has become operational. Some of Illich's critics have suggested that to deschool society would have little effect so long as the mass media, the economic system, and the other institutions of society continue to support industrial growth, materialistic development, and increased consumption. With this, Illich would appear to agree.

The Humanistic/Existentialistic Protest

Philosophy of education is sometimes defined as any reasonably coherent set of values and fundamental assumptions used as a basis for guiding and evaluating educational practice. Even under such a broad umbrella, existentialism barely qualifies as an educational philosophy. In fact, existentialism is not a philosophic school in the usual sense, and the differences between individual existential writers is often as great as between proponents of different philosophies. The contrast between theistic and atheistic existentialists looms especially large. In common is the existential acceptance of the need for introspective examination of one's own experience, the freedom and responsibility of individual choice, and the belief that existence precedes essence. The latter statement means that there is no difference between the external world of reality and the internal world of the mind. Essence refers to what a thing is intrinsically made of; while existence refers to the act by which it comes into being and is known. Only that with which the individual has experience and authentic involvement is real.

Four figures generally believed to be the founders of existentialism are Soren Kierkegaard (1813–55), Fredrich Nietzche (1844–1900), Martin Heidegger (born 1899), and Jean Paul Sartre (born 1905). None of these men has given any attention directly to education. The themes of anxiety, alienation, death, despair, and "aloneness of man" found in the existential literature seem at opposite poles from most educational theory. Nevertheless, the central idea of man and his individual being as the major concern of philosophy is classical. It is expressed in the admonition of Socrates to "know thyself" and in the works of Descartes, Pascal, and Dostoevsky.

Modern existentialists are individualists. They have little interest in the technical, analytical work of many American philosophers or in the scientific methods of pragmatism. They protest against traditional philosophy, which they believe has made man the mere servant of one system or another. They are interested in an answer to the question, "What gives meaning to the existence of Man?" Values do not have meaning apart from the freely chosen acts of human beings. The actual character of human existence makes man "condemned to be free," to determine his own nature by the choices he makes. Human beings are always thrown back upon their own resources. Meaning is not furnished by the ideas of others, by history, the church, the government, or any philosophic system. Each person's situation is unique. The manner in which choices are made always determines what man will become. The burden of consequences and responsibility also falls to each individual man, and blame for unfortunate choices cannot be shifted to anyone else.

There is almost no primary literature in existentialism which deals with education, although educational ideas are found in the works of Martin Buber, Karl Jaspers and Gabriel Marcel. There is no existentialist school which may be examined as a model. Rather, existentialism is an expression of a number of attitudes and philosophic ideas which ridicules the goals and casts doubt on the value of formal education. Since there is no fundamental set of values or established body of knowledge which existentialism supports, emphasis is placed on individual experience and the evaluation of that experience. Existentialism stresses both the freedom of choice and the necessity of choice.

Since human nature is subjective, and the individual is free to choose and become what he wills, existentialism poses a major threat to education. School values have traditionally been those of organized society and its powerful institutions. The existentialist claims that civilization is merely a thin veneer. When it is stripped away, man in his savage and brutal nature is revealed. Themes such as alienation, authenticity, the fact of freedom, and the misery of the human condition are not compatible with schools or any predetermined curriculum. The idea that man's existence is finite, that each individual must face death and non-being, and that there is nothing to give meaning to life outside of man himself, certainly challenges all systems of beliefs from which educational subjects are drawn. Existentialists call this the "age of anxiety." Man fears that his collective existence will be ended by nuclear war, starvation, or violence created by his fellows. But solving social problems and making the life space safe and secure does not remove the individual anguish. Each man must live in the knowledge that he will eventually die, whether he chooses to do so or not. It may be true that hungry people think they would be happy if they had abundant food, but when hunger is satisfied, happiness is still illusive. The pragmatic idea of groups of people working together to reach consensus about plans of action designed to improve human conditions leaves the existentialist cold. He has no faith in the ability of groups or institutions to improve the forlorn condition of human existence. Neither does the existentialist accept the standard position that the ethical life is one in which the passions are regulated and controlled by reason and the will.

Education in the existentialist view must place personal motives and preferences above social conformity. There would need to be a wide scope for individual expression. Demands and requirements such as attendance, specific courses, accumulation of credit hours, dress codes, and rules for behavior would have no place. School as a fixed program or single location would be replaced by active participation in all sorts of life experiences. The street, a seashore, a factory, or a farm, would be just as effective as any campus or school building. All of the standard pedagogical stress on logic and order would give way to honest personal evaluation and feeling. An existentialist would accept the student's emotional reaction to a piece of literature as being more valid than the scholar's systematic analysis of it. The ability to love, appreciate, respond to the environment, and communicate would be important in developing an authentic individual. The role of the teacher (if there were teachers) would be that of facilitator. Group methods would be replaced with something like the Socratic method. But even the Socratic method, if used in the classic Platonic sense to draw out ideas in the mind of the student (as in the case of the slave boy who was made by Socrates to utter the Pythagorean Theorem) would be ruled out by existentialists. Martin Buber's I–Thou relationship might be a model. Buber says that the proper educational relationship is one of pure dialogue. The student would not be sheltered from choices involving freedom and responsibility. For some existentialists, there might be room for disciplined work and hard study; but only if the choice to do this is made freely by the student without coercion. With or without a school, the existentialist would want to help the student transcend his present self and realize his full potential as a free being.

Education for Future Survival

Ever since Alvin Toffler published *Future Shock*, laymen in America have been becoming aware of what experts in certain fields have known for decades—that the rate of change in modern society is rapidly accelerating. A new group of scientists and authors, known generally as futurists, have taken issue with the standard assumptions implicit and explicit in modern civilization. They question the idea of progress leading to ever-greater production of goods, the expenditure of enormous quantities of energy, the rapid depletion of the non-renewable natural resources, and the development of a world-wide market for materialistic consumer's goods. Futurists build on the social theories of Karl Marx, Karl Mannheim, Pitirim Sorokin, Oswald Spengler, and Arnold Toynbee, among others. They are aware of the culture lag theory, which suggests that human beings cannot cope with the shattering stress and disorganization that results when materialistic invention comes too rapidly for social adjustment. Problems such as the exploding world population, the threat of nuclear war, pollution, runaway technology, the knowledge explosion, and environmental destruction, cause many futurists to doubt the survival of civilization and its institutions, unless radical adjustments can be quickly made.

In *Cybernation: the Silent Revolution*, Donald N. Michael shows how poorly prepared modern men are for the revolution now in progress. Kenneth Boulding refers to the automation/biological revolution as "The Great Transition" and ranks it as significant on human growth and development as the discovery of agriculture or the industrial revolution. In *The Coming of Post-Industrial Society*, Daniel Bell forecasts the most radical changes which have ever faced the human race. In *Overskill*, Eugene Schwartz argues that the present trend toward increased technological and materialistic expansion cannot be maintained. Lester Brown illustrates the growing economic gap between the rich and poor in *World Without Borders*. He points out that the whole world is becoming poverty stricken in terms of the earth's total ability to sustain life and predicts that a stable world order depends on meeting the basic needs of all people. Radical economists like John Kenneth Galbraith and Robert Theobald maintain that the present socio-economic system in the industrial nations like Japan, West Germany, and the United States cannot insure survival. In *The Prometheus Project*, Gerald Fineberg calls for a new and revolutionary set of long-range social goals, while Donella Meadows insists that for future survival there must be limits to growth. John R. Platt believes that a science for human survival is needed to examine social and individual priorities.

Some futurists see man as an endangered species clinging precariously to a life support system which his own actions may destroy. Others are concerned about efforts to maintain wealth and privilege in an overpopulated world, where equality of distribution of resources is badly needed. Barry Commoner believes that our technology is responsible for deterioration in the quality of the environment and that a new and better technology is needed to prevent massive biological degradation. Almost all see overgrowth, increased industrialization, urbanization, unemployment, psychological alienation, environmental destruction, polarization of rich and poor, expansion of the population, and demands for resources beyond the capacity of the earth to provide them, as major problems of the present and the future.

Most futurists are painfully aware of the danger of prediction and the terrible record of forecasting human events previous intellectuals have had. Still, most of our basic institutions and beliefs depend upon the assumption that things will remain pretty much as they are, an assumption which plainly runs contrary to fact. Electronic media and the invention of the computer have joined to produce an explosion of information unlike anything previously experienced by man. New knowledge can be quickly disseminated and applied to tasks that stagger the imagination, such as landing human beings safely on the moon. Each new technical development creates new possibilities for invention and the rapid exchange of ideas, plans, and programs, which grow at an exponential rate. Linking information systems and machines creates cybernation. The possibility of a highly refined automated, cybernated system of production is now very

real. There are also very great breakthroughs in areas of science such as biology and genetics, the results of which are not yet clear, but certainly highly significant. Every day much more is learned about human behavior and the learning process. Futurists use different terms to refer to the transformation now taking place. The unknown state into which we are passing is labeled "post-industrial, post-civilized, automated, cybernated, super-industrial, information-era, communications-era" and the like. Futuristic writers do not agree on exactly what form the great revolution will take, but they agree that it is already in process. The transformation offers great hope for achieving a higher level of human potential and "inventing the future"; however it also poses the danger that people will be unable to adjust rapidly enough to change. Obviously, futurists have little faith that education can be guided by ideas of the past, such as the collection of classics known as the Great Books of the Western World.

The Futuristic Educational Theory of Robert Theobald

Socio-economist Robert Theobald has a well developed set of theories about the nature and the problems of modern industrial society. He has also produced a statement of educational philosophy, especially in *TEG's Nineteen Ninety-four*. His ideas about education are highly futuristic and directed toward solutions for the complicated and immense difficulties which threaten survival both of the individual and the society.

A basic assumption in Theobald's thought is that modern industrial society is in an era of transition to a post-industrial state he calls the communications era. The transition period is one of profound social crisis, caused by a confusion in societal priorities and resulting in a highly normless culture. It is characterized by materialistic values in which production and consumption are dominant, intellectual and moral decay, the decline of major institutions, multi-group conflict, and cultural lag. Theobald's cultural lag theory is basically similar to William F. Ogburn's as expressed in *Social Change* and Alvin Toffler's in *Future Shock*. However, Theobald goes on to suggest that industrial-era priorities are dysfunctional for present and future society and that a new definition of societal accountability is required if American and world problems are to be solved. Survival with some degree of freedom and security, and certainly any hope for achieving a new realm of human potential, depends upon a kind of education not provided in the current industrial-military-transportation complex. Present job related educational tracks only contribute to an oversupply of specialities soon to be obsolete and useless.

Theobald maintains that modern industrial society measures success by the growth rate of the gross national product and failure by the rate of unemployment. He believes that the public assumes economists to be mere technicians who find the means to achieve goals, while in reality economists establish goals for society.

Theobald sees a major transition now beginning, which will change society from the industrial-era to the communications- or information-era. The change from automation to cybernated systems utilizing computers is evidence of the transition. While there is a major energy crisis linked to the use of fossil fuels, there is also a trend toward the production of unlimited energy. If this can be accomplished by new technology—such as harnessing solar power and converting it to electricity—even manufacturing fresh water from sea water in quantities sufficient to irrigate all the world's deserts is realistic. Man is learning how to control the building blocks of nature, even to the point of genetic engineering. Cybernation and the increased use of computers will alter all levels of human endeavor. Many jobs once performed by human hands have been given over to more efficient machines. The same logic indicates that human thought as an instrument for problem solving, will be greatly extended by more sophisticated computer technology. Already, Theobald holds, a universal language is possible through computer communication. All systems, including social and human systems, have feedback mechanisms which provide information for evaluating previous actions and making future decisions. Computerized systems (including all computer assisted extensions of human thought) operate on predetermined assumptions. If the information used in making assumptions is inaccurate or distorted, resulting actions are necessarily distorted. For example, if an automobile manufacturer makes profits its first priority, without regard for public transportation needs, energy waste, or environmental pollution, survival of the entire socioeconomic system may be endangered. No matter how sophisticated the computerized-cybernated system, the assumption that profits are of greatest priority will directly affect action. Theobald asserts that human beings in the communications-era will create their own future through the use of problem solving and unbiased information.

According to Theobald, early economic theory supposed that abundance could never be achieved and confined economics to the art of distributing scarce resources. While the modern society exhibits both scarcity and abundance, Theobald believes that it is no longer true that the basic needs of people everywhere cannot be adequately provided for. He attacks the idea that people have an unlimited desire for manufactured products. Except for food, clothing, shelter, and a little love, Theobald holds the needs people express are socially determined.

Theobald attacks neo-Keynesian economics for its assumptions that man's wants for material goods are unlimited, that work will be effectively performed only when structured into jobs with economic incentives, and that the cost of economic growth (especially in terms of environmental degradation) can be ignored as insignificant. He calls attention to the fact that information distortion is widely practiced by industry through advertising and the creation of the myth of scarcity. The monopoly which Theobald defines as a sheltered market and planned obsolescence are also objects of his attack.

According to Theobald, the cybernetic era will make it necessary for Americans to alter the Protestant work ethic. Unemployability resulting from increased automation will require a re-examination of the philosophy underlying the distribution of income and patterns of buying by consumers. Theobald does not believe that everyone can be retrained to be useful in the conventional job market. In the information-era, many more people will be used in service occupations, for which a large need will exist, but a very few highly trained individuals will be able to operate the cybernated manufacturing process. The government will become the employer of last resort, and every individual will receive a minimum income as a matter of right. This Basic Economic Security, he feels, will enable every individual to choose the way he wishes to spend his time—in work, service, or leisure. This will be helpful in overcoming the physical and psychological distress resulting from rapid change which may overload the human adaptive system and the process of adjustment. The era of cybernation will require thinking beings to integrate physical and mental activities.

Theobald feels that the present bureaucratic form of organization and structural authority was successful for the industrial period, but will become obsolete in the post-industrial era. He believes that bureaucracy fosters linear thinking and the machine metaphor as well as structural authority. In place of authority vested in the organization, Theobald suggests sapiential authority, which emerges through true communication. In a school using structural authority, the position of the teacher and textbook is used to substantiate facts, ideas, and attitudes. If sapiential authority were used, any statement or bit of information furnished by teachers or students would be justified on the basis of its validity and usefulness. Sapiential authority is based on knowledge, not rank and status. Language using the machine metaphor indicates inadequate thought processes. "Toss that idea into the hopper," or "Let's run that idea through the mill," are examples of language which makes it hard to reflect intelligently on, or analyze, proposals. Weaknesses in linear thinking are many. Linear organizations require that information must be adjusted to institutional classification systems. They are easily overloaded or underloaded with information, making good decisions difficult. Such organizations repress unfavorable information. Linear thinking leads to linear decisions, which implies extending patterns, reproducing or creating other similar institutions, and promoting individuals until they reach their level of incompetence. Theobald says that linear organizations and bureaucracies can only control people who wish to be controlled and create new linear organizations to deal with new problems. They are dysfunctional in the communications-era. Needed are systematic thought patterns which are capable of dealing with whole problems and offering alternatives. The process of achieving solutions and clarification of priorities must be emphasized more than goals. Systematic problem solving requires that each individual involved is able to see the relevance to his own needs of possible plans of action. For example, environmentalists may find that inner-city dwellers are more concerned with the elimination of rats than with the preservation of eagles. The ban on DDT in the United States, which has ample food, makes little sense to farmers in Nigeria, who fear insects and famine more than environmental pollution.

A meaningful perspective of alternative communication styles is provided in *TEG's Nineteen Ninety-four.* He describes three techniques for communication: inter, outer, and situational. Inter communication permits conclusions to be reached when both the question to be answered and the existing conditions or variables are only *thought* to be known. Marketives are often guilty of using inter communication to increase production and profits without considering variables such as the effect on the environment or the supply of natural resources. Outer communication refers to situations where the question is identified but variables are unknown or terminology is not precise. In outer communication, individuals may share limited knowledge. This kind of communication implies non-directive conversation and sapiential authority. Situational communication must be used when the question or problem itself is unknown or unclear. Sometimes it is understood that something is wrong, but the exact nature of the problem has not been identified. Situational communication is an attempt to reach the exact nature of the problem. It may also be used in a situation where the solution for a problem in one area requires modification before it can be successfully applied to another area. Hypothetically, inter communications can establish organizational priorities, outer communication can analyze the priorities as they relate to variables inside and outside of the organization, and situational communication may be used to carry out plans of action. Increasingly, situational communication will rely on reconsideration of the total situation. Therefore, the information era will be dominated by inductive thought patterns on the human level. Communication will be from specific areas of knowledge to generalized knowledge rather than by deduction from general assumptions or principles.

Theobald suggests that marketives (industrial corporations) which are formed to make profits might be replaced by consentives, which would be formed around agreed-upon purposes. The motivation which binds together a consentive is consensus on priorities. This does not rule out making profits, but making money is not the objective. Consentives would use sapiential authority and new communication styles.

Theobald on Education

Robert Theobald's educational perspectives are contained in a number of his writings, but *TEG's Nineteen Ninety-four* provides his most complete theoretical model of educational concepts. His ideas about education are logical extensions of his socioeconomic theory. Fundamental to his views are the problems of freedom, societal priorities, and future survival. Present society must be reconstructed to meet new challenges of the information era, or it will collapse, as all societies which become unsuitable to their environments must collapse. If reconstruction is not planned and orderly, there is great probability that the potential for meaningful future choice will be severely limited. Undesirable social change is that which restricts the possibilities for the individual to make his own decisions in the areas most important to him. Theobald is crisis minded. The situation is unique, urgent, and of crisis proportions. Education is the instrument which can foster evolutionary alteration of values and priorities and prevent a revolutionary change to some sort of totalitarian or fascist state which might preserve order at the price of freedom.

Broadly defined, Theobald thinks education is the process of enabling each person to live in his own society. "The education which each individual receives essentially determines which issues will be examined and which will be ignored; the areas in which society will take action and the areas where it will fail to act." It follows that educational values developed in the past must be altered to prepare the individual for the changing environment which may be expected to exist throughout his lifetime. Theobald is well aware of the social function schools perform in passing the culture from the adults to the young and uninitiated. He does not feel that change to sapiential authority and alternate modes of communication will pose a threat to the binding force of the social system. Rather, involvement of students in the examination of priorities, value clarification, and the analysis of existing beliefs against the backdrop of accelerating change will strengthen society for survival.

For Theobald, there is a major difference between education and training. Training is the process of conveying known information about a given topic or learning skills necessary for any useful process. Education is the study of principles operating within an activity in such a way as to facilitate the development of new questions and alternative answers. Education requires an environment in which students are *not* asked questions for which satisfactory answers exist, or for which priorities are predetermined. Theobald is not against training, because training is useful and is a convenient way to save time when basic skills or the acquisition of information is needed. However, industrial era schools, including colleges, are primarily constructed for training and not for education. This is clearly demonstrated by the structure of the disciplines, bureaucratic organization, linear thinking, structural authority, and inter communication and the expectation that teachers know all the answers.

The average university today is a giant Skinner Box, although nobody meant it to happen this way. If you want a good job, you need good grades. If you want good grades, you need to do well in multiple-choice questions. If you want to do well in multiple-choice questions, you need to keep discreet those nice, attractive, discreet pieces of data you are learning, because if you get them confused you cannot give a simple yes or no answer. It is therefore essential that one does not think, because if you think, you get confused.

For Theobald, the coming of cybernation will require new patterns of work and consumption. The unemployability crisis and environmental problems such as consumption of natural resources, world population growth, and pollution will force a re-evaluation of individual and societal values. With a guaranteed minimum income and ample leisure time, more people will have the choice of life-long learning as opposed to the present-day pattern of training for a job. "The cybernated era based on full education means an end of the industrial era based on full employment." Learning instead of earning will become both economically feasible and socially acceptable. This, of course, assumes that machines guided by computerized information systems will produce the goods needed for life support. It also implies that cybernation will be used for the benefit of all people and not merely for the excessive profits of a few powerful individuals.

There are three major components in the educational process for the coming age. First, provisions must be made for the study of credible information. At present, access to unbiased information is very limited because all industrial era institutions are trying to sell their particular views. False information is circulated and valid information is discarded or repressed. Theobald contends that the credibility of information increases within the auspices of sapiential authority. The second necessary component is ample opportunity to discuss and effectively examine the validity of information. The third is the opportunity for learners to derive insights from the study of information and thereby create feedback patterns for the creation of new, unbiased information. Like George Leonard, Theobald equated education with change in patterns of thought and patterns of action.

The individual needs dialogue to help him critically analyze the values of others and change his own view. Theobald suggests dialogue groups somewhat similar to Illich's learning webs. The groups are small, leaderless, and concerned with the individual differences of members. They must develop a considerable degree of trust and, of course, have access to unbiased information. There is no need for such groups to be confined to schools or other institutions. The central purpose of dialogue is to develop alternatives and responses to the problems of living in the future. They would focus on personal and community problem solving at the grass-roots level, but it should be remembered that many future problems must treat the whole world as one community if they are to be resolved. Leisure time, communication skills, un-

biased information, and a positive attitude about the possible success of alternatives are needed to make dialogue groups function as real educational tools. Theobald views education as a life-long process in which the student is an active participant in the societal and individual development. Training, narrow nationalism, materialistic growth, information distortion, and bureaucratic-linear organization must be attacked if mankind is to survive and the human potential is to be realized. Theobald has great faith in education as the instrument for reconstructing a positive future society.

What has been presented here is partly history and partly speculation about future developments. Historical analysis indicates that American schools are unlikely to accept radical alternatives which are not adopted first by the general public. Many educators do not view schools as change agents in any sense. There certainly is no major movement to deschool society or even to do away with schooling for a significant number of children. Existentialistic theories have very little influence on present educational practices, and, with the exception of some concern for ecology and the probability of mass world starvation, the concepts of the futurists have made little impact on American public schools. It is not suggested that the schools can or should jump on whatever theoretical band wagon happens by at a given moment. It is suggested that schools do not exist in a cultural vacuum and that they are not immune to change or insulated from social conflict. American educators may be working over the school system with an oil can and a screwdriver when a whole new design is needed. We may be moving at breakneck speed into the twenty-first century guided by a rearview mirror image of the nineteenth! If those who control education are unable to obtain some glimpse of the path (or trajectory) ahead, human survival on earth is indeed problematical.

10

THE SCIENTIFIC STUDY OF THE CHILD*

By John C. McCullers and John M. Love

A historical survey of the scientific study of children makes an appropriate contribution to a bicentennial review of American research in several ways. First, while we may look to Europe as the wellspring of much of psychological history, research with children has been a characteristically American enterprise. In this area, we perhaps have enjoyed a "favorable balance of trade" in the sense that we have provided a greater amount of inspiration and guidance than we have received. Second, there is no detailed history of this effort available, even though there have been several excellent histories of psychology available for fifty years or more. The present chapter will not satisfy that need for a history of scientific child study in any comprehensive sense, but it may provide some useful guidelines and generalizations toward that end. Finally, the history of the scientific study of the child is one that fits rather neatly into the two-hundred-year timespan from 1776 to the present, the period of our bicentennial review. That is not to say that there has not been a long and continuing interest in children in earlier years. As long as there have been children and adults to think about them, there probably has been a respectable amount of human thought devoted to concerns of and about children. From the time of antiquity to the Renaissance, philosophers have offered advice on the care and feeding of children, how they should be educated, and the potential evils and perils that might befall them. Most of this advice, however, stemmed from logical analysis or theological principles that did not require that the child actually be studied. That enterprise—the careful study of the child—began about two hundred years ago.

The careful and systematic study of anything probably requires that at least three preliminary conditions be met: there must be a reasonably clear conception of what is being studied, there must be meaningful questions asked, and there must be available a method or approach that presumably will yield satisfactory answers. In the case of child study, these prerequisites translate into a clear concept of the child as distinguished from the adult, some good reasons to want to study the child or infant, and a belief that careful observation of the child can provide the answers. We shall discuss these three points more carefully later, but let us note here that these necessary conditions were first satisfied about two hundred years ago. Since that time there has been an ever-growing interest in scientific child study, so much that today research with children has become one of the most active and intellectually stimulating branches of psychological science.

In the pages that follow we shall try to trace in broad outline the story of how and why we came to study the child, and what we found. We shall focus upon the principal problems, issues, and ideas that were central to this effort. We also shall consider the men who guided the effort and the methods they employed as these relate to our basic theme. Partly because of the nature of the topic, and partly because of the purpose of this volume, we shall place a major emphasis upon the contributions of American investigators. The story would not be complete, and indeed the beginning could not be told at all, however, without making note of European contributions, and so we shall not attempt to limit our discussion to American work.

THE FIRST HUNDRED YEARS: 1776–1880

An arbitrary but perhaps justifiable beginning point for our story might be the year 1787, when Dietrich Tiedemann published his observations on the development of his infant son, and thereby provided the world with the first published observational biography of a baby. We have suggested that the necessary impetus to child study depended on three conditions being met: a clear concept of childhood, important questions to be asked, and a perceived way of answering them. Let's look at these three conditions more closely. The concept of childhood as distinct from adulthood evolved rather slowly (Ariés, 1962; Kessen, 1965) and probably was not very clearly expressed until the period from about the beginning to the middle of the eighteenth century in the philosophical

*This chapter began in a very real sense about ten years ago when the authors were colleagues at Colorado Women's College, in Denver, Colorado. It was then that we began collecting notes and materials in the belief that a good, well-written account of the history of child research would be of some value to anyone who would study the child today. Our present contribution notwithstanding, we still believe that.

writings of John Locke and Jean-Jacques Rousseau. Rousseau's *Emile*, for example, was published in 1762, which was but nineteen years before Tiedemann began his observations of his son in 1781. However, as a German historian of philosophy, Tiedemann presumably was acquainted with the works of Rousseau and other philosophers of that time.

Given, then, that the child can be seen to be different from the adult, two interesting questions arise: What is the nature of the child's mind and the child's soul, and how does the child mind change into the adult form? These are the questions that occurred to Tiedemann. They are the sort of questions, one comparative and the other developmental, that should appeal to educated and intelligent men.

Given a concept of childhood and two good questions, all that was needed was a belief that empirical study of children could provide the answers. From the time of the ancients and for centuries afterward, there existed a sharp conceptual distinction between the mind of man and his body. Man's mind was eternal, limitless, perfect, and endowed with innately (indeed, divinely) given ideas and knowledge. The body, on the other hand, was just the opposite—mortal, imperfect, subject to ordinary physical limitations, and so on. According to this conception, the best avenue to truth would not be through the physical senses (eyes, ears, hands, etc.), which were subject to the limitations of the physical body, but through the mind. Given, then, that one wished to know about children, the best knowledge would be obtained only by reflection, by thinking about children, but certainly not by looking at them, listening to them, doing things to them, or taking measurements on them. However, this long-standing view was subjected to serious challenge in the century immediately prior to Tiedemann's observations. At a theoretical level, the philosophers of the seventeenth century raised major objections to the idea of the innateness and perfection of knowledge apart from experience. At the empirical level, the natural sciences were providing impressive demonstrations that much valuable knowledge could be obtained through careful, systematic observations.

Thus, the necessary prerequisites to child study were first satisfied about the time that Tiedemann began his observations. In the nearly two hundred years since, there has been an ever-increasing readiness to rely on the objective study of children as the principal means of gaining scientific information about them. At the present time, there is only one agreed-upon way to learn about children, and that is to study them.

Child study during the century immediately prior to 1880 was characterized for the most part by a few scattered naturalistic observations. These observations of the development of a single infant generally took the form of biographical accounts known as "baby biographies." Typically, the author's own child, and specifically his son, was the subject of observation. A few normative studies based on simple observations of larger numbers of children also appeared during this period. Dennis (1949) has prepared an excellent review of the literature published prior to 1880, as well as a bibliography of baby biographies (Dennis 1936). Although it is tempting to label this early work as "prescientific," Murchison and Langer (1927) in their translation of Tiedemann (1787) indicate that his study is ". . . usually regarded as the first attempt to make a series of scientific observations on the behavior of young children." Without, then, dealing with the issue of just when the "scientific study of the child" began, the highlights of the period between Tiedemann's publication and the formal beginning of the child-study movement in America in 1880 will be sketched briefly in the following paragraphs.

Baby Biographies

The baby biography was not confined to this particular period in the history of child study. As we shall see, excellent biographies continued to appear into the twentieth century; indeed, many mothers keep such records on the developmental progress of their infants even today. The baby biography, however, did typify the type of child study performed during this early period.

Although observation of young children did not originate with Tiedemann (e.g., Johann Pestalozzi, the educational philosopher, kept notes on his son's educational progress in 1774), Tiedemann (1787) is credited with the first published baby biography. Tiedemann carefully observed the progress of his son's development from the time of birth, on August 23, 1781, until the child was about two and a half years old. Tiedemann's interest was primarily in the development of the child's mind, and, to some extent, his soul. He appreciated the theoretical and scientific importance of such information, as well as its potential value for more practical, pedagogic purposes.

Tiedemann set out to observe the mind and soul and, as might be expected, managed to do so. Tiedemann's observations were made very carefully and, with respect to the physical body and its functioning, his comments appear surprisingly accurate and insightful even today. His comments on the psychological processes, on the other hand, will appear quite dated to the modern reader. Before the child was a month old, Tiedemann believed that he saw evidence of a mind that included ideas, images, affectations, and other mental phenomena, and a soul.

Tiedemann's observations became less frequent as the child grew older and finally were discontinued altogether before the child was three years old. Nevertheless, that was longer than most present-day parents who begin such projects with good intentions can manage to keep them up, and apparently longer than any of his immediate successors were able to keep at it. So, Tiedemann's biography remained for nearly a century afterward as the most conprehensive account available of an infant's development. It was not until 1835, nearly fifty years after Tiedemann, that Willard published the first baby biography in the English language. Other important baby biographies were published by Lobish and by Sigismund in the middle of the nineteenth century.

The last important baby biography to appear prior to 1880 was that of Charles Darwin (1877). Darwin's notes on his infant son were collected in 1840, but were not made public until 1873, when they were partially reported in his book, *The Expression of Emotions in Man and Animals*. The full report finally appeared in 1877, in an article in *Mind*. Darwin's record is noteworthy because his reason for observing his son was different from that which interested Tiedemann. Darwin viewed the child as a repository of evolutionary information. To the extent that the child retraces in the course of development any of the stages of his evolutionary past, observation of the child may provide some help in unraveling the mysteries of man's evolutionary history. Although *The Origin of Species* was not published until 1859, evolutionary conceptions guided Darwin's child observations in 1840. This idea that the child might retrace his evolutionary past during the course of his own individual development was known as recapitulation. We shall return to this idea later, when we discuss the work of G. Stanley Hall, in whose thinking recapitulation occupied a position of central importance. Indeed, recapitulation appears to have had its effect even in the thinking of that modern giant among developmental psychologists, Jean Piaget—but that's getting ahead of our story. As we continue, we shall see that there are a number of men who, like Darwin, are best remembered for their contributions to other areas, but who also made noteworthy contributions to the development of scientific child study.

The baby biography contained the sort of information that a modern parent might collect today—the rather easily observed milestones of walking, physical development, talking, and so on. For this reason, several early baby biographies provided contributions to the study of language development. In 1833, Feldman published one of the earliest reviews of reports of language development, based on reports of the vocabularies of thirty-three children learning to speak. He found that the typical child said his first word at about sixteen months, some six or seven months later than would be the case today. Whether this reflects a real difference in the rate of language development in the early nineteenth century, or merely a bias in his particular sample, is not known. By the middle of the nineteenth century, baby biographies were being taken that concentrated specifically on the problem of language development. Taine's (1876, 1877) early contributions to language development should be noted also. An important French philosopher and a careful observer, Taine concluded that much of initial language development (babbling, etc.) arises spontaneously through the process of maturation, and not as a consequence of special training or imitation.

Intelligence and the Heredity-Environment Issue

Several attempts to investigate and better understand the feeble-minded child were reported during this period. One of the earliest of these was Itard's (1801) account of the Wild Boy of Aveyron, a book that anticipated something of the heredity-environment controversy that was to generate so much heat a century and more later. This book also fed a long-standing interest in wild or "feral" man. Since the time of the legend of Romulus and Remus being suckled by wolves, there

have been a number of tales and an abiding curiosity about children who supposedly grew up apart from other human influence—either alone or reared by animals. A young boy of about eleven years of age was found living as a wild animal in the Caune Woods. He was captured and ultimately delivered to Itard for observation and treatment at the National Institute for the Deaf and Dumb in Paris in the latter part of the year 1800. His efforts to bring the boy to normal intelligence through special training would qualify Itard as an early voice in the environmentalist camp. However, his failure to achieve complete success according to his own criteria led Itard, but not all of his followers, to conclude that the project was hopeless.

Seguin (1864), one of Itard's pupils who pioneered work on retardation in America, provided impetus to an early movement to improve the welfare of feebleminded children. Within the next ten to twelve years, several studies were reported that explored correlates of feeblemindedness, such as the relationship between birth order and mental defect, and compared normal and feebleminded children with respect to physical growth.

The problem of intellectual development and the nature-nurture issue are closely related to each other as well as to the problem of retardation. Taine (1870), in his two-volume work on intelligence, suggested that an important influence was exerted by the environment on the behavior and intellectual development of the child, a position consonant with Itard's early notions. It was, however, a position that was not particularly compatible with the strong hereditarian orientation of the early years of the child-study movement in America. The work of Francis Galton brought the heredity-environment issue into sharper focus. For example, he gathered statistical information on English men of science (Galton, 1874), which was used to support his argument that heredity was the principal determiner of eminence. Galton also examined the distribution of eminence as a function of birth order and other variables which were later to occupy positions of central importance in child research. Through his use of twins as a means of attacking the heredity-environment problem, Galton (1876) provided what was to become one of the classic research methods for exploring this thorny problem. The study of identical twins treated differently, or reared apart, allowed the possibility of varying environmental influence while holding heredity constant. Shortly before 1880, Dugdale (1877) contributed to the literature on retardation a genealogical account of the Jukes family, which added fuel to the argument for heredity as being the main determiner of intelligence.

Early Normative Studies

By far the most common type of investigation during this early period involved the study of individual children, as exemplified by the baby biography, and occasional attempts to review and summarize such efforts, as Feldmann did in the case of infant vocabulary development. There were, however, several studies in which the investigator examined larger numbers of children in order to determine various norms of development. These studies also provided an indication of the range of individual differences, reflecting an awareness on the part of the investigator of the existence of individual differences. This type of investigation was relatively rare, however, and was focused mainly on aspects of physical development. For example, the Belgian statistician Quetelet reported measurements on children's strength of grip in 1835. Kussmaul published the first normative study of the newborn in 1859. In 1877, Henry P. Bowditch made the first important study of childhood in America with a series of physical measurements of Boston school children (Bowditch, 1877, 1879).

A different type of "normative" study also was conducted, shortly before the end of this period, that was more psychological in nature. These were the early studies that used the questionnaire technique. This method involved interviewing a number of children individually with respect to a predetermined syllabus of questions in order to find the typical or average response. These first questionnaire studies were related to the question of intellectual development in the sense that they attempted to determine the "contents of children's minds." Bartholomai (1870) and later Lange (1879) conducted these initial studies, that provided the inspiration, technique, and background for Hall's (1883) classic work. We shall consider Hall's work more carefully in the next section.

THE STUDY OF CHILDREN BECOMES FORMALLY ORGANIZED: 1880–1900

Prior to 1880, as we have seen, research efforts with children were confined mainly to individual scientists' accounts of individual children. Reports were sporadic and came almost entirely from European investigators, who also provided most of the related theory and methodology. Beginning about 1880, however, we can begin to detect the emergence of a new approach to the study of children.

Several considerations prompted the selection of the year 1880 as a major turning point. First, the beginning of the child-study movement typically is set at 1880. Also, 1880 seemed appropriate in light of the suggestion that Wilhelm Preyer's *Die Seele des Kindes* and G. Stanley Hall's "The Contents of Children's Minds," published in 1882 and 1883 respectively, marked the beginning of the scientific study of the child.

The child-study movement began largely as a parent-teacher effort, but maintained an increasing involvement on the part of psychology and other disciplines. Because of the role played by parents and teachers, the movement was a highly popular one, which gained momentum rapidly. However, as often appears to be the case with popular movements, national commitment and enthusiasm were purchased at the price of some disparagement from the scientific community.

Although the movement was initially and primarily an American undertaking, similar developments quickly took place in many other countries, notably England, France, and Germany. In addition to research activity, these two decades were important as a time for the establishing of formal organizations and the founding of technical journals devoted to the study of children.

G. Stanley Hall

Standing at the center of all this activity and providing inspiration, guidance, and possibly censorship was Granville Stanley Hall. A man of broad interests, he enjoyed the distinction of being an excellent and active public speaker who was as highly respected in education as in psychology. Hall was the prime influence in the establishment of both the American Psychological Association (APA) and the National Association for the Study of Children. He was both founder and editor of the *American Journal of Psychology* and *The Pedagogical Seminary*, the only two psychological journals in America at the time of the founding of the APA in 1892. Fernberger (1932) has noted that, "At this period, then, any man with something to publish in a psychological journal had perforce to send his manuscript to Hall as editor."

The story of the scientific study of the child during these twenty years is mainly a story of Hall's accomplishments,[1] his influence, the work of his enthusiastic followers, and to some extent, the reactions of his enthusiastic critics. It is not possible in the present space to review Hall's influence and achievements in detail.[2] Briefly, he provided the impetus and sustaining energy to found laboratories, organizations, and journals, and then often to direct them after they were established. In 1883, Hall founded what might be considered to be the first psychological laboratory in America, at Johns Hopkins University. By 1888, he had accepted an offer to become the first president of Clark University. Hall moved much of his laboratory and several staff members from Johns Hopkins to Clark, which was to become perhaps the nation's leading university in psychological research, and the focal point of the child-study movement.

Hall's theoretical leanings were evolutionary. Like Darwin, he was interested in the child as a repository of evolutionary information. Indeed, one of his aspirations was to become the "Darwin of the mind." He took the nineteenth century "law of recapitulation" rather seriously and incorporated it into his conception of child development. The idea of recapitulation is that ontogeny recapitulates phylogeny, or simply that each member of the species in the course of development from egg to maturity briefly summarizes the evolutionary history of the species. This notion was advanced by biologists and generally accepted by other disciplines at the end of the nineteenth century. It was extended by Hall and others to include social evolution. Hall saw in the childhood years a recapitulation of the development of civilization, which may have provided the principal reason for his interest in children. For example, given that Hall's basic intellectual concern was with the problem of social evolution, his otherwise seemingly unrelated interests in child study, philosophy, anthropology, and religion begin to appear more connected. Sheldon's (1946) comment concerning Hall on this point is interesting,

"While his thinking in psychology was primarily genetic and evolutionary and he showed a strong interest in anthropology, his curiosity, for some reason, seemed to stop with civilized man."

Hall's principal research effort during this time centered around his pioneering and extensive use of the questionnaire technique. Through the use of this method, he attempted to determine the nature of the child's mind and psychological development by means of a statistical averaging process. Hall's initial study was begun in 1880, with a large-scale study of Boston school children. His aim was to determine what children know and what their level of understanding is when they begin school at about six years of age. He concluded (Hall, 1883) that there was very little, if anything, that it would be safe for teachers to assume that children knew. He found that boys knew more than girls, and that country-reared children knew more than city children. However, it might be argued that his questionnaire was admirably suited to produce such results. This fascinating and now classic study has been reprinted (e.g., Dennis, 1948; 1972) and is worth a careful reading by anyone interested in the cognitive development of children, or the historical theory and method related to it.

In 1894, Hall began printing and distributing his topical syllabi. These were questionnaire leaflets of one to four pages on relatively narrow topics. They were printed privately and widely circulated among teachers, school officials, and others working with children, who completed the questionnaires and returned them to Hall for tabulation. New topics were added every year or so for several years, and by 1898 Hall had published thirty-five articles in the *American Journal of Psychology* and *The Pedagogical Seminary*, based on the results obtained from these syllabi. The syllabi served to open a number of research questions for investigation. Since many of these questions later occupied positions of central importance in the development of child psychology, it might be useful to indicate the titles of the fifteen syllabi for 1894–95. They were (1) Anger; (2) Dolls; (3) Crying and laughing; (4) Toys and playthings; (5) Folklore among children; (6) Early forms of vocal expression; (7) The early sense of self; (8) Fears in childhood and youth; (9) Some common traits and habits; (10) Some common automatisms, nerve signs, etc.; (11) Feeling for objects of inanimate nature; (12) Feeling for objects of animate nature; (13) Children's appetites and foods; (14) Affection and its opposite states in children; (15) Moral and religious experiences.

The Child-Study Movement: Action and Reaction

Essentially all the effort to study the child during the last twenty years of the nineteenth century in the United States either belonged directly to the child-study movement, or was inspired by it. Hall's role in this effort was a very central one, and the work of other investigators complemented the outpourings of his own laboratory. The purpose of the movement was to learn about the nature of the child through scientific study rather than philosophical speculation. The aim of the movement was to apply this newly gained knowledge about children to the practical business of educating them.

Hall's interests in evolutionary theory were tempered by a very practical belief that knowledge should be useful. The movement, through Hall, provided for the beginnings, therefore, of "progressive education." The guiding idea underlying progressive education was that education should be oriented toward and tailored to the developmental level of the child. This idea that education should progress according to a developmental sequence that paralleled the child's own developmental sequence was brought to its full expression in the early twentieth century under the leadership of John Dewey, an eminent educational philosopher and former student of Hall's.

The research of this period consisted of additional baby biographies and a number of large-scale studies of school children. These latter studies generally were of the questionnaire type, although a few were based on child observations. Most of this work focused on physical development and, in the case of school children, the relationship between physical development and mental development. Investigations of the social, emotional, and intellectual development of the child, particularly as these related to educational matters, were reported during this period also. Interest in the relationship between physical and mental development came partly from the educational emphasis of the child-study movement, and partly from a prevailing belief that intellectual functioning was closely tied to sensory and perceptual acuity. We shall explore the basis for this belief in the next section in our discussion of mental testing.

Several baby biographies were published during the 1890's. Miss Milicent W. Shinn of Berkeley, California, began publishing a series of notes in 1893 which eventually culminated in one of the first good baby biographies to be published in America (Shinn, 1900). Miss Shinn, Editor of the *Overland Monthly*, used naturalistic observation as her method and her young niece as her subject. Other important baby biographies of this period were those of Mrs. W. S. Hall and Mrs. K. C. Moore, both published in 1896, and Mrs. Louise E. Hogan, published in 1898. These biographies were general accounts of development. However, they contained considerable comment on language development and were the major source of information on that topic. For example, Mrs. Moore's monograph was one of the first works to seriously consider the development of sentence formation. Because of the potential relationship between language and intellectual functioning, an interest in language development was reflected in the writing of such men as John Dewey and Frederick Tracy.

At Hall's suggestion, E. H. Russell, head of the State Normal School at Worcester, Massachusetts, began a large-scale, systematic investigation of children in 1885. Using naturalistic observation, Russell collected some 35,000 records to pioneer a methodological approach to the study of children which became known as the "Russell method." The results of this work were published in 1896, under the editorship of Ellen M. Haskell, with an introduction by Russell. Much of the data were collected by students under Russell's direction and consisted of records of the verbalizations and behavior of children from one to sixteen years of age. Although not a questionnaire study, Russell's work is typical of the child-study investigations of this period, that used relatively untrained examiners to collect data on huge numbers of children.

As early as 1890, James McKeen Cattell had used the term "mental test." As the leading figure in getting the testing movement started in America in the 1890's, Cattell advocated regular testing of school children. In 1894, J. A. Gilbert published a pioneering contribution to that effort with a study of mental and physical measurements of school children. Gilbert was a former student of E. W. Scripture, who, in turn, had been associated with Hall as a Fellow at Clark University. Both Gilbert and Scripture were at Yale University.

While Scripture was still at Clark in 1891, he reported one of the earliest accounts of child prodigies in arithmetic. The study of the child prodigy was to remain a fascinating topic of investigation for many years. In 1899, E. H. Lindley and W. L. Bryan carried out investigations on a child prodigy in arithmetic with the aid of a fifty-dollar grant from APA. This was the first and apparently only grant that APA made to individuals (Fernberger, 1932).

During the 1890's there were a number of large-scale, normative studies reported. Most of these were conducted with school children, and many of the investigators, such men as W. L. Bryan, G. M. West, and Franz Boas, were rather closely associated with Hall, either as former students or as faculty colleagues at Clark. Some of these studies were based on physical, psychophysical, and anthropometric measurements of children. For example, there were studies of physical growth, motor coordination, pain and strength measurements, and the relationship between birth order and physical growth. In the last few years before the turn of the century, there was increased interest in the possible relationship between physical development and mental development. While this question produced some controversy and some conflicting evidence, there was a general agreement that mental and physical development were positively related and, indeed, that physical development could be used as a predictor of mental development.

Toward the end of the 1890's, there was also greater interest in mental development and psychological processes in general. J. C. Shaw, for example, reported one of the first American studies of memory in school children in 1895. About this same time, Earl Barnes was editing a series of volumes entitled *Studies in Education*, which reported the results of child-study movement on the West Coast. Barnes also had been investigating children's drawings since the early 1890's. In 1898 and 1899, studies of the emotional characteristics of the only child and of social consciousness and play interests in children were reported by Will S. Monroe and others; these were based on questionnaire surveys.

All this recounting of activity and apparent progress in the scientific study of the child may leave the reader with the impression that the child-study movement was widely and uncritically accepted. While that may have been the case in some quarters, it clearly was not the case among traditional psychologists. The procedure of using questionnaire methodology and relatively untrained examiners would not escape criticism today, but it was particularly difficult to accept in Hall's time, because it differed so sharply from the procedures and methods that were standard then. Reaction against Hall, his methods, and the child-study movement was centered in the orthodox psychology of the day, and in such men as William James, James Mark Baldwin, and Hugo Münsterberg. For example, in a paper published in the *Educational Review* in 1898, Münsterberg delivered a stinging criticism of the whole child-study movement. Sheldon (1946) has captured the spirit of that criticism with a quotation attributed to Münsterberg, "The data collected by questionnaires could no more result in valid scientific generalization than the counting of the leaves on a particular cherry tree could result in valid contributions to botany." Münsterberg, as the leader of the scientific opposition, in effect argued that achievements in science are the products of patient, hard work by thoughtful, well-trained individuals. He considered most of the work of the child-study movement, which was being performed by relatively untrained investigators, to be a waste of time. In addition to scientific objections to the child-study movement, there were also objections from parents and teachers on the grounds that observing the child might be harmful to the child. This latter objection, though qualified somewhat, still remains a lively issue today.

By the turn of the century, an attempt was being made to distinguish between "child study" and "child psychology." Although the distinction was not always clearly and consistently maintained, in general the former term referred to the relatively popular, educationally-oriented activity, while the latter referred to scientific activity. It was claimed among some of the disciples of the child-study movement, for example, that the principal benefit of the movement was to help the teachers who studied the children, a secondary benefit was for the children being studied, and that the last and least benefit was for science.

Organizations, Journals, and Professional Meetings

Much of the business of turning the study of children into a formally organized activity took place in the last twenty years of the nineteenth century, and in this undertaking the influence of G. Stanley Hall was readily apparent everywhere. The *American Journal of Psychology* commenced publication in 1887, under Hall's editorship. Hall founded *The Pedagogical Seminary* in 1891 and served as its first editor. This latter journal's title reflected its initial leaning toward education. As the journal came to serve the interests of psychology more specifically, the name ultimately was changed to *The Journal of Genetic Psychology*, although it carried both names for some time. The first volume reprinted Hall's "Contents" with a slightly modified title. At Hall's invitation a small group of psychologists met at Clark University in July, 1892, to discuss the organization of the American Psychological Association. The first APA meeting was held during the Christmas holidays at the University of Pennsylvania, and Hall was elected president. In 1893, Hall founded the National Association for the Study of Children, which adopted *The Pedagogical Seminary* as their official organ.

The activity that surrounded the formal organization of child study was reflected in a variety of ways. The following paragraphs are intended to provide some of the flavor and a few of the details of that development.

Formal organizations and societies devoted to the study of children were being established throughout this period. Some impetus to this activity was provided by the American Social Science Association, which, through its Committee on Education, initiated a program in 1881 to promote the general study of children. A number of state-level associations had been established by the 1890's. It is interesting to note that the states which produced some of the earliest and most active child-study associations, e.g., Iowa, Minnesota, Pennsylvania, New York, Illinois, and California, have been the same states that have maintained an active, national leadership in the scientific study of the child to the present time.

Within ten years from the founding of the *American Journal of Psychology* a number of other journals were begun that either were devoted exclusively to publishing child-study reports, or that made considerable space available for such work. Some of these, and the year that they began publication, were: *Journal of Pedagogy* in 1887, *The Northwestern Journal of Education* in 1889, *Educational Review* in 1891, *The Child-Study Monthly* in 1895, and *Journal of Psycho-Asthenics* and *Transactions of the Illinois Society for Child Study*, both in 1896.

Professional meetings related to child study were being held at this time. For example, the International Congress on Education was held in Chicago in connection with the Columbian Exposition of 1893. This congress helped to establish another state association, the Illinois Society for Child Study. Beginning in 1896, the Society published a bibliographic handbook and its journal, *Transactions*, mentioned above, under the editorship of C. C. Van Liew, the secretary of the organization. The Child Study Section of the National Education Association also held a two-day session in Chicago in 1893.

Child study as a formal activity was being reflected also in the establishment of clinics, the initiation of university courses, and the appearance of textbooks related to children. By 1895, courses on child study were included in the regular curriculum or the summer session of a number of universities, e.g., Clark, Harvard, Yale, Princeton, and Pennsylvania. Also, it is interesting to note that Lightner Witmer offered a course in Experimental Child Psychology at the University of Pennsylvania in 1896. One of the first child psychology texts appeared in 1894, authored by Frederick Tracy. Tracy summarized the principal investigations that had been published to that time and arranged his presentation according to five main topics: sensation, emotion, intellect, volition, and language. Except for volition, the same topical headings might be found in many present-day treatments of child psychology. Tracy's text was widely accepted, the seventh edition of it being published in 1910.

The first psychological clinic in America was established at the University of Pennsylvania in 1896 by Witmer. The clinic was sometimes referred to as the "psycho-pedagogical"

clinic. The second American clinic was established in 1898 at the State Institution for the Feeble Minded, in Faribault, Minnesota. R. T. Wylie, the Institution's Psychologist, was also the editor of the *Journal of Psycho-Asthenics*, which is published today as the *American Journal of Mental Deficiency*.

Concurrent Foreign Developments

The child-study movement spread to Europe shortly after its beginning in this country. It was accompanied by less fadishness and popular enthusiasm in Europe, however. This had the effect of reducing potential friction between child-study and more scientific psychology, and allowed other approaches to the study of the child to be explored. The more impressive developments occurred in England, France, and Germany, and we shall summarize some of these briefly below, but activity was evident in many countries. For example, at the third International Congress of Psychology, held in Munich in 1896, J. W. Dawid, of Warsaw, reported on the growth of ideas in children and drew comparisons between American and Polish children. Dawid was an early leader of the child-study movement in Poland, having authored a number of investigations of children with A. Szyc since 1887. Also at this Congress, Hermann Ebbinghaus and J. Friedrich reported independent investigations of intellectual tasks (memory, arithmetic calculation, etc.) and fatigue.

England. James Sully was the principal figure in the child-study movement in England and, as early as 1881, attempted to draw attention to the value of child study for scientific purposes. Sully's *Studies of Childhood* was published in 1896, a rather large volume that consisted primarily of reprints of previously published articles. The book dealt with such topics as the development of reason, the development of language, children's fears, and children's drawings. F. Warner also published works in the new child study as early as 1887.

Partly in response to Hall's stimulation at the International Congress on Education in Chicago in 1893, the British Child-Study Association was founded in 1894. Branches of the association were formed, and a journal, *The Paidologist*, was published. At the time, child-study was sometimes called "paidology," a term coined in 1893 by Oscar Chrisman, a former student of Hall's. The Childhood Society was formed in England in 1894, also.

Not all of the British work with children grew out of the child-study movement. For example, Hicks had reported the recording of fetal movements as early as 1880. Also, in 1887, Langdon Down contributed to the literature on the feebleminded a description of some of the mental defects of childhood and their correlates. Earlier, in 1866, Down had provided a description of clinical Mongolism, which today often is referred to simply as "Down's syndrome." Interestingly, Down was also contributing to the child-study literature by the late 1890's.

France. England and France were the earliest and most active followers of America's lead in the child-study movement. The leader of the French movement was Alfred Binet. His interests were broadly experimental, and, prior to the child-study movement, he had already made important contributions to the experimental study of children, particularly of infant perception. He had also made contributions to psychotherapy and the use of hypnosis as an experimental method. The journal, *L'Annee Psychologique*, began publication in 1896, and Binet contributed to it a questionnaire study of children's fears to that journal in its first year. In 1899, Theophile Simon reported the results of a series of anthropometric measurements on a large sample of abnormal boys in the age range from eight to twenty-three years. Given their interests in child research and their apparent sympathy with the educationally-oriented child-study movement, it is perhaps natural that Binet and Simon should have been the ones to develop the first successful intelligence test in the early years of the twentieth century. We shall return to a consideration of that work in the next section.

Germany. Germany followed England and France at a rather distant third place in the European child-study movement. Much of the orthodox psychology in America that was the source of major criticism of the child-study movement had its theoretical and methodological origins in Germany. It is understandable, then, that Germany would be slower and more cautious about joining the movement. Germany did join the movement by the beginning of the twentieth century, but most of the German work in the time period under discussion here belongs to a different tradition.

By far the most influential work in these last twenty years of the nineteenth century was that of Wilhelm Preyer. This work, like that of Teidemann, was in the form of a baby biography. Preyer made detailed observations on the development of his son up to the age of three years and compared his son's progress with that reported by authors of previously published baby biographies. His book, *Die Seele des Kindes*, was published in 1882. Preyer's (1882) work was translated into English as a two-volume work entitled *The Mind of the Child*. Part I, entitled *The Senses and the Will*, appeared in 1888 and dealt with physical activity and its relation to the development of the will. The second volume, Part II, *The Development of the Intellect*, was published in 1889 and focused on language development. Another book by Preyer, *Mental Development in the Child*, appeared in English in 1893. This was a somewhat more popular treatment, which combined some new material with a digest of the two earlier (1888, 1889) volumes.

Although best remembered for his monumental contribution to the experimental study of memory, Hermann Ebbinghaus published the first major writing on juvenile psychopathology in 1887. Also, one of the earliest investigations of the emotional characteristics of the only child, particularly as related to taking part in school games, was reported by E. Kolrausche in 1891. By way of organizational activity, the German child research organization, *Verein für Kinderpsychologie*, was founded in Berlin in 1899, and Carl Stumpf was elected its first president. A year later, Stumpf published a biographical account of his child's language development.

MEASURING THE CHILD'S MIND: 1900–17

The period from the turn of the century until America's entry into World War I was one of emerging new emphases and directions. Chief among these was the advent of mental testing. By far the major focus of activity during this period was on the development and use of intelligence tests. This period was also characterized by an increased scientific interest in the child, the rise of specialized educational movements such as the Montessori schools, and the beginnings of educational psychology as the science of education. These diverse interests in the child remained loosely connected through a common interest in the child's mental development and in his welfare.

The child-study movement, under G. Stanley Hall, was pre-eminent among efforts to study children at the beginning of this period. By the end of the period, the movement had ceased to function altogether. In many ways the child-study movement contained the seeds of its own destruction. From its inception, the movement had multiple aims and attempted to serve multiple interests. There had been, for example, a scientific aim, a pedagogic aim, and an aim of helping the child. As interest in children grew, each of these multiple aims of the child-study movement became the chief aim of a more specialized interest group. We alluded to some of these specialized interests above, and shall return to them later in more detail. We do not mean to leave the impression that the decline of the child-study movement was merely a natural and inevitable consequence of an expanding scholarly interest in children. We noted earlier that orthodox psychology had criticized Hall's use of untrained examiners and the questionnaire method. There were also personal attacks against Hall by persons in the fields of both psychology and education. As if these were not enough, Hall's own interests shifted to other fresher and more exciting topics. For example, Hall brought Sigmund Freud to Clark University in 1909, and subsequently showed a rather strong interest in Freud's psychoanalytic ideas. In 1904, Hall published a major, two-volume work on adolescence, which carried the imposing title, *Adolescence: Its Psychology and Its Relations to Physiology, Anthropology, Sociology, Sex, Crime, Religion, and Education*. Hall's interest in the adolescent helped to shift his focus of attention away from the young child, where it had been in the child-study movement. Also, Hall's interest in helping the child was expanded from the narrow educational form that it took in the child-study movement to a general concern for the child's welfare. Although the child-study movement was discontinued by about 1914, Hall continued to exert some influence through these new interests of his and through his former students.

The earlier trends of establishing organizations, laboratories, and journals were continued. By the middle of this period there was an active and growing interest in child welfare. Research activity continued to include baby biographies, and many of these contained important information on the development of language. Other studies of language development were conducted as well, particularly studies dealing with vocabularies and speech defects.

An interest in the religious development of the child, and the related problems of sex, moral development, and juvenile delinquency, were in evidence. For example, Havelock Ellis published his first volume on the psychology of sex in 1900. The explanations offered for juvenile delinquency were often the familiar ones of poor housing conditions, alcoholism of parents, and loss of one or both parents by death, divorce, or desertion. However, other causes given for delinquency, such as heredity, prematurity, the seductions of luxury, and illegitimacy, may appear rather odd to the present-day reader. Similarly, the child's physical condition was thought to bear an important relationship to his moral development. For example, an article was published in 1910 in the *Psychological Clinic* entitled, "Can Impacted Teeth Cause Moral Delinquency?"

The idea that the child's physical condition was related to various aspects of his psychological development produced an increased interest in studying the child's physical growth, maturation, and other physiological considerations. Part of this interest in physical development stemmed from a concern with the potentially related issue of intellectual development.

John B. Watson's appearance during the latter part of this period brought an articulate spokesman for nurture onto the heredity-environment platform, which served to bring this classic issue into sharp focus. The development of the environmental position in this controversy was accompanied by a marked increase in research into the learning process. Interest in learning was accompanied by increased research activity in other related processes. There was, for example, an active interest in children's emotions. This included study of various individual emotions, such as curiosity, pity, and fear, as well as the general problems of emotional adjustment and child rearing practices.

The three highlights of this period, however, were the development of intelligence tests, the rise of educational psychology, and the beginnings of child welfare. Let us examine each of them a bit more closely.

The Development of Intelligence Tests

As we have seen, by the end of the last century there already had developed an active interest in mental growth and development. There had been studies of the relationship between physical and mental growth, comparisons of normal and feebleminded children, and the suggestion by Cattell that children should be tested. Some of this interest in assessing the child's mind undoubtedly sprang from Hall's early attempt to determine the contents of children's minds. As Hall's methods became suspect, there was a need to find other, more reliable, methods of measuring the child's mental development.

Closely tied to the development of intelligence tests was the general question of whether heredity or environment is the more important determiner of the child's intellectual development. Because of the predominately hereditarian orientation of the leading child-research figures of the day, the heredity-environment issue in the early 1900's had not

yet become the classic controversy that was later to generate so much research and polemical effort. The groundwork for the heredity-environment argument was laid during this time, however, through research into the problem of intelligence and its assessment. Alfred Binet and Theophile Simon, in France, and Edward L. Thorndike, H. H. Goddard, and Lewis M. Terman, in America, were among the more significant contributors to the study of intelligence during this time. Although Binet's philosophy would have placed him in the environmentalist camp, America managed to import Binet's tests but not his philosophy. Rather, the hereditarian persuasion of Sir Francis Galton was reflected in the orientation of such men as Hall and Goddard and, in turn, in much of American thinking about intelligence. Hunt (1961) has provided an able discussion of this point.

Galton had more than a hereditarian philosophy. In the latter part of the nineteenth century, he had attempted to devise an early intelligence test. The philosophical viewpoint known as British Associationism held that man's ideas were not innate but came through experience, mainly as a result of combinations and associations of simple impressions received through the five senses. Galton reasoned that if intelligence is based on sensory information, then the most intelligent person should be the one with the best hearing, vision, etc. Galton set up a laboratory and carefully collected measurements of sensory data from thousands of people. Unfortunately, the measurements he collected did not prove to be related in any systematic way to what is generally regarded as intelligence. The idea was a good one, but it just didn't work.

It remained for Alfred Binet to find a better way to measure intelligence. Binet approached the problem from a different perspective. Instead of measuring sensory acuity, Binet attempted to measure symbolic or thinking ability, which he referred to as the "faculty of judgment." In 1904, Binet was named by the Minister of Public Instruction to a commission to find a way to distinguish normal from retarded children. In the following year, with Simon, Binet published the first intelligence test, the Binet-Simon scale. Related to this, Binet had established a laboratory of normal pedagogy in a primary school in Paris in 1905. The aim of the laboratory was to study the physical, intellectual, and moral aptitudes of children. In 1908, Binet and Simon published an age-graded revision of their scale. A second revision of the Binet-Simon intelligence scale was published in 1911.

It is apparent from what has been said that American psychologists were ready to accept Binet's intelligence scale when it appeared, and quick to see its potential value. The Binet-Simon tests were translated into English in 1909 by H. H. Goddard, a former student of Hall's. Since 1906, Goddard had been affiliated with the Training School of Vineland, New Jersey, as the first director of the Vineland Research Laboratory. The Training School was a pioneer institution for working with feebleminded children and the third psychological clinic to be established in this country.

Lewis M. Terman, another of Hall's former students, began revising and restandardizing the Binet-Simon scale about this same time. By 1911, the year that Goddard's translation was published, Terman had prepared a preliminary version of the revised test. Terman's revised Binet scale was published in 1916. The revision, known as the Stanford-Binet because Terman was working at Stanford University, immediately became the most popular and widely-used test of intelligence. The Stanford-Binet included the concept of Intelligence Quotient, or IQ. The IQ was based on the ratio of mental age to physical or chronological age, which ensured that a child's IQ would remain constant so long as his mental development kept pace with his physical age.

The work of Terman and Goddard were not, however, the only contributions to the questions of intellectual development and the measurement of intelligence during this period. Additional studies were reported, similar to those published in the 1890's by Bryan and Gilbert, that attempted to find a relationship between physical and mental development. W. S. Christopher collected physical measurements on Chicago school children in 1900 and searched for a relationship between these measurements and school achievement. Similarly, W. C. Bagley, in 1901, studied the relationship between mental ability, as measured by school performance, and motor ability, as measured by simple tests of coordination. Irving King, one of John Dewey's students, attempted in 1913 to determine the child's physiological age, as distinguished from chronological age, and its relation to school achievement. Several studies of the contents of children's minds were reported that more or less extended the early work of Hall. Another important intelligence test for children, the Yerkes-Bridges Point Scale, was developed by Yerkes, Bridges, and Hardwick in 1915, a year before Terman's revision of the Binet scale was published. And in 1908, in Germany, Wilhelm Stern, Wolfgang Köhler, and Max Verworn made use of children's drawings as a means of better understanding the child's intellectual development.

This was a period also for examining intellectual development in exceptional children. Important work with the gifted child was begun in 1916 by Lewis Terman. In 1914, Watkins conducted an early study of reminiscence among "bright" and "dull" children.

Much of the research and writing at this time contributed to the idea that heredity was the major determiner of intelligence. For example, Thorndike conducted an important investigation into the mental resemblance of twins in 1905. Based on data from twin births, Goddard argued in 1914 for the inheritance of feeblemindedness. Karl Pearson, a student of Sir Francis Galton remembered for his contributions to statistics, published a paper in 1912 on eugenics in which he considered the mental and physical development of children in relation to size of family. Starting with a strongly hereditarian conception of intelligence, Pearson produced a statistical argument for large families as a means of maximizing the proportion of physically and mentally superior individuals in the population. There were several family histories reported of the sort that Dugdale had pioneered in his 1877 account of the Jukes family. In 1912, H. H. Goddard contributed a classic one on the Kallikak family entitled, *The Kallikak Family: A Study in the Heredity of Feeble-mindedness*. Similarly, the family history of the Jukes was updated to 1915 by J. A. Estabrook.

Several significant works on the child's cognitive development appeared at this time. For example, in 1906 David R. Major's *First Steps in Mental Growth* was published and was important as an early longitudinal study. In the same year, James Mark Baldwin published the first volume of his three-volume work on genetic logic, which dealt with cognitive development and children's thinking. This work formed the point of departure for a large volume of research on the nature of the child's thought, work that was to be advanced later by such men as Jean Piaget and Lev S. Vygotsky. The second and third volumes of Baldwin's work appeared in 1908 and 1911 respectively.

The Rise of Educational Psychology

With the turn of the century came increased interest in applying the methods of science to the problems of education. Attempts to develop a science of education were centered in the work and writings of John Dewey and Edward L. Thorndike. No longer were the educational philosophies and prescriptions of such men as J. A. Comenius, J. H. Pestalozzi, F. W. A. Froebel, and J. F. Herbart being accepted uncritically. Perhaps the spirit of this reaction is best captured in the words of Thorndike, as quoted by Irving King (1904) in a review of Thorndike's (1903) *Educational Psychology*:

It is the vice or misfortune of thinkers about education to have chosen the methods of philosophy or of popular thought instead of those of science. We ruminate over the ideas of Pestalozzi or Herbart or Froebel as if writing a book a hundred years ago proved a man inspired . . . . We discuss the outpourings of successful college presidents . . . There is a plentiful lack of knowledge while opinions more and more abound. They are often very good of their kind but they are not science.

Thorndike's 1903 volume was a forerunner of his larger, three-volume work by the same title that began to be published in 1913. Thorndike's 1913 version of *Educational Psychology* was considered to be a landmark in both psychology and education, and hailed by some writers as the beginning of experimental child psychology. That distinction, as we have seen, has been accorded a number of luminaries in child psychology, both before and after Thorndike.

We already have noted Dewey's role in the development of the progressive education movement. Thorndike's work remained more closely tied to psychology. For example, in 1901, Thorndike and Robert S. Woodworth attacked the doctrine of formal discipline. This educational doctrine held that formal training in one class of material "improved the mind," in the sense of facilitating the learning of other classes of materials through a rather broadly generalized positive transfer effect. Thorndike and Woodworth argued that transfer within the same class of material is usually better than across different classes of material. In 1902, Thorndike co-authored an early correlational study with H. A. Aikens on the relationship between perception and association.

Maris Montessori's works were being translated into English, and Montessori schools were being established in this country by 1912. In general, the Montessori movement was received with enthusiasm in America and occupied a major place in discussions of child development during this period. It was not without its opponents, however. For example, Mrs. W. S. Stoner in her 1914 book, *Natural Education*, predicted that the Montessori method would not last because it failed to encourage imaginative play on the part of the child. In addition to the progressive education movement and the Montessori schools, other educational movements were being initiated that supposedly were founded on sound psychological principles. Among these was the nursery school movement. The first American nursery school was established in 1914. The nursery school movement in America belongs more properly to the 1920's, however. During the period from 1914 until 1918 only three nursery schools were established, but by 1930 the number of such schools had grown to 149.

Several important textbooks on child-study and child development appeared at this time. Irving King's *The Psychology of Child Development* was published in 1903. King's book grew out of John Dewey's seminars in child development conducted at the University of Chicago and carried an introduction by Dewey. Although Anderson (1956) has indicated that King's book was the first with "child development" in the title, it was not, of course, the first to deal with the psychology of children, e.g., Tracy's text of 1894. Edwin A. Kirkpatrick's *Fundamentals of Child Study* also appeared in 1903. Kirkpatrick explained the development of essentially all of the higher psychological processes of the child in terms of instinct. The appearance, development, and interrelationships among instincts was seen as the basic problem of child psychology.

The Beginnings of Child Welfare

Although the more important developments in child welfare came after and partly as a consequence of World War I, the beginnings of the welfare movement belong to this period before the war. G. Stanley Hall's role in this effort was an important one. Hall had attempted to found an interdisciplinary Children's Institute, the first of its kind, at Clark University in 1909. The aim of the Institute was to conduct and coordinate research on child development and to promote child welfare. Although the Institute was not successfully established, due primarily to a lack of funds, some important work was accomplished. An interdisciplinary, national-level Child Welfare Conference was held at Clark University in 1909.

The first of the important White House Conferences on children was called, also in 1909, by President Theodore Roosevelt. These conferences have been held regularly at ten-year intervals since then. Although the form of the Conference and the nature of the problems considered have varied widely over the years, the White House Conferences have served the important function each decade of bringing into focus the current state of affairs with respect to the major problems relating to children and helping to define the federal government's role with respect to those problems.

From the beginning, these Conferences have had a pronounced orientation toward child welfare. The early conferences, for example, were called the White House Conferences on Child Health and Protection, and the first one, in 1909, was concerned primarily with the question of child labor. Theodore Roosevelt admired G. Stanley Hall, and it is reasonable to assume that the first White House Conference was inspired by the 1909 Child Welfare Conference at Clark. The White House Conferences have been important not only for identifying major problems facing the nation's children and youth, but also for proposing solutions to those problems. For this reason, the Conferences have had the effect of prompting legislation and federal programs that in turn have exerted a guiding influence on the future course of child research and welfare. In those days, the dual goals of research and welfare were rather closely tied together and seen as mutually complementary. One of the significant outcomes of the first White House Conference was the establishment of the U.S. Children's Bureau in 1912.

Today the great bulk of financial support for child research and welfare-oriented action programs comes from the federal government. However, in this early period under discussion, and for a long while afterward, the major source of funds for child research and welfare came from private philanthropy. For example, the Child Welfare Association was incorporated in 1914 as an outgrowth of the Washington Diet Kitchen, a Washington, D.C., private charity that had been established in 1901. The Elizabeth McCormick Memorial Fund was established in Chicago in 1908 and provided active financial support for child research and welfare for more than fifty years; in 1961 the Fund reduced operations and its administration was taken over by the Chicago Community Chest. Also, in 1910, the Gatzert Fund became the Institute of Child Welfare at the University of Washington, the oldest of the presently surviving child institutes. The great wave of establishment of institutes of child welfare in this country took place in the 1920's. We shall discuss these institutes further in the next section, not for their contributions to child welfare but as America's principal research centers for the scientific study of children.

THE ESTABLISHMENT OF CHILD DEVELOPMENT RESEARCH CENTERS: 1917–30

An unprecedented flurry of organizational and research activity related to children occurred in this period from World War I through the 1920's. This activity was of such dramatic proportions as to suggest to many observers that here was the real beginning of child psychology. Clearly, if one could question the legitimacy of the discipline's existence at the beginning of this period, he could not do so by the end of it. Within the space of about ten years following World War I, child psychology became firmly established as a viable enterprise, with the United States the dominant leader in that activity. The need for a broadly-based program of child research was demonstrated in part as a consequence of the psychological testing program of World War I, and this need was underscored at the second White House Conference in 1919. The financial means for accomplishing such a large-scale endeavor was provided by the federal government, acting through the National Research Council, by private funds, notably the Laura Spelman Rockefeller Memorial, and by state legislatures and local governments.

Several institutes of child welfare and other important child research and training facilities were founded during this time. The directors of these new centers tended to possess those qualities that ensured the successful survival of their organizations. From the outset, the directors as a group tended to be competent and respected researchers who could identify and contribute to problems of fundamental importance, as well as capable administrators who could recruit and lead able staffs. They also were men who frequently held their directorships for long periods of time. As a supplement to the existing publication outlets for child research, most of the institutes initiated a series of both technical and non-technical publications of their own that reported summaries of ongoing research projects.

With the establishment of the institutes of child welfare and other centers came important increases in the volume of research activity and in the variety of problems considered. Although most of the work was done with infants and preschool children, research was conducted at every level of development from the fetus to late adolescence. Research methods became more sophisticated and more experimental, with increased emphasis upon controlled observations. Research efforts became more programmatic in nature also.

Aided by various methodological improvements, research continued on problems that had been of concern in previous decades. Interest in intelligence and intellectual development continued, consonant with the expanded interest in mental testing. Studies of intellectually gifted children were continued by such people as Terman, Goddard, Florence Goodenough, and Catherine Cox, a student of Terman's. Goodenough brought two lines of research interest together, children's drawings and intelligence testing, with her Draw-A-Man test that used the child's drawing as an index of intelligence.

The testing movement and interest in psychometrics expanded. An increased interest in ability and aptitude testing developed. Arnold Gesell's developmental tests and the so-called "baby tests" of Nancy Bayley and others were developed at this time. Some of these were used to assess physical coordination or progress along the dimension of growth and maturation; others served as nonverbal indices of intelligence.

In addition to traditional normative and observational studies, important large-scale longitudinal investigations were initiated during these years. For the most part, these were concerned with physical growth and maturation, and the effects of various special factors, such as diet, on the growth process. Several studies concerned with the heredity-environment issue attempted to assess the relative contributions of maturation and special training to overall development. The classic method of co-twin control was employed by Gesell and others as a device for separating the effects of heredity and environment.

Learning and language acquisition continued to be important research areas. These were expanded, partly as a result of Jean Piaget's influence, to include related topics such as concept learning, thinking, and problem solving. Studies of reflexes, simple motor learning, and other less complex forms of behavior were conducted at this time as well. There was research on the child's sensory and perceptual processes that included imagery, particularly Klüver's work on eidetic imagery. Harold E. Jones and Mary Cover Jones studied children's emotions, notably conditioned fear.

Important work was initiated in the area of social behavior and personality development, including Anna Freud's contributions to the psychoanalysis of the child. Children's social attitudes, interests, and imitative behavior were explored. Research continued on the general question of moral development, and Hartshorne and May examined the related issue of the development of character. In England, Cyril Burt, who is remembered for his contributions to the theory of intelligence, published a volume on juvenile delinquency. Parent-child research, the child's play activities, investigations of smiling and laughing, reflected an increased interest in the environmental determinants of behavior, particularly the social and cultural aspects of the environment. Also, several important cross-cultural studies were reported toward the end of this period, such as Margaret Mead's *Coming of Age in Samoa.*

Much of this interest in the effects of the environment, of course, was a result of John B. Watson's influence. The environmentalist position gained ground rapidly. The absolute rule of the hereditarian position began to be replaced in the 1920's by an equally absolute rule of the environmentalist. The ascendency that the environmentalist's position gained during the 1920's was not to be seriously challenged for nearly fifty years, until Arthur Jensen did so in 1969.

There is no way in the present space to adequately summarize the research explosion that occurred during this period. There were many active child research centers studying children at every age, on the widest range of topics and problems, and with a variety of both old and new methodological approaches. Perhaps something of the spirit of these times can be captured in a brief discussion of the establishment of these research centers and some consideration of the influence that Watson and behaviorism were having at the time.

Establishing America's Child Research Centers

We have already noted that G. Stanley Hall and a growing interest in child welfare provided an impetus to the establishment of child research centers in this country, and that funds to support this undertaking were provided by both government and private sources. With the aid of subsequent White House Conferences, the work of the federal government and of the Laura Spelman Rockefeller Memorial Fund was coordinated through the National Research Council. This joint labor helped bring into existence a number of important research centers and thereby create a national research effort in child development within the space of about ten years.

The Laura Spelman Rockefeller Memorial Fund was established in 1918, under the direction of Beardsley Ruml and Lawrence K. Frank. This important fund not only provided the impetus for the establishment of the institutes of child welfare during the 1920's but also helped to establish the Society for Research in Child Development. The Society had its formal beginning in 1933, and has continued actively ever since as the leading child research organization in the country.

President Wilson called the second White House Conference on Child Health and Protection in 1919. The Conference was concerned with such questions as the role of the government in aiding dependent and neglected children, outlining minimum standards for child labor, recommendations for protection of the health of mothers and children, and recommendations concerning mentally defective and delinquent children. Many of these questions were related to the deficiencies discovered in World War I soldiers through the Army's psychological testing program.

Also in 1919, the National Research Council of the National Academy of Sciences established a Division of Anthropology and Psychology. It was through the activities of this division, with the aid of the Spelman Funds, that the Society for Research in Child Development emerged. In 1920, the Division formed a Committee on Child Welfare. The Committee's function was to serve as an advisory group to the Child Welfare Association and similar organizations. The division chairman, W. V. Bingham, was appointed committee chairman, and S. I. Franz and C. E. Seashore served as members of the Committee. The Committee called a conference in January, 1924, to discuss plans for an intensive investigation of the mental and physical development of the child from birth to two years of age, in anticipation of a grant from the Laura Spelman Rockefeller Memorial. The Committee's name was changed in 1925 to the Committee on Child Development. Bird T. Baldwin became chairman of the new committee. At that time Woodworth was also chairman of the Division of Anthropology and Psychology, the parent division of the Committee. Supported by the Spelman Fund, the National Research Council called a conference on child development which brought together specialists in hygiene, growth, physiology, nutrition, anthropometry, and psychology. Although child study was well established by this time, it was by no means yet an activity restricted primarily to psychologists. For example, Jones (1956) has pointed out that in 1918 only three psychologists indicated a primary interest in children. However, this number had grown to 81 by 1937, and to nearly a thousand by 1956.

The Laura Spelman Rockefeller Memorial pledged an annual appropriation for a period of four years to support the work of the Committee on Child Development, which served as an advisory group to the Spelman Fund. The size of the annual appropriation, $10,000, was surprisingly small by present-day standards, and yet the influence of the Spelman funds at that time was enormous. John E. Anderson (1956) made the following comment on the importance of this fund,

". . . it literally created a field that was nationwide in its scope and thus advanced the work of child study by several decades."

The Spelman funds were used to sponsor research conferences and to help found or assist the several institutes of child welfare throughout the country. Although most of these institutes continue to function today, they have gone through a number of name changes over the years. In general, the term "institute" has tended to remain as part of the name while "welfare" has been replaced by terms such as "behavior" and "development." Thus the new names more accurately reflect that the principal concern of the institutes is with the discovery of knowledge rather than its application. Although initially interdisciplinary in orientation and staff composition, most of the institutes gradually evolved into the equivalent of departments of child psychology. Let us now take a brief look at the institutes and other research centers that were established at this time.

The Iowa Child Welfare Research Station at the University of Iowa began its work in 1917 under Bird T. Baldwin, its first Director. The establishment of the Iowa institute preceded by a few years the great wave of activity during the 1920's that resulted in the founding of a number of child welfare institutes throughout the country. Iowa opened its preschool laboratory in 1921, the first laboratory to be founded primarily for the scientific study of the young child. In the same year, Baldwin published a monograph on physical growth, the Iowa Station's first monograph. Baldwin summarized and reviewed the existing literature and contributed original data of his own. Containing 911 references, the monograph stands even today as an excellent reference on physical growth.

In 1927 the Iowa institute received additional support from the Spelman Fund that aided its development as a major child research center. Iowa had perhaps the greatest rate of turnover in directors among the various institutes. Nevertheless, even Iowa's directors (e.g., George D. Stoddard, Kurt Lewin, Robert R. Sears, Boyd McCandless, Charles C. Spiker) tended to hold their directorships for about ten years. In 1963 the institute's name was changed to the Iowa Institute of Child Behavior and Development, and it was so known until 1973, when it ceased to function as an institute after more than fifty years of operation.

There were five other institutes of child welfare established in the space of a few years in the mid-1920's. The first of these was at Teachers College, Columbia University, in 1924. The first director of that institute was Helen Thompson Woolley, followed by Arthur Jersild, a long-time director and investigator of children's emotions. An Institute was established at the University of Minnesota in 1925, with John E. Anderson serving as the first director. The first monograph of the Institute of Child Welfare at Minnesota was an early normative study of parent-child relations, authored by Anderson and J. C. Foster and published in 1927. Anderson continued to direct the Institute for thirty years and was followed by Dale B. Harris, Harold W. Stevenson, and Willard Hartup as later directors. Also in 1925, another institute, the St. Georges School for Child Study, was established at the University of Toronto under the directorship of W. E. Blatz, the only formal institute of child welfare to be established in Canada.

The Yale Psycho-Clinic was established in 1926, as the fourth of these five institutes. Arnold Gesell served as the first and long-term director of this institute, which subsequently was renamed the Gesell Institute of Child Development. One of Gesell's colleagues, Louise Bates Ames, succeeded Gesell as director. Gesell is best remembered for his developmental tests for infants and young children and, as a former student of G. Stanley Hall's, for his strongly hereditarian concept of development. An Institute of Child Welfare was established on the Berkeley campus of the University of California in 1927. Herbert R. Stolz was the first director of that institute, serving until 1935 when Harold E. Jones assumed the directorship. Jones served as director for twenty-five years and was instrumental in building an impressive reputation for the Berkeley institute. The Institute is perhaps best remembered for the large-scale longitudinal studies of children begun in the late 1920's and early 1930's, known as the Berkeley Growth Studies.

In addition to these six institutes at Iowa, Columbia, Minnesota, Toronto, Yale, and California at Berkeley, a number of other important centers and research projects had their beginnings at this same time. The Merrill-Palmer Institute, then known as the Merrill-Palmer School of Homemaking, was established in Detroit in 1920, with Edna White serving as the first director. The research program at Merrill-Palmer began, in 1925, with investigations into the effects of nursery school experience. This question of the effects of nursery school experience reflected a rising interest in the effects of the environment upon development and prompted considerable research activity in the fifteen years between 1925 and 1940. The Harvard Growth Studies were commenced in 1922, under the direction of W. F. Dearborn; these were important longitudinal studies, similar to those initiated later at Berkeley. Cornell's program in child development and family life began under the direction of E. B. Waring in 1925. Other important growth studies were initiated by the Child Research Council, which was established in Denver in 1927, by the Brush Foundation, which was established at Western Reserve University in 1928, and by the Fels Institute, established at Antioch College in 1929.

By the end of the 1920's what Anderson (1956) called the "Golden Age in which the Institutes were being established" had essentially passed. No longer was there a problem of getting research efforts started; the new problem became one of coordinating these projects and communicating their results to other interested child researchers.

Under the auspices of the Committee on Child Development of the National Research Council, an abstract service was initiated in 1927 that abstracted child development research from seven scientific journals. The Second Conference on Research in Child Development was held in Washington also in 1927. The Third White House Conference on Child Health and Protection was called by President Hoover in 1929, thereby firmly establishing the tradition of holding these conferences every ten years. Unlike the earlier or the later conferences, the 1929 conference reported the

results of research conducted during the previous decade and issued a number of publications based on that research. Also in 1929, the Third Conference on Research in Child Development was called by the National Research Council's Committee on Child Development and was supported by a grant from the Laura Spelman Rockefeller Memorial. The conference was held in Toronto, and H. E. Jones, T. Wingate Todd, R. E. Scammon, John E. Anderson, and Florence Goodenough were among the forty-seven members of the conference.

John B. Watson and the Rise of Environmentalism

The influence of John Broadus Watson as a behaviorist began in 1913 when his "Psychology as the Behaviorist Views It" appeared in the *Psychological Review*. The impact of this paper on psychology was immediate in helping to turn the study of behavior into a School of Behaviorism. As a "school" of psychology with an environmentalistic philosophy and an objective, experimental methodology rooted in Pavlovian conditioning, behaviorism very quickly began to exert an influence on the direction that research efforts with children were to take.

Objective methods of investigation and interest in the learning process did not originate with Watson, of course. We have seen already that W. L. Bryan and Edward Thorndike were studying children's learning in the 1890's. Other significant research was being conducted about the time that Watson's paper was published. For example, an active interest in maze learning in children was reflected in the work of Hicks and Carr in 1912, and Gould and Perrin in 1916. Robert M. Yerkes, whom we have mentioned briefly in connection with the development of intelligence tests, was doing comparative research with animals, about 1914, that included work on children's learning. In 1913, Walter S. Hunter studied delayed reactions in children, and P. B. Ballard explored remembering and forgetting in children. Woodrow and Lowell developed an early frequency table of children's word associations in 1916, which Woodrow and others used to study verbal associative learning in children. Mandel Sherman and Joseph Peterson were contemporaries of Watson who also carried on active research programs on a variety of problems related to children's learning. Nevertheless, even though instances of objective methods and research on children's learning were easy to find, Watson provided the critical emotional leadership for this effort that helped to give it a focus and direction.

Like G. Stanley Hall before him, John B. Watson was an ardent and persuasive spokesman for his beliefs. However, whereas Hall had been a champion of the traditional values of God, country, nature, and motherhood, Watson was a knight-errant, ready to tilt with a wide range of prevailing academic beliefs and social customs. Watson's personal and professional life often found him at the center of a storm of controversy.

Watson's academic career was a remarkably short one. It was interrupted by World War I and terminated precipitously by divorce in 1920. His divorce and early remarriage to his student, Rosalie Rayner, forced him to resign from Johns Hopkins University, and he never held another academic appointment after 1920. He continued to work and write for many years, but his real contribution was made during the ten to fifteen years following his paper on behaviorism in 1913. Although direct evidence of Watson's influence is difficult to find[3], Watson left behind a conceptual orientation and a string of intellectual heirs, including E. C. Tolman, Clark L. Hull, and B. F. Skinner, who were to dominate the thinking of American psychologists for the next forty years.

Watson proposed a natural science approach to psychology which argued that only what is open to objective observation can be studied. Since the mind cannot be observed directly, he argued that from the point of view of science there are no minds. Thinking, reasoning, and other "mental" phenomena were explained as peripheral, bodily movements of muscles, bones, and joints, rather than as central, cognitive, or symbolic processes. Psychological development was thought to be rooted in the learning process and, more specifically, in classical conditioning. Higher and more complex processes were viewed simply as extensions of reflexive conditioning. The building blocks of development were the organism's unlearned reflexes, and the modification and elaboration of these reflexes constituted the central problem of human development. The conditionability of animals led Watson to conclude that individual differences and even developmental differences among humans were merely the result of differential experiences and learning opportunities. It was this latter view that made Watson a formidable opponent of the hereditarian position in the nature vs. nurture issue.

At a time when psychologists were trying to decide whether Structuralism or Functionalism offered the better approach to psychology, Watson claimed that both were inadequate relative to Behaviorism. When the issue of mental development and mental testing was sweeping the country, Watson denied that we had minds at all. When the question was whether to use introspection, or observation, or perhaps Hall's questionnaires, to gather scientific information about the child, Watson argued for objective experimentation and classical conditioning as the appropriate methods.

Watson published a book on comparative psychology based on his methods and views about behaviorism in 1914. Watsonian behaviorism contained the sort of philosophy that many Americans wanted to hear, one that meshed nicely with the belief that any boy could grow up to become President of the United States. While Watson's views brought cries of outrage from his critics, they also helped to spawn an army of enthusiastic followers. In 1915, just two years after his *Psychological Review* paper, he was elected President of the American Psychological Association.

Watson published another book in 1919, *Psychology from the Standpoint of a Behaviorist*, which together with his 1914 book helped to earn him the distinction of being called by some the "father of experimental child psychology." What with Witmer, Thorndike, and others, it is clear that experimental child psychology has had many "fathers." The following year, Watson and Rayner (1920) reported the results of the now famous study of fear conditioning in Little Albert.

If a psychologist were to attempt to replicate the Little Albert study today, he probably would be hauled before the Ethics Committee of the American Psychological Association, if not into the civil courts. The study prompted criticism at the time. Nevertheless, it continues to be cited today as a reference source for infant conditioning, for emotional development, and for the fact that fear can be learned and will generalize to other stimuli—and it reflects something of Watson's daring personality.

In 1921, Watson initiated a series of studies with Rosalie Rayner Watson on the reflexes and emotional responses of the infant. His work on conditioned fear was carried on in collaboration with Mary Cover Jones. In 1925, Mary Jones reported on the use of conditioning and imitation as techniques for reducing fear in pre-schoolers. In 1928, at the Institute at California, Harold E. Jones and Mary Cover Jones reported their classic investigation on the conditioned fear of snakes in children. Watson's work appears to have prompted an increased interest in infant reflexes and infant learning, as reflected in the publications about that time of such men as Clark L. Hull, C. W. Valentine, and Mandel Sherman.

Another area in which Watson had a pronounced effect was in child-rearing advice. In 1928, he published a book of advice for mothers based on behavioristic principles entitled, *Psychological Care of Infant and Child*. Once again, his recommendations clashed with tradition and much common sense, as he advocated strict controls, rigid training and feeding schedules, and the elimination of hugging, fondling, and other "mawkish, sentimental" ways of dealing with the child. Watson's advice may sound strange in 1976, to a generation of young mothers who are rearing their children, as they were reared themselves, on the advice of Benjamin Spock. It did not sound silly in the late 1920's and throughout the 1930's to a generation of mothers who followed Watson's advice rather carefully, particularly educated mothers who were interested in their child's welfare and sought the best advice of the child experts to guide them.

THE RISE OF ENVIRONMENTALISM: 1930–60

The three decades that comprised the 1930's, 1940's, and 1950's were characterized by an increasing emphasis upon the learning process and the effects of the environment. As learning came to occupy an ever more central position in child research, interest in a number of traditional problems and topics declined. A hereditarian orientation helps to ensure interest, for example, in individual differences—differences between people that are due to genetic and biological differences in age, race, sex, and so on. Once we come to regard individual differences as merely the result of differential learning histories, as Watson had suggested, then we no longer require a special psychology of individual differences, but simply a better understanding of the learning process.

An emphasis on environmental influences does not, in itself, obviate the need to examine individual differences. A psychology of individual differences would still be useful if we agreed that such differences were not entirely the result of learning and experience, but due in part to unlearned factors such as heredity, growth and maturation, hormones, etc.; or, if we could agree that there are several different kinds of learning and that the principles involved in learning sex differences, for example, were not the same as those involved in other types of learning. As things turned out, however, many American psychologists were not ready to accept these qualifiers, claiming that learning was all important and that all learning followed the same basic principles of conditioning. This uncompromising view is best exemplified by the Stimulus-Response (S-R) tradition that came to dominate American psychology during those years.

This environmentalist orientation reached its zenith in the 1950's, when personality, motivational, racial, intellectual, and even developmental differences came to be viewed in terms of differences in learned habits. The willingness to consider developmental differences as being due primarily to differences in learning served to weaken the view that children were fundamentally different from adults. This helped to bring the child researcher into the mainstream of general psychology. By the 1950's, with the rise of experimental child psychology, the child, like the adult, like the white rat, could be considered simply an appropriate subject for exploring issues related to general behavior theory. With this trend, on the other hand, came a general decline in interest in growth and maturation, individual differences, personality development, and developmental theory. Indeed, few theoretical advances in child development were made during these years, except for those of Jean Piaget. The contributions of Piaget, however, were formulated in Switzerland, were not understood very well by most American psychologists, and had little impact on American psychology at the time.

The 1930's: Infancy and the Nature-Nurture Fracas

The child research centers that were established during the previous decade provided the arena for a head-on clash between hereditarian and environmentalist forces during the 1930's. Hereditarian interests were reflected in the continuation of work on growth and maturation, and on mental development and intelligence testing. The environmentalist orientation was reflected in experimental studies of the learning process, particularly classical conditioning. Though hereditarians and environmentalists disagreed on many things, they were agreed that the beginning of life was a period that needed to be studied. Thus the 1930's became an important decade for research on the infant, the newborn, and the unborn child.

The hereditarian approach generally consisted of normative and longitudinal studies, and relied heavily on observational and testing methods. The Oakland Growth Study, the third of three main longitudinal studies initiated at the Institute of Child Welfare, University of California at Berkeley, began in 1931. These three studies were to continue for a very long time. The Berkeley Growth Study emphasized physical, mental, and motor development and was directed by Nancy Bayley from 1928 until 1954, and after that by Dorothy H.

Eichorn. As late as 1960 these investigators were still maintaining active contact with forty-nine of their sixty-one original subjects and, indeed, were maintaining records on seventy-eight of their subjects' children. The Guidance Study emphasized personality development and parent-child relationships, and was directed by Jean W. Macfarlane for thirty years following its beginning in 1929. The Oakland Growth Study, originally known as the Adolescent Growth Study, was aimed initially at exploring physiological and psychological changes accompanying adolescence, under the direction of Herbert R. Stolz and Harold E. Jones. A reason that is sometimes given for not initiating longitudinal studies today is that such studies require great investments of time and energy by the investigator and yet offer him little potential for publication. In that connection, it may be interesting to note that by 1960 these three studies had accounted for more than half of the more than 600 publications that had issued from the Institute. A typical example was Nancy Bayley's report in 1933 on mental growth during the first three years of life, based on longitudinal data from the sixty-one children in the Berkeley Growth Study.

Mary M. Shirley, at Minnesota, studied postural and locomotor development, intellectual development, and personality development in a group of twenty-five infants. These infants, remembered as "Shirley's babies," were observed continuously for a period of two years. Shirley's results were reported in a three-volume work, *The First Two Years*, of which the first volume was published in 1931 and the other two in 1933. In 1948, Patricia Neilon published a follow-up study of the personality development of fifteen of Shirley's babies fifteen years later. Neilon's data revealed considerable stability in individual personality patterns over time.

One of the chief spokesmen for the hereditarian position was Arnold Gesell. In 1934, Gesell published his monumental two-volume normative study of infants, *An Atlas of Infant Behavior*. While conducting this and related work, Gesell pioneered several methodological innovations aimed at improving the objectivity and reliability of natural observation. One of these was "cinemanalysis," a technique that involved the sequential analysis of motion picture frames.

Other noteworthy studies of growth and maturation in this period include Myrtle McGraw's *Growth: A Study of Johnny and Jimmy*, published in 1935. This famous co-twin study examined the relative contributions of maturation and special training to total development. McGraw concluded that practice had little effect on those activities such as reflexes and locomotor activities that are necessary for normal development, but that practice was essential for acquiring "accessory skills" such as roller skating. In 1937, William E. Blatz and his colleagues at Toronto reported the best work on children of multiple birth up to that time in their *Collected Studies of the Dionne Quintuplets*.

Interest in mental testing continued, and a revised edition of the Stanford-Binet was published in 1937. This interest was extended to infants and young children as well, as reflected in Nancy Bayley's "California First-Year Mental Scale" published in 1933, and in the Merrill-Palmer scale of mental tests for preschool children published in 1931.

Meanwhile, prompted by Watsonian behaviorism, a number of studies of conditioning began to appear. Harold E. Jones reported on the conditioned fear response in a 1930 study that employed conditioning of the galvanic skin response (GSR). In 1931, Dorothy Marquis reported an experiment on conditioned sucking in the neonate that represented the first attempt by an American investigator to establish a conditioned response in the newborn. Another conditioning study of newborns was reported by M. A. Wenger at Iowa in 1936. R. W. Kantrow, also at Iowa, reported another infant conditioning study in 1937. In 1932, Ray reported an attempt to condition fetal kicking, and later, in 1938, Spelt attempted to condition the fetus *in utero*.

Ohio State University was perhaps the major center for research on the neonate until Albert P. Weiss, an early behaviorist, died in 1931. After that, research centered around Orvis C. Irwin at the University of Iowa. There was still some use of the longitudinal method to study the newborn at that time, but for the most part the trend was toward more precise control. For example, at Ohio State in 1930, Pratt, Nelson, and Sun published the design of a cabinet for studying the neonate that provided an artificial environment for controlling the stimuli impinging on the child. This, as well as Irwin's use of the stabilimeter polygraph, showed the importance of controlling external stimulation as well as the condition of the organism at the time of stimulation. These techniques were in contrast to stimulation by flashlights, rattles, bells, and telegraph snappers in the 1920's and reflected the impact that Behaviorism was having on the child psychology experiment. The use of more elaborate and precise instruments, and better control procedures, helped to turn the study of conditioned responses into a more exact science. On the other hand, these technological advances meant more complex and expensive laboratories, which put the study of conditioning phenomena out of reach of many psychologists.

By the late 1930's, the volume and nature of research on classical conditioning had begun to trouble Arnold Gesell. In a paper presented at the Congress International de Psychiatrie Infantile in Paris, in July, 1937, Gesell acknowledged the possible value of this "scientific" approach, but raised a caution:

The maturational concept suggests that the scope of natural and wholesome conditionability is always determined by the maturity of the organism. The infant's immaturity must be considered in qualitative as well as quantitative terms, as we run a certain risk when we introduce untimely artificial stimuli repeated with artificial frequency while the infant is in the formative phases of his sensorimotor organization.

A related issue that grew out of the heredity-environment clash was whether or not child psychologists should study the "whole" child. The hereditarians, with their interest in growth and maturation and emphasis upon observational methods, tended to support the "pro" side of the argument. The behaviorists, with an interest in precise experimentation and an S-R orientation, thought otherwise. For example, in 1932, George D. Stoddard, who was the director of the Iowa

Child Welfare Research Station at the time, made a plea for the experimental method in child study in, of all places, a journal called *Religious Education*. One can just imagine the reaction of religious educators to Stoddard's (1932) statement that "the concept of *the whole child* is useful to the parent, the teacher, and the clinician, but it proves to be a millstone about the neck of the exact scientist." In concluding his paper, Stoddard noted that:

. . . we need objective knowledge about children which is organized about fundamental problems of development. Undoubtedly these (experimental) techniques produce heartaches in some, just as the ways of the modern botanist or zoologist may be anathema to the older naturalist (who was essentially a romanticist). But students of the child have set their eyes toward scientific goals and they are not to be deflected.

The following comments in 1936 by Arthur Jersild and Willard C. Olsen typify those made in support of the idea of studying the whole child, which was the far more commonly held opinion. Jersild gave a progress report of work from the Columbia Teachers' College Institute, concentrating on children's fears, social behavior, development of concepts, and skills. He said that their research strived to take account of the "whole child." Siding with Jersild, in a review of research at the Child Development Laboratories of the University of Michigan, Olson (1936) noted limitations to the experimental method and said "there is a real probability that our knowledge of child development will remain unnecessarily incomplete until we have devised methods of study which take into account the development of the organism as a whole."

The thinking and writings of Kurt Lewin added an important dimension to child research during the 1930's and 1940's. Lewin was an important theoretical writer in the Gestalt tradition, who emphasized the importance of the social and cultural environment as a determiner of individual behavior. His ideas stimulated interest in personality development, and his autocratic-democratic "atmosphere" studies of the late thirties stimulated research on social factors and children's groups. Lewin's efforts also showed that there can be a close relationship between theory construction and empirical work, even though the experiments stimulated by his theory often did not achieve the level of rigor demanded by behaviorists.

Lewin's attention to the importance of social and cultural factors helped to stimulate research on a wide range of problems related to environmental influences. Surprisingly, Freudian theory was beginning to have a similar effect. For example, there was strong interest in the effects of childhood experience on adult personality, and in the effects of early experience and child-rearing variables—weaning, toilet training, etc. There were studies of home and family "atmosphere" and the effects of institutionalization. At the Iowa Child Welfare Research Station, Beth L. Wellman and her colleagues conducted a series of studies on the effects of nursery school attendance on IQ, and that generated another controversy in the next decade. John Bowlby, Rene Spitz, and others were beginning to make a case for the importance of adequate "mothering." In a related comparative study published in 1933, *The Ape and the Child*, Kellogg and Kellogg reported on the effects of human-rearing of an infant chimpanzee.

The *Handbook of Child Psychology* was published in 1931, under the editorship of Carl Murchison, and immediately proved to be an important resource volume on child research. The state of knowledge with respect to a number of important problems was reported in chapters authored by individuals who were national leaders in research on those problems. Typically, these were directors and staff members of the Institutes of Child Welfare and other research centers established in the previous decade. John E. Anderson wrote the first chapter on methodology. According to Anderson, child psychology had twelve methods at its disposal: incidental observation, biography, systematic observation, questionnaire, case history, direct measurement and simple tests, tests of complex functions, ratings, experiment, experiment involving random control groups, experiment involving paired control groups, and control by statistical devices. In 1931, all of those methods were still being used. A second edition of the Murchison *Handbook* was published in 1933.

The active establishment of laboratories and organizations continued during the early part of the decade. Two research units began operations in 1930: Research in Child Development at the University of Michigan, under the direction of Willard C. Olson, and the Mooseheart Laboratory for Child Research in Illinois, under the direction of M. L. Reymert. The most important development along these lines, however, was the establishment of the Society for Research in Child Development in 1933. In June of that year, the fourth conference on child development was held by the National Research Council, which served also as the organization meeting for the Society.

The first biennial meeting of the Society for Research in Child Development was held in November, 1934. Lawrence K. Frank, who was one of the administrators of the Laura Spelman Rockefeller fund and was instrumental in organizing the Society, pointed out (Frank, 1935) that "the new society is an attempt to provide a professional association in which all those who are concerned with the study of children can find an opportunity for pooling their needs and interests with representatives of other disciplines also engaged in studying children." The governing council of the Society was made up of men from the fields of anatomy, pediatrics, nutrition and biochemistry, sociology, psychiatry, and child psychology. Robert S. Woodworth was the first chairman of the Society.

The interdisciplinary nature of the Society and its concern with the entire life span were stressed by Woodworth in his opening address:

The words, "child development," in our Society name, are intended to cover the entire developmental period from conception to maturity. . . . The importance of child development as a field of research cannot be called in question. The physical vigor and mental health of the adult depend on the growth process of childhood and youth, as well as on the genetic constitution which also in all logic comes within the scope of our society. The social characteristics of the adult popula-

tion have to be formed in early life . . . . But . . . the growing child and the maturing youth are not mere means to an end but are entitled to full recognition in their own right.

The last sentence seems to echo the importance of the whole child, and perhaps anticipates something of the rights of children.

The *Monographs of the Society for Research in Child Development* began publication in 1935. In anticipation of this event, Frank stated that the *Monographs* would be dedicated to longitudinal studies and that he especially favored multi-discipline studies. It was hoped that this series would bridge the gap between single-discipline journals. The current editorial policy (in 1975) for the SRCD *Monographs* continues to emphasize longitudinal and cross-disciplinary studies.

The 1940's: Socio-cultural and Psychoanalytic Emphases

As a consequence of World War II, research activity declined during the early 1940's. However, the war helped to stimulate interest in applied psychology, including clinical psychology, psychotherapy, and Freudian theory. Important work was reported on a number of topics that had been studied intensively in the two previous decades—such as growth and maturation, intelligence, learning and conditioning, and language development—but these topics were not the most central ones. The major emphasis of the 1940's was upon assessing the effects of the social and cultural environment on personality development. The theories of Lewin and Freud provided important guides to research in this area. Learning theory was beginning to have its effect on child research also, and learning theory explanations were being advanced as alternatives to those of Freudian theory.

A Freudian influence in the study of children was evident in the 1930's. Melanie Klein was calling for psychoanalysis of the child in 1932. Henry Murray had developed the Thematic Apperception Test (TAT) in 1935, and by 1938 projective tests were being used with preschool children. By the late 1930's, research had been conducted on a wide range of variables related to Freudian theory, such as the effects of birth injuries, various aspects of mothering, and those elements of child rearing most closely tied to Freudian stages of development.

Prior to the 1930's, a rather marked separation existed between theory construction, on the one hand, and the empirical study of children, on the other. This separation could be seen in the 1890's, for example, when James Mark Baldwin advanced an interesting theory of development based on a minimum of empirical data, and G. Stanley Hall produced a mountain of data that had only a minimal relation to theory. To many American psychologists, therefore, the word "theory" carried a connotation of arm-chair philosophical speculation. Hardheaded psychologists had argued for years that psychology should be considered an objective and exact science, and not a branch of mental philosophy. Because of this, there was a general distaste for theoretical speculation in the 1940's, and a concern for establishing a body of empirical facts. The writings and work of Lewin, and to some extent Piaget and Freud, were influential in helping to tie theory-building and empirical investigation together. Lewin, Freud, and Piaget were all Europeans who shared a common scientific orientation that prompted them to develop broad, sweeping theories that were linked to careful systematic observations.

The heredity-environment controversy continued into the 1940's. The intensity of this dispute tended to cause the battle lines to be drawn rather sharply, and to force the participants to line up on one side or the other of the question. That, of course, would not have been necessary if a middle-ground position could have been seen that emphasized the interactive relationship between heredity and environment in determining development. Such a view was present, but apparently was not recognized by many American psychologists. For example, Jean Piaget's theory stresses the importance of the interplay between biological development and experience. Piaget's works were available in English translation from the late 1920's and throughout the 1930's. However, Piaget's point of view was generally understood in this country to be one of growth and maturation, of "ages and stages." This view that seemed to emphasize biological unfolding appeared to be very similar to Arnold Gesell's, and not compatible with the rising emphasis upon early experience and environmental influences. Since their first appearance in the 1920's, Piaget's writings have had a continuing influence on American research with children. However, Piaget's main impact had not been felt by the 1940's, and was not to be felt for another decade or so afterward.

A similar bias occurred in the American investigator's perception of Freud's theory. Although Freudian theory places heavy emphasis upon heredity and biological development, most of the research generated by the theory in this country examined the effects of various environmental influences. For example, the transition from the oral to the anal stage of development, according to theory, is largely a matter of growth and maturation. In the translation into research questions, however, the oral stage was investigated by examining child-rearing practices surrounding feeding and weaning, and the anal phase by child-rearing practices surrounding toilet training.

Both Freud and Lewin helped to stimulate a welter of research and opinion on the effects of mothering, child rearing, family atmosphere, school culture, and so on, on personality development. Some of this was frankly psychoanalytic, such as Rene Spitz' 1945 work on "anaclitic depression" that underscored the adverse consequences of maternal deprivation and infant institutionalization. A decade later, in 1955, Samuel Pinneau delivered a sharp criticism of Spitz' work that pointed out major defects in Spitz' findings and conclusions. Also, Margaret Ribble published her extremely popular book, *The Rights of Infants*, in 1943. By 1962, Ribble's book had gone through fifteen printings, and a second edition was issued in 1965 with little added. Spitz and Ribble argued that inadequate mothering leads to physical and psychological retardation in development, but their work probably had a greater influence on social workers and psychiatrists than on developmental psychologists. While Spitz and Ribble

were alerting the world to the dangers of too little mothering, David Levy was calling attention to the opposite danger in his book *Maternal Overprotection*, published in 1943.

Learning theory alternatives to Freudian explanations were pioneered by a group of young men at Yale University, beginning in the late 1930's. This group was partly responsible for the American tendency to view Freudian theory from an environmentalist perspective. The group included John Dollard, Leonard W. Doob, Neal E. Miller, O. Hobart Mowrer, Robert R. Sears, John W. M. Whiting, and Irwin L. Child, representing psychology and related disciplines. These men were interested in the broad problems and issues of personality and were strongly influenced by Clark L. Hull and his S-R behavior theory. Their approach was an eclectic one that attempted to take advantage of the best features of Hullian behavior theory, Freudian psychoanalytic theory, and ideas from cultural anthropology. In 1939, Dollard, Doob, Miller, Mowrer, and Sears published a thesis, *Frustration and Aggression*, that frustration leads to aggression, and that the presence of aggression is evidence for the existence of frustration. Much of the work of this group of men was carried on during the 1940's and published late in that decade and during the 1950's. In addition to maternal nurturance and the child-rearing variables of feeding and weaning, toilet training, and sex and modesty training, interest centered around fear, conflict, aggression, hostility, dependency, displacement, and the general problem of sex role identification. We shall return to the work of these men again in our discussion of the 1950's.

Robert R. Sears was the leader in child research within the Yale group. In the late 1940's, Sears was exploring learning explanations for thumb-sucking as alternatives to Freudian interpretations. Sears's interest in identification and personality development as a function of mothering and child-rearing practices led to his development of doll play as a method for studying these questions in the 1940's. Sears was not, of course, the only one to use children's games as an avenue to answering psychological questions. Piaget, Erikson, and Lewin had also recognized the importance of children's play by this time.

Interest in the effects of various child-rearing practices upon later personality development helped to foster a general interest in parent-child relationships. Alfred L. Baldwin, with J. Kalhorn and F. H. Breese, at the Fels Research Institute, reported a major interview study of parent-child relationships in 1945, and, in 1949, published the Fels Parent Rating Scales. Similarly, Shoben's Parent Attitude Test was also published in 1949.

Lewin's field theory provided another approach to the study of personality variables and another alternative to the Freudian viewpoint. At Iowa, with Tamara Dembo and Roger G. Barker, Lewin published in 1941 the well-known study of frustration and regression that advanced the alternate thesis that frustration leads to regression, rather than to aggression. In that same year, Jacob Kounin published experimental studies on rigidity, another aspect of Lewin's theory. Kounin's research was among the more careful to be derived from Lewin's topological and vector psychology. Lewin's theory also helped to create an interest in the psychological ecology, as reflected in the influential "habitat" studies of Barker and Herbert F. Wright that began to appear in the late 1940's.

The heavy emphasis upon psychoanalytic concepts and Freudian variables began to trouble a number of the more traditional child researchers. John E. Anderson, at Minnesota, was one of those who were concerned. The Division of Childhood and Adolescence of the American Psychological Association was established in 1946, and Anderson was elected its first president. In his presidential address the following year, Anderson did not hesitate to strike out against the psychoanalytic involvement of the discipline. Anderson (1948) indicated that Ribble's book had "become a Gospel among social workers, although almost every review in scientific journals has pointed out many misrepresentations of established fact." Anderson went on to list five popular misconceptions about the child's nature that the psychoanalytic orientation had helped to produce:

(1) Infants and young children are essentially passive recipients of stimulation who display little energy or activity on their own; (2) are very delicate and tender, and have little capacity to resist or survive and are especially sensitive to lack of affection to which they cannot adapt for even short periods; (3) are unusually susceptible to and carry the effects of traumatic episodes indefinitely; (4) carry forward all their memories and experiences, which later come out to plague them; (5) in their behavior and the products resulting, are subject to all the implications and values that inhere in adult reactions in similar situations.

In a somewhat similar vein, Harold Orlansky reviewed the literature on infant care and personality development. Orlansky cited 149 references and concluded that no specific nursing discipline has an invariant psychological impact on the child.

The Iowa studies on the effects of early experience conducted during the 1930's drew sharp criticism in the early 1940's. This work, conducted by Beth L. Wellman, Marie Skodak, Harold M. Skeels, and Ruth Updegraff, concentrated mainly on the benefits of nursery school attendance on intellectual development, but also included the effects of home atmosphere and studies of foster children. Inadequacies in this series of studies were underscored by both Quinn McNemar and Florence Goodenough in 1940. Indeed, the heredity-environment issue had generated such widespread interest that in 1940 the National Society for the Study of Education devoted its entire *Thirty-ninth Yearbook* to this problem. Also, Robert S. Woodworth, who after his influential work in founding the Society for Research in Child Development had done little work in child psychology, returned to the field with a critical survey of the heredity-environment issue in 1941. His position represented a pleasant balance between the extreme arguments.

A publication highlight of the decade was the appearance in 1946 of the *Manual of Child Psychology*, edited by Leonard Carmichael. In his preface, Carmichael indicated that psychologists had at last "established a large body of important and reliable facts" and that the period of speculative theories in child psychology was past. In the following

year, Roger Barker (1947) reviewed Carmichael's *Manual* and sounded less optimistic:

. . . The Manual gives a conservative, almost old-fashioned picture of child psychology by omitting or inadequately reporting some of the most important developments. . . . in the absence of a strong framework of theory to organize and subsume such an array of facts, and to guide further observation and experimentation, we are in danger of being engulfed.

Barker's lament did not mean that there were no theories. We have already mentioned Freud, Piaget, and Lewin. In 1948, Heinz Werner contributed an evolutionary theoretical view in his *Comparative Psychology of Mental Development*. The problem with respect to theory was the one we have mentioned earlier, namely, that often much empirical work was being done without a guiding theoretical rationale, and the existing theories often were not guiding much research. In part, this was due to the fact that some of the theories were meant only to provide a matrix within which to view specific phenomena, but not to generate testable hypotheses. Werner's theory was one of these; another was Hebb's. In 1949, Donald O. Hebb published *The Organization of Behavior*, which though not the work of a child psychologist, had a great influence upon child psychology. It was still being cited in the 1960's, especially in connection with efforts to assess the effects of early experience. Hebb's theory provided a suggestion as to how experience and the functioning of the nervous system could operate to modify the structure of the nervous system, which in turn could further modify functioning.

The 1950's: Experimental Child Psychology[4]

Things were changing in the 1950's, and those who liked the changes saw these years as progressive and exciting. Those who did not like the changes fretted about the health of the discipline. The changes were major ones, that affected the problems being studied, the theoretical orientations to those problems, and the methods used to study them.

Changes in content and conceptual orientation were reflected in an increased interest in the effects of environmental influences. In this, learning theory, particularly S-R behavior theory, and Lewinian field theory became increasingly important guides to research. There was, on the other hand, a corresponding decline in interest in growth and maturation, psychoanalytic concepts, and in developmental change and developmental theory. Many traits and abilities that had been viewed as rather permanent, genetically determined qualities were either no longer of interest or were reinterpreted to fit the environmentalist's perspective. For example, personality continued to be studied actively throughout the 1950's but began to detach itself rather early from psychoanalytic theory and to be understood more and more in terms of learning theory. As this happened, the concept of personality was changed from a "thing" that could be studied, modified, etc., to a pattern of learned behavior.

The psychoanalytic point of view was well represented in the early 1950's. Erik Erikson combined concepts from cultural anthropology with those of psychoanalytic theory in his *Childhood and Society*, published in 1950. This book proved to be enormously popular, and Erikson's "eight stages of man" became incorporated into nearly every textbook and book of readings in child psychology for years afterward. Also in 1950, a symposium on genetic psychology was held at Clark University, one of several important conferences to be held during the decade. One of the participants in that symposium, Anna Freud, expected further study would be made of the psychoanalytic processes underlying personality development. The White House Conference on Children and Youth, held in 1950, focused on personality development from a generally psychoanalytic perspective. But rumblings of discontent were being heard at this same time.

Two other participants in the Clark symposium sounded a different note. L. K. Frank appealed for the development of techniques to analyze the complex interrelationship between personality and environment, and Robert R. Sears called for an experimental approach to personality and emphasized the importance of correlations between antecedent conditions and subsequent behavior (such as, the relationship between the way a mother punishes her child and the child's expression of aggression in the doll play situation). Some reviewers of the White House Conference expressed disappointment with the approach that conceived of personality as a structured entity.

Boyd R. McCandless and Sidney Rosenblum published a review of the literature in 1952 that attempted to assess the extent to which learning theory, Lewinian field theory, and psychoanalytic theory had been supported by empirical research. They reviewed ninety-five studies published between 1933 and 1952 and concluded, among other things, that the formulations from S-R learning theory intended to account for animal behavior could be extended to research with children, and that although psychoanalytic theory had stimulated much research, the tested hypotheses had "fared little better than chance as far as support is concerned." Samuel Pinneau, who had criticized Spitz's work on methodological grounds in 1955, made a similar attack of Ribble's work in 1957, in collaboration with H. E. Hopper. By 1959, George G. Thompson (1959) was saying: "The developmentalist's filial relationship to psychoanalytic theory is nearing an end. We are becoming more critical of psychoanalytic postulates and are beginning to doubt the adequacy of much of the supporting evidence."

These changing emphases were reflected in the second edition of Carmichael's *Manual of Child Psychology*, published in 1954. In their chapter in the 1955 *Annual Review of Psychology*, Marian Radke-Yarrow and Leon J. Yarrow complained, perhaps with some justification, that the new edition of the *Manual* lacked a chapter on personality development, inadequately treated parent-child relationships, lacked a chapter on the "interdependency of various growth processes," and had taken a "highly partisan, rather than a scientifically objective, point of view concerning the contributions of psychoanalytic theory to the research and knowledge in child psychology."

There were other psychologists with a more traditional developmental orientation who did not like the way things were going. Heinz Werner, who had hosted the Clark symposium mentioned above, lamented at that meeting that child psychology had forsaken its dynamic and organismic heritage. In 1953, Dale B. Harris (1953) noted with regret that "a striking feature of current child psychology literature is the absence of discussions of growth or the use of growth concepts in an attempt to organize thinking about child behavior."

Another change that characterized the 1950's was a sharply increased level of research activity. Statements made at the beginning of the decade were no longer true a few years later. For example, in his 1951 *Annual Review* chapter, Roger Barker claimed that the field lacked vigor: "By every index available—number of publications, number of papers presented at scientific meetings, membership in scientific societies, and establishment of research institutes—child psychology shows little life." Barker complained also that research facilities and the resources to support research were inadequate, and that researchers were often poorly trained. Reports of child research were scattered throughout the technical journals of a wide range of disciplines. This indicated to Barker that, among other things, there really was no group of professional child behavior specialists. Barker also noted that the "low level of scientific output in child psychology in 1950 is in contrast with the amount of programmatic, didactic, and speculative writing." The following year, Vincent and Helen H. Nowlis endorsed "many of the negative evaluations of the area of child psychology made in this review last year." The Nowlises, like Barker before them, complained that "most research in child psychology is distinguished by a lack of reference to systematic theory."

By the joint criteria of number of pages devoted to the chapter on developmental psychology in the *Annual Review* each year and number of references cited in each chapter, an unmistakable growth trend can be seen since 1950. For example, the chapter in Volume 1, 1950, authored by Harold E. Jones and Nancy Bayley, was eight pages in length and cited 38 references. The Jones and Bayley chapter was entitled, "Growth, Development, and Decline"—the only chapter so-titled (chapters in Volumes 2 through 7 appeared as "Child Psychology," and Volume 8 and thereafter as "Developmental Psychology"). The Jones and Bayley title reflected the orientation toward growth and development at the beginning of the decade; in later volumes "decline" or aging was treated separately. Volume 25, 1974, was authored by Donald M. Baer and John C. Wright; it was 82 pages long and included 443 reference citations. Figure 1 (page 210) presents in graphic form the trend for the first 25 volumes of the *Annual Review* with respect to page length and number of references. There has been some increase in the size of the volumes themselves over the years but, for example, Volume 25 was not twice as large as Volume 1.

This spectacular growth in research activity was made possible largely through an increased availability of funds to support research. By 1954, when Radke-Yarrow and Yarrow were writing their *Annual Review* chapter, they were able to say that "research funds from the foundations and the federal government, provide abundant resources for research

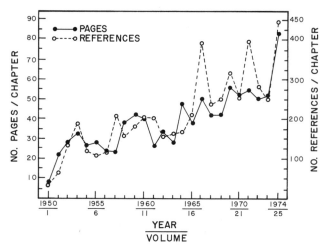

Fig. 1. Length of chapter and number of reference citations for the chapters on child/developmental psychology in the first 25 Volumes of the Annual Review of Psychology. *The solid line presents the page length of the chapters, as read against the left-hand vertical axis; the broken line gives the number of references cited per chapter and is read against the right-hand vertical axis.*

on children, far exceeding any previous period." They also noted that the National Institute of Mental Health, with which Radke-Yarrow was affiliated, had committed about a third of its total research budget between 1948 and 1954 to research relating to children. In contrast to Barker, the Yarrows painted a rather optimistic picture of the current state of the discipline. In 1963, the National Society for the Study of Education devoted the first volume (Part I) of their 62nd Yearbook to child psychology. Harold W. Stevenson, as editor of that volume, began his introduction with the statement: "The last decade has been one of the most exciting and productive in the history of child psychology."

The changes occurring in the problems being studied and in theoretical orientation produced corresponding changes in research strategy and methodology. The decreased emphasis upon developmental change and the influence of heredity helped to reduce interest in normative and descriptive studies, and in the use of longitudinal and co-twin methods. The increased emphasis upon learning and environmental influences encouraged the use of short-term experimental studies that systematically manipulated variables of general theoretical interest. The use of the child as a general experimental subject was a characteristic feature of the experimental child psychology movement that took place during the 1950's. The experimental child psychologist saw the child as an appropriate subject for answering the questions of general experimental psychology, rather than questions about developmental change or the child per se. In 1958, Glenn Terrell supported the experimental child psychology concept with a plea for the "need for simplicity" in child research.

The noble experiment was soon applied to a wide range of traditional and novel problems. For example, by 1956 Jacob L. Gewirtz was using a behavioral approach to the study of dependency, and Harriet L. Rheingold had demonstrated the modifiability of infant social behavior. Toward the end of the decade, Eleanor J. Gibson and Robert L. Fantz were independently exploring infant perception by means of different methodologies. Lewin's influence continued to be felt in research on social and personality development.

As the researcher's attention was directed more toward the child's environment, and away from the child as a developing organism, more attention was paid to racial and ethnic factors, social class and cultural differences, and the effects of child-rearing practices. These interests prompted the development of new research techniques. For example, in 1957, Harris published a new scale for measuring social attitudes in children, McCandless and Helen R. Marshall developed a sociometric technique that made use of children's photographs, and Dennis reported a technique for studying children's "cultural orientations." In 1958, Earl S. Schaefer and Richard Q. Bell published their Parent Attitude Research Instrument.

The heredity-environment argument had lost much of its heat by the 1950's, with developmental and individual differences being explained more and more in terms of environmental factors. For example, in 1951, the Hayes pointed to the effects of environmental enrichment in their book *The Ape in Our House*, an account of a home-reared chimpanzee somewhat like that of the Kelloggs, and John Bowlby underscored the effects of environmental impoverishment in an influential review of the literature on the effects of maternal deprivation. In 1958, Anne Anastasi provided a thoughtful discussion of the nature-nurture issue in her *Psychological Review* article "Heredity, Environment, and the Question 'How?'" She noted that for many psychologists the heredity-environment question had become a "dead issue." Her paper was meant to lay the old controversy of heredity versus environment to rest and prompt researchers to get on with the more meaningful question of the interrelationship between heredity and environment as joint determiners of behavior and development. She called for greater emphasis upon behavioral genetics, biological psychology, prenatal and infant development, effects of early experience, sociocultural determinants of behavior, including child-rearing practices, and longitudinal studies of development from birth to maturity. Whether it was as a result of Anastasi's urging or not, most of her suggestions were actively implemented during the next decade. Her paper did not, however, lay the old controversy to rest and probably helped to revive interest in it. At any rate, if the heredity-environment issue was dead at the end of the 1950's, there was to be a remarkable resurrection by the end of the 1960's.

The impact of S-R learning theory was particularly strong during the 1950's, and much of that influence was centered in the work of the Yale group mentioned in our discussion of the 1940's. The attempt to translate Freudian concepts into the terminology of Hullian behavior theory reached its zenith during the fifties. This effort was seen most clearly in such works as Dollard and Miller's *Personality and Psychotherapy* and Mowrer's *Learning Theory and Personality Dynamics*, both published in 1950. In a similar vein but with a focus on child development, Whiting and Child's *Child Training and Personality* employed a cross-cultural approach in 1953, using data gleaned from anthropological reports. In *Patterns of Child Rearing* in 1957, Sears, with co-authors Eleanor E. Maccoby and Harry Levin, and in collaboration with Whiting and others, continued to examine the child-rearing antecedents of personality development in terms of Freudian-type variables such as feeding and weaning, toilet training, and the like. The Sears, Maccoby, and Levin data were drawn from a large-scale interview of American mothers. All of this work to combine Freud and Hull to account for behavior stimulated considerable research (and controversy) and, in the end, pleased neither Freudians nor Hullians. It did much, however, to foster an experimental approach to the problems of child development and to establish S-R theory as an appropriate framework within which to view those problems.

This was a time when the principles of S-R theory, particularly Hullian theory, were being extended from the animal laboratory to account for complex human processes. In 1956, Alfred Castaneda, Boyd R. McCandless, and David S. Palermo co-authored the Children's Manifest Anxiety Scale, a modification of the Manifest Anxiety Scale developed for use with adults in 1953 by Janet Taylor (subsequently Janet Taylor Spence). These scales proved to be widely-used research tools for examining Hull-Spence theoretical formulations. Anxiety was viewed as a chronic emotional state, and measured anxiety provided an index of the subject's drive (D) level. According to theory, (D) interacts with available habits (H) in a simple stimulus-response fashion to determine overt behavior. Another view of anxiety was reflected in the *Test Anxiety Scale for Children* published in 1958 by Seymour B. Sarason and his colleagues, K. Davidson, F. Lighthall, and R. Waite, at Yale University. This latter scale was constructed from a Freudian psychoanalytic perspective and viewed anxiety as specific to stressful situations (tests). Nevertheless, the influence of S-R theory was strong enough to cause many behaviors and processes to be seen as being learned that formerly had been thought, from a Freudian point of view, to be largely instinctive. The work of Robert Sears was influential in this regard. In 1959, for example, Albert Bandura and Richard H. Walters published *Adolescent Aggression* and explained aggression as the result of social learning through child-rearing practices and other family relationships.

The 1950's were characterized by a declining interest in growth and maturation and in Freudianism, and a corresponding rising interest in S-R learning theory and methodology, but that is not the whole story. There was an interesting counterpoint being heard, softly at first, that was a prelude to what would become the dominant theme of the sixties and seventies. This was, in a nutshell, a dissatisfaction with S-R conceptions of behavior and development and a greater receptivity to cognitive and symbolic explanations. This attitude was expressed in many ways, but most clearly through the work of Harry Harlow and a growing appreciation of the contributions of Jean Piaget.

Harry Harlow's paper in the 1953 *Nebraska Symposium on Motivation* brought S-R drive-reduction conceptions of motivation into question and encouraged a greater interest in curiosity and exploratory behavior among child psychologists. His "Love in Infant Monkeys," published in 1959, had a similar effect on conceptions of infant attachment and af-

fection, and helped to rekindle

By the middle of the decade, th and general approach was being recog In 1957, the program of the annual Psychological Society included a "Symp tributions of Current Theories to an Under Development." One of the participants in that James Anthony, emphasized Piaget's contribu psychology of child development. Bärbel Inhelde Piaget's colleagues at the University of Geneva attention to Piaget's work in her chapter in the 1957 A *Review of Psychology*. Her chapter was the first to carry title "Developmental Psychology," and she indicated that th reason for the title change was to "bring child psychology out of its current isolation in order to reintegrate it into general psychology." These words have the ring of a learning-oriented, experimental child psychologist. What Inhelder meant was that a developmental perspective should become incorporated into the framework of general psychology—and not that developmental psychology should be subsumed within the S-R framework of general psychology, as was more nearly what happened. Lawrence Kohlberg's research on moral development in the late 1950's represented an extension of Piaget's work that also helped to call attention to Piaget's thinking.

We do not mean to imply that there was a general acceptance of Piaget's ideas at this time. For example, immediately following Inhelder's chapter we find Pauline S. Sears in the 1958 *Annual Review* saying:

The "developmental stage" approach to child behavior continues to suffer critical damage by being subjected to careful empirical test. In the 20 years since Deutsche tested Piaget's notions of children's conceptions of causality, there have been repeated indications that cognitive "stages" are no more successive than are the "libidinal stages" earlier described by Freud.

Nevertheless, disenchantment with S-R learning theory continued to grow. In 1959, Robert W. White published a theoretical discussion of motivation in a *Psychological Review* article entitled, "Motivation Reconsidered: The Concept of Competence," that was to have a strong influence on the thinking of child psychologists. White criticized drive-reduction theories, like Harlow before him, and attempted to integrate exploratory behavior and curiosity within a framework of biological survival based on learning to cope effectively with the environment. White's paper also helped to stimulate interest in Piaget's theory. The Department of Child Development at Iowa State University held a special celebration of its 35th anniversary in 1959. In an address on that occasion, William E. Martin spoke of a trend in developmental psychology toward "rediscovering the mind of the child." Martin saw as indicators of this trend: increasing recognition of consciousness, contemporary interest in the effects of early sensory deprivation on cognitive functioning, more research on children's thinking, and growing displeasure with drive reduction as the dynamism of behavior—all indicators that suggested to Martin "that at long last Watsonian behaviorism is dead."

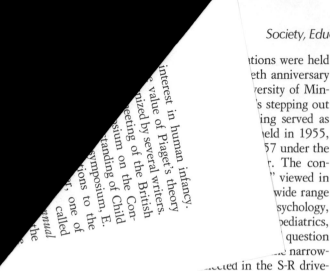

...tions were held
...eth anniversary
...versity of Min-
...s stepping out
...ing served as
...eld in 1955,
...57 under the
... The con-
..." viewed in
...wide range
...sychology,
...ediatrics,
...question
...narrow-
...cted in the S-R drive-
...ne volume proved to be a popular
...njoyed a second printing ten years later in 1967.

Another celebration was held in 1957 in Iowa City to mark the fortieth anniversary of the Iowa Child Welfare Research Station. The proceedings were published in 1959 under the editorship of Boyd R. McCandless, then director of the Station. Dorothea McCarthy reviewed research on language development, a topic that had continued to be of interest since the earliest days of child study. Robert Sears spoke on personality theory and, interestingly, suggested that our focus had become centered too exclusively in the learning process. He indicated that theory in the coming years must include the parameters of developmental change (maturation) as well as those relating to the influence of hereditary factors on development (biogenetics). Sidney Bijou reflected a growing interest in operant work with children in his plea for the use of empirical behavior theory as a guide to studying children's learning. Orville Brim spoke of parent education, and George Stoddard, the second director of the Station, outlined a number of difficulties that hamper the translation of basic research to actual practice.

The third celebration of note was held in 1959 at the National Institutes of Health, Bethesda, Maryland, to mark the twenty-fifth anniversary of the founding of the Society for Research in Child Development. The charter members and past presidents of the Society were honored guests at that meeting. The program consisted of five symposia, forty-one research papers, a series of reports on research being conducted at the National Institutes of Health that pertained to children, and an invited address by Lawrence K. Frank entitled "Future Possibilities in Child Research." Frank saw as a major research problem of child development "that of discovering how the organism-personality persists while changing, maintains a dynamic stability, with self-correcting and self-repairing processes . . . ." and reminded the Society of Einstein's reservations concerning the value of the inductive method with a quotation from a 1936 article by Einstein (1936): "We now realize with special clarity how much in error are those theorists who believe that theory comes inductively from experience." Although the program was small by present-day standards,[5] most of the participants either were at the time or subsequently became the leading figures of the discipline. Among the NIH reports were those of several investigators associated with the National Institute

of Mental Health, all of whom we have met before: Fritz Redl, Marion Radke-Yarrow, Richard Q. Bell, Jacob L. Gewirtz, Harriet L. Rheingold, Earl S. Schaefer, and Nancy Bayley. The program topics reflected research interests of the fifties as well as those that were to develop in the coming decade. For example, Roger Barker chaired a symposium on ecological methods, Charles Smock chaired one on cognitive processes, Martin L. Hoffman chaired one on moral development, and Benjamin Pasamanick chaired one on early environmental influences on infant development.

THE MODERN RENAISSANCE: 1960–1976

The closer one gets to the present, the more difficult it becomes to identify the historically important events in any scientific field. Even so far as the 1950's are concerned, we cannot speak of long-range effects, but merely indicate what events occurred and how they might have influenced work in the sixties. In dealing with the 1960's and 1970's, any attempt to identify significant events seems a bit presumptuous. Therefore, in this final section of the chapter, we shall give less attention to specific events and individual research projects as we discuss what seem to be the principal trends in child research during these most recent fifteen years.

The fortunes of child development, like those of other academic disciplines, have been influenced in a significant way by the availability of research funds and the general state of the economy. The 1960's were affluent years, and child research expanded rapidly in many directions. As Figure 1 and the related discussion implied, the growth rate in child psychology was much faster than for psychology as a whole. The expansionary years of the 1960's allowed the widest range of topics and approaches to be explored. These years did little, however, to encourage the resolution of theoretical and methodological differences within the discipline, or a broad assimilation of the results of research. Developmental psychologists were not obliged to talk to people in other disciplines, or even to each other, during the sixties and early seventies. Groups and individuals who disagreed with each other could simply part company, launch new journals, and continue right along. Perhaps the more recessionary years of the middle 1970's will prove to be a time for reviewing and consolidating the gains achieved since 1960.

Increased Publication Activity

As research activity burgeoned in the sixties, new books, serials, and journals were published in a way that was reminiscent of the heyday of child development in the 1920's. In 1960, Paul H. Mussen edited the *Handbook of Research Methods in Child Development*. Mussen's *Handbook* was a landmark volume in the history of scientific child study. Consisting of twenty-two chapters authored by distinguished investigators in the areas of their chapters, the *Handbook* gathered together in one volume for the first time the research methods and techniques of the major specializations within the field.

A number of excellent reviews of research also appeared during these years. In 1963, when Harold W. Stevenson edited *Child Psychology*, the 62nd Yearbook, Part I, of the National Society for the Study of Education mentioned in our discussion of the fifties, he noted that there had not been a general review of research in child psychology since 1954, when the second edition of Carmichael's *Manual of Child Psychology* was published. Long periods between general reviews came to an end with Stevenson's volume, however. In 1964, Martin L. Hoffman and Lois Wladis Hoffman edited Volume 1 of the *Review of Child Development Research*. This was the first of a series of volumes to be publĺshed at irregular intervals. Volumes 1 and 2 were published under the auspices of the Society for Research in Child Development and with the aid of funds from the Russell Sage Foundation. Although the Stevenson volume and the Hoffman and Hoffman volume appeared at near the same time, there was little redundancy or overlap between the two. Stevenson's volume focused mainly on experimental research on individual processes closely related to learning and cognition; the Hoffmans' volume concentrated more on correlational research relating to social and personality development.

The Hoffmans edited Volume 2 of the *Review of Child Development Research* in 1966, with a new set of topics reflecting a somewhat more applied orientation. Volume 3, edited by Bettye M. Caldwell and Henry N. Ricciuti, appeared in 1973. A fourth volume is scheduled to be published in mid-1975 under the editorship of Frances Degan Horowitz, in collaboration with Associate Editors E. Mavis Heatherington, Sandra Scarr-Salapatek, and Gerald M. Seigel, and a fifth volume is scheduled for the fall of 1975. Beginning with Volume 3, publication has been at the expense of the Society, with the aid of a grant from the National Institute of Mental Health.

In 1967, Willard W. Hartup and Nancy L. Smothergill edited another general review of research, *The Young Child*. Sponsored and published by the National Association for the Education of Young Children, the Hartup and Smothergill volume focused on research with children in the preschool and early elementary school years, but was by no means restricted to that age range. Another volume that should classify as a general review of research, although primarily intended as a textbook, is Hayne W. Reese and Lewis P. Lipsitt's *Experimental Child Psychology*, published in 1970. Reese and Lipsitt, as editor-authors, coordinated the input of sixteen other contributors. The chapters were organized around research topics of principal interest to experimental child psychologists. The contributors, with a few notable exceptions, were for the most part experimental child psychologists of the S-R persuasion—suggesting that the experimental child psychology movement was still vigorous in 1970.

The most comprehensive general review of research, however, was published in 1970 under the editorship of Paul H. Mussen. Offered as the third edition of carmichael's *Manual*, this work appeared in two volumes as *Carmichael's Manual of Child Psychology*. Volume 1 consisted of 19 chapters authored by 25 contributors, totaling 1,519 pages; Volume 2 consisted of 10 chapters authored by 12 contributors, totaling 872 pages. At the time of this writing, Mussen's *Carmichael* stands as the most current and complete summary and reference source for scientific research with children.

In addition to these general reviews, two important new serials commenced publication in the sixties. In 1963, *Advances in Child Development and Behavior* began publication as a biennial series under the editorship of Lewis P. Lipsitt and Charles C. Spiker. Lipsitt and Spiker edited Volumes 1 through 3 (1963–67). Volume 4 (1969) was edited by Lipsitt and Hayne W. Reese. Commencing in 1970 with Volume 5, the series changed to annual publication; Volume 5 was edited by Reese and Lipsitt and Volumes 6 through 9 (1971–74) have been edited by Reese. In 1966, the Institute of Child Development at the University of Minnesota began hosting the Minnesota Symposia on Child Psychology, which brought a group of distinguished child researchers to the Institute each year to discuss and summarize their work. The proceedings of each symposium have been published the following year in an annual series, *Minnesota Symposia on Child Psychology*. For example, the 1966 symposium appeared in 1967 as Volume 1. Volumes 1 through 5 were edited by John P. Hill; Volume 6 and thereafter by Anne D. Pick.

Several important new journals also commenced publication during the 1960's. The *Journal of Experimental Child Psychology* began publication in 1964 under the editorship of Sidney W. Bijou and Associate Editor Donald M. Baer. As the name implies, this journal was meant to provide an outlet for the work of experimental child psychologists. Although the *Journal* was and continues to be receptive to operant work with children, it has not been dominated by that orientation, as the names Bijou and Baer might suggest. Behavior modification and operant work with children has tended to appear in journals of the more strictly Skinnerian variety. For example, the *Journal of Applied Behavior Analysis*, which began publication in 1968, has been an important outlet for operant research with children in "real life" settings. In 1969, the American Psychological Association began to publish its own journal of child research, *Developmental Psychology*, under the editorship of Boyd R. McCandless.

A Period of Renaissance

The publication activity alluded to above simply reflects that child research has been proceeding at an unprecedented pace in recent years. As we indicated at the beginning of this section, the expansion of research activity has occurred on many fronts. Essentially all of the topics and approaches that were of interest in the fifties continued to stimulate research in the sixties and seventies. Indeed, many new topics and techniques were added during these most recent years, such as computer applications and simulations and the extension of mathematical psychology and information theory to the problems of child development. Beyond this, however, there has been a pronounced rebirth of interest in the classic problem and issues of development, and in what Martin referred to as rediscovering the mind of the child. This general trend has been perhaps the most prominent feature of the current period and seems to have brought a revival of interest in several topics with it.

We are currently witnessing a revival of the process of developmental change, including interest in physical growth and maturation. There has been a broad acceptance of cognitive and symbolic explanatory mechanisms to account for human behavior, and a readiness to explore the course of developmental change in these factors. There is a renewed interest in biological and genetic determinants of behavior and development, and a spirited revival of the heredity-environment question. During these last fifteen years there has been a major recognition and acceptance of Piaget's contribution that far overshadows whatever recognition he might have enjoyed in the preceding thirty-five or forty years. With the rising interest in Piaget has come a general interest once again in developmental theory. With this, and perhaps related to it, has been a renewed interest in historical contributions to our understanding of the child. There has been a marked revival of interest in the infant and, to a lesser extent, some renewed interest in the whole child. The following paragraphs are meant to expand briefly on some of these points and to provide a few pieces of supporting information.

Whether it was the result of a mounting dissatisfaction with the S-R conceptions and approach to development or simply that Piaget's time has arrived in the *Zeitgeist*, the ideas of Piaget and writings both by and about Piaget flooded the American child research scene in the early sixties in a way that was reminiscent of Freud's impact in the thirties and forties. The Piagetian flood is only now, in the mid-seventies, showing some signs of abatement. Piaget seems to have "landed" in England enroute to and some five to ten years earlier than his major impact in the United States. Several of our British cousins who were well known on this side of the Atlantic did much to introduce American child psychologists to Piaget. We have already mentioned E. James Anthony in this connection, in our discussion of the fifties. Daniel E. Berlyne and Martin D. S. Brain were also providing a similar service in the late fifties and early sixties.

In America, the Social Science Research Council, acting through its Committee on Intellective Processes Research, also helped to direct attention to Piaget by sponsoring a series of conferences on cognitive and intellectual development. These conferences were held in the early sixties, and the first one was devoted primarily to an understanding of Piaget. One of Piaget's colleagues, Bärbel Inhelder, spoke at the conference and helped to interpret Piaget's ideas and the work being done at Geneva to the other conference members. In 1961, J. McV. Hunt, in his *Intelligence and Experience*, presented a comprehensive English summary of Piaget's theory of intellectual development. Although Hunt's secondary treatment of Piaget was perhaps not the best one in the long run, at the time it provided the useful corrective of shattering the prevailing American image of Piagetian theory as merely one of growth and maturation, "ages and stages." Today, perhaps the best known American spokesmen for Piaget are John H. Flavell, David Elkind, and, more recently, Hans G. Furth.

The effect of increased interest in biological explanations, developmental change, and cognitive mechanisms can be found at every turn in recent child research. In terms of biology, James M. Tanner has helped to revive interest in physical growth with his proposal of a self-regulating neural "feedback" mechanism to monitor and control the growth process. Arthur R. Jensen has brought the heredity-environment issue back to the center of the stage with his 1969 *Harvard Educational Review* article, "How Much Can We Boost IQ and Scholastic Achievement?" There has been a steady growth of interest in behavioral genetics, developmental psychobiology, and the like, during these years. Renewed interest in maturation has helped to stimulate life-span approaches to human development, also.

Research in learning has continued actively at a high level of methodological rigor and experimental sophistication. However, learning studies are no longer concerned solely with the simple stimulus and response associative connections of a few years ago. For example, Morton W. Weir and Harold W. Stevenson have employed probability learning tasks to examine developmental changes in problem-solving strategies. Tracy S. Kendler and Howard H. Kendler have used discrimination learning to study developmental changes in mediational capacities. Allan Paivio has used rote verbal learning tasks to study imagery, and David S. Palermo has used such tasks to explore linguistic processes. Incidental learning and discrimination learning tasks have been used to study the development of attentional processes. There has been a major revival of interest in infancy, but many researchers today are no longer interested simply in classical conditioning for its own sake, or in motor development, as was the case in the twenties and thirties. Those who are studying the infant today often are interested in perception, cognition, curiosity, and the like. Interest in language development continues, but one no longer encounters normative and descriptive studies of vocabulary size, the appearance of various parts of speech, and the like. Current research in language development reflects the influence of psycholinguistics and is more concerned with grammatical analysis, syntax, semantics, and the relationship between thought and language.

Investigations of operant behavior and behavior modification, the stronghold of the S-R approach, also show some signs of the times. Albert Bandura and Richard H. Walters have demonstrated that considerable instrumental learning can occur through imitation and modeling—a finding which has raised a national concern since the early sixties about the amount of violence being presented to children through the mass media, primarily television. Today, by the mid-seventies, the effects of this concern have produced some changes in television programming during those hours when children most likely would be viewers.

The late fifties and early sixties were times also of introducing American investigators to research being conducted in the Soviet Union. Josef Brozek, Alexander Mintz, Gregory Razran, and others were instrumental in bringing Soviet data and viewpoints to America. Urie Bronfenbrenner and Yvonne Brackbill were helpful in this way for developmental psychology. The works and thinking of such men as Alexander R. Luria and Lev Vygotsky became well known during these years. One striking difference between the Soviet investigators of the twenties and earlier (such as Pavlov) as Americans generally understood them, and those they came to know during the late fifties and early sixties was the great emphasis given to symbolic processes by the later men. Terms such as "semantic conditioning" and "second signal system" reflected this emphasis.

Interest in Piaget has been accompanied by a general revival of interest in developmental theory. Whereas there had been no books on developmental theory for several decades, suddenly there were several. Rolf E. Muuss, Henry W. Maier, Alfred L. Baldwin, and Jonas Langer all published books on developmental theory during the sixties, and revised editions of those by Muuss and Maier appeared before 1970.

The return to developmental theory after so many years of ignoring theory in this country has had some interesting consequences. Most of the available theories are relatively old ones, and most have come from Europeans or from men trained in Europe. The theories of Fritz Heider, Kurt Lewin, Sigmund Freud, Heinz Werner, Erik Erikson, in addition to Piaget's theory, are all cases in point. All of these theorists have given a prominent place in their theories to biology and evolution, to developmental change, and to symbolic processes. Perhaps this helps to account for the recent American interest in these same factors.

Here, then, is the end of the story up to this time. It seems clear that in terms of breadth of interest, volume of research output, and rate of publication, child research has become firmly established as a hearty and viable enterprise. It is interesting, however, that in some ways we have come full circle in our effort to understand the child. Once again, we seem ready to believe that the child has a mind, that that mind shows developmental changes with age, and that the understanding of the mind and its development can be achieved through empirical study. While America has been unquestionably the leader in the scientific study of the child over the years, it is interesting that once again we are looking to Europe for theoretical guidance and inspiration—or perhaps we are simply still looking.

NOTES

1. Hall's contributions were by no means the only important ones of this period. Perhaps the most significant theoretical work was J. Mark Baldwin's (1895) theory of mental development. Baldwin took a genetic, evolutionary, approach to the problem of mental development in the child and the race. His writings anticipate so many of the terms and ideas that today are commonly associated with Jean Piaget that they should be required reading for all present-day Piagetians. Nevertheless, given the aim of this chapter, it is also fair to say that Baldwin's work was based on a maximum of logical and philosophical analysis and a minimum of empirical data derived from the actual study of children.

2. One of the authors has attempted to assess Hall's influence in developmental psychology elsewhere (McCullers, 1969). A definitive biography of Hall has been prepared recently by Dorothy Ross (1972). Interestingly, Ross is not a psychologist but a historian who is primarily interested in American intellectual history.

3. One of the present authors (Love, 1969) has searched for evidence of the influence of Watson and Behaviorism on child psychology. In spite of sweeping claims of such influence in many secondary sources, little direct evidence could be found to support those claims. Watson's influence on conceptions of mental or intellectual development seems to be virtually nonexistent. Since Watson believed there were no minds, there was no point in studying mental development. Psychologists interested in mental testing or mental development either denounced or ignored Watson, and those interested in learning and conditioning avoided the mental testing movement. Even Watson's extreme environmentalism and his conditioning methodology appear to have left few traces in terms of subsequent references to Watson's work. Perhaps this is because, like Hall, he did not conduct a great deal of research with children, and, also like Hall, probably exerted his greatest influence through emotional arguments rather than through an appeal to hard data.

4. The *Annual Review of Psychology* has included a chapter on child/developmental psychology every year since it began publication in 1950. These annual reviews of the literature greatly aided the preparation of this and the final section of this chapter. Our intent was by no means to provide a review of the *Reviews*, but to use this annual series as an aid to identifying conceptual trends in child research. Research activity has mushroomed in the years since 1950 and each succeeding *Annual Review* chapter necessarily has included an ever-smaller sample of the total work being published. Given that the authors of these chapters have generally been eminent figures within the discipline, we found it interesting to see what was considered important enough to include, why it was considered important, and what the author saw as strengths and weaknesses within the field that year.

5. The most recent meeting of the Society was held in Denver, Colorado, in April, 1975, with a program that was the largest in the organization's 41-year history. For comparison purposes, the 1975 program listed 42 symposia and 310 research papers, in addition to a variety of special meetings, discussion groups, film presentations, and three invited addresses; there were 763 participants listed in the official program. The program committee received and reviewed more than a thousand paper abstracts and symposia proposals. This means that the 1975 program, as large as it was, accommodated only about a third of the material that was submitted for consideration.

REFERENCES

We have attempted to tell the story of the scientific study of the child as simply and briefly as possible, and with a minimal use of traditional bibliographic and reference citations. We realize that this approach may prove to be a source of great frustration to those who are seriously interested in the history of child study. For that reason, we have tried to provide enough information in the text to permit easy retrieval of most sources by those who wish to do so. The dates provided throughout the text generally refer to dates of publication. Given the author, date of publication, and often the title as well, interested readers should not find the task of locating a particular reference to be as difficult as it might appear on the surface. Nevertheless, it proved impossible to dispense with references altogether. The references listed below, therefore, are highly selected ones which we felt were needed as supporting documentation or ones that might be difficult for a reader to locate without a full citation.

Anderson, J. E. "Personality Organization in Children," *American Psychologist*, 1948, *3*, 409–16.

Anderson, J. E. "Child Development: An Historical Perspective," *Child Development*, 1956, *27*, 181–96.

Airès, P. *Centuries of Childhood.* Translated by R. Baldick. New York, Knopf, 1962.

Baldwin, J. M. *Mental Development in the Child and the Race: Methods and Processes.* New York, Macmillan, 1895.

Barker, R. G. "Manual of Child Psychology: A Special Review," *Psychological Bulletin*, 1947, *44*, 162–70.

Bartholomäi, F. "The Contents of Children's Minds on Entering School at the Age of Six Years," *Report of the United States Commissioner of Education for the Year 1900–1901.* Vol. 1. Washington, D.C., United States Government Printing Office, 1902. (Translated from *Städtisches Jahrbuch, Berlin und Seine Entwicklung*, 1870, *4*.)

Bowditch, H. P. "The Growth of Children," *Massachusetts State Board of Health, Eighth Annual Report*, 1877, 273–324.

Bowditch, H. P. "The Growth of Children: A Supplementary Investigation," *Massachusetts State Board of Health, Tenth Annual Report*, 1879, 35–62.

Darwin, C. "A Biographical Sketch of an Infant," *Mind*, 1877, *2* (O.S.), 285–94.

Dennis, W. "A Bibliography of Baby Biographies," *Child Development*, 1936, *7*, 71–73.

Dennis, W. (Ed.) *Readings in the History of Psychology.* New York, Appleton-Century-Crofts, 1948.

Dennis, W. "Historical Beginnings of Child Psychology," *Psychological Bulletin*, 1949, *46*, 224–35.

Dennis, W. (Ed.) *Historical Readings in Developmental Psychology.* New York, Appleton-Century-Crofts, 1972.

Dugdale, R. L. *The Jukes: A Study in Crime, Pauperism, Disease, and Heredity.* New York, Putnam, 1877.

Einstein, A. "Physics and Reality," *Journal of the Franklin Institute*, 1936, *222*, 349–89.

Fernberger, S. W. "The American Psychological Association: A Historical Summary, 1892–1930," *Psychological Bulletin*, 1932, *29*, 1–89.

Frank, L. K. "The Society for Research in Child Development," *Journal of Educational Sociology*, 1935, *9*, 67–71.

Galton, F. *English Men of Science: Their Nature and Nurture.* London, Macmillan, 1874.

Galton, F. "The History of Twins, as a Criterion of the Relative Powers of Nature and Nurture," *Journal of the Anthropological Institute*, 1876, *5*, 391–406.

Hall, G. S. "The Contents of Children's Minds," *Princeton Review*, 1883, *11*, 249–72.

Harris, D. B. "Why an Interdisciplinary Society for Research in Child Development?" *Child Development*, 1953, *24*, 249–55.

Hunt, J. McV. *Intelligence and Experience.* New York, Ronald, 1961.

Itard, J. M. G. *The Wild Boy of Aveyron.* Translated by G. and M. Humphrey. New York, Century, 1932. Original publication, 1801; first English translation, 1894.

Jones, H. E. "The Replacement Problem in Child Development," *Child Development*, 1956, *27*, 237–40.

Kessen, W. *The Child.* New York, Wiley, 1965.

King, I. "Psychological Literature: Child Psychology," *Psychological Bulletin*, 1904, *1*, 147–60.

Lange, K. "Der Vorstellungskreis Unserer Sechsjahrigen Kleinen," *Allgemeine Schulzeitung*, 1879, *56*, 327f.

Love, J. M. "The Influence of Behaviorism in Child Psychology," in J. C. McCullers (Chair) *Historical Conceptions of Mental Development.* Symposium presented at the annual meeting of the Southeastern Psychological Association, New Orleans, 1969.

McCullers, J. C. "G. Stanley Hall's Conception of Mental Development and Some Indications of its Influence on Developmental Psychology," *American Psychologist*, 1969, *24*, 1109–1114.

Murchison, C., & Langer, S. "Tiedemann's Observations on the Development of Mental Faculties of Children," *Pedagogical Seminary*, 1927, *34*, 205–30.

Olson, W. C. "Types of Research in the Child Development Laboratories of the University Elementary School," *University of Michigan School of Education Bulletin*, 1936, *7*, 118–21.

Preyer, W. *Die Seele des Kindes.* Leipzig, Grieben, 1882.

Ross, D. *G. Stanley Hall: The Psychologist as Prophet.* Chicago, University of Chicago Press, 1972.

Seguin, E. *Idiocy: And its Treatment by the Physiological Method.* Teachers College, Columbia University, 1864. Revised, 1866.

Sheldon, H. D. "Clark University, 1897–1900," *Journal of Social Psychology*, 1946, *24*, 227–47.

Shinn, M. W. *The Biography of a Baby.* Boston, Houghton Mifflin, 1900.

Stoddard, G. D. "The Experimental Method in Child Study," *Religious Education*, 1932, *27*, 318–23.

Taine, H. *On Intelligence.* 2 vols. Translated by T. D. Haye. New York, Holt, 1889. (Original publication in French, 1870.)

Taine, H. "Note sur L'acquisition du Language chez lez Enfants et dans L'epèce Humaine," *Revue Philosophique*, 1876, *1*, 3–23. Translated as: "M. Taine on the Acquisition of Language by Children," *Mind*. 1877, *2* (O.S.), 252–59.

Thompson, G. G. "Developmental Psychology," in P. R. Farnsworth (Ed.) *Annual Review of Psychology*, Vol. 10. Palo Alto, Annual Reviews, Inc., 1959, pp. 1–42.

Thorndike, E. L. *Educational Psychology.* New York, Lemcke and Buechner, 1903.

Tiedemann, D. *Beobachtungen über die Entwickslung der Seelenfähigkeiten bei Kindern.* Altenburg, Bonde, 1787. (New York edition edited by C. Ufer, 1897.)

Watson, J. B., & Rayner, R. "Conditioned Emotional Reactions," *Journal of Experimental Psychology*, 1920, *3*, 1–14.

PART III: Philosophy

In Chapter 11, Kenneth R. Merrill traces the evolution of American philosophical thought from colonial days to the present, from Jonathan Edwards to the best-known living American philosopher, Willard Van Orman Quine.

The author presents insightful analyses of the leading philosophers of Calvinism (Edwards), the American Enlightenment (Ethan Allen and Thomas Paine), Unitarianism (William Ellery Channing), Transcendentalism (Ralph Waldo Emerson), Pragmatism (Charles S. Peirce—whom Merrill calls "America's most original philosopher, and quite possibly its greatest"—William James, and John Dewey), Ideal-

ism (Josiah Royce), and the various twentieth-century movements (George Santayana, Alfred North Whitehead, George H. Mead, Clarence Irving Lewis, Sidney Hook, and Quine).

"American philosophy" is actually a proliferation of philosophies, rooted in ancient and Western thought but indelibly marked by the unique experience of the New World. The author concludes that "there is *no* single American philosophy. There remains only the reflection—the grateful reflection—that Americans have for two hundred years enjoyed the freedom of thought and expression essential to the formation and development of a variety of points of view."

11

FROM EDWARDS TO QUINE:
TWO HUNDRED YEARS OF AMERICAN PHILOSOPHY*

By Kenneth R. Merrill

To give a comprehensive and detailed account of more than two hundred years of American philosophy in the allotted space—or even in several times the allotted space—is obviously impossible. What is possible is to convey some sense of the vitality and diversity of philosophical thought in America. But how? By giving thumbnail sketches of just about every thinker of any importance? Or by concentrating mainly on a few major (or at least representative) figures whose work, taken together, reflects the changing currents of American thought? The first alternative—the "telephone-directory" approach—is, for reasons I take to be self-evident, not a live option. However, although I have opted for the second alternative, I have tried to provide ample bibliographical sources for readers who care to look further into philosophers who are either merely mentioned or treated briefly in these pages.

When it seemed appropriate to do so, I have offered critical assessments of my own. Critical remarks occupy a very small portion of the chapter as a whole, however, and I have tried never to allow my own estimate of a philosopher to enter into the exposition of his thought. I believe that I have succeeded in this effort, but that is a judgment best left to others. I have, in general, paid only scant attention to biographical details of the philosophers covered, except where it has seemed necessary or especially interesting to focus on such details. The *Dictionary of American Biography* contains accounts of the lives of many of the persons discussed below.

In choosing the major (or representative) thinkers, I have been guided both by my own judgment and by the collective judgment of other scholars (not that there is perfect agreement on this question). The responsibility for the choices is, of course, my own; but I believe that my choices have not been idiosyncratic. I have selected philosophers for inclusion either because their work is intrinsically important or because they typify the thought of a certain school or period (or, happily, in several cases for both reasons). Thus the amount of space I devote to a philosopher does not *necessarily* reflect my own estimate of the excellence of his work.

The title of this chapter is slightly inaccurate: Jonathan Edwards, the first philosopher to be discussed, died in 1758;

thus the period to be covered is somewhat longer than two hundred years. I have divided the chapter as follows: "The Colonial Beginnings: Jonathan Edwards"; "The American Enlightenment: Ethan Allen and Thomas Paine"; "Unitarianism: William Ellery Channing"; "Transcendentalism: Ralph Waldo Emerson"; "Pragmatism: Charles S. Peirce, William James, and John Dewey"; "Idealism: Josiah Royce"; and "Various Twentieth-Century Movements and Philosophers." I have, naturally, sought to provide links among the movements and have not confined myself exclusively to the philosophers just named.

THE COLONIAL BEGINNINGS:
JONATHAN EDWARDS

In a generous but easily recognizable sense of the word "philosophical" the first European settlers in America had philosophical beliefs—about the nature and origin of the world, about the duties and destiny of human beings, about the sources of human knowledge (at least knowledge about the most important things), and about a number of other matters. The Pilgrims of New England, who came to the New World only thirteen years after Jamestown, Virginia, was settled, were by and large English Protestants, who, if not respectable by English ecclesiastical standards, still knew full well what they believed about God, sin, duty, and the way to heaven (or hell, as the case may have been).

Though arriving in Massachusetts ten years after the Pilgrims, the Puritans quickly became the dominant political and theological force in New England. The Puritans were, generally, a cut or so above the Pilgrims, both economically and ecclesiastically; but they were nonetheless out of favor with the established Church of England, and so they came to the New World to practice their own form of Protestant Christianity.[1] That form of Protestant Christianity was, generally, Calvinism. The term Calvinism refers to the theology associated with John Calvin (1509–1564), who is second only to Martin Luther among the leading figures of the Protestant Reformation. The nub of Calvinism—or the Reformed Theology, as it is sometimes called—is the utter dependence

*I wish to thank my wife, Vanita Harrod Merrill, for much help in the preparation of this chapter.

of all finite beings (including *human* beings, of course) on God.[2]

The definitive statement of orthodox Calvinism was issued by the Synod of Dort, or Dordrecht (Holland) in 1619, in the hope of bringing to an end many years of bitter controversy. (It need hardly be added that the synod failed in this noble intention.) The chief doctrines included in that historic statement may be summarized as follows:

1. All human beings, as the sinful sons and daughters of Adam and Eve, fully deserve God's awful condemnation and punishment. Nevertheless, in his infinite love and mercy, and for reasons known only to himself, God has elected some—but not all—of this guilty mass to be saved. Those who are not elected to salvation are hopelessly and everlastingly lost. This is the doctrine of *predestination.*

2. God has chosen to effect the salvation of the elect by the suffering and death of his own son, Jesus Christ. Although Christ's sacrifice is a sufficient atonement for the whole world, only those who believe in Christ can be saved, and only those whom God has elected to salvation can believe. This is the doctrine of *redemption.*

3. Although Adam and Eve were created blameless by God, through their disobedience they incurred God's wrath not only on themselves but also on all their descendants, that is, on the whole human race. Human beings after Adam have been born alienated from God, with an inherited tendency to evil. This is the doctrine of *depravity,* or *original sin.*

4. Those whom God has elected cannot be lost, even though they may not always live an exemplary life. Since their election to salvation had nothing to do with their own merit or the lack of it, neither does their preservation as children of God. This is the doctrine of the *perseverance* of the saints.[3]

It is scarcely surprising that a creed so bristling with references to God's arbitrary power and man's utter nothingness should have both tested the ingenuity of its adherents in making it palatable and evoked the moral outrage of its detractors. In Jonathan Edwards and William Ellery Channing, respectively, we shall see examples of the two responses.

The Calvinism that made its way to eastern Massachusetts in the first half of the seventeenth century had been filtered and modified by English and Dutch adherents. One widely influential form was the so-called Covenant Theology. On this reading there are several covenants (or "testaments") that reflect God's dealings with men:

1. The Covenant of Works was violated by Adam, the "federal" head of the human race, and his perfidy was passed on as original sin or depravity. For most Puritans depravity was not just a theological doctrine; it was a frightening reality that could be verified in themselves and in others. (Though written in the nineteenth century, Nathaniel Hawthorne's short story "The Minister's Black Veil" powerfully conveys the sense of sin so common among Puritans.)

2. By the terms of the Covenant of Grace, God forgives some of the children of Adam. Good works cannot save, but they do give evidence of grace.

3. The Church Covenant is the visible, institutional expression of the Covenant of Grace. It was, ideally, for the elect only, but by the eighteenth century this ideal had been substantially compromised.

4. The Civil Covenant reflects God's governance of all things: the citizens of a political community owe allegiance and obedience to civil magistrates, whose just powers derive from God himself. It is easy to see why a people governed under this model would have little patience with rebels and dissenters. To question the authority of secular rulers is, in effect, to question the authority of the Almighty. (In the interests of accuracy and fairness, it should be added that the Calvinists of New England were by no means committed to the infallibility of their civic leaders. It is only the general obligation to obey lawfully constituted authorities that they grounded in the will of God.)

The covenant view of theology and politics—especially politics—did not survive intact for very long. By the end of the seventeenth century the theocracy of the early Massachusetts Bay Colony was in theory and practice a thing of the past.[4]

To say that Jonathan Edwards (1703–58) was the greatest colonial theologian and philosopher is to understate the case. There was simply no other American thinker before Emerson who remotely approached Edwards in intellectual gifts, logical rigor, subtlety of discrimination, and range of competence. Indeed, in the respects mentioned, Edwards compares favorably with even the great post–Civil War philosophers—Charles S. Peirce, William James, and John Dewey—though no one, I suspect, would argue that he is Peirce's equal in originality.

Vernon Louis Parrington, in his *Main Currents of American Thought,* refers to Edwards as an "anachronism," and the term is apt. Edwards was to become the great and formidable champion of a religious viewpoint that was inexorably decaying. Though it received sporadic infusions of energy from Scottish and Irish immigrants, Calvinism—in its older form at any rate—was moribund. In religious circles Arminianism (an anti-Calvinist theology that we shall discuss later) had become a powerful foe of orthodox Calvinism. In philosophy rationalism—mainly in the form of English Deism—was in the air, even if its heyday was still several decades away. In politics absolutism had begun to crumble, both in England and in America: the authority of the British crown never fully recovered from the shock of Oliver Cromwell (who was, ironically, the most famous of all Puritans).

If single-minded devotion, unflagging zeal, and extraordinary intelligence could have saved the old Calvinsim that Edwards cherished, Edwards would have saved it; but even his genius could only postpone the inevitable. The most spectacular event (or, rather, series of events) of this period of reprieve was the so-called Great Awakening of the 1730's and 1740's, a religious revival in which Edwards played a major role. Though distressed by the excesses of that remarkable explosion of religious—some would say neurotic—energy, Edwards believed that the awakening was of God, and he defended its essential fruits against detractors, some of whom denounced the revival as irrational frenzy, an emotional orgy that had nothing to do with religion.[5]

Edwards was, to be sure, a terrifying preacher of hell-fire sermons; but his striking intelligence is evident even when used to present an almost psychotic picture of God's wrath. The most famous (or infamous) of this genre of sermons is his "Sinners in the Hands of an Angry God," preached at Enfield, Connecticut, in 1741. Indeed, it may well be the most famous sermon ever preached on this continent. The awful wrath of God has perhaps never been more graphically depicted:

The God that holds you over the pit of hell, much as one holds a spider, or some loathsome insect, over the fire, abhors you, and is dreadfully provoked; his wrath towards you burns like fire; . . . you are ten thousand times more abominable in his eyes, than the most hateful and venomous serpent is in ours.

Even more gory (and, one might say, psychopathic) is a sermon preached in his own church in Northampton, Massachusetts:

How dismal will it be, when you are under these racking torments, to know assuredly that you never, never shall be delivered from them; to have no hope: when you shall wish that you might but be turned into nothing, but shall have no hope of it; when you shall wish that you might be turned into a toad or a serpent, but shall have no hope of it; . . . your souls, which have been agitated with the wrath of God all this while, yet will still exist to bear more wrath; your bodies, which shall have been burning and roasting all this while in these glowing flames, yet shall not have been consumed, but will remain to roast through an eternity yet, which will not have been at all shortened by what shall have been past.

Edwards has been excoriated—no doubt justly—for such sadistic-sounding sermons as these; and there is no use denying that they express *part* of Edwards' outlook. But only part. Unfortunately, those who know just a little of Edwards invariably know "Sinners in the Hands of an Angry God" and practically nothing else. They do not know that much more typical of Edwards' preaching are sermons extolling the love and grace of God and the joy of man's experience of God. And, more to the point for our purposes, they do not know those works of Edwards that exhibit the power and subtlety of his mind. We now turn to a consideration of a few such works, but we cannot begin to do justice to a philosopher-theologian who has so many interesting and illuminating things to say about a wide range of topics: aesthetics, ethics, religious psychology, metaphysics (or theory of reality), epistemology (or theory of knowledge), faith and reason, determinism and freedom, and the nature of religious virtue—a list that is representative rather than exhaustive.

The decisive philosophical influence on Edwards was John Locke's *Essay Concerning Human Understanding* (published in 1690), which Edwards read with the greatest delight when he was fourteen. Locke's philosophy is a version of empiricism (sometimes also called sensationalism)—the view that all human knowledge is based on experience. According to Locke, all the raw materials of human knowledge are derived from the two basic modes of experience; namely, reflection (or the internal sense) and sensation (or the external sense). By reflection we are aware of ourselves as perceiving, thinking, willing, believing, doubting beings. By sensation we are aware of such "ideas" as color, odor, sound, shape, and weight. To emphasize both the passivity of perception and the absence of so-called "innate" ideas (that is, ideas that do not come from experience), Locke invented a famous simile: the mind is a blank tablet—a *tabula rasa*—on which experience writes.

Another basic—and deceptively straightforward—Lockean distinction is that between simple and complex ideas. A simple idea, said Locke, is "nothing but one uniform appearance or conception in the mind, and is not distinguishable into different ideas." Examples of simple ideas of sensation are a color seen, a sound heard, a warmth felt, or an odor smelled. Examples of simple ideas of reflection are thinking, judging, willing, and doubting. Complex ideas may be negatively defined as all those which are not simple. The idea of an apple is complex: we can analyze it into the component ideas of color, shape, odor, and so on. Another important difference between simple and complex ideas—though not strictly part of the definition of "simple idea"—is that we cannot invent or produce by imagination so much as one simple idea, whereas we can concoct all sorts of complex ideas—fairies, monsters, golden mountains, and so on. Unlike many complex ideas, simple ideas are "given," or we just do not have them. (Locke's empiricism is very far from being consistent, but that consideration need not detain us.)

Like many other philosophers and scientists of the modern period, Locke accepted the dichotomy between primary and secondary qualities. According to the more or less standard view of the time, primary qualities—such properties as shape, size, solidity, and motion/rest—enjoy a status denied to secondary qualities—such properties as color, sound, odor, and taste. That is, the primary qualities are properties of objects in themselves; but secondary qualities are merely mental reactions to certain configurations of primary qualities. To put it another way, a complete inventory of the characteristics of material objects would include the primary qualities but none of the secondary. To Edwards, Locke's position seemed half-hearted. If color exists only in the mind, as Locke and Edwards agreed, then the logic that drove us to that conclusion will force us to assign the same status to so-called primary qualities. *All* qualities whatsoever are in the mind and only there. Such is the inevitable result of consistently applying Locke's reasoning to our experience. If Locke had been consistent, he would have been an idealist too.[6]

Edwards accepted Locke's psychology and epistemology, with its emphasis on the primacy (and passivity) of perception and sensation. By accepting this view, Edwards believed that he could steer a course between the ravings and extravagances of enthusiasm (recall that his defence of revivalism was a qualified defence) and the cold, unappealing rationalism that characterized much of the "respectable" religion of his own day. He insisted on *understanding* as a vital part of genuine religious conversion, but he argued that such understanding rests on "seeing" (that is, immediately experiencing) the excellency of God and the things revealed in his word. Taking his cue from a remark of Locke that there may be senses of which we have no idea, Edwards suggested that there is a "sense of the heart" that God quickens in those who are elected to salvation. He sometimes described this intimate sense of God's goodness and excellence as a Lockean simple idea—a description consonant with the Calvinistic view of salvation as something "given," something that we cannot produce by our own effort.

The essence of true religion, for Edwards, is holy affections, primarily a love of God and holy things. In a well-known sermon of 1731, "A Divine and Supernatural Light," Edwards distinguished true religion from several things it is not but with which it is sometimes confused. By so doing, Edwards sought to set off genuine religious conversion from enthusiasm, from ordinary moral decency, and from a mere sympathetic attitude toward religion:

1. The divine and supernatural light (or the sense of the heart) is not the voice of conscience. There is a kind of general grace that God imparts to most people that enables them to lead reasonably honest and respectable lives; but a person can be morally upright and morally sensitive and still be without that special grace that God sheds only upon the elect.

2. Nor is the light any impression upon the imagination. Such an impression may or may not accompany the impartation of the divine and supernatural light; in any case, it is not essential that the imagination be affected. Edwards recalls the scriptural warning that Satan may come to us disguised as a messenger of light.

3. The divine and supernatural light is not the suggestion of any proposition or doctrine not found in the Bible. That would be inspiration or revelation. The light from God illuminates and enlivens what is in the Bible, but it does not add to the doctrinal content of scripture. (This part of Edwards' negative account seems directed against enthusiasts who frequently claimed to be the recipients of new religious truths.)

4. Finally, the divine and supernatural light is not merely an inclination toward religious things or a sympathetic attitude toward religion. One may be moved to pity by the story of Jesus' sufferings and death and yet be without that special grace transmitted by the divine and supernatural light.

In describing what the divine and supernatural light, or the sense of the heart *is*, Edwards repeatedly used the language of sensation. The light is a sense of the excellency of God, of his moral beauty, and of the things revealed in his word. It is supernaturally imparted by God in conversion; or, rather, the impartation of this light (or sense) *is* conversion. We are to *see* God's holiness, to *taste* the things of God, not merely to have a conceptual or speculative understanding of them. Edwards often spoke of the *sweetness* of this or that item of divinity. If we do not *love* divine things, if we have not *savored* the loveliness of God's holy beauty, then we do not have the supernatural sense; we have not

been illuminated by the divine and supernatural light. When the sense of the heart has been quickened in us, when we have been illuminated by God's light, we find that the old impediments to belief and holy living have been swept away. We do not need to be told; we can see and taste for ourselves.

It is in the manner just described that Edwards managed to graft a sense of the heart onto Locke's sensationalism. His insistence on the necessity of an inner conversion (appropriately manifested in one's conduct) got Edwards into trouble with his Northampton congregation. In Edwards' view, the members of his church were altogether too casual in setting the standards for church membership, and he proposed to remedy that failing. The resulting clash of wills finally issued, after a protracted struggle of several years, in Edwards' dismissal. He was obliged by financial necessity to accept the charge of a missionary church in Stockbridge, a town in western Massachusetts, where he ministered to Indians and a few white settlers.[7]

The events just recounted, which occurred late in Edwards' life, were, in some respects, foreshadowed by his experiences as a teen-ager and young man. In his *Personal Narrative*, which he never intended for publication, he described his own change of mind and heart regarding certain Calvinistic doctrines, especially the absolute sovereignty of God:

From my childhood up, my mind had been full of objections against the doctrine of God's sovereignty, in choosing whom he would to eternal life, and rejecting whom he pleased; leaving them eternally to perish, and be everlastingly tormented in hell. It used to appear like a horrible doctrine to me. But I remember the time very well, when I seemed to be convinced, and fully satisfied, as to this sovereignty of God, and his justice in thus eternally disposing of men, according to his sovereign pleasure. . . . I scarce ever have found so much as the rising of an objection against it, in the most absolute sense, in God shewing mercy to whom he will shew mercy, and hardening whom he will. . . . I have often since had not only a conviction, but a delightful *conviction. Absolute sovereignty is what I love to ascribe to God.*

. . . The appearance of everything was altered; there seemed to be, as it were, a calm, sweet, cast, or appearance of divine glory, in almost everything. God's excellency, his wisdom, his purity and love, seemed to appear in every thing; in the sun, moon, and stars; in the clouds, and blue sky; in the grass, flowers, trees; in the water, and all nature.

Edwards came gradually to identify his experiences of the inexpressible sweetness and beauty of God with salvation itself. Given such experiences, it is little wonder that he should place great store by the sense of the heart.

In spite of the truly onerous demands of his duties in Stockbridge, Edwards managed to finish, and publish in 1754, the work on which his philosophical reputation mainly rests, *Freedom of the Will*.[8] The frequently interrupted occupation of many years, the work addresses what Edwards took to be the nub of the difference between "Calvinism" and "Arminianism," namely, the question of free will.

In a prefatory note Edwards explained that he used the

terms Calvinism and Arminianism for convenience and not as accurate labels for the theologies of Calvin and Arminius. As Edwards used the term, Arminianism covers a multitude of sins; and, indeed, a great many divergent movements found shelter under that name. Beyond any doubt the Dutch theologian Jacobus Arminius (1560–1609) would have been almost as horrified as Edwards by many doctrines that were passing under the eponym Arminian. But at the core of the dispute between Edwards and the Arminians is an issue on which he and Arminius actually differed; and that is the question whether the human will is in any degree self-determining.

To Edwards the view that the will has such a power was "an almost inconceivably pernicious doctrine." In the first place, the Arminian doctrine compromises the absolute sovereignty of God; and to Edwards this derogation of God's power reduces the Almighty to the status of a partner—a senior partner, to be sure—of man. A second unhappy consequence of Arminian free-willism is, as it seemed to Edwards, to make people proudly self-reliant and forgetful of their dependence on God. The doctrine, Edwards held, tends "to encourage the sinner in present delays and neglects, and embolden him to go on in sin, in a presumption of having his own salvation at all times at his command." It is easy to see, in the light of these supposed consequences of Arminianism, why Edwards regarded it as so dangerous and why he devoted so much energy to combatting it.[9]

Another, more explicitly theological way of putting the issue is this: Edwards accepted, and Arminius rejected, the doctrines of predestination and irresistible grace. For Arminius, God elects *all* human beings to salvation, but only those who believingly accept the proffered grace are actually saved. The Arminian, no less than the Calvinist, insists on the absolute necessity of God's grace in man's salvation; but, for the Arminian, that grace is conditional, not irresistible. Christ's atonement conditionally, but not actually, effects salvation for all the fallen children of Adam; the individual must decide whether to accept Christ's atonement for himself or herself—a decision that requires free will. It is against views such as these that Edwards leveled his attack.

Freedom of the Will, then, is a polemical piece; but it is much more than that. It is, among other things, an "apology" (or defense) of a brand of theology that needed defending. Arminians were not slow to attack the vulnerable parts of the Calvinist scheme, and no doctrine seemed more exposed than the doctrine of God's absolute sovereignty. If, as Calvinists believed, a person's wishes, volitions, desires, beliefs, and actions are no more under his or her control than is the rotation of the earth, then by the plain principles of morality it is monstrous to hold anyone responsible for his or her attitudes and actions. And more: If, as Calvinists believed, God controls every detail of the natural and spiritual worlds, he is responsible for sin. Clearly, these are grave charges. If the critic can make them stick, Calvinism will stand convicted of slandering God's morality and his holiness; it will have forfeited all right to anyone's allegiance. Edwards' self-imposed task was to show that the alleged consequences do not in fact follow from Calvinist doctrines. It was a task

that Edwards performed with great brilliance, if not unqualified success.

Edwards' preoccupation with the will and its determination dates from his very earliest philosophical writing—"Notes on the Mind," a series of reflections on various subjects composed between his thirteenth and sixteenth years. By locating the essence of true religion in holy affections, Edwards pointed up the central importance of the will in his theology. Given the undoubted importance of the will in Edwards' thought, we may ask, What is the will? Edwards' answer is simple: It is that by which we choose. Though his language is occasionally misleading, Edwards did not suppose the will to be some substantial, separable *thing;* "will" is simply a word signifying the fact that people make choices.

By "determining the will" Edwards meant "causing that the act of the Will or choice should be thus, and not otherwise." The will is determined when, "in consequence of some action or influence, its choice is directed to, and fixed upon a particular object." That which determines the will is *motive,* by which Edwards understood "the whole of that which moves, excites or invites the mind to volition, whether that be one thing singly, or many things conjunctly." Further, "it is that motive, which, as it stands in the view of the mind, is the strongest, that determines the will."[10]

More specifically, the will is determined by the mind's view of the greatest apparent good. ("Apparent" here has no pejorative connotation; it refers to what appears to the mind.) Just what the greatest apparent good is, is a pretty complicated affair, or at least it may be. It includes, for one thing, the nature of the object that appears to the mind, where "object" may refer to an ordinary physical object or to some actual or possible state of affairs. But it is not just—or even mainly—the character of the object that affects the will. The clarity, the certainty, the vividness of the mind's perception of that object is of at least equal importance in determining the will. Let the object in question be as desirable as you like; if the mind's vision of it is fuzzy or superficial or distorted, the object will make little impression on the mind. By allowing a large place for the subjective factor in willing, Edwards was able to explain why many people prefer the ugliness of sin to the beauty of righteousness. They are just mistaken. Even though "the Will always is as the greatest apparent good is," it is not always as enlightened reason and good sense would dictate.

A significant part of Edwards' work on the will and its determination consists in getting clear on just what certain key terms mean. Failure to understand what is meant by such terms as "necessary" and "impossible"—or, perhaps more accurately, a tendency to confound different senses of such terms—is at the root of much confusion among philosophers and theologians. Ordinarily, when people use words such as "necessary" or "impossible," they are referring to situations in which one is forced to do something or is prevented from doing something. The terms imply something that frustrates effort or desire. That is necessary which will be despite all supposable opposition; that is impossible which will not be despite all supposable effort. The terms are *relative*—relative to the force applied and the resistance encountered. Thus, for example, it is necessary for the ordinary citizen to pay taxes, much as he might like to avoid it. (Others, apparently, can avoid it.) It is impossible for a common house cat to lift a fifty-pound sack of flour, but not impossible for an adult of normal strength.

Now philosophers and theologians sometimes depart from ordinary usage, often, it seems, without even noticing it.[11] Specifically, they sometimes use "necessary" and "impossible" when no opposition is supposed or supposable. Thus, God's existence is said to be necessary, even though there is no conceivable bar to his existing. Human actions are said to be necessary, even when there is no supposition of hindrance to the agent's doing as he pleases; or an act is said to be impossible even though the agent is free to do it if he wants. That is, philosophers and theologians sometimes use these words as "terms of art," in Edwards' phrase—what we would call "technical expressions." There is no objection to technical usage as such, but there is a danger of confounding the technical and the ordinary senses and drawing unwarranted conclusions. If the shift in meaning is subtle, much error may result and go undetected.

We have, then, distinguished two senses of *necessity;* Edwards called them "relative" (which is the ordinary sense) and "philosophical" (he might have referred to the second sense as "absolute," in the root sense of that word). "Philosophical necessity" is the name for a relationship between things that is "full and fixed." It is not entirely clear what Edwards meant by a "full and fixed connection," but he seems to have had at least two different kinds of things in mind. One kind of full and fixed connection is illustrated in the following statements: A triangle has three sides; God is infinite; all the radii of a circle are equal. Another, different type is illustrated in these statements: If a stone is dropped, it will fall; if water is heated to 212° F., it will boil; if dry gunpowder is ignited, it will explode. Statements in the second set are empirical or causal in character, and it is pretty obvious that Edwards regarded them as exhibiting a full and fixed connection no less than those in the first set. What is to be carefully noted is this: In *philosophical* necessity there is no opposition or obstacle supposed; the necessity consists in the certainty between subject and predicate or between cause and effect. In *relative* necessity some opposition or obstacle is supposed (or supposable). It is not *relatively* necessary that one perform an act that he is already inclined to perform, but the connection between such an act and its causes may be *philosophically* necessary.

Edwards divided philosophical necessity into two main species: natural and moral. To modern readers the term "moral" is likely to be misleading. In this context it has nothing to do with ethics or right and wrong. It suggests a contrast with physical or physiological necessity and is roughly equivalent to "affective" or "psychological." Human beings live under the sway of both forms of necessity. It is hardly news to be told that we are subject to physical and physiological laws: Like any other object, we fall if we lack support, and we get hot in the sun and cold in the snow. We also feel pain, hunger, thirst, pleasant sensations, and so on. But it may be news to be assured that our desires, volitions, and "voluntary" actions are governed by laws no less absolute than those that govern falling bodies. Edwards specifically endorses just such a view: "Moral necessity may be as absolute, as natural necessity. That is, the effect may be as perfectly connected with its moral cause, as a naturally necessary effect is with its natural cause." That is, a given motive will lead to a certain volition or action as surely as dropping a stone will cause it to fall.[12]

The difference between moral and natural necessity, then, is not in the strength of the connection but rather in the kind of terms related. Moral necessity relates such things as habits, motives, inducements, volitions, and actions. Natural necessity relates such things as cue sticks and billiard balls, flying rocks and broken windows, and lighted matches and gasoline. It is our ignorance, and not the way things really are, that leads us to suppose that the cause-effect relationship is stronger in the world of stones and billiard balls than it is in the world of motives and actions. And even as regards some natural events we may speak of "accident" or "chance" or "contingency"—or, of all things, an "act of God"—but the use of such words reflects only our ignorance of the true causes. In God's world *nothing* is left to chance.

Armed with the distinctions we have just explained, Edwards proceeded to explain two quite different kinds of abilities and inabilities. We are *naturally* unable to do something we will to do if we lack the intelligence or bodily strength or skill to bring it off or if some physical obstacle prevents us from doing it. We cannot, for example, work a problem in mathematics because we are not smart enough, we cannot put a shot one hundred feet because we are not strong enough, and we cannot drive a car through a mudslide. None of these incapacities has anything to do with our will.

On the contrary, will has everything to do with *moral* inability. We are morally unable to do something when we lack the motive to do it or when contrary motives outweigh the needed motive. Moral inability may be good or bad. An honest person may be unable to steal even when he has the opportunity to do so with impunity. In the movie *The Young Lions* the German soldier Christian Diestl is morally (but not physically) unable to shoot British soldiers who are trying to surrender, even though he is ordered to do so by a superior officer. On the other hand, a gluttonous man may be unable to forbear overeating, given the opportunity, and a drunkard may be unable to resist drinking. These moral—or, as we might say, psychological—inabilities, good and bad, do not make the actions (or forbearances) any the less blameworthy or praiseworthy. *Moral* inability cannot excuse bad actions, and it does not detract from good ones. (Mark Twain once facetiously said that he was morally better than George Washington. Twain argued thus: "George Washington could not tell a lie. I can, but I won't." Of course, Mark Twain knew perfectly well that Washington was speaking of moral rather than natural inability, and that his own refusal to lie and Washington's inability to lie came to precisely the same thing. Nothing but the lack of motive or inclination prevented either of them from lying.)

By contrast, natural inability *can* excuse: A person who is forced to commit an evil act, or who is prevented from doing a good one, may be blameless. Likewise, a person who *intends* to do evil but inadvertently, or through the action of someone else, does good, is still blameworthy. Suppose, for example, that someone maliciously cuts the ignition wires on a car, not knowing that someone else has attached a bomb to the starter. The serviceman notices the bomb when he replaces the cut wires, and the life of the car owner is saved. The car owner would have been killed had the wires not been cut; but the malicious intention of the wire cutter makes him guilty of an evil act.

Given these clarifications, Edwards' reconciliation of freedom and determinism is almost absurdly simple and straightforward. In ordinary usage, "freedom" or "liberty" means, in Edwards' phrase, "the power, opportunity, or advantage, that anyone has, to do as he pleases." It is freedom from "hindrance or empediment [*sic*] in the way of doing, or conducting in any respect, as he wills." The opposite of freedom is restraint or constraint: being hindered from doing what one wants to do, or being forced to do what one does not want to do. In the common (or vulgar) sense that is *all* there is to freedom or its opposite. The question how one came to want what one wants does not even come up. Edwards is admirably clear on this point: "Let the person come by his volition or choice how he will, yet, if he is able, and there is nothing in the way to hinder his pursuing and executing his will, the man is fully and perfectly free, according to the primary and common notion of freedom." In other words, the causal sequence by which one's will is determined is irrelevant to his freedom; if he can do what he wills, it does not matter how he came to will what he wills.

In Edwards' view it makes no *sense* to speak of the will as free or unfree: freedom or liberty (or the want of it) is properly ascribed only to an agent—a being that has the power of choosing. The will does not *have* the power of choice; it *is* the power of choice. It is persons or agents, not a property of persons or agents, who are free or unfree. Thus it is not so much false as nonsensical to speak of freedom of the will. [13]

The crucial implication of Edwards' reasoning is this: If one is free in the common, primary sense, one is *responsible* for his acts. As we have seen, moral inability to do good cannot excuse; indeed, it is a powerful indictment to say of someone that he is incapable of honesty or decency. Conversely, it is high praise to characterize someone as being incapable of deception or vindictiveness. Being unable to be willing to lie or slander is not a curb on one's freedom; one could lie if one chose to do so.

It is only because we confuse the ordinary and the philosophical senses of such terms as "free," "unable," "necessary," and "impossible" that we mistakenly suppose that moral inability can excuse. In the ordinary—and, for Edwards, the *primary* sense of "cannot," it is just not true that the drunkard cannot keep from drinking. No one is making him drink; he can refrain if he wills to do so. All that is lacking is the will, and for *that* lack he is responsible. Translated into theological terms, Edwards' view is that the sinner sins willingly; that is, he sins because he wills to sin. It is irrelevant that the sin can be described as *philosophically* necessary, that is,

as the result of a set of rigorous cause-effect relations. In punishing the sinner for his sin, God is doing nothing unjust. [14]

Few twentieth-century admirers of Edwards, among whom I number myself, have any interest in *Freedom of the Will* as a justification of the ways of Calvin's God to man. As a defense of Calvinism it mainly attempts to clear away certain objections supposed to be fatal to that theology. It offers little or nothing in the way of positive reasons for believing in Calvinism. (Indeed, to speak for myself, I find it hard to believe that there *are* any good reasons for believing in Calvinism.) The philosophical value of the work lies wholly in the acute analysis it offers of the supposed dilemma of determinism versus freedom. Edwards threw a great deal of light on this hard problem; but it is equally true that his vision of the moral problems surrounding this issue was myopic. His interest in moral problems was so tinted by the theology he was trying to defend that he oversimplified the answers and was closed to suspicions of doubt that otherwise might have occurred to him. His achievement, to put it briefly, is magnificent but flawed. [15]

Chiefly on the reputation earned him by *Freedom of the Will*, Edwards was offered and—rather reluctantly, it seems—accepted the presidency of the College of New Jersey (later Princeton University). He assumed office in January, 1758, and only three months later, on March 22, died of smallpox contracted from an inoculation.

THE AMERICAN ENLIGHTENMENT: ETHAN ALLEN AND THOMAS PAINE

As noted earlier, Jonathan Edwards was born out of his time. By the time of his death—indeed, a good while earlier—the theocratic viewpoint was losing its hold. A more secular view of society, with a consequent diminution of ecclesiastical authority, was displacing the Puritan vision of the Civil Covenant. In fact, there was always a tension between the theory of Protestant individualism and the repressive practices of the early colonial church and state. [16]

But it was economic success more than theological principles that issued in a greater degree of political and religious freedom. It also contributed to a less dismal picture of mankind than that found in Calvinism. A prosperous individual is less likely than is a poverty-stricken one to fall prey to doubts about his ability to survive: money in the bank provides at least some cushion against the vicissitudes of mortal life. As life in this world became more pleasant, life in the next became less alluring.

The shift in viewpoint, then, was the result more of improvements in the practical world of business and commerce than of changes in religious principles. Nonetheless, the shift was abetted by foreign writings, mainly those of the English Deists. Though not strictly Deists, Sir Isaac Newton and Locke exerted an enormous influence on American thinking. The genius of Edwards had transmuted Newton and Locke into defenders of the Calvinistic faith, but those two great Englishmen were the natural allies of Edwards' enemies.

Newton's mechanical philosophy lends itself beautifully to Deism, and Locke's empiricism was designed to be a powerful foe of various sorts of authoritarianism.

Without doubt, the best-known representatives of the American Enlightenment (as this period is sometimes called) are Benjamin Franklin (1706–90) and Thomas Jefferson (1743–1826). Although both of these remarkable men had a lively interest in philosophy and religion, their writings are not as explicitly and systematically philosophical as those of two contemporaries, Ethan Allen (1737–89) and Thomas Paine (1737–1809). We shall, therefore, take Allen and Paine as typifying the philosophy of this period of American thought. More than Allen, Paine also exemplifies the strong republicanism that characterizes much (though not all) Deistic thought in America.

Though Paine was an Englishman by birth and arrived in this country only in late 1774, his *Common Sense* helped mobilize American public opinion against further subservience to England. During the years of the American Revolution, Paine published his *Crisis* papers, a series of pamphlets designed to encourage Americans in their struggle for independence. Later, Paine wrote *The Rights of Man* as a defense of the French Revolution against the strictures of Edmund Burke. For his support Paine was made a French citizen and lived for some years in France; but when he opposed the barbarity of the extremists who assumed control of the revolution, he was put in prison and marked for execution, escaping the guillotine by a timely change in the government. He used the ten months he was in prison to write *The Age of Reason,* which is his most sustained treatment of philosophical and religious issues.

Less interesting than Paine as a political figure, Ethan Allen enjoys the distinction of having written the first Deistic work published in America, *Reason the Only Oracle of Man* (1784). The doctrinal differences between that work and Paine's *The Age of Reason* are practically nonexistent; indeed, Paine was accused of plagiarizing from Allen. The two works are alike also in the hostile reception they received. Paine dedicated his book "to my fellow citizens of the United States of America," but that thoughtful gesture did not protect him from the sustained and sometimes vicious castigation of his countrymen. Allen's book was bitterly attacked by conservative religious leaders; and when, in 1788, fire destroyed the remaining copies of the work, the orthodox regarded the fire as an act of God. (So far as I know, the orthodox never explained why God waited four years to burn the infamous book, when a more timely incineration would have prevented its distribution altogether.)

Because of their vigorous opposition to all forms of organized religion, Allen and Paine have sometimes been called atheists. The charge is, of course, ludicrous. They were no more atheists than Jonathan Edwards was; and their unswerving belief in God is so plain that one suspects the honesty of critics who made this charge.[17] (Such dishonesty may take the form either of asserting something known to be false or of claiming familiarity with a work one has not read.)

We have used the term Deism several times without making clear just what the word means. It may be useful, therefore, to state in summary form several theses that succinctly express the core of Deistic thought:

1. The existence of one supreme deity is clearly manifested in the natural world, without any need for special revelations.

2. Human beings are endowed with intellectual and moral faculties sufficient for improvement of the human lot and for the attainment of happiness.

3. The religion of nature, growing out of man's rational reflection and the moral relations of intelligent beings, is the only universal religion.

4. Human happiness and welfare must be based on the love of truth and the practice of virtue. Vice is always and everywhere destructive of happiness, both of the individual and of society.

5. Since the attainment of happiness and the avoidance of vice depend on knowledge, science and education are worthy ends for the expenditure of human effort.

6. Civil and religious liberty is essential to the true interests of man.

7. A person ought to be answerable to no human authority for his religious beliefs.

8. No religion can be of divine origin if it teaches hatred of any of one's fellow human beings or if it sanctions persecution as a means of enforcing belief.[18]

Let us now fill out a few of these tenets from the writings of Allen and Paine. (Practically any belief of consequence that we attribute to Allen can be equally attributed to Paine, and vice versa.) Both men approached their self-imposed task with something like missionary zeal. It is the solemn duty of every right-thinking person, Allen declared at the beginning of *Reason the Only Oracle of Man,* to rescue the bulk of mankind from "the torrent of superstition" that carries them along. Even in so-called civilized nations, most people have incorrect and unworthy notions of God, especially of his perfections and the way in which we may know them. Such ignorance inevitably results in unhappiness and the mistreatment of others. (The primary target of Allen's diatribe, as of Paine's, is Calvinism.)

To know God properly, Allen said, we must cast aside all putative special revelations and use our own reason. When we do so, we are forced to recognize the existence of an independent cause of the dependent, contingent beings of the world. We observe that everything in the world, ourselves included, causally depends on other things. Whether we take such causal relations singly or as a whole, we find that the things so related are *dependent.* Human beings, for example, depend for their existence on food, water, the maintenance of certain temperature ranges, and a host of other things. But it is absurd that dependent things should depend on *nothing.* It follows that there is an independent cause of all dependent things, and that cause is God.

Allen also subscribed to a slightly different proof of God's existence—the argument from design (also called the teleological argument). It is a plain fact that the universe exhibits a marvelous order: The seasons come and go, birds build nests and raise their young, the planets orbit the sun with awe-inspiring regularity, and so on. Can all this be the product of blind chance?

That wisdom, order and design should be the production of non-entity, or of chaos, confusion and old night, is too absurd to deserve a serious confutation, for it supposeth that there may be effects without a cause, viz.: produced by non-entity, or that chaos or confusion could produce the effects of power, wisdom and goodness; such absurdities as these we must assent to, or subscribe to the doctrine of a self-existent and providential being. [19]

Just as we learn of God's wisdom and power from nature, so we learn of his moral perfections from our own moral sense and rational nature. Our ability to distinguish right from wrong, justice from injustice—weak and perverted as this capacity may be—is a true reflection of God's moral character. Of course, both God and his creation are somewhat mysterious to us; that is an unavoidable consequence of our limited understanding. The mystery is not, however, an objective property of God or of his creation: though we do not understand everything about God or the universe he has created, we know that both he and his world are perfectly rational and intelligible. As Paine put it, we may find the notion of a first cause to be difficult, but we find it immeasurably more difficult not to believe that there *is* such a cause. [20]

A supposed consequence of God's munificence and power—a consequence enthusiastically embraced by both Allen and Paine—is that there are rational agents distributed throughout the universe. Allen's argument for this conclusion is reminiscent of Gottfried Leibniz's best-of-all-possible-worlds argument. The infinite goodness, wisdom, and power of God are inconsistent with the supposition that God has confined the expression of his perfection to this world. In Allen's words, "As there is no deficiency of absolute perfection in God, it is rationally demonstrative that the immense creation is replenished with rational agents, and that it has been eternally so."

God's creation, then, operates according to immutable physical and moral laws. But God's unchanging laws do not interfere with the freedom of human beings. Whatever specious arguments the necessitarians (Allen's word for determinists like the Calvinists) may present, men are free, and they know it with intuitive certainty. Those who deny free will stultify themselves: if absolutely everything is predetermined, then the beliefs that people have about freedom are also predetermined, so that dispute on the issue is pointless. The libertarians are determined to hold one opinion, and the necessitarians are determined to hold the opposite opinion. Disturbed by the conflicting demands of their predestinarian theology (on the one hand) and the plain dictates of common sense and conscience (on the other), necessitarians play a shell game in which they both assert and deny human freedom. [21]

Of the traditional beliefs generally attacked by Deists, none is regarded as more odious and illogical than the doctrine of depravity, or original sin. It is odious because it degrades man and his reason. It is illogical because it would destroy the only basis on which it could be asserted or even understood, namely, human reason. To accept or understand the doctrine of depravity, we must be able to exercise our reason, but the doctrine requires us to believe that our reason is depraved and therefore untrustworthy. The doctrine is self-disqualifying in that, if true, it ought not be believed. The defender of the doctrine is in much the same situation as one who *says,* "I am mute." By the very act of uttering the sentence, one proves that it is false: if one were in fact mute, one could not *say* that one was mute. In asserting the doctrine of depravity to be *true,* the defender of the doctrine does something that would be impossible if the doctrine were indeed true. And it does not help to say that reason is only *partly* depraved. To determine which parts are depraved and which parts are undepraved, we must have the use of *un*depraved reason.

At this point the defender of original sin is likely to say, "Your criticism is utterly wide of the mark. The doctrine of depravity is not a truth discovered by reason; it is given to us by revelation from God." But this line of defense is as futile as the others. A revelation from God presupposes a rational intelligence to receive and understand the revelation. Without reason, the recipient of God's revelation would find it unintelligible. There are, of course, varying degrees of reason, but it is not, for all that, spoiled or depraved. The closest thing we have to a proof of depravity is the gullibility of millions of people who have accepted the doctrine of original sin on the word of priests who are, if the doctrine is true, no less depraved than the people they seek to gull.

Convinced of God's infinite wisdom and goodness, Allen could not believe that prayer has any legitimate function. Prayer either amounts to an attempt to become a partner of the infinite and eternal God in the governance of the world, or it is a pointless uttering of words. God governs the universe by his infinite wisdom and power, not by reacting to our limited and self-serving requests. If God acceded to our pleas for miraculous interventions, he would be giving preference to our myopic vision over his own omniscience, and that would be irrational. We best commend ourselves to God by following the dictates of reason, not by prayer or other religious ceremonies. This position has the further consequence of divesting faith of its moral and religious connotations. When we are presented with convincing evidence for a proposition, we necessarily believe it, just as we cannot avoid seeing if we have our eyes open in sunlight. There is nothing good or evil about such matters. It *is* wrong, however, to profess faith in something that we do not actually believe.

Paine's *The Age of Reason* is doctrinally indistinguishable from Allen's *Reason the Only Oracle of Man,* but Paine spent proportionately more time attacking the specifics of certain religions (most notably Christianity) than Allen did. Paine stated his positive creed this way: "I believe in one God, and no more; and I hope for happiness beyond this life." The ethical side of his system he summed up as follows: "I believe the equality of man; and I believe that religious duties consist in doing justice, loving mercy, and endeavouring to make our fellow creatures happy." Negatively (with a positive coda): "I do not believe in the creed professed by the Jewish church, by the Roman church, by the Greek church, by the Turkish church, by the Protestant church, nor by any church that I know of. My own mind is my own church."

Now each of the churches that Paine repudiated has its own prophet, who is specially chosen by God to deliver his message to the rest of mankind. Moses, Jesus, and Mohammed are among the best known. Paine did not deny outright that God may have spoken directly to certain individuals; but since a revelation is by its nature an *immediate* communication, anyone not privy to the (alleged) revelation is free to disbelieve it. For those not getting it first hand, the revelation is hearsay. Perhaps God did give Moses the Ten Commandments on tablets of stone; but if the children of Israel had only Moses' word for it, they were under no obligation to accept Moses' claim as true. Similar considerations hold for the claims of other religions to exclusive divine sponsorship.

If we want a revelation that is freely available to all rational creatures, one that is not subject to accidental or intentional alteration, one that cannot be counterfeited—all of which are properties denied to so-called special revelations—then we must look to creation. "The word of God is the creation we behold." The revelation found in nature is not subject to the vagaries of human language or to fraud or to suppression. It is published from one end of the earth to the other: "The heavens declare the glory of God, and the firmament sheweth forth his handiwork."

As a corrective to some of the worst features of Calvinism, Deism was a salutary movement. In intention at least, it was humane and progressive. But as a system of beliefs, it was too cold and too remote to attract much of a following. The Deists we have discussed—Ethan Allen and Thomas Paine—were men of very modest philosophical abilities and learning. Compared to a genius like Jonathan Edwards, they were lightweights; and this estimate is concurred in by critics who detest just about everything Edwards stood for. Deists typically have little understanding of the faculty of reason they never tire of extolling, and Allen and Paine were depressingly typical in this respect. Their knowledge of religion, which they attacked so fervently, was often crude, simplistic, and literal-minded. Their view of the roots of evil in human society was incredibly shallow. Paine, especially, seemed to think that getting rid of priests and kings—that is, instituting religious and political freedom—would usher in a golden age of happiness and peace. To a reader living after Auschwitz, Hiroshima, and Stalinist Russia, such a conception seems wildly naïve.

"Take the system of Newton, subtract the poetry of Edwards, add the spirit of Bacon's *New Atlantis,* a strong flavor of arrogance, and you have deism." Thus did Harvey Gates Townsend sum up Deism, and it seems to me a just epitome.[22] As for Paine himself, he was a man of great courage and a passionate lover of liberty. When Benjamin Franklin said, "Where liberty is, there is my country," Paine responded, in the same spirit, "Where liberty is *not,* there is my country." For that he deserves our admiration. For his philosophical skill he deserves a much smaller share of our admiration.

UNITARIANISM: WILLIAM ELLERY CHANNING

The term Unitarian underscores the *unity* of God, as against the Trinitarian view of God as three-in-one—Father, Son, and Holy Spirit. A few American ministers and congregations had adopted Unitarian beliefs, though not the name, by the middle of the eighteenth century. But it remained for William Ellery Channing (1780–1842) to articulate a liberal (but still Bible-based) theology and to become the acknowledged, if not altogether willing, leader of that heterogeneous group who now openly called themselves Unitarians. Channing's unwillingness to become the leader of a new denomination stemmed in part from his fragile health (which was to be a lifelong burden) but also from his fear that Unitarianism would degenerate into a Unitarian orthodoxy—a fear that was borne out in the treatment of such unorthodox ministers as Ralph Waldo Emerson and Theodore Parker and in the bitter theological controversies of the 1830's and 1840's.

In Channing several diverse streams of thought meet, producing in him a curious mixture of Christian literalism, rationalism, mysticism, republicanism (his maternal grandfather, William Ellery, was a signer of the Declaration of Independence), and some mixed adumbrations of Transcendentalism. He represents a kind of halfway house between Edwards and Emerson, both in time and in doctrine. Compared to Edwards, he was quite liberal; but alongside Emerson and Parker, he was rather conservative.

In his early life Channing was under the influence of Samuel Hopkins, a disciple of Jonathan Edwards. With this conservative background and believing the Bible to be a sufficient guide to religious truth, the young Channing searched the Scriptures for confirmation of the Calvinist doctrines he had been reared to believe. But he could find no biblical basis for the doctrines of original sin, predestination, election, or the vicarious suffering of an innocent victim (Christ) for "sin" in which man's will had no part. Emancipated from these dismal beliefs, Channing proceeded to lay out a theology based squarely on God's parental love and the possibilities of human emulation of that love. He made theology a humane undertaking and in the process managed to influence such notable figures as Emerson, William Cullen Bryant, Henry Wadsworth Longfellow, Oliver Wendall Holmes, and James Russell Lowell.

In July, 1803, Channing was installed as minister of the Federal Street Church in Boston, a position he held until his death in 1842. During the thirty-nine years of his ministry he was from time to time called upon to deliver ordination sermons. On one such occasion, at the ordination of Jared Sparks in 1819, he set out succinctly and clearly the distinguishing beliefs of Unitarianism. He called the sermon, quite simply, "Unitarian Christianity." We shall use this classic statement as our chief source in what follows.

The conservative strain in Channing's thinking is nowhere more evident than in his attitude toward the Bible. The

Scriptures are, he said, "records of God's successive relations to mankind, and particularly of the last and most perfect revelation of his will by Jesus Christ." He accepted without reservation everything clearly taught in the Scriptures, though he insisted that not all books of the Bible are of equal importance. But Channing was no simple-minded literalist, as we can see in his chief rule for interpretation of Scripture: "the Bible is a book written for men, in the language of men, and . . . its meaning is to be sought in the same manner as that of other books." The truths of the Bible are consistent with, and must be constantly compared with, the truths furnished us by our own reason and experience. The language of the Bible is, as Channing put it, "singularly glowing, bold, and figurative." In interpreting that language, we must not take figures of speech literally, and we must distinguish what is permanent and universal from what was temporary and local.

In explaining his views on biblical interpretation, Channing deplored the abasement of reason found in some orthodox creeds. If reason is depraved and untrustworthy, then revelation itself becomes unintelligible—an observation reminiscent of Allen's attack on the notion of original sin. If reason is subverted, we are at the mercy of the wildest forms of fanaticism; any theory is as good as any other. But, given God's infinite wisdom and benevolence, we can be sure that he does not sport with our understanding by dealing in riddles, and we can be sure that he has made the essentials of salvation unmistakably clear.

Armed with a theory of Scripture interpretation that is—so he believed—both reasonable and reverent, Channing addressed several important doctrines. The first of these, and the one that gives Unitarianism its name, is the doctrine of God's *unity:* "There is one being, one mind, one person, one intelligent agent, and one only, to whom underived and infinite perfection and dominion belong."[23] The doctrine of the Trinity, with its "hair-breadth distinctions between being and person," reflects the sagacity of later theologians; it is not attributable to the simple and uncultivated people whom God chose as the apostles of his truth. In other words, the doctrine of the Trinity is not a biblical teaching. The language of the Bible is clear on this point: God sent his Son, Jesus does the will of the Father, and so on. Such language implies not only that Jesus is distinct from God but also that he is inferior to God. Further corroboration that the doctrine of the Trinity was not taught by the apostles is the absence of objections by the strictly monotheistic Jews and answers by the apostles. In this instance, Channing held, the argument from silence is convincing.

The Trinitarian view is, in Channing's estimate, not only unscriptural; it is illogical. According to that view, each person of the Godhead has his (its?) own particular consciousness, will, and perceptions, and each has a different role in human redemption. If differences of consciousness, will, perception, and action do not prove different *beings,* then nothing possibly could.

Another, practical objection to the doctrine of the Trinity is that it divides the attention and the affection of Christians. Rather than the one indivisible God, three beings worthy of worship and adoration are set before us, and we worry that we may be slighting one "person" of the Godhead in favor of the other two.

But the Trinitarians have not yet done with their splitting. They not only make God three beings; they make Jesus Christ two beings. Against such theological schizophrenia, Channing proclaimed the unity of Jesus of Nazareth: "Jesus is one mind, one soul, one being, as truly one as we are, and equally distinct from the one God." Channing had no use for a theory that divides Jesus into two utterly incompatible beings—one omnipotent, omniscient, and unconditioned and the other weak, relatively ignorant, and contingent. Against this two-ply, laminated Jesus, Channing posed Jesus' own words: that he is the *Son* of God, that he receives all power from God, that his authority derives from God, that he is anointed by God, and so on. Jesus claimed to be God's Christ, the long-awaited Messiah, but he did not claim to *be* God—or so Channing argued.

One motive for the Trinitarian view of Jesus as God-man is the supposed necessity for an infinite atonement—an atonement that only God himself, in some form or other, could make. But this ploy, Channing insisted, is a sleight-of-hand trick, for those who profess to find in the death of Jesus an infinite expiation for sin do not believe that Jesus' Godlike nature—his infinite and unchangeable Godhead—suffered on the cross, but only his limited human nature. Thus, even supposing—as Channing did not—that an infinite atonement were needed, it could not have been provided by finite suffering. Beyond that, the idea that an infinite atonement is needed is itself based on a fallacious argument. The reasoning is that by sinning against an infinite being we incur infinite guilt and expose ourselves to everlasting punishment. Such reasoning omits the obvious truth that guilt is proportional to a being's knowledge and powers, which in human beings are far short of infinite.

The whole idea that Jesus' suffering and death was a propitiation, infinite or otherwise, for "sin" we had no part in to placate a vengeful and tyrannical God—all this struck Channing as moral and religious nonsense. In the first place God is loving, not vengeful. The mission of Jesus is proof of God's pre-existing love. It was not undertaken to mollify God's otherwise implacable attitude toward mankind. In the second place the doctrine of depravity, or original sin, is profoundly immoral and a slander upon God's character. According to that doctrine, we are all born with an unfailing bent to evil. But if that is true, then by the plainest principles of morality we are absolved of all responsibility for our evil. For God to punish creatures born under such conditions would argue unspeakable cruelty. When we add to that repellent theory the doctrine of election, we have a system that evoked Channing's eloquent moral outrage:

This system also teaches that God selects from this corrupt mass a number to be saved, and plucks them, by a special influence, from the common ruin; that the rest of mankind, though left without that special grace which their conversion requires, are commanded to repent, under penalty of aggravated woe; and that forgiveness is promised them on terms which their very constitution infallibly disposes them to reject, and in rejecting which they awfully enhance the punishments of hell. These proffers of forgiveness and exhortations of amendment, to beings born under a blighting curse, fill our minds with a horror which we want words to express.

Compared to such a God, the most sadistically cruel human despot is a paragon of benevolence. The Calvinist picture of God, as viewed by Channing, is of a being "whom we cannot love if we would, and whom we ought not to love if we could."

Channing's own conception of God stresses his moral perfection, an attribute more important than sovereignty. All Christians agree that God is supremely just, good, and holy, but many in effect deny these properties by making God's government odious. To impute to God characteristics that we find despicable in human beings—arbitrariness, capriciousness, vengefulness, jealousy, bloodthirstiness—is to transform the Heavenly Father into a despotic and unpredictable monster. To Channing, God has not only the name but also the traits of a good parent. God punishes not for revenge or out of spite but to instruct and improve the one punished.

The most striking example of God's love, to Channing's mind, is the gift of Jesus Christ. And Channing's Christology is one of the most curious parts of his theology. As we have seen, Channing rejected the coequality of Jesus with God the Father; but he did accord Jesus a status between man and God (but closer to God), reflecting the Arian doctrine that Jesus is a unique created being who is inferior to God but superior to man.[24]

If, as we have seen, Channing rejected the "ransom" theory of the atonement, how did he construe Christ's mediation, a doctrine that he took quite seriously? The purpose of Christ's mission is "to effect a moral and spiritual deliverance of mankind; that is, to rescue men from sin and its consequences, and to bring them to a state of everlasting purity and happiness." Among the methods Jesus uses to accomplish his purpose are the following: instruction regarding God's character and government, promises of pardon to the penitent and divine assistance to the seeker of moral excellence, light thrown on the path of duty, his own spotless example, threatenings against incorrigible guilt, the Resurrection, and his power to judge, raise the dead, and confer rewards. Thus, although Channing could not accept the deity of Christ, he did accept as literally true the stories of Christ's miracles, the Resurrection, the Ascension into heaven, and Christ's sharing God's power in judgment of the world. That God raised Christ from the dead—and it was *God's* act—is the foundation of our hope of immortality. This is a far cry from the humanism that later came to be a hallmark of Unitarianism. Nonetheless, the strong conservative element in Channing's theology may be obscured by his continual insistence that love of God must be expressed in love of moral perfection and love of one's fellow human creatures—duties that too many Christians have failed to perform. Both in his conduct and in his doctrine Channing sought to be a *Christian.*

Channing was not a great philosopher or theologian, but he was a great and noble human being. Even those who differed with him respected his integrity and his moral sensitivity. Staunchly against any form of slavery, he yet drew back from plunging the nation into war—a possibility he saw more clearly than some of his more violent fellow abolitionists. He preached love, gentleness, and moral courage, and he practiced what he preached. The following tribute to Channing appears in the 1844 edition of his works: "An enlightened, disinterested human being, morally strong, and exerting a wide influence by the power of virtue, is the clearest reflection of the divine splendour on earth."

TRANSCENDENTALISM: RALPH WALDO EMERSON

The *term* Transcendentalism comes from the great German philosopher Immanuel Kant (1724–1804), but the views of most American Transcendentalists were in important ways very *un*-Kantian. Kant used "transcendental" to refer to the necessary conditions of experience—conditions that are presupposed by experience and not derived from it. In criticizing Locke, Kant argued that while all knowledge *begins* with experience it is false that all knowledge *arises from* experience. Against Locke's view of the mind as a blank tablet (*tabula rasa*) Kant contended that the mind contributes those elements that give knowledge its necessity and universality; sensation (or sense experience) provides the content of knowledge. In brief, Kant's position was that knowledge always results from a fusion of intellect and sensation. Kant's warning not to omit either aspect is embodied in his famous slogan: "Concepts without percepts are empty; percepts without concepts are blind." Applied to the history of philosophy, this dictum means that rationalists err in building grandiose philosophical schemes that are empty and that empiricists are stuck at the level of sense data. In the jargon of logic, rationalists mistakenly believe that the activity of unaided reason is a sufficient condition of knowledge, whereas empiricists fail to see that reason is a necessary condition of knowledge.

The American Transcendentalists typically ignored—if they ever read—Kant's warning against the (alleged) illicit use of reason without sensory content. They were happy with the castigation of Locke, but they had no patience with admonitions to renounce empty speculations.[25] But, as my qualifying phrase "if they ever read" suggests, most American Transcendentalists had little if any firsthand knowledge of Kant. Their exposure to German philosophy came chiefly by way of the English literary figures Samuel Taylor Coleridge and Thomas Carlyle. They were also influenced by the literary work of Goethe, Novalis, the English Romantic poets (especially William Wordsworth), and by such Indian writings as the Bhagavad-Gita. Their "Transcendentalism" is, in fact, at least as much literary as it is philosophical.

The major figures in American Transcendentalism are Emerson (1803–82), Theodore Parker (1810–60), Bronson Alcott (1799–1888), Margaret Fuller (1810–50), and Henry David Thoreau (1817–62). Among the less-well-known adherents are Orestes Brownson (1803–76), later a convert to Roman Catholicism; Frederick Hedge (1805–90); and George Ripley (1802–80). These persons were fascinating, brilliant, quixotic, and zealous to save the world. The salvation they proposed was to be effected by each person's realization that he or she is a divine incarnation. When that consciousness dawns in enough hearts and minds, wrote Emerson in his essay "Nature," "so fast will disagreeable appearances, swine, spiders, snakes, pests, mad-houses, prisons, enemies, vanish; they are temporary and shall be no more seen." The Transcendentalists' understanding of their task was no mean one. In *Transcendentalism: A Lecture,* Theodore Parker put it thus:

The problem of transcendental philosophy is no less than this, to revise the experience of mankind and try its teachings by the nature of mankind; to test ethics by conscience, science by reason; to try the creeds of the churches; the constitutions of the states by the constitution of the universe; to reverse what is wrong, supply what is wanting, and command the just.

It was such rhapsodic visions as these that led Lewis Mumford to comment: "The vast gap between the hope of the Romantic Movement and the reality of the pioneer period is one of the most sardonic jests of history."[26]

Perry Miller found three main themes in New England Transcendentalism: a search for a faith, a reaction against Unitarianism, and a revulsion against commercialism. To these three should probably be added a fourth: a faith in democracy that goes far beyond the merely political sense of that term. We shall see that Emerson, despite his pantheistic metaphysics (that is, a theory of reality that identifies God with the totality of existence), exalts the individual to a degree that, in the eyes of some critics, amounts to a *reductio ad absurdum* of his philosophy. And however the assorted Transcendentalists may differ on the details of their vision, they agree that every human being is endowed with a faculty—reason—that gives direct access to spiritual truths. This is Jonathan Edwards' sense of the heart de-empiricized, detheologized, and, above all, democratized.

Like dominoes and buttermilk, Ralph Waldo Emerson divides opinion pretty sharply. There are those who revere him as the wisest American, the greatest American philosopher, a sage of unparalleled insight. And there are those who find him a useless visionary, a denier of plain fact, a philosopher of (almost) unparalleled obscurity. And there is a third group (suggesting that the dominoes-and-buttermilk comparison is too strong) who find much to admire in Emerson but stop short of embracing his philosophical views. Among this group are some of the giants of American philosophy: William James, John Dewey, Josiah Royce, and George Santayana. Of these Santayana is probably the sharpest critic of Emerson.[27]

Whatever our final estimate of Emerson, he is a figure to be reckoned with. He is probably the only person treated in this essay with whose writings every reader will have had some contact. He is also the despair of anyone who tries to summarize his thought. For one thing, he wrote so much on so many themes. After a brief, unhappy stint as a Unitarian minister, he made his living writing and lecturing. But it is not just the sheer quantity of Emerson's writings that makes it so hard to give a capsule statement of his views. More important, Emerson was not a systematic philosopher, or at least he was not systematic in any ordinary sense. Those who read him expecting clean-cut theses and arguments are bound to be disappointed. That is not at all to say that Emerson had no identifiable philosophical position; he did and he articulated it in his own fashion, which is usually closer to poetry than to philosophy in the traditional manner. Readers who approach Emerson on his own terms, without rigid notions of what a philosopher *must* do, will find passages of great beauty, insight, and, it may be, inspiration. The most we can do is hint at something of the character and range of Emerson's writings.

It was suggested above that one of the themes of Transcendentalism is a reaction against Unitarianism. One of the things that Emerson found most distasteful about that brand of religion, especially in its conservative branches, is its excessive reliance on tradition and authority. Indeed, within Unitarianism itself a bitter struggle was raging over such questions as the role and status of Jesus Christ, the credibility of miracles, and the sacraments. Into this charged atmosphere Emerson dropped a bombshell—his "Divinity School Address," a commencement speech delivered to the graduating seniors of Harvard Divinity School, Class of 1838. The address caused a great furor, but, characteristically, Emerson remained aloof from the controversy.[28] (Oliver Wendell Holmes said that Emerson's role in the dispute was rather like that of the dead Patroclus, over whose body the Greeks and Trojans fought.)

The nub of Emerson's address is that "Historical Christianity" (an epithet for Emerson), with its sacraments, Christology, ecclesiastical machinery, and dogmas, obscured the real truth of Christ's religion: the divinity of all men. We are Christs, all of us. We need not faith *in* Christ but faith *like* Christ's. Like Christ we are all children of God; each of us has the capacity to know spiritual truths directly, without the aid of anything external, whether priests, churches, or holy books. We are able to see the beauty of spiritual, moral laws as surely as the graduating seniors could behold the beauties of the "refulgent summer" of 1838.

Historical Christianity has smothered our native capacities under a blanket of forms and dogmas. Forgetting, or denying, that God is fully in each of us (without thereby exhausting his infinite fullness), the churches point to one person (or just a few persons), one set of writings, as the only way to God. We are urged by the churches to trust this one person, this single set of writings, as leading us to God, and thereby to ignore Christ's proclamation of the divinity of the human soul. Most Unitarians wanted to humanize Christ, at least beyond the point allowed by Roman Catholic and Protestant orthodoxy. But Emerson's aim was different: he wanted to deify all of us, to raise everyone to Christ's level rather than bring him down to ours.

The Unitarians were trapped by the poverty of their philosophical outlook, which was essentially Lockean (with some new wrinkles). Trying to defend Christianity on Lockean principles proved to be impossible, as the philosophers of the Age of Reason had shown. What Emerson proposed in the "Divinity School Address" is a scrapping of Lockean sensationalism and an espousal of Transcendental Reason. As we shall see a little later, the opposition between "Understanding" and "Reason" was fundamental for Emerson, as for the Transcendentalists generally.

It is not surprising that Unitarian stalwarts such as Andrews Norton were scandalized by Emerson's address. To Norton, Emerson's views amounted to "the latest form of infidelity." But more interesting, because more perceptive and more radical, is Orestes Brownson's observation that Protestantism leads to Transcendentalism. The remark was made after Brownson's conversion to Roman Catholicism, and for him it amounted to a profound indictment of Protestantism. Given the historical fact that Protestants have often been no less willing than Catholics to imprison, exile, hang, and burn heretics, we may be surprised by Brownson's contention; but there is a fairly simple logic to it. Protestantism was originally intended to be a return to authentic Christian beginnings, to the New Testament teachings of Christ from which the Roman Catholic church had strayed. This impulse to rebirth, so characteristic of the Renaissance, was not intended to be destructive; Martin Luther wanted *reformation,* not destruction, of the church. To get back to beginnings, Protestants emphasized the primacy of Scripture, relegating priests and sacraments to ancillary roles. To reach God, one need not go through a priest in the apostolic succession; every person, no matter how lowly, is a priest before God.

Though unintended, the priesthood of all believers, with its emphasis on private judgment, raises further, more radical questions. If we do not need a human priest to approach God, why do we need authoritative, binding Scriptures or an organized church? In accepting the authority of the Bible, are we not allowing an unneeded intermediary to come between us and God? Do not the Scriptures themselves—and Christ himself—become a kind of priest or go-between? The Scriptures were written by human beings, and *we* are human beings. We do not need them to be in touch with God; we have direct access. Though the question would have horrified Edwards, is not Transcendental Reason just his "sense of the heart" shorn of its Calvinist trappings and thoroughly democratized? It is this train of reasoning that lies behind Brownson's indictment of Protestantism. To the Transcendentalist, of course, it is no indictment; it is a tribute to the germ of vital truth inherent in Protestantism.

Though not as widely read or as popular as others of Emerson's essays ("The American Scholar" and "Self-Reliance," for example), "Nature" remains perhaps the finest expression of American Transcendentalism. Readers of "Nature," published just two years before the "Divinity School Address," could hardly have been surprised to find Emerson denouncing "historical Christianity" in 1838. In the very opening lines Emerson deplored the "retrospective" character of his age. Why, he asked, waste all our energy writing biographies, history, and criticism, when we ought rather to be finding our own truths firsthand? "Why should not we have a poetry and philosophy of insight and not of tradition, and a religion by revelation to us, and not the history of theirs?" Why not indeed! "The sun shines to-day also. There is more wool and flax in the fields. There are new lands, new men, new thoughts. Let us demand our own works and laws and worship."

The person who would see nature as it is—as an expression of the Infinite Spirit—must overcome not only mundane concerns and false philosophies but also the very ubiquitousness of the evidence of the unseen world. Just as we fail to hear the music of the spheres (according to an ancient explanation) because it is omnipresent, so we may fail to see the reflection of God in the world about us, just because it *is* everywhere: "If the stars should appear one night in a thousand years, how would men believe and adore; and preserve for many generations the remembrance of the city of God which had been shown! But every night come out these envoys of beauty, and light the universe with their admonishing smile." What is needed is a childlike readiness to see and respond: "To speak truly, few adult persons can see nature. At least they have a very superficial seeing. The sun illuminates only the eye of the man, but shines into the eye and the heart of the child."

If we approach nature in the way Emerson recommends, we will find that nature is not just *there;* it subserves a final cause or purpose. This purpose can be glimpsed in the great variety of useful things and arrangements that nature provides for us, as well as in the different levels of beauty found in or pointed to by nature. A third manifestation of final cause in nature is language. Language is a vehicle of thought in three ways:

1. Words are signs of natural fact: "right" means "straight," "wrong" means "twisted," "transgression" is the "crossing of a line," and so on.

2. But language comprises more than just words; particular natural facts are symbols of particular spiritual facts. *Things* themselves are emblematic. A cunning man is a fox; a firm man is a rock; light is knowledge, and darkness is ignorance. Rivers express the flux of things: "Throw a stone into the stream, and the circles that propagate themselves are the beautiful type of all influence." Such emblems are not, Emerson insisted, just the idle fancies of poets; "they are constant and pervade nature."

3. Nature as a whole is the symbol of spirit: "The visible world and the relation of its parts, is the dial plate of the invisible." The axioms of physics translate into the laws of ethics; for example, every action has an equal and opposite reaction. This law—the third of Newton's laws of motion—was a particular favorite of Emerson, who regarded Newton as a poet. In one of his most famous essays, "Compensation," Emerson applied this law to all of reality: Every "evil" has a compensating good, but the converse is not true. (Thus, Emerson in fact applied only a truncated version of Newton's third law.)

Anyone expecting a *proof* of such assertions—or even a well-laid-out argument for them—does not know Emerson very well. If there is a proof in any sense, it is to be found in the success of Emerson's whole project. He offered us a vision, and if we do not share the vision, there is no ironclad logic by which he would force us to embrace it. Emerson did provide many illustrations of his points, but he offered very little by way of argument that the examples actually illustrate what he claimed they do.

Consider, for example, Emerson's claim that nature is a *discipline,* that is, an instructor in moral education. We learn intellectual truths from nature: similarity, difference, order, appearance, the ascent from particular to general. We may learn practical truths as well, even from such unpleasant realities as debt and poverty. In particular, we should learn that nature's dice are always loaded, that she forgives no mistakes. But we also learn that nature is made to serve, if only we exercise our mind and will. How did Emerson prove such claims? He did not; he simply made them, apparently on the assumption that the reader would *see* that they are right. (Some claims are more plausible than others. It is obvious in a pretty straightforward way that nature's dice *are* always loaded; it is not obvious, at least to many people, that nature is an emblem of spirit.)

Our first reflections on nature rest on the supposition that it is stable and substantial and that our minds are, by comparison, changing and ephemeral. But further reflection forces us to conclude that it is the mind, and not the world revealed in sense experience, that is the true center of reality. Even as simple an experience as riding on a train (not to mention an airplane, which would serve Emerson's purpose still better) may set us to thinking that, while the world changes as we change perspectives, *we* remain stable. This intimation of the reversal of orders of reality is strengthened if we consider science, poetry, and religion, all of which teach us to conform things to ideas. Such inversion of the physical and spiritual realms implies no hostility to nature. As Emerson said, he had no desire to fling stones at his "beautiful mother." Whether nature be independently real or ultimately dependent on mind, it is "alike useful and alike venerable."

Emerson's idealism saw nature in God, but nature may still be the means by which the soul is pointed to God. Unfortunately, nature is as alien to most people as God is. The root of the trouble is that most of us use only half our powers; we are stuck at the level of understanding and never reach the level of reason.[29] Understanding, with its concentration on particular observations, fractures nature into discrete pieces. The sense of the unity of the world is lost in the welter of details. Emerson put it this way:

I cannot greatly honor minuteness in details, so long as there is no hint to explain the relation between things and thoughts; no ray upon the metaphysics of conchology, of botany, of the arts, to show the relation of the forms of flowers, shells, animals, architecture, to the mind, and build science upon ideas.

What is often wanting is the synoptic vision provided by reason. Without such vision, scientists become half-sighted.[30] Even as "scientific" a philosopher as Aristotle recognized this truth when he said, "Poetry comes closer to vital truth than history."[31]

There is in all of us an almost unrecognized elemental power, which we may call reason, intuition, instinct, or conscience. There are occasional glimpses of that power unleashed, for example, in the stories of miracles in the early literature of all peoples; in the history of Jesus Christ; in the effecting of revolutions by a principle, as in the abolition of the slave trade; in hypnotism; in prayer; in self-healing; and in the wisdom of children. But these are just glimpses of light in the thick darkness. Most of us are afflicted with spiritual tunnel vision or scotoma: "The problem of restoring to the world original and eternal beauty is solved by the redemption of the soul. The ruin or blank that we see when we look at nature, is in our own eye." Spirit will resume its rightful, central place when we look again upon nature with all our powers: "The immobility or bruteness of nature is the absence of spirit."

Reading "Nature," one senses the individual being drawn into the labyrinthine reaches of the Infinite Spirit. But such was not Emerson's intention. To be sure, the individual lives, moves, and has his being in God, and without consciousness of that rootedness he is adrift and "abstracted." Emerson insisted, however, that the individual must be true to his own instincts and principles, for in doing so he will be true to the divinity within him. Thus, when Emerson wrote in "Self-Reliance" (1841), "Whoso would be a man, must be a non-conformist," he was not advocating rebellion. Still less was he preaching facile self-help formulas or extolling the power of positive thinking. He was expressing, in a concrete way, his view of the universe. God exists in every one of us. To trust our deepest self, therefore, is to trust God himself.

Why, then, is there so much *un*freedom, wretchedness, and alienation? In Rousseau's famous phrase, "Man is born free, and he is everywhere in chains." The answer is not depravity or original sin—a doctrine Emerson found blasphemous and conducive to atheism. Part of the answer lies, as Jean Jacques Rousseau argued, in the character of social institutions and practices: they often perpetuate misery and delusion. That such institutions exist and persist reflects man's limited intelligence or, more accurately, man's use of only *part* of his powers—understanding but not reason. God *does* exist in all persons, but he does not negate their finitude. To claim the birthright of knowledge—and, with it, happiness—one must renounce all sorts of external claims upon one's loyalties. In affirming one's deepest self, one realizes something universal in oneself; indeed, individual reason is of a piece with Universal Reason: "To believe your own thought, to believe that what is true for you in your private heart is true for all—that is genius." But there is still a sense in which Sören Kierkegaard was right: salvation is a lonely business. It was this realization (along, no doubt, with his temperament) that kept Emerson from entering into the "causes" of his day as enthusiastically as some of his fellow Transcendentalists. He believed in reform, of course, but the reform must come from within the individual: "Nothing can bring you peace but yourself. Nothing can bring you peace but the triumph of principles."

Self-reliance applied specifically to the world of the scholar had been the theme four years earlier (in 1837) of one of Emerson's best-known essays, "The American Scholar." The essay has been described as a kind of intellectual declaration of independence from Europe. But even a casual reading shows that Emerson finds many home-grown enemies of independence and integrity: materialism, worship of the past, timorousness before the many faces of authority, a variety of mindless enthusiasms. We need not so much scholars as *men thinking.* The phrase suggests an integral person engaged in one of the things human beings do.

The resources of the scholar—or man thinking—are nature, the mind of the past (especially in the form of books), and action. About nature we have already said enough. Books, properly used, are among the best of things; improperly used, they are among the worst. Worshiped as the main repository of truth, books are terribly mischievous; they stand between the scholar and his own thoughts. The scholar in that case degenerates into a bookworm. Action, too, is a resource, and one that Emerson was never quite able to handle satisfactorily. Action, for the scholar, provides *material* for contemplation. By getting too caught up in activity, the scholar runs the risk of losing his independence and his integrity (or centeredness) and of giving over his own judgment to the tyranny of "the popular judgments and modes of action." Emerson knew this from his own experience. Being the most famous American literary figure of his day, Emerson was constantly being pulled this way and that by individuals and groups eager to secure his participation in, or at least his blessing on, their pet schemes.

In at least one respect, Emerson did not himself exemplify the ideal of the American scholar. Though his work bears the stamp of his own genius, it also bears the clear marks of European influence. It remained for Charles Sanders Peirce (pronounced "purse"), the founder and most brilliant representative of pragmatism, to develop the first genuinely indigenous American philosophy.

PRAGMATISM: CHARLES S. PEIRCE, WILLIAM JAMES, AND JOHN DEWEY

Late in 1859, Charles Darwin published *The Origin of Species,* culminating more than a quarter-century of investigation and thought and marking one of the most important events in the history of science. In the work Darwin argued that all life, including human life, has descended from a few simple forms (possibly just one form) by way of modifications and adaptations. He proposed to account for the process of descent by the theory of natural selection. Darwin's account, resting on an impressive body of data culled from flora and fauna scattered over half the globe, challenged the belief that the hierarchy of species is fixed and unchanging. If Darwin was right, then not only the natural world but man himself would have to be viewed in a different light. Here indeed was a Copernican revolution in biology!

At first a number of scientists were skeptical of Darwin's results, especially those who took science to be the process of bringing direct observations under laws. Of course, neither Darwin nor anyone else ever *saw* the process of evolution at work. Darwin had to admit that he had never *observed* natural selection either. But criticisms of this sort were based on a rather simple-minded conception of science, and within a couple of decades most biologists had accepted the essentials of Darwin's theory.

Not so in philosophy and theology, especially the latter. The fiercest, most acrimonious disputes, which Darwin avoided as much as possible, centered on the implications of evolution for metaphysics, epistemology, ethics, sociology, and, above all, religion. The battles between Thomas H. Huxley, who called himself "Darwin's bulldog," on the one side and Bishop Samuel Wilberforce and William Gladstone on the other were spirited and caustic. (In one debate, Bishop Wilberforce inquired of Huxley whether Huxley had descended from the apes on his mother's or his father's side.) Amusing as this part of the story might be, we must pass it over. We shall also be obliged to pass over another, more philosophically important, part of the story. I refer to the work of such evolution-centered philosophers as John Fiske (1842–1901), an American disciple of Herbert Spencer. Fiske tried to show that, far from being an enemy of religion, evolution, properly understood, is its strongest ally. His lectures and writings gave Fiske a good deal of exposure and helped make the theory of evolution more palatable to many who feared its apparent antagonism to religion. Fiske's version of evolution did not appeal to tougher-minded philosophers, however, and he remains a minor, unoriginal thinker.[32]

Charles S. Peirce

The influence of evolution on Charles Sanders Peirce (1839–1914) was in a sense pervasive; but his thinking was in important ways non-Darwinian, almost anti-Darwinian. In particular, he rejected natural selection as an adequate explanation of organic evolution and, *a fortiori,* as an explanation of human consciousness. We shall see that Peirce developed an evolutionary metaphysics that is antimechanistic and antideterministic.

For several reasons—one of which is that he never held a long-term appointment at a university—Peirce never wrote a book in philosophy. Whether that circumstance is to be deplored is perhaps debatable; but in any case Peirce wrote a very large number of papers on philosophical and scientific topics. These were originally published in a variety of periodicals, such as *Popular Science Monthly,* the *Monist,* the *Nation,* and *North American Review,* and in at least one compilation, James A. Baldwin's *Dictionary of Philosophy and Psychology,* and were gathered together in eight volumes of collected papers.[33] For over fifty years Peirce wrote on just about every conceivable area of philosophy, as well as on a number of topics in logic and mathematics. Perhaps his most substantial contributions were those in logic; but he made original, provocative contributions to the theory of knowledge, the theory of meaning, the theory of signs, metaphysics, and cosmology. It is obviously impossible for us to cover, even briefly, all these areas. We shall, instead, concentrate on two topics: (1) the theory of meaning and the method for which Peirce is best known and to which he applied the term "pragmatism" and (2) an evolutionary metaphysics, which Peirce took to be a natural extension of his theory of meaning but which his critics have attacked as inconsistent with his pragmatism.[34]

Because Peirce's pragmatic analysis of meaning comes straightforwardly out of his analysis of belief, we shall look first at one of his better-known papers, "The Fixation of Belief," which appeared in *Popular Science Monthly* in November, 1877. Doubt and belief are opposite states of mind: doubt is an uneasy, agitated, unpleasant state, whereas belief is thought at rest, satisfied. When we are in doubt, we seek to assuage the irritation of that doubt, to replace it with a state of belief. Peirce called this struggle to attain belief "inquiry," though he admitted that the term is sometimes not very apt. Belief, on the other hand, represents a set of attitudes toward what we would do, how we would act, in certain situations. Belief results in the establishment of a rule of action, in *habit.* Belief is, in other words, indissolubly tied to what we do, or what we would do, in certain circumstances. Doubt has no such tendency to result in the formation of habits. If I believe that a certain ladder will support my weight, I have no hesitation in using it to climb. The belief is something I am prepared to act on. If, on the contrary, I doubt whether the ladder will support my weight, I am hesitant to use it; my action is inhibited. In this way Peirce linked doubt and belief to behavior and thereby divested them of some of their inscrutable privacy. It is this tie between belief and habit and action that led Peirce to call his theory "pragmatism" (from the Greek word *pragma,* which means "act or practice").

Although everyone seeks to get rid of doubt, to pass from doubt to belief, not everyone does so in the same way. Peirce distinguished four ways of effecting this transition—of fixing belief—but only one of them is rational. The first method is that of *tenacity,* by which one simply seizes on whatever belief is readiest to hand and holds on like a bulldog. This method is conducive to a certain stability of character (if not to a reputation for good sense), but it is unarguably irrational—if the aim of inquiry is to find the truth. The second method of fixing belief is that of *authority,* whether the authority is political, ecclesiastical, or scientific. Adopting this method may save us a lot of thought, and it may promote social cohesiveness (something that the method of tenacity does not do), but it too is irrational. To take one of many possible examples, consider the following: Suppose we define "true" as "approved by the state." Then the perfectly natural and sensible question, "Does the state approve true beliefs?" becomes the absurd question, "Does the state approve beliefs the state approves?"[35] The third method of fixing belief, and the one most admired by philosophers, is that of *a priori reason.* By this method one adopts those beliefs that are most agreeable to reason—a "reason" that usually turns out to be only the individual's reason and is often indistinguishable from personal preferences or tastes. Such beliefs do not rest on observed facts, or do so only to an insignificant degree. Though morally and intellectually superior to the first two

methods, a priori reason is also ultimately irrational. As an instance of the repressive power of this method, consider the centuries passed under the a priori "certainty" that the planets move in circular orbits. Even the revolutionary Copernicus did not question this particular "truth," and as a consequence was forced to retain that model of ad hoc irrationality, the theory of epicycles.

The reason the first three methods of fixing beliefs are irrational is this: They do not allow for the correction of mistaken beliefs, or, to put the same point differently, they do not permit a nonarbitrary distinction between truth and falsity. Once one starts with an error, he is bound to it. What is needed is a method that will subject our beliefs to the test of reality. Fortunately, we have such a method, the method of *science.* "Science" is here construed very generously, including such everyday practices as chilling milk, starting fires, and boiling water, as well as the recondite hypotheses and methods of astrophysicists and biochemists. In science our beliefs are exposed to the test of something independent of the beliefs themselves. If these beliefs are wrong, the scientific method will (eventually, anyway) show that fact. An obvious evolutionary advantage attaches to use of the scientific method: Those organisms whose beliefs stand the test of reality have better survival value than do those organisms whose beliefs rest on prejudice or personal preference.

In one of his most famous essays, "How to Make Our Ideas Clear," Peirce proceeded to develop some thoughts broached in "The Fixation of Belief." As the title indicates, Peirce was interested in a reliable method for getting clear about our ideas. ("Ideas" in this context should be taken broadly to mean concepts, beliefs, hypotheses, and so on. Some philosophers would be inclined to interpret the problem linguistically, that is, as having to do with the meanings of words or propositions.) Peirce complained that, even though science has grown stupendously during the past two to three hundred years, logicians had done practically nothing since the time of Réne Descartes (1596–1650) to help us clarify our ideas.

Descartes distinguished two levels of clarity in ideas. An idea is said to be *clear* if we have an easy familiarity with it, if we are able to recognize it whenever we encounter it. (That, at least, was Peirce's version of Descartes' view.) An idea is said to be *distinct* if, in addition to being clear, it contains nothing that is *un*clear. This latter condition—so Peirce said—amounts to our being able to give an abstract definition of the idea. Now what is wrong with Descartes' method is that it is too subjective, too dependent on introspection, which may be arbitrary and idiosyncratic. Peirce alleged that it never occurred to Descartes that an idea might *seem* clear without actually *being* so.[36] It was time for logic to catch up with science, and so Peirce proposed a third level of clarity, the pragmatic.

Recall that doubt is an irritant that is assuaged by belief and that the essence of belief is the establishment of a rule of action, a habit. This means that beliefs differ, if at all, in the different modes of action (or possible action) to which they lead. If two ostensibly different beliefs do not differ in this way—if they do not give rise to different modes of action—then they do not differ in any significant way. This truth is often obscured by nonessential verbal differences or by differences in the manner of our consciousness of two apparently different beliefs.

Peirce offered an illustration of what he had in mind. Consider the dispute between Roman Catholics and Protestants over the doctrine of transubstantiation, which has to do with the elements of the Sacrament of the Lord's Supper, the bread and the wine. Protestants generally hold that the bread and the wine become the body and blood of Jesus only in a symbolic sense: they nourish the soul as bread and wine nourish the body. But orthodox Roman Catholics believe that the bread and wine literally become the body and blood of Jesus: the substance of the elements undergoes a miraculous transformation, even though the outward appearances—the accidents—remain unchanged (hence the word transubstantiation). Peirce's verdict was that if Roman Catholics and Protestants agree on all the sensible properties of the bread and the wine, as they do, then they are deceived if they think that there is any factual issue left to argue about. To talk as if something that has all the sensible properties of wine is in reality blood is, in Peirce's blunt phrase, "senseless jargon." It is impossible that we should have in our minds any idea that is wholly disconnected from its actual or conceived sensible effects. Indeed, our idea of anything *is* our idea of its sensible effects.[37]

Peirce was then ready to state his rule for attaining the third grade of clearness of apprehension, which he sometimes referred to as the "pragmatic maxim": "Consider what effects, which might conceivably have practical bearings, we conceive the object of our conception to have. Then, our conception of these effects is the whole of our conception of the object." The repeated use of "conceive" and its linguistic relatives underlines Peirce's determination to avoid identifying the meaning of a concept with *acts.* His point is that there can be no *general* sundering of a concept from the acts to which it *would* lead under appropriate conditions. The word "practical" may be troublesome too. No one detested Philistinism, Babbittry, and the gospel of greed more than Peirce; thus there is more than a little irony in the misconception that pragmatism, Peirce's child, is a celebration of entrepreneurial success. Peirce's interests were theoretical. In fact, he went as far as to say that science is the study of useless things; useful things will get studied without the aid of scientific men. To obviate misunderstandings, Peirce began to use the term "experimental" in place of "practical" when he wrote of the pragmatic conception of meaning. Thus, for example, Peirce formulated the pragmatic maxim as follows: "If one can define accurately all of the conceivable experimental phenomena which the affirmation or denial of a concept could imply, one will have therein a complete definition of the concept, and *there is absolutely nothing more in it.*"[38]

Let us now see how Peirce applied his pragmatic maxim to a few specific cases. What does it mean to say that something is *hard?* It means simply that the object will resist being scratched by many other objects. There is nothing

mysterious about it, and there is no divorcing these effects (or *conceived* effects) from the meaning of the term.[39] A similar analysis is available for the notion of *weight*: To say that something has weight is to say that in the absence of support it will fall—that and nothing more. But the most interesting case of this kind is *force,* because the notion is often surrounded by an aura of mystery. Even competent physicists (of Peirce's day at any rate) said that we know the effects of force but we do not know what force itself is. For Peirce such a modest-sounding disclaimer was nonsense:

The idea which the word force excites in our minds has no other function than to affect our actions, and these actions can have no reference to force otherwise than through its effects. Consequently, if we know what the effects of force are, we are acquainted with every fact which is implied in saying that a force exists, and there is nothing more to know.

For the philosopher surely the notion of *reality* is the one that excites him most; and Peirce had a pragmatic clarification of that concept too. If we consider reality and its opposite, fiction, we see that the crucial difference between them is the independence of our opinions that reality enjoys. Fictions we may arrange, alter, and embellish to suit our fancy, but what is *real* defies our efforts to cut it to our own fit. So Peirce offered a tentative definition of *reality*: The real is "that whose characters are independent of what anybody may think them to be." Herein lies the advantage of the scientific method, referred to earlier.

But this account of reality is not really clear. Peirce tried to link reality to true belief, and so how do we distinguish true belief—belief in the real—from false belief—belief in fiction? The answer has to be related to the use of the scientific method. One striking difference between this method and the other methods of fixing belief (tenacity, authority, a priori reason) is that those who apply it to a common problem are bound, in the long run, to reach the same answer. This property of the scientific method is evident, for example, in studies of the velocity of light. Many researchers, starting at different times and places and with different interests and preconceptions, were driven by a force outside themselves to the same solution.

Connecting truth and reality with the prosecution of scientific inquiry, Peirce offered a modified version of his first definition of *reality*: "The opinion which is fated to be ultimately agreed to by all who investigate, is what we mean by the truth, and the object represented in this opinion is the real. That is the way I would explain reality." Of course, Peirce meant nothing superstitious by fate. He meant simply that the truth is what would be agreed upon if investigation were pressed far enough. In this way Peirce was able to make a general link between human knowledge and reality, without making reality dependent upon what anybody thinks about it and without endorsing any sanguine expectations about the *actual* course of human history. Human perversity and the limitations of intelligence may prevent us from ever finding the answers to certain questions, but the truth is still what *would* be found if inquiry were pushed far enough.

Peirce's insistence on the *social* character of knowledge

contrasts sharply with Descartes' individualistic conception. To Peirce, Descartes' picture of a solitary individual alone with his thoughts was sheer myth. The very recognition of ourselves *as* individuals takes place in a social context and is inconceivable apart from that context. Peirce's analysis of doubt and belief shows that Descartes' claim to doubt everything except his own existence is bogus to the core. Given Peirce's account of meaning in terms of "practical" consequences, there is clearly no real difference between Descartes' attitude when he was supposedly doubting and when he had supposedly overcome the doubts by the power of reason.

This scuttling of Descartes' famous voyage through the shoals of doubt illustrates how Peirce proposed to handle metaphysical problems. Contrary to what one might expect, Peirce had no animus toward metaphysics. In fact, he thought that metaphysics is inevitable; those who propose to abandon metaphysics invariably have one of their own, but they do not want to subject it to scrutiny. So far from wanting to renounce metaphysics, Peirce wanted to renovate it and make it a fit companion for the successful sciences. What disturbed him was the ill-success of metaphysics compared with the success of the other sciences. What was needed was a rigorous application of the pragmatic method to metaphysics. At least two results might be expected from such an application: (1) pseudo problems would be exposed and discarded as spurious and (2) real problems would be clarified and ways of solving them opened up.

It should be plain by now that Peirce was arguing for a *method* of attacking problems, including those we call metaphysical. For Peirce, pragmatism did not amount to a philosophical theory about this or that issue; it was, rather, a way of doing philosophy. Nevertheless, as it turned out, Peirce's pragmatism led him to certain metaphysical views. One such view is that determinism is false, that chance happenings are an objective feature of the world. Classical determinism, as represented by Thomas Hobbes, Simon Laplace, or, as we have seen, Jonathan Edwards, holds that absolutely everything in the universe is the inevitable and precise result of antecedent causes. If we had exhaustive knowledge of the world at any one moment—so the theory goes—we could (in principle) retrodict everything that had ever happened and predict everything that ever would happen in the future. Peirce argued that such retrodictive and predictive knowledge is not possible even in principle; no matter how much we knew of the world at any one time, we would encounter genuinely unpredictable events at some other time. This is Peirce's doctrine of objective chance ("tychism" is Peirce's own neologism for the theory); it embodies what Chauncey Wright, an older contemporary of Peirce's and a precursor of pragmatism, had called "cosmic weather." What is the evidence for this kind of contingency? Contrary to what William James sometimes argued, it is not a matter of moral intuition or feeling; it is a matter of applying the pragmatic (that is, scientific) method to the problem.

The first thing to notice about the theory of determinism is that it is an a priori thesis that is not based on fact or observation. No factual hypothesis can have the infallibility, exactness, and universality claimed for determinism. (Peirce often called his own view of scientific method "fallibilism," which denies that human knowledge can ever attain to absolute certainty, absolute exactitude, or absolute universality.) As a working scientist of many years' experience, Peirce was convinced that actual observations can never be ideally precise and that any pretension to the contrary is unempirical, unverifiable dogma.

If determinism were offered as a hypothesis about the world, it would be subject to decisive refutation, as we shall see shortly. But the suspicion persists that those who hold such a theory are willing to cleave to it against all the evidence. In that case it is not the sort of theory that the self-correcting method of science might verify or diversity. It is, rather, a good example of an a priori "truth" masquerading as a scientific principle. In fact, however, science makes no use of such a principle. All science needs, or could possibly make use of, are statistical regularities. Even if strict determinism were true, it would be of no value or relevance to the prosecution of scientific inquiry. For science "exact" always means "exact enough." Determinism, on the contrary, traffics in fraudulent absolutes.

But the doctrine of tychism consists of more than exposing determinism as unscientific dogmatism; it includes positive evidence for the existence of chance in the world. The most obtrusive feature of nature—so ubiquitous that we are likely to forget it—is its *variety.* Such diversity and manifoldness is direct evidence of chance or spontaneity; or, as Peirce argued, we could even say that it *is* spontaneity: "I don't know what you can make out of the meaning of spontaneity but newness, freshness, and diversity."[40] Unless all this amazing variety and diversification is an illusion, mechanistic determinism must be false, for the application of mechanical law cannot produce diversity where none was before. Mechanical law prescribes *one* determinate result; out of like antecedents only like consequents can come. Thus evolution itself—the idea that things *grew*—is inconsistent with strict determinism. For Peirce these considerations amounted to a clear confutation of determinism. They also illustrated how competing metaphysical theories can be subjected to close scrutiny in the light of facts and logic, with the verdict going to one theory and against the other. It was, to Peirce, heartening proof that philosophers can *settle* some issues. (It hardly need be added that Peirce's hopeful expectation of widespread agreement among philosophers proved to be baseless.)

The doctrine of objective chance, then, is an indispensable part of Peirce's evolutionary metaphysics. Without chance, spontaneity, the world would be at a dead level of stagnation. But it is equally obvious that the world is not a chaos. Things happen for the most part in predictable ways; even if the predictability is limited, it is real. Another crucial part of Peircean metaphysica, thus, is *lawful* change or growth. This aspect of reality Peirce called "synechism." Laws are not absolute; they reflect statistical regularities among irregularities. Further, laws themselves are growing, or, to put it another way, reality is very gradually becoming more orderly, more lawful. In a manner analogous to his earlier linking of belief to habits, Peirce accounted for the development of natural laws by the tendency of reality (both "mental" and "material") to acquire habits. This insistence on the reality of *laws* is part and parcel of Peirce's realism, and contrasts sharply with nominalism, the view that only individuals are real.

Peirce's metaphysics presents us with a picture of reality growing out of absolute chaos (at some infinitely distant past time) toward absolute order (at some infinitely distant future time). In explaining how and why such growth is possible, Peirce enunciated one of his most intriguing and boldly speculative notions: the doctrine of evolutionary love (or "agapasm," as Peirce, in characteristic indulgence of his weakness for ugly neologisms, called it). It was obvious to Peirce that growth requires a sympathetic regard for the other, that harmony is inconsistent with unchecked egoism. Thus the growth of reality toward greater order and stability is evidence of cosmic love. This Gospel of Love (as reflected in St. John's identification of God and love) is set against the Gospel of Greed, which Peirce found exemplified in the nineteenth-century conviction that progress occurs by one's trampling his neighbor under foot whenever the opportunity presents itself.[41]

Some critics have charged that Peirce's pragmatic theory of meaning is inconsistent with his metaphysical views, especially his realism regarding laws and his evolutionary metaphysics. Whether or not the charge is justified, the fact is that both his earlier pragmatism and his metaphysics exhibit a high order of genius, and both elements of his philosophy have influenced other thinkers. In particular Peirce profoundly influenced three of America's greatest philosophers, William James, Josiah Royce, and John Dewey.

Reading Peirce, one is struck with the great range of topics he took on—a reflection of his many-sided literacy. No American philosopher—unless it would be Alfred North Whitehead, who was a transplanted Englishman—can match Peirce's combination of thorough scientific training and broad knowledge of the history of philosophy. Out of the mixture of native gifts, superb training, and unremitting dedication came America's most original philosopher, and quite possibly its greatest.

William James

Among American philosophers only John Dewey begins to approach William James (1842–1910) as a figure of worldwide fame. To many James is *the* American philosopher.

No one ever wrote philosophy with more verve, freshness, and humanity than did William James. Someone has aptly observed that William James wrote psychology and philosophy like a novelist and that his brother, Henry James, Jr., wrote novels like a psychologist or philosopher. William's sister said that her brother would bring life and joy to a treadmill. Alfred North Whitehead referred to James as "that adorable genius." Even George Santayana, who detested much of James's philosophy, seemed to love James himself.

Nothing human was alien to James—the normal, the abnormal, the eccentric, the bizarre, the rational, the irrational—and his writings reflect the wide range of his interests. He wrote one of the greatest of all psychological treatises, *The Principles of Psychology,* a work that marks him as one of the founders of modern scientific psychology. But he also wrote one of the classics of religious philosophy, *The Varieties of Religious Experience.* And more than any other philosopher, James is identified with pragmatism.

Like Peirce, James took the analysis of meaning to be the fundamental philosophical problem. Indeed, there is a sense in which everything James wrote sprang from his theory of meaning. (Let it be stated at once that the links to that theory sometimes become rather tenuous.) If we want to know what a belief, an idea, or a statement means, we must look to the consequences of the belief, idea, or statement. How would my experience be different if the belief were true? If there are no practical differences between the belief's being true and being false, then the belief is without meaning: "There can *be* no difference anywhere that doesn't *make* a difference elsewhere—no difference in abstract truth that doesn't express itself in a difference in concrete fact and in conduct consequent upon that fact, imposed on somebody, somehow, somewhere, and somewhen."[42] The pragmatic method requires us to look away from putative first principles and supposed necessities to the consequences of ideas and beliefs. (It was this emphasis on the future that led George Santayana to comment on the pragmatist's "strange reduction of yesterday to tomorrow.")

So far there is nothing in James's theory to which Peirce would object. But whereas Peirce confined his pragmatic analysis to *meaning,* James went on to develop a pragmatic theory of *truth.* Though James intended nothing of the kind, some of his formulations smack of the grossest sort of relativism. For example, in his book *Pragmatism,* James defined "true" as follows: "The true . . . is only the expedient in the way of our thinking, just as the right is only the expedient in the way of our behaving." Even though James went on immediately to qualify this unfortunate statement in important ways, the linking of truth and right to expediency was enough to send shivers up and down Peirce's realistic spine. To many James's version of pragmatism seemed an invitation to cynicism, to a kind of philosophical Machiavellianism. Josiah Royce quipped that a pragmatist on the witness stand in court would, presumably, swear to tell the expedient, the whole expedient, and nothing but the expedient, so help him future experience.

It was natural that Peirce and James should have developed their pragmatic theories in different, and even opposite, directions. Peirce's scientific interests were mathematics, physics, and chemistry, the subject matter of which can be rather neatly separated from human concerns. James, on the other hand, studied physiology, medicine, and psychology, whose connections with human activities are intimate. Peirce became much more a disinterested, ivory-tower spectator than was ever possible for James. From the beginning James's conception of "practical consequences" ran to concrete, humanly important matters. It is not enough that the consequences are of an abstract, scientific sort; they must be such as to make life better, happier. For James pragmatism embodied, as it seldom or never did for Peirce, a call to action, a call to make the world better for ourselves and our fellow human beings.[43]

The concretely practical character of James's pragmatism is clear even in his defense of metaphysics: "The whole function of philosophy ought to be to find out what definite difference it will make to you and me, at definite instants of our life, if this world-formula or that world-formula be the true one."[44] This view runs counter to much of the history of philosophy, which takes the axioms of metaphysics to be self-evident truths. For James they are neither necessary rational principles (such as those found in mathematics) nor propositions of fact; they are postulates of rationality. Among the propositions James had in mind are these: "Nature is simple and invariable"; "nature makes no leaps"; "nothing is or happens without a reason"; "ex nihilo nihil fit"; "whatever is in the effect must be in the cause." Such propositions are not stopping places. They are *ideals* that keep working to reduce our world to more rational, understandable form. If nature *did* obey these laws, she would be more intelligible, and we try to show that she does obey them. But our efforts express a hope, not a self-evident truth. James went as far as to say that many so-called metaphysical principles are at bottom only expressions of aesthetic feeling.

As an illustration of James's irreverent treatment of sacred cows, consider the principle of causality: "Nothing can happen without a cause." Philosophers as different as Descartes and Locke regarded this principle as self-evident. Against such awe-struck acquiescence James contended that we do not really know what a cause is or what causality consists in. We probably do not want to go as far as David Hume (1711–76), who argued that our knowledge of causation reduces to observations of regular sequences; but we still know very little of what it is. Our use of "cause" is an altar to an unknown god. Given this undogmatic skepticism, James could attack determinism without any sense of hurling himself against an impregnable fortress of self-evident truth. And attack it he did, most notably in the essay "The Dilemma of Determinism."

Peirce attacked determinism with the tools of logic and science; James mounted his attack with the tools of moral feeling and sentiment. For James the issue between determinism and indeterminism could not be settled merely by an appeal to the facts, and we shall see why shortly. But we should state at once that for James the issue concerned what the world is really like, just as theism and atheism do. Determinism affirms, and indeterminism denies, that every event is necessitated by some other event or set of events. The indeterminist asserts that there are chance, or uncaused, events, and the determinist denies that there are any chance, or uncaused, events. The issue is a clear one: The truth must lie with one side or the other, and its lying with one side makes the other side false.

Given that just one of these competing theories can be true, and given that the theories are about the world, why can we not appeal to the facts—to science—to get an unequivocal answer? Stated briefly, James's reply was that science has to do with facts, not with possibilities, and the determinism-indeterminism dispute concerns possibilities. Suppose that a volition has occurred. Could it have been other than it is? The determinist says no, and the indeterminist says yes. But notice that the question has to do with

what *might*, or *could*, have happened. Science deals with what *does*, or *did*, happen. Thus, although the issue between determinism and indeterminism concerns what the world is really like, it cannot be resolved by an appeal to facts, that is, to what *is*.

In point of fact philosophers do not adopt determinism or indeterminism on the basis of facts, whether or not they *could* do so. They opt for one or the other of the two positions on the basis of feeling, sentiment, faith, postulates. One person *feels* that the world is more rational with possibilities excluded and becomes a determinist. Another person *feels* that the world is more rational (and certainly more habitable) with possibilities included and becomes an indeterminist. With all the flourish about facts and logic, we choose one way or another—or refuse to make an explicit choice—because of some sentiment or feeling. Each person will—and should—choose for himself or herself. James would not, therefore, try to *prove* that indeterminism is true and determinism false. He would, rather, opt for indeterminism, would act *as if* it were true, and try to show some of the undesirable consequences and problems of determinism. (As it turns out, James's polemic against determinism is considerably more than an appeal to feeling. If his arguments are sound, there are good *logical* reasons for believing determinism to be false.)

Before going any further, we should be clear that James rejected what he called "soft" determinism, the compatibilist view that freedom may coexist with determinism (that was Jonathan Edwards' position). For James, soft determinism is "a quagmire of evasion under which the real issue of fact has been entirely smothered." Some soft determinists (Edwards) identified freedom with the absence of constraint or restraint; others (Spinoza), with necessity properly understood; and still others (possibly Augustine), with "bondage to the highest." But these senses of "freedom" trivialize the whole issue in that they present no problem whatever. It is perfectly obvious that, in these senses, we are sometimes free and sometimes not. For that reason James proposed to drop the word "freedom" and substitute "indeterminism."

Readers will recall that Edwards argued that the question of determinism does not enter into the proper analysis of freedom, that the issue of freedom versus unfreedom has nothing to do with how the will is determined. James disagreed; he sided with the Arminians in holding that the excluded question must be broached. In James's view one cannot believe in both determinism and freedom because the real issue is determinism versus indeterminism. The determinist says that the world is absolutely governed by inexorable laws, and that whatever did not in fact happen *could* not have happened. The indeterminist, on the contrary, says that the world is only approximately lawful, that possibilities are real. Clearly, one cannot consistently hold to both theses, and the soft determinist who wants both freedom and determinism is muddled.

To what dilemma of determinism does the title of James's essay refer? The dilemma is illustrated, but not exhausted, by the phenomenon of *regret*, which James brilliantly exploited to make his deepest cut against determinism. When we regret something that occurred because of our choice, we must, James argued, suppose that our volition was not the inevitable outcome of earlier events. We must, that is, assume *in*determinism. (Of course, some regrets are idle, those, for example, that pertain to events that no one could have prevented. But some regrets remain, even for the wisest, most prudent of us.)

Regret is a problem for the determinist, for in his view what happened could not possibly have failed to happen. As an example James cited a famous murder case. A Brockton, Massachusetts, man became bored with his wife, lured her to a lonely spot, and shot her four times. Lying gravely wounded, she lifted her head and asked, "You didn't do it on purpose, did you, dear?" As he raised a rock and smashed her skull, he replied, "No, I didn't do it on purpose." For the determinist, we cannot isolate that grisly incident and condemn the murderer. The whole universe conspired to bring it about; it was eternally necessary.

What are we to think of such a universe? The natural and spontaneous response is that the universe would be better without such wanton cruelty; but if we are determinists, our natural response implies that the universe is tainted or flawed. Things would be better if they were, in some respects, different; but they cannot possibly be different if the determinist is right. We must, if we are determinists, regret that the universe *cannot* be what it *ought* to be. We must, as James put it, "regret . . . that whole frame of things of which the murder is one member." That is, of course, a kind of cosmic pessimism.

How is the determinist to escape from such pessimism? Abandon the judgment of regret; adopt the optimistic view that such things as the Brockton murder are, from a higher standpoint, really good. Maybe the world is better for the cruelty, treachery, and unmerited suffering that it contains.

Quite apart from being morally outrageous, this "escape" is illusory. If we try to escape our pessimism by appealing to some higher order of things, then our judgments of regret must be wrong. They are wrong because they assert, falsely, that things like murder are wrong. They are wrong, to put it another way, because they say that something impossible ought to be. But these mistaken judgments, like everything else, are necessary; *they* could not be other than they are. Thus it makes just as little sense to say that these judgments are wrong (that is, that they ought to be other than what they *must* be) as to say that murder is wrong. We cannot say either that the Brockton murder was wrong or that the judgment condemning the murder was wrong; both are equally inescapable. And yet simple logic seems to require that *one* of these judgments is wrong: If we were wrong to condemn the Brockton murder, then we must be right to judge that the first judgment was wrong. But determinism prevents us from making either judgment. The determinist is forced to embrace a flat contradiction.

The original dilemma was that we cannot have a universe in which a *wrong* (the Brockton murder) is replaced by a *right.* This reflection led to cosmic pessimism, from which we escaped only by getting into a *second* dilemma: that we cannot replace the wrong judgment of regret by the right judgment that the murder is good. We get out of one dilemma only by sinking deeper into the other. And a little reflection will show that the dilemma crops up however many removes we get from the original judgment.

James offered us a *reductio ad absurdum* argument against determinism. If a set of assumptions leads to an absurdity, we must seek out and repudiate the offending assumption, and that assumption in this case is determinism. The only plausible way out of the difficulty is to reject determinism. But, of course, there is no law saying that we must be sensible. The argument is not coercive against someone who is willing to accept a world that is not only bad but replete with absurdities—a world, for example, in which we both make judgments of regret *and* assert that nothing could possibly have been different from what it was. To such an unrepentant and illogical pessimist James has nothing more to say. The pessimist makes fewer demands on the world and on his own rationality than James does. James's world is a world of chance, of real possibilities, a world in which human action and effort make sense, a world that is at once vulnerable to evil and pregnant with possibilities for good.

In one of his most famous essays, "The Will to Believe" (a title that James later said should have been "The *Right* to Believe"), James took a somewhat different tack on moral and religious questions but reached a conclusion that in spirit is close to the one reached in "The Dilemma of Determinism." What attitude ought we take on the problem of evidence for our beliefs? A possible attitude is the one expressed by William K. Clifford, who asserted, with something approaching religious fervor, that we ought never believe anything for which we do not have positive evidence. James found this attitude puzzling in one who championed the scientific method, for, if scientists actually followed Clifford's advice, they would be confined to a few trivially apparent truths. The bold and creative scientific spirit would suffocate in such a repressive atmosphere. How can one find the truth if he is unwilling to venture beyond the evidence he has in hand? Or, more radically, how could he ever *get* any evidence if he did not already have beliefs *before* he has the evidence?

But it was not scientific or factual questions that engaged James's attention in this essay. He was interested in that large and profoundly important set of questions that admit of no scientific or logical answer—questions, for example, about the meaning of life, the existence of God, and what we ought to do. Some of these questions are simply unavoidable: Even in refusing to consider them we make a decision about them. Applied to questions of this kind, Clifford's dictum is irrational. James's own answer was that, if a question cannot be decided on "intellectual" grounds, and if it meets certain conditions, we may legitimately answer the question on emotional (or what James called "passional") grounds. We may take the answer that we find most satisfying.

James has sometimes been accused of offering a carte blanche for any kind of wild or erratic belief, but such a charge is baseless. James was perfectly clear that factual or scientific questions must be answered by scientific means. It would be insanity, not a legitimate exercise of the right to believe, to decide on emotional grounds whether a given substance is poisonous. This negative test—that the question cannot be decided on intellectual grounds (as the question of toxicity, for example, *can* be)—is crucial. But James added another condition: The option we are faced with must be *genuine.* An option is genuine only if it is momentous (as opposed to trivial), living (as opposed to dead), and forced (as opposed to avoidable). There are, to be sure, problems connected with applying these standards. Among other things the first two properties depend largely on subjective factors. And the third property can be tricky. For example, the question whether to be a Protestant or a Roman Catholic may be a burning issue to some and of no interest at all to others. On its face the option is not forced (one could be a Muslim or a Jew or an atheist), but for some people it may represent the only two real possibilities open to them. James was quite willing to allow a great deal of latitude here, but his insistence on these criteria suggests his unwillingness to extend the right to believe just any issue.

What Clifford's position ignores is, among other things, that in many important areas of human life believing something may help to make it true. If I believe that Jones likes me, and act as if I believe it, Jones will probably find it hard not to like me. More generally, there may be truths that I can discover only if I act on the assumption that they exist. There is nothing irrational or superstitious about this. On the contrary, any circumscription of belief that keeps me from seeking such truths has to be rejected. In James's own words in "The Will to Believe," "A rule of thinking which would absolutely prevent me from acknowledging certain kinds of truth if those kinds of truth were really there, would be an irrational rule." There is thus no rational precept that can keep one from believing in God if that belief makes one's life better and more hopeful. And, by the same reasoning, there is no rational precept that can keep one from being an atheist if *that* belief makes one's life better and more hopeful. The point of all this is not, of course, that both beliefs may be objectively true. It is, rather, that, having no way to tell which is objectively true, we may choose the one that better fulfils our needs. Here is a case where *holding* a belief has important "practical" consequences even though the belief itself has no consequences amenable to scientific inspection. Here also, then, is a case that illustrates clearly a difference between the pragmatism of Peirce and the pragmatism of James.

Still, both Peirce and James insisted that pragmatism is a method of doing philosophy and not a set of results or conclusions. But both of them developed metaphysical views along lines they believed to be pragmatic. The metaphysical theories James found himself developing in the last phase of his career are in important ways similar to those of Peirce. Since we have already treated some of Peirce's metaphysical insights, we can be quite brief in describing James's. (I do not mean to suggest that Peirce and James developed identical metaphysical positions, but it will be evident even in the brief account below that the two men were close in their general outlook and in several basic commitments.)

James thought of himself as perhaps above all an empiricist, that is, as one who tries all theories and doctrines by the test of experience. But the older empiricism of Locke, Berkeley, and Hume seemed to James too narrow, too static, too little aware of the dynamic quality of experience. To set off his own brand of empiricism from that of his British forebears, he called it "*radical* empiricism." The earlier representatives of this tradition came to experience with too many preconceptions, with the consequence that their vision was blinkered. Hume's analysis of causation, for example, turns on the discreteness, the disconnectedness, of the moments of experience. To James this was one-eyed empiricism, for the relations and connections of experience are just as real, just as indefeasible, as the disconnections.

Certain kinds of questions—for example, about the nature of reality or the general conditions and character of knowledge—are too "abstract" and "impractical" to receive much of an answer from common sense; and they are too comprehensive and basic to engage the attention of science. Such questions drive us, in a word, to metaphysics. But traditional metaphysics is too rationalistic, too remote from actual experience, to be credible. In his own metaphysical theories James tried to remain true to the dynamic, changing, evolving character of the world that experience reveals to us. Even in his more speculative sallies—Santayana said that James's excursions into philosophy were in the nature of raids—James repeatedly came back to the demands of human experience. This is true, for example, in his conjectures about the possibility of supraindividual experience ("compound consciousness") and in his doctrine of God, who, for James, must be finite and engaged with humanity in a struggle to bring greater order, harmony, love, and beauty into the world.[45]

Like Peirce, James was born into a literate, highly educated family. But James's family also had money, and he enjoyed the perquisites of the well to do: education, travel, fluency in foreign languages, and leisure time. And unlike Peirce, James was one of the brightest stars in Harvard's firmament. Santayana, James's most gifted student and later his colleague, recalled James as a teacher and as a man:

Even his pupils, attached as they invariably were to his person, felt some doubts about the profundity of one who was so very natural, and who after some interruption during a lecture—and he said life was a series of interruptions—would slap his forehead and ask the man in the front row "What was I talking about?". . . He liked to open the window, and look out for a moment. I think he was glad when the bell rang, and he could be himself again until the next day. But in the midst of this routine of the class-room the spirit would sometimes come upon him, and, leaning his head on his hand, he would let fall golden words, picturesque, fresh from the heart, full of the knowledge of good and evil. Incidentally there would crop up some humourous characterisation, some candid confession of doubt or of instinctive preference, some pungent scrap of learning; radicalisms plunging sometimes into the sub-soil of all human philosophies; and, on occasion, thoughts of simple wisdom and wistful piety, the most unfeigned and manly that anybody ever had.[46]

John Dewey

John Dewey (1859–1952) was not as dazzlingly brilliant as Peirce or as vivacious and personally winsome as James; but, perhaps because he *was* more "ordinary," he articulated the political and educational ideals of a democratic people more clearly and more fully than either of the other two great pragmatists. He surely worked out the implications of his philosophy more systematically than either Peirce or James—partly, no doubt, because he lived so long (into his ninety-third year) and wrote so long (almost seventy years). But there is a sense in which Dewey had no system at all. Like Peirce and James, he advocated a *method,* and through seven decades of tireless writing he applied this method to a great variety of areas.

The sheer volume of Dewey's published work is staggering: the bibliography of his writings runs to 153 pages.[47] Dewey's readers included many who were attracted to his writings on educational theory and practice but had little interest in the more traditional philosophical problems that engaged Peirce and James. For this reason Dewey is probably the most widely read of all American philosophers, with the possible exception of Emerson.

Because he took ideas to be instruments in the gaining of knowledge, Dewey's brand of pragmatism is often called "instrumentalism." This conception of ideas as instruments reflects the influence of the theory of evolution on Dewey's thought and especially the influence of James's *Principles of Psychology.*

Like Peirce and James, Dewey thought that philosophy, particularly logic, had long been out of step with the actual methods and principles of science. Dewey wrote voluminously on this subject, the best, perhaps—and the most comprehensive and systematic, certainly—being *Logic: The Theory of Inquiry.* In that work Dewey offered the following definition of "inquiry": "the controlled or directed transformation of an indeterminate situation into one that is so determinate in its constituent distinctions and relations as to convert the elements of the original situation into a unified whole."[48] An essentially identical, but less ponderous, explanation is found in *How We Think*: "The function of reflective thought is . . . to transform a situation in which there is experienced obscurity, doubt, conflict, disturbance of some sort, into a situation that is clear, coherent, settled, harmonious."[49] The similarity of Dewey's account to Peirce's theory of doubt and belief (in, for example, "The Fixation of Belief") is too obvious to require any elaboration.

What Dewey was suggesting is a general method for dealing with problematic situations. He illustrated the method by three simple cases culled from student papers (cited in *How We Think*):

Case 1. A person walking down 16th Street in New York City noticed a clock that indicated 12:20. This reminded him that he had an appointment on 124th Street at one o'clock. To decide how best to keep the appointment, the person thought of taking a taxi, the subway, or the elevated. He considered how long each vehicle would require to make the trip, how close the subway and elevated stations were to his present location, and how close they were to his destination. After a quick mental survey of his situation, he decided on the subway express and made his appointment on time. This was a case of practical deliberation.

Case 2. A regular rider of a ferryboat noticed a long white pole with a gilded ball at its tip projecting almost horizontally from the upper deck of the boat, and wondered what it was for. At first, he thought it was probably a flagpole, but three considerations told against that conclusion: (a) the pole was nearly horizontal, an attitude not normal for a flagpole; (b) it had no pulley, ring, or cord for attaching a flag; and (c) there were two vertical poles from which flags were occasionally flown. He next conjectured that it was an ornament; but since all the ferryboats and even the tugboats had such a pole, he decided that it was not ornamental. He then wondered whether it might be a radio antenna but rejected that possibility because, among other things, the best place for an antenna would be the highest point of the boat, on top of the pilot house. Finally, he hit upon a possibility that fit all the facts he knew; namely, that the pole with its gilded tip was used by the pilot to help him steer the boat properly. This was a case of reflection upon an observation.

Case 3. A person washing tumblers in hot sudsy water noticed that when he put the tumblers downward on a plate bubbles appeared on the outside of the mouths of the tumblers and then went inside. Why? The air inside the tumblers was trapped except as it escaped by means of the bubbles. But why would the air leave the tumblers? Since nothing was entering the tumblers to force the air out, the air must have expanded; but to expand, the air must be heated. Surely the air already trapped in the soap bubbles could not have been heated further upon being removed from the hot water. The only plausible explanation was that colder air entered the tumblers during their transfer from the dishwater to the plate; it was *that* air that was heated and thereby expanded. Several tests verified this hypothesis. But why did the bubbles later go inside? Simple: The tumblers and the air inside them cooled and thereby reduced the pressure, allowing the bubbles to return inside. This was a case of reflection involving experiment.

The three cases cited form a series, ranging from very simple to more complicated kinds of reflection. The first case typifies the sort of thinking one does every day; both the data and the means of reaching a solution are commonplace (at least to one who lives in a city served by subways and elevated trains). The third case illustrates a kind of reflection in which neither the problem nor the solution would have occurred to anyone innocent of scientific training. The second case is intermediate: both the problem and the solution are within the reach of people not tutored in science, but that a "problematic situation" even existed would likely occur only to someone with a theoretic turn of mind. What all three cases show is that inference—"the heart of all intelligent action"—is provoked by a doubtful, perplexing situation and that its successful issue is a resolution of the dubious situation into a settled, determinate one.

Dewey's theory of inquiry or inference answers to Peirce's scientific method in at least two fundamental respects: it is self-corrective, and it involves a community of inquirers. The truths that we discover by this means are never absolute or final; the most we can hope for—and, fortunately, all we really need—is what Dewey called "warranted assertibility." Dewey's approach, like that of Peirce, was diametrically opposite to that of Descartes, who believed that there are indubitable first truths available to the reason of the solitary thinker. Dewey rejected such supposedly certain foundations of human knowledge. He advocated, instead, looking to the consequences of our ideas, to the future. To side with Descartes on this issue is to ignore the fundamental evolutionary purpose of human intelligence.

Like James, Dewey took experience to be a fundamental—perhaps *the* fundamental—notion in his philosophy; it is a touchstone by which all parts of the philosophy are judged. Also like James, Dewey found the notion of experience in the empiricist tradition too narrow, too confining, too atomistic. When Dewey talked of experience, he did not mean merely immediate, individual experience; he meant the long-term experience of human beings as a class. Dewey came to believe that idealism, which had strongly influenced him in his younger days, was too intellectualistic, too concerned with *knowing,* to the exclusion of other ways of experiencing. Contrary to the emphasis of idealism, Dewey found experience to be basically affective or emotional, to be oriented to doing.

Again following James, Dewey developed a metaphysics of experience (most notably in *Experience and Nature,* which may be Dewey's best philosophical work). Human experience is a late-comer on the cosmic scene, but it is nonetheless of supreme importance to human beings. Before human experience, the inorganic, organic, and sensitive worlds evolved. Since human experience depends for its existence on this inorganic-organic-sensitive base, it is folly for philosophers to pretend that they are disembodied spirits or disinterested spectators of existence.

In a similar vein, Dewey worked out an aesthetic theory (in *Art and Experience,* 1934) that emphatically rejects the sharp distinction of art from life. *All* experience exhibits an aesthetic quality, and the so-called fine arts are just one expression of this pervasive quality of human life; they differ only in degree from other distillations of experience. Dewey's general characterization of knowledge as moving toward harmony, order, and coherence is decidedly aesthetic.[50]

Many of Dewey's readers have little or no interest in his metaphysics or theory of knowledge or aesthetics, but are captivated by philosophy of education. In fact, Dewey did not recognize the philosophy of education as a separate inquiry; all of philosophy—indeed, all of life—has to do with education. But Dewey did write a great deal on education, dating from the beginning of his association with the University of Chicago in 1894. Working closely with the famous laboratory school, which Dewey helped establish shortly after his arrival in Chicago, Dewey managed, over a ten-year period, both to elaborate his educational theories and to antagonize the university administration—the latter circumstance being at least partly responsible for his departure for Columbia University in 1904. It was natural for Columbia, with Dewey on its faculty, to become the world's leading center for the training of teachers.

Dewey found traditional education faulty because, among other things, it ignored the *active* role of the learner; it reflected the old spectator view of knowledge. But he was also critical of some aspects of the newer theory—often, ironically, advocated on his "authority." In particular, he did not approve of letting children do just what they want. They are too young, too immature, to know very clearly what they want. As an illustration of the judicious mixture of freedom and discipline, consider the following case cited by Dewey in *How We Think.* A teacher of mathematics was troubled by his students' carelessness in placing the decimal point when working problems involving money. They got the sequence of numbers right, but in placing the decimal point they varied widely. One would get the answer $320.16; a second, $32.016; and a third, $3201.6. While they could in one sense compute the numbers correctly, they did not *think* about what they were doing. To remedy this failing, the teacher sent the students to buy lumber for a class in manual training, the dealer having agreed to let the students figure their own bill. Not one student got the decimal point in the wrong place. The difference between mere textbook problems and a concrete situation could hardly have been more clearly illustrated. Education should cultivate *intelligence,* and that means the ability to assess and cope with actual human problems. Clearly, neither the old authoritarian education nor the new formless variety is going to help the child develop critical intelligence.

For Dewey, to say that education should nourish human intelligence is roughly equivalent to saying that it should develop skills for life in a democracy. This theme—the intimate relation between education and democracy—was a recurrent, lifelong preoccupation of Dewey. (One of the most thorough statements of his educational philosophy is *Democracy and Education,* published in 1916.) There is a close relationship between the classroom and society—not that the classroom should *mirror* the society. Rather, education should foster those habits, attitudes, and abilities that can be put to use by citizens in working toward a more harmonious, more just society. Dewey realized that there are many forces at work in a society that tend to the opposite result—to fragmentation, alienation, and loss of freedom. Such forces are inevitable in any society but especially in highly industrialized societies such as those of the United States and Western Europe (and, since Dewey's death, Japan).[51]

Dewey's moral theory is of a piece with his general philosophical outlook. A moral perplexity is like any other perplexity in that it comes to focus in a concrete situation that requires a choice of us—a choice by which some alternatives are excluded in favor of others. A moral problem ordinarily does not push us to a choice between good and evil—that is seldom a problem—but rather between conflicting goods.

We are often confronted with a situation in which we can either satisfy some immediate desire or fortify some long-term good, but not both. To make an intelligent decision, we must assess our circumstances as completely and accurately as we can, or, to use a favorite term of Dewey's, we must engage in the process of *valuation.* Our valuations are good or reasonable when they embody our developed critical intelligence. They are the opposite of good or reasonable when they fail to embody that intelligence—when they reflect haste or ignorance. True to his general attitude, Dewey held that the process of valuation is never final or complete; as long as we live we shall be called on to make moral decisions.

It should be obvious from what has been said that Dewey rejected the commonly repeated dictum that science is value-free, is concerned only with what *is.* For Dewey, this thesis runs counter to the most fundamental fact about knowledge itself, namely, that it is the effort to bring reality and human ideals into a harmonious union. Man's beliefs about what the world is like and his beliefs about values and goals must be integrated, or else civilization itself is in mortal danger. The twentieth century is a horrifying vindication of Dewey's vision—the vision of what happens when science is cut loose from its roots in human purposes.

Like Plato and Aristotle, Dewey refused to draw a sharp line between personal morality and citizenship. Our valuations are always made in a human community or in a network of human communities, and such valuations inevitably affect and are affected by our membership in these communities. Naturally, not all our decisions are equally important, either for ourselves or for the larger community. If our personal decisions are reached in isolation from our fellow human beings, we shall likely find the decisions to be unsatisfactory in the long run. On the contrary, as we contribute our own store of creative intelligence to the improvement of society, we shall find that conditions for personal satisfaction are enhanced. Although Dewey did not share the conservatism or the authoritarianism of Plato and Aristotle, he agreed with his great Greek predecessors that the conjunction of personal morality and civic irresponsibility represents something close to a contradiction in terms.

Perhaps more than any other American thinker, John Dewey epitomized in his person and in his philosophy the ideal of combining speculative boldness with concrete concern for one's world and especially for the people in that world. Epistemologist, metaphysician, ethical theorist, educational philosopher, aesthetician, teacher, man of affairs—Dewey was, in his own prosaic way, a Renaissance man.

IDEALISM: JOSIAH ROYCE

Josiah Royce (1855–1916) was the greatest and most systematic of America's idealists. ("Idealism," as we have noted earlier, is the philosophical view that reality is ultimately mental or spiritual in character.) Jonathan Edwards was an idealist, but his strictly metaphysical writings are rather meager, not remotely approaching the detail and completeness

with which Royce developed his system. Too, Edwards' idealism was closely tied to his religious Calvinism, a connection that makes it suspect to some philosophers. Though Royce was incurably religious himself, he had no patience with sectarian loyalties and squabbles. Emerson and the Transcendentalists were idealists too, but their idealism was based on intuition and feeling rather than on rigorous philosophical argument. Royce aimed to demonstrate that there must be an infinite, all-inclusive mind; and he would do this "by no mystical insight, by no revelation . . . but by a simple, dry analysis of the meaning of our own thought."[52] Royce's tools were as different from those of Emerson as one can easily imagine: Emerson used poetic feeling and a wide-ranging imagination; Royce used mathematics, logic, biology, economics—anything that his busy and capacious mind could take in. Yet the outcomes of their thought as regards reality were not so far apart.

Royce was born in Grass Valley, California, in 1855, five years after California had become the thirty-first state of the United States. After graduating from the newly founded University of California, he spent a year studying in Germany. He then returned to America, took a doctorate in philosophy at Johns Hopkins University, and went back home to teach at his alma mater. Four years later, in 1882, he was appointed to the philosophy faculty at Harvard University, where he remained the rest of his life.

On the face of it there is something anomalous and ironic about the philosophical careers of Royce and his great friends Peirce and James. Royce, a son of the wild, brawling West, devoted his life to expounding and defending his own version of a venerable European philosophical tradition. Peirce and James, the progeny of intellectual (and, with qualifications, social) Boston Brahmins, gave themselves to articulating and defending pragmatism, a philosophy much more congenial than idealism to the frontier mentality. But, odd or not, that is the way it was. James and Royce were Harvard colleagues and fast personal friends for almost thirty years, and their philosophical encounters were frequent and spirited. Neither man *fundamentally* altered his own position over the years of their association, but each whetted his mind against the other. It is some measure of James's personal greatness that he brought Royce to Harvard knowing full well that Royce would be more an adversary than an ally. Though not a colleague of Royce, Peirce strongly influenced Royce's thinking, especially through his theory of signs. Royce had a very high opinion of Peirce, and Peirce, with some qualifications, reciprocated the admiration.

Royce was, by all accounts, a formidable opponent in debate. One who knew him described Royce as "the John L. Sullivan of philosophy, ready for all comers." He was widely learned, blessed with a steel-trap memory, and indefatigable in the prosecution of his self-imposed mission. Even Santayana, whose admiration for Royce was grudging and hedged about with qualifications, granted him that much: "If you gave him a cue, or even without one, he could discourse broadly on any subject; you never caught him napping. Whatever the text-books and encyclopaedias could tell him, he knew."[53] What amazed both friend and foe was that he often knew nonphilosophical subjects—mathematics, biology, economics—as well as the specialists. It was all—"biblical criticism, the struggle for life, the latest German theory of sexual insanity" (Santayana's list)—grist for the mill.[54]

During the thirty-one years between the appearance of his first book and his death Royce wrote an unending succession of books, papers, and lectures designed to clarify, expand, and defend his basic philosophical position—a position he never really altered. The cornerstone of that position is the existence of God, who is an absolute, infinite, all-inclusive mind or spirit. In his first book, *The Religious Aspect of Philosophy* (1885), he offered a proof that such a being must exist; and in many other writings he offered additional proofs and clarifications of that thesis. His first proof rested on a rather curious foundation, the certainty of the existence of error. That error exists is absolutely indubitable. Suppose someone says, "I deny that error is indubitable." That denial, if it has any meaning at all, must mean that Royce is wrong, that is, is in error. Or suppose that someone doubts whether error is indubitable: the doubt makes sense only on the supposition that there is an error to be made. Twist as we may, we cannot escape the conclusion that error is undeniable. But if error is certain, so are the necessary conditions of error, and Royce intended to show that the indispensable condition of error is an all-encompassing mind.

To reach his ultimate conclusion, Royce examined some alternative explanations of error and found that none of them could make error intelligible. The general problem of erroneous judgments can be put this way: How can a sincere judgment be clear enough to pick out the appropriate object or relation and yet be unclear enough to be wrong? Suppose, for example, that Jones sincerely but mistakenly believes that Smith has stolen his lawnmower. Since Smith cannot literally be part of Jones's mind, and since Jones's judgment agrees with his *idea* of Smith, how can Jones be mistaken in his judgment about Smith? Clearly, he *can* be, but how? To get a clue to the right answer, imagine how Smith might react to Jones's accusation. Apart from being angry and insulted, Smith might say something like, "God knows that I didn't steal your stupid lawnmower." It would be natural for Smith to appeal to an ideal judge, to someone who knew the truth as well as Jones's sincere but false judgment. And since there is an infinite amount of error possible, the ideal judge must be infinite in his capacity to compare erroneous judgments with the truth. An error, then, turns out to be the result of our fragmentary, incomplete knowledge; an error is an incomplete thought.

Royce's insistence on the social character of knowledge recalls Peirce's dictum that truth is public. We typically have confidence in our judgments in proportion to their conformity to the judgments of others. When we say that something is really the case, we mean (so Royce thought) that others agree—or would agree—with us. This is the tack that Royce took in *The Conception of God*. If we reflect on our knowledge, and especially on scientific knowledge, we will be driven to the conclusion that our judgments of truth and falsity depend upon—draw their meaning from—an at least implicit appeal to a more stable and inclusive experience

than our own fleeting, fragmentary experiences. Now that more-inclusive experience cannot be merely the collective experience of mankind, for it is clearly possible that *everyone* could be mistaken relative to some alleged fact.

Someone may object that all we have is our impulse to a perfect, nonarbitrary standard; we have no assurance that such an absolute standard actually exists. Perhaps we can only push back the limits of our own ignorance; perhaps there is no all-inclusive subject called the Absolute—just a collection of finite minds. Let us see where that reasoning takes us. If there is no such all-inclusive, infinite mind as we have been talking about, then *that* fact must be known to some knower, must be the object of some experience. What sort of being, what sort of mind, is it who knows that there is no all-inclusive subject, that all knowers are finite? If the mind that knows this alleged fact is infinite, then the "fact" is not a fact at all. But, on the other hand, if the mind that supposedly knows that there is no all-inclusive subject is itself finite, then it cannot possibly know what it is required to know. To know that *every* experience is limited and finite would itself be the all-inclusive knowledge whose existence is being denied. To know that all experience is finite would require us to know that there is nothing that could falsify our belief, and that would amount to infinite knowledge. Only an infinite mind could know that all minds are finite—a flat self-contradiction. Such was Royce's *reductio ad absurdum* of the view that there are only finite, fragmentary experiences.

When I am right or wrong in my judgments, I am right or wrong in the presence of an all-inclusive, all-knowing mind that sees my successes or failures relative to what it is I am trying to know. In this way Royce turned to his own account the undeniable and ubiquitous experiences of frustration, fragmentariness, and error.

Someone may ask why we cannot just suppose that reality is what it is independent of our opinions of it, why *that* would not be enough objectivity to satisfy anybody. Why must we suppose an infinite mind? Royce's proof, which we have just sketched, turns on a crucial assumption, namely, that to say that something exists is to say that it is present to the experience of some subject. This assumption is common to a variety of idealist philosophies; it is also, it seems to me, the critical weakness in arguments such as Royce's. Royce insisted that what we *mean* when we assert that something exists is that it is present to the experience of some subject. As far as I can see, this claim is false. We do not mean any such thing. We may *believe* that what exists must exist as the object of some conscious experience, as implausible as such a belief on its face appears to be. But it is surely not part of what we mean by assertions of existence. If I am right on this point, Royce's argument collapses. He may, of course, have been right in believing that an all-inclusive subject (God) exists, but he was mistaken in believing that he had given a *proof* of his belief.

Royce was sensitive to a criticism often lodged against philosophies that make all finite beings dependent parts of an infinite being ("monism" is the philosophical term for such philosophies): Individuals are reduced to the status of accidents (or mere half-illusory manifestations) of the one real being. Royce devoted his great energy and ingenuity to answering such charges. The most systematic and thorough-going defense occurs in Royce's greatest work, *The World and the Individual.* Briefly stated, Royce's "solution" turns on the will or purposes of finite beings as the key to their real individuality. For this reason Royce's idealism is sometimes described as "voluntaristic." It is this emphasis on purpose that provides one of the chief links between Royce's idealism and pragmatism. In fact, Royce sometimes called himself an "absolute pragmatist." He agreed with the pragmatists that all human activity, including knowing, embodies a purpose. Even the most abstruse speculations express our purposes; if they had no purpose or point, we would not engage in them. But in the case of knowing, our purpose must be to find the *truth.* It is downright self-contradictory to reduce truth to the satisfaction of my purely personal needs, *unless* we recognize that my basic need as a rational being is that my beliefs be *true.* Royce could not abide the morass of relativism and sickly sentimentality that pragmatists occasionally fall into.[55]

Given his metaphysical views, it was natural for Royce to develop an ethics based primarily on the virtue of loyalty to the various communities of which individuals are members, the ultimate "community" being the Absolute Spirit itself. *The Philosophy of Loyalty* is the chief work in this area. One of Royce's last works, the two-volume *The Problem of Christianity,* interprets the Christian Gospel in terms of a community of interpretation.

It is hard to feel sorry for someone as hugely capable as Royce, but there is still a certain sadness in his great failure. The tides of philosophy were running too strongly in the opposite direction for even his heroic efforts to stem. Although idealism had its formidable champions, among them Francis Herbert Bradley in England, it was moribund, and no amount of dedicated nursing could restore it to health. On a somewhat happier note it is worth observing that interest in Royce has increased markedly in the past several years. Even if his "proofs" no longer convince (if they ever did), he has important and insightful things to say about problems that philosophers find endlessly fascinating.

Santayana's last word on Royce aptly expresses the splendor and the misery of the man:

His was a Gothic and scholastic spirit, intent on devising and solving puzzles, and honouring God in systematic works, like the coral insect or the spider; eventually creating a fabric that in its homely intricacy and fulness arrested and moved the heart, the web of it was so vast, and so full of mystery and yearning.[56]

VARIOUS TWENTIETH-CENTURY MOVEMENTS AND PHILOSOPHERS

George Santayana

George Santayana (1863–1952) was one of only a handful of writers—Plato and George Berkeley come to mind as ex-

amples—who combine substantial philosophical ability with consummate literary skill. Whatever our final verdict on Santayana as a philosopher—and few, I think, would put him in a class with Plato and Berkeley—we can hardly avoid the conclusion that he is one of the great stylists in the history of philosophy. Santayana himself once said that he learned English (he was not an American by birth) so that he could say plausibly in English as many un-English things as he could. It may be doubted whether he was as un-English as he supposed, but there can be no doubt that he learned English.

Most writers who have anything to say about Santayana point out that he was in several ways un-American: He was not born in America, neither parent was American (though his mother's first husband had been), he has many hard things to say about American values, and he left America permanently at his first opportunity. But, as Santayana himself acknowledged, if he belonged to any land, he belonged to America. Its impress on his mind and soul was deep and permanent. Though born in Spain, he went to Boston when he was nine and remained there forty years. He took a doctorate in philosophy from Harvard and taught there, with James and Royce, until 1912. At that time he received a legacy from his mother and immediately departed for Europe, living in England and on the Continent (the last twenty-seven years in Rome) until his death in 1952.

Santayana's influence on "professional" philosophy is weaker than that of, say, Peirce or Dewey, but he is read by many who have no taste for professional philosophy. Many of his works appeal to both classes of readers, the exceptions being "Three Proofs of Realism" (an essay published in 1920), *Scepticism and Animal Faith* (1923), and the four-volume *Realms of Being* (1927–40). These three works are the most narrowly philosophical of his entire *corpus.* We shall reverse chronological order and discuss his more traditionally philosophical works, which set out his theories of knowledge and reality, before returning to a consideration of *The Life of Reason* (1905–1906), which is the best statement of his ethics and philosophy of culture.

Scepticism and Animal Faith is different from his other books in at least one respect. There he uncharacteristically *argued* for his position. Although Santayana liberally laced his works with criticisms of other philosophers, he seldom descended into the arena to do battle with opposing views. He was generally content to state his own position and leave it to the reader to accept or reject it. But *Scepticism and Animal Faith* contains a great deal of self-conscious argument. As for skepticism, Santayana argued that the most famous modern skeptics, Descartes and Hume, were too wavering and half-hearted in their doubting. Descartes' "Cogito, ergo sum" ("I think, therefore I am"), which he took to represent absolute certainty, in fact represents no such thing. Even the "I am" is very far from expressing a certain truth. No *fact* is self-evident or certain. The empiricist Hume fared no better. His "skepticism" inconsistently allowed for the certainty of perceptions, as well as the curious doctrine that perceptions perceive themselves. Santayana's own position was that nothing "given" exists. This amounts to what he called a "solipsism of the present moment," the view that I am certain only of what is immediately before my mind. The only things that are given, and therefore certain, are what Santayana called "essences," sheer qualities of being that as such reveal nothing about what exists. Those things that exist—stones, trees, other people, our own experiences—are never given; they transcend the fleeting qualities that are given. Our knowledge of existents—and we do not strictly *know* essences—always rests on beliefs about things that are not given. Knowledge, then, is a form of faith, "faith mediated by symbols," as Santayana put it. But animal faith, a kind of instinctive belief in a world transcending immediate, momentary experience, is older and stronger than reason and doubt. This faith is justified to the extent that it works—a pragmatic element in one who detested much of pragmatism.

Santayana wrote *Scepticism and Animal Faith* as a general preface to *Realms of Being.* The purpose of this preface was, among other things, to act as a cathartic, to let us get skepticism out of our system. More positively, it served as a corrective and preventive of superstition and dogmatism, particularly of the view that knowledge is literal rather than symbolic or that we can provide proofs for any matter of fact. (In denying that we can prove any fact, Santayana was echoing the same Hume he took to task for being irresolute in his skepticism.) Like Descartes, Santayana had no intention of wallowing in skepticism; his ultimate purpose was nonskeptical. But, unlike Descartes, Santayana constructed his metaphysical "system" under the discipline of a skepticism that has been mitigated only by an appeal to the nonintellectual roots of belief. In fact, Santayana asked that his descriptions of the different "realms" of being not be called metaphysics; but that seems about as good a term as any to describe his effort. The realms—Matter, Essence, Truth, and Spirit—do not correspond to substantially separate orders of reality; they represent different ways of looking at being. In Santayana's own phrase they are "summary categories of logic."

Essences are Santayana's answer to Plato's forms, but they are not superior types of existents. Indeed, they do not *exist* at all; they are the *forms* of everything, both actual and possible. To get some idea of what Santayana means by "essence," consider the color of a pencil. Divest the color of all extraneous relations, and concentrate on the sheer quality presented. As an essence it is detached from any particular exemplification; it could be the color of an indefinitely large number of objects. The *realm* of essences is a perfect democracy; no one of them is more likely to be exemplified than any other. Just which essences are concretely embodied in actual existence depends on another realm, the realm of matter.

The realm of matter is the basic spatiotemporal reality; it is the flux of existence. It includes the ordinary objects of experience, as well as such presumed entities as electrons and neutrinos. To be precise, *matter* (or material substance) itself is presumed or inferred as a means of making our experience more intelligible and orderly. We do not have any direct experience of matter; rather, we discern patterns and rhythms of experience and postulate matter as the underlying, unifying reality.

Like everything else that exists, *spirit* is rooted in matter. Santayana's view of spirit (or consciousness or mind) is a version of "epiphenomenalism," the theory that mind is a causally inefficacious by-product of matter. Spirit is, for those organisms complex enough to generate it, of inestimable worth. That is why Santayana included it as a "realm" of being, even though it is strictly dependent on the activities of matter for its very existence. Spirit is aware of the shocks and conflicts of the material body of which it is an expression, but it also has a spontaneity by which it imagines, entertains ideas that never were true of any existing thing. Spirit may produce dissatisfaction, but it may lead to a "life of reason." The ideal of spirit is to mediate between the Realm of Essence—to which spirit has a natural affinity—and the Realm of Truth, which reflects the accidents of matter. At its zenith spirit may acquire a sympathy with all natural things and thereby attain what Santayana called "charity."

The Realm of Truth may be regarded as a subrealm of essence; namely, that part of the Realm of Essence that happens to be exemplified in the material world. Contrary to a common assumption, truth is not a property of ideas or judgments—though, of course, we intend our judgments to be true. Nor is the Realm of Truth part of the material world. It is, rather, "the standard comprehensive description of any fact in all its relations." As such, it is free from any taint of vagueness, and it is complete.

As far as causal influence goes, spirit is impotent. But it does present ideas, ideals, suggestions to the psyche, which is a material organization of responses, tendencies, and so on—what Santayana called the "automatic inward machinery." We can become rational, in several modes, if we can judiciously weave together the ideal promptings of spirit with the demands of the material world, which is the source and ground, if not the preferred "home," of spirit. Reason represents the harmonious, orderly development of man's instinctual cunning to the level of self-conscious discernment of patterns and forms and projection of ideals. The life of reason is embodied, or reflected, in five phases or areas: common sense, society, religion, art, and science—to each of which Santayana devoted a volume of *The Life of Reason.* These areas do not, of course, represent hermetically sealed compartments of human life. They can be usefully distinguished, but they do not exist in mutual exclusion.

We learn by common sense to discriminate among objects and to recognize repeated patterns of events. But this process is mixed up with a great deal of fancy and imagination, which often takes the form of superstition. The early life of all peoples is suffused with animism, the investing of inanimate things with spirits (or at least psyches) like our own. Gradually, we disentangle the two realms of nature and spirit, thereby opening the way to a fundamental division of science.

These two divisions of science are both fundamental and natural. One deals with "concretions of existence" and the other with "concretions of discourse." Alternatively, we may say that one branch treats existences, and the other treats ideas. The two branches are, respectively, "physics" and "dialectic." Dialectic includes the sciences of mathematics, logic, and ethics.

Though separate, physics and dialectic are intimately connected. Physics, like all science, is itself discourse; before any concretions in existence can be discerned, the mind must note and identify them in their recurrences. Physics, in other words, rests on *meanings* and so presupposes consciousness. The impossibility of modern science without mathematics—the chief of the dialectical sciences—is another sign of the interplay between the two types of science. Conversely, dialectic—the science of ideas—rests on fact or actual existence. The process of knowing or discovering truth is part of the real flux of existence, is an event in time. But notwithstanding their necessary connection, they must not be confused. The worst errors of philosophy and psychology have issued from confounding the functions of the two divisions of science. Natural scientists have generally been freer of this fault; they have seldom thought, for example, that a purely formal mathematical proof by itself reveals anything about actual existence. Unfortunately, philosophers and psychologists have often not shown such restraint. They have tried to prove facts about the world—for example, that the earth does not move, that an Absolute Spirit exists, or that the soul is immortal—by mere dialectic alone. Such "proofs" are always specious; no proposition about real existence is either self-evident or demonstrable.

As a materialist Santayana was bound to think that "physics" has the final, if not the only, word on what the actual world is like. He must also reject any claims of special status made on behalf of psychology or history or any humanistic science. In so far as such sciences are genuinely scientific, they are part of physiology or biology, and their explanatory principles must be mechanical. But physics, in fact, held little interest for Santayana. Though a materialist, his native sympathies lay with the world of mind or spirit, and his "scientific" interests lay in dialectic.

The part of dialectic that most intrigued Santayana was ethics, or moral theory, which he treats in *Reason in Science.* Given the impossibility of rational proofs of matters of fact, Santayana had to be careful to delimit the province of reason in ethics. To do this, he contrasted rational ethics with prerational and postrational morality. People have made moral choices for much longer than they have reflected on them or tried to introduce rational principles into them. Prerational morality rests largely on nonrational impulses and preferences; the possibility of a harmonious and coherent adjustment of conflicts hardly suggests itself at this stage. Thus, when reason is applied to morality, it deals with pre-existing preferences, values, and interests. By itself reason cannot create any value or good. (In this respect, anyway, Santayana accepted Hume's dictum that reason is and ought to be the slave of the passions.) In fact, a completely rational morality is impossible; for it would require a kind of knowledge of ourselves and a harmony of ideals that is beyond our powers. But a rational ethics is possible. That is, it is possible to get beyond the impulsive, unreflective level of prerational morality. It is possible to discover principles of adjustment and ways of choosing among competing goods that transcend the attaining of momentary and local satisfactions. When the aim of rational ethics—the achievement of satisfactions that are

truly good and durable—fails, as it is in constant danger of doing, men are tempted to throw over the whole project and seek refuge in some religious vision. The effort to find an enlightened way of living is given up in favor of a denial that such a life is possible on earth. This renunciation of rational ethics Santayana called postrational morality.

Reason manifests itself in *society* in the maintenance of conditions necessary for physical survival—the procreation and care of children and the provision for the material needs of the members of the society. Natural societies provide the primary institutions through participation in which men achieve a degree of security impossible to the solitary individual. Within such basic societies, "free," or "rational," societies may grow—societies whose members are united by common ideals and purposes. Beyond free societies of this sort are societies in which people seek the company of "ideals" in the strict sense—essences—and live the life of the spirit.

Santayana's view of religion reminds one of G. W. F. Hegel, whose *Phenomenology of Mind* Santayana acknowledged as an influence on *The Life of Reason.* Like Hegel, he regarded art and religion as essentially products of the imagination—immensely valuable, even indispensable, to human life, but not to be confused with literal truth. Nevertheless, adherents of the various religions typically believe their dogmas to be literally true, and this usually means that they regard other religions as spurious. Paradoxically, Santayana recognized that a religion is likely to lose its hold on its followers when they begin to look upon it as a free poetic creation, that is, when they cease to take it literally. What Santayana said about this problem strikes me as confused and perhaps self-contradictory, but his comments on the strengths and weakenesses of a number of particular religions seem to me interesting and insightful. Although no religion is literally true or false, each religion embodies some ideals more nearly perfectly than others in the imaginative ordering of natural life that is the essence of religion.

In our discussion, we have concentrated on Santayana's "big" works—*Realms of Being* (including *Scepticism and Animal Faith*) and *The Life of Reason.* We have been obliged to ignore his other works, some of them excellent. Readers will find that the essays "The Genteel Tradition" (1911) and "The Genteel Tradition at Bay" (1931) offer some marvelous observations on American life and thought. *The Sense of Beauty* (1896), Santayana's first book, is almost surely the most influential work in aesthetics ever written by an American. Santayana wrote an autobiography, *Persons and Places;* poetry; a novel, *The Last Puritan; Dialogues in Limbo;* and many pieces of literary criticism, most notably *Interpretations of Poetry and Religion* and *Three Philosophical Poets.* Any of these works, as well as many we have not mentioned, will repay reading.

Some critics have found Santayana's way of doing philosophy obscure and imprecise, and his style too "literary" to lend itself easily to the exacting demands of philosophy. But no one, I suspect, ever found Santayana's writing boring or wishy-washy; and no one, I should hope, ever failed to be moved by its sheer beauty.

Alfred North Whitehead

There is something odd about including in a survey of American philosophy a man who first set foot on American soil at age sixty-three. In 1924 Alfred North Whitehead (1861–1947) went to Harvard to teach philosophy after a distinguished career teaching mathematics at the University of Cambridge and the University of London. But though an Englishman all his life (he never became an American citizen), Whitehead produced most of his distinctive philosophical works in America. Thus, though it may seem odd to treat him as an American philosopher, it would be legalistic and provincial to exclude him.

Whitehead's earlier, that is, pre-American, work was mainly in mathematics, logic, and the philosophy of science. One of these works, *Principia Mathematica,* written with Bertrand Russell, ranks with the greatest ever written in logic and mathematics. But beginning with *Science and the Modern World* in 1925, Whitehead reeled off a stunning series of books dealing with a variety of traditional problems in philosophy: *Religion in the Making* (1926), *Symbolism: Its Meaning and Effect* (1927), *Process and Reality* (1929), *The Function of Reason* (1929), *Adventures of Ideas* (1933), and *Modes of Thought* (1938). Of these *Process and Reality* is easily the most important—and, alas, the most difficult.[57]

In *Science and the Modern World* Whitehead traced the development of modern science and its accompanying philosophy, which Whitehead called "scientific materialism." The confident assumption that Newtonian physics gives us an adequate and final account of the material world was rudely and decisively shattered by a series of discoveries in the late nineteenth and early twentieth centuries, culminating in Einstein's special and general theories of relativity. But philosophy has not kept pace with these changes. The ways of thinking implicit in scientific materialism, which had never been plausible when taken generally, have persisted even after their supposed legitimization by science was destroyed. It is typical of deep-rooted modes of thought to die very slowly. Whitehead proposed to administer a *coup de grâce* to this outmoded mentality.

The picture of reality offered by scientific materialism is austere. The world, according to this view, consists of bits of matter moving about in absolute space. The bodies in space have some qualities, the so-called primary qualities of figure, solidity, mass, and so on; but such qualities as color, taste, odor—the "secondary" qualities—are contributed by the mind. Whitehead's wry comment on this theory is worth quoting:

Thus the bodies are perceived as with qualities which in reality do not belong to them, qualities which in fact are purely the offspring of the mind. Thus nature gets credit which should in truth be reserved for ourselves: the rose for its scent: the nightingale for his song: and the sun for his radiance. The poets are entirely mistaken. They should address their lyrics to themselves, and should turn them into odes of self-congratulation on the excellency of the human mind. Nature is a dull affair, soundless, scentless, colourless; merely the hurrying of material, endlessly, meaninglessly.[58]

This theory, scientific materialism, proved to be remarkably efficient in organizing a part of human experience. And yet, as Whitehead observed, it is quite unbelievable. Materialistic mechanism was indeed an idea that mankind could neither live with nor live without.

Philosophers had typically consigned the material world to the mechanistic laws of physics, but they had reserved the mind for themselves. There thus emerged a kind of schizophrenia, a debilitating dualism that "bifurcated" nature into two essentially closed systems. Now the authority of science for such a split has been removed; but it is important to see why the *philosophy* of scientific materialism was mistaken even when it seemed to dovetail with the latest scientific discoveries. The trouble is that science, and physics in particular, concentrates on very limited, abstract features of the world. Its success depends on its ability to isolate and quantify those features that it finds interesting. There is nothing wrong with this as such, but it is sheer error to turn these abstractions into concrete reality. It is also exceedingly common, so much so that Whitehead coined a memorable name for the tendency—"the fallacy of misplaced concreteness." Only someone deeply infected by this tendency could take space and time to be independent realities in themselves, as Newton did. Whitehead's explanation helps us to understand why physics has been so successful and why the modern philosophy based on it is unbelievable. It is one thing to delimit our inquiry to manageable proportions; it is quite another to denounce as unreal anything that falls outside our self-imposed limits. Philosophy should be the critic of abstractions, not their chief purveyor.

The metaphysics derived from modern science, then, poses this question: How do we reconcile our belief in mind, freedom, human responsibility, and the like, with the mechanistic materialism required by modern science? Many answers have been given, but none of them attacks the legitimacy of the question itself. Whitehead's answer was that the question itself is thoroughly bogus. In the language of logic it is a complex question, like, "Have you stopped stealing from bread trucks?" "The only way of mitigating mechanism is by the discovery that it is not mechanism."[59] The dualism of mind and matter inherent in much of modern thought must be challenged by a fresh look at the actual character of our experience. Whitehead took such a look in *Science and the Modern World,* but it is in *Process and Reality* that the details of his answer are found.

Process and Reality is a difficult and important book. That it is difficult is undeniable. That it is important is not undeniable, but I shall take its importance to be clear enough that I need not argue for it. It treats in an original and provocative way practically all the basic problems of Western philosophy.[60] Whitehead was an unabashed metaphysician, beyond much doubt the greatest of the twentieth century. In *Process and Reality* he offered the most complete account of his theory of reality. We shall give a brief sketch of his system, starting with his account of "speculative philosophy."

According to Whitehead, "The true method of philosophical construction is to frame a scheme of ideas, the best that one can, and unflinchingly to explore the interpretation of experience in terms of that scheme."[61] It is a mistake to suppose that such a scheme is optional, a luxury for those with nothing better to do. On the contrary, there is always some such scheme in the various sciences, often unacknowledged and even unrecognized, but still influential in guiding the imagination. "The mentality of an epoch springs from the view of the world which is, in fact, dominant in the educated sections of the communities in question."[62] The mentality of our own epoch is characterized by the tragic split, referred to above, between common sense and the philosophy of scientific materialism. Such double-mindedness is at the root of much that is wavering and half-hearted in our civilization.

The scheme that Whitehead himself constructed is what he called the "philosophy of organism." The bare-bones outline of this philosophy is given in Chapter II of *Process and Reality,* "The Categoreal Scheme." To the first-time reader, this chapter is almost certain to seem frighteningly complex, even bewildering. Whitehead's claim to base his philosophy on the most concrete items in our experience must initially wear the face of a sick joke. But if one returns to the categoreal scheme after following Whitehead's efforts to put flesh on the skeleton, one will see that the claim is seriously intended. We are likely to be disoriented by Whitehead's approach because we are used to philosophers who take familiar but abstract categories as their starting point. In his determined attempt to crack the abstract, overintellectualized shell of our thinking, Whitehead took a concrete approach that, on initial contact at any rate, seems very abstract indeed. Whitehead's scheme, to be specific, comprises the Category of the Ultimate (with three subdivisions), eight Categories of Existence, twenty-seven Categories of Explanation, and nine Categoreal Obligations. Despite a strong sense of hopeless complexity and difficulty, the persistent reader returns to the categoreal scheme with increasing understanding and a lively admiration for Whitehead's perplexing genius.

Whitehead's position runs counter to much of Western philosophy, which has found reality in the permanent and unchanging. For Whitehead there was an element of permanence in reality, but the ultimate realities are occurrences, events, happenings—what he called "actual entities" (he used the phrase "actual occasion" as *almost* synonymous with "actual entity"). To take the unchanging as the ultimate reality, Whitehead argued, is to mistake an abstract part of the real for the concrete reality itself; it is, in other words, to commit the fallacy of misplaced concreteness.

Actual entities, then, are the ultimate "building blocks" of Whitehead's system. They exist in the full sense of the term; and behind or beyond them there is no other. All other elements in the philosophy of organism are derived by analysis from actual entities. What *are* actual entities? "The final facts are, all alike, actual entities; and these actual entities are drops of experience, complex, and interdependent."[63] Actual entities differ among themselves; indeed, it is quite impossible that any two of them should be *exactly* alike. But they all exemplify the same generic principles. For one important thing, they are all "experiences." (It is *most* important to understand that, for Whitehead, consciousness is *not* necessary to experience. Only a few highly organized actual entities attain the level of conscious mentality.) "Each actual entity is a throb of experience including the actual world within its scope. It is a process of 'feeling' the many data, so as to absorb them into the unity of one individual 'satisfaction.'"[64]

Whitehead used the term "concrescence" (literally, "a growing together") to denote the process by which an actual entity comes to be. The actual entity—and this point cannot be emphasized too strongly—is not something *in addition to* the process. "The process itself is the constitution of the actual entity; in Locke's phrase, it is the 'real internal constitution' of the actual entity."[65] If we think of the actual entity as a substantial thing independent of its experience—and to do so is a temptation that is hard to resist, given our ingrained substantialist ways of thinking—we shall never understand this crucial part of Whitehead's philosophy.

The experience that constitutes an actual entity is always *of* something; that is, it has data or objects available to it. Thus if I see a dog, the dog is the object of my experience, is a part of the experience without being the experience. Generally, the concrescing occasion (or actual entity) is built up of its appropriations of the data available to it. Whitehead called these appropriations "prehensions," a term that suggests taking hold of or grasping. (A monkey's tail is said to be "prehensile," that is, suited for grasping or wrapping around something.) By using this nonordinary term and by avoiding a term like "apprehension," Whitehead hoped to underscore the *non*intellectual character of most prehensions. Only a few extraordinary prehensions achieve the level of conscious mentality. The reaction of the mercury in a thermometer to changes in temperature exemplifies a prehension that holds no suggestion of conscious awareness.

Whitehead's own phrase for his philosophy, "the philosophy of organism," suggests the interrelatedness of the elements of reality. The crucial importance of prehension is reflected in the following passage: "An actual entity has a perfectly definite bond with each item in the universe. This determinate bond is its prehension of that item."[66] The bond may be positive or negative; hence the two species of prehension, positive and negative (Whitehead usually referred to a positive prehension as a "feeling"). In a negative prehension some possible object of experience is excluded from feeling. Now in *every* prehension, there are three factors: (1) the prehending *subject,* or the actual entity in which that prehension is a concrete element; (2) the *datum,* or the object prehended; and (3) the *subjective form* of the prehension, which is *how* the subject in question prehends that datum.[67] If the datum prehended is another (past) actual entity, the prehension is called "physical." If the datum prehended is a pure possibility (what Whitehead called an "eternal object"), the prehension is called "conceptual." Two warnings are in order: (1) "physical" is not equivalent to "material" and (2) neither physical nor conceptual prehension necessarily involves consciousness. Consciousness is a very special kind of subjective form or way of prehending. It is also worth remarking that *all* actual entities have both a physical and a conceptual "pole," though, of course, the relative importance of the two poles varies greatly from one actual entity to another.

Both words in the phrase "actual entity" are significant. An actual entity is *actual* insofar as it *acts,* or insofar as it is a being with what Whitehead called "subjective immediacy." Everything actual is something for itself; there is no such thing as "vacuous actuality," that is, an actual entity devoid of subjective immediacy. On the other hand, an actual entity is an *entity* (or an object) in that once it has come to be and perished (that is, no longer enjoys subjective immediacy), it becomes a datum for all subsequent actual entities. The distinction that Whitehead was seeking to draw is similar to Descartes' distinction between *realitas formaliter* and *realitas objective.* Indeed, Whitehead adopted these very terms for his own use. It is this sense that Whitehead had in mind when he wrote of the "*objective* immortality" of an actual entity, in other words, the influence it exerts as an *object* or datum on subsequent actual entities. By thus distinguishing the two sides of an actual entity's existence, the actual (or "formal") and the objective, Whitehead could, without paradox, describe our immediate actions as perishing and yet living for evermore.[68]

Whitehead embodied the primacy of actual entities in what he called the "ontological principle," which is, in a rather cryptic formulation, "no actual entity, then no reason."[69] This means that the final reasons for anything's being what is is and not something else are to be sought among actual entities—either in the actual past of the occasion in question or in the occasion's own "subjective aim," or over-all purpose. In other words, the conditions satisfied by the becoming (or concrescence) of an actual entity are facts about other (past) actual entities or about its own "real internal constitution." This is why Whitehead said that the ontological principle might also be called the "principle of efficient, and final, causation."[70] Though it is not strictly part of the ontological principle, Whitehead also held that no actual entity can be *wholly* explained by efficient causation, that is, by reference to causes in its past. Every actual entity exhibits some degree, however small, of final causation. This doctrine amounts to a repudiation of mechanism.[71]

For Whitehead actual entities are the functional equivalent of the traditional substance. As already noted, one basic reason for preferring actual entities to substance as the fundamental category is that "substance" carries the suggestion of a static reality whereas "actual entity" connotes process. In fact, every actual entity adds something genuinely novel to actuality; something new has been added. The question now arises how an actual entity can be novel and unique. The answer leads us to the category of *non*actual entities, the chief of which are eternal objects, or pure possibilities. These are the equivalent of what were traditionally called "universals," but Whitehead avoided that term as misleading. In Whitehead's own words, "Any entity whose conceptual recognition does not involve a necessary reference to any definite actual entities of the temporal world is called an 'eternal object.'"[72] Thus, for example, if one thinks of

the color red abstracted from any particular red thing, one is thinking of an eternal object. Without eternal objects there could be no novelty—or, for that matter, change of any sort. For change to occur, there must be possibilities that are up to the present unrealized. To Whitehead the alternative of a completely static universe was unthinkable.

Whitehead insisted that eternal objects are always potentialities *for actual entities.* He did not suppose, as Plato is often thought to have supposed, that eternal objects constitute a realm of superreality. On the contrary, they are discovered through an analysis of actual entities, and they *exist* only as elements in the constitution of an actual entity. The point of the contrast between actual entities and eternal objects is that eternal objects, considered as pure possibilities, are perfectly neutral about how, when, and by what (if anything) they will be actually exemplified. Just what possibilities are actually realized depends on the actual world, not on the possibilities themselves. (A point or two on terminology: "Ingression" is Whitehead's term for the exemplification of an eternal object by an actual entity; "objectification" is his term for the process by which one actual entity becomes a datum for a subsequent actual entity.)

Eternal objects do not "do" anything. They are absolutely passive and, as such, comprise a perfect "democracy." Considered in abstraction from the actual world, no one eternal object is more likely to be realized (or exemplified) than any other. But clearly that is not the case in the actual world. The actual world is ordered in such a way that there are regular, predictable sequences of events; just *which* sequences depends on the character of the actual entities involved. At the most general level some actual entity is required to impose limits on the boundless possibilities represented by eternal objects. This primordial actual entity is God. (In *Science and the Modern World,* Whitehead referred to God as the Principle of Concretion, that is, the principle by which *actual* possibilities, as opposed to *abstract* possibilities, are marked off.) God is necessary, in Whitehead's view, because explanation always comes to rest in something *actual.* The *real* possibilities open to actual entities reflect the *decision* of prior actual entities; and the most general limits of real possibility reflect the primordial actuality of God. God, then, mediates between the boundless abstract possibilities of eternal objects and the particularities of individual actual occasions. "By this recognition of the divine element the general Aristotelian principle is maintained that, apart from things that are actual, there is nothing—nothing either in fact or in efficacy."[73]

The agency of God in securing the required primordial limitation should not be thought of as creation *ex nihilo.* God's initial "envisagement," as Whitehead called it, is not literally *before* other actualities; it is, rather, a metaphysical necessity. As Whitehead said, God is not *before* all creation but rather *with* all creation.

The aspect of God that we have discussed was referred to by Whitehead as the "primordial" nature of God. As such it is only an abstract element in the concrete being of God. The other aspect of God—which is temporal and contingent—is the "consequent" nature of God, or that part of

God's being that arises from his participation in the temporal world. I cannot here expand on Whitehead's theory of God but will only say that the "primordial" and "consequent" natures of God are *not* two substantially independent entities. They are distinguishable aspects of *one* being. An analogous distinction can be drawn in every human being. Although our experience constantly changes, we are in some obvious sense the same person we were yesterday or ten years ago. In God the identity through time is perfect (ours is imperfect), and his changing experience is all-inclusive.[74]

As we have already noted, Whitehead sought to base his philosophy on the most concrete aspects of our experience. One basic, and, finally, inexplicable, fact of experience is that of change. It is so basic, in fact, that Whitehead included creativity under the Category of the Ultimate. By "creativity" Whitehead meant to refer to the underlying activity that is manifested in all forms of actuality. It is not—and this must be strongly emphasized—an entity separate from individual creative occasions. "It is that ultimate notion of the highest generality at the base of actuality."[75] It is impossible to characterize Creativity except by reference to its "accidents"; that is, its particular, conditioned instances. Every actual entity is an instance of Creativity. The actual entity, the concrescing occasion, has its "data," to be sure; but the particular manner in which it synthesizes those given materials is unique. Accordingly, Whitehead also described Creativity as "that ultimate principle by which the many, which are the universe disjunctively, become the one actual occasion, which is the universe conjunctively."[76] It is for this reason, too, that Whitehead includes two other notions in the Category of the Ultimate, *many* and *one*.

The tie between actual entities, the "microscopic" realities discovered by metaphysical analysis, and such ordinary "macroscopic" objects as stones and trees, is given in Whitehead's theory of *nexus* (the plural of *nexus*) and societies. Nexus are listed as one of the Categories of Existence and are characterized as "public matters of fact,"[77] as contrasted with subjective forms, which are "private matters of fact." More fully and less cryptically:

Actual entities involve each other by reason of their prehensions of each other. There are thus real individual facts of the togetherness of actual entities, which are real, individual, and particular, in the same sense in which actual entities and the prehensions are real, individual, and particular.[78]

The term "society" is introduced in the chapter "Some Derivative Notions"; societies are not included in the Categoreal Scheme. "Nexus" is the broader term: every society is a nexus, but not every nexus is a society. A society is a nexus with "social order," that is, a nexus whose characteristics are derived from earlier stages of the nexus. Thus a social nexus endures through time, a characteristic that actual entities do not have. It is by virtue of nexus—and especially social nexus—that the world is felt as a community, that there are the laws of nature discerned by the various sciences.

What is especially interesting about Whitehead's theory of *nexus* is that he made them derivative from actual entities. This is another mark of his departure from traditional substance philosophies, which fastened on *enduring* objects as the basic realities. Whitehead took events or occurrences as fundamental, thereby ensuring that change and process would not be added on as an afterthought to realities that are essentially static.

Even sympathetic readers of Whitehead are often puzzled how a writer so professedly concerned with the concrete should produce a philosophy that seems so remote from ordinary experience. It is helpful in this connection to remember that Whitehead was highly critical of traditional accounts of perception. The reason Whitehead's philosophy seems so abstract is that we are accustomed to taking as concrete elements of experience that are in fact highly sophisticated and abstract. Traditional versions of perception, of which we are heirs, or victims, proceed in a thoroughly topsy-turvy fashion. They concentrate on visual perception, in which the cruder, more basic forms of experience are almost completely obliterated by the clear-cut data of color and shape. It is understandable that philosophers have emphasized the clearer elements, but it is still catastrophic for philosophic theory. "The consequences of the neglect of this law, that the late derivative elements are more clearly illuminated by consciousness than the primitive elements, have been fatal to the proper analysis of an experient occasion. In fact, most of the difficulties of philosophy are produced by it."[79] The inevitable consequence of this inversion is skepticism, as Hume brilliantly demonstrated.

Hume's logic may be impeccable, but his account of human perception was fundamentally wrong. Against Hume, Whitehead maintained that a sound and accurate analysis reveals an element of causal efficacy. Admittedly vaguer and harder to label than the data of what Whitehead called "presentational immediacy," the data of causal efficacy refer to "our general sense of existence, as one item among others, in an efficacious actual world."[80] Examples of this latter kind of perception are memory, visceral feelings, and the sense of the "withness" of the body in perception. We see colors and shapes, for example, but we see *with* the eyes, and this sense of bodily functioning is immediate, not just an inference from physiological theory.

Perception does not normally take place in either of the "pure" modes—causal efficacy or presentational immediacy—but rather in the "mixed" mode of "symbolic reference," which results from the interaction of the two pure modes. The attempt to explain the mixed mode apart from its two more basic components has been disastrous for philosophy, but such an attempt is part of the pattern of overintellectualism that has plagued Western philosophy almost from its beginning.

In his theory of perception Whitehead tried to give proper scope both to the urgent but comparatively inarticulate sense of causal efficacy and to the more intellectualized prehensions that we often *identify* with perception. Without the sense of causal efficacy, we are cut off from our world, and we end up in Humean skepticism. Without the sharper data of clear consciousness, we would have no science, and we would not be fully human. Whitehead asked only that we remember that consciousness is the zenith of experience, not its base.

New Realism and Critical Realism

Whitehead's own label for his philosophy was "the philosophy of organism." Others have called him a realist, and a few idealists have, understandably, tried to claim him as one of their own. But the battle between realism and idealism in American philosophy goes back farther than Whitehead.

The terms "idealism" and "realism" are easily susceptible of misinterpretation. "Idealism" is often used as a label for the view that reality is ultimately mental or spiritual in character, and in this sense American philosophy is replete with idealists—from Jonathan Edwards through Emerson to Royce. We do not have space to examine the idealism of a number of other highly capable American philosophers, but we shall look briefly at two reactions to idealism: the "new realism" and "critical realism."[81]

It was to idealism as a thesis about the nature of *knowledge*, rather than as a theory about the nature of reality, that a number of American philosophers reacted. Recall, as an example of this thesis, Royce's contention that when we assert that something exists we mean that it is present to some knowing subject. The new realists and the critical realists agreed in rejecting this thesis; or, to put it otherwise, they agreed that the act of knowing does not alter the object known. In philosophical jargon, the relation of knower to known is an "external" relation as far as the object known is concerned. In attacking the idealist contention, the new realists were assaulting a position that had been widely regarded as impregnable.

In 1910 six American professors of philosophy—R. B. Perry and Edwin B. Holt, of Harvard University; W. T. Marvin and E. G. Spaulding, of Princeton University; and W. P. Montague and W. B. Pitkin, of Columbia University—published "A Program and First Platform of Six Realists" in *The Journal of Philosophy.* The same six men published a book, *The New Realism,* in 1912. Among the planks of their platform are exhortations to philosophers that they follow the example of scientists by working together and by isolating problems and tackling them separately. The substantive portion of their platform asserts that some at least of both the particulars and the essences or universals of which we are conscious are independent of our consciousness of them. The final part of their platform is the one that aroused the ire of other realists: the thesis that some at least of the particulars and essences or universals of which we are aware are apprehended *directly* rather than indirectly through copies or mental images. This is *presentative* realism, as opposed to *representative* realism.

The new realists differed among themselves about the nature of the objects known and about man's place in the world, but on the methodological and epistemological issues broached in their program and platform they were agreed. In fact, they seemed much more nearly of one mind than did another group of professors, who called themselves "criti-

cal" realists. The latter group, consisting of George Santayana, formerly of Harvard University; C. A. Strong, of Columbia University; A. K. Rogers, of Yale University; Arthur O. Lovejoy, of Johns Hopkins University; R. W. Sellars, of the University of Michigan; J. B. Pratt, of Williams University; and Durant Drake, of Vassar College, published *Essays in Critical Realism* in 1920. Though they agreed with some of the views of the "new" realists, they differed strongly on the issue of direct presentation of objects to the mind. Such a view they labeled "naïve," and accordingly they qualified their realism as "critical."

Whatever their differences on other issues, the critical realists were agreed that what the mind is directly, or immediately, aware of is never a material object but is rather a mental state or idea. Material objects are known indirectly, or mediately, as the inferred cause (direct or indirect) of ideas. The chief virtue claimed for this version of representative realism, which is a species of dualism, is its ability to account for perceptual error and for illusions. If we are directly aware of material objects, so the reasoning goes, it is hard to understand how we could be mistaken about their properties. The earlier realists were not slow to point out that, if critical realism is strong in explaining error, it is at least equally weak in explaining truth. If we are directly aware only of our own mental states, by what legitimate process can we get to the common objective world we all believe in? Of the critical realists only Santayana appreciated the force of this question and accepted the inevitable skeptical consequences of his dualistic premises.[82]

Among themselves the critical realists disagreed about the nature of what it is we are directly aware of. One group, whose most notable exponent was Santayana, held that we are directly aware of "essences" (see the earlier discussion of Santayana), which are distinct from both the material object they are supposed to characterize and the mental state that entertains the essence as its datum. The other group, which includes Sellars and Lovejoy, argue that we are directly aware of sense-data, which are momentary mental existents.

We made a point of describing the new and critical realists as professors, a description that underscores the arrival of philosophy as a *profession.* Whether this circumstance is good or bad, it is a fact. It is hard to find an important twentieth-century American philosopher who has had no academic connection. And the issues that increasingly occupied American philosophers were "academic" in the vaguely pejorative sense of that term. As far as the issues joined by the new and critical realists are concerned, even their fellow academics eventually found the fracas uninteresting and turned to other "academic" issues they found more exciting.

Naturalists

Closely allied to the realists in both outlook and doctrines are a group of philosophers often referred to as "naturalists." Indeed, the term is frequently applied to some realists, such as Santayana, Sellars, Perry, and Montague. The term "naturalism" can be used in a broad or a narrow sense. In the broad sense a philosopher is a naturalist if he or she believes that there is nothing beyond "nature," that everything can be explained without invoking any "supernatural" being or principles. (Just how unhelpful this label is can be seen in the reflection that Aristotle, Spinoza, and Whitehead have all been described as naturalists. The trouble comes in deciding just how inclusive "nature" is.) In the narrow sense a naturalist is one who believes that science offers the only genuine method of discovering the truth about anything. A third, more technical, sense of "naturalism" is found in ethics. An ethical naturalist is one who believes that statements about "good," "right," "obligation," and so on, can be translated into statements about "natural" or "empirical" properties. Thus for example, "*x* is good" means "*x* is pleasurable"; or "*x* is right" means "*x* tends to the greatest happiness of the greatest number of people." A metaphysical or epistemological naturalist may or may not be an ethical naturalist, and the converse is also true.[83]

Later Pragmatists: George H. Mead, Clarence Irving Lewis, and Sidney Hook

In addition to the "Big Three" of Peirce, James, and Dewey, American pragmatism has been ably articulated by George H. Mead (1863–1931), Clarence Irving Lewis (1883–1964), and Sidney Hook (1902–   ).

Born in the same year as Santayana, Mead published little during his lifetime; most of his works are posthumous collections of unpublished (and unfinished) manuscripts and students' notes. Nonetheless, Mead exerted, and continues to exert, some influence on philosophers and even more on philosophically inclined psychologists and sociologists.[84]

The pragmatism of Sidney Hook is essentially that of Dewey, and Hook makes no effort to conceal the fact. What is most philosophically interesting about Hook's writings is his effort to show certain affinities between pragmatism and the philosophy of Karl Marx. And we must stress that it is Marx, and *not* Soviet communism, that Hook finds congenial. As a defender of democracy and personal freedom, Hook has been a fierce and relentless foe of the Lenin-Stalin brand of Soviet totalitarianism, which invokes the authority of Marx while betraying his philosophy at every turn. Further, Hook insists that the philosophy of Marx himself has to be demythologized and dedogmatized before it is plausible.

In recent years Hook has been a severe and acerbic critic of what he regards as the irrationalism and destructiveness of some student protest movements. Always ready to do battle against the enemies of freedom or sanity and armed with what seems to be an inexhaustible supply of vitriol, Hook may well be the most formidable polemicist on the American scene today. Few have ever crossed swords with him and come away without some painful gashes.[85]

Of the three pragmatists we are discussing, C. I. Lewis was perhaps the most philosophically gifted, and certainly the most influential on "professional" philosophers. As a long-term teacher at Harvard, Lewis not only produced a sizable corpus of widely read works but also exerted a direct professorial influence on a large number of students who became capable philosophers in their own right. He made significant contributions to philosophy in logic, theory of knowledge, and moral theory.

Lewis referred to his position as "conceptual pragmatism," the adjective serving to emphasize his concern with the a priori features of human knowledge. A lifelong admirer of Kant, Lewis developed a conception of the a priori (or the nonempirical, pre-experiential element in knowledge) that reflects the influence of the German philosopher and the impact of pragmatism (especially that of Peirce). Lewis called this a pragmatic conception of the a priori, but it is easy to misinterpret his main points. Like Kant, Lewis insisted that knowledge requires a *given* element and an element of active interpretation. When we recognize or discriminate objects, we are not just passively receiving data; we are classifying and interpreting. Without the active role of mind in providing classificatory schemes, the raw given data would be unintelligible. Unlike Kant, Lewis held that the *ways* in which we classify are at bottom practical matters. What is *given* is, in some sense, absolute; it is beyond our control. But how we interpret the given, how we classify it, reflects our decision about what is most convenient and useful. Our conceptual schemes can, and do, change. The history of science affords many examples of such changes. Lewis did not suggest, of course, that our application of concepts to the given element in experience is capricious or idiosyncratic (though it may be). Such application is deeply rooted in social and linguistic conventions. But the important thing to note is that Lewis rejected the Kantian view that the conceptual structure of the human mind is fixed and eternal. The categories by which we organize our experience must, in the long run, satisfy general human needs.[86]

Logical Positivism

The movement known as "logical positivism" (or "logical empiricism") had its beginning in Europe in the 1920's. The best-known "cell" of positivists was the so-called Vienna Circle, a group of scientifically trained philosophers who met regularly to discuss problems of common interest. Another group, in Berlin, boasted some distinguished members. The rise of nazism in the 1930's forced most of them to leave the Continent, and a number of them came to the United States. Several of the better-known positivists were hired by philosophy departments in American universities. Rudolph Carnap (1891–1970), long acknowledged a leader of the positivists, taught at the University of Chicago and later at the University of California at Los Angeles. Hans Reichenbach (1891–1953), who preferred to call himself a logical empiricist, taught at the University of California at Los Angeles for about fifteen years. The great Austrian mathematician-logician Kurt Goedel went to Princeton University, as did Karl Hempel, one of the most influential philosophers of science of the last generation; Herbert Feigl went to the University of Iowa and later to the University of Minnesota. Gustav Bergmann went to the University of Iowa. Though not as philosophically inclined as the others mentioned, the great Polish mathematician-logician Alfred Tarski may be included in this group who fled the Nazi terror. Tarski has taught at the University of California at Berkeley since 1942. Whether right or wrong in their philosophical theories, these men occasioned a great deal of spirited controversy within the philosophical community.

Although positivists laid out, appropriately enough, positive programs to be accomplished, it was their attack on metaphysics that attracted the interest—and the fire—of their nonpositivist colleagues. The root of the positivists' attack on "transcendental metaphysics" is their theory of meaning, according to which there are only two classes of "cognitively meaningful" propositions: (1) the purely formal propositions of mathematics and logic (which are "tautologies" and therefore assert nothing about the actual world) and (2) those propositions that are verifiable (or disverifiable) by the methods of natural science. "The meaning of a proposition is the method of its verification" is one well-known slogan proclaiming the "verifiability" theory of meaning. Some readers will recall adumbrations of this doctrine in Peirce's pragmatic theory of meaning. (It should be stated that some members of this school, such as Reichenbach and Bergmann, never accepted the verifiability theory of meaning.)

The statements of traditional metaphysics, statements about the ultimate nature of reality or about God, are clearly not like those of mathematics or logic, nor do they admit of scientific verification. Thus, according to the positivist criterion of meaning, they are cognitively meaningless. (The adverb "cognitively" serves notice that, while metaphysical statements may be "meaningful" in the sense of having important emotional associations, they are literally senseless as putative assertions of fact.) Note that, according to this theory of meaning, metaphysical propositions are neither true nor false; they are not significant assertions at all. "The moon is larger than the sun" is a meaningful but false proposition, unlike "God is beyond space and time," which does not really assert anything at all. In this game the agnostic is as muddled as the theist or the atheist, because, like the other two, he mistakenly supposes that the question of God's existence makes sense, only we cannot find out the true answer. For all its apparent intelligibility, the proposition "God exists" is literally meaningless.

The status of ethical statements (for example, "Murder is wrong") is a point of contention among positivists; but, largely because of the widely read works of Carnap and the English philosopher Alfred J. Ayer, the ethics usually associated with the positivists is emotivism—the view that ethical statements, like those of metaphysics, are cognitively meaningless. The word "emotivism" derives from the explanation given for ethical statements—that they are expressions of emotion.[87]

The bumptious attack by the positivists on the revered citadels of traditional philosophy provoked vigorous and effective counterattacks; and, to their credit, the positivists themselves were almost painfully self-critical.[88] One of the most embarrassing questions put to the positivists—and one never satisfactorily answered—was, "What is the status of the verifiability principle itself?" It is obviously not a proposition of mathematics or logic, and just as obviously it is not itself scientifically verifiable. It appears, then, that the chief weapon of the positivists was just a piece of unsupported dogmatism; and that is precisely the verdict that a good many philosophers of various persuasions finally reached.[89]

As a movement logical positivism is very nearly dead, and no prospects of a miraculous recovery are on the horizon. Nonetheless, some salutary influences of positivism are evident. Though it can hardly be thought successful in either its own program or its polemic against metaphysics, positivism did make philosophers more cautious in stating their views, and it cast a shadow of suspicion upon certain kinds of metaphysics that still affects much of Anglo-American philosophy. In addition, positivistically inclined philosophers have done a great deal of important work in the philosophy of science.[90]

Anglo-American philosophers of the last several decades have been deeply interested in language. As we have just seen, the logical positivists were concerned to "purify" language and to admit as cognitively meaningful only those propositions that satisfy the stringent requirements of the verifiability criterion of meaning. This program issued in a view of philosophy as the logical analysis of the language of science (where "science" is construed quite broadly). Positivists were often enamored of formal or "ideal" languages, which supposedly keep us from falling into the traps set for us by ordinary language.

Ordinary-Language Philosophy

A very different attitude toward language is found among a large number of American philosophers who follow Ludwig Wittgenstein in rejecting both the possibility and the desirability of a so-called "ideal" language.[91] This school of thought is known as "ordinary-language philosophy." In opposition to the logical positivists, who hankered after "ideal" languages, adherents of this school argue that philosophers typically go wrong, that is, get themselves embroiled in puzzles and paradoxes, precisely because they ignore the ordinary contexts and ordinary restrictions of certain words. Thus, for example, the so-called problem of other minds (How do I know that someone else is in pain or even that he has a mind?) is generated by a misuse of the verb "know." The proper philosophical method consists in a kind of "therapy," that is, in showing the puzzled philosopher the source of his puzzlement. When we have exposed the roots of his problem, the philosopher will see that his original question was spurious, and he will be cured of asking senseless questions. The aim of "good" philosophy is, to change the metaphor a bit, to show the fly the way out of the fly bottle. Far from imposing narrow and arbitrary restrictions on meaning, ordinary-language philosophers of the Wittgensteinian stripe insist that we pay close attention of the great variety of ways words are actually used. If we think about the many *different uses* of language, we will not be tempted to suppose, as many philosophers have supposed, that we must be doing some *one* thing when we speak or write a language.

Perhaps the best-known American advocate of the Wittgensteinian approach is Norman Malcolm (1911–), of Cornell University. In addition to his own philosophical writings, Malcolm, who was a student and friend of Wittgenstein at Cambridge, wrote an absorbing account of Wittgenstein the man, *Ludwig Wittgenstein: A Memoir.* Another able interpreter and defender of Wittgenstein—and almost certainly the wittiest—is O. K. Bouwsma. Malcolm's colleague at Cornell, Max Black (1909–), though inclined to be more critical of Wittgenstein than Malcolm, nonetheless has been decisively influenced by Wittgenstein.[92]

Aside from Wittgenstein, who was a Cambridge man, the strongest influence on American ordinary-language philosophy has come from a group of Oxford philosophers, most notably John L. Austin (1911–60) and Gilbert Ryle (1900–). The influence of Austin, especially, has been strong in the 1960's and 1970's, but it is hard, if not impossible, to find American followers of Austin comparable to the Wittgensteinians Bouwsma, Malcolm, and (with the appropriate qualifications) Black. Two reasons for this, perhaps, are that Wittgenstein's influence has been felt for a longer time than has Austin's and that Wittgenstein was the sort of person who attracted disciples. However that may be, John R. Searle's *Speech Acts* is a continuation of the work of Austin (with other British influences clearly in evidence).[93] To what extent American philosophy will continue to bear the marks of Oxford influence is, of course, a matter of conjecture.[94]

Existentialism and Phenomenonology

Existentialism has had few well-known advocates among American "professional" philosophers, but it has attracted more attention from the public at large than any other philosophical movement during the past thirty years. With its emphasis on concrete human situations and emotions, existentialism has appealed to many people who are repelled by what they believe to be the abstractness and the triviality of much academic philosophy. Whatever the merits of that attitude, existentialism in the United States cannot boast of any advocates who begin to approach the stature of the Frenchmen Jean-Paul Sartre and Gabriel Marcel or the Germans Karl Jaspers and Martin Heidegger. (The one possible exception to this generalization is the German-American Paul Tillich, who was more nearly a theologian than a philosopher.) Two widely read books by American philosophers are William Barrett's *Irrational Man* and John Wild's *The Challenge of Existentialism.*[95]

A movement closely associated with existentialism is phenomenology, which numbers some American philosophers among its adherents. But again, no American phenomenologists have produced works approaching in importance or originality those of the major European phenomenologists (most notably Edmund Husserl, but also Sartre, Heidegger, and Maurice Merleau-Ponty). A journal, *Philosophy and Phenomenological Research,* was founded by Marvin Farber, of the University of Buffalo, in 1939 to promote discussion of philosophy from a phenomenological viewpoint. Duquesne

University Press and Northwestern University Press have published a number of original works and translations of works by phenomenologists.

Willard Van Orman Quine

Beyond much doubt the best-known living American philosopher is Willard Van Orman Quine (1908–), of Harvard University. Quine's first love, at least chronologically, was mathematical logic, and he has made significant contributions to that field. Philosophically, the strongest influence on Quine's thought was the work of Carnap, but there is also a definite and strong pragmatic influence. Unlike most positivists, Quine has never seemed embarrassed or nervous about tackling straightforwardly metaphysical questions, even if he does often rephrase the question to suit his own philosophic bent (and some may argue that Quine's brand of metaphysics was not the target of the positivists anyway). Quine's philosophical work is usually subtle and sometimes technical and for those reasons does not lend itself readily to summary statement. I shall confine this discussion of his philosophy to two issues for which he is well known.

In 1951, Quine published an article entitled "Two Dogmas of Empiricism" (*Philosophical Review,* reprinted in *From a Logical Point of View),* the two alleged dogmas being (1) the analytic-synthetic distinction and (2) reductionism, or the view that meaningful statements must be reducible to terms that refer to immediate experience (or, in even worse jargon, the view that physicalist language must be replaced by phenomenalist language).[96] We shall discuss only the first of the alleged dogmas.

Philosophers have long been given to saying that some propositions are true as a matter of fact, or that they are contingently true; for example, "Booth shot Lincoln." These are called "synthetic" propositions. But other propositions are true, so many philosophers have held, because of what the statements mean; they are necessarily true. "All mares are female" is an example of an "analytic" proposition. Now all of this seems plausible and straightforward, but Quine argues that the distinction is an "unempirical dogma," "a metaphysical article of faith."

Quine directs his fire both at efforts to explain the distinction in question and at the distinction itself. The nub of his attack on explications of the dichotomy is that they are unavoidably enmeshed in a vicious circle. To explain how and why "all mares are female" is analytic, one must invoke some notion of synonymy; but it turns out that synonymy is intelligible only if we already understand what analyticity is. And this criticism holds not only for natural languages but for artificial languages as well.

In Quine's view human knowledge in its totality may be likened to an onion (the figure is mine, not Quine's), with its many layers running from the core outward. The outermost layers may be peeled off without seriously affecting the rest of the onion; but the center can be got out only by disturbing all the other layers. Just so, we can easily revise our casually held beliefs, but revision of the core—the laws of logic or arithmetic, for example—would produce repercussions traveling to the periphery. We do, of course, occasionally revise fairly basic beliefs: Einstein superseded Newton; Kepler, Ptolemy; and Darwin, Aristotle. No belief is absolutely immune to revision, but some are so basic that we would go to great pains to keep them intact. But the boundary dividing any proposition from any other is just a matter of degree. The absolute division imbedded in the analytic-synthetic distinction is a myth, or, rather, a dogma.

Quine continues his attack on the analytic-synthetic distinction (as well as on conventional accounts of meaning) in what may be his most influential philosophical work, *Word and Object.* In that work he develops a theory of meaning (if one can say that Quine *has* a theory of meaning) closely tied to the observable behavioral responses of people who speak a given language. Thus, the meaning of the sentence, "There's a rabbit," must be sought in the responses of English-speaking people in the presence of the appropriate stimulus (in this case, the presence of a rabbit). This is what Quine calls "stimulus meaning." Synonymy is treated in parallel fashion. Two sentences are said to be "socially stimulus-synonymous" if they are individually stimulus-synonymous for most speakers of the language. Quine even offers an account of analyticity along these lines: A sentence is stimulus-analytic if a speaker would assent to it, or to nothing, following every stimulation (within the limits of a brief time that Quine calls the "*modulus* of stimulation"); and the sentence is *socially* stimulus-analytic if it is stimulus-analytic for most speakers of the language.

But this is not the traditional notion of analyticity that philosophers have cherished. It is tied to detectable verbal behavior, and it might turn out that some sentences are stimulus-analytic that would not count as analytic on the usual notion. But that circumstance, Quine argues, is no reason to reject his account. Those who criticize his view because of its divergence from their own must first of all defend their own view as the correct one; and that, in Quine's opinion, they cannot do.

The thesis of *Word and Object* that elicited most comment is what Quine calls "the indeterminacy of translation." If several people were to undertake to compile translation manuals of a language none of them has any knowledge of, it is possible for them to come up with incompatible translations of indefinitely many sentences in the language. And, what is most curious, each of the translations may be perfectly compatible with the observable speech habits of the natives who speak the language. Though it is possible to reduce the amount of disagreement, it is not possible to eliminate it altogether; or, to put it another way, there is no way to tell when we have got rid of all disagreement. Though it is less obvious, Quine believes that the same considerations apply, *mutatis mutandis,* to translations between two languages that are already known, or even to "translations" within the same language. To Quine's mind (he should pardon the expression!) these facts suggest that there are no such things as intentions or meanings or propositions conceived in the traditional way—or at least that they have no place in any philosophy that takes science as its model.

Quine has no interest in denying that there are minds or intentions in the ordinary sense, and I am not sure that he is even interested in *denying* that they may exist in the philosophical sense. What he wants to insist on is that a philosophy animated by the spirit of science can get on better, and be less tempted to bolt up dead-end streets, by concentrating on observable behavior. It is obvious that philosophy so conceived exhibits no sharp boundaries with science, and this circumstance accords well with the conception of knowledge advanced in "Two Dogmas."

Quine has original, sometimes startling, things to say about many topics. For example, he says, in discussing what there is, that to be is to be the value of a variable. But we have said enough to convey something of the stuff and the spirit of Quine's philosophy.

Quine's writings have been subjected to very close scrutiny for a long time, and some of the criticisms have been sharp and probing. One of the great virtues of Quine's work is that it has seemed worth criticizing, even when it has seemed wrong. And that is very high praise.[97]

In recent years American philosophy seems to have taken a tack away from ordinary-language analysis (though that way of doing philosophy is still widespread) and toward more formal analysis. If my sense of this direction is correct, it will turn out, I think, to owe a great deal to Quine, both by way of inspiration and by way of worthwhile target for criticism.

We began the story of American philosophy with Edwards and have ended it with Quine. In spite of outlooks that are in some ways *toto caelo* different, both men believe(d) that their philosophy was (is) in step with the latest scientific findings. And both men plead(ed) their case with eloquence and brilliance. All of which may go to enforce the conclusion that philosophy and science perform quite different functions; but *that* is itself a disputed philosophical issue.

Two hundred years of philosophical pluralism in America should convince us that while there may be a Soviet philosophy or a Chinese Communist philosophy, there is *no* single American philosophy. There remains only the reflection—the grateful reflection—that Americans have for two hundred years enjoyed the freedom of thought and expression essential to the formation and development of a variety of points of view.

Note: Where there is more than one reference to the same work, I have given full information only in the first citation.

1. It should be noted that, however odious we may find religious persecution, we should not be surprised that the Puritans practiced it. They left England not to found a religiously pluralistic society but rather to practice their own brand of intolerance. There is a certain twisted logic to their thinking. Why should they allow heretics and unbelievers to question or deny with impunity the plain truths that God had revealed in his holy word? So sure were the Puritans of their religious (and associated political) beliefs that they did not hesitate to brand as willfully dishonest or foolish and to treat with appropriate harshness anyone who challenged those beliefs. Thus the Puritans ought to be condemned not for inconsistency but for self-idolatry—for arrogating to themselves that infallibility of knowledge that belongs to God alone. For an interesting account of this side of the Puritan mentality, see Perry Miller, "Puritan State and Puritan Society," in *Errand into the Wilderness* (New York, Harper & Row, 1964; originally published in 1956 by Belnap Press of Harvard University).

2. Curiously enough, as we shall see later in connection with Jonathan Edwards, Calvinists typically insisted on human *freedom* and, therefore, on human responsibility for sin. Indeed, Edwards' major philosophical work is devoted to showing how divine omnipotence is compatible with human freedom and responsibility.

3. It is no part of my purpose here to discuss the many mutations of Calvinism since the seventeenth century. It is perhaps enough to say that, in spite of almost innumerable adaptations and modifications, the central core of Reformed theology has exhibited an amazing vitality and resiliency in a large portion of the Protestant world. Readers interested in pursuing the matter further may consult the following: "Calvinism," in *Encyclopedia of Philosophy* (New York, Macmillan, 1967), II; several articles (for example, "Calvinism" and "Confessions") in *Encyclopedia of Religion and Ethics* (ed. by James Hastings, New York, Charles Scribner's Sons, n.d.). On the transmission of Calvinism to New England, see Miller, "The Marrow of Puritan Divinity," in *Errand into the Wilderness;* and "Edwards and the New England Theology," in *Encyclopedia of Religion and Ethics*.

4. Readers interested in more details of seventeenth-century American religion and politics may consult the following: Vernon Louis Parrington, *Main Currents of American Thought* (New York, Harcourt, Brace, 1927); Miller, *Errand into the Wilderness,* Chaps. I–V; Donald Meyers, "The Dissolution of Calvinism," in *Paths of American Thought* (ed. by Arthur M. Schlesinger, Jr., and Morton White, Boston, Houghton Mifflin, 1963). Representative selections from early American writers—John Cotton, John Winthrop, and John Wise, as well as the Mayflower Compact—may be found in Gerald E. Meyers, *The Spirit of American Philosophy* (New York, G. P. Putnam's Sons, 1970).

5. I have looked at the Great Awakening rather narrowly, as an episode in Edwards' life. For a somewhat broader view, see Miller, "Jonathan Edwards and the Great Awakening," in *Errand into the Wilderness.*

6. Readers of Edwards have long been struck by the similarity between parts of his *Notes on the Mind* and the immaterialism of the great Irish philosopher George Berkeley (1685–1753). It is natural to assume that the youthful Edwards must have read Berkeley, but the evidence suggests that Edwards had no firsthand acquaintance with Berkeley's work either before or after *Notes on the Mind.* A more likely explanation is that the two philosophers reached similar conclusions as a result of applying the logic of their common source, Locke's *Essay Concerning Human Understanding,* more rigorously and persistently than Locke himself had done.

7. The story of Edwards' long struggle with his Northampton congregation is fascinating, and one in which it is hard to find clear-cut heroes and villains. It is clear that Edwards was perfectly sincere in the increasingly stringent requirements he laid on his parishioners; it is equally clear that he was, at times, obstinate, tyrannical, and blundering. Readers interested in a fuller account of this painful episode in Edwards' life may consult the following works: Harold P. Simonson, *Jonathan Edwards: Theologian of the Heart* (Grand Rapids, Mich., William B. Eerdmans Publishing Co., 1974); and Perry Miller, *Jonathan Edwards* (Cleveland, World Publishing Co., 1959). Also of great interest is Edwards' own "Farewell Sermon," delivered July 2, 1750.

8. The full title of the work, with some modernization of spelling, is *A careful and strict Enquiry Into The modern prevailing Notions of that Freedom of Will, Which is supposed to be essential to Moral Agency, Virtue and Vice, Reward and Punishment, Praise and Blame.* An inexpensive edition of this work, edited by William Frankena and Arnold Kaufman, was published by Bobbs-Merrill. The definitive edition, edited by Paul Ramsey, was published by Yale University Press, which is in the process of publishing all Edwards' works.

9. Edwards feared that even the stricter versions of Arminianism would lead inexorably to greater departures from orthodoxy, and his fears were pretty well borne out by what actually happened. The ascendancy of ethical and humane considerations was a natural consequence of giving human beings some measure of self-determination; and, although it would have scandalized Arminius, the line from Arminianism to Pelagianism is fairly straight. Pelagianism is the name associated with the views of Pelagius, a British monk and theologian of the fourth and fifth centuries, who denied original sin and affirmed freedom of the will. As a denial of original sin, Pelagianism is condemned as heretical by orthodox Protestants and Roman Catholics.

10. Edwards' position, that the will is always determined by the strongest motive, seems open to an accusation of vacuity. *Whatever* motive prevails is, by definition, the strongest. *Whatever* a person chooses—however surprising, unexpected, and unpredictable it may be—will be the result of the strongest motive. This is a fact not about the will but about the meaning of "strongest motive." Edwards was not wrong in holding such a view, but he was wrong in supposing that anything interesting or important follows from it. The view is compatible with just about any theory of how the will is determined.

11. An interesting example of this habit is Thomas Hobbes's use of "selfish." All voluntary human acts, Hobbes argued, are selfish; but it quickly becomes clear that Hobbes was not using the term in its ordinary sense. In the *usual* sense of the term some acts are selfish and some are not. When Hobbes's apparently unconscious shift of meaning is discovered, his contention loses most of its interest. The thesis, so startling at first blush, is seen to turn on an unrecognized equivocation.

12. Faced with the problem of saving human freedom and dignity in a world (allegedly) decreed by science to be mechanistic and deterministic, some modern philosophers chose to sunder the world of the mind from the world described by the physicist and to invest

that inner world with a freedom denied to the outer world. The most notable proponents of such a bifurcation are René Descartes (1596–1650) and Immanuel Kant (1724–1804). On the other hand, some philosophers, for example, Thomas Hobbes (1588–1679) and David Hume (1711–76), did not shrink from extending determinism into the inner world of the mind. Edwards belongs to the second class. However, his idealistic metaphysics has the effect of inverting the priority of matter and mind: it is God, the Infinite Spirit, who is the ultimate determiner of all things. In the jargon of philosophy matter becomes an "epiphenomenon"—a by-product—of mind. As we shall see later, some American philosophers (such as Peirce, James, and Whitehead) regarded this problem as spurious because it rests on the false assumption that the physical world is strictly mechanistic and deterministic.

13. Against Edwards we may note that "he did it of his own free will" is perfectly idiomatic ordinary English. In saying this, I do not mean to suggest that we try to trick a metaphysical theory out of this piece of ordinary language. I mean only to point out that Edwards could not appeal to ordinary language to support his argument that it is senseless to speak of the will as free or unfree.

14. Divested of its theological trappings, Edwards' solution to the problem of freedom and determinism was essentially the same as the one accepted by a good many twentieth-century philosophers. They agree with Edwards that it is a muddle to suppose that determinism is incompatible with human freedom. The true opposite of determinism is indeterminism, and the true opposite of freedom is unfreedom. For further discussion of this problem see Arnold S. Kaufman, "Responsibility, Moral and Legal," in *Encyclopedia of Philosophy,* VII. Later in this essay we shall look at two critics of the view Edwards adopts, William Ellery Channing and William James.

15. For a brief discussion of some of the difficulties in Edwards' position see William Frankena and Arnold S. Kaufman, "Introduction," in Jonathan Edwards, *Freedom of the Will* (Indianapolis, Bobbs-Merrill, 1969).

16. The struggle between Roger Williams and the rulers of the Massachusetts Bay colony illustrates this tension. It must be added, however, that Williams advocated religious freedom and church-state separation for reasons different from those of, say, Thomas Paine and Thomas Jefferson. A sloganish and oversimplified way of putting the difference is this: Williams feared that the state would contaminate the church, whereas Paine and Jefferson feared that the church would contaminate the state. The practical result, separation, would be the same in any case.

17. In the ordinary and typical acceptation of "atheist" (that is, one who denies the existence of God), it is silly to call Allen or Paine an atheist. There is a secondary sense of "atheist" that fits Allen and Paine somewhat better; namely, one who denies a *theistic* God. But it is to be doubted whether those who so criticized the two philosophers had this somewhat unusual meaning in mind. Because Paine was better known than Allen and because he outlived Allen by twenty years, he was more consistently the victim of disgraceful and barbaric treatment by some who called themselves ministers of God.

18. These statements are based on a manifesto issued by the Deistical Society of the State of New York, an organization founded by Elihu Palmer (1764–1806).

19. In all essential respects Allen's arguments are identical with a number of traditional arguments from cause and from design. Although identifiable ancestors of these arguments are as old as Plato and Aristotle, the *locus classicus* for them is the *Summa Theologica* of Thomas Aquinas (1225–74). Readers interested in further details and in bibliographical references can consult the articles on cosmological arguments for the existence of God and on teleological arguments for the existence of God in *The Encyclopedia of Philosophy.*

20. Jonathan Edwards severely criticized the Deistic claim that reason unaided by revelation can discover the truth about God and religion. To be sure, Edwards did not doubt that human reason can deduce the existence of a First Cause or some such being, but he was sure that unaided reason could never have discovered the religion of salvation, the Calvinist version of Christianity. A brilliant but uneven sample of Edwards' polemic can be found in his *Miscellaneous Observations on Important Theological Subjects,* a part of which is reprinted under the title "The Insufficiency of Reason as a Substitute for Revelation," in Walter G. Muelder (ed.), *The Development of American Philosophy* (Boston, Houghton Mifflin, 1960). The specific target of Edwards' attack was Matthew Tindal, an English Deist who in 1730 published a piece with the imposing title *Christianity as Old as the Creation.* Tindal's work was so influential and widely read that it was sometimes referred to as "the deist's Bible."

21. Readers are referred to the earlier discussion of Jonathan Edwards for an example of this alleged piece of legerdemain. On the face of it Allen appeared not to understand the distinctions that Edwards tried to draw. As we shall see later, William Ellery Channing and William James also rejected the necessitarian effort to make determinism compatible with human freedom. James avoided the dilemma by denying determinism.

22. Harvey Gates Townsend, *Philosophical Ideas in America* (New York, American Book Co., 1934), p. 67.

23. Alfred North Whitehead, the great twentieth-century mathematician and philosopher, quipped that Unitarians believe that there is at most one God. This *bon mot* is more apt for present-day Unitarians than it is for Channing, who had no doubt whatever that there is exactly one God.

24. Arianism takes its name from Arius, a fourth-century ecclesiastic, who taught that Jesus was more than human but less than divine. Arius' doctrine was condemned as heresy by the Council of Nicea in 325, but it has cropped up in various guises ever since. Channing rejected Socinianism, a sixteenth-century theory that made Jesus the greatest of men but still purely human. It turns out, however, that on the Socinian view Jesus was a *most* unusual human being. Readers interested in pursuing these topics may consult the articles on Arianism and Socinianism in the *Encyclopedia of Religion and Ethics* and in *Encyclopaedia Britannica.*

25. The change in outlook from the American Enlightenment to Transcendentalism is reflected in the respective treatments of Locke. For the Deistic philosophers of the Enlightenment (and, let it be remembered, for Jonathan Edwards as well), Locke was a patron saint. For the Transcendentalists, Locke was a favorite whipping boy, the perfect example of a philosopher who refused to make use of his greatest possession, reason. An excellent sample of this flagellation of "sensationalism" is Theodore Parker's essay "Transcendentalism." Parker accused the followers of Locke of every sin except halitosis, but it seems clear that Parker's presentation of empiricism is a caricature of any actual position.

26. Lewis Mumford, *The Golden Day: A Study in American Experience and Culture* (New York, Boni & Liveright, 1926), p. 79.

27. For a brief discussion of philosophical opinion on Emerson, see Morton White, *Science and Sentiment in America: Philosophical Thought from Jonathan Edwards to John Dewey* (New York, Oxford University Press, 1972).

28. An interesting and detailed account of one of the more famous "fights" in this struggle may be found in the following: William R. Hutchison, "Ripley, Emerson, and the Miracles Question," in *The Transcendentalist Ministers: Church Reform in the New England Renaissance* (New Haven, Yale University Press,

1959); reprinted in Brian M. Barbour (ed.), *American Transcendentalism: An Anthology of Criticism* (Notre Dame, Notre Dame University Press, 1973). Though more conservative than his cousin Emerson, George Ripley agreed with Emerson that Unitarianism placed far too much emphasis on history and too little on the individual's own religious experience. More curiously, perhaps, Ripley found an ally in Jonathan Edwards, especially the mystically inclined Edwards of "A Divine and Supernatural Light." Arguing against Andrews Norton, the "pope" of Unitarianism, Ripley invoked the authority of Edwards—"the most profound theologian whom this country has produced"—in support of the primacy of religious intuition.

29. Emerson adopted the Understanding-Reason distinction from German philosophy, as refracted through Coleridge and Carlyle. English translators have generally rendered the German *Verstand* "Understanding" and *Vernunft* as "Reason." This has always struck me as an unhappy choice, but it has been, and remains, the standard rendering. My former colleague Gustav Mueller suggested "Reason" as a better equivalent of *Verstand,* and "Comprehension" as a better equivalent of *Vernunft.*

30. An analogy may help to bring out what Emerson had in mind. The brilliant, eccentric, and irascible Danish astronomer Tycho Brahe (1546–1601) made a great many remarkably accurate observations of the movements of the planets, especially Mars. But he never really did anything with the mass of data he so assiduously collected. The real significance of his observations became clear only with the *theoretical* work of his more illustrious pupil, Johannes Kepler (1571–1630). Tycho's gathering of particular data exemplifies the work of the Understanding, whereas Kepler's laws of planetary motion reflect the synthesizing activity of Reason.

31. Emerson attributed this statement to Plato, but I think that he must be mistaken. I suspect that he has in mind Aristotle's *Poetics* 1451^b 1–8.

32. Fiske's main works are *Outline of Cosmic Philosophy Based on the Doctrine of Evolution* and *Through Nature to God,* both published by Houghton Mifflin.

33. The first six volumes of *Collected Papers of Charles Sanders Peirce* (hereafter cited as *Collected Papers*) were edited by Charles Hartshorne and Paul Weiss and published by Harvard University Press between 1931 and 1935. Volumes VII and VIII, edited by Arthur Burks and also published by Harvard, appeared in 1958. (References to this set will be by volume and paragraph, not page, number.) It is some measure of the neglect of this magnificent philosopher that it was seventeen years after his death in 1914 before any of his papers appeared in readily accessible form.

34. In the interests of historical accuracy, we should note that it was William James rather than Peirce who most effectively called attention to pragmatism. With characteristic honesty and generosity, James acknowledged his debt to Peirce, and without James's efforts, Peirce would have been even less well known than he was. There is a certain irony in the reflection that Peirce disapproved of the use James made of the pragmatic theory. Peirce went so far as to renounce the term "pragmatism," giving up his child—as he sarcastically put it—to its higher destiny. For himself he adopted the term "pragmaticism," a word ugly enough to be safe from kidnappers.

35. Peirce himself did not use this argument. Some readers may recognize the technique as similar to the one used by G. E. Moore in *Principia Ethica* to expose the so-called naturalistic fallacy.

36. As a straightforward biographical description of Descartes, Peirce's statement is not only false but perverse as well. Practically the whole of Descartes' greatest work, the *Meditations,* is devoted to elaborating and working out the distinction that Peirce said never

occurred to Descartes. But Peirce probably meant something quite different by his remark—that Descartes' individualistic, subjectivistic method does not allow for a nonarbitrary distinction between apparent and real clarity. And *that* criticism is one that Peirce argued for at considerable length and in many places, not all of them by any means in connection with Descartes.

37. It may be instructive to imagine a reply that might be made on behalf of an orthodox Roman Catholic, together with Peirce's response. The reply is this: Even though there are no sensible effects associated with the belief that the elements of the Eucharist become the body and blood of Jesus, there are important emotional results for the believer, and *these* amount to a practical difference.

Peirce's reaction to this ploy is clear: The emotional associations of a belief are not part of its "practical" consequences and therefore lie outside the scope of science. The emotions aroused are consequences of *holding* the belief, not consequences of the belief itself. For Peirce "Truth is public"; the private, affective side of belief is irrelevant to scientific truth. This issue is one on which Peirce and James differ sharply.

The widely held view that pragmatism is relativistic and "practical" in some private, emotional sense is due to its popularization by James. If Peirce had reached a wide public first—an unlikely event in any case—the general conception of pragmatism might be very different.

38. Peirce, *Collected Papers,* V, ¶412.

39. Peirce was, of course, familiar with the so-called Mohs scale of hardness, which is based precisely on the scratchability of a substance. The scale, introduced by the German mineralogist Friedrich Mohs (1773–1839), runs from talc, which is assigned the number 1, to diamond, which is 10. Unlike Mohs, Peirce was interested in the *meaning* of hardness, which he identified with resistance to being scratched.

40. Peirce, *Collected Papers,* V, ¶160.

41. Lack of space prevents me from developing Peirce's evolutionary metaphysics any further. Readers interested in a more detailed account may consult the following articles, all of which appear in Volume VI of the *Collected Papers:* "The Architecture of Theories," "The Doctrine of Necessity Examined," "The Law of Mind," "Man's Glassy Essence," and "Evolutionary Love." These papers develop more fully the three factors in cosmic evolution that we have treated briefly: tychism, synechism, and agapasm, or, if we may use plain English, chance, logic, and love. Volume VI of the *Collected Papers* also contains an account of Peirce's notion of God, which is intriguing but not thoroughly worked out.

42. William James, *Pragmatism: A New Name for Some Old Ways of Thinking,* Lecture II. Hereafter cited as *Pragmatism.*

43. James himself distinguished two varieties of pragmatism (or of philosophy generally): the "tough-minded" and the "tender-minded." Though James tended to the tender-minded species, one can detect traces of both kinds in his writings. The discussion of "The Will to Believe" will bring out something of this dichotomy.

44. James, *Pragmatism,* Lecture II.

45. The wider metaphysical implications of pragmatism, as James saw them, are set out in three books: *Essays in Radical Empiricism, A Pluralistic Universe* (which in some editions was published with *Radical Empiricism*), and *Some Problems of Philosophy.* All three works were published by Longmans, Green, & Co.

46. George Santayana, *Character and Opinion in the United States* (New York, Charles Scribner's Sons, 1924), Chap. III.

47. Milton Halsey Thomas, *John Dewey: A Centennial Bibliography* (Chicago, University of Chicago Press, 1962).

48. *Logic: The Theory of Inquiry* (New York, Henry Holt & Co., 1938), pp. 104–105. Though clear enough in context and in intention, the definition is too broad; that is, it takes in too much.

Bertrand Russell remarked that, on Dewey's account, bricklaying would be an inquiry. But even if it were logically correct, the definition sounds like a parody of a German metaphysician. It lends some credence—or the appearance of it—to those who considered Dewey a poor writer. It is only fair to add that other passages of great clarity, and even eloquence, could be cited as evidence against the charge of stylistic clumsiness.

49. *How We Think: A Restatement of the Relation of Reflective Thinking to the Educative Process* (Boston, D. C. Heath & Co., 1933), pp. 100–101.

50. Richard Bernstein noted in his article on Dewey in *The Encyclopedia of Philosophy*, II, that many readers, misled by popularized versions of Dewey's philosophy, were surprised that so "practical" a man as Dewey would regard art as worth a whole book or, indeed, that he even had any interest in art. But, as Bernstein also pointed out, careful readers of Dewey's earlier works knew that he had always made an important place for the aesthetic aspect of experience. *Art and Experience* just made explicit what had been there all along.

My friend and former colleague Gustav Mueller, while expressing admiration for Dewey's aesthetics, has argued that it is inconsistent with Dewey's general philosophical outlook, especially his metaphysics. In other words, according to Mueller, Dewey's aesthetics is too good for the rest of his philosophy. I must confess some sympathy with Mueller's astute observation. However that may be, one cannot but be delighted by the spectacle of the seventy-five-year-old Dewey springing such a pleasant surprise on the philosophical world.

51. Dewey's insistence on the central place of education in building and maintaining a good society puts one in mind of Plato's *Republic*. Although Plato's and Dewey's conceptions of what constitutes a good society are irreconcilable, there are still some interesting parallels between the educational philosophies of the two men. Readers who want to pursue this suggestion are referred to the *Republic*, the English title of which, incidentally, is an irredeemably bad translation of the Greek word *politeia*.

52. *The Religious Aspect of Philosophy* (Boston, Houghton Mifflin Co., 1885), p. 393.

53. Santayana, *Character and Opinion in the United States*, Chap. IV.

54. Readers interested in further study of the fascinating personal and philosophical relationship between Royce and James may consult either of the following books by Ralph Barton Perry, who was a student and later a colleague of both men: *In the Spirit of William James* (New Haven, Yale University Press, 1938), and *The Thought and Character of William James*, 2 vols. (Boston, Little, Brown, & Co., 1935). The second of these works is probably the best philosophical biography ever written, if, for fairly obvious reasons, we exclude Plato's Socratic dialogues.

55. For an account of Royce's relation to pragmatism see his "The Eternal and the Practical," *Philosophical Review*, 1904.

56. Santayana, *Character and Opinion in the United States*, Chap. IV.

57. Readers interested in sampling some of Whitehead for themselves might begin with *Science and the Modern World*, which is one of Whitehead's most exciting works, or with *Adventures of Ideas*, which has the advantage of coming after *Process and Reality* and thereby reflecting the definitive statement of Whitehead's metaphysics. *The Function of Reason*, though somewhat neglected, is entirely nontechnical and eminently worth reading. Yet another way into Whitehead is through *Nature and Life*, reprinted as the last two chapters (except the "Epilogue") of *Modes of Thought*. The best secondary source of an *introductory* sort is Ivor Leclerc, *Whitehead's Metaphysics: An Introductory Exposition* (New York,

Macmillan, 1958), recently issued in paperback by Vanderbilt University Press.

58. *Science and the Modern World* (New York, Macmillan, 1925), p. 80.

59. *Ibid.*, p. 111.

60. Just a word about difficult philosophical books. Some may think that we should not waste our time on philosophical works that are not readily understandable, and it is true that history is cluttered with hard-to-understand rubbish. But most of the great works in the history of philosophy are hard in some way or other, even those that give the appearance of simplicity and perspicuity. Descartes' *Meditations*, Berkeley's *Three Dialogues*, and Hume's *Treatise* come to mind as good examples of this phenomenon. And Wittgenstein's *Philosophical Investigations*, which I take to be an extraordinarily important work, does not even *appear* to be simple and lucid.

61. *Process and Reality* (New York, Macmillan, 1929), p. x.

62. *Science and the Modern World*, p. ix.

63. *Process and Reality*, p. 28.

64. *Ibid.*, p.65. It is worth noting that Whitehead did not hold that we are aware of individual actual entities in our ordinary experience. Such entities are the product of sound metaphysical analysis. The test of his philosophy is not whether we can use the basic categories to label items in our conscious experience but whether the philosophical scheme enables us to organize the *whole* of our experience better than rival schemes. Whitehead argued that the philosophy of organism is better suited to the real world of change and growth than is a static substance philosophy.

65. *Ibid.*, p. 335.

66. *Ibid.*, p. 66.

67. Cf. *ibid.*, p. 35.

68. *Ibid.*, p. 533.

69. *Ibid.*, p. 28.

70. *Ibid.*, pp. 36–37.

71. In affirming the primacy of actuality to form, Whitehead's ontological principle allied him with certain portions of the writings of Aristotle as against the more or less standard interpretation of Plato. This affinity is worth remarking because Whitehead's philosophy is often described as Platonic, a description stemming in part, no doubt, from a frequently misquoted passage from *Process and Reality*. The statement, which is seldom quoted accurately, is this: "The safest general characterization of the European philosophical tradition is that it consists of a series of footnotes to Plato" (*ibid.*, p. 63). Whitehead never said that Western philosophy consists of a series of footnotes to Plato. Whitehead was profoundly influenced by Plato, but to characterize him without qualification as a Platonist is at least as wrong as it is right.

72. *Ibid.*, p. 70.

73. *Ibid.*, p. 64.

74. Though God is of great importance in Whitehead's metaphysics, Whitehead had little interest in "theology" in the narrower sense. Nevertheless, his influence on theology has been impressive. Readers interested in learning more about so-called process theology may consult the following works: John B. Cobb, Jr., *A Christian Natural Theology* (1965) and *God and the World* (1969), both published by Westminster Press, Philadelphia; Peter Hamilton, *The Living God and the Modern World* (Philadelphia, United Church Press, 1967); and Norman Pittenger, *Alfred North Whitehead* (Richmond, Va., John Knox Press, 1969).

We must make special note of the work of Charles Hartshorne, who is by just about any test the most distinguished and creative of those philosophers who may be called Whiteheadian. A brief but reliable and fairly comprehensive statement of Hartshorne's philosophical position may be found in Andrew J. Reck, *The New*

American Philosophers (Baton Rouge, Louisiana State University Press, 1968). Pittenger's book, referred to in the preceding paragraph, has a note on Hartshorne. Full bibliographical information may be found in William L. Reese and Eugene Freeman (eds.), *Process and Divinity* (LaSalle, Ill., Open Court, 1964).

A journal devoted to process philosophy, *Process Studies,* was inaugurated in 1971 by the School of Theology at Claremont, Claremont, California.

75. *Process and Reality,* p. 47.

76. *Ibid.,* p. 31.

77. *Ibid.,* p.32.

78. *Ibid.,* pp. 29–30.

79. *Ibid.,* p. 246.

80. *Ibid.,* p. 271.

81. For readers interested in dipping further into American idealism, I offer the following note:

German idealism was systematically introduced into the United States by Henry Brokmeyer and William Torrey Harris. The latter founded *The Journal of Speculative Philosophy* and served as United States commissioner of education. For accounts of the movement they led, see J. H. Muirhead, "How Hegel Came to America," *Philosophical Review,* 1928; Charles M. Perry, *The St. Louis Movement in Philosophy* (Norman, University of Oklahoma Press, 1930); and William H. Goetzmann (ed.), *The American Hegelians* (New York, Alfred A. Knopf, 1973).

A variety of idealism known as "personalism" was vigorously expounded by Borden Parker Bowne (1847–1910), George H. Howison (1834–1916), and Edgar Sheffield Brightman (1884–1953). The work of Bowne and Brightman has had a significant effect on religious thinking in America. Brief accounts of the philosophies of these thinkers, as well as bibliographical information, may be found in *The Encyclopedia of Philosophy.*

Three idealists of a somewhat different stripe were James Edwin Creighton (1861–1924), John Elof Boodin (1869–1950), and William Ernest Hocking (1873–1966). Boodin has been labeled a realist; a fact that points up the slipperiness of the terms we are using. Stretching things even further, we may mention Elijah Jordan (1875–1953), whose work has been neglected both because it is so obscure and because it is out of style. Foremost among living idealists is Brand Blanshard (1892–), who combines in an impressive way great erudition, analytic skill, and a superb writing style. Articles on each of these thinkers except Jordan may be found in *The Encyclopedia of Philosophy.* Even more useful are two books by Andrew J. Reck: *Recent American Philosophy* (New York, Pantheon, 1964) and *The New American Philosophers,* referred to in note 74.

82. For a readable account of the two realisms written by one of the "combatants," see William P. Montague, "The Story of American Realism," *Philosophy,* Vol. XII, No. 46.

83. Among epistemological or metaphysical naturalists are several men associated with Columbia University, most notably John Dewey, Frederick J. E. Woodbridge (1867–1940), Ernest Nagel (1901–), John Herman Randall (1899–), and Justus Buchler (1914–). Morris R. Cohen (1880–1947), who taught for many years at the City College of New York, may be added to the list of noteworthy naturalists. *The Encyclopedia of Philosophy* contains articles on Dewey, Woodbridge, Nagel, and Cohen. Also useful is Reck's *The New American Philosophers,* cited in note 74. *Philosophy* (Englewood Cliffs, N.J., Prentice-Hall, 1964), a book with essays by John A. Passmore, Manley Thompson, Roderick Chisholm, and Herbert Feigl, is worth consulting on several naturalistic philosophers whose work appeared between 1930 and 1960.

84. A sketch of Mead's philosophy, together with some bibliographical information, may be found in *The Encyclopedia of Philosophy.* Reck's *Recent American Philosophy* contains a longer account. Two recent books, one devoted entirely to Mead, testify to the continuing interest in Mead. The first, *George Herbert Mead: Self, Language, and the World* (Austin, University of Texas Press, 1973), is by David L. Miller, who was a student of Mead at the University of Chicago. The second, *Four Pragmatists* (the other three being Peirce, James, and Dewey), is by Israel Scheffler (Atlantic Highlands, N.J., Humanities Press, 1974).

85. Reck has provided a highly readable account of Sidney Hook's position in *The New American Philosophers.*

86. C. I. Lewis' most important works are *Mind and the World-Order* (New York, Charles Scribner's Sons, 1929), and *An Analysis of Knowledge and Valuation* (LaSalle, Ill., Open Court, 1946). Also important are his works on logic: *A Survey of Symbolic Logic* (Berkeley, University of California Press, 1918) and *Symbolic Logic* (with C. H. Langford, New York, The Appleton-Century Co., 1932). A brief statement of Lewis' theory of the a priori is "A Pragmatic Conception of the A Priori," *Journal of Philosophy,* Vol. XX, No. 7 (1923). For concise accounts of Lewis' philosophy see *The Encyclopedia of Philosophy* and Reck, *The New American Philosophers.* For critical assessments of Lewis' philosophy the most useful work is Paul A. Schilpp (ed.), *The Philosophy of C. I. Lewis* (LaSalle, Ill., Open Court, 1968). Although this volume of *The Library of Living Philosophers* was published four years after Lewis' death, it contains Lewis' replies to his critics.

87. Emotivism is one version of critical ethics or, as it is sometimes called, metaethics. That is, emotivism is not another competing ethical theory but rather a theory about the status of ethical statements of any sort. Its best-known American defender is Charles L. Stevenson (1911–), whose *Ethics and Language* (New Haven, Yale University Press, 1944) became a classic of sorts. Stevenson's version of emotivism, which concedes that there is a descriptive component in ethical statements, is less radical than those of Carnap or Ayer. Indeed, one may argue that Stevenson's position verges on a form of ethical naturalism, which Carnap and Ayer had sought to repudiate.

88. The most illuminating account of the checkered history of the positivist theory of meaning is Carl Hempel's frequently reprinted "Problems and Changes in the Empiricist Criterion of Meaning," which originally appeared in *Revue internationale de philosophie,* 1950. The chief "internal" problem faced by the positivists was to formulate the verifiability criterion so that it was neither too broad nor too narrow, that is, in such a way that all "desirable" propositions, but no undesirable propositions, should be admitted as meaningful. The problem was never really solved.

89. In a 1950 paper, "Empiricism, Semantics, and Ontology" (*Revue internationale de philosophie*), Carnap made an interesting—one might almost say curious—attempt to answer this question. Whatever the merits of his answer, it seems to me to take most of the bite out of the positivist attack on metaphysics.

In this connection readers may be interested in a work by a nonpositivist, Stephen C. Pepper (1891–1972), *World Hypotheses: A Study in Evidence* (Berkeley, University of California Press, 1942). According to Pepper some metaphysical hypotheses can be shown to be inadequate; but among the "adequate" hypotheses, there remains an irreducible plurality, no one of the hypotheses enjoying pre-eminence over the others. One's choice of a metaphysical system is determined by which "root metaphor" one finds most compelling. The four root metaphors, or fundamental "models," that generate a variety of metaphysical views are "formism," "mechanism," "contextualism," and "organicism."

Yet another view of metaphysics was offered by Morris Lazerowitz (1907–) in his *The Structure of Metaphysics* (London, Routledge and Kegan Paul, 1955). In Lazerowitz' theory metaphysicians are actually introducing linguistic innovations, though they are not ordinarily aware of what they are *really* doing. But the metaphysician never carries through the linguistic reform implicit in his metaphysics; he leaves the project unfinished, and this because he does not want to see what a sorry mess he has made of things. Indeed, Lazerowitz asserts that the metaphysician's construction of a "better" (but fanciful) world reflects his own desire to flee from the real world. Lazerowitz' analysis is, at the least, intriguing. It is also, it seems to me, vulnerable to serious criticism.

90. Probably the most readable account of positivism written by a positivist is Alfred Jules Ayer's *Language, Truth, and Logic* (London, Gollancz, 1936, rev. ed., 1946; reissued in the United States by Dover).

A one-time positivist (of sorts) whose writings exhibit a high order of philosophical ability, if not of style, is Gustav Bergmann. His works include *The Metaphysics of Logical Positivism* (New York, Longmans, 1954)—a title chosen, one gathers, not only to make a point but also to irritate other positivists; *Meaning and Existence* (1960), *Logic and Reality* (1964), and *Realism: A Critique of Brentano and Meinong* (1967). The last three were published by the University of Wisconsin Press, Madison.

91. Ludwig Wittgenstein (1889–1951) was one of the most influential philosophers of the twentieth century. One of his early works, *Tractatus Logico-Philosophicus* (1922) had a great impact on the development of logical positivism. Later Wittgenstein repudiated his early work and developed a quite different point of view. His later thought is most fully embodied in *Philosophical Investigations,* an enormously influential book published posthumously in 1953.

92. In addition to *Ludwig Wittgenstein: A Memoir* (New York, Oxford University Press, 1958), Malcolm's chief works are *Dreaming* (New York, Humanities Press, 1959), *Knowledge and Certainty* (Englewood Cliffs, N.J., Prentice-Hall, 1963), and *Problems of Mind* (New York, Harper & Row, 1971). Several of Bouwsma's articles are collected in *Philosophical Essays* (Lincoln, University of Nebraska Press, 1965). Among Black's extensive writings the following may be singled out: *Language and Philosophy* (1949), *Problems of Analysis* (1954), *Models and Metaphors* (1962), *A Companion to Wittgenstein's "Tractatus"* (1964), and *Margins of Precision,* all published by Cornell University Press, Ithaca, N.Y. Black also edited *Philosophy in America* (London, George Allen & Unwin, 1965).

93. John R. Searle, *Speech Acts* (Cambridge, Cambridge University Press, 1969).

94. A useful anthology of work in linguistic philosophy, with an excellent introduction, is Richard Rorty (ed.), *The Linguistic Turn* (Chicago, University of Chicago Press, 1967).

95. William Barrett, *Irrational Man* (New York, Doubleday, 1958); John Wild, *The Challenge of Existentialism* (Bloomington, Indiana University Press, 1955).

96. Quine's attack on the analytic-synthetic distinction provoked many replies. The best, in my opinion, is H. P. Grice and P. F.

Strawson, "In Defence of a Dogma," *Philosophical Review,* Vol. LXV, No. 2 (1956). An elaborate reply, developed within the framework of a semantic theory of a natural language, is Jerrold J. Katz, "Analyticity and Contradiction in Natural Language" in Jerry A. Fodor and Jerrold J. Katz (eds.), *The Structure of Language: Readings in the Philosophy of Language* (Englewood Cliffs, N.J., Prentice-Hall, 1964). Gustav Bergmann responds to *both* prongs of Quine's attack, in "Two Cornerstones of Empiricism," *Synthese,* Vol. VIII (1950–51); reprinted in *The Metaphysics of Logical Positivism,* referred to in note 90.

97. Quine's writings on logic include, but are not limited to, the following: *Mathematical Logic,* rev. ed. (Cambridge, Mass., Harvard University Press, 1951), and *Set Theory and Its Logic,* rev. ed. (Cambridge, Mass., Harvard University Press, 1969). Other writings, which range over ontology, epistemology, philosophy of logic, philosophy of science, and philosophy of language, are the following: *From a Logical Point of View* (Cambridge, Mass., Harvard University Press, 1953), *Word and Object* (Cambridge, Mass., M.I.T. Press, 1960), *The Ways of Paradox* (New York, Random House, 1966), *Ontological Relativity and Other Essays* (New York, Columbia University Press, 1969), *Philosophy of Logic* (Englewood Cliffs, N.J., Prentice-Hall, 1970), and *The Roots of Reference* (LaSalle, Ill., Open Court, 1974).

Worth mentioning in connection with Quine is the work of the distinguished American philosopher Nelson Goodman (1906–), whose general philosophical outlook is close to Quine's. Among Goodman's writings are the following: *The Structure of Appearance* (Cambridge, Mass., Harvard University Press, 1951), *Fact, Fiction, and Forecast* (Cambridge, Mass., Harvard University Press, 1955); and *Languages of Art: An Approach to a Theory of Symbols* (Indianapolis, Bobbs-Merrill, 1968).

Efforts to give a behavioristic account of meaning and intention, such as the one offered by Quine in *Word and Object,* have drawn heavy critical fire. One of the most acute and effective critics is Roderick M. Chisholm. See, for example, his *Perceiving: A Philosophical Study* (Ithaca, N.Y., Cornell University Press, 1957), and "Intentionality and the Theory of Signs," *Philosophical Studies,* 1952.

Although he does not teach in a department of philosophy, Noam Chomsky (1928–) has done work in linguistics that has aroused considerable interest among philosophers. Among Chomsky's writings in linguistics are the following: *Current Issues in Linguistic Theory* (The Hague, Mouton, 1964), *Aspects of the Theory of Syntax* (Cambridge, Mass., M.I.T. Press, 1965), *Topics in the Theory of Generative Grammar* (The Hague, Mouton, 1966). Of special interest to philosophers are these two books: *Cartesian Linguistics: A Chapter in the History of Rationalist Thought* (New York, Harper & Row, 1966), *Language and Mind* (New York, Harcourt, Brace & World, 1968). To the delight of some and the chagrin of others, Chomsky has tried to breathe new life into a theory long considered dead, the doctrine of innate ideas. It hardly need be added that Chomsky's general outlook is antibehaviorist and antiempiricist.

PART IV: Science

Until the second century of its existence America relied upon Europe for new ideas and techniques in most sciences. The early American environment for basic scientific research may be described as at least indifferent and perhaps even hostile. The result was that breakthrough in scientific knowledge came from countries that presented more favorable working conditions for scientists.

In Chapter 12 "Two Centuries of Chemistry," Kenneth L. Taylor deals with the growth and development of the largest branch of science in the United States. Unlike their counterparts in other sciences, who are concentrated largely in universities, most chemists are employed in industry. This is an important indication of the influence chemistry has on the economic as well as the social life of the nation. Taylor discusses the major features of the professionalization of chemistry, its links with practical applications, and notable American contributions to advances in the science.

Americans have excelled in practical applications of scientific advances. In Chapter 13, "Physics," Thomas M. Smith deals with a science that has been thrust into the political arena, when atomic physics became an instrument of public policy. Smith examines developments in physics as both a pure and an applied science. From the findings of pure research new practical research directions have developed through federal support.

In Chapter 14, "The Evolution of Molecular Biology from Biological Science," John R. Sokatch demonstrates that molecular biology began with the deciphering of the genetic code in nucleic acids and was later expanded to almost all cell structures. American scientists played a major role in this field of inquiry and through their research influenced scientists in other countries. American industry developed various kinds of automated equipment, which freed scientists from manufacturing their own in the laboratories. In turn a wealth of scientific data was accumulated after World War II. Sokatch offers a number of reasons for the emergence of the United States as a scientific power. American leadership is illustrated by the fact that in the thirty-eight years before World War II only eight of forty-one Nobel prizewinners in medicine and physiology were Americans. From 1943 to 1973 thirty-seven of sixty-seven Nobel prizes in medicine went to Americans. A greater commitment to basic research by universities and the greater willingness of the public and private sectors to support it were partly responsible for those achievements. Only the Soviet Union among the major nations of the world devotes a higher percentage of its gross national product to research.

In Chapter 15, John C. Burnham deals with "The Growth of Scientific Medicine." At the time of American independence most medical practitioners were mostly apprentice-trained or even self-taught. Burnham reviews the development of major medical schools in the United States and the relatively slow movement of physicians into research. Public support for medical research has permitted the medical practitioner to move into iatrogenic diseases, life maintenance, environmental quality, heredity, and the borderlines of personality, life, and death.

12

TWO CENTURIES OF CHEMISTRY*

By Kenneth L. Taylor

INTRODUCTION

The science of chemistry, dealing as it does with the character of substances and the nature of their transformations, covers an extremely broad array of investigations, both theoretical and practical. Many features of chemistry impinge very directly on our daily life, whereas in other respects chemistry represents studies of unexcelled abstractness into the behavior of matter. Since materials are its subject, chemistry is naturally very strongly associated with the substantial products that abound in modern industrialized life. It is therefore not surprising that chemistry has for some time been the branch of science with the largest professional membership and with the highest proportion of members in industry.

Chemistry is woven into the fabric of American social and economic life perhaps more thoroughly than is any other major science, and for this reason alone its condition—present and future—is a matter of public concern. But even if this were not so, the quest for chemical knowledge would comprise a significant part of any comprehensive overview of American intellectual development. A brief examination of the growth of chemistry in American civilization may help not only to shed light on the current disposition of this important science but also to illustrate some issues of general interest in the history of science in the United States.

In 1776 chemistry was already a distinct and rapidly maturing science. In Paris, London, Edinburgh, and other European intellectual centers the practitioners of chemistry were eagerly pursuing investigations that promised to yield a more highly generalized and successful understanding of the transformations undergone by matter than had yet been achieved. America played no significant role in this movement. In fact, during its first century the United States was destined, in chemistry as in other sciences, to rely upon Europe for new ideas and techniques. It was only in its second century that an indigenous, self-sustaining chemical tradition came to flourish in America.

The reasons for America's subordinate role in the over-all growth of chemistry until our own century do not of course derive from the innate capacities of Americans but rather

are related to the historical circumstances of American cultural development. Until rather recently it was a widely accepted proposition that the United States was, throughout much of the nineteenth century, an inhospitable place for scientists. It is generally acknowledged that during most of the nineteenth century few original advancements in scientific knowledge were made in the United States. It has been argued that the reason for the low level of theoretical accomplishment was a prevailing indifference—even a hostility—toward science that stifled the development of a basic research tradition.[1] Indeed it does appear that, following a promising start in the late colonial era, original American contributions to science suffered a decline. After Benjamin Franklin's remarkable mid-eighteenth-century work on electrical theory, one is hard pressed to find an instance of distinguished groundbreaking science by an American before Josiah Willard Gibbs's accomplishments in thermodynamics during the 1870's. Europe remained the locus of new science, and with few exceptions Europeans needed to pay no heed to what was going on across the Atlantic.

But the fact that scientific originality was in short supply during the United States' first century does not mean that nothing important was happening in American science. Foundations were being laid for a bright future in scientific creativity. Recent historical studies have tended to show that American weakness in basic science during the first century of the Republic derived less from a pervasively indifferent attitude toward science than from the conditions natural to a young country not possessing the institutional structures present in Europe.[2] As comparable structures were established in America, conditions for scientific work of a high level improved, and early in the twentieth century the nation moved to a position where it was ready to assume a share of world leadership in science. America spent the nineteenth century catching up with Europe in science. In the meantime, however, even while American science was dependent on Europe for new ideas, science exerted a very significant influence on American life and culture. Although it was some time before America was able to do much to and for science, there was hardly ever a time when science did little to and for America.

Chemistry, as one of many scientific fields, though an es-

*I am grateful to Aaron J. Ihde for his helpful criticism of this chapter and to Cheryl Cantrell for her able research assistance.

pecially broad and important one, is in the main much like other sciences in the context of American development. While chemistry shows some historical peculiarities, owing in part to its central role in nineteenth-century scientific learning and to its susceptibility of practical application, it displays in a singularly instructive manner some of the general features of the sciences as they have developed in America over the last two hundred years. In the discussion that follows, chemistry can often be taken as an example of an American science, and even the features peculiar to itself frequently reflect upon the conditions of American civilization as much as upon the idiosyncrasies of chemistry. The focus of this chapter, then, is the place of chemistry in two centuries of American life, a focus that lends itself more readily to an examination of the institutional role of chemistry in our culture than to an analysis of chemical ideas developed by Americans.[3]

THE TEACHING OF CHEMISTRY IN AMERICA

If a retrospective search for American originality in chemistry bears little fruit until a relatively recent date, the development of the teaching of chemistry shows earlier beginnings. Formal instruction in chemistry had acquired a promising start before the Revolution, and indeed the teaching of chemistry was to prove to be an important factor in the building of a strong chemical tradition in America. In the European centers where chemistry was actively being advanced in the late eighteenth century, much of the best original work was done outside the colleges and universities. It is fair to say that new scientific ideas of the eighteenth and nineteenth centuries came more often from without than from within institutions of education. In America, however, the cultivation and dissemination of chemical knowledge, as well as its application—and not the pursuit of new chemical knowledge—long constituted the central activity of chemistry.

Chemistry was first taught in American colleges as part of natural philosophy. Such was the case at Harvard College before the end of the seventeenth century, and similar practices were followed at the College of William and Mary, the College of Philadelphia (now the University of Pennsylvania), and King's College (now Columbia University). Some instruction in chemistry seems to have become a regular part of the student's curriculum at several American colleges before 1800, for example, at Dartmouth College, Pennsylvania, and Columbia. Teaching procedures normally depended mainly on lectures and recitations from a text, sometimes accompanied by demonstrations. Student laboratory work was unknown. What was learned rarely surpassed elementary knowledge. The undergraduate was exposed to some of the fundamental ideas of chemistry as part of a survey of the rapidly growing fields of knowledge supposed to be part of an educated person's attainment.[4]

While by the end of the eighteenth century chemistry had gained only a modest and limited place in the undergraduate arts curriculum, it received a good deal greater prominence in the medical schools. The medical environment was certainly the most hospitable one for chemistry during the eighteenth and early nineteenth centuries, mainly through its association with materia medica rather than with physiology. In the early years of the Republic doctors of medicine and medical students constituted the overwhelming majority of persons actively cultivating chemistry. The Chemical Society of Philadelphia, founded in 1792, was composed mainly of medical men, and the first American professors of chemistry received their original training in medicine. A course on chemistry and materia medica was taught at King's College as early as 1767. The first person to teach a regular course devoted exclusively to chemistry in an American institution, however, was Benjamin Rush (1746–1813), of Philadelphia, who played a significant role in establishing chemistry in America.

Rush had attended the chemical lectures of Joseph Black while working toward a medical degree at the University of Edinburgh. He first gave his chemistry course in 1769 at the College of Philadelphia (later the University of Pennsylvania Medical College), and in 1770 he published a syllabus of chemical lectures, the first American book of its kind. Under Rush's leadership Philadelphia became in the late eighteenth century the most active center of chemists in America. Rush was also one of the founders of a century-long popular tradition of public chemical lectures in America, which conveyed a strong sense of chemistry's utility. When after twenty years of teaching chemistry Rush became professor of medicine, he was succeeded by a series of his own students, including Caspar Wistar, James Hutchinson, and James Woodhouse. As perhaps the most distinguished American physician of his time, Rush exemplified the strong links between chemistry and medicine.[5]

Of Rush's successors at Philadelphia, the most notable was James Woodhouse (1770–1809), who was the first American to publish a book on chemistry describing chemical experiments and apparatus (*The Young Chemist's Pocket Companion*, Philadelphia, 1797). Woodhouse also became active in the Chemical Society of Philadelphia, one of the world's first specialized chemical societies.[6] While Philadelphia held the predominant place in science during the early decades of the Republic, chemistry also made headway elsewhere. Aaron Dexter (1750–1829) was professor of chemistry and materia medica at the newly founded Harvard Medical School beginning in 1783, and Samuel Latham Mitchill (1764–1831) was from 1792 for many years professor of chemistry, natural history, and agriculture at King's College and later the first professor of chemistry in the College of Physicians and Surgeons. John Maclean (1771–1814), Scottish by birth and trained in Scotland and France, was the first chemistry professor at the College of New Jersey (later Princeton University) from 1795 to 1812, at which time he went to William and Mary, where chemistry instruction had been established as early as 1774. Maclean's professorship at Princeton was the first in chemistry established in America outside a medical school.[7]

American chemists were quick to adopt the new chemical ideas developing in Europe in the late eighteenth century. Samuel L. Mitchill taught the new chemistry of Antoine

Lavoisier from the outset of his appointment in 1792. Aaron Dexter, of Harvard, though he learned chemistry before the advent of oxidation theory, evidently was introduced to the new French doctrines through reading one of Antoine Fourcroy's works, and adjusted his teaching accordingly. The presence in America of Joseph Priestley from 1794 until his death in 1804 was surely a stimulant to an active consideration of the controversy between new and old viewpoints in chemistry, since Priestley continued energetically to defend the phlogiston theory. In fact, it appears that Priestley's arrival triggered debate where there otherwise might have been a tacit consensus favoring the new doctrines. Priestley was esteemed both as a man and as a natural philosopher—indeed he was offered the professorship of chemistry in the College of Philadelphia's Medical School, which he declined—but virtually all vocal American chemists nonetheless rejected his chemical views.[8]

During the first half of the nineteenth century gradual but significant changes were seen in the character of chemistry teaching. While the center of chemical pedagogy remained for some time in the medical schools, it gradually became available in more of the colleges; and while chemical education generally remained rather elementary, opinion increasingly favored the development of more advanced chemical training. The concomitant development of improved textbooks and the occasional introduction of student laboratory work helped raise chemical teaching by mid-century to a level where it was becoming a program of study rather than a peripheral subject merely to be touched lightly in passing. Graduate training could now become a reality. At the same time the practical uses of chemistry beyond those in medicine were becoming more manifest.[9]

The first American chemistry professor without medical training was Benjamin Silliman (1779–1864), and he became a central figure in American chemistry during the first half of the nineteenth century. A 1796 graduate of Yale College, Silliman served there as a tutor starting in 1799, meanwhile pursuing the study of law. He was admitted to the bar in 1802 but was, however, dissuaded from the practice of law by Timothy Dwight, president of Yale, who arranged Silliman's appointment in 1802 as Yale's first professor of chemistry and natural history. Unprepared for such a position, Silliman spent two winters in Philadelphia attending the lectures of Woodhouse and others and learning from association with fellow students such as Robert Hare (1781–1858), who was destined to make a name for himself as a chemistry teacher and as inventor of the oxyhydrogen blowpipe. Silliman also spent a short interval at Princeton in 1803 and was plainly more favorably impressed by Maclean than by Woodhouse. A year's journey to England, Holland, and Scotland in 1805 and 1806 to purchase scientific apparatus and pursue scientific studies capped the professional retraining of this scientific newcomer, whose subsequent achievements amply justified President Dwight's confidence in him.

In the half century until Silliman's retirement in 1853 he exercised a powerful influence on American science, primarily as a teacher and animator of support for science. A succession of influential scientists, especially geologists, emerged from his tutelage, many of whom carried forward the teaching of chemistry. One of Silliman's most remarkable students was Amos Eaton (1776–1842), a former convict, whose teaching in practical chemistry was the nucleus around which the Rensselaer Polytechnic Institute was founded. Silliman's *American Journal of Science*, founded in 1818, provided an American forum for research and soon became the American scientific journal most respected in Europe. In Silliman's journal and in his own career can be seen a significant stage in the professionalization of chemistry, the development of the science to a point where it could be mastered only by a full-time specialist.[10]

During his career Silliman's opinion changed with regard to the use of the chemical laboratory in teaching. Like most of his contemporaries he was inclined at first to think of the laboratory as a place for the professor to pursue his own studies, but he came progressively to look upon it as the student's best training ground. It was with this conviction that Silliman helped in the founding of a scientific school at Yale well equipped with laboratories. At Harvard a younger chemist who became one of the leading advocates of student laboratory work was Josiah Parsons Cooke (1827–94). To a large degree a self-taught chemist, Cooke was from 1850 until his death Erving professor of chemistry and mineralogy. He urged the inclusion of chemistry in the college curriculum as a corrective to its largely nonutilitarian courses of study. In addition to his vigorous support of laboratory work as a regular part of undergraduate chemical instruction, Cooke was successful in raising funds to construct laboratory facilities. He was also successful as a writer and public lecturer and pioneered in attempts at precise determinations of atomic weights, work later carried through with great distinction by his student, Theodore W. Richards (1868–1928).[11]

The most important educational development for chemistry in the second half of the nineteenth century was the founding of a graduate educational system based on the German ideal of active student apprenticeship in original research. This development was associated with a decline in clerical authority in the colleges and a challenge to the traditional liberal-arts curriculum, carried forward principally in the name of the sciences. It reached its most decisive turn in 1876 with the founding of the Johns Hopkins University, but the ground had been laid over several decades beforehand through extensive discussion and experimentation with graduate education.[12]

The School of Applied Chemistry at Yale (founded in 1846), which later became the Sheffield Scientific School, and the Lawrence Scientific School at Harvard (founded in 1847), embodied a mid-century conviction that scientific education ought to be supported for practical purposes. These purposes not being altogether compatible with traditional collegiate programs, each scientific school was deliberately segregated from the parent college. Sheffield, which created the first American department of graduate study in the sciences, initially appointed two faculty members with responsibilities in chemistry: John Pitkin Norton (1822–52) and Benjamin Silliman, Jr. (1816–85). Chemistry remained a central part of the Sheffield School, which was employing four chemistry professors by 1870. All faculty members were active researchers, and students at all levels engaged in regular laboratory work. No doubt the school's brightest production was Josiah Willard Gibbs (1839–1903), who in 1863 was granted the degree of doctor of philosophy, the fifth conferred by Yale. Chemistry was somewhat less important in the Lawrence School than at Sheffield, particularly since the energetic and dominating personality of Louis Agassiz soon deflected the school's emphasis toward geology and zoology.[13]

Norton, one of the first chemistry professors at the Sheffield Scientific School, had augmented his study under the senior Silliman by reparing to Edinburgh, as so many Americans had done before him. But this pattern was soon to be broken and replaced by a preference for German universities, generally acknowledged as scientifically pre-eminent in the second half of the nineteenth century. By mid-century Americans were finding a period of study at such centers as Berlin, Göttingen, Heidelberg, Leipzig, Freiberg, and Giessen obligatory for advancement in chemistry, as in virtually all the sciences. In Germany they worked under distinguished chemists like Friedrich Wöhler, Heinrich Rose, August Kekulé, Justus von Liebig, or Robert Bunsen and brought back in varying degrees a commitment to the research creativity these men exemplified.[14]

Both in Scotland and in Germany students were able to learn from distinguished and original scientists, but the pattern of instruction in the two countries was different. In their heyday the greatest Scottish chemists made ample use of demonstrations to accompany their lectures, and they favored an understanding of chemistry not only as a branch of natural philosophy but also as a source of practically applicable knowledge. The German chemists were on the whole no less interested in the practical implications of chemistry, but they taught advanced students by treating them as junior associates in research. The first appointee to the Rumford professorship in chemistry at the Lawrence School, Eben N. Horsford (1818–93), had studied under Liebig at Giessen, as did several other notable American chemists of mid-century. When Horsford resigned his professorship in 1863 to devote himself fully to his industrial work, he was succeeded by another of Liebig's pupils, O. Wolcott Gibbs (1822–1908). Despite their similarities Gibbs differed from Horsford in being less inclined toward the practical uses of chemistry, and he reoriented the Lawrence program of chemical studies more strongly toward basic research.[15]

At the new Johns Hopkins University research was placed at the center of activity for both professors and advanced students. A living example of that emphasis was Ira Remsen (1846–1927), the first professor of chemistry at Hopkins. Remsen received the degree of doctor of medicine from Columbia in 1867 and the degree of doctor of philosophy from the University of Göttingen in 1870. The central role of research in the Johns Hopkins program can be seen in a statement, prepared by Remsen's chemistry department, expressing what was expected of graduate students:

[The] dissertation . . . shall be, not a mere compilation, such as could be worked up in a good library, but a discussion of some problem on the basis of experiments undertaken by the candidate for the purpose of solving the problem. The discipline attendant upon this work will lead him to see by what means the science has been built up, and his interest will be awakened in the work done in the chemical laboratories of the world.

Remsen had a strict conception of research in the university. As long as he taught, he refused offers of consultantships, and he opposed the idea of following the German precedent of having industry-funded laboratories in the university. In 1879, Remsen founded the American Chemical Journal and acted as its chief editor until it was incorporated in the Journal of the American Chemical Society in 1911. Many graduates of the Hopkins chemistry department during Remsen's years were to be counted among the leaders of chemical education in succeeding decades. Remsen left his mark on chemistry teaching also through his textbooks, which set a new standard for their kind in America, notably Introduction to the Study of the Compounds of Carbon, or Organic Chemistry (1885) and Introduction to the Study of Chemistry (1886), each of which went through many editions and was translated into several foreign languages.[16]

The example set by Johns Hopkins was soon followed by the nation's other distinguished educational institutions, as well as by newly founded ones, such as the University of Chicago. The research ideal soon took root in American graduate education, and the doctorate was established as the normal qualification of the academic professional. A measure of the preparedness of the educational ground in America before the advent of graduate education on the German model is how rapidly American graduate education matured. By 1890 at least half the Americans earning doctorates in chemistry received their degrees from American institutions, and by 1900 American chemical education had become as good as could be found anywhere.[17] A signal of American chemistry's arrival was the invitation T. W. Richards received (and declined) to take a regular chemistry professorship at the University of Göttingen. In 1914, Richards also became the first American to win the Nobel Prize in Chemistry.

While the ideal of fundamental research was a strong motive force behind the formation of graduate chemistry programs, at the same time chemistry was manifestly part of the practical learning that in the second half of the nineteenth century was challenging the traditional, basically classical curriculum. The founding of land-grant universities following the Morrill Act of 1862, a landmark expression of popular desire for functional education, was a great stimulus to chemical education. In the latter part of the nineteenth century, with the liberalizing of the college curriculum and the introduction of an elective system, chemistry and other sciences made their way into college courses of study on an unprecedented scale.[18]

Chemistry teaching at the high-school level, interestingly enough, did not have as much catching up to do in the late nineteenth century as did college chemistry. By the 1860's chemistry was well established as an important secondary-school subject in most large cities. But the colleges, with only a few exceptions, did not recognize chemistry in their entrance requirements. A resolution to this lack of accord between secondary and higher education was sought through the 1893 report of the Committee of Ten of the National Education Association. Prepared under the chairmanship of Harvard's President Charles W. Eliot (himself a chemist), this report had a great impact in getting colleges to recognize high-school work in a wider range of subjects, especially the sciences.[19]

Indicative of the growing self-reliance of American chemistry teaching was the increase in the number of books on chemistry published by native-born American authors. Early in the nineteenth century the most abundant chemistry books in America were American editions of English books or translations from abroad. By mid-century, however, respectable numbers of books by American authors were available, and they burgeoned in the 1880's.[20] In modern times American chemistry texts are noted for their quality and are widely used throughout the world.

Virtually from the beginning of graduate education in the United States chemistry has been the leading field in the number of universities with advanced degree programs. At the end of World War I some 20 institutions were offering doctorates in chemistry. This number had increased to 90 by 1953 and reached 190 in 1974.[21] Over 22,000 doctorates were granted from 1920 to 1962. The total number awarded since then is not markedly less. The annual number of chemistry doctorates had reached 1,000 by 1950, and remained at about that figure for a decade after which it advanced rapidly during the 1960's to exceed 2,000 in 1970. Since then these numbers have declined somewhat, falling to 1,880 in 1973 and to 1,733 in 1974. Annual totals of fewer than 1,500 are anticipated in the near future. These figures do not include the number of degrees awarded in chemical engineering, biochemistry, and pharmaceutical or medicinal chemistry, fields which taken together have recently been awarding doctorates totalling over 900 annually.[22]

Even though hardly any field is more widely diffused on the campuses than chemistry, it is clear that from the earliest successes of graduate training not all the new chemists with doctorates were being absorbed into the teaching profession. An important factor in the tremendous growth of chemistry education from the late nineteenth century onward was the increasing demand for trained chemists in industry, and to a lesser extent in government as well. Of course, there is in principle more than one way to be initiated into the esoteric knowledge and techniques of almost any field, and industry and government have always employed considerable numbers of persons with limited formal training in chemistry. But it was not long after American graduate education got under way that the doctorate became the ticket to the best professional status in chemistry. An interesting illustration is that the American organization employing the most persons with doctorates, other than the federal government, is not a university but a chemical firm, E. I. Du Pont de Nemours & Company.[23]

A noteworthy twentieth-century innovation in chemical education, as in higher education generally and particularly in the sciences, has been the rise of the postdoctoral fellowship as an important means to advanced study. What amounted to postdoctoral fellowships were awarded at Johns Hopkins as early as 1876. In that year two of the twenty advanced students receiving the original fellowships there had doctorates from German universities.[24] This way of providing already highly qualified persons an opportunity to extend their expertise did not become widespread, however, until several decades later. In 1919, in a step intended to strengthen American science, the recently founded National Research Council awarded its first postdoctoral fellowships. Primarily through the support of federal agencies and private foundations, large numbers of scholars are now able to further their research skills following completion of the doctorate. In chemistry a postdoctoral fellowship is assumed to enable its recipient to expand his training into aspects of chemistry beyond that of his doctoral research. A 1967 survey of more than 10,000 postdoctoral fellows in America showed that over 15 per cent were in chemistry and over 12 per cent were in biochemistry. According to those findings about one new chemistry Ph.D. in three takes a postdoctoral fellowship, and over half the new Ph.D.'s in biochemistry do so.[25] In 1972 American universities were hosts to 2,460 postdoctoral fellows in chemistry, 1,350 in biochemistry, and 124 in chemical engineering.[26]

The lasting and influential doctoral programs in chemistry began essentially as vehicles for training in research, and that they have remained, despite the fact that many, perhaps a majority, of recipients of chemistry doctorates do little or no further research. The universities retain a central position in the chemical community to a great extent by virtue of the large amount of high-quality research they perform, but even more because they are virtually the sole suppliers of highly qualified chemists to all employers. Among the universities there is keen competition for the ablest and most articulate researchers to adorn the chemistry faculties and for the most promising students to occupy their classrooms and laboratories. As might be expected of a discipline present on practically every sizable campus, the highest-ranking institutions granting doctorates in chemistry fall almost completely into three groups: prestigious eastern universities, mainly in the Ivy League; large middle-western universities; and several select California institutions.[27] Periodic re-examination of the purposes and methods of graduate education by the American Chemical Society (ACS) has shown a continuing commitment to research by the apprenticeship system as the core of doctoral training. But recently the economic condition of the profession has spurred suggestions that graduate programs ought to be broadened, while retaining their research emphasis at the core, to reflect more fully the diverse functions other than research fulfilled by many of those who earn doctorates.[28]

The fostering of sound education in chemistry has long been an area of evident concern to professional chemists. American chemistry has never been without distinguished teachers, such as Benjamin Silliman and Ira Remsen. Two teachers of more recent times who have been noted for the excellence of their students are Gilbert N. Lewis (1875–

1946) and Roger Adams (1889–1971).[29] In 1923 the ACS set up the Division of Chemical Education, and it has published the respected *Journal of Chemical Education* since 1924. The Committee on Professional Training was created by the ACS in 1936, and since 1940 the committee has set forth minimum standards for undergraduate instruction in chemistry and published a list of schools with approved chemistry programs. The 522 schools that were on the list at the end of 1974 account for 8,712, or over three-quarters, of the baccalaureate degrees awarded that year in chemistry. The role of the ACS as arbiter of chemical-education standards was dealt a blow in 1974 by the Office of the United States Commissioner of Education, which removed the ACS from that office's list of nationally recognized accrediting agencies because of a failure to meet all the criteria set for such recognition. Despite this reverse, far from relinquishing its role in maintaining standards, the ACS is not only continuing its practice of undergraduate program approval but also looking into the advisability of instituting a similar procedure for setting standards for graduate programs as a possible response to recent overexpansion in graduate training.[30]

In the course of the twentieth century, undergraduate chemistry instruction has shifted in emphasis from a descriptive toward a theoretical approach, perhaps in recognition that within a working lifetime a trained chemist will need to cope with extensive changes in chemical concepts. Currently, however, there are signs in some quarters of a return to more descriptive chemistry. At the same time there are indications that the hard-won and long standing certitude in the paramount importance of laboratory work is weakening; some undergraduate programs are cutting down on the number of hours required in laboratory work.[31] Undergraduate chemistry obviously serves a far greater body of students than those who ultimately find work related to the field. Not only do vast numbers of students study chemistry without pursuing much beyond an introductory course but over half of those who major in chemistry in college do not remain in the field afterward. Those who do represent a large share of the approximately five thousand graduates at all levels (doctoral and masters, as well as baccalaureate) who annually have been entering the chemistry labor force in recent times.[32] Let us now turn our attention to the development of the industrial home of the majority of that labor force.

CHEMICAL INDUSTRIES AND INDUSTRIAL CHEMISTRY

The very term *chemical industry* can hardly escape signifying enterprises established upon a scientific basis, and to that extent risks being historically deceptive. For industries exploiting the manipulation of material transformations existed independently of theoretical chemical knowledge long before the advent of modern chemistry. Even following its emergence as a scientific discipline, chemistry did not immediately alter an entire class of industries but came only slowly and spasmodically to exert a governing influence. As the chemical industries irregularly acquired foundations truly derived from chemical knowledge, however, they drew from this knowledge an unprecedented potency. The most important consequence of the chemical industry's acquisition of a scientific basis has been the extraordinary potential for implementation of ideas with implications unforeseen in the absence of formalized knowledge and for rational testing of processes and products as an alternative to trial-and-error methods. In our day the central feature of the chemical and allied industries, the key to their remarkable influence in contemporary life, is the production of synthetically made materials that often serve as substitutes for products of natural origin and not infrequently fulfill new functions served before by no substance at all. No doubt trial and error have not disappeared and never will disappear from investigations toward these ends, but the production of synthetic materials has come to lie firmly on a complex of theoretical understanding.

The transition to a science-based industry did not occur all at once. In colonial America as elsewhere the business of manufacturing such useful materials as soap, salt, dyes, and bleaches went forward without being much influenced by chemical ideas until the latter part of the eighteenth century. As the Industrial Revolution partly inserted scientific understanding into the understructure of manufacture, a new dimension was added to America's dependence upon Europe. The colonial rebellion fostered American attempts at industrial independence at a time when the intellectual component of industrial procedures was increasing. The endeavor to achieve economic emancipation in chemical manufacturing was difficult enough, and was often incapable of immediate success (in gunpowder production, for example), but it was even harder for the erstwhile colonies to free themselves from dependence on European ideas and techniques.[33] Eventual American independence in industrial science coincided roughly with the maturing of a self-sustaining American scientific community, capable of generating its share (or more) of conceptual and technical innovation. Success in this maturing process was the result of many factors, and the presence of industrial interests was not negligible among them. But on the whole American industrialists came to show enthusiasm for the organized cultivation of science for commercial purposes only near the end of the nineteenth century, by which time an indigenous American scientific tradition was well under way.

In the rapid expansion experienced by the American economy during the nineteenth century, some branches of chemical manufacturing grew also, particularly those concerned with acids, black powder, and tanning materials. The growth of the American chemical industry was impressive, even if it tended to remain modest in scale, local, and decentralized. Transport was a pervasive difficulty in this industry, and most manufacturing concerns had to be located conveniently near their main consumers. The expansion of the railroad systems and the development of new devices and techniques for shipping chemicals were important in overcoming the transport problem, which helped result in the chemical industry's rise to real economic prominence in the last quarter of the nineteenth century.[34]

On the whole, American industrial chemistry remained dependent on European techniques until the twentieth century. Such a key substance as sulfuric acid, fundamental to the chemical industry, was manufactured in the United States by a series of processes imported from abroad. Late in the eighteenth century the Philadelphia druggist John Harrison (1773–1833) introduced the lead-chamber process to America, a technique that was displaced only when the contact process was brought in from Germany early in the twentieth century. World War I brought home as never before the need for national independence in the chemical industry. Following the war several thousand patents in the areas of dyes and medicines owned by German concerns were seized by the alien-property custodian and sold for a nominal fee to the Chemical Foundation, an organization founded to serve— and controlled by—American chemical industries. The Chemical Foundation then leased the patents to American firms. Through a combination of factors—the rapid development of industrial chemistry in time of need, the possession of the German organic patents, and new tariffs handicapping postwar German industry—German dominance in these areas of industry was broken, and the United States emerged as a leading nation in the chemical industry, a position it subsequently consolidated and has maintained for the last half century.[35]

As industry was becoming increasingly science-based, a new and intriguing figure rose to prominence, the industrial scientist. The American conception of the industrial scientist has tended to be dominated by two alternative models: the solitary inventor who devises a new technique or process and perhaps founds a new industry and the company scientist who makes his contributions as an employee, often as part of a team. In the development of American industrial chemistry individual illustrations of each of these models are not hard to find.

Charles Goodyear (1800–60) was the quintessentially dogged independent inventor. In 1839 he devised the process of vulcanization through extended heating of rubber and sulfur in mixture, thereby rendering rubber stable and adaptable to various uses. That Goodyear pursued the goal of making commercially useful rubber through years of experimentation in the face of personal adversity, and achieved success without technical education and essentially by accident, fits the popular mythology of independent invention. Less in accord with that myth are that Goodyear's accomplishment gained him little reward and that in spite of his work the manufacture of rubber developed reliably only after the Civil War.[36]

Other examples of achievements in practical chemistry and entrepreneurship that helped found new industries are those of Charles M. Hall (1863–1914) and Leo H. Baekeland (1863–1944). In 1886, Hall developed a commercially feasible method of obtaining aluminum from its ores by electrolysis. In contrast to Goodyear, Hall approached his problem with a sound training in chemistry, obtained at

Oberlin College, and made a fortune. Baekeland came to the United States from Belgium in 1889 and set up a photographic firm. Within a few years he had achieved financial security through invention of a photographic paper and turned to research. From 1905 onward he investigated practical methods of condensing products from phenol and formaldehyde into substances that could be molded and then hardened by heat and pressure. The successful result (in 1909) was Bakelite, one of the first useful plastics.[37]

An area of especially striking achievement in early American industrial chemistry was electrochemistry. In addition to Hall's founding of the aluminum industry, a conspicuous illustration is the case of Herbert H. Dow (1866–1930). Dow, trained at the Case School of Applied Science in Cleveland, was the first person to make a commercial success of the electrolytic manufacture of bromine from brine, in the early 1890's. One authoritative observer has compared the contribution of innovation in electrochemistry toward American expansion in chemical manufacture around the century's turn with the role of technical improvements in the dyestuffs industry in Germany's earlier rise to dominance in industrial chemistry.[38]

Chemists made their appearance as company scientists in American firms at first in narrowly technical roles as testers or samplers of raw materials or products. Most industrialists did not imagine that chemists could have a far greater impact through their potential to improve existing processes, find new uses for waste products, or create entirely new products. A notable early instance of an American company chemist who transcended the role of tester-sampler was Samuel Luther Dana (1795–1868). In 1834, after a number of years as a medical doctor and then as a private chemist and businessman, Dana took employment in a textile mill in Lowell, Massachusetts. Among his accomplishments there were the improvement of the bleaching process through modifications affording the use of cheaper materials and savings in time and labor (the "American system") and improvement of the calico-printing process by demonstrating the efficacy of phosphates as a replacement for the dung universally used beforehand.[39]

Dana's success failed to inspire much immediate emulation. The chemical industries, while sharing in the growth of the American economy during the nineteenth century, tended not to take part in the national trend toward bigness, and corporate size may have been an ally of capitalization on technical originality. In some industries, the petroleum industry, for example, the possibilities of chemical exploitation were largely neglected, and until late in the nineteenth century chemists were generally regarded as having a suitable place in industry only as technicians. A scientist who exemplified the shift of conception toward a more active industrial role for chemists was Charles B. Dudley (1842–1909). After serving in the Union army (and sustaining a severe wound), Dudley went to Yale and earned the doctoral degree in chemistry at the Sheffield Scientific School in 1874. A year later he became the Pennsylvania Railroad's first full-time chemist, and in the distinguished career that followed, he helped establish the value of the trained chemist in industry. By investigating fuels for railroad lighting and the composition of rail steel, for example, he was able to effect important savings and technical improvements, and his efforts helped make technical specification of product quality a normal part of industrial purchasing. When Dudley died, the Pennsylvania Railroad's laboratory employed thirty-four trained chemists.[40]

Industrial chemistry reached a level of unaccustomed prestige in America in the person of Irving Langmuir (1881–1957). Educated at the Columbia School of Mines and in Walther Nernst's laboratory at Göttingen, Langmuir joined the General Electric research laboratory nine years after its founding in 1900 and devoted himself fruitfully to diverse fields of chemical and physical research. His work materially contributed to such areas as technological improvements in electric lamps, the development of the condensation pump for producing a vacuum, and the understanding of electric discharges in gases and of the theory of the atomic structure. Largely for his achievements in surface chemistry, he was awarded the Nobel Prize in Chemistry in 1932 and thereby inevitably conferred some luster on the industrial laboratory as an institution.[41]

In the course of time the numbers of company chemists have greatly increased, and the solitary inventor-entrepreneur has all but disappeared. No doubt a major reason is the growing complexity of the business world. Most of those industrial chemists who have had an interest in doing serious scientific work have probably been happy to assume only a part of the responsibility of running a business enterprise— that part having to do with discoveries and techniques for their implementation. A consequence of being a company scientist, however—a member of a corporate team—has been the entrenchment of the researcher as a corporate employee, albeit an employee with professional qualifications and commitments. In a bargain that may well never have been foreseen by scientists before the twentieth century, industrial researchers gain access to the expensive tools and materials needed to further knowledge and receive salaries for spending at least a measure of time doing what interests them in return for conceding to the company the material benefits that may come from their discoveries and a degree of freedom in determining the directions and ultimate uses of their study.

Of all the features of the American chemical industry in the twentieth century none is more striking than the establishment of industrial research as a normal part of business operation, perhaps the clearest instance in modern science of an attempt to institutionalize the utilitarian potential of scientific knowledge. Organized industrial research is largely the fruit of nineteenth-century developments—the merging of the traditions of science and industry and the rise of the German style of graduate instruction. The German model of advanced education, with the execution of original research under professorial supervision as the main qualification for a doctorate, lent itself to the formation of teams of researchers working on common or related problems. This model was as influential in the American chemical industry as it was in education. Many chemists trained in German university laboratories on their return to America set up private laboratories for diverse consulting and business purposes. German professors were by no means uniformly disinterested in applied research, and a significant number of Americans were encouraged to devote themselves to practical areas of work by the example of their mentors—Eben Horsford by Liebig, for example, and, two generations later, Langmuir by Nernst.

Following occasional and irregular beginnings in the nineteenth century, the first half of the twentieth century witnessed the acceptance of organized research as a necessary object of industrial expense, without which a large chemical business would be uncompetitive. It is no coincidence that policies establishing research laboratories were effected in times when chemical industries tended toward increased diversification, since research is a means not only of improving products and processes but also of expanding into new lines of business, especially to make use of otherwise wasted by-products.

Some of the most important research laboratories in American industries were established between 1900 and World War I—for example, General Electric, Du Pont, Bell Telephone, Westinghouse, Eastman Kodak, and Standard Oil of Indiana. But the growth of industrial research laboratories was especially marked after the war. The experience of being cut off from vital supplies of German dyes, medicines, glass, and various chemicals and the resulting (and successful) mobilization of scientific work to compensate for the problems this deprivation caused, were persuasive of the need for systematic research to avoid future dependence on foreign supply of critical materials. Between 1920 and 1940 the number of industrial research laboratories grew from about 300 to over 2,200, the most rapid increase occurring during the 1920's.[42]

The chemical and electrical industries, probably more accustomed than most others to the exploitation of new discoveries, were the leaders in supporting research. Not only the major chemical manufacturers but also companies in industrial fields allied to chemistry have made major efforts in chemical research. In photography, rubber, petroleum, and elsewhere research laboratories complement the research efforts of the large chemical firms.

General Electric, moving outward from an electrical orientation, developed an important chemical department, which sponsored not only much of Langmuir's most significant work but also advances in insulating materials, the development of a new range of substances, the silicones, and the artificial creation of diamonds. While it was not until the present century that research and development in petroleum-refining methods began in earnest, once under way the contributions of American chemists and engineers made them the world's leaders in this area. A process of thermal cracking, or induced breakdown of hydrocarbon chains, was invented in 1913 by a Standard Oil of Indiana group led by William M. Burton (1865–1954). During the 1920's and 1930's the technique of fractional distillation was developed by W. K. Lewis (1882–1975) and his associates at Massachusetts Institute of Technology, and in the 1930's a catalytic-cracking method was worked out by Eugene J. Houdry (1892–1962), with the backing at first of Vacuum Oil Company and then of Sun Oil Company. Other important researches in the application of petroleum products included the development of antiknock compounds and of a polymerization process to use large quantities of cracking products to acquire hydrocarbons with desired qualities.[43] Research in the uses of petroleum products was the answer to a well-known emergency of World War II, the shortage of natural rubber experienced by America and its allies. This emergency was successfully met by chemists and chemical engineers, who produced various kinds of rubber by synthesis from petroleum products.

One of the most frequently mentioned success stories in industrial research involves the relatively undirected work done at the Du Pont laboratory at Wilmington, Delaware, under the supervision of Wallace H. Carothers (1896–1937). A new Du Pont laboratory, devoted to fundamental rather than developmental research, was created by company policy in 1927, and the following year Carothers was enticed away from Harvard to direct the work, centering on his interest in polymers. Carothers' team justified the investment of large sums on research in the area by producing nylon, a strong synthetic fiber drawn from linear condensation of a polymer of high molecular weight. This profitable Du Pont research investment came, significantly, not long after the company's transformation from a traditional concentration on explosives into a firm broadly committed to a diversity of manufactured chemical products. Not incidentally, Carothers was the first organic chemist in industry to be elected to the National Academy of Sciences, portending a broader inclusion of industrial chemists in the academy.[44]

The point has already been made that chemistry serves a very broad range of practical uses, but their breadth has perhaps not yet been indicated adequately here. As conventionally defined, the "chemical and allied products industry" is the manufacture of such things as heavy chemicals, plastics and resins, synthetic rubbers and fibers, pharmaceuticals, soaps and detergents, cosmetics and toiletries, paints and varnishes, fertilizers, and pesticides. Beyond these are many "nonchemical" industries served by chemistry, including notably petroleum refiners; paper, metal, glass, porcelain, and textile producers; and food processors. Chemistry is moreover involved not merely in the making of material products for both industrial and consumer use but equally in the processes by which these products are treated, packaged, and delivered.[45] By construing industry broadly, three additional areas may be included where chemistry has had an especially powerful influence on the American experience: medicine, military affairs, and agriculture.

Chemistry's greatest contribution to medicine in modern times has undoubtedly been in chemotherapy, particularly in the synthesis of chemical agents to control disease. Since the early 1930's useful drugs in astonishing numbers have been created, including the sulfa drugs, antibiotics, and corticosteroids. Much of the earliest work in these areas was done in Europe, although pioneering studies of corticoid drugs were conducted at the Mayo Clinic, and American investigators such as René J. Dubos (1901–   ), Selman A. Waks-

man (1886–1973), and Benjamin M. Duggar (1872–1956) have played important roles in extending our knowledge of antibiotics. The distinguished American chemist Robert B. Woodward (1917–   ) has had repeated successes in synthesizing compounds of medical and biological importance, thereby contributing both to the cause of health and to an understanding of life processes.[46]

No less obvious than its medical serviceability is chemistry's potential for military use. Although at the time of the American Revolution industries did not, by and large, look to science for procedural instruction, the manufacture of gunpowder was one essential precondition for warfare with which chemists were associated. Throughout the past two centuries chemistry has had a role in the production of various militarily useful materials. A new degree of intimacy between chemists and the military applicability of their science was arrived at, however, in World War I. The Chemical Warfare Service, formed at that time, lived on to prove its utility in World War II. In the context of warfare chemistry was naturally at first strongly associated with the use of gas, but during World War II it became more importantly connected with smoke, flame, and incendiary weapons. Industrial chemists and chemical firms were deeply involved as well in the wartime program to develop a nuclear bomb, and especially in preparation of the fissionable material. Diverse military needs have in recent decades called upon chemists to supply substances to perform special functions and to stand up to special conditions—insulators, semiconductors, rocket propellants, and a host of other materials.[47]

Practical chemistry has long enjoyed a privileged position in American eyes, in no small part owing to its aura of agricultural utility. The agricultural uses of chemistry constitute one of the main sources of American good will for the science, dating from the mid-nineteenth century onward, primarily through the implementation of new concepts of plant nutrition proposed by Liebig and others. American farmers long considered chemistry and agricultural science to be more or less synonymous. The importance of fertilizers became an agricultural mania in the mid-nineteenth century because of the new theories for the chemical basis of soil depletion and for carbon and nitrogen cycles.[48]

Chemistry acquired an institutionalized role in American agriculture through the appointment within the Department of Agriculture, from its inception in 1862, of qualified department chemists. The first was Charles M. Wetherill (1825–71), who had earned his doctorate at Giessen under Liebig. In 1901 a division within the department was redesignated the Bureau of Chemistry. Under the vigorous leadership of Harvey W. Wiley (1844–1930), who headed the Division and Bureau of Chemistry from 1883 to 1912, the constituency conceived to be served by the Department of Agriculture expanded beyond farmers to include consumers in general. This was in no small measure the result of Wiley's emphasis on the need to employ chemical knowledge to establish standards of purity and healthfulness in food and drugs and then to enforce those standards by inspection and regulation. Wiley's advocacy of legislation in this area was instrumental in the passage of the Pure Food and Drug Act of 1906.

The number of chemists employed in the Bureau of Chemistry rose sharply under Wiley, growing from a technical staff of 13 in 1888 to 425 in 1908. An organized role for chemistry in agriculture was furthered also by the Hatch Act of 1887, which mandated and funded an agricultural experiment station in each state. Such experiment stations had been started earlier at the initiative of some states, Connecticut being the first in 1875. The actual function of the chemists so employed varied from station to station, in some instances amounting to little more than inspection and regulation of fertilizers but in other instances affording at least the opportunity for research.[49]

Out of modest beginnings there grew a close relationship between the agricultural and chemical segments of the economy. Farmers came increasingly to depend on large-scale chemical production of fertilizers, insecticides, herbicides, fungicides, soil conditioners, defoliants, and growth regulators for enhanced productivity. The annual use of fertilizers by American farmers, for example, stood at about 320,000 tons by 1870, climbed to some 7.2 million tons in 1950, and by 1973 had expanded to over 40 million tons. It has been estimated that without these fertilizers current American agricultural productivity would drop a third or more.[50]

The industrial impact of chemistry is so pervasive that very few aspects of our lives are untouched by it in some way. We enjoy a style of living enhanced in countless ways by chemistry; we have also become dependent upon it. In this there are grounds for both satisfaction and foreboding.

AMERICAN CHEMISTRY'S VARIED HABITAT

For most of the two centuries of United States history education and industry have been the main sites of chemical activity. We have already seen in passing, however, that there have been other ways in which chemistry has become attached to our institutions, most importantly through government. As the chemistry profession matured in the late nineteenth century, trained chemists found new opportunities to demonstrate their worth.

Throughout most of the nineteenth century most American chemists were teachers. Their numbers were not great, but employment opportunities for chemists outside education were slighter. Even toward the end of the century, when industrial and governmental utilization of chemists was on the upswing, chemistry teaching expanded significantly as well. While chemistry teaching never lost its association with medicine, the student constituencies grew in other directions. The evident practical promise of chemistry teaching that had been important to the founding of scientific schools at Yale and Harvard was further observed by the Morrill Land-Grant Act of 1862, which provided the means for each state to create a college primarily dedicated to teaching connected with agriculture and the "mechanic arts." The Morrill Act had led by 1900 to the creation of no less than fifty-six new postsecondary institutions, most of them requiring a chemistry professor. Formal education for pharmacists, which dates from the 1820's, placed chemistry together with materia medica and pharmacy as a major segment of the curriculum. Notwithstanding these new demands for chemistry teachers, however, in time the expansion of nonacademic jobs for chemists far outstripped teaching positions. The numbers of professional chemists (including assayers and metallurgists) were reported by the decennial census as 9,024 in 1900, 16,598 in 1910, and 33,600 in 1920. Industry and government accounted for most of this rapid increase. In modern times academic chemists came to constitute a relatively small but always very influential minority within the American chemistry profession.[51]

Just as industry came to value chemical knowledge for its practical uses, so also government gradually implemented chemistry and employed trained chemists. Government followed a pattern not unlike that of industry, seeking first to use chemists as technicians and only later as discoverers. The mint hired assayers. The growing roles of chemists in the Department of Agriculture and the agricultural experiment stations have already been mentioned. During the 1880's the United States Geological Survey established chemical laboratories at Denver, San Francisco, and Washington, supporting research in addition to the routine work of chemical analysis. A division of chemistry was formed in the Bureau of Standards (founded in 1901), which in the prewar years aggressively sought new research functions and became a sort of bridge between government and industry, responding to requests from the latter for useful knowledge. Many thousands of chemists are now employed in various agencies and laboratories of the federal government, notably in the Departments of Defense; Health, Education, and Welfare; Agriculture; and Interior; and very prominently in the Atomic Energy Commission.[52]

A natural accessory to the professionalization of chemistry was the creation of professional chemical societies. Although there were ephemeral chemical societies in America from as early as 1789, lasting specialized organizations of chemists did not take shape until after the Civil War. Chemists did participate (and still do) in the American Association for the Advancement of Science, formed in 1848 from a decade-old geological association, and the Manufacturing Chemists' Association was founded in 1872. But the creation of the American Chemical Society in 1876 marked the real coming of age of chemistry as a professional scientific discipline. At the time of its founding the ACS was hardly more than a local New York organization, but in 1893 it became a truly national society, and, despite the proliferation of chemical subdisciplines and their respective societies, it has remained the premier body for the American chemical profession, acting as an umbrella for the various specialized branches of chemistry.[53]

Scientific professions keep their vitality by probing for new understanding of nature, and in chemistry as in all sciences a great deal of importance is properly attached to research. A distinction, with a somewhat vague boundary line, is made between fundamental and applied research, resting mainly on the criterion of the conceived purpose, whether for the sake of knowledge or for anticipated practical results. Industry naturally puts the overwhelming majority of its research effort into applied research but does not wholly neglect more broadly directed basic research, since it has long been a prevailing conviction that fundamental research is in the long run practical also. This belief has been supported by study of publications announcing practical chemical discoveries, showing that such publications acknowledge heavy dependence on fundamental research.[54] On the other hand, some recent studies have cast doubt on the existence of a close relationship between original scientific investigation and industrially productive results. "There seems to be general agreement," writes one observer, summarizing these skeptical inquiries, "that technological innovations are most often the result of accumulated small technical changes and are usually dictated by an intimate knowledge of market or production needs."[55] In any case, the basic research that is done in industrial settings is generally published in the same manner as that done in universities. On the other hand, much applied research, intended to provide the sponsoring firm with competitive advantage, is not immediately made public.

Investigations to produce new chemical knowledge have occurred in the United States throughout its history, but only late in the last century did they come to be regularly built into our institutions on a large scale. An indispensable element of that development was the growth of graduate education to train expert chemists and instill in them the tradition of basic research. The university became the locale of training in chemical research, but in the twentieth century a large part of the research activity has been dispersed elsewhere, in industrial research laboratories and government agencies, as well as in some private research institutes. The universities still perform the greatest amounts of basic research, however, and provide the doctoral-trained manpower. Studies during the last decade have indicated that approximately 60 per cent of basic chemical research in America originates in universities, about 30 per cent in industry, and the remaining 10 per cent in government and independent research-institute laboratories.[56] Since World War II, it is worth noting, significant portions of university-based research have been done in research institutes whose university affiliations are not so strong as to bring them wholly within the educational lives of the parent institutions.

New instruments have greatly changed the way chemists carry on their research. Problems of great complexity that only a generation ago might not have been approachable are now dealt with routinely, as phenomena once inaccessible are studied by means of new devices. This is particularly true of investigations into the structure of molecules, a key to new developments in most areas of chemistry. Prominent among these instruments are diverse kinds of spectrometers—infrared, ultraviolet, and mass spectrometers, and more recently nuclear and electron magnetic resonance spectrometers—that can provide a wide range of useful quantitative measurements concerning molecular structure. Other techniques depending on new kinds of instruments include X-ray crystallography and gas chromatography. A vitally important advance in instrumentation that has accompanied such devices is the use of high-speed electronic digital computers, without which the great volumes of data produced could not be processed and reduced to usable order. Contemporary American chemists have grown accustomed to the ready availability of electronic apparatus of many kinds on a scale unsurpassed elsewhere, and this is certainly a factor in their current world leadership.[57]

There has been a major change in the last several decades in the sources of funding for scientific research, a circumstance that applies also to other sciences. Since World War II the burden of supporting most basic research has shifted from private to federal sources. Chemists have expressed concern that in the shift to massive federal funding the amounts allotted to chemistry have not kept pace with many other sciences, particularly if measured in proportion to the number of research investigators being trained in and active in the field. One reason for the relatively low per capita level of federal support of chemistry may be that it is in organization and capital expense a "little science," highly decentralized and without requirements of immensely expensive apparatus. One thinks by contrast of the organizational and fiscal consequences for research areas that depend on devices like accelerators or large telescopes. But another factor may be that, unlike some other sciences, chemistry has no single parent agency in the federal government. While the National Institutes of Health have the responsibility of fostering medical education and research and the Atomic Energy Commission takes a direct interest in nuclear investigations, support for chemistry is shared by a large number of government agencies, each one in a capacity secondary to its main mission.[58]

A study conducted in the mid-1960's estimated that about 23,000 American chemists were engaged at that time in basic research—some 12,000 in universities and colleges (including advanced graduate and postdoctoral students), 7,800 in industrial laboratories, 2,000 in government laboratories, and 500 in private research institutions. These investigators collectively contributed over one quarter of the world's chemical papers. Examination of citations in foreign chemical journals indicates that fundamental research published by American chemists is cited out of proportion to its share of the total world publications, suggesting that it is read preferentially and presumably considered to be of high quality. This conclusion is supported by the fact that the United States, whose students a century ago flocked to Germany for advanced study, has become the place to which the largest number of foreign chemistry students go for graduate and postdoctoral training.[59] A further indicator of the international esteem in which American chemical research is held is found in the awarding of Nobel prizes. Before World War II three Americans won the Nobel Prize in Chemistry; since the war, through 1974, there have been seventeen.

Original American contributions to chemical knowledge, coming in greatest abundance in the last two or three generations, have naturally been concentrated in those areas most ripe for fruitful inquiry. For example, whereas chemical structure considered in the static sense was a dominant issue of nineteenth-century chemistry, in the twentieth century a central problem has been the dynamics of chemical change.

Many distinguished American chemists have made notable contributions to the understanding of chemical dynamics, especially through an elucidation of the chemical bond. The seminal work of J. W. Gibbs in chemical thermodynamics laid the foundations for studies of chemical equilibrium and the direction of chemical change. G. N. Lewis, building on Gibbs's work, made original contributions to chemical thermodynamics and greatly influenced the valence theory of bonding with his concept of the shared electron-pair bond, published in 1916. The shared pair bond, after a few years of neglect, was popularized by Langmuir and became a central principle of molecular structure.[60] A unified understanding of chemical bonding was outlined by Linus Pauling (1901–) in his treatise *The Nature of the Chemical Bond* (1938), and the work of Robert S.Mulliken (1896–) was important in adapting the quantum theory of electronic structure to a knowledge of molecular bonding.

Significant work in subjecting materials to very low temperatures—within a degree of absolute zero—by capitalizing on their magnetic properties, was achieved by the Dutch-born Peter J. W. Debye (1884–1966) and William F. Giauque (1895–), a student of G. N. Lewis.[61]

With the advent of nuclear chemistry early in the present century, one of the concerns of chemists was knowledge of the various isotopic forms possessed by substances. Harold C. Urey (1893–) was the discoverer in 1932 of hydrogen's heavy isotope deuterium, with important consequences for knowledge of the structure of the atomic nucleus and of molecules. A series of man-made transuranium elements was synthesized in the postwar years by Glenn T. Seaborg (1912–) and his associates, yielding valuable information on nuclear structure. The implications of radioactivity provided another American chemist, Willard F. Libby (1908–) with the means to devise, in 1949, the technique of radiocarbon dating, invaluable in archeological work.

American chemistry has benefited in both its fundamental and its applied aspects from work accomplished by immigrants and refugees. From an earlier period one need only mention Priestley and Maclean, as well as Thomas Cooper (1759–1839) and William James MacNeven (1763–1841), both distinguished teachers in early-nineteenth-century America. Frederick A. Genth (1820–93), who earned his doctorate at Marburg under Bunsen, came to the United States with many other German scientists and technologists in the migration of 1848. He was one of several chemists to operate successful commercial laboratories in Philadelphia.[62] More recent immigrants with fine accomplishments in chemistry have included Baekeland, Houdry, and Debye.

At no time has an influx of new scientific talent stimulated the sciences in America as much as in the 1930's and 1940's, and although chemistry may not have been quite as markedly affected by this development as some other sciences, it was very surely influenced by it. In 1930 the already eminent Vladimir Nikolaevich Ipatieff (1867–1952) emigrated from the Soviet Union, and in subsequent researches conducted at the Universal Oil Products Company and at Northwestern University, he extended his earlier work on high-temperature catalytic reactions and laid the groundwork for catalytic combination of hydrocarbons produced by cracking. Among the flood of scientists who came to America as refugees from fascism was a notable group of biochemists, such as Konrad E. Bloch (1912–), Erwin Chargaff (1905–), Fritz A. Lipmann (1899–), Otto F. Meyerhof (1884–1951), and Severo Ochoa (1905–). Physical chemists who gained refuge in the United States included, in addition to Debye, James Franck (1882–1964), Kasimir Fajans (1887–1975), and Eugene Rabinowitch (1901–73).[63]

Judging from recent estimates, there are presently no fewer than 130,000 professional chemists in the United States and possibly well over 200,000. Estimates of the population of chemists are complicated not merely by difficulties in fixing accurate numbers but also by the problem of defining a professional chemist. An important consideration, for example, is whether or not chemical engineers are counted, as they are in the larger figure above. According to a National Science Foundation survey conducted in 1968, about 31 per cent of American scientists are chemists, by far the largest proportion found in any one discipline. Probably this percentage would be smaller if a less restrictive criterion were used for designating someone a scientist. Various estimates of the makeup of the chemistry profession indicate that between three-fifths and four-fifths of all chemists are employed by industry. Of these industrial chemists over half are actually employed outside those industries technically understood to be chemical or pharmaceutical.[64]

Chemists often tend to think of their science as occupying a large part in the middle of a continuum whose extremities are physics at one end and the biological sciences at the other. According to this conception chemistry is a fundamental science supplying ideas to and sharing common ground with other sciences.[65] Several illustrations of historical justifications for this attitude have already been given. Another that can be mentioned is the persistently strong relationship between chemistry and mineralogy in the history of American science. Mineral analysis, with economic implications very much in the forefront, was a major preoccupation of American chemists from the days of the Chemical Society of Philadelphia through the end of the nineteenth century.[66] Strong connections between chemistry and mineralogy have by no means disappeared in the twentieth century, and meanwhile chemistry, in addition to generating many new branches from within, has forged links with other disciplines to form hybrid sciences, such as biochemistry.[67] If the sciences constitute a spectrum, the breadth of the segment that chemistry represents may be suggested by the fact that a recent study of American scientists listed two hundred special subdisciplines under the general heading chemistry.[68] Small wonder that some scientists are not certain whether they should be classified as chemists or otherwise.

Interrelatedness is a characteristic of the sciences of the later twentieth century. Another distinguishing feature of modern science well exemplified by chemistry is its convergence with technology. The history of American chemistry appears to be a clear instance of the progressive intertwining of scientific explanations for material transformations with the many ways materials are practically transformed. While this is not the place for a discussion of the modern relations of science and technology, a subject on which scholars have lively disagreements, it can be suggested here that chemistry provides good support for the thesis that much of modern scientific endeavor is neither "pure" inquiry nor application of knowledge nor technical tinkering in the craftsman tradition. Quite often it is rather a combination of all three. It seems to this writer that the terms *science, applied science*, and *technology* retain historically derived meanings which of course continue to have very definite uses but which often fail to describe the actual functioning of science in our time and bring confusion to a relatively new category created from elements of all three. If this is correct, the time is ripe for the coining of a new term, to designate the new, composite activity that "research and development" inelegantly comes closest, so far, to defining.[69]

THE FUTURE OF AMERICAN CHEMISTRY

The science of chemistry has experienced in the twentieth century a consistent vigor that is on the whole a source of gratifying confidence to American scientists. Public expectations from chemistry have nonetheless had some ups and downs. During and after World War I it seemed that chemistry was at the center of the scientific wellspring of technological change. The war itself had been called the Chemists' War, and too much was expected of chemistry in the years that followed. There was heady talk of a dawning age of chemurgy.[70] A sense of unrestrained enthusiasm for a future age of chemical technology can be found in William J. Hale's *Chemistry Triumphant*, one of many fervent tributes to chemistry published between the wars. In one passage Hale declared that skyscrapers of the future would dwarf those of the 1920's and 1930's: "Buildings will be moulded from plastic material and poured from above. A height of 10,000 feet should offer no obstacles whatsoever."[71]

With such unachievable expectations it was inevitable that chemistry's destiny should seem to decline in subsequent years to more mundane levels. Then in World War II, in spite of considerable contributions from chemists, the spectacular success of the atomic bomb and its association with physics overshadowed chemistry, and physics came in for its own period of glamor. With the biological sciences more recently gaining large measures of public appreciation, it has been some time since chemistry (biochemistry excepted) has enjoyed—or suffered from—any extravagance of popular esteem.

Under these circumstances chemistry has maintained considerable stability, although the profession is of course quickly touched by reverses in the fortunes of the economy. The recent study by the ACS entitled *Chemistry in the Economy* makes the point that professional chemists are very widely diffused throughout the nation's economic structure, fulfilling critically important functions in industrial enterprises.[72] The future demand for continued development of chemical knowledge seems assured by the practical uses it serves. One also hopes that, even in the absence of any promise of utility, chemists will carry on the lively search for new understanding of matter, its properties and changes, because knowledge is exciting and good in itself.

Chemists have of course participated from the start in the enormous rise in the consumption of goods and products in the twentieth century. Indeed, chemists have been instrumental in making available the things that embellish contemporary living, and usually are not bashful about saying so. Herein lies a problem for the future of chemistry, for the chemistry profession is, for both good and ill, associated with American habits in the use of materials, and those habits have for a long time been very wasteful and shortsighted. Good sense requires us to become less wasteful and more farsighted, to conserve useful resources, and to prevent deterioration of the environment. It is not a question of blaming chemistry for the routinely prodigal practices of Americans—that is a collective responsibility. But it is not unreasonable to call upon chemists to assume now a special obligation to help lead the way toward more judicious policies for the use of materials.

There is encouraging evidence that chemists as a group are to some degree accepting this leadership role. The founding of the monthly journal *Environmental Science and Technology* by the American Chemical Society in 1967 is one such sign. Another is a recent report of the American Chemical Society Committee on Chemistry and Public Affairs recognizing a commitment to environmental improvement.[73]

But the outside observer may hope to be forgiven for wondering whether chemists have yet gone far enough. Many chemists, probably in common with most scientists and engineers, apparently are inclined to think of mankind's modern problems as stemming mainly from technical causes and therefore susceptible of technical solutions. When chemists declare their science to be "a principal instrument in the continuing adaptation of nature to man's purposes,"[74] with a mission "to control and change the material world according to man's needs,"[75] there remains the question whether all the "adaptation" and "control" of nature is really held fully in command by those who claim to direct it. Evidently not. The wider problems of human use of the material world must be solved as much through adjustments in human values and attitudes as through improved techniques for manipulating substances. Together with a continued search for new technical capabilities, an increased sense of the need to modify the social use of materials is to be hoped for in the world of professional chemistry.

No one is likely to deny that our life is more complex than that of our ancestors. If the future looks grim, it is because of both an uncertainty in the improvability of human conduct and an anxiety that we may have come to depend too fully, to maintain a swelling population, on an intricately interconnected set of technical procedures that we may not be able to sustain indefinitely. Worries like these are very likely what lay behind the cheerless prognosis of a speaker at the recent celebration of chemistry's bicentennial. (Somewhat curiously, American chemists semiofficially fix the beginning of modern chemistry at August 1, 1774, the day Priestley isolated a gas he called dephlogisticated air, rather than at a later date, when Lavoisier assigned a new theoretical significance to this gas—a meaning Priestley always disagreed with—and thereby gave to oxygen its true historical importance.) The speaker's outlook contrasted with the buoyant optimism felt by chemists a century earlier. With rather disconcerting casualness he envisioned the probability that the tricentennial might not be observed at Priestley's home in Northumberland, Pennsylvania, because of the prior nuclear devastation of North America.[76]

Americans today obviously find it unpleasant to consider a distant and fearful future. This reluctance has at least one advantage: we may be spared some of the prophecy that otherwise would be inflicted on us. Prediction is an art seldom well executed, especially when it concerns the sciences. In looking to chemistry's future, it would be wise to assume that it will ultimately become something more than merely a grown form of its present self. The past teaches us that the chemistry of today is different from just a matured version of what it was one hundred or two hundred years ago. It has changed qualitatively, partly indeed by a great quantitative shift in its scale but also through the close alliance that has come about between theories and their implementation. We cannot know what qualitative changes chemistry will undergo in the future, but we should expect that they will occur.

NOTES

1. Richard Harrison Shryock, "American Indifference to Basic Science during the Nineteenth Century," *Archives internationales d'histoire des sciences*, Vol. XXVIII (1948), 50–65; I. Bernard Cohen, "Some Reflections on the State of Science in America During the Nineteenth Century," *Proceedings of the National Academy of Sciences*, Vol. XLV (1959), 666–77; I. Bernard Cohen, "Science in America: The Nineteenth Century," in *Paths of American Thought* (ed. by Arthur M. Schlesinger, Jr., and Morton White, Boston, Houghton Mifflin, 1963), 167–89.

2. See the papers in *Nineteenth-Century American Science: A Reappraisal* (ed. by George H. Daniels, Evanston, Northwestern University Press, 1972), especially Nathan Reingold, "American Indifference to Basic Research: A Reappraisal," 38–62.

3. For a general survey of the history of chemistry, with a concentration on developments since the eighteenth century, see Aaron J. Ihde, *The Development of Modern Chemistry* (New York, Evanston, and London, Harper and Row, 1964). A useful study of an important phase of chemistry's institutionalization is Edward H. Beardsley, *The Rise of the American Chemistry Profession, 1850–1900*, University of Florida Monographs, No. 23 (Gainesville, University of Florida Press, 1964).

4. Lyman C. Newell, "Chemical Education in America from the Earliest Days to 1820," *Journal of Chemical Education*, Vol. IX (1932), 677–95; Theodore Hornberger, *Scientific Thought in the American Colleges, 1638–1800* (Austin, University of Texas Press, 1945), 28–32; I. Bernard Cohen, "The Beginning of Chemical Instruction in America: A Brief Account of the Teaching of Chemistry at Harvard prior to 1800," *Chymia*, Vol. III (1950), 17–44; Herbert S. Klickstein, "A Short History of the Professorship of Chemistry of the University of Pennsylvania School of Medicine, 1765–1847," *Bulletin of the History of Medicine*, Vol. XXVII (1953), 43–68; Herbert S. Klickstein, "David Hosack on the Qualifications of a Professor of Chemistry in the Medical Department. With a Short History of the Professorship of Chemistry at Columbia College Medical Department (1776–1876), College of Physicians and Surgeons of New York (1807–1860), and Rutgers Medical College (1826–1830)," *Bulletin of the History of Medicine*, Vol. XXVIII (1954), 212–36.

5. Wyndham D. Miles, "Benjamin Rush, Chemist," *Chymia*, Vol. IV (1953), 37–77; Wyndham D. Miles, "Joseph Black, Benjamin Rush and the Teaching of Chemistry at the University of Pennsylvania," *Library Chronicle*, Vol. XXII (1956), 9–18; article

on Rush by Eric T. Carlson in *Dictionary of Scientific Biography* (New York, Charles Scribner's Sons, 1975), XI, 616–18. (The *Dictionary of Scientific Biography* will hereafter be cited as *DSB*. Articles in this as yet uncompleted reference work generally list the main secondary works pertaining to the subject, and throughout this chapter no attempt will be made systematically to duplicate those citations.) See also Edgar Fahs Smith, *Chemistry in Old Philadelphia* ([Philadelphia], J. B. Lippincott, 1919); and Wyndham D. Miles, "Public Lectures on Chemistry in the United States," *Ambix*, Vol. XV (1968), 129–53.

6. On Woodhouse and the Chemical Society see Edgar Fahs Smith, *Chemistry in America: Chapters from the History of the Science in the United States* (New York and London, D. Appleton, 1914), which also contains extensive biographical sketches of many other notable American chemists; and Edgar Fahs Smith, "A Look Backward," *Journal of Chemical Education*, Vol. IV (1927), 1515–21. For other sources on the Chemical Society of Philadelphia see note 53 below.

7. On Dexter see I. Bernard Cohen, *Some Early Tools of American Science* (Cambridge, Mass., Harvard University Press, 1950), Chap. 4, "The Beginnings of Chemistry at Harvard"; for Mitchill see Courtney Robert Hall, *A Scientist in the Early Republic: Samuel Latham Mitchill, 1764–1831* (New York, Columbia University Press, 1934); for Maclean see the article by Vern L. Bullough in *DSB* (1973), VIII, 612–13.

8. Denis I. Duveen and Herbert S. Klickstein, "The Introduction of Lavoisier's Chemical Nomenclature into America," *Isis*, Vol. XLV (1954), 278–92, 368–82; Robert Siegfried, "An Attempt in the United States to Resolve the Differences Between the Oxygen and the Phlogiston Theories," *Isis*, Vol. XLVI (1955), 327–36; Sidney M. Edelstein, "The Chemical Revolution in America from the Pages of the 'Medical Repository,'" *Chymia*, Vol. V (1959), 155–79; Edgar Fahs Smith, *Priestley in America, 1794–1804* (Philadelphia, P. Blakiston's Son, 1920); Cohen, "The Beginning of Chemical Instruction in America," *Chymia*, Vol. III (1950), 37–42.

9. C. A. Browne, "The History of Chemical Education in America between the Years 1820 and 1870," *Journal of Chemical Education*, Vol IX (1932), 696–728.

10. John F. Fulton and Elizabeth H. Thomson, *Benjamin Silliman, 1779–1864: Pathfinder in American Science* (New York, Henry Schuman, 1947); article on Silliman by John C. Greene,

DSB (1975), XII, 432–34; Edgar Fahs Smith, *The Life of Robert Hare: An American Chemist (1781–1858)* (Philadelphia and London, J. B. Lippincott, 1917); and article on Hare by Wyndham Davies Miles, *DSB* (1972), VI, 114–15; H. S. Van Klooster, "Amos Eaton as a Chemist," *Journal of Chemical Education*, Vol. XV (1938), 453–60; article on Eaton by Samuel Rezneck, *DSB* (1971), IV, 273–75; George H. Daniels, "The Process of Professionalization in American Science: The Emergent Period, 1820–1860," *Isis*, Vol. LVIII (1967), 151–66.

11. Article on Cooke by George S. Forbes, *DSB* (1971), III, 397–99. On early laboratory instruction see H. S. Van Klooster, "The Beginnings of Laboratory Instruction in Chemistry in the U.S.A.," *Chymia*, Vol. II (1949), 1–15; and Wyndham D. Miles, "William James MacNeven and Early Laboratory Instruction in the United States," *Ambix*, Vol. XVII (1970), 143–52. On Richards see Sheldon J. Kopperl, "The Scientific Work of Theodore William Richards" (unpublished Ph.D. dissertation, University of Wisconsin, Madison, 1970); article by Sheldon J. Kopperl in *DSB* (1975), XI, 416–18; and James Bryant Conant, "Theodore William Richards," *National Academy of Sciences, Biographical Memoirs*, Vol. XLIV (1974), 251–86.

12. Richard J. Storr, *The Beginnings of Graduate Education in America* (Chicago, University of Chicago Press, 1953); Charles Weiner, "Science and Higher Education," in *Science and Society in the United States* (ed. by David D. Van Tassel and Michael G. Hall, Homewood, Ill., Dorsey Press, 1966), 163–89. See also Laurence R. Veysey, *The Emergence of the American University* (Chicago, University of Chicago Press, 1965).

13. Russell H. Chittenden, *History of the Sheffield Scientific School of Yale University, 1846–1922* (2 vols., New Haven, Yale University Press, 1928), II, 403–405, 421; Louis I. Kuslan, "The Founding of the Yale School of Applied Chemistry," *Journal of the History of Medicine and Allied Sciences*, Vol. XXIV (1969), 430–51; Samuel Eliot Morison, *Three Centuries of Harvard, 1636–1936* (Cambridge, Mass., Harvard University Press, 1963), 279–80. On J. W. Gibbs see Martin J. Klein's article, *DSB* (1972), V, 386–93; on Norton, article by Louis J. Kuslan, *DSB* (1974), X, 150–51; and on the younger Silliman, article by Elizabeth H. Thompson, *DSB* (1975), XII, 434–37.

14. Beardsley, *Rise of the American Chemistry Profession*, 14; H. S. Van Klooster, "Friedrich Wöhler and His American Pupils," *Journal of Chemical Ecuation*, Vol. XXI (1944), 158–70, and "Liebig and His American Pupils," *Journal of Chemical Education*, Vol. XXXIII (1956), 493–97; see also Veysey, *Emergence of the American University*, 125–33.

15. Beardsley, *Rise of the American Chemistry Profession*, 7–8; Samuel Rezneck, "The European Education of an American Chemist and Its Influence in 19th-Century America: Eben Norton Horsford," *Technology and Culture*, Vol. XI (1970), 366–88; article on Horsford by Samuel Rezneck, *DSB* (1972), VI, 517–18. Much detailed information about both Horsford and Norton is in the doctoral dissertation by Margaret W. Rossiter (see note 48 below). On O. W. Gibbs see article by Nathan Reingold in *DSB* (1972), V, 393–94.

16. Hugh Hawkins, *Pioneer: A History of the Johns Hopkins University, 1874–1899* (Ithaca, N.Y., Cornell University Press, 1960), 223–24 (citing statement), 140. On Remsen see Frederick H. Getman, *The Life of Ira Remsen* (Easton, Pa., *Journal of Chemical Education*, 1940); the article by J. Z. Fullmer in *DSB* (1975), XI, 370–71; and Aaron J. Ihde, "American Chemists at the Century's Turn: S. M. Babcock, Harvey Wiley, Ira Remsen, T. W. Richards, and Edgar Fahs Smith," in *Great Chemists* (ed. by Eduard Farber, New York and London Interscience, 1961), 805–30.

17. Beardsley, *Rise of the American Chemistry Profession*, 20–21.

18. Harrison Hale, "The History of Chemical Education in the United States from 1870 to 1914," *Journal of Chemical Education*, Vol. IX (1932), 729–44; Arthur F. Scott, "Education and Training of Chemists in the U.S.," Part 1, "Putting Chemistry in Education," *Chemical and Engineering News*, Vol. XLIII, No. 13 (March 29, 1965), 82–91.

19. Paul J. Fay, "The History of Chemistry Teaching in American High Schools," *Journal of Chemical Education*, Vol. VIII (1931), 1533–62; Samuel R. Powers, "Chemical Education," in *A Half-Century of Chemistry in America, 1876–1926: An Historical Review Commemorating the Fiftieth Anniversary of the American Chemical Society* (ed. by Charles A. Browne), Golden Jubilee number of *Journal of the American Chemical Society*, Vol. XLVIII (1926), 237–54.

20. Charles A. Browne and Eva V. Armstrong, "History of Chemistry in America," *Journal of Chemical Education*, Vol. XIX (1942), 380; Wyndham D. Miles, "Books on Chemistry Printed in the United States, 1755–1900: A Study of Their Origin," *Library Chronicle* (Philadelphia), Vol. XVIII (1952), 51–62. See also John C. Greene, "American Science Comes of Age, 1780–1820," *Journal of American History*, Vol. LV (1968–69), 33–34.

21. Bernard Berelson, *Graduate Education in the United States* (New York, Toronto, London, McGraw-Hill, 1960), 35; American Chemical Society, Committee on Professional Training, "Doctoral Education in Chemistry," *Chemical and Engineering News*, Vol. XLII, No. 18 (May 4, 1964), 82; "Chemistry Graduation Data Reveal Upturn for Big Schools," *Chemical and Engineering News*, Vol. LIII, No. 17 (April 28, 1975), 30.

22. American Chemical Society, Committee on Professional Training, "Doctoral Education in Chemistry," *Chemical and Engineering News*, Vol. XLII, No. 18 (May 4, 1964), 82, 84; American Chemical Society, Committee on Professional Training, "Doctoral Education in Chemistry: Facing the '70's," *Chemical and Engineering News*, Vol. L, No. 33 (August 14, 1972), 35; "New Grads: As Many as Ever," *Chemical and Engineering News*, Vol. L, No. 40 (October 2, 1972), 18–19; "Summary of Activities of the ACS Committee on Professional Training for 1972," *Chemical and Engineering News*, Vol. LI, No. 18 (April 30, 1973), 25; "B.S. Chemistry Graduates Hit New High," *Chemical and Engineering News*, Vol. LII, No. 20 (May 20, 1974), 39–52; American Chemical Society, *Directory of Graduate Research, 1973* ([Washington, D.C.], American Chemical Society, 1974), xx, xxiii, xxiv.

23. Berelson, *Graduate Education*, 56.

24. Hawkins, *Pioneer*, 82.

25. National Academy of Sciences, National Research Council, *The Invisible University: Postdoctoral Education in the United States* (Washington, D.C., National Academy of Sciences, 1969), 54, 76; National Academy of Sciences, National Research Council, *Chemistry: Opportunities and Needs. A Report on Basic Research in U.S. Chemistry by the Committee for the Survey of Chemistry* (Washington, D.C., National Academy of Sciences, 1965), 13.

26. American Chemical Society, *Directory of Graduate Research, 1973*, xviii, xx, xxiii.

27. Kenneth D. Roose and Charles J. Andersen, *A Rating of Graduate Programs* ([Washington, D.C.], American Council on Education, 1970), 92.

28. American Chemical Society, Committee on Professional Training, "Philosophy of Graduate Training at Ph.D. Level," *Chemical and Engineering News*, Vol. XXVI (1948), 166–67; American Chemical Society, Committee on Professional Training,

"Doctoral Training in Chemistry," *Chemical and Engineering News*, Vol. XXXV, No. 6 (February 11, 1957), 56–67; American Chemical Society, Committee on Professional Training, "Doctoral Education in Chemistry," *Chemical and Engineering News*, Vol. XLII, No. 18 (May 4, 1964), 76–84; American Chemical Society, Committee on Professional Training, "Doctoral Education in Chemistry: Facing the '70's," *Chemical and Engineering News*, Vol. L, No. 33 (August 14, 1972), 35–39. See also American Chemical Society, *Chemistry in the Economy* (Washington, D.C., American Chemical Society, 1973), 440–52.

29. Lawrence Lessing, "Great American Scientists: The Chemists," *Fortune*, Vol. LXI, No. 4 (April, 1960), 256.

30. "Ph.D. Facilities Too Big, Getting Bigger," *Chemical and Engineering News*, Vol. LIII, No. 14 (April 7, 1975), 40–42; "Chemistry Graduation Data Reveal Upturn for Big Schools," *Chemical and Engineering News*, Vol. LIII, No. 17 (April 28, 1975), 27, 30.

31. Howard J. Sanders, "Era of Ferment in Chemical Education," *Chemical and Engineering News*, Vol. L, No. 41 (October 9, 1972), 20–41.

32. Arthur F. Scott, "Education and Training of Chemists in the U.S.," Part 2, "The Crises in Chemical Education," *Chemical and Engineering News*, Vol. XLIII, No. 17 (April 26, 1965), 97; "ACS Compiles Chemical Manpower Data," *Chemical and Engineering News*, Vol. LIII, No. 16 (April 21, 1975), 48–49.

33. Brooke Hindle, *The Pursuit of Science in Revolutionary America, 1735–1789* (Chapel Hill, University of North Carolina Press, 1956), 208–209, 246, 371; Brooke Hindle, *Technology in Early America: Needs and Opportunities for Study* (Chapel Hill, University of North Carolina Press, 1966), 79–82.

34. L. F. Haber, *The Chemical Industry during the 19th Century: A Study of the Economic Aspect of Applied Chemistry in Europe and North America* (Oxford, Clarendon Press, 1958).

35. Three sources have been relied on extensively in this section: Howard R. Bartlett, "The Development of Industrial Research in the United States," in National Resources Planning Board, *Research—A National Resource* (3 vols., Washington, D.C., U.S. Government Printing Office, 1938–41), II, 19–77; Kendall A. Birr, "Science in American Industry," in *Science and Society in the United States* (ed. by Van Tassel and Hall), 35–80; and Kendall Birr, *Pioneering in Industrial Research: The Story of the General Electric Research Laboratory* (Washington, D.C., Public Affairs Press, 1957), Chap. 1, "The Roots of Industrial Research," 1–27. An encyclopedic treatment is Williams Haynes, *American Chemical Industry* (6 vols., New York, Toronto, London, D. Van Nostrand, 1945–54). Other sources are American Chemical Society, *Chemistry . . . Key to Better Living,* Diamond Jubilee vol. ([Washington, D.C.], American Chemical Society, 1951); Carroll Pursell, "Science and Industry," in *Nineteenth-Century American Science* (ed. by Daniels, see note 2 above), 231–48; Courtney Robert Hall, *History of American Industrial Science* (New York, Library Publishers, 1954); Robert P. Multhauf, "Industrial Chemistry in the Nineteenth Century," in *Technology in Western Civilization* (ed. by Melvin Kranzberg and Carroll W. Pursell, Jr., 2 vols., New York, London, Toronto, Oxford University Press, 1967), I, 468–89; and Eduard Farber, "Man Makes His Materials," in *Technology in Western Civilization* (ed. by Kranzberg and Pursell), II, 183–95.

36. On Goodyear see the article by Carl W. Mitman in *Dictionary of American Biography* (12 vols., New York, Charles Scribner's Sons, 1946?–73), IV, 413–15.

37. On Hall see the article by Thomas Parke Hughes, *DSB* (1972), VI, 50–51. For Baekeland see the article by Eduard Farber, *DSB* (1970), I, 385.

38. Haber, *Chemical Industry during the 19th Century*, 144. On

Dow see Murray Campbell and Harrison Hatton, *Herbert H. Dow, Pioneer in Creative Chemistry* (New York, Appleton-Century-Crofts, 1951).

39. Article on Dana by Lyman C. Newell, *Dictionary of American Biography*, III, 61.

40. Article on Dudley by Charles E. Munroe, *Dictionary of American Biography*, III, 479–80.

41. Charles Süsskind, "Irving Langmuir," *DSB* (1973), VIII, 22–25; C. Guy Suits and Miles J. Martin, "Irving Langmuir," *National Academy of Sciences, Biographical Memoirs*, Vol. XLV (1974), 215–47; Birr, *Pioneering in Industrial Research*; Laurence A. Hawkins, *Adventures into the Unknown: The First Fifty Years of the General Electric Research Laboratory* (New York, William Morrow, 1950).

42. Bartlett, "The Development of Industrial Research in the United States," in National Resources Planning Board, *Research—A National Resource*, 19.

43. Harold F. Williamson, Ralph L. Andreano, Arnold R. Daum, and Gilbert C. Klose, *The American Petroleum Industry*, Vol. II, *The Age of Energy, 1899–1959* (Evanston, Northwestern University Press, 1963), 136–42, 612–18; American Chemical Society, *Chemistry in the Economy*, 281–86; Haynes, *American Chemical Industry*, I, 249–50.

44. Article on Carothers by Julian W. Hill, *DSB* (1971), III, 85–86; Haynes, *American Chemical Industry*, IV, Chap. 4; William S. Dutton, *Du Pont: One Hundred and Forty Years* (2d ed., New York, Charles Scribner's Sons, 1949).

45. American Chemical Society, *Chemistry in the Economy*, xi.

46. Ihde, *Development of Modern Chemistry,* 703–705; American Chemical Society, *Chemistry in the Economy*, 174; article on Duggar by Morris H. Saffron, *DSB* (1971), IV, 219–21.

47. Daniel Patrick Jones, "The Role of Chemists in Research on War Gases in the United States During World War I" (unpublished Ph.D. dissertation, University of Wisconsin, Madison, 1969); *United States Army in World War II: The Technical Services,* Vol. VI, Part 7, *The Chemical Warfare Service* (Washington, D.C., Office of the Chief of Military History, U.S. Army): I, *Organizing for War,* by Leo P. Brophy and George J. B. Fisher (1959); II, *From Laboratory to Field,* by Leo P. Brophy, Wyndham D. Miles, and Rexmond C. Cochrane (1959); III, *Chemicals in Combat,* by Brooks E. Kleber and Dale Birdsell (1966); Richard G. Hewlett and Oscar E. Anderson, Jr., *A History of the United States Atomic Energy Commission,* Vol. I, *The New World, 1939–1946* (University Park, Pennsylvania State University Press, 1962).

48. Margaret W. Rossiter, "Justus Liebig and the Americans: A Study in the Transit of Science, 1840–1880" (unpublished Ph.D. dissertation, Yale University, New Haven, 1971); Reynold M. Wik, "Science and American Agriculture," in *Science and Society in the United States* (ed. by Van Tassel and Hall), 81–106.

49. Alfred Charles True, *A History of Agricultural Experimentation and Research in the United States, 1607–1925,* United States Department of Agriculture, Miscellaneous Publication No. 251 (Washington, D.C., U.S. Government Printing Office, 1937); Gustavus A. Weber, *The Bureau of Chemistry and Soils: Its History, Activities and Organization,* Institute for Government Research, Service Monograph No. 52 (Baltimore, Md., Johns Hopkins Press, 1928); A. Hunter Dupree, *Science in the Federal Government: A History of Policies and Activities to 1940* (Cambridge, Mass., Harvard University Press, 1957), 176–81; Ernest G. Moore, *The Agricultural Research Service* (New York, Washington, London, Frederick A. Praeger, 1967); Charles E. Rosenberg, "Science, Technology, and Economic Growth: The Case of the Agricultural Experiment Station Scientist, 1875–1914," in *Nineteenth-Century American Science* (ed. by Daniels), 181–209; Oscar E. Anderson,

Jr., *The Health of a Nation: Harvey W. Wiley and the Fight for Pure Food* (Chicago, University of Chicago Press, 1958). On Wetherill see Edgar Fahs Smith, "Charles Mayer Wetherill, 1825–1871," *Journal of Chemical Education*, Vol. VI (1929), 1076–89, 1215–24, 1461–77, 1668–80, 1916–27, 2160–77.

50. American Chemical Society, *Chemistry in the Economy*, 215.

51. Beardsley, *Rise of the American Chemistry Profession*, 43–44; Glenn Sonnedecker, "The Scientific Background of Chemistry Teachers in Representative Pharmacy Schools of the United States during the 19th Century," *Chymia*, Vol. IV (1953), 171–200; Scott, "Putting Chemistry in Education," *Chemical and Engineering News*, Vol. XLIII, No. 13 (March 29, 1965), 90.

52. Jesse P. Watson, *The Bureau of the Mint: Its History, Activities and Organization*, Institute for Government Research, Service Monograph No. 37 (Baltimore, Johns Hopkins Press, 1926); F. W. Clarke, "The Chemical Work of the U.S. Geological Survey," *Science*, Vol. XXX (1909), 161–71; Dupree, *Science in the Federal Government*, 271–77; National Academy of Sciences, National Research Council, *Basic Chemical Research in Government Laboratories* (Washington, D.C., National Academy of Sciences, 1966). See also Carroll W. Pursell, Jr., "Science and Government Agencies," in *Science and Society in the United States* (ed. by Van Tassel and Hall), 223–49.

53. Wyndham D. Miles, "Early American Chemical Societies: 1. The 1789 Chemical Society of Philadelphia; 2. The Chemical Society of Philadelphia," *Chymia*, Vol. III (1950), 95–113; Wyndham D. Miles, "John Redman Coxe and the Founding of the Chemical Society of Philadelphia in 1792," *Bulletin of the History of Medicine*, Vol. XXX (1956), 469–72; Wyndham D. Miles, "The Columbian Chemical Society," *Chymia*, Vol. V (1959), 145–54; H. Carrington Bolton, "Early American Chemical Societies," *Journal of the American Chemical Society*, Vol. XIX (1897), 717–32; Marston Taylor Bogert, "American Chemical Societies," *Journal of the American Chemical Society*, Vol. XXX (1908), 163–82; Marcus Benjamin, "Organization and Development of the Chemical Section of the American Association for the Advancement of Science," *Journal of the American Chemical Society*, Vol. XXIII (1901), Supplement (*Twenty-fifth Anniversary of the American Chemical Society*, 1902), 86–98; Charles Albert Browne and Mary Elvira Weeks, *A History of the American Chemical Society* (Washington, D.C., American Chemical Society, 1952); Ralph S. Bates, *Scientific Societies in the United States* (3d ed.; Cambridge, Mass., M.I.T. Press, 1965). Publications celebrating the ACS centennial in 1976 are expected.

54. National Academy of Sciences, National Research Council, *Chemistry: Opportunities and Needs*, 3, 40–41.

55. Pursell, "Science and Industry," in *Nineteenth-Century American Science* (ed. by Daniels), 234.

56. National Academy of Sciences, National Research Council, *Chemistry: Opportunities and Needs*, 10, 150. Much of the discussion in these paragraphs relies on this study.

57. For the earlier development of chemical apparatus see Ernest Child, *The Tools of the Chemist: Their Ancestry and American Evolution* (New York, Reinhold, 1940).

58. The funding of science in an earlier period is discussed in Howard S. Miller, *Dollars for Research: Science and Its Patrons in Nineteenth-Century America* (Seattle and London, University of Washington Press, 1970).

59. National Academy of Sciences, National Research Council, *Chemistry: Opportunities and Needs*, 17, 148–49, 231–32.

60. Robert E. Kohler, Jr., "The Origin of G. N. Lewis's Theory of the Shared Pair Bond," *Historical Studies in the Physical Sciences*, Vol. III (1971), 343–76; Robert E. Kohler, Jr., "Irving Langmuir and the 'Octet' Theory of Valence," *Historical Studies in*

the *Physical Sciences*, Vol. IV (1974), 39–87.

61. On Debye see article by Charles P. Smyth, *DSB* (1971), III, 617–21; and J. W. Williams, "Peter Joseph Wilhelm Debye," *National Academy of Sciences, Biographical Memoirs*, Vol. XLVI (1975), 23–68.

62. C. A. Browne, "The Role of Refugees in the History of American Science," *Science*, Vol. XCI (1940), 203–208.

63. Carl B. Marquand and Helen H. Marquand, "Vladimir N. Ipatieff," in *Great Chemists* (ed. by Eduard Farber), 1277–98; Louis Schmerling, "Vladimir Nikolaevich Ipatieff," *National Academy of Sciences, Biographical Memoirs*, Vol. XLVII (1975), 83–140; Donald Fleming and Bernard Bailyn (eds.), *The Intellectual Migration: Europe and America, 1930–1960* (Cambridge, Mass., Harvard University Press, 1969). The *DSB* has articles on Meyerhof, by Joseph S. Fruton (1974), IX, 359; and on Franck, by H. G. Kuhn (1972), V, 117–18.

64. National Science Foundation, *American Science Manpower 1968* (Washington, D.C., National Science Foundation, 1969), 13, 32; National Academy of Sciences, National Research Council, *Chemistry: Opportunities and Needs*, 156–57; American Chemical Society, *Chemistry in the Economy*, 422–24, 458; National Academy of Sciences, *Materials and Man's Needs: Materials Science and Engineering. Summary Report of the Committee on the Survey of Materials Science and Engineering* (Washington, D.C., National Academy of Sciences, 1974), 31; Anselm L. Strauss and Lee Rainwater, *The Professional Scientist: A Study of American Chemists* (Chicago, Aldine, 1962).

65. National Academy of Sciences, National Research Council, *Chemistry: Opportunities and Needs*, 8; Lessing, "Great American Scientists: The Chemists," *Fortune*, Vol. LXI, No. 4 (April, 1960), 131.

66. Miles, "Early American Chemical Societies," *Chymia*, Vol. III (1950), 95; Smith, *Chemistry in America*, 219ff; Horace L. Wells and Harry W. Foote, "The Progress of Chemistry during the Past One Hundred Years," in *A Century of Science in America, with Special Reference to the American Journal of Science, 1818–1918* (ed. by Edward Salisbury Dana *et al.*, New Haven, Yale University Press, 1918), 288–334.

67. Russell H. Chittenden, *The Development of Physiological Chemistry in the United States* (New York, Chemical Catalog Company, 1930); Aaron J. Ihde, "An Inquiry into the Origins of Hybrid Sciences: Astrophysics and Biochemistry," *Journal of Chemical Education*, Vol. XLVI (1969), 193–96.

68. National Science Foundation, *American Science Manpower 1968*, 271.

69. Discussion of the relationships of science and technology surfaces regularly in the pages of *Technology and Culture*. See, for example, Derek J. de Solla Price, "Is Technology Historically Independent of Science?" *Technology and Culture*, Vol. VI (1965), 553–68; C. David Gruender, "On Distinguishing Science and Technology," *Technology and Culture*, Vol. XII (1971), 456–63; and Edwin Layton, "Mirror-Image Twins: The Communities of Science and Technology in 19th-Century America," *Technology and Culture*, Vol. XII (1971), 562–80.

70. Carroll W. Pursell, Jr., "The Farm Chemurgic Council and the United States Department of Agriculture, 1935–1939," *Isis*, Vol. LX (1969), 307–17; Robert M. Yerkes (ed.), *The New World of Science: Its Development During the War* (Freeport, N.Y., Books for Libraries Press, 1969 [originally published 1920]), especially Chaps. 8–10. For a general discussion of the recent history of American science see Everett Mendelsohn, "Science in America: The Twentieth Century," in *Paths of American Thought* (ed. by Schlesinger and White), 432–45.

71. William J. Hale, *Chemistry Triumphant: The Rise and Reign*

of Chemistry in a Chemical World (Baltimore, Md., Williams & Wilkins, 1932), 130.

72. American Chemical Society, *Chemistry in the Economy*, 456.

73. American Chemical Society, *Cleaning Our Environment: The Chemical Basis for Action* (Washington, D.C., American Chemical Society, 1969).

74. American Chemical Society, *Chemistry in the Economy*, 12.

75. National Academy of Sciences, National Research Council, *Chemistry: Opportunities and Needs*, 1. See also American Chemical Society, *Cleaning Our Environment*, vii, 3.

76. F. A. Long, "The Priestley Heritage: Prospects for Chemistry in Its Third 100 Years," *Journal of Chemical Education*, Vol. LII (1975), 14.

13

PHYSICS

By Thomas M. Smith

When American revolutionary radicals were resisting British oppression, the science of physics had nothing at all to do with politics and statecraft. Two hundred years later physics was hip-deep in politics and statecraft, while remaining true to its research tradition.

The altered circumstances in which the physical sciences find themselves in the twentieth century, compared with those of Benjamin Franklin's time, were brought to pass by at least three unrelated causes. In part there was the European genius for scientific originality in experiment and theory. In part there was the British genius that launched the Industrial Revolution. And in part there was the American genius for getting things organized to accomplish practical improvements in the human condition.

Although Europe was not far behind, it happened to be the United States that placed physics squarely in the political arena during the twentieth century. Only one of the fields of physics was directly involved, but physicists in all fields felt the implications, and so did the intellectual and the political leaders of American society. The particular field happened to be atomic physics, and it was American practical application of a nuclear theory constructed almost exclusively by European scientists that moved physics to the front and center of the political stage by producing the atomic bomb in the military realm and the Atomic Energy Act in the political realm. As a result, physics became an instrument of public policy, and neither science in general nor physics in particular could expect ever to be quite the same again.

In the perspective of the history of science it could be argued that there occurred no more profound change in science, since the invention of science itself twenty-five hundred years ago, than that accomplished during the first two hundred years of American independence. But whether there was indeed a causal relationship between this change in science and the American political experience has proved to be a proposition easier to assert than to demonstrate.

The "flying wedge" that opened the way for this dramatic transformation of physics was composed originally of Europeans of the sixteenth and seventeenth centuries who called themselves "experimental and natural Philosophers"—such men as William Gilbert and Robert Boyle. They were soon joined by sixteenth- and seventeenth-century mathematicians who, to a man, were convinced that God himself, the Sublime Creator, was both First Physicist and First Mathematician. Galileo Galilei, René Descartes, and Johann Kepler come readily to mind. To men such as these, masters also of the mathematical and physical science of optics, the truth of the statement in the Book of Genesis,

> *And God said*
> *Let there be light;*
> *And there was light.*

became only more profoundly true as one pursued mathematical and experimental investigations in order to comprehend the simple laws of reflection and search out the more subtle laws of refraction, as their contemporary Willebrord Snell had done.

The most illustrious member of this group, Isaac Newton, reorganized physics, including optics, once and for all, it appeared, scarcely a century before the American Revolution. Consequently, it was altogether fitting for Alexander Pope early in the eighteenth century, with his poet's perception of traditional glory and inspired by the familiar passage in the Book of Genesis, to proclaim

> *Nature and Nature's laws lay*
> *hid in night:*
> *God said, Let Newton be!*
> *and all was light.*

The actual course of events in history was, of course, more prosaic than the poet's vision and also more drastic in its impact upon Western civilization. The Scientific Revolution, in which Newton participated so heroically during the later seventeenth century, was followed by the Industrial Revolution of the next century. Spreading from England to the Continent during the eighteenth and nineteenth centuries, this revolution in the use of tools and power machinery crossed the Atlantic Ocean to the United States in the nineteenth century and leaped the Pacific to Japan in the early twentieth.

This revolution was, in considerable measure, a science-based revolution. It is true that it was not accomplished by experimental and natural philosophers or by mathematicians and mathematical physicists, and so it might appear to have little or nothing to do with the story of physics in America. But such is not the case, for the so-called Industrial Revolution was brought to pass not only by manufacturing entrepreneurs but also by engineers grounded increasingly thoroughly in the experimental and mathematical knowledge of physics. The consequence of these achievements was the emergence of a new enterprise that tapped virgin reservoirs of physical power and energy. Frequently miscalled "science," it moved to the forefront of human affairs in Western society. Private entrepreneurs, usually in business for private profit, were among the first to perceive what was going on here, then government administrators and policy makers, and finally the politicians.

In this way science, the long-time cultural ornament to society (like the fine arts or history or belles lettres), gave way to science the practical endeavor that, in American hands, offered mankind atomic power in its earliest, crudest forms and took explorers out into the untrod frontiers of space, landing them on the moon.

While the physical knowledge that was to make these events possible was thus on its way to becoming a practical social tool, from the age of Watt and Jefferson to the age of Einstein and Churchill, the theories and explanations of physical science were changing also. Research discoveries modified or displaced existing knowledge, and shifting philosophical attitudes among scientists regarding the nature of the physical world and the limitations to our knowledge of it altered their insights and their judgments about physical reality. As far as research techniques were concerned, however, the dual supremacy of mathematical and experimental investigation in physics remained unchallenged among most professors and students in generation after generation.

More important than the changing explanations or the unchanging methodology was a gradual, inexorable transformation of the scope and aims of physics and its allied sciences. This transformation went virtually unheralded principally because it occurred in the realm of practice and without any corresponding verbal, explicit policy formulations to illuminate its progress.

Thus physicists stopped referring to physics by its other, older name, "natural philosophy," during the nineteenth century, and the title of Newton's great revolutionary manifesto by which he reformed physics, *The Mathematical Principles of Natural Philosophy,* became less apt, less acute, more quaint, more antique, and increasingly irrelevant as a model of how to accomplish heroic work in physics. Besides, it was written in two foreign languages, Latin and geometry, neither of which was any longer judged necessary for the physicist to possess.

Another symptomatic indicator of the imperceptible transformation occurring in physics was the veneration accorded Galileo during the nineteenth and twentieth centuries as the ideal model of the creative, experimental physicist. This Galileo was a myth, fashioned by enthusiasts oblivious to the overwhelming evidence in Galileo's own writings and laboratory notebooks that showed him to be a mathematical physicist who found experimental knowledge useful only as it was faithfully subordinate to the overwhelming truths of mathe-

matics and significant only as it approximately pointed to these truths.

Still a third symptom of the unperceived, gradual transformation and extension of physics and its related disciplines was the failure of American schoolchildren to distinguish between Thomas A. Edison and Josiah Willard Gibbs as scientists. The former they were erroneously taught to call a "scientist," although he himself knew better and rejected the title. The latter most of them had never even heard of, although he was the only American physicist who could be ranked with the finest scientific minds that Europe had ever produced.

Simply stated, the transformation of physics and the physical sciences produced a new kind of intellectual enterprise, generated first in Europe but developed importantly under American hands. It held the scientific knowledge of physics historically at its core. Sometimes it was called "applied science," an inexact and misleading term.

By the time the nation was celebrating the Bicentennial of its Declaration of Independence, the transformed physical science had acquired still another name and was commonly accorded an inferior rank among the sciences, so hopelessly confused were the policy views regarding its nature and origins. Especially confusing were the views uttered by "leading scientists," who, as the resident experts on the subject, might reasonably be expected to appreciate perceptively what had transpired. "Research and development" (R&D) the new scientific enterprise was called. Any resemblance to physics was regarded as purely coincidental and a consequence of the historical intellectual indebtedness of a corrupted discipline which had fallen away from "pure science," the true pursuit of physical knowledge for its own sake. It was not to be construed as belonging to that class of endeavors in physics represented, for example, by the researches in electricity of Benjamin Franklin in the eighteenth century or by those of Joseph Henry in electromagnetism or Albert A. Michelson in the speed of light in the nineteenth century or by those of Edwin Hubble in astrophysics in the twentieth.

A glance at the achievements of these men will show how comfortably appropriate and fashionable it has become to emphasize the differences between physics pure and physics applied by concentrating upon the former. Indeed, this distinction can be carried to such an extreme degree that the historically more compelling resemblances between them are ignored. And when they are ignored, it is easy to entertain a beguiling, mischievous misapprehension about the condition of physics in America since first it was imported from Europe in the seventeenth century.

Consider Benjamin Franklin. Twenty-five years before he was involved in the incendiary political activities that produced the Declaration of Independence, he was spending all the time he could seize from his profitable printing business in the thoroughly apolitical and unbusinesslike study of a natural curiosity, the "amber effect." A phenomenon known to the ancient Greeks and Romans (the Latin word for amber is *electrum*), the uncanny ability of amber or glass, when rubbed with a dry cloth, to attract tiny scraps of paper or pith balls was a subject recurringly discussed in European scientific writings. In dry weather this phenomenon of electrical attraction, along with more recently observed electrical repulsion, lent itself readily to the enthusiastic experimental inquiries and thoughtful theorizing of various European gentlemen of wealth, education, and leisure during the eighteenth century.

Franklin, a self-made and self-educated man in the New World, had seen an intriguing public lecture, with experiments, on typical electrical phenomena. He found it "a subject quite new to me" and irresistibly intriguing. With a group of friends he began to read European books on the subject (there were no American ones of consequence) and to carry out various experiments as the dry seasons of the year permitted.

Between 1747 and 1751, Franklin made himself master of the subject of the electric charge. He also began to communicate his findings in letters addressed to a member of the most prestigious British scientific society of his day, the Royal Society of London. The member, Peter Collinson, considered Franklin's accounts worth publishing, and accordingly there appeared in London in 1751 a ninety-page pamphlet (price 2s. 6d.), *Experiments and Observations on Electricity Made at Philadelphia in America by Mr. Benjamin Franklin* . . . . Subsequent editions and printings, expanded and enlarged, appeared in London in 1753, 1754, 1760, 1765, 1769, and 1774. Other editions were printed elsewhere in other languages.

The book became enormously popular, as scientific works go. In 1752 an experimental demonstration of the electrical nature of thunderstorms and lightning was carried out by French investigators in accordance with the instructions in Franklin's book—the celebrated "Philadelphia Experiment" the French called it. Their report and Franklin's book transformed Franklin overnight into a famous scientist, the most famous America was to produce during that century, and one of the half-dozen greatest scientists the British-colonies-become-the-United-States were to produce during the next two and a half centuries.

Impressive as was Franklin's experimental work in electricity, it was his theoretical ingenuity and understanding that caused European scientists to recognize that here, indeed, was an outlander who understood what physical investigation was all about.

Franklin's single-fluid theory of electricity offered a new, elegant, and compelling explanation of a wide variety of phenomena involving static electricity. It explained the "amber effect," the prodigious capacity of the Leyden jar to store electricity, and the character of the thunderbolt. It encouraged Franklin to propose the use of pointed lightning rods atop barns and houses to draw off the "electric fire" before it could build up and discharge in an explosive, disastrous flash. It gave Franklin an impeccable intellectual stature in Europe, and the prestige it wrapped him in contributed to his selection as the American envoy sent to Paris to obtain French assistance during the Revolution.

Physics appeared to be mingling with politics, for American revolutionaries were fond of quoting a bit of choice political verse about Franklin:

He with a kite drew lightning from the sky,
And like a kite he pecked King George's eye.

Those whose knowledge was more sophisticated regarding the virtues of the pointed lightning rod and the apolitical truths of science, preferred:

While you, great George, for knowledge hunt
And sharp conductors change for blunt,
The empire's out of joint.
Franklin another course pursues
And all your thunder heedless views
By keeping to the point.

A contrasting Tory view of Franklin's achievements, more sober, grieving, and moralistic, was offered in the following anonymous stanzas:

Inscription on a Curious Stove in the Form of an Urn, Contrived in Such a Manner as to Make the Flame Descend Instead of Rising from the Fire, Invented By Dr. Franklin.

Like a Newton sublimely he soared
To a summite before unattained,
New regions of science explored
And the palm of philosophy gained.

With a spark which he caught from the skies
He displayed an unparalleled wonder,
And we saw with delight and surprise
That his rod could secure us from thunder.

Oh! had he been wise to pursue
The track for his talents designed,
What a tribute of praise had been due
To the teacher and friend of mankind.

But to covet political fame
Was in him a degrading ambition,
The spark that from Lucifer came
And kindled the blaze of sedition.

Let candor then write on his urn,
Here lies the renowned inventor
Whose fame to the skies ought to burn
But inverted descends to the centre.

Although physics could be made a topical subject of partisan eighteenth-century politics, it was far from being involved yet in the political arena. Rather, it was the man of varied and brilliant talents Benjamin Franklin who moved with ease in both circles. So he could remark:

The King's changing his pointed conductors for blunt is a matter of small importance to me. If I had a wish about it, it would be that he had rejected them altogether as ineffectual. For it is only since he thought himself and family safe from the thunder of Heaven, that he dared to use his own thunder in destroying his innocent subjects.

Not until Joseph Henry published in 1832 his famous paper on self-induction was there another American physicist who demonstrated that he could match European physicists at their own creative game. Like Franklin, thirty-five-year-old Henry had become thoroughly acquainted with the relevant European literature, and like Franklin he was intrigued by electrical phenomena. By Henry's time, however, the research frontier in electricity lay not in the realm of electrostatic phenomena but in a field undreamed of in Franklin's day, electromagnetism.

As in the case of electrostatic research, European experimenters and theorists dominated the field, and foremost among them when Henry was at work was Michael Faraday in London. Henry first appreciated how very original his own researches were when, to his chagrin, he read in 1831 an article by Faraday describing findings that Henry independently had made earlier but had not yet published. Faraday had not stolen Henry's discovery; he had made the same discovery and published it first, thus gaining the credit for first showing how magnetism could generate electricity in a wire. This was the principle of the dynamo, which was to underlie the technology of electric power that began to emerge during the last third of the nineteenth century.

In 1829, Henry had noticed that a strong spark occurred when he cut off the current to one of the powerful electromagnets he was building. Subsequent research convinced him that an extra burst of current seemed to be produced whenever he broke the circuit and that this extra current was self-induced in the circuit whenever the connection was broken. This was the phenomenon of "autoinduction," on which Henry published an original paper in 1832. Faraday did not publish on the subject until 1835.

Henry's originality was further demonstrated during 1830–31, when he strung nearly a mile of copper wire around the walls of a classroom and with it connected a Cruikshanks battery to one of his "intensity magnets," constructed of a continuous coil of fine wire wound around a horseshoe-shaped iron core. Then he suspended a permanent, bar magnet from its middle so that it would rotate until one end came into contact with the unelectrified intensity magnet. When Henry closed the circuit, the current flowed through the mile of wire into the intensity magnet, repelling the end of the bar magnet from the pole of the intensity magnet that it had been touching. As the bar magnet swung, it struck a bell that Henry had placed in the way. He made no effort to publish these results.

In 1831 he published in Silliman's *American Journal of Science and Arts* an article describing how electromagnetism could produce mechanical motion. The title was "On a Reciprocating Motion Produced by Magnetic Attraction and Repulsion." Samuel F. B. Morse's construction of a practical telegraph in the 1840's, after he had consulted with Henry about certain technical problems, is too well known to need more than mention here.

In 1832, Henry's originality and growing fame as an experimental investigator elicited an offer, which he accepted, to teach science in the College of New Jersey, at Princeton, which had recently been rejuvenated and saved from bankruptcy. Fourteen years later he became a scientific administrator as the first director and secretary of the newly established Smithsonian Institution, and thenceforward his fruitful research years as an experimental physicist would be forever behind him.

Josiah Willard Gibbs, the most brilliant mathematical physicist and physical chemist that America was to produce, was born in 1839. The son of a Yale graduate who was a professor of philology and sacred literature, young Gibbs entered Yale in 1854, took readily to mathematics, became a graduate engineering student in 1858, and in 1863 completed his doctoral thesis "On the Form of the Teeth of Wheels in Spur Gearing."

In 1866 he went to Europe with his two sisters. There he attended mathematics lectures at the Sorbonne in Paris and then moved on to Berlin and to Heidelberg, attending courses in physics and mathematics and reading extensively in these fields. In June, 1869, he returned to New Haven and Yale, well informed on the state of the mathematical and physical sciences in the European tradition and grounded in them beyond any measure he could have attained had he remained in the United States. He had learned how to pursue creative, abstract, theoretical research in the physical sciences in the European mode, and he found it more absorbing than engineering.

Gibbs's personal style was so quiet and unobtrusive that no one was prepared for the matchless theoretical paper that he published in two parts, between 1876 and 1878, in the obscure *Transactions of the Connecticut Academy of Arts and Sciences* under the title "On the Equilibrium of Heterogeneous Substances."

Gibbs's paper offered a novel, coherent appraisal of certain fundamental physical and chemical phenomena that never before had been so eloquently explained and interrelated. Only those who were thoroughly competent in advanced mathematics could comprehend and follow his arguments critically. As a result no American physicist or chemist was aware of what he had published until the brilliant British mathematician and physicist James Clerk Maxwell, to whom Gibbs had sent a copy, called the paper to their attention.

In this work Gibbs developed an investigative and predictive mathematical theory of extraordinary conceptual richness, rigor, and power. The theory incorporated basic physical and chemical phenomena associated with the change of state of materials from the solid-to-liquid, solid-to-gas, and liquid-to-gaseous phases into an integrated, interrelated explanatory whole of such persuasive elegance that there began to appear frequent references in later technical literature to "Gibbs's Phase Rule," to Gibbs as providing fundamental contributions to the young science of thermodynamics (a branch of physics), and to Gibbs as laying the theoretical foundations of physical chemistry and in this respect making possible the sophisticated, multimillion-dollar chemical industry of the twentieth century.

In 1901, two years before he died, the Royal Society awarded Gibbs its coveted Copley Medal for being "the first to apply the Second Law of Thermodynamics to the exhaustive discussion of the relation between electrical and thermal energy and the capacity for external work." An obituary notice referred to Gibbs's greatest achievement as "his development, into their full scope, of the fundamental principles which regulate equilibrium and the trend of transformation in inanimate matter in bulk, that is, in general chemical and physical phenomena."

In 1878, when Gibbs happened to be publishing the concluding part of his great paper, Albert A. Michelson, a twenty-five-year-old physics instructor at the United States Naval Academy, Annapolis, began to construct a new apparatus with which to measure the speed of light. This enterprise led him to postdoctoral study in Europe, at Paris, Berlin, and Heidelberg, from 1880 until 1882.

In Hermann Helmholtz' laboratory in Berlin, Michelson developed an interferential refractometer of unique and promising design to detect whether the earth was moving through the ether of space and creating an ether wind, as contemporary physical theory suggested it was. A beam of light was split into two beams, which were then bounced off mirrors to direct them at right angles to one another. If light were simply waves in the ether and if the earth were moving through the ether, then a difference in the observed times of travel of the split beams should be detectable. No difference was detected, either at Berlin or at Potsdam, although the refractometer was extraordinarily sensitive. Michelson and others concluded that experimental errors had rendered the findings inconclusive. Meanwhile, Michelson continued to prefer to believe that probably the ether was not stationary with respect to the earth.

Four years later, now at the Case School of Applied Science in Cleveland, Ohio, Michelson and a chemical colleague from Western Reserve in Cleveland, Edward W. Morley, together tackled the measurement problem once more, building an interferometer so accurate that it should measure one-fourth part per billion. Once again, in 1887, they could detect no ether drift.

While Michelson continued to prefer the explanation that light consisted of waves in a subtle, all-pervading ether, he was never able to produce convincing experimental evidence. If his is a story of failures, as this sketch would suggest, one might well ask why he subsequently received the Copley Medal and the Nobel Prize in 1907. It was partly because he was "an experimental physicist's physicist," whose interferometer and echelon diffraction grating opened up new possibilities of spectrum analysis and whose researches provided both experimental and mathematical physicists with more accurate measurements of the speed of light than had ever before been obtained. More significantly, there were those who, with Albert Einstein, George F. FitzGerald, Hendrik Lorentz, Jules Poincaré, and like-minded mathematical physicists, were heartened by Michelson's controversial null findings to abandon the ether theory for more sophisticated models. In consequence, during the twentieth century ether theory was discarded, while physicists came to perceive that the Michelson-Morley experiments were not as crucial in settling their theoretical differences as laymen generally were led to believe.

In a related field early in the twentieth century there were other American contributors of sufficient originality to lead their European peers. They were Henrietta Leavitt, Harlow Shapley, and Edwin Hubble, and their field was astrophysics.

Although at first glance their contributions might seem to fall into the astronomical tradition instead of that of physics, such was not the case. Rather, an interpenetration of disciplines had been taking place, and in this instance the initiative lay with physics. The lines of investigation that Leavitt, Shapley, and Hubble were pursuing separately proved to be typical of the manner in which questions, concepts, and techniques of physics were transforming traditional cosmology and astronomy and producing the new science of astrophysics during the nineteenth and twentieth centuries.

The international character of the fundamental-research tradition is also demonstrated in this story, for the work of the three American investigators was built upon already established European practices of measuring the speed of light and upon European formulations of the wave theory of light derived from the one Christian Huygens had proposed in the seventeenth century and Thomas Young and A. G. Fresnel had revived in the nineteenth century.

Long before Henrietta Leavitt died in 1921, it was known that a star in the constellation Cepheus regularly grew brighter and dimmer. Studies of this bright, periodically pulsating star, Delta Cephei, led to the realization that there was an entire class of such stars—Cepheid variables—scattered across the heavens.

In 1912, concentrating her attention at Harvard Observatory upon twenty-five Cepheids in the smaller of two nebulae in the northern hemisphere, the Magellanic Clouds, Leavitt found that the Cepheids' periods of pulsation could be correlated with their luminosity, or brightness, in such a way that a period-luminosity law could be mathematically formulated to demonstrate that the longer the period the brighter the star. Furthermore, the regular periods of their pulsations could be correlated with their absolute brightness, or magnitude, and their actual distances could be determined.

Subsequent investigations, carried out independently by the Danish astrophysicist Ejnar Hertzsprung and the American astrophysicist Harlow Shapley, produced absolute values that researchers were satisfied to use, and when Shapley applied them to star clusters scattered throughout the Milky Way, he found that, contrary to traditional inferences, the earth and the solar system were not near the center of the galaxy but far out on one edge.

During the 1920's, Edwin P. Hubble began to study Cepheid variables in the Magellanic Clouds. His data and calculations produced persuasive evidence, under his creative hands, that the Magellanic Clouds were much farther away than had commonly been thought. Indeed, they appeared to be so far away, according to Hubble's findings, that they could no longer be regarded as part of the Milky Way to which earth belonged.

Late in the eighteenth century William Herschel and Pierre Simon de Laplace had proposed the theory still generally accepted in Hubble's day that the sun and its planets were part of the Milky Way, that the Milky Way was a lens-shaped star cluster, or galaxy, and that the boundaries of the universe were not much larger than the Milky Way itself. But Hubble's findings placed the Magellanic Clouds outside our galaxy, and suddenly, as the American astronomer Harlow

Shapley pointed out, the galaxies were not one but perhaps many and were indeed the "island universes" that Immanuel Kant in the middle of the eighteenth century had speculated might exist in a cosmos far larger than anyone else was then willing to accept. Basing further calculations upon Shapley's findings, investigators estimated the larger Magellanic Cloud to be some 75,000 light-years away.

Hubble's studies of Cepheids in the great nebula M31, in the constellation Andromeda, led him to announce in 1924 that the nebula was some 800,000 light-years distant. The universe was indeed larger than astronomers and cosmologists had thought. Nor was this the end. In 1953, as a consequence of reappraisal of the theoretical underpinnings that made Cepheid variables both comprehensible and useful, astrophysicists concluded that their calculations had been in error. The spiral galaxy in the constellation Andromeda was recalculated to be 1.5 million light-years away.

During the 1930's, Hubble and a spectroscopist, Milton L. Humason, working together, added compelling evidence to still another insight into the nature of the universe. It was an insight that Hubble had begun to develop in the late 1920's and it came to this: there was a radial speed of distant galaxies *away* from the earth, and the more remote the galaxy the higher its speed. Ours was an expanding universe, and, depending on the values one selected, it had been expanding for some 2 billion years (subsequently the time span was increased to 10 billion years). Hubble's detection and explanation during the 1930's of the "red shift," as he called it, stimulated a fundamental reappraisal by astrophysicists of the character of the cosmos. Such was the investigative power of the unending and philosophically inspiring enterprise of physics that once again it had compelled man to reassess his place in the universe. But this time the creative physicists were to be found in the New World as well as the Old.

These profoundly revolutionary developments in astrophysical thought were part of a larger revolution in physics that grew out of such nineteenth-century European developments as extensive revisions in the theory of the atom, the explanation of the behavior of the mysterious Crookes tube, and increasing theoretical discontent with some of the fundamental assumptions and implications of Newtonian physics. By the end of the nineteenth century the pure-research area of physics had undergone a conceptual revolution that displaced Newtonian physics from center stage and introduced X rays, radioactivity, relativity theory, and quantum physics. In consequence twentieth-century physical research set off in totally new and unanticipated directions.

For the next half century the instigators and the major contributors were virtually all Europeans. After the Nazis came to power under Adolf Hitler early in the 1930's and began to prepare for the conquest of Europe and a second world war, many of the leading Continental physicists fled to the United States to escape German oppression. Their emigration does not, of course, contradict the fact that American physicists were the followers, not the leaders, in this exciting new game. Earlier, Robert A. Millikan had produced impressive contemporary measurements of the relative weight of the electron. Arthur H. Compton had invented the Compton effect to explain interactions between X rays and electrons that could be related to the more fundamental explanations of quantum mechanics. Carl D. Anderson had identified the positron as a new atomic particle. But, aside from these, American contributions to the new physics were for the most part neither as original nor as profound as the European contributions.

More significant was the wholesale migration, just mentioned, of atomic physicists to the United States. In 1939, the same year that World War II began, the Danish physicist Niels Bohr told a meeting of physicists in Washington, D.C., that two German scientists had bombarded different elements, including uranium, with neutrons, that among the by-products of the uranium bombardments lighter elements such as iodine had been discovered, and that a German woman, the Jewish scientist Lise Meitner, had quietly suggested to him (Bohr) that perhaps the uranium atom had split apart. Fission!

To this startling speculation, which hurried investigations appeared to support and certainly did not contradict, the Italian physicist Enrico Fermi added the calculation that the fission would release extra neutrons from the former uranium atom. These neutrons could split neighboring uranium atoms and thus initiate a chain reaction involving the release of stupendous energies of the sort described four decades earlier in a scientific, mathematical "fantasy" created by Albert Einstein: Multiply a unit of matter by a number so large that it equaled the *square* of the value of the speed of light, and you would have the equivalent in pure energy: $E = mc^2$. If experimental inquiries should corroborate these theoretical calculations, then a bomb of incredible destructive force could perhaps be built.

In the summer of 1939 two knowledgeable immigrant Hungarian physicists persuaded Einstein to write a confidential letter to President Franklin D. Roosevelt, indicating their concern lest the Nazis learn of the practical implications and be first to follow them up. Alerted by the physicists, top government policy makers moved cautiously at first, to the physicists' dismay. Subsequent experimental results and intense, informal quiet "lobbying" by a handful of concerned physicists and science administrators, together with the surprise Japanese attack on Pearl Harbor in December, 1941, which unified the nation for war, finally impelled Roosevelt and leading military policy makers to move secretly in 1942 to establish the supersecret Manhattan Project, in order to design and build atomic bombs before the Nazis did, if humanly possible. A brilliant young American theoretical physicist, J. Robert Oppenheimer, was placed in administrative charge of this research-and-development project, at Los Alamos, New Mexico. Enrico Fermi led the group that was building the first atomic pile at the University of Chicago, and in December, 1942, they obtained the first controlled chain reaction, indicating the feasibility of a fission bomb. Two and a half years later, on July 16, 1945, the first "experimental device" was exploded at Alamogordo, New Mexico, and twenty-one days later, on August 6, the first atomic bomb was detonated over Hiroshima. The 9,000-pound bomb exploded 1,850 feet over the city and killed over 92,000 people. Said Oppenheimer after the war, "The physicists have known sin."

Such, briefly, was the manner in which physics became deeply involved in politics. Direct involvement had begun earlier than 1945—at least as early as 1939, when the physicists assembled in Washington heard Bohr's stunning theoretical news. For they promptly agreed to discuss subsequent technical findings as quietly and informally as Bohr had and not rush into open print. Their secrecy was self-imposed, and their censorship of scientific information was voluntary. All realized that, should the Nazi leadership learn of the military research and development prospects, the political consequences might be disastrous for the free world. Six years later the atomic bombing of Hiroshima and Nagasaki by American military forces swept physics instantly into the topmost levels of national and international politics, where crucial policy was being forged. For physics had generated an issue of the profoundest political and moral concern, threatening the survival of civilization and perhaps the very existence of the human race. Physics, the *exclusively* cultural, fundamental-research ornament of society, was gone forever, and this time the statesmen, the politicians, and the men in the street knew it.

Such profound historical developments do not occur overnight, and the socialization of physics (if we may call it that) was no exception. It was the culmination of a trend that had set in, in Europe, by the end of the thirteenth century—a trend marked by a steadily rising, slowly growing interest in systematic experiment and observation among a few of the relative handful of the population who could read and write, aspire to learning for its own sake, and cultivate the life of the mind. Four hundred years later the rising interest had become an enthusiastic, double-barreled Scientific Revolution. One "barrel" took the form of the conquest of the hitherto nonmathematical field of physics by the mathematicians, and their declaration of victory was Newton's great *Principia.* The other barrel, not integrally connected to the mathematicians' triumph, was the continuing "rise of experimental science." It proved to be the opening phase of another intellectual revolution, misnamed, as I have suggested, the Industrial Revolution. This technical revolution was foreseen in the seventeenth century by practical men like Jean Baptiste Colbert, Louis XIV's chief minister, and by impractical visionaries like Sir Francis Bacon. It was undertaken before the end of the eighteenth century by such men as James Watt in Britain and Eli Whitney in America. It was consolidated in the nineteenth century and exploited extravagantly in the twentieth century, most effectively in the United States, and because it welded the basic-research tradition of the physical sciences with the sophisticated, developmental testing techniques of the engineers and with the practical aims of technology, it can more accurately be called R&D or scientific technology.

To appreciate what was happening to physics, we should recall that while the transformation that produced R&D was going on, the historic fundamental-research tradition in Europe continued also to flourish, influencing and inspiring Franklin, Henry, Gibbs, and other Americans, as we have seen. It was taken for granted in Thomas Jefferson's day that the most respectable spokesmen for physics in particular or science in general were the intellectual leaders of the basic-research tradition. Such spokesmen still prevail today. A journalist who is interested in reporting impressive achievements in physics consults members of the basic-research fraternity or a science administrator who once received his advanced degree in physics and is very likely still called a "physicist," even though he is no longer participating in research and teaching himself. Engineers and R&D administrators are less reputable sources of "properly scientific" physics information, in this traditional view. Unfortunately, the views of the basic-research spokesmen on what is most distinctive of physics in America have for the most part failed to keep pace with the larger transformations of physics dominating the past century. Instead they have continued to identify the finest and most important part of modern physics with the basic-research tradition, arguing persuasively that applied research is methodologically subordinate as well, since it requires for its continuing well-being that the wellsprings of basic research must first be kept clean and tended so that they will not dry up and cause applied science to wither on the vine, as occurred in Europe among the preoccupations and disasters of World War II.

Also, the virtues of basic research conducted purely for its own sake have been preached and extolled to us from childhood in school, with the result that a curious professional snobbery has flourished, which allows the pure researcher to look down upon the lowly engineer from a higher level of prestige and esteem. This particular habit of thought, which can be traced back to antiquity, has mistakenly encouraged us to dwell upon the "engineering failure" that occurs when a rocket fails to go into orbit or blows up on its launch pad, while we note with satisfaction that our landing upon the moon becomes another "success of space science."

Such comparisons are as erroneous as they are invidious, because they obscure the profound transformation and expansion of physics (as well as of the life sciences and medicine) that have been going on during the past two hundred years. The vitality of the transformation grows out of the *supplementary* value of basic and applied research to each other and not out of the presumed superior-inferior status of the knowledge they produce.

But in these matters habits of thought die hard, and the true measure of the American natural genius for physics still remains to be taken. Perhaps, once we perceive that physics in our time has become as devoted to both understanding and controlling natural phenomena as formerly it was dedicated only to understanding, then significant dimensions of twentieth-century physical science can begin to emerge and submit to our enlarged understanding.

One of these dimensions, already perceived in the old frame of reference, is that the economic cost to society of scientific understanding is far less expensive than is that of controlling phenomena. The relevance of such understanding to explicit practical application has not always been appreciated, but when the funds are small and obtained from private or university sources, their expenditure has seldom been questioned. When the expenses are large or supported by tax dollars, then their practical value has on occasion become a political issue. Policy attitudes have been by no means clearcut in this area. Cyclotrons ("atom smashers") and similar very expensive equipment that American physicists, led by Ernest O. Lawrence, have invented are presumed to be necessary scientific preliminaries to our control and economic exploitation of atomic energy.

As energy demands have increased and the shortage of available power has become more apparent, public policy makers have turned naturally to the recognized experts for help and once again have called upon physicists, pure and applied, to provide practical solutions based upon the scientific knowledge of physics.

While we have been reluctant to spend extravagant sums in some areas of physics ("Why spend our money on space research, when we know so little about our oceans and how they can be of value to us?"), we have remained dedicated to the general proposition that application of understanding in order to gain control should improve the human condition. Our national experience happens to support this view. Indeed, it is so obviously true in medicine that it is only debated there in the forensic areas where abortion and euthanasia represent still-unfinished business.

Another dimension of the new, expanded physics that is just beginning to be appreciated is the anonymous, social character of much of the research. This feature stands in contrast to the heroic character of the older basic-research tradition. Perhaps the most significant implication of this state of affairs is the fact that it renders part of physics accessible to those pedestrian talents which most people possess, while still cherishing as strongly as ever the accomplishments of the rarer women and men of creative genius. Thus we may assert enthusiastically that 90 per cent of all the physicists who ever lived are alive today without making the pathetic mistake of placing the average team researcher in the same class with the Einsteins and the Gibbses.

Why the Americans happened to take the world lead in the enterprise of the expanded physics that is R&D is not easy to determine. Abundant natural resources and free schooling for all presumably had something to do with it. So did the growth of accessible national wealth, which could be legitimately exploited to these ends within the framework of our politicoeconomic system.

Less clear is any possible relevance of the character of our political system and philosophy to the character of modern physics. At first glance their relevance would seem rather unlikely, since ours is a culture that leaves the specialties to the specialists: law to the lawyers, physics to the physicists (now pure and applied), and politics to the politicians. But there are curious parallels in their manner of conducting their affairs, and now that physics has become squarely involved in politics, on levels and in directions well beyond those of

atomic energy in American society, it is just possible that physics and our political system will learn something from each other.

For our physicists have been raised in a society that is a peculiarly free society in these respects: as our Founding Fathers laid it out and as we have operated it, with modifications since, we have the government as a corporate entity on one side, and we have the citizens on the other. Our Constitution and laws set out limits of action, limits of freedom, and responsibilities for each side, the government *and* the citizens.

Due process governs the relations, the tug and haul, that go on between our government and us. Furthermore, the limits to power, to action, to freedom are not graven in stone. They are not immutable. We can change them and redefine them, and we do, continually. There results a characteristically *American* pragmatic state of affairs in which we are continually re-examining and changing the rules by which we operate and the goals which we seek. We are and have been for the past two centuries a free society, in the profoundest meaning of the term. Not perfect. Not without friction or violence, as our national history attests. But free, because we are not chained to any unalterable, ultimate ideals.

Similarly, physics the basic-research tradition, along with physics the younger R&D tradition, has not been bound to unalterable, ultimate explanations or controls of phenomena. In this sense both our physics and our politics, each for their separate reasons, have been somewhat experimental and thoroughly pragmatic. Now that they have been made bedfellows, willynilly, in our time, they may prove less incompatible than some have feared. For although one has been commonly called "scientific," in both the literal and figurative senses of the word, while the other has been a most unscientific "art," the philosophies according to which they conduct their affairs have been less far apart.

To expect politics to become scientific, then, like physics, would probably be as unreasonable as to expect physics to become thoroughly politicized. Certainly, the basic-research tradition of physics would repudiate such a metamorphosis, and the R&D tradition of physics probably would find it an uncongenial, inefficient, and corrupting way to proceed, one that would subvert both the theoretical and the practical achievements sought.

What is more likely to happen is that for a while, at least, the association of physics with politics will cause the philosophy of each tradition to enrich and inform in a constructive way the philosophy and the procedures of the other. It will not be an unmixed blessing, for such associations never are. Yet each tradition may serve to invigorate and reinforce the other in ways that, while quite beyond the anticipations of our forefathers or ourselves, will yet assist the great social experiment our nation has been conducting—in government of the people, by the people, and for the people—to flourish and to endure.

READINGS AND REFERENCES

Canan, James W. *The Superwarriors: The Fantastic World of Pentagon Superweapons.* New York: Weybright & Talley, 1975.

Cohen, I. B. *Benjamin Franklin: Scientist and Statesman.* New York: Charles Scribner's Sons, 1975.

———. *Benjamin Franklin's Experiments.* Cambridge, Mass.: Harvard University Press, 1941.

———. *Franklin and Newton.* Cambridge, Mass.: Harvard University Press, 1973.

Daniels, George H. *American Science in the Age of Jackson.* New York: Columbia University Press, 1968.

———, ed. *Nineteenth-Century American Science. A Reappraisal.* Evanston: Northwestern University Press, 1972.

Dupree, A. Hunter. *Science in the Federal Government.* Cambridge, Mass.: Belknap Press of Harvard University Press, 1957.

Gibbs, Josiah Willard. *The Collected Works of J. Willard Gibbs.* 2 vols. New Haven: Yale University Press, 1948.

Henry, Joseph. *The Papers of Joseph Henry.* Washington, D.C.: Smithsonian Institution Press, 1972– .

Hindle, Brooke. *The Pursuit of Science in Revolutionary America, 1735–1789.* Chapel Hill: University of North Carolina Press, 1956.

Hubble, Edwin. *The Nature of Science, and Other Lectures.* San Marino, Calif.: Huntington Library, 1954.

Kranzberg, M. and Pursell, C. W., Jr., eds. *Technology in Western Civilization.* 2 vols. New York: Oxford University Press, 1967.

Lapp, Ralph E. *The New Priesthood.* New York: Harper & Row, 1965.

Livingston, Dorothy Michelson. *The Master of Light.* New York: Charles Scribner's Sons, 1973.

Price, Don K. *The Scientific Estate.* Cambridge, Mass.: The Belknap Press of Harvard University Press, 1965.

Reingold, Nathan, ed. *Science in Nineteenth Century America, A Documentary History.* New York: Hill & Wang, 1964.

Swenson, Loyd S., Jr. *The Ethereal Aether.* Austin: University of Texas Press, 1972.

Wheeler, Lynde P. *Josiah Willard Gibbs, the History of a Great Mind.* New Haven: Yale University Press, 1952.

14

THE EVOLUTION OF MOLECULAR BIOLOGY

By John R. Sokatch

The past quarter of a century has included the most creative and vigorous era in the history of biological science, the era of molecular biology. Molecular biology is the science of the role that the molecular structure of the cell plays in the biology of the cell. Molecular biology began with the deciphering of the genetic code in nucleic acids but now extends to almost all cell structures. A review of this period is particularly fitting for the celebration of the Bicentennial Year, for American scientists played a major role in the field, and their research strongly influenced scientists in other countries. Periodicals devoted to the history of science give little space to modern biological science even though the period just past has had an effect on civilization orders of magnitude greater than all the pre-twentieth-century science and can only be overshadowed by what is yet to come. The purpose of this chapter is to recapitulate briefly the important events of the period, to present an analysis of how this unusually productive era came to be, and to evaluate its impact on the quality of life.

PRE-TWENTIETH-CENTURY BIOLOGICAL SCIENCE

Before the seventeenth century there was more magic than science, for the tools for research and scientific philosophy were not yet available. The major discoveries of the seventeenth to the nineteenth centuries were made by Europeans. The discovery of the cellular structure of living things by Robert Hooke; the discovery of the circulation of blood by William Harvey; the description of microorganisms by Anton van Leeuwenhoek; the destruction of the theory of spontaneous generation by Lazzaro Spallanzani, Theodor Schwann, and Louis Pasteur; and the proposal of the theory of evolution by Charles Darwin were all major scientific events that occurred before the end of the nineteenth century. Biological science came alive in the time of Pasteur, who discovered and appreciated the roles of microorganisms in the biosphere. The first practical application of this knowledge led to enormous savings in the wine industry through the process of pasteurization. Pasteurization of milk prevented the transmission of tuberculosis and undulant fever,

resulting in a reduction in the incidence of those diseases. Pasteur's work led to the germ theory of disease and the identification of several etiologic agents of infectious diseases by him and others, particularly Robert Koch and his associates in Germany.

Pasteur's work influenced Joseph Lister, who applied Pasteur's ideas to the practice of surgery, effecting a dramatic reduction in postsurgical sepsis. In the pre–World War I era, Paul Ehrlich began studies that introduced the modern field of immunology and led to the discovery of antitoxins. Ehrlich also began the search for a "magic bullet," a specific antimicrobial drug that was nontoxic to man. Biological science was not advanced enough in Ehrlich's time to grasp the biochemical differences between bacteria and higher organisms, and, while Ehrlich's approach was farsighted, its success was limited. Meanwhile, American scientists were beginning to be heard. Theobald Smith, who made many solid contributions to medical microbiology and immunology, is best known for his work on the role of ticks in Texas fever. Walter Reed saved scores of lives by learning the natural history of yellow fever and applying simple sanitation procedures for the control of the mosquito vector. The first Nobel Prize in Medicine awarded to an American went to a French-born physician, Alexis Carrell, in 1912. Ironically, Carrell died in 1944 in Vichy, France, where he was director of the Carrell Foundation for the Study of Human Problems.

1928: THE START OF MOLECULAR BIOLOGY

The era of molecular biology was started in England in the late 1920's by an officer of the Ministry of Health, Fred Griffith, M.B. To set the stage, it should be emphasized that the principles of Mendelian genetics had been accepted by then, but the nature of the instrument that carried hereditary information was a complete mystery. There was no understanding of bacterial heredity—in fact, there was no evidence that bacteria even had a nucleus. There was reason to believe the genetic code was carried in a chemical, but whether the chemical was protein, nucleic acid, or some other agent was unknown.

Griffith, an epidemiologist, was curious about the occurrence of more than one serological type of pneumococcus in many cases of lobar pneumonia. He considered the possibility that one type of pneumococcus might actually change to another in the patient. To test this hypothesis, Griffith injected mice with strains of pneumococci, singly and in combinations of strains and of living and dead cultures. He added an extra dimension since he was able to isolate avirulent strains of virulent Types I and II pneumococci. The avirulent strains grew as rough colonies (RI and RII) because they lacked the capsule of the virulent parents, which grew as smooth colonies (SI and SII). When RII was injected into mice with heat-killed SIV, SII pneumococci were isolated from some mice, which suggested that RII had reverted to SII in the mouse (Griffith, 1928). Mice injected with RII alone survived. When Griffith injected mice with heat-killed SIII and live RII, the mice died, and either SIII or SII pneumococci could be isolated. The only logical conclusion was that RII had somehow transformed into SIII. He tried unsuccessfully to effect conversion of a rough strain to a smooth strain in the test tube. Griffith was careful to include the proper controls, and there was no question that his results were valid. Griffith referred to the process as the transformation of a rough strain to a smooth strain, a term that has remained.

Griffith was apparently not overly impressed with transformation since it occupied relatively little of his discussion and summary. However, others were impressed, and his results were quickly repeated both in Europe and in the United States, and M. G. Dawson and R. H. P. Sia produced transformation in the test tube in 1931 (Dawson and Sia, 1931). The significance of Griffith's results was appreciated by the scientific community: he had effected a stable, inheritable change in bacteria.

THE POST–WORLD WAR II ERA

O. T. Avery, C. M. MacCleod, and M. McCarty (1944), at the Rockefeller Institute for Medical Research, provided the historic explanation for Griffith's results. They devised a reproducible, in vitro transformation system, which they used as an assay to purify the transformation factor. The simple fact that such a process could occur in the test tube suggested that some chemical was passing from heat-killed, smooth pneumococci to living, rough pneumococci. Avery and his associates identified the substance they purified from heat-killed pneumococci as deoxyribonucleic acid (DNA) on the basis of excellent analytical data. The chemical composition of the transforming principle and the fact that it was destroyed by deoxyribonuclease established that DNA was responsible for transformation. Avery, MacCleod, and McCarty were conservative in discussion of their results and stated modestly that they had effected a stable, inheritable change with a chemical substance. What they had really done was identify DNA as the carrier of genetic information. Since any theory of protein formation required that DNA carried the code for every protein in the cell, Avery, MacCleod, and McCarty's identification of DNA as the carrier of genetic information supplied the key piece in the puzzle of protein and nucleic-acid synthesis.

The next major discovery was made by James D. Watson and F. H. C. Crick at Cambridge University in England. James Watson was only twenty-three and had received a doctorate in genetics from the University of Indiana only a year before he joined Crick to learn as much as he could about the structure of DNA. After studying X-ray diffraction patterns of purified DNA, the two men concluded that DNA was a double helix of two chains of DNA held together by weak hydrogen bonds between the bases of the two chains (Watson and Crick, 1953). The beauty and logic of their proposal was immediately evident. Their model explained the observation by Erwin Chargaff that the amount of adenine in DNA is always equal to the amount of thymine and the amount of guanine is equal to the amount of cytosine. Adenine is bound to thymine of the opposite chain and guanine to cytosine, making the two chains of DNA complementary but opposite in polarity, or antiparallel. More important, however, it explained how hereditary information could be passed from one cell to another: one of the two chains could act as the template for formation of daughter strands of DNA. Watson added another, personal dimension to biological science. He was a brash young man who by the time he was twenty-five had done the work that was later to earn him the Nobel Prize. Watson described his experiences in *The Double Helix*, a highly readable but frequently acid commentary on his work and associates in England. He modestly referred to his contribution as "perhaps the most famous in biology since Darwin's book." Nevertheless he writes well, and his refreshing style was evidence that scientists are human after all.

The Watson and Crick structure for DNA predicted that one strand of DNA would serve as the template for a new strand when chromosomes were reproduced. This prediction was proved in an elegant experiment by M. Meselson and F. W. Stahl (1958). They used as their experimental tool everybody's favorite bacterium for research, *Escherichia coli*, and grew the organism in the presence of a heavy isotope of nitrogen, ^{15}N, in order to incorporate ^{15}N into the nitrogen of DNA. They found that, after one generation of growth in ^{15}N, double-stranded DNA isolated from *Escherichia coli* was a mixture of exactly 50 per cent of the light isotope of nitrogen, ^{14}N, and 50 per cent of the heavy isotope of nitrogen, ^{15}N. The conclusion was inescapable: the chromosome was composed of one of the original strands (the template) and one newly synthesized strand (the daughter strand).

The next exciting breakthrough was deciphering of the genetic code. The discovery that led to it was made by Marshall Nirenberg at the National Institutes of Health, who found a way to produce protein synthesis in a cell-free system in the test tube. One of the important components in the system was a species of ribonucleic acid, now known as messenger RNA. Nirenberg and his associates learned that the composition of messenger RNA was critical in determining the kind of protein synthesized. Using a synthetic RNA with uracil as the only base, a polypeptide containing phenylalanine as the only amino acid was produced by the cell-free system (Nirenberg and Matthaei, 1961). It must be, therefore, that polyuridylic acid (RNA with uracil as the sole base) contained the code for phenylalanine.

Following publication of Nirenberg and Matthaei's work, the entire genetic code was quickly deciphered. The first serious suggestion for a triplet code of three bases for each amino acid came from George Gamow. Gamow, a physicist, had obtained his training with Niels Bohr and was well known for his contributions as a professor of theoretical physics at George Washington University. He was also the author of a popular, humorous, and whimsical series of books featuring the adventures of a Mr. Tompkins among atomic particles. Gamow was excited by Watson and Crick's work and invented the idea of a triplet code of the amino acids in protein. His manuscript was first submitted to the prestigious *Proceedings of the National Academy of Sciences of the United States.* Its coauthor was listed as one C. G. H. Tompkins. This bit of levity apparently did not amuse the reviewer, for the article was rejected. It was later published in the *Proceedings of the Royal Danish Academy* (Gamow, 1954a) and in *Nature* (Gamow, 1954b) but without Mr. Tompkins. See the paper by Crick (1966) for an interesting review of the events of this period.

Nirenberg's work established the existence of messenger RNA, which carried the code for amino acids from DNA to ribosomes, where proteins are synthesized. Messenger RNA is complementary in structure to a specific segment of DNA: wherever DNA contains guanine, there is cytosine in messenger RNA, and wherever there is adenine in DNA, there is uracil in messenger RNA (uracil replaces thymine in RNA). The enzyme that transcribes RNA from DNA was characterized by Jerard Hurwitz, at New York University. This enzyme uses only one strand of DNA as a template and makes RNA in its own image—again in keeping with Watson and Crick's structure for DNA. H. Goband Khorana, at the University of Wisconsin, synthesized short segments of RNA of known base composition, and from then it was simply a matter of time until the complete genetic code was known. It is a triplet code and nonoverlapping; that is, the first three bases code for one amino acid, the next three bases code for a second amino acid, and so forth. The code is "degenerate," since in most cases only the first two bases are important in determining the amino acid, and the third base can be any one of two to four bases. The code contains the symbol for the initiation of protein synthesis and for the termination of protein synthesis. *Probably most significant, however, is the fact that the code is universal.*

Other fields of biological science, in particular biochemistry and genetics, also moved ahead rapidly after World War II. Fritz Lipmann, at Massachusetts General Hospital; Severo Ochoa and Efraim Racker, at New York University; I. C. Gunsalus, at the University of Illinois; and Bernard Horecker, at the National Institutes of Health, were leading advocates of research with purified enzymes to reconstruct segments of metabolic pathways. Geneticists George Beadle and Edward L. Tatum proposed the concept that segments of DNA (genes) contain the code for enzymes. Joshua Lederberg discovered that *Escherichia coli* is capable of sexual recombination, although just a few years earlier there had been heated debate over whether bacteria had a nucleus. Arthur Kornberg, of Stanford University, was able to achieve the synthesis of biologically active DNA in the form of bacteriophage by using a purified enzyme, DNA polymerase. Kornberg's enzyme is actually a repair enzyme used to repair short breaks in DNA and not to synthesize chromosomal DNA. The true DNA polymerase is now known, but that does not lessen the significance of Kornberg's contribution. Finally, the brilliant Frenchman Jacques Monod proposed a theory for the regulation of enzyme formation which affected the thinking of biological scientists all over the world.

The contribution of American industry during the same period is not ordinarily recognized but was extremely important. The development of automated equipment, such as recording spectrophotometers and recording scintillation detectors for the measurement of radioactivity, and thousands of work-saving laboratory gadgets replaced the homemade equipment used in the 1930's and 1940's. It also became possible to purchase research biochemicals such as purified enzymes and coenzymes that had also been manufactured previously in the laboratory by graduate students and technicians. The availability of the equipment and research biochemicals freed scientists for more creative activities.

Table 1. American Nobel Prize Winners in the Pre- and Post–World War II Eras

Field	1901–39		1943–73	
	Americans	*Total Awards*	*Americans*	*Total Awards*
Physics	8	46	30	52
Chemistry	4	40	16	45
Physiology or medicine	8	41	37	67
Literature	3	31	3	38

The result of all this activity was the accumulation in the thirty years following World War II of an impressive wealth of scientific knowledge that eclipsed everything learned by man before then. The contribution of Americans was impressive by any criterion, and Americans dominated the list of Nobel laureates. In the thirty-eight years before World War II eight of the forty-one individuals receiving Nobel prizes in medicine or physiology were Americans (Table 1). In the years between 1943 and 1973 an overwhelming thirty-seven of sixty-seven Nobel prizewinners in medicine were Americans. The dominance of Americans in the physical sciences since the war is also clear from the awards in chemistry and physics.

THE EMERGENCE OF THE UNITED STATES AS A SCIENTIFIC POWER

What were the reasons for the sudden burst of scientific creativity in the United States? Clearly the nation emerged

Table 2. Expenditures for Research and Development in the United States in 1953 and 1973, in Billions of Dollars

	1953*		1973†	
	Totals	Basic Research	Totals	Basic Research
Federal government	$1.010	$0.045	$ 4.650	$0.615
Industry	3.630	0.151	20.450	0.705
College and universities	0.420	0.190	3.615	2.558
College- and university-affiliated federally funded research centers	. . . . . .	. . . . . .	0.815	0.286
Other nonprofit institutions	0.100	0.026	1.100	0.270
Totals	$5.160	$0.412	$30.630	$4.434

Statistical Abstracts of the United States (86th ed., 1965), Table 758, p. 545.

†*Statistical Abstracts of the United States* (95th ed., 1974), Table 881, p. 532.

from the war in much better shape than Europe. But while this was an important factor, it was not the only and possibly not even the major factor. There was apparently no similar increase in literary proficiency, at least as judged by the number of American Nobel prizewinners in this area. After World War II the United States was a young and growing country finally coming of age. The years of oppression had caused many of the most creative Europeans to migrate to other countries looking for a fresh start. Nobel prizewinners of the post–World War II era include Max Delbruck, Salvador Luria, H. Gobind Khorana, Severo Ochoa, Fritz Lipmann and Selman Waksman, all foreign-born and all except Khorana from Europe. Many of the best scientists in Asia also migrated to the United States, leaving behind the serious overpopulation problems that stifled progress. The flood of scientists, technicians, physicians, and other "elite" personnel from Europe and Asia was later referred to as the "brain drain."

Table 3. Expenditures for Research and Development in 1971 by the United States and Other Countries*

	Billions of Dollars	Per cent of Gross National Product
United States	$27.30	2.59
France	3.02	1.75
West Germany	4.62	2.01
United Kingdom	2.91	2.11
Japan	4.76	1.83
Soviet Union	12.88	3.00

Statistical Abstracts of the United States (95th ed., 1974) Table 889, p. 535.

With the wealth of talent available from both native-born and immigrant scientists, the United States began an impressive twenty-five-year commitment of dollars to basic research. The extent of this commitment is shown in Table 2, which compares expenditures for research and development in the years 1953 and 1973, years near the beginning and the peak of the research effort. In 1953 total expenditures for research and development were $5.16 billion of which $412 million was spent on basic research, nearly half of that in colleges and universities. In 1973, total expenditures for research and development were $30.6 billion, a sixfold increase, while the increase in spending for basic research was tenfold, to $4.43 billion. The increase in expenditures for basic research by colleges and universities was a staggering thirteenfold, to $2.55 billion. The greater commitment to basic research by colleges and universities resulted in augmented support of scholarly scientific research and research training.

The total dollar figure for the support of research and development in the United States is impressive, and taken as a fraction of the gross national product, it becomes even more impressive. Table 3 compares expenditures of several countries for the support of research as a fraction of the gross national product and includes several countries with a history of strong support for the scientific community. The only major country that contributed a higher percentage of its gross national product to research was the Soviet Union. The curious consequence of this statistic is that the Russians do not seem to have got much for their investment. Their scientific publications are considered modest, and visitors to the Soviet Union are depressed by the lack of facilities and equipment for biological scientists. A guess is that a major percentage of Russian research-and-development expenditures effort is committed to arms and space research.

A large percentage of American federal support of research and development was allocated to the National Institutes of Health (NIH) of the Department of Health, Education and Welfare. NIH dollars went to the support of research and research training and were a major source of funding of university-based research. NIH expenditures increased from $256 million in 1960 to an estimated $1.643 billion in 1974. The system of peer review used by the NIH for research proposals created in the scientific community an environment of trust that a proposal was funded on the basis of merit rather than politics. In later years, however, this system came under criticism in Congress and even among some scientists, who complained that the reviewers were a closed corporation representing colleges with the most research dollars. Nevertheless, in my opinion, NIH programs for the support of research were the single most important factor in the emergence of the United States as a strong scientific power in biological science in the post–World War II period.

The National Institutes of Health were also instrumental in the development of a national supply of biological scientists through their training-grant programs, pre- and postdoctoral fellowships, and career-development awards for young biomedical scientists. The National Science Foundation also offered pre- and postdoctoral fellowships for both biological and physical scientists. As a result, the number of medical scientists employed in the United States increased from 8,800 in 1950 to 53,000 in 1970.[1] The number of biological scientists increased from 19,900 to 71,100 during the same period. Science doctorates conferred in 1960 totaled 6,276; in 1973, 18,938.[2]

IMPACT OF BIOMEDICAL RESEARCH ON THE QUALITY OF LIFE

Are the benefits to mankind from biological research worth the expenditures? The answer to this question is yes, but the answer is frequently overlooked because it is taken for granted. The Federation of American Societies for Experimental Biology, with a membership of over 13,000, and the American Institute of Biological Sciences, with a membership of over 14,500, sponsored a joint task force to document contributions of biological sciences to human welfare (Lennette, 1972). The honorary chairman of the task force was former Senator Lister Hill (who was named by his father, Dr. L. L. Hill, for Joseph Lister, the father of antiseptic surgery). Senator Hill's father had studied under Lister, and Senator Hill was the author of several major pieces of legislature sponsoring biomedical research. The task-force members included distinguished scientists and administrators from the university community, from research institutions, and from federal research units. The task force looked at the impact of biological research not only on health but also on the quality of life, including food production, population biology, environmental hazards, marine sciences, and natural resources.

The most striking achievements have been in the treatment of infectious diseases. Antibiotics are available for the treatment of almost every infectious disease caused by bacteria. Even the treatment of tuberculosis has improved to the extent that the number of hospital beds for tuberculosis patients declined from over 100,000 in 1942 to just over 32,000 in 1969. The first antibiotic, penicillin, was discovered in Europe, as was the first successful chemotherapeutic agent, sulfanilamide. Many other antibiotics were discovered by Americans including streptomycin, discovered by Selman Waksman and used for treatment of tuberculosis. In addition, American technology showed how to mass-produce penicillin cheaply by use of the submerged-culture technique and mutants producing high yields of penicillin.

While the treatment of viral diseases is still unsatisfactory, immunization to prevent them, particularly poliomyelitis and measles, has been effective. There were 57,879 reported cases of poliomyelitis in 1952 but only 41 in 1967. The development of the polio vaccine would not have been possible without the ability to grow polio virus in tissue culture in order to study and to mass-produce the vaccine. Tissue culture is a technique derived directly from basic biological research. It has been estimated that the economic benefit of the polio vaccine in reduction of medical costs alone for the years 1955 to 1961 was $326 million. The reduction of hospital costs for treatment of measles for the five-year period 1963 to 1968 was over $200 million; reduction in loss of productivity, $531 million. The savings in hospitals costs for the treatment of tuberculosis in the years 1954 to 1969 were estimated at $3.77 billion, and increases in productivity of former tuberculosis patients were estimated at $1.2 billion. It is clear the economic benefits alone from the reduction in cases of poliomyelitis and measles and the treatment of tuberculosis would pay for the cost of all biomedical research during those years, not to mention the most important commodity, the reduction in human suffering. There are many other medical advances that would not have been possible without the foundation of basic research, among them oral contraceptives, organ transplantation, and kidney dialysis. Also the recent success in the treatment of certain kinds of cancer owes much to basic research.

In other fields there were also important developments that came from basic biological research. Agricultural efficiency in the United States increased to the extent that the American farmer now feeds forty-two people besides himself, five of whom live outside the United States. Veterinary medicine has benefited from basic research that has led to healthier livestock. Specific examples are the reduction of tuberculosis and of brucellosis in cattle.

Man's higher standard of living and advanced technology has also produced some undesirable effects, such as pollution by automobile emissions and by nondegradable pesticides and hazards of job-related chemicals. He has also depleted the supply of natural resources, and his knowledge and ingenuity will be needed to offset the loss of natural resources necessary for human civilization.

The steep rate of increase in dollars committed to research during the 1950's and 1960's obviously could not be continued. The most recent statistics show that federal funding for research and development has increased only slightly during the 1970's, probably not even enough to keep abreast of the rate of inflation. Congress, which had been the most ardent supporter of basic research in the 1950's and 1960's, in the 1970's became concerned about the large fiscal commitment to research, and the result has been a stabilization in dollars appropriated by the government for research. The stabilization was not a complete surprise, since the United States had probably achieved a somewhat larger scientific community than it could support. The competition for research dollars is keener than it should be because of an oversupply of certain kinds of scientists. Nevertheless, the achievements of the United States in biological and medical sciences in the post–World War II era will stand as the most brilliant, productive period in the history of science for many years to come.

---

[1] *Statistical Abstracts of the United States* (95th ed., 1974), 536.
[2] *Statistical Abstracts of the United States* (95th ed., 1974), Table 904, p. 541.

BIBLIOGRAPHY

Avery, O. T., C. M. MacLeod, and M. McCarty, 1944. Studies on the chemical nature of the substances inducing transformation of pneumococcal types. J. Exp. Med. *79*: 137.

Crick, F. H. C., 1966. The genetic code—yesterday, today, and tomorrow. Cold Spring Harbor Symp. Quant. Biol. *31*: 3.

Dawson, M. G., and R. H. P. Sia, 1931. *In vitro* transformation of pneumococcal types. J. Exp. Med. *54*: 681.

Gamow, G., 1954a. Possible mathematical relation between deoxyribonucleic acid and protein. Kgl. Danske Videnskab. Selsskab. Biol. Med. *22*: 1.

Gamow, G., 1954b. Possible relation between deoxyribonucleic acid and protein structure. Nature. *173*: 318.

Griffith F., 1928. The significance of pneumococcal types. J. Hyg. *27*: 113.

Lennette, E. H., 1972. Contributions of the biological sciences to human welfare. Fed. Proc. *31*: TF 13.

Meselson, M., and F. W. Stahl, 1958. The replication of DNA in *Escherichia coli* Proc. Natl. Acad. Sci. *44: 671*.

Nirenberg, M., and Matthaei, 1961. The dependence of cell-free protein synthesis in *E. coli* upon naturally occurring or synthetic polyribonucleotides. Proc. Natl. Acad. Sci. *47*: 1588.

Statistical Abstracts of the United States. 1965. Washington, D.C., Vol. 86.

Statistical Abstracts of the United States. 1974. Washington, D.C., Vol. 95.

Watson, J. D., *The Double Helix*. New York, Athenum Press. 1968.

Watson, J. D., and F. H. C. Crick, 1953. Genetic implications of the structure of deoxyribonucleic acid. Nature. *171: 964*.

15

THE GROWTH OF SCIENTIFIC MEDICINE*

By John C. Burnham

At the beginning of American independence the medical practitioners who served the population were overwhelmingly apprentice-trained and sometimes self-trained. In a day when every man was "either a fool or a physician," as Poor Richard characterized his fellow citizens, little by way of research was expectable. Yet, even before the Revolution, in some of the larger metropolitan areas institutions and conditions were developing that would later nurture medical investigators. Generations were to come and go, however, before research efforts even in the eighteenth-century tradition of natural history would materialize, much less any in the nineteenth- and twentieth-century mode.

The first American medical school was founded in 1765, in connection with the University of Pennsylvania. During the War of Independence the school faltered for a few years before getting back into operation, and the second school, founded at King's College (later Columbia University) was closed and did not reopen until 1792. Many of the founders were influenced by the Scottish tradition in medical education, and of the small minority of American doctors who held academic degrees, the largest part studied in Scotland. Scottish medical schools were attached to universities. But within a few decades, in the early nineteenth century, most medical schools in the United States had departed from the tradition and were independent, proprietary institutions aimed at producing as many health-care-delivery personnel as possible (and also profit and honor to the proprietors). Only rarely, according to critics of that day, was the profession's tradition of learning honored.[1]

In fact, the American medical practitioner was not cast in the mold of a European physician, by custom a learned man whose knowledge made him a professional and protected him from working with his hands. In Europe the manual labor of medicine was carried out by members of two other guilds, the surgeons and the apothecaries. In the English colonies the physician tended to follow the model of the second-class practitioner of the English countryside, the sur-geon-apothecary. Even into the late nineteenth century most of the American contributions to world medicine were associated with practical surgery and few with the scientific medicine rapidly developing in Europe. Only the Americans' clinical observation tied in directly with the work of the traditional, august physician.[2]

During the Revolutionary era most American medical literature was concerned with preserving the traditions of learning that marked the doctor, even of the surgeon-apothecary type, as a professional. Theses presented for the degrees of medicine at the end of the eighteenth and beginning of the nineteenth centuries were demonstrations of the abilities of the candidates to read and understand the existing literature from the time of the ancients to the Enlightenment. Mastery of what had been produced in Europe was sufficient to make a man eminent in either the Old World or the New, and Americans aspired to no more. Although the man who was the moving spirit behind the first medical school, John Morgan (1735–89), believed in medical investigation, his own most notable contribution was to bring from England a new mode of anatomical preparation for instruction of students.[3]

Like Morgan, others who published in the newly independent United States continued to play the colonial role and act as agents in the transit of civilization across the Atlantic. The first American medical journal, the *Medical Repository,* begun in 1797, carried mostly material by American authors, but with signs of deference to European physicians. The editors assumed that the readers were acquainted with European, or at least English, literature. An important section of the journal consisted of reports from other publications, especially foreign, and in 1802, for example, it presented Edward Jenner's instructions for his new technique of vaccination for smallpox. A century later most American medical journals were continuing to include large segments of reports and abstracts of the work of European investigators. One of the most important earlier American journals, published from 1810 to 1824, was entitled first the *Eclectic Repertory* and later the *Journal of Foreign Medical Science and Literature.* Having started behind, Americans had to run to keep up with the spectacular progress of the nineteenth century.

At the end of the Enlightenment and just afterward some

*The preparation of this chapter was supported in part by a National Institutes of Health Grant, No. LM 02539, from the National Library of Medicine.

medical practitioners did attempt to set up general theories comparable with those of European theorists. The most notable theorist of the United States was Benjamin Rush (1746–1813), of Philadelphia, one of the signers of the Declaration of Independence. Rush developed a theory of the tension and relaxation of particles and systems of the body much like those of his Edinburgh teacher, William Cullen, and his fellow student, John Brown. Rush and his students believed fanatically in his theories, which they used to rationalize the bleeding and purging of patients so extensively as to constitute the so-called heroic treatment for which American practitioners were famous for many decades.[4]

Other American theorists came from a tradition different from European science—empiricism—but they nonetheless expressed themselves in the Enlightenment mode of assertive certainty. One was Elisha Perkins (1741–99), who, following news of Franz Mesmer's theory of animal magnetism, came to believe that metal points, like Franklin's lightning rods, would cure the parts of the body to which the points, or "tractors," were applied. This invention and theory were carried successfully even to England in the late 1790's.[5]

Of more permanent influence was Samuel Thomson (1769–1843), the founder of botanical medicine. Although his assertions about the efficacy of emetic herbs and sweating were at first in the testimonial tradition of empirics, yet his followers soon developed a system imitative of the late Enlightenment system of Sanuel Hahnemann that flourished as homeopathy for a century in the United States. Since regular or traditional medicine was no more effective in curing patients than such "irregular" systems as Thomson's and Hahnemann's, advocates of various schemes and a large number of out-and-out quacks flourished as "doctors" in the early nineteenth century.[6]

The transformation of medicine into the modern mode came about because of developments in science. At the time of the Declaration of Independence, the relationship between medicine and science in America was extremely close, but primarily to the benefit of science, not medicine. An overwhelming proportion of Americans actively interested in science at that time were physicians. Many were curious about the natural world for the sake of curiosity, but many more perceived that the practice of medicine involved chemistry and natural history.[7]

Part of the Hippocratic tradition with which well-trained practitioners were familiar suggested that illnesses had intimate relationships to the natural environment—indeed, that particular times and places gave rise to local diseases. Presumably, too, materials from the immediate environment would have special curative powers, and for half a century after independence many American physicians were avid botanists, seeking out new plants that, they hoped, had some medical usefulness. New World botanizing received great encouragement from European scientists, who increasingly came to value the collecting activities of their American colleagues far more because of additions to systematic natural history than because of additions to the materia medica. Increasingly the physicians had to give up the field to professional botanists, who were chiefly employed in the colleges,

and adhere strictly to established medical botanical preparations. By 1850 professional botany was moving rapidly out of the medical field.[8]

During the first decades of independence medical people also recorded weather and other geographical observations that might count as part of the environment. While the works of Thomas Sydenham were a well-known part of medical knowledge and did help continue the tradition of identifying disease entities, yet until the late nineteenth century belief in local and seasonal peculiarities of illness predominated. The Cincinnati physician Daniel Drake (1785–1852), for example, opened his monumental *A Systematic Treatise, Historical, Etiological, and Practical, on the Principal Diseases of the Interior Valley of North America* (1850), with:

As no fact in etiology is more universally admitted, than the influence of climate in the production of disease, it follows that he who would understand the origin and modifications of the diseases of a country must study its meteorology.[9]

Nor was such a viewpoint about weather and natural history in general without basis in experience. One of the major illnesses of the North Central region—which is now forgotten but of which Abraham Lincoln's mother and many others died—was the milksick. Milksick was poisoning from milk of cows that had eaten particular plants, chiefly the the common weed white snakeroot. The disease was both seasonal and geographical.[10]

Chemistry, too, developed primarily as a practical course taught in the medical schools, and, like botany, the discipline was slow to become a distinct study unconnected with possible prescriptions. Except for analysis of mineral springs and other local phenomena, however, American medical chemistry tended to be entirely derivative.

In the nineteenth century the meaning of science in medicine began to change. As in the pure sciences, so in medicine a self-conscious Baconianism, or positivism, developed, encouraging physicians to think that new knowledge would develop if only enough facts were accumulated.[11] In medicine the accumulation of facts was traditional by means of the case history, publication of which was sometimes in the style of a "curiosity of nature" for one's wisdom and enlightenment or, at other times, an attempt to accumulate clinical experience from other physicians' practices. Most of the scattered Revolutionary era medical publications that were not formally natural history or natural philosophy were essentially reports of cases—usually cures.[12] But half a century later, after journals had sprung up, American doctors were still cumulating their experience in them. A variation came only in the 1820's and 1830's, when the influence of French clinicians transformed medical positivism.

During those decades a number of American physicians introduced the clinical statistical procedures of Pierre Louis in Paris, who studied numbers of cases together and added to clinical information facts gathered on autopsy. Within a few years physicians attending leading hospitals, especially in Boston and Philadelphia, were publishing aggregations of cases with conclusions based not upon an idiosyncratic curiosity but upon a numerical generality. For the most part Americans imitated the work of European colleagues and added in the Baconian manner to this growing sum of medical knowledge. But occasionally a New World contribution was carried back to the Old. The most famous instance was, typically, primarily clinical and diagnostic, the work of the Philadelphia physician, W. W. Gerhard, who distinguished between typhus and typhoid fever on the basis of cases at the Pennsylvania Hospital. Other American contributions, however useful, tended to be very modest, as that of the worker who identified the origin of rice-water dejecta in Asiatic cholera. [13]

In the rapidly proliferating journals of the first half of the nineteenth century, case reports still predominated, but in the field of surgery this mode was particularly productive on occasion. In surgery one or two cases could introduce a substantial innovation in which the test tended to be empirical and in which the techniques were set forth in the literature for replication and testing elsewhere. Unlike "cures" in more general medicine, techniques in surgery had a future. The best-known American contribution was ovariotomy, introduced by Ephraim McDowell, of Danville, Kentucky, in 1817, one of the first successful invasions of the trunk. Other surgeons reported new techniques that joined those common in surgery everywhere, and from Boston in 1846 came word of the first successful use of surgical anesthesia. This contribution—primarily an empirical development, like much of the rest of surgery—was rapidly carried all over the world after the first case report. [14]

The most famous American case history was that of Alexis St. Martin, reported by an army surgeon, William Beaumont (1785–1853). Beaumont took St. Martin as a patient in 1822, when he was wounded in the stomach by gunshot. The wound healed so that the stomach had a hole in it that opened to the outside. Through that opening Beaumont was able to perform experiments so as to contribute much new knowledge about the process of digestion. Beaumont's work symbolized changes in medicine, specifically the growing importance of physiological research and particularly what, later in the century, came to be known as scientific medicine, implying the use of experiments as well as clinical statistics and case histories. Beaumont was in fact advised by the leading physiologists of the United States who were in other areas, too, bringing new European ideas into medicine. [15] Increasingly American physicians found that the railroad and other modern means of communication and transportation were bringing American practitioners into a national and world community dominated by European scientific medicine.

By the middle of the nineteenth century there was in the profession a group of active leaders who viewed the human body as a mechanical system whose processes are reducible to physics and chemistry. So much was being learned about nerve impulses and the chemistry of physiological processes such as digestion that a large measure of the mystery of the normal processes of the body seemed to be disappearing. When, in the decade after the Civil War, the germ theory of disease, especially, tended to portray the material cause of much pathology, the mechanists felt that they had a firm basis for the advance of medicine. The emphasis on preserving traditional knowledge tended to shift to an emphasis upon new discoveries, whether in physiology or surgery.

Looking back on medicine during America's first century of independence, J. S. Billings noted that not until the 1850's did the number of American books on medicine finally exceed reprints and translations of foreign works. Yet, as the number of publications increased, the books tended to be "compends relating to the treatment of diseases and injuries," most notably textbooks and systematic treatises dealing primarily with surgery and therapeutics. Indeed, Billings concluded that the books that comprised the production of a whole century of American medicine were "for the most part compilations." Clearly, even after a century, American medicine was still largely colonial in relationship to European medicine, despite discoveries in anesthesia, digestive processes, and a large number of minor contributions. Billings' figures showed that the action lay outside the United States: of 280 regular medical journals in the world in 1876, the United States produced forty-six (many of which were largely local), and of 848 original, first-edition medical books in the major Western countries in 1874–1875, United States authors produced only thirty-six. Billings consoled himself by quoting the French sage Victor Cousin, "It is better to have a future than a past." [16]

In some respects the past had been dismal. By the 1850's licensure of doctors in the United States had almost disappeared because regular physicians had been unable to show decisively that their treatment was superior to that of homeopaths or botanics, or even to self-prescribed patent medicines. Losing faith in bleeding and purging, especially as clinical statistical research flourished, the physicians increasingly turned to "therapeutic nihilism," trusting to nature and restricting practice to diagnosis, prognosis, and gentle nurture. The best-known statement of this new tendency to abandon heroic practice was the 1836 essay "On Self-Limited Diseases" by the Bostonian Jacob Bigelow, and everyone quoted Oliver Wendell Holmes's contemporary quip that, if most medicines then in use "could be sunk to the bottom of the sea, it would be all the better for mankind—and all the worse for the fishes." This attitude increasingly characterized medicine for the rest of the nineteenth century. [17]

Abandoning most therapy except surgery, medical professionals should have been in a weak position relative to their competition. But from overseas came a whole series of innovations that gave trained doctors advantages that others lacked. The knowledge that had created the status of the physician now once again removed medicine from the grasp of just any literate person, and in some ways medical intervention for the first time was becoming demonstrably effective.

To keep up with the new knowledge, the better American physicians undertook several courses of action. They went to Europe, especially Germany and Austria, for postgraduate training. They traveled and read even more. And they often limited their practices to what by 1900 were a number of well-defined specialties, just as their German teachers (who were also researchers) did.[18] Finally, by honoring research as an integral part of medicine, the regular physicians unwittingly showed that their version of medicine embodied an element lacking in their competition, even in the increasingly good practice of the homeopaths. Regular medicine triumphed because its advocates held not only that practice must conform to scientific findings, however unpalatable, but that research was the fountainhead of medical knowledge. The conversion of both the profession and the public to this point of view was of the greatest significance.[19]

As the nineteenth century drew to a close, it became increasingly difficult to follow the European example of supporting research. Well-financed state laboratories and clinics on the Continent turned out an increasing volume of investigative studies that challenged the practitioner to keep up, much less to carry out, any research and reporting himself. The medical schools, separated as they often were from the growing research institutions of the modern universities, were not fostering investigation. Indeed, many of them did not even have substantial clinical facilities or hospital connections. No research institutes were available for the support of original work in medicine until after the turn of the century, although government-financed agricultural experimentation contributed increasingly to biological discoveries with medical implications, such as Theobald Smith's demonstration of the insect vector in Texas cattle tick fever in 1893.[20]

The dramatic demonstration of the effectiveness of medical intervention by means of surgery and the diphtheria antitoxin, plus the increasing faith in scientific public-health measures led to increasing public support of medical research in the United States.[21] The most important single development was the founding, in 1903, of the Rockefeller Institute in New York (now Rockefeller University) for the investigation of infectious diseases, in imitation of the Pasteur Institute in France.[22] Of more general importance was the rapid upgrading of American medical education, culminating in the famed Flexner report of 1910. Medical schools increasingly were forced into association with universities, where graduate schools were already fostering research and, above all, the spirit of research. The proximity of medical teachers to the universities helped legitimatize their functions as investigators, and the clinical and laboratory resources necessary just for teaching under the new standards facilitated the new emphasis.[23] Decades passed before research was fully accepted in many good medical schools, but with the increasing amount of philanthropy symbolized by the Rockefeller Institute, a substantial institutional and financial base for medical research was developing.[24]

The model institution was the Johns Hopkins Hospital and Medical School. The hospital opened in 1889, the medical school in 1893, and the latter was deeply influenced by connections with the graduate school of Johns Hopkins University, where the intention was, as it was later, when the medical school opened, to meet the very best European standards. Johns Hopkins and imitators of Johns Hopkins placed great emphasis upon basic sciences as antecedent to the study and practice of medicine.[25] One of the first symptoms of

the new spirit was the initiation of the *Journal of Experimental Medicine* in 1897, filled with accounts of laboratory, as opposed to clinical, contributions to medicine. American physicians, at least at Johns Hopkins, had come a long way from their predecessors' empiricism and aggregation of clinical experience.

Dazzling though the advances were that came from physiological investigations in both Europe and America in the late nineteenth century, progress in practical medicine tended to lie in areas somewhat removed from the interests of laboratory workers. Even bacteriology, however exciting in the realms of pathology and immunology, for many years contributed little to therapeutics (with the exceptions of rabies and diphtheria). It is remarkable that researchers in the turn-of-the-century period continued to place such extreme faith in medical research, and even more remarkable that public support through both tax-supported institutions and charitable establishments likewise continued to grow dramatically. Especially in the 1920's, when relatively few advances occurred that resulted directly in improved medical care, financial support for medical research expanded. This funding was partly the result of hope and faith in science and partly the outcome of journalistic artifice. But support grew also because turn-of-the-century people were seeing both concrete and unprecedented progress, however small the steps may appear to later generations.[26]

Particularly did progress come in the realm of surgery, and the years from about 1890 to 1910 were veritably an age of surgery. Americans had for generations worked competently in surgery, and they made important contributions to technique in the twentieth century—increasingly so as the years went on. The tradition of heroic treatment found fulfillment in the work of American operators, who more and more boldly intervened in the structures and mechanisms of the human body, reaching a pinnacle of progress in the brain surgery of the legendary Harvey Cushing (1869–1939). Areas of internal medicine were taken away from physicians by the operators, whether endocrine gland cancers or gastrointestinal diseases such as appendicitis. No area of the body was sacrosanct to these new American heroes, including the elegant W. S. Halsted at Johns Hopkins and the well-organized Mayo brothers on the Minnesota prairie.

The success of surgery initially depended upon the acceptance of the germ theory of infection and the antiseptic and aseptic techniques that permitted the introduction of many imaginative methods and devices, from rubber gloves to "buttons" to hold cut intestines together and mechanisms to protect against lung collapse.[27] This kind of surgery by and large continued to be based on the idea that the body runs like a machine.

The germ theory of disease affected relatively few other areas of treatment, but preventive medicine benefited greatly as American scientists tried to avert the spread of communicable diseases. For example, the discovery that tuberculosis is contagious and not hereditary revolutionized a significant part of American social medicine.[28] The study of bacteriology was, therefore, pursued with vigor in the United States, and often in conjunction with public health endeavors.[29] One of the early American contributions was that of the Yellow Fever Commission under Walter Reed (1851–1902), which not only established the mosquito vector but also proved that the agent in the disease is a filterable virus, a type of pathogen theretofore not proved in any but animal diseases.

Even more than in bacteriology, Americans excelled in the field of physiology, and by the turn of the twentieth century a significant percentage of the world's scientific publications in that field were coming from the United States. This was no mean achievement, for scientific medicine was established best in European physiological laboratories. Science in this context meant mainly animal experimentation, with the assumption that body functioning was the same in man as in other mammals. "For our purposes, animal experimentation, I need scarcely say, is indispensable," said a researcher in 1922.[30] From the beginning most of the articles in the *Journal of Experimental Medicine* dealt with animal physiology, although in that journal and in imitators that sprang up human experiment was also used whenever possible. All the investigators were contributing to knowledge, but the applicability of much of this work to medical practice was minimal or, at best, unclear for many decades.

Beginning about 1910 (and the date is very approximate), medicine went into the physiological stage proper as laboratory studies began to affect therapeutics directly and substantially. The hormones and vitamins were the chief substances involved, and Americans contributed fundamentally to discovery in both areas in the years up to the 1930's—including the dietary treatment of pernicious anemia.[31] A. E. Cohn, of the Rockefeller Institute, noted in 1924 that "the development of the therapeutics of infectious diseases dependent on the discovery of bacteria has for two generations been so absorbing as to dwarf the interest medicine has always displayed in conditions associated with derangement of the organs and with the ailments of advancing age." He observed, however, that a new "spirit" had come into medical research.[32]

The physiological era reflected not only concern with functional and degenerative diseases found in a longer lived generation but also a fundamental change in Americans' attitudes toward the body. Where earlier they had viewed it as a machine, now they saw body functioning in terms of the complex interaction of many independent entities and systems, including germs, genes, and groups of specialized cells, all integrated into a whole and held in balance by subtle chemical and physical means. This model persisted as the twentieth century progressed, and the extreme complexity of the various systems was worked out by ever more refined laboratory procedures and instruments.[33]

A new era abruptly superimposed itself over physiology in the 1930's. A quarter of a century earlier, Paul Ehrlich in Germany had shown that a dye derivative injected into an infected person's body could have an exclusive and fatal affinity for a particular microscopic pathogen. This was the initiation of chemotherapy, but no one on either side of the Atlantic was able to follow up the discovery with others. Then in the 1930's the sulfa drugs were introduced—again from Germany—and the era of antibiotics had begun. Within a relatively few years the incidence of infectious diseases and the seriousness of local infections were reduced dramatically in the United States. The American contribution had been to receive and confirm the sulfas and later to help develop the new penicillin into a practicable therapeutic agent. Finally workers led by Selman Waksman at Rutgers introduced a third family of antibiotics, notably streptomycin.

Nor were physiological and antibiotic medicine any longer restricted in impact to particular areas of practice. Surgery benefited greatly from both, for the control of infection and the information provided by, at the least, fluoroscopy and serological tests permitted surgeons to undertake procedures that even in 1910 had seemed impossible.[34] The psychoactive drugs introduced from France in the 1950's for the treatment of mental illnesses were developed initially on the basis of physiological theory but were quickly explored further by workers in the United States. The total result in all fields was to give science immense prestige within medicine—no longer positivistic science, but general and theoretical scientific ideas as well as experiment.[35]

Medical journals of 1876 to 1976 reflected the changing place of science in the art of medicine. In the late nineteenth century case histories continued, as earlier, to predominate. But the chief interests of the authors were less in "cures," as earlier, and more in diagnosis and pathology. Most of the physiology and bacteriology, as they came to be increasingly important, were found in the abstracts sections, summarizing literature from other, often foreign, journals. Increasingly clinical reports included more and more cases about which ever more cautious generalizations appeared. By the twentieth century there was a tendency for authors of papers in medical journals to emphasize not the case at all but generalizations: that patients with a particular set of symptoms, for example, were involved in particular physiological changes or that reactions in an organ—whether mouse or human—had definite chemical accompaniments. Even surgeons employed large numbers of cases to establish the general validity of their innovations in manipulation.

At the middle of the twentieth century the incredible complexity of the picture that medical scientists projected of both healthy and pathological processes of the body led to changes in the training and approach of medical scientists. No longer was even specialist training sufficient, for various of the scientific and medical disciplines had to be brought to bear upon the complicated interrelationships of the bodily processes. The result was the growth of team research, in which scientific work was centered on a problem, not a particular scientist, and the varieties of approaches and kinds of information embodied in team members were applied to the problem. The most that a lone researcher could aspire to be, as John H. Stokes, a Philadelphia dermatologist remarked as early as 1940, was an "informed amateur." Usually, also, vast numbers of laboratory and technical resources of all kinds were utilized by researchers, who felt obliged to have under control increasing numbers of factors that might account for events in the body systems. By the 1960's medical researchers had devised many methods of using computers to cope with the complexities that research had unearthed.[36]

Adding to the complexities of scientific medicine after the 1950's was a conviction on the part of many leaders in the profession that social factors were of substantial importance in many disease processes. One facet of this conviction went back to the growth of medical social work and interest in occupational diseases many decades earlier.[37] Another stream contributing awareness of such factors was the spectacular growth of psychiatric theory, in which Americans increasingly led the world, especially after the migration of European intellectuals to the United States in the 1930's and the growth of the subspecialty of psychosomatic medicine. The particularly generous funding of psychiatric research and training after World War II was vital in both stimulating investigation and keeping other researchers aware of psychological and social factors operating in patients.[38]

During World War II the Committee on Medical Research coordinated militarily relevant research-and-development activities and oversaw the spending of $25 million. Much of this went into the development of penicillin, insecticides, and blood components and substitutes, as well as more specific therapies.[39] The results were spectacular and well publicized, and after the war there was tremendous pressure from Congress and the public to expand federal spending for health research. The consequence was the development of a staggering expenditure by the federal government, chiefly through the National Institutes of Health, and the creation of a huge national health-research establishment. Not until 1969 was there any sign of a halt to the rapid growth of these endeavors.[40]

The most extraordinary aspect of this almost open-ended support for medical research was the amount and nature of the public interest that it reflected. The man who presided over much of the expansion, James A. Shannon, director of the National Institutes of Health after 1955, as early as 1956 spoke of "a sort of mass conversion to faith in research, including medical research. Whether this is a passing phase of our national life—a fad in thought—or an enduring, rational change in outlook remains to be seen."[41] His caution was well founded, but when he retired from the NIH in 1968 he was supervising a budget in excess of $1 billion a year.

What was probably most extraordinary about the support for health research among private proponents and congressional committee chairmen was the extent to which lay advocates understood that pure research was necessary to advance the understanding of health and disease so as to permit man to attain health and well-being. It was often difficult for medical doctors to see that clinical investigation was not all of scientific medicine, that medicine was being drawn into all science. It was much harder for lay people to see that highly abstract research, even, in later years, molecular biology, for example, could have direct payoff in health care. Medicine, in fact, was deeply involved in pure science as practiced in American laboratories and was losing the stigma of being merely an applied or technical endeavor.[42]

One of the results of having a huge establishment with talented workers devoted to health research was that a lot of questions came to be asked by those talented people. One obvious question was the relationship of research to the hospitals and medical schools and universities through which so much money for scientific medicine was being funneled. Another had to do with the increasing dependence of physicians upon technology and technologists called into existence by new scientific developments. Still another, and very sensitive, area had to do with the activities of experimenters as they came close to determining life and heredity. The medical practitioner of 1976 inherited much of the traditional role of the doctor, but science was taking him into iatrogenic diseases, life maintenance, environmental quality, experiment with heredity, unimaginable forms of warfare, and especially the question of the borderlines among personality, life, and death. Laboratory creeds had not always prepared medical scientists for the challenges of a new medical ethics and social order. The third hundred years promised not only possible progress and the certainty of increasing complexity but threats to both science and medicine in the United States.

NOTES

1. William Frederick Norwood, "Medical Education in the United States Before 1900," in C. D. O'Malley (ed.), *The History of Medical Education* (Berkeley: University of California Press, 1970), 463–99; Richard Harrison Shryock, *Medicine in America: Historical Essays* (Baltimore, Md.: The Johns Hopkins Press, 1966), 150–55.

2. Richard Harrison Shryock, *Medicine and Society in America, 1660–1860* (New York, New York University Press, 1960).

3. Whitfield J. Bell, Jr., *John Morgan, Continental Doctor* (Philadelphia, University of Pennsylvania Press, 1965).

4. Shryock, *Medicine in America*, 233–51; Carl Binger, *Revolutionary Doctor: Benjamin Rush, 1746–1813* (New York, W. W. Norton & Company, 1966).

5. Jacques M. Quen, "Elisha Perkins: Physician, Nostrum-Vendor, or Charlatan?" *Bulletin of the History of Medicine,* Vol. 37 (1963), 159–66. Joseph F. Kett, *The Formation of the American Medical Profession: The Role of Institutions, 1780–1860* (New Haven, Yale University Press, 1968), 98.

6. *Ibid.,* passim. William G. Rothstein, *American Physicians in the Nineteenth Century: From Sects to Science* (Baltimore, The Johns Hopkins Press, 1972).

7. Brooke Hindle, *The Pursuit of Science in Revolutionary America, 1735–1789* (Chapel Hill, University of North Carolina Press, 1956), especially Chap. 3.

8. Unpublished papers by G. E. Gifford, Jr., and E. D. Rudolph.

9. Henry D. Shapiro and Zane L. Miller (eds.), *Physician to the*

West: Selected Writings of Daniel Drake on Science & Society (Lexington, University of Kentucky Press, 1970), 334.

10. William D. Snively, Jr., and Louanna Furbee, "Discoverer of the Cause of Milk Sickness," *Journal of the American Medical Association,* Vol. 196 (1966), 103–108.

11. George H. Daniels, *American Science in the Age of Jackson* (New York, Columbia University Press, 1968).

12. Isobel Stevenson, "Medical Literature Produced During the War of Independence," *Ciba Symposia,* Vol. 2 (1940), 520–27.

13. Francis R. Packard, *History of Medicine in the United States* (2 vols., New York, Hafner Publishing Company, 1963 reprint), II, 1070–74; Leonard K. Eaton, *New England Hospitals, 1790–1833* (Ann Arbor, University of Michigan Press, 1957), 197–215. Edwin H. Clarke, "Practical Medicine," in *A Century of American Medicine, 1776–1876* (Brinklow, Md., Old Hickory Bookshop, 1962 reprint), 50–51.

14. A number of reports, with introductory material, are reprinted in A. Scott Earle (ed.), *Surgery in America: From the Colonial Era to the Twentieth Century, Selected Writings* (Philadelphia, W. B. Saunders Company, 1965), 38–181; Thomas E. Keys, *The History of Surgical Anesthesia* (2d ed., New York, Dover Publications, 1963); Courtney R. Hall, "The Rise of Professional Surgery in the United States: 1800–1865," *Bulletin of the History of Medicine,* Vol. 26 (1952), 231–62.

15. The original with introductory material is reprinted in William Beaumont, *Experiments and Observations on the Gastric Juice and Physiology of Digestion* (New York, Dover Publications, 1959 reprint).

16. John S. Billings, "Literature and Institutions," in *A Century of American Medicine,* 289–366.

17. Gert H. Breiger, *Medical America in the Nineteenth Century, Readings from the Literature* (Baltimore, The Johns Hopkins Press, 1972), Chap. 4.

18. Thomas Neville Bonner, *American Doctors and German Universities, A Chapter in International Intellectual Relations, 1870–1914* (Lincoln, University of Nebraska Press, 1963); Rosemary Stevens, *American Medicine and the Public Interest* (New Haven, Yale University Press, 1971).

19. Rothstein, *American Physicians in the Nineteenth Century.*

20. Charles E. Rosenberg, "The Adams Act: Politics and the Cause of Scientific Research," *Agricultural History,* Vol. 38 (1964), 3–12.

21. See, for example, A. T. Cabot, "Science in Medicine," *Boston Medical and Surgical Journal,* Vol. 137 (1897), 481–84.

22. George W. Corner, *A History of the Rockefeller Institute, 1901–1953, Origins and Growth* (New York, Rockefeller Institute Press, 1964).

23. John Field, "Medical Education in the United States: Late Nineteenth and Twentieth Centuries," in O'Malley (ed.), *The History of Medical Education,* 501–30.

24. Richard H. Shryock, *American Medical Research, Past and Present* (New York, The Commonwealth Fund, 1947), especially Chap. 4. Hereafter cited as *American Medical Research.*

25. Donald Fleming, *William H. Welch and the Rise of Modern Medicine* (Boston, Little, Brown and Company, 1954); Richard Harrison Shryock, *The Unique Influence of the Johns Hopkins University on American Medicine* (Copenhagen, E. Munksgaard, 1953).

26. Shryock, *American Medical Research.*

27. Allen O. Whipple, *The Evolution of Surgery in the United States* (Springfield, Ill., Charles C. Thomas, 1963), hereafter cited as *The Evolution of Surgery;* Helen Clapesattle, *The Doctors Mayo* (Garden City, N.Y., Garden City Publishing Co., 1943).

28. John C. Burnham, "Medical Specialists and Movements Toward Social Control in the Progressive Era: Three Examples," in Jerry Israel (ed.), *Building the Organizational Society: Essays on Associational Activities in Modern America* (New York, Free Press, 1972), 19–30.

29. Barbara Gutmann Rosenkrantz, *Public Health and the State: Changing Views in Massachusetts, 1842–1936* (Cambridge, Mass., Harvard University Press, 1972).

30. J. B. Deaver and S. P. Reimann, "Clinical Observation and Research Work," *American Journal of the Medical Sciences,* Vol. 164 (1922), 903.

31. Bernard Jaffe, *Men of Science in America* (2d ed., New York, Simon and Schuster, 1958), Chap. 17.

32. A. E. Cohn, "Purposes in Medical Research," *Journal of Clinical Investigation,* Vol. 1 (1924), 1–11.

33. Frederick G. Kilgour, "Scientific Ideas of Atomicity in the 19th Century," *Proceedings of the 10th International Congress for the History of Science* (1962), I, 329–31; Garland E. Allen, *Life Science in the Twentieth Century* (New York, John Wiley & Sons, 1975).

34. Whipple, *The Evolution of Surgery.*

35. Shryock, *American Medical Research,* Chap. 5.

36. John H. Stokes, "Changing Causal Concepts and Investigative Methods," *Journal of Investigative Dermatology,* Vol. 3 (1940), 265–66; *Medical Research: A Midcentury Survey* (2 vols., Boston, Little, Brown and Company, 1955).

37. Joseph C. Aub and Ruth K. Hapgood, *Pioneer in Modern Medicine, David Linn Edsall of Harvard* (Cambridge, Mass., Harvard Medical Alumni Association, 1970).

38. Jeanne L. Brand, "The National Mental Health Act of 1946: A Retrospect," *Bulletin of the History of Medicine,* Vol. 39 (1965), 231–45.

39. E. C. Andrus, et al. (eds.), *Advances in Military Medicine Made by American Investigators Working Under the Sponsorship of the Committee on Medical Research* (2 vols., Boston, Little, Brown and Company, 1948).

40. Stephen P. Strickland, *Politics, Science, and Dread Disease: A Short History of United States Medical Research Policy* (Cambridge, Mass., Harvard University Press, 1972), hereafter cited as *Politics, Science, and Dread Disease;* Donald C. Swain, "The Rise of a Research Empire: NIH, 1930 to 1950," *Science,* Vol. 138 (1962), 1233–37.

41. James A. Shannon, "Trends in Medical Research," *Journal of the American Medical Association,* Vol. 160 (1956), 1030.

42. Thomas M. Rivers, "Concepts and Methods of Medical Research," in Harold Brown Keyes (ed.), *Frontiers in Medicine: The March of Medicine, 1950* (New York, Columbia University Press, 1951), 120–46; Strickland, *Politics, Science, and Dread Disease.*

PART V: Ecology

Ecology is the science concerned with the interactions between organisms and their environment. The general American public became aware of its existence only in the 1960's, as a result of acute environmental problems. Because of its role in environmental affairs the relatively new science has attracted a rash of interdisciplinary programs and institutes that focus on environmental and ecological matters. Indeed, in 1973, N. Tinbergen, who in 1939 had been among the first authors to attempt to assess ecology, shared the Nobel Prize in Biology and Medicine. Ecology has expanded so rapidly in recent years that by far the greatest amount of ecological work has been done in the past twenty-five years.

A history of ecology in America is provided for the first time by Frank N. Egerton and Robert P. McIntosh. Egerton deals with the early period in "Ecological Studies and Observations Before 1900." Essentially his task is to describe the various kinds of ecological investigations that were made before 1900 and provided the foundation for the formal science. McIntosh provides a history of modern developments in "Ecology Since 1900" and identifies and evaluates the major contributions of twentieth-century scientists.

16

ECOLOGICAL STUDIES AND OBSERVATIONS BEFORE 1900

By Frank N. Egerton

The science of ecology intruded upon public awareness in America for the first time in the late 1960's as a result of acute environmental problems. Because of the context in which this awareness developed, the term *ecology* became synonymous with environment and pollution. This was a distortion of the modern historical development of the science in two respects: it placed more emphasis upon the inanimate surroundings than upon the organisms and more emphasis upon the applied than upon the pure science.

INTRODUCTION

The public perception is not much of a distortion of the earlier history of ecological interests, observations, and discussions. When ecology became a formal science at the turn of the twentieth century, however, it necessarily became less diffuse than the body of knowledge on which it was built. Thomas Kuhn has explained why this happens as a science approaches maturity. If the science is to progress beyond the level of common sense perceptions, it must identify a select group of problems that are soluble and ignore others that may be even more interesting but are less readily soluble.[1] That narrower but more profound science will be the subject of the next chapter, by Robert P. McIntosh. The purpose of this chapter is to describe the various kinds of ecological investigations that were carried out in America before 1900 and provided the foundation for the formal science.

Ecology is a science concerned with the interactions between organisms and their environment. The environment is composed of both animate and inanimate components. A rabbit's world consists of grass and foxes and also climate and soil. The history of ecology in its preformal period is similar to but not identical with the history of natural-history studies. In works on natural history written before 1900, one finds ecological discussions embedded within a context of classification and description of species. There were also many concomitant developments that were part of science but not included in most natural histories that are relevant for the history of ecology—discussions of climate and disease, for example.

The New World from the time of Columbus onward pre-sented a challenge to European explorers to describe the differences between what they found here and in their homeland. Howard Mumford Johes found, however, that new observations and experiences did not endow the Europeans with new powers of description.[2] The New World environment could stimulate interest, but for almost the entire period from 1492 to 1900 the observations made in America did not transcend in any important ways the perspectives and understanding that had developed in Europe. As Raymond Phineas Stearns has observed: "Neither scientific knowledge nor the scientific method was *sui generis* in America. Both were tender plants introduced to the new world scene by European proponents, seeded, watered, and fertilized by European patrons."[3] Only after 1850 did American naturalists take the lead in one area of ecological research, the investigation of biological control of undesirable species.

BEFORE 1800

Exploration and Inventory

The sixteenth, seventeenth, and eighteenth centuries were notable for worldwide exploration and colonization. As the maritime nations of Europe sought new products and wealth around the world, there was also a strong demand for accounts of the places explored. Ecological description and analysis would have been very useful to prospective settlers, but unfortunately the explorers had little capacity for providing them. It is true that Aristotle's and Theophrastus' writings in zoology and botany contained ecological observations, and influences of those observations can be found in natural histories by such naturalists as Conrad Gesner in the sixteenth century, John Ray in the seventeenth, and Carl Linnaeus in the eighteenth. However, few explorers were well-trained naturalists, and most of those who published accounts of their discoveries merely described new species that might be of either economic or ornamental interest to their countrymen in Europe.

The literature of exploration from the three centuries before 1800 is too extensive to survey fully its ecologically relevant accounts here. That does not seem desirable anyway, because no clear-cut ecological tradition emerged from this literature. On the other hand, some of the literature does provide an indication of the level of ecological awareness at various times, and it apparently stimulated some interest in ecological understanding. Therefore, a few of the ecologically more significant examples of this literature and their authors are discussed below.

Thomas Harriot (1560–1621) came to the first English coastal settlement on Roanoke Island with Grenville's expedition of 1585–86, and afterward he published *A Briefe and True Report of the New Found Land of Virginia . . . .* It contained descriptions of useful plants and animals that were either native to America or were European and could grow in the New World. The significance of his work lies in the fact that it has so little in it of ecological significance. It seems representative in that respect of the exploration literature of the sixteenth century. Explorers of that century seem to have had less ecological awareness than later explorers, and also they were likely to remain in the New World a shorter time and to write shorter books. Harriot's only observation of ecological interest is his brief comparison of the lands farther inland from the coast in terms of production. He found

the soyle to bee fatter; the trees greater and to growe thinner; the grounde more firme and deeper mould; more and larger champions; finer grasse and as good as ever we saw any in England; in some places rockie and farre more high and hillie ground; more plentie of their fruites; more abondance of beastes; the more inhabited with people.[4]

Because his purpose was to promote settlement, he did not attempt to ascertain why the interior was more productive. It was enough for him merely to discover that it was.

Captain John Smith (1580–1631) shared Harriot's promotional interest in America, but he also lingered longer and had more to say. His characterizations of Virginia and Massachusetts coastal regions were not detailed, but did convey an idea of the climate, the fertility of the soil, the terrain, the vegetation, and the animals. It was not yet ecology, but it was certainly an environmental picture. Sometimes he also attempted ecological interpretations of what he saw, as illustrated in this description:

Virginia doth afford many excellent vegetables, and living Creatures, yet grasse there is little or none, but what groweth in low Marshes: for all the Countrey is overgrowne with trees, whose droppings continually turneth their grasse to weeds, by reason of the rancknes of the ground, which would soone be amended by good husbandry. The wood that is most common is Oke and Walnut.[5]

It is clear that the exploration literature was stronger on ecological observations about plants than about animals. That is commonly true for the literature down to 1800 and even beyond. The dependence of plants upon soil, water, terrain, and climate was more apparent than the dependence of moving animals upon features of their environment, except for fish, whose dependence was so obvious that it provoked little comment.

John Josselyn (ca. 1608–75) was an adventurer who went to Scarborough, Maine, in 1663 to live with his brother. Eight years later he returned to London to publish his observations. His *New England Rarities . . .* (1672) is notable for being devoted primarily to the "birds, beasts, fishes, serpents, and plants." His strongest interest seems to have been in their practical uses, and many were mentioned without ecological observations. Sometimes, however, he did make such observations, particularly about the plants, which he knew more extensively than the animals. Typical is his account of White hellebore: "The first Plant that springs up in this Country, and the first that withers; it grows in deep black Mould and Wet, in such abundance, that you may in a small compass gather whole Cart-loads of it."[6] This part of his account is followed by an explanation of how the Indians used it to heal wounds.

Later in the seventeenth century, as the French moved deeper and deeper into the Great Lakes region, a young explorer, Louis Armand de Lom d'Arce, Baron de Lahontan (1666–1715) recorded in some detail his experiences in *New Voyages to North America . . .,* which became popular as a source of information and adventure. Although he was accused during his lifetime of having embellished his adventures, his interest in nature seems to have been genuine. He gave in some detail accounts of the plants and animals he observed, and his description of the Lake Erie region is at least a superficial ecological survey:

The Lake Erriè *is justly dignified with the illustrious name of Conti; for assuredly 'tis the finest Lake upon Earth. You may judge of the goodness of the Climate, from the Latitudes of the Countries that surround it. Its Circumference extends to two hundred and thirty Leagues; but it affords every where such a charming Prospect, that its Banks are deck'd with Oke-Trees, Elms, Chesnut-Trees, Walnut-Trees, Apple-Trees, Plum-Trees, and Vines which bear their fine clusters up to the very top of the Trees, upon a sort of ground that lies as smooth as one's Hand. Such Ornaments as these, are sufficient to give rise to the most agreeable Idea of a Land-skip in the World. I cannot express what vast quantities of Deer and Turkeys are to be found in these Woods, and in the vast Meads that lye upon the South side of the Lake. At the bottom of the Lake, we find wild Beeves upon the Banks of two pleasant Rivers that disembogue into it, without Cataracts or rapid Currents. It abounds with Sturgeon and white Fish; but Trouts are very scarce in it, as well as the other Fish that we take in the Lakes of* Hurons *and* Ilinese. *'Tis clear of Shelves, Rocks, and Banks of Sand; and has fourteen or fifteen fathom Water. The Savages assure us, that 'tis never disturb'd with high Winds, but in the Months of December, January, and February, and even then but seldom.*[7]

As the English settlements became more extensive, the English explorers remained longer in one area and gradually wrote more and more detailed books. John Lawson came to America in 1700 (deciding at the last moment that it would be more exciting than a trip to Rome) and remained for eight years, during which time he acquired the title surveyor-general of North Carolina. He returned to London and published his *A New Voyage to Carolina* (1709), and then came back. While continuing his explorations in 1711, he was murdered by Tuscarora Indians. As a promoter of the colony, Lawson was interested in all of its production, its climate, and its agriculture. He provided a more detailed account of the plants and animals than had any previous Englishman. His accounts of plants have much more ecological interest than do those of animals. For example, he found large oaks of four or five sorts

very common in the upper Parts of both Rivers; also a very tall large Tree of great Bigness, which some call Cyprus, *the right Name we know not, growing in Swamps. Likewise Walnut, Birch, Beech, Maple, Ash, Bay, Willow, Alder, and Holly; in the lowermost Parts innumerable Pines, tall and good for Boards or Masts, growing, for the most part, in barren and sandy, but in some Places up the River, in good Ground, being mixt amongst Oaks and other Timbers. We saw Mulberry-trees, Multitudes of Grape-Vines, and some Grapes which we eat of.*[8]

He also provided a favorable evaluation of the climate.[9]

Mark Catesby (1683–1749) traveled more broadly in the same region as Lawson, but Catesby came to America especially to study and collect plants and animals, and he provided more information than ever before about them in his two-volume *The Natural History of Carolina, Florida and the Bahama Islands . . .* (1729–47). Although a major portion of the work is devoted to descriptions and illustrations of animals, as in previous works, practically all he wrote of ecological interest concerned plants. He did, however, convey his ecological perceptions of animals by illustrating them against a background of an associated plant.[10]

After placing his region geographically, Catesby discussed the climate and pointed out some disparities between American and European climates:

The Northern Continent of America is much colder than those Parts of Europe which are parallel to it in Latitude; this is evident from the mortal Effects the Frosts have on many Plants in Virginia, that grow and stand the Winters in England, tho' 15 Degrees more North; and what more confirms this is the violent and sudden freezing of large Rivers.[11]

Although he may not have fully understood it, he also pointed out the moderating effect of the ocean upon the temperature of the adjacent land.

Catesby distinguished three main types of soil in eastern Carolina, "distinguished by the Names of *Rice Land, Oak* and *Hiccory Land,* and *Pine barren Land.*" They were distinguished partly by soil texture and partly by water content, but they were identified by the plants growing on them. "*Oak* and *Hiccory Land*" was characterized by

those Trees, particularly the latter, being observed to grow mostly on good Land. This Land is of most Use, in general producing the best Grain, Pulse, Roots, and Herbage, and is not liable to Inundations; on it are also found the best Kinds of Oak for Timber, and Hiccory, *an excellent Wood for Burn-*

ing. This Land is generally light and sandy, with a mixture of Loam.[12]

Catesby traveled inland into the Piedmont, and although he probably did not reach the Appalachian Mountains, he did collect some information about the topography, soil, and trees in both these regions.[13] In his section on agriculture Catesby discussed the species that succeeded in America and those that did not. The latter, such as the fig and the orange, were often found to be killed by the winter frosts.[14]

Although European naturalists would continue to make important explorations in America for more than a century after Catesby, native American naturalists soon joined in the explorations and gradually supplanted the Europeans in importance. The general pattern of this replacement has been well described by George Basalla.[15]

John Bartram (1699–1777) was a successful Pennsylvania farmer who became more interested in natural history and horticulture than in farming. He was America's first prominent native naturalist, and he became known and respected by European naturalists. He recorded his observations in letters and in journals that he kept during two trips, the first through Pennsylvania and New York to Lake Ontario in July and August, 1743, and the second through the Carolinas, Georgia, and Florida from July, 1765, to April, 1766. Only his first travel journal and extracts from the second were published during his lifetime. The ecological observations in his first journal are all of the same sort: indications of the species of plants that he encountered in particular kinds of places, often specified according to soil quality, moisture, and relative elevation.[16] These observations were more extensive than Catesby's but not more informative.

In his second journal Bartram occasionally offered some interpretation along with his descriptive observations, such as this one concerning soil formation:

landed on a high bluff, on the east-side of the river, at Johnson's Spring, a run of clear and sweet water, then travelled on foot along thick woody but loamy ground, looking rich on the surface by reason of the continual falling leaves, and by the constant evergreen shade rotting to soil, as the sun never shines on the ground strong enough to exhale their virtue before their dissolution, as under deciduous trees.[17]

This observation takes on ecological implications when tied to his frequent correlations between particular soil traits and plant species, but Bartram did not have a sufficiently analytical mind to pursue the subject further.

Because Bartram's farm was just outside Philadelphia and because he was respected by European naturalists, it was to be expected that when they came to America they would visit him. One who did and who drew upon Bartram's knowledge in his own writings was Pehr Kalm (ca. 1715–79). Kalm had studied natural history under the great Swedish professor Carl Linnaeus, one of the important founders of ecology. This training and his own scientific capabilities enabled Kalm to make the most extensive and perceptive ecological observations of America during the eighteenth century. His ecological perspective was further enhanced by his mission. He was sent to America by the Royal Swedish Academy of Sciences to discover useful plants that could grow in Scandinavia. He had to pay attention to soil, climate, and other environmental factors, as well as to utility.

The ecological observations in Kalm's *Travels into North America . . .*, published in Swedish in three volumes between 1753 and 1761, are so numerous that only a selection can be discussed here. His treatise was published in a German translation in 1754–64, but it did not appear in English until 1770–71. This delay may have been due to his unfavorable comments about English and Dutch settlers in America. His sympathies lay with the Swedish and French settlers, and he complained of the neglect of agriculture and inappreciation of science among the English settlers to the point that his English translator, the German naturalist John Reinhold Forster, accused him of bias.[18] Kalm's expressions of disapproval must have lessened considerably the appreciation of his work among the British and Dutch Americans.

The most extensive of Kalm's ecological observations concerned the correlation of distribution of plants with their habitat, about which he was more thorough than Bartram (he thought Bartram's book too superficial to have merited publication).[19] Kalm's book had the merit of using the Linnaean scientific names for species, enabling others, both then and now, to identify them readily. Kalm stayed in the vicinity of Philadelphia from September, 1748, until early June, 1749, when he traveled to New York City, then up the Hudson to Niagara, and on to Quebec and Montreal. About three-quarters of his observations were made in southeastern Pennsylvania and in New Jersey, but his northern trip enabled him to compare the plants and animals of the milder and colder regions.

For the Philadelphia region he made a survey of the trees and shrubs and listed fifty-eight of them according to abundance. He did not state how he determined abundance, but since this was long before the development of statistical methods of sampling, he must have depended upon his impressions. For many, but not all of them, he also stated where they grew. For example:

1. Quercus alba, *the white oak in good ground.*
6. Acer rubrum, *the maple tree with red flowers, in swamps.*
7. Rhus glabra, *the smooth leaved Sumach, in the woods, on high glades, and old corn-fields.*
9. Sambucus canadensis, *American Elder tree, along the hedges and on glades.*[20]

Often Kalm's observations on a species were detailed enough to be characterized as ecological life histories. *Rhus glabra* he found to be the commonest sumac; it seldom grew above three yards high; its berries remained on the shrub all winter; and the berries were eaten by boys with impunity. "This tree is like a weed in this country, for if a corn-field is left uncultivated for some years altogether, it grows on it in plenty, since the berries are spread everywhere by the birds."[21]

This last statement is among the earliest observations on plant succession. Brambles, he also noted, are among the first species to invade abandoned fields.[22] The Swedish settlers,

as well as Kalm, realized that it was useful to know not only which types of soil a plant came from when transplanting plants but also that certain plants can indicate by their presence the existence of good soil for crops.[23]

One of the interesting questions that Kalm asked Bartram was whether Catesby had claimed correctly that members of plant species are smaller in the northern than in the southern parts of their range. Bartram replied that there are some species suited to southern regions of which this is true, but that other species are most suited to northern regions, and among these the smaller specimens grow in the south. Kalm's subsequent experience supported Bartram's answer. Kalm found the sugar maple to be a common and tall plant in Canada, but in New Jersey and Pennsylvania it grew less than a third as high and was found only "on the northern side of the blue mountains, and on the steep hills which are on the banks of the river, and which are turned to the north." The sassafras tree, on the other hand, grew tall and thick south of forty degrees latitude, but between forty-three and forty-four degrees "it hardly reached the height of two or four feet, and was seldom so thick as the little finger of a grown person."[24]

Kalm also wrote good accounts of a number of mammals that included perceptive ecological information. In discussing the gray squirrel, he reported where they nest, the kinds of nuts they eat, the fact that hogs, Indians, and white men raid their winter stores, that after heavy snows they sometimes starve because they cannot dig down to their stores, that they are a serious pest in both maize fields and barns, that they eat not only the acorns but sometimes also the flowers of oaks, and that rattlesnakes can reputedly charm them into jumping into the snakes' mouths. It was also reported that gray squirrels migrate out of the high country before severe winters, but Kalm discounted this weather-predicting capacity and suggested instead that the occasional migrations were actually caused by a scarcity of nuts in the high country.[25]

Although America did not produce in the eighteenth century any native son who could describe ecologically the plants and animals as well as Kalm, in the second half of that century there did emerge a few capable observers who wrote notable works on the production of certain regions, and these works contained some ecological observations. William Bartram (1739–1823) was America's most capable naturalist of the eighteenth century. He followed in his father's footsteps both in his interests and in the sense that he accompanied his father on trips to Florida and elsewhere. Yet William's *Travels Through North & South Carolina, Georgia, East & West Florida* (1791) shows that he was far from a replica of his father. William had quite a different psyche, and also much more to say. William was a romantic.

His *Travels* is a famous book because it is a spellbinding adventure story about a sensitive person wandering through a tropical Garden of Eden. The book is a dazzling accomplishment because the events themselves are only occasionally exciting. Bartram's style was so nearly perfect that a high level of interest is sustained throughout. Samuel Taylor Coleridge and William Wordsworth found it a treasure chest of poetic imagery.[26] Apparently in his schooling Bartram had been as fascinated by Homer, Thucydides, Livy, Cicero, and perhaps Shakespeare, as he had been by Catesby and Linnaeus. His gift of description enabled him to carry descriptive ecological surveys to a new level of detail. Here is only a portion of his description of an island off the coast of Savannah, Georgia:

The intermediate spaces, surrounding and lying between the ridges and savannas, are intersected with plains of the dwarf prickly fan-leaved Palmetto, and lawns of grass variegated with stately trees of the great Broom-Pine, and the spreading ever-green Water-Oak, either disposed in clumps, or scatteringly planted by nature. The upper surface, or vegetative soil of the island, lies on a foundation, or stratum, of tenacious cinereous coloured clay, which perhaps is the principal support of the vast growth of timber that arises from the surface, which is little more than a mixture of fine white sand and dissolved vegetables, serving as a nursery bed to hatch, or bring into existence, the infant plant, and to supply it with ailment and food, suitable to its delicacy and tender frame, until the roots, acquiring sufficient extent and solidity to lay hold of the clay, soon attain a magnitude and stability sufficient to maintain its station. Probably if this clay were dug out, and cast upon the surface, after being meliorated by the saline or nitrous qualities of the air, it would kindly incorporate with the loose sand, and become a productive and lasting manure.

The roebuck, or deer, are numerous on this island; the tyger, wolf, and bear, hold yet some possession; as also raccoons, foxes, hares, squirrels, rats and mice, but I think no moles; there is a large ground-rat, more than twice the size of the common Norway rat. In the night time, it throws out the earth, forming little mounds, or hillocks. Opposoms are here in abundance, as also pole-cats, wild-cats, rattlesnakes, glass-snake, coach-whip snake, and a variety of other serpents. Here are also a great variety of birds, throughout the seasons, inhabiting both sea and land.[27]

This wealth of detail can sometimes be overpowering rather than enlightening.

Bartram's powers of dramatic evocation are illustrated in his account of a "forest" of century plants visited by swarms of butterflies and bees. Looking closely, he observed the drama of a spider catching and overpowering a bumblebee.[28] Whatever ecological conclusions might possibly have emerged are lost because the focus is upon drama rather than upon trying to understand how nature functions. He did not even shrink from describing smoke coming from the nostrils of a fighting alligator.[29] This focus upon drama rather than upon the meaning of interactions was enhanced by his tendency to anthropomorphize: "The bald eagle is a large, strong, and very active bird, but an execrable tyrant: he supports his assumed dignity and grandeur by rapine and violence, extorting unreasonable tribute and subsidy from all the feathered nations."[30]

Fortunately, Bartram's integrity and love of nature prevented him from embellishing his discussions with invented details, but it seems clear that his success as an enchanter diminished his significance as a scientist. His was undoubtedly a more appealing personality than Kalm's, but

Kalm's more prosaic orientation enabled him to penetrate deeper into the significance of what he saw.

Climate and Plants, Animals, People

Climate and Disease. Most of the early ecological observations were descriptive. Descriptions have remained an important part of ecology throughout its history, but a science needs a program to guide the collection of data if it is to penetrate beneath superficialities. The first ecological program that served to guide investigation was established within the context of medical research.

Since antiquity one of the most influential of medical writings was the Hippocratic treatise *Airs, Waters, and Places*. It opens with an explicitly ecological program of correlations between environmental conditions and sickness:

Whoever wishes to pursue properly the science of medicine must proceed thus. First he ought to consider what effects each season of the year can produce; for the seasons are not at all alike, but differ widely both in themselves and at their changes. The next point is the hot winds and the cold, especially those that are universal, but also those that are peculiar to each particular region. He must also consider the properties of the waters; for as these differ in taste and in weight, so the property of each is far different from that of any other. Therefore, on arrival at a town with which he is unfamiliar, a physician should examine its position with respect to the winds and to the risings of the sun. For a northern, a southern, an eastern, and a western aspect has each its own individual property. He must consider with the greatest care both these things and how the natives are off for water, whether they use marshy, soft waters, or such as are hard and come from rocky heights, or brackish and harsh. The soil too, whether bare and dry or wooded and watered, hollow and hot or high and cold. The mode of life also of the inhabitants that is pleasing to them, whether they are heavy drinkers, taking lunch, and inactive, or athletic, industrious, eating much and drinking little.[31]

This was written when diseases were generally believed caused by an imbalance of four humors—blood, phlegm, yellow bile, and black bile. Changes in climate were thought to influence the balance. For example, winter is predominantly cold and wet, and therefore there is a strong tendency for a superfluidity of phlegm. Summer is predominantly hot and dry, with a tendency for a superfluidity of yellow bile.

Beginning in the middle of the seventeenth century the humoral theory was slowly replaced by the perception of diseases as specific entities, though what these entities were was not clear. The shift away from a purely Hippocratic concept of disease did not, however, cause a loss of confidence or interest in the Hippocratic program of correlating environmental conditions with diseases. Interest in this program actually grew stronger, because, coincidentally, the barometer, thermometer, and other meteorological instruments were being developed.[32] These instruments provided the opportunity to increase the precision of the correlations and thereby increase the likelihood of obtaining a precise understanding of the environmental conditions that caused specific diseases. This program of research was encouraged in the writings of the English physicians Thomas Sydenham (1624–89) and Janes Jurin (1684–1750).[33]

The English clergyman and naturalist John Clayton (1657–1725), who came to Virginia in 1684, packed barometers and thermometers to make such studies, only to lose them at sea. Nevertheless, he reported from tidewater Virginia that in July and August the breezes ceased and the heat became "violent and troublesome." In September "The Weather usually breaks suddenly, and there falls generally very considerable Rains." When this happened, "many fall sick, this being the time of an Endemical Sickness, for Seasonings, Cachexes, Fluxes, Scorbutical Dropsies, Gripes or the like, which I have attributed to this Reason."[34]

The Scottish immigrant physician–naturalist–civil servant Cadwallader Colden (1688–1776) made much more extensive observations on weather and disease in America. In his "Account of the Climate and Diseases of New York" (written in 1723 but not published until 1811) he pointed out that spring comes to New York much later than it comes to England. The people in New York "are subject to pleurisies and inflammatory fevers, as in all other countries, upon the breaking up of hard winters; but not so much as in Pennsylvania and in the countries to the southward." He found July, August, and early September the sickliest period of the year, with intermitting fevers, cholera morbus, and fluxes being prevalent. The intermitting fevers were less prevalent than they were farther south, but the fluxes were more so, apparently because the poor of New York ate more watermelons than they did in Philadelphia. He also believed this difference in the prevalence of fluxes to be due to differences between the waters of New York and Philadelphia, New York's being more brackish and harder. Consumptions and diseases of the lungs were uncommon in New York because its air was clear and its elasticity strong. He found autumn to be America's healthiest season, the weather being mild and dry. Winter was long and often extremely cold, and the people were subject to rheumatic pains and pleurisies. In the essay he associated certain diseases with adverse qualities of the air, others with adverse qualities of water, and still others with adverse temperature.[35]

Colden stated in his "Observations on the Fever Which Prevailed in the City of New York in 1741 and 2" that the fever recurs annually in the hot months because of noxious vapors arising from "the stagnating filthy water. . . . not only different kinds of vapours are raised from a different fermentation in the stagnating fluids, but they raise likewise different fermentations in the animal fluids; hence, different kinds of fevers are produced in different constitutions of the air." He observed that the part of New York City mainly afflicted by the summer fevers was built on a swamp and also along the docks. He suggested that the city undertake the construction of a drainage system, which, in fact, was done and did lead to an improvement in the health of the area.[36]

In a letter written in 1745, Colden concluded that, while the swamps and dock areas enhanced the spread of yellow fever, the disease must initially have been imported on the ships that used the docks. He also suspected that the various malignant fevers reported from Europe were probably the West Indian yellow fever modified by climate.[37] He did not, however, go to the extreme that Benjamin Rush was to go a half century later of collapsing all fevers into different stages of one kind.[38] For Colden diseases were of different species, just as plants and animals were.

Following the lead of Dr. William Douglass, of Boston, Colden subjected an epidemic of "throat distemper" to an analysis of relevant environmental factors. He investigated its presumed origin, the geography of its dissemination, and the situations of its greatest frequency. He found it most common among children, the poor, those living in rural areas, those eating pork, those who were scorbutic, and those living on wet grounds. Sensible though this approach may have been, it did not lead to any greater understanding of the disease (now believed to have been a mixture of diphtheria and scarlet fever).[39]

On another occasion Colden drew the interesting analogy between insect galls and animal parasites, but the apparent perceptiveness of this speculation must be balanced by another of his beliefs, that scurvy is contagious.[40] Colden could ask many perceptive questions, but he could not establish causal relationships.

Another medical practitioner who emigrated from Scotland, John Lining (1708–60), settled in Charleston, South Carolina, in 1730. He made a much more thorough attempt to record weather data for correlation with disease than had been previously attempted in America, or perhaps anywhere else:

What first induced me to enter upon this Course, was, that I might experimentally discover the Influences of our different Seasons upon the Human Body; by which I might arrive at some more certain Knowledge of the Causes of our epidemic Diseases, which as regularly return at their stated Seasons, as a good Clock strikes Twelve when the Sun is in the Meridian; and therefore must proceed from some general Cause operating uniformly in the returning different Seasons.[41]

Following the examples set by Santorio Santorio in 1614 and James Keil in 1723, Lining concluded that the correlations would have to include not only incidence of disease and climatic changes but also physiological responses to climate.[42] Therefore, he recorded not only temperature, barometric pressure, and rainfall but also his weight at morning and night, his food and drink, urine and stools, perspiration and pulse rate, and daily exercise.

He began recording all these data in 1737 and continued for fifteen years. His first paper on the subject (1743) stressed the sudden changes in temperature over wide ranges at Charleston as a possibly significant factor. In following papers he refined his techniques of measurement, but without ever getting around to demonstrating the assumed correlations between weather changes and diseases. In his paper of 1753 he shifted the justification for his studies from a focus on disease to one on the environment. He included a monthly and seasonal summary of rainfall for every year from 1738 to 1752 and commented that if this series of data was extended for a half century it "might be of use in discovering to us the changes made in a climate, by clearing the land of its woods."[43]

In 1748, Charleston was struck by an epidemic of yellow fever. Lining's decade of observations enabled him to rule out the possibility that this epidemic had its origin in particular weather conditions. He concluded that it was an infectious disease because it spread throughout the city but not into the surrounding countryside.[44]

Pehr Kalm was not a physician, but the question of the relation of climate to disease interested him, and, whatever his deficiencies in medical knowledge, they were probably compensated for by his ability to reason about environmental factors. His reservations about America and Americans did not cause him to blame precipitously either climate or habits for diseases. He judged both factors as important, but only among a series of others. For example, he had heard that the air made teeth decay in America, but he pointed out that the teeth of Indians lasted longer than those of white settlers and therefore that other factors must operate. He thought that both tea drinking and eating hot food were relevant adverse factors.

There was a general belief that the climate was ameliorating, but there was also some suspicion that fevers were becoming more common. These presumed trends could be reconciled by emphasizing the increase of sharp weather changes as a cause, as in Lining's train of thought. But Kalm also found some old people who believed that fevers were not proportionately more numerous but were simply encountered more often because the population had increased. That it was unhealthy to live near stagnant bodies of water was a widespread assumption to which Kalm adhered. Since, however, there were some healthy regions near stagnant waters, he felt that the water could not be a sole cause. To him the aggravating factor seemed to be the "intemperate consumption of fruit."[45] Later he found that the French Canadians ate as many watermelons as the Pennsylvanians did, and he saved his hypothesis with the additional assumption that the greater heat of Pennsylvania made watermelons more dangerous there than in Canada.

Kalm also suspected that the consumption of tea, coffee, chocolate, sugar, and strong liquors contributed to the unhealthiness and shortness of life in America. Still another factor he considered as possibly relevant was the decline of odoriferous plants from the forests because of grazing cattle. The plant odors might have rendered harmless "the noxiousness of the effluvia from putrifying substances."[46] When he traveled to Albany, he also worried that the drinking water, containing "Monoculi," might cause diseases.[47]

From his description of the "Monoculi," they were apparently mosquito larvae, and one is inclined to imagine that at last Kalm was on the right track. Since, however, he was not prepared to verify experimentally any of his speculations, there was no way for him or his readers to know that his suspicion of mosquitoes would prove more justifiable than his fear of Pennsylvania watermelons. His observational ecology

was no more effective in solving the mystery of disease than were the ecological medical correlations of Colden or Lining.

Though Lining never demonstrated a relationship between particular diseases and changes in weather, he impressed a fellow Scottish immigrant and colleague, Lionel Chalmers (1715–77), with the value of his researches. For a time they were partners. Chalmers was to make some measurements of his own that enabled him to provide a chart of monthly maximum and minimum temperatures and rainfall data for the years 1750 to 1759. He also supplemented his own data in his *Account of the Weather and Diseases of South Carolina* (1776) by republishing one of Lining's charts.[48]

Chalmers was a less ambitious weather recorder than Lining, but he did attempt to establish a closer connection between climate and disease than Lining had. He began his book with a chapter on the climate, water, and soil of South Carolina. Having come from a cooler climate with less luxuriant vegetation, he was impressed by South Carolina's heat, stagnant waters, and fertile soils. He believed that the land had been unhealthier before the settlers cleared the land than it was in his day, because there would have been more exhalations from decaying organic matter and more moisture in the air. On the other hand, much of the cleared land had been dammed up for rice fields, indigo extraction, and mills, causing "such multitudes of fish and reptiles of various kinds [to] perish, that, for a long time after the air is tainted, with the putrid *effluvia*."[49]

Chalmers described the topography of the Charleston region and then explained the relationship between its topography and its climate:

As a south wind blows from the warmer latitudes and sweeps over a great extent of sea, it must be always hot and moist. That which comes from the south-west and west must be sultry and moist in the summer, as it passes over large spaces of heated, marshy, overflowed or wood-lands; and in the winter it will bring damps or rain, being fraught with the exhalations that are made from the above soils as well as with those vapours which are collected and condensed by the high bleak mountains that lie behind us.[50]

After describing the climate, Chalmers devoted much of his treatise to the discussion of correlations between the weather at different seasons and the diseases that were most prevalent during particular seasons. One example will show what he was able to achieve:

If the weather be either sultry and showery, or cloudy and close, and sometimes calm, intermixt with a gentle southerly wind, as often happens toward the end of summer, low and what are called nervous *and* putrid *fevers will appear, more especially among corpulent people and others who are of a weak or lax habit.*[51]

Such correlations could not lead to any causal understanding because the disease entities were too vague.

Although such studies as those by Colden, Lining, and Chalmers could not be readily published during the Revolution, a number of other physicians had similar interests, and in 1792, Dr. William Currie (1754–1828), of Philadelphia, was able to draw upon his own and their records to compile *An Historical Account of the Climates and Diseases of the United States of America.* There was no uniformity in the data, since they had been collected by different physicians with no common plan. Nevertheless, the book gave some indication of the weather and diseases state by state from Maine to Georgia. Although the conclusions to be drawn from this juxtaposition of geographical, climatic, and disease data were neither startling nor altogether clear, the book as a whole certainly reinforced the conviction that climate and general environment are relevant to the incidence of disease.

In 1793 there occurred in Philadelphia "one of the most devastating outbreaks of pestilence ever recorded on this side of the Atlantic."[52] Yellow fever carried off a tenth of the population, and a heated controversy arose over whether the disease had been imported from the West Indies or was endemic. The eminent Dr. Benjamin Rush was convinced that it was endemic. He agreed with the proponents of the West Indian origin that the epidemic started in the region of wharfs, but he attributed it to exhalations from putrified coffee on a wharf near Arch Street. The coffee was removed, but the epidemic continued. The Philadelphia College of Physicians examined the available evidence and concluded that yellow fever had never been endemic in America and appeared always to have been imported on ships.[53]

This controversy was to continue even more strongly as an epidemic of yellow fever again struck Philadelphia in 1797. Controversy, as Karl Popper has pointed out, is important to the advancement of scientific understanding, and this controversy provided the opportunity for re-examining assumptions and increasing both ecological and medical understanding.[54] In the twentieth century a research program might be designed to demonstrate the adverse effects of some environmental factor by testing the effects upon laboratory animals of variations in one environmental factor after another. In the 1790's knowledge of physiology and chemistry was not sophisticated enough for this approach to seem realistic.

In the closing years of the century America's most famous lexicographer, Noah Webster (1758–1843) joined the controversy on the side of endemic origin, and he produced a better documentation of evidence than had previously existed. His approach was systematically to collect and evaluate past evidences and to collect statistical data from American physicians. He sent a questionnaire to physicians throughout the states requesting the following information:

The time of the appearance and disappearance of any epidemic disease, with its general history.

The places where it first occurs to be described, in regard to land and water, height of land, construction of the city or streets, position as to points of compass, woods, morasses, &c. The classes of people most generally affected.

The general state of the seasons, as to heat, and cold, drought and moisture.

The time of earthquakes, meteors, lumen boreale, and all singular celestial appearances—with unusual tempests, especially when accompanied with hail—all compared with the lunar phenomena.

The appearance of unusual insects of all kinds, and any circumstance attending them.

Diseases among cattle, sheep and other animals.

Sickness and death of fish of all kinds.

Volcanic eruptions, with the phenomena preceding, attending and following them.[55]

This was a commendable effort to increase the objective data on which a decision could be made. From his returns Webster published *A Collection of Papers on the Subject of Bilious Fever, Prevalent in the United States for a Few Years Past* (1796). What he received, however, was not so much objective data as information supporting the disease theories of the responding physicians. This approach was democratic but not decisive. The available information would have to be arranged and evaluated from one point of view, and this Webster achieved in his two-volume *Brief History of Epidemic and Pestilential Diseases . . .* (1799). He stated that he had undertaken his inquiries with an impartial mind and that only after examining the evidence had he concluded that yellow fever was endemic. That may be true, but if so, he was pleased that his conclusions coincided with what he perceived to be best for American commerce. If yellow fever was endemic, it would be unnecessary to require the long periods of quarantine demanded by those, like Dr. Currie, who thought the disease was imported on ships from the West Indies.[56]

Webster's theory of disease was not original. He shared the general consensus that certain diseases can have an environmental origin and then become infectious. He believed that adverse weather changes could cause epidemics and that such changes might in turn be responses to comets, earthquakes, volcanic eruptions, and atmospheric electrical disturbances. He, like Dr. Rush, was skeptical of the trend of the time to name many different kinds of diseases. Webster believed that certain presumed disease entities were actually only mild or severe forms of other diseases or that certain diseases manifested themselves differently in different localities. He suspected that Old World plague and New World yellow fever were the same disease, which affected people differently in the different climates.[57]

Neither Webster nor his opponents were close to solving the problem of the origin of disease. Yet the debates they waged helped maintain an interest in environmental factors and influences.

Phenology. Phenology is a branch of ecology dealing with the correlation between climate and biological activity. The term itself is of comparatively recent origin, being first used in German in 1853 and in English in 1875. The term is easily confused with phrenology, the nineteenth-century term for the science of correlations between the shape of a person's head and his mental attributes. In the eighteenth and nineteenth centuries the term generally used until replaced by phenology was *calendar of flora.* This term described the form of such studies, but it was often too restricted because animals as well as plants were observed and reported.

Phenology does not occupy an important place in the

modern science of ecology because such studies today would usually be undertaken in relation to a specific question, which would necessitate providing the data in a different context. However, in the eighteenth and nineteenth centuries, when naturalists began to grope toward the organization of an ecological science, phenology held an important place in their thinking.

Two kinds of prior interests provide some reinforcement for phenological studies. Farmers' almanacs have been written for five thousand years, and throughout history one or another of them has been in demand.[58] Botanists have never been strongly motivated to contribute to this form of literature, though a few of them did so in the eighteenth century. The other interest was in drawing correlations between climate and the prevalence of diseases. This kind of study was recommended in antiquity by the Hippocratic treatise *Airs, Waters, and Places*. Nevertheless, the matter was not much investigated before the eighteenth century.

No doubt Linnaeus, who was both physician and professor of natural history, was aware of these two areas of previous study, and his own interest in phenology must have depended in part upon them. Linnaeus likely conveyed to Pehr Kalm the idea that the times of blooming, leafing, and fruiting are significant data for the life histories of plants. In addition, Kalm's mission to discover American species that might thrive in Scandinavia alerted him to the practical importance of such data. He was first to pay much heed to these phenomena in America, and his *Travels* emphasized the significance of such information.

Beginning in February, 1749, Kalm carefully noted the seasonal unfolding of biological phenomena. Purple grackles began to reappear on February 23. The flowers of the hazel began to open on March 12 and on March 13, those of the alder, *Dracontium foetidum*, and *Draba verna*.[59] This information was enhanced by meteorological tables for the Philadelphia area, which Kalm compiled for August, 1748, to September, 1749 (while he was in Canada in the summer of 1749, Bartram collected the data for him).[60]

Kalm wrote his *Travels* in chronological sequence from his diary, and sometimes he discussed a subject more than once and from different perspectives. At one point he discussed the difficulties of raising American plants in Europe in relation to climate, and later he discussed the reverse problem of raising European plants in America. The main difficulty with raising American plants in Europe was that most of them bloomed late and their fruits did not ripen before autumn frosts. Kalm evidently was speaking, or assumed he was, of plants that were being transplanted into conditions rather similar to their native situation. There were several factors that he felt were actually different and could account for the difficulty. The first was that, although the winters in Pennsylvania and northward were as severe as those in Sweden, the American winters were much shorter. Next, the summers in Pennsylvania were much longer than they were in Sweden, it being hot in the former from April to October but in the latter only in June and July. America's late-blooming flowers are correlated with its longer hot season. However, he noted that even in America some of these would not always bring their seeds to maturity before cold

weather set in. He found the wisdom of God, nevertheless, in the fact that these were perennial species. Another contributing factor in the late blooming of American species was that most of them would have grown in forests before they were cleared by the settlers, and there the dead leaves and the shade from the trees would have created seasonally late and slow-growing conditions.[61]

In a later discussion he pondered why cultivated European fruit trees imported into America bloomed earlier than similar native American species. He suggested that the key to this puzzle might lie in the more fluctuating American climate. In Europe, the plants could safely bloom as soon as it turned warm, but in America this could lead to death of the flowers, since the early warmth could be followed by a cold spell. Therefore, the late-blooming American species were better suited for the American climate than were the earlier-blooming European species.[62] Kalm did not attempt to verify his hypothesis experimentally. The removal of a problem from the field to the greenhouse or laboratory for solution was not often attempted in the eighteenth century, or even very often in the nineteenth century. Nevertheless, his discussion of his hypothesis is one of the subtlest examples of ecological reasoning in the eighteenth century.

Another interesting and innovative example of his use of phenological information occurs in a scientific paper that he published in Swedish in 1759 but that did not appear in English translation until 1911. It was on the passenger pigeon, then one of the most abundant of American birds. He discussed nine important food plants for these birds, indicating when their fruits became available in Pennsylvania or in Canada. It was possible that the movements of these birds might be correlated to some extent with the maturing of their food supply rather than only with climate, but Kalm did not have sufficient information to discuss this possibility.[63]

Meanwhile, in Sweden, Kalm's former teacher, Linnaeus, had organized the collection of information useful for determining the time to plant crops in Sweden. This information was published in 1753 under the title *Vernatio Arborum*, and it was followed in 1756 by the better-known *Calandarium Florae*, which provides phenological information for Upsala, Sweden, for the whole year. The English naturalist Benjamin Stillingfleet was impressed enough by the latter work not only to translate it into English, but also to make his own calandar of flora for Stratton, in Norfolk, and to extract from Theophrastus' *Historia Plantarum* a calandar of flora for ancient Athens. Stillingfleet included all three in a collection of Linnaean dissertations that he published in English, and it was apparently this collection and Kalm's *Travels* that introduced the idea of phenology to Americans.[64]

Thomas Jefferson (1743–1826) at times seemed more interested in natural history than in politics. He was well read in the literatures of natural history and agriculture, and he was actively interested in his crops and gardens at Monticello. He also studied the weather. In his *Notes on the State of Virginia* he based his chapter on climate upon meteorological data that his friend the Reverend James Madison, a professor of mathematics, collected at Williamsburg during

Thomas Jefferson's "Calendar of the bloom of flowers in 1782." Jefferson commented: Note they were planted this spring, and the season was very backward." From Thomas Jefferson, Garden Book, 1776–1824, *page 25. Reproduced courtesy of the Massachusetts Historical Society.*

the years 1772 to 1777 and upon some data that they collected simultaneously at Williamsburg and Monticello. Even America's Independence Day did not distract Jefferson from his observations, for he recorded the temperature on July 4, 1776, at 6:00 and 9:00 A.M. and at 1:00 and 9:00 P.M. He even bought a new thermometer that day, for 3 English pounds 15 pence. He also bought a barometer on July 8 for 4 pounds 10 pence. The War of Independence was ultimately to interrupt the coordinated weather investigation, however, because the British soldiers robbed Madison of his thermometer and barometer.[65]

Jefferson seems to have begun collecting weather data systematically in 1776, but he began entries in his *Garden Book* a decade earlier. His *Garden Book*, not published until 1944, was a combination of phenological data and planting diary. For example, the entry for March 23, 1767 was:

Purple Hyacinth & Narcissus bloom.
sowed 2. rows of Celery 9.I. apart.
sowed 2 rows of Spanish onions & 2.d°. of Lettuce.[66]

In 1782 he constructed an interesting chart to indicate the lengths of time various species of garden flowers remained in bloom.

In his *Notes on the State of Virginia*, which he completed early in 1785, he showed an awareness of the close relationship between climate and the distribution of plants. This subject became of great practical interest to him while he was serving as an American diplomat in France. He made there some investigations similar to Kalm's in America. Jefferson decided that the climate of southern France was similar enough to that of South Carolina and Georgia for it to be worthwhile to send to America seeds from French crops, particularly rice and olives. Although his attempts to establish these crops in America were not successful, his reconaissance was almost as sophisticated as Kalm's. Jefferson was elected an honorary member of the South Carolina Society for Promoting and Improving Agriculture and Other Rural Concerns, and the long letter that he sent to William Drayton of that society on July 30, 1787, is of particular interest.

One passage illustrates well his awareness of the relationship of climate and topography and distribution of plants:

My journey through the southern parts of France, and the territory of Genoa, but still more the crossing of the Alps, enabled me to form a scale of the tenderer plants, and to arrange them according to their different powers of resisting cold. In passing the Alps at the Col de Tende, we cross three very high mountains successively. In ascending, we lose these plants, one after another, as we rise, and find them again in the contrary order as we descent on the other side; and this is repeated three times. Their order, proceeding from the tenderest to the hardiest, is as follows: caper, orange, palm, aloe, olive, pomegranate, walnut, fig, almond. But this must be understood of the plant only; for as to the fruit, the order is somewhat different. The caper, for example, is the tenderest plant, yet, being so easily protected, it is among the most certain in its fruit. The almond, the hardiest, loses its fruit the oftenest, on account of its forwardness. The palm, hardier than the caper and orange, never produces perfect fruit here.[67]

Jefferson's brief experience at collecting simultaneous weather data with Madison may have given him the idea to do the same with biological phenomena. In June, 1790, while serving the federal government in New York, he sent his daughter Maria information about the reappearance of whippoorwills, swallows, and martins and the growth of peas and strawberries. He requested similar information from her about these at Monticello. She replied that

we had peas the 10th of May, and strawberries the 17th of the same month, though not in that abundance we are accustomed to, in consequence of a frost this spring. As for the martins, swallows, and whip-poor-wills, I was so taken up with my chickens that I never attented to them.[68]

He tried again the following spring this time from Philadelphia, and he finally received some information on the weather and fruit trees from his son-in-law Thomas Mann Randolph, Jr., but nothing about the robins, bluebirds, or frogs.[69]

Having many interests and activities, Jefferson never got around to publishing his phenological studies. However, he was fond of discussing his scientific interests and encouraging others to undertake the detailed investigations for which he never found the time. In a letter on phenology to the botanist Jacob Bigelow in 1818, Jefferson summarized the phenological data he had collected during the previous seven years at Monticello.[70] Those years he had spent in the White House, 1801 to 1809, had not erased his enthusiasm for the subject.

Samuel Williams (1743–1817), who for a while taught physical sciences at Harvard University, was especially interested in meteorology. He seems to have planned a comprehensive investigation of the climate and phenology of the United States, for in 1786 he sent to prospective observers a plan for collecting these data. The plan was, no doubt, interrupted by his dismissal from his professorship on grounds of forgery.[71] He moved to Vermont, where he wrote his useful *Natural and Civil History of Vermont*, first published in 1794. In the chapter on climate he gave not only a chart showing the seasonal progress of various cultivated plants in Vermont but also a capable account of the differences in climate from Charleston, South Carolina, to Rutland, Vermont. In his chapter on native animals he also provided a list of birds that are permanent residents and those that are migratory. For the latter he gave arrival and departure dates. Comparable information on birds was also published by William Bartram in 1791 and Benjamin Smith Barton in 1799.[72]

Climate and Inferiority. Captain John Smith, John Lawson, and Mark Catesby were among the early authors who praised America's climate and fertility. Pehr Kalm was unenthusiastic, but the widely read naturalist Comte Buffon initiated a controversy that lasted throughout the second half of the eighteenth century and beyond. It concerned the quality of the American climate and the possible negative influences of that climate upon its inhabitants.

Kalm's negative feelings about the English Americans have already been mentioned. Among other things he felt that their agriculture was wasteful in comparison with the intensive practices of European farmers. Yet he was not inclined to judge negligence as the sole cause of agricultural difficulties in America. Climate was obviously a potent environmental factor, though it was not always easily separated from the other factors. He reported that the Americans had failed to establish a textile industry not only because cloth could be obtained easily from England but also because "the breed of sheep which is brought over degenerates in process of time, and affords but a coarse wool." Cattle, horses, and hogs also degenerated: "The climate, the soil, and the food, altogether contribute their share towards producing this change."[73]

Even the settlers seemed affected. Kalm thought that they matured earlier than their European relatives but also were weaker and died earlier. However, Indians of old age had been known in the past—before the introduction of Old World diseases and rum—and so this degeneracy could not be blamed entirely on the weather. He also found that the Negroes had not grown lighter in color after 130 years of American slavery. But, even though Kalm could not separate the effects of weather from other factors, he did believe that the sudden changeableness of the weather and seasonal shifts from hot summers to cold winters were important health hazards.[74]

Comte Georges Louis Leclerc de Buffon (1707–88), writing at about the same time as Kalm, published the most influential pronouncements on the degenerating effects of the American environment. His first discussion relating to the subject appeared in "The Natural History of Man" (1749). In its final section, "Of the Varieties of the Human Species," he expressed the general European sense of superiority over the other peoples of the world. He supposed the cause of the differences to be environmental, believing that if white men lived long enough in the tropics and adopted the habits of black men, they would eventually become like them. Among the Indians of America it had been reported that occasionally a white child is produced, as also occurred among dark peoples elsewhere. From this fact Buffon deduced that white was the primitive color, but that skin color "may be varied by climate, by food, and by manners, to yellow, brown, and black, and which, in certain circumstances, returns, but so greatly altered, that it has no resemblance to the original whiteness . . ."[75]

Buffon later developed the idea that European animals had migrated to America and degenerated into the American species. This idea seems to have been an extension of his above assumption from people to animals. He published his speculations about human changes before Kalm published his *Travels*. However, Kalm's observations were brought to the attention of the French intelligensia by Abbé Arnaud in 1761, about the time that Buffon extended his theory to animals, and it may be that Buffon depended to some extent upon Kalm in his assertion that

All the animals which have been transported from Europe to America, as the horse, the ass, the ox, the sheep, the goat, the hog, the dog, &c. have become smaller; and those which were not transported but went thither spontaneously, those, in a word, which are common to both Continents, as the wolf, the fox, the stag, the roebuck, the elk, &c. are also considerably less than those of Europe.[76]

The same conditions that produced small, weak animals and men, he claimed produced large reptiles and insects. Those conditions were supposedly lesser heat and greater humidity, with high mountains, extensive forests, and many bodies of water. He developed this line of reasoning to the point that he could claim inferiority for all American productions, regardless of the changes in climate from one region to another.

Other European authors picked up Buffon's claim and developed their own variations of it.[77] The Americans were not convinced. Jefferson published a strong and effective rebuttal in his *Notes on the State of Virginia*. Jefferson realized that Buffon was vulnerable both in theory and in command of relevant facts. He collected his own data to show that American mammals were not usually smaller than similar European species but, indeed, were often larger. Jefferson also challenged Buffon's assumption that American species represented degenerate European species by claiming that members of any species can be modified only within limits by changes in soil, climate, and food. Jefferson could also challenge Buffon's assumption that cold and moisture caused American species to be of inferior size by citing another of Buffon's discussions, which stated that colder and more humid countries seemed better for oxen than hot dry ones.[78] Not content with the arguments in his book, Jefferson in 1786 sent back to America to obtain antlers of American deer, elk, and caribou, which he presented to Buffon in 1787. Buffon found them convincing but died before he could publish a further discussion on the subject.

Jefferson was not the only American to reply to the degeneracy arguments. Somewhat similar to his were those of Samuel Williams, who in his *Natural and Civil History of Vermont* (1794) provided additional evidence from the weight of American mammals that they were more often superior than inferior to comparable European species. He also argued that the European species would never have emigrated to America if the conditions here had not been more favorable than the ones they left.[79] Benjamin Franklin also entered the fray in a modest way by pointing out at a party in Paris that the American guests were taller and more robust than the Frenchmen present, and in 1780 he collected weather observations that seemed to indicate that England and France were more humid than America.[80]

This controversy in retrospect may seem to represent mere chauvinism argued within the realm of environmental speculation. That was certainly one aspect of the controversy, but, on the other hand, it must have served the useful function of encouraging Americans to increase their understanding of their own climate and its influences upon all forms of life in America.

Changing Environment and Changing Climate. America's climate in the seventeenth and eighteenth centuries was not simply a matter of idle conversation. It was of vital concern to settlers and would-be settlers. The early settlers in New England found the winters colder than expected, and the first settlers in the southern colonies found the summers hotter than expected. Although they soon learned to cope with the unfavorable aspects of the climate, weather remained a serious concern, for the country was strongly dependent upon agriculture, and there was a widespread belief that climate played an important role in health and sickness.

There was an understandable alertness to any changes in climate—perhaps an overalertness, for sometimes the changes appear to have been exaggerated. As early as 1688, John Clayton in tidewater Virginia was reporting, "I have been told by very serious Planters, that 30 or 40 years since, when the Country was not so open, the Thunder was more fierce."[81] He believed the climate could be favorably modified by wise agricultural planning. The existing plantations, he complained, were too large. If each planter had smaller holdings, he could clear the woods more effectively and drain the swamps, thereby imrpoving the circulation of fresh air and decreasing the unhealthy ferments in the air.[82]

Clayton's general idea that the amount of vegetation in an area would affect the climate soon received support from Dr. John Woodward, of London, a professor of medicine and cosmology. He conducted experiments on plant growth and concluded that the water evaporated from plants could cause high hunidity in heavily forested regions. That, he stated, had formerly been the condition in America, but as the forests were burned or destroyed to make way for homes and agriculture, the air became drier and more serene.[83] This conclusion met with little if any skepticism in America until the very end of the eighteenth century.

Pehr Kalm was the best historian of American land use of the mid-eighteenth century. He thought that the clearing of forests and draining of swamps must have modified the climate, and he asked elderly people whether the climate had changed since their youth. He found one old Swede who thought not, but the others felt that there had been changes. They believed that both the winter and the spring had formerly come earlier. The Delaware River had formerly froze about mid-November, but in the 1740's it did not freeze until mid-December. They generally agreed that formerly the winters had been colder but that the climate had changed less rapidly.[84]

Dr. Hugh Williamson (1735–1819), a physician who did research in the physical sciences and taught mathematics at the College of Philadelphia, had an interest in the question from the standpoints of medicine, meteorology, and patriotism. His arguments were mainly meteorological and very ingenious. He argued that as the land was cleared for cultivation it would reflect back into the immediately adjacent air more heat than would the forest, thereby increasing the warmth in the winter. On the other hand, because heat rises, he thought that the same situation would not necessarily make the summers hotter than before. He also suggested that the increasing warmth in the wintertime would decrease the difference between the land and ocean temperatures, which should also decrease the ferocity of the winds during winter.[85]

Jefferson briefly discussed the amelioration of the climate in his *Notes on the State of Virginia*, citing the fact that the rivers that were once known to freeze over in winter seldom did so any longer and that the snows that once accumulated in the mountains and caused spring floods no longer accumulated, and the rivers no longer flooded.[86]

The estimates of the changes wrought in the climate because of cultivating the land were made, up to this point, in terms of temperature and humidity, and the conclusions were favorable. During the second half of the eighteenth century chemists developed the capability of identifying different kinds of gases, and in 1772, Joseph Priestley discovered that plants restore the respirability of vitiated air.[87] Trees were not merely useful providers of fuel, lumber, and shade. The Marquis François Jean de Chastellux appreciated this point and cast doubt upon the Americans' wisdom in proceeding as rapidly as they were in eliminating their forests. He thought it beneficial to cut down forests where the swamps could be drained, but in eastern Virginia that could never be fully accomplished, and therefore the trees were needed to absorb the "mehpitic exhalations."[88] This concern for the

Ecological Studies and Observations Before 1900

value of trees to absorb noxious gases from swamps was also expressed in scientific papers read by Dr. Benjamin Rush in 1785, Dr. Thomas Wright in 1794, Dr. William Currie in 1795, and Dr. Adam Seybert in 1798.[89]

Samuel Williams decided to add precision to this discussion by quantifying the climatic influence of forests. He noted that the rainfall figures for North America were about twice those for Europe at the same latitude (he did not cite his sources of information, nor did he mention that his figures contradicted Benjamin Franklin's). This difference he assumed was caused by the great amounts of water evaporating from America's forests. He measured the evaporation rate during a six-hour period from a maple twig having two leaves and one or two buds—16 grains troy weight—and then cut down the thirty-foot tree and counted its leaves—21,192. He then estimated the density of trees in an acre of forest—640—and calculated that an acre of this forest would emit 3,875 gallons of water to the atmosphere in twelve hours. In a similar manner he measured the amount of "air" emitted by the same twig with leaves and buds (before the cutting) and calculated that an acre of forest emits 14,774 gallons of "air" in twelve hours. He pointed out, however, that not all forests would have the same density of trees as the one on which his calculations were based.

The existence of forests affects not merely the water and gases of the atmosphere but also the temperature. To ascertain the magnitude of this effect, Williams measured the temperature of the soil ten inches below the surface in an open field and in a Vermont forest for thirteen days, from May 23 to November 16:

Time		Heat in the Pasture	Heat in the Woods	Difference
May	23	50°	46°	6° [sic]
	28	57	48	9
June	15	64	51	13
	27	62	51	11
July	16	62	51	11
	30	65½	55½	10
August	15	68	58	10
	31	59½	55	4½
September	15	59½	55	4½
October	1	59½	55	4½
	15	49	49	0
November	1	43	43	0
	16	43½	43½	0

He was impressed by the ten or eleven degrees difference in June and July, because he suspected that the winters had increased in warmth by that average amount since the settlement of America. He discerned a direct correlation between the temperature of the soil and of the atmosphere because, he reasoned, the heat of the soil would heat the atmosphere to about the same temperature. As the land was cleared, the pasture temperature would come to dominate rather than the woods temperature. Unfortunately for this argument, he failed to notice that there was no difference in soil temperatures between pasture and woods for October and November. His data might support an argument for increasingly warmer summers but could not support an argument for increasingly warmer winters. Furthermore, Williams also compared pasture and woods soil temperatures on January 14, 1791, and found the pasture frozen to a depth of three feet five inches, whereas the soil in the woods was thirty-nine degrees.[90]

Down to the end of the eighteenth century there seems to have been virtually unanimous agreement that the American climate was becoming milder as the land was brought into cultivation from forests and swamps. In his study of the relationship between climate and disease, Noah Webster acquired a familiarity with the historical evidence on which that assumption was built. In 1799 he called into question the evidence for climatic change that Jefferson, Williams, and several others had offered. Webster chose to argue the issue not just for America but also for Europe, since some had also argued that the European climate ameliorated as its forests and swamps were cleared from the Middle Ages onward. Webster brought no new data to the controversy, and there were not sufficient data to show that the climate had not ameliorated. However, Webster was able to show that there were difficulties with the reasoning of Williams and other authors on the subject and that their case could not be presumed proved.[91]

The Balance of Nature

The balance of nature is the oldest ecological theory. It is a theory that has never been worked out in detail, but the basic assumptions were expressed in antiquity, beginning with Herodotus and Plato, and the theory developed by accretion throughout subsequent history. There is not much to say about it before the time of Kalm's visit to America, because the writings on American natural history had been long on observation and short on theory. In 1749, Kalm's teacher, Linnaeus, outlined an ecological science based on the balance of nature concept, though his name for it was "*oeconomia naturae.*"[92]

Although Kalm was in America when Linnaeus published his outline for a new science, Kalm would surely have learned something about it while studying under Linnaeus. In America, Kalm found that one species after another, including bear, beaver, deer, crane, duck, goose, passenger pigeon, mosquito, and grass, was known to have declined in population within the memory of the settlers. In some places the water table had also been lowered. He heard that "about sixty or seventy years ago, a single person could kill eighty ducks in a morning; but at present you frequently wait in vain for a single one." The reasons for the decline seemed clear. Before the white men arrived, there had been only a few Indians, and they lacked guns. The white men with guns had a greater ability to kill, and they indiscriminately took eggs, mothers, and young, "because no regulations are made to the contrary. And if any had been made, the spirit of freedom which prevails in the country would not suffer them to be obeyed." Other important factors he pointed out were the increasing population and the clearing of the land.[93]

Not only were certain species becoming rarer in the settled regions but some, such as the beaver, had actually disappeared. As time went on, trappers in Canada had to go farther and farther westward and northward to find them. Kalm did not predict what the ultimate fate of the beaver might be, but the situation also became known to Buffon, who in 1756 commented that "if the human species, as is reasonable to suppose, shall, in the progress of time, people equally the whole surface of the earth, the history of the beaver, in a few ages, will be regarded as a ridiculous fable."[94]

Because of his practical orientation, Kalm's ecological observations were analytical as well as descriptive. For example, when he learned that Pennsylvania farmers burned off the ground cover of leaves in the forest in March to allow the grass to grow more rapidly for their livestock, he admitted the advantage but nevertheless concluded that it was outweighed by the disadvantages:

All the young shoots of several trees were burnt with the dead leaves, which diminishes the woods considerably; and in such places where the dead leaves had been burnt for several years together, the old trees only were left, without any wood. At the same time all sorts of trees and plants are consumed by the fire, or at least deprived of their power of budding; a great number of plants, and most of the grasses here, are annual; their seeds fall between the leaves, and by that means are burnt: This is another cause of universal complaint, that grass is much scarcer at present in the woods than it was formerly; a great number of dry and hollow trees are burnt at the same time, though they could serve as fewel in the houses, and by that means spare part of the forests. The upper mould likewise burns away in part by that means, not to mention several other inconveniencies with which this burning of the dead leaves is attended. To this purpose the government of Pennsylvania have lately published an edict, which prohibits this burning; nevertheless every one did as he pleased.[95]

Among the other inconveniences that Kalm may have had in mind may have been the depletion of odoriferous plants that would counteract the noxious effluvia from putrifying substances, which elsewhere he attributed to the grazing of cattle in the forests.[96]

Implicit in the balance-of-nature concept was the assumption that different species were in some numerical proportion to each other, but it must have been clear to some that these relationships were not inflexible. It was obvious from the start that the Indians had not fully populated the New World. Free land was one of the most important factors in the immigration of Europeans to America. Kalm noted that America's white population grew rapidly, because with easily available land there was no inhibition to early marriage.[97]

Benjamin Franklin expressed the situation and its implications very well in his "Observations Concerning the Increase of Mankind, Peopling of Countries."[98] Because of the early marriages and large families he guessed that America's population might double every twenty years, and he predicted that within a century there would be more Englishmen in America than in England. One of the main objectives of his essay was to point out that the English settlers alone could easily and quickly populate the country by themselves and that the country would be more harmonious if Negro slaves and Europeans of "swarthy complexion" were excluded. Since he compared the capacity of human beings to increase to that of plants, by implication he seemed to suggest that the human population in America would eventually stabilize in the same way that plant populations had.

Franklin's ideas about stocking the country with people might in some way have been influenced by a childhood experience that he related to Kalm. His father, Josiah Franklin, had observed in the Boston area that in one river there were many herrings that swam upriver to spawn in the spring time, while in a neighboring river there were never any herrings. Kalm continued:

This circumstance led Mr. Franklin's father who was settled between the two rivers, to try whether it was not possible to make the herrings likewise live in the other river. For that purpose he put out his nets, as they were coming up for spawning, and he caught some. He took the spawn out of them, and carefully carried it across the land into the other river. It was hatched, and the consequence was, that every year afterwards they caught more herrings in that river; and this is still the case. This leads one to believe that the fish always like to spawn in the same place where they were hatched, and from whence they first put out to sea; being as it were accustomed to it.[99]

This is surely one of the earliest records of wildlife stocking in America, and it shows a belief that the rivers, like the land, might not always contain as much life as possible. This insight appears to run counter to the general assumptions of the balance-of-nature concept. The concept, however, was so loosely formulated that it was difficult to be skeptical of it on the basis of a few superficial experiences.

On a later occasion, in 1774, Franklin was pleased to learn from Joseph Priestley that vegetables restore the air that is spoiled by animals. Franklin replied that this was one more feature in a rational system of complementary relations, which included animals eating vegetables and then fertilizing them with their wastes.[100] The rational system to which Franklin referred was clearly the balance of nature, here envisioned in terms of natural cycles of matter rather than in terms of a balance in the populations of species.

While writing *Natural and Civil History of Vermont*, the mathematically minded Samuel Williams was to develop an interest in the abundance of different kinds of animals of Vermont, and when he could obtain the information, he introduced into his accounts of the mammals their periods of gestation, numbers of litters a year, and numbers of offspring a litter as means of accounting for their relative abundance. While rebutting Buffon's arguments that American mammals had degenerated from European species, Williams grew used to the assumption that American species had migrated to America, and he tied this idea explicitly to the balance of nature in his argument against Buffon's idea that America's environment was less conducive to fertility than was Europe's:

Whatever be their multiplying power, it would require a long period of time, before they would arrive at that increase of numbers, in which their progress would be checked, by the want of food. They would naturally spread over the whole continent, before they arrived to such a state. This they had done in every part of America, when it was first discovered by the Europeans. . . . what is the greatest number of quadrupeds, that the uncultivated state of any country will support, we have no observations to determine. But it seems probable, that the maximum *had already taken place. . . . if we may judge of the energy with which* [nature] *acts, from the effects of her multiplying power, the conclusion will be, that in no country has she displayed greater powers of fecundity than in America.*[101]

With Jefferson's and Williams' defense of the fertility of America and its forms of life against the slander of foreigners, it is not surprising that they did not share Kalm's and Buffon's doubts about the survival of America's wildlife. Although Jefferson and Williams must have been aware of the slaughter of America's animals and their decreasing numbers, they held tenaciously to the platonic tenent that no species can ever become extinct.[102]

THE NINETEENTH CENTURY

Exploration and Inventory

From 1590 to the time of Kalm and the two Bartrams there was a definite increase in the detail and perceptiveness of ecological observations in the literature of naturalists' travels and surveys of natural productions. By 1800 only a small portion of the North American continent had been explored in much detail by naturalists. The literature of exploration and inventory of North America continued to appear throughout the nineteenth and twentieth centuries with persisting ecological significance. This literature was useful for ecological observations but usually not, however, for ecological theory, and therefore there are diminishing returns on its significance for progress in ecological understanding.

This is evident in the *History of the Expedition under the Command of Lewis and Clark* (published in two volumes in 1814). A survey of the natural productions was one of the important objectives of the trip, and no doubt the natural-history reports would have been more extensive and of higher quality if Meriwether Lewis had not died tragically in 1809 and if Benjamin Smith Barton had been able to fulfill his subsequent agreement to prepare the scientific report of the expedition. Nevertheless, these misfortunes aside, it is not clear that the scientific reports could have added much to the progress of ecology. The expedition did make daily weather records,[103] occasional phenological notes, and observations on the kinds of trees encountered in river valleys. These data and the specimens of plants and animals they brought back were valuable additions to knowledge. Nevertheless, an exploratory expedition that traversed the continent could not

be expected to improve upon the quality of observations published from the more knowledgeable and leisurely explorations of trained naturalists like Kalm and William Bartram.

Shortly after the Lewis and Clark expedition returned to civilization, however, the possibilities for explorers to contribute to ecology was enhanced by the example set by one of the greatest scientific explorers of all times, Alexander von Humboldt. The *Personal Narrative* of his travels through Latin America (published in three volumes in Paris between 1814 and 1825) contained the same sort of ecological observations Kalm had made, and Humboldt was probably the first naturalist whose observations exceeded Kalm's both in ecological quality and quantity. His *Personal Narrative* inspired the explorations and accounts of many naturalists, including Charles Darwin, Alfred Russel Wallace, and Henry Walter Bates.[104]

Humboldt's most useful work for ecology was probably his *Essai sur la Géographie des Plantes . . .*, written with his colleague Aimé Bonpland and published in French and German editions in 1807. He urged that plants should be investigated from the standpoint of the different zones and elevations they inhabit; the degrees of atmospheric pressure, temperature, humidity, and electrical charge of the atmosphere in which they live; and their growth patterns—whether they are solitary or social species. He explained how the terrain and climate enabled the same plants to exist continuously from Canada at low elevations to Mexico at high elevations, and how the Mediterranean Sea and the Pyrenees prevented the spread of African and Spanish plants northward.[105] Accompanying the essay was a large chart of two volcanic mountains in Equador whose sides were divided into vegetation districts. On each side of the chart were columns of figures indicating elevation, gravitational attraction, barometric pressure, maximum and minimum temperature, and other physical variables. Using these columns, one could locate the magnitude of any of the environmental factors in relation to the plants listed on the sides of the mountains. One could thus presumably determine the physical requirements for any species listed.

Humboldt's correlational science of biogeography was too ambitious to be fully accepted by other naturalists of the nineteenth century. In the first place, he had not demonstrated the importance of some factors, such as atmospheric pressure and electrical charge for the distribution of species. In the second place, field studies could not yet be organized for collecting elaborate data over large areas. As the American people moved westward in the second half of the nineteenth century, however, some naturalists developed an interest in the correlation between species distribution and temperature and rainfall patterns. Some indebtedness to Humboldt appears to exist in the resulting studies.

On his return from Latin America to Europe, Humboldt stopped off for six weeks in the United States in the summer of 1804. He met Barton and included in an appendix to the *Essai* some data Barton had obtained indicating that species of plants grow farther northward on the eastern side of the Alleghany Mountains than they do on the western side, which Barton attributed to the warmer climate of the eastern side. Barton had a few pages set into galleys in 1809, but his study was never completed.[106]

After a generation went by, another American, Charles Pickering (1805–78), wrote "On the Geographical Distribution of Plants" (1830), which summarized and applied to America some of the understanding of the subject that was developing in Europe.[107] In 1838 he accompanied the United States Exploring Expedition under Lieutenant Charles Wilkes to the far Pacific, and in 1854 he published some observations on the geographical distribution of the plants and animals he had observed. He also summarized his ideas on the subject in 1859 and 1860, though some of the ideas were immediately eclipsed by arguments in Darwin's *Origin of Species*.[108]

Henry R. Schoolcraft (1793–1864) accompanied the 1820 expedition to the Great Lakes led by Governor Lewis Cass of Michigan, and in 1831 and 1832 he led expeditions of his own to the same general region. His *Narrative Journal of Travels...* of the Cass expedition can serve as a representative example of the exploration literature during the first half of the nineteenth century. He was particularly interested in stratigraphy and mineralogy, and his observations were strongest for those subjects. His observations on plants and animals appear to be reliable and useful, but they were mainly descriptive and not very detailed. For example, he characterized a sandy plain west of the Huron River as "covered principally with a growth of yellow pine. Among the shrubs and plants, the pyrola rotundifolia, or common winter green, is very abundant, and we here first noticed a creeping plant called *kinni-kinick* by the Indians, which is used as a substitute for tobacco." He was also alert for phenological changes:

On leaving Buffalo, on the 6th of May, the blossoms of the peach tree were not yet fully expanded, and the petals of the apple were just beginning to swell. On reaching Detroit, two days afterwards, the leaves of the peach blossom had fallen, and those of the apple had passed the heighth of their bloom. Gardening also, which had not commenced at Buffalo, we found finished at Detroit, and the half grown leaves of the beach, the maple, the common hickory, (juglans vulgaris), and the profusion of wild flowers on the commons, gave to the forests and to the fields the delightful appearance of spring. These facts will go farther in determining upon the differences of climate, than meteorological registers, which only indicate the state of the atmosphere, without noticing whether a corresponding effect is produced upon vegetation.[109]

While these observations were perceptive and useful, they can be considered at best as on a par with Kalm's, made seventy years earlier. Schoolcraft's later books on Indians undoubtedly did more for American literature by serving as a source of materials and inspiration for Longfellow's "Hiawatha" than his early exploration reports could do for ecology.[110]

A more ambitious effort was undertaken by Louis Agassiz (1807–73), the Swiss naturalist who came to America in 1846 and rose to a position of prominence in American science. Agassiz had come to know Humboldt in Paris in 1831 and 1832, and he was eager to follow Humboldt's example of undertaking a natural history exploration. He organized an expedition to Lake Superior for the summer of 1848, the members consisting of a few naturalists and other young "gentlemen." Although the expedition was afield for less than three months, and although Agassiz was handicapped by dogmatic and simple-minded ideas on biogeography that he owed to Georges Cuvier's influence rather than to Humboldt's, the resulting book is of ecological interest.

As a natural-history survey Agassiz'a book, *Lake Superior...* (1850), differs from previous efforts, such as Catesby's of the Carolinas or William Bartram's of Florida, in that it is more thorough because it is a joint effort of several authors of varying expertise. It also differs from the splendid survey of the natural history of New York State that James Elsworth Dekay supervised in the 1840's in that it is confined to a restricted, somewhat homogeneous region. The main emphasis in *Lake Superior* is placed upon an inventory of productions, with a catalogue of shells by Alpheus A. Gould, of birds by J. Elliot Cabot, of Coleoptera by John L. Leconte, and of Lepidoptera by Thaddeus William Harris and chapters by Agassiz on vegetation, fishes, reptiles, fossils, the lake basin, and geology. Cabot also wrote the introductory "Narrative of the Tour" but drew heavily upon materials from Agassiz in doing so. The narrative is more oriented toward plants and animals than Schoolcraft's, but it is not otherwise more ecologically notable. The book falls short of being an ecological survey of the Lake Superior region, but is a suggestive step toward such a survey.

The most interesting chapters for the history of ecology are not Agassiz's on fishes and reptiles—where his expertise lay—but rather his two chapters on vegetation. These chapters, more than anything else he wrote, show the benefit of Humboldt's influence. The first vegetation chapter discussed the environmental factors that seemed to influence the distribution of species. Unlike Humboldt, however, Agassiz did not believe that the known factors were sufficient to account for distributions, and therefore he also invoked a "Supreme Intelligence." The second vegetation chapter compared the vegetation of the northern shores of Lake Superior with that of his native Swiss Jura: "Making full allowance for the influence of the lake, and leaving out of consideration a small number of species peculiar to North America, there remains about Lake Superior a subalpine flora which is almost identical with that of Europe, with which it is here compared."[111]

The explanation for ecologically similar floras in different regions was lost upon Agassiz because he rejected Humboldt's suggestion of the possibility of historical migrations. In identifying the plants from the Lake Superior region, Agassiz obtained the assistance of Asa Gray (1810–88), the Harvard professor of botany who later became both his professional rival and his theoretical opponent concerning Darwin's theory of evolution. Gray had already become interested in the striking similarities between mountain plants in America and Japan. He was to explain these relationships successfully in the 1850's to 1870's by using the concepts of migration, competition, extinction, and evolution that had been developed in England by Charles Lyell, Charles Darwin, and

Joseph Dalton Hooker.[112] Gray thus took the first steps in America toward understanding ecological adaptation as dependent upon evolution by natural selection.

Climate and Plants, Animals, People

Climate and Germs. The theory of contagion arose in antiquity and was transmitted to Europe through a biblical discussion of leprosy and through discussions by several Roman authors. Among the Romans two possible categories of contagion were suggested. The atomic theory, preserved in Lucretius' *De Natura Rerum*, suggested infection by invisible seeds, while Varro, Vitruvius, Columella, and Palladius expressed fears of the poisons and stings of minute swamp animals.[113] During the Renaissance a number of physicians amplified the ancient speculations, most notably Girolamo Fracastoro. In *De Contagionibus* (1546) he presented cogent arguments supporting a theory of contagion by invisible seeds. He did not claim that all diseases are contagious or that contagious diseases arise only by contagion or that the agents of contagion are animate. In 1557, Jerome Cardan suggested that the agents of contagion are alive and reproduce as animals do.

In succeeding years the ideas of Fracastoro won more support than did those of Cardan. The theories of contagion and of the environmental origin of disease were generally viewed as complementary, not contradictory because the agents of contagion were thought to be inanimate. The small minority who supported the idea of *contagium vivum* were prone to wild speculations because they attempted to fit the theory to particular kinds of animals. Of the European authors defending *contagium vivum* before 1800, it will suffice to mention here only the Italian Giovanni Maria Lancisi, whose *De Noxiis Paludum Effluviis Eorumque Remediis* (1717) revived the ancient Roman idea that mosquitoes from the swamps might cause malaria. He did not pretend that he could prove this possibility, and his arguments won few adherents during the eighteenth century. Nevertheless, at the beginning of the nineteenth century some Americans developed an interest in this idea, and Samuel Latham Mitchill published a translation of Lancisi's speculations.[114]

The development of interest in *contagium vivum* in the first half of the nineteenth century can be related to an increasing awareness of parasitism in the plant and animal kingdoms. The first American to publish a defense of *contagium vivum* was Dr. John Crawford (1746–1813), an Irishman who emigrated in 1796 and settled in Baltimore. In 1800 he distinguished himself as one of the first two Americans to use the new Jenner cowpox vaccine. In 1807 and in 1809 he published in local periodicals his germ theory, based upon a presumed parallel between plant parasitism and disease. He gained no noticeable following.[115]

Among the other American physicians who either defended or seriously discussed the possibilities of *contagium vivum* during the next few decades, the most notable were Daniel Drake (1832 and 1850), Josiah Clark Nott (1848), and John Kearsley Mitchell (1849). Daniel Drake (1785–1854) was one of the leading middle western physicians of his time. He taught medicine in Ohio and Kentucky and published a constant stream of medical and other writings, many of them in a medical journal of which he was cofounder and coeditor. He began developing his ideas about pathogenic animalcules in 1832, when he observed an epidemic of cholera in Cincinnati. He thought that the animalcules might be mosquitoes or gnats whose eggs one either inhaled from the air or drank in water. This idea, not greatly different from the speculations of Kalm and Crawford, had the advantage of accounting for the fact that epidemics like cholera, malaria, and yellow fever were associated with wet places where those insects were found. This hypothesis could also account for the sudden spread of epidemics, since insects and other small animals reproduce rapidly.[116] Drake defended his hypothesis further in his *A Systematic Treatise, Historical, Etiological, and Practical, on the Principal Diseases of the Interior Valley of North America* (published in two volumes, 1850–54) which will be discussed in the next section.

Josiah Clark Nott (1804–73), from Columbia, South Carolina, received his medical degree from the University of Pennsylvania and settled in 1836 in Mobile. He soon became the leader of Alabama medicine and wrote extensively on both medicine and race. He argued the case for the animate propagation of yellow fever in the *New Orleans Medical and Surgical Journal* (March, 1848). He reasoned that some insect like the mosquito could best explain the propagation pattern of the disease and that the existence of plant parasites provides a model of possible similarity. A killing frost stops the disease and kills insects, but it should not stop miasmas. He felt sure that yellow fever was not transmitted from one person to another. Nott practiced medicine in New York City from 1868 to 1872. In 1870 a yellow fever epidemic broke out on Governor's Island. On that occasion he presented a report to the city board of health, in which he repeated his insect hypothesis. Since he did not believe that it was transmitted from one person to another, he saw no need to quarantine arriving ships.[117]

John Kearsley Mitchell (1793–1858) was a widely known and respected professor in the Jefferson Medical College in Philadelphia. He rejected the idea of infection by animalcules on the grounds of implausibility, for no poisonous animalcules were known. He found very plausible, however, the possibility that malaria and other epidemic fevers could be caused by fungi, and he developed at some length arguments supporting this hypothesis. He had got the idea in 1829, while contemplating the rapidity with which fungi can rot tree stumps, and, by the time he published his hypothesis in 1849, he could cite the known fungal diseases of corn rust, cattle hoof and horn rot, and muscardine of silk worms.[118]

Although the defense of *contagium vivum* in America can be correlated with an increasing awareness of parasitism, all the arguments were indirect, and until late in the century its defenders were a minority. Some of them defended the quarantine, and they were opposed by a free-trade anticontagion movement that followed in the footsteps of Rush and Webster. The anticontagionists did not deny that any diseases were contagious, but they placed primary emphasis upon the traditionally accepted causes of unfavorable weather, miasmas from swamps, and other sources of filth and decay.[119]

Medical Geography. The interest in correlations between weather and disease that had been so strong in the eighteenth century continued into the nineteenth century and only waned late in the century, when the European science of bacteriology began to exert an influence in America.

Constantin François Chasseboeuf, Comte de Volney (1757–1820) came to the United States in 1795 and traveled for three years through the country, making extensive notes on the rocks, minerals, fossils, physiography, geologic regions, climate, and diseases. He returned to France when a hostility toward Frenchmen arose, and he published his *Tableau du Climate et Sol des Etats Unis* in Paris in 1803. Charles Brockden Brown's English translation appeared in Philadelphia in 1804. The book is of interest for the history of ecology from various points of view, but here the focus will be upon Chapter 10, "Prevailing Diseases in the United States." In discussing the decay of teeth, he was influenced by the views of Kalm. In discussing consumption, intermittent fever, and yellow fever, he emphasized the environmental factors of sudden and violent changes of temperature and "pernicious exhalations" from swamps and from squalid low and wet areas, coupled with the hot, humid summer climate.[120] None of this was new, and it was a bit superficial, but it was related by the author of the leading study of the day on the American environment.

Early in the nineteenth century the correlations between environment and disease became the subject of a government investigation. Although it was rather modest in the amount of research that was involved, this investigation appears to be the first long-term scientific research carried out in America. On April 2, 1814, while the War of 1812 was in progress, Dr. James Tilton (1745–1822), physician and surgeon general of the United States Army, ordered all hospital surgeons to begin recording the weather at their posts. The first to comply was Dr. Benjamin Waterhouse. He had made history in 1800 by being first in America to use the Jenner cowpox in vaccinating against smallpox. He joined the army during the war, and in 1816 he made history less dramatically by submitting a meteorological journal to the surgeon general's office. In 1818, Dr. Joseph Lovell (1788–1836) was appointed surgeon general, and he had Tilton's order fully implemented, stating in his own directive that "the influence of weather and climate upon diseases, especially epidemics, is perfectly well known." His instructions were that "every surgeon should be furnished with a good thermometer, and, in addition to a diary of the weather, should note everything relative to the topography of his station, the climate, complaints prevalent in the vicinity, etc., that may tend to discover the causes of diseases, to the promotion of health, and the improvement of medical science."[121]

In 1826 the surgeon general's office published the first compilation of the evidence, for the years 1822 to 1825, and although it was not extensive enough to solve the mysteries of disease, the report did point out that the meteorological tables could serve, as time went by, to ascertain to what extent the climate changed as more and more land was being converted from forest to cultivation. Data from eighteen military posts were published.[122]

A similar compilation for the years 1826 to 1830 was published in 1840. Assistant Surgeon Samuel Forry (1811–44) compiled the official data and published his own summary accounts in 1841 and 1842. The army medical department had succeeded in obtaining the first statistical data on both climate and incidence of disease in America. Using this data, Forry could dramatically describe the wide ranges of temperature found in the country, with the moderating effects of the Great Lakes and the extremes that occurred from summer to winter in the inland regions away from large bodies of water. He also felt that he could demonstrate some correlations between climate and rates of disease, though admitting the subject was complex. Part of his caution was due to European demonstration that phthisis (tuberculosis) was not, as had been commonly supposed, caused by a changeable climate. Nevertheless, it seemed clear that a warm, dry atmosphere was therapeutic for those having the disease. It was also clear that malaria was much more prevalent in the southern than in the northern regions of the country. His statistics indicated that in many respects the Southwest was the unhealthiest region of the country. In 1840, however, the Southwest was not the presently understood region but the eastern river valleys of Texas.[123]

In retrospect it is clear that even if this was the greatest statistical study ever undertaken in America, the populations of army posts were not large enough to allow clear correlations to be drawn between diseases and climate. This was not understood by Surgeon General Thomas Lawson, however, who obtained a number of Daniell's hygrometers from Europe and also provided each military post with De Witt's conical rain gages. Forry resigned his commission in 1840, and in 1842 was replaced as meteorologist on the surgeon general's staff by James Pollard Espy (1785–1860), who was already a distinguished meteorologist. An interest continued in the correlation between climate and disease, but Espy's successes in meteorology were superior to the problematic results that were obtained from correlating these meteorological data with diseases at the army posts of America. Gradually meteorology became of more importance to the navy and other branches of the Department of War than to the surgeon general, and, although the original correlations were not quickly abandoned, they did decline in significance.[124]

Although some polarization occurred in the first half of the nineteenth century between the majority, the anticontagionist physicians, and the minority, the contagionists, both groups continued to regard as important the correlation of disease with environmental factors. Daniel Drake, an avowed contagionist from 1832, carried out the greatest investigation of this subject that had ever been made in either Europe or America.

Drake's family had migrated from New Jersey when he was a child, and he grew up in a log cabin at Mays-Lick, Kentucky. In December, 1800, at age fifteen, he went to Cincinnati to study medicine by apprenticeship. He fell in

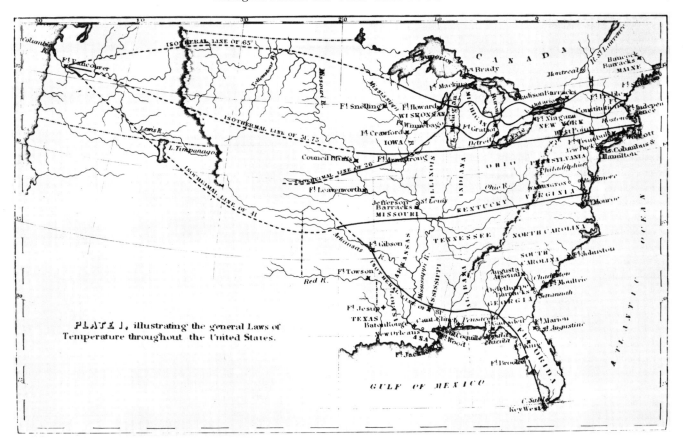

Samuel Forry's temperature map of the United States. From The Climate of the United States and Its Endemic Influences: Based Chiefly on the Records of the Medical Department and Adjutant General's Office, United States Army *(New York, J. & H. G. Langley, 1842.*

love with the town. In 1805 he attended the University of Pennsylvania, hearing the lectures of Rush and Barton. When he returned to Cincinnati, he sent Barton "Some Account of the Epidemic Diseases Which Prevail at Mays-Lick, in Kentucky."[125] This brief paper shows a faithful following of the advice given to physician observers in the Hippocratic *Airs, Waters, and Places.*

Three years later, in 1810, Drake merged his interests in medical geography and in Cincinnati in a sixty-page pamphlet *Notices Concerning Cincinnati.* This pamphlet, recently described as "an ecological survey of the Cincinnati area,"[126] began with accounts of the topography and geology. These were followed by an extensive account of the climate, including month-by-month comparisons of temperature in Cincinnati and Philadelphia, average diurnal variations in temperature, wind movement, precipitation, and frequency of different weather conditions, and a discussion of possible changes in climate between 1785 and 1810. The evidence was slight but seemed to indicate that the summers had remained constant while the winters had become colder. Drake included a "Calendarium Florae" for 1809, though he had also compiled similar observations for 1807 and 1808. Next he gave a brief account of the living conditions and

habits of the 2,320 Cincinnatians. The second half of the pamphlet was devoted to the diseases of the area, with the usual attention to the relation between climate and disease. His investigations were pursued with diligence but thus far with little originality.

Five years later, in 1815, he expanded the pamphlet into a 250-page book, *Natural and Statistical View, or Picture of Cincinnati and the Miami Country.* It was a good geographical monograph for the period and was well received. In discussing diseases, Drake continued to speak of "miasmata" and "marsh effluvia."[127] In 1832, however, his experience with a cholera epidemic convinced him that the cause of that disease was animate. He assembled evidence supporting his hypothesis and compared it with the miasmic theory in his book on cholera in 1832. He was to return to the subject with a stronger case in his greatest work, *A Systematic Treatise, Historical, Etiological, and Practical, on the Principal Diseases of the Interior Valley of North America, as They Appear in the Caucasian, African, Indian, and Esquimaux Varieties of Its Population.*[128]

In some respects this work is a vast extension of the earlier book, now encompassing the region of the Great Lakes and occasionally northward, south to the Gulf of Mexico, and from east Texas eastward along the major rivers to Quebec and Pittsburgh. He traveled this region for ten summers before publishing the first volume, and the second volume was published posthumously from his incomplete notes. *A Systematic Treatise* was more limited to medical geography than had been *Picture of Cincinnati*. He could not obtain detailed weather data for such a vast region, and so the climate was described in general terms and supplemented with data on mean, maximum, and minimum temperatures from the localities where those data had been collected. Nor could he provide phenological data for the area. He did, however, devote part of a chapter to the distributions of trees, mammals, and birds in relation to climate.[129]

Volume I was devoted mainly to detailed regional accounts of "medical topography." Drake's regions were mostly defined by river basins, and his attention was largely concentrated upon the likelihood that the terrain was conducive to fevers, mainly malaria. For example:

From Milwaukie to Racine, twenty-five miles, a belt of compact and lofty forest, nourished by the influences of the lake [Michigan], spreads to the distance of two or three miles into the country, beyond which, there are rolling prairies. The site of Racine, in N. Lat. 42° 50', is a part of this wooded plain, elevated from thirty to fifty feet above the lake. In rainy weather, small pools of water form on many parts of its surface. In digging wells, as Doctor Cary informed me, they pass through a bed of sandy loam, and then through a deposit of gravel, into another of blue clay, with pebbles, when pure but hard water is obtained. At the same level, springs burst out from the banks of Root River, which enters the lake, adjacent to the northern side of the town. The valley of this river, for two or three miles up, is about sixty rods in width, and not subject to inundation. Doctor Cary, who had resided in the place ten years, that is, from the beginning of its settlement, informed me, that for the first two years, there was scarcely a case of autumnal fever; in the next two, a number of cases occurred; and in the following year, 1839, it assumed a mild epidemic character, putting on an intermittent type, and proving fatal in a single instance only. The following year it was again epidemic. In both those years, the mouth of Root River was choked up with sand, and its waters rendered stagnant.[130]

Volume II Drake organized into five parts, reflecting his nosological understanding of fevers: autumnal (malaria), yellow, typhous, eruptive (smallpox, chicken pox, measles, scarlet fever, and so on), and phlogistic (meningitis, bronchitis, pneumonia, tuberculosis, and so on). He was interested (following in the Hippocratic tradition) not only in those diseases that were presumably caused by habits, food, and occupation. The demarkations of different diseases according to cause was not then, of course, clearly established. In investigating these diseases, he undertook ecological investigations as they seemed relevant. This was exemplified in his arguments for the animate origin of cholera and malaria.

Medical geography has continued to be an important subject, particularly in the tropics, but Drake's *A Systematic*

Treatise represented a high point for the subject in the United States. It remained definitive until rendered obsolete by the development of a definite germ theory of disease. When particular pathogens could be identified, then microbiologists studied the life cycles of the pathogens rather than the general environmental conditions. But, even so, an interest in "healthy climates" has persisted in America.[131]

Phenology. We have seen that the idea of recording the seasonal unfolding of biological phenomena was introduced into natural history by Linnaeus and Kalm in the mid-eighteenth century and that such records had been compiled in America by Jefferson, William Bartram, Williams, and Barton. The presumption was that these *calendaria florae*, as they were called even though records of animals were usually included, were useful to both farmers and naturalists. However, little by way of rationale for them appears to have been published before 1803. In that year Benjamin Smith Barton (1766–1815) discussed them in his *Elements of Botany . . .*, America's first textbook of botany. Barton, who taught botany and natural history at the University of Pennsylvania, briefly reviewed some of the *calendaria florae* that had been published, explained the kinds of data they should include, and described their various uses. While Linnaeus had sought to organize an ecological science around the balance-of-nature concept, Barton apparently believed that it could be done within the structure of *calendaria florae*:

Calendaria Florae, if they be properly kept, form some of the most interesting notices in the natural history of a country. They form, next to the living, the best, picture of the country. They show us, in the most beautiful and impressive manner, the relations of the vegetable and the animal kingdoms to each other, and to the various agents by which they are surrounded, and by which they are affected. They enable us to compare together the climates of different countries or places, which are included within nearly the same latitudes, such as Florida and Palestine, Philadelphia and Pekin, New-York and Rome.[132]

He went on to point out that if the spread of cultivation was changing the climate of America then the evidence should appear in changes in the timing of seasonal phenomena.

The urgings of Barton, along with the examples already published, led other naturalists to compile and publish *calendaria florae*. The one Daniel Drake published for Cincinnati in 1809 has already been mentioned. Barton's student, Jacob Bigelow (1787–1879), who became a prominent Boston physician and professor in Harvard Medical School, also took up the study. He published his data in a different format, however, placing notations on locale, habitat, and month of flowering in the account of each species listed in his *Florula Bostoniensis . . .* (first published in 1814 and twice revised). This was a useful reference work, but the information was not in a form conducive to theoretical conclusions. The desirability of coordinating phenological studies in different places throughout the country was mentioned to Bigelow by the Pennsylvania botanist Gotthilf Henry Ernst Muhlenberg (1753–1815), who may have been aware of

Williams' and Jefferson's interest in the project. Constantin François Chasseboeuf, Comte de Volney had also provided some data on times of blooming and harvests as he traveled in May from Annapolis across the Appalachians to Cincinnati.[133] Bigelow acted on Muhlenberg's suggestion, and in 1818 he published "Facts Serving to Show the Comparative Forwardness of the Spring Season in Different Parts of the United States."[134] This article was based upon replies received in 1817 from correspondents in Charleston, South Carolina; Richmond, Virginia; Louisville and Lexington, Kentucky; Baltimore, Maryland; Philadelphia, Pennsylvania; New York City; Albany, New York; Brunswick, Maine; Montreal, Quebec; and Geneva, Switzerland. All the data were published, and since the peach was reported from all but one location, the flowering dates of that tree were listed along with the latitude and longitude of the different locations. Temperature data were not included, but from the data given Bigelow concluded that "the difference of season between the northern and southern extremities of the country is not less than two months and a half. Difference of longitude does not seem very materially to affect the Floral Calendar within the United States."

Quite likely the floral calendars that Jacob Porter and Stephen W. Williams compiled for Plainfield and Deerfield, Massachusetts, were also prompted by Bigelow. Bigelow sent a copy of his paper to Thomas Jefferson, who responded appreciatively and sent a summary of his own phenological observations for a seven-year period.[135] It is also possible that Bigelow's paper may have alerted Schoolcraft to make his phenological observations, quoted above.

Shortly after Bigelow began to collect his data from different parts of the country, Josiah Meigs (1757–1822), commissioner of the General Land Office, petitioned Congress to authorize the keeping of meteorological records at the twenty land offices throughout the country and to provide the necessary instruments. Congress did not fulfill his request, but even without the legislative authority or instruments he had the forms printed for a meteorological register and on April 29, 1817, sent them to the land-office agents with a request that they record the temperature, wind, and weather three times a day and that they also record the following information:

1. The time of the unfolding of the leaves of plants.
2. The time of flowering.
3. The migration of birds, whether from the north or south, particularly swallows.
4. The migration of fishes, whether from or to the ocean.
5. The hybernation of other animals, the time of their going in winter quarters, etc.
6. The phenomenon of unusual rains and inundations.
7. The phenomenon of unusually severe droughts. The history of locusts and other insects in unusual numbers.
8. Remarkable effects of lightning.
9. Snowstorms, hailstorms, hurricanes, and tornadoes; their course, extent, and duration.
10. All facts concerning earthquakes and other subterranean changes.

11. Concerning epidemic and epizootic distempers.
12. The fall of stones or other bodies from the atmosphere; meteors, their apparent velocity, etc.
13. Discoveries relative to the antiquity of the country.
14. Memorable facts relative to the topography of the country.

Some of Meigs's returns were published, and no doubt more of them would have been had he not died in August, 1822.[136]

Although Congress was not yet ready to support the study of phenology beyond whatever was done in the surgeon general's office, additional institutional support appeared in 1825 from the Board of Regents of the State University of New York. It organized a state meteorological system by directing the faculty members to keep records of temperature, precipitation, winds, and other related phenomena, such as "the first appearance of flowers and leaves, the beginning of haying and harvesting, first autumnal frosts and snows, appearance and departure of birds of passage, first notice of fireflies, reptiles."[137] Annual abstracts of the returns were compiled for the Report of the Board of Regents by T. Romeyn Beck, principal of the Albany Academy. In 1855, Franklin B. Hough (1822–85) published the returns for 1826 through 1850.[138] One of the teachers under Beck at the Albany Academy was Joseph Henry, who became America's leading electrical scientist and in 1846 the first secretary of the Smithsonian Institution. Henry published in 1851 an appeal for the observation of periodical phenomena, and in 1864, Hough drew upon both New York State and Smithsonian data to publish "Observations Upon Periodical Phenomena in Plants and Animals from 1851 to 1859 . . . ."[139] This was an impressive body of data, but Hough did not attempt to draw conclusions from it—that was left to the reader.

Private individuals also continued to publish observations. Charles Peirce compiled monthly weather summaries for Philadelphia for fifty-seven years and published them, with a brief comparison with European winters, in 1847.[140]

Henry David Thoreau (1817–62) has been called the father of American phenology.[141] Although that claim has been refuted by Leo Stoller (and by the above discussion), it is true that Thoreau's phenological observations have attracted more attention in the twentieth century than those of anyone else. This is so mainly because his writings have a wide appeal and yet are somewhat enigmatic. He expressed hostility toward science at various times, but he made increasingly more and more of the kinds of observations that he disparaged. A number of capable authors have shed light upon this paradox. The interpretation followed here is by Nina Baym. She found the key to understanding Thoreau's attitude toward and interest in science as having been formed by a hope that he could unite science and Transcendentalism. He expressed hostility toward professional scientists because they were not also attempting to create this synthesis, and his hostility was reinforced by his frustration at not being able to achieve this synthesis himself. His attempted synthesis was quite largely within the realm of phenology, in which Baym sees the key to understanding his attitudes and beliefs concerning science.

It seems that Thoreau wanted to go further than Barton, creating not just an ecological science around phenology but a transcendental phenological ecology. Baym's thesis is too complex to be explained here in detail, but her explanation of the significance of this transcendental phenology for Thoreau should be expressed here in her words:

To study nature becomes the program of an action which achieves the reconciliation of man and God. The naturalist lives a saintly life because he must obey the laws he learns to know. . . .

The laws of the universe are a great rhythm, to which man at his most fulfilled moments marches. If a sense for this universal rhythm is implanted in the creature, he always moves with the music. Such a sense is instinct, possessed by animals and possibly by Indians. In most men, rhythm is not implanted, and there is substituted a capacity to learn the music. This substitution is man's curse and challenge; it is the sign that he has been expelled from the garden of Eden, but in true Miltonic fashion it is the sign that there is a peculiarly human, and therefore superior, way to regain it. The way back is through learning, which ultimately approaches instinct. When man has learned the music so thoroughly that he can anticipate it, when he knows what comes next, he will be able to keep time.

Thoreau devoted the rest of his life to learning nature well enough to "anticipate" her. In her cyclical organization he saw assurance that anticipation was possible, for in repetition lay the hope of learning, correcting, refining, and profiting from past error. Certain patterns obtruded immediately: the alternation of day and night, the succession of the seasons. These broad patterns could be quickly learned so that man might keep his life in some rough harmony, such that his ignorance did not destroy him. The next step was to sharpen perception and make out finer patterns and more precise regularities. Spring certainly follows winter, but when? This question subdivides—where, on what day, does the first crocus spring? When do the geese fly over Concord?[142]

To explain how Thoreau came to develop such a goal for his transcendental science would take us out of the history of American ecology and into the history of his psyche. However, both Stoller and Baym have uncovered some of the influences upon his phenological thoughts and the stages that these thoughts went through, and they can be mentioned. Thoreau attended Harvard while Bigelow was on the medical faculty, and Bigelow's *Florula Bostoniensis*, with its phenological data, was Thoreau's guide to the plants of the area. Also influential upon Thoreau's interest in seasonal observations was the *Book of the Seasons, or the Calendar of Nature* by the English druggist-chemist-poet-naturalist William Howitt (1792–1879). The book was published in 1831 and went through seven editions. Thoreau's manuscripts reveal an early acquaintance with this work, and he referred back to it throughout his life. Baym wrote, "Howitt is thinking of strictly practical uses for his tables, but his language is virtually identical to Thoreau's."[143]

The beginnings of Thoreau's scientific program can be found in his early essay "The Natural History of Massachusetts" (1842), in which phenological observations are pervasive:

In the autumn days, the creaking of crickets is heard at noon over all the land, and as in summer they are heard chiefly at night-fall, so then by their incessant chirp they usher in the evening of the year. Nor can all the vanities that vex the world alter one whit the measure that night has chosen. Every pulse-beat is in exact time with the cricket's chant.

In the same essay he also expressed some dissatisfaction with conventional science:

It is with science as with ethics, we cannot know truth by contrivance and method; the Baconian is as false as any other, and with all the helps of machinery and the arts, the most scientific will still be the healthiest and friendliest man, and possess a more perfect Indian wisdom.[144]

Thoreau seems to have thought that he could achieve the understanding he sought by patiently observing nature. He made many seasonal observations while living in his cabin at Walden Pond from July 4, 1845, to September 6, 1847. They were not systematic, however. As time went by, he seems to have felt that the deep insights he sought were eluding him, and he began to make systematic phenological notes in late 1851 or early 1852. In the spring of 1852 he wrote himself memoranda to "observe all kinds of coincidences, as what kinds of birds come [back from the south] with what flowers," and not to overlook the reptiles and frogs. He began a phenological chart to which he continued to add during succeeding years through the spring of 1858.[145] Wrote Baym:

But, reading the late journals and seeing what Thoreau finally did with the material he had collected for the calendar, one senses that Thoreau approached, if he did not accept, the realization that the task, as he had defined it, was impossible. Partly, he needed instruments and manuals to see what could be seen and know what he saw; partly, too, nature was simply not as regular as he had assumed.[146]

Nevertheless, his literary powers did not fail with his scientific program. Two of the last essays, "Autumn Tints" and "Wild Apples," published posthumously in 1863 by his sister, drew upon his store of phenological knowledge, and still later in the century H. G. O. Blake published extracts from Thoreau's journals arranged under the titles *Early Spring in Massachusetts* (1881), *Summer* (1884), *Winter* (1888), and *Autumn* (1892).

Thoreau's phenological observations thus continued to be published down to the time that the formal organization of ecology began to emerge. Where did phenology fit into the new science? Hardly at all. Phenology was one of the possibilities that naturalists seized as a basis for an ecological science, but it did not offer a rich enough program of investigation. Instead, therefore, ecology was founded upon phytogeography, limnology, and entomology. The secrets that eluded Thoreau were never discovered by anyone else.

Nature Appreciation and Conservation

An appreciation of the beauties of nature has been expressed in the literature of all peoples through the ages. One finds it in the exploration and natural-history literature on America from the beginning. Furthermore, Mark Catesby and any number of others who had illustrated America's plants, animals, and scenery had surely expressed through their art their appreciation for the beauty of nature. However, as a literary genre, one finds little nature writing in America before William Bartram's *Travels* (1791). Bartram and the romantic movement in Europe (inspired in part by his book) helped Americans develop a literature of nature appreciation in the nineteenth century. Bartram was also a talented artist and published some of his drawings of plants and animals in his *Travels*, others were included in Barton's *Elements of Botany* (1803), while still others have been published only in recent times.[147]

Prudence, in the early days of the Republic, was an insufficient motive for the preservation of resources because the resources seemed almost limitless. Game laws were passed in the seventeenth and eighteenth centuries to protect the deer, but there was little concern about the passing of the wolf, beaver, and buffalo from the Atlantic states because other forms of wildlife were still common. The conservation movement in America has always owed more to nature lovers than to economists. Both nature appreciation and conservation in America have their histories, and these movements will be discussed here primarily in relation to their encouragement of interest in ecological subjects.[148] Ecology is the obvious companion science to both movements.

Besides William Bartram, other eighteenth-century authors in America who were significant for influential writings expressing an appreciation of nature were St. Jean de Crèvecoeur (1735–1813), whose *Letters from an American Farmer* first appeared at London in 1782, and Philip Freneau (1752–1832), who began writing his nature poems in the 1780's.

Closer to ecological developments, however, was Alexander Wilson (1766–1813), a Scottish weaver-peddler-poet and defender of workers against oppression who found it expedient to immigrate to the United States in 1794. He developed an acquaintance with William Bartram in 1802, and under Bartram's encouragement and with access to his library, Wilson quickly developed an interest in American natural history, particularly the birds. His poetry was not stifled by this new interest. Wilson, in fact, attempted to synthesize his interests in poetry, natural history, and America in a grand epic poem, *The Foresters* (1809–10), which he also illustrated with his own drawings. His poetry was well appreciated by his contemporaries. Van Wyck Brooks observed that "Alexander Wilson's poems were continuously in print throughout the nineteenth century in Scotland, and there was no better poet in America during the years in which he lived and died here (1794–1813)."[149]

Wilson began to study American birds in earnest in 1803, and he soon began to draw them, assisted by Bartram and his niece, Nancy Bartram. Wilson found that his critical faculties, which previously had been used to write satiric verse, could also be used to collect natural histories. He also began writing poems about birds. There are in his nine-volume *American Ornithology* poems on the baltimore oriole, the blue bird, the hummingbird, the kingbird, the wood pewee, the bald eagle, and the osprey. He traveled through the states from Maine to Florida and west to the Mississippi collecting information on birds and simultaneously taking orders for his great work. *American Ornithology* contains Wilson's colored illustrations of all the birds he discussed, and it was the finest publication that had ever been produced in America. Much more than a catalogue of birds, its appeal lay not only in the high quality of Wilson's work and the attractiveness of the volumes but also in a national pride in the work and in the birds described. In several respects, such as his census in 1811 of nesting birds in Bartram's eight-acre garden, Wilson made pioneering contributions to ornithology.

Wilson consciously sought to instill a love of nature in his fellow Americans, but for those who did not respond to that appeal, he also argued for the preservation of birds on grounds of self-interest. In building these arguments, he had to investigate the ecological role of the species, as illustrated in his poem on the kingbird:

> *Yet, should the tear of pity nought avail,*
> *Let interest speak, let gratitude prevail;*
> *Kill not thy friend, who thy whole harvest shields,*
> *And sweeps ten thousand vermin from thy fields;*
> *Think how this dauntless bird, thy poultry's guard,*
> *Drove ev'ry Hawk and Eagle from thy yard;*
> *Watch'd round thy cattle as they fed, and slew*
> *The hungry black'ning swarms that round them flew;*
> *Some small return, some little right resign,*
> *And spare his life whose services are thine!*[150]

That Wilson succeeded in winning the hearts of many to the causes of bird study and preservation is evidenced by the fact that his *American Ornithology* went through nine editions in the nineteenth century.

Among those inspired by Wilson was John James Audubon (1785–1851), whose own interest in birds led to an ambition to outdo Wilson after they met at Louisville, Kentucky, in March, 1810. Although Audubon's drawings and life have become a useful symbol of conservation in the twentieth century, he himself hunted for sport as well as for specimens, and he did not develop the concern for preservation that had distinguished Wilson.

Wilson's message was clear and influential, but it was embedded within poems and natural history accounts. To become still more influential, the concern for the preservation of nature and wildlife needed philosophical elaboration. The elaboration first came from Ralph Waldo Emerson and Thoreau.

Ralph Waldo Emerson (1803–82), who in 1832 resigned from the ministry because of his doubts about Christianity, felt the need for a more comprehensive philosophy of man in nature than either Christianity or society could provide. In his lecture "The Uses of Natural History" (1833) he commented, "We feel that there is an occult relation between the very worm, the crawling scorpions, and man." No doubt this is more metaphysics than ecology, but it was evidently related to both. He was disturbed by Americans' unplanned exploitation of nature, and in 1839 he warned that "this invasion of Nature by Trade, with its Money, its Credit, its Steam, its Railroad, threatens to upset the balance of man, and establish a new, universal Monarchy more tyrannical than Babylon or Rome."[151]

Emerson's expression of a need for a new philosophy of man's relationship to nature was an important step, though couched in metaphysical language. His contact with nature was not close enough, however, for him to be able to do more than give general expression to the need. Thoreau had amused himself as a child by hunting and fishing, and although he gave up these activities as an adult, he exchanged them for that of a lifelong observer. He became friends with Emerson and was influenced by his thought, but without losing his own identity in the process.

Thoreau graduated from Harvard in 1837, with a moderate exposure to science. His interest in nature led him to read works of exploration, including those by Kalm, William Bartram, Humboldt, Schoolcraft, and Darwin. In his natural-history studies he consulted the standard references, including Bigelow's *Florula Bostoniensis* and Wilson's *American Ornithology*.[152] He was, however, discontent with the science he read. As a Transcendentalist he believed that feeling for nature and the interrelatedness between man and nature was mistakenly barred from science (if not barred by some of the above authors). His thoughts on this have been extensively discussed.[153] The discontent can be attributed largely to his insistence upon finding personal meaning in nature, but this does not seem to have been the only factor. He also demanded a science of interrelationships. Some of his ideas about that science can be surmised from the two books he published. In *A Week on the Concord and the Merrimack Rivers* (1849) he presented an essay on fishes, which included both man's impressions of the fishes and interactions with them. Among the more interesting of these accounts is this one:

The pickerel (Esox reticulatus), *the swiftest, wariest, and most ravenous of fishes, which Josselyn calls the fresh-water or river wolf, is very common in the shallow and weedy lagoons along the sides of the stream. It is a solemn, stately, reminant fish, lurking under the shadow of a pad at noon, with still, circumspect, voracious eye, motionless as a jewel set in water, or moving slowly along to take up its position, darting from time to time at such unlucky fish or frog or insect as comes within its range, and swallowing it at a gulp. I have caught one which had swallowed a brother pickerel half as large as itself, with the tail still visible in its mouth, while the head was already digested in its stomach. Sometimes a striped snake, bound to greener meadows across the stream, ends its undulatory progress in the same receptacle. They are so greedy and impetuous that they are frequently caught by being entangled in the line the moment it is cast.*[154]

The objective of the book is to convince us that nature has a valuable meaning for us—one much more of guidance than

of material gain. But nature's lessons can be learned only by attentive students.

The same message Thoreau presented, perhaps more forcibly, in *Walden, or Life in the Woods* (1854). The message he conveys effectively by a combination of exhortation and detailed observation. His technique can be illustrated by his two chapters on Walden Pond, which contain a blend of subjective description, narration of his activities, details on natural history, and philosophical comment—all conveyed in a very compelling style. As Thoreau leads us from a consideration of gardening to fishing, to scenery, to color of the pond's water, to a discussion of its bottom, its plants, animals, and man's use of the lake and its surrounding land, a sense of interrelationship is built up that is transcendental but also ecological. The ecological dimension is not merely a point of view; it also includes some precise details. Edward S. Deevey, Jr., has argued rightly that these two chapters constitute the first notable contribution to limnology from America.[155]

Besides tramping through the woods for the fun of it, Thoreau sometimes worked as a surveyor. His store of nature lore seems to have been respected locally, and sometimes while discussing the woodlots he surveyed he was asked "how it happened, that when a pine wood was cut down an oak one commonly sprang up, and *vice versa*." This question was well suited to his methods of observing nature, and after some time of patient observation and reading he wrote "The Succession of Forest Trees" (1860), a fine contribution to ecology. Kalm had discussed old-field succession and also the role of squirrels in planting acorns, and Thoreau mentioned William Bartram's observation, quoted in Wilson's *American Ornithology*, that the blue jay "is one of the most useful agents in the economy of nature, for disseminating forest trees, and other ruciferous and hard-seeded vegetables on which they feed." Thoreau felt, however, that he was the first to make a comprehensive study of the means by which forests were propagated. He rejected the spontaneous origin of trees and discussed the means by which the seeds of different species were disseminated—pines by wind, cherries by birds, and oaks and birches by squirrels. He then explained why pines are succeeded by oaks: young oaks can grow in the shade of pine trees, but young pines cannot; and why pines spring up when an oak forest is cut: young pines can grow in an open field, but young oaks grow best in shade.[156] The essay ended with some philosophical speculations, but it was not the end of Thoreau's thoughts on the matter. His journal for the same year shows that he had an interest in the practical application of his knowledge to forest management.[157] Were it not for his untimely death at age forty-five, he might have carried these studies further.

Thoreau's following has grown slowly but steadily, and although it appears to be stronger now than ever before, his influences upon nature appreciation, conservation, and ecological perspective in the nineteenth century were not negligible. More conventional approaches to the same issues were needed, however, if a science of ecology was to be developed to help Americans understand and manage their natural environment and resources.

335

George Perkins Marsh (1801–82) shared Thoreau's love of nature, but, as a lawyer-politician-diplomat, he undertook a more scholarly approach to the task of convincing Americans to conserve their natural resources. His approach demanded an ecological understanding of nature. He was a versatile and learned man who was successful at law but disliked it. He served Vermont in the United States House of Representatives from December, 1843, to June, 1849, and while there he began to express concern about the way Americans were mismanaging their resources.

In 1847 he described before the Agricultural Society of Rutland County the extent of the changes that Vermonters had wrought upon their surroundings. He was concerned about the erosion of soils and the increase of both droughts and floods that followed upon the careless destruction of forests, and he urged a concern for wise management of both forest and agricultural lands. In a letter to Asa Gray dated May 9, 1849, he outlined a proposal for a program of investigation and management of American lands. While serving as American ambassador to Turkey from 1849 to 1853, he became impressed by the long-range consequences of man's careless use of the land. Back in Vermont as railroad commissioner, he wrote a "devastating exposé of corporate irresponsibility and financial skulduggery." This was followed, in 1857, by his report, as fish commissioner, *On the Artificial Propagation of Fish*, in which he surveyed the impact of industry, agriculture, and forestry upon fisheries.[158]

In 1861, President Lincoln appointed Marsh ambassador to Italy, and he remained in that position until his death. He now had time for research and also opportunity to witness the effects of man's modifications of nature since antiquity. In 1860 he had decided to write a book about man's modification of nature, and in 1864 he published *Man and Nature; or, Physical Geography as Modified by Human Action*, which has been called "the fountainhead of the conservation movement" and "the most important and original American geographical work of the nineteenth century."[159] It also contains an elaborate account of the balance of nature and a discussion of man's upsetting of this balance. The first title Marsh proposed for the book was "Man the Disturber of Nature's Harmonies."[160]

Although Marsh wanted to make ecological studies a part of geography, like Linnaeus he saw the balance of nature as the organizing principle:

It was a narrow view of geography which confined that science to delineation of terrestrial surface and outline, and to description of the relative position and magnitude of land and water. In its improved form, it embraces not only the globe itself, but the living things which vegetate or move upon it, the varied influences they exert upon each other, the reciprocal action and reaction between them and the earth they inhabit. Even if the end of geographical studies were only to obtain a knowledge of the external forms of the mineral and fluid masses which constitute the globe, it would still be necessary to take into account the element of life; for every plant, every animal, is a geographical agency, man a destructive, vegetables, and even wild beasts, restorative powers.[161]

Marsh at one point cited Darwin's *Origin of Species*, but it is evident that he failed to appreciate Darwin's discussion of the extinction of species. This is not surprising, considering that Darwin himself failed to realize fully the implications of his own theory of evolution for the balance-of-nature concept. Darwin had, nevertheless, built a strong argument for the extinction of species through competition.[162] The reality of extinction had been accepted by most naturalists since around 1800. Marsh believed that man was the prime cause of extinctions, perhaps the sole cause.[163]

Marsh emphasized that man's impact upon nature was not confined to the direct elimination or diminution of the numbers of species. In the second chapter he discussed the effects of introduced species of plants and animals upon the economy of nature. In the third chapter he discussed the importance of forests for both man and nature and the effects of removal of forests upon the soil, climate, and rivers. In the fourth chapter he discussed the geography of marshes, lakes, and rivers, and in the fifth chapter, the sandy regions of America and Europe. The final chapter is concerned with the environmental impact of large projects, such as the Suez Canal, the draining of the Zuiderzee, and mining.

Man and Nature presented a compelling case for the development of an ecological science in relation to resource use. Marsh's message was widely read, for the book was an instant success, and was reprinted eight times, in 1865, 1867, 1869, 1871, 1874, 1885, 1898, and 1908. A number of changes were made for the 1874 edition, and the title was changed to *The Earth as Modified by Human Action*. There were also English and Italian editions.[164] Marsh also urged the support of ecological research when he was consulted in 1870 about the use of funds for the development of the University of California.[165] Marsh's book and a speech by Franklin B. Hough are credited with leading Congress to establish in 1873 the United States Forestry Commission and government forest reserves. The first forestry commissioner was Hough, who looked upon Marsh as the leader of the movement for forest conservation.[166]

The nature-appreciation and conservation movements continued to gain support in the remaining quarter of the nineteenth century, but these movements did not regularly produce ecological investigations as by-products of their concern. Stephen A. Forbes began studying the food of and interactions between species in the 1870's, and when the Division of Economic Ornithology and Mammalogy was added to the United States Department of Agriculture in 1886, it was charged with collecting such information. While doing so, however, it also carried out systematic eradication programs against rodents, coyotes, wolves, and hawks without having much quantitative information on their feeding and other habits.[167] The concern of mainstream conservationists for preserving certain species of fish and wildlife too quickly reached the desperate stage for reliance upon ecological studies. The buffalo, passenger pigeon, and Carolina parakeet had been descimated, and if other species were to be saved, it was necessary to concentrate upon obtaining legal restrictions to hunting, game preserves, and restocking programs. In the twentieth century all these programs would provide important motivation for ecological research, but when they began, there was a general conviction that good intentions, adequate funds, and common sense would make the programs work.[168]

One man who understood where good intentions without adequate knowledge could lead was John Wesley Powell (1834–1902). He spent his early years in Ohio, Wisconsin, and Illinois and then distinguished himself as a member of General Ulysses S. Grant's staff in the Civil War. He led expeditions sponsored by the Illinois State Natural History Society to the Rocky Mountains in 1867 and 1868. In 1869 he won national recognition by leading a party of ten men in four boats down the canyons of the Green and Colorado rivers, and his account of this adventure has been frequently reprinted ever since. In 1870, Congress established the Geographical and Geological Survey of the Rocky Mountain Region under Powell's supervision. He then directed the surveying and mapping of the designated region. In 1878 he published *Report on the Lands of the Arid Region of the United States*, the purpose of which was to explain the importance of matching land use with environmental conditions. He saw the settlers farming lands unfit for cultivation, and he hoped that disaster could be avoided by increasing the awareness of the conditions of the various arid lands in western America.

James S. Lippincott in 1864 had urged the importance of correlating crops with the temperature of the growing season in different regions of America. In the West, Powell urged a similar consideration for rainfall.[169] He also pointed out the interrelationship of these factors:

Primarily the growth of timber depends on climatic conditions—humidity and temperature. Where the temperature is higher, humidity must be greater, and where the temperature is lower, humidity may be less. These two conditions restrict the forests to the highlands. . . . of the two factors involved in the growth of timber, that of the degree of humidity is of the first importance; the degree of temperature affects the problem comparatively little.

He found that all western lands that might support forests did not, and this he attributed to fire:

The conditions under which these fires rage are climatic. Where the rainfall is great and extreme droughts are infrequent, forests grow without much interruption from fires; but between that degree of humidity necessary for their protection, and that smaller degree necessary to growth, all lands are swept bare by fire to an extent which steadily increases from the more humid to the more arid districts, until at last all forests are destroyed, though the humidity is still sufficient for their growth if immunity from fire were secured. The amount of mean annual rainfall necessary to the growth of forests if protected from fire is probably about the same as the amount necessary for agriculture without irrigation; at any rate it is somewhere from 20 to 24 inches.[170]

Powell was not the first to point to fire as an important environmental factor on the prairies. Caleb Atwater had argued against the idea in 1818, suggesting instead that prairies are

the remains of former lake bottoms. In response to his paper, R. W. Wells had countered with observations he had made in areas where fire had indeed destroyed forests and were replaced by grasslands.[171] Powell went further and attempted to determine with surveys the lands that could realistically be maintained under forests and those that could not. He also discussed the environmental requirements for pastureland.[172]

The Utah region was the heartland of the survey he had supervised, and he provided a summary of its lands and vegetative resources. Ecological notes are included, but only insofar as they were of practical value. For example: "*Pinus aristata* is of no commercial value, as it is much branched and spreading with limbs near the base; it grows on the crags at an altitude of from nine to eleven thousand feet."[173]

As Wallace Stegner, one of Powell's biographers, has observed, the importance of the report lies not so much in its contents or in its immediate impact, important though both of these were, but rather in the fact that the report was the beginning of Powell's sustained drive for the intelligent use of western lands based upon an understanding of the environments and the possibilities of plant and animal life within those environments.[174] Marsh had urged this procedure in a general discussion; Powell urged it from the vantage point of intimate knowledge.

Biological Control

The most important problem in applied ecology is the interaction between animal or plant parasites and agricultural plants. In the eighteenth century Leeuwenhoek, Réaumur, Linnaeus, Jefferson, and many others had discussed the possibilities of controlling insect pests through a greater knowledge of their life histories, and interest in this possibility steadily increased throughout the nineteenth century.[175] One can find parallel advances in phytopathology.[176] Attention here will be confined to only one aspect of this important and interesting story, that of biological control. This was the first area of ecological investigation in which American naturalists took the lead.

Agriculture was so important to the American economy that entomology inevitably became an important science. America imported many of its crops from Europe, and a suspicion developed that it might have imported insect pests as well. Kalm had written of having almost introduced accidentally the serious pest the "pease beetle" (pea weevil, *Bruchus pisorum*) into Sweden from America, and he also speculated about whether domestic flies, rats, mice, and other species were native to America or had been accidentally introduced from Europe.[177]

Since Alexander Wilson and others had emphasized the importance of birds as predators of insects, it was perhaps inevitable that someone would have the idea that the natural bird predators might better control European insects than American birds. Nicholas Pike in 1850 enlisted the assistance of others in Brooklyn for the purpose of introducing English sparrows (*Passer domesticus*) to combat geometrid caterpillars. The first effort was unsuccessful, but persistence led to success in 1853. On the basis of this achievement the federal government was persuaded in 1862 to provide financial assistance to a more comprehensive introduction of this bird, which has become far more conspicuous as a city resident than as a predator of agricultural insects.[178]

Asa Fitch (1809–79), state entomologist for New York, was not the first to speculate on the problem of introduced agricultural pests, but in his "Sixth Report on the Noxious and Other Insects of the State of New York" (1861) he went one theoretical step further than others had. While discussing the serious devastations caused by the spread of the European wheat midge (*Sitodiplosis mosellana*), he hypothesized that its spread in America was facilitated because its natural parasites had not also been imported. This idea had come to him during the disastrous harvest of 1854, and he had written for assistance to John Curtis, president of the London Entomological Society. Curtis read Fitch's letter to the society, but, not surprisingly, no one delivered the live parasites.[179]

Nevertheless, the idea did not disappear. Benjamin Dann Walsh (1808–69) was shortly thereafter to urge American government initiative in the importation of insect parasites. Walsh was born in Frome, England, and attended Cambridge University with Charles Darwin. In 1838 he married and emigrated to America, settling in Illinois. He had a casual interest in insects while in England, but it was only in the late 1850's that he began serious study of insect pests of agriculture. He was so effective in publicizing the dangers that the Illinois State Legislature in 1866–67 authorized the establishment of the post of state entomologist, to which he was appointed. He understood that Americans could not depend upon English altruism for the delivery of parasites of the wheat midge, and he urged the government to undertake the importation of its parasites. "But we should not stop here. The principle is of general application; and whenever a Noxious European Insect becomes accidentally domiciled among us, we should at once import the parasites and Cannibals that prey upon it at home."[180] Walsh did not persuade his state or any other to put this advice into practice, but neither was his message lost.

Charles Valentine Riley (1843–95), who was to become the second entomologist to the United States Department of Agriculture, received his professional training from Walsh. Riley also was from England and had an interest in insects before emigrating to Illinois. In 1868 with Walsh he founded the short-lived periodical *American Entomologist* and also, with Walsh's assistance, was appointed state entomologist to Missouri. Apparently Riley was the first person who actually distributed insect parasites from one locality to another. In 1870 he sent parasites of the weevil *Conotrachelus nenuphar* to various places in Missouri. In 1873 he did for France what the English had not bothered to do for Americans: he sent a predaceous mite, *Tyroglyphus phylloxerae*, to France to combat the *Phylloxera* grape-vine louse, which had been introduced accidentally into the French vineyards.[181] Although *Tyroglyphus* was not as effective in coltrolling *Phylloxera* as Riley had expected, he did not abandon the idea of transporting predatory insects to sites where their prey had accidentally been introduced.

He served as entomologist to the United States Department of Agriculture in 1878 and from 1881 to 1894. In 1883 he succeeded in arranging the importation from England of *Apanteles glomeratus* larvae to parasitize their natural host, the cabbage butterfly, *Pieris rapae*. These parasites were distributed in the District of Columbia, Missouri, Iowa, and Nebraska, where they became permanently established.[182]

The value of this technique for controlling insects was most conspicuously established, however, in the successful efforts against the cottony-cushion scale (*Icerya purchasi*), which had been introduced into California citrus groves about 1868. In 1887, Frazer Crawford wrote to Riley from Adelaide, Australia, reporting that *Icerya* was destroyed by a fly, now named *Cryptochaetum iceryae*. Riley did not take the claim seriously. Nevertheless, Crawford sent some of the flies to Waldemar G. Klee, California state inspector of fruit pests, who released them in 1888 in San Mateo County, where the species became established as an important predator of *Icerya*. Meanwhile, Riley sent Albert Koebele, an entomologist of the Department of Agriculture, to Australia, where he quickly discovered not only that *Icerya* was parasitized by *Cryptochaetum* but also that its eggs were eaten by the larvae of three other species of insects. Riley now became convinced that *Cryptochaetum* would provide the best control, and Koebele sent 12,000 of them to California. The most effective control, however, proved to be the Australian ladybird, *Vedalia (Rodolia cardinalis)*. The success of *Vedalia* in controlling the cottony-cushion scale was so dramatic that the state of California ever since has generously supported research in the biological control of insect pests.[183]

Concurrently with the rise of interest in the use of insect predators or parasites to control pest species was an even broader interest in using diseases to control insects. The idea was one aspect of the rise of the germ theory of disease, and two of the early pioneers of the germ theory, Agostino Bassi (1836) and Louis Pasteur (1874), were also early proponents of using pathogens against insects. In America the entomologist John Lawrence LeConte urged the development of this technique at the meeting of the American Association for the Advancement of Science in 1873. In 1879, Riley, J. H. Comstock, and J. H. Burns separately tested Herman A. Hagen's suggestion that yeast could infect and kill insects. Their results did not confirm it. In 1887, Stephen A. Forbes identified the fungal parasite *Beauveria globulifera* on the chinch bug (*Blissus leucopterus*), a serious cereal pest. The following year Otto Lugger in Minnesota attempted to infest these insects in the field with the disease, and F. H. Snow began to conduct investigations of the disease in Kansas. These studies continued for several years without definite success, but they did serve to publicize the possibility of this technique.[184]

The Emergence of the Ecological Sciences

Most ecological observations before 1900 fell in the domain of natural history, but this science was organized primarily according to the various groups of plants and animals, a system that was not optimal for theoretical developments. In 1749, Linnaeus had outlined an ecological science based upon the economy of nature, that is, the balance of nature; in 1803, Barton and around 1850, Thoreau had thought that phenology could provide the framework for one; and in 1864, Marsh had attempted to make room for ecological and conservation studies within the discipline of geography.

Ernst Haeckel (1834–1919), a noted German biologist, also realized the need for an ecological science, and in 1866, in his evolutionary treatise, *Generelle Morphologie der Organismen*, he coined the word *oekologie* for the science which he defined as "the whole science of the relations of the organism to the environment including, in a broad sense, all the 'conditions of existence.' These are partly organic, partly inorganic."[185] As a defender of Darwin's theory of evolution, Haeckel was in a better position to realize the theoretical implications for this science than were any of the pre-Darwinian exponents of an ecological science. The very structure and survival of species he understood to be tied to the relationships between organisms and their environments.

Walter Harding has shown (1965) that the prevalent belief that Thoreau used the word ecology in 1858 is incorrect. In his edition of Thoreau's correspondence (1958), the word geology in one letter was mistakenly read as ecology. J. S. Burdon-Sanderson (1893) and Stephen A. Forbes (1895) were the early expounders of the newly named science for British and American naturalists.[186]

During the second half of the nineteenth century four semidistinct ecological sciences began to develop as distinct from natural history. Listed in the chronological order of their self-conscious organization, they are oceanography, limnology, plant ecology, and animal ecology. A useful indicator of their formal organization is the earliest comprehensive treatises for each science. It is of interest to take note of the appearance of these treatises in relation to the development of the ecological sciences in America.

Oceanography. The English naturalist Edward Forbes (1815–54) in the 1840's made the first extensive studies on marine animals from the standpoint of their geographical distribution and environmental circumstances. He also wrote, before his early death, half of *The Natural History of European Seas,* which was completed by Robert Godwin-Austen (1859). Since Forbes's chapters discussed the animals and Godwin-Austen's chapters the physical features, the book as a whole constitutes the first general treatise on oceanography. Two of Forbes's papers on the stratification of coastal organisms (1843, 1844) were important for the concept of a biotic community, as was the study by the German zoologist Karl August Möbius (1825–1908) on oyster beds near Keil (1877). Haeckel was one of the early students of oceanic plankton (1862, 1890), and Victor Hensen (1835–1924), Möbius' colleague at the University of Keil, carried out important planktonic studies from 1870 to 1912.[187]

In America the first significant developments relating to biological oceanography came from Louis Agassiz. He carried out investigations on the Atlantic marine life of both North and South America, but more important for oceanography than his own discoveries was his role as teacher and organizer of the researches of his students and associates, including E. S. Morse, Alpheus Hyatt, B. Wilder, F. W. Putnam, Alpheus S. Packard, W. Strumpson, T. Lyman, H. J. Clark, A. E. Verrill, David Starr Jordan, and his son Alexander Agassiz. He organized a summer school on Penikese Island near Woods Hole, Massachusetts, in 1873. The school operated only two summers but provided the example for the ultimate establishment by Hyatt of the Marine Biological Laboratory at Woods Hole in 1888. Spenser F. Baird had already established the United States Bureau of Commercial Fisheries Laboratory at Woods Hole in 1885, having conducted research there since 1871.[188]

Limnology. The development of marine biology stimulated similar investigations in fresh water. German and Swiss naturalists were notable for leading the way, especially François Alphonse Forel (1841–1912). Kurt Lampert judged that Forel's "Introduction à l'étude de la faune profonde du lac Léman" (1869) was the beginning of scientific limnology. Forel's great three-volume *Le Léman, monographie limnologíque* (published between 1892 and 1904) was the first comprehensive monograph on the subject (in which he coined the word *limnologie*). He also published the first textbook on the subject.[189]

Thoreau's studies on Walden Pond in the 1840's and 1850's have already been cited as the first significant limnological work in America, but since he was not a professional naturalist or in complete sympathy with their work, he was not in a position to establish a new science.

Stephen A. Forbes (1844–1930), on the other hand, attained a very good position for furthering limnology and animal ecology. A native of Silver Creek, Illinois, he fought in the Civil War and afterward attended Rush Medical College in Chicago. He lacked both the funds and the motivation to complete a medical degree. He then taught school and studied at the Illinois State Normal University. In 1872, when Powell resigned as curator of the Museum of the State Natural History Society at Normal, Forbes was appointed to the position. He became an instructor in zoology at the university in 1875, director of the State Laboratory of Natural History in 1877, and state entomologist in 1882. He received a doctorate from Indiana University in 1884, when he also moved with the state laboratory to the University of Illinois at Urbana.

Forbes became interested simultaneously in the conservation of wildlife and the eradication of agricultural pests. Like most conservationists, he saw the wisdom of Alexander Wilson's argument that the birds of the fields did more good for the farmer by eating insects than harm from eating his crops, but as a professor of zoology and director of the State Laboratory of Natural History he could not rest content with plausible hypothetical arguments. He wanted to build a sound understanding of the situation based upon adequate data and their theoretical interpretation. The same was true for fish preservation. Many an alarmed conservationist insisted upon the need for fish hatcheries and stocking programs, but

Forbes was convinced that preservation required a basic understanding of fishery biology.

With this orientation much of his research concerned the food of insects, birds, and fish. The natural-history literature ever since Aristotle had contained this kind of information, but Forbes appears to have been the first to make it the basis of a systematic and sustained research program. Generalities were evidently no longer sufficient, anyway, because to the argument that birds eat harmful insects some skeptics replied that birds also eat parasitic and predaceous insects that might control the pest species. To combat this claim Forbes felt the need for both data and theory. The data he obtained from stomach contents from members of the species under investigation. The steady accumulation of this data over several decades finally enabled him to write an important book on the fishes of Illinois.[190]

In 1887 he used his studies on fish feeding and populations to state his ideas on the balance of nature in a well-known and often-reprinted paper, "The Lake as a Microcosm," which seems to have been the most detailed defense of a balance of nature concept within a Darwinian theoretical framework in the nineteenth century. It also represented another important step toward the biotic-community concept in ecology.[191]

Forbes persuaded the state legislature to establish under the Illinois Natural History Survey America's first river biological field station, at Havana, on the Illinois River. Charles A. Kofoid (1865–1947), who was from Illinois and had received his doctorate from Harvard University in 1894, was director of the station from 1895 to 1901, during which time he published pioneering papers on the plankton of rivers.[192]

In the 1890's limnology also became firmly established in Wisconsin, Michigan, Indiana, and Ohio, accompanied in each state by the establishment of a lake field station. The rise of limnology in these states around the Great Lakes must have been stimulated in part by the accomplishments of Forel and Forbes and their respective associates and in part by the importance of lake resources to the states.

Edward A. Birge (1851–1950) studied zoology at Harvard University and in 1876 became instructor in natural history at the University of Wisconsin. C. Dwight Marsh (1855–1932) studied at Amherst College and in 1883 became professor of natural science at Ripon College. In the 1890's both men began publishing studies on the plankton in Wisconsin lakes. In 1904, Birge began a long series of studies on the physical characteristics of Wisconsin lakes, in which studies he was joined by Chancey Juday (1871–1944) beginning in 1908. Jacob E. Reighard (1861–1942) joined the University of Michigan faculty in 1886 and became chairman of the Department of Zoology in 1892. He worked closely with the Michigan Fish Commission and directed for it an extensive investigation in 1893 and 1894 of Lake St. Clair as an ecosystem. In 1900 he recommended that the university establish a biological station, which it did at Douglas Lake in 1909, naming him as director. In 1895, Carl H. Eigenmann (1863–1927) established a biological station for Indiana University on Lake Wawasee, and the following year

David S. Kellicot established one for Ohio State University at the State Fish Hatchery on Lake Erie.[193]

Plant Ecology. Plant ecology developed into a formal science in northern Europe. It was an outgrowth of plant geography, continuing directly in the tradition established by Linnaeus, Humboldt, and Auguste Pyramus de Candolle, even utilizing at the end of the century the organization of the science established by De Candolle in 1820. The crucial works for this transition from plant geography to plant ecology were *Handbuch der Pflanzengeographie* (Stuttgart, 1890), by Oskar Drude (1852–1933), and *Plantesamfundgrundträk af den Okologiska Plantegeogre fi,* by J. Eugen B. Warming (1841–1924), (Copenhagen, 1895; German translation, 1896; English revised translation, 1909). *Pflanzengeographie auf physiologischen Grundlage,* (Jena, 1898; English translation, 1903) by Andreas W. F. Schimper (1856–1901), was also an important work in this tradition, but by the time it appeared, Americans were already busy with plant-ecology studies of their own.[194]

Some Americans were already producing similar works even before Drude's *Handbuch* appeared, because phytogeography was useful in the ongoing surveys of the plants of different regions of the country. Of particular interest in this respect is the work of John Merle Coulter (1851–1928), who grew up in Hanover, Indiana, receiving from its college his bachelor's and master's degrees and his doctorate from Indiana University. He was botanist to F. V. Hayden's geological survey of the Yellowstone country in 1872, and in 1874 he helped write *Synopsis of the Flora of Colorado.* In 1881 he was one of three authors of *Plants of Indiana,* which discussed the plants in terms of the river valleys, lake borders, prairies, and barrens. He became one of the first teachers of ecology in America.[195]

Charles Edwin Bessey (1845–1915) was from Ohio and graduated from Michigan Agricultural College in 1869. He taught botany and horticulture at Iowa Agricultural College and in 1884 accepted a professorship at the University of Nebraska. His main efforts were devoted to teaching botany, writing textbooks, and making investigations in plant phylogeny. He was also the first botanist in America to train plant ecologists. Among his students those noted for ecological studies were Conway MacMillan, Roscoe Pound, and Frederic E. Clements.[196]

Conway MacMillan (1867–1929) was born in Hillsdale, Michigan, and received his bachelor's and master's degrees from the University of Nebraska in 1885 and 1886. In 1887 he became an instructor in botany and later professor at the University of Minnesota. His *Metaspermae of the Minnesota Valley* (1892) contains a capable ecological survey of the plants of the region, following the phytogeographical tradition of Drude and other German botanists.[197]

Roscoe Pound (1870–1964), the son of a Nebraska judge, was almost lured away from his eminent career in law by the new science. He received his bachelor's, master's, and doctoral degrees from the University of Nebraska in 1888, 1889, and 1897 and also studied law at Harvard University in 1889 and 1890. He was admitted to the Nebraska bar in 1890.

Having studied botany under Bessey, he became, while a graduate student, director of the botanical survey of Nebraska. Frederic E. Clements (1874–1945) received his bachelor's, master's and doctoral degrees from Nebraska in 1894, 1896, and 1898. He also participated in the survey and published with Pound *Phytogeography of Nebraska* (1898). This was an early notable contribution to plant ecology in America, and it marked the beginning of Clements' career as one of the leading ecologists of the early twentieth century.[198]

Meanwhile, in 1896, Coulter had become head of the Department of Botany at the new University of Chicago. Warming's text convinced him of the importance of plant ecology, and he encouraged one of his students, Henry Chandler Cowles (1869–1933) to undertake doctoral research in the subject. Cowles was from Kensington, Connecticut, and had graduated from Oberlin College before going to the University of Chicago. He wrote his dissertation on the vegetative communities on the sand dunes of southern Lake Michigan, and he published a series of influential papers on the subject (1899–1901). Both Clements and Cowles did pioneering work on the description and dynamics of succession in plant communities. Cowles joined the University of Chicago faculty and was a prominent ecology professor during the first four decades of the twentieth century.[199]

Some young American botanists adopted the new perspective on their own. One of the first to do so was William Francis Ganong (1864–1944), of St. John, New Brunswick. He received his bachelor and master's degrees from the University of New Brunswick, and was at Harvard University, from 1887 until 1891, when he went to the University of Munich for his doctorate (1894). His paper "On Raised Peat-Bogs in New Brunswick" (1891) is not profound, but it does show his ecological orientation before he went to Munich and before he could have read Drude's *Handbuch*.[200]

Another who apparently developed an ecological interest on his own was John W. Harshberger (1869–1929), a lifelong resident of Philadelphia. He received his bachelor's and doctoral degrees from the University of Pennsylvania and then taught biology there throughout his career. His doctoral dissertation (1893) was a botanical and economic study of maize, but he became interested in the new science and soon published "An Ecological Study of the New Jersey Strand Flora" (1900–1902) and "An Ecological Study of the Flora of the Mountainous North Carolina" (1903). He continued throughout his career to conduct studies in both agricultural botany and plant ecology.[201]

Animal Ecology. Animal ecology was built partly upon limnology and plant ecology and partly upon pure and applied zoology. The diversity of its early years is nicely illustrated by the topical bibliographies in Charles C. Adams' *Guide to the Study of Animal Ecology* (New York, 1913). The German zoologist Karl G. Semper (1832–93) published the earliest comprehensive account of animal ecology—his Lowell Institute Lectures, *Animal Life as Affected by the Natural Conditions of Existence* (New York and London, 1881). He had become interested in animal geography and ecology during a research trip to the Philippine Islands.

Semper's book does not appear to have stimulated anyone in America to commence studies in animal ecology comparable to the influence that Forel's limnological writings and Drude and Warming's plant-ecology writings apparently exerted. America's leading investigator in animal ecology at that time was undoubtedly Stephen A. Forbes, who acknowledged a debt to Herbert Spencer's *Principles of Biology* (1867) in the formation of his own balance-of-nature concept,[202] but his ecological orientation appears to have developed out of the kinds of problems that seemed important to an economic zoologist rather than from the influence of programatic writings by others.

Since no single pattern is detectable in the animal-ecology studies of the 1880's and 1890's, a brief survey of different kinds of studies is the best way to indicate the ways in which the science was developing in America. Probably the commonest ecological observations were still being recorded in natural-history studies, which were too numerous to be cited here individually. Forbes set an example for others on food studies, and Ralph Dexter's survey of such studies in northeastern Ohio from 1879 to 1899 is probably representative of the observations being published. Few of these reports could equal the high standards of Forbes and Riley, but an exception was Leland O. Howard's study on the parasites of the white-masked tussock moth (1897). Howard (1857–1950) studied entomology under J. H. Comstock at Cornell and then served as Riley's assistant in the Division of Insects of the United States Department of Agriculture. Upon Riley's resignation in 1894, Howard succeeded him as head of the division, and in the twentieth century Howard became one of America's leading entomologists, particularly in the study of insects in relation to disease.[203]

The advance of natural-history studies of invertebrates, the germ theory of disease, and parasitism eventually led to an understanding of the role of insects and other invertebrates as vectors of certain diseases. Patrick Manson discovered in 1878 that filariasis is caused by the worm *Wuchereria bancrofti* transmitted to man by the mosquito *Culex fatigans*. In 1893 two physicians of the United States Bureau of Animal Industry, Theobald Smith and F. L. Kilbourne, demonstrated that Texas cattle fever is caused by a protozoan, *Babesia bigemina*, which is transmitted by the tick *Boöphilus annulatus*. The work of Ronald Ross on malaria and Walter Reed on yellow fever followed in 1897 and 1900.[204] Although these studies often were viewed as within the providence of medicine or parasitology rather than of animal ecology, the demand for eradicating vector species would often lead to a demand for ecological investigation.

Darwin's theory of evolution provided an important stimulus for ecological investigation. Examples of this stimulus in American animal ecology are Alpheus S. Packard's monograph "The Cave Fauna of North America" (1888), studies on protective coloration by Abbott H. Thayer (1896) and Sylvester D. Judd (1898), and John A. Ryder's theoretical paper "A Geometrical Representation of the Relative Intensity of the Conflict between Organisms" (1892).[205] Darwin's influence is also indirectly evident in many other studies. The direct stimulus for American insect-pollination studies came largely from Hermann Müller's *Die Befruchtung der Blumen durch Insekten* (1873, English translation, 1883). George Valentine Riley (1892) and William Trelease (1893) published notable studies on the pollination of yucca by the yucca moth. Charles Robertson published "Flowers and Insects: Contributions to an Account of the Ecological Relations of the Entomophilous Flora and the Anthophilous Insect Fauna of the Neighborhood of Carlinville, Illinois" in 1897, and John Harvey Lovell began in the same year to study the fertilization of flowers and the color preferences of insect pollinators.[206]

The applied ecological investigations by Bashford Dean on the oyster (1890) and by Charles T. Simpson on "The Pearly Fresh-Water Mussels of the United States; Their Habits, Enemies, and Diseases; with Suggestions for Their Protection" (1898) were undoubtedly inspired by Möbius' study, as well as by the practical needs of the fisheries.[207]

C. Hart Merriam (1855–1942), who in 1888 became the first head of the Division of Economic Ornithology and Mammalogy of the United States Department of Agriculture, had a strong interest in the geographical ranges of American birds and mammals, and he and his field naturalists gathered larger amounts and more precise data on the distributions and habits of American mammals than had ever before been collected. This information was mostly published in a series of reports, beginning in 1890, entitled *North American Fauna*. In 1889 he led an expedition to the San Francisco Mountains, near the Grand Canyon in Arizona, to study the relation between temperature and geographical distribution. Since childhood he had had some awareness of Humboldt's work and an interest in this question. The data he and his associates collected on the distribution of plants and animals at different elevations enabled him to describe a series of "life zones," each of which contained characteristic species. He published these results in 1890 and attempted through the 1890's to establish the general application of his life zones for all of North America. Ever since, some naturalists in the mountainous West have found his life zones of practical convenience. Close scutiny by others, however, showed that the theoretical foundations of his scheme were never well established and cannot be sustained. Nor did his life zones have even practical utility farther eastward and northward.[208]

One of the unique American ecological studies in the nineteenth century was Murray G. Motter's "Study of the Fauna of the Grave" (1898). He examined 150 bodies that were disinterred at different stages of decomposition to determine the different species of saprophytic organisms associated with each stage. Perhaps this was a definitive study, since ecologists in the twentieth century seem not to have felt it necessary to continue this line of research.

CONCLUSIONS

This survey shows that throughout American history naturalists and others have had an interest in ecological questions. As is characteristic of a poorly organized science, many of the important questions came from without science rather than from within. This survey leads to the question why ecology was not formally organized earlier than it was, particularly in light of the suggestions for such a science from Linnaeus, Barton, and Marsh. Even after Haeckel's formal definition of it in 1866, more than two decades went by before there was a good response. Presumably naturalists found descriptive natural history—an inventory of the world—of higher priority and easier to carry out than most ecological investigations would have been. Second, the importance of ecology to the world lies in its value for resource management, and America was prodigal of its resources until they began to become scarce. Wilson, Thoreau, and Marsh were voices crying in the wilderness, and the value of ecological research depended to some extent upon how many Americans could hear them. Furthermore, the germ theory of disease undermined the medical importance of environmental studies, and, although a few people became concerned about the health hazards of pollution even in the nineteenth century, this concern was not substantial enough to raise the importance of ecology.[209] Only at the end of the century with the trend toward formal organization did ecological knowledge become well organized from a theoretical standpoint. Even so, the science was mainly descriptive rather than theoretical.

Nevertheless, Darwin's theory of evolution, the practical needs of agriculture and wildlife management, and the progress of natural history all led to the establishment of four ecological sciences—oceanography, limnology, plant ecology, and animal ecology—during the second half of the nineteenth century. Before 1900 American naturalists had already taken the lead in biological control of insect pests, and the investigation of ecological questions was already so diverse and competent that Americans were competing well with Europeans in advancing ecological understanding.

NOTES

1. Thomas S. Kuhn, *The Structure of Scientific Revolutions* (Chicago, University of Chicago Press, 1962), Chaps. 2–4.

2. Howard Mumford Jones, *O Strange New World: American Culture: The Formative Years* (New York, Viking Press, 1964), Chap. 1.

3. Raymond Phineas Stearns, *Science in the British Colonies of America* (Urbana, University of Illinois Press, 1970), 4. Hereafter cited as *Science.*

4. Thomas Harriot, *A Briefe and True Report of the New Found Land of Virginia, of the Commodities and of the Nature and Manners of the Naturall Inhabitants . . .* (Frankfurt am Main, Theodor de Bry, 1590), 31. Stearns, *Science,* 68–71.

5. John Smith, *The Generall Historie of Virginia, New-England, and the Summer Isles . . .* (London, Michael Sparkes, 1624), 25. On Massachusetts see *ibid.,* 209ff.; Stearns, *Science,* 71–74.

6. John Josselyn, *New Englands Rarities Discovered: in Birds, Beasts, Fishes, Serpents, and Plants of that Country. Together with the Physical and Chyrurgical Remedies wherewith the Natives Constantly Use to Cure Their Distempers, Wounds, and Sores . . .* (London, G. Widdowes, 1672), 43; Stearns, *Science,* 139–50.

7. Louis Armand de Lom d'Avce, Baron de Lahontan, *New Voyages to North-America . . .,* (tr. anon., 2 vols., London, H. Bonwicke, 1703); cited from reprint ed. (ed. by Reuben Gold Thwaites, 2 vols., Chicago, A. C. McClurg, 1905), I, 319–20. The first French edition (3 vols.) also appeared in 1703.

8. John Lawson, *A New Voyage to Carolina* (ed. by Hugh Talmage Lefler, Chapel Hill, University of North Carolina Press, 1967), 74, hereafter cited as *A New Voyage;* Stearns, *Science,* 305–15.

9. Lawson, *A New Voyage,* 93–94.

10. For the identification of Catesby's birds and plants see W. L. McAtee, "The North American Birds of Mark Catesby and Eleazar Albin," *J. Soc. for the Bibliog. Nat. Hist.,* Vol. 3 (January, 1957), 177–94; Frans A. Stafleu, *Taxonomic Literature: A Selective Guide to Botanical Publications with Dates, Commentaries and Types* (Utrecht, International Bureau for Plant Taxonomy and Nomenclature, 1967), 78–79; George Frederick Frick and Raymond Phineas Stearns, *Mark Catesby: The Colonial Audubon* (Urbana, University of Illinois Press, 1961), Chap. 6.

11. Mark Catesby, *The Natural History of Carolina, Florida and the Bahama Islands: Containing the Figures of Birds, Beasts, Fishes, Serpents, Insects, and Plants: Particularly, the Forest-Trees, Shrubs, and Other Plants, Not Hitherto Described, or Very Incorrectly Figured by Authors . . .* (2 vols., London, Author, 1731–43), I, ii, hereafter cited as *Natural History.*

12. *Ibid.,* iii–iv.

13. *Ibid.;* v; Frick and Stearns (*Mark Catesby,* 29) judge that he did not reach the mountains.

14. Catesby, *Natural History,* I, xxi.

15. George Basalla, "The Spread of Western Science," *Science,* Vol. 156 (May 5, 1967), 611–22. For material to illustrate his model, see Stearns, *Science,* and Brooke Hindle, *The Pursuit of Science in Revolutionary America, 1735–1789* (Chapel Hill, University of North Carolina Press, 1956), hereafter cited as *The Pursuit of Science.*

16. John Bartram, *Observations on the Inhabitants, Climate, Soil, Rivers, Productions, Animals, and Other Matters Worthy of Notice . . . in Travels from Pensilvania to Onondago, Oswego and the Lake Ontario . . .* (London, J. Whiston and B. White, 1751); Stearns, *Science,* 575–93; Ernest P. Earnest, *John and William Bartram: Botanists and Explorers* (Philadelphia, University of Pennsylvania Press, 1940), hereafter cited as *John and William Bartram.*

17. John Bartram, *Diary of a Journey Through the Carolinas, Georgia, and Florida from July 1, 1765 to April 10, 1766* (ed. by Francis Harper, American Philosophical Society Transactions, Vol. 33, Pt. 1 [Dec. 1942]), 37, hereafter cited as *Diary.* The quotation, December 27, 1765, is from a portion of the *Diary* first published in 1769.

18. Pehr Kalm, *Travels into North America; Containing Its Natural History, and a Circumstantial Account of Its Plantations and Agriculture* (trans. by John Reinhold Forster (3 vols., Warrington, William Eyres, 1770–71), III, iii–iv, hereafter cited as *Travels.* For Kalm's negative judgments see II, 194–95, 262–63; III, 7, 135. Adolph B. Benson edited a revised edition of Kalm's *Travels* (2 vols., 1937; New York, Dover, 1964), which contains important additions; however, all citations in this paper are from the first English edition. Carl Skottsberg, "Pehr Kalm, Levnadsteckning," *Levnadsteckningar över Kungl. Svenska Vetenskapsakademiens Ledamöter,* Vol. VIII, No. 139 (1951), 221–504.

19. For his general estimate of Bartram, which is favorable, see Kalm, *Travels,* I, 112–14.

20. *Ibid.,* 65–66.

21. *Ibid.,* 75.

22. *Ibid.,* 162.

23. *Ibid.,* II, 90.

24. *Ibid.,* I, 142–43.

25. *Ibid.,* 311–20.

26. John Livingston Lowes, *The Road to Xanadu: A Study in the Ways of the Imagination* (Boston, Houghton Mifflin, 1927). Nathan B. Fagin, *William Bartram: Interpreter of the American Landscape* (Baltimore, Johns Hopkins Press, 1933), Part 3.

27. William Bartram, *Travels Through North & South Carolina, Georgia, East & West Florida, the Cherokee Country, the Extensive Territories of the Muscogulges, or Creek Confederacy, and the Country of the Chactaws; containing an Account of the Soil and Natural Productions of Those Regions . . .* (Philadelphia, James Johnson, 1791), 7–8, hereafter cited as *Travels.* The authoritative reprint, with commentary, is by Francis Harper (ed.), *The Travels of William Bartram, Naturalist's Edition* (New Haven, Yale University Press, 1958), 4–5. See also Earnest, *John and William Bartram;* Fagin, *William Bartram,* Parts 1, 2.

28. Bartram, *Travels* (1st ed.), xxvii–xxxi; (Harper ed.), lviii–lix.

29. *Ibid.* (1st ed.), 118; (Harper ed.), 75.

30. *Ibid.* (1st ed.), 8; (Harper ed.), 5.

31. *Airs, Waters, and Places,* in *Hippocrates* (trans. by W. H. S. Jones, Cambridge, Mass., Harvard University Press, 1923), I, 71.

32. William E. Knowles Middleton, *The History of the Barometer* (Baltimore, Johns Hopkins Press, 1964); William E. Knowles Middleton, *A History of the Thermometer and Its Use in Meteorology* (Baltimore, Johns Hopkins Press, 1966); William E. Knowles Middleton, *Invention of the Meteorological Instruments* (Baltimore, Johns Hopkins Press, 1969).

33. Genevieve Miller, "'Airs, Waters, and Places' in History," *J. Hist. Med. and Allied Sciences,* Vol. XVII (1962), 129–40; Kenneth Dewhurst, *Dr. Thomas Sydenham (1624–1689)* (Berkeley and Los Angeles, University of California Press, 1966), 65–67; Gordon Manley, "The Weather and Diseases; Some 18th Century Contributions to Observational Meteorology," *Notes and Records of the Roy. Soc. London,* Vol. IX (1952), 300–307; James H. Cassedy, "Meteorology and Medicine in Colonial America: Beginnings of the Experimental Approach," *J. Hist. Med. and Allied Sciences,* Vol. XXIV (1969), 193–204, especially 194–96, hereafter cited as "Meteorology and Medicine."

34. John Clayton, "A Letter from Mr. John Clayton Rector of Crofton at Wakefield in Yorkshire to the Royal Society, May 12, 1688, giving an Account of several Observables in Virginia, and in his Voyage thither, more particularly concerning the Air," *Phil. Trans. Roy. Soc. London,* Vol. XVII (1693), 781–89; reprinted in Edmund Berkeley and Dorothy Smith Berkeley (eds.), *The Reverend John Clayton, a Parson with a Scientific Mind: His Scientific Writings and Other Related Papers, Edited, with a Short Biographical Sketch* (Charlottesville, University Press of Virginia, 1965), 45, hereafter cited as "Concerning the Air," *Clayton;* Stearns, *Science,* 183–95.

35. Cadwallader Colden, "An Account of the Climate and Diseases of New-York," *Amer. Med. and Philos. Register,* Vol. I (1811), 304–10; Saul Jarcho, "Cadwallader Colden as a Student of Infectious Disease," *Bull. Hist. Med.,* Vol. XXIX (1955), 99–115, especially 102, hereafter cited as "Colden as a Student." Colden had discussed the nature of smallpox and other diseases in 1716–19 in letters published by Saul Jarcho, "The Correspondence of Cadwallader Colden and Hugh Graham on Infectious Fevers," *Bull. Hist. Med.,* Vol. XXX (1956), 195–211. See also Hindle, *The Pursuit of Science,* 39–48 et passim; Stearns, *Science,* pp. 559–75; Cassedy, "Meteorology and Medicine," *J. Hist. Med. and Allied Sciences,* Vol. XXIV (1969), 197–98.

36. First published anonymously in *New-York Weekly Postboy,* December 26, 1743–January 9, 1744; reprinted in *Amer. Med. and Philos. Register,* Vol. I (1811), 310–30. Jarcho, in "Colden as a Student" (*Bull. Hist. Med.,* Vol. XXIX [1955], 102–103), observed that about half of this essay was paraphrased from Giovanni Maria Lancisi's *De Noxiis Paludum Effluviis* (1717).

37. Letter to Dr. John Mitchell, Urbanna, Va., November 7, 1745, Jarcho, "Colden as a Student," *Bull. Hist. Med.,* Vol. XXIX (1955), 105.

38. James Thomas Flexner, *Doctors on Horseback: Pioneers of American Medicine* (New York, Viking, 1937; Dover reprint, 1968), 93–94.

39. "Extract of a Letter from Cadwallader Colden, Esq., to Dr. Fothergill concerning the Throat Distemper, Oct. 1, 1753," *Med. Observations and Inquiries,* Vol. I (1757), 211–29. Jarcho, "Colden as a Student," *Bull. Hist. Med.,* Vol. XXIX (1955), 106–109.

40. [Cadwallader Colden], "The Cure of Cancers. From an Eminent Physician at New-York," *Gentleman's Magazine,* Vol. XXI (1751), 305–308; on scurvy see letters to Dr. John Mitchell (ca. 1745) and Pehr Kalm (1751), Urbanna, Va., Jarcho, "Colden as a Student," *Bull. Hist. Med.,* Vol. XXIX (1955), 109–10.

41. John Lining, "Extracts of Two Letters . . . giving an Account of Statical Experiments made several times in a Day upon himself, for one whole Year, accompanied with Meteorological Observations; to which are subjoined Six General Tables, deduced from the whole Year's Course," *Phil. Trans. Roy. Soc. London,* Vol. XLII (1743), 491–509, especially quotation on 492. Joseph Ivor Waring, *A History of Medicine in South Carolina, 1670–1825* (Charleston, South Carolina Medical Association, 1964), 254–60, hereafter cited as *History.*

42. Santorio, *Medicina Statica: Being the Aphorisms of Sanctorius, Translated into English, with Large Explanations. To which is added Dr. Keil's Medicina Statica Britanna . . .* (London, 1723).

43. John Lining, "A Letter from . . . Charles-Town, South Carolina . . . Concerning the Quantity of Rain Fallen There from January 1738, to December 1752," *Phil. Trans. Roy. Soc. London,* Vol. XLVIII (1753), 284–85 and table.

44. John Lining, "A Description of the American Yellow Fever . . .," *Essays and Observations, Physical and Literary,* Vol. II (1756), 370–95. This report was reprinted at Philadelphia in 1799. Robert Croom Aldredge, "Weather Observers and Observations at Charles-

ton, South Carolina, 1670–1871," *Year Book of the City of Charleston for the Year 1940,* pp. 190–257, see especially 204–18, hereafter cited as "Weather Observers"; Everett Mendelsohn, "John Lining and His Contribution to Early American Science," *Isis,* Vol. LI (1960), 278–92. Cassedy, "Meteorology and Medicine," *J. Hist. Med. and Allied Sciences,* Vol. XXIV (1969), 199–201.

45. Kalm, *Travels,* I, 361–68, especially quotation on 368; II, 120.

46. *Ibid.,* I, 371–72; see also 369–71, 376–78.

47. *Ibid.,* II, 253–54.

48. Lionel Chalmers, *Account of the Weather and Diseases of South Carolina* (2 vols., London, 1776), I, charts at 42 and at end of vol., hereafter cited as *Account;* Waring, *History,* 188–97 and portrait; Aldredge, "Weather Observers," *Year Book of the City of Charleston for the Year 1940,* 219–22.

49. Chalmers, *Account,* I, 6.

50. *Ibid.,* 33–34.

51. *Ibid.,* 150–51.

52. Charles-Edward Amory Winslow, *The Conquest of Epidemic Disease: A Chapter in the History of Ideas* (Princeton, Princeton University Press, 1943), 193, hereafter cited as *Conquest.*

53. Benjamin Rush, *An Account of the Bilious Remitting Yellow Fever as It Appeared in the City of Philadelphia in the Year 1793* (Philadelphia, 1794). The conclusion by the College of Physicians is quoted by Winslow, *Conquest,* 198.

54. Karl Popper, *Conjectures and Refutations; the Growth of Scientific Knowledge* (New York, Basic Books, 1962).

55. Quoted from Benjamin Spector, "Noah Webster, His Contribution to American Medical Thought and Progress," in Noah Webster, *Letters on Yellow Fever Addressed to Dr. William Currie* (first published 1797; ed. by Benjamin Spector, Baltimore, Johns Hopkins Press, 1947), 11, hereafter cited as "Webster," *Letters.* See also Charles-Edward Amory Winslow, "The Epidemiology of Noah Webster," *Conn. Acad. Arts and Sciences,* Vol. XXXII (1934), 21–109; see 45 showing the date of the questionnaire as October 31, 1795.

56. In a letter to Benjamin Rush, 4 Dec. 1798 Webster complained that the theory of imported disease "is a serious attack on the commercial interests of the country." Quoted from Spector, "Webster," in Webster, *Letters,* 15.

57. Noah Webster, *Brief History of Epidemic and Pestilential Diseases, with the Principal Phenomena of the Physical World, Which Precede and Accompany Them, and Observations Deduced from the Facts Stated* (2 vols., 1799), II, Secs. 15–16; I, x.

58. Samuel Noah Kramer, *The Sumerians: Their History, Culture, and Character* (Chicago, University of Chicago Press, 1964), 340–42 for the almanac and 105–109 for a discussion of it.

59. Kalm, *Travels,* II, 76, 90–91.

60. *Ibid.,* 318–52.

61. *Ibid.,* I, 105–12.

62. *Ibid.,* II, 167–68.

63. Kalm, "Beskrifining pa de vilda Dufvar I Norra America," *Kongl. Vetenskaps-Akademiens Handlingar,* Vol. XX (1759), 275–95, cited from S. M. Gronberger (trans.), "A Description of the Wild Pigeons Which Visit the Southern English Colonies in North America, During Certain Years, in Incredible Multitudes," *Auk,* Vol. XXVIII (1911), 53–66, especially 61–64, hereafter cited as "A Description of the Wild Pigeons."

64. Benjamin Stillingfleet, *Miscellaneous Tracts relating to Natural History, Husbandry, and Physick, To which is added: The Calendar of Flora* (2d ed., London, R. & J. Dodsley, 1762), 229–327. The bibliography of Linnaean works is complex; see B. H. Soulsby, *A Catalogue of the Works of Linnaeus . . .* (2d ed., London, British Museum, 1933).

65. Alexander McAdie, "A Colonial Weather Service," *Popular Science Monthly,* Vol. XLV (1894), 331–37; Edward T. Martin, *Thomas Jefferson: Scientist* (New York, Henry Schuman, 1952), Chap. 5.

66. Thomas Jefferson, *Garden Book, 1766–1824, with Relevant Extracts from His Other Writings* (ed. by Edwin Morris Betts, Philadelphia, American Philosophical Society, Memoir 22, 1944), 4, hereafter cited as *Garden Book.*

67. *Ibid.,* 129; see also Thomas Jefferson, *Notes on the State of Virginia* (ed. by William Peden, Chapel Hill, University of North Carolina Press, 1955), 75, hereafter cited as *Notes.*

68. Quoted in *Garden Book,* 151.

69. *Ibid.,* 161–62.

70. *Ibid.,* 578–79.

71. The plan was briefly described by Samuel Vaughan in a letter to Humphry Marshall dated May 22, 1786 quoted in William Darlington (ed.), *Memorials of John Bartram and Humphry Marshall, with Notices of Their Contemporaries* (Philadelphia, 1849), 558; facsimile (ed., with introduction and indices, by Joseph Ewan, New York, Hafner, 1967); Hindle, *The Pursuit of Science,* 332 et passim; *National Cyclopaedia of American Biography* (1891), I, 257.

72. Samuel Williams, *Natural and Civil History of Vermont* (1794; enlarged ed., 1809), 44–56, 78, 112–13 (all citations from 1st ed.), hereafter cited as *Vermont.* Bartram, *Travels* (1st ed., 286–302; (Harper ed.), 179–91. Benjamin Smith Barton, *Fragments of the Natural History of Pennsylvania . . .* (Philadelphia, Author, 1799). Witmer Stone, "Bird Migration Records of William Bartram, 1802–1822," *Auk,* Vol. XXX (1913), 325–58 and 3 plates.

73. Kalm, *Travels,* I, 58, 102–103 (on degeneration); II, 194–95 (on American farming).

74. *Ibid.,* I, 104, 390; II, 189; III, 8–9.

75. Comte Georges Louis Leclerc de Buffon, "The Natural History of Man," in *Natural History, General and Particular* (trans. by William Smellie, 9 vols., Edinburgh, William Creech, 1780), III, 181, 164–65, hereafter cited as *Natural History.*

76. *Ibid.,* V, 129; Clarence J. Glacken, *Traces on the Rhodian Shore: Nature and Culture in Western Thought from Ancient Times to the End of the Eighteenth Century* (Berkeley and Los Angeles, University of California Press, 1967), 663–85, hereafter cited as *The Rhodian Shore.*

77. Antonello Gerbi, *The Dispute of the New World: the History of a Polemic, 1750–1900* (trans. by Jeremy Moyle, Pittsburgh, University of Pittsburgh Press, 1973); Gilbert Chinard, "Eighteenth Century Theories of America as a Human Habitat," *Amer. Philos. Soc. Proc.,* Vol. XCI (1947), 27–57, hereafter cited as "Eighteenth Century Theories."

78. Jefferson, *Notes,* 48; he cited Buffon, *Histoire naturelle,* VIII, 134; Martin, *Thomas Jefferson: Scientist,* Chaps. 6–7.

79. Williams, *Vermont,* 105–107.

80. Benjamin Franklin, *Writings* (Memorial ed.), XVIII, 170 on the Paris party; "Letter to Mr. Nairne, of London, on Hygrometers," *Amer. Philos. Soc. Trans.,* o.s. II (1786), 51–56 on climate data. Both citations from Chinard, "Eighteenth Century Theories," *Amer. Philos. Soc. Proc.* Vol. XCI (1947), 43.

81. John Clayton, "Concerning the Air," in Berkeley and Berkeley (eds.), *Clayton,* 48.

82. Reprinted in *ibid.,* 80–81.

83. John Woodward, "Some Thoughts and Experiments Concerning Vegetation," *Phil. Trans. Roy. Soc. London,* Vol. XXI (1699), 193–227, especially 208–209. Woodward's speculations on the evolution of the environment were explained in *An Essay Towards a Natural History of the Earth* (1695), which has been discussed by Glacken, *The Rhodian Shore,* 409–11.

84. Kalm, *Travels,* II, 119, 127–30; III, 258.

85. Hugh Williamson, "An Attempt to Account for the Change of Climate, Which Has Been Observed in the Middle Colonies in North America," *Amer. Philos. Soc. Trans.,* Vol. I (1771), 272–80; Whitfield J. Bell, Jr., *Early American Science: Needs and Opportunities for Study* (Williamsburg, Institute of Early American History and Culture, 1955), 77–78, hereafter cited as *Early American Science.*

86. Jefferson, *Notes,* 80.

87. On the history of photosynthesis studies in the eighteenth century see Leonard K. Nash, *Plants and the Atmosphere,* Harvard Case Histories in Experimental Science, No. 5 (ed. by James B. Conant, Cambridge, Mass., Harvard University Press, 1966); Howard S. Reed, "Jan Ingenhousz, Plant Physiologist, with a History of the Discovery of Photosynthesis, *Chronica Botanica,* XI, Nos. 5–6 (1949).

88. Marquis François Jean de Chastellux, *Travels in North America in the Years 1780, 1781, and 1782* trans. by George Grieve, rev. and ed. by Howard C. Rice, Jr., 2 vols., Chapel Hill, University of North Carolina Press, 1963, II, 395–96.

89. Benjamin Rush, "An Enquiry into the Cause of the Increase of Bilious and Intermitting Fevers in Pennsylvania, with Hints for Preventing Them," *Amer. Philos. Soc. Trans.,* Vol. II (1786), 206–12; Thomas Wright, "On the Mode Most Easily and Effectually Practicable of Drying Up the Marshes of the Maritime Parts of North America," *Amer. Philos. Soc. Trans.,* Vol. IV (1797), 243–46; William Currie, "An Enquiry into the Course of the Insalubrity of Flat and Marshy Situations," *Amer. Philos. Soc. Trans.,* Vol. IV (1797), 127–42; Adam Seybert, "Experiments and Observations on the Atmosphere of Marshes," *Trans. Amer. Philos. Soc.,* Vol. IV (1797), 262–71; all cited from Gilbert Chinard, "The American Philosophical Society and the Early History of Forestry in America," *Amer. Philos. Soc. Proc.,* Vol. LXXXIX (1945), 444–88, especially 454–55.

90. Williams, *Vermont,* 50, 74–76, 60–61, 54.

91. Noah Webster, "On the Supposed Change of Temperature in Modern Winters," in *A Collection of Papers on Political, Literary and Moral Subjects* (New York, 1843; facsimile ed., New York, Burt Franklin, 1968), 119–62; Glacken, *The Rhodian Shore,* 560–61, 660–63.

92. Herodotus, *History,* Book III, Chaps. 108–109; Book II, Chap. 68; Plato, *Protagoras,* 320d–321b; Plato *Timaeus,* 30c–d; Carl Linnaeus, *Specimen Academicum de Oeconomia Naturae* (I. J. Biberg, respondent, Upsala, 1744); Frank N. Egerton, "Changing Concepts of the Balance of Nature," *Quart. Rev. Biol.,* Vol. XLVIII (1973), 322–50, hereafter cited as "The Balance of Nature."

93. Kalm, *Travels,* I, 291, 116–17, 143–45, 289–92, 343–44, 353–54; II, 59–60, 72, 196, 200; III, 296–97; "A Description of the Wild Pigeons," *Auk,* Vol. XXVIII (1911), 59.

94. Buffon, "The Wild Animals," in *Natural History,* IV, 73; Kalm, *Travels,* II, 59–60.

95. Kalm, *Travels,* II, 135.

96. *Ibid.,* I, 371–72.

97. *Ibid.,* II, 3.

98. Franklin's "Observations Concerning the Increase of Mankind, Peopling of Countries" was written in 1751 and first appeared as an appendix in William Clarke, *Observations on the Late and Present Conduct of the French, with Regard to Their Encroachments upon the British Colonies in North America* (Boston, 1755); reprinted in *The Writings of Benjamin Franklin* (ed. by Albert Henry Smyth, 10 vols., New York, Macmillan, 1905–1907), III, 63–73. See also Conway Zirkle, "Benjamin Franklin, Thomas

Malthus and the United States Census," *Isis,* Vol. XLVIII (1957), 58–62.

99. Kalm, *Travels,* I, 294.

100. Benjamin Franklin, *Works* (ed. by John Bigelow) (New York: G. P. Putnam's Sons, 1904), VI, 334.

101. Williams, *Vermont,* 110–11, 84ff.

102. Jefferson, *Notes,* 53–54; Williams, *Vermont,* 103.

103. Paul Russell Cutright, *Lewis and Clark: Pioneering Naturalists* (Urbana, University of Illinois, 1969), 56. The first edition of the report of the Lewis and Clark Expedition was edited by Nicholas Biddle. His text was later the basis for Elliott Coues (ed.), *History of the Expedition Under the Command of Lewis and Clark . . . A New Edition, . . . with Copious Critical Commentary . . .* (4 vols., New York, Francis P. Harper, 1893; reprinted, 3 vols., New York, Dover, 1965).

104. Humboldt's influence on Darwin is discussed in some detail in Frank N. Egerton, "Humboldt, Darwin, and Population," *J. Hist. Biology,* Vol. III (1970), 325–60.

105. Alexander von Humboldt and Aimé Conpland, *Essai sur la Géographie des Plantes; accompagné d'un Tableau physique des Régions équinoxiales, Fondé sur des Mesures Exécutées, depuis le Dixième Degré de Latitude boréale jusqu'au Dixième Degré de Latitude australe, pendant les Années 1799, 1800, 1801, 1802 et 1803* (Paris, Levrault, Schoell, 1807), 14–18.

106. *Ibid.,* 154–55; Benjamin Smith Barton, "Specimen of a Geographical View of the Trees and Shrubs, and Many of the Herbaceous Plants of North America, Between the Latitudes of Seventy-one and Twenty-five" (a set of galley proofs is in the Yale University Library, New Haven, Conn.).

107. Charles Pickering, "On the Geographical Distribution of Plants," *Amer. Philos. Soc. Trans.,* n.s., Vol. III (1830), 274–84 and map.

108. Charles Pickering, *Geographical Distribution of Animals and Plants,* Vol. XIX in *U.S. Exploring Expedition* (Boston, Little, Brown, 1854); "On the Geographical Distribution of Species," *Amer. Acad. Arts and Sci. Proc.,* 4 (1859), 192–94; "Relative to the Geographical Distribution of Species," *ibid.,* 5 (1860), 81–82. On Pickering see Asa Gray, *Scientific Papers* (ed. by Charles S. Sargent, 2 vols., Boston, 1889), II, 406–10.

109. Henry R. Schoolcraft, *Narrative Journal of Travels, Through the Northwestern Regions of the United States Extending from Detroit Through the Great Chain of American Lakes, to the Sources of the Mississippi River . . .* (Albany, N.Y., E. & E. Hosford, 1821), 71 on phenology, 161 on the Huron plain. For a guide to the literature of his and other American expeditions see Max Meisel, *A Bibliography of American Natural History: the Pioneer Century, 1769–1865* (3 vols., New York, Premier, 1924–29; reprinted, New York, Hafner, 1967).

110. Chase S. Osborn and Stellanova Osborn, *Schoolcraft—Longfellow—Hiawatha* (Lancaster, Pa., Jacques Cattell, 1942), contains Schoolcraft's biography and bibliography.

111. Louis Agassiz, *Lake Superior: Its Physical Character, Vegetation, and Animals, Compared with Those of Other and Similar Regions . . .* (Boston, Gould, Kendall and Lincoln, 1850), 153; Frank N. Egerton, "Louis Agassiz and Biogeography," to be published in a volume commemorating the centennial of Woods Hole Marine Biological Laboratory (ed. by Harold L. Burstyn); Edward Lurie, *Louis Agassiz: A Life in Science* (Chicago, University of Chicago Press, 1960).

112. Asa Gray, review of Philip Franz von Siebold, *Flora Japonica,* in *Amer. J. Sci.,* Vol. XXXIX (1840), 175–76; "Analogy Between the Flora of Japan and That of the United States," *Amer. J. Sci.,* n.s., Vol. II (1846), 135–36; "Diagnostic Characters of New Species of Phaenogamous Plants, Collected in Japan by Charles Wright, Botanist of the United States North Pacific Exploring Expedition. With Observations upon the Relations of the Japanese Flora to That of North America, and of Other Parts of the Northern Temperate Zone," *Mem. Amer. Acad. Arts and Sci.,* Vol. VI (1859), 377–452; Asa Gray and Joseph Dalton Hooker, "The Vegetation of the Rocky Mountain Region and a Comparison with That of Other Parts of the World," *Bull. U.S. Geol. and Geogr. Survey of the Territories,* Vol. VI (1881), 1–77; Asa Gray, *Darwiniana* (1st ed., 1876; reprinted, Cambridge, Mass., Harvard University Press, 1963), Art. 4 and 5. A. Hunter Dupree, *Asa Gray, 1810–1888* (Cambridge, Mass., Harvard University Press, 1959).

113. Leviticus 13–14; Lucretius 6. 1090–1137; Varro 1. 12; Vitruvius 1. 4. 11. Columella 1. 4; Palmer Howard Futcher, "Notes on Insect Contagion," *Bull. Hist. Medicine,* Vol. IV (1936), 536–58, esp. 544–45; Winslow, *Conquest,* Chap. 5.

114. Jerome Cardan, *De Rerum Varietate* (Basel, 1557); Charles Singer and Dorothea Singer, "The Development of the Doctrine of Contagium Vivum, 1500–1750," *XVIIth International Medical Congress, Section XXIII* (London, 1914), 187–207; Winslow, *Conquest,* Chaps. 7–8; Giovanni Maria Lancisi, "On the Noxious Exhalations of Marshes" (trans. by Samuel Latham Mitchill), *Medical Repository,* Vol. XIII (1809–10), 9–18, 126–35, 237–45, 326–30; n.s., Vol. IV (1818), 201–12, 322–32, 442–67. More recently William C. Gorgas and Fielding H. Garrison have translated the most significant passages in "Ronald Ross and the Prevention of Malarial Fever," *Sci. Monthly,* Vol. III (1916), 133–50, esp. 135–36. Their translation is also quoted by Futcher, "Notes on Insect Contagion," *Bull. Hist. Med.* Vol. IV (1936), 547–48.

115. John Crawford published "Remarks on Quarantine" and "Dr. Crawford's Theory and an Application of It to the Treatment of Disease," *Observer,* Vols. I–II (1807), and "Observations on the Seats and Causes of Disease," *Baltimore Medical and Physical Recorder,* Vol. I (1809), 40–52, 81–92, 206–21. See also Raymond N. Doetsch, "John Crawford and His Contribution to the Doctrine of *Contagium Vivum,*" *Bacteriological Reviews,* Vol. XXVIII (1964), 87–96.

116. Daniel Drake, *A Practical Treatise on the History, Prevention, and Treatment of Epidemic Cholera, Designed for Both the Profession and the People* (Cincinnati, Corey & Fairbank, 1832); Raymond N. Doetsch, "Daniel Drake's Aetiological Views," *Medical History,* Vol. IX (1965), 365–73.

117. Josiah Clark Nott, "Yellow Fever Contrasted with Bilious Fever—Reasons for Believing It a Disease Sui Generis—Its Mode of Propagation—Remote Cause—Probable Insect or Animalcular Origin," *New Orleans Med. Surg. J.,* Vol. IV (1848), 563–601; Josiah Clark Nott, "Report on Yellow Fever," *Memorial Record,* Vol. VI (1871), 451–59; Emmett B. Carmichael, "Josiah Clark Nott," *Bull. Hist. Medicine,* 22 (1948), 249–62 and portrait; William Leland Holt, "Josiah Clark Nott of Mobile, an American Prophet of Scientific Method" [based on researches of Bayard Holmes], *Medical Life,* Vol. XXXV (1928), 487–504; Robert Wilson, "Dr. J. C. Nott and the Transmission of Yellow Fever," *Annals of Medical Hist.,* n.s. Vol. III (1931), 515–20.

118. John Kearsley Mitchell, *On the Cryptogamous Origin of Malarious and Epidemic Fevers* (Philadelphia: Lea & Blanchard, 1849), reprinted in his *Five Essays* (ed. by S. Weir Mitchell, Philadelphia, J. P. Lippincott, 1859), 13–140; Raymond N. Doetsch, "Mitchell on the Cause of Fevers," *Bull. Hist. Med.,* Vol. XXXVIII (1964), 241–59.

119. Erwin H. Ackerknecht, "Anticontagionism Between 1821 and 1867," *Bull. Hist. Med.,* Vol. XXII (1948), 562–93. Phyllis Allen [later Richmond], "Etiological Theory in America Prior to the Civil War," *J. Hist. Med. and Allied Sci.,* Vol. II (1947), 489–520; Phyllis Allen [Richmond], "Some Variant Theories in

Opposition to the Germ Theory of Disease," *J. Hist. Med. and Allied Sci.*, Vol. IX (1954), 290–303; Phyllis Allen [Richmond], "American Attitudes Toward the Germ Theory of Disease (1860–1880)," *J. Hist. Med. and Allied Sci.*, Vol. IX (1954), 428–54; Charles Rosenberg, "The Causes of Cholera: Aspects of Etiological Thought in Nineteenth Century America," *Bull. Hist. Med.*, Vol. XXXIV (1960), 331–54.

120. Constantin François Chasseboeuf, Comte de Volney, *A View of the Soil and Climate of the United States of America . . .* trans. by C. B. Brown, Philadelphia, J. Conrad, 1804), Chap. 10 (facsimile ed., Intro. by George W. White, New York, Hafner, 1968), hereafter cited as *Soil and Climate.*

121. Joseph Lovell, *Regulations for the Medical Department, by Order D. Parker, Adj. & Insp. Gen.* (September, 1818, 31 pp.); Quoted from Edgar Erskine Hume, "The Foundations of American Meteorology by the United States Army," *Bull. Inst. Hist. Med.*, Vol. VIII (1940), 202–38, esp. 206, 208, hereafter cited as "Foundations."

122. *Meteorological Register for the Years 1822, 1823, 1824, & 1825 from Observations Made by the Surgeons of the Army at the Military Posts of the United States* (prepared under the direction of Joseph Lovell, M.D., Surgeon General of the United States Army, Washington, D.C., Edward de Krafft, 1826).

123. *Meteorological Register for the Years 1826, 1827, 1828, 1829, and 1830; from Observations Made by the Surgeons of the Army and Others at the Military Posts of the United States* (prepared under the direction of Thomas Lawson, M.D., Surgeon General of the United Sates Army, Philadelphia, Haswell, Barrington, and Haswell, 1840); Samuel Forry, "Statistical Researches Elucidating the Climate of the United States and Its Relation with Diseases of Malarial Origin; Based on the Records of the Medical Department and Adjutant General's Office," *Amer. J. Med. Sci.*, n.s., Vol. I (1841), 13–46; Samuel Forry, *The Climate of the United States and Its Endemic Influences: Based Chiefly on the Records of the Medical Department and Adjutant General's Office, United States Army* (New York, J. & H. G. Langley, 1842), 244, cites "Cowan's Additions to Louis on Phthises."

124. Hume, "Foundations," *Bull. Inst. Hist. Med.*, Vol. VIII (1940), 214–38. Donald R. Whitnah, *A History of the United States Weather Bureau* (Urbana, University of Illinois Press, 1961), Chaps. 1–2.

125. Published in *Philadelphia Medical and Physical J.*, Vol. III (1808), 85–90; reprinted by Henry D. Shapiro and Zane L. Miller (eds.), *Physician to the West: Selected Writings of Daniel Drake on Science & Society* (Lexington, University of Kentucky Press, 1970), 1–4, hereafter cited as *Physician*; Emmet Field Horine, *Daniel Drake (1785–1852): Pioneer Physician of the Midwest* (Philadelphia, University of Pennsylvania Press, 1961).

126. Shapiro and Miller, *Physician*, p. 5. They reprinted the entire *Notices*, pp. 6–56.

127. Selections are reprinted by Shapiro and Miller (eds.), *Physician*, 66–124. Adolph E. Waller, because of his unfamiliarity with the history of ecology before Drake, has overstated Drake's originality in this book ("Daniel Drake as a Pioneer in Modern Ecology," *Ohio State Archeological and Historical Quarterly*, Vol. LVI [1947], 262–73).

128. Drake's cholera book is cited above, n. 116. Drake's evidence for *contagium vivum* [in *A Systematic Treatise, Historical, Etiological, and Practical, on the Principal Diseases of the Interior Valley of North America, as They Appear in the Caucasian, African, Indian, and Esquimaux Varieties of Its Population* (2 vols., 1850–54), hereafter cited as *A Systematic Treatise*] occurs in Book 2, Part I, Chap. II, which, confusingly, is included near the end of Vol. I and also near the beginning of Vol. II. This chapter is in-

cluded in the extracts from *A Systematic Treatise* in Shapiro and Miller (eds.), *Physician*, 366–79. The chapter is also reprinted by Norman D. Levine (ed.), *Malaria in the Interior Valley of North America: a Selection from a Systematic Treatise . . . by Daniel Drake* (Urbana, University of Illinois Press, 1964), hereafter cited as *Malaria*.

129. Drake, *A Systematic Treatise*, I, 455–59 on weather, 623–36 on distributions of trees, mammals, birds (these pages are not reprinted by either Shapiro and Miller [eds.], *Physician*, or Levine [ed.], *Malaria*).

130. *Ibid.*, 341.

131. For example: Manning Simons, "Report on the Climatology and Epidemics of South Carolina," *Amer. Med. Assoc. Trans.*, Vol. XXIII (1872), 275–331; Billy M. Jones, *Health Seekers in the Southwest, 1817–1900* (Norman, University of Oklahoma Press, 1967); John E. Baur, *The Health Seekers of Southern California, 1870–1900* (San Marino, Calif., Huntington Library, 1959).

132. Benjamin Smith Barton, *Elements of Botany: or Outlines of the Natural History of Vegetables* (3 parts, Philadelphia, Author, 1803), Part I, 300; Francis W. Pennell, "Benjamin Smith Barton as Naturalist," *Amer. Philos. Soc. Proc.*, Vol. LXXXVI (1942), 108–22; William Martin Smallwood and Mabel Sarah Coon Smallwood, *Natural History and the American Mind* (New York, Columbia University Press, 1941), 289–93. See also above, n. 72.

133. Jacob Bigelow, *Florula Bostoniensis; a Collection of Plants of Boston and Its Environs, with Their Generic and Specific Characters, Synonyms, Descriptions, Places of Birth, and Time of Flowering* (Boston, 1814, 268 pp.; 2d ed., 1824, 423 pp.; 3d ed., 1840, 468 pp.), hereafter cited as *Florula Bostoniensis*; Volney, *Soil and Climate*, 120–21. On Muhlenberg see Bell, *Early American Science*, 67–68; see also Constantine S. Rafinesque, "A Journal of the Progress of Vegetation near Philadelphia, Between the 20th of February and the 20th of May, 1816, with Occasional Zoological Remarks," *Amer. J. Sci.*, Vol. I (1818), 77–82.

134. *Amer. Acad. Arts and Sci. Mem.*, Vol. IV (1818), 77–85; George E. Ellis, "Memoir of Jacob Bigelow, M.D., L.L.D.," *Mass. Hist. Soc. Proc.*, Vol. XVII (1880), 383–467 and portrait.

135. Jacob Porter, "Floral Calendar for Plainfield, Massachusetts, 1818," *Amer. J. Sci.*, Vol. I (1818), 254–55; Stephen W. Williams, "Floral Calendar Kept at Deerfield, Massachusetts, with Miscellanious Remarks," *Amer. J. Sci.*, Vol. I (1819), 359–73. Jefferson to Bigelow, April 11, 1818, in Jefferson, *Garden Book* (ed. by Betts), 578–79.

136. Quoted from Alfred J. Henry, "Early Individual Observers in the United States," *U.S. Dept. Agriculture, Weather Bureau Bull.*, Vol. XI (1895), 291–302, esp. 300; William M. Meigs, *Life of Josiah Meigs, by His Great-Grandson* (Philadelphia, J. P. Murphy, 1887).

137. Franklin B. Hough, *Historical and Statistical Record of the University of the State of New York During the Century from 1784 to 1884* (Albany, N.Y., Weed, Parsons, 1885), 767; Leo Stoller, "A Note on Thoreau's Place in the History of Phenology," *Isis*, Vol. XLVII (1956), 172–81, esp. 177, hereafter cited as "Thoreau's Place."

138. Franklin B. Hough, *Results of a Series of Meteorological Observations Made in Obedience to Instructions from the Regents of the University at Sundry Academies in the State of New York, from 1826 to 1850 Inclusive, Compiled from the Original Returns of the Annual Reports of the Regents of the University* (Albany, N.Y., Weed, Parsons, 1855); reviewed in *Amer. J. Sci.*, Vol. XXI (1856), 149.

139. [Joseph Henry], "Smithsonian Institution—Registry of Periodical Phenomena," *Amer. J. Sci.*, Vol. XII (1851), 293–95; Franklin B. Hough, "Observations upon Periodical Phenomena

in Plants and Animals from 1851 to 1859, with Tables of Opening and Closing of Lakes, Rivers, Harbors, &c.," 36th Cong., 1st Sess., *House Ex. Doc. 55* (Washington, D.C., 1864); Romeyn B. Hough on Hough in Howard A. Kelly and Walter L. Burrage, *American Medical Biographies* (Baltimore, Norman, Remington, 1920), 562–63; Edna L. Jacobsen, "Franklin B. Hough, a Pioneer in Scientific Forestry in America," *New York History*, Vol. XV (1934), 310–25.

140. Charles Peirce, *A Meteorological Account of the Weather in Philadelphia, from January 1, 1790, to January 1, 1847, Including Fifty-Seven Years; with an Appendix, Containing a Great Variety of Interesting Information . . .* (Philadelphia, 1847).

141. Aldo Leopold and Sara Elizabeth Jones, "A Phenological Record of Sauk and Dane Counties, Wisconsin, 1935–1945," *Ecological Monographs,* Vol. XVII (1947), 81–122, esp. 83. Their claim has been repeated often, as by Philip Whitford and Kathryn Whitford in "Thoreau: Pioneer Ecologist and Conservationist," *Scientific Monthly*, Vol. LXXIII (1951), 291–96, esp. 292.

142. Nina Baym, "Thoreau's View of Science," *J. Hist. Ideas*, Vol. XXVI (1965), 221–34, esp. 224, 226.

143. *Ibid.*, 225. On Howitt see George C. Boase in *Dict. Nat. Biog.*; Wendell Glick, "Three New Early Manuscripts by Thoreau," *Huntington Lib. Quart.*, Vol. XV (1951), 59–71, esp. 61–68.

144. Henry David Thoreau, "Natural History of Massachusetts," *Dial*, Vol. III (July, 1842), 19–40, esp. 23, 40.

145. Various memoranda are in Henry David Thoreau, *The Journals* (ed. by Bradford Torrey and Francis H. Allen, 14 vols., Boston, Houghton Mifflin, 1906, New York, Dover, 1962), III, 364, 377, 438; IV, 8, 15, 66; IX, 158. These memoranda and the chart (in Henry and Albert A. Berg Collection, New York Public Library) are discussed by Stoller in "Thoreau's Place," *Isis*, Vol. XLVII (1956), 173–74.

146. Baym, "Thoreau's View of Science," *J. Hist. Ideas*, Vol. XXVI (1965), 227.

147. On Bartram's influences upon literary authors, see Lowes, *Road to Xanadu*, and Fagin, *William Bartram*, Part 3; Joseph Ewan (ed.), *William Bartram: Botanical and Zoological Drawings, 1756–1788, Reproduced from the Fothergill Album in the British Museum (Natural History)*, (Philadelphia, American Philosophical Society, 1968).

148. Hans Huth, *Nature and the American: Three Centuries of Changing Attitudes* (Berkeley and Los Angeles: University of California Press, 1957); Robert Henry Welker, *Birds and Men: American Birds in Science, Art, Literature, and Conservation, 1800–1900* (Cambridge, Mass., Harvard University Press, 1955); Philip Marshall Hicks, *The Development of the Natural History Essay in American Literature* (Philadelphia, 1924); Arthur A. Ekirch, Jr., *Man and Nature in America* (New York, Columbia University, 1963); Roderick Nash, *Wilderness and the American Mind* (New Haven, Yale University, 1967); *The American Environment: Readings in the History of Conservation* (Reading, Mass., Addison-Wesley, 1968); Donald Fleming, "Roots of the New Conservation Movement," *Perspectives in Amer. Hist.*, Vol. VI (1972), 7–91; Frank Graham, Jr., *Man's Dominion: The Story of Conservation in America* (New York, M. Evans, 1971); Henry Clepper (ed.), *Origins of American Conservation* (New York, Ronald Press, 1966); Henry Clepper (ed.), *Leaders of American Conservation* (New York, Ronald Press, 1971).

149. Van Wyck Brooks, *The World of Washington Irving* (New York, E. P. Dutton, 1944), 87. Alexander Wilson, "The Foresters, Descriptive of a Pedestrian Journey to the Falls of Niagara, in the Autumn of 1804," *The Port Folio*, n.s., Vols. I–III (1809–10), and four later separate editions; *The Poems and Literary Prose . . .*, (ed. by Alexander B. Grosart, 2 vols., Paisley, Scotland, 1876);

Robert Cantwell, *Alexander Wilson: Naturalist and Pioneer* (Philadelphia, J. B. Lippincott, 1961); Emerson Stringham, *Alexander Wilson: A Founder of Scientific Ornithology* (Kerrville, Texas, Author, 1958); James Southall Wilson, *Alexander Wilson, Poet-Naturalist: A Study of His Life with Selected Poems* (New York, Neale, 1906); Gordon Wilson, "Alexander Wilson, Poet-Essayist-Ornithologist" (unpublished Ph.D. dissertation, Indiana University, 1930).

150. Alexander Wilson, *American Ornithology; or, the Natural History of the Birds of the United States . . .* (9 vols., Philadelphia, Bradford and Inskeep, 1808–14), II, 72, on kingbird; I, 27, on Baltimore oriole and 59–60 on blue bird; II, 29, on hummingbird and 79 on wood pewee; IV, 96, on bald eagle; V, 24–26 on Osprey. On his bird census, see *ibid.*, IV, v–x, and Frank L. Burns, "Alexander Wilson in Bird Census Work," *Wilson Bulletin*, Vol. XIX (1907), 100–102.

151. Ralph Waldo Emerson, *The Early Lectures, 1833–1836* (ed. by Stephen E. Whicher and Robert E. Spiller, Cambridge, Mass., Harvard University Press, 1959), 10; Ralph Waldo Emerson, *Journals* (ed. by Edward W. Emerson and Waldo E. Forbes, Boston, Houghton Mifflin, 1909–14), V, 285.

152. Thoreau's readings are well documented by John A. Christi, *Thoreau as World Traveler* (New York, Columbia University Press, 1965); Walter Harding, *Thoreau's Library* (Charlottesville, University of Virginia Press, 1957); Kenneth W. Cameron (ed.), *Thoreau's Fact Book,* 2 vols. (Hartford, Conn., Transcendental Books, 1966).

153. Baym, "Thoreau's View of Science," *J. Hist. Ideas*, Vol. XXVI (1965), 221–34; Raymond Adams, "Thoreau's Science," *Scientific Monthly*, Vol. LX (1945), 379–82; Charles R. Metzger, "Thoreau on Science," *Annals of Sci.*, Vol. XII (1956), 206–11; Whitford and Whitford, "Thoreau: Pioneer Ecologist and Conservationist," *Scientific Monthly*, Vol. LXXIII (1951), 291–96; James McIntosh, *Thoreau as Romantic Naturalist: His Shifting Stance Toward Nature* (Ithaca, N.Y., Cornell University Press, 1974).

154. Henry David Thoreau, *A Week on the Concord and Merrimack Rivers* (1849), cited from 1906 edition (Boston, Houghton Mifflin, 1906), 29.

155. Edward S. Deevey, Jr., "A Re-examination of Thoreau's *Walden*," *Quart. Rev. Biol.*, 17 (1942), 1–11.

156. Henry David Thoreau, "The Succession of Forest Trees," *Excursions* (1863, cited from reprint, Boston, Houghton, Mifflin, 1893), 225–50. Thoreau read this essay before the Middlesex Agricultural Society in Concord in September, 1860; Kalm, *Travels*, I, 75, 162, 312; Wilson, *American Ornithology*, I, 17; Kathryn Whitford, "Thoreau and the Woodlots of Concord," *New England Quart.*, Vol. XXIII (1950), 291–306; Leo Stoller, *After Walden: Thoreau's Changing Views on Economic Man* (Stanford, Calif., Stanford University Press, 1957), 72–88. For a survey of studies on plant succession before 1860 see Frederic E. Clements, *Plant Succession: An Analysis of the Development of Vegetation* (Washington, D.C., Carnegie Institution, 1916), 8–17.

157. Thoreau, *The Journals*, XIV, 94–95, 125–27, 130–33, 145–46, 203–205, 211.

158. David Lowenthal, *George Perkins Marsh: Versatile Vermonter* (New York, Columbia University Press, 1958), 251–53, hereafter cited as *Marsh*; David Lowenthal (ed.), "Introduction," xvii–xviii, in George Perkins Marsh, *Man and Nature; or, Physical Geography as Modified by Human Action* (ed. by David Lowenthal, Cambridge, Mass., Harvard University Press, 1965); *ibid.*, 102–105, hereafter cited as *Man and Nature*.

159. Lewis Mumford, *The Brown Decades: A Study of the Arts in America, 1865–1895* (New York, 1931), 78; Lowenthal,

Marsh, 246.

160. Lowenthal (ed.), "Introduction," in Marsh, *Man and Nature*, xiii.

161. Marsh, *Man and Nature*, 53.

162. *Ibid.*, 247; Darwin, *On the Origin of Species by Means of Natural Selection, or the Preservation of Favoured Races in the Struggle for Life* (London, John Murray, 1859), Chaps. 3–4, 10; Egerton, "The Balance of Nature," *Quart. Rev. Biol.*, Vol. XLVIII (1973), 341–42.

163. Marsh, *Man and Nature*, 36–37, 76–78, 82–87, 99–102, 105–108.

164. Lowenthal (ed.), "Introduction," xxi–xxiii, xxvii–xxviii, in *ibid.*; George Perkins Marsh, *The Earth as Modified by Human Action* (New York, Scribner, Armstrong, 1874; facsimile ed., New York, Arno, 1970).

165. Letters of E. P. Evans to Marsh, November 24, 1870, January 20, 1871, letter of Marsh to Evans, December 5, 1870, Marsh Collection, University of Vermont. Lowenthal (ed.), n. 51, in Marsh, *Man and Nature*, 49–50.

166. Lowenthal (ed.), "Introduction," xxii, in *ibid.*; Clepper (ed.), *Leaders of American Conservation*, 172–73, 217–18; Herbert A. Smith, "The Early Forestry Movement in the United States," *Agricultural History*, Vol. XII (1938), 326–46, esp. 326–31.

167. On Forbes see below. On the Division of Economic Ornithology and Mammalogy see Jenks Cameron, *The Bureau of Biological Survey: Its History, Activities and Organization* (Baltimore: Johns Hopkins University Press, 1929; New York: Arno, 1974), hereafter cited as *Biological Survey*; Keir B. Sterling, *Last of the Naturalists: The Career of C. Hart Merriam* (New York, Arno, 1974), Chaps. 3–4, 7.

168. A. Starker Leopold, "The Conservation of Wildlife," in *A Century of Progress in the Natural Sciences, 1853–1953* (ed. by Edward L. Kessel, San Francisco, California Academy of Science, 1955), 795–807; Norman G. Benson (ed.), *A Century of Fisheries in North America* (Washington, D.C., American Fisheries Society, 1970); Frank G. Roe, *The North American Buffalo: A Critical Study of the Species in Its Wild State* (2d ed., Toronto, University of Toronto Press, 1970); A. W. Schorger, *The Passenger Pigeon* (Madison, University of Wisconsin Press, 1955); James C. Greenway, Jr., *Extinct and Vanishing Birds of the World* (2d ed., New York, Dover, 1967), 35–48, 304–11, 322–27.

169. James S. Lippincott, "Geography of Plants," *Agricultural Report of the United States Commissioner of Patents for 1863* (Washington, D.C., Government Printing Office, 1864), 464–525.

170. John Wesley Powell, *Report on the Lands of the Arid Region of the United States, with a More Detailed Account of the Lands of Utah* (ed. by Wallace Stegner, Cambridge, Mass., Harvard University Press, 1962), 25, hereafter cited as *Report*; William Culp Darrah, *Powell of the Colorado* (Princeton, Princeton University Press, 1951); Wallace Stegner, *Beyond the Hundredth Meridian: John Wesley Powell and the Second Opening of the West* (Boston, Houghton Mifflin, 1954).

171. Caleb Atwater, "On the Prairies and Barrens of the West," *Amer. J. Sci.*, Vol. I (1818), 116–25; R. W. Wells, "On the Origin of Prairies," *Amer. J. Sci.*, Vol. I (1819), 331–37.

172. Powell, *Report*, 30–31.

173. *Ibid.*, 114.

174. Stegner (ed.), "Editor's Introduction," xxiv, in Powell, *Report*.

175. F. S. Bodenheimer, *Materialien zur Geschichte der Entomologie* (2 vols., Berlin, W. Junk, 1928–29); Leland O. Howard, *A History of Applied Entomology (Somewhat Anecdotal)* (Smithsonian Miscellaneous Collection, Vol. LXXXIV, 1930), 207–12; Harry B. Weiss, "Thomas Jefferson and Economic Entomology,"

J. Economic Entomology, Vol. XXXVII (1944), 836–41.

176. John A. Stevenson, "The Beginnings of Plant Pathology in North America," in *Plant Pathology: Problems and Progress, 1908–1958* (ed. by C. S. Holton, G. W. Fischer, R. W. Fulton, Helen Hart, and S. E. A. McCallan, Madison, University of Wisconsin Press, 1959), 14–23. Despite the limited scope indicated by the title of the volume, Stevenson surveys the whole history. E. C. Large, *The Advance of the Fungi* (London, Jonathan Cape, 1940; New York, Dover, 1962).

177. Kalm, *Travels*, I, 177; II, 46–48; III, 60.

178. Cameron, *Biological Survey*, 12–13.

179. Fitch, "Sixth Report on the Noxious and Other Insects of the State of New York," *New York State Agricultural Society Trans.*, Vol. XX (for 1860, pub. 1861), 745–868, esp. 824; Richard L. Doutt, "The Historical Development of Biological Control," see *Biological Control of Insect Pests and Weeds* (ed. by Paul DeBach, New York, Reinhold, 1964), 26–27, hereafter cited as "Control"; Arnold Mallis, *American Entomologists* (New Brunswick, N.J., Rutgers University Press, 1971), 37–43 et passim; Samuel Rezneck on Fitch, *Dictionary of Scientific Biography* (1972), V, 11–12.

180. Walsh, "Imported Insects; the Gooseberry Sawfly," *Practical Entomologist*, I (September 29, 1866), 117–24; Doutt, "Control," *Practical Entomologist*, I (September 29, 1866), 27–31; Mallis, *American Entomologists*, 43–48 et passim.

181. Large, *Advance of the Fungi*, Chap. 11; Mallis, *American Entomologists*, 69–79 et passim; Alpheus S. Packard, "Charles Valentine Riley," *Science*, n.s., Vol. II (1895), 745–51; G. B. Goode, "Charles Valentine Riley (1843–95)," *Science*, n.s., Vol. III (1896), 217–25.

182. Riley, "Parasitic and Predaceous Insects in Applied Entomology," *Insect Life*, Vol. VI (1893), 130–41.

183. Doutt, "Control," *Practical Entomologist*, I (September 29, 1866), 31–38.

184. Edward A. Steinhaus, "Microbial Control—The Emergence of an Idea: A Brief History of Insect Pathology Through the Nineteenth Century," *Hilgardia*, Vol. XXVI (1956), 107–60.

185. Ernst Haeckel, *Generelle Morphologie der Organisme. Allgemeine Grundzüge der organischen Formen-Wissenschaft, mechanisch begründet durch die von Charles Darwin reformirte Descendenz-Theorie* (2 vols., Berlin, Reimer, 1866), II, 286–87; trans. in Robert C. Stauffer, "Haeckel, Darwin, and Ecology," *Quart. Rev. Biol.*, Vol. XXXII (1957), 138–44, esp. 140; Georg Uschmann on Haeckel, *Dictionary of Scientific Biography* (1972), VI, 6–11.

186. Walter Harding, "Thoreau and 'Ecology': Correction," *Science*, Vol. CXLIX (1965), 707; J. S. Burdon-Sanderson, "Biology in Relation to Other Natural Sciences," *Nature*, Vol. XLVIII (1893), 464–72, reprinted in *Smithsonian Institution Annual Report for 1893* (Washington, D.C., 1894), 435–63, esp. 439; Stephen A. Forbes, "On Contagious Disease in the Chinch-Bug (*Blissus leucopterus* Say)," *Illinois Dept. Agriculture Trans.*, Vol. XXXII (1896), 16–176, esp. 16–18.

187. Edward Forbes, "Report on the Molluscs and Radiata of the Aegean Sea, and on Their Distribution Considered as Bearing on Geology," *British Assoc. Advancement of Sci. Report*, Vol. XIII (1843), 130–93, esp. 173; Edward Forbes, "On the Light Thrown on Geology by Submarine Researches," *Edinburgh New Philos. J.*, Vol. XXXVI (1844), 318–27; Frank N. Egerton on Forbes in *Dictionary of Scientific Biography* (1972), V, 66–68; Karl August Möbius, *Die Auster und die Austernwirtschaft* (Berlin, 1877); trans. by H. J. Rice, "The Oyster and Oyster-Culture," *U.S. Commission of Fish and Fisheries Report for 1880* (Washington, D.C., 1880), 683–751; Hans Querner on Möbius, *Dictionary of Scien-*

tific Biography, IX (1974), 431–432; John Lussenhop, "Victor Hensen and the Development of Sampling Methods in Ecology," *J. Hist. Biology*, Vol. VII (1974), 319–37, hereafter cited as "Hensen"; Stauffer, "Haeckel, Darwin, and Ecology," *Quart. Rev. Biol.*, Vol. XXXII (1957), 141–42.

188. Edward Lurie, *Nature and the American Mind: Louis Agassiz and the Culture of Science* (New York, Science History, 1974), 37ff.; Ralph W. Dexter, "From Penikese to the Marine Biological Laboratory at Woods Hole—the Role of Agassiz's Students," *Essex Institute Historical Collections*, Vol. CX (1974), 151–61; Frank R. Lillie, *The Woods Hole Marine Biological Laboratory* (Chicago, University of Chicago Press, 1944), Chaps. 2–3; Paul S. Galtsoff, *The Story of the Bureau of Commercial Fisheries Biological Laboratory, Woods Hole, Massachusetts* (U.S. Fish and Wildlife Service, Bureau of Commercial Fisheries, Circular 415, 1962); Donald J. Zinn, "Study of Marine Life," *Dictionary of American History* (new ed., New York, Charles Scribner's Sons, 1976).

189. Kurt Lampert, *Das Leben der Binnengewässer* (2d ed., Leipzig, Tauchnitz, 1910), 13; Frank N. Egerton, "The Scientific Contributions of François Alphonse Forel, the Founder of Limnology," *Schweizerische Zeitschrift für Hydrologie*, Vol. XXIV (1962), 181–99; W. C. Allee, "Ecological Background and Growth Before 1900," in W. C. Allee, Alfred E. Emerson, Orlando Park, Thomas Park, and Karl P. Schmidt, *Principles of Animal Ecology* (Philadelphia, W. B. Saunders, 1949), 13–43, esp. 40–42.

190. Stephen A. Forbes and Robert E. Richardson, *The Fishes of Illinois* (Urbana, Illinois State Laboratory of Natural History, 1908, 2d ed., 1920); Leland O. Howard, "Stephen Alfred Forbes, 1844–1930," *National Academy of Sciences Biographical Memoirs*, Vol. XIV (1932), 3–25; H. C. Oesterling, "Bibliography of Stephen Alfred Forbes," *National Academy of Sciences Biographical Memoirs*, Vol. XIV (1932), 26–54; Harlow B. Mills, "Stephen Alfred Forbes," *Systematic Zoology*, Vol. XIII (1964), 208–14; Harlow B. Mills, "From 1858 to 1958," *Illinois Natural History Survey Bull.* (special issue, *A Century of Biological Research)*, Vol. XXVII (1958), 85–103, esp. 94–98; Thomas G. Scott, "Wildlife Research," *Illinois Natural History Survey Bull.*, Vol. XXVII (1958), 179–201, esp. 183–84; Mary P. Winsor on Forbes, *Dictionary of Scientific Biography* (1972), V, 69–71.

191. Stephen A. Forbes, "The Lake as a Microcosm," *Peoria Scientific Assoc. Bull.*, 1887, 77–87; Egerton, Balance of Nature," *Quart. Rev. Biol.*, Vol. XLVIII (1973), 342–43.

192. Gerald E. Gunning, "Illinois," in *Limnology in North America* (ed. by David G. Frey, Madison, University of Wisconsin Press, 1966), 163–89, esp. 166–71, hereafter cited as *Limnology*; George W. Bennett, "Aquatic Biology," *Illinois Nat. Hist. Survey Bull.*, Vol. XXVII (1958), 163–78, esp. 163–68; Pierce C. Mullen on Kofoid in *Dictionary of Scientific Biography* (1973) VII, 447. Lussenhop, "Hensen," *J. Hist. Biol.*, Vol. VII (1974), 334.

193. G. C. Sellery, *E. A. Birge, a Memoir*, with "An Appraisal of Birge the Limnologist, an Explorer of Lakes," by C. H. Mortimer (Madison, University of Wisconsin Press, 1956); Florence W. Marsh, "Professor C. Dwight Marsh and His Investigation of Lakes," *Wisconsin Acad. Sci. Arts Letters Trans.*, Vol. XXXI (1938), 535–43; David G. Frey, "Wisconsin: the Birge-Juday Era," in Frey, *Limnology*, 3–54; David C. Chandler, "Michigan," in *ibid.*, 95–115, esp. 98–99; Shelby D. Gerking, "Central States," in *ibid.*, 239–68, esp. 239.

194. Auguste Pyramus de Candolle, "Géographie botanique," *Dictionnaire des science naturelles* (ed. by F. G. Levrault (1820), XVIII, 359–422. William J. Hooker published a modified translation, "Geography Considered in Relation to the Distribution of Plants," in Hugh Murray, *An Encyclopaedia of Geography: Comprising a Complete Description of the Earth* . . . (London, Longman,

1834), 227–46. See also A. G. Tansley, "The Early History of Modern Plant Ecology in Britain," *J. Ecology*, Vol. XXXV (1947), 130–37, esp. 130; Howard S. Reed, "A Brief History of Ecological Work in Botany," *Plant World*, Vol. VIII (1905), 163–70, 198–208, esp. 198–201.

195. Andrew Denny Rodgers III, *John Merle Coulter: Missionary in Science* (Princeton, Princeton University Press, 1944); William Trelease, "John Merle Coulter, 1851–1928," *Nat. Acad. Sci. Biog. Mem.*, Vol. XIV (1932), 97–108 and portrait, J. C. Arthur, "Bibliography of John Merle Coulter," *Nat. Acad. Sci. Biog. Mem.*, Vol. XIV (1932), 109–23.

196. Raymond J. Pool, "A Brief Sketch of the Life and Work of Charles Edwin Bessey," *Amer. J. Botany*, Vol. II (1915), 505–18, and portrait; Joseph Ewan on Bessey, *Dictionary of Scientific Biography* (1970), II, 102–104; Richard A. Overfield, "Charles E. Bessey: The Impact of the 'New' Botany on American Agriculture, 1880–1910," *Technology and Culture*, Vol. XVI (1975), 162–81.

197. Conway MacMillan, *The Metaspermae of the Minnesota Valley. A List of the Higher Seed-Producing Plants Indigenous to the Drainage-Basin of the Minnesota River* (Minneapolis, Harrison and Smith, 1892); Conway MacMillan, "Observations on the Distribution of Plants Along Shore at Lake of the Woods," *Minnesota Botanical Studies*, Vol. I (1897), 949–1023 and pls. 70–81; Harry Baker Humphrey, *Makers of North American Botany* (New York, Ronald, 1961), 159–60, hereafter cited as *Makers*.

198. Raymond J. Pool, "A Memorial, Frederic Edward Clements," *Ecology*, Vol. XXXV (1954), 109–12; Roscoe Pound, "Frederic E. Clements as I Knew Him," *Ecology*, Vol. XXXV (1954), 112–13; J. Phillips, "A Tribute to Frederic E. Clements and His Concepts in Ecology," *Ecology*, Vol. XXXV (1954), 114–15; David Wigdor, *Roscoe Pound: Philosopher of Law* (Westport, Conn., and London, Greenwood, 1974), Chap. 3.

199. Cowles, "The Ecological Relations of Vegetation on the Sand Dunes of Lake Michigan," *Botanical Gazette*, Vol. XXVII (1899), 95–117, 167–202, 281–308, 361–91; "The Physiographic Ecology of Chicago and Vicinity," *Botanical Gazette*, Vol. XXXI (1901), 73–108, 145–82; "The Plant Societies of Chicago and Vicinity," *Bull. Geographical Soc. Chicago*, Vol. II (1901), 1–76; William S. Cooper, "Henry Chandler Cowles," *Ecology*, Vol. XVI (1935), 281–83 and portrait.

200. William Francis Ganong, "On Raised Peat-bogs in New Brunswick," *Botanical Gazette*, Vol. XVI (1891), 123–26; "The Vegetation of the Bay of Fundy and Diked Marshes: an Ecological Study," *Botanical Gazette*, Vol. XXXVI (1903), 161–86, 280–302, 349–67, 429–55; Humphrey, *Makers*, 91–92.

201. John W. Harshberger, "An Ecological Study of the New Jersey Strand Flora," *Acad. Nat. Sci. Philadelphia Proc.*, 1900, 623–71, 1902, 642–69; John W. Harshberger, "An Ecological Study of the Flora of Mountainous North Carolina," *Botanical Gazette*, Vol. XXXVI (1903), 241–58, 368–83; John W. Harshberger, *Life and Work of John Harshberger, Ph.D.: An Autobiography* (Philadelphia, 1928); G. E. Nichols, "Obituary Notice: John William Harshberger, 1869–1929," *Ecology*, Vol. XI (1930), 443–44.

202. Stephen A. Forbes, "On Some Interactions of Organisms," *Illinois State Lab. Nat. Hist. Bull.*, Vol. I (1880), 3–17, esp. 6; "The Food of Birds," *Illinois State Lab. Nat. Hist. Bull.*, Vol. I (1880), 80–148, esp. 85; Herbert Spencer, *The Principles of Biology* (2 vols., London, 1865–67; New York, D. Appleton, 1866–67), II, 397–478.

203. Ralph Dexter, "Birds and Insects in Relation to Horticulture in Northeastern Ohio, 1879–1899," *Biologist*, Vol. XLIV (1961), 1–6; Leland O. Howard, "A Study in Insect Parasitism: a

Consideration of the Parasites of the White-Masked Tussock Moth, with an Account of Their Habits and Interrelations, and with Descriptions of New Species," *U.S. Dept. Ag., Technical Series*, Vol. V (1897), 5–57; Leland O. Howard, *Fighting the Insects: The Story of an Entomologist, Telling of the Life and Experiences of the Writer* (New York, Macmillan, 1933); Mallis, *American Entomologists*, 79–86 et passim.

204. Winslow, *Conquest*, Chap. 17; Jean Théodoridès, "Les grandes Étapes de la Parasitologie," *Clio Medica*, Vol. I (1966), 129–45, 185–208, esp. 196–204; William B. Herms, *Medical Entomology, With Special Reference to the Health and Well-being of Man and Animals* (3d ed., New York, Macmillan, 1939), Chap. 1.

205. Alpheus S. Packard, "The Cave Fauna of North America, with Remarks on the Anatomy of the Brain and Origin of the Blind Species," *National Acad. Sci. Mem.*, Vol. IV (1888), 3–156 and 27 plates; T. D. A. Cockerell, "Biographical Memoir of Alpheus Spring Packard, 1839–1905," *Nat. Acad. Sci. Biog. Mem.*, Vol. IX (1920), 181–236; Abbott H. Thayer, "The Law Which Underlies Protective Coloration," *Auk*, Vol. XIII (1896), 124–29, 318–20; S. D. Judd, "The Efficiency of Some Protective Adaptations in Securing Insects from Birds," *American Naturalist*, Vol. XXXIII (1899), 461–84; Mary Fuertes Boynton, "Abbott Thayer and Natural History," *Osiris*, Vol. X (1952), 542–55; Sterling, *Merriam*, 332–35; Hugh Cott, *Adaptive Coloration in Animals* (London, Methuen, 1957); J. A. Ryder, "A Geometrical Representation of the Relative Intensity of the Conflict Between Organisms," *American Naturalist*, Vol. XXVI (1892), 923–29.

206. George Valentine Riley, "The Yucca Moth and Yucca Pollination," *Missouri Botanical Garden Annual Report,* Vol. III (1892), 99–158; William Trelease, "Further Studies of Yuccas and Their Pollination," *Missouri Botanical Garden Annual Report,* Vol. IV (1893), 181–226; Charles Robertson, "Flowers and Insects: Contributions to an Account of the Ecological Relations of the Entomophilous Flora and the Anthophilous Insect Fauna of the Neighborhood of Carlinville, Illinois," *Acad. Sci. St. Louis Trans.*, Vol. VII (1897), 151–79; Frank N. Egerton on Lovell, *Dictionary of Scientific Biography* (1973), VIII, 518; On Trelease see Humphrey, *Makers of North American Botany*, 251–53, and Joseph Ewan, *Dictionary of Scientific Biography* (1976), XIII, 456.

207. Bashford Dean, "The physical and Biological Characteristics of the Natural Oyster Grounds of South Carolina," *U.S. Fish Commission Bull.*, Vol. X (1890), 335–61; Charles T. Simpson, "The Pearly Fresh-water Mussels of the United States; Their Habits, Enemies, and Diseases; with Suggestions for Their Protection," *U.S. Fish Commission Bull.*, Vol. XVIII (1898), 279–88.

208. C. Hart Merriam, "Results of a Biological Survey of the San Francisco Mountain Region and Desert of the Little Colorado, Arizona," *North American Fauna*, Vol. III (1890), 1–136, 14 plates and 5 maps. This and other writings by Merriam on the subject have been reprinted in facsimile, *Selected Works of Clinton Hart Merriam* (ed. by Keir B. Sterling, New York, Arno, 1974); Sterling, *Merriam*, Chap. 6.

209. But see Robert Clarke, *Ellen Swallow: The Woman Who Founded Ecology* (Chicago, Follett, 1973).

17

ECOLOGY SINCE 1900

By Robert P. McIntosh*

In 1938 the distinguished philosopher of science Rudolph Carnap recognized a logical need for a branch of biology dealing with the interactions of individual organisms, groups of organisms, and their environment (Allee et al., 1949). He apparently was not aware that this logical need had been felt by biologists for over half a century and that the already thriving young science of ecology was filling the logical niche he recognized. Carnap's lapse was particularly striking because ecology in the United States was, in considerable degree, a product of the Middle West, notably his own institution, the University of Chicago.

THE RISE OF SELF-CONSCIOUS ECOLOGY, 1900–20

Ecology began to be formalized as a discipline in Europe in the late 1800's, when biology was becoming well established as a professional and scientific area discrete from medicine and was still largely dominated by taxonomy, anatomy, morphology, physiology, and controversies over the new the-

ory of natural selection. The same logic that struck Carnap must have been apparent to European biologists, for in 1866, E. H. Haeckel, the leading proponent of Darwinian thought in Germany, christened the science "oekologie" (Egerton, 1976). Stauffer (1957) asserted that the logical justification for the introduction of the term was a notable consequence of Darwin's thought. Lynn White (1968) attributed the "crystallization of the novel concept of ecology" to the recognition that scientific knowledge means technological power over nature that developed principally in the mid-nineteenth century. Haeckel was not so much the founder of a science as he was the first to name and define a logically consistent area of biology bringing together an extremely heterogeneous mix of natural history, physiology, hydrobiology, biogeography, and evolutionary concerns of nineteenth-century biology. He raised a standard around which biologists of similar mind could gather, thus providing a focus for a previously inchoate area of science (Egerton, 1976).

Among the seminal European ecological works that exerted major influence on the genesis of ecology in the United States were E. Warming's *Oecological Plant Geography* (1895), A. F. W. Schimper's *Plant Geography on a Physiological Basis* (1898), both of which stressed the relation of plants to environment (Goodland, 1975), and F. A. Forel's (1892) monograph on Lake Leman introducing the term *limnology* (Egerton, 1962). Prominent among American biologists of the nineties were J. M. Coulter and C. E. Bessey, professors of botany at the University of Chicago and the University of Nebraska, respectively; E. A. Birge, zoologist of the University of Wisconsin; and S. A. Forbes, entomologist associated with the University of Illinois, the Illinois State Laboratory of Natural History, and its successor, the Illinois Natural History Survey. In 1887, Forbes wrote *The Lake as a Microcosm,* which later came to be recognized as a classic of ecology. The work of these four biologists forms something of a watershed in the history of ecology in the United States. Although not themselves trained as ecologists, they became interested in the new science of ecology and were influential in the careers of many of the biologists who established ecology as a science in America.

"Oekologie" was formally considered at the Madison Botanical Congress of 1893, where the "O" was dropped and the

*Ecology has expanded so rapidly in recent years that by far the greatest amount of ecological work has been done in the past twenty-five years. Thus a history of ecology since 1900 is soon involved in what may better be called current events. Entry into this area is fraught with dangers of omission and commission because of the vast amount of material, much of it not yet assimilated into a clear conceptual framework. My efforts to boil down ecology in the United States to an essence suitable for publication in a short article were greatly aided by the kindness of several colleagues in reading the commenting on preliminary drafts of the manuscript. I express my appreciation to Carl von Ende, Grant Cottam, Robert Whittaker, Orie Loucks, and Frank Egerton. I am also grateful for the interest and comments of Paul B. Sears, a premier practitioner and expositor of ecology, whose lucid writing did much to bring ecology to the attention of scientists and the lay public. I do not intimate that all of the above persons necessarily agree with my selection or interpretations or that they share any onus for the inevitable omissions or errors. The real appreciation for any history of ecology goes to those whose work established a body of ecological concepts and facts long before ecology became a familiar word in the household, councils of government, and funding agencies. It seems a nice example of scientific preadaptation that ecology was there when it was needed.

Anglicized spelling, "ecology," adopted, a source later of confusion and controversy. The early development of ecology as a named and recognized science is commonly attributed to botanists. Charles Elton (1933), a prominent British animal ecologist, commented, "Animal ecology began as a science by following rather closely the lines laid down by the earlier work of plant ecologists"; and the American animal ecologists, R. N. Chapman (1931), and Allee and his associates (1949), also acknowledged the early leadership of botanists.

At the University of Chicago, H. C. Cowles transferred his interests from geology with T. C. Chamberlin, to botany with J. M. Coulter and received his doctoral degree in 1898 for studies entitled "Ecological Relations of the Sand Dune Flora of Northern Indiana." This, and his subsequent studies of the vegetation and physiographic ecology of the Chicago region, constituted the pioneer studies in America of succession—the process of change in ecological systems—that preoccupied ecologists in subsequent decades and remains one of the central concepts of modern ecology. Perhaps Cowles's major contribution was his impact on the first generation of ecology students.

In the same year, 1898, F. E. Clements completed his doctoral work with Bessey, a distinguished mycologist, at the University of Nebraska. Clements had previously published on fungi, but his doctoral dissertation was a study of the phytogeography of Nebraska, later published with Roscoe Pound, who abandoned ecology for a distinguished career in law. By virtue of his prolific research and writing (in 1901 he presented five of the twelve papers on the program of the meeting of the Botanical Society), Clements became the major codifier and theorist of early-twentieth-century plant ecology, and in 1905 he produced the first American book on ecology, *Research Methods in Ecology*. In this volume he evidenced the tendency that was to earn for ecology the pejorative definition "that part of biology which has been totally abandoned to terminology." Its glossary contained the classical definition of *geotome* (complete with Greek derivation): "An instrument for obtaining soil samples"—that is, a shovel. The bibliography of Clements' book suggested the newness of ecology in America, for it referred mostly to European works, and only two references (by Cowles) used the word "ecology."

Ecology, one of the newest branches of biological science, slightly antedating the formalization of genetics, was taken up rather quickly, particularly in botanical circles. By 1902 it was incorporated without comment in a high-school botany book, although still suspect as a bastard version of physiology in some circles and unknown in others. Even Haeckel described ecology as a part of physiology, an unfortunate classification (Haeckel, 1898). Indeed, ecology was still so new that in 1902 a letter to *Science* from a well-known editor was critical of the word being used without explanation when it did not appear in the standard dictionaries. A number of respondents pointed out that the word was in the dictionaries as *oecology,* and an extended discussion ensued concerning its origin, etymology, and proper spelling. William Morton Wheeler (a distinguished entomologist and later the first

vice-president of the Ecological Society of America) complained that botanists had usurped the word, had eliminated the *o* improperly, and were distorting the science. He urged that zoologists adopt the word "ethology" instead (Wheeler, 1902). There is in the exchange a suggestion of the split between plant and animal ecologists that pervaded ecology from its beginnings and only recently shows signs of closing.

Those who find recent ecology difficult to comprehend may be relieved to know that this has long been so. Cowles (1904), attempting to review the work in ecology for 1903, said: "It is almost impossible to do such a task for the field of ecology since the field of ecology is chaos. Ecologists are not agreed even as to fundamental principles or motive; indeed no one at this time, . . . is prepared to define or delimit ecology." Early ecologists apparently did agree on the central role of evolution, for Cowles also said, "If ecology has a place in modern biology, certainly one of its great tasks is to unravel the mysteries of adaptation." In the same issue of *Science*, W. F. Ganong (1904), an early Canadian ecologist, listed "seven cardinal principles of ecology," all concerned with adaptation. This central concern with evolution, which was widespread in early ecology, was not as intensely pursued as it might have been, for many years later John Harper (1967) complained that ecology had abandoned evolution to genetics, although evolution is predominantly an ecological subject. Allee et al. (1949), in their review of the history of ecology, also noted the tendency of some ecologists to "veer away from an evolutionary viewpoint," a tendency clearly reversed in recent textbooks of ecology. The diffuseness of ecology that often drew critcism of its publications was also noted early. Ganong (1904) commented:

Ecological publications in American are too often characterized by a vast prolixity in comparison with their real additions to knowledge, by a pretentiousness of statement and terminology unjustified by their real merits, and by a weakness of logic deserving the disrespect they receive. The subject suffers, I fear, from a phase of the "get-rich-quick spirit."

Although the real rise of the get-rich-quick spirit in ecology was many years in the future, with the rise, in the 1960's, of the popularity and status of ecology in an era of large-scale funding and public concern for the environment, perhaps the earliest funding of ecology in America appeared in 1903, as both Cowles and Ganong noted. The Carnegie Institution supported a proposal to establish a desert laboratory on a hill overlooking Tucson in the then munificent sum of eight thousand dollars, which in those days built a substantial building (which continues to serve its purpose) and funded its first year's operation. The institution also supported early investigations of transpiration of plants by B. E. Livingston (inventor of one of the earliest instruments used by ecologists, the atmometer, a clay bulb for measuring water loss to the atmosphere) and other significant studies in physiological ecology. Forest Shreve, a major student of desert ecology, was on the staff of the Carnegie Institution from 1908 to 1945 and Clements, the premier American plant ecologist, from 1917 to 1946.

Already well into his long career as zoologist, student of

zooplankton, and university administrator, E. A. Birge made his debut as an aquatic ecologist, or limnologist, in 1895 (Mortimer, 1956; Frey, 1963). Like Forbes, he had earlier been interested in taxonomy of aquatic organisms *(Cladocera).* His distinguished career as a limnologist began with studies of plankton, but this led him into significant work in the physics and chemistry of lakes in the very first formative years of limnology. The Wisconsin Geological and Natural History Survey, the counterpart of Forbes's department in Illinois, afforded him a similarly strategic position to influence the development of aquatic ecology. In 1900, Chancey Juday joined the survey, and the partnership of Birge and Juday, which was substantially to lay the foundations of limnology in America, was formed. Birge established in detail the physical phenomenon of lake stratification and mixing resulting from change in temperature and density of water.

In the long collaboration of Birge and Juday (their joint publications exceeded the total of those published separately) they considered the "lake as a microcosm," to borrow Forbes's apt phrase. The processes of photosyntehsis, respiration, and decay and the attendant changes in dissolved gases were primary concerns of this synergistic pair, who also developed the earliest assays of biological productivity of lakes and studied the key factors controlling it. It may well be that the view of the lake as a whole, as a complex of physical and biological processes, articulated by Forbes and developed by Birge and Juday, is the reason that the moderate concept of the ecosystem and its functioning leans so heavily on aquatic studies. Chapman (1931) commented: "These relationships and processes are to be found everywhere in nature, though they may be less susceptible to analysis in other environments (than aquatic). The student of terrestrial synecology may do well to study the results of the aquatic synecologists."

Around and shortly after the turn of the century the pioneers of formal animal ecology in America also appeared. Charles C. Adams and Victor Shelford were both influenced by Cowles and Davenport at the University of Chicago. Adams (1917) said that he gave the first course in general animal ecology at Chicago in 1902, and he subsequently worked with S. A. Forbes at the Illinois Natural History Survey. Shelford completed his doctoral thesis in 1907 on "Tiger Beetles of Sand Dunes," describing the parallels of beetle populations and vegetational succession shown earlier by Cowles. In 1913, Adams published the first text on animal ecology, *Guide to the Study of Animal Ecology,* and Shelford published one of the monuments of ecology, *Animal Communities in Temperate America,* which was somewhat mistitled, for it stressed the relations of plants and animals in the Chicago region. Shelford emphasized the community concept clearly developed, before ecology was named, by the geographer-explorer Alexander von Humboldt and the marine biologist Karl August Möbius, which became the essence of ecology. According to Shelford:

Ecology is the science of communities. A study of the relations of a single species to the environment conceived without reference to communities and, in the end, unrelated to

the natural phenomena of its habitat and community associated is not properly included in the field of ecology.

Shelford underplayed the study of single-species populations, their properties, and relations to the environment *(autecology),* which actually came to be a major focus of ecology along with the central concern with the community and its properties. The relative contemporariness of ecology is seen in the fact that Shelford, one of its founders in America, published his last book in 1963.

It is perhaps unfair to mention only a few of the personalities in the early development of ecology in America, for others are surely worthy of note. C. H. Merriam (1894) had propounded his famous (if inadequate) doctrine of the distribution of animals related to temperature based on his extensive studies of mammals. H. A. Gleason, later to abandon ecology for taxonomy, was formulating his "individualistic concept," which would make him the first apostate to the overwhelming Clementsian credo of the climax association as an organism (McIntosh, 1975). Joseph Harshberger was pursuing his extensive surveys leading to the *Phytogeographic Survey of North America* (1911), the first summary description of the major communities of North America. Forrest Shreve was well into his studies of the American deserts, J. E. Weaver was beginning the work that would make him the foremost student of the American grassland, while E. N. Transeau was beginning to formulate his ideas of vegetational distribution leading to his well-known phrase "the Prairie Peninsula," describing the eastward extension of grassland into the deciduous forest. E. W. Hilgard was developing the idea of plants as indicators of soils, and C. MacMillan, one of the first to use the new word "ecology," was studying Minnesota's bogs.

The early part of the century also saw the rise of the professional areas of applied ecology, forestry, range management, wildlife management, and fisheries management; the related sciences of soils and meteorology; and the great tradition of conservation in America with its notable successors to John Wesley Powell and George Perkins Marsh. Carrying on the interlocking traditions of natural history, love of the out-of-doors and the aesthetic, almost mystical, appreciation of nature earlier seen in American poets, writers, and artists such as Walt Whitman, Henry David Thoreau, William Cullen Bryant, and Thomas Cole, were John Burroughs, John Muir, and the key figures of the American conservation movement, Gifford Pinchot and Theodore Roosevelt. The common cultural heritage of ecology and conservation and their joint development in the early 1900's were the beginning of a continued and fruitful interaction.

By 1915 a body of scientists had risen in America who regarded themselves as ecologists, although their areas of interest in biology ranged widely over plants, insects, aquatic organisms, and terrestrial vertebrates; and their approaches to these diverse taxonomic groups and different habitats were, similarly, wide-ranging, from the ecological physiology and morphology of the several taxa to their biogeographical distributions and aggregation in communities. Ecologists were notably concerned with the phenomena of succession and population and environmental changes. Following in the midlands tradition, R. H. Wolcott, professor of zoology in the University of Nebraska, wrote to Shelford, at the University of Illinois, suggesting the formation of a society of ecologists. Shelford consulted with Cowles, who agreed, and in December, 1915, the Ecological Society of America was founded, with Shelford as its first president. At the end of the year there were 307 members (Shelford, 1938).

Ecologists, then as now, were a heterogeneous group. The second president of the new society was Ellsworth Huntington, a pioneer of human ecology and an early proponent of the profound impact of the environment on human beings. Unfortunately, this early hybrid of general and human ecology was not viable; and at intervals since, particularly in recent years, there have been earnest, if only partly successful, efforts to merge human sociology and ecology in a science of human ecology.

The early American ecologists were not unduly modest. Adams (1917) saw the United States as the world leader in the "new Natural history," as he called ecology. He commented in a very modern vein, ". . . we look upon science as a tool to aid us in securing better human living in the broadest and best sense." He and Barrington Moore (1920), the first editor of the journal *Ecology,* which was established in 1920 by the Ecological Society, asserted that ecology represented the synthetic phase of biology with the function of bringing together myriads of isolated facts. Moore, along with Adams and Forbes, the latter two occupying strategic positions as directors of the state natural history surveys of New York and Illinois, respectively, stressed the importance of ecology as the basis for applied ecology and natural-resource management, a consideration that persisted throughout the development of ecology as a science.

By 1920 self-conscious ecology was reasonably well established and recognized as an academic discipline in America, although it was hardly known to the general public. It had accumulated extensive surveys and descriptions of communities, both aquatic and terrestrial (mostly qualitative though primitive quantitative methods were developing), extended the tradition of "relations physiology" as *autecology* (the relation of the organism to the physical environment), produced a limited number of specifically ecological books and references, and developed in some detail one major concept—succession. It had also established its own professional society and publication outlet and had a number of notable spokesmen in the biological community. Ecology was still notoriously heterogeneous. As one of them, Adams (1913), stated, "At present ecology is a science with its facts out of all proportion to their organization or integration." Adams (1917) also noted that the hostile opponents had mellowed with time, agnostics had been convinced and the younger generation accepted ecology, as a matter of course, like physiology.

ECOLOGY, 1920–50

From 1920 to about 1950 ecology developed rapidly. Far from the synthetic ideal of its early proponents, it prolif-

erated its own set of special interests and remained an eclectic science that frustrates writers of ecological history. Gleason (1936) correctly described ecology as "extraordinarily polymorphic." The distinction between plant and animal ecology persisted, and there was little commonality between aquatic and terrestrial aspects of ecology. It was not uncommon for authors dealing with either plants or animals to apply the word "ecology" to their particular interests without bothering with the limiting descriptor plant or animal (Nichols, 1928). Thus Gleason (1936) considered *Twenty-five Years of Ecology 1910–1935* without reference to animals, and Victor Shelford (1929) published *Laboratory and Field Ecology* as a methods book for animal ecology, although he did include references to plants as food for animals.

The first formal textbooks of ecology that might establish a "normal" science of ecology in the sense of Kuhn (1962) were Pearse's *Animal Ecology* (1926), W. B. McDougall's *Plant Ecology* (1927), Weaver and Clements' *Plant Ecology* (1929), R. N. Chapman's *Animal Ecology* (1931), and R. S. Welch's *Limnology* (1935). Pearse, for example, considered the major subdivisions of animal ecology to be physical and chemical factors, biological factors, succession, animals of the ocean, fresh-water animals, terrestrial animals, relations of animals to plants, relations of animals to color, intraspecific relations, and economics aspects of ecology. Weaver and Clements included chapters on methods of studying vegetation, plant succession, units of vegetation, causes of succession, migration, ecesis (establishment) and aggregation, competition and invasion, soils, reaction (effects of plants on environment) and stabilization, coaction (effects of organisms on each other) and conservation, a series of chapters on the environment—humidity, temperature, light, water, plants as indicators of the environment, and a description of the climax-vegetation formations of North America.

Major European influents were Charles Elton's *The Ecology of Animals* (1927) and R. Hesse's *Tiergeographie auf oekologischer Grundlage* (1924), which, translated into English as *Ecological Animal Geography* (1937), had major impact on American as well as European ecologists. It emphasized the importance of ecological aspects of animal geography, much as Warming's earlier (1895) *Oecological Plant Geography* had done for plant ecology, and, according to its translators, Allee and Schmidt, marked a new phase in the development of animal ecology. This phase emphasized the geographical distribution of animals and communities, the structural features of communities, and the feeding relations and quantitative makeup of the animal community. The nature of animal aggregations was pursued extensively, notably by Allee in a series of articles and books (1927, 1931, 1938) that emphasized studies of experimental populations and of social organization and cooperation among animals.

A significant development early in this middle period was the rise of paleoecology. Paleoecology, based largely on the study of the layers of fossil pollens (palynology) preserved in peat bogs or lake sediments, began in Scandinavia about 1916 and was rapidly adopted in America. Clements, the encyclopedist of American plant ecology, published *Methods and Principles of Paleo-ecology* (1924) and pollen studies by C. L. Fenton, Paul B. Sears, J. Potzger, Henry Hansen, and others in the 1930's and 1940's traced the history of vegetation and associated climates as they had changed with successive advances and recessions of the Pleistocene ice sheets. These studies made clear the significance of history in any consideration of the distribution of plant and animal communities and, along with the concept of succession, required that ecology develop a dynamic view of communities. Communities continued as major objects of study for ecologists and, in 1935, were rechristened and incorporated in an expanded concept "ecosystems" by Sir Arthur Tansley, a prominent British plant ecologist. *Ecosystem,* defined as the complex of living organisms (the community) and its nonliving environment, was, however, to remain in the wings until called forth by dramatic post–World War II developments in ecology. Although the actual study and analysis of the entire ecosystem was, until recently, only a gleam in the intellectual eye of ecologists, the "holistic" ideal was clearly evident much earlier. According to W. F. Taylor (1936), the key words for ecology were integration, correlation, coordination, synthesis, holistic, emergent, and relationship, all of which are prominent in the lexicon of recent ecologists. The extension of this ideal of ecology into the realm of the human environment, with its economic and political overtones, was foreshadowed in Taylor's quotation from Henry Wallace, then secretary of agriculture and left-of-center political leader, "There is as much need today for a declaration of interdependence as there was for a Declaration of Independence in 1776."

A particularly significant event that occurred about 1920 was the flourishing of population ecology, stemming from demography, which was primarily associated with animal ecology. It was notable in that it represented the first attempt to use a mathematical and theoretical approach in ecology, and the tradition continues in current ecology at an accelerated pace. Treatments of populations (demography) have a distinguished lineage most familiarly from Thomas Malthus' famous *Essay on Population,* first published in 1798, and the famed logistic equation, the most ubiquitous mathematical model of population growth, was devised in the early nineteenth century (Verhulst, 1838). Like many another promising scientific idea, the logistic equation lay fallow until rediscovered and extensively exploited in the 1920's and 1930's by several authors in Europe and, in America, notably by Raymond Pearl (Pearl and Reed, 1920; Pearl, 1925). Although Allee and his associates (1949) commented that "theoretical population ecology has not advanced to a great degree in terms of its impact on ecological thinking," the background was established for subsequent expansion of analytic population studies. Theoretical, experimental, and field studies of populations were to become a major part of ecology and, along with the study of communities, constitute those aspects of biological phenomena which are most distinctively ecology. Animal-population studies explored the theoretical form of growth of populations, the effects of population density on growth and development of individual organisms, reproduction and mortality, and the factors controlling population growth and community organization. Pearl's contribution

was salient in that it represented the impact of the new biometric, or statistical, methods, which were then being developed and incorporated into ecological theory and practice. One of the cornerstones of modern ecology is the concept of a population as a group of individuals with a set of attributes to be considered in terms of the population, not of the individuals (for example, mortality rates); and the gradual recognition of the power of statistics to describe and, more particularly, to assess probable error in the numerical estimates of population characteristics and measures of association and correlation between species was necessary for the population concept to develop.

An important corollary of the logistic equation and mathematical theory in ecology derived from the classical work in theoretical and experimental population ecology by G. F. Gause in Europe, and in America the extended studies of Thomas Park with flour beetle *(Tribolium)* populations were a significant extension of this work. These and similar studies led to the formulation of "Gause law," or the "competitive exclusion principle" (Hardin, 1962), which became a cornerstone of ecological thought. The general thesis of the competitive exclusion principle is that two species that compete for a common and limiting resource cannot coexist and one will be eliminated. Thomas Park corroborated Gause's findings, showing that one of two competing species normally becomes extinct. From this kind of study, and observations in the field, it was assumed that species that coexisted in nature inhabited somewhat different niches, the niche being the organism's place in the community. Recent formulations of competitive exclusion agree that two species, to survive in the same stable community, must have different controls on their populations, but not necessarily resource limitation. Few aspects of ecological theory or experimentation have a more involved, or even convoluted, history than the study of populations, the phenomenon of competition and their offspring, the *niche.* The niche concept, first specifically named by Joseph Grinnell in the United States in 1917 and built into community interpretation by Charles Elton, blushed substantially unseen until the 1950's, when it was seized upon and moved into place with the hope that it would be a major tenet of modern ecological theory. The famous individualistic concept of Gleason (1917, 1926) was also an early statement of the species niche.

Although theoretical-mathematical aspects of ecology were largely confined to considerations of populations, ecologists in America were aware of the need for quantitative approaches to communities. The earliest attempts to apply rigorous quantitative sampling and statistical methods to field populations were made by a European marine biologist, V. Hensen, about 1880 (Lussenhop, 1974). Aquatic sampling was extended to fresh waters in Illinois about 1897; and Clements and Pound, as early as 1898, used sample areas called "quadrats" in terrestrial studies. They noted the difficulty of estimating numbers of individuals and urged the need for actual counts. W. L. McAtee (1907) censused animal populations in four square feet, and in the same year Forbes (1907) introduced the idea of a coefficient of association designed to show the frequency with which one species was found with another. Forbes (1909) also published a survey of bird populations in an E-W transect 150 feet wide across the entire state of Illinois (191.86 miles) and analyzed the relative abundance of bird species in the different habitats, mostly corn fields, that were encountered. Early proponents of statistics in ecology assumed that populations were uniformly (evenly) distributed in nature; later, randomness was accepted as a possibility. Although ecology has been widely criticized as being largely a descriptive and qualitative science, there has been a continuity of interest in quantitative approaches from the pioneers in the field to the present. Statistical sophistication on the part of ecologists grew slowly, however, and as late as 1935 even as astute an individual as Gleason could assert that plant species were distributed at random, and therefore, he said, it was possible to determine densities (number of individuals) from frequency (the number of samples in which a species occurred). It would be unfair to allow this uncharacteristic lapse of judgment to obscure the fact that Gleason was one of the major proponents of the use of mathematical methods in ecology. He was in the 1920's an early student of species-area curves (the increase in number of species with increasing sample size), and he noted that attempts to determine number of species by empirically developed equations had failed. In this area he anticipated the recent interest in species diversity. Gleason correctly predicted the continuing development of quantitative and mathematical methods in ecology, although, as late as 1944, Stanley Cain (1944), another proponent of quantitative methods in ecology, worried, with considerable justice as it now appears, that ecological systems might be difficult, or even too complex, to treat mathematically. It is only in the past decade that the validity of Cain's apprehension is being tested. Quantitative ecologists, particularly plant ecologists and marine ecologists, were extensively concerned with sampling methods and statistical analysis of the resulting data. These aspects of quantitative ecology, which were largely used in field studies of population and communities, were carried on quite independently of the theoretical mathematical concerns of population growth and population interactions that were developing concurrently.

Ecologists, plant and animal, aquatic and terrestrial, were expanding their horizons from studies of communities as lists of species to assessments of numerical abundance and measures of relations among species. In this they followed in the wake of applied areas of ecology, such as fisheries, which had been concerned with numerical assessment, at least of commercial species, for many years. Differences in techniques of sampling and in ease of catching various kinds of organisms obscured the general similarity of the means and ends of quantitative approaches to ecology. Animal ecologists generally were assured that they could recognize individuals for sampling; plant ecologists worried about recognition of individuals. Plant ecologists and marine benthic ecologists, dealing with relatively stationary organisms, were most confident of their estimates, while animal ecologists generally experienced more difficulty in arriving at accurate estimates of abundance. The quantitative interests of ecologists focused on a number of central concerns:

1. Single-species distribution and the dispersion of individuals that complicated sampling and statistical analyses by being nonrandom or distributed in patterns (usually clumped) for varied reasons, contrary to early assumptions of uniform or random distribution.

2. The number of species and their relative abundances in an area or community.

3. Association or correlations between species that were suggestive of common reactions to the environment or of interactions among species.

4. Measures of similarity between areas or communities.

5. Assessment of the pattern or homogeneity of an area. Homogeneity had been widely assumed to be a criterion of a natural ecological community. In fact, the nature and scale of pattern or heterogeneity under a series of new terms (heterogeneously diverse, patchiness, grain) continues as a major concern of sampling technique and of recent theoretical ecology.

Ecology, like biology generally, proved relatively difficult to fit into a numerical or mathematical framework, and the model of the so-called hard sciences like physics was not readily followed (Haskell, 1940). This was, in substantial part, due to the difficulty of isolating single ecological variables for study and to the difficulty of recognizing, or at least arriving at a consensus on, the objects for ecological study, essentially the population and the community (the aggregation of populations) and their interaction with the environment. Much of the first fifty years of self-conscious ecology in America was spent in describing, largely qualitatively, the complex mantle of environments, vegetation, and animal communities that blended in subtle and ill-understood ways over the landscape and were rapidly being modified or eliminated by the activities of man and his animals even as ecologists sought to study them. The composition, structure, distribution, successional status, classification, and terminology of the plant community were a pervasive concern of American plant ecologists (phytosociologists). The theoretical concepts of Clements dominated American plant ecology, largely isolating it from the several European schools and producing a provincial tone lamented by F. E. Egler (1951), then as now a perceptive, if acerbic, critic of the needs and failings of ecology.

Ecology was, to a large degree, a descriptive and empirical science in 1920. As late as 1939, Allee and Thomas Park wrote, "The statement is frequently made that ecology deals mainly with facts which are organized around relatively few principles." Recognizing this limitation, they attempted to summarize distinctly ecological principles from the literature. In this endeavor they followed Ganong, who in 1904 had recognized seven ecological principles, all dealing with adaptation; and they anticipated K. E. F. Watt, who in 1973 recognized an unwieldy thirty-eight principles, starting with the laws of thermodynamics. Allee and Park recognized about nine sets of principles, which they said dealt with "interrelations between an organism or one or more groups of organisms and its or their environment." They serve to characterize ecology at approximately the midpoint in its formal existence in the United States:

1. *Law of the minimum,* or, more generally, the capacity of an organism to tolerate the minimum or maximum extreme of environment. Familiarly, some organisms have narrow, others broad, ranges of tolerance.

2. *Adaptation,* which was so prominent in Ganong's principles (1904), appeared also as a fundamental principle of Allee and Park, who cited as an example the familiar "Bergman's rule," which suggested an adaptive relation of body size of related warm-blooded animals to temperature.

3. *Community,* at that time often thought of as the major, or even the only, ecological concern, particularly by some plant ecologists.

4. *Succession,* the process of maturation of the community towards a "climax," in those days usually thought of as a regional formation recognized by its dominant organisms, substantially self perpetuating under the control of the regional climate according to the ideas of Clements.

5. *Population growth,* particularly the quantitative aspects summarized in the logistic curve.

6. *Cooperation* and *competition* among organisms suggested a whole set of ecological principles centering about evolution. Allee and Park noted that the factors of natural selection are definitely ecological and laid claim to evolutionary dynamics as a province of ecology, but they noted that this was a field that ecologists had avoided.

7. *Niche separation,* a principle which was based on the observation that related species occupy separate niches and thus are in less direct competition. This principle has been seized on by recent ecological theorists and extensively exploited.

8. *Geographic distribution.* Among these they noted the tendency for tropical species to have fewer individuals per species than temperate species, an aspect of another central concern of current ecological thought under the name diversity.

9. *Emigration* and *dispersal* of organisms.

The 1939 statement of ecological principles was very loosely structured, and Allee and Park recognized its inadequacy. It serves to illustrate the very tentative thinking of two leading animal ecologists, who said, "We believe that focusing attention on a theoretical framework will lead to more important work in ecology."

Another landmark of ecology in midcourse was *Plant and Animal Communities* (Just, 1939), which was the result of a 1938 conference described as "the first ambitious attempt to arrange a general public stocktaking of ecology" (Allee, 1939). It marked, according to Allee, a change from the earlier evangelical tone of ecologists to "frank scepticism about every aspect of ecology except the value of the subject itself." The general stocktaking included the following titles and authors:

Plant Associations on Land, H. S. Conard
Littoral Marine Communities, G. E. McGinitie
Fresh-Water Communities, F. E. Eggleston
The Biome, J. R. Carpenter
The Individual Concept of the Plant Association, H. A. Gleason

The Unistratal Concept of Plant Communities (The Unions), Theodore Lippma
The Climax and its Complexities, S. A. Cain
Social Coordination and the Superorganism, A. E. Emerson
On the Analysis of Social Organization Among Vertebrates with Special Reference to Birds, N. Tinbergen
Analytical Population Studies in Relation to General Ecology, T. Park

The list of authors included many of the ecological luminaries of the day, but Allee noted that the conference was dominated by the ideas of those who were not present, such as Clements, Shelford, J. Braun-Blaunquet, Juday, Elton, and K. Lorenz. The reviewer, a distinguished animal ecologist, commented "The papers on plant sociology seemed at times to be fuller of words than meat," which suggested that the traditional plant-animal ecology schism still persisted; and he noted that the concept of the *biome* (biocommunities considering both plants and animals) received lip service only. He also deplored the continuing problem of proliferating terminology, which continues unabated to the present, and called for more effective means of collecting, analyzing, and interpreting data.

The symposium was distinctive in that in included plant and animal, terrestrial and aquatic, fresh-water and marine aspects of ecology. Aquatic ecology had developed along somewhat distinct lines from terrestrial ecology, and in 1936 the Limnological Society of America had been founded with 221 members and Juday as its first president. In 1948 it became the American Society of Limnology and Oceanography. Fitting all the taxonomic and habitat interests into one ecological bed was not notably successful, and the several aspects of ecology continued to develop in parallel. Since most limnologists were trained as zoologists, there was more interaction between terrestrial animal ecology and limnology. Plant ecology, especially *phytosociology* (the study of plant communities), largely dominated by the views and terminology of Clements, went substantially its own way (Egler, 1951). Sears (1956) provided an apt phrase, "the ecology of ecologists," to describe the environmental reasons why ecologists and ecology continued to be divided into parochial interests.

A striking aspect of the 1938 conference was the inclusion of the famous animal behaviorist N. Tinbergen, and the reference to Lorenz as one of the notable absentees. The chronology of the development of animal behavior parallels that of ecology, and in the United States outstanding work, such as that of Margaret Morse Nice (1937) on the song sparrow, emphasized the significance to ecology of aspects of animal behavior such as territoriality and social hierarchy, concepts which were being developed in this period.

Another important publication of 1939 was *Bio-ecology,* by Clements and Shelford, then among the major figures in American ecology. As the hyphenated title implies, *Bio-ecology* was an attempt to achieve the synthetic ideal ecologists often talked about but rarely practiced. It incorporated animal, plant, and aquatic ecology but recognized that the desirable addition of human ecology would be delayed until the feeling of the need for synthesis became more general. *Bio-ecology* may in some ways mark a turning point in ecology. In a review, G. E. Hutchinson (1940), one of the titans of modern ecology, noted the failures of the book and pointed the way ecology should go and, indeed, has gone (Hutchinson, himself, usually in the lead). Hutchinson criticized the book's emphasis on classification and terminology. He specifically deplored (1) its failure to use statistics and mathematics in dealing with ecological problems, (2) the insistence of *Bioecology* on the community, and (3) a complete lack of the biogeochemical approach, which integrates the living community with the nonliving environment. At this time Hutchinson was beginning his famous studies on Linsley Pond and developing his interests in limnology (Hutchinson, 1957b), biogeochemistry, and theoretical ecology, which have had major influence on subsequent developments in ecology by virtue not only of his own enormous research output but of his impact on a large number of the leading figures in modern ecology (Edmondson, 1971; Kohn, 1971; Riley, 1971). Some of the needs of ecology urged by Hutchinson in 1940 had been foreshadowed in the world of E. N. Transeau, who, as early as 1926, worked out a reasonably detailed energy budget of a cornfield; and by 1940, Juday had worked out an energy budget of a lake, and Raymond Lindeman (1941, 1942) had elaborated in detail the subject of tropic (nutritional) relationships and developed the framework of the metabolism of biological communities.

The latter part of this middle period in the growth of ecology was marked by the appearance of a number of significant publications. Plant ecology, previously dominated by Weaver and Clements' premier textbook, *Plant Ecology,* was subdivided into *Plants and Environment: A Textbook of Plant Autecology,* by R. F. Daubenmire (1947), and H. J. Oosting's *The Study of Plant Communities* (1948), emphasizing *synecology* (plant communities). Another milestone was the appearance of the first encyclopedic attempt to review animal ecology, *Principles of Animal Ecology* (1949), which was written, appropriately enough, by five distinguished second-generation ecologists from Chicago: Allee, A. E. Emerson, Thomas Park, Orlando Park, and K. P. Schmidt. The major sections of this volume were: (1) The history of ecology (to 1940), (2) the environment; (3) populations, (4) the community, and (5) ecology and evolution. The authors' major interest was in the documentation of the general ecological principles that Allee and Thomas Park had discussed earlier. However, principles are nearly buried in the wealth of detail amassed by these ecologists, although they disavowed detail for the sake of detail. Nevertheless, the explicit exposition of ecological concepts, which had been developing in the notoriously diffuse subject ecology had become, served to summarize the state of animal ecology about 1949 and to anticipate the dramatic developments of the next two decades. The delineation in the book of the essence of trophic ecology, the quantitative treatment of population and energy budgets, the emphasis on biomass and the re-emphasis on natural selection and evolution as ecological subjects point to what came to be called "the wave of the future" in the full flush of post–World War II ecology.

Ecologists in the consolidation period of ecology continued the strong impetus toward an important role for ecology in the management and conservation of natural resources that had been given it by Forbes, Clements, and Adams and that was the basis for the establishment of a committee on the preservation of natural conditions in 1917 as one of the first acts of the newly formed Ecological Society of America. The reciprocal effects of ecology and various professional areas of management were represented in H. L. Stoddard's *The Bobwhite Quail* (1932), Aldo Leopold's *Game Management* (1933), H. J. Lutz and R. F. Chandler's *Forest Soils* (1946), J. Kittredge's *Forest Influences* (1948), and other similar books. The early-warning system of the current ecological crisis, which unfortunately had little influence, was seen in Paul B. Sears's *Deserts on the March* (1935), William Vogt's *Road to Survival* (1948), Fairfield Osburn's *Our Plundered Planet* (1948), and Aldo Leopold's *Sand County Almanac* (1949). The last, in the 1960's, would become the bible of the new converts to the land ethic.

It is not possible in the short compass of this paper to suggest the important impacts on ecology of contemporary developments in other sciences, such as meteorology, geology, soils, and chemistry, as well as other facets of biology. Preeminently a field science, ecology depends on many sources of information about the physical environment, as well as living organisms, which it hopes to integrate into its effort to understand the complex of populations, communities, and environment that is the distinctive goal of ecology.

By midcentury ecology was established widely, if not universally, in the academic world of the United States as a science with its own concepts, techniques, and objects of study—the population and community. It had its own societies, publication outlets, basic specialized literature, influential textbooks, and an embarrassment of terminology for which it was roundly criticized. Ecology had progressed and improved on the work of its founders, whose active professional lives continued up to, and even past, the half-century mark, but it had not much transcended them. There had been few if any of what in modern scientific jargon are called "breakthroughs." Perhaps the diffuse subject matter of ecology does not lend itself to the quantum jump of insight or the revolutionary new interpretation that has marked the dramatic turning point of other scientific disciplines. Or, as so often is the case, the promising but unconventional idea is ignored. This was true of Gleason's "individualistic concept" of the species and of the association that he developed in three papers between 1917 and 1939 and were almost totally ignored in the standard ecological texts and references before 1950. Late in the 1940's Gleason's concept was resurrected, in the early 1950's it was supported by a substantial body of quantitative evidence, and since it has become a standard idea in most ecological textbooks and references, often being taken as almost axiomatic (McIntosh, 1967, 1975).

Ecology had in its ranks critics and prophets who tried to interpret it for other ecologists, to extend its insights to wider horizons, and to lead it into the role of public service and utility that had been envisioned by its founders, particularly Adams, Forbes, and Clements. Up to 1950, however, ecology was little known, and its worth as a basis for management of natural resources was poorly exploited. Notable among those ecologists of the pre–World War II generation striving to bring its name and ideas out of the academic shadow were Frank Egler, Paul B. Sears, and Aldo Leopold. Egler worked both sides of the street, introducing abstract and formal aspects of philosophy into interpretations of vegetation study (Egler, 1942) and, on the other hand, urging the empirical use of ecological ideas upon practical men of affairs.

Paul Sears was the master of the lucid essay, intriguing specialist and nonspecialist alike, in seeking a wider audience for ecological ideas inside and outside the scientific community. He was one of the few ecologists whose writing gave a glimpse of what ecology was and, moreover, what it ought to be. It was Sears who, as late as 1944, wondered about the factor that had retarded the development of ecology and suggested as a partial answer the failure of ecology to recognize its ancestors in biology whose work pointed toward "organized elaborations of the energy and material cycle." He called attention then to the early work in energetics and nutrient dynamics, and in 1949 he stressed the absence of information on "unifying dynamic principles that may apply to the community process." He noted the relevance of the laws of thermodynamics, the concept of entropy, complex channels of energy flow, and number of species in community development as some of the things ecologists should attend to.

Aldo Leopold, apart from being the founder of game management as an extension of ecology, extrapolated ecological ideas and placed them in the framework of the human conscience. He took the ordinary stuff of the farmer, woodsman, naturalist, and scientist and spun it into the web of ethics and aesthetics (Leopold, 1949).

Ecology had not yet achieved the public acclaim accorded its sister science, genetics, as Sears (1949) noted, nor had it become the synthetic science that its advocates in 1950, as in 1920, wished it to be.

THE RISE OF THE NEW ECOLOGY, 1950–76

The immediate post–World War II period provides a convenient and reasonably logical break in the continuum of the history of ecology. Many ecologists who were to bring to fruition concepts of ecology born in its first half century in America and add new ones were trained in the postwar flush in higher education and on the G.I. Bill. The war period had seen the development of some radically new techniques in other scientific disciplines that had filtered into ecology, and the concept of the relation of science to society had begun to undergo significant changes, which were suggested in Vannevar Bush's *Science the Endless Frontier* (1946). It can as truly be said of ecology of 1950 as Allee and his associates (1949) had said of ecology of 1900: "Scientific attention in general was focused on nonecological phases of biology, and the science of ecology, now well and firmly rooted, could continue to develop outside the distorting influences often accompanying high popularity." In the early

postwar period scientific and popular attention was drawn largely to the dramatic developments in molecular biology, especially molecular genetics, and ecology progressed quietly, undisturbed by public adulation. It was a not unmixed blessing to ecology later, in the 1960's, to be thrust onto center stage with the rise of the environmental movement, and the consequent distorting influences attendant upon high popularity, foreseen by Allee and others (1949) became apparent.

As Adams had described ecology in 1913 as "the new natural history," so ecologists by the 1960's were referring to the "new ecology," a phrase suggesting that ecology had undergone a sharp break with its prewar "classical" past (Odum, 1964; Darnell, 1970). This was, in fact, the case. Although much ecological work in the postwar era continued and expanded the earlier traditions, there were a number of significant departures. In the space remaining, the emphasis will be placed on what seem to be distinctive aspects of the break with traditional ecology. It must, unfortunately, omit references to very extensive and excellent work in ecology that extended and improved on the information base and insights of "classical" ecology. I have selected some aspects of ecology for emphasis because of their notoriety as well as because of their solid accomplishment, since some of the most recent developments in ecology are in a state of flux, and their impact on the future of ecology may be problematical. Some of the impacts are more cultural or sociological than scientific.

One of the striking changes in the postwar years was that ecology emerged as "big science" compared with its early traditions (McIntosh, 1974b). Most pre–World War II ecologists were university faculty members working as individuals with a few students and minimal funding. The advent of large-scale federal funding and an era when "Grant Swinger" became an apocryphal figure in science greatly changed the expectations of ecologists, as well as those of other scientists. The comparatively ample funds available helped spread ecology inside and outside the academic arena and carried ecological studies extensively into arctic and tropical regions. The National Science Foundation (NSF), established in 1950, began funding ecological work in 1952 and by 1956 was supporting many awards in the newer thrusts of ecology, such as trophic structure, productivity, energetics, and nutrient cycling of ecosystems. Foundation-financed training programs helped support the new generation of ecologists. About the same time the United States Atomic Energy Commission (AEC) became aware of the health and environmental hazards of radiation. As early as 1955 ecological studies were underway at several AEC installations, and the ecology program at Oak Ridge National Laboratory was begun. It expanded rapidly after 1958, and under the able leadership of Stanley Auerbach it became the largest single ecological-research enterprise in the United States, pioneering in the development of radiation ecology and other aspects of the new ecology.

A consequence of large-scale funding was a new approach to ecological research made possible by the conjunction of new and expensive instrumentation and techniques, the money to exploit the possibilities of these, many more ecologists, and logistical support to do the work. The classical ecologist was described as working with apparatus which, "if not just a ruler and a piece of string, was seldom much more complex than a thermometer and a rain gauge" (Darnell, 1970). The new ecologists, as time went on, confidently looked for the tools of the trade, to include radioisotopes and counting equipment, gas analyzers, chromatographs, respirometers, spectrophotometers, neutron probes, colorimeters, biotelemetry, automatic recording devices, computers, controlled-growth chambers, and biotrons. An old-fashioned car-window ecology was in some instances replaced by airplanes or helicopters. This and other elements of a richer diet for ecologists sometimes led to a rather smug air about the limitations of earlier ecologists. It would be well for the new breed of ecologists to ponder the words of Thomas H. Huxley: "It is easy to sneer at our ancestors, . . . but it is much more profitable to try to discover why they, who were really not one whit less sensible than our own excellent selves, should have been led to entertain views which strike us as absurd" (Huxley, 1903).

In addition to the availability of more complex instrumentation and an extended capacity to collect data, ecology in the last twenty-five years has seen a great increase in the use of quantitative techniques to analyze data. The earlier, somewhat grudging, acceptance of quantitative methods gave way to an almost unbridled enthusiasm for applying numbers, sometimes calculated to unwarranted numbers of significant digits. Nevertheless, ecologists have devoted much attention to sampling methods and quantitative analyses of populations and communities of diverse kinds of organisms, from redwood forests to minute fresh-water or marine plankton. Earlier, often naïve approaches have given way to increasingly sophisticated and rigorous use of sampling and statistical methods stimulated by the appearance of books that made quantitative methods more readily available to ecologists (Greig-Smith, 1957; Pielou, 1969; Patil et al., 1971).

The basic problems of many aspects of ecology, however, remained: securing reasonably accurate estimates of numbers of species and individuals (abundance), assessing their distribution in space (pattern), and determining their associations or correlations with other organisms and the environment. The static view of populations or communities increasingly gave way to studies of population and community dynamics as plant ecologists followed the lead of animal ecologists, and both studied such characteristics of populations as age structure and birth or mortality rates and their effects on population growth and distribution or, reciprocally, the effects of abundance on population characteristics or interspecific interactions such as predator-prey relations, parasitism, or competition.

Quantitatively minded plant ecologists improved their sampling methods in the postwar era, introducing point or distance techniques that increased the efficiency of sampling (Cottam and Curtis, 1949; Goodall, 1952). The traditional preoccupation of plant ecologists with community classification, reviewed by Whittaker (1962), was continued, and numerical methods of ordination and classification were intro-

duced in the United States that rekindled the long-term dispute concerning Gleason's "individualistic concept," which argued that the vegetational community varied continuously and that therefore classifications were necessarily arbitrary. Studies in the 1950's of vegetation by J. T. Curtis in Wisconsin (Curtis, 1959) and R. H. Whittaker (Whittaker, 1967) converged in supporting Gleason's contention, and the continuum, or gradient, concept of the plant, and in some cases the animal, community has been widely if not universally accepted as a useful concept (McIntosh, 1967). Simple empirical methods of numerical analysis were rapidly supplanted by more elaborate mathematical techniques, especially principal components and discriminant analysis, which are still being explored. However, recent studies have raised questions about the utility of these presumably more powerful methods because they presume linear relations, and organisms and environment are not linearly related (Austin and Noy-Meir, 1971; Gauch, Chase, and Whittaker, 1974; Beals, 1973). The interst of animal ecologists in the community has been rekindled in recent years, and they are also using gradient analysis and numerical techniques to examine the animal community (Terborgh, 1970; Green, 1974).

During most of its history ecology held to the holistic approach, that is, the study of the entire complex of nature as a unit. In practice ecologists usually studied single species or single environmental variables, taxonomic groups, particular functions or specific relations between organisms, for example, parasitism or competition predation. The study of the whole complex of organisms and environment, the ecosystem, had been deferred, probably because most prewar ecologists agreed with Egler (1942), who said of the ecosystem, "Although the concept is intellectually more acceptable than any of the preceding, the natural phenomena appear at present too complicated for study and development as a separate science." Among the most far-reaching changes in postwar ecology was a determined effort to produce a science of ecosystems—"ecosystem ecology." The ecosystem was said to be to the ecologist what the cell is to the molecular biologist (Odum, 1964). The rise of the ecosystem concept in ecology was paralleled by a reduction in the traditional distinction between plant ecology and animal ecology and by the development of research teams, bringing together experts in various aspects of ecology and other fields necessary to deal with the complexities of the ecosystem.

This change of emphasis was stimulated in ecological education by the appearance of several textbooks of general ecology in the early 1950's (Odum, 1953; Woodbury, 1954; Clark, 1954). These, particularly the "green book" of E. P. Odum and H. T. Odum, were influential in leading the way to courses in general ecology in addition to the traditional courses in plant ecology, animal ecology, and limnology. Perhaps the most significant emphasis in Odums' popular book was its stress on basic principles of ecology and on the ecosystem as a functional entity. These had been called for in prewar ecology by Hutchinson, and Sears, who had urged the need for a biogeochemical and metabolic approach to the ecosystem. The ground for these ideas had been laid by the work of Juday (1940) and Lindeman (1941, 1942) and in the monumental animal ecology text by Allee and others (1949), but they were introduced to a new generation of ecologists substantially by the Odums' book and their effective campaign for the functional view of the ecosystem in their other writing and research.

The "new ecology"—functional ecology, trophic ecology, ecosystem ecology, to cite a few of its aliases—had a number of distinctive emphases. Beginning with the study of aquatic ecosystems, it emphasized productivity, and ecologists devised new methods to measure the rate of formation or organic material (primary productivity) and the accumulated amount of living material (biomass) in plants and its transfer to other components (consumers) of the trophic (food) web, such as herbivores and carnivores and, eventually, from all of these to decomposers (microorganisms) that returned the materials back to the inorganic state, making them again available to plants, thus completing the biogeochemical cycle. These studies were aided by some of the new techniques developed during the war, for example the use of radioisotopes and new instrumentation that had become available after 1950. Associated with productivity were studies of ecological energetics and nutrient cycling.

The quantitative measurements of essential nutrients in various trophic levels, their pathway or cycle through the ecosystem, and, in some cases, loss from the ecosystem were significant developments in the 1950's and early 1960's. Widespread recognition of the vital importance of biogeochemical cycles to human welfare and concern about losses of essential plant nutrients or unfortunate concentrations of toxic substances stimulated scientific interest in mineral cycles. Recognition of widespread distribution of radioactive iodine and strontium, excessive phosphorus from sewage outfalls and detergents and its deleterious effects on lakes and streams, or the occurrence of toxic levels of nitrogen from fertilizer runoff brought nutrient cycles into the public domain.

Ecosystem energetics seized on the calorie as a common denominator to assess the function of ecosystems, and studies of ecological thermodynamics proliferated in various guises. E. P. Odum (1968) asserted, "Ecoenergetics is the core of ecosystem analysis." Studies of the energy dynamics of ecosystems are an important aspect of ecosystem ecology. The ultimate energy source for the earth's ecosystems, the sun, provides a nearly constant amount of energy, but its availability and use varies greatly over the earth's surface. Energy ultimately limits the productivity of ecosystems, and some ecologists (Gates, 1968; Gates and Schmerl, 1975) have urged the application of physical, micrometeorological, and mathematical techniques in ecology to produce detailed energy budgets that would allow the workings of the ecosystem to be understood.

H. T. Odum (1971), another notable proponent of ecological energetics, urges an engineering approach to ecology. In his view all phenomena are based on energy flows and can be expressed in the common denominator of energy and the language of electrical circuitry to allow a quantitatively integrated approach to ecology and to human affairs in general.

Other ecologists have reservations and question the faith in the calorie as the common denominator of ecology (Goldman, 1968; Paine, 1971). The ecosystem, like all other systems, obeys the first and second laws of thermodynamics, but it is not as yet clear that it does not have idiosyncracies that introduce complications. Some organisms simply do not eat or cannot digest perfectly good calories in the wrong package. A deer does poorly on balsam needles, while a moose thrives on them; or, as Goldman (1968) put it, "Animals are not bomb calorimeters."

A development that was to have a dramatic effect on ecology was the International Biological Program (IBP). It grew from the widespread concern in the 1950's about rapidly intensifying resource-related and environmental problems facing mankind. These problems, recognized by earlier ecologists, were brought into sharper focus by rapidly increasing human populations, incipient food shortages, and increasingly obvious environmental degradation. The IBP was initiated an an international undertaking around 1960, and the United States National Committee for the IBP was appointed in the National Academy of Sciences in 1965. A somewhat distinctive American twist was given to the American IBP at a meeting at Williamstown, Massachusetts, in 1966 (U.S. National Committee for the IBP, 1974). The proposals emanating from this meeting led to the analysis-of-ecosystems program, a valiant and unprecedented effort to develop large-scale, relatively well-funded, closely-linked, cooperative studies of whole ecosystems. The operational phase of the IBP began in 1967 with a group of Integrated Research Programs (IRP) as its primary concern. Perhaps the major impact of the IBP program was that it drastically revised the way ecology was done, and it produced a managerial class in ecology. A new era was clearly indicated when an ecological article described the deployment by a manager of a staff of mathematical modelers in an ecological research program (Pielou, 1972). These programs have not only supported but directed the course of ecology, and it is not entirely clear where they may lead. The travail of breaking the trail in the wilderness of management of large-scale ecological research is effectively described by Van Dyne (1972), the program director of the earliest and largest of the United States IBP ecosystem studies.

The IBP had multiple goals, including: (1) understanding the interactions of the many components of complex ecological systems, (2) exploiting this understanding to increase biological productivity, (3) increasing predictive capacity of the effects of environmental impacts, (4) enhancing human capacity to manage natural resources, and (5) advancing the knowledge of human genetic, physiological, and behavioral adaptations. It had made substantial progress in advancing understanding of ecosystems, particularly the physical and biological processes operating in them: photosynthesis and productivity, water and mineral-nutrient cycling, competition, predation, and, particularly, decomposition processes and the role of detritus in the ecosystem. It has certainly changed the way in which ecology is pursued, and some have proposed that a substantial restructuring in the education of ecologists is in order to train people to cope with the demands of the new ecology (Van Dyne, 1969a; Watt, 1966;

Council on Environmental Quality, 1974). Although the IBP ended as a nationally coordinated program in June, 1974, the substance of its results has yet to be fully appreciated. A synthesis of the results is to be published in a series of a dozen book-length monographs. A continuing impact will likely be felt in large-scale and long-term ecosystem studies and in applications of ecological research to management of natural resources and environmental concerns.

Modeling

One of the major aspects of the new ecology, particularly of the IBP, was a greatly increased emphasis on modeling. A striking departure from most of ecological tradition, except for population ecology, was the introduction of substantial numbers of mathematically sophisticated persons, in some cases physicists, mathematicians, or engineers, either as individuals or as members of teams. It was their function and interest to make models amenable to analytic or digital treatment that would transfer the myriad variables and properties of populations, processes, or even of entire ecosystems into an abstract image that, it was hoped, would fit or elucidate the "real world" of ecology. Models were designed to be dynamic and to possess in varying degrees: (1) realism—to correspond accurately to the "real-world" ecosystem, (2) precision—to predict quantitative changes, (3) generality—to be widely applicable, and (4) resolution—to show detail. It is not possible to achieve all these goals in a single model, and the recent trend in ecology has been to emphasize limited models when more ambitious dreams of whole ecosystem models proved difficult to realize. Nevertheless, the new breed of modelers in ecology believe that more general models will be useful in ecology as they have in other sciences. Robert May (1974), a prominent proponent of the potential of models in ecology, stated:

In ecology, I think it is true that tactical models . . . applied to specific individual problems of resource and environmental management have been more fruitful than has general theory and they are likely to remain so in the near future. But in the long run, once the "perfect crystals" of ecology are established, it is likely that a future ecological engineering will draw upon the entire spectrum of theoretical models, from the very abstract to the very particular, just as the more conventional (and more mature) branches of science and engineering do today.

May was likely speaking metaphorically, but the contrast of a "perfect crystal" model with the entire tradition and realities of ecology brings the ecologist up sharply. Crystals and living cells or organisms are commonly considered as two distinct classes (Blackburn, 1973), and the rigidity of crystal structure, even as a metaphorical model, is difficult to perceive in the organization of an ecosystem.

In the attempt to develop the perfect-crystal model for ecology, myriads of models, large and small, have appeared, and there is even some dispute over what constitutes a model. It harks back to an earlier day, when Allee and his associates

(1949) warned: ". . . for all our emphasis on the need of ecological principles it must be emphasized again that in the formulating of principles, as in testing and extending them, evidence is basic." Some ecologists, concerned about the proliferation of models, suggest the need for more testing of models (Pielou, 1972), Schoener (1972) warns of a "constipating accumulation of models," and there is some suggestion that old models never die (McIntosh, 1962). A good example of the resilience of a model is the "broken-stick" model of Robert MacArthur (1957) which purported to represent the way relative abundance of individuals was distributed among the species of a community. It generated great interest among animal ecologists and was tried in a variety of communities, fitting some (mostly birds) but not others. After Pielou (1966) pointed out a mathematical deficiency, MacArthur (1966) described his intellectual offspring "an obsolete approach to community ecology which should be allowed to die a natural death." Far from being allowed a decent burial, the model was widely used until Hairston (1969) reviewed its inadequacies and asserted that "no biological significance can be attributed to the fact that a collection does or does not show a fit to the broken-stick model, and its usefulness in any ecological context is challenged." Nevertheless, as recently as 1974 the broken-stick model was in use, not even bent, much less broken, by these several attacks. It was still appealed to as an adequate model that showed consistent patterns in real communities, all without acknowledgment of the many criticisms of the model or even its author's request that it be allowed to die. Mathematical models of ecological processes and ecosystems proliferate, and articles and books about models in ecology appear with disquieting regularity, all suggesting that modelers have not yet finished with ecology and ecologists have not finished with models (Kadlec, 1974; Jeffers, 1972; May, 1973; Smith, 1974). It is not clear how much longer it will be true that "ecology is still a branch of science in which it is usually better to rely on the judgement of an experienced practitioner than on predictions of a theorist" (Smith, 1974).

Ecosystems Analysis

The extreme complexity and diversity of ecological systems, which had long made ecology a notably prolix subject, proved a challenge to a new generation of nontraditional ecologists. Stimulated by recent demands on ecology to provide more effective bases for resource management and attacking environmental problems, many ecologists have seized upon systems analysis as the wave of the future (Odum, 1971). Certainly, systems analysis washed over ecology during the last decade and thoroughly saturated some aspects of it, but whether the tide is still rising or ebbing is not clear. One of the reasons that the World War II era is an apt break in the history of ecology is that operations research and systems analysis were spawned during the war. Subsequently, systems analysis flourished in the physical sciences and engineering, and, more recently, was introduced into ecology. The systems approach has been one of the most heralded of the postwar entries into ecology, and Spurr (1964) commented on the etymological connection with the ecosystem: "And how should such a system be studied if not by systems analysis and the computer"? E. P. Odum (1971) noted several pioneers of systems analysis (G. Van Dyne, J. Olson, B. Patten, K. Watt, C. Holling and H. T. Odum) who were "revolutionizing the field of ecology." Systems analysis involves some formal methods that were introduced to the ecologist, for example, linear and nonlinear programming, game theory, decision theory, queuing theory, and extensive use of mathematics and computers. The methods of systems analysis were developed to apply to man-dominated, "complex aggregates of simpler components that interact to produce a desired result" and in which "the components are under design control" (Bode, 1967). Their application to biological systems that have a "mind" of their own may call for new developments in systems analysis (Reichle and Auerbach, 1972), much as Johnson (1970) suggested that description of living things would require modification of information theory. It is, however, a thesis of the new ecology that the time is ripe for advances in ecology through systems analysis, and the wave of the future rolls on, ignoring any commands to the sea to stand still uttered by ecological counterparts of King Canute.

One of the difficulties of the neophyte in systems ecology is to find out just what it is. A system as defined as "a set of objects together with relations between the objects and between their attributes" (Young, 1956). Systems ecology is pre-eminently the application of advanced mathematical techniques and computer technology to the analysis of ecosystems, but it is not a lineal descendent of traditional quantitative ecology or even cousin to other quantitative and mathematical approaches that have been more recently introduced into ecology. According to Rosen (1972), systems theory "amounts to a profound revolution in science—a revolution which will transform human thought as deeply as did the earlier ones of Galileo and Newton." Rosen noted further that systems analysis is in the eye of the beholder and that it is different things to different people, an observation that is amply born out in a review of the literature on systems analysis in ecology.

The first linking of ecology with systems theory seems to have been a publication of a Spanish marine biologist and theoretical ecologist, R. Margaleff (1958). It was not until the mid-1960's, however, that systems analysis, as a more-or-less explicit approach, became a force in ecology. Strikingly, systems analysis, the mostly extravagantly heralded development in the history of ecology, is poorly represented in the ecological research literature. It is difficult to identify its beginnings because, like modeling, it came in so many guises and largely appeared outside the conventional ecological research publications in *Memo Reports of the IBP Biomes* and several recent books (Watt, 1966, 1968; Van Dyne, 1969; Patten, 1971).

The techniques and concepts of systems analysis derive substantially from engineering (Bode, 1967), and the future linking of ecology and engineering is commonly indicated. Odum (1971) comments on systems ecologists who are "pro-

viding a vital link with engineering where systems analysis procedures have been in use for some time." Patten (1971) noted that systems ecology is a hybrid of biology and engineering and predicted that if ecologists "open the door ever so slightly" a shotgun marriage, if not a rape. In either case he anticipates an inevitable kinship between engineers and ecologists helped by demonstrating how ecology can be cast into *"their terms"* (italics added). Levins (1968) viewed at least one approach to systems ecology as a "school of ecological engineering," and engineers, notably electrical engineers, have entered into ecology through systems analysis. Some ecologists have embraced systems analysis wholeheartedly and see in it the wave of the future for ecology; others are less confident that systems ecologists can stay afloat. Deevey (1968), for example, said ". . . it is not certain that the systems approach, powerful though it is, can be made general enough to handle the many weak interactions involved in community organization." Slobodkin (1968), however, predicted that systems analysis "will be a major area of intellectual concern 20 years from now." Given the inertia of scientific developments, this seems a safe prediction.

Quite apart from the emphasis on ecosystem ecology, but with the similar effect of breaking down the distinction between plant and animal ecology, a significant development in postwar ecology was a renewal of interest in the plant-animal interface. The importance of the interaction of plant and animal in community control was argued by Hairston, Smith, and Slobodkin (1960), followed by an extended interchange exploring the question. Harper (1969) examined the role of herbivores in modifying or controlling vegetation. Jansen (1970) placed major importance on the role of animals in controlling plant populations in the tropical forest. Studies of food preferences, nutritional quality, and factors that influence herbivory are causing a reassessment of the role of secondary substances in plant metabolism. These had long been considered waste products, but in the light of the renewed interest in chemical interactions of plants and animals this evaluation is being reinterpreted (Whittaker and Feeney, 1971; Dethier, 1970). Chemical interactions of plants (allelopathy) had been known since 1881, but the years since World War II have produced effective demonstrations of its importance in certain communities (Rice, 1964; Del Moral and Muller, 1970), and it may play an important role in community organization and evolution (Muller, 1970).

Theoretical Ecology

One of the most frequently encountered criticisms of ecology throughout its early years and up to the present was the extensive collection of data in the absence of organizing principles or theory. Yet in one aspect of ecology—populations—there was a long history of mathematical treatment that was available to begin a theoretical framework for ecology. These analytic mathematical treatments of populations did not have substantial influence on ecology generally until recently (Allee et al., 1949; Cole, 1954; Watt, 1962). Among the noteworthy changes of the last decade are increased calls for and interest in mathematical and theoretical approaches to ecology; and in animal ecology at least there has been an extension of the early mathematical theory of populations to the community.

There had been one premature effort (Haskell, 1940) to provide for ecology a mathematical systemization of *environment, organism,* and *habitat*—terms that about sum up ecology. Its author was critical of the structure of ecological concepts and terminology and asserted, "It is no more possible to make present ecological theory produce accurate predictions than to make a wild cherry tree produce fancy dessert cherries." He called somewhat patronizingly for a drastic linguistic transformation of ecology, saying, "For ecology to become an exact science, . . . all its basic notions will have to be redefined and stated in such ways as to be fairly functionally constant and amiable to progressive regularization." In a prescient discussion anticipating recent theoretical interests in ecology (for example, ordination and niche), he said that the only kind of geometry that would encompass the environment-organism relation is an *N*-dimensional geometry, and he referred to "hyperbodies" as spaces representing the effective regions of various processes of an organism. He also posed the concept of entropy as "the first contribution to a unified ecological theory." Although Haskell's paper left no ripple in ecology in the 1940's, redefinition of old concepts (such as niches) in terms of set theory, the concepts of entropy, and multidimensional or *N* hyperspaces all came to the fore in the 1950's and 1960's in a dramatic resurgence of the search for a theoretical ecology.

The earliest postwar entrant into ecological theory was information theory in the work of R. Margalef (1958). The concepts of information, entropy, and cybernetics were briefly intriguing to ecologists, and Patten (1959) proposed a general theory of ecosystem dynamics elucidated by information theory. Information theory has not been generally productive in biology (Johnson, 1970), and it has largely disappeared from ecology, leaving behind a residue in the form of the Shannon-Weaver equation, which has been widely applied to quantify anything that came to hand, particularly species diversity and niche breadth.

Ecologists had long been intrigued by the variation in the number of species in certain areas and by the variation in the number of individuals per species. Plant ecologists from Gleason on had been interested in species-area curves or species-individual curves. The relation between number of species and number of individuals per species in a community, under the rubric diversity, has become an active area of theoretical ecology. Diversity was regarded as a fundamental attribute of a community, has been variously related to productivity, niche, successional development, and particularly stability, and was the subject of a wide-ranging but inconclusive symposium in 1969 (Brookhaven Symposia in Biology, 1969). The conventional wisdom of ecology held that diversity enhanced ecosystem stability by increasing the number of links in the ecological web. This idea became almost axiomatic to some biologists despite indications that diversity of trees in relatively stable or climax forests was less than that in seral or changing forests, and recently May

(1974) has argued against the tradition on theoretical-mathematical grounds.

A more fruitful effort in theoretical ecology, at least bibliographically, was the formalization of the niche concept in terms of set theory by G. E. Hutchinson (1957a). The concept of the niche as an *N*-dimensional hyperspace was avidly seized on, especially by animal ecologists, has gone through a series of modifications (Maguire, 1973; Whittaker, Root, and Levin, 1972; Vandemeer, 1972), and is incorporated in ecological theory (Levins, 1968). Darnell (1970) said that nomenclature in ecology "has subsided into a few useful handles for the most basic concepts." This is somewhat wishful thinking, for new terms spring up as frequently as ever. Niche alone has already generated a number of terms peculiar to its discourse (among them fundamental, realized, included, partial, actual, virtual, and envelopes) in addition to the confusion about the meaning of the term niche itself (Whittaker, Levin, and Root, 1973). Notwithstanding, there has developed a considerable literature on niche mensuration by use of several numerical indices (Levins, 1968; Colwell and Futuyma, 1971), which have given rise to a number of theoretical generalizations. Niche has been said to suggest a "predictive practical ecology" (Lewandowsky, 1972) that would substantially fulfill the dream of a theoretical ecology. What is intriguing is the spurious accuracy to which niche measures are sometimes determined to four significant digits in violation of elementary canons of quantitation.

The 1960's was the decade in which theoretical-mathematical ecology burgeoned. The IBP was seen as a step toward developing a new field of theoretical ecology, allowing predictions about natural and man-made ecological changes (U.S. National Committee for IBP, 1974). R. Lewontin (1970) commented that ecology was being transformed from a descriptive science to a quantitative and theoretical one. He attributed the change to a union of mathematics and evolution and said that the theoretical framework for ecology was *"the concept of the vector field in N-dimensional space,"* citing particle physics as a model for ecology. *Science* (Kolata, 1974) published a commentary, "Theoretical Ecology: Beginnings of a Predictive Science," which reviewed the thrust of theoretical ecology produced by the late Robert MacArthur, his associates, and his students. It seems to be a misfortune of ecology that several of its most productive and imaginative personalities (such as Robert MacArthur, Raymond Lindemand, and John Curtis) died prematurely following major contributions to ecology. MacArthur's work is perhaps the outstanding example of a mathematical-theoretical approach to ecology, and he initiated or stimulated theoretical ecological work in species diversity, island biogeography, community organization, niche structure, *r*- and *k*-selection, and the effect of pattern (coarse and fine grain) on community organization. Whether this thrust of theoretical ecology is a major breakthrough of modern ecology (Fretwell, 1975) or "a public relations web," as one ecologist suggested (Mitchell, 1974), remains to be seen.

The revolutionizing of a science is not accomplished without breaking a few eggs, and the infusion of mathematics and new theoretical approaches was no exception. During the 1960's mathematically and theoretically oriented persons complained bitterly that they were unable to get their work published in the usual ecological journals (Ecology Study Committee, 1965). In 1969 Wilson expressed a fear of an "unholy alliance between the population model builders and molecular biologists to exclude systematists and descriptive ecologists." In 1974, Van Valen and Pitelka voiced a complaint that mathematical ecologists, having entered the ecological establishment, were pursuing a policy of intellectual censorship against ecologists who studied real organisms. The suggestion of a schism or a divisive power struggle in ecology with some sacred cows endangered is not unique in the history of science, but it is hoped that this can be avoided.

Mathematical and theoretical ecology is in full cry in the 1970's, and, like many active scientific areas, there are differences of opinion, some honest, some not so honest, and even basic differences in philosophy. Lewontin (1968) called for a reductionist approach to ecology and evolution and deplored "biologists who reject the analytic method and insist that the problems of ecology and evolution are so complex that they cannot be treated except by holistic statements." Lane, Levins, and Lauff (1974) take a diametrically opposed position, saying:

In ecology there has been too much reliance on the assumption that once small portions of the system are studied, the whole can be reconstituted from the part. . . . While reductionist approaches have always been more popular in all areas of science, we believe it is possible and indeed desirable to develop holistic approaches for ecosystem analysis.

There are those who look on the physicists, mathematicians, and engineers recently entering ecology and bringing new types and levels of mathematical approaches with them as carpetbaggers. Others are more hospitable, but many questions are raised. Slobodkin, an active student of population mathematical and theoretical ecology, commented that "the normal criteria of scientific quality which we use as biologists, are not the same as those of the physicists and mathematician" (Slobodkin, 1962). Ten years later, when the full force of mathematical ecology was impinging on ecology, Slobodkin (1974) offered a list of ten caveats to mathematicians involved in population biology and ecology. Among the more trenchant of these are the second and the fifth:

2. I wish they would not build theories that involve extremely precise exponential functions. . . . The ecological world is a sloppy place.

5. I wish mathematical ecologists would stop rediscovering the wheel. . . . All would-be mathematical modelers should read the extant works on mathematical ecology, and three other books, at a minimum, on descriptive ecology.

This particular criticism of theoretical ecology had been voiced earlier in a review of a book (one of a prominent series on theoretical ecology) presenting a theory of forest structure and succession:

Much of this type of canopy analysis has been done before in a much more sophisticated manner; reading this book is therefore rather like discovering a tribe lost to civilization that has quite independently discovered a primitive form of the internal combustion engine. Does one praise the originality or sympathize with the ignorance? [*Harper, 1972*].

Slobodkin's sixth caveat is:

6. I wish they would stop developing biological nonsense with a mathematical certainty.

One of the major criticisms of mathematical-theoretical approaches in ecology is that they commonly rest on simplifying assumptions, often unstated, that make them tractable mathematically but nonsense biologically. The problem is basically the same one raised by Stanley Cain (1944): whether the complexities of ecology are amenable to mathematical treatment. If not, it will not be for want of trying, and there is a danger that ecology may be cut or stretched to fit not a bed of Procrustes but a rectangular matrix. Theorists have been accused of building unfalsifiable hypotheses into untestable theories and of cooking up the ecological omelet by their own recipe. A more optimistic hope is that new mathematics may be called forth by the challenge of ecological phenomena:

There is every reason to hope that original and creative mathematics will be developed by mathematicians who will become well versed in biology as a discipline, rather than attempting to force biological phenomena into a mold created by hydrodynamics, economics, physics or what have you [*Slobodkin, 1974*].

Perhaps the best advice for bruised egos and stepped-on toes comes from one of the most active of mathematical-theoretical ecologists, Robert May (1974), who counsels the need for a full spectrum of theoretical activity from abstract to specific *"with sympathetic handling"* (italics added). May, however, repeats the familiar comment that ecology is "immature," by which he means it is not mathematical in the manner of physics. This may be a questionable generalization, as Slobodkin's comments suggest.

Whatever the case for the new ecology or any of the elements of the new look in ecology—modeling, systems analysis, theoretical ecology—the relatively ugly duckling of biological science of the 1920's and the 1950's has emerged with a new vitality and a new authority. With the influx of very large sums of money many additional hands and minds and a new visibility and public image, ecology has fulfilled some of the ideals claimed by its early practitioners. It has increased understanding of the functioning of both natural and human-controlled ecosystems, has begun really effective work on the role of decomposer organisms in the maintenance of cycles of nitrogen and other vital nutrients, has made substantial progress in the study of population mechanisms (for example, competition, predation) and their role in the organization of communities, and has developed an impressive range of techniques for ordering large amounts of data to analyze communities and niche relationships of species in communities. There has been significant increase in the knowledge of the physiological properties of organisms as these relate to ecological attributes and response to environmental stress and of the genetic mechanisms involved in these properties. Ecology has returned to the emphasis of its founders in their concern for the centrality of evolutionary biology with the emergence of a comparative approach to species and even community evolution. The new look in ecology is seen in the very existence of a document entitled *The Role of Ecology in the Federal Government,* which begins with the unequivocal assertion, "Ecology as a science has come of age" (Council on Environmental Quality and Federal Council for Science and Technology, 1974).

The Environmental Movement

In 1950 ecology was fairly well established in the academic world, although it was still peripheral in many biology departments. Outside of academic and limited professional circles ecology was little known, and its potential importance for human well-being was not recognized, although it had been a tenet of ecologists from its very beginnings in America. Perhaps the really significant development in ecology was its emergence from obscurity in the shadow of molecular biology into the limelight. This clearly was a consequence of the rapidly mounting concern of the American public about the quality of its environment. The awakening was stimulated by early concerns about the effects of radioactive fallout and by Rachel Carson's book on the hazards of pesticides, *Silent Spring* (1962), which succeeded where earlier cries of alarm had failed to arouse much interest (Fleming, 1972).

Once aroused, concern with the environment grew exponentially, in proper fashion, and myriads of articles and books in the popular press belabored the point that the world's ecosystems were in serious trouble. There were ample expressions of concern about radiation, the spread of industrial and urban decay, the population explosion, and attendant consequences, including the food crisis and the ultimate reality of starvation. Ecology was dubbed the subversive science and was itself in danger of subversion and incorporation into various ideologies associated with the environmental movement. As Allee and others had warned (1949), high prosperity and the accompanying notoriety had distorting influences as well as stimulating a rapid and turbulent growth of ecology. If the ecology of 1903 as seen by Cowles was chaos, that of 1970 was *Chaos chaos,* making it an amoeba, which is not an inapt term, for ecology grew and spread in many directions, sometimes propelled by its inner intellectual motivations, at other times simply drawn into a vortex of environmental questions with which it was ill-prepared to deal. Instant ecologists like Barry Commoner came to the fore to fill the rhetorical gap not adequately filled by working ecologists. The environment movement threatened to turn ecology from science to ideology, and the long-held dogmas of ecology could, without undue distortion, be linked with those of Zen (Barash, 1973). The terms "revolution" and "explosion" have frequently been applied to developments in ecology and environmental concerns in recent years, and

perhaps the greatest burden placed on ecology was the revolution in expectations about its role in the development and management of natural resources and maintenance of the quality of the human environment (Slobodkin, 1968; McIntosh, 1974a; Council on Environmental Quality and Federal Council for Science and Technology, 1974).

Ecology had always been closely aligned with the traditional conservation movement as its scientific arm. The environmental movement is basically an enormous expansion of the conservation movement with many enlarged, scientific, economic, historical and political consequences. In effect, it has become the central issue of modern society. Thus it is not surprising to find a resurgence of interest in human ecology, which was a primary interest in early ecology but was too indigestible for the limited conceptual structure of ecology to embrace. In spite of abortive efforts in the 1930's and 1950's, it is only in the 1970's that there seems to be a determined effort to develop a general ecology incorporating the complex of human affairs, including urban ecosystems.

Ecologists, and the Ecological Society of America from its inception, were involved in alerting America to concerns of the environment and what has come to be called the "environmental crisis." As individuals ecologists have devoted much time and effort to providing professional expertise in questions of waste disposal; resource management; the impact of human use of the environment; erosion effects and control; the effects of strip mining and revegetation of mined areas; the effects and role of fire, herbicides, pesticides, and pollutants generally in ecosystems; and innumerable other environmental concerns. Ecologists have increasingly become involved in matters that are beyond their ecological training and are called upon to interact with other scientists, engineers, lawyers, economists, and other social scientists, as well as diverse governmental agencies at local, state, federal, and even international levels.

Because of his expertise the ecologist often finds that he can no longer stick to his last but must frequently enter the public arena. The Ecological Society of America has recently proposed adoption of a code of ethics for ecologists, and a more conspicuous person on the environmental scene is the ecologist as a practitioner applying his ecological knowledge to practical problems. Only in the past few years have ecologists been hired by consulting firms, banks, and utilities. The result has been a substantial commercial enterprise of consulting ecology. The principal stimulus was the National Environmental Policy Act (NEPA) of 1970, which calls for environmental impacts for major federally financed developments to provide a statement of environmental consequences. Ecologists necessarily cooperate with other scientists and nonscientists in preparing these statements.

An institutional approach to these same ends is the Institute of Eology (TIE), founded in 1971 by ecologists. TIE is an international consortium devoted to ecological research to meet human needs and, particularly, to incorporation of ecological analyses in policy formation and education of the public on environmental issues. It deal with problems beyond the scope of individuals, single institutions, or even of ecologists as specialists, and its structure incorporates individuals and organizations not restricted to professional ecologists. TIE is the latest and, in some respects, the most encompassing effort to make ecological science relevant in human affairs.

Perhaps as a consequence of the increasing role of ecology in environmental affairs, there has appeared in the last decade a rash of interdisciplinary programs, institutes, and other academic aggregations focusing on environmental and ecological concerns, embracing, at least rhetorically, the essential precepts of ecology as a way of dealing with the environment and, as Slobodkin (1969) notes, attracting the attention of academic vice-presidents. Not the least significant indication of the new visibility of ecology is that the august National Academy of Sciences (NAS) has seen fit to increase its representation of ecologists from two (G. E. Hutchinson and Alfred Emerson) to a modest number. The lack of representation of ecologists in the NAS was noted by W. F. Taylor (1936), who counseled ambitious ecologists, "If you want to get elected to the National Academy, . . . select an old established science and stay right in the middle of it!" It may be a slight stretch to note that the distinguished animal behaviorist N. Tinbergen, who was among the authors in the first ambitious attempt to assess ecology in 1939, in 1973 shared (with K. Lorenz and K. von Frisch) the Nobel Prize in Biology and Medicine. This marks a dramatic change in eligibility for that award recently lusted after largely by molecular biologists. A new era is also evidenced in the institution in 1972 of the Tyler Ecology Award. It is the largest monetary award for science. In 1974 it was shared by G. E. Hutchinson with A. Haagen-Smit and M. F. Strong. In 1975 it was bestowed on Ruth Patrick, a leading aquatic ecologist.

The essence of the modern environmental movement is that it is now clear at all levels of human concern—scientific, sociopolitical, and religious—that man's fate, on earth at least, is intimately and ultimately integrated with the natural and managed ecosystems of the earth, their biogeochemical processes, nutrient cycling, transformation of energy, and productive capacity. While all sciences contribute to the factual describing of the universe in which man functions, it is essentially biology, particularly ecology, that integrates the information available into an understanding of the ecosystems of which man is a part, which he in part creates, which he can readily destroy, and the rules of which he must live by however he manipulates them. Aldo Leopold (1949) expressed this eloquently in his land ethic, and there has been ecological feedback into philosophy and ethics:

Ecology provides a model to philosophy and to the other human sciences of a new way of viewing the interrelationships between the phenomena of nature. Central to its perspective is the idea of ecosystem analysis and the concepts of the balance of Nature. . . . The answer to the value question then from an ecological point of view is this: human values are founded in objectively determinable ecological relations within Nature [Colwell, 1970].

It is fortunate that this passage was written not by an ecologist but by a philosopher, for ecologists have been accused of having visions of grandeur, and so broad a claim would simply confirm that accusation.

A philosophical overtone in ecological thought is not entirely new, nor is an ecological overtone in philosophical thought; but a concept that allows nature or scientific consideration of nature to inform philosophy contradicts a long-argued precept of philosophy. Clearly, early American writers and philosophers like Thoreau and Emerson were influenced by nature in their philosophical discourse. Ecologists have often ventured into aspects of value and ethics but have rarely argued from ecological grounds to aesthetic or ethical conclusions. Something of a departure from this is seen in the writings of Aldo Leopold (1949) and, from the philosophical camp, in *Man's Responsibility for Nature* (Passmore, 1973). What is most interesting is to see interpretations by philosophers such as that quoted above and more guardedly discussed in the pages of *Ethics,* by Rolston (1975). Rolston poses a new and difficult axis to the ecologist's *N*-dimensional space where "the topography is largely uncharted; to cross it will require the daring and caution of a community of scientists and ethicists who can together map both the ecosystem and the ethical grammar appropriate for it."

Perhaps the greatest of challenges to the new ecologist is on the horizon of Charles Darwin's and Aldo Leopold's vision.

BIBLIOGRAPHY

Adams, C. C. 1913. Guide to the study of animal ecology. MacMillan Co., New York, 183pp.

Adams, C. C. 1917. The new natural history-ecology. Am. Mus. J. 7:491–94.

Allee, W. C. 1927. Animal aggregations. Quart. Rev. Biol. 2:367–98.

Allee, W. C. 1931. Animal aggregations. A study of general sociology. Univ. Chicago Press, Chicago, 431pp.

Allee, W. C. 1938. The social life of animals. Norton, New York, 293pp.

Allee, W. C. 1939. An ecological audit. Ecology. 20:418–21.

Allee, W. C., and T. Park. 1939. Concerning ecological principles. Science. 89:166–69.

Allee, W. C., A. E. Emerson, O. Park, T. Park, and K. P. Schmidt. 1949. Principles of animal ecology. W. B. Saunders Co., Phila., 837pp.

Austin, M. P., and Noy-Meir. 1971. The problem of nonlinearity in ordination: experiments with two gradient models. J. Ecol. 59:763–73.

Barash, D. P. 1973. The ecologist as Zen master. Am. Mid. Nat. 89:375–92.

Beals, E. W. 1973. Ordination: mathematical elegance and ecological naivete. J. Ecol. 61:23–36.

Blackburn, T. R. 1973. Information and the ecology of scholars. Science. 181:1141–46.

Bode, H. W. 1967. The systems approach. pp. 73–94. In Applied science and technological progress. Report to the Committee on Science and Astronautics by the National Academy of Sciences, Washington, D.C.

Brookhaven Symposia in Biology. 1969. Diversity and stability in ecological system. No. 22. Brookhaven Nat'l. Lab., Upton, New York, 264pp.

Bush, V. 1945. Science the endless frontier. U.S. Govt. Printing Office, Washington, D.C., 184pp.

Cain, S. A. 1944. Foundations of plant geography. Harper and Brothers, New York, 556pp.

Carson, R. 1962. Silent spring. Houghton Mifflin Co., Boston, 368pp.

Chapman, R. N. 1931. Animal Ecology. McGraw-Hill Book Company, Inc., New York, 463pp.

Clarke, G. L. 1954. Elements of ecology. John Wiley and Sons Inc., New York, 534pp.

Clements, F. E. 1905. Research methods in ecology. Univ. Pub. Co., Lincoln, Nebr., 334pp.

Clements, F. E. 1924. Methods and principles of paleo-ecology. Year Book. Carnegie Inst. Wash. 32.

Clements, F. E., and R. Pound. 1898–1902. A method of determining the abundance of secondary species. Minnesota Bot. Stud. 2:19–24.

Clements, F. E., and V. Shelford. 1939. Bio-ecology. J. Wiley and Sons Inc., New York, 425pp.

Cole, L. C. 1954. The population consequences of life history phenomena. Quart. Rev. Biol. 29:103–37.

Colwell, R. K., and D. J. Futuyma. 1971. On the measurement of niche breadth and overlap. Ecology. 52:567–76.

Colwell, T. B., Jr. 1970. Some implications of the ecological revolution for the construction of value. pp. 245–58. In E. Lazlo and J. B. Wilbur (ed.). Human values and natural science. Gordon and Breach Sci. Publ., New York.

Cottam, G., and J. T. Curtis. 1949. A method for making rapid surveys of woodlands by means of pairs of randomly selected trees. Ecology. 30:101–104.

Council on Environmental Quality and Federal Council for Science and Technology. 1974. The role of ecology in the federal government. Report of the committee on ecological research. December 1974, 78pp.

Cowles, H. C. 1904. The work of the year 1903 in ecology. Science 19:879–85.

Curtis, J. T. 1959. The vegetation of Wisconsin. Univ. of Wisconsin Press, Madison, 657pp.

Darnell, R. M. 1970. The new ecology. Bioscience. 20:746–48.

Daubenmire, R. 1947. Plants and environment. J. Wiley, New York, 424pp.

Deevey, 1964. General and historical ecology. Bioscience 14:33–35.

Del Moral, R., and C. H. Muller. 1970. The allelopathic effects of *Eucalyptus camaldulensis*. Am. Mid. Nat. 83:254–82.

Dethier, V. 1970. Chemical interactions between plants and insects. pp. 82–102. In E. Sondheimer and J. B. Simeone (Eds.) Chemical Ecology. Academic Press, New York.

Ecology Study Committee, 1965. Summary report with recommendations for the future of ecology and the Ecological Society of America [15 April 1965].

Edmondson, Y. H. 1971. Some components of the Hutchinson legend. Limnol. Oceanog. 16:157–61.

Egerton, F. N. 1962. The scientific contributions of Francois Alphonse Forel, the founder of limnology. Schweizerische Zeitschrift Fur Hydrologie. 214:181–99.

Egerton, F. N. 1976. Ecological studies and observations in America before 1900. In B. J. Taylor and T. J. White (eds.). Evolution of issues and ideas in America, 1776–1976. Univ. of Oklahoma Press, Norman, 1976.

Egler, F. E. 1942. Vegetations as an object of study. Phil. of Sci. 9:245–60.

Egler, F. E. 1951. A commentary on American plant ecology based on the textbooks of 1947–1949. Ecology. 32:673–95.

Elton, C. 1927. Animal ecology. Macmillan, New York, London, 209pp.

Elton, C. 1933. The ecology of animals. John Wiley and Sons Inc., New York, 97pp.

Fleming, D. 1972. Roots of the new conservation movement: Perspectives. Am. Hist. 6:7–94.

Forbes, S. A. 1887. The lake as a microcosm. Bull. Ill. Nat. Hist. Survey. 15:537–50.

Forbes, S. A. 1907. On the local distribution of certain Illinois fishes: An essay in statistical ecology. Bull. Ill. Lab. Nat. Hist. 7:1–19.

Forbes, S. A. 1909. An ornithological cross-section of Illinois in autumn. Bull. Ill. State Lab. Nat. Hist. 7:305–35.

Fretwell, S. D. 1975. The impact of Robert MacArthur on ecology. Ann. Rev. Ecol. Syst. 6:1–13.

Frey, D. (ed.) 1963. Limnology in North America. Univ. of Wisconsin Press, Madison, 734pp.

Ganong, W. F. 1904. The cardinal principles of ecology. Science. 19:493–98.

Gates, D. M. 1968. Toward understanding ecosystems. Adv. Ecol. Res. 5:1–36.

Gates, D. M., and R. B. Schmerl. 1975. Perspectives of biophysical ecology. Springer-Verlag, New York, 609pp.

Gauch, H. G., Jr., G. B. Chase, and R. H. Whittaker. 1974. Ordination of vegetation sample of Gaussian species distributions. Ecology. 55:1382–90.

Gleason, H. A. 1917. The structure and development of the plant association. Bull. Torrey Bot. Club. 44:463–81.

Gleason, H. A. 1926. The individualistic concept of the plant association. Bull. Torrey Bot. Club. 53:1–20.

Gleason, H. A. 1936. Twenty-five years of ecology, 1910–1935. Mem. Brooklyn Bot. Gard. 4:41–49.

Goldman, C. R. 1968. Aquatic primary production. Am. Zool. 8:31–42.

Goodall, D. W. 1952. Quantitative aspects of plant distribution. Biol. Rev. 27:194–245.

Green, R. H. 1974. Multivariate niche analysis with temporally varying environmental factors. Ecology. 55:73–83.

Greig-Smith, P. 1957. Quantitative plant ecology. Butterworth's Sci. Publ., London, 198p.

Grinnell, Jr. 1917. The niche relationships of the California thrasher. Auk. 34:427–33.

Haeckel, E. 1891. Planktonic studies: a comparative investigation of the importance and constitution of the pelagic fauna and flor. (Trans.) Rept. U.S. Fish Comm. 1889–91. pp. 565–641.

Haeckel, E. 1898. The evolution of man. 2 vols. Kegan Paul, London.

Hairston, N. G. 1969. On the relative abundance of species. Ecology. 50:1091–94.

Hariston, N. G., F. Smith, and L. B. Slobodkin. 1960. Community structure, population control and competition. Am. Nat. 94:421–25.

Hardin, G. 1962. The competitive exclusion principle. Science. 131:1292–97.

Hardin, G. 1968. The tragedy of the commons. Science. 162:1243–48.

Harper, J. L. 1967. A Darwinian approach to plant ecology. J. Ecol. 55:247–70.

Harper, J. L. 1969. The role of predation in vegetation diversity. pp. 48–62. In Diversity and stability in ecological systems. Brookhaven National Laboratory, New York, No. 22.

Harper, J. L. 1972. Review of H. S. Horn. The adaptive geometry of trees. Science. 176:660–61.

Harshberger, J. 1911. Phytogeographic survey of North America. G. E. Stechert, New York, 790pp.

Haskell, E. F. 1940. Mathematical systematization of "environment," "organism" and "habitat." Ecology. 21:1–16.

Hesse, R. 1924. Tiergeographie auf oekologischer grundlage. Fischer, Jena, 613pp.

Hesse, R., W. C. Allee, and K. P. Schmidt. 1937. Ecological animal geography. H. Wiley and Sons, New York, 597pp.

Hutchinson, G. E. 1940. Review of Clements F. E. and V. E. Shelford. 1939. Bio-ecology. Ecology. 21:267–68.

Hutchinson, G. E. 1957a. Concluding remarks, Cold Spring Harbor Symp. Quant. Biol. 22:415–27.

Hutchinson, G. E. 1957b. A treatise on limnology. Vol. I. J. Wiley and Sons Inc. New York. 1015pp. Vol. II. 1967. 1115pp.

Huxley, L. 1903. Life and letters of T. H. Huxley. Macmillan Company, New York, 3 vols.

Jeffers, J. N. R. 1972. Mathematical models in ecology. Blackwell Sci. Publ., Oxford, 398pp.

Johnson, H. A. 1970. Information theory in biology after 18 years. Science. 168:1545–50.

Juday, C. 1940. The annual energy budget of an inland lake. Ecology. 21:438–50.

Just, T. (ed.). 1939. Plant and animal communities. Am. Midl. Nat. 21:1–255.

Kadlec, J. A. 1971. A partial annotated bibliography of mathematical models in ecology. Analysis of Ecosystems I.B.P. Univ. of Michigan, Ann Arbor. Unnumbered.

Kuhn. 1962. The structure of scientific revolutions. Univ. of Chicago Press, Chicago, 210pp.

Kittredge, J. 1948. Forest influences. McGraw-Hill Inc., New York, 394pp.

Kohn, A. 1971. Phylogeny and biogeography of Hutchinsonia: G. E. Hutchinson's influence through his doctoral students. Limnol. Oceanog. 16:173–76.

Kolata, G. G. 1972. Theoretical ecology: beginnings of a predictive science. Science 183:400–401 (cont. p. 450).

Lane, P. A., G. H. Lauff, and R. Levins. 1974. The feasibility of using a holistic approach in ecosystem analysis. pp. 111–11 in S. A. Levins (ed.). Ecosystem analysis and prediction. Proc. SIAM-SIMS Conference, Alta, Utah, July 1–5, 1974.

Leopold, A. 1933. Game management. Scribners, New York, 481pp.

Leopold, A. 1949. A Sand County almanac. Oxford Univ. Press, New York, 226pp.

Levandowsky, M. 1972. Ecological niches of sympatric phytoplankton species. Am. Nat. 106:71–78.

Levins, R. 1968. Evolution in changing environments. Princeton Univ. Press, Princeton, N.J., 120pp.

Lewontin, R. C. (ed.). 1968. Population biology and evolution. Syracuse, Univ. Press Syracuse, N.Y., 206pp.

Lewontin, R. C. 1970. The meaning of stability. pp. 13–23 in Diversity and stability in ecological systems. Brookhaven Nat'l. Lab. Symp. Biol. 22.

Lindeman, R. 1941. Seasonal food-cycle dynamics in a senescent lake. Am. Mid. Nat. 26:636–73.

Lindeman, R. L. 1942. The trophic-dynamic aspect of ecology. Ecology. 23:399–418.

Lussenhop, J. 1974. Victor Hensen and the development of sampling methods in ecology. J. Hist. Biol. 7:319–37.

Lutz, H. J., and R. F. Chandler. 1946. Forest soils. John Wiley and Sons Inc., New York, 514pp.

MacArthur, R. H. 1957. On the relative abundance of bird species. Proc. Nat. Acad. Sci. U.S. 43:293–95.

MacArthur, R. H. 1966. Note on Mrs. Pielou's comments. Ecology. 47:1074.

MacArthur, R. H. 1972. Geographical ecology. Harper and Row, New York, 269pp.

Maguire, B. Jr. 1973. Niche response structure and the analytical potentials of its relationship to the habitat. Am. Nat. 107:213–46.

Margaleff, R. 1958. Information theory in ecology. Gen. Syst. 3:36–71.

McDougall, W. B. 1927. Plant ecology. Lea and Febiger, Philadelphia, 326pp.

McIntosh, R. P. 1962. Raunkiaer's "law of frequency." Ecology. 43:533–35.

McIntosh, R. P. 1967. The continuum concept of vegetation. Bot. Rev. 33:130–87.

McIntosh, R. P. 1974a. Commentary—an object lesson for the new ecology. Ecology. 55:1179.

McIntosh, R. P. 1974b. Plant ecology 1947–1972. Ann. Miss. Bot. Gard. 61:132–65.

McIntosh, R. P. 1975. H. A. Gleason—"individualistic ecologist," 1882–1975. Bull. Torrey Bot. Club. 102:253–73.

Merriam, C. H. 1894. Laws of temperature control of the geographic distribution of terrestrial animals and plants. Nat. Geogr. Mag. 6:229–38.

Mitchell, R. 1974. Scaling in ecology. Science. 183:1131.

Moore, B. 1920. The scope of ecology. Ecology. 1:3–5.

Mortimer, C. H. 1956. E. A. Birge: an explorer of lakes. pp. 163–211. In Sellery, G. C. 1956. E. A. Birge: a memoir. Univ. Wisconsin Press, Madison.

Muller, C. H. 1970. The role of allelopathy in the evolution of vegetation. pp. 13–31. In P. R. Ehrlich (ed.). Biochemical coevolution. Oregon State Univ. Press, Corvallis.

Nice, M. M. 1937. Studies in the life history of the song sparrow I. Trans. Linn. Soc. 4:1–247.

Nichols, G. E. 1928. Plant ecology. Ecology. 9:267–70.

Odum, E. P. 1953. 1st ed. Fundamentals of ecology. 1st ed. W. B. Saunders Co., Philadelphia, 546pp. 2d. ed., 1958. 3d ed., 1971.

Odum, E. P. 1964. The new ecology. Bioscience. 14:14–16.

Odum, E. P. 1968. Energy flow in ecosystems. A historical review. Am. Zool. 8:11–18.

Odum, H. T. 1971. Environment, power and society. Wiley-Interscience, New York, 331pp.

Oosting, H. J. 1948. The study of plant communities. W. H. Freemand and Co., San Francisco, 389pp.

Osburn, F. 1948. Our plundered planet. Little, Brown and Co., Boston, 217pp.

Paine, R. T. 1971. The measurement and application of the calorie to ecological problems. Adv. Ecol. Syst. 2:145–62.

Passmore, J. 1974. Man's responsibility for nature. Charles Scribner's Sons, New York, 213pp.

Patil, G. P., E. C. Pielou, and W. E. Waters. 1971. Statistical

Ecology. 3 vols. Pennsylvania State Univ. Press, University Park.

Patten, B. C. 1959. An introduction to the cybernetics of the ecosystem: the trophic dynamic aspect. Ecology. 40:221–31.

Patten, B. C. 1971. Systems analysis and simulation in ecology. Vol. I. Academic Press Inc., New York, 610pp.

Pearl, R. 1925. The biology of population growth. Knopf, New York, 260pp.

Pearl, R., and L. J. Reed. 1920. On the rate of growth of the population of the United States since 1790 and its mathematical representation. Proc. Nat. Acad. Sci. 6:275–88.

Pearse, A. S. 1926. Animal ecology. McGraw-Hill Book Co., Inc., New York, 417pp.

Pielou, E. C. 1966. Comment on a report by J. H. Vandermeer and R. H. MacArthur concerning the broken stick model of species abundance. Ecology. 47:1073–74.

Pielou, E. C. 1969. An introduction to mathematical ecology. Wiley Interscience, New York, 286pp.

Pielou, E. C. 1972. On kinds of models. Science. 171:981–82.

Reichle, D. E., and S. I. Auerbach. 1972. Analysis of ecosystems. pp. 260–80. In J. A. Behnke (ed.). Challenging biological problems. Oxford Univ. Press, New York.

Rice, E. L. 1964. Inhibition of nitrogen-fixing and nitrifying bacteria by seed plants. Ecology. 45:824–837.

Riley, G. A. 1971. Introduction. Limnol. Oceanog. 16:177–79.

Rolston, H. Jr. 1975. Is there an ecological ethic? Ethics 85:93–109.

Rosen, R. 1972. Review of: Trends in General Systems Theory. Klir (ed.) Wiley-Interscience, New York. Science. 177:508–509.

Schimper, A. F. W. 1898. Pflanzengeographie auf physiologischer Grundlage. Jena., Fischer, 870pp. Trans. by Wm. A. Fischer. 1903. Plant geography upon a physiological basis. Clarendon Press, Oxford, 839pp.

Schoener, T. W. 1972. Mathematical ecology and its place among the sciences. Science. 178:389–91.

Sears, P. B. 1935. Deserts on the march. Univ. Oklahoma Press, Norman, 231pp.

Sears, P. B. 1944. The future of the naturalist. Am. Nat. 78:43–53.

Sears, P. B. 1949. Integration at the community level. Am. Sci. 37:235–42.

Sears, P. B. 1956. Some notes on the ecology of ecologists. Sci. Monthly. 83:22–27.

Shelford, V. E. 1913. Animal communities in temperate America. Univ. Chicago Press, Chicago, 368pp.

Shelford, V. E. 1929. Laboratory and field ecology. Williams and Wilkins Co., Baltimore, 608pp.

Shelford, V. E. 1938. The organization of the ecological society of America. Ecology. 19:164–66.

Shelford, V. E. 1963. The ecology of North America. Univ. Illinois Press, Urbana, 610pp.

Slobodkin, L. B. 1965. On the present incompleteness of mathematical ecology. Am. Sci. 53:347–57.

Slobodkin, L. B. 1968. Aspects of the future of ecology. BioScience. 18:16–23.

Slobodkin, L. B. 1969. Pathfinding in ecology. Science. 164:817.

Slobodkin, L. B. 1974. Comments from a biologist to a mathematician. pp. 318–29. In S. A. Levin (ed.). Proc. SIAM-SIMS Conference, Alta, Utah, July 1–5, 1974.

Smith, J. M. 1974. Models in ecology. Cambridge Univ. Press, New York, 146pp.

Spurr, S. M. 1964. Forest ecology. Ronald Press Co., New York, 352pp.

Stauffer, R. C. 1957. Haeckel, Darwin and ecology. Quart. Rev. Biol. 32:138–44.

Stoddard, H. L. 1932. The bobwhite quail. Scribners, New York, 559pp.

Taylor, W. P. 1936. What is ecology and what good is it? Ecology. 17:333–46.

Terborgh, J. 1970. Distribution on environmental gradients: theory and a preliminary interpretation of distributional patterns in the avifauna of Cordillera Vilcabama, Peru. Ecology. 52:24–40.

Transeau, E. N. 1926. The accumulation of energy by plants. Ohio J. Sci. 26:1–10.

U.S. National Committee for the International Biological Program. 1974. U.S. participation in the International Biological Program. Report No. 6. National Academy of Sciences, Washington, D.C., 166pp.

Vandermeer, J. H. 1972. Niche theory. Ann. Rev. Ecol. Syst. 3:107–32.

VanDyne, G. M. 1969a. Implementing the ecosystem concept in training in the natural resource sciences. pp. 327–367. In G. M. Van Dyne (ed.). The ecosystem concept in natural resource management. Academic Press, New York.

Van Dyne, G. M. (ed.). 1969b. The ecosystem concept in natural resource management. Academic Press, New York, 383pp.

VanDyne, G. M. 1972. Organization and management of an integrated ecological research program. pp. 111–172. In I.N.R. Jeffers (ed.). Mathematical models in ecology. Blackwell's Scientific Publications, Oxford.

Van Valen, L., and F. Pitelka. 1974. Commentary: Intellectual censorship in ecology. Ecology. 55:925–26.

Verhulst, P. F. 1838. Notice sur la loi que la population suit dans son accroissement. Corresp. Math. et Phys. 10:113–21.

Vogt, W. 1948. Road to survival. William Sloane Assoc., Inc., New York, 335pp.

Warming, E. 1895. Plantesamfund-grundtrak of den okologiska plantegeogrefi. Copenhagen. Trans. 1909 as Oecologie of plants. Oxford, Clarendon Press, 422pp.

Watt, K. E. F. 1962. Use of mathematics in population ecology. Annu. Rev. Entomol. 7:243–60.

Watt, K. E. F. ed. 1966. Systems analysis in ecology. Academic Press, New York, 276pp.

Watt, K. E. F. 1968. Ecology and resource management: A quantitative approach. McGraw-Hill Book Co., Inc., New York, 450pp.

Watt, K. E. F. 1973. Principles of environmental science. McGraw-Hill Book Co., Inc., New York, 319pp.

Weaver, J. E., and F. E. Clements. 1929. Plant ecology. McGraw-Hill Book Co., Inc., New York, 601pp.

Welch, R. S. 1935. Limnology. McGraw-Hill Book Co., Inc., New York, 471pp.

Wheeler, W. M. 1902. Natural history, "Oecology" or "Ethology"? Science. 15:971–76.

White, L., Jr. 1968. Dynamo and virgin reconsidered. Massachusetts Inst. Tech. Press, Cambridge, Mass., 186pp.

Whittaker, R. H. 1962. Classification of communities. Bot. Rev. 28:1–239.

Whittaker, R. H. 1967. Gradient analysis of vegetation. Biol. Rev. 42:207–64.

Whittaker, R. H., and P. P. Feeney. 1971. Allelochemics: chemical interactions between species. Science. 171:757–70.

Whittaker, R. H., S. A. Levin, and R. B. Root. 1973. Niche, habitat and ecotope. Am. Nat. 107:321–38.

Wilson, E. O. 1969. The new population biology. Science. 163:1184–85.

Woodbury, A. M. 1954. Principles of general ecology. The Blakiston Co. Inc., Toronto, 503pp.

Young, O. R. 1964. The impact of general systems theory on political science. General Systems. 9:239–53.

THE CONTRIBUTORS

JOHN C. BURNHAM is Professor of History and Lecturer in Psychiatry at Ohio State University, Columbus, Ohio. He received the Ph.D. from Stanford University. He is the author of several books.

RAYMOND DACEY is Associate Professor of Management at the University of Oklahoma, Norman, Oklahoma. He received the Ph.D. from Purdue University. He has been a member of the faculty of the University of Iowa. He has published articles in professional journals, including *Kyklos,* and has made many presentations before professional societies. He is a member of a large number of professional organizations.

FRANK N. EGERTON is Associate Professor of the History of Science at the University of Wisconsin, Parkside, Wisconsin. He received the Ph.D. from the University of Wisconsin, Madison. He has served as a member of the faculty of Boston University and of Carnegie-Mellon University. He is the author of many articles, which have appeared in such publications as the *Journal of History of Biology.* He has had an interest of long standing in the field of ecological ideas.

MURRAY CLARK HAVENS is Professor and Chairman of the Department of Political Science, Texas Technological University, Lubbock, Texas. He received the Ph.D. from Johns Hopkins University. He has been a member of the faculty of Duke University and of the University of Texas at Austin and was Visiting Professor at the University of Sydney, Sydney, Australia. He is the author of several books and articles. He is a member of several professional societies, including the American Political Science Association and the Southern Political Science Association.

RICHARD HILBERT is Professor of Sociology at the University of Oklahoma, Norman, Oklahoma. He received the Ph.D. from Pennsylvania State University. He has been a member of the faculty of Southern Illinois University, of Allegheny College, and of Albright College and was Visiting Professor at the University of Kansas. He is a member of the American Sociological Association and the Southwestern Sociological Association.

JOHN M. LOVE is Director of the Research Department of High/Scope Educational Research Foundation, Ypsilanti, Michigan. He received the Ph.D. from the University of Iowa. He has been a member of the faculty of Colorado Women's College. His articles have appeared in the *Journal of Genetic Psychology, Child Development,* and other jounals.

JOHN C. McCULLERS is Professor and Chairman of the Department of Psychology at the University of Oklahoma, Norman, Oklahoma. He received the Ph.D. from the University of Texas at Austin. He has written extensively on subjects related to his field. He is a member of a number of associations, among them the American Psychological Association and the Society for Research in Child Development.

ROBERT P. McINTOSH is Professor of Biology at the University of Notre Dame, Notre Dame, Indiana. He received the Ph.D. from the University of Wisconsin. He has been a member of the faculty of Middlebury College and of Vassar College. He has written many articles on ecology, which have appeared in such publications as *Ecology* and the *Quarterly Review of Biology.* He is a member of the Ecological Society of America, the British Ecological Society, the American Association for the Advancement of Science, and the American Society of Naturalists.

KENNETH R. MERRILL is Associate Professor of Philosophy at the University of Oklahoma, Norman, Oklahoma. He received the Ph.D. from Northwestern University. In addition to American philosophy, his academic interests include logic; the philosophies of Descartes, Berkeley, and Hume; and twentieth-century analytic philosophy.

H. WAYNE MORGAN is George Lynn Cross Research Professor of History, the University of Oklahoma, Norman, Oklahoma. He received his Ph.D. from the University of California at Los Angeles. He has held professorial rank at San Jose State College, San Jose, California, and the University of Texas at Austin. He has written many books, articles, and reviews for scholarly journals on various historical subjects.

W. NELSON PEACH is George Lynn Cross Research Professor of Economics at the University of Oklahoma, Norman, Oklahoma. He received the Ph.D. from Johns Hopkins University. He has been a member of the faculty of the University of Texas at Austin and of Syracuse University. He has served in the federal government, holding posts in the Federal Reserve Bank of Dallas, the United States Department of State, and the Agency for International Development. He is the author of many books and articles. He is a member of the American Economic Association, the American Finance Association, and other associations.

JOHN D. PULLIAM is Professor of Education at the University of Oklahoma, Norman, Oklahoma. He received the Ed.D. from the University of Illinois. He has been a member of the faculty of the University of Texas at Austin. He is the author of books and articles on various aspects of education. He is a member of the History of Education Society and the John Dewey Society.

THOMAS M. SMITH is Professor of the History of Science at the University of Oklahoma, Norman, Oklahoma. He received the Ph.D. from the University of Wisconsin. He has held the position of Scientific Historian with the United States Air Force. He has published in the areas of the management of scientific research and development and the applied physical sciences associated with scientific technology. He is a member of the History of Science Society and the Society for the History of Technology.

JOHN R. SOKATCH is Professor of Microbiology and Immunology, Biochemistry and Molecular Biology and Associate Dean of the Graduate College of the University of Oklahoma Health Sciences Center, Oklahoma City. He received the Ph.D. from the University of Illinois. He is the author of many books and research articles in science. He is a member of many associations, among them the American Society for Microbiology and the American Chemical Society.

WILLIAM F. SWINDLER is John Marshall Professor Law, the College of William and Mary, Williamsburg, Virginia. He received the Ph.D. from the University of Missouri, and the LL.B. from the University of Nebraska. He has been a member of the faculty of the University of Idaho and of the University of Nebraska. He has published a number of books and articles on legal issues. He is a member of various organizations, including the Selden Society, Phi Delta Phi, the American Law Institute, and Coif.

BENJAMIN J. TAYLOR, the coeditor of this book, is Professor of Economics at the University of Oklahoma. He received the Ph.D. from Indiana University, Bloomington, Indiana. He has been a member of the faculty of Oakland City College, Oakland City, Indiana, Indiana University, and Arizona State University. He is the author of many books, monographs, and articles. He is a member of the American Economic Association, Phi Kappa Phi, and Beta Gamma Sigma.

KENNETH L. TAYLOR is Associate Professor of the History

of Science at the University of Oklahoma. He received the Ph.D. from Harvard University. He has held a postdoctoral research fellowship at Centre National de la Recherche Scientifique, in Paris. He is a member of a large number of organizations, including the History of Science Society, the Society for the History of Technology, and the British Society for the History of Science.

DANIEL A. WREN is Professor and Division Director of Management and Curator of the Harry W. Bass Business History Collection at the University of Oklahoma, Norman, Oklahoma. He received the Ph.D. from the University of Illinois. He has been a member of the faculty of the University of Illinois and of Florida State University. He is the author of two books and articles that have appeared in the *Academy of Management Journal* and the *Business History Review.* He received an Outstanding Educator of America Award in 1972 and is listed in *American Men and Women in Science.*

THURMAN J. WHITE, the coeditor of this book, is Professor of Adult Education and Vice-President for Continuing Education and Public Service at the University of Oklahoma, Norman, Oklahoma. He received the Ph.D. from the University of Chicago. Among his publications are contributions to the *Journal of the American Physical Therapy Association* and the *Handbook of Adult Education in the United States.* In addition to his duties as Vice-President, he serves or has served as a member of many associations, foundations, commissions, boards, and committees. He is a member of Phi Beta Kappa, Phi Delta Kappa, Psi Chi, Pi Kappa Alpha, and Omicron Delta Kappa.

ROBERT R. WRIGHT is Professor of Law, Dean of the College of Law, and Director of the Law Center of the University of Oklahoma, Norman, Oklahoma. He received the J.D. from the University of Arkansas and the S.J.D. from the University of Wisconsin. He has been a member of the faculty of the University of Arkansas and was a Visiting Professor at the University of Iowa. In addition to maintaining a private practice, he has been a corporate lawyer. His publications include a number of books and articles. He engages in many professional activities and is a member of the Arkansas Bar Association, the Oklahoma Bar Association, and the American Bar Association. He is a member of Phi Beta Kappa, Omicron Delta Kappa, and Coif.

INDEX